LANCASHIRE page 184
Haworth
LEEDS
HUMBERSIDE page 164
PRESTON
BRADFORD
WEST YORKSHIRE page 322
KINGSTON UPON HULL
GREATER MANCHESTER page 136
SOUTH YORKSHIRE page 320
MERSEYSIDE page 200
LIVERPOOL
MANCHESTER
SHEFFIELD
Chester
CHESHIRE page 44
Chatsworth
DERBYSHIRE page 74
Lincoln
LINCOLNSHIRE page 194
CLWYD page 332
WREXHAM
STOKE-ON-TRENT
Alton Towers
NOTTINGHAMSHIRE page 224
NOTTINGHAM
STAFFORDSHIRE page 254
DERBY
STAFFORD
LEICESTERSHIRE page 190
NORFOLK page 204
Norwich
SHREWSBURY
Iron Bridge
SHROPSHIRE page 238
BIRMINGHAM
WEST MIDLANDS page 298
LEICESTER
ENGLAND
COVENTRY
CAMBRIDGESHIRE page 32
POWYS page 360
WARWICKSHIRE page 292
NORTHAMPTONSHIRE page 212
WARWICK
Stratford-upon-Avon
NORTHAMPTON
BEDFORD
Cambridge
SUFFOLK page 260
Worcester
HEREFORD & WORCESTER page 150
BEDFORDSHIRE page 16
Lavenham
IPSWICH
Bourton-on-the-Water
HERTFORDSHIRE page 158
ESSEX page 106
GLOUCESTER
GLOUCESTERSHIRE page 112
AYLESBURY
BUCKINGHAMSHIRE page 26
HERTFORD
St Albans
CHELMSFORD
GWENT page 346
Oxford
OXFORDSHIRE page 230
SWINDON
GREATER LONDON page 120
Tower
Greenwich
Kew
NEWPORT
CARDIFF
AVON page 10
BRISTOL
Bath
BERKSHIRE page 20
READING
Windsor
WILTSHIRE page 302
SURREY page 268
GUILDFORD
SEVENOAKS
Canterbury
KENT page 174
Glastonbury
SOMERSET page 246
TAUNTON
Salisbury
HAMPSHIRE page 140
WINCHESTER
WEST SUSSEX page 280
Weald Museum
EAST SUSSEX page 274
LEWES
SOUTHAMPTON
CHICHESTER
Arundel
Brighton
Portsmouth
DORSET page 94
DORCHESTER
Lymington
Yarmouth
Fishbourne
NEWPORT
Abbotsbury
Weymouth
ISLE OF WIGHT page 170
CHANNEL ISLANDS page 40
Portsmouth
Weymouth
Torquay
Alderney
FRANCE
Guernsey
Sark
Jersey
FRANCE
Alderney
Guernsey

Places To Visit In Britain

ALTON TOWERS, STAFFORDSHIRE
For key to this illustration,
see page 256

AA

PLACES TO VISIT IN BRITAIN

A county-by-county guide to more than 2400 castles, stately homes, gardens, theme parks, museums and other places of interest throughout England, Wales and Scotland

Published by Drive Publications Limited
for the Automobile Association
Fanum House, Basingstoke, Hampshire RG21 2EA

CONTRIBUTORS

The publishers would like to thank the following people for major contributions to this book:

Writers

John Burke Russell Chamberlin
Ross Finlay Ned Halley Tim Healey
Belinda Hunt Keith Spence
Roger Thomas

Photographers

Nigel Cassidy Barry Hitchcock
Neil Holmes Anthony Lambert Skyscan
Eric Meacher Richard Surman John Vigurs
John Wyand

Artists

Richard Bonson Ronald Maddox
Peter Morter

We would also like to thank English Heritage, the National Trust, the National Trust for Scotland, Cadw (Welsh Historic Monuments) and Scottish Historic Buildings and Monuments for advice concerning the properties they administer; the owners of all properties listed in the book for checking material; and local authorities and Tourist Boards for their cooperation.

PLACES TO VISIT IN BRITAIN
was edited and designed by
The Reader's Digest Association Limited
for Drive Publications Limited
Berkeley Square House, London W1X 5PD

Designer: Bob Hook
First Edition Copyright © 1988
Drive Publications Limited

All rights reserved. No part of this book may be reproduced, stored in a retrieval system, or transmitted in any form or by any means, electronic, electrostatic, magnetic tape, mechanical, photocopying, recording or otherwise, without permission in writing from the publishers.

Printed in Great Britain
The typeface used for text in this book is
9pt Garamond

Cover: Chatsworth, Derbyshire
Page 1: Chinese peacock,
at Butterfly House,
Syon Park, Gtr London
Pages 2-3: Alton Towers, Staffordshire
Pages 6-7: Ironbridge Gorge, Shropshire

CONTENTS

An A-Z guide to the 66 counties, regions and islands areas of England, Wales and Scotland, together with the Isle of Man and the Channel Islands

Little Moreton Hall, Cheshire

PAGES 8-329

ENGLAND

Special Features

St Botolph's Church
Boston, Lincolnshire

Caerlaverock Castle
Dumfries and Galloway

PAGES 330-363

WALES

Special Features

PAGES 364-423

SCOTLAND

Special Features

Where to enjoy Britain

The first cast-iron bridge in the world arches gracefully across a tree-banked gorge on the beautiful River Severn. The combination of engineering marvel and natural wonder at Iron-Bridge in Shropshire – named by an international committee as a World Heritage site – typifies the quality and variety of attractions that Britain offers the traveller. In these small islands it is never necessary to drive far to find something that makes the journey worth while; and man-made spectacles such as castles and stately homes are often set in untouched countryside which makes the journey to visit them part of the pleasure of the excursion.

From all the attractions that the British countryside and the enterprise of its inhabitants can offer, our writers have selected the Places to Visit described and illustrated in this book. They range from a walk among alpine plants on a Scottish mountainside to a close-up view of the flight-deck of Concorde . . . from a ride up a Welsh valley by steam train to a whirl on a Victorian fairground roundabout in Norfolk. What they have in common is that all go out of their way to welcome visitors; and in our opinion every one of them is worth going out of your way to see.

HOW TO USE THIS BOOK

To help you make the most of your visit, the paragraph in *italics* at the end of each entry gives the following information:

EH, NT, etc Organisation administering the property. *Cadw* = Welsh Historic Monuments; *EH* = English Heritage; *FC* = Forestry Commission; *HBM* = Scottish Historic Buildings and Monuments; *NCC* = Nature Conservancy Council; *NT* = National Trust; *NTS* = National Trust for Scotland; *RSPB* = Royal Society for the Protection of Birds.

All year, daily, etc Times of opening can change from year to year, so if you are planning a journey round a visit to a particular property it is advisable to telephone to confirm that the property will be open. Note that 'daily' usually excludes Christmas Day and often other days during the Christmas and New Year period, and some half days at other times.

Adm charge/Free entry Charges vary greatly, and can change from year to year.

Refreshments Facilities provided range from full meals to simple snacks.

Shop Includes kiosks selling guide books and postcards, as well as more elaborate shops selling souvenirs, craft goods and plants.

P Cars may be parked reasonably close to the property.

Toilets Toilets are available for visitors' use.

♿ Enough of the property is accessible to a handicapped visitor in a wheelchair to make a visit worth while. Specially adapted toilets are often provided.

Tel Telephone this number to confirm that a property will be open, or to obtain further details. Use the code when telephoning from outside the area.

ENGLAND

Cathedrals, stately homes and castles offer a glimpse of England's history through buildings that have changed little over the centuries, while new 'living museums' re-create for visitors the sights and sounds of Viking township, Canterbury pilgrimage, Georgian mill and Victorian river port. By contrast, other displays involve visitors in the wonders of modern technology. In Bradford, visitors watch themselves as television newscasters; at Goonhilly they listen to radio signals bounced through space by satellite; at Sellafield they learn the mysteries of nuclear power. Traditional museums preserve and display a range of exhibits from steam locomotives to teddy bears, and in addition to man-made marvels there beckon the splendours of nature in caves, high mountains and wildlife sanctuaries.

Canterbury Cathedral, Kent

AVON

GEORGIAN CITY AND HISTORIC PORT AMONG MELLOW HILLS

Bristol, at the heart of this small county, has been a crossroads of world exploration and trade ever since John Cabot left its quay for the New World in 1496. Bristol Historic Harbour and Blaise Castle House Museum tell the port's story, and Battery Point is a good place to view its modern trading ships. The Bristol Exploratory maintains the questing tradition in a modern, scientific context.

The American connection is the strongest of Avon's ties, and a large American Museum is housed at Claverton Manor. Several of the county's other fine country houses were preserved or built by Bristol wealth, including Clevedon Court and Beckford's Tower. The Regency period, when Bristol was prospering from the slave trade, saw Bath develop into the fashionable spa whose legacy enriches the modern city. Avon has natural beauty too. Steep Holm lies off the coast, and plains are studded with areas of quiet water such as Chew Valley Lake.

THE AMERICAN MUSEUM

On A36, 3¼ miles east of Bath (Ea)

To walk into Claverton Manor, an English neo-classical mansion designed in 1820 by Sir Jeffry Wyatville, is to step back 250 years and into another continent. For the manor contains a series of furnished rooms which bring to life the history, everyday affairs and arts of the American people. Many of its rooms contain panelling and floorboards taken from houses across the Atlantic and reinstalled here.

The earliest room is a 17th-century New England Puritan 'keeping room', which served as a living room. Its massive beams, huge fireplace – around which the housewife's herbs are drying – and sturdy furniture give it an air of permanence in striking contrast with the wattle-and-daub cabins of the earliest settlers. A hefty Bible rests at the head of the table.

An austere, sparsely furnished living room once belonged to a Shaker family – members of a sect so called because of the shaking movements involved in their religious dancing. Brightly coloured coffee pots and tea chests and elaborately veneered and patterned furniture grace a room in the style of the Pennsylvania-Germans (also called Dutch) who were originally Protestant refugees from Germany and Switzerland.

Displays cover the exploration of America, the life of the American Indians, and transport by river and sea. Others show what it was like to be a pioneer on one of the trails, such as the 2000 mile Oregon Trail that opened up the Wild West, to sail a 19th-century whaler or clipper, or to ride the range as a cowboy. Conkey's Tavern dates from 1776 – the year the Declaration of Independence was signed – while a 19th-century country store acts as a souvenir shop, selling jams and sweets made to American recipes.

The garden which George Washington laid out at his home at Mount Vernon is re-created in the manor grounds. There is also a herb garden, a milliner's shop of the last century, an Indian tepee from the Prairies, and a folk art gallery.

End Mar-end Oct, pm Tues-Sun, and Bank Hol Mon. Adm charge. Refreshments. Shop. P *Toilets. Tel Bath (0225) 60503.*

AVON GORGE NATIONAL NATURE RESERVE

Off A369, on west bank of River Avon (Cb)

This reserve includes more than a mile of the craggy, almost 300ft high limestone cliffs of the Avon Gorge, and is noted for its rare plants. These include the Bristol whitebeam, which grows nowhere else in the world. There are magnificent views of the Gorge and of the graceful 702ft span of the Clifton Suspension Bridge, built in 1831-59 to the designs of Isambard Kingdom Brunel.

NCC. All year, daily.

BATTERY POINT

Off A369, 1 mile north of Portishead (Bb)

Land and water fuse in the magnificent views from the viewpoint at Battery Point, reached by a few steps up from a car park. A broad sweep of the Severn Estuary stretches below, spanned to the north-east by the Severn road bridge. The main shipping lane comes close to the shore, and watchers have a close-up view of craft approaching and leaving Avonmouth.

All year, daily.

BECKFORD'S TOWER

Off Lansdown Road, 1 mile north of Bath (Db)

In 1769, at the age of nine, William Beckford inherited a fortune from his father's sugar plantations in Jamaica. After travels abroad he settled at Fonthill Abbey in Wiltshire and there built a 276ft high Gothic tower. This collapsed in 1825, but by then Beckford was living in Bath and had begun a new tower near the city to house his furniture, books and paintings.

The two-storey Italianate building, with a 154ft tower topped by an octagonal lantern, now contains a museum devoted to Beckford. A climb of 156 steps is rewarded by magnificent views over Bath.

Apr-Oct, Sat and Sun pm. Adm charge. Shop. P *Tel Bath (0225) 336228.*

BITTON STEAM RAILWAY

On A431, 5 miles east of Bristol (Db)

A band of volunteers has resurrected part of a line built by the Midland Railway in 1864-9 to join the Birmingham-Bristol route with Bath. Passenger services from Bitton ceased in 1966, freight services were withdrawn in 1971, and the track itself was removed the following year. The volunteers restored Bitton station, relaid the track, and started collecting steam locomotives and carriages. Steam trains now run to School Road Bridge and Oldland Common. The pride of the collection is a restored 126-ton LMS Stanier Black Five locomotive, rescued in 1973 from a scrapyard at Barry.

All year, Sat, Sun and Bank Hol; Mar-Dec, steam days 1st Sun each month and Bank Hol. Refreshments. Shop. P *Toilets.* ♿ *Tel Bristol (0272) 327296.*

BLAISE CASTLE HOUSE MUSEUM

Off A4018, 3½ miles north of Bristol (Cb)

Life in and around Bristol over 300 years makes the theme of this museum. Displays of furnishings, costumes, textiles, toys and farm implements give vivid insights into everyday life; while other collections, including watches and chocolate packaging, portray some of the city's trades.

The museum is housed in a neoclassical mansion built of mellow Bath stone by John Harford, a wealthy Bristol Quaker, at the end of the 18th century. He employed Humphry Repton to lay out the grounds, and it was he who introduced John Nash to Harford. Nash designed the conservatory for the house and then designed Blaise Hamlet – nine 'rustic' cottages, half a mile to the west, grouped around a green in a harmonious whole. Harford built the hamlet to house his older servants and tenants; it is now owned by the National Trust.

All year, Sat-Wed. Free entry. Shop. ♿ *(ground and first floors). Tel Bristol (0272) 506789.*

BRISTOL EXPLORATORY

Victoria Rooms, Clifton, Bristol (Cb)

Children are overjoyed by this 'Hands on Science Centre' and rush excitedly from one 'plore' – experiment, something to explore – to another, under the guidance of the centre's 'pilots'. Its purpose is to introduce basic principles of science and technology by means of fun experiments.

EXPLORATORY LIGHTHOUSE *The secrets of light are revealed to young experimenters in this house of Light Rays. Wall slots show the unerring straightness of rays projected from a point of light inside, and mirrors, prisms and lenses reflect, refract and focus them.*

Visitors start by getting to know about their own perception of the world about them. Look at a hollow mask long enough, and it becomes a positive one, with the nose pointing outwards. Try to trace a pattern reflected in a mirror: most people can hardly pencil a line. Reach to touch an electric light bulb, only to find there is nothing there but a reflection from a mirror of a Second World War searchlight. The curious can play with lasers, with a large ball balanced on a column of air, or with disorienting mirrors and visual illusions; they can 'see' both sounds and impossible objects.

At The Exploratory visitors can find out that the way balls behave on an elliptical snooker table is similar to the motions of the planets, while racing model cars down straight and curved tracks relates to Einstein's theory that space is curved.

The Exploratory can be enjoyed by young or old as serious science or just fun with a serious undertone.

All year, daily. Adm charge. Shop. P *Toilets. Tel Bristol (0272) 634321.*

IRON LADY *Brunel's restored masterpiece SS* Great Britain *(top) is now back in Bristol Harbour, where she was built in 1843. The contemporary painting shows her sailing under steam and sail at the beginning of her first voyage to Australia, in 1852. By far the largest ship of her time, the* Great Britain *was converted to full sail in 1882, and was driven onto the Falkland Islands in a storm only four years later.*

BRISTOL HISTORIC HARBOUR

In Bristol, near city centre (Cb)

'Shipshape and Bristol-fashion' has long been a term of high commendation among seafarers, and was also the standard *(continued on page 14)*

GRANDEUR FROM THE WATERS

Celts revered the healing springs at Bath as sacred to their goddess Sulis. The Romans knew them and began to create a city there in the 1st century AD which they called Aquae Sulis, 'Waters of Sulis'. A Saxon town was followed by a medieval city, which blossomed as an elegant Georgian spa under the dandy Beau Nash, its 'uncrowned king'. John Wood began the city's transformation with his designs for Queen Square and The Circus. His equally gifted son, John Wood the Younger, designed Royal Crescent and the Assembly Rooms.

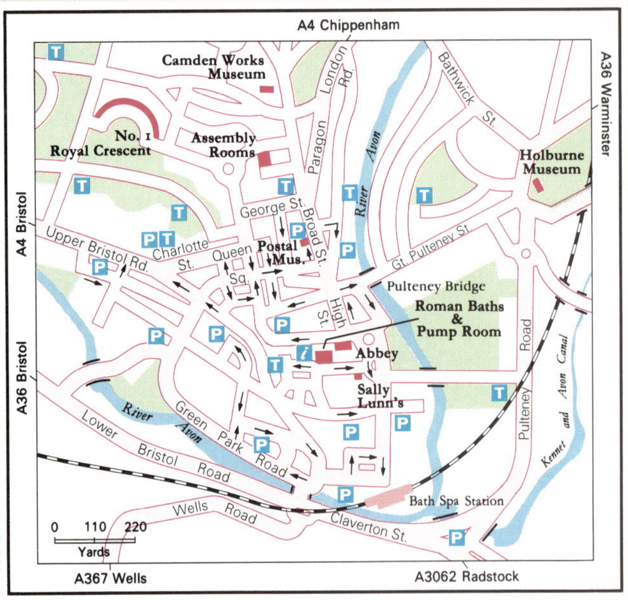

Roman Baths and Museum *All year, daily. Adm charge. Shop. Toilets. Tel Bath (0225) 61111.*

Pump Room *All year, daily. Free entry. Refreshments. Shop. Toilets. ♿ Tel (0225) 61111.*

No 1 Royal Crescent *Mar-Oct, Tues-Sat, Sun pm and Bank Hol Mon. Adm charge. Shop. Tel (0225) 28126.*

Bath Postal Museum *All year, Mon-Sat; also Sun pm in summer. Adm charge. Refreshments. Shop. P Toilets. ♿ Tel (0225) 60333.*

Camden Works Museum *Feb-Nov, pm daily; Dec-Jan, Sat and Sun pm. Adm charge. Refreshments. Toilets. Tel (0225) 318348.*

Sally Lunn's Museum *All year, am Mon-Sat. Adm charge. Refreshments. Shop. Toilets. Tel (0225) 61634.*

Bath Abbey Church of St Peter and St Paul *All year, daily. Free entry. ♿*

Holburne Museum *Mid Feb-mid Dec, Mon-Sat, and Sun pm; closed Mon mid Feb-Easter. Adm charge. Refreshments (Easter-Oct). Shop. P Toilets. ♿ Tel (0225) 66669.*

Assembly Rooms and Museum of Costume *All year, daily. Adm charge to museum. Shop. Toilets. ♿ Tel (0225) 461111.*

ROMAN BATHS AND MUSEUM

The main spring at Bath produces 250,000 gallons of water each day at a temperature of 46.5°C (116°F). The Romans built a reservoir around the spring to create a head of water to feed their baths complex. Now known as King's Bath, the reservoir is overlooked by the Pump Room, and its overflow (left) can be seen in the museum. King's Bath was sacred, and the museum has a fascinating collection of objects dropped into it by pious Romans. They include more than 12,000 coins, four of them of gold, metal cups, and a fine bronze brooch.

HOLBURNE MUSEUM

Decorative arts, paintings and work by 20th-century artist-craftsmen are housed in the Holburne Museum and Crafts Study Centre. The small teapot (below) was made in Bristol around 1775. The larger teapot dates from about 1935.

THE GREAT BATH

The 70ft long Great Bath (left), was part of the complex at the heart of Roman Bath. Nearby the builders raised a temple dedicated to Sulis-Minerva – the Celtic god and their own goddess of healing. Water still enters the bath by Roman plumbing from King's Bath.

ASSEMBLY ROOMS

A Museum of Costume in Bath's Assembly Rooms has fashions from Tudor times to the present, and includes this exquisitely embroidered lady's doublet made in about 1615. The building was erected in 1769-71.

SALLY LUNN'S MUSEUM

In the bakery of Bath's oldest house, built in 1480, Sally Lunn evolved her brioche buns around 1700. The delicacies are still made to her secret recipe, and eaten in the coffee house there now. The cellar holds a kitchen museum.

PUMP ROOM

A statue of Beau Nash (1674-1762) surveys the Pump Room built some 30 years after his death. Today's visitors may take tea or coffee and a Sally Lunn bun as in olden days, or sample the spa water from the elegant pump or fountain (right).

BATH ABBEY

The tower of Bath Abbey soars to 162ft, high above a Roman statue standing over the Great Bath. The abbey, the third on the site, was begun in 1499 by Bishop Oliver King, and is a masterpiece of airy Perpendicular Gothic style, with exquisite fan vaulting. A ladder to heaven (above right), with angels ascending and descending, graces both west front turrets, and illustrates a dream of the bishop's. Abbey Churchyard is surrounded by lovely 18th-century buildings – so a flute player in Regency dress (above) is no surprise there.

CAMDEN WORKS MUSEUM

In a building of Bath's 18th-century heyday, a Victorian family business has been re-created. J.B. Bowler set up in Bath in 1872 as a brass founder and engineer. He later produced mineral waters, and it was in the mineral water factory office (right) that deliveries were checked out, and workers paid. The firm closed in 1969, and its premises were demolished. Incredibly none of its contents had ever been thrown away so exact reconstructions were possible. The museum also traces the story of golden Bath stone, used for Roman and Georgian Bath.

NO 1 ROYAL CRESCENT

A majestic sweep of 30 houses, fronted by 104 graceful Ionic columns, makes Royal Crescent one of the most elegant streets in Britain. It is the work of John Wood the Younger, and was built in 1767-74. No 1 has been restored and furnished to re-create its 18th-century appearance.

BATH POSTAL MUSEUM

The training of the Post Office Rifles at Cuckfield, in Sussex, before leaving for France in 1917 was commemorated by a postcard (far right) in the museum. Another card shows a Victorian song sheet. The museum charts the means by which the written word has been carried, from the clay tablets of ancient times to the electronic methods used by postal services today.

(continued from page 11) adopted by the city when it set about the re-creation of its near-derelict dockland as a leisure centre. There are water sports and water tours, old ships, an ancient bridge, a warehouse converted into a cinema and art gallery, museums, old pubs and places to eat and drink.

To capture the authentic flavour of the old docks, it is a good idea to begin at the Maritime Heritage Centre. This gallery was originally built to house the ship models, paintings, prints and other maritime relics bequeathed by Charles Hill & Sons, for more than two centuries Bristol's most distinguished shipwrights. Much has been added to the collection, including a replica of Isambard Kingdom Brunel's dredger *BD6* that for generations hauled the mud out of Bristol harbour.

The Centre is also the door to the star of the whole complex – Brunel's SS *Great Britain*, hauled back in triumph from the Falklands in 1970 for a refit in the dock where she was built in 1843. Her 38ft funnel and 100ft-plus masts tower above the flush decks, the coat of arms on her stern is gilded, her great six-bladed propeller in place. *Great Britain* was the transatlantic revolution of her day. In 1845 she became the largest vessel to cross the Atlantic, and the first to do so driven by propeller. Later, she carried troops to the Crimea and thousands of emigrants to Australia, until a storm ended her career on a Falklands beach in 1886.

A walk along the quay past yachts, houseboats, old coasters, tugs and a ponderous steam crane of 1876 leads to the Industrial Museum. This features Bristol-made products that contributed to the city's industrial fame down the years; Bristol cars, Douglas motorcycles, Rolls-Royce aero engines and Concorde, represented by a mock-up of a nose section. A steam-driven carriage of 1875 is believed to be the world's oldest self-propelled vehicle still in working order. A superb model railway layout makes a good introduction to the restored engine and rolling stock of the Bristol Harbour Railway outside. Another major exhibition reviews the story of the City Docks and includes a reconstructed 19th-century marine workshop.

Next to the Industrial Museum along the quay is the National Lifeboat Museum. Among its exhibits are an oared lifeboat of 1904, a modern Atlantic 21, and one of the earliest of the outboard motor inshore dinghy lifeboats. Several of the boats on view have taken part in dramatic rescues.

Maritime Heritage Centre: All year, daily. Free entry. P *Toilets.* ♿ *Tel Bristol (0272) 20680. SS* Great Britain*: All year, daily. Adm charge. Refreshments. Shop.* P *Toilets.* ♿ *(part). Tel (0272) 20680. Industrial Museum: All year, daily exc Thur and Fri. Free entry. Shop. Toilets.* ♿ *(part). Tel (0272) 299771. Lifeboat Museum: Apr-Sept, daily. Adm charge. Shop.* P *Toilets.* ♿ *(part). Tel (0272) 213389.*

BRISTOL ZOO

On A38, Clifton Down (Cb)

Visitors to Bristol Zoo may find themselves standing within arm's length of a gorilla or a lion – but with armour-plated glass safely between them and the animals. Many animals, including monkeys and nocturnal animals such as bushbabies and armadillos, are housed under cover. To enter the reptile house is to walk into a tropical forest, with tumbling waterfalls, lighted pools policed by crocodiles, and an array of orchids and other rare plants.

All year, daily. Adm charge. Refreshments. Shop. P *Toilets.* ♿ *Tel Bristol (0272) 738951.*

BURRINGTON COMBE

Off B3134, 4 miles north of Cheddar (Ca)

This Cheddar Gorge in miniature cuts a swathe down the 'softer' northern side of the Mendip Hills – but it is spectacular for all that, with towering craggy sides. Like Cheddar, it was the haunt of Stone Age men, who used caves such as Aveline's Hole, near the bottom of the combe, as shelters around 12,000 years ago. Another cleft was the inspiration for Augustus Toplady's hymn 'Rock of Ages'. A short walk from the car park at the top of the gorge leads up to Burrington Ham, a ridge with a delightful view over Blagdon and Chew Valley Lakes, Bristol, and on a clear day, the shadowy Welsh hills across the Bristol Channel.

All year, daily.

CHEW VALLEY LAKE

Off B3114, 1 mile south of Chew Magna (Ca)

Reed-fringed banks and an island rising from the waters belie the fact that Chew Valley Lake is a reservoir supplying water to Bristol. It covers 1200 acres in a lovely wooded setting on the northern flanks of the Mendip Hills, and is a nesting ground for many species of water birds. These are especially plentiful in winter, but permanent residents include great crested grebes, kingfishers, woodpeckers, little owls and kestrels. Two landscaped picnic and parking areas on the north-eastern side of the lake offer excellent views of the birds, and there is an information centre with a bird identification chart. The southern part of the lake is a nature reserve, with four birdwatching hides for which permits may be obtained at Woodford Lodge.

All year, daily. Free entry. Refreshments. Shop. P *Toilets.* ♿ *Tel Bristol (0272) 665881.*

CLEVEDON COURT

Off B3130, ½ mile east of Clevedon (Bb)

It is remarkable that a mansion built as early as 1320 should have survived intact to the present day, but it was in that year that Sir John de Clevedon grafted a new manor house of mellow local stone onto an even earlier tower and hall standing at the foot of Court Hill. He incorporated a 'hanging chapel' on the first floor, with a window looking down on the Great Hall – perhaps to allow the lady of the house while at Mass to oversee the household.

Abraham Elton, a wealthy merchant-venturer from Bristol, bought the court in 1709, and his family owned it until the National Trust took it over in the 1950s. The Eltons were gifted merchants and scholars who helped to develop the Victorian resort of Clevedon. Visitors to Clevedon Court included William Makepeace Thackeray, who came there to sketch but stayed to draft most of *Vanity Fair*.

The house contains a collection of exquisite glassware from the works which flourished at nearby Nailsea from 1788 to 1873. There is also Eltonware produced between 1880 and 1921 at the enterprise established by Sir Edmund Elton, a gifted potter, inventor and captain of the local fire brigade. Outside are terraced gardens laid out in the 18th century.

At the Clevedon Craft Centre in Moor Lane, about 1 mile south-west, a variety of craftsmen work in the buildings of a 17th-century farm. Their skills include cabinet making, weaving, leather working, glass blowing and engraving, silversmithing and porcelain making.

Clevedon Court. NT. Apr-Sept, Wed, Thur, Sun and Bank Hol Mon pm. Adm charge. Refreshments. P *Toilets. Tel Clevedon (0272) 872257. Craft Centre: All year, daily. Free entry. Refreshments. Shop.* P ♿ *Tel (0272) 872867.*

DYRHAM PARK

On A46, 8 miles north of Bath (Db)

The country mansion and medieval Church of St Peter beside it lie amid a deer park in a superb setting in the Cotswold Hills. The grand house in baroque style was built between 1692 and 1704 for William III's Secretary of State, William Blathwayt, and Dyrham's panelled rooms are little changed since his day. Many of their contents, including Delft china and a series of bird pictures by the Dutch artist Hondecoeter, were acquired by William while he was in the diplomatic service, and are recorded in surviving housekeepers' inventories of 1703 and 1710. There are also tapestries, furniture, pictures and books which he inherited from his uncle, William Povey, a friend of the diarists Samuel Pepys and John Evelyn.

The garden front was built in 1692 by the Dutch architect Hauduroy. It overlooks the church, and a peaceful lake refuge for waterfowl.

NT. Park: pm daily. House and garden: Apr, May and Oct, pm daily exc Thur and Fri; June-Sept, pm daily exc Fri. Adm charge. Refreshments. P *Toilets.* ♿ *(garden, ground floor). Tel Abson (027582) 2501.*

PRISTON MILL

Off A367, 4 miles south-west of Bath (Da)

A corn mill with a water wheel has stood on or near this site since Saxon times. It was one of more than 5600 English mills listed in Domesday Book, and one of the handful still in operation today. It is now part of Priston Mill Farm and lies tucked away in the hills on Conygre Brook.

The present water wheel, 21ft in diameter, was installed in the 1850s. A channel and trough direct water from the mill pond over the top of the wheel into its iron buckets. In the 18th century the water wheel drove mallets which fulled, or pounded, the loosely woven woollen cloth to strengthen it. Priston Mill now produces stone-ground wholemeal flour for sale in the mill shop. There is also a nature trail, a collection of farm animals and an adventure play area.

Easter-end Sept, pm daily. Adm charge. Refreshments. Shop. P *Toilets. Tel Bath (0225) 23894.*

ROOFTOP VIEW *The gables of Clevedon Court and the fertile green fields of Clevedon Moor stretching to the misty Mendips fill the view southwards from the terraced gardens behind the house. The 13th-century tower at the east end is the mansion's oldest part.*

STEEP HOLM

Island 5 miles off Weston-super-Mare (Aa)

A trust set up in memory of the naturalist and author Kenneth Allsop bought this small cliff-girt island in the Bristol Channel in 1976 to preserve it as a nature reserve. The island covers only 50 acres at high tide – yet provides a home for more than 260 plant species, including the deep-pink wild peony and stagshorn plantain, found nowhere else in Britain.

Breeding gulls dominate the scene in summer, with cormorants, ducks, ravens and doves, and in 1977 the peregrine returned after an absence of more than 20 years. Shy muntjac – small deer introduced in the same year – are sometimes glimpsed in the undergrowth, and grey seals sport offshore.

Steep Holm was fortified in Victorian times, and in the Second World War it bristled with artillery. A 19th-century barracks (now used to house visitors) and gun batteries remain. There are also the remnants of the priory built by Augustinian monks in the 12th century, and the ruins of a refuge built for sailors in 1786 and a farmstead established in 1865. A 2 mile nature trail visits most of the island's places of interest.

Apr-Oct, Sat and Bank Hol Mon, day-trips from Knightstone Causeway, Weston-super-Mare. Adm charge. Refreshments. Shop. P *(at Causeway). Toilets. Tel (0963) 32583 (Fri evening).*

WOODSPRING MUSEUM

In centre of Weston-super-Mare (Aa)

A re-creation of everyday life at the turn of the century is one of the main themes of this small museum. Visitors walk around an old chemist's shop, with its curatives, elixirs and colourful potions, see an Edwardian dentist's surgery, visit a farm dairy or cider-making room, or enter into the spirit of a Victorian day at the seaside.

A display conjures up life – and death – in the Iron Age hill-fort at nearby Worlebury some 2000 years ago, and another brings Mendip mining to life. The collections range from costumes and dolls to cameras and penny-farthing bicycles. There is also an indoor nature trail, complete with a running stream and a freshwater and seawater pond.

The building was used by the Weston-super-Mare Gaslight Company as workshops from 1912 to 1970. It opened as a museum in 1975.

All year, Mon-Sat. Free entry. Refreshments. Shop. P *(limited). Toilets.* ♿ *Tel Weston-super-Mare (0934) 21028.*

WOODSPRING PRIORY

Off A370, 3½ miles north of Weston-super-Mare (Bb)

The graceful Perpendicular style of this small priory church recalls the great age of medieval church building. It lies in a rural setting above Woodspring Bay at the end of a leafy green lane.

The priory was founded between 1210 and 1220 by William de Courtenay, a grandson of one of the knights who murdered Thomas Becket in 1170; but the present building dates mainly from the 15th century. After the Dissolution of the Monasteries in the mid-16th century the priory church was used as a farmhouse.

The National Trust acquired the estate in 1968, and later the priory passed into the care of the Landmark Trust and was restored.

All year, daily. Free entry. Shop. P *(limited). Tel Weston-super-Mare (0934) 512728.*

COUNTY CALENDAR

Easter Tuesday Bristol, Church of St Michael on the Mount Without: Two Penny Starvers (traditional distribution of buns).

May Badminton: Horse Trials.

Whit Sunday Bristol, St Mary Redcliffe: Rush Sunday Service.

Spring Bank Hol Bristol, Ashton Court: North Somerset Agricultural Show.

May (last week) - **June** (first week). Bath: International Festival of Music and Arts.

June Bristol Docks: Power Boat Grand Prix.

August Bristol, Ashton Court: International Balloon Fiesta.

Christmas Eve and Boxing Day Marshfield: Mumming.

Tourist information: Bristol (0272) 293891; Bath (0225) 62831; Weston-super-Mare (0934) 26838.

BEDFORDSHIRE

TREASURES ON A PILGRIM'S PROGRESS BESIDE THE GREAT OUSE

Associations with John Bunyan are strong in a green and peaceful county where water meadows flank the meandering River Great Ouse and rolling downs climb towards the Chilterns. The author of *The Pilgrim's Progress* was born in the village of Elstow and imprisoned for his religious views in the county town of Bedford, and both places have many reminders of him.

Wildlife, native and exotic, has a favoured place in Bedfordshire. At Whipsnade Park Zoo more than 2000 animals roam free, and there is a Wild Animal Kingdom at Woburn Abbey, showplace home of the Dukes of Bedford. The Royal Society for the Protection of Birds is based at Sandy where visitors can tour a nature reserve, and there is a garden of rare birds at Stagsden. Other homegrown attractions include a lace museum at Luton and a treasure house at Luton Hoo.

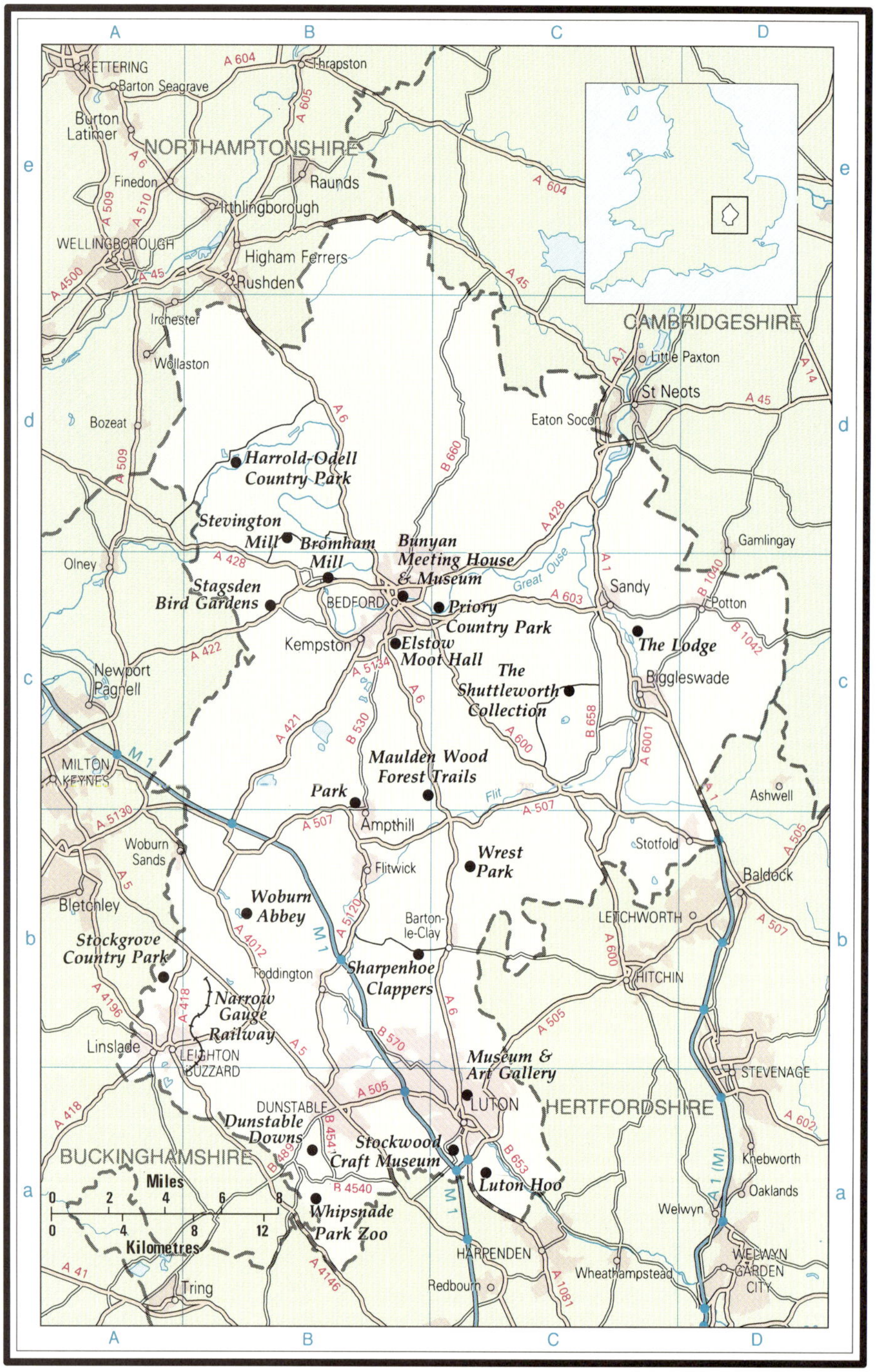

AMPTHILL PARK

Near centre of Ampthill (Bc)

Capability Brown laid out Ampthill's splendid landscape park, just to the west of the Georgian town centre. Among its features are ancient pollarded oaks, perhaps survivors of the 15th-century Ampthill Great Park enclosed by the uncle of Henry V, and a small reservoir surrounded by mature trees. It was in Ampthill Castle, long since vanished, that Henry VIII imprisoned Catherine of Aragon in the 1530s, during his divorce proceedings against her. She is commemorated in the park by Catherine's Cross, set up on the site of the castle in 1774.

All year, daily.

BROMHAM MILL

Off A428, 2½ miles west of Bedford (Bc)

The mysteries of spur wheel, wallower, silk dresser and sack hoist are explained at this four-square water mill beside the River Great Ouse, restored by Bedfordshire County Council as a museum of milling history and a countryside exhibition centre. A mill has stood here since the Domesday Book, though the present building is far later, part brick-built around 1700, and part stone-built in 1858. The water meadow round it has been turned into a picnic area, where visitors may see dragonflies and kingfishers.

Apr-Oct, Wed, Thur, Sat, Sun and Bank Hol Mon pm. Adm charge. Shop. P *Toilets. Tel Bedford (0234) 228330.*

BUNYAN MEETING HOUSE AND MUSEUM

In centre of Bedford (Bc)

Though little is left of the Bedford that John Bunyan knew, his presence lives on in the streets of the town. A 9ft tall bronze figure of the great preacher and writer stands at the end of the High Street farthest from the River Great Ouse, and a plaque on a house in nearby St Cuthbert's Street marks the place where his cottage stood. Another plaque in the High Street pavement is on the site of the old Bedford County Gaol, demolished in 1801, where Bunyan was imprisoned in the 1660s and 1670s for his religious beliefs and wrote *The Pilgrim's Progress*.

Elsewhere in the town there are more links with Bunyan. A church in Mill Street, known as the Bunyan Meeting Free Church, stands on the site of the barn where he officiated as pastor after his release from prison. It has fine bronze doors illustrating scenes from *The Pilgrim's Progress*. The adjacent Bunyan Museum contains many relics of the author, including his metal violin and flute and some 170 translations of *The Pilgrim's Progress*, in languages ranging from Cambodian to Gaelic.

The Bedford Museum, housed in a converted

brewery in Castle Lane, has displays of Bedfordshire geology, archaeology and natural history, with exhibits of 19th-century rural life.
Bunyan Museum: Apr-Sept, Tues-Sat pm. Adm charge. Shop. Toilets. Tel Bedford (0234) 58075. Bedford Museum: All year, daily exc Mon, and Bank Hol. Free entry. Shop. P *Toilets.* ♿ *Tel (0234) 53323.*

DUNSTABLE DOWNS

On B4541, 2 miles south-west of Dunstable (Ba)

These gentle, rolling hills form the northern end of the Chilterns chalk escarpment, and from them there are wide views over the Vale of Aylesbury and beyond. Thousands of years ago they were a highway for prehistoric man, who trudged along the Icknield Way (now the B489) at their foot. Ancient rituals took place at the grassy barrows known as Five Knolls, on the outskirts of Dunstable, where a Bronze Age burial was excavated in 1928. On fine summer afternoons the shadows of today's gliders flicker over these relics of the past, soaring effortlessly upwards on the thermals.

Some 300 acres of downland are left untreated by chemical weedkillers or fertilisers. As a result, many rare plant species flourish, including fairy flax and chalk milkwort. Little muntjac deer browse among the scrub, and whinchats and grasshopper warblers dart over the hillside.

At Whipsnade Heath is the Tree Cathedral, a sun-dappled grove laid out to a plan of nave, transepts and chapels. It was planted in the 1930s by Edmund Kell Blyth, in memory of friends killed in the First World War.
NT (part). All year, daily.

ELSTOW MOOT HALL

Off A5134, 1½ miles south of Bedford (Bc)

Brick-filled between its sturdy timbers, this fine late 15th-century building is closely linked with John Bunyan, who was born in the village of Elstow in 1628. The hall was built in about 1500, in connection with the famous May Fair at Elstow, held by the nuns of Elstow Abbey, and was used both for storing goods for the fair, and as a court (or 'moot') house. Bunyan may have had Elstow Fair in mind when he described the worldly 'Vanity Fair' in *The Pilgrim's Progress.*

After the abbey was dissolved at the Reformation, the Moot Hall (or Green House, as it was called, from its position on the village green) continued as a local court house; and in the 19th century the upper floor was used for worship and as a village school. After a period of neglect, the Moot Hall was restored in 1951. The upper floor has been opened up to display the superb medieval roof, with massive beams and graceful uprights.
Apr-Oct, Tues-Sun and Bank Hol Mon, pm. Adm charge. Shop. P *(limited). Toilets. Tel Bedford (0234) 228330.*

HARROLD-ODELL COUNTRY PARK

Off A6, 10 miles north-west of Bedford (Bd)

More than 140 acres of water meadows and disused gravel pits beside the River Great Ouse have been turned into a varied country park, which gets its name from two nearby villages. At least half of it is water, which attracts birds ranging from kingfishers to Canada geese. Among the mammals are the shy muntjac or barking deer, while wild mink, which have escaped from farms on the east coast, are a menace to the fish and smaller mammals. The small nature sanctuary is the haunt of goldfinches, feeding on the seeds of teasels which grow abundantly there.
Apr-Oct, daily exc Mon, and Bank Hol; Nov-Mar, Sat and Sun pm. Free entry. P *Toilets.* ♿ *Tel Bedford (0234) 228330.*

LEIGHTON BUZZARD NARROW-GAUGE RAILWAY

On A4146, ½ mile south-east of town centre (Bb)

An average speed of 5½mph may not seem much by modern Intercity standards, but it is quite enough for the locomotives of the Leighton Buzzard Railway. This 2ft gauge line, built in 1919 to carry sand from the quarries north of the town to the main London and North Western Railway, runs for 2¾ miles through modern housing estates and open countryside. Due to be scrapped at the end of the 1960s, it was saved by a band of enthusiasts who have acquired steam and diesel engines from as far away as India and the Cameroons, constructed rolling stock, and built an engine shed for maintenance.
Easter-Oct, Sun and Bank Hol. Adm charge. Refreshments. Shop. P ♿ *Tel Leighton Buzzard (0525) 373888.*

THE LODGE, SANDY

Off B1042 1½ miles south-east of Sandy (Cc)

More than 140 species of bird have been recorded round The Lodge – not surprising perhaps, since this Victorian mansion has been the headquarters of the Royal Society for the Protection of Birds since 1961. The 104 acres of heathland round The Lodge are run as a nature reserve, with the encouragement of bird life as the main object. In most years some 45 species breed there, among them the three varieties of native woodpecker (green, great spotted and lesser spotted), nuthatches and tree pipits. Visitors who follow the waymarked nature trails beyond the formal gardens may spot a fascinating range of other types of wildlife, from foxes to natterjack toads.
RSPB. All year, daily. Refreshments. Shop. P *(limited). Toilets.* ♿ *Tel Sandy (0767) 80551.*

FAMILY HOME *Simple wooden furniture and household possessions of John Bunyan's day make up this replica of a 17th-century Bedfordshire living room. It is on show in the Moot Hall in Bunyan's birthplace, Elstow.*

LUTON HOO

Off B653, 1 mile south of Luton (Ca)

Though Luton's housing estates are just to the north, the M1 to the west and the railway to the east, Luton Hoo's 1200 acre Capability Brown park manages to keep an atmosphere of rural remoteness. At its heart is the large stone mansion, whose plain exterior hides a glittering treasure house within. The house was begun in

TSAR'S BOX *Among the treasures displayed at Luton Hoo (below) is a gold and enamel cigarette box (right) made by the Russian goldsmith Fabergé for Tsar Nicholas II.*

1767 by Robert Adam for Lord Bute, Prime Minister under George III, but his designs were never completed, and the house suffered a disastrous fire in 1843.

It owes its present appearance, both inside and out, to Sir Julius Wernher, a diamond tycoon who made a fortune in South Africa. He bought it in 1903 and filled it with medieval carved ivories, Limoges enamels, Renaissance jewels, and French furniture, porcelain and tapestries. His son, Sir Harold Wernher, added to the collection, but was equally interested in horseracing. A room is devoted to the Wernher family's bloodstock successes. Sir Harold's wife, Lady Zia Wernher, was the daughter of a Russian Grand Duke and added Russian items to the collection, including delicate flower sprays made of gold and jewels by Fabergé, the jeweller to the Russian royal family.

Mid Apr-mid Oct, daily exc Mon but open Bank Hol. Adm charge. Refreshments. Shop. P *Toilets.* ♿ *Tel Luton (0582) 22955.*

LUTON MUSEUM AND ART GALLERY

On A6, north of Luton town centre (Ca)

Buckinghamshire Point Ground and Bedfordshire Maltese are not small dogs, as some might guess, but the two main types of lace made in Bedfordshire in the 19th century. A number of the displays in Luton's fine museum, housed in a Victorian mansion set in a 40 acre park, are devoted to such local crafts, which included hat-making. The museum is unusual in being registered as a goldsmith, and it produces replicas of some of its items in conjunction with local craftsmen.

All year, daily exc Sun am. Free entry. Shop. P *(limited). Toilets.* ♿ *Tel Luton (0582) 36941.*

MAULDEN WOOD FOREST TRAILS

Off A6, 8 miles north of Luton (Bc)

Observant walkers following the waymarked trails in this 460 acre Forestry Commission wood may spot pine cones torn open by crossbills in search of the seeds inside, or the sharp print of a grey squirrel's foot at the edge of a pond. The northern half of Maulden Wood is boulder clay, ideal for oak, ash and other broadleaved trees, while the southern section is on Lower Greensand, which produces a lighter soil suitable for conifers. Uncommon birds sometimes to be seen include tawny owls in the northern part and goldcrests in the southern part.

FC. All year, daily.

PRIORY COUNTRY PARK

Off A428, just east of Bedford (Cc)

Set within a sweeping curve of the River Great Ouse, the park's 200 acres of woods, grass and water provide a marvellous open-air 'lung' only 1½ miles from the centre of Bedford. An 80 acre lake attracts winter migrants from Russia and Scandinavia, as well as providing a breeding ground for mallard and other native birds. Visiting birds include great grey shrikes and little egrets. There are fishing and sailing, and a visitor centre with displays illustrating the site.

All year, daily.

TRAVEL VETERANS *Two of the prized exhibits at The Shuttleworth Collection are this early car, a 1903 de Dietrich, behind which stands a 1933 Avro Tutor, used as a training plane by the RAF.*

SHARPENHOE CLAPPERS

Off A6, 6 miles north of Luton (Bb)

The men of the Iron Age saw the strategic value of this northern outpost of the Chilterns and built a hill-fort here, dominating the flat Midlands plain below. Rising to 525ft, Sharpenhoe Clappers is crowned by the beech trees of Clappers Wood, where paths wind along the ridge. In summer, the open ground where the trees thin out is covered with chalkland flowers, among them the rock-rose, musk thistle and yellow-flowered tansy.

NT. All year, daily.

THE SHUTTLEWORTH COLLECTION

Off A1, 3 miles west of Biggleswade (Cc)

On the last Sunday of every month, from April to September, the engine drone of Spitfire and Sopwith Pup, Gloster Gladiator and De Havilland Moth fills the air above Old Warden Aerodrome's grass runways. These are a few of the 30 historic aircraft of The Shuttleworth Collection, founded in the 1930s by Richard Ormonde Shuttleworth, a young racing driver and pilot who was killed while training with the RAF in 1940. He bought his first aircraft in 1932, and after the Second World War his mother set up a trust to continue his work. The oldest aircraft in the collection is a Blériot XI of 1909, similar to the machine that made the first crossing of the Channel. The collection also includes horse-drawn and motor-driven vehicles built between 1860 and 1954.

Next door to the aerodrome is the Old Warden Park estate, which formerly belonged to the Shuttleworth family. The building is now an agricultural college, but visitors can explore the attractive Swiss Garden, one of the finest examples in existence of the romantic gardening tastes of the 1820s. The garden gets its name from the rustic Swiss cottage which forms its centrepiece. With its superb specimen trees, its ornamental ponds and islands, and its grotto combined with a glass fernery, it gives a unique insight into our gardening past.

Shuttleworth Collection: All year, daily. Adm charge. Refreshments. Shops. P *Toilets.* ♿ *Tel Northill (076 727) 288. Swiss Garden: Apr-Oct, Wed, Thur, Sat, Sun and Bank Hol Mon pm. Adm charge. Shop. Toilets. Tel Bedford (0234) 228330.*

STAGSDEN BIRD GARDENS

Off A422, 4½ miles west of Bedford (Bc)

Visitors who might be hard put to it to tell a guan from a gallinule or a Chinese golden from a Himalayan monal pheasant will have their horizons widened at these attractive gardens, a major centre for the preservation and breeding of more than 150 species and varieties of birds. Apart from pheasants and waterfowl, which in summer wander among displays of shrub roses, Stagsden is preserving for posterity old breeds of domestic birds common in farmyards half a century ago.

All year, daily. Adm charge. Refreshments. Shop. P *Toilets.* ♿ *Tel Oakley (023 02) 2745.*

STEVINGTON WINDMILL

Off A428, 4 miles north-west of Bedford (Bd)

Until about 50 years ago, the cloth-covered sails of this mill – the only complete mill in Bedfordshire – whirled busily on a ridge above the River Ouse. Built around 1770, it is of post-mill type, in which the whole upper part of the mill revolves around a central post to turn the sails into the wind. It was restored in 1921 and again in 1951. Though still in working order, it is no longer operated.

All year, daily. Key from Royal George, Stevington. P *(limited). Tel Bedford (0234) 228330.*

DINTON PASTURES COUNTRY PARK

Off B3030, 4 miles east of Reading (Da)

An expanse of open countryside on the River Loddon, this peaceful country park is well laid out with picnic areas, nature trail and lakes. Visitors can fish along the riverbank or on White Swan Lake, while Black Swan Lake offers windsurfing, dinghy sailing and canoeing. The visitor centre occupies a converted Edwardian farmhouse, where equipment for water sports can be hired.

All year, daily. Free entry. Refreshments. Shop (weekends only). P *Toilets.* ♿ *Tel Twyford (0734) 342016.*

DONNINGTON CASTLE

Off B4494, 1 mile north of Newbury (Ba)

Standing atop its grassy mound with twin round-towers etched against the sky, Donnington Castle has the faintly implausible look of a Victorian folly. Yet this is an authentic ruin: the gatehouse, built in 1386, of a once much larger medieval house. In truth it was never quite a castle – more of a fortified manor.

Besides the solitary gatehouse, visitors can still admire the elaborate earthwork defences dug by the Royalists in 1644 to defend their stronghold against a large Parliamentarian army. Angled bastions radiate from the centre so that artillery, positioned in them, had a wide angle of fire. This helped the Royalist colonel Sir John Boys to hold out for two years. By the time he and his garrison eventually surrendered, on Charles I's orders, in 1646, Cromwell's cannons had razed most of the castle to the ground. Today the ruins of Donnington Castle overlook the village of Donnington, and there are fine views south.

At the tiny hamlet of Bagnor, $1\frac{1}{2}$ miles west, a mill built in 1839 has been converted into the attractive little Watermill Theatre. The theatre straddles the millstream, and visitors pass the 20ft cast-iron water wheel on their way into the tiny auditorium.

Castle: EH. All year, daily. Free entry. P *Tel London (01) 211 8828. Watermill Theatre: Summer season of plays. Tel Newbury (0635) 46044.*

ETON COLLEGE

In centre of Eton (Eb)

The Battle of Waterloo was won on the playing fields of Eton, according to the Duke of Wellington. No matter that he was unhappy there as a pupil, and left at the age of 15: Eton College remains world-renowned for its historic pedigree. The school has bequeathed 20 prime ministers to the nation – not to mention the Eton jacket and collar, the Eton crop and the *Eton Boating Song*. The 18th-century poet and scholar Thomas Gray was among innumerable literary Old Etonians, and his epigram on schooling, 'where ignorance is bliss'/ 'Tis folly to be wise', appears in his nostalgic *Ode on a Distant Prospect of Eton College*.

A museum of Eton Life traces the history of the college from its foundation by Henry VI in 1440. Some of the buildings seen by visitors date back to the same period, including the beautiful

REGAL FIGURE *The founder of Eton, Henry VI, stands in front of the school's Lupton's Tower, completed in 1520 by provost Roger Lupton. Names of former eminent Etonians carved on a desk panel at Upper School include the statesmen Walpole and Pitt (the Elder).*

Chapel, with exquisite 15th-century wall paintings inside. The Chapel was, in fact, conceived by Henry as no more than the choir in the much larger church which he envisaged, but the king was deposed before he could fulfil his ambitious plan for a cathedral-size building.

Other notable buildings were added in the 16th century, including the west range of the Cloisters and Lupton's Tower, completed in 1520 by Roger Lupton, provost of the time. This is a noble piece of brickwork which looks down to the cobbled school yard.

End Mar-early Oct, most days. Adm charge. Shop. Toilets. ♿ *Tel Windsor (0753) 863593.*

FINCHAMPSTEAD RIDGES

On B3348, 3½ miles south of Wokingham (Da)

An avenue of giant conifers lines the road to Finchampstead Ridges. The trees are Wellingtonias, redwoods from the Californian Sierra which owe their name to the Duke of Wellington, who lived at Stratfield Saye not far away. The wooded slopes of the ridges have 100-year-old Scots pines among the beeches and oaks, and from the bracken-clad heights are views over the valley of the River Blackwater.

NT. All year, daily.

INKPEN HILL

Off A338, 4 miles south of Hungerford (Aa)

A double gibbet looms from the 954ft summit of Inkpen Hill. The macabre landmark was originally erected in 1676, when the corpses of a child-murdering couple were suspended from its arms. Today the relic continues to confer its sinister aura on the hilltop, competing for chill effect with the winds which gust around the escarpment.

The views are tremendous, and a short walk along the ridge leads to Walbury Hill, at 974ft the highest upswell of chalk downland in England. The panorama takes in four counties, plunging northwards into the quilted woods and meadowlands of the green Kennet Valley, sweeping south to the Hampshire Downs and west to the Wiltshire Downs. Ancient man knew these commanding heights. Inkpen Hill's summit has a Neolithic long barrow, while the top of Walbury Hill is contoured with the rampart of an 82 acre hill-fort dating back to the Iron Age.

All year, daily.

MUSEUM OF ENGLISH RURAL LIFE

At Reading University (Ca)

Bygone Britain is well represented in Reading. The Museum of English Rural Life, founded in 1951, recalls the days when lives were lived closer to the rhythm of the seasons. Scythes and churns, farm wagons and ploughs, are just a few of the exhibits which help to evoke the rural past, and the photographic library contains over 500,000 prints and negatives. Particular emphasis is placed on the historic changes of about 1840, when the individually crafted products of rural workshops started to give way to factory-made goods. Vintage tractors help to illustrate the evolution of mechanised farming, and domestic life is evoked with farmhouse bakery and laundry equipment.

Down by the Thames, housed in a brick-built Victorian pumping station, Blake's Lock Museum recalls Reading's vanished waterway life, trades and industries. The museum includes reconstructions of local *(continued on page 24)*

WORKERS OF THE SOIL *A 19th-century poster for a seed-drill merchant sets the theme for a museum illustrating the farming methods of yesteryear. Some of the horse-drawn and hand-steered ploughs displayed were in use little more than 30 years ago.*

ROYAL TOWN BY THE THAMES

Seen from a distance, Windsor Castle seems to ride above the Thames like some immense and stately galleon. William the Conqueror originated it, and the great fortified residence covering 13 acres has been a home of British monarchs for almost 900 years; it was George IV who was responsible for much of what is seen today. The town of Windsor owes its existence to the famous castle, and its fascination to its proud royal heritage.

Windsor Castle Precincts *All year, daily exc Garter Day. (East Terrace closed when Queen in residence.) Free entry. Shop. Toilets. Tel Windsor (0753) 868286.*

St George's Chapel *Feb-Dec, daily exc Sun am. Adm charge. Tel (0753) 865538.*

Queen Mary's Doll's House; Exhibition of Drawings; Royal Mews *All year, daily exc Good Fri, Garter Day and Christmas period. Adm charges. Tel (0753) 868286.*

State Apartments *All year, daily exc when Queen in residence. Adm charge. Tel (0753) 868286.*

The Household Cavalry Museum *All year, Mon-Fri. Free entry. Toilets. Tel (0753) 868222.*

Royalty and Empire Exhibition *All year, daily. Adm charge. Shop.* P *Toilets.* ♿ *Tel (0753) 857837.*

Parish Church *All year, daily.*

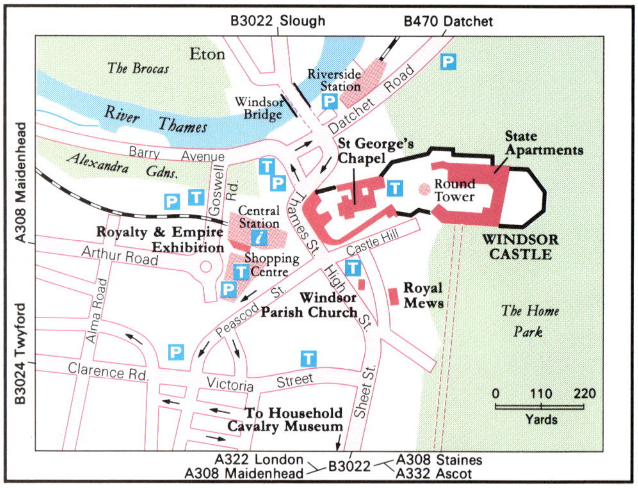

ST GEORGE'S CHAPEL

The banners of the Knights of the Garter hang over their helms in the choir of St George's Chapel, the chapel of the Order, which Edward III founded in 1348. Built between 1475 and 1528, the present chapel is a glorious example of late Gothic architecture, with soaring piers breaking into graceful fan vaulting. Ten monarchs are buried there.

STATE APARTMENTS

The magnificently furnished rooms on the precipitous north flank of Windsor Castle are still used on official occasions. The Queen's Presence Room remains as decorated in 1675-83 for Charles II, who employed the Neapolitan painter Antonio Verrio for the superb ceiling. Its figures seem to spill onto the panelled walls, which are adorned by fine Gobelins tapestries and royal portraits in a flood of colour.

The outsize suit of gleaming armour overlooking the Grand Staircase was made in 1540 for the portly Henry VIII.

WINDSOR CASTLE PRECINCTS

Three wards, or enclosures, make up Windsor Castle. The Round Tower in the Middle Ward was built in the 12th century by Henry II to replace the Norman fortress of wood; George IV added its upper half in 1828-32. The Lower Ward contains St George's Chapel, and the Upper Ward has the State Apartments.

THE HOUSEHOLD CAVALRY MUSEUM

Colourful uniforms of the Blues and Royals are on view at the Household Cavalry Museum in Combermere Barracks, on the B3022. Exhibits cover the history of the Regiments of Household Cavalry – bodyguards and escorts of the sovereign – from their beginnings in Charles II's reign through to the age of armoured and motorised transport.

QUEEN MARY'S DOLL'S HOUSE

Displayed near the State Apartments, the doll's house was built in 1921-4 to designs by Sir Edwin Lutyens at a scale of one-twelfth life size, so its occupants are about 6in tall. Miniature paintings grace its walls, and the little books in the library were written in by Rudyard Kipling, G.K. Chesterton and others. Drawings from the castle's superb collection are on view nearby.

THE ROYAL MEWS

The elegant Scottish State Coach of 1830 holds pride of place in the Royal Mews Exhibition in St Albans Street. Burford House beside it was built for Nell Gwyn in the 1670s and now displays gifts presented to the royal family.

ROYALTY AND EMPIRE EXHIBITION

Queen Victoria and her daughter the Empress Frederick of Germany, followed by the Empress's daughter-in-law and son, board their landau for the drive to Windsor Castle. The year is 1897, and the foreign guests have come to celebrate the Queen's Diamond Jubilee. The life-size tableau – with a guard of honour more than 70 strong – is in the exhibition mounted by Mme Tussaud's of London in the restored Eton and Windsor Central Station, which was specially built for the Jubilee. The royal train in which the visitors have arrived, drawn by a locomotive gleaming with brass, stands in the station. 'Stars' of the exhibition include computer-controlled models of the Queen, Florence Nightingale, Charles Dickens and other celebrities moving and speaking in a spectacular display designed to recall 'Sixty Glorious Years'.

Royal connections are strong in Windsor's parish church, just along the High Street from the castle. It contains the 15ft by 14ft painting *The Last Supper* by Francis Clein, James I's court painter, which once formed the reredos in St George's Chapel. The church was begun in 1820, on the site of an earlier church, and its building was supervised by Jeffry Wyatt, who later, as Sir Jeffry Wyatville, designed the castle's Waterloo Chamber for George IV. The chancel is embellished with mosaics by Salviati, who also decorated the ceiling of the Albert Memorial Chapel in the castle.

(continued from page 21) shops as they were around 1900, and there is a model railway.

Reading Museum and Art Gallery takes visitors into a more distant past. The prime exhibits here are antiquities from the great Roman site of Silchester, south of Reading. They include the bronze eagle which inspired *Eagle of the Ninth*, the novel by Rosemary Sutcliffe.

Museum of English Rural Life: All year, Tues-Sat. Adm charge. Shop. P *Toilets.* ♿ *Tel Reading (0734) 875123. Blake's Lock Museum: All year, daily exc Mon and Tues. Free entry. Shop.* P *(limited). Toilets.* ♿ *Tel Reading (0734) 55911. Reading Museum: All year, daily exc Sun and Bank Hol. Free entry. Shop. Tel Reading (0734) 55911.*

NEWBURY DISTRICT MUSEUM

In the Wharf, off Newbury Market Place (Ba)

In centuries past the Berkshire Downs were great sheep hills, and Newbury was a thriving cloth town. The district museum is situated in the town's beautiful Jacobean Cloth Hall and extends into a picturesque 18th-century Granary. The varied displays include material connected with the history of local weaving. There are also items related to the making of the Newbury Coat of 1811: a garment converted from raw wool on a sheep's back to a coat worn by Sir John Throckmorton in 13 hours and 20 minutes.

Among other displays are fossils, archaeological exhibits, costumes, pewter, pottery and jewellery. Vintage cameras, hot-air ballooning and the story of the Kennet and Avon Canal provide further themes for displays. Visitors can admire the old town stocks, and there is an audiovisual show dramatising events of the Civil War at Newbury.

Apr-Sept, daily exc Wed; Oct-Mar, daily exc Wed and Sun. Free entry. Shop. P *(limited).* ♿ *Tel Newbury (0635) 30511.*

REME MUSEUM, ARBORFIELD

Off A327, 5 miles south of Reading (Da)

Life-size tableaux and large model dioramas are used at Arborfield to show the history and many-sided work of the Royal Electrical and Mechanical Engineers. From them the visitor learns how the corps sprang out of the rapid growth of military technology from the outset of the Second World War; this meant that a single, unified body of soldier engineers and technicians was required to maintain equipment.

REME was set up in October 1942 and made responsible for equipment ranging from radar systems to tanks, lorries and guns. Today the Corps continues its role, but now repairs army aircraft and seagoing ships, electronic equipment, vehicles, weapons, railway locomotives, medical equipment and so on. This is all reflected in the museum, which also contains displays on REME activities worldwide.

All year, Mon-Fri. Free entry. Shop. P *(limited). Toilets.* ♿ *Tel Twyford (0734) 760421.*

SNELSMORE COMMON COUNTRY PARK

Off B4494, 3 miles north of Newbury (Ba)

Open heathland covering 146 acres offers attractions for walker, picnicker and naturalist alike. Pale-stemmed birches, heather, gorse and bracken all entangle the slopes, providing cover for foxes, lizards and adders. Butterflies abound in season and bird life, too, is plentiful. Grasshopper warblers are among the summer guests and on evenings in June, visiting nightjars can be heard churring from the trees at the common's edge. Among the permanent residents are woodcocks, and at dusk during spring and early summer visitors may see male birds defending their territory in 'roding' flight: they fly in circuits with bill pointing downwards uttering a shrill 'tsiwick' followed by a guttural croaking.

A belt of mature, deciduous woodland known as Withy Copse marks the west side of the common. To the east is a valley bog offering its seductions to enthusiasts for peaty wetlands. Cotton grass, bog asphodel and heath spotted orchids here set the scene, and here too visitors may recognise the spoon-leaved, white-flowering sundew. This is a carnivore among plants. It makes up for mineral deficiencies in the soil by trapping and digesting insects in secretions from its furred leaf blades.

A nature trail allows visitors to observe all aspects of the park's wildlife.

All year, daily. Free entry. P *Toilets.* ♿

STANLEY SPENCER GALLERY

In centre of Cookham (Db)

Perhaps no painter ever had a more intense affection for his birthplace than Sir Stanley Spencer (1891-1959). Born in a semi-detached villa called 'Fernlea' in Cookham's High Street, the artist developed a passionate, lifelong devotion to the Thameside village of his childhood. At the Slade Art School in London he was referred to as 'Cookham' by his fellow students. The Stanley Spencer Gallery, devoted exclusively to the artist's works, is housed in a former Wesleyan chapel to which he was taken as a child by his mother. It contains both naturalistic landscapes and portraits (done chiefly to earn a living) and some of the more imaginative pieces for which Spencer is especially remembered.

Whatever the theme, Cookham itself almost always provided the setting for Spencer's paintings.

He saw the village as a place of 'heavenly visitations', and throughout his life it remained central to his art. Cookham High Street, the parish church, the River Thames and its flanking meadows are all recognisable in Spencer's work.

Pride of place in the gallery is held by the immense, unfinished *Christ Preaching at Cookham Regatta*. There are, in addition, many relics of the artist including his spectacles, easel, palettes, brushes, sunshade and folding chair – and even the baby's push-chair in which the artist used to convey his equipment when out on painting expeditions.

A fine copy of Spencer's celebrated painting of *The Last Supper* now hangs in Cookham's Church of the Holy Trinity.

Easter-Oct, daily; Nov-Easter, Sat, Sun and Bank Hol. Adm charge. Shop. P *(limited). Toilets.* ♿ *Tel Bourne End (062 85) 20043.*

SWALLOWFIELD PARK

Off B3349, 6 miles south-east of Reading (Ca)

The house was built in 1690 for the 2nd Earl of Clarendon but much remodelled in the 18th century, when the red-brick stables were added. Notable features include a charming little oval vestibule, restored to its original appearance and containing the arms of the Clarendon family. The original doorway, elegantly designed by architect William Talman, was removed during later alterations and now serves as a feature of the walled garden.

The beautifully landscaped garden covers 4 acres. It contains a variety of flowering shrubs

AIRBORNE ANTICS *Water explodes from the Seaworld Pool at Windsor Safari Park as a killer whale lifts its mighty tonnage into the air, before flopping back in the same easy movement.*

COOKHAM CHRIST
A basket-chair in an old horse ferry barge by Cookham Bridge is the pulpit for Christ Preaching at Cookham Regatta, *in the Stanley Spencer gallery. The artist (right) was still working on the canvas at the time of his death.*

and roses, as well as many fine specimen trees, including cedars. Among the other features are an ancient yew-tree walk, a small lake, and banks of massed rhododendrons in season.
May Sept, Wed and Thur pm. Adm charge. P ♿ *Tel Reading (0734) 883815.*

WINDSOR GREAT PARK

Off A332, south of Windsor (Eb)

Sprawling for 4800 acres south of Windsor Castle, Windsor Great Park is the remnant of a much vaster royal hunting forest which once covered much of southern Berkshire. Nevertheless, the park remains large enough to satisfy the most energetic visitor, with marvellous walking and some fine views which include the vista up the famous Long Walk – a 3 mile avenue leading from a statue of George III on horseback, known as the Copper Horse, to the walls of the castle.

The Long Walk was originally lined by elms planted by Charles II in 1685, but in 1945 the trees were stricken with disease and were replaced by London planes and chestnuts. In the forest and park, many ancient oaks still flourish, together with pines, cedars and beeches. Among the outstanding specimens are the King's Oak, the largest tree in the park, and the Four Queens – made up of three oaks and a beech.

The park, at its south-east corner, stretches into Surrey, where two beautiful gardens – Savill Garden and Valley Gardens – spill to the shores of Virginia Water. This fine sheet of water had an unlikely creator. It was the work of William, Duke of Cumberland, an early Ranger of Windsor Great Park – but better known as 'Butcher' Cumberland for his slaughter of the Jacobites after the Battle of Culloden in 1746.
All year, daily. Adm charge for Savill Garden only. Refreshments. Shop (Savill Garden). P *Toilets.* ♿ *Tel Windsor (0753) 860222.*

WINDSOR SAFARI PARK

On B3022, 2 miles south-west of Windsor (Eb)

A 1 mile motor route through Windsor Safari Park takes visitors through reserves of giraffes, zebras, camels, baboons, lions, tigers, elephants, wolves and bears. To drive among so many of the world's larger predators is an astonishing experience; nevertheless, even the creatures with the fiercest reputations present no problems for the properly cautious motorist. Baboons are the true offenders: they are fantastically inquisitive, and woe betide any motorist with raised aerial or a faulty petrol cap who loiters too long in their enclosure.

The Safari Park's setting is immensely attractive, with long views from its steep green slopes. Besides the drive-through circuit there is a forest where visitors can mingle on foot with deer, and in the children's zoo youngsters can pet and feed the nuzzling goats and other farmyard animals. Among displays, the park's grand setpieces are the famous killer-whale, sea-lion and dolphin shows held in the open-air Seaworld complex. Aficionados of falconry will enjoy the flying displays by birds of prey, while macaws – the exotic comedians of the Parrot House – put on a colourful indoor show which includes displays of roller-skating, charioteering and high-wire bicycle riding.

Recent additions include a chimpanzee enclosure and a walk-through Tropical Plant and Butterfly House where alligators lurk, log-still, in the artificial pools. For any youngster who may tire of the animal fare there are plentiful amusements including the African Tiki Show, a musical entertainment with animated jungle figures, mounted in a small theatre.

The white turrets and battlements that command the high ground at Windsor Safari Park belong to St Leonard's Mansion. The building was put up in the 1930s by an American motorcar manufacturer, and its hilltop castellations seem almost to pay tribute to those of the gigantic royal castle not far away.
All year, daily. Adm charge. Refreshments. Shop. P *Toilets.* ♿ *Tel Windsor (0753) 869841.*

COUNTY CALENDAR

April (2nd Tues after Easter). Hungerford: Hocktide Ceremony ('Tutti Day'), commemorating gift of fishing and grazing rights to town by John of Gaunt in 1364.

May (mid-month). Newbury: Spring Festival. Reading: Arts Festival. Windsor: Royal Windsor Horse Show.

June (mid-month). Windsor Castle: Garter Service.

June (3rd week). Ascot: Royal Ascot Meeting.

July (mid-month). Windsor: Royal Windsor Rose Show.

August (mid-month). Ascot: World Carriage Driving Championships.

Tourist information: Windsor (0753) 852010; Reading (0734) 592388; Newbury (0635) 30267.

BUCKINGHAMSHIRE

MANSIONS AND POETS' HOMES AMONG LEAFY HILLS AND VALES

If counties were colour-coded, Buckinghamshire might be designated green and gold for the seasonally changing beechwoods that clothe the Chiltern Hills. The county's leafy seclusion lies close to London and has long been favoured by wealthy commuters. The Rothschild family of financiers made no fewer than three homes there – at Ascott, Mentmore and Waddesdon.

Many other famous names are associated with the county. The Temples lived at Stowe and the Russells at Chenies. The prime minister Disraeli chose Hughenden as his home, and Sir Francis Dashwood, founder of the notorious Hell Fire Club, owned West Wycombe. The Chiltern beechwoods are seen in their greatest glory at Burnham Beeches, and the thriving furniture industry based on their timber is the theme of Wycombe Chair Museum.

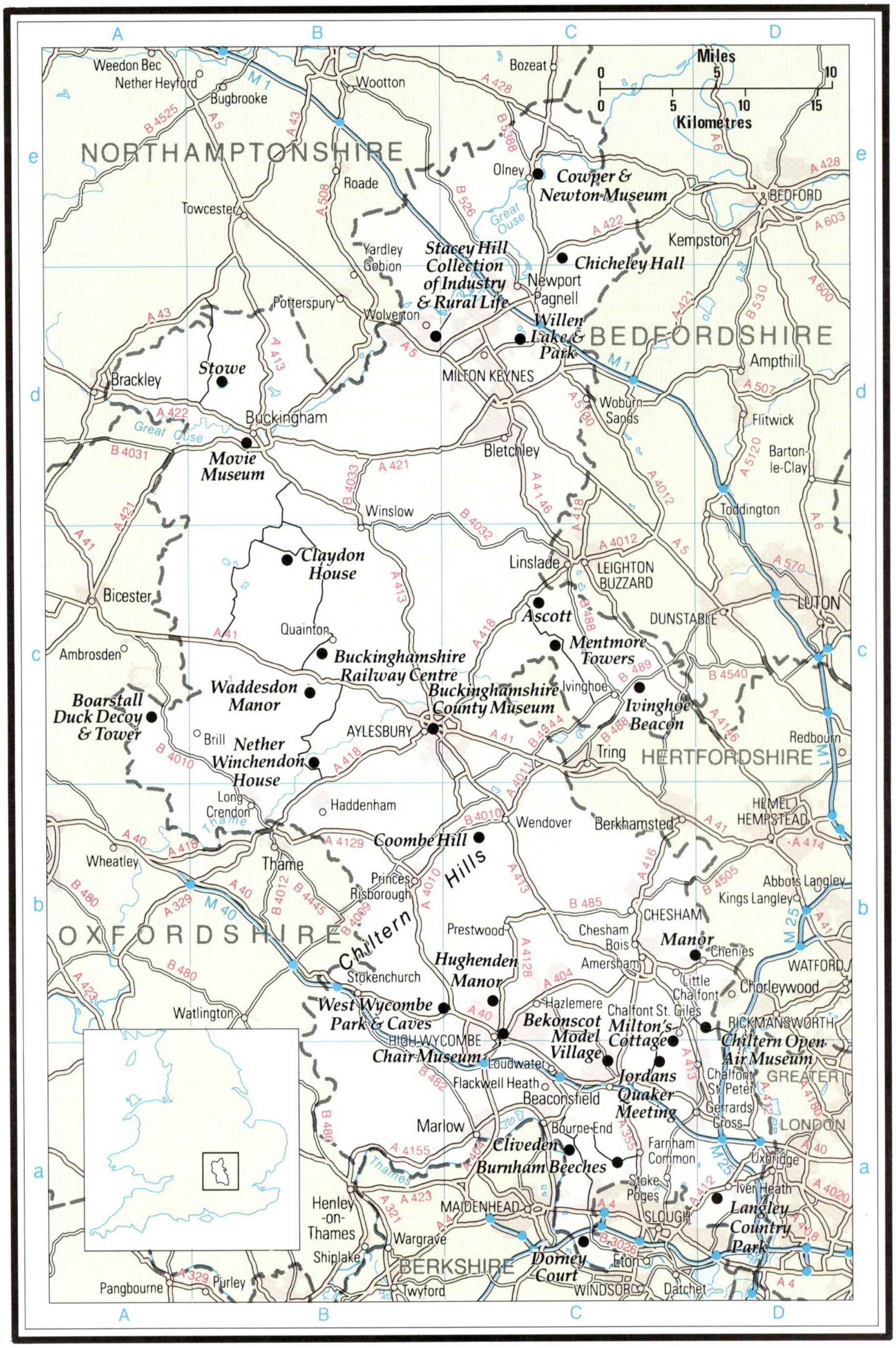

ASCOTT

Off A418, 2½ miles south-west of Leighton Buzzard (Cc)

The house is a largely 19th-century construction of mock Tudor half-timbering, but it contains an outstanding art collection assembled by Leopold de Rothschild and his son Anthony. Dutch painters of the 17th century are especially well represented, and there are many fine English and Italian paintings as well as Persian carpets and magnificent examples of Chinese Ming porcelain.

The 30 acre gardens include a lily pond, sunken garden and, on the grassy terraces, an immense topiary sundial sculpted from golden box and yew. There are sweeping views over the Vale of Aylesbury.

Late July-late Sept, Tues-Sun and Aug Bank Hol pm; Garden only: April-mid July, Thur and last Sun in month pm. Adm charge. ♿ (part). Tel Aylesbury (0296) 688242.

BEKONSCOT MODEL VILLAGE

Off A355, in Beaconsfield (Ca)

This is the oldest model village in the world; one of Britain's more eccentric 'firsts'. Bekonscot was the brainchild of Roland Callingham, a London accountant whose passion for model-making led him to build a miniature wonderland in the field opposite his home in the 1920s. The name is a merger of Beaconsfield, where Callingham lived, and Ascot, his former home in Berkshire.

The village was first opened to the public in 1929. The young Princess Elizabeth was brought there many times, and today Bekonscot remains a delightful period piece which recalls a bygone Britain. The miniature blacksmith is still at his forge; the golfers wear plus fours, and the local cinema première is Disney's *Snow White*, made in 1937.

The village has expanded over the years, and today covers 1½ acres with its lakes, zoo, airport, coal mine and racecourse. There are many working models, and Bekonscot's proudest exhibit is its model railway. Twenty-two locomotives run on 500yds of gauge-1 track, and each engine covers well over 300 miles during the summer season. The greenery serving as backdrop for the houses is made up chiefly of some 8000 dwarf conifers.

Mar-Oct, daily. Adm charge. Refreshments. Shop. P Toilets. ♿ (part). Tel Beaconsfield (049 46) 2919.

BOARSTALL DUCK DECOY AND TOWER

Off B4011, 10 miles west of Aylesbury (Ac)

A decoy in its original sense was an enclosed place – often a pond – into which wildfowl were lured for capture. At Boarstall the National Trust maintains an 18th-century specimen in working order. There is an exhibition hall, and the decoy is situated in 13 acres of natural woodland where a nature trail has been laid out. Boarstall Tower, in the same village, is the 14th-century moated stone gatehouse of a now-vanished fortified house.

Across the B4011, at the hilltop village of Brill, stands one of the oldest post mills in the country. A post mill is a windmill whose whole body revolves around a central post to face the wind (rather than just the top), and all the early windmills were of this type. Brill's mill dates from 1689, was worked until 1916 and has been fully restored. It stands on an exposed site 603ft above sea level, commanding splendid views into Oxfordshire.

Duck decoy: NT. Good Fri-Aug Bank Hol, Wed pm and Sat, Sun and Bank Hol Mon. Adm charge. Toilets. ♿ Tel Brill (0844) 237488. Tower: NT. May-Sept, Wed pm by written appt. Adm charge. Brill Windmill: Apr-Sept, Sun pm. Adm charge. 🅿 (limited). Tel (0844) 237659.

BUCKINGHAM MOVIE MUSEUM

In Buckingham town centre (Bd)

The town of Buckingham is twinned with Joinville, the home of Pathé of France. Charles Pathé was the great pioneer of home-movie making, producing safe apparatus from 1912, so it is appropriate that Buckingham should house a museum devoted to home cinema. The exhibits include many vintage cinecameras, projectors and accessories including such historic items as the pathfinding *Pathé Baby* cinecamera of 1922, and the English *Midas* of 1934 – the first cinecamera with a battery-run motor. The museum contains a private cinema where old films are shown and equipment is demonstrated.

All year, Wed-Sun and Bank Hol Mon. Adm charge. Shop. 🅿 (town centre). Toilets. Tel Buckingham (0280) 816758.

BUCKINGHAMSHIRE COUNTY MUSEUM

In Aylesbury town centre (Bc)

Aylesbury, not Buckingham, has been the county town of Buckinghamshire since 1725, and the county museum occupies two buildings on Church Street: a grammar school of 1720 and the 18th-century house next door. Inside, displays cover the history, archaeology, geology and wildlife of the county. Exhibits range from Bronze Age weapons to modern studio pottery. Old costumes are well represented, and there is a gallery of rural life. The Aylesbury Gallery, opened in 1985, shows aspects of past life in the town.

All year, Mon-Sat. Free entry. Shop. Tel Aylesbury (0296) 82158.

BUCKINGHAMSHIRE RAILWAY CENTRE

Off A41, 5 miles west of Aylesbury (Bc)

A mile outside the prettily thatched village of Quainton is one of Britain's largest private railway collections. The Buckinghamshire Railway Centre is situated at Quainton Road Station – once a thriving railway junction where the Great Central and Metropolitan lines met. The station closed to passengers in 1963.

The station has been restored to recall its appearance in Victorian times, and its exhibits range from the gigantic *King Edward I*, a main-line express of the Great Western Railway, to the little *1900*, Britain's smallest standard-gauge locomotive. Visitors can ride in a steam-hauled vintage train, and on certain Sundays can take tea in a dining car of 1901 which once formed part of the Royal train. There are workshops in which restoration work by volunteers of the Quainton Railway Society can be seen in progress. A museum offers glimpses of local railway life during the station's heyday.

End Mar-end Oct, Sat and Sun; also Wed in June-Aug, and Bank Hol Mon. Adm charge. Refreshments. Shop. 🅿 Toilets. ♿ Tel Quainton (029 675) 450.

BURNHAM BEECHES

Off A355, at Farnham Common (Ca)

Buckinghamshire is a beechwood county, and these native trees have cloaked the chalk slopes of the Chilterns since time immemorial. They remain distinctive features of the landscape today, and are seen in their greatest majesty at Burnham Beeches.

The area covers some 600 acres of woodland and common which the City of London had the foresight to buy in 1879 and continues to maintain as an area of recreation. Six miles of forest drives have been laid out, and there are many footpaths and bridleways. East Burnham Common makes a good starting point for exploration, and information boards with maps, displayed at the main intersections, make route-planning easy.

Ancient pollards – misshapen beeches often 300 years old – loom like splendid gargoyles in the cathedral grandeur of the woods. The pollards were produced by repeatedly lopping trunks somewhat above head-height to yield clusters of straight young poles. By no means all the trees are beeches: holly and rhododendron lend evergreen tones, and there are oaks too. But the beeches are everywhere, giving Burnham's woods a chameleon character. In spring, as the pale green leaves start to break, the glades have an emerald brightness. In summer they darken under a heavy canopy, and in late autumn the whole leafy covering turns gold. And then, in winter, when the vast freight of foliage is shed, the carpet of leaf litter continues to colour the woods with russet.

Squirrels and jays are among the creatures which feed eagerly on beech mast – the fallen triangular brown nuts of the beech tree. There are deer, too, in the woods: the tracks of muntjac often appear in the soft mud by woodland streams and ponds.

All year, daily. Free entry. Refreshments. 🅿 Toilets. ♿

CHENIES MANOR

Off A404, in Chenies (Db)

This brick-built manor was owned by the Russell family from the 16th century until 1955. Earls and Dukes of Bedford, the Russells rose under the patronage of Henry VIII and in 1526, when John Russell acquired the estate through marriage to a rich widow, he built a whole wing at Chenies to accommodate the monarch and his court. There is a notable 16th-century staircase, and the house makes an imposing backdrop for the gardens, noted for their old-world flowers and species roses.

Apr-Oct, Wed and Thur pm. Adm charge. Refreshments. Shop. 🅿 Toilets. ♿ (gardens). Tel Little Chalfont (024 04) 2888.

BEECH BOWER *Shafts of sunshine strike through the thick canopy of foliage at Burnham Beeches. In the 19th century, the woods were the source of timber for the county's thriving furniture industry.*

CHICHELEY HALL

Off A422, 2 miles east of Newport Pagnell (Ce)

The façade is grand English Baroque: tapering pilasters and a florid carved frieze are set against the Georgian brickwork, while the doorway is topped by a dramatic fan-shaped gable. Inside, though, Chicheley's scale is human and the tone more restrained. The entrance hall, in particular, is classically serene, with a cool arcade of marble columns opening onto the staircase.

Chicheley Hall was built in 1719-23 for Sir John Chester, and the main rooms contain many good examples of 18th-century craftsmanship in plaster and panelled oak. Sir John's library is ingenious: the panels are hinged, swinging open to reveal the bookshelves hidden behind.

The present owners descend from Admiral Beatty, whose son bought Chicheley in 1952. There is a collection of memorabilia associated with the admiral, including portraits, naval pictures, and the flag taken from HMS *Lion* after the 1916 Battle of Jutland, in which Beatty commanded the Grand Fleet's battle-cruiser squadron.

Easter-Sept, Sun and Bank Hol pm. Adm charge. Refreshments. Shop. P *Toilets.* ♿ *(ground floor). Tel North Crawley (023 065) 252.*

CHILTERN OPEN-AIR MUSEUM

Off A413, 2 miles north of Chalfont St Peter (Db)

The collection laid out on a north-facing slope of the chalk hills displays buildings which reflect centuries of life in the Chiltern area. Some have been built up from scratch, like the Iron Age and Saxon dwellings reconstructed by enthusiasts according to archaeological evidence from Chiltern sites. Most, though, are rescued buildings of historical interest from elsewhere: they have been dismantled, transported and re-erected at the open-air museum. These buildings include a 19th-century smith's forge from near Watford. One of the most ambitious current projects is the re-erection of Elliott's Furniture Factory, a Victorian building from the centre of High Wycombe.

The buildings are set among 45 acres of parkland where a nature trail winds through open grassland, mixed woodland and hawthorn scrub. Cowslips bloom on the open ground in spring, and in summer butterflies abound. The walk leads beneath the boughs of a splendid horse chestnut tree whose arched branches, tugged and smothered by twining stems of wild clematis, form a jungly tunnel of shade.

Apr-Sept, Sun, Bank Hol Mon and Wed pm; also Thur and Fri in August. Adm charge. Refreshments. Shop. P *Toilets. Tel Chalfont St Giles (024 07) 71117.*

CLAYDON HOUSE

Off A413, 13 miles north-west of Aylesbury (Bc)

The house has no front entrance: visitors enter by a side door in the north wall. For although Claydon has been the home of the Verney family since 1620, the original building was rebuilt in monumental style – then largely demolished – in the 18th century. What survives today is only the west wing, classically correct in its outward appearance, but missing a formal entrance – and giving no external hint of the rococo extravagance within.

Rococo is a light and elegant decorative style characterised by profusions of S-shaped curves. Claydon's North Hall, for example, has extraordinary doorcases, chimneypiece and wall niches adorned with curling leaves and fabulous birds. The ironwork balustrade of the staircase is miraculous in its delicacy, with gilded husks and ears of corn. But the most fantastic creation is the Chinese Room where rococo blends in with 18th-century chinoiserie. Black lacquer and bamboo furniture is disposed around, and the centrepiece is an astonishing pagoda-like alcove, with tiny bells hanging from the roof, which encloses a divan of Chinese yellow silk.

MEDIEVAL TRANSPLANT *The cruck-framed barn from Arborfield near Reading in Berkshire was re-erected at the Chiltern Open-Air Museum in 1980. It dates from about 1500, and has wall panels of woven oak laths and a wheat thatched roof.*

Florence Nightingale lived at Claydon for some years with her sister, and her bedroom survives, furnished in Victorian style. The Museum Room includes relics of her Crimean mission.

NT. Apr-end Oct, Sat-Wed and Bank Hol Mon pm. Adm charge. Refreshments. P *Toilets.* ♿ *(ground floor and garden). Tel Steeple Claydon (029 673) 349.*

CLIVEDEN

Off 4094, 3 miles north of Maidenhead (Ca)

Breathtaking views over the wooded reaches of the Thames are Cliveden's supreme attraction. The first great house to command the scene was built there in 1660 for the 2nd Duke of Buckingham, and the present Italianate building dates from 1851. It was designed by the architect Charles Barry for the 2nd Duke of Sutherland, and later sold to the millionaire Astor family. The house is now leased as a hotel, but the magnificent grounds are open to the public, and parts of the house can be visited on certain days.

The high terrace on the south front drops to a vast formal lawn beyond which the curving Thames glistens amid woods plunging steeply at its banks. The diarist John Evelyn, who came here in 1679, wrote of a 'circular view to the uttermost verge of the Horison, which with the serpenting of the Thames is admirably surprising'. More admirable surprises are to be had elsewhere in the grounds: the most famous vantage point is an aged oak tree known as Canning's Oak after the Georgian statesman who often loitered under its boughs. The Thames here is theatrically framed by foliage; Garibaldi, visiting the house in 1864, likened the vista to 'some of the mightiest river prospects of South America'.

Other features include temple, pavilion and water garden. William Waldorf (later 1st Viscount) Astor had a keen interest in statuary, and installed the Roman sarcophagi, and the Greek and Italian sculptures which adorn the grounds.

NT. Grounds: Mar-Dec, daily. House: Apr-Oct, Thur and Sun pm. Adm charge. Refreshments and shop (Apr-end Oct). P *Toilets.* ♿ *(grounds). Tel Burnham (062 86) 5069.*

COOMBE HILL

Off B4010, 1½ miles west of Wendover (Cb)

The Chiltern Hills form one link in the great chain of chalk uplands which extend from Dorset to Yorkshire. At 852ft above sea level, blustery Coombe Hill is the Chilterns' highest point, providing spectacular vistas across the Thames Valley and as far as the smudged lines of the Cotswolds to the north-west and the Berkshire Downs to the south-west. South-westerly too, but much closer at hand, lies the wooded estate of Chequers, official country home of British prime ministers since 1921, when Lloyd George was the occupant.

The summit of Coombe Hill itself is scattered with broom, heather and gorse and capped by a tall granite monument to the Buckinghamshire men who fell during the Boer War. Around the turn of the century the hill was in private hands, and the owner tried to fence the public off; irate townsfolk of nearby Wendover responded by tearing the barriers down and public access was eventually guaranteed by law. Today, 106 acres of the hill are owned by the National Trust and a nature walk has been laid out. Not far along the Upper Icknield Way (marked today by the A4011) are Wendover Woods, where there is a forest park with waymarked walks.

NT. All year, daily.

COWPER AND NEWTON MUSEUM

In Market Place, Olney (Ce)

The poet William Cowper (1731-1800) lived in this brick-faced house for 18 years with his housekeeper Mary Unwin. Here he composed *John Gilpin, The Loss of the Royal George* and much more besides. The house contains many intimate mementos of his life and work: including the porthole through which his pet hares gained access to the kitchen from the hall.

Cowper came to Olney to be near his friend the Reverend John Newton, who is also commemorated in the museum. Newton had been captain of a slave ship before entering the church, and was the author of *Amazing Grace*. There is also a collection devoted to lace-making.

Easter Mon-end Oct, Tues-Sat and Bank Hol Mon; also Sun pm, June-Sept; Nov-Easter Tues-Sat pm. Adm charge. Shop. P *(exc Thur). Toilets. Tel Bedford (0234) 711516.*

DORNEY COURT

Off B3026, 2 miles west of Eton (Ca)

The first pineapple grown in England is said to have been raised at this pink brick Tudor manor, and presented to Charles II in 1661. The king used to come here to visit Barbara Palmer, Countess of Castlemaine (later Duchess of Cleveland). She was long his most favoured and influential mistress, and bore him several children.

Beautifully timbered and gabled, the house itself was built around 1440, and successive generations of Palmers have occupied it for almost 400 years. Memorable rooms include the intimate low-beamed parlour, the panelled Great Chamber which now serves as principal bedroom, and the splendid Great Hall where paintings crowd the walls. There is a portrait by Lely of the gallant Countess of Castlemaine and a large carved stone pineapple commemorating the royal presentation.

The name Dorney is an ancient one meaning 'Island of Bees', and the manor's small shop sells Dorney Court honey, still made locally. Hard by is the parish church of St James, notable for its tomb of Sir William Garrard (died 1607) and his wife Elizabeth, curiously ornamented with mourning children bearing skulls.

Easter weekend then Sun and Bank Hol Mon pm to 2nd Sun in Oct; also Mon and Tues pm, June-Sept. Adm charge. Refreshments. Shop. P *Toilets. Tel Burnham (062 86) 4638.*

HUGHENDEN MANOR

Off A4128, 2 miles north of High Wycombe (Cb)

Benjamin Disraeli first proposed to buy Hughenden in 1847, believing that as the possible future leader of the Conservative Party he should possess a substantial landed estate. The purchase took some time, but by the summer of 1848 he could write to his devoted wife, Mary Anne: 'It is all done, you are the Lady of Hughenden.' The house was to remain the statesman's home until his death in 1881, and with the help of the architect E.B. Lamb, the couple deliberately 'gothicised' what had been a plain, three-storeyed Georgian building by refacing it with brick and adding the Jacobean-style parapets seen today.

The interior was restyled too, and Hughenden survives today much as in Disraeli's time. Books, letters, portraits and original furnishings recall the statesman's career, and there are many personal touches, too: locks of hair, for example, and the black-edged writing paper which he always used after Mary Anne's death in 1872.

The house is situated in a sloping park whose woods Disraeli loved especially in autumn. 'The limes all golden', he rhapsodised one October, 'the beeches ruddy brown . . . But not a leaf has fallen; they want the first whisper of frost, and then they will go out like the lamps when the dawn breaks on a long festival.' The garden is planted today with bedding plants in the authentic Victorian fashion.

NT. Apr-Oct, Wed-Sun and Bank Hol Mon pm; also Sat and Sun in Mar. Adm charge. P *Toilets.* ♿ *(ground floor). Tel High Wycombe (0494) 32580.*

TRIM GREENSWARD *The silvery Thames lies beyond the magnificent parterre in this view from the roof balustrade at Cliveden. The geometrical garden, with flowerbeds edged with box, replaced 'a huge field of grass and wild flowers' in the 19th century, much to the grief of the children of the house.*

IVINGHOE BEACON

Off B489, 1 mile north-east of Ivinghoe (Cc)

Downland, common, wood and farmland covering 6 square miles on the ridge of the Chilterns climb to a peak at Ivinghoe Beacon, a bold chalk hill rising to 756ft. Like other such landmarks across the nation, it was established as a beacon site under Elizabeth I to summon men in case of Spanish invasion.

The hill is virtually bare of tree or shrub, but on a warm summer day the scent of wild thyme loads the air. And the summit provides a sweeping panorama which takes in the chalk-cut image of a lion at Whipsnade Zoo to the east.

Half a mile south of Ivinghoe, and in view of the Beacon, stands the Pitstone windmill, built to profit from the exposed position. One of its timbers, dated 1627, makes it the oldest dated windmill in the country. It is of the post-mill type, its whole body revolving round a post to face the wind, and was in operation until 1902. Once badly neglected, it has since been restored and its two pairs of grindstones are in full working order.

Ivinghoe Beacon. NT. All year, daily. Windmill. NT. May-Sept Sun and Bank Hol pm. Small charge. Shop. Tel Cheddington (0296) 668227.

JORDANS QUAKER MEETING

Off A40, 2 miles east of Beaconsfield (Ca)

Jordans is not the oldest surviving meeting place of the Quakers, but it is probably the best known. For this was the burial place in 1718 of William Penn, founder of Pennsylvania, who often attended meetings here during his lifetime.

Built in 1688, the meeting house is a simple construction of local brick overhung by a tiled roof. Inside, the building has changed little since the 17th century: the wood, glass and unmortared brick paving are merely more worn. The burial ground itself is as simple as the meeting house: more than 400 Quakers lie here, but the headstones like that of Penn are plain and many of the shallow mounds are entirely unmarked. Close by is the Mayflower Barn, dating from

TREASURED COLLECTION *Disraeli looks down on the present library at Hughenden Manor from a portrait painted in 1852, the year he first became an officer of state. Many of the books were his, and he once wrote 'I have a passion for books and trees. I like to look at them'. At Hughenden he had plenty of both.*

1624. Many of its venerable timbers are alleged to have come from the famous *Mayflower* which took the Pilgrim Fathers to America and which was broken up in Ipswich.

All year, daily exc Mon pm and Tues. Free entry. P *Toilets. Tel Chalfont St Giles (024 07) 4146.*

LANGLEY PARK COUNTRY PARK

Off A412, 3 miles north-east of Slough (Da)

This park and Black Park Country Park just to the north, on the other side of the A412, form part of the estate purchased in 1738 by the 3rd Duke of Marlborough, who built the present 18th-century mansion (not open). Langley Park, covering 130 acres, has old woodlands, parkland and a lake, and is noted for its rhododendron gardens and arboretum.

Black Park is more heavily wooded, with conifer and mixed plantations. Its 500 acres include an information centre and 13 acre lake, where there is swimming, canoeing and fishing. Both parks have numerous rides and paths, and there are self-guided trails.

All year, daily. Free entry. Refreshments.

MENTMORE TOWERS

Off B488, 5 miles north of Tring (Cc)

With its mighty corner towers of grey-gold Ancaster stone, Mentmore is one of Victorian architecture's fabulous shams. The mansion was built in 1855 for Baron Meyer Amschel de Rothschild, a member of the wealthy banking family. And the style is so-called 'Jacobethan', recalling in particular the authentic Elizabethan towers of Wollaton Hall in Nottinghamshire.

Sir Joseph Paxton, architect of the Crystal Palace, designed the building. Its main rooms are grouped around a Grand Hall two storeys high, with arcaded gallery and a balustrade of marble and alabaster. All speaks of opulence, which is evoked most powerfully in the gilded ornamentation and sumptuous velvet of the dining room.

Mentmore won national fame in 1977 when its entire contents were sold at auction for over £6 million. But there are still many immovable artefacts to admire, in particular a huge black and white marble fireplace said to have been designed by Rubens for his house in Antwerp.

Mentmore is now the national headquarters of a Transcendental Meditation organisation, and also houses the Maharishi Ayurveda Health Centre. It rises from an area of parkland at whose edge is a model village, which Baron Rothschild also created in Jacobethan style.

All year, Sun and Bank Hol Mon pm. Adm charge. P *Toilets. Tel Cheddington (0296) 662183.*

POET'S CORNER *Writing materials lie ready for use on the table in Milton's room in his cottage home. It was here in 1667 that the poet, already blind, finished the mammoth task of dictating the 10,566 lines of* Paradise Lost *to his daughter.*

MILTON'S COTTAGE

Dean Way, Chalfont St Giles (Cb)

John Milton came to this timber and brick cottage in 1665 with his third wife and daughter, seeking refuge from London's Great Plague. The poet, already blind, stayed here only two years, but the house is important as Milton's sole surviving home. It contains portraits, busts and relics as well as nearly 100 rare books; they include a first edition of *Paradise Lost*, the epic poem which he completed at the cottage.

Outside, a pretty little garden bursts with cottage flowers in summer. The mulberry tree was taken as a cutting from an old one growing at Christ's College, Cambridge, when Milton was a student there.

Mar-Oct, Tues-Sat, Sun and sometimes Spring and Summer Bank Hol Mon pm. Adm charge. Shop. P *(limited).* ♿ *Tel Chalfont St Giles (024 07) 2313.*

NETHER WINCHENDON HOUSE

Off A418, 6 miles south-west of Aylesbury (Bc)

A medieval house with Tudor and Georgian alterations, Nether Winchendon was once owned by the Abbey of Notley. Sir John Daunce, whose likeness can be seen carved in a drawing room frieze, carried out much of the Elizabethan work, and the house later passed to the Bernard family, whose home it remains today. There is some good 18th-century furniture, as well as maps belonging to Sir Francis Bernard, who was Governor of New Jersey and Massachusetts Bay in the 18th century. The pleasant gardens run down to the River Thames.

May-Aug Thur pm, and certain other days. Adm charge. P ♿ *Tel Haddenham (0844) 290101.*

STACEY HILL COLLECTION OF INDUSTRY AND RURAL LIFE

At Wolverton, north-west of Milton Keynes (Bd)

Milton Keynes is one of Britain's newest cities, but the Stacey Hill Society, founded in 1972, is dedicated to preserving the area's past. Initiated by enthusiastic volunteers and set among farm buildings, the collection has exhibits ranging from farm carts to a fire engine; from tractors to tram. A laundry has been converted into a Victorian kitchen and, besides the many displays, live demonstrations of rural crafts such as thatching, woodcarving and bee-keeping are given during special open weekends. A blacksmith works at his forge and a printer at his press; a special highlight is the old threshing machine in action.

May-Oct, first Sun pm in each month. Working displays at certain weekends. Adm charge. Shop. P *(limited).* ♿ *Tel Milton Keynes (0908) 316222.*

STOWE

Off A422, 4 miles north of Buckingham (Bd)

Templa Quam Dilecta – 'How delightful are thy temples!' – was the family motto of Sir Richard Temple, who became Viscount Cobham in 1714. As if to illustrate the text, he embellished his gardens at Stowe with a profusion of classical temples – and pavilions, monuments, arches and bridges. There are 32 today (at one time there were 50); a grand total unmatched in any other British garden.

Well known now for its public school, the house at Stowe is an imposing late 17th-century building put up by Sir Richard's father. But it was the 1st Viscount Cobham who was chiefly responsible for developing the estate. A distinguished soldier and politician, he married a millionairess in 1715, and for the next 30 years devoted himself to improving Stowe. The work was continued by his nephew and successor Richard Grenville (1711-79), reputedly the richest man in Britain, so funds were never lacking. Three great landscape designers, Charles Bridgeman, William Kent and Capability Brown, were brought in to achieve the natural look so admired in the 18th century. An artificial lake known as the Octagon was re-shaped to make the informal sweep of water seen today. And the temples, of course, were laid out. Perhaps the best known is the Temple of British Worthies, designed by Kent in about 1735, and containing busts of 16 great Britons including Shakespeare.

Easter, then end July-early Sept, daily. Adm charge. Refreshments. Shop. P *Toilets. Tel Buckingham (0280) 813650.*

WADDESDON MANOR

On A41, 6 miles west of Aylesbury (Bc)

There is nothing quite like Waddesdon elsewhere in England: it looks like one of those 16th-century French châteaux whose fairy-tale towers grace the banks of the Loire. In fact, the manor was built in 1874-89 for Baron Ferdinand de Rothschild. But there are many French connections. The architect and landscape gardener were both imported from France, and French art of the 18th century forms the heart of the splendid collection inside.

Waddesdon is one great treasure box. It has paintings and drawings by Boucher and Watteau, statuettes by Clodion, Sèvres porcelain, Savonnerie carpets, furniture made for the French royal family, gilt bronzes and ormolu clocks. To complement the French works there are magnificent paintings by Gainsborough, Romney and Reynolds, as well as Dutch artists of the 17th century.

Waddesdon's gardens offer notable attractions in their own right. There are fine blue cedars and silver limes; fountains and much statuary. Deer roam a special enclosure, and the garden's pride is its elegant 19th-century aviary with rare and exotic birds.

Late Mar-late Oct, Wed-Sun pm, and Good Fri and Bank Hol Mon; closed Wed after Bank Hol. Adm charge. Refreshments. Shop. P *Toilets.* ♿ *Tel Aylesbury (0296) 651211.*

WEST WYCOMBE PARK AND CAVES

On A40, at west end of West Wycombe (Cb)

Approach by the ruler-straight road from High Wycombe and the scene is dominated by the hilltop Church of St Lawrence, with its adjacent mausoleum. A golden ball surmounts the church tower and in sunlight it can be seen from miles around, flashing like some fantastic lighthouse. The gilded globe encloses a room with seating for eight people. And inside, at one time, met members of the 'Knights of St Francis of Wycombe' – better known as the Hell Fire Club.

This notorious fraternity was founded in 1746 by Sir Francis Dashwood (1708-81), a man who has completely imprinted West Wycombe with his character. It was he who rebuilt the church and gave it its golden ball. He too was responsible for the mausoleum, a hexagon of columns, arches and friezes, open to the sky. Across the little valley in which the attractive brick-built village is cupped, lies West Wycombe Park – the Dashwood family home also built by Sir Francis, and almost unaltered since his day.

Inside the house's warm Georgian gold walls are superbly decorated rooms with especially fine ceilings painted by the Italian Borgnis family. The columned hall has an elegant staircase, and other fine rooms include the tapestry room, hung with Flemish arras, the red drawing room and the saloon. These three rooms all look north, and the saloon commands lordly views to the hilltop church and mausoleum, with the landscaped lake closer at hand.

North of the park, below the church hill, are the West Wycombe caves. These were mined for road-building materials, at Sir Francis's suggestion, to help relieve local unemployment. The Hell Fire Club is said to have conducted secret revels in these underground grottoes.

The alcoves today are electrically lit and adorned with artificial stalagmites and stalactites, as well as many life-size tableaux recalling Sir Francis and his time. The taped voice of the present Sir Francis Dashwood guides visitors through to the so-called inner temple, a quarter of a mile into the hill, where gallants in periwigs and lace ruffles banquet with female companions.

NT. Grounds only: Easter, May Day and Spring Bank Hol Sun and Mon pm. House and grounds: June, Mon-Fri pm; July and Aug, pm daily exc Sat. Adm charge. P ♿ *(grounds only). Tel High Wycombe (0494) 24411.*

WILLEN LAKE AND PARK

At Milton Keynes, off M1 (Junction 14) (Cd)

There is something for all the family in this 260 acre leisure centre, with its woods and gardens, adventure playground and lakeside walks. The North Lake is a wildlife reserve, the home of mallard, tufted duck, curlew and plover. The South Lake of more than 100 acres is used for dinghy sailing, windsurfing and canoeing, and all the craft can be hired. Fishing is also permitted on the lakes, which are well stocked with roach, perch and pike.

All year, daily. Free entry. Refreshments. Shop. P *Toilets.* ♿ *Tel Milton Keynes (0908) 670197.*

CARRIAGE WAY *The lovely Palladian Bridge at Stowe spans an arm of the Octagon Lake. Built around 1740, it was a copy of the graceful footbridge at Wilton House in Wiltshire which was highly praised as a flawless essay in the style of the great Italian architect Andrea Palladio. But the bridge at Stowe, unlike its model, was built without steps so that it could form part of the route for the grand carriages of the household when they conveyed guests on tours of the park.*

ELEGANCE PRESERVED *Fine red damask lines the walls of the red drawing room at West Wycombe Park, and its lovely painted ceiling is one of several in the house. Generations of the Dashwood family have lovingly cared for the mansion, which remains much as it was when rebuilt in the 18th century.*

WYCOMBE CHAIR MUSEUM

Priory Avenue, High Wycombe (Cb)

In everyday speech, a 'bodger' is someone who botches things through carelessness. The Wycombe Chair Museum reveals an altogether nobler meaning. To bodge in the literal sense is to make chair legs out of beechwood. And in the chalk hills around Wycombe, where beechwoods abound, bodging was a traditional craft.

The museum is devoted almost exclusively to a single theme: the history, development and production of the Windsor Chair. This is the well-known English wooden cottage chair, typically with a high, curved back, arms, and splayed legs joined by a crossbar. But as the exhibits demonstrate, the Windsor Chair came in many other forms. During the 19th century curious one-armed chairs were manufactured; they were ordered by the War Office and lacked a left arm so that officers wearing dress swords could rise without impediment to a toast. The museum displays tools used in chair-making, and also illustrates cane and rush work. There are also exhibits of lacemaking and thatching.

All year, daily exc Sun, Wed and Bank Hol. Free entry. Shop. P *Toilets.* ♿ *(ground floor). Tel High Wycombe (0494) 23879.*

COUNTY CALENDAR

February Olney: Shrove Tuesday Pancake Race.

February (late, to March). High Wycombe: Arts Festival.

May (end of month). High Wycombe: Weighing the Mayor Ceremony.

June (3rd Sat). Marlow: Amateur Regatta.

September (1st Thur). Hartwell House Grounds, nr Aylesbury: Buckinghamshire County Show.

September (1st Sat). High Wycombe: Agricultural Show.

November 11 Fenny Stratford: Firing the Fenny Poppers, a 6-gun salute.

Tourist information: Aylesbury (0296) 395000; High Wycombe (0494) 461000; Milton Keynes (0908) 691995; Wendover (0296) 623056.

CAMBRIDGESHIRE

CATHEDRALS, COLLEGES AND GREAT HOUSES BESIDE THE FERTILE FENS

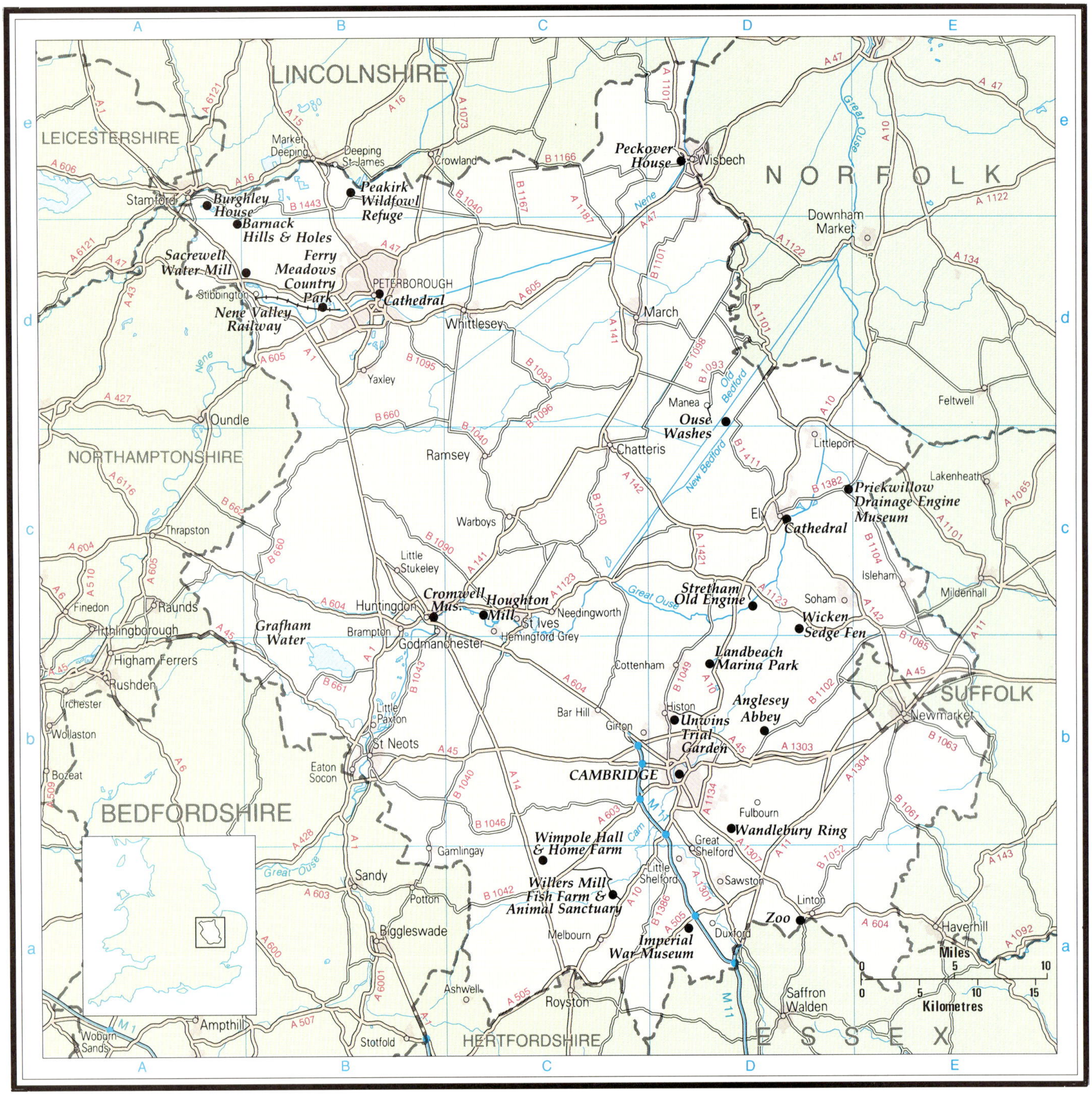

'The shire for men who understand', said the poet Rupert Brooke of Cambridgeshire, no doubt thinking of his beloved university's dreamy beauty. The shire has long encouraged quality; it is seen in the sublime craftsmanship of Ely and Peterborough cathedrals, and in the relics of its great men. Burghley House declares the power of Elizabeth I's chief minister, Wimpole Hall's Home Farm recalls the innovative policies of the 3rd Earl of Hardwicke, while the Cromwell Museum remembers a revolutionary of another kind. However, the greatest monument to Cambridgeshire genius is its landscape of rich flat acres won from the primeval swamps by centuries of skilled toil. Some of the pumping engines that held the fenland waters in check, like that at Stretham, survive, and in Wicken Fen there is a glimpse of the swampy wilderness that Hereward the Wake knew.

ANGLESEY ABBEY

On B1102, 6 miles north-east of Cambridge (Db)

It has nothing to do with the Isle of Anglesey, nor was it ever an abbey. About the middle of the 12th century, the Augustinians founded a small priory on the spot, then in the middle of wild fen country, and named it after the nearby hamlet of Angerhale, long vanished from the map; 'abbey' was a later and unjustified promotion. The black-robed canons were expelled during the Dissolution of the Monasteries in the 1530s, after which the building passed to a succession of owners, who pulled down part of it and grafted a Tudor house onto the remains.

In 1926 Anglesey was purchased by Huttleston Broughton, later Lord Fairhaven, as a showcase for his paintings, porcelain, statuary, furniture, tapestries, snuffboxes and much else besides. And to the medieval and Tudor building he added a library, a hall and staircase and picture galleries linked to the older parts of the house by a bridge. The result is not the jumble it sounds, but a charming and harmonious whole.

The riches begin at the entry by the 1930s Tapestry Hall, with a great Egyptian porphyry vase, gilt phoenixes from the Summer Palace at Peking, medieval carvings and cabinets and a collection of gold and silver crosses. The next room, whose massively vaulted ceiling is supported on marble columns, was the old canons' Common Room, and Lord Fairhaven adopted it as his dining room. Every room is full of masterpieces of one kind or another, attractively displayed in a lived-with sort of way.

In his youth, Lord Fairhaven served with the Life Guards at Windsor, an event which so impressed him that he later gathered together several hundred paintings, drawings and prints of the place, presenting a remarkable portrait of Windsor Castle over 350 years.

The garden, also created by Lord Fairhaven, is among the most splendid in the country. The problem of achieving the grand effect in the flat fen country was solved by contrasting majestic walks, beds and clipped hedges of the utmost formality with swathes of naturalised planting. Like the house, the garden is a setting for treasures: busts of Roman emperors, a temple containing a 6ft 4in wide porphyry urn, a statue of Narcissus reflected in a pool, a lovely group of Graces from Stowe. There is even a water mill on the old Roman lode, or waterway. On the first Sunday of every month when the house is open, the mill grinds corn and sells stone-ground flour to visitors.

NT. Mid Apr-mid Oct, Wed-Sun and Bank Hol Mon pm. Gardens only, also early Apr and July-mid Oct, daily. Adm charge. Refreshments. Shop. P *Toilets.* ♿ *(gardens only). Tel Cambridge (0223) 811200.*

BARNACK HILLS AND HOLES

Off B1443, 9 miles north-west of Peterborough (Ad)

Bury St Edmunds Abbey and the cathedrals at Ely and Peterborough were all built of Barnack stone; so were a number of Cambridge colleges and many churches and other medieval buildings of Eastern England. Most of the usable stone was gone by the 16th century, and the quarrymen moved away, leaving Hills and Holes – their spoil heaps and excavations.

Vegetation spread over the rubble and shattered limestone until the bumps and hollows became entirely carpeted with turf from which, in spring and summer, lime-loving wild flowers emerge. The old quarry, now a nature reserve, launches its annual display with a pale-gold dappling of cowslips, and then brings forth the rarish pasqueflower, rock rose and orchid.

All year, daily.

FACES OF AN IMMORTAL *An 18th-century French statue, believed to depict an Etruscan deity holding a symbolic mask of tragedy, stands in the wooded gardens of Anglesey Abbey.*

BURGHLEY HOUSE

Off B1443, 11 miles north-west of Peterborough (Ae)

Situated in a tiny promontory of Cambridgeshire between Northamptonshire and Lincolnshire is the most grandiose of all Elizabethan houses. Its 200ft Barnack stone front is topped by spires, cupolas with gilt weather vanes, tall, ornamental chimneys and a balustrade. The building was constructed in the form of an enormous E, no doubt a tribute to Elizabeth I from its builder, William Cecil, Lord Burghley, one of the most brilliant men of a brilliant age and friend and adviser to the queen for most of her life. He began building the house on land left to him by his father in the 1570s, and his descendants have lived there ever since.

The Elizabethans were not modest. Great men were expected to advertise, and Lord Burghley zestfully declared himself by his house and its contents, richly added to in later years. There are 18 State Rooms on view, crammed with rare furniture, tapestries, ceramics, and some 400 old master paintings. The Italian paintings are regarded as the finest, though they are liberally punctuated by the works of such other giants as Van Dyck, Lely, Gainsborough, Rembrandt and Bruegel. The Heaven Room has walls and ceiling decorated with mythological scenes by the 17th-century Italian painter Verrio.

The Deer Park offers fine views of the house and is a good place in which to stroll or picnic.

Easter-early Oct, daily. Adm charge. Refreshments. Shop. P *Toilets.* ♿ *Tel Stamford (0780) 52451.*

CROMWELL MUSEUM, HUNTINGDON

In centre of Huntingdon (Bc)

The future Lord Protector was born in Huntingdon High Street, in a house whose site is now occupied by a private clinic. He attended the Grammar School a few yards up the road – as did Samuel Pepys some 20 years later. The school-house, a fragment of the 12th-century Hospital of St John, is now the Cromwell Museum.

Considering his unpopularity with the succeeding Stuart regime, it is remarkable that any relics of Oliver Cromwell survived at all, and this museum houses many of those that have. On view is Cromwell's dispatch box, a cabinet given to him by the Duke of Tuscany, his hat and other personal belongings. There are also numerous portraits of himself and of his family and friends.

ROUNDHEAD'S HAT *The hat worn by Oliver Cromwell when he dissolved Parliament in 1653, the decisive moment in his rise to supreme power as Lord Protector, is displayed at the Cromwell Museum, Huntingdon.*

Cromwell enthusiasts can also see nearby Hinchingbrooke House, the family's ancestral home which is now a school, Huntingdon's All Saints' Church where Oliver's father is buried, and the village church at Wicken. There lies Henry, Oliver's most capable son, a distinguished soldier and one-time Lord Lieutenant of Ireland.

Cromwell Museum. All year, Tues-Sun and Bank Hol. Free entry. Shop. Tel Huntingdon (0480) 425830. Hinchingbrooke House: Apr-Aug, Sun and Bank Hol Mon pm. Adm charge. Tel (0480) 51121.

ELY CATHEDRAL

In centre of Ely (Dc)

No other building in England dominates its landscape in the way that Ely Cathedral does. On summer mornings its tower and lantern climb like wraiths above the mist, and in the evening the cathedral's black bulk is like a great ship anchored in the shoals of the wide fenland sunset.

A monastery for both monks and nuns was founded in Ely in AD 673 by St Etheldreda. In the centuries that followed, it blazed to the sky in a Danish raid and was later besieged by the Normans; Hereward the Wake put up a heroic defence there, but was betrayed and disappeared from history. It was in about 1080 that the present building, one of the triumphs of Norman architecture, began to rise. It was completed by 1200, but in 1322 the tower fell down. Rather than replace it, the sacristan, Alan of Walsingham, built in its stead the Octagon, an enormous lantern that is acknowledged as one of the wonders of medieval engineering.

There are many good things to see in and around Ely Cathedral. Don't miss the painted ceilings, the mosaics in Prior Crauden's Chapel, the wonderful medieval carving on, for example, the Monks' Door and in the Lady Chapel. Many buildings in the precincts are *(continued on page 36)*

SERENE BEAUTY IN CAMBRIDGE

Today Cambridge is inseparable from its university, whose superb buildings help to make it one of the world's loveliest cities. But there was a settlement there 1000 years before the university. A Roman fort crowned Castle Mound, near a crossing of the River Cam, and later there was a Saxon castle, market town and port. William the Conqueror and Oliver Cromwell both defended the hill, but nothing remains of their forts. The oldest structure today is the Saxon tower of St Bene't's Church, built around 1020. Peterhouse, the first college, was founded in 1284. The tower of Great St Mary's Church yields fine views over the city, whose university area retains an air of seclusion despite new industries beyond. There are many museums to explore; these range from the University Museum of Archaeology to the Cambridge Art and Holographic Centre in Magdalene Street.

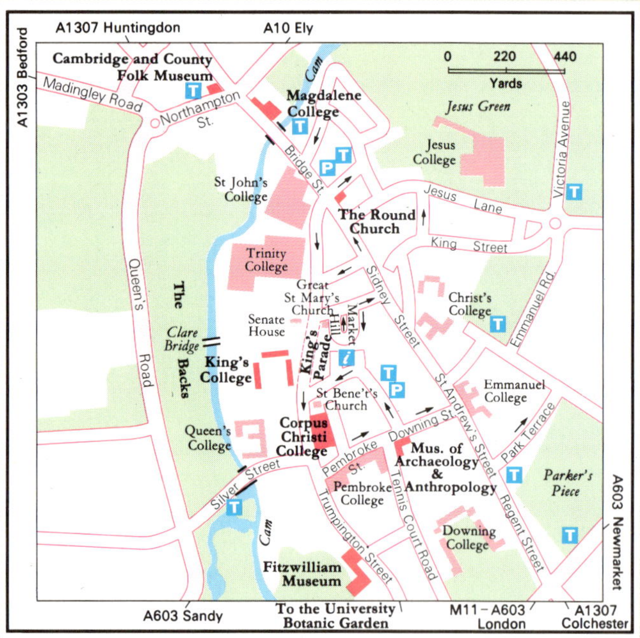

Colleges *Most open daily pm. Adm charge in some colleges. Tel Cambridge (0223) 322640.*

Fitzwilliam Museum *All year, Tues-Sat, and Sun pm; also Easter Mon, Spring and Summer Bank Hol. Free entry. Refreshments. Shop. Toilets. ♿ Tel (0223) 332900.*

Great St Mary's Church *All year, daily. Adm charge (tower). Tel (0223) 350914.*

Cambridge and County Folk Museum *All year, daily exc Sun am. Adm charge. Shop. Toilets. ♿ (ground floor). Tel (0223) 355159.*

St Bene't's Church *All year, daily. Tel (0223) 353903.*

The Round Church *All year, daily.*

Art and Holographic Centre *All year, daily. Adm charge. Shop. ♿ Tel (0223) 460349.*

University Botanic Garden *All year, Mon-Sat; also Sun pm, May-Sept. Free entry. Toilets. ♿ Tel (0223) 336265.*

University Museum of Archaeology and Anthropology *All year, Mon-Fri pm and Sat am. Free entry. Shop. Toilets. ♿ Tel (0223) 333516.*

FITZWILLIAM MUSEUM

Today one of the chief treasure houses of the nation, the university's own museum was founded in 1816, and acquisitions over the years have built up fine collections of Egyptian, Greek and Roman antiquities, arms and armour, ceramics, coins, manuscripts, paintings and textiles. The 'three loggerheads' on a dish (left) made at Burslem in the 1720s – possibly for an inn of the same name – include the viewer as the third drinking figure. The story of Adam and Eve is depicted on the page from a 13th-century psalter (below left), and J.M.W. Turner painted the atmospheric watercolour *Venice, Calm at Sunrise* (below) in the 1840s.

CAMBRIDGE AND COUNTY FOLK MUSEUM

A Victorian child's embroidery, a work basket, and an early sewing machine are among the bygones housed in a former coaching inn. The inn, the White Horse, was built on Castle Street, the city's oldest street. The collections reflect the domestic and working life of the city and surrounding countryside, including the Fens, down the centuries.

KING'S COLLEGE

Henry VI granted King's College its charter in 1441 and laid the foundation stone of the chapel (above) – the glory of King's – in 1446; it was left to Henry VIII to complete it, in 1515. Despite its vast size – it is 289ft long, 94ft high and 40ft wide – it has an ethereal quality. Inside, delicate columns soar 80ft to a riot of fan vaulting, and light filters in through some of the finest 16th-century stained glass in England. One window (right) depicts the betrayal of Christ.

BOTANIC GARDEN

A tranquil lake and water garden provide a refreshing oasis not far from the city centre. The Botanic Garden was established primarily for botanical research, but has become a delight to the layman. There are rock, scented and winter gardens, and a 'chronological' bed in which the plants are arranged in the order in which they were introduced into Britain.

THE ROUND CHURCH

The Church of the Holy Sepulchre dates from the 12th century. It was founded by one of the Crusading military monastic orders pledged to protect the Holy Land and the Holy Sepulchre itself – supposedly a circular structure.

CORPUS CHRISTI

A statue of Matthew Parker, Master of Corpus Christi in 1544-53 and later Archbishop of Canterbury, looks down on the college's New Court. The nearby Old Court, completed in 1377, has been little altered since.

THE BACKS

A punt glides lazily on the Cam near Clare Bridge. The college is one of several whose back lawns roll down to the river and are known simply as 'The Backs' – one of the delights of Cambridge, affording magnificent views of the colleges. Clare Bridge, built in the 17th century, is approached by beautiful wrought-iron gates. Queens' Mathematical Bridge was built in 1749 on mathematical principles, and needed no nails.

KING'S PARADE

This short street is part of one of the world's most pleasing thoroughfares. Among its fine buildings are St Catherine's, King's and Corpus Christi colleges. The University Church, Great St Mary's, dates mostly from the 15th century. Behind it is Market Hill (above). The Senate House (left), completed in 1730, is the University's 'parliament'.

PEPYS LIBRARY

A portrait of the diarist Samuel Pepys (1633-1703) looks down on the treasures of his library in his old college, Magdalene. The 3000 volumes include 70 medieval manuscripts, early printed books, seven of them by Caxton, and Pepys' diaries for the years 1660 to 1669. These are written in shorthand, which it took experts some 10,000 hours to decipher.

(continued from page 33) those of the old Benedictine monastery and are still in use, mostly by the pupils of the King's School, founded in AD 970 and given its charter by Edward the Confessor, who was educated there.

The cathedral has its own museum, devoted to the history of stained glass from medieval to modern times. The exhibits, beautifully displayed and lit, are mostly from redundant churches.

Cathedral: All year, daily. Museum: Mar-Oct, daily. Adm charge. Refreshments. Shop. P *Toilets. Tel Cambridge (0223) 67735.*

FERRY MEADOWS COUNTRY PARK

Off A605, 3½ miles south-west of Peterborough (Bd)

The principal theme of the 500 acre Ferry Meadows Country Park is water, and the sports concerned with it. There is good fishing, and Gunwade Lake is the scene of sailing, canoeing and sailboarding.

For those who prefer non-aquatic activities, there is a river cruiser, a bird reserve with hides, children's ponies and pony and trap rides, footpaths and cycleways, and a visitor centre. Younger visitors will be thrilled by the adventure playground and the miniature steam railway – and awed perhaps by the full-size steam locomotives of the Nene Valley Railway that runs through Nene Park (which includes Ferry Meadows) between Orton Mere and Wansford.

All year, daily. Refreshments. Shop. P *Toilets.* ♿ *Tel Peterborough (0733) 234443.*

GRAFHAM WATER

Off B661, 6 miles south-west of Huntingdon (Bb)

A great reservoir which supplies about a million and a half people daily in the south-east Midlands covers some 2½ square miles. It is based upon the shallow valley of the Diddington Brook, and therefore required no mighty dam to contain it. An embankment of rolled clay contains its waters, which are actually pumped in from the Great Ouse, about 3 miles to the east.

Grafham Water also provides entertainment. Its trout are plump and famous, and many people come in pursuit of them. Sailing is another attraction, and non-members of the Grafham Water Sailing Club may sail by paying daily membership and sailing fees. There is public access to most of the 10 mile perimeter of the lake, including picnic sites galore and nature trails. These include viewpoints and two hides from which an enormous variety of birds may be observed.

At Kimbolton Castle, 2 miles west, Henry VIII's divorced queen, Catherine of Aragon, was kept prisoner by Sir Richard Wingfield, a confidant of the king. The Tudor mansion built by Wingfield was entirely remodelled by the early 18th-century giants Vanbrugh and Hawksmoor. There are sumptuous interiors with fine murals, especially on the staircase. The building is now a school, so opening times are limited.

Grafham Water: All year, daily. Refreshments. P *Toilets.* ♿ *Tel Huntingdon (0480) 810247. Kimbolton Castle: Easter, Spring and Summer Bank Hols, Sun and Mon pm; also late July-Aug Sun pm. Adm charge.* P *Toilets. Tel (0480) 860505.*

HOUGHTON MILL

Off A1123, 2 miles east of Huntingdon (Cc)

This is one of those water mills that, as Kipling put it, 'has ground her corn and paid her tax ever since Domesday Book', except that Houghton Mill was already getting on a bit when that first great income tax return was compiled. In AD 974 it provided a good income for the Benedictine monks of Ramsey Abbey, since the locals were forbidden to get their corn ground anywhere else, and it may have been working long before that. The original building has long vanished, but the present five-storey, brick and tarboarded structure that dates from the 17th to the 19th centuries still stands on the same backwater of the lazy, spreading Great Ouse; and until about 1930, it performed much the same task as its predecessors.

NT. Mid Apr-mid Sept, pm daily exc Thur and Fri; mid Sept-mid Oct, Sat and Sun pm. Adm charge. Tel St Ives (0480) 301494.

IMPERIAL WAR MUSEUM, DUXFORD

On A505, 9 miles south of Cambridge (Da)

RAF Duxford began as a bomber base in 1918, spent the inter-war years as a fighter station and launched its Spitfires, commanded by Douglas Bader, against the German Luftwaffe in 1940. Later, USAAF Mustangs and Thunderbolts flew from the field, escorting Flying Fortresses on their daylight raids deep into Germany. Demobbed in 1961, Duxford starred a few years later as both the British and German airfields in the film *Battle of Britain*; during the filming, one of its 1917 hangars was accidentally destroyed.

Now a part of the Imperial War Museum, Duxford reflects not only its own colourful history but also that of aviation in general in a superlative collection of classic aircraft. Military representatives range from a veteran BE2c fighter of 1916 to a Vulcan V-bomber of the 1960s. In between are such workhorses as the Anson, the Dakota and the Junkers 52; the whole range of Boeing Fortresses from the B17 to the gigantic B52; and the two planes that will always be associated with Duxford, the Spitfire and the Mustang. Between the aeroplanes are fighting vehicles of the Second World War, an enormous coastal defence gun from Gibraltar, midget submarines and coastal craft.

In one hangar Duxford's volunteer workforce restores planes that have lain derelict, or, as in the case of the Sunderland, spent many years as a nightclub in Brittany. A Concorde prototype was flown into Duxford just before the M11 was built across the end of the runway, making it impossible for the aircraft ever to leave the museum by air. The Red Arrows and Parachute Regiment display team are frequent visitors to the Flying Days in summer, when many of the aircraft in the museum take to the air again.

Mid Mar-end Oct, daily exc Good Fri and May Day Bank Hol; parts also open Nov-mid Mar. Adm charge. Shop. P *Toilets.* ♿ *Tel Cambridge (0223) 833963.*

LANTERN LIGHTS *The superb, eight-sided lantern of Ely Cathedral towers above the Fens. Above the crossing (right) soars a 400 ton mass of lead, timber and glass.*

LANDBEACH MARINA PARK

On A10, 4 miles north-east of Cambridge (Db)

The fenland sky is reflected in some 120 acres of flooded gravel pits that have been given a splendid new lease of life as a centre for fishing, sailing, canoeing, windsurfing and water-skiing. Visitors can hire equipment for all these pastimes or, for a modest fee, launch their own. Landlubbers can occupy themselves on putting greens, tennis courts and adventure playgrounds.

Apr-mid Oct, daily. Adm charge. Refreshments. Shop. P *Toilets.* ♿ *Tel Cambridge (0223) 860019.*

LINTON ZOO

On B1052, 9 miles south-east of Cambridge (Da)

Though occupying no more than 12 acres, Linton Zoo has a considerable reputation as an animal breeding centre. Among the species successfully bred there are lions, leopards, eagle owls, bird-eating spiders and binturongs (near relations of the civet). Some of the offspring are kept by the zoo to maintain its breeding stock, while others are sent to other menageries in Britain and abroad. The grounds have been beautifully landscaped with trees, shrubs and flowerbeds, and the mammals, birds, reptiles and insects have been housed in conditions as close to their natural habitat as possible.

All year, daily. Adm charge. Refreshments. Shop. P *Toilets.* ♿ *Tel Cambridge (0223) 891308.*

NENE VALLEY RAILWAY

Wansford Station, Stibbington, on A1, 7 miles west of Peterborough (Bd)

The Northampton & Peterborough Railway opened in 1845 to the combined execrations of the Dean and Chapter of Peterborough Cathedral, local landowners and stagecoach proprietors. Strange, when you come to see with what affection it is now regarded by steam buffs. The line was closed in 1972, its rails pulled up, its buildings and stock scrapped or sold. But even before the closure, the 7 mile stretch between Wansford and Orton Mere, running through the lovely Nene Park, was being negotiated for by the Peterborough Railway Society.

The whole line, which runs from Wansford to Peterborough, had to be re-created. Wansford's turntable came from Peterborough East, and its station building from Barnwell, 12 miles up the line. The footbridge was adapted from a Lowestoft harbour bridge, and the buffet was created out of an old GWR parcels brake.

This is the only railway in the country that runs foreign as well as British stock. There are locomotives that started life on the railways of France, Sweden, Italy, Denmark, Germany and Norway, as well as such British classics as *City of Peterborough*, *Britannia* and the Battle of Britain class *92 Squadron*. Even those left unmoved by the reek of steam and the churn of pistons may be touched by the idea of lunching in a 1927 restaurant car that spent most of its working life on the line from Scandinavia through Switzerland to Italy. Understandably, the Nene Valley's locomotives, rolling stock and even stations are frequently used by film directors. Productions in which it featured include *Secret Army*, *Octopussy*, *Patton*, *Jenny's War*, *Biggles* and *Lime Street*.

Wansford Station all year, daily. Trains Apr-Oct, weekends and Bank Hols; June-Aug, weekdays also. Adm charge. Refreshments. Shop. P *Toilets.* ♿ *Tel Stamford (0780) 782854.*

SILVER ARROW *The nose of the Anglo-French Concorde 101 towers 37ft above the ground at the Imperial War Museum at Duxford. A forest of controls faced the three-man crew of the airliner, which achieved 1450mph in tests in 1974. The Junkers Ju52 transport craft was built in 1937, and is similar to the model Hitler used as his personal plane.*

OUSE WASHES

Off B1093 at Manea, 5 miles south-east of March (Dd)

'Wash' is the old East Anglian term for a meadow that floods in the winter and dries out sufficiently in summer to provide grazing for sheep and cattle. The Ouse Washes form one of the few such areas left. They were created in the 17th century when the Earl of Bedford and his Dutch engineer Cornelius Vermuyden reclaimed 20,000 acres of perpetually soggy fen north-west of Ely by driving two great drains – called the Old and New Bedford Rivers – some 25 miles long and a few hundred yards apart, to bypass the slow meanders of the Great Ouse.

The desired effect was achieved and, in time, surpassed. The strip between the drains is still the valuable pasture it was intended to be, but when it floods in winter it attracts wildfowl, waders and marsh birds, while the river banks provide permanent homes for other species. Among birds that breed there are mallard and shoveler ducks, shelducks, coots, reed buntings, goldfinches and black-tailed godwits.

But it is the winter visitors that are the stars, arriving in their tens of thousands, mostly from Scandinavia or Russia. The most glamorous of the visitors, perhaps, is the Bewick's swan, whose maximum count (in 1984) was 4550, an estimated 15 per cent of the world's entire population of these birds. Visitors may watch the birds from a number of hides.

RSPB. All year, daily; visitor centre Sat, Sun and Bank Hol. Free entry. P *Toilets. Tel Manea (035 478) 212.*

PEAKIRK WILDFOWL REFUGE

Off B1443, 6 miles north of Peterborough (Bc)

Flooded gravel workings are now a home for some 650 wildfowl from all over the world. There are ducks from Carolina, New Zealand, the Bahamas, South Africa and Argentina, and geese from Ethiopia, Egypt, the Orinoco and the Falklands.

An important part of the Wildfowl Trust's work at Peakirk is the succour of endangered species, among them the Hawaiian goose, or nene. At one time its numbers had dwindled to less than 50 in the world, but with the help of birds bred at Peakirk it has been possible to return hundreds of the birds to their home.

All year, daily. Adm charge. Refreshments. Shop. P *Toilets.* ♿ *Tel Peterborough (0733) 252271.*

PECKOVER HOUSE

In centre of Wisbech (Dc)

The streets that flank the River Nene as it runs its dreamy course through Wisbech are called The

Brinks. Both streets are attractive, but North Brink is surely one of the most elegant Georgian streets in the country. The best of its buildings is Peckover House, which from about 50 years after its construction in 1722 until 1943 was the home of the Peckovers, a family of Quaker bankers. The furniture and paintings in the house have been gathered from elsewhere by the National Trust, its new owners, but the magnificently carved mantlepieces, the panelling, and the glorious plasterwork are all original. The garden has a Victorian air, with a fine collection of plants and trees; the fruiting orange trees in the conservatory are reputed to be 300 years old.

On the other side of the river, in Ely Place, is the Wisbech and Fenland Museum. Dating from 1847, it is one of the oldest purpose-built museums in the country. Folk life and local history feature among its collections, and there are exhibitions by local artists and craftsmen.

Peckover House. NT. Apr-Oct, Sat, Sun and Bank Hol Mon pm; May-Sept, Sat-Wed pm. Adm charge. Refreshments. Toilets. ♿ (part). Tel Wisbech (0945) 583463. Wisbech and Fenland Museum. All year, Tues-Sat. Free entry. Shop. 🅿 (limited). Tel Wisbech (0945) 583817.

PETERBOROUGH CATHEDRAL

In centre of Peterborough (Bd)

Though its majesty is apparent from a distance, Peterborough Cathedral is somewhat blurred closer to by the modern shops and offices around it. But once through the partly Norman Great Gate and into the cathedral precinct, there is nothing to obscure the glory of the west front with its three mighty arches, each reaching up to a rose window and a 13th-century statue of an apostle – St Peter, St Paul and St Andrew, to all of whom the cathedral is dedicated.

The present building was begun in 1118, but the foundation goes back to AD 654 and to Peada, the first Christian king of Mercia, who established a monastery on the site. This and the surrounding town endured a succession of sackings, burnings and slaughterings, first by the Danes and then by Hereward the Wake, and a second abbey was destroyed in an accidental fire in 1116. The present building, with the unique painted wooden ceiling in the nave, was consecrated in 1238. The abbey was dissolved in 1539, and re-founded as a cathedral in 1541. The cathedral is perpetually filled with light due to the plain glass in most of its windows; the original stained glass was smashed by Parliamentarian troopers during the Civil War.

Peterborough was ancient long before Peada built his monastery. New Stone Age people had a settlement on the site 6000 years ago. These were followed by Bronze and Iron Age farmers, Roman legionaries and, eventually, the Anglo-Saxons whose king was Peada. Relics of them all may be seen in the Museum and Art Gallery in Trinity Street. Also on display are ship models made by French prisoners during the Napoleonic Wars, and a Victorian corner shop.

Cathedral: All year, daily. Museum: All year, Tues-Sat and Bank Hol Mon (pm only Oct-Apr). Free entry. 🅿 Tel Peterborough (0733) 43329.

PRICKWILLOW DRAINAGE ENGINE MUSEUM

On B1382, 4 miles east of Ely (Dc)

Winning farmland from the Fens by drainage has been the chief preoccupation of the area since Roman times. Paradoxically, the process was easier in earlier days, before the mid-17th century and the vast drainage schemes of the Earl of Bedford and his engineer Cornelius Vermuyden.

As large areas were drained, the peat of which the Fens are composed dried out and shrank. Rivers had to be embanked and consequently flowed, as they do now, at a higher level than the surrounding countryside. The drains could no longer run into them, and to maintain drainage, a means had to be found to raise the water to the rivers' level. Wind pumps were the first solution, then steam beam engines. In the early 1920s some of these were replaced by giant diesel engines, and it is one of these, a five-cylinder Mirrlees, still lovingly maintained by the Prickwillow Engine Trust, that takes pride of place in the museum. The building was constructed in 1880.

Apr-Oct, daily. Free entry. 🅿 (limited). Tel Prickwillow (035 388) 230.

SACREWELL WATER MILL

Off A47, 7 miles west of Peterborough (Bd)

Like most of the water mills in this part of the country, Sacrewell has a long history. There was a mill on this site when Domesday Book was compiled, and possibly even earlier, in Romano-British times. Sacrewell is still a working water mill and is the central feature of a Farming and Country Life Centre. In the mill and 18th-century farm buildings there are displays of farming, domestic and rural bygones, of country crafts and skills, of farming tools and transport during the last century or so, and of archaeological discoveries made while ploughing the nearby fields. There are tours of the farm and a nature trail.

Apr-Oct, Sun and Bank Hol. Adm charge. Refreshments. Shop. 🅿 Toilets. Tel Stamford (0780) 782222.

STRETHAM OLD ENGINE

On A10, 4 miles south of Ely (Dc)

Uncompromisingly utilitarian, the tall-chimneyed brick engine house stands by the wind-flicked Old West River, as the Great Ouse is called at this point. For those who relish relics of the Cast Iron Age, the beauty lies within – a

EXTINGUISHED FIRES *Like huge diving bells, the massive coal-fired boilers that once raised steam to power Stretham Old Engine lie disused today in the workshop. They were superseded by diesel engines in 1925.*

great beam engine of 1831. Its job was to drive a 37ft diameter scoop wheel that lifted water out of a main fen drain and dumped it into the river that flowed 4ft above, or 12ft in times of flood. Some 30 tons of water were lifted at each revolution of the wheel, or about 120 tons a minute. During the floods of 1919, the old engine worked non-stop for 47 days and nights, and it was still running sweetly when last operated in 1941.

All year, daily. Adm charge (small). 🅿 (limited). Tel Stretham (035 389) 236.

UNWINS TRIAL GARDEN, HISTON

On B1049, 3 miles north of Cambridge (Db)

Visitors to Cambridge in summer frequently pause between colleges to admire the flowers in the city's parks and gardens. Many of these were grown from seeds given by Unwins, the seedsmen, whose headquarters is at Histon. There, from mid-July to mid-September, they put on their own display in their 4 acre trial garden, a truly incredible composition made up of more than 30,000 annual garden flowers and over 1000 varieties of vegetables.

Mid July-mid Sept, daily. Adm charge (to charity). Refreshments. 🅿 Toilets. ♿ Tel Histon (022 023) 2270.

WANDLEBURY RING

Off A1307, 4 miles south-east of Cambridge (Db)

This Iron Age hill-fort on the crest of the Gog Magog Hills lies near the ford over the Cam where Cambridge now stands and commanded the ancient trackway that ran westwards through the chalk. The hills are named after the mythical giants Gog and Magog, who were the last survivors of Albion (ancient Britain), and ancient legends also tell of a ghostly knight who dwelt in the ring.

None of this deterred the Earl of Godolphin, who in the early 18th century built a house within the half-mile circumference of the defences and planted trees to form a sporting estate. The site of the house is marked now by a raised lawn with a sundial, but a stable block with a clock in a cupola still stands. It has been converted into private houses, and a small shop and exhibition centre.

A nature trail skirts the defences. It offers beechwoods, chalk downland vegetation and flowers, picnic spots and fine views.

All year, daily (shop and centre, Sun only).

WICKEN SEDGE FEN

On A1123, 6 miles south of Ely (Dc)

With its odd loneliness, whispering reeds and slow-moving water, the reserve at Wicken Fen is part of the Great Levels that cover 2000 square miles between Lincolnshire and Suffolk. The reserve covers 605 acres and is made up of Sedge Fen, St Edmund's Fen and Adventurers' Fen – an adventurer being an investor in the 17th-century fen drainage.

Sedge Fen is one of the few tracts in the Great Levels where drainage has had little effect, so it is an important site for preservation. Local people for centuries have harvested its peat for fuel and sedge for thatching. More recently, reeds were cut for thatching and litter gathered for animal feed and bedding. Such 'cropping' ceased at the end of the last century, but has been resumed to conserve the range of habitats it helped to create: open water, reedbeds, sedge fields, woodland and 'carr', or alder buckthorn scrub.

The drainage and cultivation of peat causes it to shrink and decompose, and the 330 acres of Sedge Fen now stand 8ft above the level of the surrounding drained areas. It was necessary to build a flood bank around the fen to help maintain the water table and thus prevent it from drying out.

The fen is crossed by droves – paths cut by fenmen as a means of access. Sedge Fen Drove is 300 to 350 years old, but the others date from the 1920s. It is bounded on the south by Wicken Lode, one of the ancient waterways that carried water across the Fens into the River Cam, and were the principal means of access to the remote Fenland villages.

Sedge Fen is one of the great wetlands of Europe, full of rare marsh plants. Some 5000 insect species live there, with numbers of large birds. A tower hide gives wide views of the reserve and its birds, and on clear days Ely Cathedral can be seen.

A nature trail of just over 2 miles starts at the entrance to Sedge Fen. Visitors are recommended to wear rubber boots, and must keep to the paths. A boardwalk trail of just under a mile is suitable for wheelchairs and can be walked in all conditions. The William Thorpe building at the entrance has displays about the fen, and tourist information.

The windpump a few yards from the entrance once pumped water from Adventurers' Fen, and was installed on its present site in 1956. Now restored to full working order, it can be used to help maintain the water table of Sedge Fen.

NT. All year, daily. Adm charge. P *Toilets.* ♿ *Tel Ely (0353) 720274.*

WILLERS MILL FISH FARM AND ANIMAL SANCTUARY

Off A10, 8 miles south-west of Cambridge (Ca)

Large carp that will eat from the fingers are on view here. There is a hatchery, and fish for aquarium or pool are on sale. Animals are brought to the sanctuary for a variety of reasons. Some are the victims of road accidents or the shotgun; others are unwanted pets or specimens from closed down menageries. They include foxes, chipmunks, marmosets, otters, monkeys, raccoons, a llama, owls and wolves. There are pony rides on summer weekends.

Mar-Oct, daily; Nov-Mar, Sat and Sun. Adm charge. Refreshments. Shop. P *Toilets.* ♿ *Tel Royston (0763) 61832.*

WIMPOLE HALL AND HOME FARM

Off A14, 8 miles south-west of Cambridge (Ca)

In the flat landscape, Wimpole Hall stands out from far off, and the 2 mile avenue that runs straight as a ruler to the classical red brick and stone South Front enhances rather than dwarfs it.

The original central block was built for Sir Thomas Chicheley in the 1640s, and later owners

LYING IN STATE *The 3rd Earl of Hardwicke, the owner of Wimpole Hall who died in 1834, lies clad in his Garter robes in the nearby Church of St Andrew. The effigy by Richard Westmacott stands amid a wealth of other monuments by major sculptors*

have rebuilt or added to the house and its out buildings. The last private owner was Mrs Elsie Bambridge, Rudyard Kipling's daughter, who spent almost 40 years restoring the house to its proper splendour; when she died in 1976 she left it, and its 3000 acre estate, to the National Trust.

Wimpole's architects and designers read like a Roll of Honour of the craft – Philip Gibbs, Sir John Soane, Capability Brown, Humphry Repton. It was Gibbs who planned the richly painted chapel and the library, built about 1730 to house Lord Harley's vast collection of books and prints. Known as the Harleian Miscellany, the collection became the nucleus of the British Museum Library. Soane contributed the wondrous Yellow Drawing Room, flooded with light from the glazed dome, and relined in yellow silk by Mrs Bambridge. Particularly charming are Mrs Bambridge's own apartments, left with magazines and books laid aside as though she had just gone out for a moment, and with collections of costume and coaching paintings and prints.

Close by the house is the mid-19th century stable block and the Church of St Andrew, much remodelled in the 18th and 19th centuries. Lapping the buildings about are the gardens and park, which have seen constant change since the late 17th century. To begin with, they were highly formal, with parterres, fountains, ponds and walks; the great South Avenue belongs to this period. Then came Capability Brown who grassed over the beds, brought pasture up to the windows of the house, changed the ponds into a lake and added a 'ruined' tower. Humphry Repton planted new gardens around the house and pushed the pasture back with lawns and railings. The 19th century added shrubberies and trees. Mrs Bambridge put in drifts of daffodils.

In the late 18th century, under the 3rd Earl of Hardwicke, the Home Farm was famous for its advanced methods of agriculture. Sir John Soane did not feel it beneath him to design the farm buildings, and his grand touch is especially apparent in the abbey-like Great Barn, covered with reed thatch and housing a museum of farming methods down the centuries.

The remainder of Home Farm combines museumship with working establishment. There are huge, longhorn cattle, doe-eyed Guernseys, goats and mighty-thewed workhorses. There is also a collection of rare and ancient breeds of farm animals from which it is hoped to raise future herds. For younger visitors there is a Children's Corner with goslings and woolly lambs.

NT. Mid Apr-late Oct, daily exc Mon and Fri; open Bank Hol Mon. Adm charge. Refreshments. Shop. P *Toilets.* ♿ *(limited). Tel Cambridge (0223) 207257.*

COUNTY CALENDAR

January (mid-month, Sat and Sun). Whittlesey: Straw Bear Festival (ancient fertility rite).

March Alwalton, nr Peterborough: National Shire Horse Show.

May (end of month). Ely: Festival.

Whit Tuesday St Ives: Dicing for Bibles (17th-century tradition).

June Cambridge: Midsummer Fair.

July Cambridge: Folk Festival.

July Alwalton, nr Peterborough: East of England Show.

July Cambridge: Arts Festival.

July Wisbech: Rose Fair.

Tourist information: Cambridge (0223) 322640; Ely (0353) 2062; Huntingdon (0480) 52181; Peterborough (0733) 63141; Wisbech (0945) 583263.

CHANNEL ISLANDS

DEFIANT CASTLES AND OCCUPATION RELICS NEAR THE COAST OF FRANCE

A visit to the Channel Islands is rather like taking a continental holiday on British soil. Yet each island has its own character and appeal. Alderney's only town has the character of a Normandy village; Guernsey nurtures tomatoes and displays its links with fishing and the sea; Jersey has two proud castles and a zoo of international repute; Herm and Sark are places to wander on foot.

The two main islands contain poignant reminders of the German Occupation in the Second World War, and both also have strong fictional associations. Victor Hugo set and wrote his novel *Toilers of the Sea* in Guernsey, while Jersey is the home of the TV detective Bergerac.

ALDERNEY

The island's history since Iron Age times and its role in two wars can be traced in the Alderney Museum, housed in the old town school building in Lower High Street, St Anne. The island's only town, St Anne is a pleasing mixture of colour-washed houses and cobbled streets. The island, only $3\frac{1}{2}$ miles long and $1\frac{1}{2}$ miles wide, is circled by boat trips which visit the bird sanctuary island of Burhou, a pleasant picnic spot.

Alderney Museum: Apr-Oct, Mon-Sat am. Adm charge. Shop. Tel Alderney (048 182) 3222.

GUERNSEY

CASTLE CORNET

St Peter Port (Bc)

The castle once stood defiantly isolated on a rocky island, but it is now joined to St Peter Port by a causeway and overlooks a cluster of yachts in the harbour. Its tiered grey walls are softened by clusters of palm trees, and the nearby Sutler's Garden creates a vivid blaze of colour around the old town jail in summer.

The earliest known reference to Castle Cornet was in 1206, and the surviving buildings date from the 13th to the 20th century. The Barbican is one of the oldest parts, built by the French during their six-year occupation which ended in 1345. During the Civil War, Castle Cornet was the last Royalist stronghold to fall to the Parliamentarians, after an eight-year siege. In 1672, lightning detonated gunpowder stored in the central tower and demolished it.

Guernsey's maritime and military history museums are housed in the castle together with weapons ranging from pikes to machine guns. The RAF's 201 Squadron Museum is also in the castle; the squadron's connection with Guernsey goes back to the 1920s, when test flights on a new flying boat were carried out there.

Apr-Oct, daily. Adm charge. Refreshments. Shop. P *(limited). Toilets. Tel Guernsey (0481) 26518.*

FORT GREY MARITIME MUSEUM

5 miles west of St Peter Port (Ac)

Built in 1804 as one of several towers to defend Guernsey against Napoleon's forces, Fort Grey has had a chequered history. It was manned in both World Wars – in the Second by the occupying Germans. In 1975 it was converted into a maritime museum specialising in exhibits of local shipwrecks. It stands on a tidal islet, and its white-painted tower is a landmark for seamen.

For light relief the museum tells the story of the steamship *Briseis*, which hit a rock and sank in Vazon Bay in 1937. Its crew got ashore in lifeboats. Shortly afterwards, the ship's cargo of wine barrels floated ashore – and a local newspaper reported 'amazing scenes of drunkenness'.

Apr-Oct, daily. Adm charge. Shop. Tel Guernsey (0481) 26518.

GERMAN MILITARY UNDERGROUND HOSPITAL

2½ miles south-west of St Peter Port (Bc)

This hospital and ammunition store, built in concrete under a hill, is the biggest structure left by the occupying Germans anywhere in the Channel Islands. It also has some of the grimmest associations. Hundreds of slave workers of many nationalities took three and a half years to build and equip it. The hospital, designed for 500 patients, was used only briefly, taking in German soldiers wounded in France after the Allies' invasion in 1944. The $1\frac{1}{4}$ miles of corridors and rooms which can now be seen were excavated out of solid rock at the cost of many lives. There are still beds in three of the wards, and occupation relics such as rifles, pistols and uniforms as well as a collection of wartime newspapers.

Apr-Oct, daily. Adm charge. Shop. P *Tel Guernsey (0481) 39100.*

GERMAN OCCUPATION MUSEUM

At Forest (Bb)

In its skilful unfolding of the wartime story of Guernsey, this museum recalls first of all the German air raid on St Peter Port harbour on June 28, 1940, in which 34 islanders were killed when planes bombed tomato lorries which had been mistaken for military transport. Two days later the occupying forces arrived, marching through

St Peter Port to the strains of a band – and there is a painting depicting the scene.

To show how islanders lived in those troubled times, there is a reconstructed kitchen complete with the crystal set on which the BBC news was secretly heard, and displays of eagerly awaited Red Cross food parcels. In the map and bunker rooms are illustrations of the wartime defences, including mighty battleship guns with a 37 mile range.

Apr-Oct, daily; Nov-Mar, Sun and Thur. Adm charge. Refreshments. Shop. P *Toilets.* ♿ *Tel Guernsey (0481) 38205.*

GUERNSEY FOLK MUSEUM

2½ miles north-west of St Peter Port (Bc)

Life in a Guernsey farmhouse more than a century ago is strikingly reconstructed in this museum. The kitchen, traditionally the centre of family life, had a fire of seaweed, dung and furze which never went out. There is a domed brick oven, a variety of kitchen utensils and a dresser stocked with china. In the costume room is a fine collection of clothes, and the traditional local doll, Côbo Alice or Côbo Sue, colourfully dressed in odd bits of material, is in the kitchen.

Mar-Oct, daily. Adm charge. Refreshments. Shop. P *Toilets. Tel Guernsey (0481) 55384.*

GUERNSEY MUSEUM

Candie Gardens, St Peter Port (Bc)

In 1811 a young man named Frederick Corbin Lukis walked home from a Guernsey excavation with a skull under his arm. The skull became the nucleus of a collection by Lukis and his sons, archaeologists like himself, on which this museum was founded.

Exhibits tell Guernsey's story through the ages, while the adjoining art gallery contains works by two local 19th-century painters, Paul Jacob Naftel and Peter Le Lievre. The museum and gallery are set in the Candie Gardens, where exotic plants are attractively laid out.

All year, daily. Adm charge. Refreshments. Shop. P *Toilets.* ♿ *Tel Guernsey (0481) 26518.*

GUERNSEY TOMATO CENTRE

½ mile south-east of Vazon Bay (Bc)

Tomato cultivation is Guernsey's main industry, so there could be no better place for a centre and museum dedicated to the 'love apple'. Films and displays chart the progress of the island's tomato history, since its introduction in the early 17th century. Aztecato, Guernsey's tomato wine, can be seen in the making and is on sale.

Apr-Oct, daily. Adm charge. Refreshments. Shops. P *Toilets.* ♿ *Tel Guernsey (0481) 54389 (summer).*

GUERNSEY ZOO

3 miles south-west of St Peter Port (Bc)

The speciality of this collection belonging to the Zoological Trust of Guernsey is smaller and lesser-known mammals and birds. The two-toed sloth, for instance, has hair growing 'in reverse' to enable the rain to drain off when it is hanging upside down.

The smallest ape, the gibbon, is represented, and there are small monkeys such as the marmoset and the tamarin. More than 40 Parma wallabies have been bred at the zoo; the species was believed to be extinct until some were found on a New Zealand island in 1960.

All year, daily. Adm charge. Refreshments (summer). P *Toilets.* ♿ *Tel Guernsey (0481) 39176.*

LITTLE CHAPEL

3 miles south-west of St Peter Port (Bc)

This jewel of a building, with an interior measuring 19ft by 10ft, may be the smallest church in the world. It was built largely of discarded odds and ends by the dedicated and tireless Brother Déodat, one of a group of French teaching monks who established themselves in Guernsey in the early 20th century.

First Brother Déodat built a grotto, which was completed just before the outbreak of the First World War. After volunteering for the French Army and being rejected on health grounds he set about building a chapel. This stood until 1923, but because a portly bishop could not squeeze through the door to consecrate it, Déodat destroyed it and started work on the 'do-it-yourself' chapel that now stands.

All year, daily. Free entry. P *Shop.*

SAUSMAREZ MANOR

1½ miles south of St Peter Port (Bc)

Built on the site of a Norman house, and richly added to in Queen Anne and Regency times, Sausmarez Manor is an excellent example of a hereditary feudal home. The house is still occupied by the de Sausmarez family, which has had a long association with the Channel Islands.

The magnificent dining room has portraits of four generations of the family. They include Thomas de Sausmarez, who built the spacious drawing room in 1820 to accommodate his large family.

Spring Bank Hol-Sept, Wed-Sat. Adm charge. Refreshments. Shop. P *Toilets. Tel Guernsey (0481) 35611.*

VICTOR HUGO'S HOUSE

Hauteville, St Peter Port (Bc)

Woodcarvings, tapestries and tiles decorate a house which is just as much a creation of Victor Hugo as any of the novelist's works. The richly decorated interiors, which took years to complete, incorporate Turkish carpets, pirates' treasure and even a stall thought to come from Chartres Cathedral. Hugo used pieces of old carving to create new furniture, often in surprising ways: the enormous fireplace in the tapestry drawing room is in fact three carved chests supported by 'columns' of table legs.

The glass room on the third floor was added by Hugo in 1861 on what was previously the roof of the house. It has a spectacular view across St Peter Port, part of Guernsey, and on clear days, to the French coast. Hugo worked here every morning, and the corner tables were built to accommodate his habit of writing while standing up. A small library and Hugo's bedroom are also on this floor.

Apr-Sept, daily exc Sun. Adm charge. Toilets. Tel Guernsey (0481) 21911.

ONE MAN'S CHAPEL *The Little Chapel on Guernsey was built by a French monk, Brother Déodat, out of patiently collected broken teapots, unwanted ornaments, and pebbles and shells.*

HERM

A 20 minute motorboat trip from Guernsey brings the visitor to this tiny island with a surprising variety of natural scenery and a warm 'continental' atmosphere. There are rugged cliffs with safe walks and spectacular views; sandy beaches such as Fisherman's and Bears'; sheltered coves such as Belvoir Bay; a grassy plain to the north; and a Mediterranean-style village near the harbour.

Herm measures 1½ miles from north to south and half a mile across, and there is a coastal walk

THE HOUSE THAT HUGO BUILT *The French novelist Victor Hugo designed the richly decorated interior of his house at St Peter Port, including the red salon. He bought its large Charles II table in London.*

around the entire island, whose highest point is some 230ft above sea level.
Summer, hourly boat from St Peter Port, Guernsey.

JERSEY

BATTLE OF FLOWERS MUSEUM

Off B34, 2 miles north-west of St Peter (Ab)

At one time the beautiful floats made of flowers taking part in Jersey's annual carnival were torn to pieces at the end of the day so that people could pelt each other with blossoms. Since 1964 there has been no actual 'Battle of Flowers', and the outstanding floats have a prolonged life in this museum. Among them are '101 Dalmatians', a 1968 prizewinner depicting a scene from the Walt Disney film, and some magnificent Arctic, Alpine and African scenes.
Mar-Nov, daily. Adm charge. Refreshments. Shop. P *Toilets. Tel Jersey (0534) 82408.*

ELIZABETH CASTLE

In St Aubin's Bay, off St Helier (Ba)

Set on an islet in the sea, this rugged fortress guards St Aubin's Bay and St Helier harbour. It can be reached by amphibious craft, or on foot at low tide. In the mid-16th century, as the growing town of St Helier became a strategic point, work began on fortifying the islet. It was to take more than 50 years. Sir Walter Raleigh, governor of Jersey from 1600 to 1603, complimented Queen Elizabeth by calling the castle 'Fort Isabella Bellissima', and the name Elizabeth Castle remains.

Throughout the 18th century the castle was defended against expected attack by the French. In the Second World War the occupying German forces refortified the castle, using slave labour to put up gun emplacements and bomb-proof shelters. Two of the guns they installed can still be seen, as can many of the castle's earlier buildings and defences.
Late Mar-Oct, daily. Adm charge. Refreshments. Shop. Toilets. Tel Jersey (0534) 23971.

ISLAND FORTRESS OCCUPATION MUSEUM

Esplanade, St Helier (Ba)

The history of the German wartime occupation is recalled in this seafront museum. As well as displays and showcases containing Second World War relics, there are uniformed dummies in hospital field station and armoury scenes; a vehicle compound; and a large arms collection ranging from pistols to howitzers.

Civilian exhibits include ration books for dogs, home-grown tobacco, and crystal radio sets used for listening to the BBC. Pride of place goes to the surrender document, signed in 1940.

At St Lawrence, 3 miles west of St Helier, is the German Underground Hospital – a vast complex bored deep into a hillside by forced labour from all over Occupied Europe. It has an extensive display of relics and memorabilia of the island's five years of German occupation.
Museum: Mar-Nov, daily. Adm charge. Tel Jersey (0534) 34306. Hospital: Mar-Oct, daily; Nov, Dec and Feb, Thur and Sun pm. Adm charge. Shop. P *Toilets.* ♿ *Tel (0534) 63442.*

HIDDEN HOSPITAL *Built to take 500 patients, the German Underground Hospital in Jersey has been faithfully re-created – including its wards, operating theatre, doctors' quarters and Kommandant's office.*

JERSEY MUSEUM

Pier Road, St Helier (Ba)

When Le Quesne's chemist's shop in St Helier was modernised in 1972, the old fittings and equipment were taken to the Jersey Museum to make a reconstruction of a Victorian chemist's shop. This and other period rooms, full of artefacts given by islanders, convey a vivid impression of Jersey life in earlier days. One room is dedicated to the Jersey-born actress Lillie Langtry, mistress of Edward VII, and contains many of her personal possessions.

Traditional island trades – many of which have now disappeared – are a feature of the museum. There are cider flagons and pipkins, made from medieval times until recently, and a collection of Victorian and Edwardian bottles. A wooden figure of a Highland soldier taking snuff used to stand outside a local tobacconist's shop as a symbol of his trade. The collection of coins and bank notes is extensive, and there are sea-worn stones, once used for weighing market produce according to Jersey's own system of weights.
All year, daily exc Sun. Adm charge. Shop. Toilets. Tel Jersey (0534) 75940.

JERSEY ZOOLOGICAL PARK

Off B31, 2¾ miles north of St Helier (Ca)

More than 1500 endangered animals – including families of orang-utans, snow leopards, spectacled bears and babirussas, or wild hogs – live in peace and safety at this zoo founded by the author and naturalist Gerald Durrell. Its symbol is the long extinct dodo – a reminder of the increasing threat of extinction for many of the world's wild creatures.

One of the zoo's major attractions is the gorilla family in its own large enclosure. One of the silver-backed gorillas – Jambo – became an international celebrity in the summer of 1986 when a five-year-old boy fell into the compound and lay unconscious. Jambo protected the injured child from the natural curiosity of the other gorillas until human aid arrived.

Breeding is a feature of the zoo and, since his act of mercy, Jambo has fathered more than a dozen fine gorillas and is now a grandfather.
All year, daily. Adm charge. Refreshments. Shop. P *Toilets.* ♿ *Tel Jersey (0534) 61949.*

KEMPT TOWER CENTRE

On B35, 1½ miles west of St Peter (Aa)

Les Mielles, a nature area overlooking St Ouen's Bay, is rich in flora and wildlife. Its sand dunes – *mielles* in Norman French – along with scrub, ponds and other types of habitat, are the home of some 5000 insect species and a wide variety of birds. There are also many reminders of man's history – from Neolithic tombs to fortifications set up by the Germans in the Second World War. At the Kempt Tower Interpretation Centre, visitors are given expert advice and information.
May-Sept, pm daily; Apr and Oct, Thur and Sun. Free entry. Shop. P *Toilets. Tel Jersey (0534) 83651.*

L'ETACQ WOODCRAFTS

Off B35, 2½ miles north-west of St Peter (Ab)

Cabbages 10ft tall – and sometimes more – provide Jersey with an unusual industry: they are cut and made into walking sticks. How the cabbages first reached Jersey is uncertain, but they grew in practically every garden on the island in the early 19th century. Since the Second World War, walking-stick production has been carried on solely by L'Etacq Woodcrafts, whose craftsmen also turn the giant stalks into a variety of other articles – including shoehorns and corkscrews.
All year, daily exc weekends Nov-Mar. Adm charge. Refreshments. Shop. P *Toilets. Tel Jersey (0534) 82142.*

LA HOUGUE BIE

On B28, 3 miles east of St Helier (Ca)

A giant prehistoric tomb with two Christian chapels on top gives an awesome atmosphere to this site and its museum complex. The burial mound, one of the finest in Western Europe, is thought to be about 7000 years old. A great pile of earth and rubble, 40ft high and 180ft across, covers the tomb itself, and inside there is a passage 33ft long leading to a central burial chamber with side chambers branching from it. The first chapel built on the mound was that of Notre Dame de Clarté (Our Lady of the Light), probably by the Paisnel family, lords of Hambye, in the 12th or early 13th century. The Jerusalem Chapel was added in about 1520 by Richard Mabon, Dean of Jersey.

La Hougue Bie was acquired in 1919 by the Société Jersiaise, a voluntary organisation devoted to preserving the island's heritage. In 1924 the mound was excavated and the chapels were extensively restored. In July 1940 German occupying forces set up a communications centre in a concrete bunker at La Hougue Bie and for a time this was linked to a dugout in the tomb mound itself. Now the bunker houses a museum of the German Occupation.
Mar-Oct, Tues-Sun. Adm charge. Refreshments. Shop. P *Toilets. Tel Jersey (0534) 53828.*

LA MARE VINEYARDS

Off B33, 1½ miles west of St John (Ba)

Vines have been grown in Jersey for centuries, probably since Roman times. The scene at La

Mare, home of the Blayney family, is green and tranquil; in addition to the avenues of vines there are beautiful gardens, a cider orchard and one of the island's finest farmhouses, originally built in 1797. The cider orchard has some 150 trees, and there is an old cider press. Another speciality is Jersey mustard flavoured with wine or cider.
May-Oct, Mon-Fri. Adm charge. Refreshments. Shop. P *Toilets. Tel Jersey (0534) 81178.*

MONT ORGUEIL

At Gorey, 4 miles north-east of St Helier (Ca)

The castle of Mont Orgueil, on a headland overlooking Grouville Bay and the Normandy coast, presents a dramatic picture. It was built as a bastion against invasion in the early 13th century after King John had lost Normandy to France. Between then and the 16th century the French attacked Jersey no fewer than 15 times, and nearly always Mont Orgueil was the main target.

Arrow slits and openings made later for cannon can be seen in the walls. In the 15th century the castle began to fall into disrepair, and among those who later had restoration carried out was Sir Walter Raleigh, Jersey's governor from 1600 to 1603. Mont Orgueil survived the Napoleonic Wars without invasion, and returned temporarily to a military role when the German occupying force refortified it in the Second World War.
End Mar-Oct, daily. Adm charge. Refreshments. Shop. Toilets. Tel Jersey (0534) 53292.

QUETIVEL MILL

Off A11, 3½ miles north-west of St Helier (Ba)

In St Peter's Valley a number of water-mill sites remain, but only one mill, Quetivel, now operates. Milling began on this site in 1309, and it continued until the late 19th century. The mill was set in action again during the German Occupation in the 1940s to grind locally grown corn when supplies ran low. A new wheel made then is a fine piece of craftsmanship. After the war, milling stopped again; but in recent years the National Trust for Jersey has rebuilt and re-equipped the mill.
May-Oct, Tues, Wed, Thur. Adm charge. Shop. P *Toilets. Tel Jersey (0534) 83193.*

ST PETER'S BUNKER

Off A12, in St Peter's village (Ba)

The Germans built the seven-room bunker in 1942, using Russian and other slave labour, to guard a vital crossroads giving access to Jersey Airport. More than 30 men slept in the bunker, now an Occupation Museum in which one room has been reconstructed to show what it looked like when occupied; a soldier is seen sleeping, and a picture of Hitler stares from the wall.

Other rooms house collections of uniforms and technical equipment – including the famous Enigma encoding machine which the Allies 'cracked'. There are reminders of the grim atmosphere in which islanders lived in the posters announcing proclamations and death warnings issued by the occupying forces.

The Jersey Motor Museum, opposite the bunker, presents an impressive array of vehicles. Some of these, too, have a military interest – such as the Rolls-Royce Phantom III which was used by General Montgomery during the run-up to D-day. Others – such as the Austin Seven, the 'bullnose' Morris and the Morris Eight – evoke the atmosphere of jolly jaunts between the wars.
Both museums: Mar-Nov, daily. Adm charge. Refreshments. Shop. P *Toilets. Bunker Mus: Tel Jersey (0534) 81048; Motor Mus: (0534) 82966.*

SAMARES MANOR

St Clements Inner Road, St Clement (Ca)

A herb maze based on the design of a medieval knot garden is an unusual feature of the herb garden at Samarès. More than 100 herbs are clearly labelled with their names and uses. The manor dates from Norman times, when herbs were an essential part of everyday life. All that remains of the original manor is the crypt, which now houses a collection of dairy and agricultural implements. An oriental flavour was introduced to the 14 acre grounds when a pagoda and Japanese summerhouse were built in 1930. An artificial hill was constructed to create the Japanese garden with its series of cascading waterfalls.

Each morning a guided tour of the manor takes in the William and Mary drawing room and the magnificent walnut-panelled dining room. The 11th-century dovecote in the grounds had nesting places for more than 500 pigeons.
Apr-Oct, daily. Adm charge. Refreshments. Shop. P *Toilets.* ♿ *(part). Tel Jersey (0534) 70551.*

SARK

The island is still a haven of peace where cars are banned: travel is by horse and carriage or bicycle – or on foot. It consists of two peninsulas, Great and Little Sark, joined by a narrow isthmus called La Coupée. The coast is rocky and the cliffs are high, but there are enchanting bays, caves and pools.

Travellers from Guernsey usually arrive at Maseline harbour, on the east coast. From Maseline they climb on foot or by tractor-drawn bus to the top of a steep hill, where they can transfer to a horse-drawn carriage. In the main settlement, called the Village, are shops, a church and an inn – as well as Sark's prison, built in 1853 for only two inmates.

Since Elizabethan times Sark has been a feudal state governed by a seigneur – as it is today. The grounds of his residence, the seigneury, are open to the public. They contain a superb walled garden, a *colombier*, or dovecote, which only the seigneur may own, a signalling tower, a bronze cannon presented by Elizabeth I, and two restored 12th-century chapels.
Apr-Oct, boats from St Peter Port, Guernsey. Gardens: Easter-Oct, days vary. Adm charge. Toilets. ♿ *Tel Sark (048 183) 2345.*

ISLANDS' CALENDAR

April (late). Jersey Airport: International Air Rally.

May 8/9 Guernsey/Jersey: Liberation Day Thanksgiving Services.

June (mid-month). Midsummer Flower and Garden Show.

July (mid-month). Jersey: Floral Island Week.

July (end). Guernsey: Harbour Carnival.

August (1st Mon). Alderney: Cavalcade.

August (early). Guernsey: Rocquaine Regatta.

August (2nd Thur). St Helier: Jersey Battle of Flowers.

August (mid-month). Sark: Water Carnival.

August (3rd or 4th Thur). Sausmarez Park: Guernsey Battle of Flowers.

Sept (early). Guernsey: International Power Boat Week. Sark: Horse Show.

Tourist information: Alderney (048 182) 2994; Guernsey (0481) 23555; Herm (0481) 22377; Jersey (0534) 78000; Sark (048 183) 2345.

LIT UP WITH PRIDE *The fortress of Mont Orgueil – French for 'Mount Pride' – was given its name by Henry V's brother, Thomas, Duke of Clarence, early in the 15th century. It is also known as Gorey Castle.*

CHESHIRE

MAGPIE HOUSES AND MILL MUSEUMS ON A PLAIN CUT BY CANALS

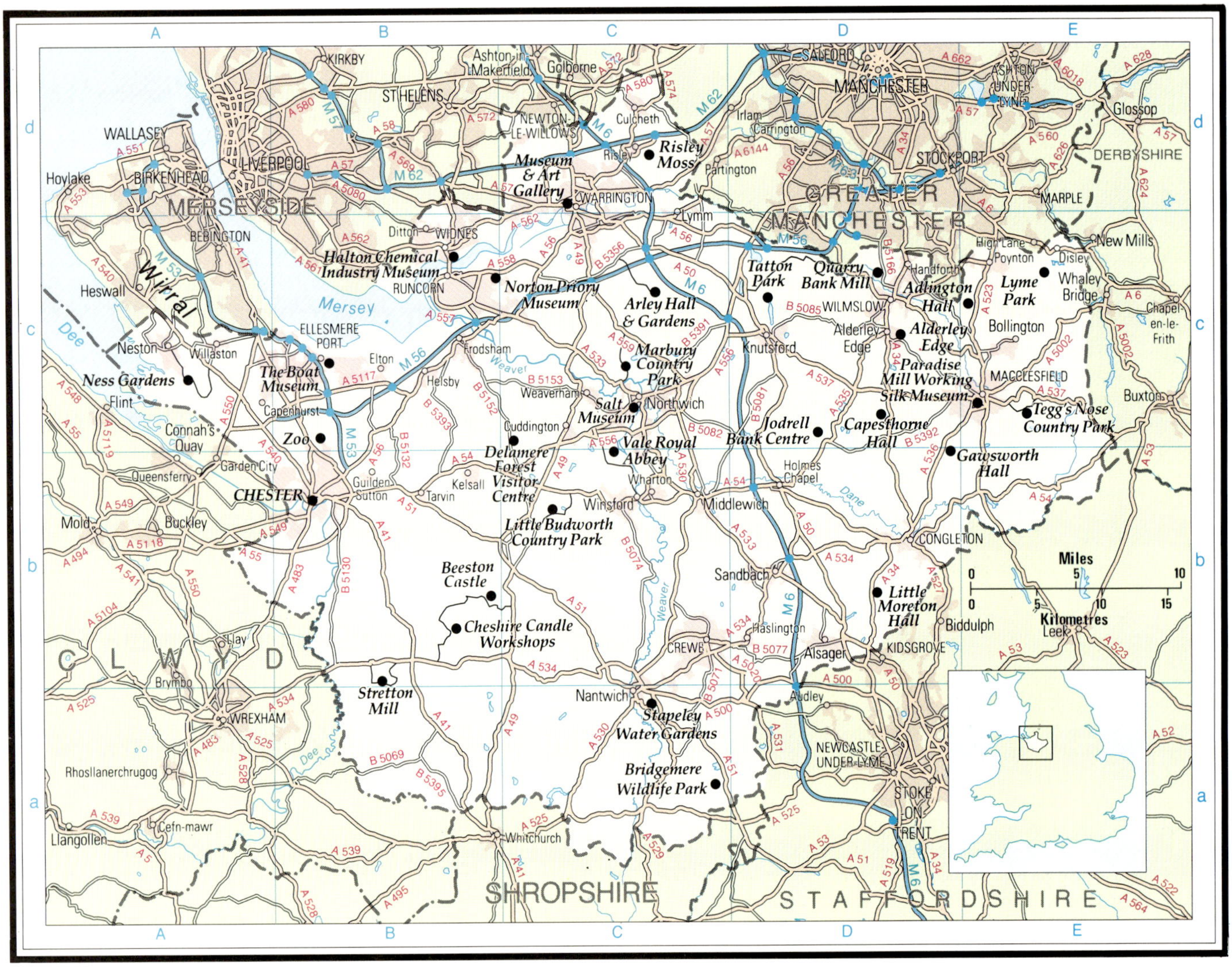

Salt and silk were the foundations of Cheshire's industrial wealth, and their stories are recalled in museums across the county. The Industrial Revolution which led to the building of Quarry Bank Mill and its pioneering model village for mill workers also saw the development of the county's canals, which are the theme of the Boat Museum at Ellesmere Port.

The Cheshire Plain has for centuries been rich dairy farming country. Wealth from the land built a profusion of country houses, and Gawsworth and Little Moreton Hall show how the traditional half-timbering used for cottages was equally successful for mansions. Their owners, unlike those of Tatton Park and Capesthorne, resisted the urge to rebuild in the grander styles of later centuries. The plain offered few natural defensive sites for castles, and those at Chester and Beeston are rare survivors from medieval times.

ADLINGTON HALL

Off A523, 5 miles north of Macclesfield (Ec)

When George Frederick Handel stayed at Adlington in 1741 and 1751 he played on England's largest 17th-century organ; and the organ still stands in the Great Hall, between two huge carved oak timbers. These timbers, the remains of a Saxon hunting lodge, support the east end of the hall, which was completed in 1505 with a magnificent hammerbeam roof and fine murals. The black-and-white portions of the house, in Cheshire's finest tradition, date from 1581, and the red-brick front from 1757.

Good Fri-Sept, Sun and Bank Hol; also Wed and Sat pm in Aug. Adm charge. Refreshments. Shop. P *Toilets. Tel Macclesfield (0625) 829206.*

ALDERLEY EDGE

On B5087, south-east of Alderley Edge village (Dc)

A beautiful wooded escarpment rising to 650ft, Alderley Edge gives panoramic views across Manchester to the Pennines beyond, and across the green Cheshire Plain. A pile of stones marks the spot on the summit where beacons have announced great events in the nation's history, such as victory at Waterloo in 1815.

Only bird songs break the serenity now, but in past times the hillside was a busy industrial centre. Copper was mined there before the Romans came to Britain, and cobalt and lead workings, used well into the 19th century, riddle its pink sandstone.

Stone Age and Bronze Age people sought the refuge of the scarp's caves, and inevitably such an ancient place has its legends. One tells of a troop of horsemen who will ride out of Wizard Cave to save their country in time of need.

Nether Alderley Mill, $1\frac{1}{2}$ miles south, dates from the 15th century and has two water wheels powered by water from a reservoir. The mill is tucked up against the wall of the reservoir, and its blanket of stone roofing slates sweeps low on both sides. The Victorian corn-grinding machinery stood derelict from 1939 until it was restored to working order in 1967.

NT. Alderley Edge: All year, daily. Mill: July-Sept, Tues-Sun and Bank Hol pm; Mar-June, and Oct, Wed, Sun and Bank Hol Mon pm. Adm charge. Tel Alderley Edge (0625) 584412.

ARLEY HALL AND GARDENS

Off B5356, 5 miles south-east of Warrington (Cc)

This is one of the few large gardens in Britain which are still maintained as they were before the Second World War – as part of a family home. The same family has lived at Arley since 1469, and it was the newly married Roland and Mary Egerton-Warburton who between 1840 and 1860, created in all essentials the exquisite garden of today. Its 8 acres include some of the earliest herbaceous borders and an avenue of 14 ilexes kept clipped into giant cylinders, more than 20ft tall.

In the 1970s a woodland garden containing more than 100 varieties of rhododendron was laid out; it leads to a woodland walk. There are also walled, scented and herb gardens, and a collection of shrub and species roses.

The present house, in Victorian Jacobean style, was built between 1832 and 1845. The Ride – a tithe barn built on great wooden arches in about 1450 – was used as a riding school in the 19th century. A Tudor barn also survives from earlier days.

Easter-early Oct, Tues-Sun and Bank Hol Mon. Adm charge. Refreshments. Shop. P *Toilets.* ♿ *Tel Arley (056 585) 353.*

BEESTON CASTLE

Off A49, 11 miles south-east of Chester (Bb)

A party of Royalists held out at Beeston Castle until November 1645 – six months after their king's final defeat at the Battle of Naseby – and Parliamentary forces virtually destroyed the castle a year later. Its remains stand dramatically on top of an isolated red-sandstone outcrop rising to 500ft. There are magnificent views across the Cheshire Plain to the Mersey and Wales, and to the Pennines in Derbyshire.

Remains of the inner ward and its gatehouse crown the highest point. They date from the 13th century. On two sides of the castle is a dry moat, hewn out of solid rock. Displays in the site museum tell the castle's story.

EH. All year, daily. Adm charge. Shop. P *Toilets. Tel Bunbury (0829) 260464.*

THE BOAT MUSEUM

At Junction 9 on M53, Ellesmere Port (Bc)

The subject of the award-winning Boat Museum is canals: canal boats, horses, machinery, people, history. The museum is set in the old Shropshire Union Docks which linked the Shropshire Union Canal with the Manchester Ship Canal and the Mersey. Some of the warehouses, workshops and locks date from the 1790s and continued in use until well after the Second World War.

The Old Stables now house a horse and canal exhibition. Nearby is the Blacksmith's Forge where half a dozen forges stand and sometimes work, fed by gigantic bellows; their main purpose was to make and repair chains for cranes and dockside railway wagons.

The one-time Pattern Shop houses a nostalgic display of photographs of the docks in former days, their industries and workpeople, their sports and entertainments. The theme is pursued in Porters Row, where rooms in four dockworkers' cottages built in 1833 have been restored to show how they would have looked at various times between 1840 and 1950. In the Hydraulic Pumping Station, two steam engines produced the 60hp needed to run the dock's cargo-handling gear; the engines are once more in full working order.

The main exhibition, in the Island Warehouse, is concerned with cargoes and craft on the nearby rivers and waterways since early times. Exhibits include a dugout canoe from an unspecified period, coracles and a Dee salmon boat. There are barge builders' and painters' workshops and examples of canal folk art – cans, kettles, lanterns, foghorns – all traditionally decorated with motifs of castles and roses. No one knows why these symbols were chosen, but the most likely explanation seems to be that they were copied from cheap Black Country enamelware of the last century. The central display is the canal longboat *Friendship*, partly converted into an audiovisual theatre. Built in 1925, she hauled coal on the Oxford Canal.

The stars of the show are the boats afloat in the basin – the dayboats and the wide boats, the tugs, icebreakers and weedcutters, the 'Starvationers', so called because their ribs show, the steamers, the motors and the horse-drawn boats, the Joshers and the old Clyde puffer. Many people's favourite is the narrowboat *Gifford*, whose cabin, 6ft by 8ft, gleams with paint, china and rag rugs and is cosy with the glow from its cast-iron stove. All very well until you remember that this tiny space was home for skipper, wife and maybe four or five children.

All year, daily. Adm charge. Refreshments. Shop. P *Toilets.* ♿ *Tel Liverpool (051) 355 5017.*

BRIDGEMERE WILDLIFE PARK

On A51, 6 miles south-east of Nantwich (Ca)

Big cats, including a Bengal tiger and puma, live alongside wolves, dingos, foxes and monkeys in this 40 acre park. Their enclosures and paddocks lie among meadows where daffodils bloom in spring. A collection of birds of prey includes eagles, a snowy owl from the Arctic and an eagle owl from Central Europe. Penguins, elegant Andean flamingos and several species of swan live in the four landscaped pools. There are craft, falconry and taxidermy displays in the new heritage centre, which also has traditional farm tools and machinery and rare British farm breeds on show.

Mar-Nov, daily. Adm charge. Refreshments. Shop. P *Toilets.* ♿ *Tel Bridgemere (093 65) 223.*

CAPESTHORNE HALL

On A34, 4 miles south of Alderley Edge (Dc)

A great fire in 1861 gutted the red-brick mansion which had been remodelled in Jacobean style only 24 years earlier. The architect Anthony Sal-

TWO WHEELER *The restored Nether Alderley Mill is once more grinding corn. Unusually, it has two stepped water wheels: water from the upper wheel drives the lower, and both drive millstones.*

vin was employed for the rebuilding, and he kept to the Jacobean style, with its turrets, pinnacles, stepped gables and ornate windows.

Capesthorne has been owned by the Bromley-Davenport family and their ancestors since the Conqueror's time. It contains fine furniture, sculptures and paintings, and an 'American room' furnished with items brought by Lady Bromley-Davenport from her home in Philadelphia. A Victorian theatre in the stable wing is still in use, and services are still held in an elegant Georgian chapel to the south of the hall.

The extensive park is drained by a lake and chain of pools overlooked by colourful gardens. These and the arboretum are on Mill Wood Walk, a circular route past an old ice house, a water mill, and a summer house set in a golden, leafy glade. There is also a herb garden, nature trail and children's adventure playground.

Apr, Sun; May and Sept, Wed, Sat and Sun; June-Aug, daily exc Mon and Fri; also Bank Hol. Adm charge. Refreshments. Shop. P *Toilets.* ♿ *Tel Chelford (0625) 861221.*

CHESHIRE CANDLE WORKSHOPS

Off A41, 10 miles south-east of Chester (Bb)

The ancient art of hand sculpting candles has been revived and expanded at the Cheshire Candle Workshops, and visitors can watch colourful candles being made and carved into intricate abstract designs. Wax figurines and wall plaques are also carved, and wooden name plaques and candle holders made. A film of the processes is shown, and a shop sells items from the workshops and a variety of locally handmade gifts.

Mar-Dec, daily; Jan and Feb, Sat and Sun. Free entry. Refreshments. Shop. P *Toilets.* ♿ *Tel Tattenhall (0829) 70401.*

CHESTER ZOO

Off A41, 2½ miles north of centre of Chester (Bc)

To walk into the Tropical House here is to enter one of the world's fast-dwindling habitats – a steamy, equatorial forest, with luxuriant vegetation up to 40ft tall, snakes, lizards and free-flying birds. The zoo provides as natural a setting as possible for its animals. *(continued on page 48)*

WALLED CITY ON THE DEE

The fair city of Chester has had many roles. First it was Deva, a Roman legionary fortress and naval base. This was succeeded by Saxon township, Norman border fortress, medieval walled town and seaport, Royalist stronghold, and finally modern cathedral city and county town. The marks that its history has left on Chester's architecture, and the present-day work of conservation, are described in displays at Chester Heritage Centre. Although Chester's Norman castle has disappeared, the 12th-century Agricola's Tower survived the city's rebuilding of 1788-1822. The area's army associations are recalled in The Cheshire Military Museum, which traces the history of four regiments which have their historic home in Chester or in Cheshire.

Chester Cathedral *All year, daily. Free entry. Refreshments. Shop.*

Chester Heritage Centre *Apr-Sept, daily exc Wed; Oct-Mar pm daily exc Wed. Adm charge. Shop. Tel Chester (0244) 317948.*

Toy Museum *All year, daily. Adm charge. Shop. Tel (0244) 316251.*

The Rows *All year, daily.*

Castle *EH. All year, daily exc Sun am. Free entry. ♿ (part).*

Grosvenor Museum *All year, daily exc Sun am. Free entry. Shop. Toilets. Tel (0244) 21616.*

King Charles' Tower *Apr-Oct, daily; Nov-Mar, Sat and Sun pm. Adm charge. Shop. Tel (0244) 21616.*

Chester Visitor Centre *All year, daily. Adm charge. Refreshments. Shop. Toilets. ♿ Tel (0244) 318916.*

Cheshire Military Museum *All year, daily. Adm charge. P (Sat and Sun). Tel (0244) 27617.*

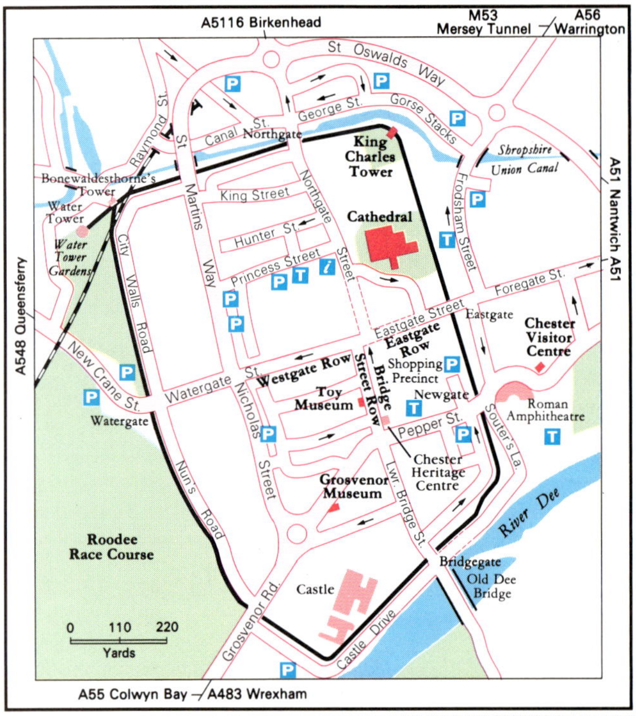

CHESTER CATHEDRAL

The glory of Chester Cathedral is its 13th-century choir (far left). Beneath the lofty vault stand magnificently carved and canopied wooden choir stalls; an elephant-and-castle figure (left) adorns one bench end. Hugh Lupus, the Norman Earl of Chester, refounded the Saxon church dedicated to St Werburgh of Mercia as a Benedictine abbey in 1092. After the Dissolution of the Monasteries the abbey became a cathedral. It was extensively restored in Victorian times.

TOY MUSEUM

A mechanical roundabout made in Germany in 1912 is one of more than 5000 items in Chester's Toy Museum. Exhibits date from 1830 to the present day, and range from tinplate cars, aeroplanes and lorries to dolls and teddy bears, and from pedal cars and games to battery toys and puppets. There is a re-created toyshop window from the 1950s, and a dolls' hospital.

GROSVENOR MUSEUM

Bygone Chester is vividly brought to life in the Grosvenor Museum. Paintings of local scenes include *Watergate Street* (above) by Louise Rayner (1829-1924), and the elegant Georgian drawing room (above right) is one of several period rooms re-created in the museum. There are displays of glass and of silver, much of it made and assayed in Chester. Pottery includes the slipware dish of 1671 (right), made by Thomas Toft and showing the Arms of Charles II. The museum's main theme, however, is Roman Chester. Dioramas, models and local finds tell the story of the XXth Legion *Valeria*, which began the great Deva fortress in AD 76 and defended it for 200 years.

THE ROWS

This handsome Victorian brick and timber-frame building stands on the corner of Bridge Street and Watergate Street at The Cross, the meeting place of Chester's main streets. These are lined by Chester's unique Rows – lines of buildings, some medieval and others Victorian remodellings, which have shops on galleried walkways at first-floor level.

KING CHARLES' TOWER

It was from this tower (above left) that Charles I watched the defeat of his army at Rowton Moor in 1645. It now contains displays re-creating the time of the Civil War (above). The tower is part of Chester's city walls; these are unique in Britain, for the 2 mile circuit dating from Roman and medieval times survives virtually intact. The Eastgate (left) stands on the site of Roman Chester's east gate. It was rebuilt in 1769, and its clock was added to commemorate Queen Victoria's Diamond Jubilee in 1897. Beyond is Foregate Street, outside the medieval city.

CHESTER VISITOR CENTRE

A reconstruction of one of Chester's Rows as it would have looked in the 1850s is one of the ways in which Chester Visitor Centre gives newcomers an introduction to the city. A video film takes visitors on an armchair tour, and describes the city's history and customs. The centre also offers guided tours of the city, including a daily Pastfinder Tour and a Ghost Tour, in which visitors are introduced to the city's spooks, witches and demons. Opposite the centre is the half-excavated Roman amphitheatre – the largest in Britain.

(continued from page 45) The orang-utans and chimpanzees live on grassy islands, with only water-filled moats between them and visitors. The elephants' outdoor island is surrounded only by a flower border and dry ditch, and indoors a dry ditch makes their enclosure.

The penguin pool has a sandy beach, and caves where the birds breed, and there are large windows to provide watchers with close-up views of them swimming underwater. Waterbuses take visitors for rides along the zoo's canals, and these give fine views of the penguins.

All year, daily. Adm charge. Refreshments. Shop. P *Toilets.* ♿ *Tel Chester (0244) 380280.*

DELAMERE FOREST VISITOR CENTRE

On B5152, 8 miles east of Chester (Cc)

'The forest of the meres' is a remnant of the vast royal hunting preserve of the Earls of Chester which covered central Cheshire in Norman times, and the Forestry Commission's centre has displays telling of Delamere's history and management. The area is now mostly planted with conifers, and is noted for kestrels, sparrowhawks, crossbills, goldcrests, foxes and badgers.

Besides the ancient public footpaths, there are waymarked walks, including a 1½ mile trail from the centre. This is also passed by the 31 mile Sandstone Trail, which follows a sandstone ridge from Frodsham 5 miles to the east.

All year, daily. Refreshments (weekends only). Shop. P *Toilets.* ♿ *Tel Northwich (0606) 882167.*

GAWSWORTH HALL

On A536, 2½ miles south of Macclesfield (Db)

The 'Fighting Fittons' held the manor of Gawsworth from 1316 to 1663, and the present superb, long, low, half-timbered house was built in 1480. In the following century, Sir Edward Fitton built a great wall to enclose the mansion and its park with lake and medieval tilting ground, which remains largely unchanged today. Mary Fitton, the daughter of another Sir Edward, was known as a great beauty, and is possibly the 'Dark Lady' of Shakespeare's sonnets. She was appointed Maid of Honour to Elizabeth I in 1596, but was disgraced six years later when found to be pregnant. Her lover, the Earl of Pembroke, refused her marriage, and their son died soon after birth.

Among the famous visitors to Gawsworth was the Duke of Monmouth, who was 'royally' entertained in 1682 when some 4000 people came to the park to see him. The house has fine furniture, sculpture and paintings.

End Mar-end Oct, pm daily. Adm charge. Refreshments. Shop. P *Toilets.* ♿ *(gardens). Tel North Rode (026 03) 456.*

HALTON CHEMICAL INDUSTRY MUSEUM

Gossage Building, Mersey Road, Widnes (Bc)

The name of Spike Island on which this museum stands is derived from a local slang word for a lodging house, many of which once stood on the island. The museum lies among the relics of the chemical industry that played a key role in the Industrial Revolution, and life-size reconstructions, photographs, working machines and slide shows tell the industry's story.

The Gossage Building itself was erected by John Hutchinson in 1860, and used by him as an office and laboratory. In 1908 it was bought by Gossage's soap company, and later it belonged to Imperial Chemical Industries. A glassed-in platform on top of the museum provides wide views over Widnes and Runcorn, whose chemical installations are explained by interpretive displays. A history trail leads around some of the local sites.

All year, daily exc Mon. Adm charge. Shop. P *Toilets.* ♿ *Tel Liverpool (051) 420 1121.*

SPACE AGE SYMBOL *The sky at sunset makes an appropriate backdrop for an instrument made by man to probe the secrets of space. The 250ft dish belongs to Manchester University's Mark 1A radio telescope at Jodrell Bank, in the Pennine foothills.*

JODRELL BANK SCIENCE CENTRE

On A535, 2½ miles north-east of Holmes Chapel (Dc)

The Mark 1A telescope designed by Sir Bernard Lovell for Manchester University is one of the world's largest fully steerable radio telescopes, and its reflector – 250ft across – towers above the centre. Like all radio telescopes, it vastly outdistances optical telescopes in the extent of space which it can 'view'. Nearby is its more wieldy fellow – a 25ft telescope which visitors can steer to pick up radio waves from the Sun.

The Jodrell Bank centre provides an excellent introduction to modern astronomy. Visitors can start by seeing a preliminary film before passing into the main exhibition area, with its displays devoted to satellite communications, weather monitoring, space research, and light and optics. There are several working space models, and 30 minute presentations in the planetarium.

Outside, a tree park covers more than 30 acres, and contains more than 20,000 trees and shrubs, including fine collections of crab apples, whitebeam and rowan.

Easter-Oct, daily; Nov-Easter, Sat and Sun pm. Adm charge. Refreshments. Shop. P *Toilets.* ♿ *Tel Lower Withington (0477) 71339.*

LITTLE BUDWORTH COUNTRY PARK

Off A49, 7 miles south-west of Northwich (Cb)

Visitors to this park on Little Budworth Common enter a time capsule of prehistoric Britain, for the landscapes here survive almost untouched by Man. The barren sands have limited the area's use to hunting and the occasional grazing of cattle. There are heaths covered by heather, gorse and bracken; woods of graceful silver birches, and some of Cheshire's unique mosses – bogs in which islands of sphagnum moss float. The woods are noted for fungi, insects and birds, including coal tits, great spotted woodpeckers, tree pipits and nuthatches. There is an information board in the main car park, and there are tracks and paths for walkers and horse riders.

All year, daily.

LITTLE MORETON HALL

On A34, 4 miles south of Congleton (Db)

It is something of a miracle that this magnificent, very English house survives intact. It was begun by William Moreton, who built a moated, timber-framed house around a courtyard in the 15th century. His son added the gatehouse. It was William's grandson who, like all fashionable Elizabethan gentlemen, felt it essential to have a large but friendly room for formal entertaining and displaying his paintings, and so built the panelled, 68ft Long Gallery over the gatehouse. Fortunately later Moretons resisted fashionable trends and preserved the Tudor extravaganza; its jumbled gables and slightly leaning, timbered walls are superb monuments to the arts of Tudor woodcarvers and plasterers. There are fine wall paintings and intricately leaded windows, and a 16th-century chapel.

An Elizabethan herb garden and a knot garden based on a design of 1688 lie within the moat.

MAGPIE MAGNIFICENCE *A dazzling jigsaw of white plaster and black timber makes Little Moreton Hall one of the most decorative houses in Britain. Despite its leaning walls, the house has survived for more than 400 years. The inside is just as ornate. The Long Gallery (left) retains its original panelling and floor; here Elizabethans displayed their paintings and entertained guests.*

NT. Apr-Sept, pm daily exc Tues; Mar and Oct, Sat and Sun. Adm charge. Refreshments. Shop. 🅿 *(limited) Toilets. Tel Congleton (0260) 272018.*

LYME PARK

Off A6, ½ mile west of Disley (Ec)

This house is not what it seems, for its elegant Palladian exterior conceals an Elizabethan mansion. The Legh family owned the estate from 1397, and in 1541 Sir Piers Legh swept away the original medieval house to make way for a new one. Its grand gatehouse, and 120ft Long Gallery and drawing room, both with fine wood and stone carving, still survive intact.

Peter Legh commissioned the classical exterior and other alterations in 1720, and the entrance hall, grand staircase and saloon remain as he planned them – the saloon embellished with finely carved wall panels by Grinling Gibbons. The house contains beautiful tapestries and furniture, including four chairs made by Thomas Chippendale for the parlour. These are reputedly upholstered with cloth from the cloak which Charles I wore at his execution in 1649.

The 'mansion within a mansion' overlooks a lake and stream more than 1100ft up on the Pennine moors. There are extensive gardens, and a surrounding 1300 acre walled country park, with ancient limes, fallow deer and the descendants of the red deer prized by huntsmen in Elizabeth I's time. The park can be explored by a nature trail or guided walks. There is a pitch and putt course, and there are facilities for fishing, horse riding and orienteering.

NT. Park all year, daily. Hall: June-Sept, pm daily exc Mon; Apr and May, Tues-Thur, Sat and Sun pm; Oct, Sat and Sun pm. Adm charge. Refreshments. Shop. 🅿 *Toilets. Tel Disley (066 32) 62023.*

MARBURY COUNTRY PARK

Off A533, 2½ miles north of Northwich (Cc)

This 200 acre park remains a gracious country estate, although its great house – Marbury Hall – was pulled down in 1968 after years of dereliction. An old ice house and avenues of limes planted in the 1840s survive. Terraces lead down from the house site to Budworth Mere, where a bird hide overlooks Marbury Reed Bed and grebes, coots, moorhens and reed warblers abound.

Several footpaths cross the park, and one beside the mere has splendid views across to Great Budworth village. A 2 mile 'Fact or Fiction Walk' explores some of the legends associated with the area, and there is a waymarked horse ride. The Trent and Mersey Canal forms the park's eastern boundary.

All year, daily.

NESS GARDENS

Off A540, 10 miles north-west of Chester (Ac)

A rose collection laid out to show the development of the rose in England, from those chosen as emblems by the Houses of Lancaster and York in medieval times to modern varieties, is an unusual feature of the Ness Gardens. The gardens are laid out on the Wirral's sandstone ridge, with magnificent views across the Dee estuary to the Welsh hills.

Ness Gardens were begun in 1898 by Arthur Kilpin Bulley, a wealthy Liverpool cotton broker. He sent out plant collectors, who between 1904 and 1931 introduced to Britain hundreds of oriental plants, many of which Bulley developed commercially for his firm Bees Ltd. Six years after Bulley died in 1942 his daughter gave the estate to Liverpool University as a botanic garden.

The gardens are colourful all the year, with fine rock, terrace, herb, shrub and heather areas, and herbaceous and rhododendron borders, all sheltered by trees. A visitor centre presents exhibitions, slide shows and lectures.

All year, daily. Adm charge. Refreshments (Easter-Sept). Shop. 🅿 *Toilets.* ♿ *Tel Liverpool (051) 336 2135.*

NORTON PRIORY MUSEUM

Off A558, 2 miles east of Runcorn (Bc)

Only 20 years before he dissolved Norton Priory in 1536, Henry VIII gave 30 great oaks from nearby Delamere Forest to repair fire damage to the building. In 1545 the Brooke family bought the 400-year-old priory and its estates, and turned part of it into a Tudor house. A Georgian mansion replaced this in about 1750, but this was demolished in 1928 and only the medieval undercroft survives.

Excavations of the site began in 1971, and in 1982 a museum opened to explain the site's story, and show what its buildings looked like. Displays give a clear insight into the everyday life of the Augustinian canons who lived and worshipped at Norton, and of the craftsmen who made the priory. There are 16 acres of woodland and

COLOURFUL COMMEMORATION *The glorious yellow flowers of* Primula bulleyana *brighten the rock garden at Ness. The plant, a native of China, was named after Arthur Bulley who created the garden.*

CHEQUERED WEB *The jacquard hand looms which once wove intricately patterned silk cloth for men's ties are preserved at Paradise Mill in Macclesfield. The Victorian mill reached its heyday in the 1930s. Today's visitors can see the design room in which artists worked out the patterns on squared paper, and the room in which workers cut the punched cards which 'programmed' the looms.*

STYLISH WORKPLACE *Quarry Bank cotton mill at Styal was founded in 1784 among woods beside the River Bollin. Inside, the giant water wheel, which was the kingpin of the mill and of the valley's power system, is now restored to full working order.*

gardens, including a tranquil glade with a stream and a shady pool, and a Victorian rock garden.

All year, pm daily. Adm charge. Refreshments. Shop. P *Toilets.* ♿ *Tel Runcorn (092 85) 69895.*

PARADISE MILL WORKING SILK MUSEUM

Near centre of Macclesfield (Ee)

The town of Macclesfield is almost synonymous with silk, for the industry has dominated the town from the 17th century almost to the present day. The weaving of silk cloth on hand looms began in the 1750s in skylit weavers' garrets and mills. Gradually the home weavers moved into the great, burgeoning mills, where in the 19th century power looms replaced hand looms. However, the best quality cloths continued to be hand woven.

Macclesfield's last hand-loom workshop closed in 1981 but is preserved in Paradise Mill. There are machines from the whole process of cloth production, from the arrival of raw silk from the Orient, to the finished article. An exhibition tells the history of the firm.

Macclesfield Heritage Centre, five minutes' walk from Paradise Mill, is housed in the former Macclesfield Sunday School. Here displays trace the history of the Sunday School movement and of Macclesfield, and a museum and library are devoted to the history of silk.

Paradise Mill: All year, pm Tues-Sun and Bank Hol. Adm charge. Shop. ♿ *Tel Macclesfield (0625) 618228. Heritage Centre: All year, pm Tues-Sun and Bank Hol. Adm charge. Refreshments. Shop. Toilets.* ♿ *Tel (0625) 613210.*

QUARRY BANK MILL

Off B5166, 2 miles north of Wilmslow (Dc)

As the Industrial Revolution gained momentum in the 1780s, two men of conscience and vision created factory communities in rural settings. One was Robert Owen, who established his cotton-mill village at New Lanark near Glasgow. The other was Samuel Greg, who inherited the Styal estate in the deep Bollin valley and founded his water-powered cotton-spinning mill at Quarry Bank in 1784.

Greg went on to build a model village around the mill, with workers' cottages, a manager's house, a school, a village shop and two chapels. There was also an Apprentice House, where children – many of them from Poor Houses – lived from the age of nine under a master and mistress. They worked for 13 hours each weekday, but on Sunday they went to chapel in the morning and to school in the afternoon, and at least two of the boys rose to be mill managers.

The village, which grew to house nearly 500 people, survives almost unaltered. The mill has been restored as a working museum, with spinning room and weaving shed. When the spinning room was officially opened in 1985, the honours were done by a lady, descended from pauper apprentices, who had herself worked there around 1900.

The 240 acre Styal Country Park in which the village lies is noted for its varied river life and wildlife. There are miles of woodland walks, including the Apprentice Walk linking Twinnies Bridge with Wilmslow, 2½ miles away, and a riverside path to Oversley Ford.

NT. June-Sept, daily; Oct-May, Tues-Sun and Bank Hol. Adm charge. Refreshments. Shop. P *Toilets.* ♿ *(parts). Tel Wilmslow (0625) 527468.*

RISLEY MOSS

Off A574, 3 miles east of Warrington (Cd)

This piece of serene but truly wild country lies on the very edge of Warrington, with its industries and urban bustle. Besides preserved mossland – the raised bogs of the Mersey valley – the area now includes fine woodland with grassy glades, ponds and delightful pathways. A slide show in the visitor centre tells the story of Risley Moss and its people, including those in the peat industry, which flourished until early this century. There is an observation tower, and a woodland hide from which great spotted woodpeckers may be seen. Other attractions include a nature trail and guided walks.

All year, daily exc Fri.

SALT MUSEUM

Near town centre of Northwich (Cc)

A desert studded with small salt lakes some 250 million years ago occupied most of the area of present-day Cheshire. As the lakes dried up, rock salt formed in the depressions, laying the foundation for one of the county's major industries since Roman times.

Displays and an audiovisual presentation at the Salt Museum describe the extraction of salt through the centuries, and its preparation and uses, especially in the chemical industry. Everyday life in the 'salt towns' such as Northwich between 1889 and 1910 is brought vividly to life, and photographs show how buildings were sometimes left with walls, windows, roof and chimneys askew when subsidence followed the collapse of old salt mines. There is a model of a works where as late as 1966 salt was extracted from brine in great, open evaporating pans.

All year, pm Tues-Sun and Bank Hol. Adm charge. Shop. P *Toilets. Tel Northwich (0606) 41331.*

STAPELEY WATER GARDENS

On A51, 1 mile south-east of Nantwich (Ca)

Beautifully coloured Koi carp up to a yard long glide beneath the surface of a lake amid 30 acres of water gardens. Around the lake are landscaped waterfalls and pools with some 60 varieties of water lilies.

Inside a gigantic heated glass house called The Palms, covering more than an acre, visitors pass through a variety of environments from dense rain forest to palm-fringed beaches. There are tropical aquaria and cold-water fish tanks, while the colours and spray patterns of a computer-controlled fountain change in time to music.

All year, daily. Free entry. Refreshments. Shop. P *Toilets.* ♿ *Tel Nantwich (0270) 623868. The Palms: Adm charge. Tel (0270) 628628.*

STRETTON MILL

Off A534, 9 miles south of Chester (Bb)

There had been a mill on the site for at least 200 years when the Leche family took over this water mill in 1596, and it continued to grind corn until 1959. The Leches relinquished the property in the 1970s, and it has been restored as a working museum. There are two water wheels, and a system of sluices allows the mill to operate even when the level of water in the mill pond is low.

The mill was a thatched, timbered building in the 16th century, but this was given a face-lift in the 1770s, when slates replaced the thatch and the timber frame was covered with weatherboarding and stone.

Apr-Oct, pm Tues-Sun and Bank Hol Mon. Shop. P *(limited). Toilets.* ♿ *(ground floor). Tel Northwich (0606) 41331.*

TATTON PARK

Off A50, 2 miles north of Knutsford (Dc)

A double avenue of beeches, older than the 18th-century mansion, leads to an entrance, guarded by gilded railings and sheltered by a great porch that enabled visitors to dismount from their coaches without getting wet. The interior is sumptuous; a handsomely columned entrance hall, a Music Room and Great Drawing Room filled with carved, gilded furniture and hung with cherry silk, an austerely splendid library. If it all seems a little familiar, it is because several of the rooms starred as the interior of Marchmain House, the Flytes' London mansion, in the television serial *Brideshead Revisited*.

Little has changed at Tatton Park since the house was built by Samuel Wyatt for the Egertons towards the end of the 18th century. The only innovation is in Tenants' Hall, which contains a museum of hunting trophies, vintage vehicles and curios collected by the last Lord Egerton.

Perhaps the greater glories are outdoors, in the 1000 acre park where herds of deer wander, and where grand vistas were planned by Humphry Repton at about the time that work was beginning on the house. Its controlled wilderness is a frame for the exquisite gardens, best introduced by the view from the terraces at the south front, where beds of massed perennials flower among ornamental vases and fountains. Beyond is the highly formal parterre, and beyond that lie the misty distances of the park. Tatton is famed for its azaleas and rhododendrons, and for its Japanese garden complete with Shinto temple.

There is plenty to see and do at Tatton. Rooms in the pre-Reformation Old Hall, where the Egertons lived for two centuries before they built their mansion, have been restored in the manner of their appropriate periods. So has the Home Farm which, though still a working entity, largely employs the methods of half a century ago. Visitors can fish, bathe and sail in Tatton Mere. Marked walks include a lakeside walk round Melchett Mere, a Forester's Walk which describes how the estate managed its woodlands down the years, and a Medieval Village Trail. On this, illustrated panels and bumps in the ground recall the village swept away in the remodelling of the park.

There is also a Wartime Tatton Trail. During the Second World War, secret agents, commandos and some 60,000 paratroops made their initial training parachute jumps at Tatton. By an odd coincidence, one of the men who jumped there was Evelyn Waugh, author of *Brideshead Revisited* – he broke his leg.

NT. Park and garden: all year, daily. Mansion, Old Hall and Home Farm: various times. Adm charge. Refreshments. Shop. P *Toilets.* ♿ *Tel Knutsford (0565) 54822.*

TEGG'S NOSE COUNTRY PARK

Off A537, 2 miles east of Macclesfield (Ec)

This park in Cheshire's 'high country' in the Pennine foothills extends along a ridge of Millstone Grit. The stone makes excellent building material, and the park is studded with old quarries, with geology and quarrying displays near one of them. Heather, bracken and gorse crown the highest part, which was once known as Tegga's Naze, after a Norse landowner. There are dramatic views over the Cheshire Plain, Macclesfield and Manchester. Waymarked trails start at the visitor centre and car park, and the $18\frac{1}{2}$ mile Gritstone Trail crosses the park.

All year, daily.

VALE ROYAL ABBEY

Off A556, $2\frac{1}{2}$ miles south of Northwich (Cb)

A storm gave birth to Vale Royal Abbey – and another storm 83 years later nearly destroyed it. Edward I laid the altar foundation stone of the abbey in 1277, 14 years after vowing during a savage storm at sea to found an abbey if he survived the tempest. Cistercian monks laboured alongside 92 masons and a host of other craftsmen to raise the building, using local red sandstone and timber from Delamere Forest. In 1346, however, a violent storm destroyed the abbey, and the rebuilding was not completed until 1360.

After the Dissolution of the Monasteries, a local landowner acquired the property for £450. He demolished the abbey church and used its stone to create a new house, incorporating the abbey's surviving buildings. The Cholmondeley family, owners of the estate from 1616 until 1947, altered the Tudor mansion, and in the 1830s the Victorian architect Edward Blore enlarged it.

The house has now been converted into apartments, but visitors can still see the state rooms, including the armoury, great hall, dining hall and library. In the grounds there are walks beside the River Weaver, a fountain, a walled garden, and the Nun's Grave – a fragment of the abbey church.

All year, Sat, Sun and Bank Hol Mon. Adm charge. P *Toilets.* ♿ *(ground floor and grounds). Tel Sandiway (0606) 888684.*

WARRINGTON MUSEUM AND ART GALLERY

Near town centre of Warrington (Cd)

An actor's mask found at Wilderspool on the outskirts of Warrington is one of many Roman items in a museum which covers the life of man in the district from prehistoric times to the present day. Glass has been made in Warrington since the 2nd century AD, and the museum has fine examples of the work of local 18th and 19th-century glassmakers. Ceramics and folk material and dress from all over the world feature in other sections. There are some 1000 paintings, including fine Victorian oils, and early English watercolours by masters such as Peter de Wint and David Cox. Geology and wildlife are also covered.

All year, daily exc Sun. Free entry. Tel Warrington (0925) 30550/35961.

COUNTY CALENDAR

January (nearest Sat to 25th). Nantwich: Holly Holy Day (Re-enactment Battle of Namptwyche).

May (1st Sat). Knutsford: Royal May Day Festival.

May (mid-month). Nantwich: Festival of Music and Drama.

May (late). Chester: Regatta, and Beating Retreat.

June (late). Tatton Park: County Show.

June/July Chester: Sport and Leisure Festival. Gawsworth Hall: Open-air theatre season.

July (early). Warrington: Walking Day (religious procession, with bands).

July (mid-month). Chester: Music Festival.

July (late). Nantwich: South Cheshire Show.

August (Sun after Aug 12). Macclesfield: Rushbearing Service.

October (31st, and following two weekends). Antrobus: Soul Caking Play (village custom)

Tourist information: Chester (0244) 40144; Congleton (0260) 271095; Crewe (0270) 583191; Knutsford (0565) 2611; Macclesfield (0625) 21955; Nantwich (0270) 623914; Warrington (0925) 36501

MAGNIFICENT PAST *Fine wall hangings adorn the Great Hall (left) at Tatton Old Hall. The dimly lit hall is arranged as it would have looked in the late 15th century, when it was built: the lord's table is set with cloth and candles, and wood smoke from the central fireplace rises to the high, carved oak roof. One of the estate's gamekeepers lived in the Old Hall around 1900, and his rooms, including the Victorian parlour (above), have been restored.*

CLEVELAND

MARITIME HISTORY ON TEESSIDE, WHERE AN EXPLORER WAS BORN

The North Sea is never far away in Cleveland, whose spectacular coast culminates in the towering Boulby Cliff. Here a young haberdasher's apprentice named James Cook walked and dreamt of running away to sea; the feats of exploration that made him famous are recalled today at his birthplace. Hartlepool remembers its heyday in the 1880s as England's third busiest port, while set amidst pastoral country inland are architectural gems such as Guisborough Priory and Ormesby Hall.

BOULBY CLIFF

Off A174, 3 miles east of Loftus (Db)

Cleveland means 'land of cliffs', and in this land Boulby reigns supreme. It is a spectacular rock rising 666ft above the sea, the highest cliff on England's east coast. A footpath to the summit provides an exhilarating walk, culminating in a magnificent view. At the foot of this wild but benign giant lies the little fishing village of Staithes, full of steep, narrow alleys with intriguing names such as Gun Gutter and Dog Loup. There is also a beach from which Boulby Cliff can be surveyed in all its towering splendour.

All year, daily.

CAPTAIN COOK BIRTHPLACE MUSEUM

Off A172, 3 miles south of Middlesbrough (Bb)

Few stories of personal achievement against overwhelming odds can compare with that of Captain James Cook RN. Born in 1728 the son of a Scottish farm labourer in the village of Marton, now part of Middlesbrough, he lived to become the greatest explorer of his day and probably the greatest navigator of all time. Middlesbrough has not forgotten its favourite son, and a museum in Cook's honour stands close to the site of the cottage in which he was born. It contains displays relating the story of his remarkable life, together with exhibits from the areas with which his name is most closely associated – Canada, Australia, New Zealand and the South Pacific islands.

Visitors to the museum can explore Cook's story further by following the Heritage Trail, which starts at Marton and leads to Whitby 30 miles away, where the young seaman set sail on his extraordinary career. The trail can be followed on foot or by car through some of Northern England's most beautiful countryside.

All year, daily. Adm charge. Refreshments. Shop. P *Toilets.* ♿ *Tel Middlesbrough (0642) 311211.*

GUISBOROUGH PRIORY

In Guisborough town (Cb)

To visit Guisborough Priory is to step back into medieval England. The abbey was founded in 1119 by Robert de Brus, the most powerful Norman lord in north-east Yorkshire, and rebuilt in Decorated Gothic style in the late 13th century after a disastrous fire. Following the destruction wrought by the Dissolution of the Monasteries in Tudor times, there remains only the Norman gatehouse, and the east end of the abbey church. The abbey was once the fourth richest in Yorkshire, after York, Fountains and Selby, and even in decay it recalls the enormous skill, energy and resources committed in the Middle Ages to the Christian faith.

EH. All year, daily exc Sun am. Adm charge. Shop. ♿ *Tel Guisborough (0287) 38301.*

HARTLEPOOL MARITIME MUSEUM

On Hartlepool Headland (Bc)

Standing upon a ship's bridge, with radar signal bleeping and ship-to-shore radio crackling, the visitor to this museum can appreciate some of the problems that beset real-life captains at sea. The setting is appropriate, for Hartlepool has a history as a port going back to medieval times. In the 1880s it was England's third busiest port, and many of its people worked in building ships as well as in manning and servicing them.

The museum gives a vivid glimpse of what life in such a thoroughgoing maritime community was like. What are the ganseys and clippie mats which local fisherwomen were once so industriously engaged in making? The museum explains. How did the local fisherfolk and their families live? The museum includes a complete reconstruction of a fisherman's cottage. There are beautifully made shipbuilder's models, ship portraits and other marine paintings, boat-builder's tools, a working model of a ship's engine, model fishing cobles and a display from a 19th-century nautical instrument maker's shop window. It all makes for a fascinating, free – and completely safe – voyage.

All year, Mon-Sat. Free entry. Shop. Tel Hartlepool (0429) 272814.

KIRKLEATHAM OLD HALL MUSEUM

Off A174, 2 miles south-west of Redcar (Cb)

Set in a village which is itself an architectural gem, the charming Queen Anne house known as Old Hall is full of history. It was built in 1710 as a free grammar school with money left by a local boy, Sir William Turner, who became Lord Mayor of London after the Great Fire and played a leading part in the rebuilding. In 1738 it became a museum and lending library – one of the first in the country. Today the Old Hall and its Pavilion have 14 exhibition rooms showing different aspects of local life and industry, and a changing programme of exhibitions in the main hall. There is also a bird garden. A few yards away, the Church of St Cuthbert has the Turner Mausoleum designed by James Gibbs, which contains work by the 18th-century London sculptor Peter Scheemaker.

All year, daily exc Mon. Free entry. Refreshments. Shop. P *Toilets.* ♿ *Tel Middlesbrough (0642) 479500.*

MIDDLESBROUGH ART GALLERY

In Linthorpe Road, ½ mile from town centre (Bb)

The building may be Victorian, but it houses one of the most important collections of British 20th-century art in north-east England, including work by Lowry, Augustus John, Gwen John, Victor Pasmore and many more. There are lively, changing exhibitions, and an attractive outdoor sculpture garden. The nearby Dorman Museum tells the history of Middlesbrough, which encapsulates so much of the history of Britain's Industrial Revolution. Its displays cover local iron and steel and pottery industries. Middlesbrough is also noted for its bridges. The Transporter Bridge is probably Teesside's most distinctive landmark – a unique structure built in 1911 and still in operation. The Newport Bridge is the largest remaining vertical lift bridge in the world.
All year, daily exc Sun. Free entry. Shop. **P** *(limited).* ♿ *Tel Middlesbrough (0642) 247445 (Art Gallery); 813781 (Dorman Museum).*

NEWHAM GRANGE LEISURE FARM

Off B1365, 3½ miles south of Middlesbrough (Ba)

The mystery surrounding country skills such as hay making, dry-stone walling and sheep dipping is lifted for the town dweller by demonstrations at this leisure farm. Other attractions include rare breeds of farm animals, a museum of regional farming, farm workshops and other exhibits designed to show in a tangible, realistic way, the traditional farming processes in the Cleveland area. To complete the rural picture visitors can follow one of the farm's waymarked wildlife or geology trails.
Easter-Oct, daily; Nov-Easter, Sun. Adm charge. Shop. **P** *Toilets. Tel Middlesbrough (0642) 245432.*

ORMESBY HALL

Off A171, 3 miles south of Middlesbrough (Bb)

The rich interior of this fine 18th-century country house is an impressive example of the work produced by the craftsmen of York, which was then a great centre of the decorative arts. Sir James Pennyman, the 6th baronet of the family which built and occupied Ormesby Hall, finished its expensive interior in the 1770s. The dining room, drawing room, principal bedrooms and above all the Palladian hall and gallery are supreme examples of craftsmanship. Sir James, a great spendthrift, did obtain one item at a bargain price – his portrait by Sir Joshua Reynolds over the fireplace in the dining room, for which he paid the artist £20.
NT. Apr-end Oct, Wed, Thur, Sat, Sun and Bank Hol Mon pm. Adm charge. Refreshments. Shop. **P** *Toilets.* ♿ *Tel Middlesbrough (0642) 324188.*

PRESTON HALL MUSEUM

Yarm Road, 1½ miles south of Stockton-on-Tees (Bb)

The faded, sepia-toned postcards of Victorian high streets spring to life in this museum, which contains an entire Victorian cobbled street complete with shops. Seen at dusk, with the gas street lamps alight and the shop windows illuminated with a warming magnetic glow, the street creates a powerful, magical impression of one of the most appealing aspects of Victorian life.

PRICE OF PERFECTION *The lavishly decorated interior of Ormesby Hall was achieved at great cost. After this Adam-style drawing room was completed in the 1770s, bailiffs seized the house.*

This museum street is typical of Stockton's high street, or that of any similar town of north-east England, in the 1890s. One of its most striking features is its range of specialist shops, which includes a pawn shop. In 1890 Stockton had 15 such shops which acted rather like banks for poorer townsfolk; only one remains today. The museum also contains displays on Victorian industrial and domestic life.

The hall itself was built in 1825. Other museum displays include pewter, arms and armour, snuff boxes and an attic full of toys.

More of the history of Stockton itself can be gleaned from a visit to the Green Dragon Museum in the centre of the surviving Georgian area of the town, next to the recently restored Georgian Theatre. Displays show the administrative, commercial and domestic growth of Stockton, both as a town and as a port.
Preston Hall Museum. All year, daily exc Sun am. Free entry. Refreshments. Shop. **P** *Toilets.* ♿ *Tel Stockton-on-Tees (0642) 781184. Green Dragon Museum. All year, Mon-Sat. Free entry. Shop.* **P** *Toilets.* ♿ *Tel (0642) 602474.*

ZETLAND LIFEBOAT MUSEUM

On seafront at Redcar (Cb)

The oldest lifeboat in the world, made by the man who built the world's first lifeboat, still looks out across the rocky coast of Redcar at the wild North Sea. Built in 1800 by Henry Greathead, the *Zetland* saw active service for 80 years, and saved more than 500 lives. On one January day in 1830 she was launched three times, saving first seven, then six and finally a further 14 lives. She ended her career in 1880 with the rescue of seven crewmen from the brig *Luna*.

Zetland is the last survivor of 31 lifeboats built by Greathead. After his first boat was launched at South Shields in 1790 Parliament voted him £1200, and the Emperor of Russia presented him with a diamond ring. Made of English oak seasoned for 20 years, the *Zetland* originally had a thick layer of cork on the outside for buoyancy; this was later replaced by copper-lined air cases. She was very shallow, and waves which swamped her escaped through eight valves in the bottom of the boat.

The sturdy old *Zetland* is still helping to save lives, for the collecting boxes at the museum provide funds for the Royal National Lifeboat Institution. In the gallery there is a reconstruction of a local fisherman's cottage at the end of the 19th century – complete with fishing equipment – and displays relating to local history.
Easter-Sept, daily; weekends in winter. Free entry. Shop. ♿ *(ground floor). Tel Redcar (0642) 471813.*

COUNTY CALENDAR

July (mid-month). Redcar: Folk Festival.

August (early). Saltburn: Victorian Festival.

August (mid-month). Billingham: International Folklore Festival.

August (mid-month, alternate years). Middlesbrough: International Eisteddfod.

Tourist information: Hartlepool (0429) 68366 (winter 66522); Middlesbrough (0642) 243425; Redcar (0642) 471921 (summer); Guisborough (0287) 35240.

CORNWALL

LAND OF LEGEND, MOORLAND AND MANORS BETWEEN TWO SEAS

A dramatic coast is never far away in Cornwall, where the jagged promontory of Land's End divides granite cliffs facing the wild Atlantic from the softer Channel shore. Legends of King Arthur cling to Tintagel in the north and St Michael's Mount in the south, while a less-shadowy monarch built the castles at St Mawes and Pendennis Point. The long coastline has its full stock of stories of fishermen, smugglers and wreckers, and these are vividly recalled in museums at Charlestown, Falmouth and Polperro.

Moving inland, Launceston Castle guards the road to high Bodmin Moor, and green lanes entice the traveller to mellow manor houses and bright gardens such as Cotehele, Lanhydrock, Trelissick and Trengwainton. The Cornish have long been miners: the boom years of tin mining and slate quarrying are recalled at Poldark and Delabole, while Wheal Martyn gives an insight into one industry that continues to expand. Cornwall entered the space age with an Earth Station for satellite communications, while the latest technology supplements traditional skills in theme parks at Dobwalls and Flambards.

ANTONY HOUSE

Off A374, at Torpoint (Eb)

One of the attractions of this house is its continuous association with a single family – the Carews – since it was built in the 18th century. Much of the furniture bought for the house when it was built is still there – and still in use. To walk into the pastel painted, pine-panelled bedrooms, or the oak-panelled dining room or salon, is to step back into the 18th century, and into the atmosphere of gracious country living.

Family portraits and other paintings include many by Sir Joshua Reynolds. In the green bedroom is a portrait of Rachel Carew, the 17th-century lady who inspired Daphne du Maurier's novel *My Cousin Rachel.* Outside is a woodland garden, with mulberry, walnut and plane trees as well as an immense cork oak. Clumps of evergreen oak, planted about 1760, frame the view down to the beautiful River Lynher.

Apr-Oct, Tues, Wed, Thur and Bank Hol Mon pm; also Sun pm June-Aug. Adm charge. Shop. P *Tel Plymouth (0752) 812191.*

AUTOMOBILIA

On A3058, 4½ miles west of St Austell (Cb)

The first overland trip from Britain to Australia was completed in 1927 in a Bean – a motor car which few people now remember, but which has its place in motoring history and in this motor museum. It was a long trip – the Bean 14hp Tourer's maximum speed was 50mph. It is one of over 50 vehicles on show in the museum, from famous names such as early Lagondas, Bentleys, Bristols and Rolls-Royces to lesser-known marques such as the Skinner Union Roll-Top Coupé, the Rhode and the Swift. Among the older models to be seen are a 1914 Ford Model T and a 1904 De Dion Bouton.

Apr-Oct, daily. Adm charge. Refreshments. Shop. P *Toilets.* ♿ *Tel St Austell (0726) 823092.*

BARBARA HEPWORTH MUSEUM

St Ives, near town centre (Ab)

Barbara Hepworth was one of the major sculptors of the 20th century, and the progress of her work can be followed in the house in St Ives that was the artist's home and studio for 26 years. On a turntable are the stone blocks on which she was about to start work when she died in a fire in 1975, while in the garden are many of the finished sculptures which helped to make her name known throughout the world.

St Ives was also the home of Britain's greatest potter, Bernard Leach, until his death in 1979. The Leach Pottery contains a showroom housing Janet Leach's collection of her husband's work. She is herself a distinguished potter, who works daily at the pottery.

Hepworth Museum: All year, Mon-Sat; also Sun pm in July and Aug. Adm charge. Shop. Tel Penzance (0736) 796226. Leach Pottery: All year, Mon-Fri; also Sat in summer. Shop. Tel (0736) 796398.

BODMIN FARM PARK

Off A38, 2 miles east of Bodmin (Dc)

It is not every farm which now stocks a British Lop, a Buff Orpington or a Jacob. This farm has decided to stick with traditional breeds of farm animal, and attract visitors to help pay its way. Here are horses ranging from enormous Shires to little Shetlands; cattle from all the main breeds; pigs, including the original Cornish British Lop; sheep, including the black-and-white spotted Jacob; and a wide range of poultry including the Buff Orpington. There is an assortment of ducks, rabbits and goats, including the Toggenburg – a large brown goat from Switzerland which produces excellent milk and is friendly to visitors.

Mid May-end Sept, daily exc Sat. Adm charge. Refreshments. Shop. P *Toilets. Bodmin (0208) 2074.*

BODMIN MOOR

Crossed by A30 (Dc)

High on this wild moor, the 'roof' of Cornwall, the landscape has remained almost untouched by man for thousands of years. It is a rolling, treeless landscape, with pockets of bog and marsh, and scattered with granite boulders. Giant tors rise in isolated splendour, like islands from a seabed of grass.

In prehistoric times the moor was the most heavily populated part of Cornwall, before metal tools were developed to clear the wooded valleys. Evidence of early man's presence is all around in the form of hut circles, sacred sites and burial grounds.

The granite tors offer spectacular views over the moor and are well worth the sometimes fairly steep scramble needed to reach them. Brown Willy (1375ft) is the highest point in Cornwall, and Rough Tor (1311ft) the second highest. In the middle of Bodmin Moor is the tiny hamlet of Bolventor, with its Jamaica Inn which Daphne du Maurier made famous in her novel about that popular old Cornish industry – smuggling. The inn houses an unusual collection of animal tableaux made by the Victorian naturalist Walter Potter.

All year, daily.

BUDE STRATTON FOLK MUSEUM

On Lower Canal Wharf, Bude (De)

Now a sedate holiday resort, Bude was once a notorious centre for Cornish wreckers. Much of the dramatic history of this coast is recorded in the Folk Museum. Some of the ships' figureheads on display, if they could talk, would have hair-raising stories to tell: 47 ships were lost trying to enter Bude harbour in the last 38 years of the 19th century, and 85 came to grief on the short stretch of coast between Henna Cliff and St Gennys in the same period.

The museum is in what used to be a blacksmith's forge beside the Bude Canal. The canal itself can be explored either by the towpath, which extends 2 miles inland, or by hired rowing boat.

Another exhibition, in Lansdown Road, vividly portrays the varied natural life of the Bude area. 'A World of Nature' was devised by the warden of a local nature reserve and depicts life on the seashore, estuary, marshes and cliffs.

Folk Museum: Apr-Sept, daily. Adm charge. Refreshments. Shop. P ♿ *Tel Bude (0288) 2861. World of Nature: All year, shop hours. Tel Bude (0288) 2423.*

CAMBORNE SCHOOL OF MINES GEOLOGICAL MUSEUM

Off A30, on Pool Road, at Camborne (Bb)

One of the glories of this world-famous school of mining is its geological museum, which houses in attractive modern displays a unique collection of rocks and minerals. Much of the material has been given to the museum by ex-students of the school now working in mines all over the world. More has been gathered by students in the course of their field studies, and a great deal has come from private collections given to the school since its foundation in the late 19th century.

Among the items on display are gems and ornamental stones; crystals; a model of a volcano section, with samples; radioactive materials, complete with a Geiger counter; and fossils illustrating the geological time scale.

After this glimpse into the earth's history over thousands of millions of years, the traces of early

BODMIN ROCK *The logan, or rocking stone, at the 1311ft summit of Rough Tor on Bodmin Moor can be moved by hand. Its precarious balance is the result of long weathering of the rock beneath it.*

man on the nearby hill of Carn Brea seem relatively recent. Yet Stone Age settlements discovered at the east end of the hill date from 3000 BC and are among the earliest found in Britain. More visible are the Iron Age ramparts round the hill, circular huts from the same period and, from later periods, the remains of a Roman fortress and a 15th-century castle.
All year, Mon-Fri, exc Bank Hol. Free entry. Shop. P *Tel Camborne (0209) 714866.*

CAPE CORNWALL

Off B3306, 1 mile west of St Just (Aa)

The granite cliffs of Cape Cornwall miss by barely a mile the distinction of being the westernmost point of mainland England, but they also miss the great mass of tourists who descend on Land's End in the summer, and the scenery is even more beautiful. It is the only headland in England and Wales to bear the title 'Cape'. But although made of granite, the relentless Atlantic breakers have worn it away until it is now almost an island.

A tall chimney standing in splendid isolation in the middle of this wild natural scene is the last relic of the Cape Cornwall tin mine, which closed in the late 1870s. Until then the Cape and the surrounding area was a thriving centre of the tin-mining industry. Less than 2 miles away along a spectacular coastal path are the ruins of the old tin mine of Botallack, with its engine houses perched precariously on the edge of 200ft cliffs.
All year, daily.

CHARLESTOWN VISITOR CENTRE

Off A3061, 1½ miles south-east of St Austell (Db)

Ships' bells, gold doubloons, guns, casks and chests rescued from the seas round Cornwall's coasts are on display in Charlestown. The village is itself a living museum, almost unchanged since the 18th century. Starting as a tiny fishing hamlet, when pilchards were abundant, Charlestown became a thriving port in the 18th century, when a dock was built to provide a safe harbour for ships on Cornwall's stormy southern coast. With the discovery of copper in the area in the 1800s, trade through Charlestown boomed – not only in copper, but also in hides, tallow, iron ore, timber, oak bark for sail tanning, and hemp for rope making. By the 19th century, boom times were over. Many of these products were available more cheaply elsewhere; steam had come to replace sail; fewer ships were needed; and there was less demand for ropes. Then the abundant pilchard disappeared and the making of barrels ceased. This quick decline had one benefit – it has preserved a port which is fascinating to visitors interested in stepping back in time. But it would be wrong to think of Charlestown as only a museum. One local industry has continued to expand – the shipping of china clay to Europe.
Apr-Oct, daily. Adm charge. Refreshments. Shop. P *Toilets.* ♿ *Tel St Austell (0726) 73332.*

CHYSAUSTER ANCIENT VILLAGE

Off B3311, 4 miles north of Penzance (Ab)

The oldest identifiable village street in England runs through the centre of this 2000-year-old Iron Age settlement. Four pairs of oval stone houses, with 15ft thick walls, are set on opposite sides of the street. Each house consists of a number of circular rooms opening onto a central courtyard, with stone-lined terrace gardens. Now open to the sky, the houses were originally roofed with turf or thatch. One house, twice as big as the rest, probably belonged to the chief.
EH. All year, daily. Adm charge. P *Toilets. Tel Penzance (0736) 61889.*

HIGH LEVELS *Terraced gardens descend from the front of Cotehele to woods beside the Tamar. The simple strips of lawn, hedges and flowerbeds were laid out in the 19th century.*

CORNISH ENGINES

On A3047 at Pool, 2 miles west of Redruth (Bb)

Two of the most impressive relics of the great days of Cornish engineering can be seen on adjoining sites near Redruth. At East Pool Whim stands the most impressive beam engine in Cornwall, designed to lift miners and ore from a depth of 1300ft. Across the road is the East Pool pumping engine at Taylor's Shaft – the largest and latest of all the engines left in Cornwall, representing the peak of development in this type of engine at the end of the 19th century.
NT. Apr-Oct, daily. Adm charge. Shop. Tel Redruth (0209) 216657.

COTEHELE

Off A390, 6 miles north of Saltash (Ec)

The house, one of the finest medieval and Tudor manor houses in England, has been the home of the Edgcumbe family for 600 years, and its rooms are filled with the family's furniture, passed down through the generations, unaltered and carefully preserved. The hall where in medieval times the whole household dined is one of the most splendid interiors in the West Country. Many rooms are decorated with tapestries.

By the river is Cotehele Quay, a bustling port in the days when river transport was the main line of communication for the whole of the Tamar valley. A museum in one of the restored warehouses on the quay commemorates this period in the Tamar's history. Half a mile up the valley is the restored manor mill of Cotehele.
NT. Apr-Oct, garden and mill daily, house daily exc Fri; Nov-Mar, garden daily. Adm charge. Refreshments. Shop. P *Toilets.* ♿ *(parts). Tel Liskeard (0579) 50434.*

DAIRYLAND FARM PARK

On A3058, 2½ miles south-east of Newquay (Cc)

For people who have never machine-milked a cow and feel it is about time they did, this is the place to go. Dairyland is a modern farm in action, and visitors can also see a constantly changing variety of baby animals including calves, lambs and piglets. A country life museum houses a number of working exhibits including a horse-driven corn mill, butter churn and cider press; a poacher's den, complete with man-traps; a wheelwright's shop and a millstream garden.
Easter-Oct, daily. Adm charge. Refreshments. Shop. P *Toilets.* ♿ *Tel Mitchell (087 251) 246.*

DELABOLE SLATE QUARRY

Off B3314, 3 miles south-east of Tintagel (Dd)

Man has made many holes in the ground, but few as big as Delabole. More than 500ft deep and a mile in circumference, it is the work of men quarrying for centuries. Delabole slate is blue-grey in colour, with a sheen seldom found in slate from other quarries.

Dumper trucks instead of beam-type steam engines today draw the slate from the giant hole, as can be seen from a public viewing platform. Some aspects of the operation, however, remain the same. Roof slates are still split by hand in the traditional way, using a small wooden mallet and a chisel with a wide, thin blade. And the various sizes of slate are still known by their traditional names, such as 'wide counters'.
All year, Mon-Fri. Free entry. P *Toilets. Tel Camelford (0840) 212242.*

DOBWALLS THEME PARK

Off A38, 2 miles west of Liskeard (Dc)

The park's first major theme is a train set of 15-20ft long steam and diesel locomotives that haul carriage-loads of visitors round an extensive track system. The locomotives are scaled-down replicas of US transcontinental giants – a steam Union Pacific 'Big Boy', for example, and a UP diesel 'Centennial'. The American theme continues into the landscaping of the railway part of the park; the area called Wyoming has Red Indian tepees, while Colorado is thickly planted with pines. Riding the railroad, passengers pass over Windy Ridge, through Horseshoe, Marshall and several other passes, Lost Soul Canyon and a number of tunnels. The Union Pacific and Rio Grande railroads are the subject of the Model Train Exhibition: two splendid dioramas, one depicting a mountain railroad, and the other a long stretch of desert track.

The second major theme at Dobwalls is very different in character. Its core is an exhibition of the paintings of Archibald Thorburn, who died in 1935, and was one of Britain's greatest wildlife artists. This is not, however, a straightforward picture gallery. Instead, the tour begins in London's Jermyn Street as it was at the turn of the century, complete with authentic sounds and a Victorian tearoom. It was there that Thorburn's agent had his premises, and in wandering through his gallery the visitor wanders, as it were, into Thorburn's life. This is presented in a series of tableaux of the settings in which Thorburn worked: Stag Hall, Grouse Moor, Woodland, Garden, Potting Shed and Studio. Thorburn's paintings, together with photographs and stuffed birds and animals, are presented against appropriate backgrounds accompanied by appropriate sounds such as stags roaring, a cock pheasant's bark, a grouse's alarm call, garden birdsong – and even by appropriate smells. As with everything else in the park, it is done with style and imagination.

For children Dobwalls has a vast range of slides, swings and adventure playgrounds strongly reminiscent of assault courses.

All year, daily. Adm charge. Refreshments. Shop. P *Toilets.* ♿ *Tel Liskeard (0579) 20325/21129.*

FALMOUTH MARITIME MUSEUM

In Falmouth town centre (Ca)

The prize attraction of this museum is the steam tug *St Denys*, which spent all its working life at Falmouth, from 1929 until 1980 when it was honourably retired. Children – and adults, if they have a mind to – can stand on the bridge, as the captain once did, and issue orders to the engine room via the ship's telegraph or the voice pipe. All parts of the ship are open, and a different exhibition is set up on board each year.

On shore, the museum illustrates the maritime history of Cornwall, including shipbuilding, the famous Falmouth Packet service, and maritime trade and ports.

Building: all year, daily. 'St Denys': late Mar-early Nov, daily. Adm charge. Shop. P *(limited).* ♿ *(parts). Tel Falmouth (0326) 250507.*

PAINT AND STEAM *The artist Archibald Thorburn is seen working on one of his celebrated wildlife paintings, in one of the tableaux depicting Thorburn's life on show at Dobwalls Theme Park. Through the park run scaled-down replicas of classic American trains, such as the Rio Grande Railroad locomotive (right) being tended by a devoted slave in the engine shed.*

FLAMBARDS TRIPLE THEME PARK

On A394, 1 mile east of Helston (Ba)

Devised and operated by a retired Royal Navy pilot, the aero collection in this varied theme park offers a special attraction: visitors can do more than just stand and look at the aircraft on show, they can climb aboard several of them, including a Shackleton and a Widgeon helicopter, to inspect the flight deck, sit in the pilot's seat and operate the flying controls.

Flambards Village, in the same park, is a realistic re-creation of a Victorian village, complete with gent's and ladies' outfitters, a village sweet shop, chemist, grocer, haberdasher and pub. There is also a complete Victorian kitchen. All the shops are filled with authentic Victorian furniture, fixtures and fittings, clothing and bric-a-brac. Britain in the Blitz, another attempt to re-create the past, shows what ordinary life was like in Britain during the Second World War, from the housewife in her kitchen to the family in their air-raid shelter.

Easter-Oct, daily. Adm charge. Refreshments. Shop. P *Toilets.* ♿ *Tel Helston (0326) 574549.*

WILL THAT BE ALL, MADAM? *The grocer weighs out goods for a customer in his re-created Victorian shop in Flambards Village. Some of the brand names on show are still well known today.*

GLENDURGAN GARDEN

Off A39, 4 miles south-west of Falmouth (Ba)

The great tulip trees at Glendurgan were planted by the original owner, Alfred Fox, in the 1820s and 1830s. As a member of the family who were the principal shipping agents in Falmouth, he was able to order plants from all over the world, Falmouth being the first port of call for shipping returning from overseas. His son continued the tradition, planting many conifers, deodars and Atlas cedars, swamp and Mexican cypresses, Monterey pines and weeping spruces. The family tradition has continued into a third generation under Cuthbert Lloyd Fox, who planted many of the specimens now at their best – rhododendrons, magnolias, cornuses, camellias, hydrangeas and eucryphias, as well as more unusual plants such as aloe, persimmon and evergreen oleasters.

The gardens are in a lovely setting, rolling down in torrents of colour to the Helford River.
NT. Mar-end Oct, Mon, Wed and Fri. Adm charge. **P** *Toilets. Tel Bodmin (0208) 4281.*

GODOLPHIN HOUSE

Off B3302, 7 miles north-west of Helston (Ba)

This impressive early Tudor and Elizabethan house on the slopes of Godolphin Hill was home until the end of the 18th century of the Godolphin family, who could trace their ancestry back to the Normans. It's most striking feature is the great north front, supported on massive granite columns. The house was built around two main courtyards, with large windows facing inwards and small ones – providing less of an invitation to raiders from the sea – facing out. There is a fine 'King's Room' in which Prince Charles, later Charles II, is believed to have stayed after his escape from Pendennis Castle on his way to the Isles of Scilly, of which Sir Francis Godolphin was then Governor.
May and June, Thur pm; July-Sept, Tues and Thur. Adm charge. **P** *(limited). Toilets. Tel Penzance (0736) 762409.*

GOONHILLY EARTH STATION

On B3293, 7 miles south of Helston (Ba)

The great dishes of Goonhilly's ten aerials, rising from the bleak moorland of the Lizard and cocked slightly towards the sky to listen to millions of voices reflected from space, give the visitor a slight twinge of unease. It is a feeling not unlike that experienced when contemplating the prehistoric standing stone by Goonhilly's eastern boundary. It too points to the sky, but the voices of the men who erected it have been stilled for thousands of years.

Goonhilly Earth Station was born, appropriately, out of an idea put forward in 1945 by Arthur C. Clarke, the doyen of science fiction writers, who envisaged the possibility of extra-terrestrial relays hovering above the planet exchanging radio signals, and sending the signals onward to receiving stations on Earth. The 'extra-terrestrial relays' are now known as communication satellites, and Goonhilly is Britain's major station for receiving and transmitting the signals relayed through them.

The general principles of the station's operations, and the sheer wonder of it all, are demonstrated on guided tours. At the first stop, an audiovisual display tells of the different roles of each aerial – how one links the world's stock exchanges, how some handle maritime and airline communications, and how others are engaged in satellite tracking. The largest of all, the 105ft diameter Aerial 6, transmits and receives TV signals 24 hours a day across the Atlantic. Another display shows the course of a transatlantic telephone call, from local exchange to Telecom Tower in London, then via repeater stations to Goonhilly, whence it is bounced off a satellite to an American earth station and so onward to its destination, giving instant voice communication in both directions.

At the next stop, the Observation Tower, there is an overall view of the station, and a diorama that shows how it developed. In the Control Room, coloured lights sparkle from a range of consoles day and night, watched by the controller and an assistant, who also keep an eye on the electricity monitors and half a dozen TV screens, checking the quality of the films coming and going between Britain and the USA.

Finally the tour makes a circuit of the station, visiting the aerials and the gigantic diesel engines that would cut in to run emergency generators should the electricity supply fail. The whole great complex of space-age monuments, ancillary buildings and roads is lapped about by moorland which contains a number of rare plant and insect species and provides a sanctuary for many birds, reptiles and mammals.
Easter-end Sept, daily. Adm charge. Refreshments. Shop. **P** *Toilets. Tel Truro (0872) 78551.*

KYNANCE COVE

Off A3083, 1 mile west of Lizard (Ba)

It is possible to enter the Kitchen, the Parlour and the Drawing Room at Kynance – but only at low tide. They are caves, just three of many tunnelled out of the rock at Kynance by a restless sea. The rock is serpentine, mottled like snake-skin, in lovely grey-green and red-brown colours.

Kynance has the misfortune of being at the top of almost every visitor's list of favourite Cornish coves, because it is so beautiful. This means that at the height of the holiday season it can become extremely crowded. It is best visited well before low tide to ensure a good position for the cove's most spectacular display – the Devil's Bellows. This fissure in the cliff sucks in the incoming tide with an enormous roar then spews it out in a gargantuan spray.
All year, daily.

THE ANGRY SEA *Atlantic rollers break on the rocks of Kynance Cove. The cliffs above it form a nature reserve which is noted for its birds, lichens and dwarf varieties of plants such as betony and oxeye.*

LAND'S END

On A30, 8 miles west of Penzance (Aa)

England comes to a dramatic conclusion of sheer granite cliffs approached by steep, boulder-strewn slopes of rabbit-shorn grass. This is the troubled meeting place of the Atlantic, the Irish Sea and the English Channel, and the water, even on quite calm days, claws greeny-white and lacy up the sides of the jagged granite stack called The Armed Knight. A mile and a half out to sea, the Longships light stands over Carn Brâs – 'great rock' – and 9 miles out is the Wolf Rock light.

For some, Land's End is the most spectacular section of the South-west Peninsula Coastal Path; to others it proffers craft shops, Cornish cream fudge, a restaurant, ice cream, and an amusement arcade. The Mariner's Chest, with its brightly illustrated walls, sells things made out of shells, sea urchins and starfish. Penwith House sells Land's End souvenirs and postcards, which may be posted in England's very last postbox. Visitors can have a photograph taken against the signpost whose arms indicate the distances to the Scillies, Wolf Rock, the Longships and John o'Groats (874 miles); another arm has space to spell out the name of any place one may choose.

The Land's End Heritage Centre admirably illustrates the more serious aspects of the place. The geological display, for example, explains that Land's End is one of three related granite outcrops thrust up from the Earth's core 270 million years ago, the other two being the Scillies and Bodmin Moor. How Man came to the peninsula is told in displays on the Iron Age village of Chysauster and other prehistoric sites, and there are other exhibitions dedicated to the natural history of the area and to farming and mining.

The theme that underlies everything at Land's End is the sea and its dangers. There is a dramatic series of photographs of Land's End wrecks, and another on the history and heroism of the local lifeboatmen. There is an audiovisual display on the work of Land's End Radio Station, which maintains contact between ships in the Western Approaches and others all over the world.

On a lighter note there is an exhibition on what is apparently the secret yearning of every Briton, to travel from John o'Groats to Land's End, or vice versa. It seems people have done so backwards, for charity (often), on stilts, a penny-farthing bicycle, in a fire engine, an invalid chair, and stark naked on bicycles.

Land's End Exhibition Centre: Easter-end Oct, daily. Adm charge. Refreshments. Shops. 🅿 *Toilets. Tel Penzance (0736) 87501.*

OUT OF THE ASHES *The north wing (right) of Lanhydrock House survived a great fire in 1881. The rebuilt mansion is approached through formal gardens where 38 clipped yews stand sentinel.*

LANHYDROCK

On B3268, 2 miles south of Bodmin (Dc)

The sumptuous scale on which people lived in houses like Lanhydrock in Victorian times is today hard to imagine. Originally a 17th-century house, much of it was badly damaged by fire in 1881. It was rebuilt in grandiose style by the owner, Lord Robartes. The 36 'upstairs and downstairs' rooms open to today's visitors include the kitchen, the main bedrooms and the north wing gallery, 116ft long, with a magnificent plaster ceiling showing scenes from the Old Testament.

The house stands amid beautiful shrub gardens and formal gardens, and its immaculate parkland falls down to the valley of the River Fowey, with some splendid woodland walks.

NT. Apr-Oct, daily; Nov-Mar, gardens only daily. Adm charge. Refreshments. Shop. 🅿 *Toilets.* ♿ *(ground floor). Tel Bodmin (0208) 3320.*

LANREATH FARM AND FOLK MUSEUM

Off B3359, 5 miles north-west of Looe (Db)

What are a Codd bottle or dubbing scissors? A great many minor mysteries of country life and language are explained in this museum. The bottle was invented by Hiram Codd and had a glass marble in the top. It was used for soft drinks – hence the phrase 'Codd's wallop'. The dubbing scissors were used to extinguish lighted candles. The vacuum cleaner on display is, unusually, powered by hand.

Easter-Oct, daily. Adm charge. Shop. 🅿 *(limited). Tel Lanreath (0503) 20321.*

LAPPA VALLEY RAILWAY

Off A3075, 4½ miles south of Newquay (Cb)

The original railway carried ore from the East Wheal Rose silver lead mine to Newquay. The wagons were first pulled by horses helped, in the steeper sections, by rope hoists, then from 1874 by steam locomotives. The present narrow-gauge steam railway is therefore carrying passengers for just over a mile along one of the oldest railway track beds in Cornwall. The engine house of the old mine still stands. Once it contained the Great Hundred-Inch pumping engine – the biggest in Cornwall and so big that when it was first commissioned 13 people sat down to dinner inside its cylinder. This great machine was sold off when the mine closed in 1885. There is also an ingenious maze based on the design of Richard Trevithick's 1804 steam locomotive – the first in the world to run on rails, ten years before George Stephenson's first locomotive.

Mid Apr-Sept, daily. Adm charge. Refreshments. Shop. 🅿 *Toilets.* ♿ *Tel Mitchell (087 251) 317.*

LAUNCESTON CASTLE

In Launceston town centre (Ed)

The principal castle of Robert of Mortain, half brother of William I, Launceston overlooked the ford at Polson, which was the chief landward entry into Cornwall. Although now much reduced, with only the stone keep, gatehouses and some of the curtain walling surviving, the castle still towers over the roofs of the town and provides a fine view of it.

The keep stands on a high mound built on a natural steeply sloping ridge, which falls sharply to the River Kensey in the north. It consists of an outer stone wall, used as a fighting platform against attacks, a shell keep which once had rooms inside it, and the High Tower, which was used as a prison in the late Middle Ages. The surrounding bailey, or courtyard, would once have been crowded with the principal buildings of the castle, including the Great Hall in which the Black Prince and his council met in 1353.

Just down the hill from Launceston Castle is the station of the Launceston Steam Railway, providing a step back in time to Victorian England and the heyday of steam. The 2ft gauge line runs for 1½ miles through the picturesque Kensey Valley, following part of the old North Cornwall Railway route which was closed in 1966. Some of the locomotives used are over 100 years old.

There is a museum of vintage transport at Launceston Station, while Lawrence House, in Castle Street, is a typical country town house, now a local museum.

Castle: EH. All year, daily. Adm charge. 🅿 *Tel Launceston (0566) 2365. Steam Railway: Easter, then end May-Sept, daily; also Sun, Christmas to Easter. Adm charge. Refreshments. Shop.* 🅿 ♿ *(part). Tel (0566) 5665. Lawrence House: NT. Apr-Sept, Mon-Fri. Free entry. Tel (0566) 2833.*

LIZARD POINT

Off A3083, near village of Lizard (Ba)

The southernmost tip of England offers spectacular views of the great sweep of Mount's Bay, while closer at hand are the great rocks whose very names – Bumble Rock, Enoch Rock, The Yellan Drang and many others – filled sailors with dread in the days of sailing ships. Before the lighthouse was built in 1792, a fire was kept burning on the Point as a warning to ships. Today the lighthouse has a single light of 5 million candle-power – one of the most powerful in the world. The cliff-top walk northwards to Predannack

LONELY LIGHT *The oil lamps of the lighthouse at Lizard Point were replaced by an electric beacon in 1903. The building now includes a small museum.*

Head and Mullion is superb, the cliffs faced with lichen and the grassy slopes sweeping down to them filled with wild flowers and grasses.
Lighthouse: All year, pm daily exc Sun or in fog.

LONGSTONE HERITAGE AND LEISURE CENTRE

In Hugh Town, St Mary's, Isles of Scilly (Ac)

The Isles of Scilly are more than an astonishing concentration of pretty sea views and flower-covered fields, as a visit to this centre will show. Set on a $3\frac{1}{2}$ acre site which was once part of the largest farm on St Mary's, the centre houses an exhibition on the history of the Scillies and on local industries ranging from flowers to ship-building. A section on shipwrecks describes the loss in 1707 of three ships from Admiral Sir Cloudesley Shovell's fleet, including his flagship the *Association*.

The gardens are filled with tropical and sub-tropical plants seldom seen growing outdoors on the mainland.
Apr-Nov, daily. Adm charge. Refreshments. Shop. P *Toilets. Tel Scillonia (0720) 22924.*

LOOE ISLAND

By boat from Looe (Eb)

There are no roads on the island, no traffic and no shops. It is also very small – a mere 22 acres, rising at its highest point to a mere 150ft. But it does offer a range of magnificent sea and coastal views from Prawle Point in Devon to the Lizard peninsula. Daffodils bloom at Christmas, and in spring the wood is full of wild flowers and the cliffs covered with nesting birds. There is bathing, a natural rock swimming pool, rocky coves, cliff and woodland walks, a craft shop and a café. The income from visitors is devoted to preserving the natural beauty of the island.
May-Sept, boats daily from East Looe Quay. Landing fee. Refreshments. Toilets. Tel Looe (050 36) 2728.

MEVAGISSEY FOLK MUSEUM

On quayside in Mevagissey (Cb)

Even the building is part of Mevagissey's history, since it was once a boatyard used from 1745 by the town's first firm of boatbuilders. The roof supports are made from old ships' masts. Inside, on the ground floor, an old Cornish kitchen has been re-created, complete with oil lamps and a giant cider press and apple crusher, hand-carved out of solid granite. On the first floor a tableau depicts work in progress on the construction of a traditional Cornish wooden boat, complete with 200-year-old wooden pins and pieces of oakum for caulking seams.

In nearby Meadow Street is the Mevagissey Model Railway, containing more than 2000 models, not only of great British railway engines, but also from other parts of the world. About 50 trains are operated automatically and controlled in sequence through finely detailed scenery, including a harbour, with moving boats and a lifting bridge, and a china clay works.
Folk Museum: Easter-end Sept, daily. Adm charge. Shop. P *Toilets.* ♿ *Tel Mevagissey (0726) 843568. Model Railway: Easter, then end May-Oct, daily; Oct-end May, Sun pm.*

MONKEY SANCTUARY

Off B3253, 4 miles east of Looe (Eb)

The first protected breeding colony of Amazon woolly monkeys in the world can be seen at this sanctuary. The founder, Leonard Williams, tried to create as natural an environment as possible for the monkeys. The trees are linked by thick ropes to enable the monkeys to get about more easily. Visitors can wander about the sanctuary, and several informal 'meetings' are arranged each day, at which visitors can get better acquainted with both adult and baby monkeys and learn more about their behaviour.
Two Easter weeks, Spring Bank Hol week, July and Aug, Sun-Thur, and Easter Fri and May Day; other weeks Apr-Sept, Sun, Wed and Thur. Adm charge. Refreshments. Shop. P *Toilets.* ♿ *(part). Tel Looe (050 36) 2532.*

MOUNT EDGCUMBE COUNTRY PARK

Off B3247, 8 miles south of Torpoint (Eb)

The great Dr Samuel Johnson, who was not easily impressed, thought this landscaped park, then privately owned, had one of the finest situations in the country. Queen Victoria, who visited it much later, was inclined to agree. The park covers 865 acres of formal gardens, unspoilt coast and miles of footpaths, from which the magnificent scenery can be explored and enjoyed.

The coastline offers spectacular views over Plymouth Sound and out to the Eddystone Lighthouse 10 miles offshore. The park even includes two fishing villages, Kingsand and Cawsand, which were founded on the pilchard trade. But Cawsand also developed a reputation at the beginning of the last century as a notorious smuggling village. From the car park at Cawsand there is a splendid walk along the Earl's Drive to Penlee Point.
All year, daily. Free entry. Refreshments. Shop. P *Toilets.* ♿ *Tel Plymouth (0752) 822236.*

NEWQUAY ZOO

Near Newquay town centre (Cc)

This zoo is not only a place to see animals, but also a place where younger members of the family can expend their energy in such places as an activity play park and a Tarzan Trail assault course. The zoo is set in 8 acres of landscaped gardens, and the leisure park which is attached to it includes swimming pools, squash and tennis courts and a golf driving range.

The nearby Trenance Cottages Museum houses a collection of antiques and curios from all over the world. It is set in an attractive leisure park.
Zoo: Apr-Oct, daily. Adm charge. Refreshments. Shop. P *(limited). Toilets. Tel Newquay (0637) 873342. Museum: May-Oct, daily. Adm Charge.* P *Toilets.* ♿ *(ground floor). Tel Crantock (0637) 830478.*

PADSTOW TROPICAL BIRD GARDENS

In Padstow, near town centre (Cc)

A regular non-paying visitor to these gardens is the peregrine falcon, which paying visitors can often see gliding overhead in the hope of snatching one of the tastier inhabitants – the fantail dove. The gardens are also home for the chough, a bird which is sadly extinct in the wild in the West Country. But the gardens' chief attraction is the colony of tropical birds, with their brilliant technicolour plumage. These include South American macaws, the big touracos from Africa, the Indian tree pie and the Australian kookaburra or 'Laughing Jackass'.

The gardens also contain an exhibition of butterflies from all over the world, including many live specimens.
All year, daily. Adm charge. Refreshments. Shop. Toilets. Tel Padstow (0841) 532262.

PARADISE PARK

In Hayle, near town centre (Bb)

Beautiful birds to be seen at Paradise Park range from giant parrots and eagles to pink flamingos. More than 70 pairs of rare birds, gathered mainly from tropical countries where they are threatened with extinction, have started breeding at the park – some of them, like the white-eared pheasant and the wattled crane, breeding in Britain for the first time. The park has 35 different species of parrot, an otter sanctuary, and rare breeds of pigs, sheep, goats and poultry. There is a small brewery where visitors can see how Cornish real ale is made – and taste the results.
All year, daily. Adm charge. Refreshments. Shop. P *Toilets.* ♿ *Tel Hayle (0736) 753365.*

PAUL CORIN'S MAGNIFICENT MUSIC MACHINES

Off B3254, 2 miles south of Liskeard (Dc)

The peaceful Cornish village of St Keyne is not the obvious place for a visitor to go who is longing to hear the mighty roar of a 1929 Wurlitzer

SOUND AND SIGHT *Elaborate decoration adorns a fairground organ made by the French firm of Limonaire early this century. It is one of the 'magnificent machines' in the Paul Corin collection.*

cinema organ. But at this unusual museum there are live, and very lively, daily performances on this machine through the summer months. It is part of one of Europe's finest collections of automatic musical instruments, which includes fairground organs, continental café organs, orchestrions and pianolas, worked by perforated paper rolls, which reproduce performances of famous pianists such as Rachmaninov.
May-Sept, daily. Adm charge. P *Toilets.* ♿ *Tel Liskeard (0579) 43108.*

PENCARROW

Off A389, 3½ miles east of Wadebridge (Dc)

This elegant Georgian country mansion contains one of the finest collections of paintings, furniture and china in the West Country. It also has 50 acres of woodland gardens, a Palm House, an ice house, and a children's corner. The house, which has been occupied by the Molesworth-St Aubyn family since it was built, has some outstanding rooms, including the music room with its rococo ceiling, the panelled entrance hall, and the dining room which has a series of family portraits painted by Sir Joshua Reynolds.
Easter-mid Oct, daily exc Fri and Sat. Adm charge. Refreshments. Plant shop. P *Toilets.* ♿ *Tel St Mabyn (020 884) 369.*

PENDENNIS CASTLE

Pendennis Point, 1 mile south-east of Falmouth (Ca)

Henry VIII built Pendennis Castle on Pendennis Point as part of his coastal defences against the Pope's threatened reprisal for refusing to bow to his authority. Together with St Mawes Castle on the opposite shore, it guards the entrance to the Carrick Roads. Only the inner keep and curtain wall were built by Henry. The large enclosure and its bastions are Elizabethan, built to guard against the later threatened full-scale invasion from Spain which foundered with the Armada. There are fine views from Pendennis Point of Falmouth Bay and the Carrick Roads.
EH. All year, daily. Adm charge. Shop. P *Toilets.* ♿ *Tel Falmouth (0326) 316594.*

POLDARK MINE

On B3297, 3 miles north of Helston (Ba)

The best way to learn about Cornwall's most ancient and famous industry – tin-mining – is to go down a real mine. At Poldark the mine, which has been worked since Roman times, has been converted into an underground museum, in which visitors descend by a walkway and steps to a depth of more than 200ft. The site of the main tin lode can be clearly seen; here 18th-century miners worked by candlelight, breaking the rock by hand. The nine underground museum chambers contain many relics found in the mine, including the seal of an 18th-century beer bottle.

Women played an important part in processing the ore when it was brought to the surface. They operated the heavy stamps which were used to crush the ore, and were known as bal maidens; a model of one, dressed in her 19th-century working clothes, is in the museum. On the surface are several Cornish beam and hoisting engines.

Next to the mine is Ha'penny Park – a fun park with a variety of amusements including a mini-car race track, radio-controlled boats and a giant climbing frame.
Apr-Oct, daily. Adm charge. Refreshments. Shop. P *Toilets. Tel Helston (0326) 73173.*

RESTORMEL CASTLE

Off A390, 1½ miles north of Lostwithiel (Dc)

Crowning a hill overlooking the River Fowey and surrounded by a deep 60ft wide moat, Restormel is one of the oldest and most romantic ruins in Cornwall. Built in the 12th century, on ground falling steeply away on three sides, it had formidable defences which were last tested in the Civil War, when it was garrisoned by the Parliamentarian army of Lord Essex and fell to the Royalists led by Sir Richard Grenville. The remains include the gate, keep, kitchens, great hall, private rooms and bed chamber and private apartment of the lord of the castle.
EH. All year, daily. Adm charge. P *Tel Bodmin (0208) 872687.*

ST AGNES LEISURE PARK

On B3277, 1 mile south-east of St Agnes (Bb)

For the visitor who wants to touch the spire of Truro Cathedral without leaving the ground, or examine a working tin mine without venturing below the surface, this 7 acre park offers unrivalled facilities. Both the tin mine and the cathedral are, of course, models, though on a substantial scale. Other Cornish scenes represented include Restormel Castle and the Royal Naval Air Station at Culdrose. In the landscaped gardens, far from miniature model dinosaurs can also be seen, together with Cornish piskies and other fairies, all floodlit at night. Another attraction for children is a creepily atmospheric haunted house.
Mid Mar-Mid Oct, daily. Adm charge. Refreshments. Shop. P *Toilets.* ♿ *Tel St Agnes (087 255) 2793.*

ROCK OF AGES *St Michael's Mount has been in turn a Roman trading station, a church, priory, fortress and private house. In 1588, a beacon on the church tower warned of the approaching Spanish Armada.*

ST MAWES CASTLE

On A3078, in St Mawes (Ca)

'St Mawes lieth lower and better to annoy shipping, but Pendennis standeth higher and stronger to defend itself.' So wrote Carew in his Survey of Cornwall written in the reign of the first Queen Elizabeth. He was referring to the two castles built by Henry VIII guarding the opposite sides of the entrance to Falmouth Harbour. His assessment proved right, for later, in the Civil War, Pendennis withstood a Parliamentarian siege for five months, while St Mawes yielded without a shot. Each of the eight recesses in the gun room has its own ammunition cupboard and overhead smoke vent. Carved inscriptions in praise of King Henry girdle the keep, and there are fine gardens and lawns.
EH. All year, daily. Adm charge. P *Toilets.* ♿ *(part). Tel St Mawes (0326) 270526.*

ST MICHAEL'S MOUNT

At Marazion, near Penzance (Aa)

Walking out along the causeway, which at low tide links St Michael's Mount to the mainland village of Marazion, is like stepping into a scene from a fairytale. The little island rises like a giant sandcastle 300ft from the waters of Mount's Bay, capped with real castle buildings dating from the 12th century. The Mount was an important trading station in Roman times; it is said to have been the home of the giant of Jack the Giant-killer fame and also part of the legendary king-

QUIET HAVEN BY 'ST PETER'S POOL'

Polperro must surely be everyone's vision of a Cornish village come true. Its narrow lanes of cottages wander down the steep sides of a creek to a tranquil, small harbour, and the little River Pol chatters briskly through the midst of it all. But below this picturesqueness lies a tough little fishing and smuggling port. Pilchard fishing was its chief occupation for centuries, but around 1900 the pilchards mysteriously stopped coming to Cornwall. Now the fishermen take visitors shark fishing, or on trips down the coast. Some commercial fishing, however, still goes on, nowadays mainly for mackerel, crab and lobster.

The village lanes are not for motorists, so park in the car park and descend to the village by horse bus.

Land of Legend and Model Village: June-Oct, daily. Adm charge. Shop. Toilets. ♿ Tel Polperro (0503) 72378. Museum of Smuggling: Easter-mid Oct, daily. Adm charge. Toilets. ♿ Tel Tiverton (0884) 860847.

LAND OF LEGEND *A blacksmith plies his trade in the attractively restored Old Forge, which today houses animated tableaux depicting Cornish traditions. One shows Merlin producing Excalibur, King Arthur's magical sword; another shows a gathering of witches and piskies.*

HOLY HAVEN *The name of Polperro means 'St Peter's Pool', presumably a reference to its delightful small harbour, almost walled in by cottages, many of them lime-washed and with outside stone stairs. They stand on narrow lanes, such as the Warren, which climb the steep sides of the coomb. The harbour dries out at low tide. Despite its sheltered aspect, the harbour is susceptible to damage by south-east gales and the piers have needed replacing several times in the last 200 years. In 1978 the situation was much improved by the installation of the 22 ton New Gate, which can seal off the Inner Harbour in bad weather.*

As many pleasure craft as fishing boats now use the harbour. Many of the crustaceans caught locally finish up in the attractive seafood restaurants that crowd the harbour with their quaint signs (right), along with artists' studios and craft shops. The Shell House (left), in the Warren, was decorated by a retired fisherman.

YO-HO-HO AND A YACHTFUL OF POT *A smuggler checks his haul in the Museum of Smuggling, which traces the story of British smuggling from its golden age (from around 1750 to 1850) to the present. In 1979, a yacht landed cannabis worth £2 million at nearby Talland Bay – a favourite haunt of brandy and tobacco smugglers in the 18th century.*

POCKET BOROUGH *Polperro is reproduced in miniature in the Model Village next to the Land of Legend museum. Kept up to date by local craftsmen, the model includes the 16th-century House on Props, a restaurant leaning on fragile-seeming beams. A recording of the singing of the Fishermen's Choir issues from St John's Church – and the Model Village even contains a reduced model of itself.*

dom of Lyonnesse, where King Arthur's knights once rode. It was given to monks from Mont St Michel in Normandy in 1070, and a Benedictine priory built on the summit in 1135 became an important place of pilgrimage in the Middle Ages.

The priory, rebuilt in the 14th century, became the home of the St Aubyn family in 1659 and a member of the family still lives there, although the property is now owned by the National Trust. The connection with its monastic past is most strikingly recalled in the Chevy Chase Room, which was originally the monks' refectory. The Blue Drawing Rooms, found in what was once the Lady Chapel, are exquisitely pretty, containing some very fine early rococo Gothic plasterwork and Chippendale chairs.

NT. Apr-May, Mon, Tues, Wed and Fri; June-Oct, Mon-Fri; Nov-Mar, Mon, Wed and Fri. Adm charge. Refreshments. Shop. P (mainland). Toilets. Tel Penzance (0736) 710507.

SEAL SANCTUARY

At Gweek, off B3293, 3 miles east of Helston (Ba)

Life for the grey Atlantic seal round Cornwall is not all basking on sun-drenched Cornish rocks. They breed in the autumn, when fierce gales can sweep the new-born pups off their nursery ledges and far out to sea, or pound them mercilessly against the cliffs. In either case there is little a seal mother can do to help. But this sanctuary, in a beautiful natural setting at Gweek on the Helford River, is a hospital and convalescent home for battered seals found exhausted, injured and starving on beaches all round Cornwall.

Every baby seal brought to the sanctuary spends from 6 to 12 weeks in hospital, during which injuries and infections are treated. It is then transferred to one of the sanctuary's five pools where it is taught to catch its own food, and is then returned to the sea.

Some seals are so badly injured that they can never fend for themselves again, and these are kept permanently at the sanctuary.

All year, daily. Adm charge. Refreshments. Shop. P Toilets. ♿ Tel Mawgan (032 622) 361.

SHIRE HORSE FARM AND CARRIAGE MUSEUM

Off A3047, 1½ miles south-east of Camborne (Bb)

There are few farmyard sights more impressive than a line of full-grown heavy horses, especially if the parade includes, as it does at this farm, a Champion Suffolk Punch. The farm has 15 of these extremely high, wide and handsome horses, including Clydesdales as well as Suffolks and shires, which are actively involved in ploughing in winter and haymaking in summer. They are not cheap to run, each needing in winter a daily diet of three buckets of oats, barley and sugar beet, mixed with cod-liver and linseed oil, together with unlimited quantities of hay. But the result is far more spectacular than any tractor. The farm also has a wheelwright's workshop, a blacksmith's shop, where farm carts and machinery are repaired, and a carriage museum.

Apr-Oct, daily. Adm charge. P Tel Camborne (0209) 713606.

TAMAR OTTER PARK

Off B3254, 4 miles north-west of Launceston (Ed)

Visitors to the park and Wild Wood, a branch of the Otter Trust, can see otters playing in large natural enclosures. Deer roam free, and peacocks and golden pheasants strut by the waterfowl lake. The British or European otter is bred at the park for release into the wild wherever suitable habitats remain. Attractions for visitors include picnic areas and an illustrated nature trail from which the animals and birds can be observed in their natural surroundings.

Apr-Oct, daily. Adm charge. Refreshments. Shop. P Toilets. ♿ Tel Launceston (0566) 85646.

TINTAGEL CASTLE

At Tintagel, 5 miles north-west of Camelford (Dd)

Even on the sunniest day, the ruins of this famous castle seem to be swathed in a mist of legend and romance like no other in Britain. Out of the mist, the ghost of King Arthur looms large, conjuring up pictures of brave knights in shining armour and England's dim and distant past. Legend has it that King Arthur was born here, which is by no means impossible, since the earliest identifiable settlement is Celtic, and dates from about AD 400.

The remains now standing on the splendidly rugged cliffs, connected by a broad footpath to the village, are of a royal castle built in the 12th century, with later additions in the 13th and 14th centuries by Richard, brother of Henry III, and Edward, the Black Prince. Even without King Arthur, therefore, whose very existence, let alone his connections with Tintagel, cannot be proved, the castle has a considerable history.

The village has two other buildings of particular interest. The Old Post Office is a medieval house, now furnished as it was in Victorian times as a Post Office. The other building, King Arthur's Hall, is much more recent and is devoted to depicting the legend of the Knights of the Round Table in a series of 73 stained-glass windows. Paths descend from the village to a shingle beach and another fragment of the Arthurian legend, Merlin's Cave.

Castle: EH. All year, daily. Adm charge. Shop. Toilets. Tel Camelford (0840) 770328. Old Post Office: NT. Apr-Oct, daily. Adm charge. Shop. ♿ Tel Camelford (0840) 770256.

TRELISSICK GARDEN

On B3289, 4 miles south of Truro (Cb)

These gardens planted in the 1820s sweep down to the water's edge of the Carrick Roads, the deep water anchorage of Falmouth Harbour. In the distance, across the water, Pendennis Castle can be seen, facing its sister castle St Mawes across the great estuary. Dense clusters of brilliant white yachts are gathered, like migrating geese, along the far shore.

The creator of this haven of visual delights was Ralph Allen Daniell, known as 'Guinea-a-minute Daniell' on account of the torrent of money made from tin-mining in the 19th century. He saw to the planting of the hanging woods of beech, oak and pine, and he laid out the carriage drives along which a lovely Woodland Walk now runs. Later owners have planted rhododendrons, and many other species of plants which, when sheltered, respond well to the mild Cornish climate.

NT. Mar-Oct, Mon-Sat and Sun pm. Woodland Walk also open Nov-Feb. Adm charge. Refreshments. Shop. P Toilets. ♿ (parts). Tel Truro (0872) 862090.

MOST CORNISH OF FLOWERS *Many-hued hydrangeas bloom in Trelissick Garden in late summer, in tranquil havens protected from the savage westerly winds by conifers, holm oaks and mature beeches.*

TRELOWARREN

Off B3293, 3½ miles south-east of Helston (Ba)

The earliest-known owner of the Manor of Trelowarren was Earl Harold, who later achieved lasting fame as the king killed at the Battle of Hastings. It passed in 1086 to Robert Mortmain, half brother of William the Conqueror. The Vyvyan family, who still occupy part of the manor house, have lived on the site since 1427. It is a family with a long history, since tradition has it that a Vyvyan was the last governor of the lost legendary land of Lyonnesse when it sank beneath the waves somewhere between Mount's Bay and the Scillies.

The earliest part of the present building is 15th century. It is a handsome house, full of family portraits of people who were part of the local history of Cornwall down the centuries.

House: Easter-end Oct, Wed pm (guided tours only); also Bank Hol Mon pm, and Sun pm in Aug. Chapel: All year, daily. Adm charge. Shop. P *Toilets. Tel Mawgan (032 622) 366.*

TRENGWAINTON

On B3312, 2 miles north-west of Penzance (Aa)

One outstanding feature of this garden is the stream garden, which starts under a canopy of beech and sycamore then spreads its banks wide to embrace masses of primulas, daffodils and other moisture-loving plants. Another is the enticing view of St Michael's Mount seen from the lawn in front of the house.

A number of great Cornish gardeners have worked at Trengwainton over the years, and the collection of exotic and tender plants is unsurpassed. Many of the glorious rhododendrons were raised from seeds brought from Assam and Burma in the late 1920s by the noted collector Frank Kingdon-Ward.

NT. Mar-Oct, Wed-Sat; also Bank Hol Mon and Good Fri. Adm charge. Toilets. ♿ *Tel Penzance (0736) 63021.*

TRERICE

Off A3058, 2½ miles south-east of Newquay (Cc)

This lovely Elizabethan manor house is one of the few in Cornwall which has not suffered substantial alteration over the centuries. It lies, half-hidden by trees, in a quiet valley in which a tributary of the River Gannel runs down to the sea. Features of the house include a great mullioned hall window with 576 panes of mostly 16th-century glass; much fine plasterwork; and a façade with highly decorative scrolled gables.

NT. Apr-Oct, daily. Adm charge. Refreshments. Shop. P *Toilets.* ♿ *Tel Newquay (0637) 875404.*

TRESCO ABBEY GARDENS

Tresco, Isles of Scilly (Ac)

On a small island out in the Atlantic, one of the most interesting gardens in the world has been developed over 150 years. The island was once one of the least accessible places in Britain to visit, but now has a heliport. The gardens were created by Augustus Smith, who in 1834 was made Lord Proprietor of the Isles of Scilly, and the development of the gardens has been continued by succeeding generations of his family. They contain an enormous variety of beautiful plants from all over the world, which grow out of doors on Tresco because of its exceptionally mild climate.

SUBTROPICAL BRITAIN *Palms and cycads flourish around the abbey ruins in Tresco Abbey Gardens, where temperatures below 10°C (50°F) are very rare. The figureheads (right) in the 'Valhalla' collection are from ships wrecked around the Isles of Scilly.*

The gardens also contain, in the so-called 'Valhalla', an outstanding collection of ships' figureheads from vessels wrecked on the vicious reefs of the Scillies in the 19th century.

All year, daily. Adm charge. Refreshments. Shop. Toilets. Tel Scillonia (0720) 22849.

TREWITHEN GARDENS

On A390, 5 miles east of Truro (Cb)

This beautiful woodland garden is internationally famous for its rare trees and shrubs from all over the world. In all, 28 acres of mature garden surround an elegant 18th-century mansion which has been home for generations to a succession of keen gardeners. The result of their efforts, and many plant-hunting expeditions, is a superb display of trees, shrubs and flowers which varies from season to season. But perhaps the chief glories are the magnolias, rhododendrons and camellias. The giant Himalayan pink tulip tree took 20 years to flower, but now opens its lily-shaped buds each February and March.

Adjoining Trewithen is the County Demonstration Garden at Probus which covers more than 7 acres. There are displays of plants of many kinds, and examples of designs for small and large gardens. Wild flowers, culinary and medicinal herbs, a children's nature trail and a nature reserve are also included.

Trewithen: Gardens, Mar-Sept, daily exc Sun; House: Apr-July, Mon and Tues pm. Adm charge. P *Toilets.* ♿ *(gardens only). Tel St Austell (0726) 882585. Probus: All year, Mon-Fri; May-Sept, Sun also. Adm charge.* P *Toilets. Tel Truro (0872) 74282.*

TRURO CATHEDRAL

In centre of Truro (Cb)

The three great spires of Truro Cathedral rise dramatically from the surrounding cluster of narrow streets filled with elegant Georgian houses, as if they had dominated the town for hundreds of years. The building is, in fact, a recent creation, completed in 30 years between 1880 and 1910 with typical Victorian energy and industry, but its architectural inspiration is unmistakably that of the great medieval churches. It was the first cathedral to be built in England since St Paul's and was in a sense an assertion of the county's independence, since it had previously been part of a joint Cornwall and Devon diocese.

The fascinating history of Cornwall is impres-

sively displayed in the County Museum in Truro, where exhibits ranging from early Bronze Age collars of beaten gold to the hard clay porcelain which was the product of the Cornish china clay industry are displayed.
Cathedral: All year, daily. Shop. Museum: All year, daily exc Sun and Bank Hol. Adm charge. Shop. Tel Truro (0872) 72205.

WESLEY'S COTTAGE

Off A30, 10 miles west of Launceston (Dc)

John Wesley, the founder of Methodism, spent most of his life on preaching tours, staying with friends and fellow Methodists, as he did at Trewint on at least six occasions. The cottage is now a place of pilgrimage for thousands, and an open-air service is held every year outside the cottage on Wesley Day, May 24, to commemorate the reopening of the cottage in Wesley's honour in 1950. Inside the cottage are many items of 'Wesleyana' and the room in which the preacher slept.

A carved stone head of John Wesley can be seen over the doorway of the old Methodist chapel at Altarnun. The 15th-century parish church of St Nonna of Altarnon is known locally as 'the cathedral of the moors', because of its great tower – one of the highest in Cornwall. At the gate of the church is a fine Celtic cross, dating from the 6th century, the time when the Celtic St Nonna passed through Cornwall from Wales on her missionary work.
Cottage: All year, daily. Shop. P *(limited). Tel Pipers Pool (0566) 86811.*

WHEAL MARTYN CHINA CLAY MUSEUM

On A391, 1½ miles north of St Austell (Cb)

The history of Cornwall's largest industry is recorded in this museum built on the site of two old china clay works – the Gomm Clay Works and Wheal Martyn. The Wheal Martyn pit – wheal means 'mine' in Cornish – was started in 1820 by Elias Martyn, and was reopened in 1971, but its clay is now piped down to modern works at Blackpool and Goverseth.

An audiovisual display and a series of working models help visitors to understand some of the processes involved. Among the highlights of the tour of Wheal Martyn are the famous 35ft diameter water wheel which was originally used to operate a pump in the clay pit, and an 18ft diameter water wheel and bucket pump which was used to lift clay up to the settling pits. The various stages of the refining process can then be followed to the settling tanks, which cover a third of an acre. The enclosed drying floor, called a pan kiln, is more than 200ft long, with a travelling bridge to distribute the wet clay from the settling tanks.

The nearby storage bay is now used for displays of various other aspects of china clay production, including cask and barrel making and a clay worker's cottage kitchen. There is also a 1¼ mile nature trail, passing a viewing platform from which the operations in two modern clay pits can be seen, and a working pottery.
Easter-Oct, daily. Adm charge. Refreshments. Shop. P *Toilets.* ♿ *Tel St Austell (0726) 850362.*

WORLD IN MINIATURE

At Goonhavern, 5 miles south-west of Newquay (Cb)

Even in the age of supersonic travel, it might be thought to be asking a lot to expect to see the Leaning Tower of Pisa, the Great Sphinx and the Parthenon in a single afternoon. But all these great monuments, and many more, can be seen in the form of large-scale models at Goonhavern. Set in 12 acres of gardens, with more than 70,000 plants and trees, the models range from Stonehenge to Tombstone – a complete, full-size Wild West town with jail, bank, saloon, livery stable and funeral parlour.
Mid Mar-Mid Oct, daily. Adm charge. Refreshments. Shop. P *Toilets.* ♿ *Tel Truro (0872) 57828.*

ZENNOR QUOIT

Off B3306, 4½ miles west of St Ives (Ab)

The Land's End peninsula is one of the richest areas in Britain not only in natural beauty but also in Neolithic and Bronze Age remains, from longstones to hut circles. Zennor Quoit is the largest stone quoit, or burial chamber, in the country. It has seven stones, each 10ft high, capped with a massive slab 6yds long. Originally it may have been covered with earth, to form a barrow or mound. Remains found in the chamber indicate that it was built during the Stone Age, between 3200 and 2500 BC.

In the nearby village of Zennor, the Wayside Museum houses implements and relics of life in the area over the last 5000 years. Zennor Head, half a mile north-west of the village, is a wild, lonely spot, 300ft above the Atlantic, with a narrow gorge cutting into the headland.
Quoit: All year, daily. Museum: Easter-Oct, daily. Refreshments. Shop. P *Tel Penzance (0736) 796945.*

GIANT PRESERVED *Cornwall's largest working water wheel, 35ft across, was built in the 1880s. It once drove a pump in Wheal Martyn Pit, which is working again and produces some 3000 tons of china clay each week.*

COUNTY CALENDAR

February (early in month). St Ives: Hurling the Silver Ball (traditional game).
Shrove Tuesday (and Sat after). St Columb Major: Hurling the Silver Ball.
May 1. Padstow: Hobbyhorse ceremony.
May 8. Helston: Furry Dance.
June (early in month). Wadebridge: Royal Cornwall Agricultural Show.
June 23. Carn Brae: Midsummer Bonfire.
June 29. Mevagissey: Feast Week.
August (early in month). Bude: Blessing of the Sea. Bodmin: Sealed Knot Civil War re-enactment.
August (Mon after 12th). Marhamchurch: Revels.
August (mid-month). St Ives: Harbour Day.
September (early in month). Helston: Harvest Fair.
September (first Sat). Different site each year: Cornish Gorsedd (Celtic traditional ceremonies).
Tourist information: Bodmin (0208) 4159; Bude (0288) 4240 (summer); Falmouth (0326) 312300; Looe (050 36) 2072 (summer); Newquay (063 73) 71345/6/7; Penzance (0736) 62207/62341; Isles of Scilly (0720) 22536; St Ives (0736) 796297; Truro (0872) 74555.

TOWERING KINGPIN *From every approach to the city, Truro's cathedral is seen at its very centre, as here from Chapel Hill. The city gained its landmark only at the turn of the century.*

CUMBRIA

WRITERS' HOMES IN A LAND OF LAKES AND MOUNTAINS

The mountains, valleys and lakesides of Cumbria are as beautiful and awe-inspiring today as they were in the early 19th century, when Wordsworth wandered through them 'lonely as a cloud'. The poet's spirit and genius live on in his homes: Grasmere's Dove Cottage and nearby Rydal Mount.

Wordsworth's homes are now places of pilgrimage for admirers from all over the world. So also is the home of the Lake District's other famous writer, Beatrix Potter. She created Squirrel Nutkin, Samuel Whiskers and all her other much loved animal characters at her stone farmhouse, Hill Top, Near Sawrey. An exhibition of her fantasy world can be seen at Brockhole, near Windermere, the headquarters of the Lake District National Park.

Centuries earlier, the Roman legions left their traces at the fort below Hardknott Pass. During the Middle Ages, monks settled at St Bees and Furness and barons controlled the turbulent Border region from castles at Appleby, Carlisle and Sizergh. Victorian technology can be admired at Windermere's Steamboat Museum, while modern nuclear power production is explained at the exhibition centre at Sellafield.

APPLEBY CASTLE CONSERVATION CENTRE
In Appleby, near town centre (Dc)

The Norman builder of Appleby's frowning keep would have been amazed at some of the livestock that now grazes below its lofty walls. He would probably have been familiar with the White Park cattle, brought to England by the Romans, and perhaps with Soay sheep, which may have been here since the Stone Age. But he would certainly never have seen the Bagot goat, brought back from the Crusades, or the grotesque-looking Vietnamese pot-bellied pig, with a stomach almost touching the ground. These are just a few of the threatened species kept at Appleby, a Rare Breeds Survival Trust Centre, which also maintains a stock of birds from many parts of the world.

Easter week, then early May-Sept, daily. Adm charge. Refreshments. Shop. P *Toilets.* ♿ *Tel Appleby (076 83) 51402.*

BELLE ISLE
In Windermere lake (Cb)

This attractively wooded island, about 40 acres in extent, stretches diagonally across Windermere opposite Bowness, and almost appears to cut the lake in two. Occupied by the Romans and the Norsemen, and defended in the Civil War by a Royalist colonel against the Roundheads, for the last 200 years it has been famous for Belle Isle House, a completely circular country house built in 1774 for a certain Mr English. Inside the house are a number of portraits by George Romney, including one of Miss Isabella Curwen, a leading beauty of her day who owned it. Belle Isle has given its name to a recently invented liqueur, made of butterscotch and whisky. A 'sight and sound' animated museum depicts below-stairs life on Belle Isle in the 1920s, and there is a nature trail and adventure playground.

May-Sept, Sun-Thur. boat from Bowness. Adm charge. Refreshments. Shop. Tel Windermere (096 62) 3353.

BIRDOSWALD ROMAN FORT
Off B6318, 8 miles east of Brampton (De)

The massive stone lower courses of the fort's eastern gate reveal the strength and permanence of the Emperor Hadrian's great wall. Built around AD 125, Birdoswald Fort (known to the Romans as Banna) covers 5 acres and would have been manned by a garrison of 300 cavalry or 500 foot soldiers. It guards a Roman bridge over the River Irthing, which sweeps round behind it in a deep gorge. At Birdoswald, one of the most remote of all the forts along the Wall, it is easy to imagine the legionaries gazing north towards the bleak Scottish hills and longing for the warm south. Among the discoveries that have been made there is a Roman 'arm purse' containing 28 silver denarii. The farmhouse on the site was built largely of stones taken from the fort.

An exhibition on site has displays on the fort's history and the life of its garrison, and photographs of finds excavated from the site.

EH. All year, daily. Adm charge.

BRANTWOOD
Off B5285, 1½ miles south-east of Coniston (Cb)

For the last quarter of the 19th century Coniston Water could boast two Grand Old Men – the 2600ft peak known as Coniston Old Man which dominates the fells on the western side of the lake, and John Ruskin, who lived at Brantwood on the eastern shore. From Brantwood, Ruskin could look across the lake to the hills, green in spring and summer and snow-covered in winter, and it is easy to imagine him gazing from his study window at the view he called 'the finest I know in Cumberland or Lancashire'.

Ruskin bought Brantwood for £1500 in 1872 and lived there until his death in 1900. Earlier in his life he had won fame as an art critic and social reformer, championing the pre-Raphaelite school of painting, and attacking the evils of the Victorian industrial system. Later in life he became one of the pioneers of conservation, putting forward such ideas as smokeless zones and green belts, and inspiring the founders of the National Trust.

Built in 1797, Brantwood started out as little more than a large cottage, but was added to by various 19th-century owners and finally by Ruskin himself. His study, dining room and bedroom are much as he left them, full of artistic treasures including many of his own drawings. A nature trail leads through the gardens, which in early summer are brilliant with azaleas and rhododendrons.

Ruskin no doubt pottered up and down the lake aboard the steam yacht *Gondola* – which still plies the lake in summer, calling at Brantwood.

Brantwood: Mid Mar-mid Nov, daily; Winter, Wed-Sun. Adm charge. Refreshments. Shop. P *Toilets.* ♿ *(ground floor). Tel Coniston (0966) 41396.* Gondola: *NT. Apr-Oct, daily. Tel (0966) 41288.*

BROCKHOLE
On A591, 2 miles north of Windermere (Cb)

More than 140 years before the Lake District National Park was designated in 1951, the poet Wordsworth described the Lakes as 'a sort of national property, in which every man has a right and interest who has an eye to perceive and a heart to enjoy'. Suitably enough, the Lake District National Park's headquarters is only a few miles from Wordsworth's own Grasmere, in a large, gabled, turn-of-the-century mansion on the eastern side of Windermere. Looking over terraced gardens to a magical view of the lake, Brockhole was established in 1969 as the first National Park Visitor Centre.

A Living Lakeland exhibition explains the history, geology, botany and wildlife of the Lake District in tableaux ranging from a Roman legionary in full battle gear to realistic woodland scenes complete with stuffed animals and recorded birdsong.

A World of Beatrix Potter exhibition re-creates scenes from *Squirrel Nutkin, Jeremy Fisher* and a further half-dozen of the children's classics. Young people's knowledge of the countryside is increased by following the waymarked 'Squirrel Nutkin Trail' through Brockhole's parkland and along the edge of Windermere.

Among the events held at Brockhole are guided walks through the landscaped gardens, talks and demonstrations by National Park rangers, crafts such as dry-stone walling and woodturning demonstrated by local experts, and courses on birdwatching and other outdoor hobbies. The lake can be enjoyed aboard the boats from Brockhole pier to Bowness or Ambleside.

Visitors who want a more energetic type of activity can take a recommended hour-long walk from Brockhole into the hills. At its highest point, the walk offers a magnificent view of Windermere and the fells beyond, and is an easy introduction to more strenuous hill walks.

Late Mar-early Nov, daily. Adm charge. Refreshments. Shop. P *Toilets.* ♿ *Tel Windermere (096 62) 6601.*

LAKELAND GONDOLA *The steam yacht* Gondola, *launched in 1859, can carry up to 86 passengers in her luxurious saloons as she cruises Coniston Water. She is the only boat owned and run by the National Trust.*

GRASMERE: LAKESIDE HOME OF A POET

The name of Grasmere – both village and lake – is inextricably linked with the poet William Wordsworth, who lived there in the first half of the 19th century; and who, along with his sister, Dorothy, and his wife, Mary, is buried in the village churchyard.

The area, with its rolling fields and gently rising hills, inspired much of Wordsworth's finest nature poetry. And in his long, unfinished work, *The Recluse*, he expressed the serenity and contentment he felt at Grasmere, referring to its 'crags and woody steeps . . . its one green island and its winding shores'. Wordsworth was a great walker, and his favourite paths have changed little since his days there.

Dove Cottage and Museum: All year, daily; closed mid Jan-mid Feb. Adm charge. Refreshments. Shop. P (limited). Toilets. ♿ Tel Grasmere (096 65) 544. Rydal Mount: All year, daily exc Tues in winter. Adm charge. Shop. P Toilets. Tel Ambleside (053 94) 33002.

POET'S PARADISE *The placid expanse of Rydal Water (above) was one of Wordsworth's favourite local views. Slightly smaller than neighbouring Grasmere, and hemmed in more closely by hills, the lake is set among reeds and shore-line trees. Only some 55ft deep, it is the first of the Cumbrian lakes to freeze over in winter – and the poet loved to watch the speeding skaters who glided gracefully over it.*

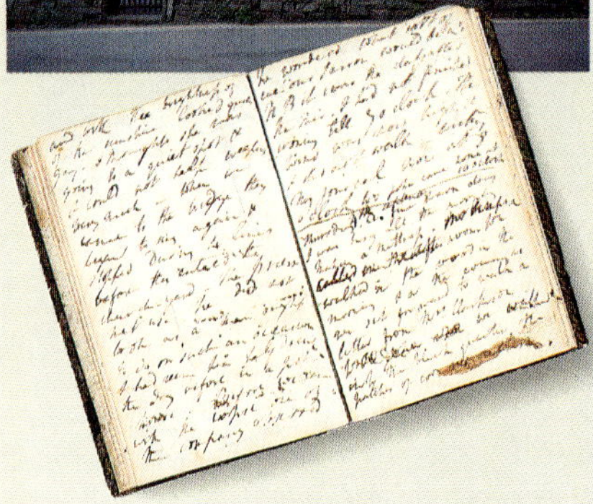

COTTAGE INDUSTRY *William Wordsworth called the terraced grounds behind Dove Cottage his 'little domestic slip of a garden', and laid the stone steps leading to the upper, tree-shaded levels (above). From 1799 to 1808 he shared the cottage (left) with his sister, Dorothy, who found the 17th-century building, with its stone-flagged floors, cold and draughty. She lined one of the upstairs bedrooms with newspapers for insulation, and they are still there. While William worked on his poetry, she kept her* Journal, *in which, on September 3, 1800 (lower left), she records the death of a poor woman who was 'buried by the parish'.*

Next door to the cottage is a long stone barn which houses The Grasmere and Wordsworth Museum. The lower floor is largely given over to displays of Lakeland life as it was in Wordsworth's days, while upstairs the Wordsworth Room provides an all-round picture of the poet.

HILLSIDE HOME *Built on a hillside overlooking Rydal Water, and set in 4 acres of wooded gardens, Rydal Mount (above) was Wordsworth's last home. He moved there in 1813 as he needed a larger house for himself, his wife, Mary, their three children – as well as his sister, Dorothy. He died there in 1850 aged 80. The house is still filled with his furniture and personal possessions, including his picnic box and top hat.*

SWIFT FOOT, SWEET TOOTH *Each August sees one of the highlights of the Lakeland summer calendar: the outdoor sports meeting held at Grasmere. No event is more popular and well-attended than the Junior Guides' Race (right) in which local youngsters enthusiastically compete in scrambling up and down a 1500ft fell. As preparation for such strenuous occasions, the young people – like their parents before them and visitors today – often eat the locally made Kendal Mint Cake. Together with gingerbread, the mint cake is one of the best-selling items in Grasmere. Climbers value its high sugar content, and it has sustained British expeditions on Everest.*

CARLISLE CASTLE
On A595, near city centre (Cd)

The squat strength of the castle keep, crouching on a low hill, symbolises Carlisle's turbulent history as a frontier town between the warring Scots and English. The site was first fortified by William Rufus in 1092, while the keep and defensive walls were built in the 12th century by the successive efforts of the Scots and the English. In the 16th century Henry VIII adapted the keep for the heavy guns of the day, which accounts for the low, wide battlements, quite unlike the usual medieval type.

The later history of warfare is summed up in one of the castle towers, which houses the Museum of the King's Own Royal Border Regiment. The museum illustrates the regiment's outstanding fighting record from 18th-century campaigns to the Second World War.

Carlisle's more peaceful aspects can be studied in the City Museum and Art Gallery, in Tullie House, a fine 17th-century mansion. Stones from Hadrian's Wall, natural history and geological displays, toys and dolls, musical instruments and an extensive collection of English paintings are on show. The city's civic pride is displayed in the magnificent 15th-century Guildhall, now a museum of guild, local and civic history.

Carlisle: EH. All year, daily. Adm charge. Refreshments. Shop. P *Toilets. Tel Carlisle (0228) 31777. City Museum: Apr-Sept, daily; Oct-Mar, daily exc Sun. Free entry. Tel (0228) 34781. Guildhall: All year, daily exc Sun and Mon. Adm charge.*

CUMBERLAND PENCIL MUSEUM
In Keswick, near town centre (Cc)

The wood of the incense cedar from America, and graphite from Mexico and Korea, are put through a complex manufacturing process before emerging as the humble pencil that everyone takes for granted. The history behind the process is explained at this museum at the Cumberland Pencil Company's factory. The world's first pencils were made in Keswick in the 16th century, after graphite was discovered in nearby Borrowdale around 1500. A cottage industry grew up, making pencils laboriously by hand, and the original factory was established about 1830. The museum traces the history of pencil making from its primitive beginnings to the latest high-speed methods.

All year, daily. Adm charge. Shop. P *Toilets.* ♿ *Tel Keswick (076 87) 73626.*

DENT CRAFTS CENTRE
Off A684, 4½ miles south-east of Sedbergh (Db)

For centuries the picturesque cobbled village of Dent was famous for its handknitted woollens. Resident knitters are still at work in Dent today, and their products are on view and for sale at this enterprising Crafts Centre. Apart from its knitwear, the Centre has a gallery of oil paintings, watercolours and etchings by local artists, toys made from the bobbins used in the machinery of the Pennine cotton mills, and an unusual sales line in antique printing blocks, which can be used either for printing or simply as ornaments.

CARVED IN CAPTIVITY *Prisoners in Carlisle Castle in the Middle Ages made these ornate carvings on the cell walls. They include religious pictures – such as a crucifixion – and some inspired by legend, such as a mermaid with a mirror and a dragon being slain.*

Mid Mar-Dec, daily. Free entry. Refreshments. P *Shop. Toilets. Tel Dent (058 75) 400.*

ESKDALE CORN MILL
In Boot village, 6 miles north-east of Ravenglass (Bb)

The fast-flowing Whillan Beck tumbles down from Barnmoor Tarn, near Scafell, joining the Esk below Boot village and there driving a water mill which has a history going back some 600 years. Reached by a 17th-century packhorse bridge from the village, the present mill dates from Elizabethan times. It has been restored and houses a permanent exhibition illustrating the techniques of milling grain of different types. There are also displays of Eskdale's farming history.

The mill was powered by an unusual double water wheel, both wheels of which were overshot (driven by water from above). Visitors can appreciate the mill's tranquil setting from a woodland walk and picnic area.

Easter-Sept, daily exc Sat. Adm charge. P *(limited). Tel Eskdale (094 03) 335.*

FELL FOOT PARK
Off A592, 8 miles south of Windermere (Cb)

Set in gently wooded countryside at the southern tip of Windermere, Fell Foot shows the National Trust as actively encouraging leisure pursuits, as well as preserving their surroundings. This 18 acre country park has facilities for every type of water sport, with a beach for swimming and fishing, slipways for boat-launching and rowing-boat hire. There are also an information centre, picnic areas and an adventure playground.

NT. Park: All year, daily. Shop (Easter-Oct). P *Tel Newby Bridge (053 95) 31273.*

FURNESS ABBEY
Off A590, 1½ miles north of Barrow-in-Furness (Ba)

Hidden away in a valley, the red-sandstone remains of Furness Abbey are among the grandest monastic ruins in the north. Founded in 1123 by Count Stephen (later King Stephen of England), it was during the Middle Ages second in importance only to Fountains Abbey, in Yorkshire, among the Cistercian abbeys of England.

Enough of the abbey survives to give an idea of its scale. The dormitory was 200ft long, and the refectory 150ft. A small chapel attached to the infirmary contains two 13th-century effigies of knights in armour, among the oldest of their type in this country. A small exhibition gives a good introduction to monastic life at Furness.

EH. All year, daily. Adm charge. Refreshments. Shop. P *Toilets.* ♿ *Tel Barrow-in-Furness (0229) 23420.*

GRIZEDALE FOREST VISITOR CENTRE
Off B5285, 8 miles east of Coniston (Cb)

From the eastern shore of Coniston Water, a rolling expanse of tree-covered fell, interspersed with meadows full of grazing cattle and sheep, stretches for 5 miles towards Windermere. This is the 8700 acre Grizedale Forest Park, run by the Forestry Commission as a partnership between forestry and farming.

The Visitor and Wildlife Centre, at the heart of the forest, occupies the outbuildings of Grizedale Hall, a mansion demolished in 1956. Permanent displays, films and booklets explain the history of the forest, and show steps taken to reconcile the interests of commercial forestry and farming with wildlife conservation and recreation.

From the Centre, various waymarked trails lead through the forest. The longest is the 9½ mile Silurian Trail, which introduces the walker to the whole history and ecology of the forest. Today's forestry concentrates on fast-growing conifers such as larch and spruce, but in former centuries Grizedale consisted largely of oak. Coppiced every 12-15 years, it was turned into charcoal for the iron furnaces in the forest. Here and there the Commission is now replanting felled areas with oak and other broadleaved trees.

Among the animals that visitors can see are roe and red deer and red squirrels, while greylag geese, teal and tufted duck have been encouraged to return to the small lakes that dot the forest.

FC. All year, daily.

HARDKNOTT ROMAN FORT
On minor road, 9 miles west of Ambleside (Bb)

The legionaries who garrisoned Hardknott must have hated it even more than the Roman Wall itself, since it lies remote in western Lakeland, far from the comradeship of Hadrian's great rampart. It was built to guard the access to the central lakes by way of Eskdale. From it, a single-track road snakes up to Hardknott Pass, leading via Wrynose Pass and the valley of the Duddon to the gentler country round Coniston Water and Windermere.

The Romans called it Mediobogdum, meaning 'in the middle of a bend in the river' (the

SMALL WORLD *In a bedroom at Beatrix Potter's home, Hill Top, is this doll's house similar to the one featured in* The Tale of Two Bad Mice. *It shows the food stolen by Tom Thumb and Hunca Munca.*

River Esk). Built at the same time as the Wall, soon after AD 120, the fort covers about 3 acres, and even after more than 1800 years is an impressive reminder of the far-reaching might of Rome. It was constructed to the typical fort pattern, in the form of a rectangle, with a turret at each corner. The stone lower courses of the outer wall can be easily traced, as can the main administrative buildings – the commandant's house, the headquarters with its weapon stores and pay office, the granary with its loading bays still clearly visible.

Outside the walls are the bath house and the flattened-out parade ground. The wooden barrack blocks have long since vanished, but parts of the legionaries' kit have been discovered, in the form of sandals and a large piece from a leather jerkin.

EH. All year, daily.

HERON MILL

At Beetham, off A6, 1 mile south of Milnthorpe (Da)

Just north of the Lancashire border the waters of the little River Bela tumble over a shelf of rock, which forms a natural weir. The power generated was used as long ago as 1220 to drive a corn mill, known as Heron Mill from the heronry which existed nearby until the 1720s. Its successor, built about 1750, was grinding corn until 1955. The simple foursquare building, containing four pairs of millstones, has been restored, and the mill machinery brought back into working condition. The 19th-century water wheel is 14ft in diameter.

Apr-Sept, daily, exc Mon, and Bank Hol. Adm charge. Shop. P *Toilets.* ♿ *(ground floor). Tel Carnforth (0524) 734858.*

HILL TOP

In Near Sawrey, 7 miles east of Coniston (Cb)

Lovers of the ever-fresh animal tales of Beatrix Potter who come to the little village of Near Sawrey step straight into the world of Peter Rabbit and Pigling Bland. For Beatrix Potter stayed here at intervals over almost 50 years, and brought the village and the country round into the delicate watercolour illustrations of her books.

Born in 1866, Beatrix Potter first came to Near Sawrey on holiday in 1896. In 1905, she bought Hill Top with the royalties from *The Tale of Peter Rabbit,* her first book. Hill Top is a typical sturdy Lakeland farmhouse, with slate roof and rough-hewn stone walls, remaining much as Beatrix Potter left it. The cottage garden bright with phlox, Michaelmas daisies and roses, the rhubarb patch where Jemima Puddleduck hid her eggs, and the clock that features in *The Tailor of Gloucester* are still there.

After her marriage in 1919 Beatrix Potter moved to Castle Cottage but still kept Hill Top as a private retreat. For the next 30 years she devoted herself to preserving the Lake District from development, buying as much property as she could afford. At her death in 1943 she left 4000 acres to the National Trust, along with Hill Top and her collection of china, furniture and drawings.

In 1987 the National Trust acquired the Hawkshead office of William Heelis, Beatrix Potter's solicitor husband. It is being converted into a gallery for her watercolours and drawings.

NT. Apr-Oct, Mon-Thur, Sat; also Sun pm. Shop. P *(limited). Toilets. Tel Hawkshead (096 66) 269.*

HOLKER HALL

On B5278, 1 mile north of Flookburgh (Ca)

Great banks of azaleas and rhododendrons make a colourful early-summer setting for this stately home on the north side of Morecambe Bay. The house is an unusual mixture of the 17th century, Georgian and Victorian styles, and was largely rebuilt after a disastrous fire in 1871. The 7th Duke of Devonshire then commissioned two local Lancaster architects to design a new west wing in the Elizabethan style, and it is this part of the house that is open to the public.

Holker is unusual among great houses for the fact that it has never been bought or sold. Since it was built about 1604, on land which once belonged to nearby Cartmel Abbey, it has been handed down by inheritance. Only three families have ever owned it – the Prestons, who built the original mansion, the Lowthers, who largely rebuilt it in the early 18th century, and the Cavendishes (the family of the Dukes of Devonshire), who inherited it in 1756.

Among Holker's exhibitions is the Lakeland Motor Museum, housed in the old stable block. The collection consists of over 80 vintage cars, motorcycles and bicycles, including a replica of Sir Malcolm Campbell's record-breaking *Bluebird.* A typical filling station of the 1920s still advertises petrol at a few pence a gallon.

Easter-Oct, daily, exc Sat. Adm charge. Refreshments. Shop. P *Toilets.* ♿ *Tel Flookburgh (044 853) 328.*

LAKESIDE AND HAVERTHWAITE RAILWAY

On A590, near Newby Bridge (Cb – Ca)

A glimpse of a buzzard soaring overhead, a roe deer stepping daintily among the trees, sometimes even a fox walking along one of the rails – these are among the sights that make this short length of line a constant delight to its passengers. The $3\frac{1}{2}$ mile railway, restored to life and once more powered by steam, runs from Lakeside, at the southern end of Windermere, to

HALL OF TREASURE *Majestic on the outside and richly ornate within, Holker Hall is noted for its splendid west wing, a treasure house of ornate plaster ceilings, sparkling chandeliers and parquet floors. But the highlight is its superb grand staircase (left), cantilevered from the wall with no visible support.*

the village of Haverthwaite, in the Leven Valley. It was originally part of a 7 mile branch line, built by the long-vanished Furness Railway to carry passengers and coal for the Windermere steamers, which were in operation by the 1850s.

The railway was closed in the 1960s, but the northern section was saved by a group of steam enthusiasts, who bought their first locomotive in 1967 and reopened the line in 1973. Rolling stock in operation consists of 21 locomotives, mainly small tank engines saved from the scrapyard, and 11 carriages, including the sumptuous royal saloon of the Princess of Wales (later Queen Alexandra), built in 1897. The 3½ mile journey takes 18 minutes, and trains connect with the Windermere cruise boats, thus reviving the Victorian tradition.

Good Fri to early Oct, daily. Fares. Refreshments. Shop. P *Toilets.* ♿ *Tel Newby Bridge (053 95) 31594.*

LEVENS HALL

On A6, 5 miles south of Kendal (Da)

For three centuries the patient gardeners at Levens Hall have been climbing on ladders and trestles to trim yew and box into cones, pyramids and a variety of fantastic shapes, carefully tending an open-air museum of green sculpture. The garden was laid out around 1700 by Guillaume Beaumont, a Frenchman who had been gardener to James II.

The grey stone Hall itself is far older, going back at least another 400 years, and has been considerably added to since then. Inside it has superb Elizabethan plasterwork and elaborate carved panelling. The fine Charles II furniture was acquired by Colonel James Grahme (or Graham), who employed Beaumont to lay out the garden, and is said to have accepted Levens – on a superb site by the River Kent – in settlement of a gambling debt.

Levens used to brew its own strong 'Morocco beer', drunk to the toast 'Luck to Levens whilst t' Kent flows'. Today the brewhouse has been made into a display area for a collection of working steam engines, illustrating the development of industrial steam power from 1820 to 1920.

Easter Sun-early Oct, Sun-Thur. Adm charge. Refreshments. Shop. P *Toilets.* ♿ *(gardens). Tel Sedgwick (053 95) 60321.*

GREEN SHAPES *The gardens at Levens Hall, with their fanciful topiary, have been maintained as they were when laid out around 1700. The hall dates from 1250.*

LOWTHER PARK

Off A6, 4 miles south of Penrith (Dc)

Picnickers in this spacious country park may be nuzzled by graceful Japanese sika deer in search of a bite of their sandwiches, or startled by the autumn roar of red deer stags challenging rivals for the hinds. Red deer have bred here for more than 700 years, since Edward I granted Sir Hugh de Louther permission to create a 200 acre deer park in 1283. The park is part of the vast 72,000 acre Lowther estate.

Nature trails lead through undulating parkland and mixed woodland containing a rich variety of wild flowers, birds and animals. For children Lowther has an adventure playground, indoor amusements, and a miniature railway.

Easter-mid Sept, daily. Adm charge. Refreshments. Shop. P *Toilets.* ♿ *Tel Hackthorpe (093 12) 523.*

MARYPORT MARITIME MUSEUM

By harbour in Maryport (Bc)

The sea chest belonging to Fletcher Christian, leader of the mutineers aboard HMS *Bounty*, who was born in nearby Cockermouth in 1764, is one of the prize exhibits of this museum. It also has a collection of birds and fishes carved from the wood of the *Bounty* by descendants of the mutineers living on Pitcairn Island, and a facsimile of the ship's log kept by Captain Bligh. Visitors may also look over three steam vessels, including the tug *Flying Buzzard*, restored to working order and moored in Elizabeth Dock. The engine of the tug is particularly impressive.

Museum: May-Sept, daily; Oct-Apr, daily exc Wed and Sun. Shop. P *Toilets.* ♿ *Tel Maryport (0900) 813738. Steamboat (0900) 815954.*

MUNCASTER CASTLE

On A595, ½ mile east of Ravenglass (Bb)

The pink granite battlements of Muncaster face inland towards Eskdale and Hardknott Pass, guarding one of the key routes to central Lakeland, while to the west they look out over the Ravenglass estuary to the sea. This strategic position made it a natural site for the peel tower that was built on the banks of the Esk in the 13th century, and which still survives embedded in the Victorian castle visible today.

The home of the Pennington family for 700 years, Muncaster is set in one of the finest rhododendron gardens in Europe. The shrubs, collected from many parts of the world, have been chosen to give a succession of bloom throughout the year, made possible by the mild winters of Cumbria's west coast.

Muncaster's greatest treasure is the so-called 'Luck of Muncaster' – a glass bowl given to Sir John Pennington by the defeated Henry VI after the Battle of Towton in 1461, as a reward for giving him shelter. Legend has it that as long as the bowl stays unbroken, the family's good fortune will endure. The unusual octagonal library contains 6000 books, and family portraits.

Good Fri-Sept, pm daily exc Mon; also Bank Hol Mon. Adm charge. Refreshments. Shop. P *Toilets.* ♿ *Tel Ravenglass (065 77) 614.*

MUSEUM OF LAKELAND LIFE AND INDUSTRY

In Kendal, near town centre (Db)

As the centuries-old gateway to the Lake District, Kendal is in an appropriate setting for the Museum of Lakeland Life and Industry. Housed in the stable block of Abbot Hall, beside the placid waters of the River Kent, the museum was set up to save the last relics of traditional Lake District life from the inroads of the modern world. It features the work of the blacksmith, wheelwright, brewer and printer, a spinning and weaving display centred on a cottage weaver's loom, and implements and historic photographs of the bygone farming scene. One room is devoted to Arthur Ransome, the author of the *Swallows and Amazons* books.

Abbot Hall itself is an elegant 18th-century mansion, designed probably by John Carr of York. It is now an art gallery, with paintings by Romney and Turner, and also contains a collection of 18th and 19th-century furniture.

On the other side of the town, in Station Road, Kendal's Museum of Archaeology and Natural History sets the region in a wider context. It tells the story of the people who have lived in Cumbria since the Stone Age, taking in the Romans and the medieval development of the wool trade, and explains the natural scene in a series of displays of birds, animals and insects.

Abbot Hall: All year, daily. Adm charge. Refreshments. Shop. P *Toilets.* ♿ *(parts). Tel Kendal (0539) 22464. Museum of Archaeology: All year, daily exc Sun. Tel (0539) 21374.*

ROOM WITH A LOOM *A local loom with flying shuttle is among the exhibits in the Museum of Lakeland Life and Industry. There are also displays of hand-worn craft tools and implements.*

RAVENGLASS AND ESKDALE RAILWAY

On A595, 15 miles south of Whitehaven (Bb)

For sheer scenic beauty, the 7 mile route followed by the Ravenglass and Eskdale Railway is unrivalled by any small railway in the country. From Ravenglass on its tidal estuary, with the man-made bulk of the Sellafield nuclear power complex looming to the north, the trains chug up the beautiful valley of the River Mite, past woods, farms and the remains of Cumbria's stone-quarrying industry, to Dalegarth in the heart of Eskdale.

Known familiarly as 'Ratty', this is England's oldest narrow-gauge railway, built in the 1870s to service Eskdale's short-lived iron-mining industry. From the 1920s to the 1950s it carried granite from the quarry at Beckfoot, in Eskdale, as well as passengers. The quarries closed in 1953 and the line was in danger of closing. It was bought by enthusiasts in 1960, and a new company was formed which now runs the railway, supported by a preservation society.

The railway now has six steam locomotives and several diesels, which have plenty of power in spite of their small size, and can haul ten coaches laden with 200 passengers up gradients of 1 in 36 – steep in railway terms. At Ravenglass Station there is a small railway museum which displays models, photographs and railway relics, and a former British Rail building has been turned into a pub called the Ratty Arms.

At Muncaster, a mile up the line from Ravenglass, the Ravenglass and Eskdale Railway owns a small water mill on the banks of the Mite, one of the three rivers that meet in the Ravenglass estuary. A mill was working here by 1470, and the present stone building dates from three centuries later. It has been restored to full working order, and sells a range of stone-ground flour.

Railway and Museum: All year, daily. Fare according to journey. Refreshments. Shop. P *Toilets.* ♿ *Tel Ravenglass (065 77) 226. Mill: Apr-Sept, daily exc Sat. Adm charge. Shop.* P *Tel (065 77) 232.*

ST BEES HEAD

Off B5345, 3 miles south of Whitehaven (Ac)

Gulls, kittiwakes, razorbills and fulmars shriek and jostle on the narrow ledges of St Bees Head, while puffins skim over the sea below. This bastion of red sandstone, towering more than 460ft above the shoreline, holds the largest seabird colony on the west coast of England. Rarest of the 5000 pairs of birds that breed here is a small colony of black guillemots. Large sections of the cliff are owned by the Royal Society for the Protection of Birds, which maintains a number of observation hides for visitors.

St Bees gets its name from St Bega, an Irish girl missionary who landed on the coast around AD 900 and settled there as a hermit. Some time after 1120 a small priory was founded on the site, but all that is left of it today is the church, built of the red St Bees sandstone. Its magnificent west doorway is a fine survival of Norman times, carved with a riot of zigzags, birds and animals.

RSPB. All year, daily.

STEAM POWER *Despite their small size, the vividly painted steam and diesel engines of the Ravenglass and Eskdale Railway can pull ten coaches fully laden with 200 passengers up gradients of 1 in 36.*

SELLAFIELD EXHIBITION CENTRE

Off A595, 6 miles south of Egremont (Bb)

The gently steaming cooling towers, the dome and the massive square blocks of the Sellafield complex loom over the golden sands of the west Cumbria coast. There are two parts to the complex – the Calder Hall nuclear power station, and the nuclear reprocessing plant, which recycles the spent fuel rods used in nuclear reactors. British Nuclear Fuels have set up an exhibition centre outside the perimeter fence. This explains the processes of nuclear power, including the reprocessing of the spent nuclear fuel, and the steps that are taken to ensure the safety of workers at the plant and the public outside.

All year, daily. Free entry. Refreshments. P *Toilets.* ♿ *Tel Seascale (0940) 27735.*

SIZERGH CASTLE

Off A591, 3½ miles south of Kendal (Db)

Sizergh began life as a peel tower, built about 1350 as a defence against the marauding Scots. Owned by the Strickland family from 1239 until they gave it to the National Trust in 1950, it still has very much the feel of a family home, being full of Strickland portraits and relics such as a giant two-handed sword made about 1340. In the later Middle Ages, a typical medieval hall house was added to the peel tower, and in Elizabethan times, two wings were built on, giving the castle its present U-shape. The grounds are notable for a superb rock garden, rose gardens and a newly restored Dutch garden.

NT. Apr-Oct, Sun, Mon, Wed, Thur pm. Adm charge. Refreshments. Shop. P *Toilets.* ♿ *(garden only). Tel Sedgwick (0448) 60070.*

STOTT PARK BOBBIN MILL

Off A590, 1 mile north of Newby Bridge (Cb)

The clattering cotton mills of Victorian Lancashire could not have functioned for a day without wooden reels and bobbins for their spinning and weaving machinery. These were provided by a host of small Lake District mills, which made use of cheap water power and coppiced wood grown on the spot. The Stott Park mill, which began operations in 1835 and did not close until 1971, has been restored as an industrial monument, with its lathes for turning the bobbins and flapping leather driving belts still in working order. Run by the bobbin-master, in its heyday it employed about 25 men and turned out 28,000 bobbins a day.

EH. Apr-Sept, daily. Adm charge. Shop. P *Toilets. Tel Sedgwick (0448) 31087.*

TALKIN TARN COUNTRY PARK

Off B6413, 1½ miles south of Brampton (Dd)

The name of this delightful and popular stretch of water a few miles south of Hadrian's Wall comes from the Celtic *tal can*, meaning 'white brow'. The 65 acre tarn, together with more than 100 acres of wood and farmland round it, has been a country park since 1962. It provides the only water playground in this part of Cumbria, with rowing, sailing, windsurfing, and fishing for pike, perch, eel and dace. Walkers on the waymarked nature trail can see a wide range of trees, from western hemlock to mountain ash, while red squirrels and roe deer may be spotted.

All year, daily

TOWNEND

Off A591, 3 miles north of Windermere (Cb)

For centuries, Lakeland farmers lived remote from the outside world, self-sufficient in almost every respect. Townend, on the outskirts of Troutbeck village, gives a unique insight into their lives over a stretch of 300 years. The sturdy, white-painted stone house, with a substantial slate roof, was built in the 1620s for the Browne family, prosperous yeoman farmers who lived there without interruption until the 1940s. The Brownes carved their own furniture, cured their own meat, and made their own rushlights. About the only items that came to Townend from outside were books, collected slowly over the years. The National Trust preserves the house as a time capsule of a vanished way of life.

NT. Apr-Oct, pm daily exc Mon and Sat; also Bank Hol Mon. Adm charge. P *(limited). Toilets. Tel Ambleside (0966) 32628.*

WHINLATTER VISITOR CENTRE

Off B5292, 5 miles west of Keswick (Bc)

Lying between the massive bulk of Grisedale Pike to the south and the Forestry Commission conifers of Thornthwaite Forest to the north, the Whinlatter Pass, 1043ft above sea level, is among the most dramatic of Lakeland's high-level passes. Just north of the road, the Forestry Commission's Visitor Centre provides an introduction to the surrounding countryside. With working models, displays and slide shows, it tells the story of the forest, from the geology that underlies the wild landscape to the different types of conifer and the animals that live among them. The Centre is the starting point for several waymarked walks.

Mar-early Nov, daily; Nov-mid Dec, Sat and Sun. Free entry. Refreshments. Shop. P *Toilets.* ♿ *Tel Braithwaite (059 682) 469.*

WINDERMERE STEAMBOAT MUSEUM

On A592, ¼ mile north of Bowness (Cb)

Moored in a lakeside floating dock, a dozen survivors of more than a century of lake travel gleam with polished woodwork, glittering brass and spotless white paint. All the boats have been restored to working order. Pride of the collection is the little steam launch *Dolly*, 41ft long. Built about 1850, she sank in Ullswater during the great frost of 1895, and lay mouldering at the bottom of the lake until 1962, when she was raised by divers of the Furness Sub-Aqua Club. The *Dolly* and the *Bertha*, built in 1844 and now in Exeter Maritime Museum, are the world's oldest propeller-driven mechanically powered steamboats.

Among the gems of the collection is the *Esperance*, built in 1869, which was the model for the houseboat in Arthur Ransome's children's classic *Swallows and Amazons*. Another well-loved children's author is recalled by the rowing boat in which Beatrix Potter used to row round the small tarn near where she lived, wearing clogs and munching cheese sandwiches.

When Prince Charles opened the museum in 1977, he took a trip aboard the *Branksome*, a luxurious steam launch built in 1896, which includes among its equipment a Victorian lavatory that still works, and a beer-pump handle in the galley.

The museum runs pleasure trips aboard the *Osprey*, a steam launch built in 1902. A number of operators run trips from Bowness aboard more modern pleasure cruisers, stopping at Windermere's lakeside villages.

End Mar-end Oct, daily. Adm charge. Refreshments. Shop. P *Toilets.* ♿ *Tel Windermere (096 62) 5565.*

WORDSWORTH HOUSE

At Cockermouth, in town centre (Bc)

The Georgian house facing the main street of Cockermouth, and with a garden running down to the sparkling waters of the Derwent, was the birthplace of Lakeland's greatest poet. William Wordsworth was born here in 1770, and in later life remembered it fondly as the place where he first felt the 'intimations of immortality' inspired by the beauty of the natural scene. In 1939 it was given to the National Trust as a permanent memorial to the poet, after being threatened with demolition to make way for a bus station. Nine rooms are furnished in 18th-century style, with some personal effects of the poet, and outside is Wordsworth's childhood garden, with a terraced walk.

Near the Market Place across the river is Cockermouth's Doll and Toy Museum, with exhibits ranging from dolls in ethnic costumes to model trains dating from prewar days.

Wordsworth House. NT. Apr-Oct, daily exc Thur. Refreshments. Shop. Toilets. Tel Cockermouth (0900) 824805. Doll and Toy Museum: Mar-Oct, daily. Tel (0900) 85259.

WYTHOP MILL

Off A66, 4 miles east of Cockermouth (Bc)

Tucked away in a coomb beside the fast-flowing Wythop Beck, Wythop Mill is typical of the sturdily built water mills that formerly ground the Lake District's corn supply. It seems likely that there was a mill here in pre-Norman times. There was certainly a mill on the site by 1300, as part of the extensive Wythop estate. However, the present stone building probably dates from the 18th century. About 1860 it was converted from grinding corn to sawing wood, and it was probably at this time that the overshot water wheel was installed. In the 1970s the mill buildings were developed into a museum of vintage woodworking machinery, complete with the hand tools used in past centuries.

End Mar-Oct, daily exc Mon; Winter, Sat and Sun. Adm charge. Refreshments. P *(limited). Toilets. Tel Bassenthwaite Lake (059 681) 394.*

GREAT LITTLE BOATS *Craft in the Windermere Steamboat Museum include the* Canfly *(centre front), built in 1922 with a speed of 30mph. On the right are the* Dolly *(front) and* Branksome *(back).*

COUNTY CALENDAR

Good Fri, Easter Tues and following Sat. Workington: Uppies and Downies (street football).
May (early). Ravenglass: Fair.
May (late). Coniston: Water Festival. Holker Hall: Carriage Driving and Country Show.
June (early). Appleby: Horse Fair.
June (late). Warcop: Rush-bearing.
July (1st Sat). Ambleside: Rush-bearing.
July (early). Lake Windermere Festival.
July (late). Carlisle: Cumberland Show.
July (last weekend). Flookburgh: Cumbria Steam Gathering.
August (mid-month). Grasmere: Sports.
August (late). Carlisle: Great Fair. Kendal: Gathering.
September (early). Kendal: Westmorland County Show.
September (Sat nearest Sept 18). Egremont: Crab Fair and World Gurning Championships.
Tourist information: Carlisle (0228) 25517; Kendal (0539) 25758; Keswick (076 87) 72645; Maryport (090 081) 3738; Windermere (096 62) 4561.

DERBYSHIRE

MANSIONS ON THE HILLS AND MAGICAL CAVERNS IN THE ROCKS BELOW

The rocky grandeur of the Peak District seems to dominate Derbyshire; but the county is softened by ravishing stretches of green, such as Dove Dale with its sparkling river. The harnessing of water power gave Derbyshire a leading role in the Industrial Revolution, and this is recalled today at Cromford Mill – where Richard Arkwright built his cotton town – and at Derby Industrial Museum. Trains and trams have their own shrines at the Midland Railway Centre and the National Tramway Museum.

Out in the countryside, natural wonders range from the heights of Black Rock and High Tor Grounds to the depths of fantastic caverns such as Blue John and Treak Cliff, where the beautiful, translucent mineral called Blue John is found. Above ground, stately homes such as Hardwick Hall and Melbourne Hall maintain their grandly aristocratic atmosphere.

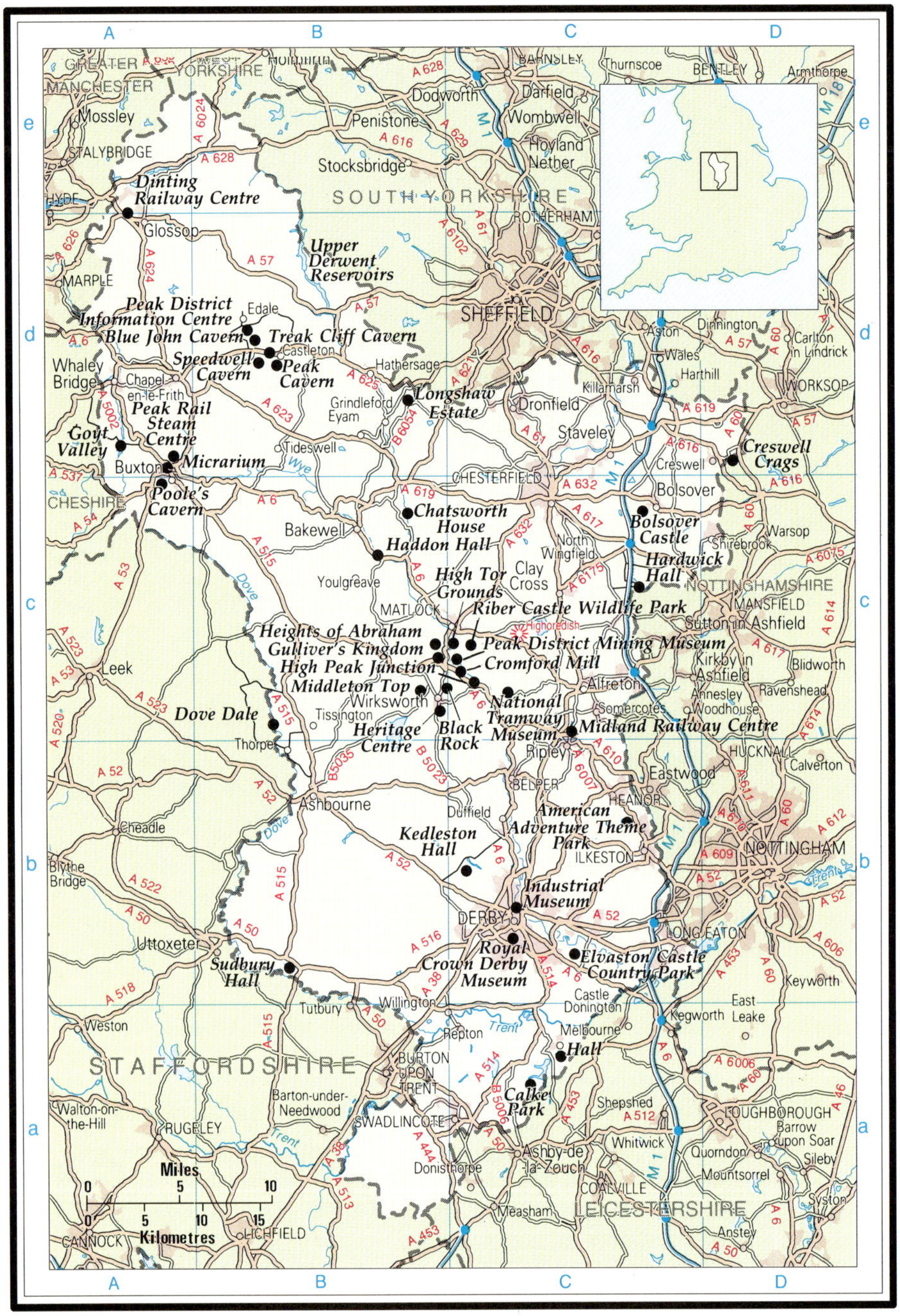

AMERICAN ADVENTURE THEME PARK

On A6007, 2 miles north-west of Ilkeston (Cb)

The days of the Wild West are re-created in this park established on a restored open cast coal site on the edge of the Derbyshire hills. Visitors may try their hand at cowboy arts, or watch rodeos held in the Alamo Arena. There are rides on Mississippi paddle-steamers, a runaway train and similar attractions, and Wild West Shows inspired by those of Buffalo Bill Cody and Chief Sitting Bull at the end of the last century. A trading post, Indian village and Silver City Cowboy Town stand beside a 32 acre lake.

This re-creation of the Wild West adjoins the very English scenery of Shipley Country Park, nearly 1000 acres of meadow, woods, lakes and open spaces with more than 18 miles of bridlepaths and footpaths.

Theme Park: Spring Bank Hol-Sept, daily; Oct, weekends. Adm charge. Refreshments. Shop. P *Toilets.* ♿ *Tel Langley Mill (0773) 769931. Country Park: All year, daily.*

BLACK ROCK

Off B5036, 3 miles south of Matlock (Cc)

From a distance, the visitor might mistake this dark, jagged rock for the romantic remains of some great Norman fortress set on top of a grassy wooded mound. The approach up the rock's steep, winding paths is rewarded by splendid views over Matlock and the Peaks, only a little marred by the fearsome scar of the Middleton quarries in the foreground. The picnic area is well furnished with rustic tables and benches. There are waymarked walks, and behind Black Rock passes the line of the old Cromford and High Peak Railway, now a 17½ mile High Peak trail.

All year, daily.

BLUE JOHN CAVERN

Off A625, 1 mile west of Castleton (Bd)

There are spectacular vases made of the translucent, multicoloured, semiprecious mineral called Blue John not only in nearby Chatsworth, but in Windsor Castle, the Vatican, the White House and in many galleries and museums round the world. Most were carved in the 18th and 19th centuries, but one Blue John vase was unearthed from buried Pompeii, and another from the debris of Imperial Rome. These were particularly interesting, since there is only one known source of the material in the world – the mineral veins in the limestone Treak Cliff, on the north side of Winnats Pass just outside Castleton.

Another remarkable feature of Treak Cliff is its systems of caverns, hollowed out of the limestone tens of thousands of years ago by torrents of meltwater from succeeding Ice Ages and broken into by 18th-century miners in search of Blue John or lead. The name 'Blue John' is thought to have been provided by French craftsmen who worked on a blue-yellow form of the mineral, and called it '*bleu jaune*'.

Large-scale, commercially viable deposits of Blue John are virtually exhausted, and in the last

50 years or so, some of the spectacular mine/cavern systems have been turned into tourist attractions. Deep in the enormous caves, it is possible to see how the limestone was laid down by ancient seas, the bucklings of the Earth's crust, the scars left by the titanic scouring of post Ice Age torrents, and the fretted patterns of stalagmites, stalactites and lacy curtains of limestone deposited by the slow drip and flow of calcium-bearing water over thousands of years.

All these features may be seen in the Blue John Cavern, which dives hundreds of yards into the hillside. There, eight out of the known 14 deposits of Blue John were mined. Beyond a display of 18th and 19th-century mining equipment lies the Crystallised Cavern, whose calcined roof, stained by various minerals, sparkles red, blue, green and purple.

Next comes the Waterfall Cavern, one of whose walls is a frozen waterfall of limestone deposit, infinitesimally added to each year, and past that a round chamber scoured out by a whirlpool long, long ago. The climax of the tour is the Variegated Cavern, so called from the differently coloured patches of minerals interspersed with creamy stalactite on the walls. A stream falls from the ceiling, an incredible 200ft overhead, bringing in air from the outside world. The floor is covered by huge boulders scattered by the raging torrents that created the caverns.

All year, daily. Adm charge. Refreshments. Shop. P *Toilets. Tel Hope Valley (0433) 20638.*

BOLSOVER CASTLE

On A632, near centre of Bolsover (Cc)

The building rising majestically from a hilltop and dominating the countryside is not strictly speaking a castle, but rather what remains of a mansion built by the Cavendish family in the 17th century. Bolsover was the conception of Sir Charles Cavendish, who bought the manor in 1613, and his designer, Robert Smythson. One of their delightful creations was the keep-like Little Castle, built as a folly, which retains its fairy-tale charm today, with its corner turrets, pinnacles and battlements. Both Sir Charles Cavendish and Smythson died when the work was in its early stages, but Sir Charles's son, Sir William, continued the work with Smythson's son John and grandson Huntingdon. Sir William, who became the 1st Duke of Newcastle, was an authority on horsemanship, and the riding school in the castle was designed for him by Huntingdon Smythson.

EH. All year, daily exc Sun am. Adm charge. Shop P *Toilets.* ♿ *(exc keep). Tel Chesterfield (0246) 823349.*

BUXTON MICRARIUM

The Crescent, Buxton (Ad)

Monsters of the microscopic world are startlingly revealed in this amazing museum. Banks of microscopes are focused onto tiny living creatures and plants and their images are projected onto large screens – magnified up to 150 times. Hundreds of objects normally invisible to our eyes are on view, including miniature fleas within whose bodies offspring can be seen developing or even being born; a brilliant green and perfectly spherical plant that perpetually rolls through water like a bizarre football; the astonishing beauty and symmetry of a simple snowflake.

Exhibits more orthodox in scale are on show at the Buxton Museum and Art Gallery in nearby Terrace Road. Displays covering the various aspects of the Peak District include a collection of Blue John ware, made from the locally mined translucent stone.

Micrarium: Apr-Oct, daily. Adm charge. Shop. P *Tel Buxton (0298) 78662. Museum: All year, daily exc Sun and Mon. Free entry. Shop.* P *Toilets.* ♿ *Tel (0298) 4658.*

CALKE PARK

On A514, 9 miles south of Derby (Ca)

This magnificently landscaped park covers 750 acres around Calke Abbey, a mansion built in 1701-3. The grounds were laid out about 1800, and a fine avenue of limes leads from the Ticknall entrance to an area of ancient oaks and bracken surrounding a series of attractive ponds. The house is being restored.

NT. All year, daily. Free entry. P *Toilets. Tel Melbourne (033 16) 3822.*

CRESWELL CRAGS VISITOR CENTRE

Off A616 and A60, 1 mile east of Creswell (Dd)

Bison, bears, hyaenas, reindeer, wolves, woolly rhinos and cave lions twice the size of modern lions once sheltered in the limestone caves of Creswell Crags, where their bones and the tools of the people who hunted them have been excavated.

Prehistoric men occupied the caves as early as 45000 BC, and by 13000 years ago makers of sophisticated stone tools and bone and antler implements such as needles had arrived. These so-called 'Creswellians' were artists, as is shown by a horse finely carved on a fragment of bone found in Robin Hood's Cave. The visitor centre's display which tells the story of these peoples, and of the early farmers who followed, makes a good prelude to the discovery trail around the caves.

Feb-Oct, daily exc Mon; Nov-Jan, Sun. Free entry. Shop. P *Toilets.* ♿ *Tel Worksop (0909) 720378.*

CROMFORD MILL

Off A6, 2½ miles south of Matlock (Cc)

Visitors can see the five-storey, water-driven cotton mill built in 1771 by Richard Arkwright to house his 'water frame' – a spinning machine which, unlike James Hargreaves' earlier spinning jenny, did not need highly skilled operators.

By 1776, the mill employed 650 people, mostly women and children, who worked 12 hour shifts around the clock. Local labour proved insufficient, so workers were brought in from outside and Arkwright created Cromford, the first town in Britain purpose-built to house factory workers. Rows of stone cottages soon went up and were followed by a hotel, a chapel, a lock-up and a market place. The new museum features a tour of the mill buildings and an audiovisual display about Arkwright and Cromford.

In 1790 Arkwright built himself a Gothic-style mansion called Willersley Castle nearby, though he died before he could move in. It is now a Methodist college, and not open to the public.

Nov-Easter, Wed, Thur, Fri, Sun, Summer, daily exc Mon, Tues. Adm charge. Refreshments (Thur-Sun). Shop. P *Toilets. Tel Wirksworth (062 982) 4297.*

DERBY INDUSTRIAL MUSEUM

In centre of Derby (Cb)

Derby was a pioneering centre of the Industrial Revolution, and this museum is appropriately

POWER SOURCE *Two streams of water meet in the basin by the sluice gate at Cromford Mill yard. The water powered the cotton mill in Richard Arkwright's industrial complex and flowed into the River Derwent.*

GRAND AND GRACIOUS CHATSWORTH

Though it conceals the remains of an Elizabethan house deep within it, present-day Chatsworth dates largely from 1687 and is the work of three Dukes of Devonshire – the 1st duke, champion of William of Orange, the Georgian 4th duke and the 6th duke, who died early in Victoria's reign. It is not the largest house in England, but it is certainly one of the grandest. It gives the impression more of a palace than of a stately home, and it is easy to imagine that the surroundings are not an estate but a Grand Duchy, ruled by an enlightened and intelligent dynasty.

The impression of grandeur is intensified as soon as the visitor passes through the Entrance Hall into the 64ft long Painted Hall. This is the grand overture to the State Rooms that lie, via the Great Stairs, two floors above. With its marble floor, gilded ironwork, writhing gold ormolu and exquisite 17th-century flower paintings, the Painted Hall is an effective introduction indeed. But it is the upper walls and ceiling that draw gasps of astonishment. Painted by Louis Laguerre in 1694, the walls depict scenes from the life of Julius Caesar, while the ceiling shows his reception among the gods in the next world. If the Painted Hall is an overture, then the State Rooms are like the scenarios of a Grand Opera – richly furnished and decorated throughout, with painted walls and ceilings, woodcarvings and wall hangings of superb tapestries and stamped leather.

After the wonders of the house there is still the garden to explore, much of it the work of Sir Joseph Paxton, architect of the Crystal Palace. Covering more than 100 acres, it includes a rose garden, secluded walks, the Emperor Fountain thrusting its jet 290ft into the air and the remarkable Cascade, a dramatic staircase of water flowing down a hillside.

Off B6012, 8 miles north of Matlock (Bc). Apr-Oct, daily. Adm charge. Refreshments. Shop. P *Toilets.* ♿ *(garden only). Tel Baslow (024 688) 2204.*

TUMBLING WATERS *The waters of the Cascade, built in 1696 by the Frenchman, Grillet, flow over 24 groups of steps. These are unequally spaced, so that the sound of falling water varies at each point.*

BOOKWORM'S PARADISE *Some 17,000 books line the walls of the Library, created in 1815. It includes the collection of Henry Cavendish, who in 1777 discovered the constituents of water.*

ROOMS WITH A VIEW *The 1000 acre grounds of Chatsworth were landscaped by Capability Brown. The design involved changing the course of the River Derwent so that it flowed in view of the house.*

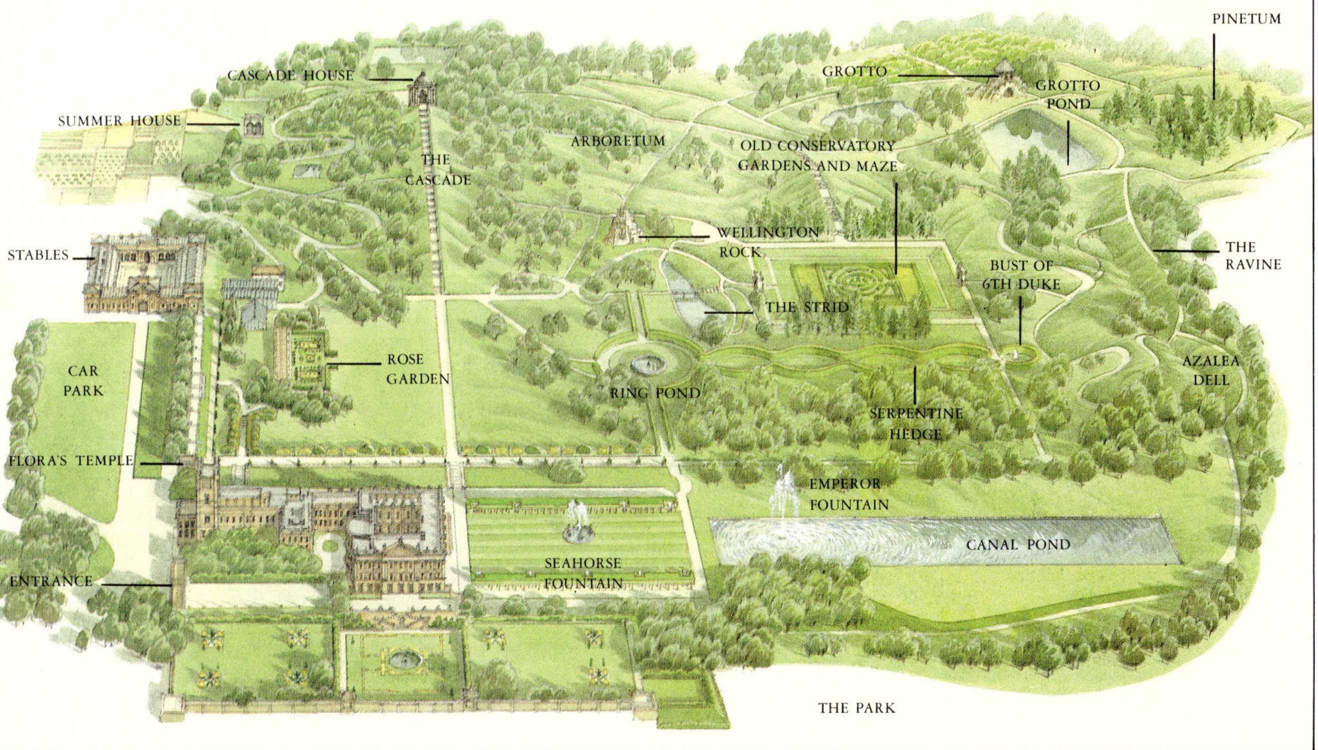

housed in Britain's first factory. This was the water-powered, silk-spinning mill that the local engineer George Sorocold built for Thomas Lombe in 1717-21. It was rebuilt after a fire in 1910. The ground floor is devoted to Rolls-Royce aero engines made in Derby since 1915, and has models and sectioned working engines.
All year, Tues-Sat. Free entry. Shop. P (limited). Toilets. ♿ Tel Derby (0332) 31111 ext 740.

DINTING RAILWAY CENTRE

Off A57, 1 mile west of Glossop (Ae)

Utter dereliction and a site overgrown with weeds faced the 70 enthusiasts who began work on this centre in August 1968. The site was the old Great Central Railway steam locomotive depot at Dinting, which had closed four years earlier. The engine shed was re-roofed and a small locomotive called *Jacob* was installed.

The centre has gone from strength to strength. Part of Dinting Station was acquired in 1970, and volunteers built the exhibition hall – 200ft long and 40ft wide – in the late 1970s. The pride of the collection is *Bahamas*, an LMS 4-6-0 Jubilee class express locomotive, for it was to save this old lady from the scrap heap that the Bahamas Locomotive Society was founded in 1966. It was this society which built and runs the centre where on steam days there are brake-van rides behind express locomotives or tank engines. There is also a miniature railway with 300yds of track.
All year, daily. Steam days Mar-Nov, Sun and certain weekdays. Adm charge. Refreshments. Shop. P Toilets. ♿ Tel Glossop (045 74) 5596.

DOVE DALE

Thorpe, off A515, 3 miles north-west of Ashbourne (Bc)

In the twilight, when the crowds have gone home, it may be that two gentle ghosts come to Dove Dale. They would be those of Izaak Walton, author of that 17th-century delight, *The Compleat Angler, or the Contemplative Man's Recreation,* and his friend, Charles Cotton. To neither of them could the world offer anything more glorious than the River Dove. They might be a little puzzled nowadays by the worn footpaths, but the rest they would recognise.

Today's visitor would be wise to come to Dove Dale in late spring or early autumn, so helping to spread out the human weight upon the valley; besides, it looks better then. Start near Thorpe, at St Mary's Bridge, where old Izaak has an hotel named after him. The River Dove marks the county boundary, and at the entry to the dale stand two tall sentries – Thorpe Cloud on the Derbyshire bank, and Bunster Hill in Staffordshire. Both are about 1000ft high and offer splendid views over the dale, but they are stiffish scrambles and most people follow the path along the valley floor. From the car park this goes along the Staffordshire shore to the Stepping Stones, which lead across into Derbyshire.

The path almost immediately begins to climb to Lover's Leap, leaving the Dove in its gorge far below. The height is named after a girl who, for unrequited love, threw herself into the abyss, but was thwarted by her clothes catching in the bushes. The opposite shore presents Dove Dale Castle, the Twelve Apostles, Jacob's Ladder and Church Rocks, while Derbyshire ripostes with Tissington Spires – all great limestone massifs named with imagination but tackled only by experienced rock climbers.

EYE OF THE VALLEY *Peering out of the ash and alder woods is Dove Hole, one of the many hillside caves of Dove Dale. The River Dove winds through the green valley, past banks thick with meadowsweet.*

The most impressive single feature, again on the Derbyshire shore, is Reynard's Cave, a shallow cavern 30ft high and 15ft wide, fronted by an even larger natural arch, caused by part of the cave roof falling in. Beyond is a crag called Lion's Head, which does look a little bit like a lion. Across the river is the great monolith of Ilam Rock, and after that, the dale begins to lose something of its drama.

After about 4 miles the path comes to the hamlet of Milldale. From here walkers can retrace their steps, or cross the river and make a longer half circle through the Staffordshire hills back to the car park.
All year, daily.

ELVASTON CASTLE COUNTRY PARK

Off A6 and A6005, 5 miles south-east of Derby (Cb)

The life of a close-knit rural community in 1910 has been re-created here in the old stable block of Elvaston Castle. Attendants wear the clothing of the period, and a wheelwright, a blacksmith, a saddler, a cobbler and other craftsmen demonstrate their work. The life of the womenfolk is re-created in cottage, wash house and dairy.

James Wyatt drew up the plans for the pale, stuccoed, neo-Gothic castle which was built in 1817 to replace an earlier mansion at Elvaston. The castle is not open, but its 200 acres of grounds, laid out around 1830, now form the Elvaston Castle Country Park. The formal gardens include a parterre and an Italian garden with stately yew topiary. An Old English Garden with rose and herb gardens has been created in the former walled kitchen garden.

Woods, of oak, birch, ash and ornamental conifer cover much of the park. In spring they are thick with rhododendrons, and there are daffodils on the castle lawns. A 1 mile nature trail leads through the woods, and past a lake.
Park: All year, daily. Museum: Apr-Oct, Wed-Sat pm, Sun and Bank Hol. Adm charges. Refreshments. Shop. P Toilets. ♿ Tel. Derby (0332) 71342.

GOYT VALLEY

Off A5002, 3 miles north-west of Buxton (Ad)

Little more than 110 years ago this peaceful valley had a different appearance. Steam trains laboured along the eastern side and there were coal mines, quarries, a mill, gunpowder plant, paint factory and 15 sheep farms. After the railway closed in 1877, a slow economic decline set in, and today only the sheep remain. A new use for the valley has been found in this century: Fernilee and Errwood Reservoirs now supply some 8 million gallons of water a day to the Stockport area.

Shining Tor, 1833ft, stands back from the Goyt's steep, wild slopes, and chattering streams fringed by bracken run down the rocky ravines. There are vast areas of grass, heather, bilberry and peaty moorland, which is the home of red grouse. Some ancient oak woodland survives, and conifers clothe the western slopes.

Information is given on boards at sites throughout the valley. There are six walks, including a woodland path which passes the stark ruins of Errwood Hall, built in 1830. The road from The Street to Derbyshire Bridge is closed to cars on Sundays and Bank Holidays from May to September.
All year, daily.

GULLIVER'S KINGDOM

On A6, 1½ miles south of Matlock (Bc)

A picnic at the OK Corral, a safari in the land of dinosaurs or a stroll down an Elizabethan street are three of the many activities possible in this world of fantasy. It takes its name from the 12ft figure of Gulliver which towers over a water garden with cascades, fountains and ponds.

In the Royal Cave, full-size replicas tell the story of man underground, from the times of cavemen and Roman miners. Gulliver's Kingdom also has a model railway, a puppet theatre, a roller-coaster and a children's fairground. There are vintage cars, canoes, jeeps, paddle boats, children's motorcycles and an 'astroliner' for rides.

Easter-Aug, daily; Sept, weekends; Dec, certain days. Adm charge. Refreshments. Shop. P *Toilets.* ♿ *Tel Matlock (0629) 580540.*

HADDON HALL

Off A6, 1½ miles south-east of Bakewell (Bc)

This romantic mansion, one of the best preserved medieval houses in Britain, is built of local gritstone around two courtyards, on a wooded slope overlooking the lovely Wye Valley. Haddon Hall is noted for airy, panelled rooms and for the medieval wall and ceiling paintings in its chapel and dining room. Exquisite tapestries, including a set of five made at Mortlake in the early 17th century, probably for Charles I, grace its rooms.

GALLERY OF LIGHT *Sunshine streams in from windows on three sides, emphasising the beauty of the oak panelling and the boldly carved ceiling of the 110ft Long Gallery at Haddon Hall, built around 1590.*

The building was begun in the 11th century by William Peverel, an illegitimate son of the Conqueror. The estate passed to the Vernons in 1170, and the hall was added to over the centuries. After 1703, however, Haddon was not lived in again until the 20th century, so it escaped the frenetic rebuilding that overtook many great houses in the intervening years. A faithful restoration took place between 1912 and 1939.

Apr-Oct, Tues-Sun and Bank Hol Mon; closed Sun in July and Aug, exc Bank Hol Sun. Adm charge. Refreshments. Shop. P *Toilets. Tel Bakewell (062 981) 2855.*

HARDWICK HALL

Off A617, 9½ miles south-east of Chesterfield (Cc)

This beautifully preserved Elizabethan mansion was the creation of a remarkable lady, Elizabeth, Countess of Shrewsbury, whose initials, 6ft high, shout from its tower parapets. She had a knack of marrying wealthy husbands, and after the death in 1590 of her fourth spouse, the 6th Earl of Shrewsbury, she returned to Hardwick Hall where she was born and began a new house about 100yds from the Old Hall. By this time 'Bess of Hardwick' was 70 years old, and 'proud, furious, selfish and unfeeling, a builder, a buyer and seller of estates'. Her furious energy inspired her architect, Robert Smythson, and his craftsmen to complete the house in seven years.

Its windows increase in size with height, and reflect the 'upside down' arrangement of the interior, with offices on the ground floor, family apartments on the first, and state rooms for grand entertaining on the second. Bess filled the splendidly decorated house with fine furniture and priceless tapestries and embroideries, and many of the items listed in her own inventory of 1601 survive.

The Old Hall fell into disrepair in the mid-18th century. Today both halls, with restored Elizabethan enclosed gardens, stand in a country park in which two rare breeds roam: Whiteface Woodland sheep and Longhorn cattle.

NT. Hall: Apr-Oct, Wed, Thur, Sat, Sun and Bank Hol pm. Garden: Apr-Oct, pm daily. Adm charge. Refreshments. Shop. P *Toilets. Tel Chesterfield (0246) 850430. Old Hall (EH) and Park: pm daily*

HEIGHTS OF ABRAHAM

Off A6, 1 mile south of Matlock (Bc)

The dramatic south side of Masson Hill overlooks the wooded gorge of the Derwent. It has been known as the Heights of Abraham since one of General Wolfe's officers likened it to the Quebec battlefield of 1759.

A fleet of 'bubble' cable cars climbs from a base beside Matlock Bath station slowly upwards, high above railway, road and river, to the Tree Tops Visitor Centre. The views are breathtaking, and a climb to the 1000ft top of Victoria Prospect Tower gives even finer vistas.

The limestone hill is riddled with fissures and caves in which minerals have been found, and lead ore was mined from prehistoric times until about 1810. Later, Great Masson Cavern, which has a Roman staircase, and the Great Rutland Cavern – Nestus Mine complex were opened to visitors. A multivision display in the new pavilion entrance to Great Masson Cavern shows the world in which the limestone was laid down 300 million years ago.

Cable car, caverns etc, Easter-Oct, daily; winter weekends, but closed Jan. Adm charge. Refreshments. Shop. Toilets. ♿ *Tel Matlock (0629) 2365.*

HIGH PEAK JUNCTION

On A6, 4 miles south of Matlock (Cc)

Here the 19th-century Cromford and High Peak Railway met the Cromford Canal and transferred its cargoes to barges for the $14\frac{1}{2}$ mile journey along the waterway to the Erewash Canal, gateway to the Midlands and the Mersey valley. In the late 1960s the railway was converted into a footpath, the High Peak Trail, by removing its rails, tidying it up and providing car parks, information centres and picnic sites along its $17\frac{1}{2}$ mile course through the glorious countryside.

At the Junction, a number of railway and canal buildings remain, variously restored and looked after by the County Council and the Cromford Canal Society. The most impressive of them are the single-span aqueduct built over the River Derwent in 1792, and the tall, rock-faced

HOUSE OF GLASS *The numerous huge windows of this mansion inspired the comment, 'Hardwick Hall, more glass than wall', when it was built in the late 16th century. It was the brainchild of the wealthy widow 'Bess of Hardwick' – Elizabeth, Countess of Shrewsbury (right), who built it as her 'retirement home'.*

Leawood Pumphouse, whose 1849 pumping engine still raises water from the river to the canal. The railway workshops, including the forge, have been restored and opened as an exhibition centre. The Canal Society provides trips along the waterway in horse-drawn narrowboats, one of which, the *John Gray*, appeared in a TV production of *Silas Marner*.

Upline, or uptrail, from the Junction is the 1320yd Sheep Pasture Incline. Wagons were hauled up and down the 1 in 8 gradient by cable, and the catch pit to catch runaway trucks on the incline can still be seen.

Junction workshops: Weekends; also midweek in school hol and Bank Hol weeks. Adm charge. P *Shop. Toilets. Steam train rides: Apr-Oct, Sun and Bank Hol; also Sat in July and Aug. Boat rides: Apr-Sept weekends, Aug daily. Pumphouse: Apr-Sept, Bank Hol and some Sun. Adm charges.* P *Tel Wirksworth (062 982) 2831 (workshops); 3727 (pumphouse and canal).*

HIGH TOR GROUNDS, MATLOCK

Off A6, 1 mile south of Matlock (Cc)

Below the majestic 380ft High Tor, 60 acres of grounds offer lovely walks and breathtaking views. They were landscaped in the 18th century by Richard Arkwright, the pioneer of mechanised textile manufacture.

Visitors entering by the Matlock Bath gate can walk up steps and woodland terraces to reach the entrance of caves from which lead was extracted in Roman times. The narrow gorges and fissures which tunnel through the limestone are deep in places but always open to the sky, making exploration easy. Another entrance to the grounds, from Dale Road, offers a more gradual ascent past the glorious Switzerland View.

All year, daily. Adm charge. Refreshments. Shop. Toilets. Tel Matlock (0629) 3289.

KEDLESTON HALL

Off A52, 4 miles north-west of Derby (Cb)

This was Robert Adam's first great work, and remains miraculously unaltered after more than 200 years. It is the third house on the site where the Curzon family have lived for 850 years; Adam was fresh from his Grand Tour of Europe when in 1759 he began work on the present house, a supreme example of the neoclassical style. Behind the north front, with grand portico and curving wings overlooking the lake, are the marble entrance hall, library, state rooms and elegant domed saloon.

The interior decor is Adam's too, as is some of the furniture. The house also contains old master paintings, and a collection of Indian silver, ivories, weapons and other items collected by Lord Curzon during his time as Viceroy of India, from 1898 to 1905.

NT. Apr-Sept, Sat, Sun and Mon pm. Adm charge. Refreshments. Shop. P *Toilets. Tel Derby (0332) 842191.*

LONGSHAW ESTATE

Off A625, 7½ miles south-west of Sheffield (Bd)

The unspoilt beauty of this country park makes it hard to realise that it lies less than 10 miles from the industrial cities of South Yorkshire. It consists of 1500 acres of open moorland, plantations and grazing land, and includes the lovely Padley Gorge, clothed with ancient oakwoods.

The estate lies near the edge of the gritstone Dark Peak, and there are several curious natural rock formations. One of these is the Rocking Stone, a huge boulder which balances breathtakingly on a group of rocks in Lawrence Field, not far from the stark remains of an ancient village. The gritstone was highly prized for building and for millstones, unfinished examples of which still lie scattered about.

A visitor centre contains displays tracing the history of Longshaw. There are also leaflets describing walks through the varied habitats. There are fine views from the heights above the River Derwent.

NT. All year, daily. Visitor centre: Apr-mid Dec, weekends; also Wed, Thur, Fri and Bank Hol mid July-mid Dec. Free entry. Refreshments. Shop. P *Toilets.* ♿ *Tel Hope Valley (0433) 31708.*

MELBOURNE HALL

Off A514, 8 miles south of Derby (Ca)

The formal gardens of Melbourne Hall are a 'mini-Versailles', for they were laid out by Henry Wise, an admirer of the work of André le Nôtre, Louis XIV's gardener. Stepped, velvet lawns sweep down from the east front of the hall to a lake called the Great Basin. They are crossed by treelined vistas which focus on fountain pools or statues. The grounds also include a rose garden, a walled fruit garden, woodland walks, a shell grotto, and an ancient avenue of sombre yews.

The greystone mansion took its present form in the early 18th century, when Sir Thomas Coke, vice-chamberlain to Queen Anne and George I, enlarged the original 16th-century house. The estate passed by marriage to the Lamb family. William Lamb, 2nd Viscount Melbourne, was Queen Victoria's first prime minister, and his sister's second husband was Lord Palmerston, another of Victoria's prime ministers. Relics of both premiers are preserved at Melbourne, which also has a collection of superb paintings.

June-Sept, Wed pm. Gardens: Apr-Sept, Wed, Sat, Sun, Bank Hol pm. Adm charge. Refreshments. Shop. P *(limited). Toilets.* ♿ *Tel Melbourne (033 16) 2502.*

MIDDLETON TOP ENGINE HOUSE

On B5035, 1 mile north-west of Wirksworth (Bc)

Opened in 1831, at the dawning of the Railway Age, the Cromford and High Peak Railway was built to link the Cromford Canal with the Peak Forest Canal at Whaley Bridge, picking up goods from various quarries and factories on the way. On its first surveying, this line too was intended to be that of a canal, but due to lack of water and the bumps in the terrain it became a railway instead, on which wagons were at first hauled by horses over the flat sections and up the steeper inclines by steam windlasses.

Of the nine engine houses along the way, only Middleton Top remains, with its tall brick smokestack, two cavernous boilers and great pulley wheels which haul the rope and wagons up the 708yd, 1 in $8\frac{3}{4}$ gradient of the Middleton Incline. Though scarcely warranting the use of

OPEN TO THE SKY *The delicate, wrought-iron pergola known as the Birdcage stands in the grounds of Melbourne Hall. It was built in the 18th century by the renowned ironsmith Robert Bakewell of Derby.*

alpenstocks by present-day walkers, it is nevertheless steep, a point that is given emphasis by a wagon poised on the summit above the now railless track. The magnificent, ponderous engine house lit by tall, Gothic windows was built in 1825 and continued to do its job until 1963. When the line was closed in 1967, the rails were removed and the track converted into the High Peak Trail. A visitor centre tells the story of the railway, and occasionally the engine is reawakened; though run now by compressed air, it still suggests the power it possessed when it hauled two filled wagons up the slope.

Visitor centre. Easter-Oct, daily; Nov-Easter, Sat and Sun. Free entry. Engine house: Apr-Oct, Sun and first Sat in month. Adm charge. Shop. P *Toilets.* ♿ *Tel Wirksworth (062 982) 3204.*

MIDLAND RAILWAY CENTRE

On B6179, 1 mile north of Ripley (Cc)

The sight, sound and smell of steam trains stir emotions among older folk, while providing a thrill for those too young to remember them as part of everyday life. As well as running a regular steam passenger service, the Midland Railway Centre displays a fine collection of locomotives, the oldest of which was built in 1866.

The centre is based on a restored station at Butterley, on a line built in 1875 to serve local coal mines. The line was closed in 1947 and the station building at Butterley demolished. When volunteers reopened the line they acquired a similar station at Whitwell in north Derbyshire, dismantled it and rebuilt it in Butterley.

Mar-Dec, Sat, Sun and Bank Hol; also Wed end Mar-mid July; daily Easter week, Spring Bank Hol weekend and mid July-early Sept. Adm charge. Refreshments. Shop. P *Toilets.* ♿ *Tel Ripley (0773) 47674*

NATIONAL TRAMWAY MUSEUM

At Crich, off B5035 6 miles south-east of Matlock (Cc)

Two-thirds of the way up a Derbyshire peak may seem an odd place to establish a tramway, but there are other oddities at Crich more startling still. The museum features an 18th-century façade that used to be that of Derby's Assembly Rooms. Beyond lies a street in some northern city – Leeds, say, or Liverpool – of a period vaguely before the First World War. In fact, it is a bit of both; the granite setts in the roadway came from Liverpool and the pavement from Leeds. Oldham supplied the gas lamps, and Glasgow the tramlines.

The period advertisements and more street furniture were obtained from other sources, and the shop fronts and the café from the fertile imaginations of the museum's administrators. Some of the fronts are attached to the workshops and offices of George Stephenson's narrow-gauge quarry railway that originally occupied the site.

The museum is a re-creation of the Tram Age, a backdrop to suit the 40-odd vehicles in the collection, which range from horse-drawn cars of the 1870s to streamlined trams of the 1950s. About a third of them are in working order, and prove it on the mile-long track; armed with an entrance ticket, the visitor can ride up and down all day. All the cars have been restored to their original liveries, and the crews wear the uniforms of the appropriate corporations.

Whatever their backgrounds, one thing all the trams show in common is the care and craftsmanship that went into their building. Though designed as a cheap form of urban transport, all bear some little touch of pride – engraved glass, carved panels, chandeliers or art deco lighting.

The ride to the end of the line is splendid. The tram leaves the cobbled street under a cast-iron bridge, then runs at the foot of the soaring cliff of a working quarry. There is a halfway halt beside a little café and a lead-mining museum before the tram plunges through a wood, then out along a ledge with views over the Derwent Valley.

Easter-Sept, daily exc certain Fri; Oct, weekends. Adm charge. P *Shops. Refreshments. Toilets.* ♿ *Tel Ambergate (077 385) 2565.*

WELL-TRAVELLED TRAM *Built in Preston, this open-balcony tram at the National Tramway Museum was shipped to Johannesburg in 1905 and has signs in Afrikaans. The tram stop came from Liverpool.*

DEVIL WATER *Deep in Peak Cavern, the River Styx – named after one of the rivers of Hades – flows under Five Arches, a series of perfect hoops worn by thousands of years of water erosion. Between the last two arches, the ceiling soars up some 100ft. The cavern system is more than 2 miles long – but for most of its length it is penetrable only by experienced potholers, who aqualung their way along flooded passages.*

PEAK CAVERN

Off A625 at Castleton (Bd)

The entrance to Peak Cavern, 102ft wide and 60ft high, was carved out, like the ravine in which it is set, by a river far bigger and immeasurably more ancient than the Peakshole Water which runs along its base today. Maintaining height and width, the first part of the cavern runs back for some 300ft, in a great chamber that was for centuries the abode of beggars and tinkers. Later, the entrance to the cavern was terraced into rope-walks by rope makers.

From the entrance, the visitor walks beneath stalactites and by electric light to a little chamber called the Bell House. Beyond, a low tunnel called Lumbago Walk leads to Little Styx, a pool inhabited by white, eyeless shrimps. From this point another tunnel leads to the Great Cave, 150ft wide, 90ft long and 60ft high. Off it is Roger Rains' House, loud with the pouring of a cascade that has made its way down from a spring in the floor of Cave Dale.

Then there is the Orchestra Chamber, where visitors were once entertained by Castleton village choir, Pluto's Dining Room and Devil's Staircase leading to the River Styx which eventually emerges into daylight as Peakshole Water.

Easter to second Sun in Sept, daily. Adm charge. Refreshments. Shop. P *Tel Hope Valley (0433) 20285.*

PEAK DISTRICT MINING MUSEUM

On A6, 1½ miles south of Matlock (Cc)

Mining began in Derbyshire before Roman times and Derbyshire miners still retain medieval privileges, such as the right to seek and mine lead anywhere except churchyards, gardens, orchards and public roads. Such rights are among the topics covered by the Peak District Mining Museum in the Pavilion at Matlock Bath.

The miners' lives were hard, and water seeping through the limestone rock posed a constant danger. A huge water-powered engine designed in 1819 by the Cornish engineer Richard Trevithick to drive water pumps stands in the museum. A complex of twisting tunnels through which visitors may crawl re-creates the cramped world of the miners.

Visitors can really go underground at the nearby Temple Mine. This mine was worked in the 1920s and 1950s to produce fluorite, a mineral used in the iron and steel industry.

Museum: mid Feb-mid Nov, daily; winter weekends. Adm charge. Shop. ♿ *(ground floor). Tel Matlock (0629) 3834. Mine: Apr-Oct, daily; most winter weekends. Adm charge.*

PEAK DISTRICT NATIONAL PARK INFORMATION CENTRE

Off A625, 5 miles north-west of Castleton (Bd)

Established on neutral ground in Edale, between the Dark Peak, composed of hard Millstone Grit, and the White Peak, made up of more amenable limestone, is the Peak District National Park Information Centre. Its displays are a 'must' for any visitor who wishes to understand the character, terrain and life of the area.

A number of exhibits are devoted to history, archaeology, geology and wildlife. Other exhibitions explain the story of the park and the work of the Mountain Rescue Team and the Ranger Service, both of which are based in the information centre. Edale is also the start of the Pennine Way, the toughest long-distance path in Britain, running for 250 gruelling miles to Kirk Yetholm over the Scottish border.

Information centre: All year, daily. Free entry. P *Toilets. Tel Hope Valley (0433) 70207.*

PEAK RAIL STEAM CENTRE

Station Road, Buxton (Ad)

Steam trains run again on 350 yds of track re-laid by enthusiastic volunteers in the abandoned Buxton station of the old LMS line. The aim is to reopen the scenic 20 mile line between Buxton and Matlock which joined the London (St Pancras) to Manchester line and closed in 1968.

A display of photos in the rebuilt engine shed tells the history of the Buxton site, and engines on view include *Harry*, a 1924 0-4-0 saddle tank, the last conventional steam engine regularly used in Britain; it retired only in 1984.

All year, daily. Rides: Easter weekend; May-Oct, Sun and Bank Hol weekends, also Sat in July and Aug. Adm charge. Refreshments. Shop. P *(limited). Toilets. Tel Buxton (0298) 79898.*

POOLE'S CAVERN

Off A53 and A515, 1 mile south of Buxton (Ac)

Derbyshire's River Wye has its source in Poole's Cavern, a spectacular limestone cave with festoons of icicle-like stalactites and armies of stalagmites. It is now illuminated to display the subtle colourings of its eerie formations.

The cavern lies in Buxton Country Park, 100 acres of woodland planted in 1820 to cover the ravages caused by quarrying and lime burning. The woods contain clearings where rare flowers grow, including frog orchids and celandine. A visitor centre has displays relating to Poole's Cavern and the park, Stone Age and Roman relics from the cave, and a video film about the cavern. A crenellated round tower known as Solomon's Temple crowns the 1440ft grassy summit of Grin Low, adjacent to the park. Inside, a spiral staircase leads to a platform with superb views over Buxton to the hills beyond.

Cavern and visitor centre: Easter-May and Oct, daily exc Wed; June-Sept, daily. Adm charge. Refreshments. Shop. P *Toilets.* ♿ *Tel Buxton (0298) 6978. Country Park: All year, daily.*

RIBER CASTLE WILDLIFE PARK

Off A615, 1 mile south-east of Matlock (Cc)

Ruined Riber Castle, with four tall corner towers, is a striking landmark high above Matlock. Its grounds are now a wildlife park specialising in the breeding of rare birds and animals. The lynx collection is most successful, and it was to Riber that the French government and the World Wildlife Fund turned when they sought to reintroduce lynxes to the Vosges mountains in 1983. An interpretive centre tells the story of the successful operation. There is also a motorcycle collection and a children's playground.

All year, daily. Adm charge. Refreshments. Shop. P *Toilets.* ♿ *Tel Matlock (0629) 2073.*

ROYAL CROWN DERBY MUSEUM

In Derby, 1 mile south of city centre (Cb)

Some of the finest works produced by the Royal Crown Derby Porcelain Company, in existence for more than 200 years, are on display in the company's museum. The factory was set up by William Duesbury in 1748 to produce china of unrivalled beauty. Royalty and rich landowners soon realised the quality of his wares, and George III granted him the right to mark them with a crown. Since 1890, by command of Queen Victoria, the factory's products have been stamped 'Royal Crown Derby'. Today's visitors can tour the factory and see every stage in the production of fine tableware.

All year, Mon-Fri. Adm charge. Refreshments. Shop. P *(limited). Toilets.* ♿ *(museum). Tel Derby (0332) 47051.*

SPEEDWELL CAVERN

Off A625, ½ mile west of Castleton (Bd)

A floodlit underground canal runs straight as an arrow for half a mile into the hillside. Guides take visitors along it in powered boats, which they help to propel by pushing the tunnel sides with their hands.

The canal, cut by lead miners soon after 1771, leads to the Bottomless Pit Cavern, where visitors disembark onto a railed platform 600ft below ground level. A murky lake lies some 70ft below, its bottom invisible although, despite its name, divers have found it to be only 30ft deep. The lake is fed by a thundering torrent of water from the 'far canal' beyond the cavern, which collects water from seepage and from swallow holes in the limestone hills above. Water leaves the lake only by seepage. The cavern roof curves out of sight above the platform, and rockets fired upwards have shown that it is more than 450ft high.

Speedwell Cavern is entered through the former mine-agent's house; this is now a shop selling Blue John jewellery and ornaments.

All year, daily. Adm charge. Refreshments. Shop. P *Toilets. Tel Hope Valley (0433) 20512.*

SUDBURY HALL

Off A50, 6 miles east of Uttoxeter (Bb)

Intricately carved stonework and walls patterned in pale and dark red brick decorate the exterior of this magnificent house built in the reign of Charles II. The mansion is E-shaped, with a roof surmounted by an elegant cupola, and the tall windows with their tracery give it a Jacobean air.

Sudbury and its idiosyncrasies were created in 20 years by one man – George Vernon, who in 1659 inherited the estate owned by his family since 1513. Vernon was almost certainly his own architect, and miraculously the exterior and state rooms remain as he left them.

The interior is a late 17th-century extravaganza of the decorative arts – perhaps a reaction after the austerity of Cromwellian times. Vernon employed the finest craftsmen, among them Grinling Gibbons and Edward Pierce, for carving and joinery. Perhaps their best work was the staircase and the saloon, which also has fine plasterwork and a series of Vernon portraits.

Sudbury's informal lake dates from the late 18th century, and the southern garden terraces were laid out in the 1830s. The former servants' wing now houses the Museum of Childhood.

NT. Apr-Oct, Wed-Sun and Bank Hol pm. Adm charge. Refreshments. Shop. P *Toilets.* ♿ *Tel Sudbury (028 378) 305.*

TREAK CLIFF CAVERN

Off A625, 1 mile west of Castleton (Bd)

Two of the old workings in Treak Cliff, from which miners extracted the translucent fluorspar known as Blue John, have been opened to the public; presumably to avoid confusion, one is called Blue John Cavern and the other Treak Cliff Cavern. Access to Treak Cliff Cavern is by way of a steepish climb up the hillside to a gift shop and café which offers splendid views down the Hope Valley. Behind the café is a 40ft tunnel chipped through the solid rock by 18th-century miners in search of lead. There was no lead, but their efforts were rewarded when the tunnel broke through to a vast cave system carved by post-Ice Age floods, revealing rich veins of Blue John.

The tour through the caverns begins in Fossil Cave, where the fossilised remains of sea creatures can be seen, then passes onto the eerie Witch's Cave; to Fairyland, with its grotto of delicate stalactites, and to Dream Cave, which has a forest of larger stalactites. Finally a flight of steps lit by electric lights which have gathered delicate growths of plants leads to a door that opens onto the hillside, high above the entrance.

All year, daily. Adm charge. Refreshments. Shop. P *Toilets. Tel Hope Valley (0433) 20571.*

UPPER DERWENT RESERVOIRS

Off A57, 10 miles west of Sheffield (Bd)

The natural-looking finger lakes that stretch for 7 miles along the Derwent Valley were created between 1912 and 1945 to provide water for cities to the east and south. The lowest and largest is the two-pronged Ladybower Reservoir. Its shores are dotted with picnic areas and car parks, and conifers clothe the slopes above its western bank. The villages of Derwent and Ashopton lie beneath its waters.

The upper valley, with the Derwent and Howden Reservoirs, is a wilder, remoter place. The away-from-it-all feeling is preserved even in the high season by the closing of the scenic valley road to cars beyond the Derwent Dam on Sundays and Bank Holidays from Easter to October, when there is a minibus service. Walks above the lakes include exhilarating climbs up Derwent Edge to the east.

All year, daily. Free entry. P *Tel Hope Valley (0433) 50953.*

WIRKSWORTH HERITAGE CENTRE

Off Market Place, in centre of Wirksworth (Bc)

This storehouse of local history in the foothills of the Peak District is housed in a former silk velvet mill. Many old buildings have been splendidly restored. The old blacksmith's shop now houses a display of locally made furniture.

Many old crafts and customs survive in Wirksworth, including the Ascension-tide well-dressing. A traditional butcher's shop remains in the Old Market Place where there was once a shambles – an arcade of such shops.

Apr-Oct, Tues-Sun and Bank Hol; Nov-Mar, daily exc Wed and Thur. Adm charge. Refreshments. Shop. Toilets. Tel Wirksworth (062 982) 5225.

COUNTY CALENDAR

Shrove Tues, Ash Wed Ashbourne: Shrovetide Football.

May 29 (if Sunday May 28) Castleton: Garland Day (commemorating Charles II's escape from Cromwell).

May (Ascension Day). Tissington: Well-dressing.

June (mid-month). Derby: Derbyshire County Show.

June (Sat nearest June 24). Tideswell and Youlgreave: Well-dressing.

July (Sun nearest July 12). Grindleford: Padley Pilgrimage (in remembrance of Roman Catholic martyrs).

July (late, to Aug) Buxton: Music and Arts Festival.

August (last Sun). Eyam: Plague Memorial Service.

Tourist information: Alfreton (0773) 833199; Ashbourne (0335) 43666; Bakewell (0235) 22711; Buxton (0298) 5106; Chesterfield (0246) 207777; Derby (0332) 290664; Glossop (045 74) 5920; Ilkeston (0602) 301104; Matlock Bath (0629) 55082.

DEVON

TALES OF THE SEADOGS, AND GREAT HOUSES BELOW TWO MOORS

A county whose 2000 square miles include two national parks and two quite different coastlines has much to offer the lover of scenic splendour. Devon's history is bound up with the sea: memories of Drake, Hawkins, Raleigh and Gilbert are strong in Plymouth and Dartmouth, while Buckland Abbey is a memorial to Drake.

Boats of all ages and nationalities float at Exeter Maritime Museum, while Exeter's glorious cathedral presides over a city whose attractions extend underground. Morwellham's Victorian prosperity as a port is re-created for today's visitors, and the days of the great fishing fleets are recalled at Brixham and Appledore.

Great houses have exhibitions of paintings and costumes; and gardens such as Bicton and Overbecks thrive in Devon's kindly climate.

A LA RONDE

Off A376, 2 miles north of Exmouth (Dc)

This fairy-tale cottage was designed in 1795 by two spinsters, Jane Parminter and her young cousin Mary, who aimed to combine the charm of a 'rustick' cottage with the Byzantine splendour of the Church of San Vitale, which they had visited in Ravenna. Eight doors lead from the octagonal hall. High above it a narrow staircase containing two 'Gothic grottoes' leads to a gallery with shell-and-feather panelling resembling the mosaics of San Vitale.

The cottage still has much of its original furniture, and contains almost every kind of Regency handicraft. The feather frieze and dado in the drawing room were patiently pieced together by the two spinsters. No less delightful are their sand-and-seaweed collages and delicate paper silhouettes, each cut out from a single sheet.

June-Sept, Sun-Thur; also Easter and May Bank Hol. Adm charge. Refreshments. Shop. P *Toilets.* ♿ *Tel Exmouth (0395) 265514.*

ARLINGTON COURT

On A39, 7 miles north-east of Barnstaple (Be)

Around this elegant Regency mansion, Shetland ponies and Jacob sheep graze in parklands, which were owned by the Chichester family for more than 500 years. Much of the furniture on the ground floor was specially made for the house when it was built in 1820, and in several rooms silk hangings or wallpaper have survived from the 19th century.

One of the delights of the house is the variety of objects collected by Rosalie Chichester – the last member of the family to live here. These range from prettily arranged seashells and enamelled boxes to model ships made by French sailors imprisoned on Dartmoor during the wars with Napoleon. The daughter of a keen yachtsman, she shared her love of the sea with her step-nephew, Francis; he frequently visited Arlington as a child, and a silver model of his yacht *Gipsy Moth IV* can be seen here. The stable block is now a carriage museum.

NT. End Mar-Oct, Sun-Fri and Bank Hol Sat. Adm charge. Refreshments. Shop. P *Toilets.* ♿ *(garden and grounds). Tel Shirwell (027 182) 296.*

AXMINSTER MUSEUM

Church Street, Axminster (Ec)

A little south Devon town has given its name to a style of carpet weave prized throughout the world. It was Thomas Whitty who, in 1755, began the production of fine hand-tufted carpets. The process was slow, and completion of each carpet was celebrated by a peal of bells from the parish church of St Mary. This factory closed in 1835, after which some of the looms were moved to Wilton, near Salisbury. In 1937 a new Axminster Carpet company was set up on the outskirts of the town and its factory is open to visitors daily in summer.

Displays in Axminster Museum tell the story of Axminster carpets, and of the Axminster area from the Stone Age to the present day.

May, Thur; June-Sept, Mon, Tues, Thur, Fri, also Sat am. Free entry. P *Toilets. Tel Axminster (0297) 3486.*

BECKY FALLS

On B3344, 4 miles north-west of Bovey Tracey (Cb)

Melting snows or heavy rain can turn the burbling Becka Brook into a torrent as it plunges down from the moors, northwards through a wooded valley to the River Bovey. A gentle half-hour nature trail passes through the Dell, where 6ft tall ferns follow the bluebells, and glow golden red in autumn. A more strenuous one hour walk takes a rocky route beside the falls, where the fern-fringed brook drops 70ft in a rocky ravine.

Apr-Oct, daily. Refreshments. Shop. P *Toilets. Tel Manaton (064 722) 259.*

BICKLEIGH CASTLE

Off A3072, 4 miles south of Tiverton (Dc)

Only the tiny chapel remains of the original Norman castle on a wooded slope facing the River Exe. But from later centuries there survive thatched cottages and a 17th-century farmhouse, surrounding a peaceful courtyard, and a massive gatehouse, which contains fine collections of armour and Tudor furniture.

In the barn across the courtyard there is a museum with an enchanting range of exhibits. These include dolls' houses and Victorian rocking horses, which children can ride, a display devoted to the Tudor warship *Mary Rose*, and a collection of gadgets used by spies during the Second World War.

Easter week, then Wed, Sun and Bank Hol to Spring Bank Hol, then to early Oct, daily exc Sat, pm only. Adm charge. Refreshments. Shop. P *Toilets.* ♿ *Tel Bickleigh (088 45) 363.*

BICKLEIGH MILL

Off A396, 4 miles south of Tiverton (Dc)

A restored and working water mill also houses a craft centre, where visitors can watch weaving, pottery and glass engraving and buy the finished products. The adjoining farm is run as a living example of 19th-century agricultural methods. Shire horses and oxen can be seen at work, and there are demonstrations of milking and butter making.

Easter-Christmas, daily; Christmas to Easter, Sat and Sun. Adm charge. Refreshments. Shop. P *Toilets.* ♿ *Tel (088 45) 419.*

MANOR GUARDIAN *In the 1300s the great gatehouse of Bickleigh Castle guarded the entrance to a moated, fortified manor house. Tudor windows were later fitted into the original arched openings.*

BICTON PARK

Off A376, 3 miles north of Budleigh Salterton (Dc)

Visitors to Bicton Park can shoot forward into the future, drift back into the past – or simply enjoy the park's 50 acres of woodland and gardens. A futuristic World of Tomorrow display features a mock-up space station and a simulated rocket ride for younger visitors. The pace slackens in The World of Yesterday, a countryside museum with implements and machines of the past, magic lantern shows and genuine old penny-in-the-slot machines in a Victorian setting.

The Italian garden with its formal lawn, colourful flowerbeds and beautiful fountain was laid out in 1735 to designs by the French gardener Andre le Notre, who created the gardens at the Palace of Versailles. Close by is an American garden, containing trees and shrubs imported during the 1830s. The Bicton Woodland Railway, the only 18in gauge railway in Britain, takes visitors to the more distant Hermitage garden, where an exotic summer-house stands among heather, small conifers and rockery plants.

Mid Apr-Sept, daily. Adm charge. Refreshments. Shop. P *Toilets.* ♿ *Tel Colaton Raleigh (0395) 68465.*

BRAUNTON BURROWS

Off B2321 or A361, 6 miles west of Barnstaple (Bd)

This area of sand dunes beside the Taw-Torridge Estuary is one of Britain's largest, and the 1500 acre national nature reserve has more than 400 species of flowering plants. The wind-blown shell sand is constantly on the move as it is eroded, then 'fixed' again by stout marram grass. In summer the dunes are heady with the scent of wild thyme, and bright with flowers such as pansy and sand toadflax. In the damp 'slacks' between, marsh marigolds are followed by marsh orchids and marsh helleborines. An ecology trail starts at the car park.

The Braunton and District Museum in Church Street focuses on local farming, seafaring and crafts. There is a display about the Saxon open field system, worked until recently in Braunton Great Field.

Reserve: NCC. All year, daily exc when army training in progress. Free entry. P (limited). Tel Braunton (0271) 812552. Museum: Easter, then mid May-Sept, Tues-Sat. Adm charge. Tel (0271) 816218.

BRITISH FISHERIES MUSEUM

The Quay, Brixham (Db)

The small museum in Brixham's Old Market House re-creates 500 years of the deep-sea fishing which was long the town's livelihood. Documents, paintings, prints and photographs show the hard lives of fishermen and their families through the ages. The details are fascinating: in 19th-century Scotland, for example, the women carried the men out to the boats on their shoulders so that they could start their working day with dry clothes.

There are models and pictures of fishing boats ranging from Brixham mumblebees to Scottish zulus and Manx nickeys – so called because boat-builders on the Isle of Man copied the design of visiting Cornish luggers and every boat they looked at seemed to be called 'Nicholas'. Another section traces changes in fishing methods, from traditional hooks, lines and sinkers to the sophisticated gadgetry of the latest fishing vessels fitted with satellite navigation systems and electronic fish-finding equipment.

Brixham Aquarium, on the Quay, displays a wide range of the creatures found in British waters, including octopuses, conger eels, rays, crayfish and lobsters.

Museum: Late May-early Oct, daily; Nov-Apr, Tues-Sat. Adm charge. ♿ Tel Brixham (080 45) 2861 Aquarium: Easter-Sept, daily. Adm charge. ♿ Tel (080 45) 2204.

BUCKFAST ABBEY

Off A38, 1 mile north of Buckfastleigh (Cb)

Almost incredibly, the whole of the present Benedictine abbey at Buckfast was built by six monks, only one of whom had worked as a mason before. The original abbey founded in 1018 beside the River Dart had sunk into decay after its Dissolution in 1539. The six began their work in January 1907 and laboured for 31 years, re-creating the lofty 12th-century Cistercian abbey.

The abbey church is noted for its fine stained glass and mosaic floors, all made at the abbey. The reredos behind the high altar, using silver figures on a copper-gilt background to depict Christ in Glory, is a replica of a 12th-century reredos in Koblenz, West Germany. There is an audiovisual show, and an exhibition about the abbey in the crypt. Today's monks pursue numerous activities including teaching, farming and making stained glass. Tonic wine and honey produced at the abbey are on sale.

All year, daily. Free entry. Refreshments. Shop. P Toilets. ♿ Tel Buckfastleigh (0364) 43723.

ALTAR MASTERPIECE *Restored to medieval splendour, Buckfast Abbey church has at its heart a High Altar of Belgian marble. The reredos above, which took four years to complete, shows Christ in Glory as the Holy Spirit descends on the apostles beneath.*

BUCKLAND ABBEY

Off A386, 11 miles north of Plymouth (Bb)

This peaceful Cistercian monastery founded in 1278 became the home of Sir Francis Drake for the last 15 years of his life, and still contains many relics of the great seaman. In a case in the Great Hall stands Drake's drum, which was with him when he died at sea in 1596. At the beating of this drum, Drake's sailors mustered on the decks of the *Revenge* in preparation for the battle with the Spanish Armada. Elsewhere are documents concerning the Armada, Drake's last will – written in a shaky hand the night before he died – and his silver-cased compass inscribed with precise bearings for landing points on the Spanish Main and the ports of Europe.

To mark the 400th anniversary of the defeat of the Spanish Armada in 1588, a new exhibition illustrates the building's monastic origins and its reconstruction in Tudor times.

NT. July-Oct, daily; Nov-Mar, Wed, Sat and Sun. Adm charge. Refreshments. Shop. P Toilets. ♿ Tel Yelverton (0822) 853607.

CASTLE DROGO

Off A30, 10 miles west of Exeter (Cc)

This masterpiece of melodramatic architecture, built on a windswept crag above the wild Teign gorge, was the joint creation of a self-made tycoon and a prominent architect. After making a fortune from the grocery business, Julius Charles Drewe commissioned Sir Edwin Lutyens to build him a mansion resembling a medieval fortress. In 1930, a year before his death, Drewe and his family were at last able to move in; his castle had taken 20 years to complete.

The main entrance is guarded by a heraldic beast known as 'Mr Drewe's Lion'. Inside, the impression of Gothic grandeur is sustained by vaulted or timbered ceilings, arched passages and massive walls of shimmering white granite, pierced by mullioned windows looking down on the gorge below. Terraced gardens surrounded by woods and parkland provide a fitting setting.

NT. Apr-Oct, daily. Adm charge. Refreshments. Shop. P Toilets. ♿ Tel Chagford (064 73) 3306.

COBBATON COMBAT VEHICLES MUSEUM

Off A361, 5 miles south-east of Barnstaple (Bd)

The formidable array of armoured vehicles on show at this military museum include two veteran tanks that saw service in the Second World War. They are the Centaur Mark IV, the first self-propelled armament to land on the beaches of Normandy on D-Day, and a monster Churchill Mk VII 'Crocodile' infantry tank weighing 44 tons. Among the other combat vehicles there are armoured trucks and personnel carriers of every kind.

Apr-Oct, daily. Adm charge. Shop. P Toilets. ♿ (most parts). Tel Chittlehamholt (076 94) 414.

COMPTON CASTLE

Off A3022, 4 miles west of Torquay (Cb)

With portcullis entrances and buttressed walls pierced by arrow-slits and chutes through which intruders could be pelted with stones, Compton Castle has retained much of its medieval character. It was built around 1329 and enlarged during the 15th and 16th centuries by the Gilbert family, whose home it still is. The family has produced a number of distinguished soldiers and seafarers – among them Sir Humphrey Gilbert, half-brother of Sir Walter Raleigh and colonist of Newfoundland in 1583.

The solar, or medieval living room, and 15th-century withdrawing room both have small windows through which the family could watch services in the chapel. In the kitchen a cavernous hearth has ancient bread ovens on either side.

NT. Apr-Oct, Mon, Wed, Thur. Adm charge. Refreshments. P *(limited). Toilets.* ♿ *Tel Kingskerswell (080 47) 2112.*

DARTINGTON CIDER PRESS CENTRE

On A384, 1½ miles north-west of Totnes (Cb)

Beneath a beautiful vaulted ash roof, a cluster of shops in a rural setting provides a showcase for a variety of British craftsmen. Shops sell handmade toys, rugs, clothes and glass, country food and plants and herbs. The old stone buildings that form part of the complex once housed a cider-making business, started in the 1920s, which continued until after the Second World War; the wooden cider press still stands in the courtyard.

The imposing entrance to Dartington Hall leads to a series of lovely gardens on different levels around the 14th-century hall (not open). Lawns give broad vistas, and there are great banks of flowering shrubs.

Cider Press Centre: All year, daily exc Sun; also Sun end July-early Sept. Free entry. Refreshments. Shop. P *Toilets.* ♿ *Tel Totnes (0803) 864171. Dartington Gardens: All year, daily. Adm charge. Refreshments. Shop.* P *Toilets.* ♿ *Tel (0803) 862367.*

DARTINGTON GLASS

School Lane, Great Torrington (Bd)

Molten glass, red-hot from the furnace, is transformed into fragile goblets, vases, jugs and many other kinds of lead crystal glassware, under the wondering gaze of visitors in the viewing galleries of Dartington Glass. It takes as many as 11 glassblowers to shape an intricate piece, but even the simplest tumbler requires the labours of a team of six under the supervision of a master blower. Visitors can see all stages of the process, then view and buy the finished glassware. The Glass Centre includes a video theatre, a re-creation of an 18th-century glass-making workshop and displays on the history of glass.

All year, Mon-Fri. Adm charge. Refreshments. Shop. P *Toilets. Tel Torrington (0805) 23797.*

DARTMOOR WILD LIFE PARK

Off A38, 11 miles north-east of Plymouth (Bb)

In the 'Close Encounters of the Animal Kind' that are organised here every afternoon, visitors are allowed to handle a selection of creatures including lambs, rabbits, calves and even snakes and raccoons. The 30 acre park lies amid lovely countryside, with fine views. There are enclosures for timber wolves, lions, Siberian tigers, pumas, monkeys and many other animals. Displays with hawks are given on most days.

All year, daily. Adm charge. Refreshments. Shop. P *Toilets.* ♿ *Tel Cornwood (075 537) 209.*

DARTMOUTH MUSEUM

The Butterwalk, Dartmouth (Ca)

Dartmouth's fortunes have echoed the great days of British maritime history. Crusaders, the explorers Sir Walter Raleigh and Sir Humphrey Gilbert, and the Pilgrim Fathers in the *Mayflower*, all used the harbour on the Dart estuary. This history is depicted in Dartmouth Museum which is housed in four adjoining houses built by wealthy merchants in the 17th century.

There is a fine collection of ship models, including Sir Francis Drake's *Golden Hind*, and many paintings, drawings and photographs of ships. The town stocks now stand in the lovely panelled room where the mayor entertained Charles II after the maiden voyage of his yacht *Cleveland* in 1671. A room is devoted to Thomas Newcomen, inventor of the atmospheric pressure steam engine, who was born in Dartmouth in 1663.

At Bayard's Cove a small, early 16th-century artillery fort stands above the cobbled cove. Dartmouth Castle, a much grander artillery base, was built in 1481 and enlarged in the 16th century to protect the entrance to the Dart estuary. It lies off the B3205, 1 mile south-east of the town.

Museum: All year, daily. Adm charge. Shop. P *Tel (080 43) 2923. Fort: EH. All year, daily. Castle: EH. All year, daily. Adm charge.* P *(limited). Toilets. Tel (080 43) 3588.*

DART VALLEY RAILWAY

Station on A38 near Buckfastleigh (Cb)

The gleaming engines and coaches of the Dart Valley Railway recall the excitement and bustle of the Great Western Railway in the heyday of steam. The line runs between Buckfastleigh and Totnes through beautiful countryside close to the River Dart. The banks and cuttings are dotted with wild flowers, and from the train it is sometimes possible to see buzzards and herons. At Buckfastleigh, engines and coaches can be seen in the railway yard or being repaired in the workshops.

At the adjoining Buckfast Butterfly Farm a 9000sq ft glasshouse encloses a tropical garden where exotic butterflies and moths live and breed in the freedom of their natural habitat. A colony of honey bees can be seen in a glass-sided hive, and there are also scorpions and tarantulas – safely behind glass.

Railway: June-Aug, daily; Apr, May, Sept and Oct, certain days. Fares. Refreshments. Shop. P *Toilets.* ♿ *Tel Buckfastleigh (0364) 42338. Butterfly Farm: Apr-Oct, daily. Adm charge.* P *Toilets.* ♿ *Tel (0364) 42916.*

DAWLISH WARREN

Off A379, 2 miles north-east of Dawlish (Db)

More than 1500 dark-bellied Brent geese can be seen – and heard – on the mud flats of the Dawlish Warren Local Nature Reserve in winter. They and countless other wildfowl and waders, including long-billed black-tailed godwits, can be seen from a hide overlooking the main high-tide roosting area.

Most of the 1½ mile long sandspit reaching into the Exe estuary is a nature reserve. Sandy shore and dunes, salt marsh, mud flats and freshwater marsh attract a great variety of wildlife. There are some 180 species of birds and 450 flowering plants, including the pretty lilac-blue warren crocus, which grows nowhere else in mainland Britain.

BATHROOM VIEW *The inventive hand of Sir Edwin Lutyens in the design of Castle Drogo is evident even in the bathroom. Steps lead to window seats on either side of the mullioned window.*

Dawlish Museum in Barton Terrace, Dawlish, has a collection of Victoriana from the town's heyday as a resort, with toys, dolls and costumes.
Reserve: All year, daily. Free entry. P *Tel Dawlish (0626) 863980. Museum: May-Sept, daily exc Sun am. Adm charge.* P *(limited). Toilets. Tel (0626) 862633.*

DONKEY SANCTUARY

Off A3052, 2 miles north-east of Sidmouth (Ec)

More than 3000 donkeys, from geriatrics to newborn foals, have found a refuge here since 1969, when Elisabeth Svendson began the enterprise. They usually arrive in a pitiable condition, after much suffering, and none is turned away. Here they find security for life, for they are never sold, though a few are loaned to suitable homes.

An information centre tells the story of the Sanctuary, which has quiet paddocks, warm winter quarters and a hospital with an operating theatre. Besides the Sanctuary staff, there are six full-time inspectors and 52 voluntary staff who check on markets and follow up reports of cruelty to donkeys.
All year, daily. Free entry. Shop. P *Toilets.* ♿ *Tel Sidmouth (039 55) 6391.*

EXETER CATHEDRAL

In centre of Exeter (Dc)

Cathedral Close is a green and cobbled atoll in Exeter's sea of traffic, surrounded by a pretty collection of buildings of many periods. Over all stand the twin Norman towers of the Cathedral of St Peter. Entrance is by the west front, carved with tier upon tier of worn stone angels, prelates, knights, kings and queens. The nave and choir are 300ft long and roofed by the longest single run of Gothic vaulting in the world, like a glade in a cream-and-gold stone forest. On the north side is the Minstrels' Gallery, fronted with coloured angels, each playing a different kind of medieval instrument, including bagpipes.

The nave is divided by a screen erected in 1325, which is topped by the huge organ case. Behind is the choir, in effect a church within a church, intended for the daily services of those who serve the cathedral. It has a lively range of misericords, one of which is perhaps the first representation of an elephant carved in England. The Bishop's Throne of 1312, its spire towering 60ft to the ceiling, was the gift of Bishop Stapledon, lynched by a London mob as a court official of the unpopular Edward II. The cathedral library's treasures include a book of Anglo-Saxon poems written in AD 950, the West Country section of the Domesday Book, and the cathedral's charter, awarded by Edward the Confessor in 1050.
All year, daily. Free entry. Shop. Toilets. ♿ *Tel Exeter (0392) 55573/74779.*

EXETER MARITIME MUSEUM

The Quay, south of centre of Exeter (Dc)

It is not too easy to distinguish where the museum begins and ends, in a canal basin which is crammed with all manner of craft. But once within the museum there lie ahead many happy hours of messing about in boats. And what a variety to mess about in. There is the kolek, for example, a slim, high-ended craft from Malaysia, two jukungs from Indonesia, a shewe from Bahrain, and a sardine boat from Portugal impossibly called a xavega. Here too is a clean-lined racing prahu from Brunei.

Some of the exhibits are presented afloat, like the *Sotero*, a sailing lighter from Lisbon whose decoration makes that of British canal boats seem almost dowdy. Tied up nearby is the world's oldest surviving working steamship, the Bridgwater dredger *Bertha*, designed by Isambard Kingdom Brunel in 1844, and still in working order. Most endearing exhibit in the floating show is the lofty funnelled steam tug *St Canute* which spent her working life as an ice-breaker, firefighter and harbour tug in Odense, Denmark.

Other exhibits are housed in the old canal warehouses. Among these is the Arab collection which includes coracle-like craft made of straw and pitch whose design has not changed since it was commented upon by Herodotus in 450 BC, boats made of date-palm fronds, and a swift, slim umla fishing boat of South Arabia.

Another part of the museum lies across the River Exe and is reached by a ferry worked by one man hauling on a cable. The early 19th-century quays and stone warehouses seem to yearn for the days of sail, a point appreciated by the makers of TV's *Onedin Line*, who set several early episodes there. In the warehouses and quayside cellars there are still more boats – fishing boats, coracles, an old lifeboat, a Venetian gondola dressed for a wedding. A section devoted to ocean rowing contains the transatlantic rowing boat *Puffin* from which David Johnstone and John Hoare disappeared in mid-Atlantic in 1966; it is hard to look into the tiny cabin without an eerie twinge.
All year, daily. Adm charge. P *Refreshments. Shop. Toilets. Tel Exeter (0392) 58075.*

EXETER UNDERGROUND PASSAGES

Princesshay, in centre of Exeter (Dc)

A raised flowerbed surrounded by a neat stone wall running down the middle of Exeter's busy modern shopping precinct of Princesshay marks the entrance to an extraordinary system of tunnels, stone-built or cut through the rock, that lies beneath the city. This was a system of conduits, built to bring water to Exeter from springs at the head of the Longbrook valley. The canons of Exeter Cathedral built the first passages to bring water to Cathedral Close. They were added to in 1420 by the City Fathers, who ran a tunnel beneath the High Street to take water to a public fountain.

Some of the tunnels have been lost, some collapsed in the Blitz, others are too dangerous to enter. But tours are offered in the section that runs beneath Princesshay and the surrounding streets, a fascinating and steamy-breathed journey through the ancient and modern roots of the city. This section of the system is a series of slits hacked through the solid red rock to about shoulder width and anything from 3-18ft in height. Silence closes in only a yard or so from the entrance, and for most of the half-hour tour the only sounds that can be heard are the crunching of gravel beneath your feet and the voice of the guide as he unravels the mysteries.

Here and there are fragments of mouldering timber, part of the timber lining that carried the water in the Middle Ages. High up at one point is the curve of a stone door, probably the remains of the Roman Eastgate, all traces of which on the surface were obliterated centuries ago. Just as evocative of the past are the blocked-up holes in the roofs of the tunnels through which

A FORGE REVIVED *Two tilt hammers and a pair of metal-cutting shears driven by water wheel are preserved in working order at the Finch Foundry Museum. The hammers were used to forge farming and mining tools.*

householders in the basements of long-vanished houses used to lower buckets for water.
All year, Tues-Sat, tours 2-4.30pm. Adm charge. Tel Exeter (0392) 265858.

EXMOOR BIRD GARDENS

Off B3226, 6 miles north-east of Barnstaple (Ce)

Wooded banks clothed in spring with wild violets and primroses shelter landscaped gardens in a valley of tumbling streams on the edge of Exmoor. Exotic birds, including parrots and cockatoos, brightly coloured pheasants and ornamental poultry selected for their fine plumage are housed in spacious aviaries among shrubs and trees. Owls and rheas have domains of their own, while the gardens echo with the cries of laughing thrushes and whistling ducks.

But birds are not the sole inhabitants. Shetland ponies, wallabies and guanacos (woolly coated llamas from the Andes) run free in grassy paddocks, and there is a pets' corner.
Apr-Oct, daily. Adm charge. Refreshments. Shop. P *Toilets.* ♿ *Tel Parracombe (059 83) 352.*

FARWAY COUNTRYSIDE PARK

Off B3174, 4 miles south of Honiton (Ec)

There are superb views over the Coly Valley from this park, which contains 189 acres of open hillside, woodland, pasture and scrub, with the traces of prehistoric burial mounds. Animals from a rare breeds farm, including shaggy West Highland Cattle, roam freely, and there is an animal sanctuary and a pets corner. The park has several waymarked nature trails, and there are donkey-cart and pony rides.
Easter-Sept, daily exc Sat. Adm charge. Refreshments. Shop. P *Toilets.* ♿ *Tel Farway (040 487) 367/224.*

FINCH FOUNDRY MUSEUM

Off A30, 4 miles east of Okehampton (Cc)

Harnessing the fast-flowing waters of the River Taw, 19th-century Sticklepath became a village of water wheels, with as many as six or seven wheels providing power for a variety of mills and rural industries. Among these was the foundry run by the Finch family, which from 1814 to 1960 produced agricultural hand tools and tools for the tin and copper mines and china clay industry of Devon and Cornwall.

In 1966 a trust was set up to preserve the foundry, and today its buildings and machinery, mill leat (watercourse) and launder (a wooden aqueduct used to wash out debris), have all been restored to working order. Three great water wheels drive the forges, cutting shears, grindstone and polishing wheel, and a pair of heavy tilt hammers can still be seen in motion.
All year, daily. Adm charge. Shop. P *Toilets. Tel Okehampton (0837) 840286.*

HARTLAND QUAY MUSEUM

Off B3248, 2 miles west of Hartland (Ad)

The beautiful coast around Hartland Point is one of Britain's most treacherous. At least 36 ships were wrecked on the 4 miles centred on Hartland Quay alone between 1800 and 1920. They included the French brigantine *Souvenance*, which a hurricane drove onto rocks below Upright Cliff in 1868 – watched by a host of helpless spectators on the shore. This small museum tells it all, and also has displays on the little port itself and its smuggling days, natural history, and the incredibly contorted rock layers hereabouts.

Six circular walks start from the museum, one of which covers a gentle 2 miles. The others, 1½ miles long, involve steeper climbs. The routes follow high cliffs past secluded coves, rocky coombs, waterfalls, and the Church of Stoke St Nectan, whose 128ft tower was a landmark for sailors.
Easter, then Spring Bank Hol-Sept, daily. Adm charge. Shop. P *Tel Morwenstow (028 883) 353.*

FROM TAGUS TO EXE *A number of Portuguese boats in the Exeter Maritime Museum include the sailing lighter* Sotero *from Lisbon, once used to tranship cargoes from ship to shore on the River Tagus.*

ILFRACOMBE MUSEUM

On Ilfracombe seafront (Be)

The six rooms of this versatile little museum house an amazing 20,000 exhibits – ranging from a turtle to a turret clock, from butterflies to a Breeches Bible of 1584. As well as local moths and butterflies, the museum's collection also includes tropical specimens of outstanding beauty.

The local history section recalls a frustrated invasion by the French on February 22, 1797. Four French men-of-war sailed up the Bristol Channel after scuttling several ships off the Devon coast. Since few men remained to defend the town, the women of Ilfracombe are said to have paraded on War Hill with their scarlet petticoats draped around their shoulders, so that from a distance they looked like an army of Redcoats. As a result, the French never attempted a landing there. The tattered remains of one of the petticoats, together with the drum banged by Betsy Gammon to rally the women of the town, are proudly displayed in the museum.
All year, daily (closed Sun, Oct-Easter). Adm charge. Shop. P *Toilets.* ♿ *Tel Ilfracombe (0271) 63541.*

KENT'S CAVERN

Wellswood, 1 mile east of Torquay centre (Db)

Some of the earliest man-made tools known in Britain have been found in the limestone caves that honeycomb the hillside overlooking Tor Bay. Stone Age hunters sheltered in these caves 250,000 years ago – and today's investigators have found their flint hand-axes and the bones of the cave bears, sabre-toothed tigers and other prehistoric animals they hunted. Guides take visitors through the maze of natural stone passageways that connect high-roofed halls and tiny grottoes. Floodlighting picks out the red, green and white stalactites and stalagmites to give a display of eerie magnificence.

Finds from Kent's Cavern are on show in the Torquay Museum in Babbacombe Road. Other items from prehistory include Celtic works of art, such as a fine stag in bronze, and artefacts from Australia, India, China, Japan and Egypt.
Kent's Cavern: All year, daily. Adm charge. Refreshments. P *Toilets. Tel Torquay (0803) 24059. Museum: All year, Mon-Fri; also Sat, Easter-Oct and Sun, mid June-mid Sept. Adm charge. Shop.* P *(limited). Toilets. Tel (0803) 23975.*

KILLERTON

Off B3185, 4 miles north-east of Exeter (Dc)

Set amid beautiful hillside gardens, with magnificent views of the Clyst and Culm valleys, Killerton House was built in 1778 and occupied by a single family, the Aclands, for more than 150 years. As well as fine furniture, silver and paintings, the house contains a costume collection started by the theatrical designer Paulise de Bush. This contains some 3000 items ranging from the 18th to the 20th century.

MORWELLHAM QUAY

In the Middle Ages, the River Tamar was the easiest means of transport through the hilly Devon countryside, and Morwellham became a port to serve the market town of Tavistock. Prosperity grew in the 18th century with the discovery of copper on the Duke of Bedford's land around Tavistock, then boomed in the 1840s when some of the richest deposits in Europe were found in Blanchdown Woods. Acres of new docks were built, and cottages and an inn were provided for the miners and quay workers, who during the next 60 years shipped 700,000 tons of copper ore out of Morwellham. By 1900, however, the seam was worked out, and the once busy quays were deserted.

During the last couple of decades the port has been resuscitated as a museum by the Dartington Hall Trust. To mirror the great days, the staff wear Victorian dress and assume the roles they might have had in the 1860s. Visitors can chat to the cooper, the blacksmith and the assayer, and call in at a miner's cottage. A tour of the village includes a visit to the restored quays and buildings, the Port and Mining Museums and the Victorian farmyard. Among the attractions is a train ride through the old George and Charlotte copper mine, an audiovisual display on the lives and labours of 18th and 19th-century miners, and a ride in a horse-drawn wagonette along the carriageway laid for the Duke of Bedford in 1833.

Off A390, 3 miles south-west of Tavistock (Bb). All year, daily. Adm charge. P *Refreshments. Shop. Toilets. Tel Tavistock (0822) 833808.*

DUAL ROLE *Though an important port, Morwellham never quite forgot its rural past; the Victorian farm, complete with old-fashioned animal breeds, has been lovingly restored. Nearby, the assayer (left), a senior mine technician working in his laboratory, analyses the copper content in the ore taken from the Devon Great Consols mines.*

ROLLING OUT *A present-day cooper demonstrates the craft of barrel-making. In old-time Morwellham, casks were made to contain arsenic, a by-product of copper-mining and widely used in the manufacture of paints and insecticides.*

The house is surrounded by 1000 acres of park and woodland. On Dolbury Hill there are stone quarries and the earth works of an Iron Age fort dating from around 400 BC.

NT. Apr-Oct, daily. Adm charge. Refreshments. Shop. 🅿 *Toilets.* ♿ *Tel Exeter (0392) 881345.*

KNIGHTSHAYES COURT

Off A396, 2 miles north of Tiverton (Dd)

A grandiose Victorian mansion, with a richly decorated interior and one of the most beautiful gardens in Devon, stands high above the Exe looking out over the river valley. Knightshayes Court was built for the Heathcoat-Amory family in the 1870s and has a flamboyant Gothic façade designed by the architect William Burges – eventually sacked for extravagance and delay. Inside, much of the original decor, removed or covered up as fashion altered, has been restored and there are two of Constable's rare flower paintings, a Turner seascape and a Rembrandt self-portrait.

A paved garden, with pale grey and silver foliage and soft pink blossoms, contrasts with the dark yew hedges planted in the 1880s. An alpine terrace leads down to the 'Garden in the Wood', where masses of flowers and shrubs grow beneath large forest trees and roses clamber up into the branches.

NT. Apr-Oct, pm daily exc Fri; open Good Fri. Adm charge. Refreshments. Shop. 🅿 *Toilets.* ♿ *Tel Tiverton (0884) 254665.*

LYDFORD GORGE

Off A386, 7 miles north of Tavistock (Bc)

The 200ft deep gorge carved by the River Lyd is a beautiful but eerie place – thickly wooded with oaks and sycamores, and with dense ground cover of ferns and low branches festooned with moss. Its caverns and vegetation once sheltered the notorious Gubbins gang between their pillaging, murdering forays into the surrounding countryside. Now the gorge is left to herons, dippers and woodpeckers.

The main entrance is by the bridge over the chasm at the west end of Lydford village. A 1½ mile walk follows the river through woods to the White Lady Waterfall. Paths lead from it up to the other gorge entrance and car park near Manor Farm. The path zigzags back along the river past the Devil's Cauldron, where there is a walkway over the churning water.

The remains of Lydford Castle top a rise between village and gorge. Lydford was once an important town controlling most of Dartmoor, then a prosperous tin-mining area. In its massive 12th-century square tower offenders against local laws were held prisoner.

Gorge: NT. Apr-Oct, daily; Nov-Mar, waterfall only, daily. Adm charge. Refreshments. Shop. 🅿 *Toilets. Tel Lydford (082 282) 320. Castle: EH. All year, daily.*

LYN AND EXMOOR MUSEUM

Market Street, Lynton (Ce)

In St Vincent's Cottage, one of the oldest houses in Lynton and once reputed to be haunted, local enthusiasts have collected relics, craftwork and implements illustrating the history of Exmoor. Exhibits range from powder horns to Elizabethan oak pitchers, and there is a typical Exmoor kitchen of 1800.

GREEN RAMPARTS *A lily pond occupies a former bowling green at Knightshayes Court, and clipped hedges surround it like castle battlements. Strong shapes are the keynote of the gardens, softened by shrubs and trees.*

A Victorian cliff railway offers a spectacular ride between the twin towns of Lynton on the cliff and Lynmouth on the shore, 500ft below. The two cars are operated by water ballast and run on a track cut through the wooded cliffside. In Lynmouth, the 18th-century quay and the pretty cottage, house and inns behind it survived the disastrous flood of 1952.

Museum: Apr-mid Oct, daily. Adm charge. Railway: mid Mar-Boxing Day, daily.

MUSEUM OF DARTMOOR LIFE

West Street, Okehampton (Bc)

Two restored 19th-century cottages, a mill of 1811 and an old printer's workshop set around a charming courtyard house this museum. Its displays tell the story of Dartmoor from its formation to the present day. Equipment from the area's industries – farming, mining, quarrying, peat cutting, china clay and glass – is on show, and a Cradle to Grave exhibition features the life of ordinary folk last century. An information centre, opal studio, craft shops and Victorian tearooms are also set around the courtyard.

The remains of Okehampton Castle lie 1 mile south-west. A nephew of the Conqueror began the castle in 1068, and the Courtenays, Earls of Devon, held it for several centuries until one of them fell foul of Henry VIII, who had the fortress dismantled soon after 1529. Parts of the Norman keep, and 14th-century hall, chapel lodgings and gatehouse, still stand tall amid fine grounds.

Museum: All year, Mon-Sat; also Sun in July and Aug. Adm charge. Refreshments. Shop. 🅿 *Toilets. Tel Okehampton (0837) 3020. Castle: EH. All year, daily exc Sun am. Shop.* 🅿 *(limited). Tel (0837) 2844.*

NATIONAL SHIRE HORSE CENTRE

Off A379, 8 miles east of Plymouth (Ba)

From stables dating back to 1772, some 30 Shire horses emerge for three parades a day in an arena that holds 5000 people. In the 1920s there were 2 million heavy work horses in Britain, but with increased mechanisation on the farms their numbers dwindled, until survivors were protected and allowed to breed in special centres such as this one. In the Old Stables is a display of shining horse brasses and show harnesses; these include a 15 stone Cornish decorated harness with more than 1500 brasses, plumes and bells. The centre also has a *(continued on page 92)*

FALLING WATERS *The White Lady Waterfall drops as a 100ft silver ribbon down the side of Lydford Gorge. Remains of potholes carved by Ice Age meltwaters pit the gorge sides.*

CITY OF THE SEAFARERS

To walk the narrow, cobbled streets of Plymouth's Barbican, to visit its ancient houses and to wander beside the quays of its historic Sutton Harbour is to tread in the wake of England's most intrepid seafarers. From here, in 1577, Drake sailed to circumnavigate the world, and 11 years later to defeat the Spanish Armada. In 1620 the Mayflower *carried the Pilgrim Fathers to the New World, and in 1768 James Cook left in search of a southern continent. On Plymouth Hoe stands the Royal Citadel built, it is said, on the site where Drake played his game of bowls, and nearby is Smeaton's Tower, the lighthouse that once marked the Eddystone Rocks.*

Smeaton's Tower *All year, daily. Adm charge.* P *Tel Plymouth (0752) 66800.*

Aquarium *All year, daily. Adm charge.* ♿ *Tel (0752) 21761.*

Prysten House *Apr-Oct, daily exc Sun. Adm charge. Tel (0752) 661414.*

Royal Citadel *All year, pm daily (tours). Free entry.* P *Tel (0752) 772312.*

Merchant's House and Elizabethan House *All year, daily. Adm charge. Tel (0752) 264878.*

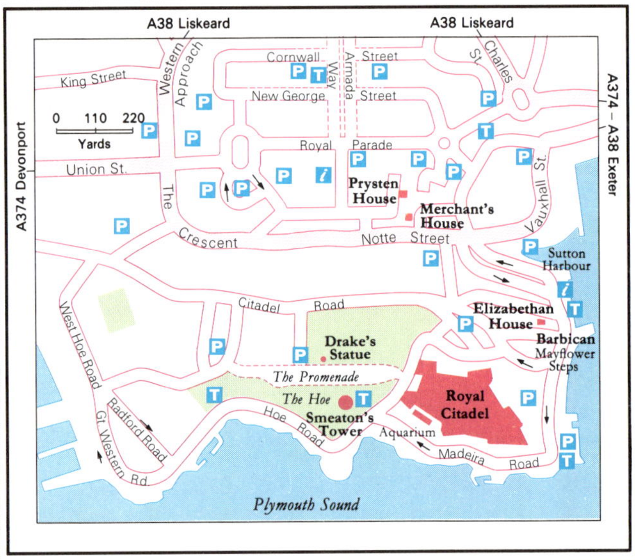

ROYAL CITADEL

The royal coat of arms above the gate (left) and the date 1670 signify that the Royal Citadel was built by Charles II. Its purpose, the king claimed, was to guard against a French invasion, but although some of the cannon (below) faced seawards, others pointed across the city – to subdue the citizens who had supported Parliament during the Civil War. Close by the Royal Citadel is the aquarium of the Marine Biological Society.

SMEATON'S TOWER

The view (above) from the top of Smeaton's Tower takes in a wide sweep of Plymouth Sound, with Drake's Island just offshore and the Cornish coast beyond. The tower (left) was the third lighthouse to be erected on the Eddystone Rocks, 14 miles out to sea, and was designed by John Smeaton in 1755. It set the pattern for all other lighthouses built after it, and stood on the reef from 1759 until 1882. When it was replaced by the light that still stands there today, the upper part of Smeaton's Tower was re-erected on Plymouth Hoe.

THE BARBICAN

The lights of shops, pubs and restaurants on the Barbican's quayside daub the still, purple waters of Sutton Harbour – departure point for many voyages of discovery, exploration and colonisation. Once these buildings were busy warehouses, and on the end wall of one of them is a gigantic mural (below) painted by a local artist in 1972. The figures in the painting depict Elizabethan culture from 1580 to 1620.

ELIZABETHAN HOUSE

The Elizabethan House in the Barbican was built about 1584, and its rooms, furnished in period style, show what life was like in Plymouth in the days of Drake. The staircase is built around a great pole that was once a ship's mast, and the house is filled with dark oak furniture, including a magnificently carved box bed.

PRYSTEN HOUSE

MERCHANT'S HOUSE

Raiding ships on the Spanish Main was a favourite Elizabethan pastime; the Plymouth privateer William Parker used some of his loot to modernise this Tudor residence, now called the Merchant's House. It is the largest and finest building of this period in Plymouth, and today serves as a museum of the city's social and economic history, arranged according to the themes of tinker, tailor, soldier, sailor, rich man, poor man, apothecary, thief.

DRAKE'S STATUE

In Prysten House, a tapestry (above) displays some of the plants and herbs the colonists took with them to the New World. The gravestone (right) commemorates two American naval officers killed in 1813 in a battle in Plymouth Sound.

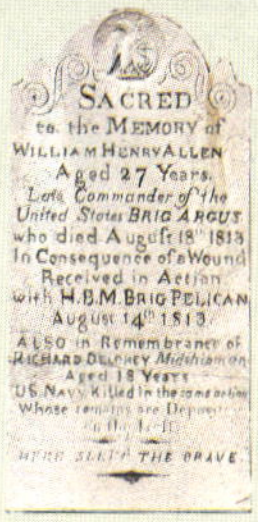

A bronze statue of Sir Francis Drake on Plymouth Hoe honours the explorer and sailor whose brilliant tactics played a major role in crushing the Spanish Armada in 1588.

(continued from page 89) blacksmith's forge; a crafts centre where a saddler, wheelwright, potter and glass engravers can be seen at work; and an aviary which contains exotic birds and Old English Game Fowl. Ploughs, wagons and antique farm machinery are on display, and a nature trail leads along the River Yealm, past a weir and salmon leap.

All year, daily. Adm charge. Refreshments. Shop. P *Toilets.* ♿ *Tel Plymouth (0752) 880268.*

NORTH DEVON MARITIME MUSEUM

Odun Road, Appledore (Bd)

Shipowners, merchants and master mariners once lived in Odun House – an old house with a view of sailing boats on the river and now the home of the North Devon Maritime Museum. On the ground floor, pictures, models and shipwrights' tools tell the story of local boatbuilding, and there are scenes of smuggling, Viking raids and Tudor adventures.

Upstairs, dioramas re-create Appledore's bustling quayside of 1900 and the drama of lifeboat rescue operations, while other displays show what life was like on barges, coasters and fishing boats in the days of sail. The kitchen has been restored to give an idea of household life at the turn of the century.

Easter-Sept, daily. Adm charge. Shop. P *Toilets.* ♿ *(ground floor). Tel Bideford (023 72) 74852.*

OVERBECKS MUSEUM AND GARDEN

Off A381, 1½ miles south-west of Salcombe (Ca)

On a sunny day, the lush subtropical vegetation and magnificent view of the sea give the garden of this Devon country house a Mediterranean appearance. Palm trees lead from the entrance gates to the garden, where plants seldom found in Britain flourish. In March the flamingo-pink blooms of a giant Himalayan magnolia are visible almost a mile away; and in June a tall echium shrub from Madeira puts out spires of lavender-blue blossom 8ft tall.

The house itself contains many collections, ranging from birds' eggs and butterflies to man-traps and handcuffs. Among the curiosities is an 'electrical rejuvenator' invented by Otto Overbeck, the last owner of the house, who was an avid collector. Under the stairs is a secret room filled with toys and dolls, together with dolls' houses, clothes and furniture.

NT. Apr-Oct, daily. Adm charge. Shop. P *(limited). Toilets. Tel Salcombe (054 884) 2893.*

PARKE RARE BREEDS FARM

On B3344, 1 mile west of Bovey Tracey (Cb)

Covering 240 acres on either side of the wooded valley of the River Bovey as it flows down from Dartmoor, the Parke estate offers a series of splendid walks through woodlands, by the river, and along the route of the former South Devon Railway. The Rare Breeds Farm was the home farm of Parke manor, which accounts for the massive grandeur of its barns and buildings and for the vastness of its stone-walled kitchen garden. The scream of peacocks and the glory of a great copper beech beside the house are quite appropriate to the general air of opulence.

Some of the animals and birds on display are descended from the first creatures domesticated by man. The horses, naturally, include Exmoor ponies, descendants of the old Celtic type that hauled the war chariots of the Iron Age. Some of the cattle breeds are just as ancient: the long-horns, with their forward-sweeping, inward-curving horns, look exactly like the cattle depicted in Stone Age cave paintings.

The early 19th-century Parke House is the headquarters of the Dartmoor National Park Authority, and not open to the public; but information about the National Park can be obtained from the joint National Park and National Trust interpretation centre housed in a barn.

Apr-Oct, daily. Adm charge. Refreshments. Shop. P *Toilets.* ♿ *Tel Bovey Tracey (0626) 833909.*

PECORAMA

Off B3174 at Beer (Ec)

From a *Golden Arrow* Pullman car – back in service as a restaurant – to model locomotives that hoot and whistle as they race round table-top tracks, engines and coaches of all sizes make this railway complex built around a disused Victorian station a playground for enthusiasts of all ages.

The surrounding pleasure gardens contain some 80,000 plants, and a miniature railway takes passengers for a half-mile ride through cuttings excavated from the hillside, with magnificent views across Lyme Bay. There is an aviary, a crazy golf course and a picnic area.

All year, Mon-Sat; also Sun, Spring Bank Hol-Oct. Adm charge. Refreshments. Shop. P *Toilets.* ♿ *Tel Seaton (0297) 21542.*

POWDERHAM CASTLE

Off A379, 8 miles south-east of Exeter (Dc)

From the terrace of Powderham Castle herons and wildfowl can be seen landing on the River Kenn or winging their way over a deer park towards the estuary of the River Exe. The castle dates from 1390 but was converted during the 18th century into a grandiose manor with towers and battlements. It has been the home of the Courtenays for nearly 600 years, and still retains the atmosphere of a family home.

Many of the rooms have elaborate rococo ceilings, magnificent marble fireplaces and fine Stuart and Regency furniture. From the China Room – the beautiful French china on the shelves was in everyday use until the 1930s – a sumptuous Staircase Hall with ornate panels set against a turquoise background leads to the Marble Hall, its walls hung with delicately worked Brussels tapestries. By contrast the Victorian chapel – in earlier times the grange or storehouse – has a quiet simplicity.

End May-mid Sept, Sun-Thur pm. Adm charge. Refreshments. Shop. P *Toilets.* ♿ *Tel Starcross (0626) 890243.*

ROSEMOOR GARDEN

On B3220, 1 mile south-east of Great Torrington (Bd)

This 8 acre garden was created by Lady Anne Palmer around her country house between 1959 and 1987. It includes species from all over the world, including alpines and dwarf conifers, many of which are on sale. Rosemoor also specialises in roses.

Lawns and shrubs surround a lake, and dwarf rhododendrons provide brilliant cover. There is an aboretum, and conifers and rhododendrons clothe the slopes. In 1987, the owner gave Rosemoor to the Royal Horticultural Society.

Apr-Oct, daily. Adm charge. Refreshments. Shop. P *Toilets.* ♿ *Tel Torrington (0805) 22256.*

ROUGEMONT HOUSE MUSEUM

Castle Street, in centre of Exeter (Dc)

John Patch, an Exeter surgeon who had attended the various Jacobite Pretenders to the British throne in France, built Rougemont House in the 1760s. Its wrought-iron balconies were added in 1810. As the Museum of Costume and Lace, its rooms have been redecorated and furnished in the style of different periods. The collection of lace has been gathered together from all over the world. One room is devoted entirely to lace from Honiton, famed for its light, delicate lace since it was introduced to the town by the Huguenots in the 16th century.

All year, daily. Adm charge (free on Fri). Refreshments. Shop. Toilets. Tel Exeter (0392) 265858.

ROYAL ALBERT MEMORIAL MUSEUM

Queen Street, in centre of Exeter (Dc)

Behind the museum's Victorian exterior, a lively, modern series of exhibitions paints a portrait of Devon in a succession of highlights. The displays begin with the story of the excavations at Kent's Cavern near Torquay in the 1850s. The discovery that humans had lived in the caves when woolly rhinos, mammoths and cave bears were stalking the Earth threw traditional thinking about the date of Man's origins into disarray.

An exhibition on the Roman occupation of what is now Exeter tells how the Second Legion raised the first buildings on the site.

Devon's preoccupation with the New World is reflected in displays of the arts, crafts, weapons and skills of the native peoples of the Americas, while crafts of the stay-at-homes are represented in a gallery of mostly West Country silver, ceramics and glass. Finally there are the picture galleries, devoted to the works of painters who lived or worked in the West Country – a distinguished gathering that includes Turner, Joshua Reynolds, Nash, Sickert and Stanley Spencer.

All year, daily. Free entry. Shop. Toilets. Tel Exeter (0392) 265858.

SALTRAM

Off A38, 3½ miles east of Plymouth (Ba)

Visitors to Saltram step back in time to the heyday of the English country house. For the house and its contents have changed little since Fanny Burney, the diarist and author, wrote in 1789: 'The house is one of the most magnificent in the kingdom; its view is noble.' Saltram has two particularly splendid rooms, the saloon and the dining room, designed by Robert Adam, and many portraits by Sir Joshua Reynolds, who was born at nearby Plympton St Maurice.

The Great Kitchen contains relics of downstairs life two centuries ago. An array of 600 copper utensils includes moulds for making blancmanges, jellies and ices, while the unusual food trolley was at one time heated by gas supplied by a private gas works in the woods. Outside, an avenue of limes leads to an octagonal 'castle' built in 1772.

NT. House: Apr-Oct, Sun-Thur, Good Fri and Bank Hol Sat pm. Garden: daily all year. Refreshments. Shop. P *Toilets.* ♿ *Tel Plymouth (0752) 336546.*

TIVERTON MUSEUM

In centre of Tiverton (Dd)

Exhibits ranging from a 200-year-old smithy to model soldiers representing Devon regiments give the visitor to Tiverton Museum a broad picture of West Country history. Displays devoted to local industries include the first lacemaking machine. Across the courtyard there is a railway gallery where would-be engine drivers can mount the footplate of the *Tivvy Bumper*.

The earlier, turbulent history of Tiverton and the surrounding area is recalled by the thick-walled towers and great stone gatehouse of Tiverton Castle, on the outskirts of the town. Henry I ordered Tiverton and other castles to be built after dreaming that the Lords, Church and Commons would rise against him. Each of these groups is visible in a depiction of his dream painted near the castle entrance.

Museum: All year exc Jan, Mon-Sat. Free entry. Shop. P *Toilets.* ♿ *(ground floor). Tel Tiverton (0884) 256295. Castle: Easter-Sept, Sun-Thur pm. Adm charge. Shop.* P *(limited). Toilets. Tel (0884) 253200.*

TORBAY AIRCRAFT MUSEUM

Off A385, 3 miles west of Paignton (Cb)

In this enterprising museum, which is built on a hillside with fine views of Torbay and Dartmoor, full-size replicas of Second World War fighters that starred in films such as *The Battle of Britain* stand alongside jet warplanes that saw active service. Besides some 18 historic aircraft, there are indoor exhibitions telling the story of the men who flew them. They include the 'Dambusters' and the 'Red Baron', Manfred von Richthofen, who shot down more than 80 aircraft.

The museum also has a large '00' gauge model railway, with rolling stock ranging from Victorian steam trains to the electric and diesel locomotives of the 1980s. Next to the helipad are flower gardens dedicated to the film actor Kenneth More, who spent many hours here during the making of a television film about the development of helicopters.

Apr-Oct, daily. Adm charge. Refreshments. Shop. P *Toilets.* ♿ *Tel Paignton (0803) 553540.*

TORRE ABBEY

The King's Drive, Torquay (Db)

Behind the stuccoed façade of the classical Georgian mansion lie the remains of a medieval abbey, once the wealthiest of the 40 monasteries belonging to the Premonstratensian Order, called the White Canons from the colour of their habit. Today the house contains fine collections of terracotta and oriental snuff bottles, as well as glass, silver, sculpture, drawings and paintings – among them William Blake's engravings illustrating the Book of Job. In the clock tower is an exhibition concerning the writer Agatha Christie, who lived in Torquay.

Much of the abbey now lies in ruins, but a massive gatehouse has survived almost intact. So has the old tithe barn in which Spanish sailors were imprisoned after the defeat of the Armada.

Apr-Oct, daily. Adm charge. Refreshments (May-mid Sept). P *Toilets. Tel Paignton (0803) 23593.*

TOTNES CASTLE

Near centre of Totnes (Cb)

The hollow keep of this Norman stronghold overlooking the River Dart dates from the 13th century, but was much rebuilt over the next 200 years. The parapet includes two arched stairways built within the 6ft thick walls to enable archers to reach the circular wall-walk.

Two museums in Totnes offer contrasting glimpses of the past. The Elizabethan Museum in Fore Street is a 16th-century merchant's house with period furniture and costume and a Victorian grocer's shop. Totnes Motor Museum, on Steamer Quay, houses vintage, sports and racing cars.

Castle: EH. All year, daily exc Tues, and Wed am. Adm charge. Tel Totnes (0803) 864406. Elizabethan Museum: Apr-Oct, Mon-Fri and Bank Hol. Adm charge. Tel (0803) 863821. Motor Museum: Easter-Oct, daily. Adm charge. Shop. P *(limited).* ♿ *Tel (0803) 862777.*

WATERMOUTH CASTLE

On A399, 2 miles east of Ilfracombe (Be)

Although adorned with battlements and turrets, Watermouth is in reality a grand 19th-century manor house completed in 1825, though the labyrinth of tunnels beneath it is much older.

Most of the castle is today the setting for a remarkable range of displays. There are Victorian and Edwardian handcarts, mechanical musical instruments, old kitchen, dairy and cider-making equipment and even a collection of early vacuum cleaners.

Spring Bank Hol-Sept, daily; also Sun-Thur pm from Easter to Spring Bank Hol, and in Sept and Oct. Adm charge. Refreshments. Shop. P *Toilets.* ♿ *Tel Ilfracombe (0271) 63879.*

WHEEL CRAFT WORKSHOPS

In Chudleigh, off A38, 8 miles south-west of Exeter (Cb)

The old mill at Chudleigh once ground grain into flour. Today, the outbuildings around the courtyard have been converted into workshops where visitors can see craftsmen and craftswomen at work. Their output includes stained glass, pottery, furniture, jewellery, shoes and clothes, all of which are sold at the mill. The iron-framed water wheel, 20ft in diameter, and the machinery are all in working order.

All year, daily. Free entry. Refreshments. Shop. Toilets. Tel Chudleigh (0626) 852698

SETTING FOR SONG *Powderham Castle's richly decorated Music Room was designed by James Wyatt in 1794. Its walls are divided by Corinthian pilasters and in the alcoves are alabaster vases on marble stands.*

COUNTY CALENDAR

May (mid-month). Exeter: Devon County Show.

May (late, to early June). Exeter: Festival.

June (mid-month). Dartmouth: Britannia Royal Naval College Open Day.

July (1st Tues after 19th). Honiton: Fair.

August (early). Exeter: Air Show.

August (Bank Hol). Plymouth: Navy Days.

September (early). Plymouth: Powerboat Race.

September (2nd Tues). Widecombe in the Moor: Fair.

September (mid-month). Barnstaple: St Giles's Fair.

October (2nd Wed). Tavistock: Goose Fair.

October (last week). Bampton: Pony Fair.

Tourist information: Barnstaple (0271) 72742; Brixham (080 45) 2861; Dawlish (0626) 863589; Exeter (0392) 72434; Ilfracombe (0271) 63001; Lynton (0598) 52225; Paignton (0803) 55833; Plymouth (0752) 264849; Teignmouth (062 67) 6271; Torquay (0803) 27428.

DORSET

ANCIENT HILL-FORTS ABOVE A LAND OF GREAT GARDENS AND ABBEYS

Dinosaurs, the hill-fort of Iron Age warriors and a re-creation of Tutankhamun's tomb are among the unexpected discoveries to be made around Dorchester, the county town at the heart of Thomas Hardy's Wessex. Farther afield are more surprises: subtropical gardens at Abbotsbury and Compton Acres, thriving in the gentle coastal climate; the stately Italianate palazzo of Kingston Lacy; and sublime Tudor houses at Athelhampton, Parnham, Sandford Orcas and Sherborne.

Rare birds and red squirrels find sanctuary in reserves such as Durlston and the strange island of Brownsea, enclosed within Poole's huge natural harbour. Other wildlife wonders include Abbotsbury's unique swannery, where hundreds of birds gather, and the gorgeous specimens on the wing at Worldwide Butterflies in Sherborne.

Martial history of different ages finds substance in the Bovington Tank Museum and the atmosphere-laden castle ruin at Corfe. The majesty of Sherborne's abbey and the great churches at Christchurch, Milton Abbas and Wimborne contrast with the simplicity of Hardy's birthplace and the cottage of Clouds Hill, the last home of Lawrence of Arabia.

ATHELHAMPTON

On A35, 5½ miles north-east of Dorchester (Cb)

This lovely country house retains a happy air of what it has been for 500 years – a private family home, albeit in the grand manner. Built in 1485, when Henry VII ascended the throne and ended the Wars of the Roses, Athelhampton illustrates

TOUCH OF ELEGANCE *Athelhampton's lovely gardens – the velvet lawns, the delicately matched herbaceous borders, the strategically placed statuary – show centuries of loving good taste.*

the new style of architecture heralded by the coming of peace. The battlemented entrance front and porch, for example, are romantically decorative and not at all the businesslike defences of the fortified manors of earlier times. And the south-west wing, the fine gabled end of which faces the drive, is attached to the main house not at the 90 degrees classical taste would dictate but at a wider angle. This was very probably to minimise the shadow the two parts of the building would cast on each other – letting the sunshine into the bright new Tudor interiors.

The Great Hall is among the finest examples of 15th-century domestic architecture in the country, complete with its original timbered roof and stained glass. English furnishings, paintings and other treasures dating from the 14th century remain in their original settings.

Strolling in the formally laid-out gardens, catching glimpses of the manor's ancient gables, it is not hard to imagine the pleasure that five centuries of Athelhampton's fortunate owners must have derived from this beautiful place.

Easter-mid Oct, Wed, Thur, Sun and Bank Hol pm; also Mon and Tues pm in Aug. Refreshments. Shop. P *Toilets.* ♿ *Tel Puddletown (030 584) 363.*

BLUE POOL

Off A351, 3 miles south of Wareham (Da)

In tranquil seclusion within its pinewood fringe,

SWANS AND PALMS AT ABBOTSBURY

Lying in a sheltered green valley, Abbotsbury is a quiet place of honey-coloured stone cottages, many of them thatched with reeds from the nearby Fleet lagoon. The village owes its existence to the Benedictine abbey that prospered here for centuries before the Dissolution of 1539. Only scant ruins of the abbey remain, with some medieval masonry in the walls of village houses; but the chapel and tithe barn, with its great, buttressed gable, are impressive reminders of past glories. Abbotsbury is also noted for its fine subtropical gardens and its ancient swannery.

St Catherine's Chapel: All year, daily. Free entry. P *(limited). Tithe Barn (exterior only): All year, daily. St Nicholas' Church: All year, daily. Free entry. The Gardens: Easter-Oct, daily. Adm charge. Refreshments. Shop.* P *Toilets.* ♿ *Tel Abbotsbury (0305) 871228. Swannery: May-mid Sept, daily. Adm charge.* P *Toilets.* ♿ *Tel (0305) 871228.*

CHAPEL BY THE BEACH *A mile south of Abbotsbury the vast bank of shingle called Chesil Beach stretches towards the Bill of Portland, rising up to 40ft in parts. The 15th-century Chapel of St Catherine – a seafarers' landmark – stands away from the village overlooking green fields and the English Channel.*

STANDING TALL *Dwarfing the trees around it, the Church of St Nicholas – in rich, honey-coloured stone – was built in the 15th century and is noted for its sturdy west tower. It contains a 13th-century marble monument of an abbot.*

LAGOON LIFE *Hundreds of wild mute swans nest in The Swannery, a marsh at the head of the Fleet lagoon. The colony feeds on a rare grass –* Zostera marina *– that has grown in the area for at least 600 years.*

ABBEY STOREHOUSE *Built in the 15th century, the huge tithe barn – 272ft long and 31ft wide – was used to store the dues paid in kind to the abbot by his tenants in and around the village. It is now used as a store for thatching reed, harvested from the Fleet.*

AMONG THE SHELTERING PALMS *Palm trees, eucalyptus, acacias and bamboos are among the subtropical flora that flourish in The Gardens on the Beach Road west of Abbotsbury. During the spring and summer the tree-sheltered gardens – with their 20 acres of rare plants and shrubs – are ablaze with camellias, magnolias and roses.*

this extraordinary lake takes its brilliant colouring from the action of light on the clay and minerals suspended in the water. Changes in light bring transformations in hue from greeny-blue to turquoise to sapphire. The colours are most impressive on overcast days.

The 300yd pit was dug in the 1840s for its Purbeck ball clay – a highly prized potter's clay. The pit soon filled with rainwater, and has been a source of fascination ever since. The most dramatic views of the water are from the woodland paths that encircle the pool.

Mar-Nov, daily. Adm charge. P *Toilets. Tel Wareham (092 95) 51408.*

BROWNSEA ISLAND

Poole Harbour (Da)

The woodland of Brownsea is one of the few places where red squirrels still thrive, protected in a tranquil and largely wild environment which offers many attractions to visitors. Not the least of these are the safe, sandy beaches, broad views of the Dorset coast to Studland and Corfe Castle, and many idyllic spots for picnics. Now owned by the National Trust, the island formerly had a long succession of private owners, who bequeathed to it a curious array of buildings and imported plant and animal life.

Boats land at the quay, which is handsomely lined with the castellated houses built in the 18th and 19th centuries for the coastguard station established to counter the smuggling for which Poole was notorious. At the quay's west end stands the extravagant turreted landing stage for the castle; the great mock-Gothic pile itself, just behind, is not open to the public.

Most of Brownsea's 500 acres are composed of woodland, with some marsh, two small lakes created by peat-cutting and reed beds. The northern half of the island is a nature reserve run by the Dorset Trust for Nature Conservation, and public access is by guided tour or nature trail only. Besides the red squirrels, other mammals include a colony of the tiny Japanese sika deer – introduced in 1896 – and several members of the bat family. More than 200 bird species have been seen on the island. A public hide overlooks the lagoon, which provides views of the thousands of migrating ducks and waders, geese and gulls that feed here in spring and autumn. Many birds, too, remain to breed.

HERO'S SHRINE *Clouds Hill, the cottage home of Lawrence of Arabia, is now a shrine to his memory. He loved its wooden beams, leather-covered furniture and sombre colour scheme, and called it his 'earthly paradise'.*

Inshore, as many as 120 pairs of herons nest in the pines, and there are glimpses of woodpeckers feeding on insects that infest the conifer trunks. Golden pheasants and rare silver pheasants roam the island glades, and there are numerous semi-wild peacocks.

On the south side of Brownsea, a commemorative stone records the holding of the first experimental boys' camp here in 1907, under the instruction of Robert Baden-Powell. The success of that ten-day gathering of 20 boys led to the founding of the Boy Scout movement.

NT. Apr-Sept, daily by ferry from Poole Quay or Sandbanks. Landing fee. Refreshments. Shop and information centre. Toilets. ♿ *Tel Bournemouth (0202) 707744. Ferries: Tel Poole (0202) 674063 and 700120.*

CERNE ABBAS ABBEY AND GIANT

Off A352, 10 miles south of Sherborne (Cb)

The 10th-century Benedictine abbey that once dominated the village is now recalled only by the scant ruins of a gatehouse, added in the 15th century. Much more ancient is the celebrated Cerne Abbas Giant – the 180ft, club-wielding naked man cut starkly into the chalk of the hillside just north-east of the village. Believed to be 1500 or more years old, the frankly phallic figure is the near-miraculous testimony to the countless succeeding generations who have saved him from disappearing under the encroaching grassland.

All year, daily. Free entry.

CHRISTCHURCH PRIORY

In centre of Christchurch (Eb)

All the great styles of architecture are represented in the priory church, as its construction spanned four and a half centuries. Founded in 1094, it has a superb Norman nave and transepts, an Early Gothic porch of about 1200, and Decorated Gothic screens from the following century. The tower, soaring to 120ft, is pure Perpendicular of about 1460 and the chantries represent the Renaissance style of the 1520s.

The church measures 311ft from east to west and is the longest parish church in England. It has many remarkable carvings and monuments. The altar screen, sculpted with the Tree of Jesse, looks modern but dates from 1350. The beautiful statue facing the font commemorates the poet Shelley, who drowned off the coast of Italy in 1822. The tower has a peal of 12 bells, two of which were made in 1370 and are the oldest still to be regularly rung anywhere in Britain.

North of the church, high on a mound, stand the ruins of Christchurch Castle's once-massive keep, built around 1100, with walls 9ft thick. Opposite, backing onto the mill stream, is the constable's house. Built around 1160, it remains amazingly intact, the walls reaching their full height in places, and retaining their elaborately arched and carved Norman windows.

Priory Church: All year, daily. Adm charge. Castle and Norman House: EH. All year, daily. Free entry.

GARDEN GROTTO *The Roman Garden at Compton Acres is a circular grotto with a miniature pool, lead fountain and a charming set of lead statuettes. Through the handsome, wrought-iron gates are intriguing glimpses of the terrace of the main Italian garden.*

CLOUDS HILL

Off B3390, 9 miles east of Dorchester (Cb)

It was on his way home by motorcycle to this cream-coloured little cottage that T.E. Lawrence was killed on May 13, 1935. Clouds Hill has been preserved just as he had left it earlier on that day – an intimate memorial to the enigmatic soldier and author, better known as Lawrence of Arabia. The cottage is filled with his books and wartime photographs, and the furniture Lawrence bought secondhand or made.

He used Clouds Hill as a retreat from Army life when serving as 'Private Shaw' in the Tank Corps at Bovington Camp, a mile to the south.

NT. Apr-Sept, Wed, Thur, Fri, Sun and Bank Hol pm; Oct-Mar, Sun pm. Adm charge. P *(limited). Tel Bindon Abbey (0929) 463824.*

COMPTON ACRES

Canford Cliffs Road, Poole (Db)

Pagodas and arched bridges, temple and tea house blend harmoniously with the beautiful and mature specimen trees and plants of the Japanese garden – one of a series of seven self-contained gardens of this horticultural pleasure-ground, conceived as a living museum of garden styles. The formal Italian garden, symmetrically arranged around a lake and decorated with fine statuary, is framed by the colour of a thousand rose bushes. There is a rock and water garden with carp-filled, lily-covered pools; a heather dell with bloom all the year round; and a subtropical glen of exotic palms and shrubs.

Apr-Oct, daily. Adm charge. Refreshments. Shop. P *Toilets. Tel Canford Cliffs (0202) 700778.*

CORFE CASTLE

On A351, 4 miles south-east of Wareham (Da)

Corfe is everything an ancient castle should be. The 12th-century keep and its massive outer fortifications are steeped in history, for kings were not only born and bred here but imprisoned – and murdered – too. And though a ravaged ruin now, the castle is the very stuff of fairy tales, looming over the picturesque village that has grown up around its feet, and now reaches right to the medieval moat-bridge.

It was to the Saxon royal castle that in March 978 the popular teenage King Edward came to visit his half-brother Ethelred – and was assassinated by his young host's ambitious mother. Thus began the disastrous reign of St Edward the Martyr's 'Unready' successor. Ever since, Corfe has witnessed many epic chapters in the nation's history.

The last of these took place in the Civil War, when the castle stood as the last Royalist stronghold anywhere between London and Exeter. Then it was the home of Charles I's Chief Justice, Sir John Bankes, whose place was with the king, and so to his wife fell the task of defence. From 1643 to 1645, Lady Bankes resolutely held out – and looking even at today's remains it is easy to imagine how impregnable Corfe must have seemed to its besiegers. The castle finally succumbed only through the treachery of one of Lady Bankes's officers, and was then looted and blown up on the orders of a vengeful Parliament.

To see just how the castle looked in its prime, visit the excellent model village just off the square in West Street. There, in full view of the ruins, stands a pristine 1:20 scale reconstruction of the original fortress and its village, among delightful gardens.

GUARD DUTY *The ruins of Corfe Castle rise from a great natural mound on which strongholds have stood for more than a thousand years, guarding a strategically important gap in the Purbeck Hills.*

Castle: NT. Mar-Oct, daily; Nov-Feb, Sat and Sun pm only. Adm charge. Refreshments. Shop. P *Toilets. Tel Corfe Castle (0929) 480442. Model village: Easter-Sept, daily; Oct, Sun-Thur. Adm charge. Refreshments. Shop.* ♿ *Tel (0929) 480091.*

DORSET COUNTY MUSEUM

High West Street, Dorchester (Cb)

Durnovaria to the Romans who founded it in AD 70 and Casterbridge to Thomas Hardy who lived here and wove the town into his 'Wessex' novels, Dorchester takes a pride in its past that is delightfully conveyed in its marvellous museums and ancient monuments.

Beautiful mosaics from Roman Dorchester are among the exhibits in the award-winning Dorset County Museum. Along with other antiquities, there is an exhibition of the archaeological findings made in the 1930s at nearby Maiden Castle, the Iron Age settlement stormed by a Roman legion in AD 43.

The main part of the museum, an airy and brightly decorated Victorian galleried hall, displays the large collection of Thomas Hardy's possessions, bequeathed by the author. As well as much fine furniture, there is a complete reconstruction of the study from Max Gate, Hardy's Dorchester home. In this richly atmospheric room, the world's most important library of original Hardy manuscripts is on display.

A notorious episode in Dorchester's history is recalled in the Old Crown Court, just along High West Street in the Old Shirehall. This was the scene of the trial of the Tolpuddle Martyrs in 1834, and the courtroom today is just as it was when the savage sentence of transportation to Australia was pronounced on the six local farmworkers who had formed what amounted to Britain's first trade union. Visitors can roam the court and even sit on the bench – where a visitors' book invites comments.

Some of the more glorious chapters from Dorchester's history are recorded at the Dorset Military Museum in The Keep – a towered and battlemented pile built in 1879. There are displays of uniforms, medals and weaponry spanning three centuries of regimental life in peace and war. Deeds of derring-do are depicted in battle-scene dioramas, and there are some intriguing items of memorabilia – including Hitler's desk from the wartime Chancellory in Berlin.

County Museum: All year, daily exc Sun. Adm charge. Shop. P *Tel Dorchester (0305) 62735. Old Crown Court: All year, Mon-Fri. Military Museum: All year, daily exc Sun. Adm charge. Shop.* P *Toilets. Tel (0305) 64066.*

DORSET HEAVY HORSE CENTRE

Off B3081, 1 mile north of Verwood (Eb)

Joss, one of the finest Shire horses in the world, is among several magnificent members of his noble breed living and working at this nostalgically tractorless farm on the edge of the New Forest. The centre holds daily parades of the horses, and there are demonstrations of the farm work that made the animals such a familiar sight in our countryside as late as the 1950s.

Among other gentle giants to be seen here are the Clydesdale, the Suffolk Punch and the Percheron – the latter being the French breed that pulled the original London omnibuses.

Apr-Oct, daily. Adm charge. Refreshments. Shop. P *Toilets.* ♿ *Tel Verwood (0202) 824040.*

DURLSTON COUNTRY PARK

On Lighthouse Road, 1 mile south of Swanage (Da)

The Great Globe, a 40 ton sphere of local Portland stone intricately sculpted with a map of the world, is among the unexpected sights of this wild and unspoilt coastland at the south-eastern tip of the Isle of Purbeck. It was erected in 1887 by George Burt, a local stonemason, and is etched with the names of many former British colonies. On its high point by Durlston Head, it is a poignant reminder of the Empire.

Along the cliffs to the west, colonies of sea birds nest in this important sanctuary. Fulmars and kittiwakes, guillemots and razorbills are among the species which can be watched from an observation point, just below a folly built by George Burt and known as Durlston Head Castle (now a cafeteria).

In Durlston Bay, the exposed Purbeck stone beds show many fossils, and are frequently visited by geologists. More recent history is recalled by the Tilly Whim Caves – man-made caverns in the cliffs where, until the last century, Portland limestone was quarried and lowered from ledges into barges below. The wooden cranes used for the purpose were called whims, and the name Tilly was probably that of a local quarryman. The caves are closed to the public, but there is a fine view of them from the nearby Anvil Point lighthouse.

The information centre has details of several walks and trails, one of which takes in Anvil Point lighthouse.

Park: All year, daily. Information centre: Apr-Oct. Free entry. Refreshments. Shop. P *Toilets. Tel Swanage (0929) 424443.*

HAMBLEDON HILL

Off A350, 4 miles north-west of Blandford Forum (Cc)

Crowned by an Iron Age hill-fort, the stark, summit of Hambledon Hill rises to 604ft amid lush green farmlands. There are superb views of the Stour valley which runs below the hill, and of Hod Hill just to the south where defenders of the hill-fort there were routed by a Roman legion – probably the 2nd Augusta led by the Roman general Vespasian – in AD 43. South of the summit is a much older 20 acre causewayed camp, where Stone Age farmers lived and kept their herds 4500 years ago.

Both settlements were strategically placed and saw much strife down the years. Excavations in the 1970s revealed a skeleton with an arrowhead in the chest, and it was on Hambledon Hill that 2000 war-weary villagers held out against both sides in the Civil War before being overcome by 50 Parliamentarians in 1645. The hill is privately owned, but there is a public path to the summit.

All year, daily.

HOME TIES *Long after he had moved out of his cottage birthplace, the novelist Thomas Hardy maintained his links with it. He helped the next tenant to replant the garden with a 'floral knot' of flowerbeds, and paid his last visit there in 1926, at the age of 86.*

HARDY'S COTTAGE

Off A35, 3 miles north-east of Dorchester (Cb)

Crouching low under its handsome thatch, the cottage at Higher Bockhampton today looks very much as it did when Thomas Hardy was born here in 1840. Sheltered by the majestic beeches his great-grandfather planted when building the cottage in 1800, it was in the garden during the summer of 1873 that Hardy started to write *Far From the Madding Crowd*, the novel that was to make him famous. Hardy married in the following year and moved away, but he returned to Higher Bockhampton all through his life.

NT. Apr-Oct, daily exc Tues. Adm charge. **P** *(limited).*

KINGSTON LACY

On B3082, 1½ miles west of Wimborne Minster (Db)

Paintings by Rubens and Titian, Van Dyck and Velázquez are among scores of masterpieces that hang in this extraordinary house. Kingston Lacy is, to all intents and purposes, an extravagant Italian palazzo – set somewhat incongruously within its vast estate of mellow Dorset woods and rich farmland.

The property was left to the National Trust in 1981 by Ralph Bankes, whose ancestor Sir John originally bought it from Charles I, whom he served as Chief Justice. The house was built at the time of the Restoration, but assumed its present palatial aspect after William John Bankes, MP, inherited in 1834. An avid connoisseur of Italian architecture and fine art, Bankes was in the midst of transforming the house when he became involved in an unsavoury case and fled Kingston Lacy, never to return. From exile in Italy, Bankes continued to send detailed drawings and instructions to his builders at home – along with boatloads of art treasures – right up to his death in Venice in 1855.

The fruits of those long-distance endeavours include not only the fabulous collection of paintings but countless other works of art. There are sculptures from Venice, furnishings from Florence, even a pair of exquisite carved doors said to be from the Vatican. The spectacular white staircase is of Carrara marble.

In the garden, the cedars stand as a testament to the respect Bankes commanded, despite his disgrace – for the great trees were planted by, among others, Edward VII and Bankes's own lifelong friend, the Duke of Wellington.

NT. Apr-Oct pm, daily exc Thur and Fri. Adm charge. Refreshments. Shop. **P** *Toilets. Tel Wimborne (0202) 883402.*

MAIDEN CASTLE

Off A354, 2½ miles south-west of Dorchester (Ca)

Thomas Hardy likened this ancient hill-fort to 'an enormous many-limbed organism of an antediluvian time'. The huge, isolated mound of Maiden Castle does indeed call to mind some primitive life form lying down in the green and treeless surrounding fields.

Its tremendous fortifications, begun around 300 BC, make this one of the most important settlements of British prehistory. Three great ditches, each rising up to 90ft, surround the hilltop's 2 mile perimeter. The entrances at each end are guarded by labyrinths of earthworks, through which attackers would have had to pick their way under a hail of missiles from the ramparts above before reaching the wooden gates to the 47 acre town within.

The end of Maiden Castle as a settlement came suddenly with the arrival of the Romans in AD 43. By this time the most important town for miles around, it became a target for the legion led by Vespasian, who was to become Emperor of Rome in AD 69. The legionaries stormed the fortress and massacred or enslaved unknown numbers of the population.

An archaeological dig in the 1930s headed by Sir Mortimer Wheeler revealed the graves of 34 people, their skeletons showing the wounds inflicted by Roman swords and ballista bolts. Also discovered were mounds of the defenders' ammunition, 22,000 beach pebbles for sling shots – effective weapons to ancient Britons, but no match for the armour and artillery of Rome.

Now entirely grassed over, except for the foundations of a curious Romano-Celtic temple of about AD 380, the breezy heights of Maiden Castle command fine views all round. Display boards provide historical information, and further knowledge can be gained from the exhibition on the castle at the Dorset County Museum in Dorchester.

EH. All year, daily. Free entry. **P**

MILTON ABBEY

Off A354, 9 miles south-west of Blandford Forum (Cb)

The 15th-century abbey church is virtually all that remains of Middleton, a once-thriving town that was demolished in the 1770s by Lord Milton, Earl of Dorchester. He replaced it with an architect-designed small village of uniform thatched cottages nearby and renamed it Milton Abbas. A former Benedictine monastery founded in AD 934, the Gothic, cathedral-like abbey church contains a marble monument to Lord and Lady Milton by Agostino Carlini. Another monument, to John Tregonwell, lord of the manor until his death in 1680, commemorates a remarkable incident. As an infant, 50 years earlier, Tregonwell had fallen from the church roof – but was miraculously uninjured, apparently saved by the parachute-effect of his voluminous clothing.

Lord Milton employed the architect Sir William Chambers to design his enormous Gothic-style mansion beside the abbey church. James Wyatt and Robert Adam worked on the interior, which incorporates the Abbot's Hall of 1498, complete with its original hammerbeam roof and screen. The house is now a boys' boarding school, and was the setting for BBC TV's serial *To Serve Them All My Days*.

At Park Farm there is a museum which displays a pictorial history of the village, and has a collection of early stone bottles and old brewery equipment.

Abbey Church: All year, daily. Free entry. Abbey House: Easter and Summer school holidays. Adm charge. Refreshments. **P** *(limited). Toilets. Tel Milton Abbas (0258) 880258. Museum: All year, daily. Adm charge. Tel (0258) 880216.*

PARNHAM

On A3066, 1 mile south of Beaminster (Bb)

Sir Arthur Conan Doyle, awoken by the baying of dogs during a night's stay at Parnham, is said to have been inspired by the sound to write his 1902 classic *The Hound of the Baskervilles*. It is easy to understand how the old house might prompt such a flight of imagination. However, inspiration of a more tangible kind is Parnham's new lifeblood, for it houses the workshop of the furniture-maker John Makepeace.

The first house at Parnham was built around 1400, but today's Renaissance-cum-Gothic structure of warm Hamdon stone and fine mullioned windows is largely Elizabethan. The battlements, which blend happily with the Elizabethan gables, were added in 1810 by the Regency architect John Nash. Inside, the rooms have been restored to their 16th-century style. The Great Hall has its beautiful original oak screen and minstrels' gallery from 1554. Here and in other fine rooms there are displays of Makepeace's work, along with exhibitions of contemporary works of art.

The lovely grounds at Parnham include formal terraces and gardens, and riverside walks and picnic areas where kingfishers, dippers and wagtails may be glimpsed.

Apr-Oct, Sun, Wed and Bank Hol. Adm charge. Refreshments. Shop. P *Toilets.* ♿ *Tel Beaminster (0308) 862204.*

POOLE QUAY

Old Town, Poole (Db)

Poole's great natural harbour has served for centuries as a seafarers' sanctuary from storms, and today the port offers many all-weather attractions to shorebound visitors. These are concentrated along the quay – still very much a working waterfront for commercial vessels as well as leisure craft – and in the splendidly preserved Old Town that lies behind it.

The unblinking predatory eyes of two dangerous-looking sharks, circling their enormous tank, welcome you to the Natural World, an enthralling aquarium and 'serpentarium' in one of the quay's fine old warehouses. This well-kept miniature zoo's collection includes alligators and crocodiles, iguanas and dinner-plate-size frogs, and an awe-inspiring collection of venomous and constricting snakes.

There are less hair-raising delights at the Great Poole Model Railway, one of the largest 'oo' gauge layouts in Britain, with up to 20 computer-controlled trains running along 1000ft of track. Set in a well-designed landscape, the locomotives convincingly recall the age of steam.

The nearby Poole Pottery is heir to a local tradition for the craft dating from Roman times, and has a museum, video displays and demonstrations of pottery painting.

Poole makes something of a speciality of museums, for the Old Town has three. The Maritime Museum is housed in the magnificent Town Cellars in Paradise Street off the quay. Largely devoted to Poole's salty 600 year history as a seaport, the museum also has lively displays on such themes as the Mutiny on the *Bounty*, the Spanish Armada and the more localised custom of smuggling.

Directly behind the Town Cellars in the High Street is the medieval merchant's house, Scaplen's Court. This is a gem of a museum, full of the items of everyday life that were used in such a home from the 16th century onwards. The building is constructed around a courtyard and has been faithfully restored; the kitchen is complete with all manner of cooking and cleaning equipment dating from medieval times to the early 20th century.

Recalling the great mercantile prosperity Poole has enjoyed in the past is the old Guildhall, in Market Street. It is approached up symmetrical, sweeping staircases, and its Georgian brick façade is modestly Palladian. The guildhall now serves as a museum devoted to Poole's colourful history. Its ground floor displays an audiovisual presentation of 19th and early 20th-century Poole built up from collections of old photographs.

In Poole Park, off Parkstone Road, there are enough attractions – including a zoo, miniature railway, windsurfing lake, mini marina and swimming pool – to provide a family day out.

Natural World: All year, daily. Adm charge. Refreshments. Shop. Toilets. Tel Poole (0202) 686712. Model Railway: All year, daily. Adm charge. Shop. Tel (0202) 687240. Pottery: All year, Mon-Sat; also Sun, May-Oct. Free entry. Refreshments. Shop. Toilets. Tel (0202) 672866. Maritime Museum, Scaplen's Court and Guildhall: All year, daily. Adm charges. Shops. Toilets (at Scaplen's Court). Tel (0202) 675151 ext 3550.

PORTLAND CASTLE

On A354, 4 miles south of Weymouth (Ca)

St Paul's Cathedral, Buckingham Palace and the Cenotaph are among many famous landmarks partly built from the Isle of Portland's pale-coloured stone. The narrow and rather barren peninsula, once an island, extends 4½ miles to the Bill of Portland – so called after its beak-like shape. The stone has been put to local use, too, in building the three castles on the Isle.

Oldest is the Norman Bow and Arrow or Rufus Castle, now ruined, above Church Ope Cove. Close by is the newest, Pennsylvania Castle, built in romantically Gothic style in 1800 by John Penn, grandson of the founder of the American State of Pennsylvania. It is now a hotel. Portland Castle itself is the squat, tough-looking fortress down in the harbour, beside the Royal Navy helicopter base. The castle was built in the 1520s by Henry VIII, has 14ft thick walls and once bristled with artillery.

Portland's history is told in the Portland Museum at 217 Wakeham in Easton. It was founded in 1930 by Dr Marie Stopes, the birth-control pioneer, who donated the two 17th-century cottages that house it. Thomas Hardy made one of these the home of his heroine Avice in *The Well-Beloved*, and it has been known as Avice's Cottage ever since. Among the museum's attractions are a large collection of local paintings, prints and photographs, and a picture-history of the scores of shipwrecks the Isle has witnessed over the centuries.

The 135ft Portland Bill lighthouse was built of the local stone in 1906, and has wide views. Its 3 ton lantern revolves freely on a bath of mercury, and emits a beam of light from a 3000 watt bulb which is seen 29 miles away.

Castle: EH. Apr-Sept, daily exc Tues and Wed and Sun am. Adm charge. P *Tel Portland (0305) 820539. Museum: All year, daily, exc Sun and Mon Oct-Apr. Adm charge. Lighthouse: All year, Mon-Sat pm (weather permitting). Tel (0305) 820495.*

ROYAL SIGNALS MUSEUM

Off B3082, 1 mile east of Blandford Forum (Db)

From the carrier pigeon that won a VC to the long-range technology of the Falklands campaign, the museum brings to life the history of extraordinary ingenuity – and courage – behind army communications. The museum is housed in the School of Signals of the Royal Corps of Signals, and illustrates army signalling methods used both before and after the regiment's formation in 1920. Displays include the signalling lamps and heliographs that came into use with the invention of Morse code in 1838. The first use of a military electric telegraph, in the Crimean War of 1854, is recalled, as are many exploits of both World Wars, including those of the motorcycle dispatch riders.

All year, Mon-Fri. Free entry. Shop. P *Toilets. Tel Blandford (0258) 52581 ext 2248.*

DRY DOCK *Tall-masted sailing craft, including the* Mistletoe *of 1909, are a feature of Poole Maritime Museum. The galleried building, with its beamed ceiling, was a warehouse in the 15th century.*

RUSSELL-COTES ART GALLERY

East Cliff, Bournemouth (Eb)

Favoured by film-makers as a classic Victorian location, the grand mansion at East Cliff was given to Bournemouth in 1908, along with its collections, by the traveller and connoisseur Sir Merton Russell-Cotes. Among the paintings on show are French Impressionists and some fine Victorian oils and watercolours. Furniture includes Tudor and Jacobean pieces, and an unusual item is the octagonal table used by Napoleon on St Helena. Collections include relics of the Victorian actor-manager Sir Henry Irving, and three rooms devoted to Japanese art. The Victorian gardens are as gracious as the interiors.

Nostalgia is the theme of the Transport and Rural Museum at the Mallard Road Depot. On display are more than 30 of the venerable tram cars, trolley buses and buses that trundled through Bournemouth from Victorian times. The Big Four Railway Museum at the back of 81 Christchurch Road likewise recalls an almost-forgotten era of public transport. Its name derives from the Big Four rail networks that were created in 1921 out of the 250 independent companies operating lines at that time. The four were finally absorbed into British Railways in 1948. The museum has many models of the steam locomotives of those days and a collection of the name plates from some of the great engines.

Russell-Cotes: All year, Mon-Sat. Adm charge. Shop. Toilets. Tel Bournemouth (0202) 21009. Transport and Rural Museum: June-Sept, Wed. Adm charge. Tel (0202) 21009. Big Four: All year, Mon-Sat exc Bank Hol. Adm charge. Shop. Tel (0202) 22278.

CHANGING TIMES *The moulded ceiling in the handsome Green Drawing Room of Sherborne Castle bears the arms of Sir Walter Raleigh, first owner of the castle. The chimneypiece bears the arms of the Digbys, owners since 1617.*

SANDFORD ORCAS MANOR HOUSE

Off B3148, 4 miles north of Sherborne (Bc)

The serene Tudor house's owner, a member of the Medlycott family whose home this has been for 250 years, personally shows visitors around his enchanting domain. Built in the 1550s around a central courtyard, the small manor retains several superb panelled rooms, medieval heraldic glass in its fine mullioned windows, fine paintings, and furniture of the Jacobean and Queen Anne periods.

Wisteria and honeysuckle festoon the house's honey-coloured walls of Ham Hill stone, and the gardens beyond are bright with roses, lilac and laburnum in May and June.

Easter Mon, then May-Sept, Sun pm and Mon. Adm charge. P *Toilets. Tel Corton Denham (096 322) 206.*

SEA LIFE CENTRE, WEYMOUTH

In Lodmoor Country Park, Preston Beach Road (Ca)

Conger eels and leopard sharks loom large in this aquarium complex, where a major attraction is the Ocean Tunnel – a walkway entirely surrounded by the glass of a huge tank shimmering with shoals of fish. Another aquarium is designed as a shoreline habitat, home to octopus, lobster and many other fascinating sea creatures. An even closer acquaintance with marine life is offered by the shallow 'touch' pools, where visitors can scramble over rocks in search of crabs, shrimps and sea anemones.

Mar-Nov, daily. Adm charge. Refreshments. Shop. P *Toilets.* ♿ *Tel Weymouth (0305) 788255.*

SHERBORNE ABBEY

In centre of Sherborne (Cc)

The golden Ham Hill sandstone of Sherborne's beautiful medieval buildings has its most sublime use in the stately Abbey Church of St Mary the Virgin, built between the 12th and 15th centuries. Weathered to a mellow honey colour outside, the effect within is one of warm welcome. In the cathedral-scale nave, ingenious mobile mirrors give a thrillingly detailed view of the exquisite fan-vaulting overhead. The oak choir stalls merit close inspection, too, for the 15th-century misericords – on the underside of the tip-up seats – feature enchanting carved tableaux such as a doctor portrayed as a monkey (an indication of the esteem in which some of the profession were held at the time) and a stern-faced schoolmaster birching a schoolboy. Close to the abbey are its almshouses, set around a tiny cloistered courtyard and a roofed conduit house, where monks washed and shaved their heads.

Nearby, the 19th-century Abbey Gatehouse is home to a museum devoted to Sherborne's history – largely from the year 705, when St Aldhelm chose to set his bishop's stool here and built a cathedral on the site of the present abbey. The museum's diverse attractions include a large and richly detailed Victorian doll's house, an exhibition recalling the town's prosperous 18th-century silk industry, and a scale model of Sherborne's Norman castle in its original state.

The old castle itself, half a mile east and commandingly situated on a rise overlooking the River Yeo, is now a ruin. But the towering south-west gatehouse, built in the 12th century and still mostly intact, offers a good idea of just what a formidable fortress this must have been. It stood for 500 years until the Civil War when it was stormed, after two bitter sieges, by Parliamentarian forces whose second-in-command, Oliver Cromwell, complained what a 'malicious and mischievous castle' it was.

The old castle had once known happier times when Sir Walter Raleigh made it his family home in 1592. But the great adventurer preferred to build a new house on the site of a hunting lodge in the south of the park. This he extended into the large, Dutch-style Elizabethan manor that is the Sherborne Castle of today. Further developed by the Digby family, who have owned it since 1617, the house and grounds are a delight to visit.

The castle's several drawing rooms and dining rooms are filled with treasures: glorious furniture from the 17th century onwards, including some fine examples of Hepplewhite; oriental porcelain dating back 500 years; fine paintings and interiors spanning every period from Elizabethan to Victorian.

The grounds, landscaped by Capability Brown 200 years ago, sweep down to a great lake, across which there is a fine view of the Old Castle through the giant cedars planted by Raleigh. Nearby is Raleigh's Seat, the stone platform where the great man could sit and contemplate his castles both old and new – the domain he dubbed his 'fortune's fold'.

Abbey: All year, daily. Free entry. ♿ *Tel Sherborne (0935) 812452 (weekday mornings). Museum: Apr-Oct, Sun pm and Tues-Sat; Nov-Mar, Tues and Sat. Adm charge. Shop. Tel (0935) 812252. Old Castle: EH. All year, daily, exc Sun am Oct-Mar. Adm charge. Shop.* P *Toilets. Tel (0935) 812730. Castle: Easter-Sept, Sat, Sun, Thur and Bank Hol Mon pm. Adm charge. Refreshments. Shop.* P *Toilets. Tel (0935) 813182.*

SWANAGE RAILWAY

Swanage Station in town centre (Da)

Steam trains are again plying the century-old track that once linked the seaside town of Swanage with Corfe Castle. Enthusiasts have restored the handsome stone buildings of Swanage station, closed along with the line in 1972, and have relaid 2 miles of the railway. Passengers travel in nostalgic style on 25 minute round trips to Harman's Cross Halt, through some glorious Purbeck countryside. The railway is being extended all the way to Corfe Castle, with plans to provide a regular passenger service.

Mid July-mid Sept, daily; also Sat mid Apr-Sept and Sun Apr-Oct and Dec. Fare. Refreshments. Shop. **P** *(limited). Toilets. Tel Swanage (0929) 425800 (weekends).*

TANK MUSEUM

Off A352, 7 miles west of Wareham (Ca)

A massive 48 ton Centurion tank, cut in half along its length to expose the menacing secrets of its interior, is one of more than 180 armoured vehicles on display here. They date from the first true tank, built in 1915, and include Second World War veterans such as British Churchills, America's ubiquitous Shermans and Germany's awesome Jagd Tiger, with massive 128mm gun.

The collection was started in 1924 following a visit to Bovington Camp by Rudyard Kipling. By then a distinguished chronicler of war, he suggested that some of the First World War tanks parked at the camp awaiting scrapping should be preserved for posterity.

All year, daily. Adm charge. Refreshments. Shop. **P** *Toilets.* ♿ *Tel Bindon Abbey (0929) 463953.*

TUTANKHAMUN EXHIBITION

25 High West Street, Dorchester (Cb)

The sights, sounds and even the smells that greeted Howard Carter and his colleagues in 1922 when they entered the 3200-year-old tomb of the boy pharaoh Tutankhamun have been re-created with meticulous care in a spectacular addition to Dorchester's outstanding array of museums. Facsimiles of fabulous treasures such as the golden mask and the statue of the jackal-god Anubis were made by craftsmen employing the same methods and materials used by the ancient Egyptians. The acoustics and aromas of the burial chamber are based on notes taken by Howard Carter.

Even earlier times come spectacularly to life in the nearby Dinosaur Museum, in Icen Way, which as well as many locally found fossils has full-size models of such gigantic species as *Tyrannosaurus rex* and *Stegosaurus*. There are ingenious demonstrations of how dinosaurs lived, looked and even felt to the touch. The museum is designed with children in mind, with display cases at low levels, video and 'interactive' presentations and live iguana lizards – whose habits give clues to those of their prehistoric forebears.

Tutankhamun: All year, daily. Adm charge. Shop. ♿ *Tel Dorchester (0305) 69571. Dinosaurs: All year, daily. Adm charge. Shop. Toilets.* ♿ *Tel (0305) 69880.*

WIMBORNE MINSTER

In town centre, off B3082 (Db)

A library of ancient books, each chained to prevent theft, an astronomical clock that predates the astronomer Copernicus (1473-1543), and a Saxon treasure chest more than a thousand years old are among the many marvels of this imposing twin-towered church. Built on what is believed to be the site of an 8th-century Benedictine nunnery, the minster dates from the 1100s and retains its magnificent Norman nave and arches. The west tower – added in 1464 to accommodate an extra peal of bells – has a Quarter Jack, a carved figure brightly painted as a grenadier which strikes a pair of bells every quarter hour. Monuments include the tombstone of a smuggler named Gulliver, famed for his audacious exploits and narrow escapes from the Excise men.

The Priest's House Museum in High Street traces Wimborne's earliest history, and there are collections illustrating the town's life in the 18th and 19th centuries. Dorset crafts of all kinds are displayed – and demonstrated by the experts – at the Walford Mill Craft Centre on its own island in the River Allen, just a quarter-mile walk from the minster.

Minster: All year, daily. Free entry. Shop. **P** *(limited). Tel Wimborne (0202) 884753. Museum: Easter-Sept, Mon-Sat. Adm charge.* ♿ *Tel (0202) 882533. Craft centre: All year, daily. Free entry.* **P** *Tel (0202) 841400.*

WORLDWIDE BUTTERFLIES

On A30, 2 miles west of Sherborne (Bc)

Close encounters with the world's most exotic insects await visitors to Compton House. The gardens, specially planted to provide ideal butterfly habitats, are alive with countless British species in summer. And in the house's handsome panelled rooms there are many more to be seen.

The Breeding Hall has a display demonstrating the metamorphosis of butterflies and moths from egg to caterpillar to pupa to flying adult. There are live insects to be seen at each stage. In the Palm House, there is a chance to walk among lush vegetation where tropical species are on the wing. Among them are the astonishing Giant Atlas moths, gaudily patterned and nearly a foot across, and Brazil's Passion Flower butterflies with their unique and intriguing in-flight courtship rituals.

The first floor of Compton House is the home of the Lullingstone Silk Farm – so called because it was started at Lullingstone Castle in Kent in the 1930s. The farm has produced silk for the bridal dresses at several royal weddings, including that of the Princess of Wales in 1981.

A living exhibition shows how the silk moth caterpillar, or silkworm, gorged on its diet of mulberry leaves, spins a golden monkey-nut-like cocoon in which to pupate. It is this cocoon, composed of half a mile or more of continuous superfine thread, that is unravelled and reeled for spinning into silk.

Apr-Oct, daily. Adm charge. Refreshments. Shop. **P** *Toilets. Tel Yeovil (0935) 74608.*

COUNTY CALENDAR

May (Spring Bank Holiday). Abbotsbury: Garland Day.

June (mid-month). Lyme Regis: Pitchfork Rebellion (pageants to commemorate landing of Duke of Monmouth in 1685). Bournemouth: Flower Festival; International Music Festival.

July (mid-month). Weymouth: Folk Festival.

July (3rd Sunday). Tolpuddle: Rally.

August (1st week). Dorchester: County Fair.

September (1st Saturday). Dorchester: Agricultural Show.

Tourist information: Dorchester (0305) 67992; Bournemouth (0202) 291715; Weymouth (0305) 772444; Blandford Forum (0258) 51989.

STONE AND GLASS *The two stone towers of Wimborne Minster are a Dorset landmark. Inside (top picture), the nave leads towards a glorious Early English east window, with three slender lancets; the centre light contains 15th-century glass.*

DURHAM

CATHEDRAL, CASTLES AND TREASURE HOUSES OF ART AND INDUSTRY

The Prince-Bishops of Durham once ruled the north-east virtually supreme from their cathedral in Durham and their castles in Durham and Auckland. In the 12th century, King Stephen granted them the mineral rights of Weardale, starting a long history of mining in the area which is told today at the Killhope Centre and the Weardale Museum.

A major aspect of Durham's later industrial greatness is preserved at the Darlington Railway Centre, while both industrial and farming life in the county in bygone days are vividly re-created at Beamish.

The arts are not neglected in Durham. The Bowes Museum is a treasure house of works of art from all over Western Europe, and the city of Durham, among its many treasures, has Britain's only exclusively Oriental museum.

AUCKLAND CASTLE

In the centre of Bishop Auckland (Cb)

Standing commandingly above the River Wear, Auckland Castle has been a residence of the Bishops of Durham for the past 800 years. The visitor's first sight is of the battlemented gateway leading from the Market Place of Bishop Auckland – a piece of mock medievalism built in the 1760s. The castle itself, also decorated with pinnacles and battlements, looks similarly mock-Gothic, but has a 12th-century core.

The castle is now the only residence of the Bishops of Durham who, until 1836, were Prince-Bishops. Their role in the Middle Ages as powerful warrior-prelates defending the Border regions against Scottish marauders is shown by their coat of arms, which has a sword as well as a bishop's crook and mitre.

The oldest part of the castle is the magnificent St Peter's Chapel, built by Bishop Hugh Pudsey about 1190 as his great banqueting hall, complete with central hearth, minstrel gallery and cellars. In 1665 it was converted into a chapel by Bishop John Cosin. The interior appearance of the castle today is due mainly to Bishop Shute Barrington, who in the 1790s commissioned James Wyatt to remodel it in the Gothic revival style.

Beyond the castle stretches a rolling 800 acre deer park, with an unusual 'deer shelter' built in 1760.

Castle: Mid May-mid Sept, Sun and Wed pm; chapel, also Thur am. Adm charge. Shop. P Toilets. ♿ (chapel only). Park: All year, daily. Tel Bishop Auckland (0388) 602576.

BOWES MUSEUM

In Barnard Castle (Bb)

A massive French-style chateau presents an incongruous sight looming up on the outskirts of a small northern market town. The Bowes Museum at Barnard Castle was built in 1869-75 by John Bowes, a wealthy local magnate, and his French wife Josephine.

Measuring 300ft long, and 130ft high from its formal gardens to the summit of its mansard roof, it was built specifically for Bowes' art collection, housed in 40 rooms on three storeys. Paintings by Goya, El Greco, Canaletto and other masters, European furniture, pottery and porcelain, even complete rooms taken from demolished buildings – all these add up to a fascinating insight into the taste of an enlightened Victorian collector.

All year, daily exc Sun am. Adm charge. Refreshments. Shop. P Toilets. ♿ Tel Teesdale (0833) 690606.

BOWLEES VISITOR CENTRE

On B6277, 3 miles north-west of Middleton-in-Teesdale (Bb)

Rising high in the bleak Pennine moorland, the Tees in its upper reaches is fast-flowing and restless, forming a succession of rapids and waterfalls that are among the most spectacular in the country. A good starting point for a tour of the area is the Bowlees Visitor Centre, housed in a disused chapel, which explains the ecology, agriculture and history of Teesdale.

Across a small stream, a footpath leads from the Bowlees picnic area car park through an idyllic waterside landscape up to Gibson's Cave. Here a shallow pool below enormous slabs of overhanging rock is fed by a small waterfall.

On the other side of the road from the visitor centre, Low Force provides a good introduction to the major waterfalls of Upper Teesdale. The action of water over the centuries has worn the underlying volcanic rock into strange many-sided pillars. Reached across a couple of fields and a swaying suspension bridge across the river, Low Force is like a series of small rapids.

High Force, 1 mile upstream, is reached in ten minutes or so along a peaceful path under tall conifers and beech trees. The cataract hurtles down a succession of rock steps, with the pillar-like Whin Sill formation on either side.

Cauldron Snout is reached at the end of a 2 mile nature trail from the car park beside the Cow Green Reservoir. Where the Tees and Pennine Way meet, the river explodes through an outlet at the foot of the dam. A few hundred yards lower, the mighty cascade drops some 200ft in a boiling foam of peaty water, falling away in a series of steps into the valley below.

Visitor centre: Easter-Oct, daily; also winter weekends. Adm charge. Shop. P Toilets. ♿ Tel Teesdale (0833) 22292.

BEAMISH: A JOURNEY BACK IN TIME

Life in the north-east around the beginning of the century is re-created on 200 acres of gently sloping hillside in the Beamish North of England Open-Air Museum. A clanking tram takes visitors to the museum's centrepiece, The Town. Here a general store has been brought from nearby Annfield Plain and stocked with the goods of the day, from Liberty bodices to biscuit tins. A row of town houses built around 1830 has been brought brick by brick from Gateshead, and people in contemporary costume talk to visitors about the life of the times.

A north-eastern railway station from the village of Rowley revives a vanished world of hissing steam locomotives, oil lamps, and signal boxes crammed with red-painted levers. Exhibits include a massive black-painted locomotive built by George Stephenson in 1822 and a monster Ruston Bucyrus 'steam navvy' built in 1931 and weighing 100 tons.

Agricultural life is displayed at Home Farm, little changed in layout for 200 years. Among its exhibits are old farm implements, a section devoted to farm horses and their harness, and a working blacksmith's forge. In a reconstructed colliery, visitors can put on hard hats and follow a former miner down the narrow, dripping tunnel of a drift mine to experience the conditions under which coal was extracted.

Off A1(M), 4 miles west of Chester-le-Street (Cc). All year, Nov-Mar, daily exc Mon. Adm charge. Refreshments. Shop. P *Toilets. Tel Stanley (0207) 231811.*

HEAVY GOING *Maintained in gleaming working order, this Mann steam tractor of 1928, on display at Home Farm, was built to pull a plough. But it proved too heavy to be a great success.*

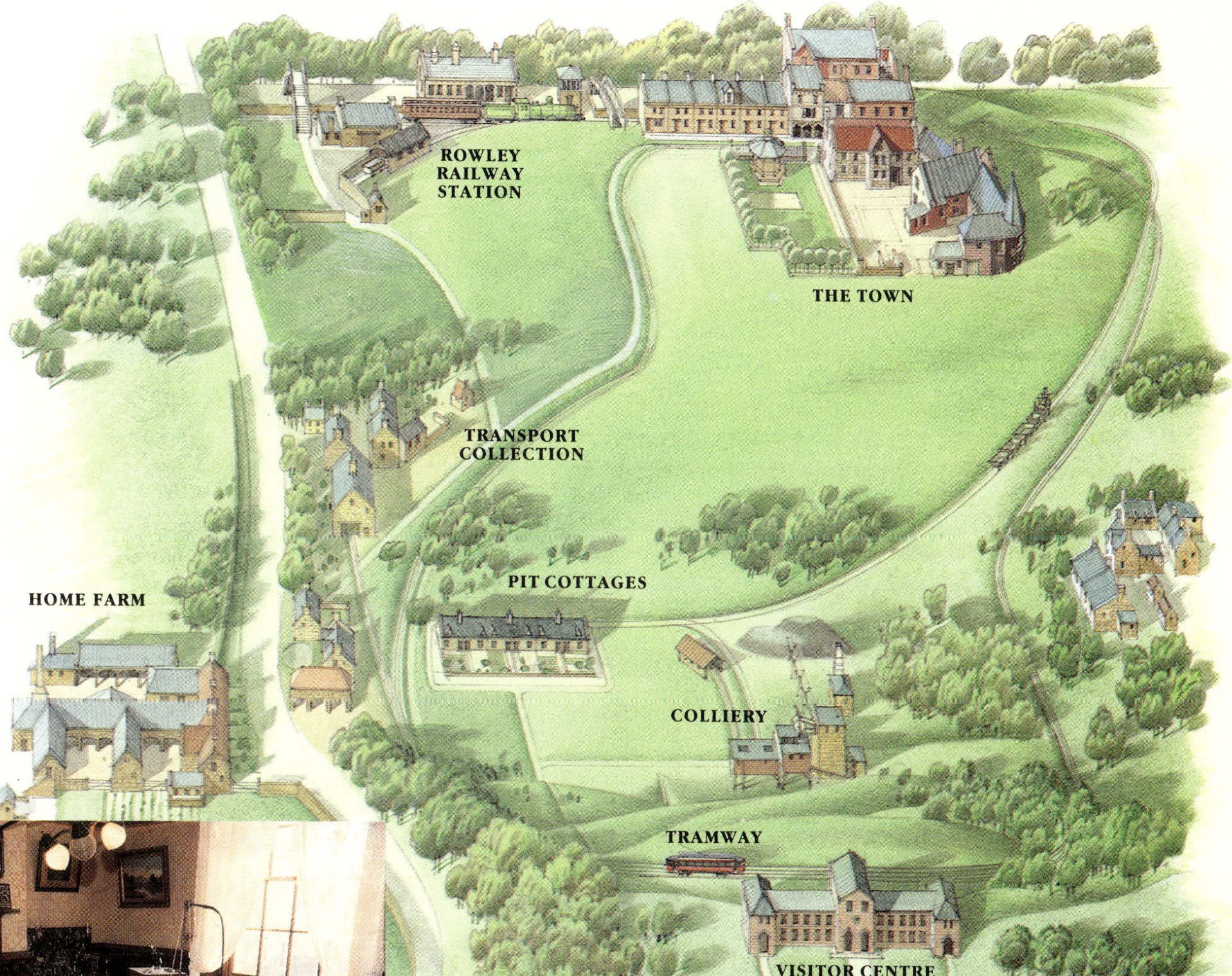

INTO MY PARLOUR *This dentist's surgery of the 1920s in The Town lulls the patient with its cosy atmosphere and glowing coal fire. The cast-iron dental chair has a foot-operated treadle drill.*

CASTLE EDEN DENE

Off A1086, 1 mile south of Peterlee (Db)

The coast from Seaham south to Hartlepool is deeply cut by a succession of denes – wooded ravines gouged out by the waters of the glaciers as they melted at the end of the last Ice Age some 10,000 years ago. The largest and finest of these denes, running inland for 4 miles, takes its name from the village of Castle Eden and is a designated National Nature Reserve. There is a visitor centre and car park at Oakerside Dene Lodge, Peterlee.

Visitors can enjoy the beauties of the dene from a network of footpaths on either side of the Castle Eden Burn. The rocks through which the stream has carved its channel are light yellow and white Permian limestones, which were exploited in previous centuries to make lime for building and agriculture. Trees of many varieties flourish along the valley, among them the yew trees for which the dene is famous.

As many as 70 species of birds have been recorded here, including pied, grey and yellow wagtails, goldcrests, kestrels and nuthatches. The dene has even given its name to a rare subspecies of butterfly, known as the Eden Argus.

NCC. All year, daily.

CAUSEY ARCH

Off A6076, 2 miles north of Stanley (Cc)

The mile-long gorge of the Causey Burn is spanned by the world's oldest railway bridge. A century or more before the advent of the steam locomotive, horse-drawn wagons laden with coal were being pulled along wooden 'wagonways' from inland coal mines to the Tyne, where the coal was transferred to barges. The Causey Arch, a graceful stone structure 100ft long and 80ft above the gorge, was built in 1725-6 to carry the wagonway which ran from the mining village of Tanfield north to the Tyne at Gateshead.

All year, daily.

DARLINGTON RAILWAY CENTRE AND MUSEUM

Off A167, 1 mile north of town centre (Cb)

With its sash windows, cream-painted walls and elegant colonnade, Darlington's North Road Station looks more like a small country mansion than one of the world's first railway stations. Dating from 1842, it declined into an unstaffed halt in the 1960s and became derelict. Just in time it was saved by the campaigning of a group of railway enthusiasts, and was restored and turned it into a museum commemorating the birth of the railway.

The museum was opened on September 27, 1975 – 150 years to the day after the historic opening of the Stockton and Darlington Railway. The railway was built to take coal from the South Durham coalfields near Shildon down to the River Tees at Stockton, via Darlington. But the railway company soon realised that the future lay with passengers as well as goods and in 1833 introduced regular steam-hauled passenger trains. The collection is built round two of the world's pioneer locomotives – the little *Locomotion*, built by Robert Stephenson & Company, which hauled the first-ever steam train on a public railway, in 1825, and the *Derwent* of 1845, designed by Timothy Hackworth, George Stephenson's successor as engineer to the Stockton and Darlington Railway.

The so-called 'Coffee Pot', which looks like a stove upended on a platform, was an efficient locomotive which hauled coal for almost a century. Railway paintings and photographs, posters and nameboards hang round the walls, and there are a number of superbly detailed scale models, some built by Darlington's rail workshop staff in their spare time. Train speeds may have increased from the *Locomotion*'s 12mph, but as this museum shows there is an unbroken continuity from George Stephenson to Inter-City.

All year, daily. Adm charge. Shop. **P** *Toilets.* ♿ *Tel Darlington (0325) 460532.*

DERWENT WALK COUNTRY PARK

Off A694, 1½ miles north of Consett (Bc)

A Roman fort, a ruined medieval chapel, a Statue of Liberty and an 18th-century furnace where wrought iron was heated in charcoal are among the relics of the past that lie in and around this fascinating country park. The walk from which it gets its name is along the former track of the Derwent Valley Railway, which closed in 1962, and in the 1970s was developed by Durham County Council as a footpath, bridleway and cycle track. Keeping close to the windings of the Derwent, it runs for 10½ miles from Shotley Bridge to the site of Swalwell Station, near Gateshead.

All year, daily.

DURHAM CATHEDRAL

In centre of city (Cc)

Towering majestically above a loop in the River Wear, Durham's cathedral, with the castle close by, makes an unforgettable picture of Norman splendour. During the Middle Ages the Prince-Bishops of Durham were the uncrowned kings of the north-east, and their twin strongholds recall the days when a bishop would wear a suit of armour one day and his religious vestments the next.

Inside the cathedral, the mighty columns of the nave, carved with zigzag Norman decoration, march with solemn tread towards the lofty bishop's throne and the high altar, behind which the body of St Cuthbert has been enshrined since 1104. At the western end, the many-pillared Galilee Chapel contains the tomb of the Venerable Bede below its graceful arches.

South of the nave, the cloisters provide a delightfully quiet green oasis. Opening off them is the Treasury, rich in silver-gilt chalices and church furnishings, together with St Cuthbert's 7th-century carved wood coffin, and the delicate gold cross buried with his body. Also off the cloisters is an audiovisual display on the saint.

Across the open space of Palace Green, the Norman castle is now given over to Durham University, though parts of it are open to the public. The only castle in northern England that was never captured by the Scots, it was the palace of the Prince-Bishops of Durham from 1072 to 1836. The chapel survives from Norman times, while the great hall was built about 1280.

NORMAN SANCTUARY *The west towers of Durham Cathedral rise to 144ft and the central tower is 11ft taller. The 12th-century knocker in the Treasury once graced the north door, and criminals could clasp it for sanctuary.*

Overshadowed by the great east end of the cathedral, the modest church of St Mary-le-Bow has been converted into Durham's Heritage Centre. Audiovisual displays cover facets of the city's history, architecture and natural history.

A beautiful tree-shaded riverside walk leads to the Archaeological Museum, below the western end of the cathedral. Housed in a former fulling mill, the collections span the earliest history of Durham, from the Stone Age, through the Romans, to the trades of the Middle Ages.

Cathedral: All year, daily. Free entry. Refreshments. Shop. Toilets. ♿ Tel Durham (091) 386 4266. Castle: All year, Mon, Wed and Sat pm; also Easter and Spring Bank Hol pm, and daily July-Sept. Adm charge. Tel (091) 386 5481. Heritage Centre: Late May-mid Sept. Adm charge. Archaeological Museum: All year, daily. Adm charge. Tel (091) 374 3623.

DURHAM LIGHT INFANTRY MUSEUM

Off A691, north of city centre (Cc)

The museum is a treasure house of souvenirs from historic battles, such as the chocolate box presented to the Durham Light Infantry by Queen Victoria after the Siege of Mafeking – with the original chocolates still inside. The museum covers the history of the British Empire from the 18th century onwards, for the DLI have been involved in almost every major military action over the last 200 years. Here is the musket ball that wounded Ensign Stretton at Vitoria, during the Napoleonic Wars; and there are souvenirs of the Indian Mutiny and relics of the two World Wars.

All year, daily exc Mon. Adm charge. Refreshments. P *Toilets. ♿ Tel Durham (091) 384 2214.*

DURHAM UNIVERSITY ORIENTAL MUSEUM

Off A1050, south of city centre (Cb)

This museum – the only one in Britain wholly devoted to Oriental art – houses a superb collection of Chinese ceramics from 2000 BC to the 18th century, including many outstandingly beautiful pieces of the Tang, Song and Ming dynasties. The collection of Chinese jade is unique in size and range. The art of Ancient Egypt and the Near East is also well represented, along with that of India, Asia and Japan.

Mar-Oct, daily; Nov-Feb, weekdays. Adm charge. P *Toilets. ♿ Tel Durham (091) 374 2911.*

FINCHALE PRIORY

Off A167, 3 miles north-east of Durham (Cc)

The monks of Durham Cathedral who chose Finchale (pronounced 'Finkle') as a holiday home certainly had an eye for their surroundings, for the priory stands in beautiful countryside on a bend in the River Wear, only 3 miles from Durham yet peaceful even today. A good proportion of the 13th-century buildings still stand to roof height, and make it easy to see the typical monastic layout. In the ruined church a cross on the floor marks the tomb of St Godric, a former pirate and merchant, who saw the error of his ways and retired to a hermitage at Finchale.

EH. All year, daily. Adm charge (summer only). Shop. P *Toilets. ♿ Tel Durham (091) 386 3828.*

LEAD RUSH *The overshot water wheel at Killhope in Upper Weardale measures 34ft across. It dates from the 1870s when the dale was as noted for its lead as the Klondyke was to become for gold.*

HAMSTERLEY FOREST

Off A68, 9 miles west of Bishop Auckland (Bb)

West of Bishop Auckland, rolling moorland rises to more than 1500ft. Here, most of the Forestry Commission's 5000 acre Hamsterley Forest is open to the public, who can enjoy it from a 4 mile Forest Drive or waymarked walks.

The six walks range in length from 1½ to 8 miles, and take in an enormous variety of terrain and scenery, along the streams, across the ridges between them and among plantations and woodland glades. Visitors who keep their eyes to the ground may see the 'slots' or footprints of the roe deer that roam the forest. Up in the trees, the cones of the pines and larches are attractive to red squirrels and also to crossbills. There is an information centre at the eastern end of the forest with displays of wildlife and forest management.

All year, daily. Toll for Forest Drive.

KILLHOPE WHEEL LEAD MINING CENTRE

On A689, 12 miles west of Stanhope (Ac)

High in the North Pennines, not far from the Cumbrian border, a giant iron water wheel looms over the bleak moorland of Upper Weardale. It supplied power to a crushing mill, where lead ore from the nearby Park Level mine was pulverised so that the metal could be extracted.

The mine and mill buildings have been restored as they were in the 1870s, complete with railways and primitive machinery. This is an open-air museum, for along a three-quarter-mile trail are displays of mining through the ages. Visitors may pan for lead, work the machinery – or play quoits.

Easter-Oct, daily. Adm charge. Shop. P *Toilets. Tel Weardale (0388) 537505.*

RABY CASTLE

On A688, 7 miles south-west of Bishop Auckland (Cb)

Herds of red and fallow deer graze in Raby's 200 acres of rolling parkland, which provides a peaceful foreground to the castle's massive battlemented walls and towers. The present castle was built towards the end of the 14th century by the powerful Nevill family, and remained largely unaltered until the 18th century, by which time it had come into the possession of the Vane family, ancestors of the present owner.

From about 1760 the interior was largely remodelled by the architects James Paine and John Carr. At the same time the park was landscaped and the formal gardens were laid out. A further building phase in the 1840s saw the addition of the unusual Octagon Drawing Room and the large dining room, both unexpectedly elegant for their period. Medieval Raby survives in the high, vaulted kitchen, the servants' hall (originally the guardroom) and the chapel.

The 18th-century coach yard contains a fine collection of horse-drawn vehicles, including two travelling chariots, a large state coach, and two fire engines complete with hoses. Among the features of the Walled Gardens are two yew hedges which may date back to the castle's foundation.

Easter, May and Spring Bank Hol weekends, Sat-Wed pm; May and June, Wed and Sun pm; July-Sept, pm daily exc Sat, but open Sat of Bank Hol weekend. Adm charge. Refreshments. Shop. P *Toilets. ♿ (park). Tel Staindrop (0833) 60202.*

WEARDALE MUSEUM

On A689, 8 miles west of Stanhope (Bb)

Built in 1760, High House Chapel is the second oldest Methodist chapel still in use. It is now a museum illustrating the rugged past life of the upper Wear valley. In the second half of the 18th century John Wesley often preached at Ireshopeburn nearby, and one room is given over to the history of religion in Weardale. Another room gives a picture of the life of a typical working family in the 1870s, while displays are devoted to farming, mining, landscape and wildlife.

July and Aug, daily; also Bank Hol, and Wed, Thur, Sat and Sun in May, June and Sept. Adm charge. Toilets. Tel Weardale (0388) 537417.

COUNTY CALENDAR

April (late). Barnard Castle (Lartington Park): Teesdale Country Show.

June (mid-month). Durham: Regatta.

July (mid-month). Durham: Miners' Gala. Lampton Park (off A183, 2 miles east of Chester-le-Street): Durham County Show.

August (mid-month). Darlington: Show. Durham Folk Festival.

September (early). Durham: Beer Festival.

September (mid-month). Stanhope: Show. Durham and Chester-le-Street: St Cuthbert's Fair.

Tourist information: Barnard Castle (0833) 3700; Darlington (0325) 469858; Durham (091) 384 3720; Peterlee (091) 586 4450.

ESSEX

CASTLES OLD AND NEW BETWEEN THE FORESTS AND THE SEA

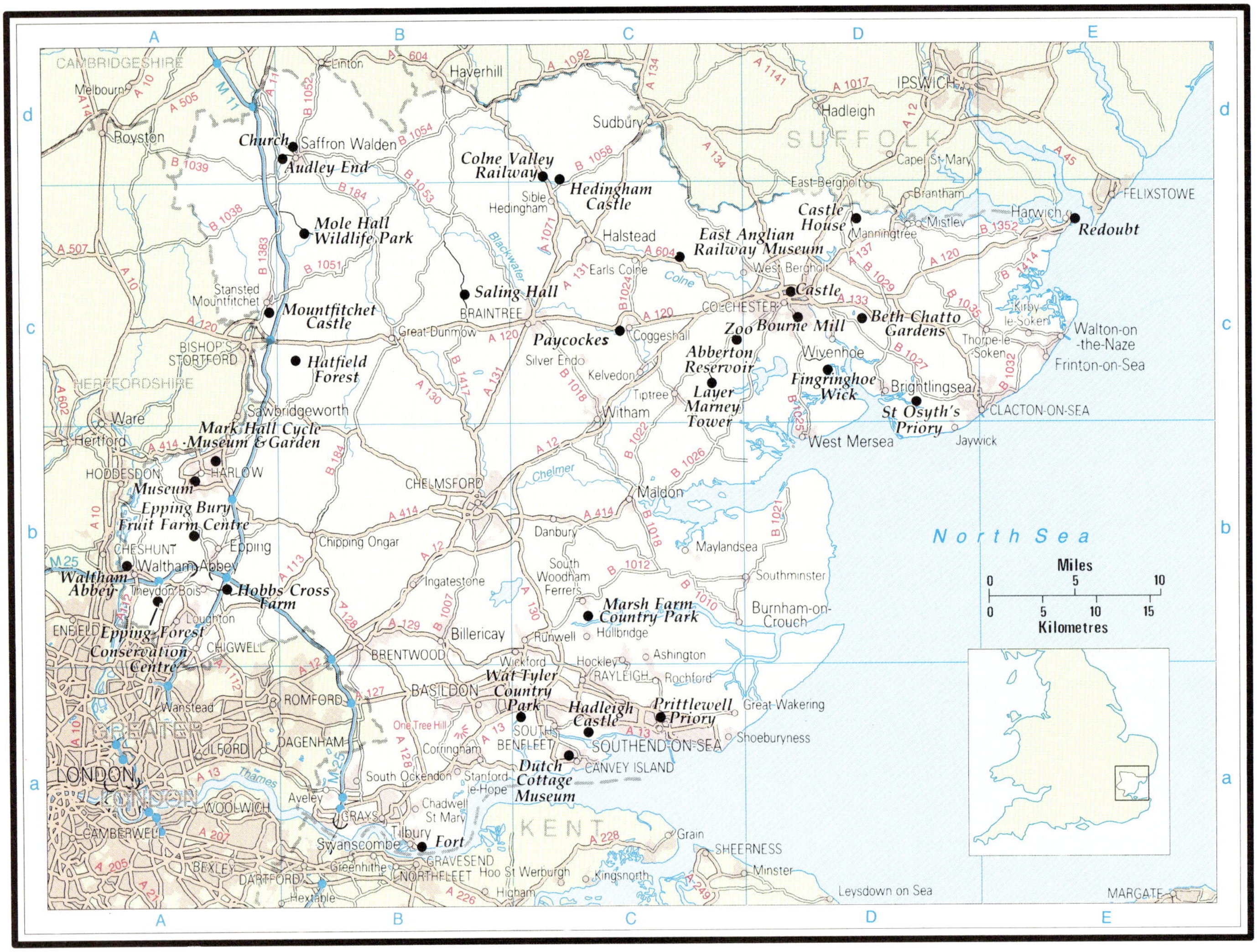

London's suburban fingers penetrate deep into the heart of Essex, but only a few miles beyond their tips are salt marshes where the only sound is that of seabirds, country towns whose centres have scarcely changed over the centuries, and gardens lovingly tended for generations.

Essex is a rich agricultural county and more and more farmers offer open days to give visitors the chance to see the seasonal round of activities. But there are, too, traditional attractions: great houses, represented by the Jacobean splendours of Audley End; fascinating smaller houses such as Paycocke's merchant's house in Coggeshall, with its wealth of carved woodwork so characteristic of the county; medieval castles, some long reduced to romantic ruin, such as Hadleigh, others still family homes such as Layer Marney Tower.

At the heart of Essex is the great forest of Epping, where trees have provided green shade and tranquillity since before the Romans came.

ABBERTON RESERVOIR

Off B1026, 4 miles south of Colchester (Dc)

Tufted ducks, pochards, mallards, goldeneye and shovelers are among the ducks that flock to Abberton Reservoir in their thousands in winter. The reservoir is also a natural resting place for birds on their way to or from their breeding grounds in north-west Europe and Asia, and rare grebes and divers can sometimes be seen. The public are admitted to three specially constructed birdwatching sites in the bird sanctuary. The two causeways are also good points for birdwatching. *All year, daily. Adm charge.* P *Toilets.*

AUDLEY END

On B1383, 1 mile west of Saffron Walden (Bd)

'Too large for a king – but might do for a Lord Treasurer', King James I said when his Lord Treasurer Sir Thomas Howard proudly showed him round the house of Audley End that he had just completed. The king had probably contributed – unwittingly – to the building of the house, for in 1619 Howard was found guilty of embezzlement and committed to the Tower of London. He was later released, and died in disgrace – but back in his splendid house – in 1626. What is visible today is barely half the original building, for it was too expensive to maintain and much of it was demolished in the 18th century; even the remains form one of the biggest houses in Britain.

Audley End was a family home for nearly 400 years, and successive occupants altered it to conform with current fashions – sometimes with confusing results. In the 18th century, for example, Robert Adam was commissioned to turn some old-fashioned rooms on the ground floor into a suite of reception rooms. The 19th-century owner of the house, however, had a poor opinion of 18th-century taste and turned these handsome rooms into bedrooms, transferring the reception suite to the first floor. The Jacobean appearance of the Great Hall was re-created by furnishings and pictures placed there only in the late 1820s.

If the visitor emerges a little bewildered by the riches in the house, the beautiful grounds are a place for relaxation. They were laid out by

Capability Brown in 1762, and though there have been many subsequent adaptations they still conform to his idea. Dotted around the park are ornamental buildings in the classical style, such as the Temple of Concord, erected in 1790 to celebrate George III's recovery from his first attack of insanity, and an exquisite Palladian bridge.

A 20th-century addition to Audley End's attractions is the Audley End Railway, a $10\frac{1}{4}$in gauge line built entirely by members of the estate and farm staff in the early 1960s. Starting from a station near the coach park, trains take passengers on a $1\frac{1}{2}$ mile circular route, passing through a woodland garden and over the River Cam.

EH. Apr-mid Oct, daily exc Mon, and Bank Hol Mon. Adm charge. Refreshments. Shop. P *Toilets.* ♿ *(ground floor and gardens). Tel Saffron Walden (0799) 22399. Railway: Apr-Oct, Sat, Sun and Bank Hol pm. Tel (0799) 22354.*

BATTLESBRIDGE ANTIQUES CENTRE

Off A130, 8 miles south of Chelmsford

Five buildings which have stood beside the River Crouch since the 17th and 18th centuries have been carefully restored and adapted to modern use. The Old Granary, for example, has been reclad in traditional Essex boarding instead of the tin cladding that once covered it, and there is a craft centre on the ground floor with a showroom above. Nearby stand Cromwell House, the Haybarn, Bridgebarn and Muggeridge Farm.

The 45 dealers represented at Battlesbridge sell a wide range of antiques, from jewellery to militaria and including even coin-operated amusement machines. There are two pubs, and tearooms.

All year, Wed-Sun. Free entry. Refreshments. Shop. P *Toilets. Tel Wickford (0268) 734005.*

BETH CHATTO GARDENS

On A133, ¼ mile east of Elmstead Market (Dc)

Until 1960 the site of these gardens was simply an overgrown wilderness. Farmers saw no use for land which was too dry on the gravel slope, or too waterlogged in the hollow. Over some 21 years, however, its owners turned its apparent disadvantages to good use. Native plants died on the gravel bed – but Mediterranean plants, with their preference for dry hot soils, flourished. The waterlogged area proved ideal for water gardens and their moisture-loving plants, and now presents a linked chain of pools.

More than 1000 different species of herbaceous plants present a glowing, living catalogue which garden lovers can enjoy for their own sake or study to glean ideas for the improvement of their own gardens.

Mar-Oct, Mon-Sat; Nov-Feb, Mon-Fri. Adm charge. P *(limited). Tel Colchester (0206) 222007.*

BOURNE MILL

Off B1025, 1 mile south of Colchester (Dc)

Curved and stepped gables and stone mullioned windows give Bourne Mill more the look of an elegant Tudor mansion than a workaday mill. Indeed, its builder in 1591, Sir Thomas Lucas, may well have intended it as a fishing lodge before he decided to use it for grinding corn, like its predecessor which had stood on the site since the 12th century. After the Civil War, the mill was taken over by Dutch refugees who converted it to clothmaking. The wool trade declined in the 1820s and the mill was converted back to grinding corn, but by 1914 all operations had ceased. The National Trust has restored the mill machinery to working order.

NT. Mid Apr-mid Oct, Sat, Sun and Bank Hol Mon pm; July-Sept, Tues pm also. Adm charge. Tel Colchester (0206) 572422.

SCALED DOWN *Demolition work in the 18th century reduced Audley End to its present still impressive size and turned it into a manageable country house. Its magnificent interior was remodelled in the 19th century, when the oak-panelled Great Hall (right) was hung with pictures of the nobility – including the house's owners in the 16th and 17th centuries.*

CASTLE HOUSE

Off B1029, 7 miles north-east of Colchester (Dc)

In 1919 the East Anglian artist Alfred Munnings purchased Castle House, 'the house of my dreams', where he was to live until he died in 1959. In 1965 a Trust took over the house and extensive grounds, and arranged the house as a gallery for the many important paintings of this most English of artists.

Munnings had a profound contempt for 'modern' art, believing that painting should be realistic, and took little trouble to hide his beliefs. As the paintings in this gallery show, he exulted in landscapes, and in portraying events in East Anglian life such as horse fairs and racecourses. In the courtyard, look for the drawings Munnings made with a sharp piece of wood on the newly plastered wall before it was dry.

May-Sept, Sun, Wed and Bank Hol Mon; also Thur and Sat in Aug. Adm charge. P *Toilets. Tel Colchester (0206) 322127.*

COLCHESTER CASTLE

In centre of Colchester (Dc)

The massive keep of Colchester Castle as it appears today was built by the Normans about 1076; but its history goes much farther back, for it stands on the immense stone podium or base of the Roman Temple of Claudius. The Saxons probably knew it as King Coel's Palace – the Old King Cole of the nursery rhyme. The Normans dug a ditch around it and threw the excavated earth on top of the Roman foundations to make a mound. Subsequently, they used the stones of the temple to build their keep.

Throughout most of the Middle Ages the castle was a royal fortress. During the Civil War Colchester was held for the King, and after its surrender two Royalist commanders were shot in the castle bailey; the spot is now marked with an obelisk. The castle today houses the Colchester and Essex Museum, which traces the castle's long history.

All year, daily. Adm charge. Shop. Tel Colchester (0206) 712481.

FULL STEAM AHEAD *The signal box at the end of Platform 3 at the East Anglian Railway Museum (top right) controls operations on steam days, when visitors can watch the signalman at work. Like many of the museum's exhibits it was saved from demolition and is now a listed structure. The red-brick station buildings and covered footbridge (above) are fine examples of Victorian architecture. The bridge's double staircase links the approach road and parking and picnic areas with the railway platforms and the restored booking hall. Two tank engines stand outside the former goods shed (left), which has been restored to its original 1880 appearance and is used to demonstrate the handling of freight and to house exhibitions and special events.*

COLCHESTER ZOO

Off B1022, 3 miles south-west of Colchester (Cc)

Set in 40 acres of beautiful parkland belonging to Stanway Hall this privately owned zoo specialises in rare and endangered species such as Cape hunting dogs, snow leopards and Siberian tigers. Other animals include bears, zebras, deer, antelopes, otters and chimpanzees. In summer there are falconry displays, sea-lion shows and penguin parades.

Children are particularly well catered for with their own 'Familiar Friends' enclosure, full of all kinds of small, friendly animals, and the Safari Express Miniature Railway runs alongside the park's lake, past bird, wolf and rhino enclosures. Visitors can become 'Friends' of the zoo and, for an annual donation, adopt their own animals.

All year, daily. Adm charge. Refreshments. Shop. P *Toilets.* ♿ *Tel Colchester (0206) 330252.*

COLNE VALLEY RAILWAY

On A604, 1 mile north of Sible Hedingham (Cd)

Painstaking care by local railway enthusiasts has restored part of the old Colne Valley and Halstead Railway, abandoned by British Rail in 1962. Trains set out from a newly built station, composed of authentic Victorian buildings threatened with destruction where they stood and moved to this site. Along the two platforms are a bookshop, and a reconstruction of an early 19th-century ticket and booking office. There are also a platform dock where cattle and merchandise could be handled, a signal box and a water column.

The locomotives and other rolling stock can be inspected daily, and there are rides along a mile of track on many summer weekends. The Pullman car *Gwen* has been restored to its Edwardian elegance. Near the station complex is a wildlife conservation area, with a picnic site.

Easter-Dec 23, daily; rides Easter-Oct, 1st and 3rd Sun of each month, and Bank Hol Sun and Mon; also each Sun in June, July and Aug. Adm charge. Refreshments. Shop. P *Toilets. Tel Hedingham (0787) 61174.*

DUTCH COTTAGE MUSEUM

On A130 at Canvey Island (Ca)

The cottage is a reminder of the endless battles that have been fought against the sea along all this low-lying coast of England. Built in 1618, it was probably used as a workman's cottage while land was being reclaimed from the water to join the five islands of Canvey into one. It owes its name to the fact that the work of reclamation was done by Dutch workmen under the direction of the engineer Cornelius Vermuyden, whose portrait hangs in the museum.

Entering the cottage, a visitor's first impression is of the lowness of the ceiling. In fact, it is the floor which has risen: originally the floor was made of beaten earth and shells, but since then five separate layers have been spread over the first layer, the topmost one being of rough brick. Exhibits reflect the life and work of the Essex coastline. Ancient eel spears lie on the window-ledge of the living room, as if ready for instant use.

Upstairs, a tiny bedroom has been furnished in the style of the period. The long, narrow Dutch cradle is a replica, but the Dutch bonnet in it was made by a refugee at the time of the French Revolution. It was presented to the museum by a descendant of its original owner.

Spring Bank Hol-Sept, Wed and Sun pm; Bank Hol all day. Free entry. Shop. Tel South Benfleet (0268) 794005.

EAST ANGLIAN RAILWAY MUSEUM

On A604, 6 miles west of Colchester (Cc)

The smell of steam and hot metal and the rhythmic chuffing of vintage locomotives bring back the age of steam, in a genuine working museum run by volunteers. Based on a Victorian country station called Chappel and Wakes Colne, the museum has a collection of passenger and freight coaches tracing the development of railways over 100 years.

Relics from many closed stations have been brought together in re-creating one platform as a typical East Anglian halt, of the type that was once so much a part of our railway scene. Visitors can see restoration work in progress, from the reconstruction of vintage wooden coaches to heavy engineering overhauls on the locomotives. On steam days the entrance charge includes quarter-mile rides on the trains.

All year, daily. Adm charge. Refreshments. Shop. P *Toilets. Tel Earls Colne (078 75) 2571.*

EPPING BURY FRUIT FARM CENTRE

Off B182, 2 miles north of Epping (Ab)

Unlike most 'pick-your-own' fruit farms, Bury Farm is an organic farm with an educational function. Displays and working models show how such a farm is maintained. Visitors can learn

how a mole helps to drain a field; how the beds in which the fruit and vegetables grow are made up; and what a 'gooseberry sawfly' does. A mile-long 'herbal fruit trail' identifies plants which have been used since the 17th century to make beauty aids, alcoholic drinks and medicinal cures.
Late June-end Sept, daily. Adm charge. Refreshments. Shop. P *Toilets. Tel Epping (0378) 78400.*

EPPING FOREST CONSERVATION CENTRE

Off A104, 3½ miles south-west of Epping (Ab)

Barely 12 miles from central London lies one of Europe's oldest forests. Epping Forest runs in an immense green crescent covering some 6000 acres, from the town of Epping in the north to Wanstead in the south. Densely populated built-up areas press against its eastern flanks like the seas against a peninsula. It is crisscrossed by roads, but it is still a genuine forest, and so large that first-time visitors who want to leave the highway and explore its hidden depths would be well advised to make first for the Conservation Centre at High Beach to get their bearings.

The centre, a modest collection of single-storey buildings buried deep in the forest, has displays giving a bird's-eye view of the forest's history, as well as details of the animals and birds which inhabit it and its rich plant life. Particularly valuable are the easy-to-follow 'trail guides'. Each of these covers a different section of the forest, guiding the walker through the labyrinth of footpaths and bridleways, and also drawing attention to natural and man-made features seen on the route.
Easter-Oct, daily; Nov-Easter, Sat-Sun.

FINGRINGHOE WICK

Off B1025, 3 miles south of Colchester (Dc)

Set in a 125 acre disused gravel pit near the estuary of the River Colne is one of the richest wildlife sanctuaries in Essex, particularly noted for its huge gatherings of Brent geese, dunlins and curlews in winter. At the heart of the sanctuary is the Fingringhoe Centre, headquarters of the Essex Naturalists' Trust which created the reserve by purchasing the worked-out pit in 1961. The centre, though modern in design, incorporates farm buildings which have survived from the 19th century. Displays illustrate the range of Essex wildlife, and there are a number of nature trails through the reserve, including one for disabled visitors.
All year, daily. Free entry (donations). Refreshments. Shop. P *Toilets. Tel Colchester (0206) 28678.*

HADLEIGH CASTLE

Off A13, 5 miles west of Southend-on-Sea (Ca)

The approach to Hadleigh Castle is dramatic. After negotiating the narrow streets and heavy traffic of residential Leigh-on-Sea, the visitor suddenly finds himself on the open downlands, with a tremendous view across the marshes and the Thames Estuary. The castle was built by Hubert de Burgh, Earl of Kent, in 1230, but was seized by Henry III nine years later. Thereafter it remained in the hands of the Crown.

The castle was last occupied in the mid-16th century, and had become a total ruin by the end of the 17th century. But there are still sufficient remains from the 13th and 14th centuries to remind visitors of its powerful past.
EH. All year, daily.

HARLOW MUSEUM

In Harlow, near town centre (Ab)

The museum is housed in a handsome Georgian building known as Passmores House, after the Passemer family who lived in an earlier house on the site in the Middle Ages. Although most of the present house was built in 1727, it incorporates parts of a much older building, and one arm of a medieval moat survives at the back of the house. The exhibitions tell the history of Harlow from Roman times onward. A model showing the area as it looked before the building of the new town is the central feature of a room devoted to the medieval history of the locality.
All year, daily. Free entry. Shop. P *Toilets. Tel Harlow (0279) 446 422.*

HARWICH REDOUBT

Off main road, near centre of Harwich (Ec)

As many as 300 soldiers could live under siege conditions in this huge fortress, built in about 1810 to protect the port of Harwich against the threat of invasion by Napoleon. The redoubt was armed again in the World Wars, but later it was abandoned and deteriorated into little more than a rubbish dump until, in 1969, volunteers of the Harwich Society began to restore the site to its 19th-century state.

Today, visitors cross a bridge over a 20ft deep dry moat to enter the redoubt. At its heart is a central parade ground 85ft across. The walls of the redoubt are 3ft thick, and within them can be seen the mountings of the hoists used to raise shells from the ammunition store to the gun positions. A 12 ton cannon, found among the rubbish in the moat, has been remounted.
Easter-end Oct, Sun. Adm charge. Refreshments. Tel Harwich (0255) 503429.

HATFIELD FOREST

Off A120, 4 miles east of Bishop's Stortford (Bc)

The long, straight avenues or 'rides' that cut through Hatfield Forest, interspersed with a number of open 'chases', are a reminder of the time when the forest was a royal hunting preserve. While many of England's former hunting forests have changed their nature over the years, Hatfield came into the hands of a family who maintained its medieval features, and its new owners, the National Trust, are restoring the forest as closely as possible to its original appearance.

A National Trust shop has been established in the unusual Shell House, built in 1757 beside a lake. Designed as a grotto, its walls are decorated with flints, shells, clinker and fragments of glass. There is good fishing on the lake, where great crested grebes nest, and kestrels and sparrow-hawks can be seen in the woodland. The red deer died out during the First World War, but fallow deer are common.
NT. All year, daily.

HEDINGHAM CASTLE

On B1058, 4 miles north-west of Halstead (Cd)

Towering up from its great green mound or 'motte', Hedingham is a remarkably unspoilt example of a Norman keep. Dating from about 1140, it had a fine new house built in the Outer Bailey in 1719. The keep has maintained most of its 12th-century features including its four floors and roof, and the minstrels' gallery overlooking the great Banqueting Hall, which itself has the largest surviving Norman arch in Europe. The bridge which spans the dry moat is early Tudor – built in about 1496 to replace the original drawbridge. There was probably once a well in the keep, and a tunnel which emerged near the fishponds.

The castle was built by the De Veres, Earls of Oxford – one of whom is claimed by some to have been the true author of the plays usually attributed to Shakespeare.
Easter then May-Oct, daily. Adm charge. Refreshments. Shop. P *Toilets. Tel Hedingham (0787) 60261.*

HOBBS CROSS FARM

Off A113, 1½ miles east of Theydon Bois (Ab)

Three times every day, at 5am, 2pm and 8pm, the pretty black-and-white Friesian cows come into the milking parlour at Hobbs Cross Farm to be milked and fed. There is a viewing gallery from which the visitor can see the afternoon milking, and afterwards follow the process of bottling and preparing the milk for distribution. Among other farm animals to be seen are calves, chickens, ducks, geese, hens, piglets and sows.
All year, daily. Adm charge. Refreshments. Shop. P *Toilets.* ♿ *Tel Theydon Bois (037 881) 2882.*

LAYER MARNEY TOWER

Off B1022, 7 miles south-west of Colchester (Cc)

Compared with a modern office block or even a medieval church, Layer Marney Tower is not particularly high – just 90ft. But its total unexpectedness in the flat countryside and the fact that it is flanked by relatively low domestic buildings give it a commanding presence.

Henry, 1st Lord Marney, who built the tower in 1520, doubtless intended it to be simply the gatehouse to a far grander building. But with his death in 1523 and that of his son two years later, the short-lived barony became extinct. Lord Marney had accompanied Henry VIII to the fabulous Field of the Cloth of Gold, and there had seen and been influenced by the new Italian style of architecture that was entering France. Terracotta was an outstanding feature of this new style, and Lord Marney used it extensively when designing his grand new house.

The lavish use of glass on the tower betrays its purpose: it was built for prestige, not defence. A number of these tower houses were springing up all over England in the 15th and early 16th centuries. The second floor of the tower is set out as an exhibition area where documents relating to the history of the house are on display.
Apr-Sept, Thur and Sun pm, and Bank Hol, also Tues in July and Aug. Adm charge. Refreshments. P *Tel Colchester (0206) 330202.*

MARK HALL CYCLE MUSEUM AND GARDENS

In First Avenue, Harlow, off A414 (Ab)

More than 70 beautifully restored exhibits in this unusual museum show the development of the bicycle over more than 150 years. The oldest exhibit is a 'hobby horse', built in 1818. It consists simply of a frame, two wheels and a saddle on which the rider sat and propelled himself by striding along the ground. Though today it looks like a child's toy, it is in fact the forerunner of the modern bicycle. Other exhibits include penny-farthings and early safety bicycles. Behind the museum are three superb walled gardens.

All year, daily. Free entry. Shop. P *Toilets.* ♿ *Tel Harlow (0279) 39680.*

MARSH FARM COUNTRY PARK

Off B1012, at South Woodham Ferrers (Cb)

On the very edge of the new town of South Woodham Ferrers, sea, sky and marshland melt into each other in an immemorial pattern. Marsh Farm Country Park is helping to preserve this beautiful, but fragile, balance of nature. Visitors can see over the stock farm of some 320 acres, on low-lying reclaimed marshland, and view the cattle, sheep and pigs at close range, under cover; to make this possible the animals are kept housed, and fed on hay, longer than in more traditional farms.

All year, daily. Free entry. Refreshments. Shop. P

MOLE HALL WILDLIFE PARK

Off B1383, 4½ miles south of Saffron Walden (Bc)

Exotic creatures such as wallabies, chimps and guanacos from South America are among the residents of this privately owned park. There are also otters, fallow deer and Highland cattle – and even an entire 'village' for guinea pigs. In the moat that separates the 13th-century Mole Hall manor house from the rest of the estate, wildfowl make their home. The butterfly pavilion houses exotic species including tarantulas, scorpions and hissing cockroaches, as well as rare species of native British butterflies.

All year, daily. Adm charge. Refreshments. Shop. P *Toilets. Tel Saffron Walden (0799) 40400.*

MOUNTFITCHET CASTLE

Off B1051, 2 miles north of Bishop's Stortford (Ac)

To visit this snug complex of crude wooden buildings on their hilltop is to step back 800 years into the past. Everything has been reconstructed in the last few years – but the painstaking research that preceded the construction guarantees that the visitor is exploring a Norman castle just as it would have appeared only a few years after the Norman Conquest.

Most of the original Mountfitchet Castle disappeared in 1215, when King John razed the fortifications and the local villagers lost no time in carrying off the valuable stone. Thereafter the site was overgrown and forgotten by all but local folk and archaeologists, until the present owner decided to rebuild the castle.

It consists simply of a mound, crowned with a wooden palisade inside which are separate wooden buildings. Although the present palisade looks deeply rooted, it is in fact freestanding, for the earthworks on the mound are protected by law and may not be disturbed.

Reeds and wheatstraw were used for the thatching, and the walls are of wattle-and-daub plastering. Among the displays in the reconstructed buildings is a blacksmith's forge and a brewery.

Mid Mar-mid Nov, daily. Adm charge. Refreshments. Shop. P *Toilets. Tel Bishop's Stortford (0279) 813237.*

PAYCOCKE'S

Near centre of Coggeshall (Cc)

The casual visitor to Coggeshall could easily pass by this handsome timber-framed building, so modestly does it line up with its neighbours along the street. It is, however, not only a remarkable example of a medieval house, the home of a wealthy merchant, but also an example of how chance can decide the fate of a priceless part of our heritage.

The house was built about 1500 by a local clothier, John Paycocke. By 1890, after passing through various hands, it needed a new roof and front windows and the owner decided to demolish it; the beautifully carved woodwork, which today is so outstanding a feature of the house, was actually sold. Then, just in time, a local antiquary got the sale of the woodwork cancelled; the house was restored, and later it was presented to the National Trust. Following its policy of giving its residential properties a 'lived-in' look, the house is let out to a tenant, but the public are admitted at certain times.

The National Trust has provided contemporary furniture for the house. The woodwork, an outstanding example of Tudor woodcarving, has also been restored so that, both inside and outside, Paycocke's today looks much as it would have done nearly 500 years ago.

NT. Mid Apr-mid Oct, Tues, Thur, Sun and Bank Hol Mon pm. Adm charge. Tel Coggeshall (0376) 61305.

PRITTLEWELL PRIORY

In Priory Park, Southend-on-Sea (Ca)

At first sight, Prittlewell Priory and its surroundings look like an attractive, but not particularly unusual, public park, with a couple of ornamental lakes and what appears to be an early 19th-century building. The lakes, in fact, are fishponds created by monks more than 800 years ago to stock the carp upon which they fed on fasting days. And behind the early 19th-century façade, a substantial part of a 12th-century Cluniac priory survives. The Refectory, where the monks ate their communal meals, is a particularly impressive hall, and the prior's chamber is notable for its magnificent timber roof.

Another remarkable survival in the heart of modern Southend is the moated medieval manor house of Southchurch Hall. Built in the 13th century it later became a farmhouse and passed through many hands until, in 1927, the Borough of Southend turned it into a museum. The Great Hall is exactly as it would have appeared in the 13th century, rising straight up to the roof without an upper floor. It has been set out with furnishings in the medieval manner, surrounding an open hearth in the centre.

Both museums: All year, Tues-Sat; closed Bank Hol. Free entry. Shop. P *Tel Southend (0702) 330214.*

SAFFRON WALDEN CHURCH

In centre of Saffron Walden (Bd)

The spire of St Mary's gazes down on the ancient tiled roofs, the maze on the common and the Norman castle of this pretty market town. In fact, the spire is much younger than any of these surroundings, since it was built in the 1830s. The church beneath it, however, dates from at least 400 years earlier. Its abbey-like proportions – 184ft long by 50ft high – reflect the town's prosperity in the late Middle Ages. Much of this was due to the saffron flower, *Crocus sativus*, from which a golden-yellow dye was produced. It is remembered in the name of the town and in the carvings high up in the arches of the church.

Prominently on view is the Banner of the Order of the Garter which belonged to the politician Lord Butler of Saffron Walden ('Rab' Butler) who died in 1982, and is buried in the churchyard. Nearby a black slate monument commemorates Lord Audley, Chancellor of England, who presided over the court that sentenced Sir Thomas More to death.

Tucked away just behind the church are Bridge End Gardens, a delightful survival from Victorian England. The area they occupy is small, but they are designed to give the visitor the impression of a series of gardens, each with its own vista. The Dutch Garden, with its formal clipped yews and fountain, is best seen from the special viewing platform. Poets' Corner, Jacob's Well and the entrancing little Grotto each has its own atmosphere. Just beyond a wrought-iron gate a Victorian maze has been replanted.

All year, daily. Free entry. P

ST OSYTH'S PRIORY

Off B1027, 3 miles west of Clacton-on-Sea (Dc)

Peacocks proudly flaunting themselves before a massive medieval gatehouse; a tranquil water garden glowing with multicoloured water lilies; a beautiful house crammed with art treasures and a sense of hundreds of years of history – all these combine to make St Osyth's Priory an unforgettable landmark. The visitor enters it through the immensely strong gatehouse, richly decorated with carvings, which stoutly protected the original priory from the outside world. Inside the walled precincts are the Great Barn, built in the 16th century, the dramatic Abbot's Tower and the sumptuous Bishop's Lodgings, all set in beautifully maintained grounds.

Easter, then May-Sept, daily. Adm charge. Refreshments. P *Tel Clacton-on-Sea (0255) 820242.*

SALING HALL

Off A120, 6 miles north-west of Braintree (Bc)

There is a church in the grounds of Saling Hall, and approaching the house the visitor passes a duck pond which was evidently the original village horse pond before the 18th-century enclosure of the village green. The present house was built about 1570 and was then altered and improved by a lawyer, Martin Carter, in 1698. It was Carter who built the beautiful walled garden which is a distinctive feature of Saling Hall.

The garden and surrounding grounds were rather run down when the present owner acquired the house in 1972, but have now been lovingly restored and given additional features. The huge elms of Saling which were recorded two centuries ago fell victim to Dutch elm disease, but the Lombardy poplars that link village to church and were planted in 1936 continue to flourish. Much of what is visible are new plantings in an ancient framework, with such inspired additions as a Japanese garden whose pattern of rock-work is taken from a Kyoto monastery.

Mid May-July, and Sept-mid Oct, Wed, Thur and Fri pm. Adm charge. P *(limited). Toilets.* ♿ *Tel Great Dunmow (0371) 850141.*

TILBURY FORT

Off A126, ½ mile east of Tilbury (Ba)

An immense modern concrete embankment, part of the Thames tidal control, now separates Tilbury Fort from the river, but behind the embankment the fort looks much as it would have done when built more than 300 years ago. The dominant feature on the river side is the handsome Watergate, which originally allowed direct access to the river. Ranged on either side of it are gun lines, sited to provide, together with the sister fort at Gravesend, a withering crossfire over the Thames.

Tilbury is today probably the best surviving example of 17th-century military engineering in Britain. Although there have been fortifications on this site since 1539, the present building dates mostly from the 1670s and its low, squat construction was the response to improved artillery. An ingenious system of triple moats surrounds it on three sides. Apart from the Watergate there is only one other entrance, the Landport Gate, which is approached over a series of drawbridges. Inside, powder magazines are buried deep inside the bastions and covered with earth. The heart of the fort consists of an immense parade ground, with officers' quarters along one side. The chapel and guardhouse remain intact, and a small military museum is established in one of the magazines.

All year, daily. Adm charge. P *Toilets. Tel Tilbury (037 52) 78489.*

A FORT REBUILT *One of the principal Norman fortresses in Essex was Mountfitchet Castle, destroyed by King John to revenge himself on Richard de Montfitchet, one of the barons who forced the king to set his seal to Magna Carta. The fort has been re-created on its original site, historically accurate in both shape and size, with a whitewashed Grand Hall (top) and a fenced falconry in front of it. The stone throwing catapult (above) would have been used to defend the fort against attackers using the wooden siege tower (right).*

WALTHAM ABBEY

Off A112, in Waltham Abbey (Ab)

Dominating this small attractive town is an immense church built of white stone which seems to glow even on a dull day. Large though the church is, it represents only the surviving part of a huge abbey founded by Harold, the last Saxon king of England, around the year 1060. The monks were dispersed by Henry VIII in 1540, and new owners used much of the abbey's stone to build a large house. The abbey church itself became the parish church.

Today, the site of the abbey is a public park, dotted with the ruins of the great building. The gatehouse, a massive, isolated tower, survives on the edge of a little stream. Built of brick, it was originally the main entrance into the abbey grounds. Most of the encircling walls of the abbey remain, and a circuit of these walls gives some idea of the size of the original building.

All year, daily.

WAT TYLER COUNTRY PARK

Off A13, 1 mile south of Basildon (Ca)

The 120 acres of this beautiful and richly varied park are dedicated to the people of Essex and Kent who, under Wat Tyler, took part in the Peasants' Revolt of 1381. Until a few years ago the land was literally a blasted heath, but since its official opening in 1984 the park has undergone extensive development, offering country-loving visitors nature trails set in peaceful, natural surroundings.

Watersports, including a 100-berth marina and the world's first motorboat museum, are an appropriate theme of the park, as it is bounded on three sides by water. There is also opportunity for birdwatching and a folk custom museum is planned illustrating local history

All year, daily. Tel Basildon (0268) 550088.

COUNTY CALENDAR

June Great Dunmow: Flitch Trial (test of happy marriage).

June (mid-month). Chelmsford: Essex County Show.

June (end of month). Colchester: Summer Show.

July (mid-month). Manningtree (Lawford House Park): Tendring Hundred Show.

August Layer Marney Tower: Jousting and Country Fair.

August (end). Burnham-on-Crouch: Regatta Week.

October 20 Colchester: Oyster Feast.

Tourist information: Clacton-on-Sea (0255) 423400; Colchester (0206) 46379; Maldon (0621) 56503; Saffron Walden (0799) 24282; Southend-on-Sea (0702) 355122.

GLOUCESTERSHIRE

VILLAGES IN THE COTSWOLDS AND A CITY BESIDE THE SEVERN

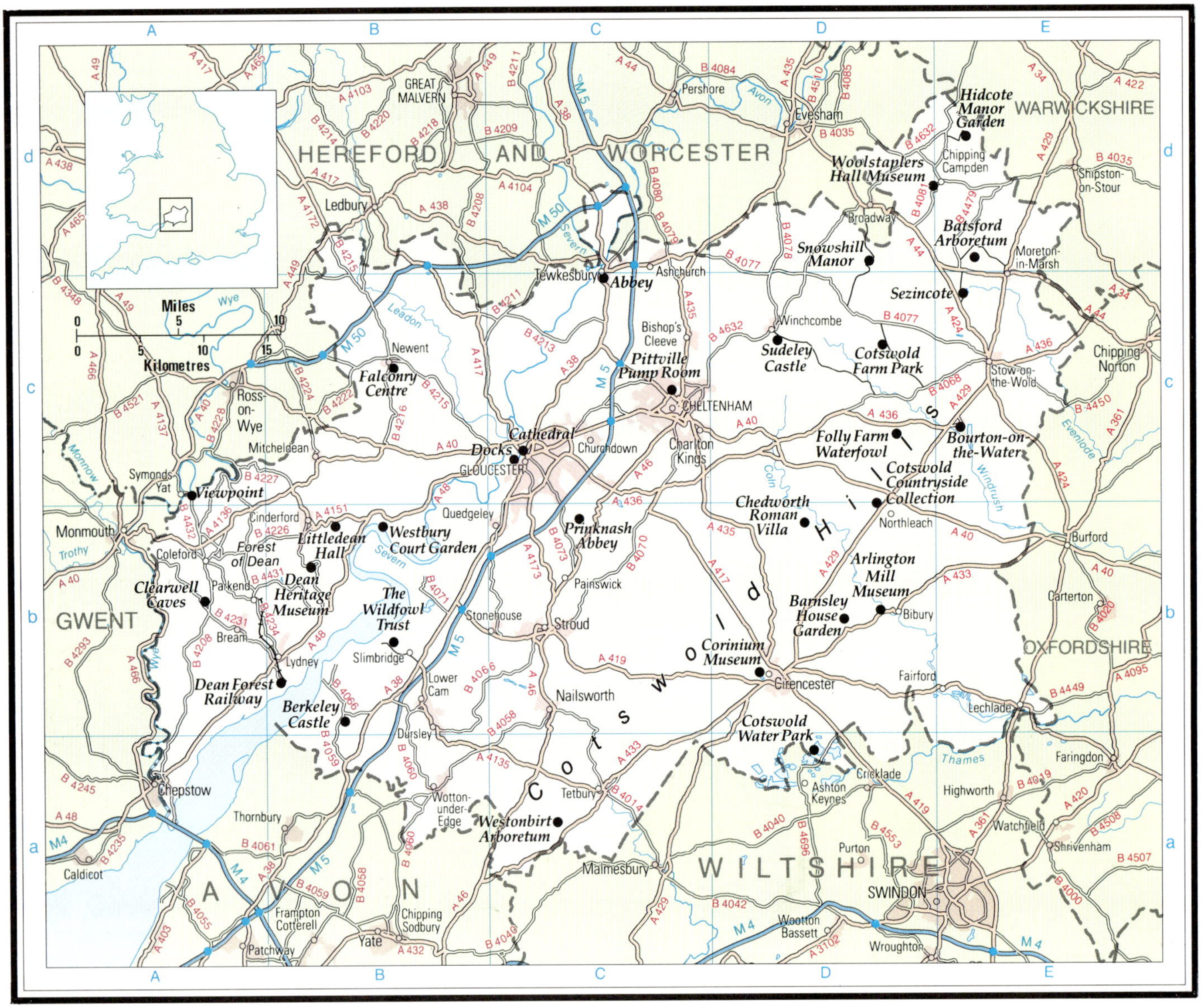

The Cotswolds roll across the eastern half of Gloucestershire, and from their honey-coloured limestone has been wrought a wealth of lovely towns and villages, such as Bibury, Chipping Campden and Bourton-on-the-Water. At Hidcote Manor, Barnsley House and Westbury Court are some of the country's most pleasing gardens.

In the Forest of Dean, old iron workings can be seen at Clearwell Caves and Puzzle Wood, and a Heritage Centre tells the story of the Forest folk who grazed their stock in the glades. At Norchard the revived Dean Forest Railway has a Steam Centre, and trains run the $1\frac{1}{2}$ miles to Lydney.

The county has many relics from Roman times. The Roman villa at Chedworth is exceptionally well preserved, and at Cirencester the Corinium Museum has fine mosaics. Busy Gloucester city on the banks of the River Severn is dominated by its fine cathedral, a superb example of the Perpendicular style that began in the 14th century. There is elegance of a different period at Cheltenham, where Regency architecture abounds and the town's famous spa water can be tasted in the Pittville Pump Room.

A brutal episode from Gloucestershire's heritage is evoked in the murder room at Berkeley Castle, where Edward II was horribly done to death. There are gentler attractions at the Wildfowl Trust nature reserve at Slimbridge, at Bourton-on-the-Water's model village and motor museum, Cotswold Farm Park and the Westonbirt Aboretum.

ARLINGTON MILL MUSEUM

On A433, in Bibury (Db)

Part of the enchantment of the village of Bibury derives from a terrace of 17th-century weavers' cottages called Arlington Row which overlooks the old mill stream. The stone-tiled corn mill dates back to the same period and now houses a rural museum with exhibits ranging from toys to traps, from old lace to vintage machinery.

One of the 17 exhibition rooms is fitted out as a cobbler's shop, another as a blacksmith's and another as a weaving room. Special displays are devoted to William Morris and to the Arts and Crafts movement. Demonstrations by traditional craftsmen are given on some summer weekends, and the mill machinery is intact and capable of turning the grinding stones.

The slow waters of the River Coln which feed

the mill stream also serve Bibury Trout Farm. It has 40 rearing ponds, with further tanks and troughs for breeding trout fry. Fish are sold to visitors.

Museum: Mid Mar-mid Nov, daily; winter, Sat and Sun. Adm charge. Shop. P *(limited). Toilets. Tel Bibury (028 574) 368. Trout farm: All year, daily. Adm charge. Shop.* P *(limited).* ♿ *Tel (028 574) 215.*

BARNSLEY HOUSE GARDEN

On A433, 4 miles north-east of Cirencester (Db)

A 17th-century house of mellow Cotswold stone forms the backdrop to these 4 acre gardens created in recent decades by the gardening writer Rosemary Verey and the late David Verey, architectural historian. Features include a Doric temple with lily pool, knot and herb gardens, and a kitchen garden laid out as a decorative potager with roses, lavender and trained fruit trees for ornamental effect. The borders in the main garden area are crowded with interest all the year round; the great seasonal attraction is the laburnum tunnel, seen in golden splendour during the first two weeks of June.

All year, Mon-Fri; also 1st Sun in May, June and July. Adm charge. Shop. P *Toilets. Tel Bibury (028 574) 281.*

BATSFORD ARBORETUM

Off A44, 1½ miles west of Moreton-in-Marsh (Ed)

A large bronze Buddha contemplates infinity from a knoll in the 50 acre park. The effigy was brought to Batsford by Lord Redesdale, who laid out the arboretum in the 1880s. Other far-eastern touches include bronze deer and a Japanese rest house, as well as a wealth of oriental trees and shrubs. There are more than 1200 different species in the arboretum, which is set on the slope of a Cotswold spur, with splendid views over the Evenlode vale.

Apr-Oct, daily. Adm charge. Refreshments. Shop. P *Toilets. Tel Moreton-in-Marsh (0608) 50722*

BERKELEY CASTLE

Off A38, 13 miles south-west of Gloucester (Bb)

White doves coo among the rafters of the outer gatehouse, and the castle's ancestral stones are tinged a warm grey-pink. Though mightily buttressed, this is a fortress which speaks of domesticity. Tall chimneys overtop the battlements and mullion windows are set snug into the walls. Not even the little cannon, grouped at the castle entrance, convey a real sense of menace. Berkeley Castle has been the home of the Berkeley family since it was built more than 800 years ago, and no one could guess its taint of ancient horror.

In 1327, Edward II was imprisoned in the dungeons and vilely dispatched by his jailers. Visitors to the murder room can see the hole in one corner leading down to a pit where the carcasses of putrefying cattle were once thrown so that their foul vapours would asphyxiate prisoners in the cell. The castle was besieged and captured by Roundheads during the Civil War, and a huge breech in the wall of the keep gives evidence of the event.

Otherwise, however, the medieval building is remarkably well preserved. The many apartments open to the public include bedroom, picture gallery, dining room, kitchen and beer cellar. Two drawing rooms contain gilded furniture of the 18th century, and the Great Hall ceiling, supported by splendidly arched timbers, rises to more than 30ft.

The terrace gardens were planted in this century by Captain R.G. Berkeley. Wisteria clusters the walls, and many another plant has seeded itself in crevices of the ancient masonry. Adjoining the castle is the lovely parish church of St Mary the Virgin containing the 14th-century tomb of Lord Thomas Berkeley (the lord when Edward II was murdered) and his wife.

The physician Edward Jenner (1749-1823) is also buried in the church. A Berkeley man, he is famed for inventing vaccination and so conquering the lethal scourge of smallpox. Jenner lived in the Chantry, a shapely, white, 18th-century building which rises from its gravel forecourt only a stone's throw from church and castle. It is maintained today as the Jenner Museum.

Castle and Museum: Apr-Sept, daily exc Mon, and Bank Hol Mon; Oct, Sun. Adm charge. Refreshments. Shop. P *Toilets. Tel Dursley (0453) 810332 (castle); 810631 (museum).*

CHEDWORTH ROMAN VILLA

Off A429, 6 miles north of Cirencester (Db)

Dating back to about AD 120, the villa was clearly built for a rich landowner and equipped with all the comforts typical of the Roman invaders, including hot-air underfloor heating and two forms of bath. The villa stood close to the Roman road to Corinium (Cirencester), so that however tranquil as a retreat, it had access to bustling urban centres.

Around AD 400, as the Empire crumbled, such villas were abandoned. Chedworth was no exception, but enough relics have been excavated to reveal a building with three wings enclosing a rectangular courtyard which was open to the east. The bath suites and one dining room are particularly well preserved, with good mosaics. Visitors can also see a Nymphaeum, a water shrine, still filled by the ancient spring which supplied the inhabitants with fresh water. A museum displays varied household objects.

Nearby, Denfurlong Farm Trail provides a tour round a working dairy farm of the present day. Milking may be watched, and there are taped commentaries on farm life. The main trail conducts visitors through fields, by streams, and across hawthorn-tufted Cotswold slopes.

Roman Villa: NT. Mar-Oct, daily exc Mon, and Bank Hol Mon; Nov-early Dec, Wed-Sun. Adm charge. Shop. P *Toilets.* ♿ *Tel Withington (024 289) 256. Farm trail: All year, daily. Adm charge. Tel (024 289) 215.*

CLEARWELL CAVES

Off B4228, 1 mile south of Coleford (Ab)

The ghost of an old miner is said to frequent these caves, clad in medieval mining costume with helmet, pick and hod. But Clearwell Caves need no spectral lore, for there is a haunted aura in their very antiquity. These are old, old workings – iron ore was being mined by the

FORTRESS HOME *Since 1153, Berkeley Castle has been transformed from grim fortress to stately home. The Great Hall dates from 1340, and on its site in 1215 the West Country barons met before going to Runnymede to force King John to put his seal to Magna Carta.*

BIRDS AND BYGONES AT BOURTON

The grass-edged waters of the River Windrush flow through the showpiece Cotswold village of Bourton-on-the-Water. Low stone bridges span the river's tranquil course, and among the buildings are some surprise delights for visitors. In the gardens of the Old New Inn is a miniature replica of Bourton. The model village was built in 1936 by the then innkeeper, and everything is re-created at one-ninth life-size, including the inn itself and a model of the model village. Other attractions include a motor museum and village life exhibition, a perfumery and Birdland.

Cotswold Motor Museum and Village Life Exhibition, The Old Mill: Feb-Nov, daily. Adm charge. Tel Bourton-on-the-Water (0451) 21255. Model Village: All year, daily. Adm charge. Tel (0451) 20467. Model Railway: Apr-Sept, daily; Oct-Mar, weekends. Adm charge. Tel (0451) 20686. Cotswold Perfumery: All year, daily. Tel (0451) 20698. Birdland: All year, daily. Adm charge. Shop. Toilets. Tel (0451) 20480.

RURAL BYGONES *An Edwardian village shop, with bright enamelled advertisements for soap, tea and cocoa, has been re-created in the Old Mill at Bourton, a picturesque streamside building which houses relics of Cotswold country life. There is also a fully equipped blacksmith's forge, and a model of the mill as it looked in the 18th century; a water turbine later installed there was amongst the earliest suppliers of electricity in the Cotswolds. Smaller exhibits include vintage radios, crested china, baby carriages and period toys.*

MORE THAN MOTORS *A pretty little 1922 Rover van in OXO livery is one of the collection of 30 vintage cars, motorcycles and vans in the Cotswold Motor Museum. Invicta, Swallow, BSA and Calthorpe are among the venerable names no longer seen on the road which are represented, and besides the vehicles there are more than 600 vintage advertising signs. The museum re-creates the motoring atmosphere of the 1920s, with shops, caravans dressed in the style of the period, vintage pedal cars, and pedal aeroplanes which were as much curiosities then as now.*

TRACK EVENTS *A turnstile in Bourton's High Street toyshop leads to a low-beamed back room – and a miniature wonderland for railway enthusiasts. The model trains run through carefully re-created settings, and British and continental locomotives are represented in HO/OO and N gauge.*

A COTSWOLD LILLIPUT *The slates and stonework in the model village have mellowed with lichens over the years, adding natural realism to this perfect replica of Bourton-on-the-Water. Visitors can walk among the houses and then stand on a viewpoint to take in the enchanting panorama.*

POOL PERFORMERS *One of Britain's largest collections of penguins can be seen at Birdland, and their underwater antics can be observed through the windows of a glass-walled pool. Parrots and macaws are also among the 320 species of birds in this 3 acre sanctuary in the grounds of an old manor house.*

Celts from deep in their limestone innards some 2700 years ago.

The caves are a system of waterworn cavities wrought out of carboniferous limestone. The eight large caverns open to the public reach 100ft below ground level, but these mark only the beginning of the system which descends a further 500ft. The name of Clearwell derives from the underground pools, crystal clear and overhung with stalactites, which once served local people with drinking water. The pick marks of the old miners can still be seen in the caves. A museum contains minerals and mining equipment, while vintage mining engines are displayed in the Engine House.

At nearby Puzzle Wood, more ancient iron workings have mazed the forest with grotto, boulder, chasm and dell. During the 19th century, the owners of Perrygrove Farm laid out paths, bridges and seats, making the woodland labyrinth seen today. It takes about an hour to walk the circuit.

Clearwell Caves: Mar-Oct, daily. Adm charge. Refreshments. Shop. P *Toilets. Tel Dean (0594) 23700. Puzzle Wood: Easter-Oct, daily exc Mon, and Bank Hol Mon. Adm charge. Refreshments. Shop.* P *Toilets. Tel (0594) 33187.*

CORINIUM MUSEUM

In Cirencester, near town centre (Db)

Founded by the Romans as an administrative centre for the local Dobunni tribe, Cirencester grew to become the second largest Roman town, after London, in the whole of Britain. Corinium Museum, named after the Roman name for Cirencester, displays an impressive collection of relics in modern galleries. Prize exhibits include two beautiful mosaics, one depicting the Four Seasons which was found in Dyer Street, Cirencester, in 1849, and another bearing the motif of a Hare, discovered much more recently in Beeches Road in 1971. To illustrate how such mosaics were crafted, the museum has a life-size replica of a stone-cutter's shop.

Cirencester has many fine old buildings, but its supreme glory is its parish church of St John the Baptist, built on the wealth of the wool trade in the 15th and 16th centuries. Grey and gold are the colours of its mellow stonework: the soaring tower is hugely buttressed and the pinnacled three-storeyed south porch has a fairy-tale loveliness out of keeping with its original functions – it was built as a suite of offices for the abbot, and was later used as the town hall. It has a dole table where bread was given to the poor.

Museum: Apr-Sept, daily; Oct-Mar, daily exc Mon. Adm charge. Shop. Toilets. ♿ *Tel Cirencester (0285) 5611.*

COTSWOLD COUNTRYSIDE COLLECTION

On A429, in Northleach (Dc)

The museum is housed in a former house of correction – an 18th-century country prison whose grey, rather forbidding exterior belies the wealth of interest within. Displays illustrate rural life in the region, with some fine old Gloucestershire harvest wagons, reconstructed workshops

ROMAN AUTUMN *The head of a goddess, her hair decorated with berries, depicts autumn in the Four Seasons mosaic floor in the Corinium Museum. The mosaic dates from the 2nd century AD.*

of the blacksmith and wheelwright, and a country kitchen. The 19th-century courtroom, used until recently, has been preserved, and visitors can see a restored cell block, complete with life-size effigies of the inmates.

Apr-Oct, daily. Adm charge. Refreshments. Shop. P *Toilets.* ♿ *Tel Cotswold (0451) 60715.*

COTSWOLD FARM PARK

Off B4077, 5 miles west of Stow-on-the-Wold (Dc)

Film and TV companies needing historic farmyard animals for location work often obtain them from the Cotswold Farm Park, which boasts the most comprehensive collection of rare farm breeds in the country. Occupying 25 acres, the farm park was founded as a 'shop window' for the Rare Breeds Survival Trust – a body set up to protect breeds threatened with extinction by modern commercial farming.

There are, for example, specimens of White Park cattle, beautiful creatures once sacrificed by the Druids and used in Roman rites, and dark little Soay sheep, prehistoric survivors from the St Kilda islands. The collection also includes specimens of the Cotswold Lion breed, whose fleeces wove the wealth of the medieval wool trade and funded the noble churches and manors for which the Cotswold Hills are renowned.

Good Fri-Sept, daily. Adm charge. Refreshments. Shop. P *Toilets.* ♿ *Tel Guiting Power (045 15) 307.*

COTSWOLD WATER PARK

Off A419, 3 miles south-east of Cirencester (Da)

Nearly 100 lakes created by gravel workings in the Upper Thames Valley form two miniature 'lakelands', one centred on Ashton Keynes and the other on Fairford and Lechlade. Where gravel extraction has ceased, the waters have been turned over to recreational pursuits ranging from lakeside walks and picnic sites to angling, sailing, windsurfing, water-skiing and powerboat racing.

Keynes Country Park is one major centre, having a nature reserve, a children's beach and an adventure playground. Somerford Lakes Reserve offers a guided tour of its 100 acres on an Edwardian-style launch: the pre-booked hour-long circuit takes in an eel and trout farm, as well as an island with pheasants and animals.

Keynes: All year, daily. Adm charge in summer. Refreshments. P *Toilets.* ♿ *Tel Cirencester (0285) 861459. Somerford: Apr-Oct, daily. Adm charge. Shop.* P *Tel (boat trips) Kemble (028 577) 226.*

DEAN FOREST RAILWAY

On B4234 at Norchard, 1 mile north of Lydney (Bb)

The first steam railways reached the Forest of Dean in the 1850s, and with a booming local coal industry the forest became mazed with track. The Severn and Wye was the principal railway company, and it ran locomotives romantically named after Old England's forest outlawry: *Robin Hood, Will Scarlet* and *Friar Tuck*.

A sense of railway romance has not left the forest, and in 1970, when the last remaining section of the old Severn and Wye, from Lydney to Parkend, was threatened with closure, the Dean Forest Railway Preservation Society was formed. The wooden station building at Norchard is an original Severn and Wye station from Drybrook Road Junction in the forest, restored with the addition of a Midland Railway ticket office. The first of the society's acquisitions to steam in public display was the chunky little *Uskmouth 1*, an industrial shunting engine of 1952.

All year, daily; steam days Bank Hol Sun and Mon, Sun May-Sept, Wed pm mid June-Aug, and occasional Sun in Mar, Apr, Oct and Dec. Adm charge. Refreshments. Shop. P *Toilets.* ♿ *Tel Dean (0594) 43423.*

DEAN HERITAGE MUSEUM

On B4227, 2 miles south of Cinderford (Bb)

A great green triangle spread between the Severn and the Wye, the Forest of Dean has never been idle: it wears innumerable scars in the quarries or 'scowles' where from Celtic times Foresters dug for iron ore. Trees were felled in great number to provide metalworkers with charcoal, and to keep the Tudor fleets afloat. Then, in Victorian times, the whole area became pitted with coal mines.

BIRD IN THE HAND *A white-bellied sea eagle perches on the gloved hand of a falconer at the Birds of Prey Conservation and Falconry Centre, where there are regular demonstrations of this medieval sport.*

Centred on a restored mill building, Dean Heritage Museum contains a wealth of exhibits telling the Forest story. They include a steam-powered colliery beam engine and a reconstructed miner's cottage complete with the inevitable zinc bath.
All year, daily. Adm charge. Refreshments. Shop. P *Toilets.* ♿ *Tel Dean (0594) 22170.*

FALCONRY CENTRE

On B4216 at Newent (Bc)

The sight of a hawk on the wing and of a golden eagle flying to fist are among the spectacles at the Birds of Prey Conservation and Falconry Centre, dedicated to the ancient hunting art and its feathered exponents. Trained eagles, buzzards and falcons can be seen in action daily on the flying ground whenever the weather is favourable. The centre has one of the world's largest collections of birds of prey, and there is a 'Hawk Walk' where trained specimens can be seen in open enclosures. Visitors can also watch birds nesting and rearing young in the aviaries.

Winged wonders of a different type offer their colourful fascination at the Newent Butterfly Centre. Here giant butterflies fly free in a landscaped tropical setting, among pools and exotic vegetation. The menagerie contains varied insects and invertebrates ranging from giant bird spiders to stick insects and praying mantises.
Falconry Centre: Mar-Oct, daily. Adm charge. Refreshments. Shop. P *Toilets.* ♿ *Tel Newent (0531) 850286. Butterfly Centre: Good Fri-Oct, daily. Adm charge. Refreshments. Shop.* P *Toilets.* ♿ *Tel (0531) 821800.*

FOLLY FARM WATERFOWL

On A436, 2½ miles west of Bourton-on-the Water (Dc)

A cacophany of honking echoes up to hilltop Folly Farm at evening time. Enfolded by the rolling Cotswolds, the valley sanctuary below has been created around a chain of spring-fed pools, and more than 120 breeds of domestic fowl are tended on the site. They include a wealth of rare and endangered species and come in a bewildering assortment of shapes. Pride of place is surely held by the stately Toulouse goose, a massive, jowled creature with a look of inquisitive concern.
All year, daily. Adm charge. Refreshments. Shop. P *Toilets.* ♿ *Tel Cotswold (0451) 20285.*

GLOUCESTER CATHEDRAL

In centre of Gloucester (Cc)

The afternoon sun shining through Gloucester Cathedral's west window throws splashes of coloured light onto the giant piers of the nave arcade. These immense stone columns convey an impression of solid, uncomplicated strength characteristic of the work of Norman builders. But passing through to the choir and Presbytery, the visitor enters another world where on either side vertical shafts rise more than 90ft to a vault of intricate stone tracery and delicate flying arches. Over the high altar a celestial orchestra of carved angels plays a triumphant *Gloria.* Dominating the scene is the famous east window of around 1350, measuring 78ft by 38ft – the size of a tennis court. Erected as a memorial to those who died at the Battle of Crécy, it shows the coronation of the Virgin Mary. Beyond, at the easternmost extremity of the cathedral, is the lovely Lady Chapel completed in 1483, a last flowering of the Perpendicular style.

Founded in 1089, Gloucester Cathedral contains some of the most beautiful Perpendicular architecture in existence. In fact, it is said that the Perpendicular style was invented here in about 1330, when masons in the South Transept replaced the Norman windows with larger ones containing vertical tracery. The adjoining cloisters are equally fine: built between 1367 and 1400 they were the focus of domestic life in the old abbey and are decorated with fan vaulting as delicate as a spider's web.

SOARING SPLENDOUR *Built in the 15th century, Gloucester Cathedral's South Porch and 225ft high tower are a glorious profusion of graceful parapets, slender pinnacles and lacy stonework.*

Apart from its architectural splendours, the cathedral is rich in historic memorials. Here, for example, is a 13th-century wooden effigy of Robert, Duke of Normandy, eldest son of William the Conqueror, reclining in an expressive, courtly pose. Here, too, is the tomb of Edward II, foully murdered at Berkeley Castle in 1327, whose beautiful alabaster likeness lies beneath a many-pinnacled canopy. The Treasury glitters with Holy Communion plate, and there is a fascinating exhibition, depicting the long history of the building from monastic times to the present, in the gallery round the east end.

Gloucester itself is a city of great antiquity, founded by early Britons as the lowest practicable crossing point on the Severn. The City Museum and Art Gallery has the old Roman wall running through its basement, and exhibits include the Birdlip Mirror, a beautifully crafted Celtic bronze dating from the 1st century AD.

Gloucester Folk Museum, housed in a delightful timber-framed Tudor building, recalls changing patterns of farm life, trades and crafts.
Cathedral: All year, daily. City Museum and Folk Museum: All year, Mon-Fri. Free entry.

GLOUCESTER DOCKS

Near centre of Gloucester (Cc)

Gloucester was long important for its inland port, and the city's dockside area is currently being redeveloped for recreation. The old customs house contains the Museum of the Gloucestershire Regiment: an armoured vehicle stands outside, and within is memorabilia of a regiment famed for its heroic stand against the French in the Battle of Alexandria, 1801.

Also in the docks, housed in a tall Victorian warehouse, is the Robert Opie Collection. This is a marvellous treasure house of advertising and packaging ephemera ranging from tins and cartons to hoardings and flickering blue neon lights. Laid out in a series of illuminated alcoves, one sequence demonstrates how packaging styles have changed, decade by decade, from the 1880s to the 1970s. 'Watson's Matchless Cleanser', 'Ogden's Demon Flake', 'Jazz-time Toffees', 'Zoological Biscuits'. There is a nostalgic poetry even in the products' names. Altogether, more than 200,000 items are on display.

Another dockside warehouse has been restored as a new National Waterways Museum. Canal boats are on show and working displays tell the story of Britain's canals, while craftsmen give demonstrations.
Glos Regt Museum: All year, Mon-Fri. Adm charge. Tel Gloucester (0452) 22682. Robert Opie Collection: All year, daily exc Mon, and Bank Hol Mon. Adm charge. Refreshments. Shop. P *Toilets.* ♿ *Tel (0452) 302309. Waterways Museum: All year, daily. Adm charge. Refreshments. Shop.* P *Toilets.* ♿ *Tel (0452) 25524.*

HIDCOTE MANOR GARDEN

Off B4632, 4 miles north-east of Chipping Campden (Ed)

One of Britain's most influential gardens, Hidcote was laid out by Major Lawrence Johnston who bought the 17th-century estate in 1905 and developed its 10 acres over the next 40 years. The site, high on the Cotswolds, is laid out in a series of compartments often likened to open-air rooms. Brick walls and clipped hedging serve as the dividers, also helping to screen off the wind. Within the orderly framework, planting is often informal and designed to evoke the pleasing turmoil of cottage gardens, the scrambling and intermingling of plants in rural hedgerows and woodlands.

Every compartment has its own theme. One, for example, is given over to reddish flowers; another to lilacs and hellebores. The so-called Theatre Lawn is a sheet of primary green overlooked by beeches, while the Pool Garden is almost filled by its circular mirror of water. The variety of plantings and effects guarantees interest from spring to autumn, and the main vista ends at wrought-iron gates with fine views beyond.

COUNTER ATTRACTIONS *In Gloucester Docks, the Robert Opie Collection is a history of packaging. It recalls the days when the best biscuits came in colourful tins, and washday blues came in bags.*

Neighbouring Kiftsgate Court Gardens is another garden of distinct corridors and boudoirs. The yellow border is one of the most striking features, its golden euphorbias accentuated by vivid blue spires of delphiniums.
Hidcote: NT. Apr-Oct, daily exc Tues and Fri. Adm charge. Shop. P *Toilets.* ♿ *(part of garden). Tel Mickleton (0386) 438333. Kiftsgate: Apr-Sept, Sun, Wed and Thur pm and Bank Hol Mon. Refreshments.* P *Toilets.*

LITTLEDEAN HALL

On A4151, 1½ miles east of Cinderford (Bb)

The front of the house is 17th century but its origins go back much further. Littledean Hall was the home of the Lords of Dene from before the Norman Conquest, and contains in the cellar the only remains of a Saxon hall known in England. A 'Ghost Tour' takes in a host of apartments woven with spectral lore, from phantom bloodstains in the dining room to the Black Boy on the landing. The grounds contain many trees of great age as well as the recently discovered and restored site of a major Roman temple. A Panorama Walk culminates in magnificent views over the horseshoe bend of the Severn.
Apr-Oct, daily. Adm charge. Toilets. Tel Dean (0594) 24213.

PITTVILLE PUMP ROOM

In centre of Cheltenham (Cc)

The famous spa waters at Cheltenham can be sampled from a paper cup at the Pittville Pump Room. They taste smoothly salty, and it is to this healthful liquid that Cheltenham owes its glorious heritage of Regency architecture. Medicinal springs were first discovered in 1716, and the little market town's gradually increasing popularity as a spa was boosted in 1788 with a visit by George III.

Joseph Pitt, a self-made lawyer and banker, sought to capitalise on the building boom by creating an entirely new 100 acre community at the northern edge of the city. It was to be called Pittville, and its focus would be a great Pump Room for dispensing spa water.

Pitt's grandiose scheme was never fully realised, but the Pump Room was opened in 1830 and became a rendezvous for nobility and gentry. Green-domed and with a colonnaded facade of golden stone, it remains perhaps the finest of all Cheltenham's Regency buildings. Inside is a spacious pillared hall, two storeys high, with a balcony running round the upper level. Spa waters are still available at the ornate pump on the ground floor. Upstairs, a costume collection illustrates changing fashions from 1760 to 1960, and a jewellery collection includes cameos, frontlets and tiaras which recall the elegant Regency age.

The Pump Hall overlooks a green lawn sloping to ornamental lakes, with a glimpse of the rough Cotswold escarpment to the east. A walk through Pittville Park leads past some very grand houses, but close to the ironwork gates is the Holst Birthplace Museum where the scale of things is much more intimate. In this plain Regency terrace building, the composer Gustav Holst (1874-1934) was born. Memorabilia laid out on the ground floor include his Victorian grand piano, while rooms upstairs and down have been restored as period pieces. The sitting room is in the plush Regency style.

Pump Room: Apr-Oct, daily exc Mon; Nov-Mar, daily exc Sun and Mon; also Easter, Spring and Aug Bank Hol. Adm charge. Shop. P *Toilets. Tel Cheltenham (0242) 512740. Holst Museum: All year, daily exc Sun and Mon. Shop. Toilets. Tel (0242) 524846.*

PRINKNASH ABBEY

On A46, 3 miles north of Painswick (Cb)

The Old Abbey dates back to the 14th century, when it served as a manor for the Abbots of Gloucester. After the monasteries were dissolved in 1540 Prinknash passed to a succession of lay owners until 1928 when it was given back to the Benedictines to serve as a monastery. Many centuries of its history are still imprinted on the greystone building. The medieval chapel, for example, has a carving of the badge of Edward IV, and in the East Court is a basrelief portraying a young man said to be Henry VIII.

The New Abbey is a strikingly modern building consecrated in 1972 and designed to meet the needs of today's monks. Prinknash's community has become famed for its pottery wares crafted from local clay, and visitors can watch the potters at work. The two abbeys stand amid wooded parkland which includes a 9 acre bird park with medieval fish ponds as well as birds, waterfowl and farmyard animals.
Abbey: All year, daily. Adm charge to pottery. Refreshments. Shop. P *Toilets.* ♿ *Tel Painswick (0452) 812239. Bird Park: Apr-Oct, daily. Adm charge. Refreshments. Shop.* P *Toilets. Tel (0452) 812727.*

GARDEN GREENERY *Formality and informality blend at Hidcote Manor. Clipped box and yew hedges surround a series of gardens each with its own theme, including this White Garden.*

SEZINCOTE

On A44, 1½ miles west of Moreton-in-Marsh (Ec)

Onion domes and peacock-tail arches adorn the house which might have been transported to Gloucestershire on some outsize magic carpet. Sezincote was completed in 1805 for Charles Cockerell, a former functionary of the East India Company, and is probably unique in Europe as a complete example of Mogul architecture. It influenced the Prince Regent in his Indianisation of Brighton Pavilion, and is described in *Summoned by Bells*, the autobiographical poem by John Betjeman who used to visit the house as an Oxford undergraduate. The water garden has oriental features which include an Indian bridge, Brahmin bulls and a temple to the Hindu sun god, Surya.

Garden: All year exc Dec, Thur, Fri and Bank Hol Mon pm. House: May, June, July and Sept, Thur and Fri pm. Adm charge. P *(limited). Toilets.*

SNOWSHILL MANOR

Off A44, 3 miles south of Broadway (Dd)

A shapely manor set high in its Cotswold village, Snowshill dates mainly from the 17th century, and is known especially for its contents: a fantastic assortment of handmade curios gathered by the former owner, Charles Wade, between 1900 and 1951. Samurai armour, mousetraps, cuckoo clocks, Flemish tapestries, vintage bicycles, lacquer cabinets, narwhal tusks, kettle drums – the assemblage is astonishing and colonised the house even in Wade's time (he lived in an outbuilding, without electric light).

The terraced garden, with ponds, was also laid out by Wade, an extraordinary character of whom Queen Mary once said that he himself was the most remarkable part of his entire collection.

NT. May-Sept, Wed-Sun; Apr and Oct, Sat and Sun. Adm charge. Shop. P *(limited). Toilets.* ♿ *(ground floor and part of garden). Tel Broadway (0386) 852410.*

DRESSED TO KILL *Arms and armour of samurai warriors fill the Green Room at Snowshill Manor. The samurai were the military aristocracy of feudal Japan and the only class permitted to bear arms.*

SUDELEY CASTLE

On B4632, 6 miles north-east of Cheltenham (Dc)

George Brydges, 6th Lord Chandos, held Sudeley for the Royalists during the Civil War, and although he later defected to Cromwell's side, the victorious Parliamentarians nevertheless demolished his castle so that it could never again serve as a hostile stronghold. Surviving from the medieval fortress are the chapel, the ruined banqueting hall and a 15th-century octagon tower holed by a cannon shot.

Though much of the imposing building seen today is a 19th-century restoration, it remains richly evocative and crowded with interest. The chapel has the tomb of Catherine Parr, sixth wife of Henry VIII, who managed to outlive him and become mistress of Sudeley. Arms, armour and antique furniture are on display. Sudeley was the model for Blandings, the stately home in the novels of P.G. Wodehouse. The little town of Winchcombe, at whose edge the castle lies, contains buildings constructed from the demolished masonry of the original castle. The town hall has a Folk Museum with displays illustrating Winchcombe's history, and in an adjoining room is a Police Museum with exhibits ranging from a Peeler's uniform to an original press cutting about Jack the Ripper. Winchcombe also has a Railway Museum with memorabilia from the age of steam.

Sudeley Castle: Apr-Oct, daily. Adm charge. Refreshments. Shop. P *Toilets. Tel Cheltenham (0242) 602308. Folk Museum: Mar-Oct, daily exc Sun. Adm charge. Toilets. Tel Winchcombe (0242) 602925. Railway Museum: All year, daily.*

SYMONDS YAT VIEWPOINT

On B4432, at Symonds Yat (Ac)

One of the loveliest river views in England is to be had from this 400ft high bluff. Around it the curving Wye performs a glorious 5 mile loop, returning almost to encircle the vantage point. To either side wooded slopes fall precipitously away, and the views north extend far beyond the spire of Goodrich church to a blue mist of hills.

The word *yat* in Old English means 'gate', and there was once a pass through Iron Age fortifications near the summit. Forest paths lead down to the Wye and to a ferry connecting with Symonds Yat village on the opposite bank.

All year, daily.

TEWKESBURY ABBEY

On A38, just south of Tewkesbury (Cc)

The abbey church of St Mary the Virgin at Tewkesbury has every appearance of a cathedral. It is not – but with its great square tower and high fan-vaulted ceiling, this splendid building survived the Dissolution, and is one of the largest parish churches in England. Built by Benedictine monks in about AD 1100, the abbey was saved by local townspeople who, at the Dissolution, bought it from Henry VIII.

Measuring 46ft square and 148ft high, its Norman tower is the largest in existence. The Norman nave is a wonder too, with 14 giant cylindrical columns supporting the plain rounded arches. There is some fine medieval stained glass, and an immense high altar made of Purbeck marble. John Milton is said once to have played at the 17th-century organ, and the church contains many notable memorials including a burial plaque of Prince Edward, son of Henry VI, who was murdered in the abbey.

Tewkesbury appeared as 'Nortonbury' in Mrs Craik's *John Halifax, Gentleman*, and memorabilia connected with the book are among the exhibits in the John Moore Museum of the Countryside, housed in a 15th-century cottage. The neighbouring Little Museum has been restored to represent a medieval shop.

Abbey: All year, daily. Free entry. Shop. P *(limited).* ♿ *Tel Tewkesbury (0684) 292896. Museums: Easter-Oct, Tues-Sat and Bank Hol. Tel (0684) 297174.*

WESTBURY COURT GARDEN

On A48, 9 miles south-west of Gloucester (Bb)

When William of Orange ascended to the throne of England a craze for all things Dutch swept the nation. Westbury Court possesses a very rare example of a formal Dutch-style garden surviving from that era and the earliest of its kind remaining in England. Many others were obliterated by Capability Brown's natural landscape school. The 5 acre garden was laid out between 1696 and 1705 by Colonel Maynard Colchester with straight-cut canals and neatly trimmed hedges of yew. It has been restored to its original condition, including its tall, unmistakably Dutch summerhouse shaped like a square lantern.

NT. Apr-Oct, Wed-Sun and Bank Hol Mon. Adm charge. P *(limited). Tel Westbury-on-Severn (045 276) 461.*

FLAMINGO SUNDOWN *Late on a winter's day the feeble rays of the setting sun cast long shadows over Slimbridge, and tint the roseate plumage of stately flamingos from South America.*

WESTONBIRT ARBORETUM

Off A433, 3 miles south of Tetbury (Ca)

These 500 woodland acres contain one of Europe's finest collections of trees and shrubs, with specimens drawn from all over the temperate world. There are 15,000 of them in total, bewildering in the variety of their leaf tones and in their living architecture of domed canopies, soaring spires and hanging boughs.

The arboretum was begun in 1829 by Robert Holford of Westonbirt House. The building itself is now a girls' school, but the wooded park is managed by the Forestry Commission and includes plantings of Holford's time. Some 17 miles of paths wind through the woods.

Trees have often been massed for seasonal effect. Visitors can come in January to enjoy the groves of witch hazel and scented viburnum. In April the flowering cherries come into their own, while in May the woods burst with rhododendron and azalea. October is the month of the Japanese maple, widely planted at Westonbirt for its vivid autumn colours.

The story of the arboretum is told in the visitor centre, a building which is something of an exhibit in itself, being made of many different timbers to recall the international character of the collection.

FC. All year, daily. Adm charge. Refreshments. Shop. P *Toilets.* ♿ *Tel Westonbirt (066 688) 366.*

THE WILDFOWL TRUST

Off A38, at Slimbridge (Bb)

Many a summertime attraction for visitors lacks interest in winter. Slimbridge, the headquarters of the Wildfowl Trust, is a different case. Here, under chill grey skies, the salt marsh comes alive with white-fronted geese in flocks sometimes 7000 strong. From the Arctic, formations of Bewick's swans settle in their hundreds on the waters. The wetland site on the Severn estuary has always offered wildfowl a natural wintering ground. But the additional collection of rare species, the conservation work and the viewing facilities make Slimbridge a wonder among bird reserves.

The Wildfowl Trust was founded in 1946 by the naturalist Sir Peter Scott, both to aid conservation and to focus public interest on the beauty of wildfowl and their habitat. The 100 acre enclosure has pens, paddocks and lakes containing the world's largest collection of ducks, swans, geese and other water birds. Species have been drawn from all over the world and several of them, including the Hawaiian goose, were threatened with extinction before the Trust stepped in. The permanent collection includes all six types of flamingos, and a Tropical House contains delicate creatures such as hummingbirds.

All year, daily. Adm charge. Refreshments. Shop. P *Toilets.* ♿ *Tel Slimbridge (045 389) 333.*

WOOLSTAPLERS HALL MUSEUM

High Street, Chipping Campden (Ed)

With timeworn buildings of warm Cotswold stone, the High Street at Chipping Campden is among the most beautiful main streets in England. The town's wealth was founded on wool, and the Woolstaplers Hall, built in 1340, was where medieval dealers bought and sold fleeces. The building now houses a museum with an unusual collection of curios ranging from early dental instruments to vintage cine apparatus, sewing machines and typewriters.

The bow-fronted premises of Campden Pottery specialise in glazed wares, many of which are hand-thrown on the potter's wheel.

Woolstaplers Hall: Apr-Oct, daily. Adm charge. Shop. Tel Evesham (0386) 840289. Pottery: July-Oct, daily; Nov-June, daily exc Sun, and Easter Sun. Free entry. Shop. P *(limited). Tel (0386) 840315.*

COUNTY CALENDAR

April Gloucester: St George's Day Celebrations.

May (Ascension Day). Bisley: Well Blessing.

May (Spring Bank Holiday). Cooper's Hill: Cheese Rolling.

July Cheltenham: Music Festival.

August (3rd week). Gloucester (every third year from 1989): Three Choirs Festival.

September (Sunday nearest Sept 19). Painswick Church: Clipping the Yews.

Tourist information: Cheltenham (0242) 522878; Cirencester (0285) 4180; Gloucester (0452) 421188; Moreton-in-Marsh (0608) 50881; Stow-on-the-Wold (0451) 30352; Stroud (045 36) 4252.

GREATER LONDON

'WHEN A MAN IS TIRED OF LONDON HE IS TIRED OF LIFE' – DR JOHNSON

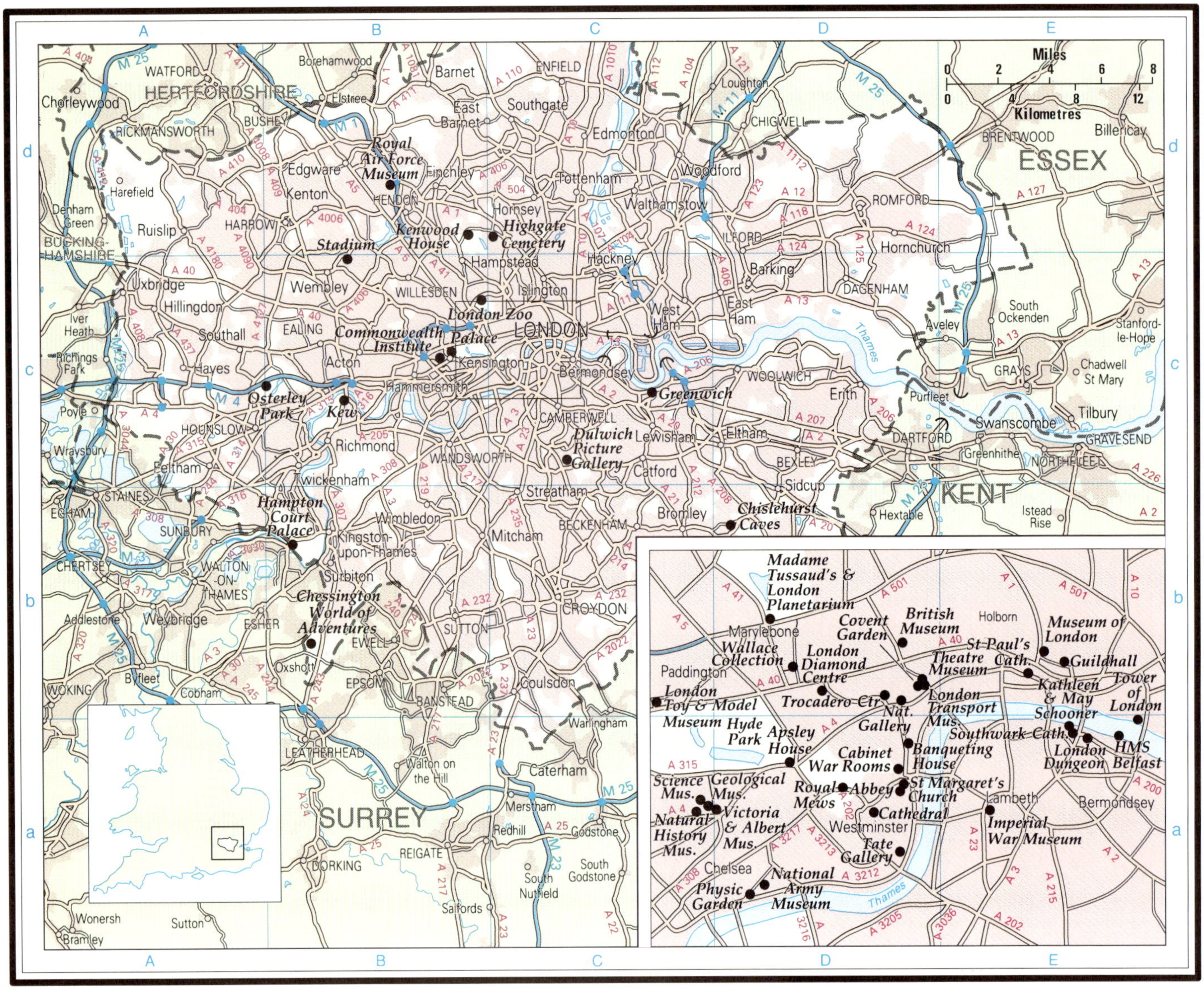

London is a kaleidoscope: shake it every week or so to behold new plays, films, concerts and exhibitions. But there are also aspects of the capital that do not change, and these range from the grand spectacle to the fascinating particular: from the incomparable view of London presented at the Old Royal Observatory, Greenwich, for instance, to the bed in which Queen Victoria was born in Kensington Palace.

If London itself is the lure then begin at the London Museum, move on to the Tower and later visit the houses of the great – the Duke of Wellington, Charles Dickens and Dr Johnson. If royalty is the attraction, there is no more regal tour than around the palaces of Kew, Greenwich, Hampton Court and Kensington. Epitaphs, tombs and other reminders of mortality crowd St Paul's Cathedral and Westminster Abbey. And when the visitor is sated with stone and bricks and mortar, he can blow the dust away in London's countryside: Kensington Gardens, airy Hampstead Heath and Regent's Park.

The diversity of London's museums and exhibitions is enormous. The British Museum is one of the world's great institutions, and seems to get livelier each year. Other perennial favourites include Madame Tussaud's, the Zoo and the *Cutty Sark* at Greenwich. Devotees of battles long and not so long ago are indulged on board HMS *Belfast*, at the National Army Museum, the Imperial War Museum and the Cabinet War Rooms, and there are all kinds of specialist museums such as the Diamond Centre, the Transport Museum and the Theatre Museum.

APSLEY HOUSE, THE WELLINGTON MUSEUM

149 Piccadilly, W1 (Da)

An unpretentious 18th-century mansion by Robert Adam, later extended and covered in Bath stone, Apsley House was the London home of the 1st Duke of Wellington. The house is often known as 'No 1, London', because a tollgate a little to the west once separated Piccadilly from the suburb of Knightsbridge. Within, the Plate and China Room contains a silver-gilt shield of incredible ornateness, presented by grateful City bankers to the victor of Waterloo.

At the foot of the Grand Staircase is a colossal nude statue of Napoleon by Canova, while on the first floor are the splendid reception rooms – three drawing rooms, the Dining Room and the Waterloo Gallery, covered from floor to ceiling with paintings. The most important of

ROYAL GIFTS *Two candelabra of porphyry, decked with flowers, stand in the Waterloo Gallery at Apsley House. They were presented to the 1st Duke of Wellington by Tsar Nicholas I of Russia.*

these were looted by the French in Spain, rescued by the duke, restored to the Spanish and courteously returned to him as honourable spoils of war. Chief among this glorious group is the *Water Seller of Seville*, by Velázquez.

In the Dining Room a huge table is adorned by a silver-gilt centrepiece of cavorting nymphs, the gift of Portugal. The great gallery, with its moulded and gilded ceiling, great chandelier and sumptuous paintings, is literally palatial.

All year, daily exc Mon. Adm charge. Shop. Toilets. Tel (01) 499 5676.

BANQUETING HOUSE

Horseguards Avenue, Whitehall, SW1 (Da)

Designed in 1619 by Inigo Jones for James I as an auditorium for court masques, the Banqueting House was the first building in London to be constructed in the classical Italian style. Its Whitehall façade, two storeys of seven windows each, supported by Ionic columns below and Corinthian above, still looks remarkably distinguished.

So does the interior, a two-storey single chamber of perfect proportions, 110ft long by 55ft high and wide. Though the great hall has been used for many purposes it stands dramatically empty now, apart from four great chandeliers and a crimson throne on a dais at one end. The most startling feature is the ceiling, which is divided by gilded ribs into nine huge panels, each panel filled by a huge painting. The painter of the whole vast undertaking was Sir Peter Paul Rubens, working to the command of Charles I who conceived it as a memorial to his father James I and as an allegory of the benefits conferred upon the nation by the Stuart dynasty. Thus the central oval panel depicts James being wafted up to Heaven as the just recompense for his labours on Earth. Charles was delighted with the work, and perhaps it comforted him when he walked out of one of the Banqueting House's windows to the scaffold and death.

All year, daily exc Sun am and Mon. Shop. Tel (01) 930 4179.

HMS BELFAST

Vine Lane, Tooley Street, SE1 (Ea)

The last of the Royal Navy's big ships, HMS *Belfast* is a survivor of the days when cruisers were the backbone of the fleet. Visitors to this veteran of the Second World War and the Korean War can follow a marked route, taking about two hours to complete, to see every aspect of how a fighting ship operated, from the massive turbine engines that could propel her at 32 knots to the gun turrets that could hurl a shell 14 miles.

The bridge, with its bewildering array of instruments, the Operations Room and the fire control equipment are all as they were when the *Belfast* last saw action. Below decks can be seen how the crew lived when at sea, with model figures posed to show how bakery, sick bay, dental surgery and NAAFI canteen operated.

All year, daily. Adm charge. Refreshments. Shop. Toilets. Tel (01) 407 6434.

COVER GIRL *The effigy of a bride of the 2nd century BC rests on the lid of this Etruscan sarcophagus in the British Museum.*

BEAK AND CLAW *Once part of a circular wooden shield, this menacing bird of prey in gilt and bronze is part of the Sutton Hoo treasure in the British Museum.*

PAST PRIESTESS *This wooden coffin in human form (left) in the British Museum contains the mummy of a Theban priestess of about 1000 BC. A floral shawl and red braces cover the breast.*

BRITISH MUSEUM

Great Russell Street, WC1 (Db)

Behind the mightily pillared portico of the British Museum the monumental style of architecture is continued in marble and granite pillars and doorways and lofty, opulent ceilings. But the atmosphere is very friendly, the more so since the bright modernisation of recent years. To capture the general flavour of the place and see its best-loved treasures en route, go first to the Manuscript Rooms on the ground floor, where such treasures as Magna Carta, the Lindisfarne Gospels, the Beatles' *Yesterday* and the first draft of *Alice in Wonderland* lie in surprising juxtaposition. Also on the ground floor is that wondrous procession of stone horsemen and mythical battles known collectively as the Elgin Marbles. Not far off is the Assyrian Saloon with its brutally realistic reliefs of a lion hunt, and in the Roman Art room is the lovely glass Portland Vase, whose design was the inspiration for Wedgwood pottery. Also on the ground floor is the Rosetta Stone, whose identically worded inscriptions in two kinds of Greek and Egyptian hieroglyphs facilitated the first modern translations of ancient Egyptian.

Essential viewing on the upper floor includes Coins and Medals, for portraits of the great as their contemporaries saw them, Clocks and Watches – see especially the automaton ship clock of 1580 that fires guns and rings bells on the hour – and the Egyptian Galleries, for their mummies and amazingly lifelike early Christian portraits. In the Prehistoric and Romano British Galleries look out for the gold alloy torque that belonged to an ancient British chieftain, and the Mildenhall silver plates made for a Roman official in Britain. Round the tour off with a visit to the Early Medieval Room and relics from the Sutton Hoo Ship Burial, the grave goods of an Anglo-Saxon king.

All year, daily exc Sun am. Free entry. Refreshments. Shop. Toilets. ♿ Tel (01) 580 1788.

CABINET WAR ROOMS

King Charles Street, SW1 (Da)

A flight of basement steps tucked away behind a mighty buttress in Great George Street leads to an underground complex of nearly 70 rooms, built in 1938-9 as a bomb-proof base from which the Cabinet and the Chiefs of Staff could continue conducting the war against Germany whatever the storms overhead. As it happened, the capabilities of the Luftwaffe had been considerably exaggerated; the Cabinet met only about 100 times in the War Rooms, mostly during the Blitz of autumn 1940 to spring 1941, and the V1 and V2 raids of June 1944 to March 1945. The rooms' more vital role was as an intelligence, communications and planning headquarters.

Today, some 15 of the War Rooms are presented as a time capsule in which nothing has changed since 1945. Corridors and rooms both declare the spartan values of the period – yellowish-cream brick walls and brown linoleum floors, sighing ventilators, signs telling the inmates what the weather is like in the outside world. The simple furniture of the Cabinet Room is baize-covered metal, apart from Winston Churchill's wooden chair, and the tables are dotted with tin ashtrays. Generals, guards, typists and telephonists alike slept on army cots covered by rough blankets; only Churchill had the luxury of a green eiderdown.

All year, daily. Adm charge. Shop. Toilets. ♿ *Tel (01) 930 6961.*

CHELSEA PHYSIC GARDEN

66 Royal Hospital Road, SW3 (Da)

Between the razzmatazz of the King's Road and the avalanche of traffic along the Embankment, red-brick walls and overtopping leafy growth enclose a 4 acre oasis established by the Worshipful Society of Apothecaries in 1673.

There are few more fruitful plots on Earth. Chelsea sent the seeds that launched the cotton industry in the southern states of the USA, and Dr Ward, Master of the Apothecaries in the 1850s, invented a special case in which to dispatch the first tea plants from China to India and the first rubber plants from Brazil to Malaya. The garden remains a serious botanical laboratory to this day, but casual visitors are more likely to be entranced by the magnificent old trees – those that survived the gale of October 1987 – the Fernery and the magnolias. There are kitchen herbs such as fennel, thyme, rosemary and sage mingled with the fragrances of lavender, lily of the valley and lemon verbena.

Apr-Oct, Wed and Sun pm; also pm during Chelsea Flower Show. Adm charge. Refreshments (Sun). Shop. Tel (01) 352 5646.

CHESSINGTON WORLD OF ADVENTURES

On A243, at Chessington (Bb)

There are several worlds to be enjoyed at Chessington: the world of America's wild west, the eastern world of Buddhas and pagodas, the charm of an English village, the unknown world beyond the computer screen and the world of the animals.

A replica of an American frontier town offers a thrilling ride on the Runaway Mine Train through tunnels and gorges, while a river ride through the Mystic East ends with an exhilarating plunge down a water chute. The ruins of an old Norman castle and a mill with a water wheel overlook the village square with its Georgian shops and a pub – a good place to rest or eat in the castle courtyard before tackling the journey through a giant computer screen into a fantasy world called the Fifth Dimension. Also riding in space, but closer to the Earth, are the acrobats and trapeze artists of Circusworld.

All these attractions are set among the enclosures of the zoological gardens. Wild animals, birds and reptiles from all over the world can be seen by wandering among the gardens, or viewed from the height of the Safari Skyway, a monorail that gives panoramic views of the animals with a commentary by Johnny Morris.

All year, daily (Nov-Mar, zoo only). Adm charge. Refreshments. Shops. P *Toilets.* ♿ *Tel Epsom (037 27) 27227.*

WAR REPORTS *In the Map Room in the underground Cabinet War Rooms, the latest information on front-line fighting in the Second World War was collected, for presentation to the King and the War Cabinet.*

CHISLEHURST CAVES

Off A222, near Chislehurst Station (Db)

A guided tour of part of Chislehurst's 22 mile system of man-made caverns casts some light on the caves' inhabitants over the centuries. The caverns and passages have been hewn out of the chalk over 8000 years, but they contain rare traces of even earlier times: fossils found in the caves include the thighbone of a prehistoric ichthyosaurus. Altars allegedly used for human sacrifices by Druids remain.

The guided tour, which lasts 45 minutes, shows where, during the Civil War, Royalists used to hide themselves and their valuables. The labyrinth became Britain's biggest air-raid shelter, housing more than 15,000 people nightly during the air raids of the Second World War.

Easter-Sept, daily; Oct-Easter, weekends and school hols. Adm charge. Refreshments. Shop. P *Toilets. Tel (01) 467 3264.*

COMMONWEALTH INSTITUTE

Kensington High Street, W8 (Bc)

The polyglot collection of races and peoples called the Commonwealth accounts for a quarter of the world's population. Colourful samples of the varied cultures of more than 40 Commonwealth countries and dependencies are displayed on three floors of the Institute. Among the permanent features of the exhibitions is the Gagalo stiltman, a towering model of a dancer from West Africa. The Sri Lanka exhibition has delightful water-lily gardens dominated by a serene Buddha.

Behind the Commonwealth Institute lie the lawns and shaded walks of Holland Park, and in nearby Holland Park Road stands Leighton House, the home of the 19th-century classical painter Lord Leighton. Its centrepiece is the Arab Hall, added in 1877-9 to house the artist's collection of Islamic tiles. The House also contains paintings by Leighton, Burne-Jones and Millais.

Commonwealth Institute: All year, daily exc Sun am. Free entry. Refreshments. Shop. P *Toilets.* ♿ *Tel (01) 602 3257. Leighton House: All year, daily exc Sun. Free entry. Toilets. Tel (01) 602 3316.*

COVENT GARDEN

Central London, WC2 (Db)

Bistros, restaurants, wine bars and pubs line the most un-English Square in England. Covent Garden began as the convent garden that supplied vegetables to Westminster Abbey, and for centuries it was London's principal market for farm produce. In 1980 it reopened as a combined shopping precinct and pleasure garden. In the old covered market there are rows of handsome little shops: boutiques, confectioners, bookshops, art galleries, food shops, a toy theatre shop, an old-fashioned tobacconist's. Buskers provide entertainment.

St Paul's Church, a great sumptuous parallelogram of a building, was described in 1638 by its builder, Inigo Jones, as 'the handsomest barn in England'. The painter Sir Peter Lely is buried there, and also the woodcarver Grinling Gibbons. But most of all, St Paul's is famed as the Actors' Church. Ellen Terry's ashes repose there and wall panels and monuments read like a roll call of the theatre.

All year, daily. Church: all year, daily exc Sun pm. Free entry. Tel (01) 836 5221.

DR JOHNSON'S HOUSE

17 Gough Square EC4 (Eb)

In the garret of this red-brick early 18th-century house the scholar and lexicographer Dr Samuel Johnson compiled his *Dictionary*. With revisions it remained the standard English dictionary for some 100 years. In the other rooms are relics and mementos of Johnson, including the first edition of the *Dictionary*. All around the house there are paintings of his many friends, among them his biographer James Boswell.

All year, daily exc Sat. Adm charge. Tel (01) 353 3745.

DULWICH PICTURE GALLERY

College Road, SE21 (Cc)

A display of some 320 British and European pictures is housed in a building that was the first in England to be designed specifically as an art gallery; its foundations were laid in 1811, ten years before the National Gallery was established. The gallery's lantern top inspired the design of the original K2 telephone box in 1924, and to mark this, one of the classic red boxes has been installed in the grounds.

One of the most famous pictures in the gallery is *The Linley Sisters*, painted by Thomas Gainsborough around 1772. There is a wide range of works by continental masters, particularly of the 17th century and including Rembrandt, Murillo, Poussin, Van Dyck and Hobbema. Opposite the gallery gates is Dulwich Park, which has displays of rhododendrons and azaleas in season.

Picture Gallery: All year, daily exc Sun am and Mon. Adm charge. Shop. P *Toilets.* ♿ *Tel (01) 693 8000. Park: All year, daily.*

GUILDHALL

Gresham Street, EC2 (Eb)

The City's seat of municipal government was built in the second decade of the 15th century, but suffered considerably in the Great Fire of London and again in the Blitz. Among the numerous restorations, the porch, the undercroft and other fragments remain of the original building. The 152ft long Great Hall is decorated with the arms and banners of the livery companies and has a gravity that befits the venue for the City's great ceremonies. Monuments to the Duke of Wellington, the two Pitts and Winston Churchill look down on the historic chamber where the City's Lord Mayor presides over the Court of Common Council. At the west end of the hall is the post-war gallery bearing the 9ft 3in high images of Gog and Magog, carved by David Evans to replace the 18th-century figures burnt in the Blitz. These replaced yet earlier images, but no one knows who the original Gog and Magog were. Perhaps they were gigantic slaves of Brutus, London's legendary founder, or simply effigies carried in medieval processions.

In the Guildhall's modern library is the museum of the Worshipful Company of Clockmakers, which illustrates the development of clockmaking from the 15th century. There are exquisitely decorated English, Swiss and French pocket watches, long-case clocks, and an Italian gas-operated clock dating from 1835.

All year, Mon-Fri. Free entry. Shop. Toilets. Tel (01) 606 3030.

HAMPTON COURT PALACE

East Molesey (Bb)

The mighty red-brick mass, under wide skies and by the sweet curve of the River Thames leading down to Kingston, remains every bit as impressive as its builder, Cardinal Wolsey, intended it to be. The visitor enters by the bridge and the Great Gatehouse, patched and restored at various times, into the Base Court: parts of this area featured in the film *A Man for All Seasons*. Next, through Anne Boleyn's Gateway, is Clock Court, to which all Hampton's owners have made a contribution – including Henry VIII, to whom Wolsey handed over the building soon after its completion in 1520. Above are the gorgeous Tudor chimneys, seemingly carved out of dark strawberry biscuit, and the Astronomical Clock which since 1540 has announced such data as the time, the date, month, phases of the moon and the state of the tide at London Bridge.

From the colonnade in the Court, the King's Staircase climbs to the first floor. An allegorical painting of breathtaking size swarms up the walls and over the ceiling, accompanying visitors to William and Mary's State Apartments, designed by Sir Christopher Wren. Here is a collection of more than 3000 muskets, pistols and bayonets arranged in whirls and patterns in the King's Guard Chamber, followed in the Communication Gallery by the 'Windsor Beauties' – the beautiful women, sly and voluptuous, of Charles II's court, painted by Lely. In the Queen's Guard Chamber, William III replies with his favourites painted by Kneller. Next door, the Presence Chamber is a splendid room designed by Vanbrugh, with a heroic fireplace supported by huge, laughing Beefeaters.

Towering tapestries and paintings flank visitors as they move through the intersecting rooms, passing here a stately fireplace by Grinling Gibbons, there a State Bed the size of a small room. In the Queen's Drawing Room a crimson-canopied, ostrich-plumed bed is regarded from the ceiling by Queen Anne, as the Spirit of Justice, and from the wall by her consort, Prince George. The windows look upon the focal point of Wren's design for palace and park; the view of the Great Fountain Garden, the Long Water and the three radiating avenues.

Hampton Court's immaculately tended gardens are a delight to stroll in. There is the Maze, if not so mystifying as originally intended, still baffling enough, and The Vine in its greenhouse, planted in 1768 and now measuring 7ft plus round the stem. Then there are the Tudor and 18th-century gardens, the Hornbeam Arch, and the delicious waterside walks. Gardeners in search of inspiration might like to consider the beds in which ornamental cabbages, rhubarb and chard are grown among the flowers.

All year, daily exc Sun am Oct-Mar (certain areas closed in winter, or at short notice). Adm charge. Refreshments. Shop. P *Toilets.* ♿ *Tel (01) 977 8441.*

HIGHGATE CEMETERY

Swains Lane, N6 (Cd)

The Old (Western) Cemetery in Highgate was opened as a private business venture in 1839, complete with Egyptian Avenue, Terrace Catacombs and Lebanon Circle, all massive combinations of monument and receptacle for the dead. Between 1839 and the early 1970s some 166,000 people were buried there; they included the novelists Radclyffe Hall and Mrs Henry Wood and the scientists Michael Faraday and Jacob Bronowski.

Then the company that owned the cemetery began to run out of money. Maintenance was neglected, paths disappeared, saplings thrust up through graves, and stone angels, children, faithful dogs and horses stood half-concealed in ivy and brambles. Foxes, badgers and other animals and birds found haven there, and the place took on a wild and melancholy splendour all its own. Unfortunately, it also attracted vandals, and in 1975 it was decided to close it permanently. Soon, however, the Friends of Highgate Cemetery repaired the worst of the damage without spoiling the cemetery's forlorn and overgrown charm or its appeal as a wildlife sanctuary. There are frequent conducted tours to the more notable resting places.

CEILING SPLENDOURS *The decorative ceiling of the Queen's Bedchamber (above) in Hampton Court Palace depicts Aurora, the Dawn Goddess, rising in her chariot from the sea. It was painted by Sir James Thornhill in 1715. The Great Hall (right), built by Henry VIII, is noted for its ornate wooden ceiling.*

GIANTS IN KENSINGTON

Four of the most famous museums in London – and the world – stand close together in South Kensington. In Cromwell Road, the Natural History Museum has a Whale Hall and a gallery devoted to the work of Charles Darwin, while the Victoria and Albert Museum covers the art and design of all nations and all periods. The Geological Museum in Exhibition Road is noted for its collections of gemstones and minerals; the Science Museum surveys all aspects of technology.

Four Museums: All year, daily exc Sun am. Natural History: Adm charge. Refreshments. Shop. Toilets. ♿ Tel (01) 938 9123. Victoria and Albert: Free entry. Refreshments. Shop. Toilets. ♿ 938 8500. Geological: Adm charge. Refreshments. Shop. Toilets. ♿ 938 8765. Science: Free entry. Refreshments. Shop. Toilets. ♿ 938 8000.

STONE LILY *Graceful and intricate patterns like the creations of an abstract artist decorate this crinoid, or stone lily, in the exhibition of British fossils in the Geological Museum. It was found at Lyme Regis in Dorset and dates from the Jurassic period, around 200 million years ago.*

HEAVENLY TIME *This astrological watch in the Science Museum was made in the 18th century by George Margetts. As well as telling the time, it shows the months of the year and their zodiacal signs. The museum's displays tell the story of technological change, from the Industrial Revolution to the Space Age.*

DRAGON COAT *Embroidered in coloured floss silks, this Chinese lady's coat in the Victoria and Albert Museum has a traditional design of dragons among clouds, above a deep hem of stylised waves. The dragons' scales are made of seed pearls and coral beads. The coat dates from the 1870s.*

MODEL MONSTER *The life-size model of a blue whale is on show at the Natural History Museum. It is about 85ft long and the original whale weighed some 100 tons – as much as about 1350 heavy men. Blue whales are toothless and have fringed sheets of baleen, or whalebone, hanging from their upper jaws. These sheets form a sieve through which the whales ingest plankton and phosphorescent shrimps called krill. Suspended above the blue whale model is the skeleton of a Greenland right whale.*

MUSEUM MISCELLANY

Other museums in London's rich treasury include:

Baden-Powell House, Queen's Gate, SW7. Life of founder of Scout movement. All year, daily. Tel (01) 584 7030.

Barnet Museum, Wood Street, Barnet. Local history, military artefacts. All year, Tues-Thur and Sat pm; also Sat am Mar-Nov. 449 0321.

Bethnal Green Museum of Childhood, Cambridge Heath Rd, E2. Toys, dolls, dolls' houses, puppets, games. All year, daily exc Sun am and Fri. 980 2415.

Carlyle's House, 24 Cheyne Row, SW3. Home of Scottish writer Thomas Carlyle and wife Jane. Furniture, clothes and trinkets. Apr-Oct, Wed-Sun and Bank Hol Mon. 352 7087.

Dickens House and Museum, 48 Doughty St, WC1. Dickens' home 1837-9; study, desk, chair and writing table. All year, daily exc Sun and Bank Hol. 405 2127.

Fenton House, Windmill Hill, NW3. Keyboard instruments and period furniture. NT. Apr-Oct, Sat-Wed; Mar, Sat and Sun pm.

Forty Hall, Forty Hill, Enfield. Furniture of 17th and 18th centuries, ceramics and pictures. All year, Tues-Sun and Bank Hol Mon. 363 8196.

Freud Museum, 20 Maresfield Gdns, NW3. Home of psychoanalyst Sigmund Freud 1938-9; library, desk, couch and souvenirs. All year, Wed-Sun pm. 435 2002.

Geffrye Museum, Kingsland Rd, E2. Furniture, furnishings and domestic appliances from Elizabethan times to late 1930s. All year, daily exc Sun am and Mon; also Bank Hol. 739 8368.

Grange Museum, Neasden Lane, NW10. Local history of Brent, including Victorian parlour, 1930s lounge and Edwardian draper's shop. All year, daily pm, exc Sun. 908 7432.

Horniman Museum, London Rd, Forest Hill, SE23. Man and his environment; also musical instruments. All year, daily exc Sun am. 699 1872.

Keats House, Keats Grove, NW3. Home of John Keats 1818-20; manuscripts, letters and relics of the poet, and his fiancée Fanny Brawne. All year, daily exc Sun am. 435 2062.

Museum of Mankind, 6 Burlington Gdns, W1. Different cultures and peoples, including Africa, the Americas, Australia and Pacific Islands. All year, daily exc Sun am. 437 2224.

National Postal Museum, King Edward St, EC1. World's largest stamp collection, with stamps issued since 1878. All year, daily exc 1st week Oct and Bank Hol. 432 3851.

North Woolwich Old Station Railway Museum, Pier Rd, E16. Exhibits of Great Eastern Railway, including rolling stock. All year, daily exc Sun and Bank Hol am. 474 7244.

Pollock's Toy Museum, 1 Scala St, W1. Toys from all over the world. All year, Mon-Sat. 636 3452.

Sir John Soane's Museum, 13 Lincoln's Inn Fields, WC2. Antiquities and works of art, including paintings by Turner and Hogarth. All year, Tues-Sat; closed Bank Hol. 405 2107.

William Morris Gallery, Lloyd Park, Forest Road, E17. Collections of Morris's decorative art. All year. Tues-Sat; also 1st Sun in month. 527 5544.

Wimbledon Lawn Tennis Museum, Church Rd, SW19. History of tennis; trophies and films of famous matches. All year, daily exc Sun am and Mon (spectators only during championships). 946 6131.

On the other side of Swains Lane is the New (Eastern) Cemetery, opened in 1854. Not so romantic as the old one, it has just as high a quota of famous residents. The most famous of these is Karl Marx, whose massive monument attracts reverent parties of Russians and Chinese.

All year, daily (tours every hour on the hour). Free entry. Shop. P *Tel (01) 348 0808.*

IMPERIAL WAR MUSEUM

Lambeth Road, SE1 (Ea)

Two gigantic naval guns, each weighing 100 tons and capable of throwing a 17cwt shell some 18 miles, stand before the Georgian portico of the building which once housed the Bethlem, or 'Bedlam', hospital for the insane. Inside, the museum's galleries begin with a recruiting office of 1914 featuring a poster: 'Women of Britain say Go!' and appeals to join the Public Schools Brigade, the Pals' Battalions, the Bantams and other hastily raised units.

Then to a muted concert of battle noises and songs of the period, visitors walk through a trench system under camouflage nets, wherein are displayed uniforms, trench furniture, periscopes, grenades, mortars, clubs, daggers, artillery and machine guns. There is a dinosaur-like Mk V tank of 1918 and a kite-like F2B fighter, while relics of heroes include the cap and battered cigarette case of Captain Albert Ball, and Lawrence of Arabia's head ropes and rifle. From the Home Front, there are memories of Zeppelins, posters and fading photographs matched to War Office telegrams and last letters.

From the early days of the Second World War there is a fishing boat that helped to lift troops off the Dunkirk beaches and a Spitfire that took part in the Battle of Britain. Life in wartime Britain is represented by displays on the Blitz, air-raid shelters, ration books and gas masks.

Wars did not finish in 1945, and there are displays on Korea, Suez, Malaya, Aden, Cyprus and the Falklands. The museum's art galleries house paintings by famous artists, who have seized upon moments in battle with far more immediacy than any photograph. From the autumn of 1988 until the following summer, parts of the museum will be closed while displays are redeveloped and mounted. Four new floors will then illustrate the major aspects of the two World Wars.

All year, daily exc Sun am. Free entry. Refreshments. Shop. P *(meters). Toilets.* ♿ *Tel (01) 735 8922.*

KATHLEEN AND MAY SCHOONER

St Mary Overy Dock, Cathedral Street, SE1 (Ea)

For some 60 years the *Kathleen and May* sailed the coastal waters of Britain, working mostly out of Appledore in Devon where she was built in 1900. She is the last of hundreds of wooden-built, three-masted schooners that plied between the coastal ports carrying coal, iron, wheat, pitprops, bags of cement and fertiliser. In the 1930s the ship had an auxiliary engine fitted and the topsails removed because of the shortage of crews with sailing experience. Now, however, she has been restored to her original condition, and gives an insight into how the six-man crew existed.

All year, daily. Adm charge. Shop. Tel (01) 403 3965.

KENSINGTON PALACE

Kensington Gardens, W8 (Bc)

Of all the people associated with Kensington Palace since William and Mary bought it as a royal residence in 1689, to escape the damp riverside airs of Whitehall Palace, it was Queen Victoria who left the most vivid impression. Just inside the entrance is the Red Saloon – red pillars, red carpet and red cloth on huge table – where the young Queen held her Accession Privy Council on June 20, 1837. A little farther on is the North Drawing Room, surprisingly furnished as a bedroom; the Duchess of Kent made the alteration in May 1819, a few days before giving birth there to her daughter Victoria. Upstairs, next to the duchess's dressing room, is Victoria's own bedroom where, in the small hours of June 20, 1837, she learned that William IV had died, and that she was now Queen. The room is filled with memorabilia of Victoria – her favourite paintings and souvenirs, the cot occupied by each of her nine children in succession.

The State Apartments, dark-panelled and filled with glorious paintings, were built to impress. Here, on behalf of George I, William Kent excelled himself. His allegorical painting on the ceiling of the King's Drawing Room is breathtaking, while the King's Staircase is decorated with a huge trompe l'oeil depicting spectators leaning over balustrades to watch George I's courtiers.

The King's Gallery, however, is the province of William III. The enormous chamber was built to house his collection of paintings, but to show that he never forgot he was a soldier, a repeater weather vane above the fireplace continuously indicates the direction of the wind across a map of north-western Europe.

At various points on the tour of the palace there is an exhibition of Court Dress from about 1750 onwards, displayed on models posed against contemporary backgrounds and furniture. And beyond the palace's windows lie the magical glades of Kensington Gardens, laid out in their present form by George II, but sadly scarred by the great gale of October 1987. Peter Pan's statue attracts generation after generation of young admirers, while small boys and old gentlemen sail their boats on the Round Pond.

All year, daily exc Sun am. Adm charge. Shop. Toilets. Tel (01) 937 9561.

KENWOOD HOUSE

Hampstead Lane, NW3 (Bd)

Kenwood is a lovely Georgian wedding cake of a house, all tall white pillars and pediments; within, it is cream, pale grey and gold and filled with light. The loveliest room is the Adam library, a confection in pink, blue and gold, set off by crimson and gold furniture. The tall gilt mirrors designed by Robert Adam are still in place, reflecting the view of the surrounding park and lake seen through the windows. But the principal treasures are the paintings. There is a Rembrandt self-portrait, a Van Dyck, a Franz Hals, delicate Boucher pastorals, Vermeer's luminous *Guitar Player*, and a view of Old London Bridge painted in 1639 by Claude de Jongh. The portrait that stops even the most casual strollers in their tracks is Gainsborough's *Mary, Countess Howe*. Coolly beautiful, she is shown in a wide-brimmed hat and a dress of shimmering pink beneath a shawl of transparent lace, and looks as if about to speak. *(continued on page 128)*

COURTLY ONLOOKERS *Realistic figures crowd the illusionist gallery painted by William Kent on the walls of the King's Staircase in Kensington Palace in the 1720s. They are depicted watching the comings and goings of George I's courtiers. A court dress of cream silk (right) of 1870 is in the palace collection.*

MARITIME TREASURES AT GREENWICH

London could have no finer gateway than the Thames at Greenwich, with its breathtaking vistas and royal, nautical heritage. On the south bank is the Royal Naval College, twin-domed and divided to give unbroken views of the elegant Queen's House, now part of the National Maritime Museum. The steep sward behind, topped by the Old Royal Observatory, is Greenwich Royal Park, laid out in 1662 to designs by André Le Nôtre, the landscaper of Versailles. Along the delightful riverside walk, the *Cutty Sark* clipper ship is preserved in dry dock, and a foot tunnel leads under the Thames to the lovely Island Gardens. *Observatory: All year, daily. Adm charge. Shop.* 🅿 *Tel (01) 858 4422. Museum: All year, daily. Adm charge. Refreshments. Shop. Toilets.* ♿ *Tel (01) 858 4422.* Cutty Sark*: All year, daily exc Sun am. Adm charge. Shop.* ♿ *(part). Tel (01) 853 3589. Ranger's House: EH. All year, daily. Free entry. Shop.* 🅿 *(limited). Toilets.* ♿ *(part). Tel (01) 853 0035. College: All year, pm daily exc Thur. Free entry.* 🅿 *Tel (01) 858 2154. Thames Barrier Visitor Centre, Woolwich: All year, daily. Adm charge. Refreshments. Shop.* 🅿 *Toilets.* ♿ *Tel (01) 854 1373.*

OLD ROYAL OBSERVATORY *Charles II founded the observatory at Greenwich in 1675, and Sir Christopher Wren designed living quarters for the first Astronomer Royal, John Flamsteed. Now topped by a time ball which drops at 1pm every day, Flamsteed House, on the left, is dwarfed by the telescope domes of the Altazimuth Pavilion, in the foreground, and the Great Equatorial Building. Displays about astronomy and timekeeping in Flamsteed House include (below) an hour glass, a* Nautical Almanac *and a nocturnal – used for measuring time by observation of stars.*

NATIONAL MARITIME MUSEUM *Among the treasures of Britain's naval heritage on show at the National Maritime Museum is the coat that Nelson wore at Trafalgar; the hole on the shoulder made by the musket shot that killed him can be clearly seen. Another is the chronometer (below) made by John Harrison in 1736. Much more accurate than existing timepieces, the chronometer revolutionised navigation, by enabling longitude to be calculated accurately from the difference in time around the world.*

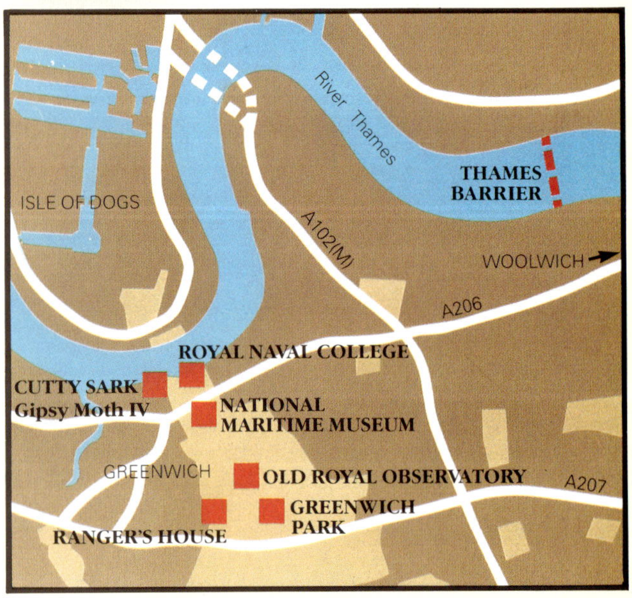

CUTTY SARK AND GIPSY MOTH

A grand old lady of the tea-clipper era, Cutty Sark *still has the power to stir the blood as she stands high and dry in dock, restored in appearance to her 19th-century glory (artist's reconstruction, above left). Her mainmast towers 145ft, and 10 miles of rigging and huge crosstrees once carried nearly an acre of sail, to give speeds of more than 17 knots. Yet her graceful hull is only 212ft long and her beam 36ft.*

Cutty Sark, *named after the short shift worn by the witch who chased Tam in Robert Burns' poem* Tam o'Shanter, *was built in Dumbarton in 1869 as a rival for* Thermopylae, *then the fastest tea clipper, and fully justified expectations. In 1871 she sped from Shanghai to the Thames in 107 days, and in 1885, while engaged in the Australian wool trade, she raced from the Lizard to Sydney via Cape Horn in 72 days.*

Close by is another proud vessel, Gipsy Moth IV *(above), in which Sir Francis Chichester sailed single-handed around the world in 1966.*

NO SHELTER *The helmsman at the wheel on the poop deck was exposed to the elements, and 'rode' the ship like a jockey.*

BUNK BEDS *Straw-filled mattresses once covered the wooden bunk beds that line the walls of the crew's quarters in the fo'c'sle.*

WAY FINDERS *The mate and his officers pored over charts on tables in the saloon to plan the fastest and safest route.*

FRESH FOOD *Chickens and pigs were carried to supplement the seamen's regular diet of salt meat, beans and biscuits.*

TWO CARGOES *At first, chests of tea were carried from China. Later,* Cutty Sark *brought bales of Australian wool to England.*

FIGUREHEAD *The witch wears a 'cutty sark', or short chemise, and bears the tail torn from Tam o'Shanter's fleeing mare.*

RANGER'S HOUSE *The Dolmetsch Collection of early musical instruments is housed in a late 17th-century red-brick villa in Greenwich Park. The house, once the official residence of the park's Ranger, is also home to the magnificent Suffolk Collection with royal portraits by Sir Peter Lely (1618-80).*

ROYAL NAVAL COLLEGE *A superb chapel, rebuilt after a fire in 1779, is part of a complex of baroque buildings which began as the King's House, built for Charles II. William and Mary commissioned Wren to enlarge it as a hospital for naval pensioners. It became home to the college in 1873.*

THAMES FLOOD BARRIER *Giant roofs covered with stainless steel house the mighty machinery needed to raise the ten massive gates from the riverbed. London's flood protection – necessary because the sea level off south-east England is rising – is 580yds long, cost £535 million and was first used in 1983.*

(continued from page 125) The Kenwood estate, landscaped in the 18th century, includes a gigantic oyster shell beside a small lake from which orchestras and bands play anything from trad jazz to Mozart. Beyond lie the 800 acres of Hampstead Heath, a hilly, wooded landscape of unexpected viewpoints and valleys.
EH. All year, daily. Free entry. Refreshments. Shop. P *Toilets. Tel (01) 348 1286.*

LONDON DIAMOND CENTRE
10 Hanover Street, W1 (Db)

Behind an elegant Georgian façade lies a world that begins with a realistic reconstruction of a diamond mine and ends with a glittering display of jewellery. A life-size model of a miner boring into a rockface with his pneumatic drill sets the scene for a tour of the workshops where skilled craftsmen cut, shape and polish the most coveted of all gemstones. A goldsmith demonstrates how the finished stones are set. Display cases contain replicas of famous diamonds, including the Cullinan, the largest diamond ever found. At the other end of the scale is the smallest brilliant-cut diamond, with 58 facets, which has to be viewed through a magnifying glass.

In the showroom it is possible to buy diamonds and other unset precious and semi-precious stones, and a designer is on hand to create a unique piece of jewellery.
All year, Mon-Fri, Sat am. Adm charge. Toilets. Tel (01) 629 5511.

LONDON DUNGEON
28-34 Tooley Street, SE1 (Ea)

Anyone who doubts the popularity of public executions as a spectator sport in days of yore should see the queues outside the London Dungeon, and the expressions of happy anticipation. Though the Dungeon is actually situated in the arches of a Victorian railway viaduct, the site is of impeccable pedigree, since it occupies that of the business premises of Roland Topcliffe, torturer by appointment to Elizabeth I.

The exhibition consists mainly of a tour through the nastier moments of our island story, illustrated by bloodstained, life-size models. There is Boudicca butchering a Roman, Harold and the arrow, the execution of Anne Boleyn, the burning of Latimer and Ridley, a headless Mary, Queen of Scots pumping gore, and numerous hangings, gibbetings, drawing and quarterings, rackings, pressings, brandings and boilings. A few bloodthirsty foreigners are admitted, such as Vlad the Impaler and Gilles de Rais.
All year, daily. Adm charge. Refreshments. Shop. Toilets. ♿ *Tel (01) 403 0606.*

LONDON TOY AND MODEL MUSEUM
21-23 Craven Hill, W2 (Cb)

Amid the plane trees, large Victorian houses and little shops and restaurants of Lancaster Gate lies an amazing collection of toys evidently gathered by people in love with childhood and intent on establishing the finest nursery in the world. Among its greater glories are the model railway displays, which include such stars as the giant 1932 Bassett-Lowke LMS *Royal Scot* and the *Evening Star*, steam model of the last steam locomotive specially built for British Rail.

ALL ABOARD *School children eagerly explore a modern bus at London Transport Museum. The poster (far right) dates from 1908; a year earlier, the Hampstead Tube had opened up to city workers the rural delights of living in north-west London.*

A huge collection of model soldiers includes a fascinating display on 19th-century wars, gathered together when sailors wore straw hats, soldiers khaki topees, and the enemy was Boxer, Zulu or Mutineer. The 'civilian' collection includes station personnel, cowboys and Indians, farms, police, Little Red Riding Hood in nine scenes, and a village christening.

Children's preoccupation with teddy bears is traced back to the first publication of *Goldilocks and the Three Bears* in 1836. Then came the Teddy Bear, named after a bear cub that Theodore Roosevelt forebore from shooting on a hunting trip in 1902, and originally called Roosevelt Bear. Since Paddington Station is five minutes' walk away, it is only right that there should be a display devoted to Paddington Bear, including the manuscript of *A Bear Called Paddington.*
All year, daily exc Mon. Adm charge. Refreshments. Shop. P *(meters). Toilets. Tel (01) 262 7905.*

LONDON TRANSPORT MUSEUM
Covent Garden, WC2 (Db)

The way in which London Transport is woven deep into the life of the capital is splendidly reflected by the displays in this museum. Early means of moving Londoners about are represented by a model of a 17th-century wherry that used to ferry passengers across the river between Brentford and Kew. On show is a reconstruction of the first true London bus – George Shillibeer's horse omnibus that ran from Paddington to Bank in 1829. The first electric trams ran on London streets in 1901, and continued to do so for 51 years, though accompanied by motor buses from 1904 and trolley buses from 1931. Representatives of all these forms of transport are on show; among the stars are a 1910 B Type bus, one of the kind that, dressed in khaki, carried troops to the Western Front, and an LT Type, still wearing Second World War blast netting on its windows and black-out hoods on its headlamps.

Young visitors can operate points and signals in a full-scale mock-up of a Tube tunnel, or sit at the controls of a Circle Line train. There are video films on the history of London Transport, and an exhibition of its posters, many by famous artists, that have informed and entertained Londoners for the best part of a century.
All year, daily. Adm charge. Shop. Toilets. ♿ *Tel (01) 379 6344.*

LONDON ZOO
Regent's Park, NW1 (Bc)

Elephants led by their keepers parade the broad paths, ambling past the bronze statue of Guy the Gorilla – the zoo's most famous recent inhabitant, who died in 1978 aged 31. More than 8000 animals – from aardvarks to zebras – occupy the north-east corner of Regent's Park, in a zoo that is constantly changing so that the 900 species of animals live in conditions as near natural as possible.

Visitors can see Chia Chia, the giant male panda; orang-utans which swing from pole to pole like trapeze artistes; dinner-suited penguins waddling pompously in line; sea lions catching raw fish in their mouths at feeding times; reptiles and insects patrolling their own special houses; and lions and tigers lazing majestically in glassed-in dens.

Sheep, cows, rabbits, pigs, ducks and cream ponies inhabit the jolly Children's Zoo, which also has a collection of night animals, including bush babies and porcupines, living in dimly lit enclosures that turn daylight into darkness. There is also an aquarium with freshwater, seawater and brilliantly coloured tropical fish, and an outdoor pool in which graceful pink flamingos rest on one leg.

A tunnel leads under the Regent's Canal to the Snowdon Aviary, the home of up to 200 tropical birds including egrets, ibis, touracos and gallinules. A cantilevered bridge spanning the aviary gives visitors close-ups of the birds nesting and flying.

Next to the zoo lies the level green oasis of Regent's Park, developed as a public park in the early 19th century when two broad terraces and two sweeping, circular roads were designed by John Nash. Today it has tennis courts, football and cricket pitches, a delightful rose garden in Queen Mary's Gardens, a boating lake, military bandstand and an open-air theatre in the summer months which specialises in Shakespeare.

A waterbus service runs along Regent's Canal, which forms the northern boundary of the park. The long, brightly painted canal boats ply the 2¼ miles from Camden Lock to Little Venice in West London, with a stop at the zoo.

Zoo: All year, daily. Adm charge. Refreshments. Shop. P *(limited). Toilets.* ♿ *Tel (01) 722 3333. Park: All year, daily. Free entry. Refreshments.* P *(limited). Toilets.* ♿ *Tel (01) 486 7905. Waterbus: Easter-Sept, daily. Ticket fare. Tel (01) 482 2550.*

MADAME TUSSAUD'S AND LONDON PLANETARIUM

Marylebone Road, NW1 (Db)

Madame Tussaud's is a national institution, and though much has changed over the years some of the old favourites are still there; they include such tableaux as *When did you last see your Father?*, Guy Fawkes, the Sleeping Beauty who has been breathing gently since 1837, and the Little Princes in the Tower.

From the late 18th century on, the figures become more and more convincing. Excellent likenesses include the young Queen Victoria, Picasso, Lord Lichfield, Mrs Thatcher, Joan Collins and Ken Livingstone. The 'Super Stars' Gallery features giants of pop and sport, and in the Grand Hall members of the Cabinet gaze enviously upon the crowd-pulling Royal Family, fronted by the Duke and Duchess of York.

The Chamber of Horrors has been enlivened by the addition of audiovisual effects. Every few minutes there are noisy executions by firing squad and the electric chair, while round about there are more static dispatchings via the gallows, the garrotte and the guillotine. George Joseph Smith's Bride in the Bath blows bubbles through the bath water, and in a highly realistic alley in Victorian Whitechapel lies an eviscerated victim of Jack the Ripper.

Moving on, visitors come to the lower gun deck of HMS *Victory* at the height of the Battle of Trafalgar. Impressionistic figures serve the monster 24 and 32-pounder guns, which every few minutes belch thunder, flame and smoke. Orders and screams punctuate the din, and shafts of sunlight from the gratings overhead move to and fro across the deck, giving the impression of the ship's ponderous roll. Down below, in the red-painted orlop deck, Lord Nelson is dying.

The London Planetarium, part of the Madame Tussaud's complex, offers half-hourly star shows in which the audience leans back and gazes up to the dome which is transformed into the night sky. Planets, stars and galaxies wheel across the heavens, projected by a massive star projector which itself looks like something from a science-fiction film.

Special gearing is used to simulate the effect of the Earth's rotation, and the sky can be shown from any part of the Earth's surface; revealing stars not seen from Britain. In the evening, the Planetarium turns itself into a Laserium, in which beams of light dance and form patterns to current rock and pop music.

All year, daily. Adm charge. Refreshments. Shop. Toilets. ♿ *Tel (01) 935 6861.*

ANNUAL OUTING *The ornate crimson and gold Lord Mayor's State Coach, built in 1757, can be seen at the Museum of London. The coach is still used every year in the Lord Mayor's Show in November.*

HIGH LIFE, LOW LIFE *Spectators at the London Planetarium gaze up at a night sky dominated by Jupiter, the largest of the planets. It is noted for its oval-shaped Great Red Spot, whose vivid colour may be caused by phosphorus. In the neighbouring Madame Tussaud's is an eerie re-creation (left) of a dank alley in London's East End in the 1880s, when Jack the Ripper prowled the shadows in search of victims for his knife.*

MUSEUM OF LONDON

London Wall, EC2 (Eb)

Like the imagined cross-section of a City excavation shown in the foyer, the galleries of the London Museum are presented as layers of London time. The story begins with the prehistoric exhibits, which include a flint hand axe used by a hunter in the Thames Valley some 250,000 years ago, and a replica of a Celtic shield found in Battersea. The Roman gallery has reconstructed rooms furnished with articles imported from other parts of the Roman Empire, or made by a local craftsman. A large window turns the real Roman wall outside the museum into an exhibit.

Medieval London is represented by, among other exhibits, a model of William the Conqueror's Tower, a 15th-century London interior and lead crosses buried with victims of the Black Death. Business and craftsmanship flourished in Tudor London, as can be seen from a collection of jewels found in Cheapside, while the troubled days of the Stuarts are recalled by Cromwell's death mask, a plague bell and a realistic diorama of the Great Fire, with a commentary from Samuel Pepys' Diaries.

So the galleries continue, presenting the changing ages of London, each with its own talisman: a door from Newgate Prison, a Georgian doll's house, a model of the Crystal Palace that housed the Great Exhibition of 1851, a Victorian schoolroom. There are shops, offices and a pub from Edwardian London, Selfridge's bronze lifts, a Woolworth's counter, a BBC studio from the inter-war period, and an Anderson air-raid shelter from the Second World War.

All year, daily exc Sun am and Mon. Free entry. Refreshments. Shop. P *Toilets.* ♿ *Tel (01) 600 3699.*

NATIONAL ARMY MUSEUM

Royal Hospital Road, SW3 (Da)

The brick-and-concrete blockhouse accommodating the National Army Museum is defended by a Centurion tank, a pair of 5.5 guns and some armoured cars. Inside are two galleries. The first tells the story of the British and Imperial armies from Henry VII's raising of the Yeomen of the Guard in 1485 to the eve of war in 1914. The second is concerned with the citizen, Commonwealth and professional soldiers who have fought our battles ever since, from Flanders to the Falklands.

In the first gallery are the jerkins of Cromwel-

THE CONQUEROR'S MIGHTY FORTRESS

The Tower of London has in its time been a palace, a zoo, an arsenal, a treasury and a mint: but it is as a state prison for awkward subjects that it is most famous. Prisoners were brought in secretly by river and then through Traitors' Gate. The 'Little Princes' (the sons of Edward IV) are said to have been murdered in the Bloody Tower. Sir Thomas More was held in the Bell Tower in 1534-5, and from the tower named after him Elizabeth I's erstwhile favourite, Robert Devereux, Earl of Essex, was taken to the block on Tower Green in 1601. On Tower Green is the site of the block where died Anne Boleyn and Catherine Howard, and others whom it would have been impolite to execute publicly on Tower Hill. The Tower's last prisoners, its ravens, hop about the Green now; they cannot leave for their wings are clipped – and if they did, it is said, the Tower would fall.

The building that dominates the whole fortress is the massive, square White Tower – the original Tower of London begun by William the Conqueror, and more or less completed by 1097. It contains the Royal Armouries, a collection of arms and armour from Saxon times to the near-present. The Chapel of St John, pure Norman, plain and perfect, is on the first floor. Mary Tudor was married by proxy in it in 1554, and there young men kept vigil before becoming Knights of the Bath. The New Armouries contain Oriental armour, and the Heralds' Museum, which covers everything from coin design to the grant of armorial bearings to Miss Sarah Ferguson.

Beside Tower Green is the Chapel Royal of St Peter ad Vincula ('in chains'), a pretty Tudor building where executioners' victims, including Sir Thomas More and Henry VIII's wives, lie buried. The Crown Jewels are kept beneath the Waterloo Block next door.

Soaring above Tower Wharf is Tower Bridge, its ironwork brightly painted to contrast with the Gothic spires of its piers. It is today the instantly recognised symbol of London, though it was opened only in 1894. Visitors can admire the mighty machinery which raises the bascules carrying the road, and walk the high, glazed walkways to see the spires and skyscrapers of the City upstream, and the renascent Docklands downstream. Nearby St Katharine Dock, once busy with tall ships, is now a complex of business facilities, hotel, shops, restaurants, houses, offices and a marina where old Thames barges may be seen.

Tower: Mar-Oct, daily exc Sun am; Nov-Feb, Mon-Sat. Adm charge. Shops. Toilets. P *Tel (01) 709 0765.*
Bridge: All year, daily. Adm charge. Shop. Toilets. ♿ *Tel (01) 407 0922.*

CROWN AND JAIL *Centrepiece of the Crown Jewels, the Imperial State Crown is set with 2800 diamonds. In the Bloody Tower (left), Raleigh was held for 13 years.*

EAGLE FLASK *Holy oil for the monarch's anointing is held in this ampulla, which was first used for the coronation of Henry IV in 1399.*

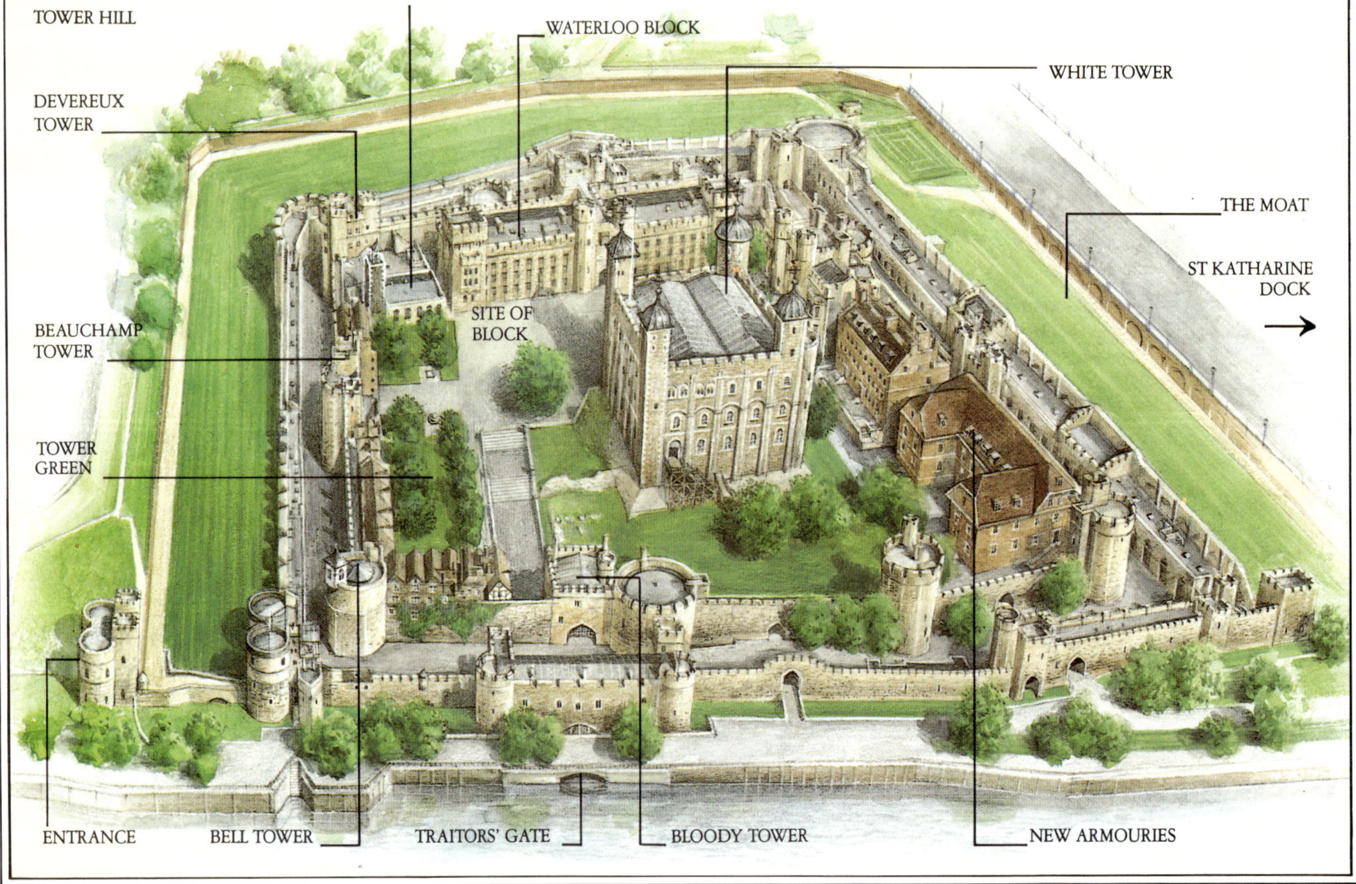

lian troopers, Highland broadswords from the Jacobite Rebellions, Marlborough's saddle cloth, and dioramas and relics of the American Wars. The Napoleonic Wars contribute captured French colours, helmets, eagles and the skeleton of 'Marengo', the emperor's charger, while the Crimea has bequeathed early war photographs, Lord Raglan's telescope (for one-armed use) and the note that launched the Charge of the Light Brigade.

Between the galleries there is martial music, and on the walls photographs of the armies of Europe being reviewed by their respective emperors in 1914. Past recruiting posters the route leads to a full-scale section of trench, complete with dugout, shell hole and a glimpse of No Man's Land. There is a sullen rumble of artillery, bursts of machine-gun fire, and a soldier's voice, quoting from a letter telling of the appalling conditions.

The period between the wars is summed up by a guard room, weapons of ever-growing sophistication, trouble on the North-west Frontier. Hostilities are resumed with a noisy evocation of the Dunkirk beaches, and subsequent exhibitions and dioramas follow British and Empire troops all the way through the Second World War to the demob suit. National Servicemen are shown at kit layout and battle in Korea and Malaya, and a final display shows paratroops in action in the Falklands.

A contrasting military presence in Royal Hospital Road is the Royal Hospital, home of the Chelsea Pensioners. Founded by Charles II, it is a red-brick Wren masterpiece with a huge lantern perched on top, and surrounded by velvety lawns and a few dignified old cannons. The Chapel and the Great Hall, where the Duke of Wellington lay in state, are open to the public, as is the Museum which contains paintings, documents, uniforms and medals reflecting the Royal Hospital, its pensioners and staff. The Chelsea Flower Show is held annually in the grounds.

Museum: All year, daily exc Sun am. Free entry. Refreshments. Shop. 🅿 *Toilets.* ♿ *Tel (01) 730 0717. Royal Hospital: All year, daily exc Bank Hol weekends and Sun, Oct-Mar. Free entry. Tel (01) 730 0161.*

NATIONAL GALLERY

Trafalgar Square, WC2 (Db)

Stretched elegantly across the north side of Trafalgar Square, the National Gallery was opened in 1838 to house the nation's growing collection of art masterpieces. Today it contains more than 2000 outstanding European paintings, dating from the 13th to the early 20th centuries. They include Velázquez's *The Toilet of Venus*; Hans Holbein the Younger's *The Ambassadors*, with its sinister and symbolic reminders of death; and Leonardo da Vinci's *The Virgin of the Rocks*, a strange and haunting portrayal of the Virgin Mary and the Christ Child resting outside a grotto.

A 'quick tour' takes in 16 masterpieces, including Constable's *The Hay Wain*, Seurat's *Bathers*, Rembrandt's *Self Portrait aged 63* and Turner's *The Fighting Téméraire*. There are also hour-long guided tours.

Just around the corner, in Charing Cross Road, stands the National Portrait Gallery, which contains some 10,000 likenesses of famous British men and women – any 1000 of which are on show at any given time. Among the faces on view are Chaucer, Shakespeare, Cromwell, Nell Gwyn, Captain Cook, Florence Nightingale, Charles Darwin, Beatrix Potter, Lord Mountbatten and the Prince and Princess of Wales.

National Gallery: All year, daily exc Sun am. Free entry. Refreshments. Shop. Toilets. ♿ *Tel (01) 839 3321. Portrait Gallery: All year, daily exc Sun am. Free entry. Shop. Toilets.* ♿ *Tel (01) 930 1552.*

RIVERSIDE IMPRESSION *The French artist Claude Monet was little known when in 1871 he painted* The Thames below Westminster, *now in the National Gallery. It was the result of a winter in the capital.*

OSTERLEY PARK

Off A4, 2 miles north of Hounslow (Bc)

A splendid example of the 18th-century classical style, Osterley was originally built in the late 16th century by the merchant Sir Thomas Gresham, founder of the Royal Exchange; what stands today is largely the creation of Robert Adam between 1761 and 1780 for the banker Robert Child. Adam retained the Elizabethan layout, based around a courtyard with towers at the corners, but in Italian style he put the chief apartment on the first floor; the approach by a broad flight of steps is spectacular.

The interior today is remarkable for the richness of its 18th-century decorations, statues and wall paintings, and for its grand Georgian furnishings. The antechamber of the state apartment is one of the few rooms anywhere to have remained entirely as it was in the 18th century. The eating room, as it is called, displays the emblems of Bacchus. The design of the ceiling plasterwork is attributed to William Chambers and is rich in hop leaves and vine garlands. The library walls display brightly coloured portraits of classical literary figures.

NT. All year, daily exc Mon. Adm charge. Refreshments. 🅿 *Toilets.* ♿ *Tel (01) 560 3918.*

ROYAL AIR FORCE MUSEUM

Grahame Park Way, Hendon, NW9 (Bd)

For more than 70 years Hendon has been identified with the Royal Air Force, so it is fitting that the RAF Museum should stand in what was a corner of the aerodrome that saw the development of Britain's military air power. The main building is as historic as many of the aircraft it contains, being made up of two hangars dating back to 1915.

Exhibits range from the tiny Bleriot XI, one of the first aircraft used by the Royal Flying Corps in the First World War, to the mighty English Electric Lightning which, with its powerful jet engines, could fly at twice the speed of sound. In between are names that brought fame and glory to the RFC and RAF in two World Wars – the Sopwith Pup, SE 5a, Gloster Gladiator, Spitfire, Typhoon and Tempest. There are also some of their adversaries, such as the Russian MIG-15 which opposed Allied fighters during the Korean War.

Pride of place in the adjoining Bomber Command Museum goes to the indefatigable Lancaster bomber of the Second World War. The aircraft on display took part in more than 120 raids over Germany. Beside it stands its American ally – the B17 Flying Fortress, used in daylight raids by the US Air Force. Both these magnificent aircraft, however, are overshadowed by the vast wings of two of Britain's post-war V bombers – the Valiant and the Vulcan.

A separate building contains the Battle of Britain Museum, evocative of the summer of 1940 when the Spitfires and Hurricanes defied and conquered the Messerschmitts, Junkers and Heinkels of Hitler's Luftwaffe.

All year, daily exc Sun am. Adm charge. Refreshments. Shop. 🅿 *Toilets.* ♿ *Tel (01) 205 2266.*

ROYAL MEWS
Buckingham Palace Road, SW1 (Da)

Some of the Queen's horses and most of her state carriages can be seen in the Royal Mews, with pride of place going to the magnificent Gold State Coach which has been used at every coronation since that of George IV. It was built in 1762 and is gilded all over, with side panels painted by the Florentine painter Giovanni Battista Cipriani.

Also on show are the Irish State Coach, which the Queen uses for the State Opening of Parliament, and the Glass Coach used for royal weddings – including those of Prince Charles and Prince Andrew. Adjoining the coach house are the stables, where the lovely greys that draw the coaches stand patiently in their stalls. The saddlery is a hall of gleaming brass and polished leather in tall, glass-fronted cases.

A little way along the road from the Royal Mews is the Queen's Gallery, a changing exhibition of works from the royal collection. Apart from many fine works of art, including paintings by Canaletto, there are photographs collected by Queen Victoria and Prince Albert.

Royal Mews: All year, Wed-Thur pm. Adm charge. Toilets. ♿ *Queen's Gallery: All year, daily exc Sun am and Mon. Adm charge. Shop. Tel (01) 930 4832.*

ST MARGARET'S CHURCH
Parliament Square, SW1 (Da)

While Westminster Abbey belongs to the world, St Margaret's belongs to London, and most especially to the City of Westminster. It is the parish church of the House of Commons, and since before the Civil War has had a strongly Protestant bias. The poet John Milton was married there, and has a memorial window in the church; William Caxton, the first English printer, is buried in the churchyard; Samuel Pepys was married in the church and so too, in 1908, was Winston Churchill. The glorious east window shows Henry VIII and Catherine of Aragon beside the Crucifix. John Piper's windows, of abstract design, replace glass blown out in the Second World War. Beneath the altar lie the headless remains of Sir Walter Raleigh. He was executed in Old Palace Yard outside, and buried on the same day, October 29, 1618.

All year, daily. Free entry. Tel (01) 222 6382.

ST PAUL'S CATHEDRAL
Ludgate Hill, EC4 (Eb)

The monumental grandeur of St Paul's subdues the modern office blocks that loiter around it like beggars at a rich man's gate. Built on the site of Old St Paul's – destroyed in the Great Fire of London in 1666 – the building was designed by Sir Christopher Wren and took 25 years to complete. Wren is buried in the Crypt and the inscription above his simple tomb reads, in part: *Si monumentum requiris, circumspice* – 'If you seek his monument, look around you.'

Entering the cathedral, which is 515ft long and 365ft high to the top of the cross, visitors move along the Nave past a massive memorial to the Duke of Wellington and Holman Hunt's full-length portrait of Christ, lantern in hand, *The Light of the World.* Overhead at the heart of the building is Wren's great Dome, decorated with large monochrome paintings of incidents in the life of St Paul.

Straight ahead lies the Ambulatory which opens onto three small chapels: the Chapel of Modern Martyrs, the Lady Chapel and the American Memorial Chapel, commemorating the 28,000 Americans based in Britain who lost their lives in the Second World War. The walk back along the South Choir Aisle passes the entrance to the Crypt, a lofty undercroft running the entire length of the cathedral. As well as Wren's tomb, it contains the graves of Wellington – a vast sarcophagus of Cornish porphyry resting on an immense block of Peterhead granite – and of Lord Nelson. Nearby is Painters' Corner, where Sir Thomas Lawrence, Sir Joshua Reynolds and J.M.W. Turner are buried.

From the foot of the South Transept, stairs curve up to the Whispering Gallery and the Dome. The gallery's unusual acoustics allow a whisper at one side to be clearly heard at the other side, more than 100ft away. A further scramble leads to the Dome and the circular, open-air Viewing Gallery, with breathtaking views of London and beyond.

All year, daily (Sun, services only). Free entry (adm charge for ambulatory, crypt and galleries). Shop. Tel (01) 248 2705.

SOUTHWARK CATHEDRAL
London Bridge, SE1 (Ea)

A cathedral only since 1905, the Church of St Saviour and St Mary Overie has some 2½ million people – inner London citizens, suburbanites and commuter villagers in Surrey – in its diocese. The building, like so many others in this ancient gateway to London, has had its ups and downs, as is apparent in the variety of its stonework, ranging from 12th-century fragments to the mostly late-Victorian nave.

Public subscriptions in 1911 paid for an alabaster reclining monument to William Shakespeare, actor and playwright at the nearby Globe Theatre. His brother Edmund, 'a player', is buried in the cathedral, and close by are the names of John Fletcher and Philip Massinger, Shakespeare's fellow-playwrights.

All year, daily. Free entry. Shop. Tel (01) 407 2939.

TATE GALLERY
Millbank, SW1 (Da)

In 1892 the old Millbank Prison, looking out onto the steel-grey waters of the Thames, was demolished to make way for a new art gallery given to the nation by the sugar tycoon Sir Henry Tate and opened in 1897. It is a cool, airy, spacious building with green-and-black marble floors and stone walls the colour of meringue. It houses two main collections: the Historic British Collection, ranging from the 16th century to about 1900, and the Twentieth Century Collection, including Léger, Matisse, Miró and Picasso, and taking in Dada, Minimal Art and Pop Art.

Passing through the pillared entrance, visitors receive their first shock of delight: Rodin's large marble sculpture, *The Kiss.* A short distance ahead are more statues – by Henry Moore, his *King and Queen* and *Family Group* – just as shocking in their stark, angular way as Rodin's voluptuous work was some 60 years before. The main body of pictures is hung in the rooms on either side and beyond, where Hogarth, Gainsborough, Reynolds, Stubbs, Blake and the Pre-Raphaelites are well represented. For calm, reflective viewing there are works by Bonnard, Gauguin and Van Gogh; and conventions are flaunted by the controversial American painter Julian Schnabel, whose *Humanity Asleep* (1982) consists of a paint-smothered collage of saucers, cups and bits of broken crockery.

On the east flank of the Tate, discreetly masked by trees, is the Clore Gallery. It was opened in 1987 and contains some 300 oil paintings and about 19,000 watercolours and draw-

UNDER WREN'S DOME *In the Nave of St Paul's Cathedral, lines of arches and saucer domes draw the eye eastwards to the High Altar and the stained-glass windows beyond. Light floods the space below Sir Christopher Wren's 200ft high Dome.*

Riverside Homes and Gardens

The lovely banks of the Thames, as it glides majestically past Richmond and Kew, have attracted mansion-builders down the ages. Here monarchs have had their private residences, and nobles have created elegant homes within easy reach of the court in London. Today, a wealth of modern attractions add to the delights of their spacious grounds.

Ham House: NT. All year, daily exc Mon. Adm charge. Refreshments. Shop. P Toilets. ♿ Tel London (01) 940 1950. Kew Bridge Steam Museum: All year, daily. Steam days: Sat, Sun and Bank Hol Mon. Adm charge. Refreshments (steam days only). Shop. P (limited). Toilets. ♿ (part). Tel (01) 568 4757. Kew Gardens: All year, daily. Adm charge. Refreshments. Shop. P Toilets. ♿ Tel (01) 940 1171. Kew Palace, Kew Gardens: Apr-Sept, daily. Adm charge. Shop. Toilets. ♿ Tel (01) 940 3321. Marble Hill House: EH. All year, daily exc Fri. Free entry. Refreshments. Shop. P Toilets. ♿ Tel (01) 892 5115.

Syon Park: All year, daily. Free entry. Refreshments. Shop. P Toilets. ♿ Tel (01) 560 0881. Gardens: Apr-Oct, daily. Adm charge. House: Apr-Sept, Sun-Thur pm; Oct, Sun pm. Adm charge. Shop. ♿ Motor museum and butterfly house: All year, daily. Adm charges. Shops. ♿ Tel (01) 560 1378 (museum), 560 7272 (butterfly house).

GLASS MOUNTAINS *The futuristic Princess of Wales Conservatory, opened in Kew Gardens in 1987, encloses the plant life of ten different climates. Conditions are maintained by computer, and the effects are dramatic: at one point, a path leads through a door from desert on one side to rain forest on the other.*

STEAM POWER *A twin-beamed pumping engine of 1867 is on show at the Kew Bridge Steam Museum. Displays tell of London's water supply down the ages.*

CHIMNEY CORNER *Ham House reflects the exuberance of Restoration times, when the Countess of Dysart and her husband, the Duke of Lauderdale, created its lavish interiors. An elegant corner chimneypiece is a feature of the White Closet.*

QUEEN'S MUSIC *Built in Dutch style for a London merchant in 1631, Kew Palace was bought by George III in 1781. The Queen's Drawing Room, with its 18th-century harpsichord, remains as it was when his wife Charlotte died at Kew in 1818.*

CUBE ROOM *The white-and-gold Great Room at Marble Hill House, contained within a 24ft cube, was modelled on a similar room by Inigo Jones at Wilton. The classical house, set in a lovely park, was built for George II's mistress Henrietta Howard in the 1720s.*

MANY-SIDED SYON *At the heart of Syon Park stands Syon House, a fort-like mansion built in 1547. In 1762 the 1st Earl of Northumberland engaged Robert Adam to create its gorgeous interiors, among them the Great Hall (above right). The gardens include a vast conservatory with an aquarium. The park has other attractions. In the London Butterfly House are species from all over the world, including the Chinese peacock (right). The British Heritage Motor Museum has more than 85 British-made cars, including a 1923 Austin 7 Chummy Tourer. Art and garden centres complete the attractions.*

ings by J.M.W. Turner. The canvases include *Peace*; *Burial at Sea*; *The Decline of the Carthaginian Empire*; *Heidelberg*; and a series of delicate Venetian scenes, shimmering with light.
All year, daily exc Sun am. Free entry. Refreshments. Shop.
P *(limited). Toilets.* ♿ *Tel (01) 821 7128.*

THEATRE MUSEUM
Russell Street, WC2 (Db)

With the Royal Opera House and the Theatre Royal, Drury Lane, just over the way, and half a dozen other theatres within easy reach, no better site could have been chosen for the Theatre Museum than Covent Garden. It remains open until 7pm so that theatregoers may while away the odd hour before curtain-up; to help establish the mood, the area about the ground-floor café is laid out as a pretty combination of foyer, auditorium and back-stage machinery.

The museum itself is housed in bright showcases in dim galleries. The exhibits are frequently rotated, though the theme remains constant. It is the story of the performing arts – theatre, opera, ballet, variety, circus, pop – from about Shakespeare's day to our own. Early plays are illustrated by the matching of programmes with manuscript cast lists, property lists, portraits and drawings of the productions. These displays involve notable feats of historical detective work, especially where costume is concerned, as in the case of the apron worn by Polly Peachum in the first production of *The Beggar's Opera* in 1728.

Among the memorabilia in the museum's collection are Sarah Siddons' dressing table, Jenny Lind's wedding veil, costumes from early productions of *Peter Pan*, Henry Irving's 'invisible' spectacles for wearing on stage, and a skull that Victor Hugo gave to Sarah Bernhardt. A costume display ranges widely through ballet, theatre and opera, and includes such relics of pop as the rock costumes of Adam Ant and Mick Jagger's jump suit of 1972. Also among the museum's treasures are 200 designs for ballets performed at the court of Louis XIII between 1614 and 1634, and Oliver Messel's 15,000 designs for plays, operas, ballets, films, fabrics and interiors.
All year, Tues-Sun. Adm charge. Refreshments. Shop. Toilets. ♿ *Tel (01) 836 7691.*

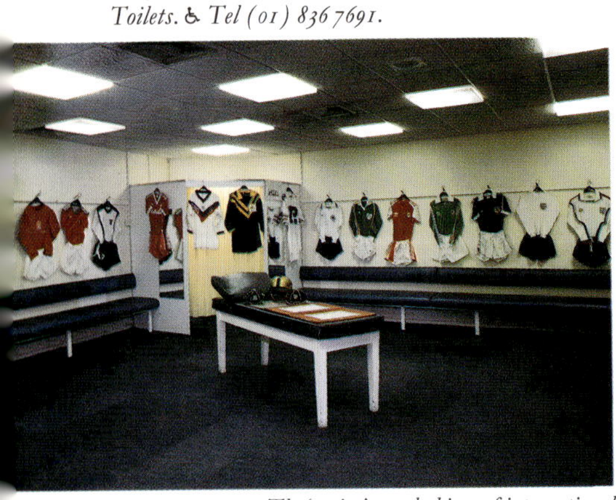

TEAM COLOURS *The 'strips', or clothing, of international teams adorn the walls of one of Wembley Stadium's show dressing rooms.*

SMALLER BY DESIGN *A model of a set made by Oliver Messel in 1956 for Mozart's comic opera* The Seraglio *is part of the Theatre Museum's large collection of designs, costumes, programmes and portraits.*

THE TROCADERO CENTRE
Piccadilly Circus, W1 (Db)

When Piccadilly Circus and Leicester Square are hot and dusty, or damp with rain, the Trocadero is a cool, undercover haven of shops, cafés and unusual attractions. Its heart is a vast courtyard, 80ft high, with three floors of polished marble walkways and a centrepiece of trees, shrubs and waterfalls. An escalator leads to three displays, widely contrasting in character.

The Guinness World of Records brings pages from the famous book to life with the aid of videos, lifelike models, sound effects and dioramas. Here are the men, women and animals who were born great, achieved greatness or had greatness thrust upon them – the 8ft 11in tallest man and the 23½in lady who was the smallest human; the 6ft 4in mountain gorilla and the 21in tall Argentinian horse; the sporting greats and the showbiz greats. Dioramas display the world's highest natural and man-made features.

The London Experience takes visitors on a 35 minute journey through the history of the capital, re-creating tragedies such as the Great Plague, the Great Fire and the wartime Blitz on a five-screen audiovisual display. The lighter side of London life is also portrayed, from a tour of the sights with a taxi-driver to the fervour of a Last Night at the Proms. Light Fantastic is a display of more than 100 holograms – three-dimensional images that appear to float in space.
All year, daily. Free entry (adm charges for Guinness World of Records, London Experience and Light Fantastic). Toilets. ♿ *Tel (01) 439 1791.*

WALLACE COLLECTION
Manchester Square, W1 (Db)

The 18th-century town house bought by the 2nd Marquess of Hertford houses a superb collection of paintings and furniture collected by the Hertford family over several generations. It was brought to England in the 19th century from Paris by Richard Wallace, natural son of the 4th marquess, and given to the nation in 1897.

Paintings in the collection include *The Laughing Cavalier* by Franz Hals, Rembrandt's *Titus,* and *Lady with a Fan* by Velázquez, as well as English pictures by Reynolds, Gainsborough and Lawrence. Furniture includes pieces from Louis XV's bedroom at Versailles and others made for Queen Marie Antoinette. There is a large collection of Sèvres porcelain, and fine gilt-bronzes, clocks and snuffboxes.
All year exc Sun am, daily. Free entry. Shop. Toilets. ♿ *Tel (01) 935 0687.*

WEMBLEY STADIUM
Stadium Way, Wembley (Bc)

Some idea of how the players feel as they walk onto Wembley Stadium's football pitch on Cup Final day can be obtained by an hour-long conducted tour of the stadium, the highlight of which is a walk along the players' tunnel and out onto the pitch. The sound of 100,000 voices singing 'Abide with Me' echoes down the broad concrete tunnel, and as visitors step into the open the hymn becomes a thunderous roar, pouring from loudspeakers around the stadium and reverberating among the empty terraces.

The tour starts with a short film show illustrating the history of the stadium and showing some of the great events that have taken place there. Then there is a visit to one of the dressing rooms, with the football kits of many countries arranged around the walls, followed by that awe-inspiring walk onto the hallowed turf. Another emotional moment that can be experienced is that climb up the steps to the royal box, where the players receive their trophies – and visitors can even sit in the royal box.
All year, daily. Five or six tours each day, except when stadium in use. Adm charge. Shop. P *Toilets. Tel (01) 903 4864.*

WESTMINSTER ABBEY
Parliament Square, SW1 (Da)

Two emotions draw the crowds to Westminster Abbey; love for a medieval church of great beauty and majesty, and admiration of a building that embodies the history and spirit of the nation in a way no other building does. The last but one of the Saxon Kings of England is buried in it, and the first of the Norman kings was crowned in it; so has been every monarch of England since, except Edward V and Edward VIII. Early Parliaments shared the Chapter House with the Benedictine monks who served the abbey, and the first royal treasury was established in the Pyx Chapel. Nearly everyone who was anyone was buried in the abbey, generally grouped by profession or occupation: monarchs, statesmen, musicians, scientists, poets, soldiers, sailors, lords and ladies.

At the west door visitors are greeted by the 14th-century portrait of Richard II in the Chapel of St George, and memorials to Lloyd George, Clement Attlee, David Livingstone, Isaac Newton, Ramsay MacDonald, Winston Churchill and other great men and women. There, too, is the grave of the Unknown Warrior, surrounded by poppies, 'Buried among Kings' and in the soil of the First World War battlefields. The north transept has an array of older statesmen – Pitt, Canning, Gladstone, Castlereagh, Disraeli – mostly in oratorical attitudes. The south aisle contains the ever-popular Poets' Corner, gathered about the tomb of Geoffrey Chaucer.

POMP AND PREMIERS *Henry VII is buried in the chapel named after him in Westminster Abbey, among the heraldic banners of the living Knights Grand Cross of the Order of the Bath. Monuments (right) to great statesmen such as Sir Robert Peel, in the foreground, line the abbey's North Transept.*

Behind the High Altar is the St Edward the Confessor Chapel, containing the rather battered shrine of St Edward that is the true heart of the abbey and the reason for the great building conceived by Henry III in the 13th century. Here stands the plain Coronation Chair, surprisingly scarred with the initials of 18th-century schoolboys, and carrying the Scottish Stone of Scone in a shelf beneath the seat. All around are the tombs of kings and queens whose names are the very essence of our medieval history.

Chief glory of the abbey is the Henry VII Chapel, with its astonishing fan-vaulted ceiling with exquisitely carved pendants and tracery, its walls ablaze with the arms and banners of the Knights Grand Cross of the Order of the Bath. Henry VII and his queen, Elizabeth of York, lie in the chancel, while in the north aisle, Elizabeth I and Mary Tudor share a single tomb.

The Chapter House, the old monastic council chamber and part of Henry III's great rebuilding in the 1250s, contains medieval tiles, wall paintings and statues. Next door, the massively pillared Pyx Chamber or Chapel is even older, probably dating from shortly after the Norman Conquest. It has three large medieval chests, and showcases containing the largely 17th-century Abbey Plate.

The Undercroft, perhaps the oldest part of the building, houses the abbey's museum, containing remarkable effigies of the type that used to be carried in the funeral processions of the rich and great. Often the faces were constructed from death masks and so must be considered excellent likenesses. Henry VII looks more humorous and more sensitive than history relates, Lord Nelson much tougher than depicted in his ethereal portraits, while Charles II looks rather like a film actor of the 1930s.

All year, daily. Free entry (adm charge to Royal Chapels and Chapter House). Refreshments (summer). Shop. Tel (01) 222 5152.

WESTMINSTER CATHEDRAL

Ashley Place, SW1 (Da)

Almost entirely fronted now by concrete-and-glass shops and offices, the Roman Catholic cathedral in its wide piazza looks even more like a wanderer from Siena or some other Tuscan city. Completed only in 1903, its roofs are a succession of domes, its walls are of banded stone and red brick, and its slender campanile soars 284ft to its domed lantern.

The interior is Byzantine rather than Italian in feeling, 342ft long, 149ft wide and 117ft to the tops of the domes. It was the intention to line the interior entirely with mosaics and marbles. This has been carried out in the chapels and to about halfway up the nave; above is the contrasting rough brick of the shell. The ceiling is dim, and from the dome above the altar hangs a huge Crucifix, its base almost touching the pillared roof of the Sanctuary canopy.

In the Chapel of St George and the English Martyrs, embalmed and in a glass case, are the remains of St John Southworth, hanged, drawn and quartered in 1654 under the laws that forbade Catholic priests to minister in England. Probably the cathedral's greatest artistic treasure is Eric Gill's Stations of the Cross, carved just before the First World War in a modern, linear style.

A lift takes visitors to the top of the campanile, from which there are dizzying views over or around the surrounding new buildings to Greenwich on one side and Hampstead and Highgate on the other, with the Houses of Parliament seemingly close enough to touch.

All year, daily. Free entry. Shop. ♿ *Tel (01) 834 7452.*

LONDON CALENDAR

Daily Buckingham Palace: Changing the Guard, Apr-July, 11am daily; Aug-Mar, alternate days. Horse Guards Parade, Whitehall: Changing the Guard, 11am Mon-Sat; 10am Sun.

January (early). Earl's Court: International Boat Show.

January (last Sun). Banqueting House, Whitehall: Charles I Commemoration (parade and service).

February (first Sun). Holy Trinity Church, Dalston, E8: Clown Service (for Grimaldi).

February (mid-month). Earl's Court: Cruft's Dog Show.

March (mid-month). Earl's Court: *Daily Mail* Ideal Home Exhibition. Chelsea Old Town Hall: Antiques Fair. Church of St Clement Danes, Strand: Oranges and Lemons Service (for children). River Thames: University Boat Race

Easter Day Battersea Park: Easter Parade. Tower of London: Church Parade (Yeoman Warders).

April (mid-month). Westminster Bridge: London Marathon (finish).

April (last Sun). Old Bailey: Tyburn Walk (to Marble Arch in memory of Catholic martyrs).

May (late). Royal Hospital, Chelsea: Chelsea Flower Show. Tower of London: Ceremony of Lilies and Roses (laying flowers on spot where Henry VI was murdered).

June (early). Royal Hospital, Chelsea: Founder's Day (Chelsea Pensioners). Horse Guards Parade, Whitehall: Beating Retreat (second Sat). Horse Guards Parade: Trooping the Colour.

June (late). Wimbledon: Lawn Tennis Championships.

July City of London Festival (mainly music).

July (mid-month). Earl's Court: Royal Tournament.

July (late). London Bridge: Doggett's Coat and Badge Race (sculling, to Chelsea Bridge).

August (first Sun). Rotten Row, Hyde Park. London Riding Horse Parade.

August Bank Hol. Hampstead Heath Fair.

September (early). Westminster Bridge: London to Brighton Walk (7am start). Westminster Abbey: Battle of Britain Week (Thanksgiving Service).

September (late). Mansion House: Election of Sheriffs. Guildhall: Election of Lord Mayor.

October (early). Wembley: Horse of the Year Show.

October (first Sun). St Martin-in-the-Fields, Trafalgar Square: Costermongers' Harvest Festival.

October Trafalgar Square: Trafalgar Day Service.

October (late). State Opening of Parliament.

November (first Sun). Hyde Park Corner: London to Brighton Veteran Car Run (8am start).

November (second Sat). Lord Mayor's Show.

November (second Sun). Cenotaph: Remembrance Sunday Service.

November (mid-month). Regent Street and Oxford Street: Christmas lights.

December (mid-month, to Christmas Eve). Trafalgar Square: Carol singing around Christmas tree.

Christmas Day The Serpentine, Hyde Park: Peter Pan Cup Swimming Race.

Tourist information: London Tourist Information Centre, Victoria Station Forecourt, SW1, Tel (01) 730 3488; City of London Information Centre, St Paul's Churchyard, EC4, Tel (01) 606 3030.

GREATER MANCHESTER

A CITY WHERE COTTON WAS THE SPUR TO INVENTION

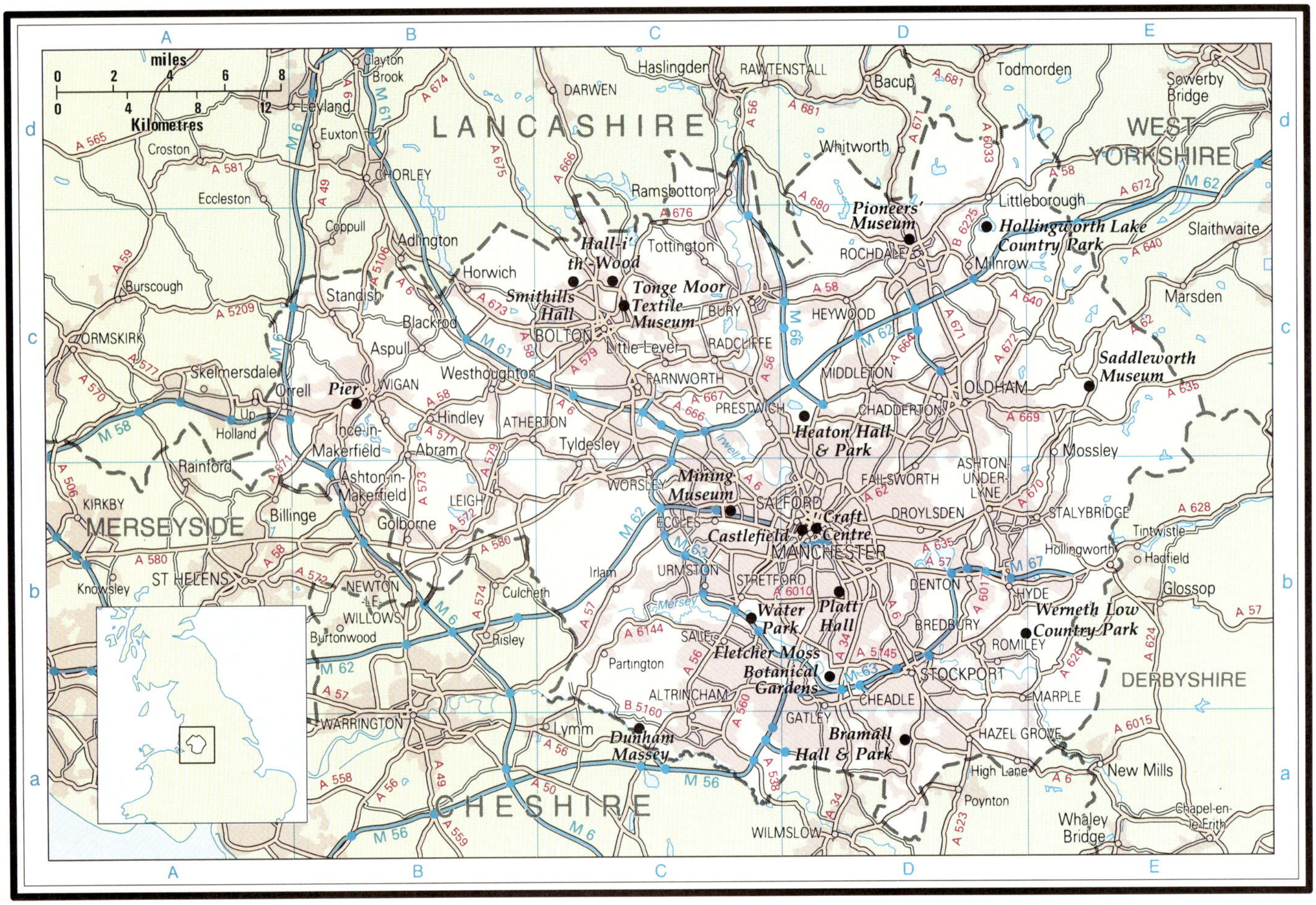

Cotton created Manchester. In the 14th century Flemish weavers came to Britain and set up their trade in such places as Uppermill where, in the Saddleworth Museum, their primitive looms can still be seen. Four centuries later their trade was revolutionised by men like Samuel Crompton, Richard Arkwright and James Hargreaves. Crompton's spinning mule, Arkwright's spinning frame and Hargreaves' spinning jenny are among the exhibits at Tonge Moor Museum, and Crompton's home at Hall-i'th'-Wood is much as it was when he lived there.

Progress brought prosperity, resulting in great houses such as Dunham Massey, Heaton Hall and Platt Hall. Progress also brought the need for transport, soon provided by canals and railways; at Castlefield a station of the Liverpool and Manchester railway is today part of a heritage park. The railways carried coal from the pits, vividly re-created at the Salford Mining Museum. So, too, did the canal barges, often loading at Wigan where Wigan Pier is now a heritage centre re-creating life in the 1900s.

BRAMALL HALL AND PARK

On A5102, 2 miles south of Stockport (Da)

Some 60 acres of gardens, lakes, lawns and woodland surround Bramall Hall, one of England's finest Elizabethan houses. Built in traditional black-and-white style, it has many memories of the Davenports who were lords of the manor of Bramall for 500 years before selling the estate in 1877. Remarkable wall paintings, believed to date from about 1600, were discovered when a more recent owner repaired a wall in the ballroom. They depict a winged figure riding a horse with a cock's head, a wild boar hunt, and a demon playing a drum and flute. The ballroom has a splendid timber roof, and high above the door are two figures in early 16th-century dress.

The Paradise Room, with its 16th-century plasterwork and 17th-century bed, is said to be haunted by Dame Dorothy Davenport, who lived at Bramall Hall during the Civil War. The family supported King Charles, but a Royalist force marched off with what livestock had not been stolen by Parliamentarian troops.

Feb-Dec, daily exc Mon, and Bank Hol. Adm charge. Refreshments. Shop. P *Toilets. Tel Manchester (061) 485 3708.*

CASTLEFIELD

Near centre of Manchester (Db)

Roman soldiers, Victorian engineers and characters from TV's *Coronation Street* rub shoulders on a colourful, house-high mural that illustrates the 2000 years spanned by Britain's first urban heritage park. Its attractions include an aerospace museum, a pioneering canal and the world's first passenger railway station.

The visitor centre in Deansgate provides a good 'entry point' for an exhibition that covers numerous sites in a network of streets between Deansgate and the River Irwell. Reconstructions and special displays on the various sites combine to build up an impression of the development of Manchester since Roman times.

Railway viaducts now cross the land where, towards the end of the 1st century AD, the Romans established a fort and civilian settlement – the 'castle in the field' which gives the area its modern name. The stronghold's north gateway has been reconstructed on its original site, and its guardroom is furnished as it might have been when occupied by Agricola's troops.

Nearby runs the Bridgewater Canal – one of the arteries that helped to make Manchester one of the great 'workshops of the world' during the

Industrial Revolution. Today, commercial traffic has ceased and the canal is used for leisure traffic.

The attractive exterior of Castlefield's Liverpool Road station has remained remarkably unchanged since 1830, when the Liverpool and Manchester Railway, built by George and Robert Stephenson, was opened to meet the fast-growing city's need for more efficient transport. Figures dressed in 19th-century costumes stand in the restored first-class booking hall, now the entrance to the Museum of Science and Industry, which presents a wide array of the machines that revolutionised industry in the Western world.

In the museum's Power Hall, locomotives, steam engines, cars and motorcycles glisten. The most impressive locomotive is an articulated GL – class Beyer – Garratt built for South Africa in 1930. Nearly 90ft long, it weighs 214 tons and carried 7000 gallons of water. The museum also includes the National Electricity Gallery, housed in a former railway warehouse. Displays telling the story of Michael Faraday, Benjamin Franklin and other pioneers in electricity are reached by walking through a huge, cutaway steam condenser built in 1923 for a power station in Bolton.

In the Air and Space Gallery, on the opposite side of Lower Byrom Street, is a replica of the triplane built by Alliott Verdon 'Hopper' Roe in 1909. Roe founded the Avro company, whose famous aircraft included the four-engined Shackleton which dominates the collection.

Heritage Park: All year, daily. Free entry. Tel Manchester (061) 832 4244. Museum of Science and Industry: All year, daily. Adm charge. Refreshments. Shop. 🅿 *Toilets.* ♿ *Tel (061) 832 4211. Air and Space Museum; All year, daily exc Mon. Adm charge. Refreshments. Shop.* 🅿 *Toilets. Tel (061) 833 9555.*

DUNHAM MASSEY

On B5160, 3 miles south-west of Altrincham (Ca)

The path from the car park runs beside a broad moat, then turns over a bridge to the front of the low, plain red-brick house, for over 300 years the seat of the Earls of Stamford and Warrington. Within, more than 30 rooms are open to the public, evoking the way of life for those who lived and worked here in past centuries. Outside, visitors can walk for hours through 250 acres of parkland, watch the herd of fallow deer, sit on an Elizabethan mound or wander alongside an Edwardian water garden.

Dunham Massey dates from Tudor times, but was rebuilt by George Booth, 2nd Earl of Warrington, in the 18th century. His portrait shares the chintz drawing room with paintings, prints and photographs devoted to the history of the Booth and Grey families, united by marriage in 1736.

A set of seven watercolours in the rose gallery reveal how Dunham Park was landscaped at the end of the 18th century. The 3000 acre estate, where George Booth is said to have planted 'no less than 100,000 oaks, elms and beech', includes an Elizabethan mill in working order and an 18th-century deer barn.

NT. Apr-Oct, daily exc Fri. Adm charge. Refreshments. Shop. 🅿 *Toilets.* ♿ *(grounds). Tel Manchester (061) 941 1025.*

FLETCHER MOSS BOTANICAL GARDENS

On A5145, 4 miles south of Manchester city centre (Db)

Sheltered from cold winds, many specimen trees and shrubs grow in the park that Alderman Fletcher Moss presented to the City of Manchester early this century. One garden is devoted to heathers while another, the peat garden, has delightful miniature conifers and rhododendrons. There is also an alpine house, and a wild garden bright with roses and other flowers native to Britain and Europe. The Parsonage, where Alderman Moss lived, has a walled garden with an orchid house where cymbidiums bloom from Christmas until early summer. Peaches have also been grown in the gardens.

All year, daily. Free entry. Refreshments. 🅿 *Toilets. Tel Manchester (061) 434 1877.*

HALL-I'TH'-WOOD

Off Green Way, 2 miles north-east of Bolton (Cc)

In this manor house in 1779 Samuel Crompton, a farmer's son, invented the spinning mule – a machine which revolutionised the textile industry by producing yarn that, while still strong, was fine enough to make muslin. Links with Crompton, to be seen in the house where the Cromptons lived from 1758 until 1782, include a model of the 'mule' – a traditional Saxony spinning wheel – and hymn tunes composed when Crompton was choirmaster at a Bolton chapel.

The oldest part of Hall-i'th'-Wood is half-timbered and dates from the 15th century. Nothing has been altered since the 'new' wing of dressed stone was added in 1648. A typical 18th-century Lancashire kitchen is one of the most striking rooms in the house.

Apr-Sept, daily exc Thur; Oct-Mar, daily exc Thur and Sun. Adm charge. 🅿 *Tel Bolton (0204) 51159.*

HEATON HALL AND PARK

At Prestwich, 6 miles north of Manchester (Dc)

An income of £5000 a year enabled the young Sir Thomas Egerton, who later became the 1st Earl of Wilton, to set about building Heaton Hall in 1772. His architect, 26-year-old James Wyatt, gave the house a Palladian façade, with a domed central block flanked by colonnaded wings and octagonal pavilions for the library and kitchen. An orangery was added and other alterations made in the 1820s by James Wyatt's nephew, Lewis Wyatt. Heaton Hall was then owned by the 2nd Earl of Wilton, a vain character whose guests included the Duke of Wellington, Benjamin Disraeli and the actress Fanny Kemble.

Portraits and landscape paintings, furniture in satinwood and mahogany, and an organ built for the music-loving 1st Earl give a vivid impression of what Heaton Hall was like in its glittering heyday. The Cupola Room's painted walls and ceiling are vivid reminders of the 'Etruscan' style that became popular when 18th-century archaeologists excavated the Roman cities of Pompeii and Herculaneum.

Sir Thomas Egerton also had Heaton Park's 600 acres landscaped by William Emes, a follower of Capability Brown. Its attractions today include a boating lake, a farm interpretation centre, a vintage tram and bus service and a public, 18-hole golf course. A boulder marks the place where Pope John Paul celebrated Mass during his visit to Manchester in 1982.

Park: All year, daily. Hall: Apr-Sept, daily exc Tues. Free entry. Refreshments. Shop. 🅿 *Toilets.* ♿ *(ground floor). Tel Manchester (061) 773 1231.*

HOLLINGWORTH LAKE COUNTRY PARK

Off B6225, ½ mile south of Littleborough (Dc)

The 120 acre Hollingworth Lake has been a popular day-out destination ever since the Manchester-Leeds railway was opened during Queen Victoria's reign. Links with that period still maintained today include a funfair held each Easter at Lakebank, a ferry service, and boat trips. A 2¼ mile waymarked trail starting at the information centre follows the lake shore. From it there are fine views across the lake and up to Blackstone Edge, which rises to 1550ft. The trail passes a bird sanctuary where great crested grebe breed.

All year, daily.

MANCHESTER CRAFT VILLAGE

Oak Street, near city centre (Db)

Markets selling fish, fruit, vegetables and other produce made Smithfield one of central Manchester's most lively areas for more than a century. The markets moved to a new site in 1973, but a £230,000 investment saved one of Smithfield's handsome Victorian buildings and turned it into a colourful craft centre.

The buildings are now studios occupied by potters, silversmiths, weavers, enamellers and many other exponents of traditional crafts that now tend more often to be associated with rural areas. All the goods on sale are produced in the village.

All year, daily exc Sun and Mon. Refreshments. Tel Manchester (061) 832 4274.

PLATT HALL

Off A6010, 2 miles south of Manchester city centre (Db)

A hall built in 1762 for a wealthy textile merchant is an appropriate setting for one of the world's outstanding collections of clothes. Male and

GREEN ROOM *Family portraits, including one by Romney, grace the walls of Dunham Massey's saloon. Its designer said that the colour red must never enter the room, 'even on the dresses of them that inhabit it'.*

female fashions span the centuries, from Tudor times to the age of Laura Ashley, Zandra Rhodes and the 'punk rocker'. Beautiful gowns made for great ladies contrast with the woollen shawls and wooden clogs of Lancashire's 19th-century mill-workers. The Gallery of English Costume also has handbags, umbrellas, fans and other accessories, costumed dolls, and a large library for serious students of fashion.

The surrounding Platt Fields Park contains a Coronation Rose Garden, a boating lake and a Shakespearean Garden in which are grown many plants mentioned in Shakespeare's plays.

All year, daily exc Tues. Free entry. Shop. P *(limited). Toilets. Tel Manchester (061) 224 5217.*

FASHION FINERY *Richly embroidered pockets and tails decorate this gentleman's silk coat made in the late 18th century. It is one of the exhibits in the Gallery of English Costume at Platt Hall.*

ROCHDALE PIONEERS' MEMORIAL MUSEUM

In Toad Lane, near centre of Rochdale (Dc)

The modern co-operative movement – the 'Co-op' – traces its roots back to 1844, when the Rochdale Equitable Pioneers Society opened a shop in Toad Lane. The building containing the shop is now a memorial museum. The Pioneers were working men who formed the society to provide a fair trading service and social and educational amenities. Starting with £28 capital, they paid £10 a year to rent the ground floor of the building, where sugar, butter, flour, oatmeal and candles were sold. Whitewashed walls and a stone floor make the shop as stark and simple as it would have been in 1844, when purchases were recorded with a quill pen. The worldwide movement that grew from the venture now has 500 million members.

All year, daily exc Mon. Adm charge. Shop. P *Toilets. Tel Manchester (061) 832 4300.*

SADDLEWORTH MUSEUM

Off A670, 5 miles east of Oldham (Ec)

A reconstruction of a traditional clothier's cottage, complete with spinning wheels and a hand-operated loom, recalls what life was like in this part of the Pennines 200 years ago. The dramatic changes that revolutionised the textile industry during the 19th century are epitomised by a power loom from the nearby village of Dobcross, where John and James Platt established what became the world's largest machine-making business in the 1850s. A Victorian parlour, laundry and bedroom have also been re-created in the museum. It occupies a former cotton mill in Uppermill, one of several industrial villages that grew up in the middle of the 19th century. An adjoining art gallery stages exhibitions of paintings and sculpture.

Trips on the Huddersfield Narrow Canal start from the museum's car park. The colourful, 70ft long narrow boat is named after the original canal company's engineer, Benjamin Outram. North-east of Uppermill, the canal enters the Standedge Tunnel. Just over 3 miles from end to end, it is the longest canal tunnel in Britain, and at 645ft the highest above sea level. The visitor centre on the canal between Uppermill and Dobcross is a starting point for many walks.

Museum: All year, daily. Adm charge. Shop. P *(limited). Toilets. Tel Saddleworth (045 77) 4093.*

SALE WATER PARK

On outskirts of Sale (Cb)

Lakes formed when gravel was excavated to build the M63 motorway now attract anglers, birdwatchers, walkers and boating enthusiasts. Sale Water Park, which is visited by grey heron, has a nature reserve and an area where model aircraft are put through their paces. The western end of the park's 35 acre lake is overlooked by an impressive embankment that carries the canal built by the Duke of Bridgewater in 1761. This 'cut', engineered by James Brindley, was used by barges carrying coal from the duke's collieries at Worsley to Manchester. Footpaths beside the River Mersey link Sale Water Park to its neighbour, Chorlton, where Canada geese breed. Both lakes are stocked with perch, carp, bream and other fish.

All year, daily; watersports Apr-Sept. Toilets. ♿ *Tel Manchester (061) 881 5639.*

SALFORD MINING MUSEUM

Buile Hill Park, near centre of Salford (Cb)

The days when women and young children hauled heavy tubs through workings too low for pit ponies are recalled in north-west England's only museum devoted to the history of 'King Coal'. Pit scenes that take visitors back to the 1840s have been re-created in the basement of Buile Hill Park, a neoclassical mansion built in 1827. It was 1842 before an Act of Parliament raised the minimum age for mineworkers to ten, and made it illegal to employ women.

The old workings make it easy to understand why many 19th-century miners suffered from eye problems. They toiled in virtual darkness, because the safety lamp invented by Sir Humphry Davy in 1815 produced less light than a single candle.

The museum's ground floor features scenes from a small drift mine of the 1930s. Drift mines were developed in places where coal seams came close to the surface, and there was no need to sink a vertical shaft. The bird on the cabinet in the manager's office is a reminder that collieries bred canaries and mice to test the atmosphere after a fire or explosion. They react very quickly to carbon monoxide and other dangerous gases. South Lancashire pioneered the provision of pit-head baths, but they were not free. A pay slip from 1935 reveals that the equivalent of 2p was deducted for the amenity. A miner then earned little more than £2 a week. Another display covers all aspects of coal-mining, from geology to health, welfare and social history.

Buile Hill Park was built for Sir Thomas Potter, the first Mayor of Manchester. He was one of 11 men whose financial backing enabled the *Manchester Guardian* newspaper to be launched in 1821.

All year, daily exc Sat. Free entry. Shop. P *Toilets. Tel Manchester (061) 736 1832.*

SMITHILLS HALL

Off A58, 1½ miles north-west of Bolton (Cc)

This medieval manor house on the lower slopes of Smithills Moor has memories of two 16th-century Protestants who died for their beliefs during Queen Mary's turbulent reign. Tudor glass in the chapel's east window depicts the heraldic arms of Thomas Cranmer, Archbishop of Canterbury, who was burnt at the stake at Oxford in 1556. The passage leading to the chapel has a mark said to have been left by a local man who stamped his foot, and defiantly proclaimed his Protestant faith, before meeting an identical fate in 1555.

The chapel was rebuilt after a fire in 1856, but the oldest part of Smithills Hall dates from the 14th century. The withdrawing room, added during the Tudor period, has a wealth of beautifully carved oak panelling.

Apr-Sept, daily exc Thur; Oct-Mar, daily exc Thur and Sun. Adm charge. Shop. P *Toilets. Tel Bolton (0204) 41265.*

TONGE MOOR TEXTILE MUSEUM

Off A676, 1 mile north of Bolton (Cc)

This museum's most important exhibit is the only surviving example of the spinning 'mule' invented by Samuel Crompton in 1779, when he was living at Hall-i'th'-Wood, a short walk from Tonge Moor Road. Other machines that helped to revolutionise the textile industry in the 18th century were also invented by Lancashire men. They include the spinning 'jenny' perfected by James Hargreaves, a Blackburn weaver, and the water-powered spinning frame produced by Richard Arkwright in 1769.

Traditional spinning methods are recalled by a 14th-century Jersey wheel, operated by hand, and a foot-powered Saxony wheel which left both hands free for stretching the yarn. At the other end of the time scale are steam-powered

PIER SHOW *At Wigan Pier's The Way We Were, life as it was in the 1900s is re-enacted. The grocer serves in his shop, well stocked with cheese, bread, eggs and bacon, and in the schoolroom Mr Hargreaves flexes his supple cane as he reminds pupils of the need for discipline. Life in Wigan at the turn of the century revolved around coal mines and cotton mills, and at nearby Trencherfield mill (right) the thrusting pistons of a giant steam engine still set a flywheel as tall as a house in throbbing motion.*

machines that made Lancashire the world's greatest textile producer in the 19th century.
All year, daily exc Wed and Sun. Free entry. P *(limited).* ♿ *Tel Bolton (0204) 21394.*

WERNETH LOW COUNTRY PARK

Off A626, 1½ miles south-east of Hyde (Db)

Landmarks that include sandstone cliffs 30 miles away on the Mersey estuary, Liverpool's two cathedrals, and mountains 50 miles away in North Wales can be seen from this 200 acre country park between Hyde and Marple. More than 20 landmarks are indicated on an Automobile Association plaque in the car park, 820ft above sea level, from which five counties are visible.

The memorial on the hilltop is a reminder that most of the land – and the farmhouse now used as a visitor centre – was bought with money raised to commemorate Hyde men who were killed in the First World War.
All year, daily.

WIGAN PIER

Near centre of Wigan (Bc)

Part theatre and part museum, Wigan Pier's The Way We Were display provides a remarkable insight into the life of Wigan, Leigh and other local communities at the turn of the century. Amid authentic sets re-creating cottage, colliery and schoolroom, actors and actresses assuming the clothes and occupations of 1900 stand ready to talk to visitors about their day-to-day lives. Visitors can sympathise with a collier's widow, chat to a canal boatman or 'pit brow' lass, exchange political views with a suffragette and pass the time of day with a visiting theatre company's immaculate actor-manager.

The pier, immortalised by George Formby senior's jokes, and later by George Orwell's book *The Road to Wigan Pier*, was a 'tippler' where coal was loaded into barges on the Leeds and Liverpool Canal. The original was scrapped in 1929 – seven years before Orwell's visit – but a replica now stands on the site. Formby's music hall jokes mocked the pleasure piers at Blackpool and Southport, resorts that were popular Wakes Week destinations. They were nothing to Wigan's pier, he told his audiences. Appropriately, a figure depicting the entertainer in a battered bowler hat and boots laced with string stands at the entrance to The Way We Were.

The display starts by taking a light-hearted look at the brief seaside holidays enjoyed by people from Lancashire's industrial towns. They are seen strolling along the sands, watching Punch-and-Judy shows, posing for souvenir photographs, and slotting hard-earned pennies into What The Butler Saw machines on the pier. By contrast, a coal mine complete with pit pony dramatically illustrates workaday Wigan.

A background babble of recorded voices adds atmosphere to the market, where one of the busiest stalls was run by Ellen Santus, maker of Uncle Joe's Mint Balls. They were very popular with coalminers, and are now sold in Wigan Pier's shop. A collier's home reveals what life was like at one end of the social scale. At the other end, Wigan's mayor is seen trying on the ceremonial robes ordered for Edward VII's coronation. All the characters in the exhibition have been modelled on photographs of people who lived in Wigan at the turn of the century.

A pub named The Orwell occupies a former warehouse next to The Way We Were. Its decorations include an 'E.A.Blair and Co. Ltd' barge sign; Eric Arthur Blair was George Orwell's real name.

Trencherfield cotton mill, on the opposite side of the canal, is reached on foot or by waterbus. Built in 1907, it houses the world's biggest steam-powered mill engine.
All year, daily. Adm charge. Refreshments. Shop. P *Toilets.* ♿ *Tel Wigan (0942) 323666.*

COUNTY CALENDAR

February (late). Manchester: Manchester and Salford Boat Race.

Spring Bank Hol Manchester: Whit Walks.

June (early). Manchester: Vintage and Veteran Car Run, to Blackpool.

June (mid-month, to early July). Manchester Free Trade Hall: Hallé Proms.

August (early). Manchester: Show.

September (early). Castlefield: Carnival.

September (mid-month). Manchester: Festival.

Tourist information: Bolton (0204) 22311; Manchester (061) 234 3157/8; Oldham (061) 678 4654; Stockport (061) 480 0315.

HAMPSHIRE

PALACES AND PARKS, AN ANCIENT FOREST AND A HERITAGE COAST

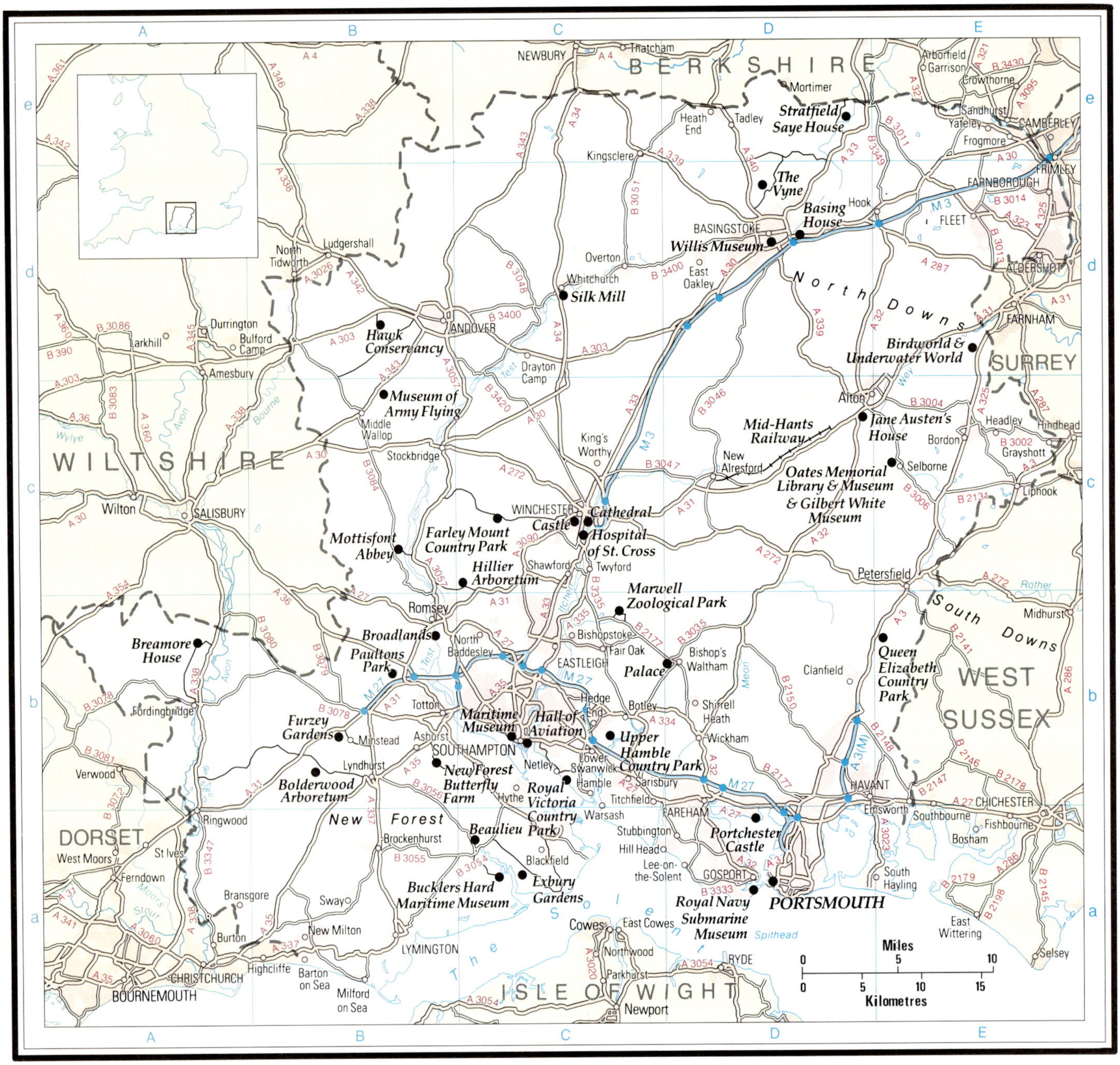

A great forest, designated 'New' by William the Conqueror, is the scene of attractions as diverse as herds of deer at Bolderwood, a butterfly farm at Ashurst, and motor cars of yesteryear at Beaulieu. William hunted in the forest when England's capital was Winchester, still a city of medieval charm with its long, grey-backed cathedral and the remains of the Conqueror's castle. Hampshire's coast, too, is awash with history. At Bucklers Hard the ships of Nelson's day were built; at Gosport the Royal Navy has its Submarine Museum; and in Southampton's Maritime Museum the days of the great ocean liners are recalled. Portsmouth has had a Royal Naval Dockyard for nearly 500 years, and fittingly Nelson's flagship HMS *Victory* is preserved there.

Downs and leafy valleys are the settings for several great houses. Broadlands was home to Earl Mountbatten of Burma, while the aura of the Iron Duke still pervades Stratfield Saye House. Downs and woods combine in the Queen Elizabeth Country Park, whose rolling acres include the unusual spectacle of a re-created Iron Age farm.

BASING HOUSE

Off A30, 2 miles east of Basingstoke (Dd)

Dovecotes still in working order and the walls of a Tudor garden remain as clues to a past of wealth and extraordinary power. Basing was the domain of the Paulet family, who held the manor from 1428. Two centuries later their fortified Tudor mansion was razed to the ground by Cromwell's troops after a bitter siege lasting two years.

An exhibition in the 19th-century Lodge House guides visitors through the ruins on a historical detective trail. It begins with the remains of the Norman castle protected by massive earthworks, and follows through to the Tudor period and the rise of Sir William Paulet (1485-1572). He survived as Lord Treasurer to the last four Tudor monarchs, and amassed a fortune, which paid for his massive 'tithe barn' at nearby Grange Farm and his grandiose red-brick mansion, whose foundations and cellars are now excavated.

Apr-Sept, Wed-Sun and Bank Hol Mon pm. Adm charge. Shop. P *Toilets. Tel Basingstoke (0256) 467294.*

BEAULIEU

On B3054, 5 miles north-east of Lymington (Ca)

At a discreet distance behind the ancient walls of Palace House a futuristic monorail glides at tree-top level above the gleaming display of cars in the National Motor Museum. Palace House began its life as the 14th-century Great Gatehouse of a Cistercian abbey, and was adapted and extended over the centuries into the present comfortable manor house. Splendid 14th-century fan-vaulting survives in the lower drawing room and dining hall, its graceful curves highlighted by brightly coloured ceilings. There are portraits of the ancestors of Beaulieu's owner, Lord Montagu – among them Henry Wriothesley, 3rd Earl of Southampton and probably the patron who inspired Shakespeare to dedicate his sonnets to 'W.H.'

Behind Palace House are the ruins of the remainder of the abbey, where monks worked and worshipped for 300 years. After the Dissolution their refectory, or dining room, was converted for use as the parish church, and it still serves this role today.

The National Motor Museum surveys a century of motoring history, and the monorail provides an exciting bird's eye view of the entire site – passing at one point right through the main exhibition hall. Descending to ground level, the visitor has more than 200 cars to inspect: pioneering Peugeots and Daimlers, record-breakers such as Malcolm Campbell's two Sunbeam racers and Donald Campbell's Bluebird, vintage roadsters as diverse as the Austin Seven and the Rolls-Royce Phantom. 'Wheels', a sound-and-vision spectacular, carries visitors in moving 'pods' through exhibits that illustrate the social changes that have accompanied the rise of the motor car.

All year, daily. Adm charge. Refreshments. Shop. P *Toilets.* ♿ *Tel Beaulieu (0590) 612345.*

BIRDWORLD AND UNDERWATER WORLD

On A325, 5 miles north of Bordon (Ed)

Birds ranging from tiny hummingbirds to the great ostrich can be seen in the pens and aviaries of Birdworld, and there are lakes where flamingos strut and penguins dive. On the Sea-shore Walk, waves lap a sandy beach, shags and cormorants perch on a beached dinghy, and waders dabble at the water's edge. In the Underwater World are fierce piranhas, a myriad tiny tropical fish and oddities such as the gruesome scorpion fish and the puffer fish.

All year, daily. Adm charge. Refreshments. Shop. P *Toilets.* ♿ *Tel Bentley (0420) 22140.*

BEAULIEU BYGONES *British-made vehicles of all ages stand in the Hall of Fame of the National Motor Museum at Beaulieu: a 1909 Rolls-Royce Silver Ghost makes a striking centrepiece. An imposing Victorian fireplace (right) adorns the Lower Drawing Room of Beaulieu's Palace House, once the Great Gatehouse of a 13th-century abbey.*

BISHOP'S WALTHAM PALACE

In Bishop's Waltham (Db)

Ruined palace walls rising majestically above green turf are a stark memorial to the days when bishops were princes, and lived accordingly. The palace was built in the 12th century by Henri de Blois, brother of King Stephen and Bishop of Winchester. It remained – with much rebuilding – the seat of Winchester's bishops until the Dissolution. Final destruction came during the Civil War a century later, but some melancholy grandeur still lingers by the walls of the bishop's massive Banqueting Hall, which are pierced by tall windows.

EH. All year, daily. Adm charge. P *Toilets.* ♿ *(grounds). Tel Bishop's Waltham (048 93) 2460.*

BOLDERWOOD ARBORETUM

Off A31, 6 miles north-east of Ringwood (Bb)

On the edge of the New Forest's densest woodlands, waymarked walks, deer sanctuaries and ornamental drives introduce the visitor to some of the forest's main glories. From the car park a clearly marked path drops downhill through a cathedral-like natural aisle of forest giants planted in 1860. Many of the species had not long been introduced from their native home in north-west America, and some specimens here are still the tallest or finest in Britain. Clear labelling enables even the least tree-conscious walker to pick out the 130ft redwood, the 145ft noble fir and the 115ft Weymouth pine. The route passes two observation platforms from which some of the New Forest's 600 fallow deer may be observed at close quarters.

Two other woodland walks start from the Bolderwood car park, which is also the northern starting point of the Bolderwood Ornamental Drive. This 2 mile motor route passes through the so-called Inclosures – plantations of trees enclosed from 1700 onwards to safeguard supplies of timber for building and fuel. Near the southern end of the drive stands the Knightwood Oak, a stately veteran of more than 350 years, its multi-branched crown an early example of the practice of pollarding, or beheading young trees to produce many branches instead of a single stem.

FC. All year, daily. P

BREAMORE HOUSE

Off A338, 2½ miles north of Fordingbridge (Ab)

The many-gabled Elizabethan manor of pink brick is set in a sweep of parkland on the edge of the New Forest. The building enshrines four centuries of change, although its structure has hardly altered since 1583. Sir Edward Hulse, physician to Queen Anne, bought the estate in 1748 and his descendants live there still. The treasures collected over centuries reflect the

MEN OF ACTION *The Palmerston Room at Broadlands is a memorial to the Victorian prime minister whose aggressive policies made Britain's power felt abroad, and brought victory in the Crimean War. During the Second World War another owner of Broadlands, Lord Mountbatten, later Earl Mountbatten of Burma, exercised an influence abroad as Supreme Commander, South-east Asia. His insignia, cap and a war map (right) are on show in the Mountbatten Exhibition.*

changing tastes of nine generations, and the decorations and furnishings range from sturdy Tudor simplicity to ornate Regency elegance.

The 17th-century stable block has a superb collection of carriages and early fire-fighting equipment. The nearby Breamore Countryside Museum reconstructs aspects of bygone rural life – a dairy, forge, a brewery and even a farmworker's cottage. It also has a gleaming array of vintage tractors.

Aug, pm daily; May, June, July, Sept, pm daily exc Mon and Fri; Apr, Tues, Wed, Sun and Easter pm. Adm charge. Refreshments. Shop. P *Toilets.* ♿ *(ground floor). Tel Downton (0725) 22270.*

BROADLANDS

On A31 at Romsey (Bb)

Visitors enjoying the beauty of river-girt lawns and rolling parkland at Broadlands may be tempted to echo the verdict of the 1st Viscount Palmerston in 1736, the year he bought the estate: 'This place altogether pleases me above any place I know.' At the centre of the landscaped stage stands a square, white brick mansion with two impressive porticoes. In the 1760s the 2nd Viscount Palmerston employed the designers Capability Brown and Henry Holland to transform the original 16th-century house. The result was this Palladian masterpiece, and its romantically 'natural' park.

Broadlands is best known as the home of Lord Mountbatten, the last Viceroy of India. Another famous statesman who lived here was Lord Palmerston, prime minister to Queen Victoria, and portraits and personal possessions of both men abound in the house. Breathtaking plasterwork adorns whole rooms, or provides a delicate framework for the superb collections of sculpture, pictures and furniture gathered by the 2nd Viscount Palmerston.

An exhibition is devoted to Lord Mountbatten's career in the navy and as a statesman and diplomat. It includes audiovisual displays, uniforms and many of the gifts he received.

Broadlands once belonged to the nuns of nearby Romsey Abbey. The abbey church survives, and is among the finest examples of late Norman architecture in the country, tier upon tier of rounded arches rising above the choir. Lord Mountbatten was buried here in 1979.

Broadlands: Apr-Sept, daily exc Mon; also Late Summer Bank Hol Mon. Adm charge. Refreshments. Shop. P *Toilets.* ♿ *(ground floor). Tel Romsey (0794) 516878. Abbey: All year, daily.*

BUCKLERS HARD MARITIME MUSEUM

Off B3054, 2½ miles south of Beaulieu (Ca)

Step through a front door halfway down Bucklers Hard's single street and walk into the parlour of an 18th-century shipwright, returning from work with adze on shoulder to be greeted at the door by his young son. Peer through a window lower down the street and look into the face of Henry Adams, the Master Builder who made Bucklers Hard one of the busiest shipbuilding quays on Britain's coast; he sits in a hanging seat, discussing with an overseer the building of *Agamemnon*, Nelson's favourite ship.

Both displays, featuring life-size effigies, are adjuncts of the Maritime Museum at the top of the village, in which the visitor can walk through further wondrously re-created scenes from the past. A labourer sits at his supper table, waiting for his wife to ladle soup from the fireside pot, while two children play in the corner and, upstairs, a baby cries in the bedroom to which he has been banished. Turn a corner in the museum and walk into the village alehouse, where shipwright, blacksmith and sawyer sit carousing in the dim light, their cries and laughter ringing out all around.

These vivid tableaux, like everything in Bucklers Hard, are done with such care for detail and such evident pride in the community's past that the effect is wholly entrancing. The village today consists of nothing more than two terraces of red-brick houses facing each other across a wide green that slopes gently down to the edge of the Beaulieu river. Its preservation is so complete (cars are banished to an out-of-sight car park at the top of the village) that the visitor feels genuinely transported back in time. It is as well that those houses the visitor cannot enter are protected with a discreet notice saying 'Resident'.

The riverside below the Master Builder's Hotel is the starting point of a $2\frac{1}{2}$ mile path that leads upriver to Beaulieu.

All year, daily. Adm charge. Refreshments. Shop. P *Toilets. Tel Bucklers Hard (059 063) 203.*

EXBURY GARDENS

Off B3054, 3 miles south-east of Beaulieu (Ca)

This woodland garden is a dream world of flowering shrubs from March until July. Paths lead off into glades and hollows and with every turn the colours change – from cream and yellow to mauve and deep throbbing reds. Exbury was created by the banker Lionel de Rothschild, who during the 20 years starting in 1919 filled the 250 acres with his beloved rhododendrons. Many were sent by plant-hunters from the wildest regions of the Far East; others Rothschild produced himself as hybrids. Camellias, magnolias and azaleas are here in their plenty, underplanted with spring flowers.

Early Mar-late July and mid Sept-late Oct, daily. Adm charge. Refreshments. Shop. P *Toilets.* ♿ *Tel Fawley (0703) 891203.*

FARLEY MOUNT COUNTRY PARK

Off A3090, 3 miles west of Winchester (Cc)

Sarum Road – the old Roman road from Winchester to Salisbury – cuts straight as a die through the downs in this beautiful country park of more than 1000 acres, where the rare bastard toadflax and lovely pyramidal orchid are found. A network of tracks leads through woods and open grasslands, and some routes are signposted as waymarked trails. The views from Beacon Hill, which rises to 572ft, are breathtaking.

Not far from the Roman road are the rounded

hummocks of a prehistoric burial ground, and nearby in West Wood is the site of a Roman villa, where a mosaic now in Winchester Museum was excavated. A pyramid to the west is the 18th-century tomb of a successful racehorse, buried here by a grateful owner.
Part FC. All year, daily.

FURZEY GARDENS
Off A31 at Minstead (Bb)

Its hillside site adds interest to Furzey's floral displays and gives long views across the surrounding New Forest. Grassy paths swoop and twist among banks of azaleas and heathers; and wild flowers such as foxgloves, bluebells and anemones pop up to complement the planned displays. Trees from Australia and South America flourish in sheltered spots, and English birches surround a lake stocked with carp. At the entrance to the gardens, white doves perch precariously on the steeply sloping thatched roof of a cottage built in 1560. The shape of its timber beams indicates that they were cut for shipbuilding in the Tudor boatyards at Lymington. Today's visitors creep cautiously through tiny rooms which at the turn of the century were home to a family with 14 children.
All year, daily. Adm charge. Shop. P *Toilets. Tel Southampton (0703) 812464.*

HAWK CONSERVANCY
Off A303, 4 miles west of Andover (Bd)

Birds of prey exercise a strange fascination, and men have long fought to harness their speed and wild strength. The Hawk Conservancy offers a rare opportunity to see magnificent hawks, falcons, eagles and even owls at close quarters, while a careful breeding programme is designed to lead to the releasing of birds to the wild. The birds can be seen in aviaries and on open perches in the grounds, and on dry days flying demonstrations are given. Injured birds of prey found by the public and brought to the Hawk Conservancy are here nursed back to health.
Mar-Oct, daily. Adm charge. Refreshments. Shop. P *Toilets.* ♿ *Tel Weyhill (026 477) 2252.*

HILLIER GARDENS AND ARBORETUM
Off A31, 2 miles north-east of Romsey (Cc)

As many as 10,000 different species of shrubs and trees adorn the slopes of a windy hill looking north to the Hampshire Downs. The display of flowers, foliage and fruit changes with each season, against a constant backdrop of evergreens, and several routes have been mapped out to enable the visitor to see the best of the collection at every season. Spring presents the most colourful spectacle, bringing a blaze of camellias, azaleas, magnolias and rhododendrons, with the occasional flash of scarlet from a *Pieris formosa* 'Forest Flame', glimpsed through the trees. The Late Summer Walk wanders past borders of Himalayan honeysuckle and ruby-red escallonias, while autumn brings its own fiery displays as the maples in Acer Valley turn crimson and gold.
All year, Mon-Fri; also Sat and Sun, Mar-mid Nov. Adm charge. P *Toilets.* ♿ *Tel Romsey (0794) 68787.*

HOSPITAL OF ST CROSS
Off A333, 1 mile south of Winchester (Cc)

In quiet meadows beside the River Itchen stands one of the finest surviving groups of medieval buildings in Britain. They date from 1136, during King Stephen's reign, a time of civil war and famine. The king's brother, Bishop Henry of Blois of Winchester, founded the hospital as a home for 'thirteen poor men, feeble and so reduced in strength that they can scarcely, or not at all, support themselves'. He also instituted a daily meal for 'one hundred other poor persons, as deserving as can be found'.

Today 17 successors of the original 13 brethren live at St Cross, together with eight brothers of the Almshouse of Noble Poverty, which Cardinal Beaufort added in 1446. They wear distinctive 15th-century caps and gowns. The charitable institution has experienced periods of ease and plenty, but also times of corruption and financial need – as in the mid-19th century, when it provided the novelist Anthony Trollope with the basis of *The Warden*.

A magnificent 15th-century gateway – the Beaufort Tower – leads into the main court, and at the porter's lodge near the tower travellers may ask for the Wayfarer's Dole – a 'horn' of wine and a little bread – just as Bishop Henry planned. However, the daily dole is now limited to a gallon of wine and two loaves. The flats of the brethren, with tall, sentinel chimneys, line one side of the court and, opposite, the ambulatory, or covered way, leads to the chapel – the jewel among the buildings. Built between 1160 and 1290, with a squat, sturdy tower, it contains finely carved windows and lovely medieval glass.
All year, Mon-Sat. Adm charge. Shop. P *Toilets.* ♿ *Tel Winchester (0962) 51375.*

WRITER'S GARDEN *The lawns and flowerbeds of Jane Austen's home at Chawton have changed little since the novelist lived there. There are many old varieties of plants she would have known.*

JANE AUSTEN'S HOUSE
Off A32, 1 mile south-west of Alton (Dc)

The large red-brick house in which the novelist Jane Austen spent the last years of her life was once a 17th-century posting inn, and still wears an air of welcoming comfort. Today the building has been carefully restored to its appearance in 1809 – the year in which Jane moved here with her widowed mother and her sister Cassandra.

A gate in the garden wall leads to the entrance at the side of the house. Inside, a tour of the drawing room, parlour and five bedrooms reveals a very private world – a lock of hair, a dress, a patchwork quilt made by Jane and Cassandra for the double bed they shared. Some of Jane's letters have been framed, giving vivid reminders of the lively wit which sparkles through all her writings. The novels *Emma, Persuasion* and *Mansfield Park* evolved in this atmosphere of discreet elegance, and first editions are on display. Jane wrote in the dining parlour, whose creaking door gave warning of company. The bakehouse at the rear still contains its old oven and wash tub, and Jane's donkey-cart.

Just a mile to the north is Alton, where the Curtis Museum has an amusing collection of Victorian toys, and an exhibition on the local brewing industry. The Allen Gallery nearby displays fine ceramics, and a silver collection.
Jane Austen's House: Apr-Oct, daily; Nov, Dec and Mar, Wed-Sun; Jan and Feb, Sat and Sun. Adm charge. Shop. P *(limited). Toilets.* ♿ *(garden). Tel Alton (0420) 83262. Curtis Museum and Allen Gallery: All year, Tues-Sat. Free entry. Shop.* P ♿ *(ground floor). Tel (0420) 82802.*

MARWELL ZOOLOGICAL PARK
On B2177, 5 miles south-east of Winchester (Cb)

An exotic world of leopards and lynxes, zebras and gazelles lies hidden behind a dense curtain of trees just off the main road. Some 100 acres of pastures and pens provide a haven at Marwell for

almost 1000 varieties of animals and birds. The zoo's primary concern is the conservation of endangered species. A large number of each species are kept, to encourage breeding.

Rare inhabitants include the Asiatic lion, smaller than its African cousin but no less proud; only 300 now survive in the world. Marwell's large collection of big cats includes Siberian tigers, snow leopards, jaguars and cheetahs.

Marwell can be explored on foot or by car. A 2 mile road meanders through a fantasy world of red pandas, rhinos, llamas, wallabies, gibbons, ostriches and flamingos. There are large picnic sites, and a restaurant with a children's play area.
All year, daily. Adm charge. Refreshments. Shop. P *Toilets.* ♿ *Tel Owslebury (096 274) 406.*

MID-HANTS RAILWAY

Off A31, at Alton or New Alresford (Dc)

From spring to autumn, steam engines amble through 10 miles of the Hampshire countryside, making their way down the 'Watercress Line'. Passengers joining at Alton or New Alresford make a half-hour return journey through rich farmland and deep chalk cuttings, between banks bright with wild flowers and up steep inclines dubbed 'the Alps'. Along the way the train stops at two stations, lovingly restored to their steam-age glory.

The line between Alton and Winchester opened in 1865 as a branch of the main London-Southampton route, and local watercress growers used it to get their produce to market. Watercress beds can still be seen near New Alresford, and fresh watercress can be bought on the train. In 1973 British Rail closed the line, but a group of enthusiasts rescued it, restoring passenger services in 1985.
July-Sept, daily; Mar-July, weekends and Bank Hol; Sept-Oct, Sat and Sun. Adm charge. Refreshments. Shop. P *Toilets.* ♿ *Tel Alresford (0962) 733810.*

HOT POT *What appears to be an alcove, with a smoking urn draped in an ermine stole, is one of Rex Whistler's painted illusions at Mottisfont Abbey. The artist decorated the room named after him in the 1930s.*

MOTTISFONT ABBEY

Off A3057, 4½ miles north-west of Romsey (Bc)

Venerable trees and close-mown lawns, smooth as striped satin, make a magical setting for an Augustinian priory of 1201, which became a private house after the Dissolution. Outside, the north and south façades present a contrast in styles: the north front is of flint, the south of brick. Inside, two main areas of the house are open to the public. The impressively vaulted cellars were once the Augustinian canons' offices and storerooms. Upstairs is a large sitting room, whose apparent ornamental plasterwork on ceiling and walls is in fact a masterpiece of trompe l'oeil painting by the artist Rex Whistler, who was killed during the Second World War.
NT. Grounds: Apr-Sept, pm daily exc Fri and Sat. House: Apr-Sept, Wed and Sun pm. Shop. P *Toilets.* ♿ *Tel Lockerley (0794) 40757.*

MUSEUM OF ARMY FLYING

Off A343 at Middle Wallop (Bc)

The army first took to the skies when the Royal Engineers flew balloons in Africa during the 19th century. Improvements in artillery meant that missiles could be fired beyond the range of the gunners' eyesight, so spotters with a bird's eye view played a vital role in reporting to the gunners where their shells were landing. The Museum of Army Flying re-creates 100 years of army flying in pictures and dioramas, uniformed models, weapons and equipment.

Pride of place goes to the aircraft themselves, from First World War biplanes to the missile-carrying helicopters of today. The fighting role of the Royal Flying Corps gradually passed to the Royal Air Force, formed in 1918, and reconnaissance became the main task of army flying. Its Second World War spotter planes seem dangerously insubstantial, and so too does the frail Horsa glider which flew troops to Normandy in the D-Day landings.
All year, daily. Adm charge. Refreshments. Shop. P *Toilets.* ♿ *Tel Andover (0264) 62121.*

NEW FOREST BUTTERFLY FARM

Off A35, 1½ miles south-east of Ashurst (Bb)

The butterflies are kept in cavernous glasshouses, surrounded by 2000 acres of woodland. The visitor steps through the door into a tropical garden of passion flowers, heliotrope and sweet-scented choisya. The humid air vibrates with colour as butterflies dip and hover – purple emperors, red helens and hundreds more. Next door, British butterflies such as red admirals enjoy the milder climate of a cottage garden. Bees can be seen at work in their hive.

WINGED WONDER *A native of South-east Asia, the lovely atlas moth, with a 12in wingspan, is one of the many exotic moths and butterflies seen in flight at the New Forest Butterfly Farm.*

The insectarium introduces scorpions and tarantulas – safely behind glass – and there is a chance to see butterflies hatching from their chrysalises in special cages. The garden also has a dragonfly pond and an aviary. Visitors can take horse-drawn wagon rides through the woods.
Apr-Oct, daily. Adm charge. Refreshments. Shop. P *Toilets.* ♿ *Tel Ashurst (042 129) 3367.*

OATES MEMORIAL LIBRARY AND GILBERT WHITE MUSEUM

On B3006 at Selborne (Ec)

Gilbert White, the 18th-century naturalist and clergyman, brought fame to Selborne with his classic work *The Natural History and Antiquities of Selborne,* first published in 1789, which describes the natural world around the village. He lived at The Wakes, a 16th-century house, and died there in 1793 at the age of 72. The building is now a museum, with an exhibition devoted to White's studies and accounts. Many of his possessions are gathered together in the old part of the house, including notebooks with sermons written in his own clear hand and two watercolours by S.H. Grimm, whose work was used to illustrate the first edition of White's book.

Exhibitions on the first floor tell the stories of two very different explorers, both relatives of the museum's benefactor. Captain Lawrence Oates joined Scott's tragic 1911 expedition to the Antarctic, and a story of almost unbelievable courage emerges from letters and personal belongings. The captain was one of Scott's party, which reached the Pole but perished on the return journey to base camp.

Exotic birds and tribal weapons were some of the objects collected by the captain's uncle, Frank Oates, in the 19th century. The exhibition charts his travels in Africa and the Americas. Behind the house White's delightful garden retains some of its original features – such as the sundial and sunken fence, or ha-ha. Enthusiasts may follow in White's footsteps on the zigzag path up the Hanger, a steep slope clad with beech trees behind the house.
Mar-Oct, Tues-Sun and Bank Hol pm. Adm charge. Shop. Toilets. Tel Selborne (042 050) 275.

PAULTONS PARK

On A31, 3 miles south-west of Romsey (Bb)

A lake forms a gleaming horseshoe where coral-pink flamingos browse sedately among busier wildfowl. Large aviaries house exotic creatures such as parrots, toucans and scarlet ibis, while rare breeds of sheep and cattle, and ponies, llamas and wallabies, graze in grassy paddocks by the lake.

The Romany Museum displays a collection of caravans and wagons, beautifully carved and brightly decorated, and depicts the gypsies' nomadic life. A Village Life Museum exhibits the workshops and tools of the blacksmith, wheelwright, cooper, carpenter and dairymaid.

Mar-Oct, daily. Adm charge. Refreshments. Shop. P *Toilets.* ♿ *Tel Southampton (0703) 814442.*

PORTCHESTER CASTLE

Off A27, 2½ miles east of Fareham (Da)

On a low headland overlooking Portsmouth Harbour, the flint walls of Portchester Castle, with D-shaped bastions, form a vast quadrangle and the longest intact Roman wall in Northern Europe. Built in the 3rd century AD to defend the shore against Saxon pirates, the fort's strength was recognised 900 years later by Henry II, who built his own castle within. Richard II adapted this as a small palace, whose remains include the hall, kitchen and great chamber.

In the south-west corner the tall, square tower of the Norman keep still stands, and an exhibition on the ground floor describes the castle's colourful history. Troops were mustered here before leaving Portsmouth for historic battles such as Agincourt in 1415. In the 17th and 18th centuries the castle was used as a prison, as carved graffiti still testify.

EH. All year, daily. Adm charge. Shop. P *Toilets.* ♿ *(parts). Tel Portsmouth (0705) 378291.*

QUEEN ELIZABETH COUNTRY PARK

On A3, 4 miles south of Petersfield (Eb)

The main road slashes dramatically through the South Downs and divides this 1400 acre park into two quite different halves. To the west, open grassy slopes grazed by sheep culminate in Butser Hill – the westernmost summit and highest point of the South Downs, rising to 888ft. It is topped by a slender radio mast and has breathtaking views all round. Woods with ancient, shadowy yews clothe the deep coombs below.

East of the road, man-made forest covers the hills, and at its edge a Park Centre offers film shows about the park, a relief model of the area, and an exhibition showing how the land has been worked from Stone Age times to the present day. At weekends the centre hums with the sound of craftsmen at work, or with the jingle of morris dancers.

The leisurely way to explore the park is by car, following the Forest Drive from the Park Centre through the woods to the Juniper Car Park, near which foresters give regular displays of skills such as hurdle-making. A little more energy is required for the three marked walks, from 2½ to 3½ miles long. Two forest trails, starting near the Park Centre, are magical in their spring and autumn colours. The Butser Trail, starting at a hilltop car park, affords spectacular views over the Downs, with hang-gliders hovering overhead and grass-skiers careering down the slopes below.

A highlight of the park is Butser Ancient Farm, a few minutes walk from the Park Centre

ANCIENT FARM *The Pimperne House in Queen Elizabeth Park is based on the evidence of an excavated Iron Age site in Dorset; it is the largest Iron Age building ever reconstructed.*

on the slopes below Butser Hill. This remarkable collection of circular huts with conical thatched roofs – much like an African village in appearance – is a unique attempt to re-create a working Iron Age farm. Its centrepiece is a vast house built from 200 trees, its dim interior filled with replicas of Iron Age tools. Outside there are pens for livestock – old breeds such as Soay sheep and Dexter cattle – while early forms of cereals are enclosed by hurdle fences.

Park: All year, daily; centre, Mar-Oct, daily; Nov-Feb Sun. Free entry. Refreshments. Shop. P *(charge). Toilets.* ♿ *Tel Horndean (0705) 595040. Farm: Apr-Sept, daily. Adm charge. Shop. Tel (0705) 595040.*

ROYAL NAVY SUBMARINE MUSEUM

Off B3333 at Gosport (Da)

Five submarines were introduced into the navy in 1901 to be greeted by traditionalists with amazed contempt. One of those prototypes, *Holland I*, is on view at this museum which chronicles the history of submarines in pictures and in a collection of models which range from a full-size replica of the one-man submersible craft *Turtle*, built in 1776 to attack the British fleet off New York, to today's nuclear-powered submarines.

Outside the museum, cradled above the water, stands the museum's principal exhibit, the sleek grey hull of the submarine HMS *Alliance*, completed in 1947. Doors cut into her side open up a cramped metal world of pipes and gauges.

All year, daily. Adm charge. Refreshments. Shop. P *Toilets. Tel Gosport (0705) 529217.*

ROYAL VICTORIA COUNTRY PARK

Off B3397, 1 mile north-west of Hamble (Cb)

A screen of trees shelters a wide grassy amphitheatre sloping down to a lovely beach by Southampton Water. A Victorian church stands centre stage – all that remains of what was once Britain's largest military hospital, its main buildings a quarter of a mile long.

The chapel is now a Heritage Centre, where the hospital's past is re-created in pictures and tableaux using costumed models. The hospital was built in the 1850s to accommodate soldiers wounded in the Crimean War, after Florence Nightingale had drawn public attention to their grim suffering. In 1966 it was demolished and the grounds turned into terraced lawns and peaceful woods.

All year, daily.

SOUTHAMPTON HALL OF AVIATION

Albert Road South, Southampton (Cb)

The hall celebrates some of the most exciting and romantic years in aviation history – the inter-war years of the Schneider Trophy, which Britain won outright in 1931 in competition with the USA, Italy and France. R.J. Mitchell, designer of the Spitfire, also designed many of the Schneider Trophy racing floatplanes, and his work is commemorated in a section of the museum which includes a Mark 24 Spitfire and a Supermarine S6A. The centrepiece of the museum is a Sandringham 'Beachcomber' flying boat – one of a series of flying boats for which Southampton and Cowes became famous.

All year, daily exc Mon (also Mon in school holidays). Adm charge. Refreshments. Shop. P *Toilets.* ♿ *Tel Southampton (0703) 635830.*

ACTION STATION *The control room of HMS* Alliance*, now at the Royal Navy Submarine Museum, is dominated by the periscope, on the left, and the large circular depth gauge.*

HAVEN OF NAVAL HISTORY

The history of Portsmouth is the history of England's naval heritage. It was Henry VII who, in the late 15th century, first fortified Portsmouth's sea walls. Behind them he built England's first permanent dry dock, and about 50 years later Henry VIII expanded it into the country's first royal dockyard. Relics of Portsmouth's history include three of the great ships that once sailed from the port – HMS Victory, Mary Rose *and HMS* Warrior. *Museums tell the story of the Royal Navy, of the Royal Marines and of the D-Day landings, and the quiet streets of Old Portsmouth still have their ancient fortifications. Here, too, is the birthplace of the son of a navy pay clerk, christened Charles Dickens; the house is now a museum.*

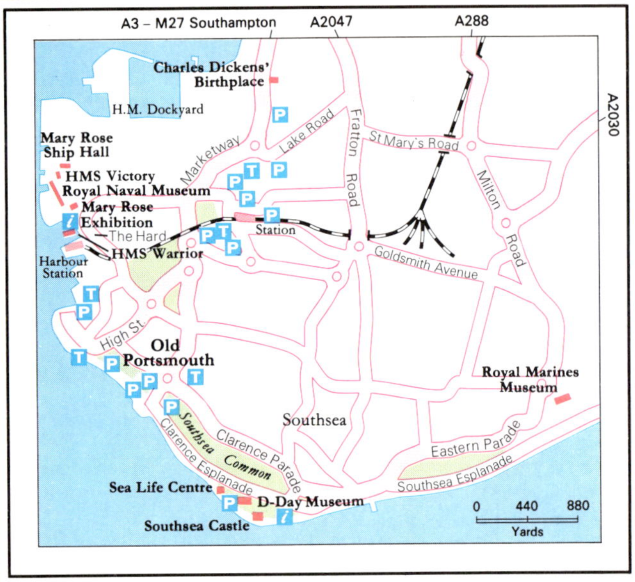

HMS *Victory*, *Mary Rose*, RN Museum *All year, daily. Adm charge. Refreshments. Shop.* P *Toilets. Tel Portsmouth (0705) 839766.*

Dickens' Birthplace *Mar-Oct, daily. Adm charge. Shop. Toilets. Tel (0705) 827261.*

Southsea Castle, D-Day Museum *All year, daily. Adm charge. Shop.* P *Toilets. Tel (0705) 827261.*

Royal Marines Museum *All year, daily. Adm charge. Shop.* P *Toilets.* ♿ *Tel (0705) 819385.*

Sea Life Centre *All year, daily. Adm charge. Refreshments. Shop.* P *Toilets.* ♿ *Tel (0705) 734461.*

HMS *Warrior* *All year, daily. Adm charge.* P *Tel (0705) 291379.*

THE MARY ROSE SHIP HALL AND EXHIBITION

On a calm summer day in 1545 the *Mary Rose*, pride of Henry VIII's fleet, set out from Portsmouth to engage a French invasion fleet anchored off the Isle of Wight. As the *Mary Rose* sailed defiantly into The Solent a horrified crowd on shore, including the king, saw her heel over and sink, taking with her 700 men. More than four centuries later, in 1982, the ship's hull was raised and taken back to Portsmouth. Objects recovered include several massive bronze guns – a reconstruction (right) shows where the guns might have been set – a pewter tankard (left) and a pocket sundial (below). In the Ship Hall today, water jets keep the hull cool and damp (below left).

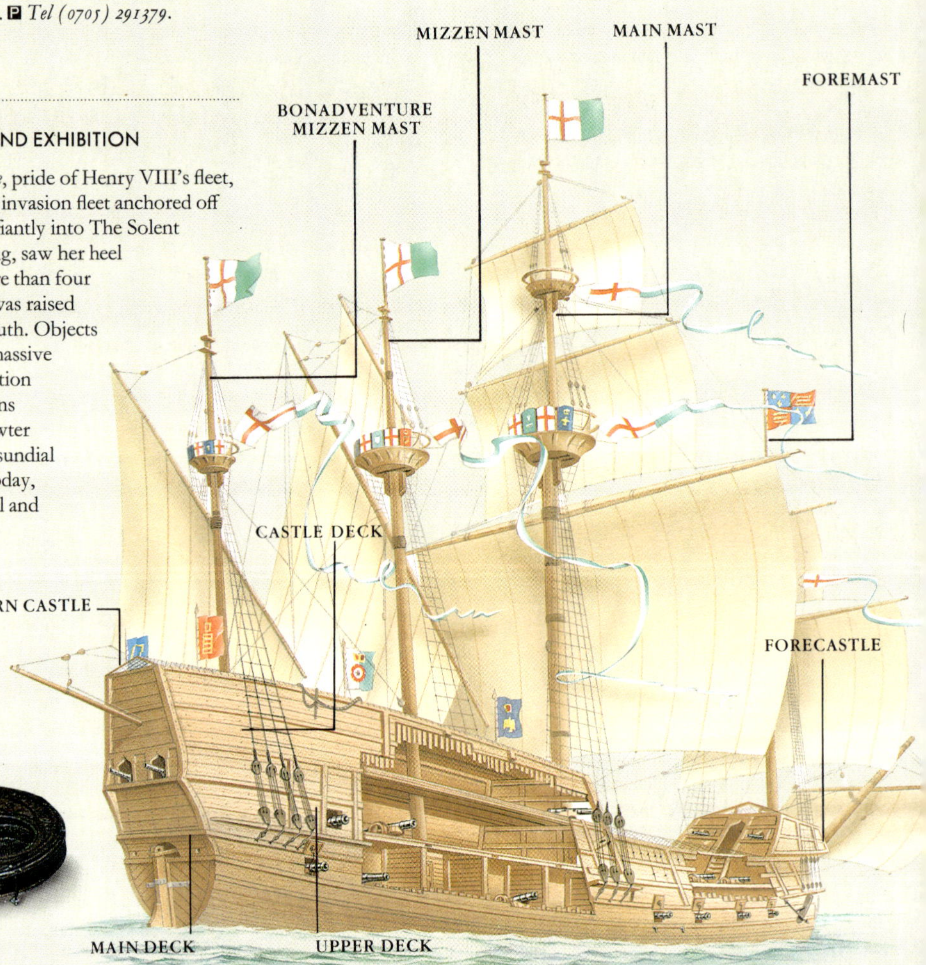

CHARLES DICKENS' BIRTHPLACE

The novelist Charles Dickens was born at 1 Mile End Terrace, now 393 Old Commercial Road, on February 7, 1812. The Georgian house is now a Dickens Museum, furnished in the style of a middle-class family of the early 1800s. Possessions of the novelist on view include his inkwell (above) and the couch on which he died.

ROYAL NAVAL MUSEUM

Fine Georgian storehouses contain exhibits telling the story of the Royal Navy from Tudor times to the present day. There are many relics and mementos of Nelson, ranging from a Staffordshire china figure portraying his death (above), to the State Barge that carried his body up the River Thames for burial in St Paul's Cathedral. In an upper gallery are figureheads of 19th-century ships, including that of HMS *Bellerophon* (right).

SEA LIFE CENTRE

Shoals of fish and a variety of other sea creatures inhabit the Sea Life Centre's Ocean Reef display – a 13ft deep enclosure with toughened glass walls.

D-DAY MUSEUM

An embroidered tapestry more than 270ft long is the focal point of the D-Day Museum on Clarence Esplanade, Southsea. In muted colours of blue, grey, green and brown, its 34 panels tell the story of 'Operation Overlord', code name for the invasion of France on June 6, 1944. The Royal School of Needlework spent seven years on the tapestry.

ROYAL MARINES MUSEUM

Silver memorial drums and trumpets in the Bands History Room commemorate the members of Royal Marine bands who died in two World Wars.

SOUTHSEA CASTLE

A swivel-mounted cannon points across The Solent from the walls of Southsea Castle, which houses a museum devoted to Portsmouth's military history. The castle was built in 1545 by Henry VIII; tradition says that it was from the walls of the castle that the king watched as the *Mary Rose* sank.

OLD PORTSMOUTH

The view from the Round Tower, part of Old Portsmouth's fortifications, takes in fine Georgian houses, including the weatherboarded Quebec House on Portsmouth Point, built in 1754 for seawater bathing.

HMS WARRIOR

Launched at Blackwall, London, in 1860, HMS *Warrior* was Britain's first iron-hulled warship, armed with 44 guns and driven by steam or sail power, or both. When she became obsolete in 1883 she became a depot ship and then a floating jetty. Now she is anchored at Portsmouth on permanent display as the navy's first, and last remaining, battleship.

HMS VICTORY

Proudly towering over the dockside buildings, HMS *Victory* symbolises the supremacy of British sea power in the 19th century. As Admiral Lord Nelson's flagship, *Victory* carried him to a decisive victory over the French fleet at Trafalgar on October 21, 1805. A plaque on the quarter-deck marks the spot where Nelson fell to a sniper's bullet, and the cockpit in which he died has become a shrine. The 32-pounder guns on the lower gun deck (top right) show the ship's enormous firepower.

SOUTHAMPTON MARITIME MUSEUM

Bugle Street, Southampton (Cb)

Carved on the beams of the 14th-century wool warehouse on the waterfront, which houses the Maritime Museum, are the names of French prisoners of war who were held there in the 18th and 19th centuries. Another sombre memory from the past is a display devoted to the *Titanic*, which sank on its maiden voyage from Southampton to New York in 1912. There is also a 22ft model of the *Queen Mary*. The museum also celebrates the many triumphs of local shipbuilding, including the powerboat *Miss Britain III*, which set a new 100mph speed record in 1934.

All year, daily exc Mon. Free entry. Shop. P ♿ *Tel Southampton (0703) 224216.*

STRATFIELD SAYE HOUSE

Off A33, 6 miles north-east of Basingstoke (De)

A grateful government presented this lovely mansion to the Duke of Wellington in 1817 as a tribute for his victory over Napoleon at Waterloo two years earlier. From the main gates, the narrow drive leads straight to the low 17th-century building with cupola and simple portico. The original white stucco has worn away, leaving the brickwork beneath a mellow, tawny yellow.

For 170 years the Dukes of Wellington have preserved the house as a monument to their illustrious ancestor. The hall is hung with paintings of Wellington's battles. Many of Europe's monarchs, grateful to be free of the Napoleonic menace, gave gifts, and these included a green malachite *tazza*, or urn, from Tsar Alexander I of Russia. The Roman mosaic floors were excavated at nearby Silchester by the 2nd Duke. The library has scarcely changed since Wellington sat there surrounded by leather-bound books, many of which belonged to Napoleon.

An exhibition on Wellington's life has been set up in the stable block. Each stall covers a different period or campaign. The victory over the French at Vittoria in 1813 is recalled by the great trunk captured from Napoleon's retreating brother Joseph. It contained spoils of war including valuable paintings now hanging in the drawing room, and at Apsley House, the Duke's London home. More prosaic are the famous 'Wellington Boots', and the hero's false teeth. The exhibition ends – in 1852 – on an awesome note with Wellington's massive funeral carriage, made of bronze guns taken at Waterloo and weighing 18 tons. There are beautiful walks through the grounds by the River Loddon, and near the old ice house lies the grave of Wellington's horse, Copenhagen.

Part of the estate is now the Wellington Country Park, reached from the B3349, 2 miles north-east of the house. Boating, fishing and windsurfing are major attractions on its lake, and in the surrounding deer park there are nature trails and a miniature steam railway. The National Dairy Museum, housed in the Park Centre, offers regular demonstrations of skills such as butter-modelling amid a display of Victorian milk churns and delivery carts.

House: May-Sept, daily exc Fri; also Easter and weekends in Apr. Adm charge. Refreshments. Shop. P *Toilets.* ♿ *Tel Basingstoke (0256) 882882. Park: Mar-Oct, daily; Nov-Feb, weekends. Adm charge. Refreshments. Shop.* P ♿ *Tel Reading (0734) 326444.*

UPPER HAMBLE COUNTRY PARK

Off M27 (exit 8) 4 miles east of Southampton (Cb)

As the tidal waters of the River Hamble push northwards they leave behind the yachtsmen's world of the lower river and enter a rural landscape little changed by the hand of man. On the west bank the Upper Hamble Country Park covers a wide area of woods and farmland, offering the visitor a choice of shaded river walks or paths across the open fields.

One of the park's many delights – the Hampshire Farm Museum – re-creates life on a Hampshire farm as it was lived from 1850 to 1950. Original farm buildings preserved at the museum include a large 18th-century barn supported on mushroom-shaped staddle stones. Visitors can wander round a traditional farmhouse, its rooms furnished with the sparse belongings of a bygone age, a forge and a wheelwright's shop, and see rare shorthorn cattle, saddleback pigs and other livestock.

Park: All year, daily. Free entry. Museum: All year, daily. Adm charge. Refreshments. Shop. P *Toilets.* ♿ *Tel Botley (048 92) 87055.*

HALL OF BANNERS *The banner of the 7th Duke of Wellington hangs in the hall of Stratfield Saye House, flanked by embroidered Napoleonic tricolours given to the Iron Duke after the Battle of Waterloo.*

THE VYNE

Off A340, 4 miles north of Basingstoke (Dd)

Lord Sandys, Henry VIII's Lord Chamberlain, built this low E-shaped house in a hollow by the River Loddon. The façade is of rose-pink brick with a lattice design in darker plum. The north front overlooks a lake, and its classical portico built in the 1650s was the first to be added to an English country house. Exquisite interior decoration includes fine linenfold panelling in the oak gallery, and a theatrical staircase of fluted columns and intricate plasterwork.

NT. Apr-mid Oct, pm daily exc Mon and Fri; also Bank Hol Mon. Adm charge. Refreshments. Shop. P *Toilets.* ♿ *(parts). Tel Basingstoke (0256) 881337.*

WHITCHURCH SILK MILL

Winchester Street, near centre of Whitchurch (Cd)

The red-brick mill buildings are square and plain, with shallow slate roofs topped by a graceful cupola – the whole making a practical, elegant simplicity. The River Test flows alongside between even lawns, and the old millwheel and machinery are still in evidence. Whitchurch Mill was built in about 1800 and is one of the few silk mills in the country still undefeated by foreign competition. Traditional techniques are still used, and visitors can watch the painstaking process as fine threads are wound, warped and woven to create the rich silks used in ceremonial gowns for QCs and university dons, flags and exclusive fashion collections.

Easter-Oct, Tues-Fri; also Sun, June-Oct and Dec. Adm charge. Shop. Toilets. ♿ *Tel Whitchurch (0256) 892065.*

BISHOP'S TOMB *William of Wykeham, one of Winchester's greatest bishops, lies in a chantry in the cathedral nave. Students of the college he founded nearby are still known as Wykehamists.*

WILLIS MUSEUM

Market Place, Basingstoke (Dd)

The old market town of Basingstoke largely disappeared in the 1960s under a mountain range of homes and offices. In the Old Town Hall the Willis Museum guards the town's rich past. George Willis, a local watchmaker, set up the museum in 1931 with his outstanding collection of watches and clocks. Numerous exhibits have been added since then. The museum's survey of the history of Basingstoke begins in prehistoric times with a 6½ft long mammoth's tusk found near Odiham, and displays from later times include children's toys and embroidery.

In Harrow Way is another remarkable outpost of the past – the Viables Craft Centre. Traditional crafts represented include spinning, weaving, joinery and pottery.

Willis Museum: All year, Tues-Sat. Free entry. Shop. Tel Basingstoke (0256) 465902. Viables Centre: All year, daily exc Mon. Free entry. Refreshments. Shop. P *Toilets. Tel (0256) 473634.*

WINCHESTER CASTLE

In centre of Winchester (Cc)

The Great Hall of Winchester Castle is one of the finest medieval halls in England, with a lofty timbered roof resting on slender marble columns. An elaborate bronze – a glorification of Queen Victoria made to commemorate her Golden Jubilee in 1887 – stands in one corner. The hall is the sole remnant of the royal castle begun by command of the Conqueror in 1067 on the site of a Saxon royal fortress, and rebuilt by Henry III, who was born there in 1206. The remainder of the castle was destroyed by Cromwell in 1645.

To medieval and Tudor monarchs Winchester was traditionally the Camelot of King Arthur, from whom they claimed descent, and the Round Table that now hangs in the hall was made for Edward I in about 1265. Made of oak, it is 18ft across and weighs more than a ton. It bears a portrait of Arthur and the names of his 24 knights, painted for Henry VIII. Later, the hall was used as a court where, in 1603, Sir Walter Raleigh was convicted of treason. Judge Jeffreys held a 'Bloody Assize' there in 1685, after the Monmouth Rebellion.

Sir Christopher Wren began a sumptuous palace for Charles II on the site in 1683. However, the king died two years later and the scheme was dropped. The completed buildings and later additions eventually became a barracks, which now houses the regimental museum of the Royal Hussars, who mount a dramatic display with real tanks and lifelike model horses. In nearby Southgate Street, the regimental museum of the Royal Green Jackets – an amalgam of three famous infantry regiments – traces the regiment's battle honours back to the Peninsular Wars and Waterloo.

The medieval castle was built on a hill in the south-west angle of the city walls, and nearby is the Westgate. Its tower room has an exquisitely painted wooden ceiling and contains a collection of armour.

Great Hall: All year, daily. Free entry. Shop. ♿ *Tel Winchester (0962) 841841. Royal Hussars Museum: Easter-Oct, Tues-Sat and Bank Hol. Adm charge. Shop. Toilets. Tel (0962) 63751. Royal Green Jackets Museum: All year, Mon-Fri; also Sat pm Apr-Sept, exc Bank Hol weekends. Free entry. Shop. Tel (0962) 63658. Westgate Museum: All year, daily exc Mon, Oct-Mar. Adm charge. Shop. Tel (0962) 68166.*

WINCHESTER CATHEDRAL

In centre of Winchester (Cc)

Royal capital of Saxon Wessex and of England until the late 12th century, Winchester has had a cathedral for 13 centuries, but the present building was begun in Norman times. It appears massive, skirted by smooth lawns, its square tower brooding and low. Norman architecture survives in the crypt, and in the transepts, where the splendid Epiphany Chapel has been restored.

The rest of the building is in pure Gothic style – a breathtaking 556ft procession of soaring arches, ribbed vaulting and graceful windows with fine stained glass making one of the longest churches in Europe. It was built in the 13th century, and in the 14th century under Bishop William of Wykeham. The 15th-century reredos is a masterpiece of stone carving, and more than 500 faces carved in wood above the choir stalls smile in common delight. Exquisite medieval wall paintings have come to light in the Holy Sepulchre and Guardian Angels' chapels. The simple tomb of the novelist Jane Austen lies in the nave.

Just north-west of the cathedral, in The Square, the City Museum has exhibits dating from Winchester's past including the 9th-century Winchester Reliquary of gilded bronze, which once held the hair or bone of a saint. An exhibition on local trades has an original Victorian chemist's shop. South-eastwards across the lovely cathedral close, the Pilgrims Hall – now part of the choir school – offers a glimpse of one of England's oldest hammerbeam roofs, built in about 1290.

In College Street south of the Close is Winchester College, founded in 1382 by Bishop William of Wykeham. The 70 black-gowned scholars among some 600 pupils at the school still roam the medieval cloisters.

Cathedral: All year, daily. City Museum: All year, daily exc Mon, Oct-Mar. Free entry. Shop. Tel Winchester (0962) 68166 ext 2269. Pilgrims Hall: All year, daily exc when used by school. Free entry. Tel (0962) 54189. College: All year, daily. Adm charge. Toilets. Tel (0962) 64242.

COUNTY CALENDAR

March 25 Tichborne: Dole Ceremony.

May (early). Calshot: Small Boat and Marine Festival.

June (late). Beaulieu: Country Sports and Craft Fair.

July (early). Southampton: Show.

July (mid-month). Southampton: Balloon Festival.

July (Sun nearest 19th). Bucklers Hard: Village Festival.

July (late). Brockenhurst: New Forest and Hampshire County Show. Winchester: Southern Cathedrals Festival (every third year, from 1990).

August (early). Southampton: Carnival. Southsea: Show.

August Bank Hol Portsmouth Naval Base: Navy Day.

September (mid-month). Eastney: Royal Marine Tattoo. Broadlands: Romsey Show.

Tourist information: Lyndhurst (042 128) 2269; Portsmouth (0705) 826722; Southampton (0703) 221106; Winchester (0962) 840500.

HEREFORD AND WORCESTER

BEACONS ON THE MALVERNS AND CATHEDRAL CITIES ON TWO RIVERS

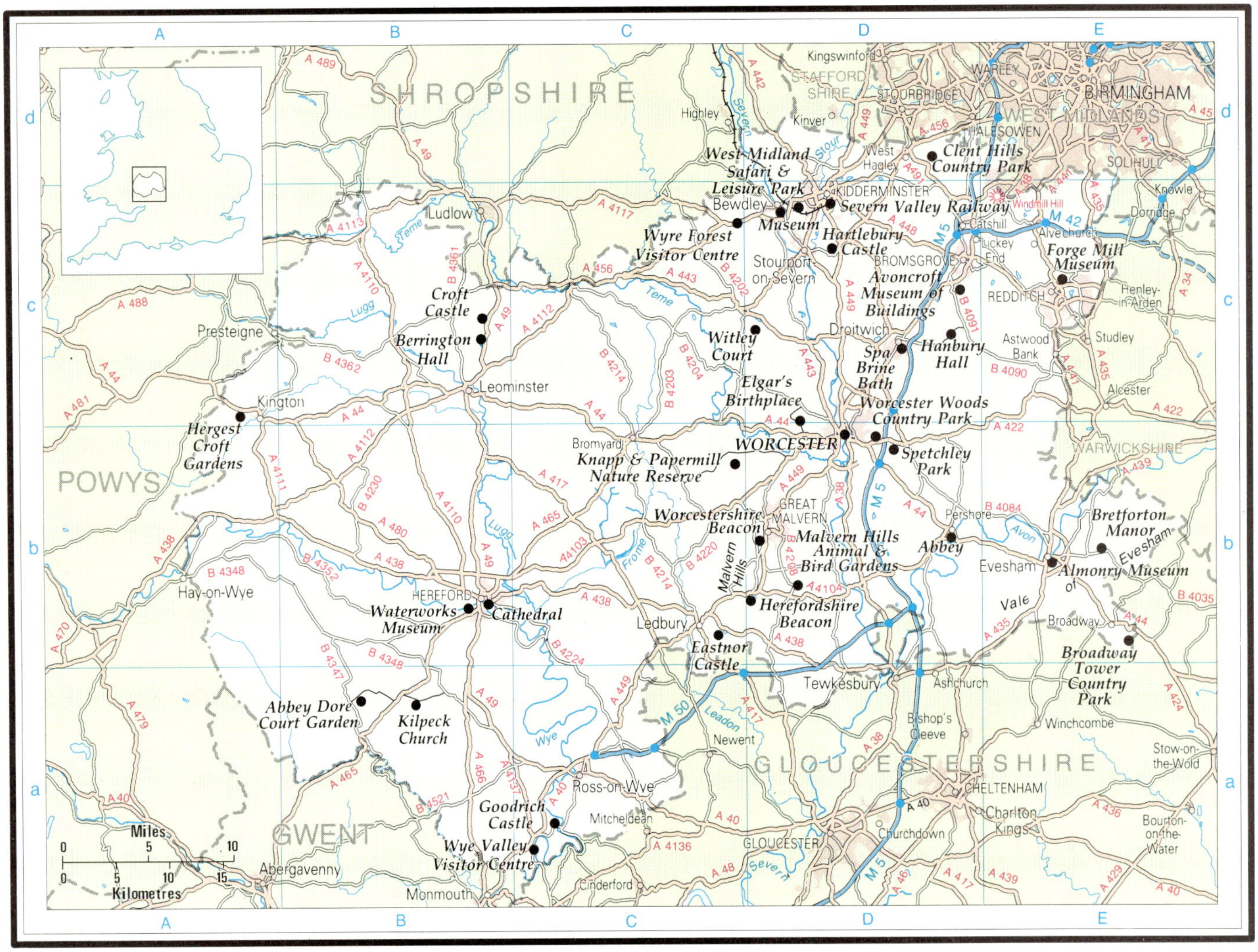

The sinuous ridge of the Malvern Hills divides this county – formed in 1974 by the merger of Herefordshire and Worcestershire – into two lowland plains. The Malverns and the countryside around them were loved by the composer Sir Edward Elgar, who wrote his two great symphonies here.

The musical theme is continued in the cathedral cities of Hereford and Worcester, which share the annual Three Choirs Festival with Gloucester. They both stand in rich farmland which contains, in the Vale of Evesham, one of Britain's main fruit-growing and market-gardening centres. Each city has its own special associations: Hereford is famed for its breed of cattle and its cider industry; Worcester is noted for its porcelain and spicy sauce.

The River Severn flows down from the north, and one of its prettiest stretches is followed by the steam-powered Severn Valley Railway.

ABBEY DORE COURT GARDEN

Off B4347, 11 miles south-west of Hereford (Ba)

The walled and riverside garden at Abbey Dore Court covers some 4 acres containing a notable fern border, rock garden and pool, and a circular herb garden. Many unusual plants are grown and sold, and the garden is the home of the national sedum and euphorbia collections. Nearby is Dore Abbey Church, built from the chancel of a 12th-century Cistercian abbey church.

Abbey Dore stands at the gateway to the tranquil Golden Valley where the River Dore flows between meadows, farmlands and little villages overlooked by the Black Mountains.

Mid Mar-Oct, daily exc Wed. Adm charge. Refreshments. Shop. P *Toilets. Tel Golden Valley (0981) 240419.*

ALMONRY MUSEUM, EVESHAM

Near Abbey Park, in centre of Evesham (Eb)

Set in 7½ acres of riverside parkland, and fronted by the old town stocks, the almonry is a rambling stone and half-timbered building which grew from the 14th century onwards on or near the site of the ruined Evesham Abbey. Food and clothing for the poor were once dispensed from there, and it is now a museum of local history, with exhibits ranging from prehistoric times to the present day.

There are many Romano-British and Saxon exhibits and other displays include a 14th-century illuminated psalter and the Great Chair of Evesham Abbey, elaborately carved from oak. In the precinct, other monastic remains include the great gateway and the superb, pinnacled bell tower of 1532. One room in the museum is devoted to Simon de Montfort, father of England's Parliament, who was killed in the Battle of Evesham (1265) and is buried in Abbey Park.

The River Avon flows past the park, which has a children's playground with boating and paddling pools which have been converted from the old abbey fishponds.

Mar-Nov, daily exc Mon, Wed. Adm charge. Refreshments. Shop. Tel Evesham (0386) 6944.

AVONCROFT MUSEUM OF BUILDINGS

Off A38, 2 miles south of Bromsgrove (Dc)

How did people store ice before the invention of refrigerators? What was it like inside a prefab of the 1940s? The Avoncroft Museum of Buildings offers fascinating insights into the past. Some 20 buildings spanning seven centuries of English history have been rescued from destruction and re-erected on this 15 acre, open-air site in the Worcestershire countryside.

The museum's first acquisition was a timber-framed 15th-century merchant's house from Bromsgrove, opened to the public in 1967, and since then the collection has steadily expanded. There is an 18th-century cockpit theatre from the Crown Inn at Bridgnorth – and a windmill from Warwickshire which still grinds flour. The prefab is an Arcon Mk V from Yardley in Birmingham, dating from 1946 and restored with period furnishings. There is an Ice House from the 18th-century Tong Castle in Shropshire: it is a huge, brick-built domed cylinder formerly sited underground. Sawn ice blocks were either stored in layers interspersed with straw, or crushed and crammed in to form a compacted mass so that its wealthy owners could enjoy iced drinks in midsummer.

Besides its buildings, Avoncroft has a display of carts and caravans. On certain days a Shire horse gives wagon rides, and there are train rides on a miniature track.

June-Aug, daily; April, May, Sept and Oct, daily exc Mon; Mar and Nov, daily exc Mon, Fri; open Bank Hol. Adm charge. Refreshments. Shop. 🅿 *Toilets.* ♿ *Tel Bromsgrove (0527) 31886/31363.*

BERRINGTON HALL

Off A49, 3 miles north of Leominster (Bc)

The square-shouldered house with its porticoed front is almost severe in its classical simplicity. Built in 1781 of reddish local stone, Berrington Hall was designed by the architect Henry Holland for Thomas Harley, a banker and privy councillor who was Lord Mayor of London at the age of 37. Though austere outside, the house has much elegant detailing inside, including plaster friezes and painted ceilings.

The square-shaped hall on the ground floor is patterned with black, white and greeny-grey marble, which partly reflects the ceiling design. French furniture and works of art furnish the drawing room and boudoir. The parkland, which includes an extensive artificial lake, was landscaped by Capability Brown, father-in-law of the Hall's architect.

NT. Apr-Oct, Sat and Sun pm; May-Sept, Wed-Sun pm; also Bank Hol. Adm charge. Refreshments. Shop. 🅿 *Toilets. Tel Leominster (0568) 5721.*

BEWDLEY MUSEUM

In centre of Bewdley (Dc)

The Severnside town of Bewdley on its steep, wooded hillside displays its history in a museum housed in the Shambles – an 18th-century butcher's row. The past life, trades and industries of the townspeople are the museum's concern: Bewdley was once a thriving little inland port

RISING GLORY *The magnificent staircase at the centre of Berrington Hall is lit by a delicate, glass-domed lantern. The marble pillars set off the richly designed ceiling, decorated in several pastel shades.*

and a centre for the craftsmen of the Wyre Forest. Displays in the historical galleries include charcoal-burning, basket-making, coopering and the making of besoms, or birch-twig brushes. Rope-making was another important concern, and hand-turned machinery from an old local ropeworks demonstrates how ropes were made.

In a restored foundry, complete with forge, grinding wheel and finishing shop, brass founding may be seen on most days. The museum also makes workshops available to present-day crafts-people – and visitors can sometimes see a professional pewterer, glass-blower or lacemaker at work. There is a small brass-rubbing centre in an annexe of the museum, and at the end of a cobbled row is the old town lock-up, whose stone cells can be examined.

Mar-Nov, daily, Sun (pm only). Adm charge. Shop. Tel Bewdley (0299) 403573.

BRETFORTON MANOR

On B4035, 4 miles east of Evesham (Eb)

Built on the site of a ruined monastery, this gabled 450-year-old mansion is reputedly haunted. Inside there is much carved oak, some said to come from a Spanish ship wrecked at the time of the Armada, and there is a priest-hole in the library. The grounds contain the old village stocks and a thatched barn with a horse-drawn cider mill. There is also a 15th-century stone dovecote – one of five in the village.

In the village square, the half-timbered Fleece Inn contains Stuart pewter, among other antiquities. A farmhouse in medieval times, the Fleece is one of a small number of inns owned by the National Trust.

All year, daily. Adm charge. Refreshments. Shop. 🅿 *Toilets. Tel Evesham (0386) 830216.*

BROADWAY TOWER COUNTRY PARK

Off A44, 5 miles south-east of Evesham (Eb)

No folly in Britain is more gloriously sited, or more splendidly preserved. Broadway Tower was built by the 6th Earl of Coventry in the 1790s – simply, it seemed, to have something to look at from his family seat at Worcester, some 20 miles away. Crenellated in sham medieval style, the building was designed by the architect James Wyatt. It was erected on Broadway Hill – at 1024ft above sea level the second highest natural point on the Cotswolds – and climbing the spiral staircase, 65ft further, to the summit of the tower, the visitor can enjoy a stupendous panorama.

Westward, the Cotswolds fall sharply away and the eye ranges unimpeded over the green, quilted vastness of the Vale of Evesham as far as the Black Mountains of Wales and even, on a clear day, to the Shropshire Wrekin. Worcester Cathedral, Tewkesbury Abbey and Warwick Castle are three of the landmarks to be discerned amid the distant specklings of stone-built towns and villages.

William Morris, the Victorian artist-craftsman, used to spend holidays in the tower – bringing with him Pre-Raphaelite painter friends, including Dante Gabriel Rosetti and Sir Edward Burne-Jones. Three exhibitions are mounted in the building: one to Morris, another to sheep farming and a third to the story of the tower itself. In the country park around there are rural walks.

Apr-early Oct, daily. Adm charge. Refreshments. Shop. 🅿 *Toilets.* ♿ *Tel Broadway (0386) 852390.*

HIGH-RISE HOME *Broadway Tower, notable for its three crenellated towers and three wedge-shaped sides, was lived in until 1972, when its last tenant left after almost 40 years in lofty splendour.*

CLENT HILLS COUNTRY PARK

Off A491, 7½ miles east of Kidderminster (Dd)

Space for the people of Birmingham to breathe and roam is provided in plenty at the Clent Hills Country Park, a splendid tract of grassy hills and farm land covering more than 500 acres. It includes High Harcourt Farm, a recent acquisition whose outbuildings are being restored to make a countryside interpretation centre.

There are magnificent views from the steep hill slopes: north and east to the Black Country's urban spread, and in the other direction over a great green patchwork to the Cotswolds, the Malverns and Kinver Edge. The hills rise to 1000ft at the summit, where the four gigantic stones are not (as sometimes thought) a prehistoric monument but an 18th-century sham, erected for picturesque effect by the local poet William Shenstone.

All year, daily.

CROFT CASTLE

Off A49, 5 miles north of Leominster (Bc)

A fortress built on the once turbulent Welsh border, Croft Castle stands in ancient parkland and woods. The Croft family has occupied the land almost without interruption since the time of Domesday. Their castle, built of warm pinkish-brown Herefordshire stone, contains evidence of its original defensive intent in the four circular corner towers, dating to the 14th century, which guard the inner courtyard.

In later centuries, Croft grew from a stronghold to a house. Windows replaced arrow slits, and in the 18th century many Gothic-style alterations were made for picturesque effect, both inside and outside the house. Chippendale furniture, oak panelling and portraits by Sir Thomas Lawrence and Thomas Gainsborough all contribute to the civilised air.

The little church beside the castle contains a portrait monument to Sir Richard Croft, who died in 1509, and his wife Eleanor.

The parkland contains rare plants such as branny liverwort, many aged, majestic oaks and a half-mile avenue of gnarled and twisted Spanish chestnuts estimated to be 350 years old. A chain of fishpools lies in a steeply banked, wooded valley, while above the woods looms the Iron Age hill-fort of Croft Ambrey, from which there are views over much of Wales.

NT. Apr and Oct, Sat, Sun and Bank Hol Mon (pm only). May-Sept, Wed-Sun (pm only). Adm charge. P *Toilets. Tel Leominster (056 885) 246.*

DROITWICH SPA BRINE BATH

In centre of Droitwich (Dc)

Deep under Droitwich are deposits of rock salt from which briny waters well up. Before the Romans came Ancient Britons produced salt from these waters by evaporation, but it was the health-conscious Victorians who built the first brine baths for therapeutic purposes. Droitwich brine is ten times as salty as normal seawater, and taking a dip in it is comparable to relaxing in the Dead Sea: the water is amazingly buoyant, making it possible to float without effort. From 1836, Droitwich became a fashionable spa town where visitors came in throngs to relieve back trouble or rheumatism or simply to relax.

After its Victorian heyday the spa trade languished for many decades, but it revived in the 1980s with the opening of a new brine bath using modern technology to pump cleaned and filtered brine to a pool kept at a steady 33°C (92°F). The nearby heritage centre has a display devoted to Droitwich's ancient salt industry.

All year. Adm charge. Refreshments. P *Toilets.* ♿ *Tel Droitwich (0905) 776782.*

EASTNOR CASTLE

Off A438, 2 miles east of Ledbury (Cb)

Posing dramatically in its beautiful park, Eastnor Castle is an architectural impostor. Shaped like a medieval fortress with massive towers at each corner, the building was erected for the 1st Earl Somers between 1810 and 1816 as part of the vogue for things Gothic. Its designer was Sir Robert Smirke, architect of the British Museum.

It has a good collection of armour, pictures, carvings and tapestry, laid out in six spacious ground-floor rooms. The ornate drawing room was decorated to designs by Augustus Pugin, well known for his interiors in the Houses of Parliament, and in the grand staircase hall hang works by his equally renowned Victorian contemporary, the painter G.F. Watts. Eastnor's terraces command fine views of the Malvern Hills, and there is a varied collection of specimen trees in the grounds.

Bank Hol Mon; late May-Sept, Sun; July-Aug, Wed and Thur. Adm charge. Refreshments. Shop. P *Toilets. Tel Ledbury (0531) 2305.*

ELGAR'S BIRTHPLACE

Off A44, 3 miles west of Worcester (Dc)

Cottage flowers crowd the garden of the little Georgian house at Upper Broadheath where Sir Edward Elgar was born in 1857. It is maintained today as a museum, and has manuscripts, scores, photographs and much other memorabilia associated with the composer, whose works include the *Enigma Variations* and five *Pomp and Circumstance* marches. Elgar was passionately attached to the surrounding countryside, often seeking musical inspiration in the Malvern Hills which face the cottage. A 45 mile Elgar Trail is signposted for motorists, connecting sites associated with the composer.

Mid Feb-Apr pm; May-Sept all day; Oct-mid Jan pm; Wed closed, all year. Adm charge. P *Toilets. Tel Cotheridge (090 566) 224.*

FORGE MILL MUSEUM

Off A441, in north-east Redditch (Ec)

Redditch is a town famous for its needle industry, which began locally in the 17th century. The brick-built Forge Mill, the home today of the National Needle Museum, is itself an old water-driven mill adapted for making needles and similar items such as fish-hooks and hatpins. The original 18th-century machinery is intact and working, and displays illustrate the stages

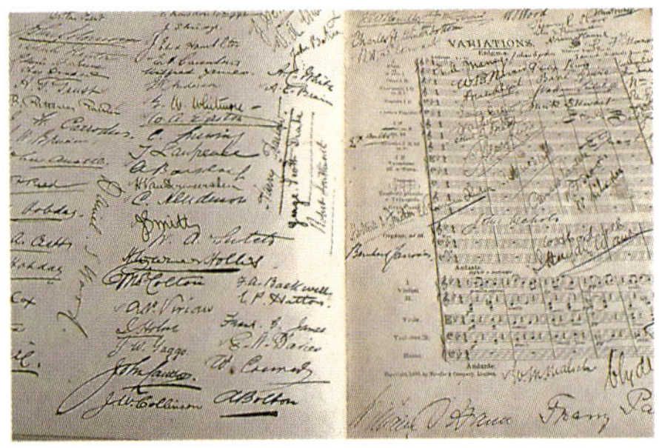

MUSIC ROOM *Visitors to Elgar's Birthplace can see the desk (below) at which he composed. Among the displays is a book (right) with a score of the* Enigma Variations *and the signatures of players and friends who attended an early performance.*

involved, including pointing, eyeing, hardening and polishing. A final gallery shows the variety of uses to which the humble device of the needle can be put, with surgical needles, gramophone needles, a giant 6ft 1in mattress needle and even – set in clear acrylic plastic – a needle used to stitch in place the thermal barrier of the space shuttle *Columbia*.

Apr-Oct, daily (Sat, pm only); Mar and Nov, weekdays only. Adm charge. Refreshments. Shop. 🅿 *Toilets.* ♿ *Tel Redditch (0527) 62509.*

GOODRICH CASTLE

Off A40, 5 miles south of Ross-on-Wye (Ca)

A red-sandstone ruin looming over green water meadows, Goodrich Castle seems almost to grow from the living rock of its spur. This once mighty stronghold commanded a crossing of the River Wye and dates back to the 12th century. It was a Royalist bastion during the Civil War, and in 1646, when the garrison was forced to surrender, Cromwell's mortars rendered it uninhabitable. Enough survives, though, to recall its former grandeur – including the deeply gouged moat, the hulk of the Norman keep and the great 13th-century corner towers guarding the inner ward.

EH. All year, daily. Adm charge. Shop. Tel Monmouth (0600) 890538.

HANBURY HALL

Off B4090, 2½ miles east of Droitwich (Dc)

'A sweet place and a noble estate', is how an 18th-century visitor described Hanbury Hall. The red-brick Queen Anne house was built for Thomas Vernon, a prosperous barrister, and has its completion date, 1701, carved above the front door. Not much has changed since then. The house has fine furniture and eye-catching staircase murals and ceilings by the master decorator Sir James Thornhill (1675-1734). The Long Room contains English porcelain from the Watney Collection, and there is an orangery in the garden.

NT. Apr-Oct, Sat-Sun, Bank Hol Mon pm; May-Sept, Wed-Sun pm. Adm charge. Refreshments. Shop. 🅿 *Toilets. Tel Hanbury (052 784) 214.*

HARTLEBURY CASTLE

Off A449, 3 miles south of Kidderminster (Dc)

For more than a thousand years the Bishops of Worcester have lived at Hartlebury Castle. But except for a remnant of the old moat, nothing remains of the medieval exterior – for the original fortress was sieged, looted and ruined by Roundhead troops in 1646.

The present three-wing mansion was built 30 years later, with 18th-century alterations including many arched windows in Gothic style. The Bishop's House is in the south wing by the chapel, the north wing holds the Worcester County Museum and the central block contains the State Rooms, which are used for various public and religious events.

The entrance to the State Rooms is by a handsome, pedimented doorway leading directly into the Great Hall. With its hammerbeam roof, this room does recall something of medieval Hartlebury. Here Bishop Nicholas Bullingham received Elizabeth I in 1575, and the picture gallery has episcopal portraits going back to the 14th century. Very different in mood are the elegant rococo saloon, with furniture by Chippendale, and the superb Hurd Library built in the 18th century by Bishop Richard Hurd to hold his collection of 7000 volumes.

Hereford and Worcester County Museum, in the north wing, has exhibits of local crafts and industries. These include an old cider press and a collection of carriages, gypsy caravans and farm wagons.

Easter-Aug, Wed pm and first Sun pm each month; also Bank Hol Mon pm and Tues and Wed pm immediately following. Adm charge. Refreshments. Shop. 🅿 *(limited). Toilets. Tel Hartlebury (0299) 250410. Museum: Mar-Nov, Mon-Fri pm and Sun pm; Bank Hol all day; closed Good Fri. Adm charge. Refreshments. Shop.* 🅿 *Toilets. Tel (0299) 250416.*

DESK-BOUND *Chained to the desks in Hereford Cathedral library are some 1500 books and manuscripts, some dating back to the 8th century. The chains were installed to deter thieves.*

HEREFORD CATHEDRAL

In centre of Hereford (Bb)

The former county of Herefordshire is a red earth area, its rock being an Old Red Sandstone which gives a ruddy hue to ploughed fields and building materials alike. Hereford Cathedral shares the land's warm aura: though the cathedral evolved over many centuries, successive generations of builders used the same red-tinged stone, so giving a unity to the whole.

Much of what is seen today is early Norman, the great rounded arches of the nave, patterned with decisive zigzags, at once striking the eye. Other features, though, are of later date – including the 13th-century Lady Chapel with its elaborate lancet windows, and the exquisite little chantry of Bishop John Stanbury, built in the 15th century.

The cathedral has two exceptional treasures in its medieval world map and chained library. The world map, dating from about 1290 and measuring some 5ft square, is a fanciful creation on vellum, showing a flat world surrounded by a circular ocean, with Jerusalem at the very centre. The British Isles, thoroughly misshapen, are squashed down at the bottom left and a weird bestiary of creatures covers the continents: unicorn, satyr, sphinx and even a one-legged humanoid who uses his giant foot as an umbrella to shield himself from the sun.

Facing the cathedral, in Broad Street, is Hereford's small City Museum and Art Gallery, whose exhibits range from inscribed Roman stones to a beekeeping display, complete with glass-walled observation hive in which live bees can be see working.

The Old House, a few minutes walk away, is a black-and-white Jacobean building, once part of a butchers' row, which now rises in solitary splendour from the heart of a modern shopping precinct. A carved angel above the entrance bears the date 1621, and inside are three beautifully restored floors with period kitchen, hall, bedrooms and attic. Good oak furniture can be seen throughout, and there is a striking carved overmantel on the first floor. Upstairs, besides imposing four-poster beds, are two delightful 17th-century babywalkers.

Cathedral: All year, daily. Free entry. Refreshments. Shop. Toilets. Tel Hereford (0432) 59880. City Museum: All year, daily exc Sun, Mon; also Bank Hol Mon. Free entry. Old House: All year, daily exc Sun; also closed Mon pm all year, and Sat pm in winter. Adm charge. Shop. Tel (0432) 268121.

HEREFORD WATERWORKS MUSEUM

By Riverside Walk, Hereford (Bb)

Lying at the foot of Broomy Hill in meadows by the River Wye, this unusual museum occupies the site of a Victorian pumping station. It tells the story of 19th-century water supply, from river to tap, using the original buildings, reservoirs, filter beds and equipment.

In the pumping station itself, surmounted by its 70ft chimney, visitors can explore in succession the coal store, boiler houses and engine houses – where working exhibits, agleam with polished brasswork, can be seen in steam on Bank Holidays. Many of the smaller hand pumps and gauges can be operated by visitors. A horse-drawn fire engine of the Napoleonic period is on display, and there is a short length of narrow-gauge line outside, with skip wagons once used to haul dirty sand from the filter beds. The original reservoir survives at the upper works on Broomy Hill, surrounded by ornamental gardens and with an Italianate water tower of 1883.

Nearby, the Cider Museum in Pomona Place, off Whitecross Road, occupies a former cider factory and illustrates the traditional art with a huge beam press and the original champagne cider cellars. Opposite, the Bulmer Railway Centre houses some steam locomotives and a small collection of rolling stock.

Waterworks Museum: Apr-May, 1st Sun; June-July (Sun); Aug, daily; also Bank Hol. Adm charge. Refreshments. Shop. P *Toilets. Tel Hereford (0432) 273635. Museum of Cider: Apr-Oct, daily; Nov-Dec, Mon-Fri; Jan-Mar, Wed and Sat. Adm charge. Refreshments (summer). Shop.* P *Toilets. Tel (0432) 54207. Railway Centre: Easter-end Sept, Sat and Sun. Adm charge. Tel Bristol (0272) 834430.*

CATHEDRAL LOOK-ALIKE *The superb lantern tower of Pershore Abbey, built around 1330, is strikingly similar to the tower below the spire of Salisbury Cathedral. Made of local limestone, the abbey has been added to and restored until well into the 20th century.*

HEREFORDSHIRE BEACON

Off A449, 4 miles south-west of Great Malvern (Db)

The swirling ramparts of a 32 acre Iron Age hill-fort, known as British Camp, contour the summit of Herefordshire Beacon. Built around 200 BC, the stronghold commanded a pass at the southern end of the Malvern Hills and supported some 2000 people. Today a metalled path leads steeply up from the car park, above a small reservoir and almost to the top of the beacon.

The swooping, soaring crest of the Malverns themselves gives the vistas their beautiful perspectives. The hilly ridge runs from north to south between the flat Vale of Severn and the rumpled terrain of the Welsh borderland, and gazing out from the 1114ft vantage point of the beacon, the divide is dramatically laid out. Eastward the ridge drops sharply to vast, level spaces extending to the Cotswold skyline, with Bredon Hill looming in front. Westward the ground is higher and choppier. A walk along the ridge leads to an obelisk erected by Lord Somers of Eastnor Castle, the battlements of which are prominent in the views south.

Little Malvern Priory, under the beacon, is a tiny parish church adapted from the tower and choir of a once large cruciform Benedictine building. Former glories are recalled in the high ceiling, fragments of statuary and a damaged east window containing medieval royal portraits. Little Malvern Court next door incorporates the old Prior's Hall and has a 14th-century timber roof.

All year, daily.

OUTLOOK CLOUDY AND FINE *From the top of Herefordshire Beacon, on even the cloudiest day, can be enjoyed what the 17th-century diarist John Evelyn called 'one of the goodliest views in England'.*

HERGEST CROFT GARDENS

Off A44, ½ mile west of Kington (Ac)

For four generations one family – the Banks – has tended the gardens at Hergest Croft. Planting began in 1867 and since then specimen trees and shrubs have been gathered from temperate regions throughout the world. Special features include an azalea garden seen at its colourful best in May and June, and an old-fashioned kitchen garden planted with spring and summer borders. In the secluded oak valley of Park Wood, rhododendrons grow up to 30ft tall. The gardens cover some 50 acres, with views to the distant Black Mountains of Wales.

Late Apr-mid Sept, pm daily; mid Sept-Oct, Sun. Adm charge. Refreshments. Shop. Toilets. Tel Kington (0544) 230160.

KILPECK CHURCH

Off A465, 8 miles south-west of Hereford (Ba)

One of the most perfect small Norman churches in England, Kilpeck stands remote and secluded in a rural setting. It was built in the 12th century, and its fascination derives partly from its array of intricate carvings in red sandstone. The south doorway has a stylised tree of life with serpentine monsters and other fantastical creations, while running around the whole exterior of the building are many lively and often comic figures. There is an example of a Sheila-na-gig, or female fertility figure; the Victorians removed some other bawdy images, which accounts for certain gaps. Carving of a more spiritual nature can be seen inside, especially in the fine chancel arch.

All year, daily.

KNAPP AND PAPERMILL NATURE RESERVE

Off A4103, 6 miles west of Worcester (Cb)

Covering some 62 acres in the foothills of the Malverns, this secluded reserve is threaded by the Leigh Brook. Near the visitor centre is a hide overlooking a pool where kingfishers nest most years. Mink have colonised the brook, and trout can sometimes be seen leaping the weir upstream. In the spring, bluebells and marsh marigolds grow wild on one bank of the stream, facing a daffodil field on the other. A solitary cottage, set by a meadow in coppice woodlands, is all that survives of the old paper-mill complex from which the reserve takes its name.

All year, daily. P *(limited). Toilets. Tel Leigh Sinton (0886) 32065.*

MALVERN HILLS ANIMAL AND BIRD GARDENS

On B4208, 5 miles south of Great Malvern (Db)

Visitors to these gardens are encouraged to approach its animals and birds closely – and even handle them under supervision. The never-failing attraction is the snake-handling demonstration, held three times daily. There is a pets' corner with goats and a miniature pony, and a $7\frac{1}{4}$in gauge steam railway carries passengers through a wallaby and deer paddock.

All year, daily. Adm charge. Refreshments. Shop. P *Toilets.* ♿ *Tel Malvern (0684) 310016.*

PERSHORE ABBEY

In centre of Pershore (Db)

People have worshipped on the site of this handsome abbey since AD 689, when Ethelred, King of Mercia, endowed a monastery there. Much of what is seen today is Early English work, dating from the 13th century, but there are also the remains of a Norman building, including a window and a corner of the original tower.

When the monastery was surrendered to Henry VIII in 1540, the townspeople paid £400 to save part of it as a parish church. The font is also Norman, and other relics include a handsome monument bearing the arms of Thomas Hazelwood, who died in 1624, with mourning figures in Jacobean dress.

All year, daily. Free entry. Shop. P *(limited). Toilets.* ♿ *Tel Pershore (0386) 552071.*

SEVERN VALLEY RAILWAY

Kidderminster Station (Dc)

A coal fire still warms the ticket office on chilly mornings at Kidderminster Town railway station, northern terminus of the Severn Valley line. Vintage posters advertise the sunny attractions of Torquay, Paignton and Looe. Leather suitcases stand in one corner, and on the platform beyond hang the fire buckets of the Great Western Railway in their bold primary red.

A superbly preserved standard-gauge line, the new Severn Valley Railway was founded in 1965 and its 16 mile steam-hauled trip runs from Kidderminster to Bridgnorth. The route follows the quiet, curving course of the River Severn for most of the way, through sheep-grazed hills, the wooded heathland of the Wyre Forest, and past restored country stations.

SANTA SPECIAL *At Christmas, the Severn Valley Railway runs special trains from Kidderminster and Bewdley to Santa's Grotto at Arley. There each child receives a present from Santa Claus – and each adult is given a cup of hot punch.*

There is magic in the pent, emphatic thunder of the engine as it first builds up steam to leave Kidderminster Town. The train clatters through a tunnel, and there are glimpses of bison in enclosures beyond, for the track skirts the West Midland Safari Park. Ahead lies the historic Severnside town of Bewdley, whose station has carriage and wagon workshops, as well as a fine little model railway. Beyond Bewdley the line crosses the river on the 200ft span of the Victoria Bridge, something of a wonder when it was built in 1861, for it then incorporated the largest cast-iron span in the world.

The country stations at Arley, Highley and Hampton Loade are all set in tranquil countryside, pretty Arley making an especially enchanting place to stop off and picnic or walk by the river. Sheep scamper back from the line as the locomotive with its billowing smoke and snaking line of carriages steams on to the terminus at Bridgnorth, a market town scrambling down a red-sandstone ridge. Bridgnorth is the railway's main locomotive depot: its shed is open to visitors and houses many of the engines which work the line. There are more than 40 locomotives ranging from steam veterans of the passenger lines to industrial and diesel locomotives.

A one-way trip takes roughly an hour, and with five engines working on some days it is possible to plan a full day's enjoyment around a return journey with stops at different stations. The return ticket allows passengers to join and rejoin all trains at all stops on the day, and there are buffet and restaurant cars.

All year, daily (stations); trains, Mar-Nov, certain days. Adm charge. Refreshments. Shops. P *(limited). Toilets.* ♿ *Tel Bewdley (0299) 403816 (info); 401001 (timetable).*

SPETCHLEY PARK

On A422, 2 miles south-east of Worcester (Db)

Green lawns sweep down from a Georgian mansion to a lake, and the park is little changed since the 17th century. Though the house itself is not open, Spetchley's gardens have a wealth of formal and informal plantings. These include a walled garden sheltering many tender plants including the silvery leafed Moroccan broom – a yellow flowering shrub curiously scented with pineapple. Elsewhere there are Victorian-style borders planted with irises and peonies; a yew-hedged fountain garden; a rose lawn and a heather bed.

Apr-Sept, Mon-Fri, Sun pm. Refreshments (Sun and Bank Hol). P *Toilets. Tel Spetchley (090 565) 213.*

WEST MIDLAND SAFARI AND LEISURE PARK

Off A456, 2 miles west of Kidderminster (Dc)

Giraffes as tall as double-decker buses loom over car roofs, and monkeys sometimes clamber onto vehicles. The West Midland Safari and Leisure Park is one of the English heartland's most popular pleasure complexes, covering 200 acres and with drive-through reserves.

The winding route leads through enclosures of rhinoceroses, tigers, bison, wolves, elephants, zebras and lions, among other animals. There is also an amusement park whose attractions

WORCESTER, CITY OF FINE CRAFTS

Set on either side of the curving River Severn, Worcester is known throughout the world for three prize products: gloves, a local craft since the 13th century; fine and handsome china; and Worcestershire sauce, a tasty concoction of the late 1820s. The city is also noted for its magnificent medieval buildings, the queen of which is the cathedral, begun in 1084 and largely completed some 300 years later. Nearby are the historic Commandery – in its time a hospice, country house and glove-maker's workshop – and two museums: the Tudor House Museum in Friar Street and the City Museum and Art Gallery in Foregate Street, next to the 19th-century Shire Hall. In High Street stands the grandiose brick-built Guildhall of 1721-2.

In Severn Street the Worcester Royal Porcelain Works, founded in 1751, is still producing fine bone china and porcelain. The adjacent Dyson Perrins Museum contains an exhibition representing all periods of production and including a cream boat, possibly one of the first pieces made, and the gigantic Great Exhibition Vase made for the Chicago World Fair of 1893.

Tudor House Museum: All year, Mon-Wed, Fri and Sat; closed Good Fri. Free entry. Shop. P *Tel Worcester (0905) 20904. Cathedral: All year, daily. Free entry. Refreshments. Shop.* P *Toilets.* ♿ *Tel (0905) 723471. Commandery: All year, Mon-Sat; Sun pm. Adm charge. Refreshments.* P *Tel (0905) 355071. Dyson Perrins Museum: All year, Mon-Sat. Free entry. Refreshments. Shop.* P *Toilets.* ♿ *Tel (0905) 23221. City Museum: All year, daily except Thur and Sun. Free entry. Tel (0905) 25371.*

BATHING BY GASLIGHT *A reconstruction of a 1910 bathroom, complete with hot-water geyser and gas lamp, is displayed at the timber-framed Tudor House Museum. The museum's period rooms also include an Edwardian schoolroom.*

TOWERING SIGHT *Rising majestically on the site of a monastery founded by St Oswald in AD 983, Worcester Cathedral was begun by Wulstan – the only Saxon bishop after the Norman Conquest.*

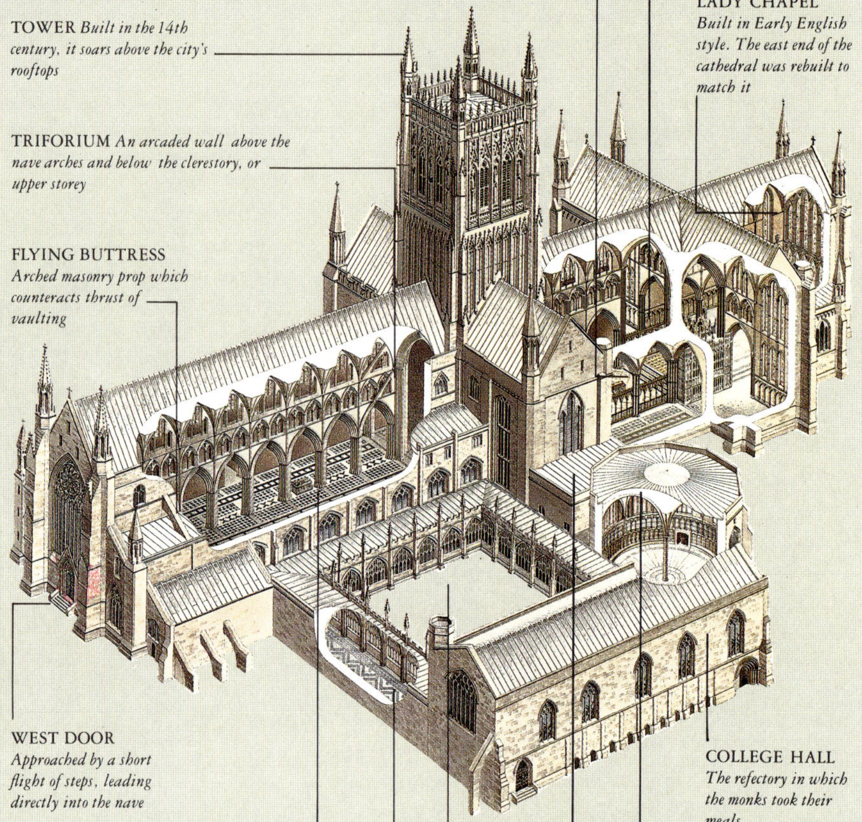

ROYAL RESTING PLACE *The marble-topped tomb of King John, who died in 1216, lies before the high altar in Worcester Cathedral. The figure – with its miniature carvings of Oswald and Wulstan, Worcester's two great religious figures – is said to be the oldest royal effigy in England.*

COMMAND ZONE *The half-timbered, medieval Commandery was the scene of Charles II's war council before the Battle of Worcester in 1651. An audiovisual display about the battle is mounted in the Great Hall, under its splendid hammerbeam roof.*

include a roller coaster, a pirate ship, rocket rides, a sea-lion show and a pets' corner. The futuristic Cinedome houses a 180 degree cinema screen which evokes the thrill of switchback and motor-racing rides. The park also has boating lakes and picnic areas.

Early Apr-Oct, daily. Adm charge. Refreshments. Shop. P *Toilets. Tel Bewdley (0299) 402 1141.*

WITLEY COURT

Off A443, 7 miles south-west of Kidderminster (Dc)

An astonishing ruin, Witley Court is the shell of an immense, Italian-style mansion created by the 1st Earl of Dudley in the 19th century around a much earlier house. A wing was gutted by fire in 1937, and the rest fell victim to vandals and decay. The most striking ornament in the surrounding garden is the great Perseus Fountain, showing the Greek mythological hero riding 26ft high on a prancing horse.

The adjacent parish church of St Michael is among the finest Baroque churches in Britain, containing 18th-century stained glass and ceiling paintings by Antonio Belluci.

EH. All year, daily. Free entry. P

WORCESTERSHIRE BEACON

Off B4232, ½ mile west of Great Malvern (Db)

The Malvern Hills' drama lies in their suddenness. Surging abruptly from the Midland Plain, they form a 9 mile long, narrow chain of ancient lavas and granites folded under such pressure that they seem to ripple with contorted energy.

Situated at the northern end of the chain and rising to 1394ft above sea level, Worcestershire Beacon is the Malverns' highest point. Zigzag paths of pinkish gravel lead steeply up from the edge of Great Malvern through a valley lightly wooded with birch. The enfolding hillsides conceal the grandeur of the views to come, and it is not until the summit is reached that the vast panorama unfolds. The views extend westward to the Black Mountains, north to the Wrekin, east to Edge Hill, and south down the bony spine of the Malverns themselves to Herefordshire Beacon – and, far beyond, to the blue mist of the Mendips in Somerset.

The polished stone view indicator at the summit was erected in 1897 to commemorate 60 years of Queen Victoria's reign. Tucked away just under the summit is a log-built refreshment hut also dating to Victorian times, which was later visited by Edward VII (who drove up a carriage path in his Daimler) and more recently by the mountaineer and conqueror of Everest, Sir Edmund Hillary.

Scattered outcrops of raw rock pierce the turf at this height: it is Precambrian, dating back at least 600 million years, and its hard, crystalline fabric is not dissolved by rainwater – which helps to account for the local springs' purity. Down in the little valley near the start of the walk is a Regency cottage housing one famous source, St Ann's Well, built in 1815 to dispense water to visitors.

Great Malvern itself owes its prosperity to the 19th-century vogue for taking medicinal waters and water cures, and survives as a fine example of a Victorian spa town, with handsome buildings and tidy evergreens. The supreme attraction, though, is its great church, the Priory, built of chequered stonework with greenish, yellow, pink and grey blocks. The nave is Norman and the rest 15th century, containing some glorious medieval stained glass. The north transept has an impressive window given by Henry VII and showing the Coronation of Mary, who is seen in a golden sunburst.

In Priory Park, under the wild hummock of the Beacon, the nobility and gentry used to promenade after taking the waters.

All year, daily.

WORCESTER WOODS COUNTRY PARK

Off A422, 1 mile east of Worcester (Db)

Two ancient woodlands, Nunnery and Perry Woods, together make up this country park just outside the cathedral city of Worcester. In Perry Wood are earthworks probably erected by Roundhead troops during Worcester's Civil War battle. Land in Nunnery Wood has a conspicuous 'ridge and furrow' patterning, showing that it was being farmed in the early Middle Ages.

The park's new Worcester Countryside Centre has an exhibition hall, information desk and picnic tables. There are guided walks from the centre lasting for 1½ to 2½ hours.

All year, daily.

WYE VALLEY VISITOR CENTRE

Off A40, 6 miles south-west of Ross-on-Wye (Ca)

Performing a graceful loop around Symonds Yat rock, the River Wye flows through a landscape of farmland, wood and meadow. Under the hummocks of the Doward hills lies the Wye Valley Visitor Centre, developed around an award-winning maze made by the brothers Lindsay and Edward Heyes. This was first planted in 1977 to celebrate the Jubilee of Queen Elizabeth II, and opened on the wedding day of the Prince of Wales in 1981.

A little temple of stone columns and domed ironwork tracery marks the centre, and at the entrance one of the brothers, clad in Victorian boating costume, introduces visitors to the baffling green corridors. A raised viewing gallery looks down on the puzzle from above, and there is a pavilion with displays telling the story of mazes and labyrinths through history.

Also at the visitor centre is a Butterfly House where paths wind through a young indoor jungle of luxuriant plants and landscaped pools. The butterflies dart about and chase one another through the foliage on their own mysterious maze of flightpaths. Different stages in the life of butterflies can be seen in the glass-walled hatching boxes; as well as beauties there are beasts in the shape of caged locusts, tarantulas and bird-eating spiders.

Four craft workshops are open to the public, and a path leads from the visitor centre to the pretty little riverside church of St Dubricius, dating back to the 12th century. The churchyard has a fine old tulip tree, and a tiny landing stage at which, on occasions, brides still arrive to be married. From there, a riverside path follows the Wye into a dramatic wooded gorge. A ferry goes to Symonds Yat Rock on the Gloucestershire side of the river, and farther downstream is Fair View Rock with its own splendid vistas of the gorge.

Symonds Yat Bird Park, next to the visitor centre, has 160 species of birds from all over the world, from tiny nectar-feeders to the colourful parrots of Australia and the Amazon. High in the woods above, about 1½ miles eastwards, off the A40, the Herefordshire Rural Heritage Museum has a collection of historic farm machinery and vehicles, including vintage tractors, a gypsy caravan and cider-making equipment.

Visitor centre: Easter-Oct, daily. Free entry. (Maze and Butterfly house, adm charge.) Refreshments. Shop. P *Toilets.* ♿ *Tel Monmouth (0600) 890360. Bird Park: Easter-Oct, daily. Adm charge. Shop.* P *Toilets.* ♿ *Tel (0600) 890989. Museum: All year, daily. Adm charge. Refreshments.* P *Toilets. Tel (0600) 890474.*

WYRE FOREST VISITOR CENTRE

On A456, 3 miles west of Bewdley (Cc)

Covering some 6000 acres west of the River Severn, Wyre Forest is the remnant of a much larger royal hunting forest mentioned in Domesday Book. Fallow deer still haunt its quieter depths – and though much of the woodland is privately owned, some 2800 acres are managed by the Forestry Commission. Modern plantations of fir, larch and pine mingle with old oakwoods and beeches. One tree, known as the Seckley Beech, is 90ft in girth and consists of 26 trunks grown together.

The visitor centre illustrates forest crafts, as well as plants and animals. Nature trails and forest walks of differing lengths have been laid out, leading at one point to fine views over the woods and the outlying Clee Hills. To the east, the Hawkbatch Forest area has its own set of walks leading to the Seckley Beech, as well as to viewpoints overlooking the Severn and Trimpley Reservoir.

All year, daily. Free entry. Shop. P *Toilets.* ♿ *Tel Rock (0299) 266302.*

COUNTY CALENDAR

May (3rd week). Great Malvern: Music and Drama Festival.

May (Spring Bank Holiday). Hereford: Regatta.

June (2nd and 3rd weeks). Kington: Carnival and games.

June (mid-month). Great Malvern: Three Counties Show.

June (end of month). Upton upon Severn: Jazz Festival.

July (mid-month). Malvern: Victorian Week.

July (end of month). Weobley: Trotting Races.

July (end of month). Bewdley: Regatta.

August (end of month). Hereford (1988): Three Choirs Festival (alternating with Gloucester, 1989, and Worcester, 1990).

August (Bank Hol weekend). Ross-on-Wye: Regatta.

Tourist information: Hereford (0432) 268430; Kington (0544) 230202; Malvern (0684) 892289; Ross-on-Wye (0989) 62728; Worcester (0905) 723471.

HERTFORDSHIRE

RURAL BEAUTY AROUND THE HOMES OF STATESMEN AND WRITERS

Memorials to the famous abound in Hertfordshire. The cathedral at St Albans is dedicated to the Roman soldier who became England's first Christian martyr. The astute Robert Cecil, Secretary of State to Elizabeth I and James I, built Hatfield House, in whose park in 1558 the young Princess Elizabeth learnt she had become queen. Elizabeth had lived with Henry VIII's other children at Ashridge House, which later became the home of the 3rd Duke of Bridgewater, pioneer of Britain's inland waterways.

The Victorian novelist Edward Bulwer-Lytton owned Knebworth House, and Bernard Shaw found a haven of peaceful inspiration at Shaw's Corner. The birthplace of the statesman Cecil Rhodes is preserved at Bishop's Stortford.

The county is predominantly rural, and its traditional farming life is featured at Standalone Farm. The Aldenham and Lee Valley parks conserve Hertfordshire's leafy countryside, and Northaw Great Wood and Whippendell Wood are reminders of the ancient forest that once covered the area. Hertfordshire has lovely man-made landscapes too, at such places as Benington Lordship Gardens and the Gardens of the Rose.

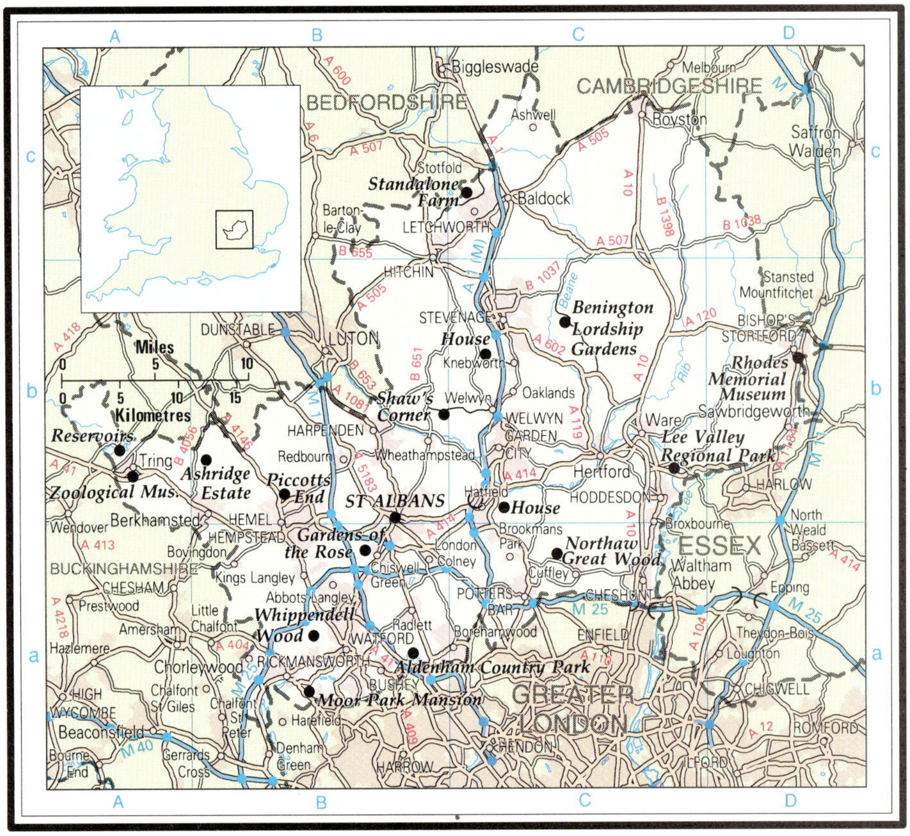

ALDENHAM COUNTRY PARK

Off A41, 3 miles east of Watford (Ba)

Meadows, woods and a 65 acre lake provide a delightful setting for a family day out in this country park, with much to see and do both for the energetic and the seeker of peace and tranquillity. Small-boat enthusiasts can sail their own boats on the lake. There are lakeside walks, a children's corner, with small animals and a playground, a picnic area and a nature trail. Special events include craft shows and exhibitions. A herd of rare-breed Longhorn cattle roams the park, and the lake attracts visiting wildfowl and waterside birds.

All year, daily. Sailing: May-Sept, Tues. Adm charge. Shop. P *Toilets.* ♿ *Tel London (01) 953 9602.*

ASHRIDGE ESTATE

Off B4506, 2 miles north of Berkhamsted (Bb)

The high point of Ashridge's 4000 acres of wood, heath and downland is the Bridgewater Monument, a fluted, urn-topped column that towers 108ft above the beechclad Chiltern Hills. It was erected in 1832, in memory of the 3rd Duke of Bridgewater, the canal pioneer who once lived at nearby Ashridge House, now a private college. For the energetic, the climb of 172 steps to the top of the monument is rewarded by views stretching north to where the wooded hills give way to the grassy humps of Dunstable Downs, and west across the Vale of Aylesbury.

There are miles of paths and bridleways. For those who prefer a gentle stroll through shady woodland, a 1½ mile nature trail starts near the foot of the monument and winds northwards among magnificent beeches, oaks, silver birches and sycamores. Grey squirrels scamper among the branches, goldcrests and warblers flit in the treetops, and occasionally a colourful Lady Amherst's pheasant may scurry across the trail. Where the undergrowth is thick there are fallow deer and muntjac deer, most likely to be seen at dusk when they come out of cover to feed.

NT. All year, daily; monument, shops and Information Centre, Apr-Oct. Adm charge (monument). Refreshments. P *Toilets.* ♿ *Tel Aldbury Common (044 285) 227.*

BENINGTON LORDSHIP GARDENS

Off B1037, 5 miles east of Stevenage (Cb)

An arched stone gateway, with twin weatherworn towers, a crumbling castle wall and a broad moat create a medieval approach to Benington Lordship Gardens. Though looking as if it has stood for 900 years, the 'castle' is, however, a folly built in 1832. There was a Norman castle here once, and parts of it still stand within the grounds, but Benington Lordship's glories are the superb gardens skilfully created around the part-Georgian, part-Edwardian house.

Inside the gateway in a sheltered courtyard is a splendid magnolia tree, while a formal rose

BEAUTIFUL BORDER *The massed plants of a colourful herbaceous border are set off by the mellow brick wall of the kitchen garden at Benington Lordship Gardens. The variety of plants is such that the border is in constant bloom from March to October.*

garden provides a colourful contrast to the red-brick façade of the house. There is nothing formal about the gardens at the rear, however. Here paths and steps lead through the sunken Shylock Garden, ablaze with summer flowers, the tumbling rockery whose pools are fed by natural springs, and herbaceous borders.

May-Aug, Wed and Bank Hol, also Sun pm exc Aug; Sept and Oct, Wed only. Adm charge. Refreshments. P *Toilets. Tel Benington (043 885) 668.*

GARDENS OF THE ROSE

Chiswell Green, off B4630, 2 miles south of St Albans (Ba)

A rose by many thousand names is the theme of the Royal National Rose Society's gardens, said to be the greatest collection of roses in the world. The 12 acre garden contains some 30,000 roses of all types, ranging from the well-known 'Peace' to the newest award-winning varieties.

Massed in beds set among spacious lawns are the shrub and bush roses, while pink and white climbers cascade over a pergola flanking a pool. One bed is devoted to scented roses, where the heavy fragrance of 'Fragrant Cloud' mingles with the delicate bouquet of 'Michèle Meilland'. Set aside from the gardens are the trial grounds, where visitors can see the latest developments in the world of rose-breeding.

Mid June-Oct, daily. Adm charge. Refreshments. Shop. P *Toilets.* ♿ *Tel St Albans (0727) 50461.*

A GARDEN ENCLOSED *A fountain stands at the heart of the lovely West Gardens at Hatfield House. Beyond the yew hedges are leafy bowers, in one of which (left) a stone carving of 1823 depicts the opening of the Royal Exchange in London by Elizabeth I in 1570. The queen is accompanied by courtiers.*

HATFIELD HOUSE

At Hatfield, on A1000 (Cb)

Few houses in England can match the impressive dignity of this Jacobean house. Though from the outside its towering red-brick walls and stone mullioned windows look forbidding, once inside the house that first impression is soon forgotten.

Immediately next to the entrance hall, where the guided tours of the house begin, lies the first and perhaps most spectacular of Hatfield House's splendours – the magnificent Marble Hall. This is the Jacobean version of a medieval Great Hall, and occupies two floors and almost the full width of the house. The marble which gives the hall its name forms the gleaming black-and-white chequerboard floor. The ceiling, a screen and a minstrels' gallery are of richly carved oak, relieved only by paintings in the ceiling panels and panels under the gallery, and superb tapestries that fill the upper half of one wall.

There is more carved oak to admire on the Grand Staircase, where cherubs and heraldic beasts top the pillars. A newel post at the head of the staircase is carved with the figure of John Tradescant, the 17th-century botanist who laid out the gardens of the house.

On the upper floor, splendour follows splendour – from the King James Drawing Room, where a life-size statue of the king stands above the mantelpiece, to the 180ft Long Gallery with its gold-leaf ceiling; and from the Winter Dining Room, hung with full-length pictures of kings, to the Library, where some 10,000 books flank a mosaic portrait of the 1st Earl of Salisbury.

Fittingly the tour ends in a room where the black-and-white flooring of the Marble Hall is repeated – the long, colonnaded Armoury, bedecked with breastplates and lined with suits of armour worn by men of the Spanish Armada.

Hatfield House was built by Robert Cecil, 1st Earl of Salisbury, between 1607 and 1611. It stands close to the remains of the Old Palace, which the earl had taken from James I in exchange for his house at Theobalds. Here at the palace the Princess Elizabeth was made a virtual prisoner by her sister, Mary Tudor, and it was in the grounds that she heard of her accession to the throne. Part of the oak tree under which she was sitting is displayed in the souvenir shop in the Old Palace stables.

Between the Old Palace and the house are the West Gardens, re-created in the formal style of the 17th century and planted with rare and unusual plants.

Mar-Oct, daily exc Mon. Adm charge. Refreshments. Shop. P *Toilets. Tel Hatfield (070 72) 62823.*

KNEBWORTH HOUSE

On A1 (M), 1 mile south of Stevenage (Cb)

The house and its 250 acre parkland are full of surprises, the first coming shortly after leaving the entrance gate. To the right of the long driveway, and in the middle of a wide expanse of grass, stands a stockade. Its rough-hewn timber walls and corner towers look bizarre and incongruous in the Hertfordshire countryside – where, so far as is known, there are no Red Indians except in the imagination of the children who find in Fort Knebworth a paradise of things to climb, swing on or slide down. The house itself is hidden until the last moment, and then comes suddenly into view – an extravaganza of Gothic turrets, pinnacles and towers encrusted with gargoyles, and battlements studded with griffins.

On the surface all is Victorian fantasy, yet behind the stuccoed walls lies a Tudor house where, not surprisingly, Elizabeth I is said to have slept. Knebworth has been the home of the Lytton family since 1492, and it was the novelist Edward Bulwer-Lytton, best known for *The Last Days of Pompeii*, who employed architects and builders to transform the house into a Gothic palace. Fortunately the legacies of earlier generations were not entirely obliterated, as can be seen in the magnificent banqueting hall with its 17th-century oak screen, and the Queen Elizabeth Room dominated by a great four-poster bed with carved wooden figures supporting its massive canopy.

From room to room the mood and style change, from Bulwer-Lytton's library where even the doors are fashioned to look like bookshelves, to the State Drawing Room – Victorian again, but a superb example of the Gothic revival, with a full-length stained-glass window depicting Henry VII and a ceiling painted with 44 coats of arms.

At the rear of the house are formal gardens, a deer park and a narrow-gauge steam railway.

Mid May-mid Sept, daily exc Mon; Apr and May, weekends and Bank Hol. Adm charge. Refreshments. Shop. P *Toilets. Tel Stevenage (0438) 812661.*

HOUSE WITHIN A HOUSE *The riotous Victorian Gothic stucco of Knebworth House hides a red-brick mansion which was begun in 1490 by Sir Robert Lytton, a favourite of Henry VII. The Lytton arms appear beneath one of the intricately embellished windows.*

LEE VALLEY REGIONAL PARK

Off A1170, along Hertfordshire/Essex border (Cb)

At Ware the River Lea (or Lee) turns southwards, and for 5 miles of its 20 mile course to join the Thames there are country and riverside walks, picnic spots, a lido and a boating centre, all within a few minutes' drive of each other.

About 1 mile north of Stanstead Abbots, on the road to Ware, is the Amwell Walkway, a narrow track that was once the railway branch line to Buntingford. Steps lead down to it from a humpback bridge, and immediately the sheen of water catches the eye; not the river, though that flows under the walk a few yards away, but a broad lake in disused gravel pits that is now the home of swans, coots and other waterfowl.

In the opposite direction the walk meanders through peaceful countryside, between hedgerows sprinkled with wild flowers, green meadows and wooded vales.

Half a mile east of Hoddesdon the river turns sharply and dramatically at Dobb's Weir, sliding and hissing over the concrete weirs and then tumbling noisily through a sluice gate to the weirpool.

The lido at Broxbourne is a vast, glass-sided building containing a swimming pool with a wave-maker, fountain, underwater lighting and a 'beach' bordered by exotic tropical plants. Outside there are sunbathing terraces and a solarium. Close to the lido is the Broxbourne Boat Centre, with rowing boats or motorboats for hire and river trips on a motor launch.

Amwell Walkway: All year, daily. Dobb's Weir: All year, daily. P *Toilets. Lido: All year, daily. Adm charge. Refreshments. Toilets. Tel Hoddesdon (0992) 442841. Boat Centre: Apr-Sept, daily.* P *Tel (0992) 462085.*

MOOR PARK MANSION

Off A404, 1½ miles south-east of Rickmansworth (Ba)

Few golf clubs can boast a clubhouse as fine as Moor Park, a superb 18th-century mansion in Palladian style which is open to visitors as well as being the golfers' '19th hole'. The greens and fairways of the two golf courses lend emphasis to the perfect symmetry of the three-storey house. Rising to more than 50ft it stands four-square in an uncluttered setting, its Portland stone facing gleaming on even the dullest day. On the west front a noble portico of Corinthian columns supports a massive pediment at rooftop height.

Inside are beautiful carved and painted ceilings, paintings by the Venetian artist Amiconi, carved fireplaces and pedimented doorways of white veined marble. During the Second World War the house was occupied by the 1st Airborne Corps, and it was here that the Arnhem landings were planned.

All year, daily exc Sun and Bank Hol. Free entry. P *Toilets. Tel Rickmansworth (0923) 776611.*

NORTHAW GREAT WOOD

On B157, 1 mile west of Cuffley (Ca)

In Norman times great forests covered what is now Hertfordshire and Essex, and Northaw Great Wood is a remnant of those forests. It now covers only 400 acres, 290 of which are designated a Country Park. Oaks, hornbeam and birch grow in the natural woodlands, and ash trees are watered by a trickling brook.

Three nature trails, ranging from three-quarters of a mile to 2½ miles in length, lead through avenues of tall trees to grassy glades and wide clearings where wild flowers grow in profusion. Deep in the woods the air is filled with birdsong – with blackbirds, thrushes and, in spring, nightingales competing for star attraction with chaffinches and warblers. Occasionally a bright flash of wings may mark the passage of a jay or woodpecker, or a woodcock may rise from its cover of dead leaves and disappear in twisting flight among the trees.

All year, daily. Adm charge. Toilets. P *Tel Cuffley (0707) 872213.*

PARADISE PARK

Off A10, 3 miles west of Broxbourne (Ca)

Bobby, a lion born in this woodland zoo, is the star attraction of Paradise Park. He shares it with llamas, wallabies, Vietnamese pot-bellied pigs and many other animals and birds. A miniature railway runs through a woodland nature trail.

All year, daily. Adm charge. Refreshments. Shop. P *Toilets.* ♿ *Tel Hoddesdon (0992) 468001.*

PICCOTTS END

Off A4146, ¾ mile north of Hemel Hempstead (Bb)

Six layers of wallpaper and a layer of linen covered medieval wall paintings in this house for some 500 years. Now revealed, they depict in remarkable detail Christ in Majesty, the Baptism of Christ and the Pieta – the Virgin holding the dead Christ in front of the Cross. Other panels show St Peter, St Clement, St Catherine of Alexandria and St Margaret of Antioch.

In 1826 the house became England's first cottage hospital, under Sir Ashley Paston Cooper who was surgeon to George IV. It contains a fine collection of carved oak furniture, a range of early kitchen equipment and a collection of historic medical equipment.

Mar-Nov, daily. Adm charge. Shop. P *Tel Hemel Hempstead (0442) 56729.*

RHODES MEMORIAL MUSEUM

At Bishop's Stortford, on B1003 (Db)

The life and times of the empire-builder Cecil Rhodes are vividly portrayed in this museum, part of which is the house where he was born in 1853. In the birth-room, Rhodes' cot stands beside the four-poster bed and his Bible and his father's prayer book are nearby.

Rhodes lived in this house until he was 17; photographs and documents of the local grammar school give an impression of his schooldays. A model showing what Bishop's Stortford was like at the time is on display in one of the 15 rooms of exhibits in the house. The

MARTYR AND MILL IN ST ALBANS

Remains of the Roman city of Verulamium, including its theatre and city wall, lie on a grassy site south-west of the centre of St Albans. Many finds, including superb mosaics, are in the Verulamium Museum nearby.

The cathedral on the hill across the River Ver began as an abbey founded before AD 800 to hold the shrine of St Alban, a Roman citizen martyred on the spot in the 3rd century for his Christian beliefs. Close by, Georgian buildings line a street leading down to the river and a water mill.

Roman Theatre: All year, daily. Adm charge. Shop. P (limited). ♿ Tel St Albans (0727) 54051. Museum: All year, daily. Adm charge. Shop. P Toilets. Tel (0727) 54659. Cathedral: All year, daily. Free entry. Refreshments. Shop. Toilets. ♿ Tel (0727) 60780. Clock Tower: Easter-mid Sept, Sat, Sun and Bank Hol. Adm charge. Water mill: All year, Wed-Sat; also Sun pm. Adm charge. Refreshments. Shop. P Toilets. ♿ Tel (0727) 53502.

KINGSBURY WATER MILL *Now restored as a working museum, the mill stands on a tranquil stretch of the River Ver at St Michael's, where there has been a mill since Saxon times. The present Tudor building, with Georgian façade, is part of the Gorhambury Estate, which was owned by the lawyer, philosopher and scientist Sir Francis Bacon, Baron Verulam (1561-1626). The mill ground the estate's corn until 1936. The great water wheel drives the millstones and also a hoist which raises sacks of corn to the top floor. The grain then feeds through wooden hoppers to the stones below (left).*

LONE COLUMN *A modern reconstruction shows the type of pillar that once supported the roof of the stage at the Roman theatre at Verulamium.*

KEEPING TIME *In medieval times a curfew bell in the 77ft high Clock Tower aroused the citizens of St Albans at 4am – and sent them to their beds at 8pm. Since Victorian times a clock has told the time of day, and its mechanism (right) can be seen on the second floor.*

FLOWERS ON HIGH *The roses of York and Lancaster adorn the tower ceiling of St Albans Cathedral (above). The Normans began the building for a Benedictine abbey in 1077, retaining some pillars of the earlier Saxon building. They used red Roman bricks from ruined Verulamium for the tower. After the Dissolution, the abbey church continued in use as a parish church, and the great gatehouse also survives. Restoration work in 1877, when the present bishopric was created, revealed the building's exquisite medieval wall paintings.*

most fascinating are the exhibits that plot Rhodes' life in South Africa, where he went in 1870 and became a diamond tycoon. He was elected to the Cape Colony Parliament in 1881, and later founded the company that obtained mineral rights in the whole of the territory to be named Rhodesia (now Zambia and Zimbabwe).

RHODES RELICS *The room in which Cecil Rhodes was born in 1853 and his gun-metal cigarette case are carefully preserved in the Rhodes Memorial Museum.*

WRITER'S RETREAT *Hats and walking sticks in the hall at Shaw's Corner and writing materials at the ready in the summerhouse give the impression that the writer lives there still, and has perhaps only gone out for a stroll in the garden he loved.*

Rhodes, ever a visionary, saw this as part of a block of the British Empire stretching from Cairo to the Cape. During the Second Anglo-Boer War, Rhodes was besieged in the town of Kimberley in 1899 and 1900, and his cigarette case in the museum is inscribed with that name and the dates. He died in Capetown two years later and was buried in the Matopo Hills he loved.

All year exc first two weeks in Aug, weekdays exc Tues pm and Bank Hol. Adm charge. P *Toilets. Tel Bishop's Stortford (0279) 51746.*

SHAW'S CORNER

Off B651, 2 miles north of Wheathampstead (Bb)

The modest Edwardian house in which the writer George Bernard Shaw died in 1950 at the age of 94 is still today much as he left it. His hats still hang in the hall, beside his walking sticks, shoes and gaiters, and in his study the desk by the window is set out with his pens, typewriter and dictionaries. Here, and in the revolving summerhouse in the garden, Shaw wrote *Pygmalion, St Joan* and *The Apple Cart*. In the drawing room and dining room are mementos of his extraordinary life – his bronze bust, by Rodin; the Oscar awarded for the film version of *Pygmalion*; his membership card of the Cyclists' Touring Club, and photos of Gandhi, Lenin and Stalin.

In the kitchen, kettles and pans stand on the cast-iron kitchen range, the dresser is stacked with plates and an old-fashioned knife cleaner stands on the table. A typical kitchen of the 1920s and 1930s – except that Shaw's influence is again present, in the pile of his vegetarian recipes on the table.

On the outskirts of Ayot St Lawrence, north of Shaw's Corner, stands St Lawrence's Church, its Greek temple portico and open colonnades making it a conspicuous oddity in the Hertfordshire countryside. The church was built in 1778 by Sir Lionel Lyde, who had started to demolish the old church because it spoilt his view from

HORSE POWER *The mighty Shire horse at Standalone Farm weighs three-quarters of a ton. He is descended from the horses upon which medieval knights rode into the fray of battle and tournament.*

Ayot House, but was stopped by the Bishop of Lincoln. Sir Lionel had the new church built nearby, in the classical style then in vogue. Its great portico, with massive columns and colonnaded wings, was modelled on the temple of Apollo at Delos. The ruins of the old church, a little to the east, has wrought-iron gates that were ceremonially opened by Shaw in 1949.

Shaw's Corner: NT. Apr-Oct, pm daily exc Fri and Sat. Adm charge. Tel Stevenage (0438) 820307.

STANDALONE FARM

Letchworth, 1 mile north of town centre (Cc)

Milking demonstrations, a blacksmith's forge, old farm wagons, farm implements and a variety of cattle, sheep, pigs and poultry are all part of a day's visit to Standalone Farm. While operating as a working farm, Standalone has been designed to show visitors what life is like, and was like in the past, on a typical farm of some 170 acres.

Though the farm produces some crops, animals are its main attractions. Black-and-white Friesian cows and gentle-eyed Jerseys stand placidly in the milking parlour, where there are regular demonstrations of modern milking methods. Two breeds of sheep, the Suffolk and Hampshire Downs, goats, Large White pigs, a magnificent Shire horse named Warrant, and Light Sussex and Rhode Island hens make up the rest of the farm's livestock. In the spring there are calves to stroke and lambs to fondle, while the ducks on the farm pond are on constant lookout for a morsel or two.

The pond is part of the Pix Brook which runs through the farm and, at its northern end, forms a series of lakes that are the home of wigeon, mallard, shoveler and tufted ducks. In summer they are joined by pintails, ringed teals and pochards, and along the brook kingfishers burrow into the banks to build their nests. All these activities can be watched from hides, including one designed for disabled people.

The farm buildings are a mixture of traditional eastern counties and south-east Midlands barns and modern outbuildings. One barn houses old wagons and a horsedrawn fire engine.

Apr-Oct, daily. Adm charge. Picnic area. Refreshments. Shop. P *Toilets.* ♿ *Tel Letchworth (0462) 686775.*

TRING RESERVOIRS

On B489, 1 mile north of Tring (Ab)

Patient anglers line the banks of the Grand Union Canal near its 400ft summit in the Chiltern Hills. Nearby, steep grassy banks hold back the waters of four reservoirs, and these, their banks and surrounding woodlands make up a National Nature Reserve. From hides beside Tringford Reservoir, a watcher may spot a heron rising from the reeds on slow-beating wings, or see flocks of mallard, teal, wigeon and pochard darting across the still waters. In spring, pairs of great crested grebe perform their stately courtship dance, and common terns hover and plunge to catch fish. Lucky watchers may see a high-gliding marsh harrier or, most spectacular of all, the plummeting dive of an osprey.

The reservoirs store water for the canal, which passes through a flight of six locks as it descends from the hills. Each time a boat passes through the locks, about 50,000 gallons of water are lost downhill, and are replenished at the summit by a pumping station. The reservoirs themselves are topped up by natural springs, and on busy summer days when gleaming pleasure craft and brightly painted narrowboats pass to and fro, the water level is constantly changing.

NCC. All year, daily. Free entry. P *Tel Tring (044 282) 2379.*

WHIPPENDELL WOOD

Off A411, in Watford (Ba)

To the west of Watford's Cassiobury Park are 200 acres of glorious woodlands, with picnic sites, quiet walks, an orienteering course and a nature trail. From the woods, footpaths meander across a golf course to the River Gade and the Grand Union Canal where, at Iron Bridge Lock, there are canal trips in summer on a genuine narrowboat. There are also lovely riverside or canalside walks, a children's play area, paddling pool and miniature railway.

All year, daily.

ZOOLOGICAL MUSEUM

At Tring, off A41 (Ab)

To enter the red-brick portals of the museum is to enter a fantasy world of stuffed animals, birds, fish, reptiles, moths, butterflies and insects. From great apes and lordly lions to exotic butterflies and grotesque beetles, a kaleidoscope of wildlife is displayed here – all inanimate, yet portrayed as they must have looked when they inhabited the world's forests, hills, plains and seas.

Six galleries on two floors house the exhibits, with the 'big cats', gorillas and polar bear providing a grand overture in the main hall. Each gallery offers outstanding examples of the taxidermist's art, including a unique collection of domestic dogs.

The museum is based on the collection of Lionel Walter, 2nd Baron Lord Rothschild, who bequeathed it to the nation in 1938. At the time of his death, Rothschild's collection included more than 2000 mammals, a similar number of birds and more than 2 million butterflies and moths. The museum is now an annexe of the Natural History Museum, in London.

All year, daily. Adm charge. Shop. P *Toilets. Tel Tring (044 282) 4181.*

WINGED BEAUTY *The Tring Zoological Museum is the home of this* Gonimbrasia zambesiana *moth. The preserved specimen, from Africa, has a wingspan of nearly 5in.*

COLOUR ON THE CANAL *A brightly decorated narrowboat waits in a lock on the Grand Union Canal near Tring Reservoirs. The waterway, which linked London with Birmingham, was started in 1795.*

COUNTY CALENDAR

April (mid-month). Stevenage: East Herts Festival.

May (mid-month). Redbourn: Herts Show.

May (Spring Bank Hol). Hertford: County Day Fair.

June (mid-month). Hatfield House: Festival Gardening. Redbourn: Country Fair.

June (late). Capel Manor, near Waltham Cross: National Horticultural Show. Hatfield House: Folk Dance Festival.

July (early). St Albans: International Organ Festival (biennial, 1989). St Albans: British Rose Festival.

Tourist information: Berkhamsted (044 27) 4545; Hertford (0279) 55261; Hitchin (0462) 34738; St Albans (0727) 64511; Stevenage (0438) 69441.

HUMBERSIDE

MANSIONS, A MINSTER AND A BRAVE NEW BRIDGE

The graceful new Humber Bridge linking the two halves of Humberside crosses an estuary which has dominated the area from earliest times. On its bank rose the great port of Kingston upon Hull, whose story is told today in the Hull Town Docks Museum. Much of the old city is being preserved as it was when William Wilberforce, the great campaigner against slavery, walked its streets as a boy in the 1760s, and his birthplace is now a museum. A meeting place of sea and land routes, Hull appropriately has its own Transport Museum, and the county boasts three more: the Lincolnshire and Humberside Railway Museum, the Museum of Army Transport and the Sandtoft Transport Centre.

Estuary and coast attract a wealth of wildlife, as seen at Bempton Cliffs, Blacktoft Sands and Spurn Head. Inland, gentle country has nurtured religious establishments such as Thornton Abbey and Beverley Minster, and wealthy estates such as those at Burnby, Burton Agnes, Burton Constable and Sewerby. Around the estuary lies excellent farming country. Aspects of village and farm life 100 years ago are re-created at Hornsea Museum and Skidby Windmill Museum.

BEMPTON CLIFFS

Off B1229, 3½ miles north of Bridlington (Cc)

A wall of chalk up to 400ft high stretching for 4 miles along the coast affords magnificent views. Seabirds rear their young in every nook and cranny, and some 33 species of birds breed there, including kittiwakes, guillemots, razorbills and puffins. This is also Britain's only mainland site where gannets breed. There are viewing platforms and descriptions of the birds to aid identification.

RSPB. All year, daily.

GOTHIC LANDMARK *The twin western towers of Beverley Minster, built around 1400, rise above the red-roofed town and green countryside like a huge, fretted confection coated in icing sugar.*

BEVERLEY MINSTER

On south side of Beverley (Cb)

The minster's grandeur and craftsmanship are apparent from miles away; within the building they are awe-inspiring. The interior seems endless – actually 332ft long – and is supported by a forest of columns reaching up to a rib-vaulted ceiling of cream and gold. There are delightful carvings everywhere; see the little stone medieval portrayals of knights, ladies, musicians and demons that squeeze out of every cranny, and the 68 misericords – ornate wooden shelves for the clergy to rest on in the choir stalls yet appear to remain standing.

The tale of the life and works of St John of Beverley, Bishop of York, is told in a series of embroideries supplied by the Hull School of Art. He it was who founded the minster in about AD 690, though what with Danish raids, a fire and a tumbling tower, the present building is the fourth to stand on the site since then; it was completed in the early 1400s.

All year, daily.

BLACKTOFT SANDS

Off A161, 8 miles east of Goole (Bb)

A spit of land where the Ouse and Trent rivers meet and flow into the Humber provides a haven for people as well as birds. Common reeds growing up to 10ft high provide natural protection for many nesting birds including the bearded reedling. A public hide overlooks the reserve, where reed buntings, reed warblers and water rails may also be seen. Redshanks nest in the salt marshes, as well as mallards, teal and shelduck and occasional marsh harriers.

RSPB. All year, daily.

BURNBY HALL GARDENS

At Pocklington off A1079, 14 miles east of York (Bb)

In the middle of these lovely gardens are two lakes which contain one of the finest collections of water lilies in Europe – more than 50 varieties, seen in their full glory in summer. The lakes look natural but are in fact man-made. They are set at different levels and connected by a stream which runs through a delightful rock garden. Sur-

TRIAL OF STRENGTH *This 'Mills perfect muscle developer' in the Penny Arcadia museum at Pocklington was made in 1904. Users pulled two handles at its base to test their strength.*

rounding the lakes are 6 acres of garden filled with lilacs and laburnums, Japanese maples, 20 varieties of holly and many rare trees. There is a rose garden and a scented garden for the blind, and also a museum housing the mementos and trophies assembled by the gardens' creator, Major Percy Stewart, in many years of travel.

Another remarkable collection to be seen in Pocklington is the array of fruit machines and other amusement machines in the Penny Arcadia museum. On display are classic machines such as the Mills Poinsettia and the Vest Pocket – the smallest fruit machine ever made; a whole range of ballgum vendors; and many working mechanical models, ranging from the Floating Lady to the Chinese Torture.

Burnby Hall: Easter-early Oct, daily. Adm charge. Refreshments. Shop. P *Toilets.* ♿ *Tel Pocklington (075 92) 2068. Penny Arcadia: May-Sept, daily. Adm charge. Shop.* P *Toilets.* ♿ *Tel (075 92) 303420.*

BURTON AGNES HALL

On A166, 6 miles south-west of Bridlington (Cc)

The architect of this outstanding Elizabethan house was Robert Smythson, Master Mason to Elizabeth I. It was completed in 1598 and has survived with remarkably few changes. Almost everything about the house is exceptionally pleasing, from the handsome gatehouse, bearing the arms of James I, to the Great Hall, with its superb carving, plasterwork and panelling. One of the most remarkable features of the house is the staircase, in which the newel posts are linked by a series of lavishly carved arches.

Next to Burton Agnes Hall are the remains of a Norman manor house built in 1173. The undercroft of the house is intact, with stone piers supporting a vaulted roof. The hall and manor house are surrounded by 42 acres of fine gardens.

Hall: Apr-Oct, daily. Adm charge. Refreshments. Shop. P *Toilets.* ♿ *(ground floor). Tel Burton Agnes (026 289) 324. Manor house: EH. All year, daily. Tel York (0904) 22902.*

BURTON CONSTABLE

On B1238, 11 miles north-east of Hull (Cb)

With its soft red brickwork, castellated towers and mullioned oriel windows, Burton Constable is one of the great Tudor architectural glories of Humberside. Inside, however, the character of the house is almost entirely Georgian, the product of an astonishing number of distinguished 18th-century architects and craftsmen.

Among the finest rooms are the Hall and Long Gallery, designed by Thomas Lightoler; the Ballroom designed by James Wyatt with furniture by Chippendale; and the Dining Room, again designed by Lightoler, with its gilded ceiling and oval stucco wall reliefs by William Collins.

The mansion lies in an equally splendid country park. It includes a 25 acre lake for boating, fishing and sailboarding. The park also contains motorcycle and carriage museums, a model railway and an adventure playground.

Hall: Easter-Sept, pm daily, exc Fri and Sat. Adm charge. Refreshments. Shop. P *Toilets.* ♿ *Tel Skirlaugh (0401) 62400. Country park: Easter-Sept, pm daily.*

FLUTTERS NATURAL WORLD

Off B1255 in Pinfold Lane, Bridlington (Cc)

Scorpions, tarantulas and giant moths are not creatures generally associated with Bridlington. But in this exotic corner of a Humberside town these and many more spectacular examples of tropical fauna and flora can be seen. British and tropical butterflies fly freely in an enclosed garden, among vines and tropical flowers. An insect gallery contains a variety of formidable creatures, from hissing cockroaches to praying mantises.

Easter-Oct, daily. Adm charge. Refreshments. Shop. P *Toilets.* ♿ *Tel Bridlington (0262) 671897.*

HORNSEA MUSEUM

In Newbegin, near centre of Hornsea (Cb)

A building dating from the 16th century that was the home of a single farming family for 300 years is furnished throughout as it might have been 100 years ago. The kitchen of this delightful museum of village life is filled with Victorian cooking utensils and fittings. The parlour and bedroom are also furnished in authentic Victorian style. One room is devoted to local history, and there is also a dairy, a workshop and a blacksmith's shop.

Museum: Good Fri-Oct, pm daily. Adm charge. Shop. P *Toilets. Tel Hornsea (040 12) 3443.*

HORNSEA POTTERY LEISURE PARK

Off B1242, Rolston Road, Hornsea (Cb)

Thousands of people visit Hornsea each year to buy tableware, vases and other products of its noted pottery. Gradually, over the years, the pottery has come to provide more and more diversions for its visitors, and these now form a complete leisure park. One of the chief attractions are the birds of prey – owls, hawks and eagles. The park also contains a collection of 300 live tropical butterflies housed in an indoor garden, a 1 acre model village and an adventure playground.

Apr-Oct, daily. Nov-Mar, Wed-Sun. Free entry (grounds). Refreshments. Shop. P *Toilets.* ♿ *Tel Hornsea (040 12) 2161.*

HULL TOWN DOCKS MUSEUM

Queen Victoria Square, Hull (Cb)

An intimate portrait of the relationship between a city and the sea is presented in the late Victorian headquarters of the old Hull Dock Company. Fishing is the subject closest to Hull's maritime heart, and there are models of the different types of fishing boats that sailed out of the city, mingled with photographs and fishing gear.

Ghostly whistles, grunts and howls – the recorded conversation of whales – accompany the museum's whaling exhibition. Though whaling ceased to play a part in the city's economy in the late 1860s, for two centuries before that Hull sent its ships to the Arctic in pursuit of whales. It is difficult to look at the weapons used against these creatures – the harpoons, lances, crossbows and grenade-headed gun harpoons – without wincing, as the schoolchildren's framed essays in the gallery testify. But it is also difficult to withhold admiration for the tough old-time whalers who charged their open rowing boats into the 60ft giants before driving the harpoons home. All aspects of whaling are reflected in the displays, as is the whaler's traditional pastime of scrimshaw work – surprisingly delicate pictures and designs etched into whalebone or walrus ivory with a sailmaker's needle, then highlighted with ink or blacking.

THAR SHE BLOWS *A reproduction of a 19th-century whaling boat in Hull Town Docks Museum is armed with a formidable array of harpoons and lances. Such boats were used in the waters off Greenland.*

FASHION PLATE *A 4th-century Roman lady, her hair stylishly coiffeured, stares out from a mosaic in Hull's Transport and Archaeology Museum. The mosaic was found at Brantingham Tyche, west of the city.*

Upstairs, further exhibitions tell the story of Hull and the Humber, of the growth of the docks, shipbuilding, and the vessels that used the port. There is the reconstructed saloon of a topsail schooner, and displays of famous ships that were built in the city – such as the *Bethia,* for example, that became HMS *Bounty.*

All year, daily. Free entry. Refreshments. Shop. Toilets. ♿ Tel Hull (0482) 222737.

HULL TRANSPORT MUSEUM

High Street, Hull (Cb)

Ancestors of the bicycle, velocipedes, ancient cars, carriages and trams provide massed evidence of the enormous ingenuity man has expended down the years in his efforts to avoid walking. Among favourite exhibits in this museum are the world's oldest tram, beautifully carved and veneered, built in 1871 for Ryde Pier; a six-horse road coach of 1860; and a hansom cab. The museum also contains a collection of archaeological discoveries made in the area.

Immediately opposite the Transport Museum is the 18th-century Maister House. Only the hall and the staircase are open to the public, but these are well worth seeing for their splendid stucco and delicate ironwork.

Transport Museum: All year, daily. Free entry. Shop. Toilets. Tel Hull (0482) 222737. Maister House: NT. All year, Mon-Fri. Adm charge. Tel (0482) 24114.

HUMBER BRIDGE COUNTRY PARK

Off A15, on northern side of Humber Bridge (Cb)

The Humber Bridge may as yet lack the romantic associations which the Golden Gate Bridge of San Francisco inspires, but it already has one clear, undisputed claim to fame: it is the longest single span suspension bridge in the world At 4626ft, it is 366ft longer than its closest rival, the Varrazano Narrows Bridge, New York, and 426ft longer than the Golden Gate Bridge.

The country park which lies beside the bridge's northern end offers a good vantage point from which to view the bridge. The park comprises 48 acres of meadows, woodlands, ponds, cliffs and an old mill. Footpaths crisscross the area, and wheelchairs can reach the viewpoint at the north end by using the entrance from the bridge car park. The park also has a picnic area and a nature trail.

All year, daily.

LINCOLNSHIRE AND HUMBERSIDE RAILWAY MUSEUM

On B1398, 7 miles south of Scunthorpe (Ba)

The old clock ticks above the little iron fireplace in the Station Master's office, while from the platform come the dramatic sounds of a steam train stirring into life and moving off. The train is a 'ghost', existing only in sound fed through hidden speakers, but the platform is filled with authentic railway furnishings from the heyday of steam, even down to the notices decorating the walls.

A narrow-gauge railway carries visitors to a viaduct from which there is a panoramic view of the Trent Valley. By the station is Mount Pleasant Mill which, while lacking sails, is complete internally and still used for grinding corn, powered by an 1893 portable steam engine

Easter-Aug, Sat and Sun; Aug, Wed-Sun; Sept-Dec, Sun. Adm charge. Refreshments. Shop. P Toilets. ♿ Tel Kirton in Lindsey (0652) 648251.

MUSEUM OF ARMY TRANSPORT

Flemingate, near centre of Beverley (Cb)

A large slogan greets the visitor: 'Logistics is the Art of Moving an Army and Keeping it Supplied. This museum shows how the Royal Corps of Transport, and its predecessors dating back to 1794, have faithfully practised that art.

The Corps has its own air force, represented by a de Havilland Beaver, a helicopter and a figure wearing the equipment of an air dispatcher inside a gigantic Blackburn Beverley, which is set out as a museum of the army's air supply operations. It also has a navy, which has contributed amphibious vehicles and a hovercraft. An entire gallery is devoted to military railways which have moved the army about since the Crimean War.

As well as a fine collection of tanks, armoured cars and scout cars, there are fire engines, mobile command posts, workshops and surgeries, a veterinary ambulance for wounded horses and a mobile bakery used in the Falklands campaign. A number of well-mounted tableaux show some of the vehicles in action: a recovery vehicle taking a half-track in tow in the Western Desert, amphibious craft unloading supplies on the Normandy beaches, an advanced HQ in Germany. Vehicles are put through their paces outdoors on the last Sunday in May, June, July and August, and on Bank Holidays in May and August.

All year, daily. Adm charge. Refreshments. Shop. P Toilets. ♿ Tel Hull (0482) 860445.

NORMANBY HALL COUNTRY PARK

On B1430, 4½ miles north of Scunthorpe (Ba)

The great attraction of Normanby Hall is the thoroughness with which it re-creates the taste and atmosphere of a Regency country house. The manor of Normanby is much older, dating back to 1086 and the Sheffield family have lived there since 1589. But the house was rebuilt in 1830.

Normanby Hall is set in 350 acres of gardens and parkland, including a deer park with large herds of red and fallow deer.

All year, daily exc Sat. Adm charge (Hall only). Refreshments. P Toilets. ♿ Tel Scunthorpe (0724) 720215.

PATRINGTON CHURCH

In centre of Patrington (Cb)

St Patrick's Church, Patrington, is probably unequalled as an example of the Decorated period of English church architecture. The perfectly proportioned spire is ringed by a delicate octagonal corona, and the roof of the nave is surrounded by smaller pinnacles. One of the outstanding features of the church is its fine stone carving – there are more than 200 carved faces of humans and animals. In the chancel stands a rare Easter Sepulchre, with carvings of sleeping Roman soldiers. But perhaps the church's greatest glory is the fact that it is so completely of

DESERT RATS *A tableau in the Museum of Army Transport in Beverley shows how field workshops of the Royal Army Service Corps kept the vehicles of the Seventh Armoured Division running in the Western Desert battles of 1941.*

an age, and has survived virtually unchanged since its completion in 1410.
All year, daily.

SANDTOFT TRANSPORT CENTRE

Off A18, 14 miles west of Scunthorpe (Ba)

There are people who still mourn the passing of the last trolleybus, in Bradford in 1972. In fact the trolleybus had positive advantages over the diesel-engined buses which succeeded it, because it was pollution-free. This may account in part for the popularity of the Sandtoft Transport Centre, which houses the largest collection of trolleybuses in the country – more than 60 vehicles – operating on the centre's own circuit.
Spring and Summer Bank Hol weekends, and certain other days. Adm charge. Refreshments. Shop. P *Toilets. Tel Doncaster (0302) 842948/771520.*

SEWERBY HALL PARK AND ZOO

Off B1255, 2 miles north-east of Bridlington (Cc)

The grounds of Sewerby offer magnificent views over Bridlington Bay, from Flamborough Head in the north-east to Spurn Head in the south. The hall itself is Georgian, built on the site of a medieval manor house, and has many fine rooms. It was purchased by Bridlington Corporation in 1934 and opened to the public two years later by Amy Johnson. One of the most popular features of Sewerby now is the Amy Johnson museum, containing relics of the pioneer airwoman.

The Oak Room and the Green Room have particularly fine early Georgian panelling. An outstanding feature of the house is the cantilevered oak staircase. The grounds are a mixture of woodland and gardens, including the formal garden, noted for its giant monkey-puzzle trees, and the Old English walled garden. There is also a zoo and a 6 acre paddock containing deer, wallabies and Shetland ponies.
Park and zoo: All year, daily. Hall: Good Fri-end Sept. Adm charge. Refreshments. Shop. P *Toilets.* ♿ *(Park, zoo and ground floor of Hall). Tel Bridlington (0262) 687255.*

SKIDBY WINDMILL MUSEUM

On A164, 4 miles south of Beverley (Bb)

Windmills, like steam engines, attract their own groups of devoted supporters. Skidby Mill has a special claim to their attention in that it is the only complete example of an East Riding windmill still working. Built in 1821, it was worked by wind until 1954, when electrically driven plant was installed. This has been retained and the original windmill completely overhauled, providing a contrast between old and new. The mill also contains a museum.
May-Sept, daily exc Mon. Adm charge. Refreshments. Shop. P *Toilets. Tel Hull (0482) 882255.*

SLEDMERE HOUSE

On B1251, 6 miles north-west of Great Driffield (Bc)

In building, as in many other things, the English landed gentry of the 18th century did not believe in half measures. Shortly after this house was completed in 1751, the Sykes family – who still live there – decided to ask Capability Brown to landscape the surrounding 2000 acres. As part of the plan, the old village was demolished and rebuilt on the eastern boundary of the park.

The house and park are full of visual delights. The decorative plasterwork is superb. The library is a magnificent room, 100ft long, with splendid views over Capability Brown's landscapes. The house is filled with Chippendale, Sheraton and French period furniture.
Easter; Apr, Sun; May-Sept, pm daily, exc Mon and Fri; Bank Hol. Adm charge. Refreshments. Shop. P *Toilets.* ♿ *Tel Driffield (0377) 86208.*

SPURN HEAD

Off B1445, 9 miles south-east of Patrington (Da)

Spurn is formed from sand and shingle washed from the cliffs of Holderness. The tip of the headland is reached along the beaches surrounding a nature reserve, which is itself closed to the public. Many stones and fossils can be found on the beaches, including corals and ammonites.

An enormous variety of migrating birds stop at Spurn – wheatears, whinchats, redstarts, pied and spotted flycatchers and many more. Among the bigger birds seen are curlews, oystercatchers, Brent geese and terns. Seals and porpoises occasionally approach the shore.
All year, daily.

THORNTON ABBEY

Off A1077, 8 miles north-west of Immingham (Ca)

According to local legend, a party exploring the ruins of Thornton Abbey in the 18th century discovered the remains of a monk, seated at a table with a book, pen and ink by his side. The ancient ruins provide a credible setting for such a discovery. The abbey was founded in 1139 for a community of Augustinian canons and became one of the richest houses of the Order. The 50ft high gatehouse was built in 1382. It includes a large hall and an elaborate system of wall passages and small chambers, some with fireplaces.
EH. Apr-Sept, daily; Oct-Feb, Sat and Sun. Adm charge. Shop. P *Tel Immingham (0469) 40357.*

WILBERFORCE HOUSE

High Street, Hull (Cb)

Several of the High Street's elegant houses bear witness to the wealth of Hull's merchant princes. In one of them, a very handsome Jacobean building, the anti-slavery campaigner William Wilberforce was born in 1759; it is now a museum. The panelled Banqueting Room, filled with dark 17th-century furniture, is the room that is least changed. Charles I dined in it in April 1639, and a large pair of boots, in a surprisingly good state of repair, leaning against a chair, belonged to his standard bearer, Sir Edmund Verney, who was killed at the Battle of Edgehill in 1642.

The main part of the museum is devoted to Wilberforce and the slave trade. Because of the opposition of a large number of vested interests Wilberforce's dream of abolishing slavery throughout the Empire was by no means easy to fulfil. He achieved it only in 1833, three days before he died at the age of 73. There are posters, paintings and prints relating to the trade, as well as shackles, whips and branding irons. An effective diorama with sound portrays conditions on the 'tween-decks of a slave ship.

Wilberforce is also commemorated by a statue on a 90ft column standing at the eastern end of Queens Gardens.
All year, daily. Free entry. Shop. P *(limited). Toilets.* ♿ *(ground floor). Tel Hull (0482) 222737.*

OLD CAMPAIGNER *Wilberforce House, birthplace of the slavery abolitionist William Wilberforce, contains a fine 17th-century Banqueting Room and a display of slave auction posters. Wilberforce waged his campaign, against bitter resistance, for more than 50 years.*

COUNTY CALENDAR

January 6 Haxey: Hood Game (commemorating 13th-century deed of chivalry).

March (3rd Thur). South Dalton: Kiplingcotes Derby (ancient horse race).

June (early). Burton Constable Hall: Country Fair.

June (closest Sun to Midsummer). Walkington: Victorian Hayride.

July (early). Humberside Airport: International Air Fair.

August (mid-month). Great Driffield: Steam Fair.

October (early). Kingston upon Hull: Fair.

Tourist information: Beverley (0482) 867813; Bridlington (0262) 673474; Cleethorpes (0472) 697472; Hull (0482) 223559; Hull Dock (0482) 702118; Humber Bridge (0482) 640852.

ISLE OF MAN

RELICS OF A VIKING PAST, AND A RAILWAY TO A SUMMIT VIEWPOINT

Tailless cats and motorcycle racing make up the popular image of the Isle of Man. Both have their places among the island's attractions: the cats are bred at Noble's Park, and an entire museum is devoted to motorcycles. But the visitor soon becomes aware of other aspects of island life through the ages, recalled in museums or displayed in stone battlements and thatched cottages. Above all, Manxmen have been seafarers, and their story is told in Castletown's Nautical Museum. Ancient castles such as Rushen and Peel, and the Manx Museum in Douglas, recall the island's Viking past, while the life of the crofter is re-created at Cregneish, and The Grove depicts life on the larger farm.

Manxmen were quick to adopt the techniques of the Industrial Revolution. A railway network soon covered the land, and parts of it today survive as the Isle of Man Steam Railway and Manx Electric Railway. And when Laxey Water Wheel first turned in 1854, it was the biggest in Europe.

CASTLE RUSHEN

At centre of Castletown (Ba)

This splendidly preserved medieval fortress, its four square limestone towers rising 70ft above a sturdy curtain wall, dates from about 1153 and was the home of Man's Norse rulers, the Kings of Man, until 1265. The sovereignty of Man was then disputed between England and Scotland,

PROUD HERITAGE *The 12th-century fortress of the Norse Kings of Man towers over Castletown harbour. Inside Castle Rushen is a tapestry woven this century to mark 1000 years of Tynwald, the Manx parliament.*

but from 1329, all Lords of Man were English.

Until 1710 Castle Rushen was the meeting place of the Manx parliament's House of Keys. It then served as a jail and asylum before being presented to the Manx people by George V in 1929. The one-handed clock on the outer wall is said to have been presented by Elizabeth I.

June-Sept, daily exc certain Sun; Oct-May, daily exc Sun. Adm charge. Refreshments. Shop. Toilets. Tel Castletown (0624) 823326.

CREGNEISH VILLAGE FOLK MUSEUM

Off A31, 4½ miles west of Castletown (Ba)

The most truly Manx village, Cregneish, stands at the top of a steep hill and commands a magnificent view of land and sea. It was one of the last places where the traditional crofters' skills were practised. Features of that past way of life have been retained or re-created within the essentially 19th-century village.

The Folk Museum embraces a number of different buildings. The starting point is Cummal Beg 'Little Dwelling', where the story of the local community is explained. The journey continues to the thatched and whitewashed Harry Kelly's Cottage, which dates from the early 18th century. Harry, a crofter and a fluent Manx speaker, died in 1934. The furnishings of the restored cottage provide a picture of the old days when the family gathered around the open hearth – the *chiollagh* – for warmth and conversation.

May-Sept, daily. Shop. P *Tel Douglas (0624) 75522.*

CURRAGHS WILDLIFE PARK

Off A3, 4½ miles west of Ramsey (Cc)

Creatures from all over the world roam the 26 acres of a large nature reserve. Among the inhabitants are llamas, monkeys and lynx – as well as the rare loghtan sheep of Man, whose rams grow two or three pairs of horns. There are pools for penguins, sea lions and otters, and among the exotic birds are flamingos, parakeets, crested touracos and golden and silver pheasants.

All year, daily. Adm charge. Refreshments. Shop. P *Toilets. Tel Sulby (062489) 7323.*

GROVE RURAL LIFE MUSEUM

On A9, 1 mile north of Ramsey (Cc)

Life on a prosperous Manx farm in the 19th century is recalled at The Grove, an early Victorian house built onto an earlier cottage in 1849. Its period rooms show the family's lifestyle, and there are displays of costume, toys and games, beekeeping and gardening. Outbuildings are used to display machinery, including the farm's original horse-powered threshing mill, which is still in working order.

May-Sept, daily, exc Sat. Adm charge. Refreshments. Shop. P *Tel Ramsey (0624) 75522.*

ISLE OF MAN STEAM RAILWAY

From Port Erin to Douglas (Ba-Cb)

The Isle of Man's longest-running transport

system – older even than the horse trams of Douglas – is that of the Isle of Man Steam Railway. Its first stretch of track was opened in 1874, and some of the narrow-gauge engines and coaches in use in the 19th century still carry summer visitors through lovely countryside on the one-hour journey between Port Erin and Douglas.

The Railway Museum at Port Erin tells the history of the line and displays a fine collection of steam engines, coaches and other Victorian and Edwardian memorabilia. Among the sights of the route are Crogga Woods, and the clifftop views above Port Soderick before the 200ft descent into Douglas.

Late Apr-early Oct, daily exc Sat. Fares. Shop. P *Toilets. Tel Douglas (0624) 74549.*

LAXEY WATER WHEEL

Off A2, ¼ mile north of Laxey (Cb)

The mighty wheel bearing the decorous name of Lady Isabella is a spectacular memorial to a mining industry which once yielded lead, copper and iron ore. The wheel originally had a strictly practical purpose – to pump water from the shafts of the Laxey mines, and in the mid-19th century Manxmen saw the installation of what was then the largest water wheel in Europe – 72½ft across and 6ft broad, and carrying 168 buckets.

In September 1854 the Lieutenant-Governor, the Honourable Charles Hope, started the mechanism and the wheel – named after his wife – pounded into action. In 1929 the Laxey mines closed down, and the wheel was left to decay. In 1965 the Manx government took it over, and in 1970 the wheel started turning again.

Easter-Sept, daily. Adm charge. Shop. P *Tel Laxey (0624) 26262.*

MANX ELECTRIC RAILWAY

Derby Castle Station, Douglas (Cb-Cc)

A living memorial to the technological skills of Victorian times, the Manx Electric Railway opened in 1893, and two of its original cars are still in use on the service between Douglas and Ramsey. Just out of Douglas, passengers enjoy a fine panorama of Douglas Bay. Farther on, sea views give way to the wooded approach to Groudle Glen, and after a stop at Laxey there is a long climb to the highest point of the journey – Bulgham clifftop, 588ft above sea level.

A branch line, open in summer, takes trains from Laxey to the summit of Snaefell, at 2036ft the highest point on the island. A museum at Ramsey houses historic locomotives and rolling stock.

Electric Railway: Early Apr-early Oct, daily exc some Sun. Fares according to journey. P *Museum: Mid-May to mid-Sept, Mon-Fri. Adm charge. Shop.* P *Toilets. Snaefell Railway: Early May-early Oct, daily exc some Sun. Tel Douglas (0624) 74549.*

MANX MUSEUM

In centre of Douglas (Cb)

A Viking warship with a dragonhead prow and a great square sail gives visitors to the Manx Museum an idea of the sea power that once spread fear around the coasts of Britain. Built in Norway in 1939, the large-scale model is based on a Viking ship discovered there in 1880. Other exhibits range from intricate Celtic and Viking stone carvings to a 4½ ton skeleton of a sei whale, and from stuffed birds to Art Nouveau silver. There is an art gallery, and a library incorporating the national archive.

All year, daily exc Sun. Free entry. Shop. Toilets. Tel Douglas (0624) 75522.

MARINE BIOLOGICAL STATION

Near centre of Port Erin (Ba)

Glass tanks – many set at children's eye level – vividly display the wonders of the deep to visitors to the Marine Biological Station. It is a department of the University of Liverpool, but its aquarium and museum are open to the public and cover a broad range of marine topics, from towering icebergs to the humble cod.

Apr-Oct, Mon-Fri, and Sat am. Free entry. P ♿ *Tel Port Erin (0624) 832027.*

MURRAY'S MOTORCYCLE MUSEUM

On A18, 5 miles south-west of Ramsey (Cb)

A motorcycle museum could find no more appropriate setting than the island of Tourist Trophy racing. Moreover, the Murray collection is housed at a well-known point on the TT course – Bungalow Corner on the slopes of Snaefell. The collection was begun in 1955 by a local enthusiast, Charles Murray. The oldest motorcycle on view is a 1902 Kerry, while machines dating from before the First World War include the 1910 Wynn Ladies' Model.

Late May-late Sept, daily. Adm charge. Refreshments. Shop. P *Toilets. Tel Laxey (0624) 781.*

NAUTICAL MUSEUM

Bridge Street, Castletown (Ba)

Tucked in beside Castletown's harbour, this museum is actually a three-storeyed boathouse dating from the late 18th century. The first-floor cabin room – with balcony and wooden railings – resembles the stern cabin of a ship of Lord Nelson's time. But the museum's centrepiece is an 18th-century schooner-rigged yacht, the *Peggy*. Built in 1791 by Captain George Quayle, who also built the boathouse for her in the shadow of his home, Bridge House, the *Peggy* is the oldest known surviving vessel of her type.

Mid May-late Sept, daily. Adm charge. Refreshments. Shop. P *Tel Castletown (0624) 75522.*

COLOURFUL CLIMBER *Car SMR No 1 climbs the 1 in 12 gradient of the Snaefell branch of the Manx Electric Railway, built in 1895. From the summit there are magnificent views across the island.*

ISLAND FORTRESS *Sunset silhouettes Peel Castle's 10th-century watch tower and battlemented cathedral ruins. Scots, Irish, English and French raiders all plundered the castle in the Middle Ages.*

NOBLE'S PARK

Near centre of Douglas (Cb)

The Manx cat – the only completely tailless breed in the world – may be seen in Noble's Park breeding cattery. Kittens born here are sent at about 12 weeks old to many parts of the world as pets. Tailless cats are thought to have been first bred about 300 years ago, but legend gives them a much older origin: a fable tells how a pair of cats rushed into the ark at the last moment and Noah, shutting a door, cut their tails off.

Mid May-Sept, daily. Adm charge to cattery. Refreshments P *Toilets. Tel Douglas (0624) 21132.*

PEEL CASTLE

St Patrick's Isle (Bb)

The impressive fortress of Peel Castle stands on St Patrick's Isle – which is joined to Peel by a causeway – and within its walls is a cathedral. According to tradition, St Patrick landed on the islet on his way to Ireland in AD 444; the cathedral, dating mainly from the 13th century, is dedicated to his follower St German. The present castle was built mostly by the Lords of Man in the 15th century. In the Civil War it was held for the king by the Earl of Derby.

May-Sept, daily. Adm charge. Shop. P *Toilets. Tel Douglas (0624) 26262.*

ISLAND CALENDAR

Easter weekend Douglas: Easter Play Festival.

May (1st week). Douglas: Music Festival.

May (late, to early June). International TT Motorcycle Races.

June (late, to early July). Port Erin: Festival.

July 5 Tynwald Hill: Tynwald Ceremony. (New laws proclaimed in Manx and English.)

July (late). International Football Festival.

August (early). Douglas: Carnival.

August (late, to early September). Manx Grand Prix Motorcycle Races.

September (mid-month). International Car Rally.

Tourist information: Castletown (0624) 823518; Douglas (0624) 74323; Peel (0624) 842341; Ramsey (0624) 812228.

ISLE OF WIGHT

JAIL OF A DEFEATED KING AND REFUGE OF A LONELY QUEEN

Inland from the beaches that lure the summer visitor, the Isle of Wight offers a wealth of year-round attractions that between them span England's history. At Brading and Newport the Romans have left their mark; Arreton Manor has been owned by eight English monarchs, and the castle at Yarmouth was built by Henry VIII to defend the south coast against the French. The medieval Carisbrooke Castle became Charles I's jail, while in later times Osborne House was the favourite residence of Queen Victoria and Prince Albert.

Memories of less illustrious episodes in the island's past are recalled by a well-stocked museum of smuggling. In Wight's gentle climate vineyards thrive and trees and flowers blossom in Ventnor Botanic Garden, while more exotic forms of wildlife are on view at Flamingo Park and at Robin Hill.

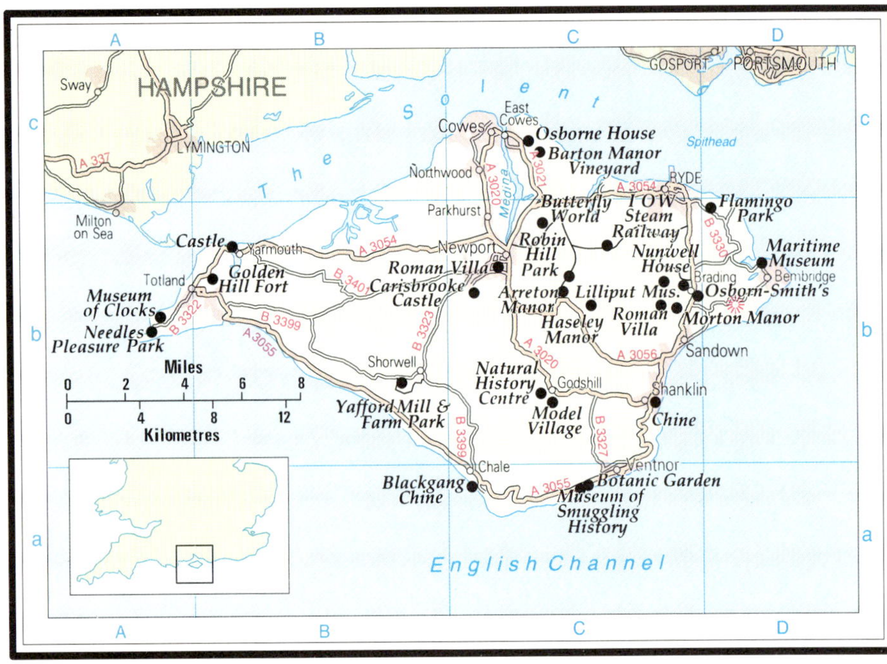

DOORWAY TO THE PAST *Two projecting wings frame a central porch in the south front of Arreton Manor, and time-worn steps lead up to the door of a house which has been lived in for nearly 400 years. Today the manor also houses a museum, Echoes of Childhood, a collection of dolls, toys and dolls' houses. One exhibit is the pedlar doll (left) of 1795, her tray overflowing with miniature wares.*

ARRETON MANOR

Off A3056, 3½ miles south-east of Newport (Cb)

No fewer than eight English monarchs have owned Arreton Manor and given it a heritage of historical and architectural treasures. The house was built in late Elizabethan and early Jacobean times, but still has traces of a 14th-century building on the site. In rooms walled with fine Jacobean panelling relics including Charles I's snuffbox and a 300-year-old candlestick are on display, as well as an exquisite 19th-century woodcarving of *The Last Supper*. There is a collection of sand paintings made from the different coloured sands found on the Isle of Wight.

The manor is home to various exhibitions. In the Fabric and Fashion Accessories Museum visitors can see fine Victorian lace, baby gowns and smocking, while radio buffs can inspect dozens of wireless sets, dating back to the First World War, in the National Wireless Museum. The surrounding Arreton Manor Farm is the setting for a collection of craft studios, housed in former barns.

Easter-end Oct, daily exc Sat. Adm charge. Refreshments. Shop. 🅿 *Toilets. Tel (0983) 528134.*

BARTON MANOR VINEYARD

On A3021, ½ mile south of East Cowes (Cc)

Grapes used to produce English wine are carefully tended in this vineyard in the grounds of Barton Manor, once owned by Queen Victoria. Depending on the season, visitors can watch the harvesting and pressing of the grapes, fermentation or bottling. A 20 acre garden adjoins the vineyard, and springtime visitors walk through woodland among a quarter of a million daffodils. The Scented Secret Garden has a collection of fragrant plants, and a cork tree plantation. The Water Garden was created out of what used to be Queen Victoria's skating rink.

Easter; Apr, weekends; May-mid Oct, daily. Adm charge. Refreshments. Shop. 🅿 *Toilets.* ♿ *Tel (0983) 292835*

BEMBRIDGE MARITIME MUSEUM

Off B3395, in Bembridge (Db)

A deep-sea diving suit designed in 1840 is one of the most solid exhibits in this museum dedicated to sailing craft and salvage from shipwrecks. The suit weighs some 140lb – of which the boots alone weigh 40lb. Photographs show what life was like aboard a 19th-century square rigger, and there are ship models, navigation instruments and models of lifeboats.

Apr-end Sept, daily. Adm charge. Refreshments. Shop. 🅿 *Tel (0983) 872223/872734.*

BLACKGANG CHINE

Off A3055, ½ mile south of Chale (Ca)

A ride on a Wild West stagecoach in a 'cowboy town', an encounter with a 20ft high dinosaur and an expedition through the jungle are among the unusual experiences offered in the Fantasy Theme Park at Blackgang Chine. For younger visitors there is a Fairy Castle, a Gnomes Garden and a Nursery-Land with larger-than-life-size models of nursery rhyme characters. St Catherine's Quay is the re-creation of a 19th-century quay, complete with a Victorian bathing machine. Automated models saw and transport logs at the Blackgang Sawmill, a display telling the story of the use of timber by man.

Early Apr-late Oct, daily. Adm charge. Refreshments. Shop. 🅿 *Toilets.* ♿ *Tel (0983) 730330.*

BRADING ROMAN VILLA

Off A3055, ½ mile south-west of Brading (Cb)

In Roman times this villa on the southern side of Brading Down was the centre of a large, prosperous estate, its living quarters, barn and workshops grouped around a central courtyard.

Excavations have revealed elaborate mosaic floors, some abstract in design, others illustrating myths including Perseus slaying Medusa. A reminder of the villa's agricultural past is provided by a T-shaped oven used in Roman times to dry grain before threshing. In one of the rooms there are traces of an underfloor heating system.

Apr-end Sept, daily. Adm charge. Shop. P *Toilets.* ♿ *Tel (0983) 406223.*

BUTTERFLY WORLD

Off A3054, 1 mile north-east of Newport (Cb)

Around the exotic plants in this indoor garden flit butterflies of more than 90 different species, from places as far apart as India, Peru and Fiji. The bright colours and elaborate patterns of unusual tropical butterflies mingle with those of British species such as the swallowtail and red admiral. The garden's smallest butterfly, the small tortoiseshell, has a 2in wing span, while the largest, the giant owl, is 5½in across.

Good Fri-end Oct, daily. Adm charge. Refreshments. Shop. P *Toilets.* ♿ *Tel (0983) 883430.*

CARISBROOKE CASTLE

Off B3401, 1 mile south-west of Newport (Cb)

The excitement of medieval battle is easy to envisage at this 12th-century castle. The keep, set high on a 58ft mound and reached by 71 steps, must have formed a daunting target for any attacker, while the gatehouse has a row of machicolations or openings in the floor through which missiles could be dropped onto the enemy below, and slits through which bowmen could send volleys of arrows. The castle was also a daunting prison for Charles I, who tried to escape through a window but became wedged between the bars.

In a 16th-century wellhouse visitors can see donkeys working a treadwheel, to raise water from a well, sunk in 1150, which is 161ft deep. The St Nicholas Chapel was built in 1904 on the site of a ruined 12th-century chapel.

EH. All year, daily. Adm charge. Refreshments. Shop. P *Toilets. Tel (0983) 522107.*

FLAMINGO PARK

Off B3330, 1½ miles east of Ryde (Db)

Elegant flamingos, haughty peacocks and ornamental pheasants are among the 100 species of birds seen at this park. There are black-necked swans, cranes, finches, canaries and budgerigars, as well as green-winged macaws and sulphur-crested cockatoos. Birdsong is accompanied by the sound of flowing water, for the park contains several waterfalls. In the largest of these, the water drops 15ft over the lip of rocks forming a graceful half-circle 60ft across. There are fountains and a lake fringed by willows.

Easter-end Oct, daily. Adm charge. Refreshments. Shop. P *Toilets.* ♿ *Tel (0983) 612153.*

GODSHILL MODEL VILLAGE

On A3020, in Godshill (Cb)

The real world is cut down to size to make a fascinating spectacle at Godshill's Model Village, a carefully reproduced miniature version of the village in which it stands. Each model house, complete with thatched roof and tiny flowerbed, took 250 hours to make, and more than 600 hours were spent on the model of the 15th-century All Saints' Church. The small village's imitation of the real one is so authentic that it even contains a model of the model, as well as a model of *that* model, all standing in 1½ acres of the Old Vicarage Garden.

More miniatures are on show in Godshill's Toy Museum. Housed in a 17th-century thatched cottage, the collection includes clockwork toys, dolls with their cats, and a reconstruction of a Victorian toyshop window.

Model Village: Apr-end Sept, daily. Adm charge. Shop. ♿ *Toy Museum: Easter-end Sept, daily. Adm charge. Shop.* P *Toilets.* ♿ *Tel (0983) 840790.*

GODSHILL NATURAL HISTORY CENTRE

On A3020, in Godshill (Cb)

An aquarium with 60 species of tropical fish, including the deadly piranha, is one feature in a museum dedicated to the wonders of nature. There are more than 40,000 seashells from all over the world; the textile cone, Pacific triton, and chambered nautilus are particularly collectable. Phosphorescent minerals, precious and semiprecious stones vie in brilliance with replicas of the Crown Jewels.

HILLTOP PRISON *The formidable stronghold of Carisbrooke Castle once housed an involuntary royal guest: Charles I was imprisoned there for a year in 1647-8, and played bowls in the outer bailey.*

SCALED-DOWN SPORT *Cricketers enact a timeless summer scene on the village green – but visitors must stoop to see them, for they are among the miniature figures in Godshill Model Village.*

More wildlife is on display on the nearby Old Smithy Garden, where aviaries contain parrots, macaws and talking cockatoos.

Natural History Centre: Mar-Nov, daily. Adm charge. Shop. P *Toilets.* ♿ *Tel (0983) 840333. Old Smithy: Mar-Nov, daily. Adm charge. Shop.* P *Toilets.* ♿ *Tel (0983) 840242.*

GOLDEN HILL FORT

Off A3054, 1 mile west of Yarmouth (Bb)

Bygone military days are honoured at a fort which was built between 1863 and 1867 as part of the coastal defence of southern England against a possible invasion by France. Rooms restored and

on view in the two-storey hexagonal building include the commander's offices, the mess and a tap room, cells, a guardroom and a powder store. A Military Museum contains uniforms and weapons used throughout the fort's history, and the fort also houses a bustling craft centre.
All year, daily. Free entry. Refreshments. Shop. P *Toilets.* ♿ *Tel (0983) 753380.*

HASELEY MANOR

Off A3056, 4½ miles south-east of Newport (Cb)

This manor set in a fertile valley has seen many changes since it was built in the 11th century as a royal residence for King Harold. In 1139 Haseley – the name means 'hazel wood' – was turned into a sheep farm under the ownership of the nearby Quarr Abbey, and after the Reformation the estate became a family home. The façade of the house is Georgian, but inside there are Tudor timbers and a 22ft Tudor fireplace. An Adam fireplace and an 18th-century crystal chandelier can be seen in the withdrawing room.
All year, daily. Adm charge. Refreshments. Shop. P *Toilets.* ♿ *Tel (0983) 865420.*

ISLE OF WIGHT STEAM RAILWAY

On A3054, 3 miles east of Newport (Cb)

Traditional wooden railway carriages, some dating from 1864, are one attraction of this old-time railway, which conveys passengers over a section of track used by Queen Victoria on her way to Osborne House. The locomotives, which date from 1876, puff along through 3 miles of woodland and fields. Visitors can watch the engines take on coal and water, and tour, by prior arrangement, the workshops and signal box. A museum displays locomotives and carriages once used on the Isle of Wight.
Easter-end Sept, Sun and Bank Hol; July and Aug, Thur; week before Aug Bank Hol, daily. Adm charge. Refreshments. Shop. P *Toilets.* ♿ *Tel (0983) 882204.*

LILLIPUT ANTIQUE DOLL AND TOY MUSEUM

High Street, Brading (Cb)

Dolls made from materials that range from wax, wood and china to a crab's claw span thousands of years of history in this glimpse of childhood through the centuries. The oldest figure, dating from 2000 BC is in fact not a toy but an Egyptian stone figure found in a tomb, where it was placed in the belief that it would act as the dead person's servant in the next world. There are talking dolls and an Edwardian doll's house family, all dressed in elaborate period costume.
Mid Mar-Christmas, daily. Adm charge. Shop. P ♿ *Tel (0983) 407231.*

MORTON MANOR

Off A3055, ½ mile south of Brading (Cb)

Elizabethan sunken gardens, a rose garden and ornamental ponds surround Morton Manor, a Tudor house with additions dating from 1680 and Victorian times, and filled with Georgian furniture. In the adjoining vineyard seven varieties of grape are grown for use in the winery which visitors can tour, along with a Winemaking Museum containing antique filters and corking machines.
Early Apr-Oct, daily exc Sat. Adm charge. Refreshments. Shop. P *Toilets.* ♿ *Tel (0983) 406168.*

MUSEUM OF CLOCKS

On B3322, 1 mile south-west of Totland (Ab)

Time passes in countless ways in a museum whose exhibits range from a replica of an inclined plane clock of 1600 that rolls slowly down a slope in 24 hours, to an early 20th-century clock run on batteries. Longcase clocks include one of Dutch marquetry with a moving dial showing the moon, day, and dates. A Chinese fire dragon boat clock of 1800 incorporated an unusual timing device: an incense stick was lit at one end and, as it burnt, balls clattered into the metal boat.
Good Fri-end Sept, daily exc Sat. Adm charge. Shop. P ♿ *Tel (0983) 754193.*

MUSEUM OF SMUGGLING HISTORY

On A3055, 1 mile west of Ventnor (Ca)

Smugglers are 'frozen' for all time in their illegal deeds of daring in this museum devoted to smuggling memorabilia. Life-sized models show smugglers taking their punishment, which could range from having a hand cut off to being hanged. The museum illustrates ways in which brandy and tobacco were smuggled in past centuries: for example, contraband balls of tobacco were covered with dirt to resemble potatoes and a barrel was made to fit into a top hat. Other displays bring the history of smuggling up to date by illustrating how ordinary objects, including cigars, crutches and even ice-cream cornets, are used to hide smuggled goods today.
Easter-end Sept, daily. Adm charge. Refreshments. Shop. P *Toilets. Tel (0983) 853677.*

NEEDLES PLEASURE PARK

Off B3322, 1½ miles south-west of Totland (Ab)

Rock formations and multicoloured sands provide the backdrop for this park, with attractions that include a chairlift on which riders are carried 165ft down a cliffside to the beach at Alum Bay. Launches operate from the beach to the jagged chalk pinnacles of the Needles and their lighthouse, in use since 1859. On land, a clifftop walk leads to Needles Old Battery, the remains of a fort built in 1863 and now a museum containing 19th-century guns, magazines and searchlight positions, while a 200ft tunnel leads to splendid views over the Needles.
Pleasure Park: Apr-Oct, daily. Adm charge. Refreshments. Shop. P *Toilets.* ♿ *Tel (0983) 752401. Old Battery. NT: Apr-end Oct, daily exc Fri and Sat; also Fri and Sat in July and Aug. Adm charge. Tel (0983) 754722.*

NEWPORT ROMAN VILLA

Off A3020, ¼ mile south of Newport (Cb)

More than 16 centuries ago Romans enjoyed heated baths at this villa, reconstructed from remains found in 1926. The single-storey villa, made of timber, clay daub and limestone, had a verandah and two projecting wings, one of which was used as the bath wing, or caldarium. There is a hypocaust, or underfloor heating system, surviving from Roman times. Another relic from Roman days is a plunge bath with a lead drainage pipe.
Easter-end Sept, daily exc Sat. Adm charge. Shop. P *Toilets.* ♿ *Tel (0983) 522324.*

NUNWELL HOUSE

Off A3055, ½ mile west of Brading (Cb)

In its mixture of architectural styles, Nunwell shows the development of the English house over the centuries. The Jacobean west wing is connected to the Georgian east wing by a central hall; the curved wall at the north end of the west wing was built by John Nash, the Regency architect, while the tiled brick façade dates from the time of Queen Anne. The rooms are filled with period furniture and paintings.
Late May-late Sept, Sun-Thur pm. Adm charge. Refreshments. Shop. P *Toilets. Tel (0983) 407240.*

OSBORNE HOUSE

Off A3021, ½ mile south-east of East Cowes (Cc)

The seaside retreat to which Queen Victoria retired after the death of Prince Albert, and in which she died in 1901, has the scale of a royal palace but the intimacy of a domestic home. Built in the 1840s and 1850s, the house has a 107ft flag tower, a clock tower, and a loggia extending across the first floor, while the terrace gardens are adorned with fountains and sculptures.

Osborne's intimate character is most evident in the Queen's sitting room. The room, crowded with bric-a-brac and chintz-upholstered furniture, contains Queen Victoria's spinning wheel and a musical-box shaped like a castle.

In Prince Albert's suite, pictures painted by the prince and marble models of the royal children's limbs can be seen, and the prince's umbrella stand remains just as he left it.

In the grounds, the innocent flavour of Victorian childhood lingers on in the Swiss Cottage, built for the Queen's children and grandchildren. The cottage – a miniature Swiss chalet – is filled with child-sized furniture, miniature charcoal ranges and cooking implements.
EH. Apr-end Oct, daily. Adm charge. Refreshments. Shop. P *Toilets. Tel (0983) 200022.*

OSBORN-SMITH'S ANIMAL WORLD

On A3055, in Brading (Cb)

Visitors can stand before the gaping jaws of a lion at this museum displaying animals preserved by the art of the taxidermist. The animals come from all over the world and are snown in re-creations of their natural settings; they include an elephant, a camel, a mongoose and a kangaroo, as well as British coastal birds. A display shows the work of the taxidermist, from the skinning of the animal to mounting or modelling the exhibit.
All year, daily. Adm charge. P ♿ *Tel (0983) 407498.*

OSBORN-SMITH'S WAX MUSEUM

On A3055, in Brading (Cb)

Personalities from the past ranging from Henry VIII to George Bernard Shaw seem to live again at this museum of life-sized wax models. Humble

figures, too, have their place in the museum; for example, a model of a child sweep named Valentine Grey represents all the children who toiled to clean the chimneys of Victorian Britain. A Chamber of Horrors includes re-creations of torture implements, among them a spiked cradle which pierced the victim's body with needle-sharp spikes.
All year, daily. Adm charge. **P** *Toilets. Tel (0983) 407286.*

ROBIN HILL ZOOLOGICAL AND ADVENTURE PARK

Off A3056, 1 mile east of Newport (Cb)

Woodland water gardens, a children's obstacle course, a fort playground and many other amusements have been added to this park since it opened in 1970 as a zoo. Animals, however, are the main attractions. Coyotes, deer, baboons, raccoons and strutting peacocks can all be seen. Parrots and cockatoos perform tricks, including using a telephone, in the Parrot Playschool, and small prairie marmots from the North American plains peep out of the burrows where they live.

Corsican pines line a walk leading to a tree-house and to the water gardens; planted in 1905. Lively red squirrels – rare in most parts of Britain – often leap among the branches.
Mar-Nov, daily. Adm charge. Refreshments. Shop. **P** *Toilets.* ♿ *Tel (0983) 527352.*

SHANKLIN CHINE

Off A3055, in Shanklin (Cb)

Water cutting through sandstone over the last 10,000 years formed this deep and narrow ravine which drops 105ft to the sea, with two waterfalls. At least 150 varieties of wild plants and more than 50 species of mosses and liverworts can be found in the woodland surrounding Shanklin Chine. Ferns, wild garlic, golden saxifrages, fuchsias and heliotrope grow in profusion, and an aviary houses budgerigars and cockatiels.
Mid Apr-mid Oct, daily. Adm charge. Refreshments. Tel (0983) 866432.

VENTNOR BOTANIC GARDEN

On A3055, 1 mile west of Ventnor (Ca)

Palm trees, pomegranates and cypresses flourish in this 22 acre garden, which, being sheltered from north winds by the downs behind it, possesses an almost Mediterranean climate. There are an Asian camphor tree, banana trees, a rare oak from China, and five cashmiriana – Indian trees bearing large white berries. Exotic plants include the Mexican *Beschorneria yuccoides*, its dramatic 6ft spikes bearing green and red flowers, and shrubs from Burma and eucalyptus trees.
All year, daily. Free entry. Refreshments. Shop. **P** *Toilets.* ♿ *Tel (0983) 853254.*

YAFFORD MILL AND FARM PARK

On B3399, ½ mile west of Shorwell (Bb)

The water wheel still turns at this mill, which was used in the 19th century to grind feed for animals and is still in working order today. There is also a collection of farming equipment from bygone days. A path lined with bluebells in season and spanned by footbridges wends along the banks of the Mill Stream, home to moorhens and ducks.
Easter-Oct, daily. Adm charge. Refreshments. Shop. **P** *Toilets.* ♿ *Tel (0983) 740610.*

ROYAL HOME *Tall towers help to give Osborne House (above) the appearance of an Italian villa. The intricate decoration in the Durbar Room (left) includes a plaster peacock over the fireplace. Two brass-edged writing tables (below) were used by Queen Victoria and Prince Albert as they worked on official papers.*

YARMOUTH CASTLE

Off A3054, in Yarmouth (Bb)

Washed on two sides by the sea, this castle was built by Henry VIII in 1545 to defend the coast against French invasion. In 1669 the Captain of the Island, Sir Robert Holmes, had the moat filled and the earthworks demolished to adapt Yarmouth to the defensive needs of a later age. The master gunner's house, built in the late 16th century, contains a baker's brick oven.
EH. Late Mar-Sept, Mon-Sat and Sun pm. Adm charge. Shop. Tel (0983) 760678.

COUNTY CALENDAR

May (late in month). Ventnor: Crab Fair.

June (mid-month). Cowes: Round the Island Race. Bembridge: Digital Schneider Air Trophy Race. Ventnor: Smugglers' Pageant.

July (mid-month). Cowes: Royal Isle of Wight County Show.

August (1st week). Cowes Week; also Admiral's Cup Race (alternate years, from 1989).

August (mid-month). Sandown Bay: Regatta.

August (Bank Hol weekend). Cowes: International Power Boat Race.

Tourist information: Cowes (0983) 291914; Newport (0983) 525450; Ryde (0983) 62905; Sandown (0983) 403886; Shanklin (0983) 862942.

KENT

CASTLES AND GREAT HOUSES IN THE GARDEN OF ENGLAND

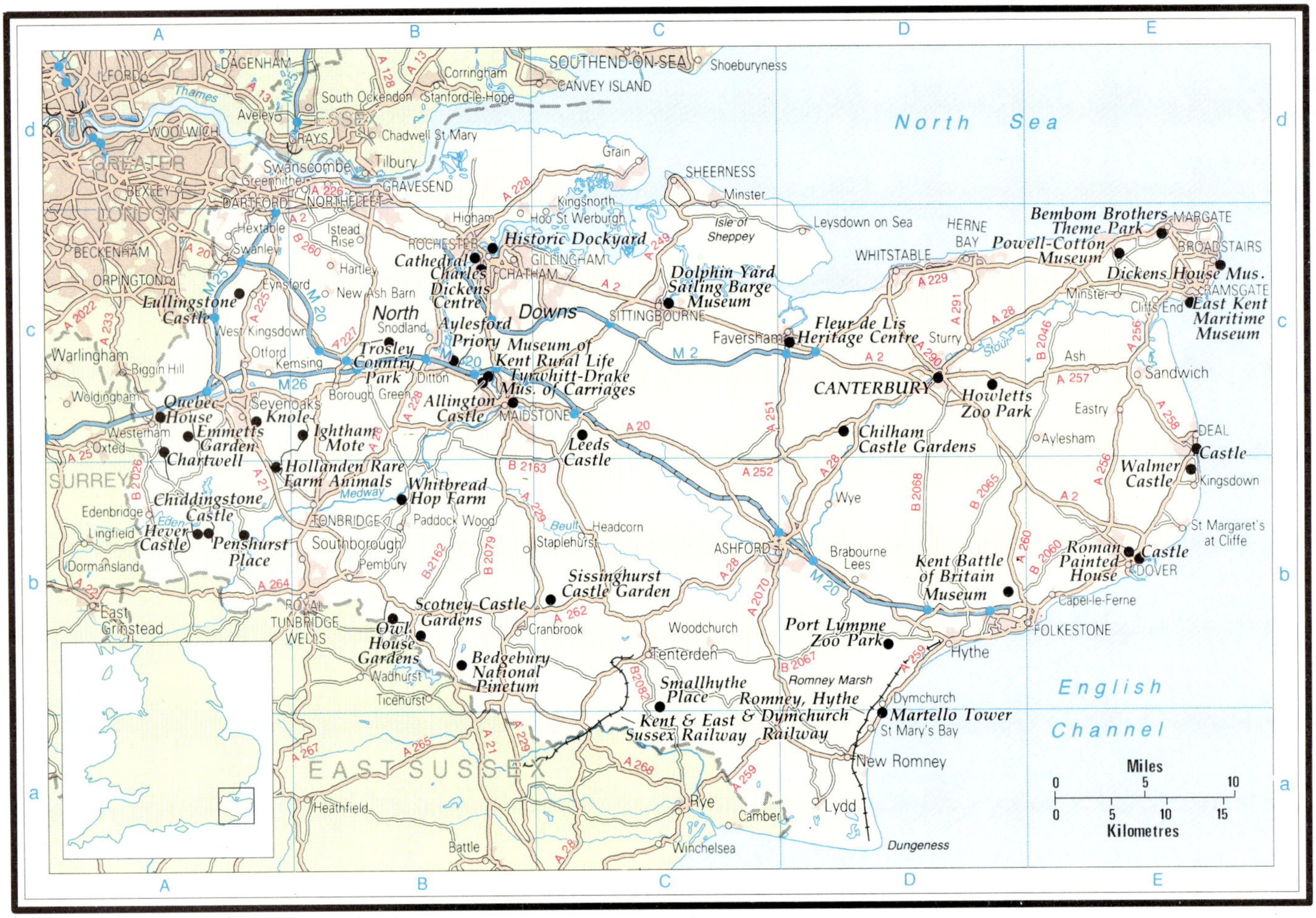

The great castles at Dover, Deal and Walmer were built to guard the invaders' traditional gateway to England. Even earlier, the Romans came this way, and built a lighthouse on Dover's eastern heights to mark their harbour below. St Augustine followed the same route when he landed in AD 597 to establish Canterbury as the 'Mother Church of England', and pilgrims later travelled to Canterbury's shrine of the martyred St Thomas Becket. Kent's second cathedral city, Rochester, keeps alive its association with the writer Charles Dickens, while nearby Chatham has turned its dockyard into a permanent commemoration of Britain's maritime past.

Kent is also the Garden of England, where orchards dot the landscape, a hop farm displays its historic oasts and its Shire horses, and gardens such as Sissinghurst are among England's finest. The county's nearness to London has given it a wealth of country houses including Knole, Penshurst Place and Hever Castle, together with the famous Chartwell, which was the home of Sir Winston Churchill for much of his life.

ALLINGTON CASTLE

Off A20, 2½ miles north of Maidstone (Bc)

Only a few hundred yards from the busy M20, the 13th-century moated castle on the banks of the River Medway still keeps a sense of tranquillity and remoteness from the 20th century. Its squat stone walls are crenellated and pierced with arrow slits, and a massive gatehouse leads to the central courtyard. The building contains fine furniture and works of art. Once owned by Sir Thomas Wyatt, the Tudor poet and diplomat, Allington is now the home of friars of the Carmelite order, who run it as a centre for religious retreats and conferences.

All year, pm daily. Adm charge. Shop. P *Toilets.* ♿ *Tel Maidstone (0622) 54080.*

AYLESFORD PRIORY

Off A20, 3 miles north-west of Maidstone (Bc)

Swans glide beneath the stone walls of this quiet religious retreat by the Medway. The Carmelites founded a priory here in 1242. Dissolved at the Reformation in 1538, it fell into decay, but was reoccupied by the Carmelites in 1949. They have restored the medieval buildings, including the 13th-century Pilgrims' Hall, and built a large open-air shrine capable of holding 5000 pilgrims. Several smaller shrines have been decorated with ceramic panels by the Polish artist Adam Kossowski. The buildings include a pottery.

All year, daily. Free entry. Refreshments. Shop. P *Toilets.* ♿ *Tel Maidstone (0622) 77272.*

BEDGEBURY NATIONAL PINETUM

On B2079, 2½ miles south of Goudhurst (Bb)

Conifers in all their variety grow tall and slender, spread wide branches, or droop towards the ground, their foliage ranging from pale green to dark silvery-blue.

Some of the trees, such as the giant Wellingtonias planted in 1870, date from the time when Bedgebury was a private estate. But most have been planted since 1924, when the pinetum was founded as a joint venture by the Forestry Commission and the Royal Botanic Gardens at Kew. Many rare specimen trees were lost in the storm of October 1987. Among the survivors, swamp cypresses from America flourish in the waterlogged soil of a small lake – originally a hammer-pond that provided waterpower for ironworking. There is a waymarked route for visitors.

FC. All year, daily. Adm charge. Shop. P *Toilets.* ♿ *Tel Goudhurst (0580) 211044.*

BEMBOM BROTHERS THEME PARK

Marine Terrace, Margate (Ec)

A stone's throw from the sunbathers on Margate beach, parents and their children crowd aboard the stomach-churning Looping Star, experience astronauts' G-forces in the spaceship 'Enterprise', and survey the coast from the top of Britain's tallest Big Wheel. The Bembom Brothers Theme Park understandably describes the thrill of its rides as 'white knuckle'.

Among Margate's quieter indoor attractions, the most unusual is the Shell Temple, in Grotto Hill, also known as the Grotto. Discovered in 1835 by schoolboys digging in a field, it consists of a network of passages and rooms hollowed out of the chalk, and covered with seashell decoration. The fanciful designs of stars, figures and abstract motifs probably date from the 18th century.

Exhibits at the restored Tudor House in King Street cover the human occupation of Thanet to the end of the Tudor period. The extensive caves in Northdown Road were hacked out of the chalk more than 1000 years ago and used by smugglers in the 18th century.

Park: End May-mid Sept, daily. Adm charge. Refreshments. Shop. Toilets. ♿ Tel Thanet (0843) 227011. Grotto: Apr-Oct, Sat am and Mon-Fri; also Sun in high season. Adm charge. Shop. P Toilets. Tel (0843) 220008. Tudor House: May-Sept, Tues-Sat. Adm charge. Shop. Tel (0843) 225511. Caves: Apr-Sept, daily. Adm charge. Refreshments. Shop. P (limited). Tel (0843) 220139.

CHARLES DICKENS CENTRE

High Street, Rochester (Bc)

Every May the people of Rochester put on Dickensian costume and hold street entertainments, processions, readings and other events based on the novelist's life and creations. Many of Rochester's fine old buildings are described in his novels and feature in a 'Dickens Trail' through the city. The Elizabethan Eastgate House, in the High Street, is the home of the Charles Dickens Centre, where the rooms have been laid out in a series of tableaux illustrating scenes from the lives of Little Nell, Oliver Twist, Fagin and other Dickens characters. In the grounds of Eastgate House is the chalet where Dickens wrote many of his books. It was moved here from Gads Hill, outside Rochester, where he lived for the last 14 years of his life.

At the other end of the High Street, the magnificent 17th-century Guildhall is the city's main museum. Its exhibits include the splendid civic plate and regalia of Rochester, Chatham and Strood, Bronze Age and Anglo-Saxon relics, model ships and Victorian dolls and toys.

Dickens Centre: All year, daily. Adm charge. Shop. Tel Medway (0634) 44176. Guildhall Museum: All year, daily. Free entry. Shop. Tel (0634) 48717.

CHARTWELL

Off B2026, 2 miles south of Westerham (Ac)

Soldier, statesman, artist, author, bricklayer, garden-planner – all these aspects of Sir Winston Churchill's wide-ranging genius are revealed at Chartwell, his country home from 1924 until his death in 1965. Built on a south-facing slope with magnificent views across the Kentish Weald, it is an unpretentious house largely remodelled for Sir Winston by the architect Philip Tilden.

When Churchill bought it, he was in the political wilderness, and he spent much of his time in retirement at Chartwell until he was recalled to lead the country during the Second World War. It still has very much the feeling of a family home, with everyday objects lying around. Upstairs some of the bedrooms have been converted to display his various uniforms and his famous wartime 'siren suit', photographs and gifts from foreign heads of state.

Outside is the long wall Churchill built round the kitchen garden during the 1920s and 1930s, and the rose garden planted with golden roses to mark the Churchills' golden wedding in 1958.

NT. Apr-Oct, Tues, Wed and Thur pm, and Sat, Sun and Bank Hol Mon (closed Tues after Bank Hol Mon and Good Fri); Mar and Nov, Sat, Sun and Wed. Adm charge. Refreshments. Shop. P Toilets. ♿ Tel Edenbridge (0732) 866368.

CHATHAM HISTORIC DOCKYARD

Dock Road (A231), north of town centre (Bc)

For more than 400 years a muddy stretch of riverbank near the mouth of the Medway was one of the powerhouses of the Royal Navy. The great days of British naval supremacy can be relived at Chatham Historic Dockyard, where vessels from the tubby wooden warships of Henry VIII's time to today's nuclear submarines have been built and serviced. By far the finest example of a royal dockyard from the age of sail, it has many surviving buildings, among them the vast Ropery, more than 1140ft long, and covered slipways where 'wooden walls' (ships) were built; they included Nelson's *Victory*.

Approached through the imposing Main Gate built in 1719, the dockyard includes a visitor centre in the old Galvanising Shop, where the story of Chatham as a naval base, from its beginnings in the 16th century to its final closure in 1984, is told by video, film, models, displays and maps. A museum in what was once the Lead and Paint Mill has dockyard relics, and visitors may watch the traditional art of rope-making, which has been revived in the original Ropery.

A few hundred yards away in Dock Road, the Medway Heritage Centre tells the story of the river from prehistoric to modern times, from the mud flats and sandbanks at its mouth upstream as far as Allington. Opposite the centre a short road leads up to Fort Amherst, part of the Great Lines built to protect the dockyard peninsula in Georgian times. Begun in 1756, the 14 acre fort's bastions, redoubts and tunnels are being restored to form a military complement to the dockyard.

Dockyard: Apr-Oct, Wed-Sun; Nov-Mar, Wed, Sat and Sun. Adm charge. Refreshments. Shop. P Toilets. ♿ Tel Medway (0634) 812551. Heritage Centre: Easter-Oct, Wed-Sat; winter, Wed; also Sun pm all year. Adm charge. Shop. P (at fort). Toilets. Tel (0634) 407116 or 408437. Fort: Apr-Oct, Wed, Sat and Sun pm; school hols, pm daily; Nov-Mar, Sun pm. Adm charge. Refreshments. Shop. P Toilets. Tel (0634) 47747.

CHIDDINGSTONE CASTLE

Off B2027, 3 miles east of Edenbridge (Ab)

This battlemented, mock-baronial country house now stands aloof from the picturesque National Trust village of Chiddingstone, though it once formed part of it. The first house on the site was built by the Streatfeild family of ironmasters in Tudor times. In the 1680s this was pulled down and a Charles II mansion was built in its place. Around 1800, Henry Streatfeild encased this in a Gothic Revival exterior, diverted the High Street round his property, and dug an artificial lake.

Apart from its external trimmings, the castle is still basically 17th century. From 1955 to 1977 it was owned by the art connoisseur Denys Eyre Bower, who filled it with *(continued on page 178)*

DARLING CLEMENTINE *Family photographs, including one of his adored wife Clementine Hozier (back, right) crowd Sir Winston Churchill's desk at Chartwell. It was at this desk that Churchill wrote his* History of the English Speaking Peoples.

A TALE OF CANTERBURY

Eight centuries after the first pilgrims made their way to Canterbury, the city attracts visitors from all over the world. They may come to pray in the cathedral that is the mother of the Anglican Church, marvelling at its superb stained glass, or merely to wander in the city that grew around it.

Within its massive medieval walls, Canterbury is a bustling modern city which never forgets its colourful and historic past. This can be relived in the Canterbury Heritage museum or in the vivid new Pilgrims Way experience. It can also be savoured in the medieval Old Weavers House, in the Roman ruins or among the crumbling remains of St Augustine's Abbey, on the site where English Christianity began in AD 597.

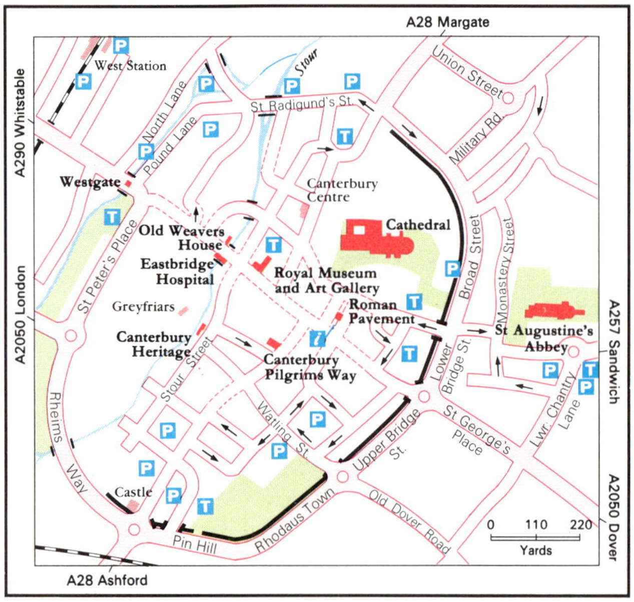

Canterbury Cathedral *All year, daily. Free entry. Shop. Toilets. ♿ Tel Canterbury (0227) 762862.*

Canterbury Pilgrims Way *All year, daily. Adm charge. Shop. Toilets. ♿ Tel (0227) 454888.*

Eastbridge Hospital *All year, daily. Free entry. Tel (0227) 451767.*

Old Weavers House *All year, Mon-Sat. Free entry. Shop. Refreshments. Toilets. River tours, Easter-Oct. Tel (0227) 462329.*

Canterbury Heritage *All year, Mon-Sat. Adm charge. Shop. ♿ Tel (0227) 452747.*

St Augustine's Abbey *EH. All year, daily exc Sun am. Adm charge. ♿ Tel (0227) 67345.*

Roman Pavement *All year, Mon-Sat; pm only in winter. Adm charge. Shop. Tel (0227) 452747.*

Westgate *All year, Mon-Sat; pm only in winter. Adm charge. Shop. Tel (0227) 452747.*

Royal Museum and Art Gallery *All year, Mon-Sat. Free entry. Shop. P Tel (0227) 452747.*

CANTERBURY CATHEDRAL

The magnificent brass effigy of the Black Prince – Edward, Prince of Wales – lies in the cathedral's Trinity Chapel (right). The prince, who died in 1376, was an admirer of Thomas Becket, who was brutally murdered in the cathedral in 1170. Becket, Archbishop of Canterbury during the reign of Henry II, was cut down by four of the king's knights after defying the king's efforts to control the power of the Church. The scene of Becket's murder in the north-west transept is marked by a modern metal sculpture (below), dedicated in 1986.

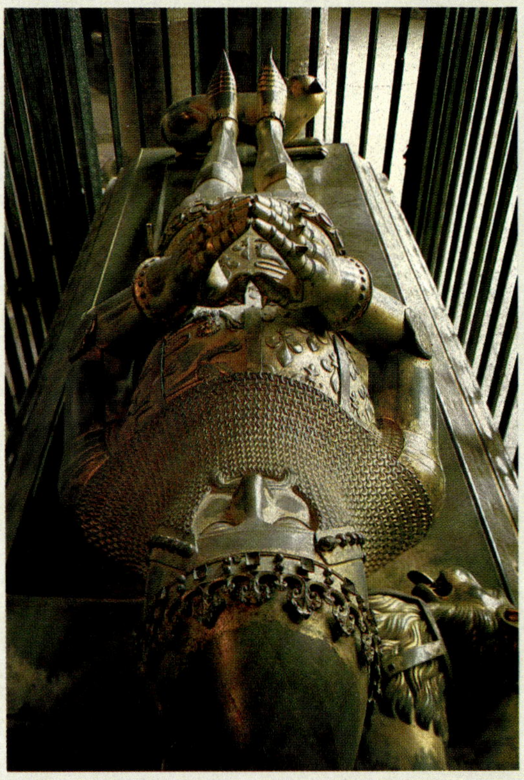

OLD WEAVERS HOUSE

Rising sheer from the River Stour, the house dates from the late 15th century and takes its name from the Protestant weavers who settled in the city to escape religious persecution on the Continent. Their raw materials were brought up river by barge, and the tiny jetty where they moored is still in use as a departure point for river tours. The house is now a shop selling handicrafts and knitwear. Jutting over the river is the ducking stool, which was used in medieval times to punish scolding wives.

CANTERBURY PILGRIMS WAY

After Becket's murder, Canterbury became a place of pilgrimage; the poet Geoffrey Chaucer, in his *Canterbury Tales* of 1380, described a typical pilgrims' journey. Visitors to the Canterbury Pilgrims Way travel with Chaucer's characters, including the Wife of Bath (left), past tableaux and audiovisual interpretations of their tales.

EASTBRIDGE HOSPITAL

Though inhospitable-looking by today's standards, the Eastbridge Hospital was a welcome refuge for poor pilgrims for 400 years. Built about 1175 as the Hospital of St Thomas (Becket) the Martyr, it consists of a chapel, a refectory, and a crypt or undercroft in which the pilgrims slept. A large mural in the refectory shows Christ giving his blessing.

CANTERBURY HERITAGE

A model of a Huguenot silk weaver at her loom (below) is one of the many models that bring the city's history to life in the Canterbury Heritage museum. The models and other displays show Canterbury from Roman times until the Second World War, when one-third of the city was destroyed by German bombs. The museum is in the 14th-century Poor Priests' Hospital, built to house retired clergy.

ST AUGUSTINE'S ABBEY

From the abbey he founded in 598, the ruins of which can still be seen, St Augustine and his followers spread the Gospel. Augustine came to Britain from Rome in 597, and his first convert to Christianity was King Ethelbert of Kent. The Norman abbey church and the abbey were destroyed at the Dissolution in 1538.

ROMAN PAVEMENT

In Roman times, Canterbury was the city of Durovernum Cantiacorum, and excavations have revealed many artefacts of the time which are now displayed in the Canterbury Heritage museum. In Butchery Lane, however, still lies this superb mosaic pavement, part of a large courtyard house built around AD 100.

THE BUFFS MUSEUM

The Museum of The Buffs, part of the Royal Museum, contains uniforms, weapons and medals of the regiment which was nicknamed after the colour of its uniform. Raised in 1572 it officially became The Buffs, East Kent Regiment in 1881, as the belt buckle shows.

THE WESTGATE

The imposing Westgate was built in 1380 by Archbishop Sudbury, at the time of the first stirrings of unrest that led to the Peasants' Revolt a year later. Until 1829 it was used as the city jail. Now a museum, its walls are hung with leg-irons and other grisly relics. There is a fine view of the city from the roof.

ROYAL MUSEUM AND ART GALLERY

The view of Canterbury as seen by John Pardon in 1819 has changed – but the cathedral's dominance endures. Founded by St Augustine, the cathedral has been enhanced down the centuries; its crowning glory is the soaring Bell Harry Tower completed about 1504. The painting is one of many fine works in the Royal Museum and Art Gallery, which also has displays of local archaeology and natural history.

(continued from page 175) his superb collections of Japanese works of art, and relics of the Stuarts and the Jacobites.

May-Sept, Wed-Sat pm, also Tues pm mid June-mid Sept, and Sat, Sun and Bank Hol Apr and Oct. Adm charge. Refreshments. Shop. P *Toilets.* ♿ *Tel Penshurst (0892) 870347.*

CHILHAM CASTLE GARDENS

On A252, 6 miles south-west of Canterbury (Dc)

Below the Jacobean gables and tall chimneys of Chilham Castle, terraced lawns and flower-filled borders fall away towards the peaceful valley of the Stour. Laid out by the famous 17th-century botanist John Tradescant, Chilham's gardens include an evergreen oak planted when the house was built, and mulberries thought to be 500 years old. On summer weekends the Middle Ages live again in mock tournaments by the Jousting Association of Great Britain, which has its home at the castle.

Apr-Oct, daily. Adm charge. Shop. P *Toilets. Tel Canterbury (0227) 730319.*

DEAL CASTLE

On the seafront (A258), south of town centre (Ec)

Within sight and sound of the waves breaking on Deal's shingle beach, this small castle is a reminder of an invasion scare four and a half centuries ago. In the late 1530s the Pope preached a Crusade against Henry VIII because of his divorce from Catherine of Aragon and his defiance of papal authority; Henry's response was to build a chain of coastal castles, of which Deal is the finest and best-preserved.

The castle is shaped like a six-petalled Tudor rose, with no right angles anywhere – a better shape for deflecting cannonballs than the typical square medieval castle. It was garrisoned by a Captain, answerable to the Lord Warden of the Cinque Ports, and about 20 soldiers or gunners. The Pope's threatened invasion did not take place, and so the castle was never put to the test, though it changed hands twice in the Civil War.

A short way along the seafront towards the pier is a fascinating relic of pre-radio days, when accurate time signals could be given only by visual means. In the 19th century the ships anchored in The Downs – the natural anchorage off Deal – used to get the correct time from the 'time-ball' on top of the square, four-storey Time-ball Tower. Sharp at 1pm each day, the large black-painted metal ball, installed in 1854, would drop down a mast on top of the tower. In 1985 the tower rooms were made into a museum of maritime communications, from signal fires to satellites. The time-ball still falls at 1pm.

The Museum of Maritime and Local History in St George's Road includes cannons, figureheads, paintings and examples of the sturdy 'beach boats' used to carry passengers ashore from ships anchored in The Downs.

Castle: EH. All year, daily exc Sun am. Adm charge. Toilets. Tel Deal (0304) 372762. Tower: Spring Bank Hol-Sept, Tues-Sun and Bank Hol. Adm charge. Shop. Tel (0304) 360897 or 201066. Maritime Museum: Spring Bank Hol-Sept, pm daily. Adm charge. Toilets. Tel (0304) 362896.

DURABLE DEFENDER *Square cut and uncompromising, for 800 years Dover Castle guarded the English Channel at its narrowest point. Begun in the 12th century, it was continuously garrisoned until 1956.*

DICKENS HOUSE MUSEUM

Victoria Parade, Broadstairs (Ec)

Summer visits which the novelist Charles Dickens used to pay to the sands of Viking Bay are recalled in a charming double-fronted house overlooking the bay. This is now a small museum, containing many of the novelist's letters and personal possessions, together with costumes and other Victoriana. In Dickens's day the house was owned by Miss Mary Strong, model for the character of Betsey Trotwood in *David Copperfield*. The parlour has been refurnished in Dickensian style.

Apr-Oct, daily. Adm charge. Shop. Tel Thanet (0843) 62853.

DOLPHIN YARD SAILING BARGE MUSEUM

Off Crown Quay Road, Sittingbourne (Cc)

Between Sittingbourne and The Swale (the channel separating mainland Kent from the Isle of Sheppey), the muddy waters of Milton Creek flow sluggishly through a landscape of factories and reed-filled inlets. For centuries the creek was an important waterway, reaching its heyday in the late 19th century when it was crowded with red-sailed Thames spritsail barges, carrying the products of the Sittingbourne brickfields down to the Thames and beyond. Many of the barges were actually built on Milton Creek, and since 1970 the Dolphin Yard – the only such yard to survive out of a total of 11 – has housed a museum devoted to the old barges. Alongside the yard, several vessels lie at anchor. The former sail loft is now a museum, with models, photographs and shipwrights' tools.

The Sittingbourne and Kemsley Light Railway was built to service Sittingbourne's other major industry, papermaking, which is still carried on there. Built in 1906 to a gauge of 2ft 6in, the line originally ran for 4 miles from its own station to a dockyard on The Swale. Leaving the suburbs by way of a viaduct, it runs through orchards and farmland, and now sets its passengers down after 2 miles at Kemsley Down Station at the giant Kemsley Papermill.

Barge Museum: Easter-mid Oct, Sun and Bank Hol. Adm charge. Refreshments. Shop. P *Toilets. Tel Maidstone (0622) 62531. Railway: Trains Easter-mid Oct, Sun and Bank Hol; also Sat late July and Aug, and Wed in Aug. Refreshments. Shop.* P *(limited). Toilets. Tel Medway (0634) 32320.*

DOVER CASTLE

Castle Hill Road, Dover (Eb)

The looming bulk of Dover Castle dominates the town from the Eastern Heights above the harbour. The massive keep, outer curtain wall and inner bailey were built mainly by Henry II in the 1180s, as the key to England's gateway. Inside, the keep consists of two enormous main storeys, with a basement below. On its walls hang pikes, muskets and other relics of bygone warfare, while down below is a scale model of the Battle of Waterloo. An exhibition 'All the Queen's Men' tells the story of the Queen's Regiment, in a series of lifelike tableaux illustrating campaigns from the Crimean War, through both World Wars, to present-day operations.

On a grassy mound inside the outer curtain wall are two buildings that were already old when the castle was built. The Church of St Mary-in-Castro was restored in the 19th century and has a Victorian look, but possibly goes back to Roman times. A stumpy octagonal tower some 40ft high formed the lower half of a lofty Roman lighthouse or pharos, built about AD 45.

EH. All year, daily. Adm charge. Refreshments. Shop. P *Toilets.* ♿ *Tel Dover (0304) 201628.*

DYMCHURCH MARTELLO TOWER

On seafront at Dymchurch (Da)

During the Napoleonic invasion scare of the early 1800s, more than a hundred of these chunky little fortresses were built to guard England's south and east coasts. At Dymchurch, one of the main towns of Romney Marsh, Tower No 24 has been restored as a museum showing the preparations to repel an invasion that never happened.

Martello towers – named after a similar tower at Mortella in Corsica – had a storage basement with a magazine for gunpowder within the 13ft thick walls, a first floor where the 24 men and their officers lived, and a gun platform, mounted with a powerful 24-pounder muzzle-loader, which had a range of more than a mile. Nelson's victory at Trafalgar in 1805 made them redundant before they were completed.

EH. Apr-Sept, daily exc Sun am. Adm charge. Tel Dymchurch (0303) 873684.

EAST KENT MARITIME MUSEUM

Royal Harbour, Ramsgate (Ec)

In dignified contrast to the small boats scudding in and out of Ramsgate's marina, the stone classical bulk of the Clock House stands squarely at the eastern end of the harbour. It was completed in 1817, and for almost 30 years, until Greenwich took over the role of timekeeper to the nation in 1848, South-coast sailors set their chronometers by 'Ramsgate Mean Time'. In the Clock Room on the upper floor a north-south meridian line was used to observe the sun's transit, and the Ramsgate clock was adjusted accordingly.

The Clock House was restored and opened as a maritime museum in 1984. The exhibits include navigational instruments from 1700 onwards, lifeboat models and objects from wrecks.

On the Westcliff Promenade to the west of the harbour, land transport is commemorated in Ramsgate Motor Museum. Ranging from the Ford Model T to the Sinclair C5, exhibits include bicycles and even a child's pedal car.

Maritime Museum: Apr-Sept, Tues-Fri; also Sat and Sun pm; Oct-Mar, Tues and Thur. Adm charge. Shop. P *(limited). Tel Thanet (0843) 587765. Motor Museum: Easter-mid Nov, daily; also winter weekends. Adm charge. Shop. Toilets. Tel (0843) 581948.*

EMMETTS GARDEN

On B2042, 3 miles south-west of Sevenoaks (Ac)

The mighty 100ft Wellingtonia which towers over this fascinating 5 acre National Trust garden has the loftiest treetop (though it is not the tallest tree) in the whole of Kent. The garden is planted on the highest point in Kent, some 700ft above sea level, and on a clear day the Wellingtonia is visible from Crowborough Beacon, 12 miles away. Emmetts is a garden of tree shapes, where low-spreading or rounded specimens contrast with tall columnar forms. In autumn the varied foliage gives spectacular displays of colour. The rock garden is being restored, but Emmetts' bluebell wood was severely damaged in the great storm of October 1987.

NT. Apr-Oct, Sun, Tues-Fri and Bank Hol pm. Adm charge. P *Toilets.* ♿ *Tel Lamberhurst (0892) 890651.*

FLEUR DE LIS HERITAGE CENTRE

Preston Street, Faversham (Dc)

With its wide streets of ancient buildings, beautifully maintained, Faversham is one of the gems of north Kent. Its history and civic pride is revealed in the Fleur de Lis Heritage Centre opened in 1977 in a restored 15th-century inn. The centre uses audiovisual presentation, artwork, photographs and museum material to give a vivid picture of life in Faversham down the centuries, from its schools and domestic buildings, to its fire service and industries.

All year, daily exc Thur, Sun and Bank Hol. Adm charge. Shop. Tel Faversham (0795) 534542.

HEVER CASTLE

Off B2026, 3 miles south-east of Edenbridge (Ab)

The sad ghost of Anne Boleyn must surely haunt Hever Castle, where she spent her childhood and was wooed by Henry VIII. Hever is like a perfect child's drawing of a castle, approached by a drawbridge across a neatly squared-off moat, then under a portcullis into an entrance courtyard. It was built and fortified by the De Hever family about 1300, and came into the hands of the Bullen (or Boleyn) family about 1460.

Anne Boleyn's 'Thousand Days' of marriage to Henry, which ended with her execution in 1536, were largely engineered by her ambitious father, Sir Thomas Bullen. He greatly enlarged the original castle, and encouraged Henry in his attentions to Anne.

After centuries of decay, Hever Castle was bought in 1903 by the American millionaire William Waldorf Astor. He refurbished the interior of the castle, filled it with fine furniture and works of art, and added a 'Tudor Village' for his weekend guests. His greatest achievement was the creation of the landscaped gardens, which involved diverting the River Eden and digging a 35 acre artificial lake. Especially fine is the Italian Garden, full of statues from Roman times to the Renaissance. In 1983 the Astor family sold Hever to a property company, which has turned the Tudor Village into a conference centre, while keeping the castle, gardens and maze open to the public.

Apr-Oct, daily. Adm charge. Refreshments. Shop. P *Toilets.* ♿ *Tel Edenbridge (0732) 865224.*

HOLLANDEN RARE FARM ANIMALS

Off B245, 4½ miles south-east of Sevenoaks (Ab)

Sheep of a breed said to have swum ashore to England from the battered galleons of the Spanish Armada are among the rare farm animals on view at Great Hollanden Farm, set in peaceful countryside in the heart of the Kentish Weald. This breed, the Portland, has superb spirally

TRAGIC QUEEN *A portrait of Anne Boleyn, Henry VIII's second wife, and the prayer book she carried to her execution in 1536 are displayed in her room at Hever Castle, the Boleyns' family home. The 100ft Long Gallery (below) contains a lifelike reconstruction of a visit by the king to see Anne at Hever.*

curved horns and was well established in Britain for several centuries, though it is not found on farms today. Hollanden's other sheep include a four-horned breed from the Isle of Man. Rare varieties of cattle, pigs and ponies have also been established, and there is a display of ancient farming equipment.
May-Oct, daily. Adm charge. Refreshments. Shop. P *Toilets.* ♿ *Tel Hildenborough (0732) 832273.*

HOWLETTS ZOO PARK

Off A257, 5 miles east of Canterbury (Dc)

Howletts is a beautiful 18th-century house with a fine entrance portico, but it is the animals in the park that visitors come to see. After building up a collection of animals from all over the world, John Aspinall opened his Zoo Park in 1975 with the purpose not only of displaying rare animals in ideal conditions, but also of breeding them. Nearly 50 species roam Howletts' ancient parkland, among them the dhole (Asiatic wild dog), the bongo (a shy and elusive striped antelope), and the Calamian deer from the Philippines.
All year, daily. Adm charge. Refreshments. Shop. P *Toilets.* ♿ *Tel Canterbury (0227) 721286.*

IGHTHAM MOTE

Off A227, 6 miles north of Tonbridge (Bc)

A few miles south of the picture-postcard village of Ightham, a narrow lane opens suddenly onto the romantic vista of a moated manor house tucked away in a hollow on the hillside. Though it does indeed have a moat, the house's name probably derives from the Saxon *moot*, or 'place of assembly'.

Built in a mixture of architectural styles, Ightham has weathered the centuries to form a harmonious blend of half-timbering, mellow brickwork and stone. At its heart is a small courtyard, dominated by the windows of the lofty Great Hall, built about 1340.
NT. Apr-Oct, daily exc Tues and Sat. Adm charge. Shop. P *Toilets. Tel Plaxtol (0732) 810378.*

KENT AND EAST SUSSEX RAILWAY

Off High Street, Tenterden (Cb)

For more than half a century this delightful little single-track railway carried passengers and freight along the Rother valley and through the hop-gardens and orchards of Kent. In late summer the trains were packed with hop-pickers down from the East End on their annual working holiday, enjoying the sight of sheep-filled water meadows and the gentle, green hills rising behind them.

After the Second World War the line became uneconomic and was closed to passenger services in 1954, when much of the track was pulled up. Since the 1960s a group of enthusiasts have restored 5 miles of the line between Tenterden and Hexden Bridge, and there are regular summer services, the return trip from Tenterden taking nearly an hour. The locomotives are kept at Rolvenden.
Trains: Easter-New Year, Sat and Sun; also Tues, Wed and Thur in June and July, and daily in Aug. Adm charge. Refreshments. Shop. P *Toilets.* ♿ *Tel Tenterden (058 06) 2943.*

PILLARED STAIRS *The richly decorated Great Staircase leading to the state rooms at Knole was built around 1606. The plaster figure below it depicts Gianetta Baccelli, the mistress of an 18th-century owner.*

KENT BATTLE OF BRITAIN MUSEUM

On A260, 2½ miles north of Folkestone (Db)

From August to October 1940, Hawkinge was the front line of defence in the Battle of Britain, as it was the RAF fighter station nearest to occupied France. The planes of the Luftwaffe were only a few minutes' flying time away, and it was within range of cross-Channel German artillery.

After falling derelict, Hawkinge has taken on a new lease of life with the opening of an RAF museum in its disused control tower and other buildings. The centrepiece of the collection is Britain's largest assembly of recovered remains of aircraft, both British and German, that took part in the epic struggle.

Together with the fragments of Hurricanes, Spitfires and Messerschmitts, the museum displays the equipment and uniforms worn by both sides. There are also aircraft built for the film *Battle of Britain*. The story of war in the air is taken back in time with displays of Zeppelin and aircraft items from the First World War.
Easter-Oct, daily. Adm charge. Shop. P *Toilets.* ♿ *Tel Hawkinge (030 389) 3140.*

KNOLE

On A225, in Sevenoaks (Ac)

Reached across rolling parkland, and set among the tree-clad 'knolls' or hillocks which give it its name, Knole is one of the most mysteriously fascinating houses in the south of England. It is fancifully linked to the passage of time by having 365 rooms, seven courtyards, 52 staircases and 12 entrances.

Knole was mainly built in the mid-15th century by Thomas Bourchier, Archbishop of Canterbury, as a country palace for himself and successive archbishops. The covetous Henry VIII acquired it from Archbishop Cranmer in 1538 simply by saying he liked it. In 1566 Queen Elizabeth gave Knole to the Sackville family, whose portraits, painted by Reynolds and other artists, hang on the walls. The furniture includes the first of the famous Knole drop-end settees, made in the time of James I, while the chairs in the Brown Gallery still have their 17th-century brocade upholstery. Rarest of all the furnishings are the silver-decorated mirror, table and candlesticks in the King's Room.
NT. Apr-Oct, Wed-Sat and Bank Hol; also Sun pm. Adm charge. Shop. P *Toilets. Tel Sevenoaks (0732) 450608.*

LEEDS CASTLE

On B2163, 4½ miles south-east of Maidstone (Cc)

Black swans glide serenely across the lake that mirrors Leeds Castle's mellow stone walls, in a romantic setting of water, trees and gently rolling parkland. For more than 300 years the castle was the favourite country retreat of the medieval queens of England, escaping to its peaceful serenity from the bustle of court.

Standing on two islands in a lake fed by the River Len, Leeds was first fortified by a Saxon called Leed or Ledian, who built a wooden castle on the site. In 1119 a Norman knight, Robert de Crevecour, rebuilt it in stone, and traces of his castle survive in the form of a vaulted cellar. Its royal connection began in 1278, when it was given to Edward I and Queen Eleanor of Castile. Edward greatly enlarged its defences, building the outer curtain wall and strengthening the gate-tower. Henry VIII turned Leeds from a castle into a palace, and after 1552 it passed from royalty to a succession of families, who altered it down the years. In 1822, the main building was completely rebuilt in its present four-square medieval style, and in 1976 Lady Olive Baillie, its last personal owner, gave Leeds to the nation as a conference centre.

Leeds Castle is as magnificent inside as it is externally. Typical of its splendour is the Henry VIII Banqueting Hall, 75ft long, with carved oak ceiling, a massive 16th-century stone fireplace, and superb tapestries including one portraying the Adoration of the Magi. The Middle Ages have been re-created in two rooms known as Les Chambres de la Reine, which are now as they would have been in the 1420s, in the time of Henry V and his queen, Catherine of Valois.

Inside the gatehouse is a unique collection of dog-collars, ranging back over 400 years and made of silver, brass and leather. In the grounds are aviaries with parakeets and many other exotic birds, a garden planted with flowers and herbs, a maze, a grotto and a vineyard.
Apr-Oct, daily; Nov-Mar, Sat and Sun. Adm charge. Refreshments. Shop. P *Toilets.* ♿ *Tel Maidstone (0622) 65400.*

LULLINGSTONE CASTLE

On A225, 5 miles north of Sevenoaks (Ac)

A sturdy brick Tudor gatehouse leads to the spacious mansion of Lullingstone Castle, set in wide lawns beside the sparkling River Darent.

Though it looks from the outside like a dignified Queen Anne country seat, the façade hides a Tudor house, built about 1500 by Sir John Peche. A trusted adviser of Henry VIII, Sir John was a noted jouster at tournaments, and not far from the gatehouse is the grassy jousting ground where he kept himself in training.

Internally the house was largely remodelled in the early 18th century, when a new staircase was built for a visit from Queen Anne, with the treads made shallow so that the overweight queen could climb them without difficulty.

Off A225, half a mile north of the castle, the remains of a superb Roman villa reveal the extent of domestic luxury in the Darent valley 1800 years ago. Probably rebuilt as a country retreat by a government official in the 2nd century AD, the villa has the usual baths and underfloor heating system, and two fine mosaics, depicting scenes from classical mythology. What is unusual is the evidence of early Christian worship.

Castle: Apr-Oct, Sat, Sun and Bank Hol pm. Adm charge. Refreshments. Shop. P *Toilets. Tel Farningham (0322) 862114. Villa: EH. All year, daily exc Sun am Oct-Mar. Adm charge.* P *Toilets.* ♿ *Tel (0322) 863467.*

MUSEUM OF KENT RURAL LIFE

Off A229, 2 miles north of Maidstone (Bc)

Between the roaring traffic of the M20 and the placid waters of the Medway, a cluster of oast-houses and other traditional farm buildings have been turned into a living reminder of Kent's country past. Set amid farmland, the museum includes comprehensive displays of farm tools and machinery, and exhibitions on the people of rural Kent. The land is being planted with crops such as hops and is used for grazing a variety of livestock. There are beehives and a herb garden.

Apr-Oct, Mon, Tues, Thur, Fri; also Sat and Sun pm. Refreshments. Shop. P *Toilets.* ♿ *Tel Maidstone (0622) 63936.*

OWL HOUSE GARDENS

Off A21, 7 miles east of Royal Tunbridge Wells (Bb)

From the daffodils of spring to the glowing maple foliage of late autumn, the Owl House Gardens provide constant changes and contrasts of colour. Spreading lawns, woodland walks and sunken water gardens form the setting for the small tile-hung Kentish house (not open to the public), which gets its name from the 'owlers' – wool smugglers who would warn one another of the approach of excisemen by hooting.

The Heaver Model Museum (at Forstal Farm, on A262, just north-east of Lamberhurst) is a collection of model scenes and dioramas housed in a Kentish oast complex. There is also a model fairground, a craft village and a puppet theatre.

Gardens: All year, daily. Adm charge. P *Toilet. Tel Lamberhurst (0892) 890230. Museum: All year, daily. Adm charge. Refreshments. Shop.* P *Toilets. Tel (0892) 890711.*

PENSHURST PLACE

On B2176, 4½ miles north-west of Royal Tunbridge Wells (Ab)

This palatial country house, tucked away in quiet countryside where the Eden joins the Medway, was the birthplace of Sir Philip Sidney, the Elizabethan poet and courtier. Approached across a superb formal garden through the sturdy medieval Garden Tower, the building lies spread out before the visitor like a study in architectural history. The centrepiece is the magnificent Great Hall, built about 1340 by Sir John de Pulteney, four times Lord Mayor of London. Hardly altered since it was built, the hall soars uninterrupted to its roof of massive chestnut beams some 60ft from the stone-flagged floor.

Next to the hall is the State Dining Room, lined with portraits of the Sidney family, including Sir Philip, who was mortally wounded in battle in 1586. Other rooms on view to the public include the Elizabethan Long Gallery, built for exercise in bad weather, and the Tapestry Room, named from the colourful tapestries on its walls. A room across the stable courtyard houses a Toy Museum, while in the rolling parkland north and east of the house are a nature trail, an adventure playground and a farm museum in a traditional Sussex barn.

Apr-Oct, Tues-Sun and Bank Hol. Adm charge. Refreshments. Shop. P *Toilets. Tel Penshurst (0892) 870307.*

PORT LYMPNE ZOO PARK

Off B2067, 3½ miles west of Hythe (Db)

A bend in a green country footpath reveals a field ahead occupied not by cattle or sheep but by African buffaloes. Another meander through banks of wild flowers and shrubs brings the visitor face to face with rhinoceroses grazing the grassy slopes ahead. One of the main attractions of Port Lympne Zoo Park is the broad swathes of natural vegetation which have been left as miniature nature reserves between the animal enclosures, so that a walk round the 300 acre estate combines the pleasures of a day in the English countryside with a close view of exotic wildlife. Among the rare and beautiful animals in the park are tigers, Indian elephants, bison, leopards, timber wolves and monkeys.

Cars must be left in the car park, for this is a 'walk-through' park; however, a tour can be made by safari trailer.

FIT FOR A QUEEN *The main part of Leeds Castle lies on an island. Henry VIII built the Maiden's Tower, on the left, for the royal maids-of-honour. Behind the castle and over a bridge is a separate fortress, the Gloriette, which contains a bedroom and bathroom (left) restored as they might have been prepared for Catherine of Valois, Henry V's queen.*

EXOTIC KENT *The Dutch-style mansion at Port Lympne was built in 1911, and has superb views over the terraced gardens and the broad flatlands of Romney Marsh to the English Channel. Animals in the surrounding Zoo Park, such as the Siberian tiger (right), live in conditions as near their natural habitat as possible.*

The Port Lympne estate was bought by John Aspinall to take the overflow of animals from his Howletts Zoo Park, near Canterbury. It includes a Dutch-style mansion built by Sir Herbert Baker for the local MP, Sir Philip Sassoon, who entertained royalty and world statesmen between the wars. Rex Whistler was among the designers of the interiors, which include a Moorish patio.

All year, daily. Adm charge. Refreshments. Shop. P *Toilets.* ♿ *(not house). Tel Hythe (0303) 64646.*

POWELL-COTTON MUSEUM

On B2048, 4 miles south-west of Margate (Ec)

A family of stuffed white rhinoceroses plods through realistic bush country, nyala and kudu graze in a clearing and a giant tusker gazes down on the visitor to this amazing museum. It was the creation of Major Percy Horace Gordon Powell-Cotton, a big-game hunter turned conservationist before the Second World War. He displayed his trophies from Africa and the Far East in meticulously re-created habitats. Weapons, costumes and musical instruments collected on his travels are also displayed.

The large museum is built onto Quex House, a country home built between 1805 and 1813.

Museum and house: Apr-Sept, Wed, Thur, Sun and Bank Hol pm; also Fri pm in Aug; Museum: also Sun pm in winter. Refreshments (summer only). Shop. P *Toilets. Tel Thanet (0843) 42168.*

QUEBEC HOUSE

At east end of Westerham (Ac)

This red-brick mainly Jacobean building is famous for its connection with General James Wolfe, who spent his early years there. Four rooms are full of portraits, prints and memorabilia devoted to his soldiering life and heroic death, which took place in 1759 on the Plains of Abraham above Quebec, at the moment of his victory over the French.

NT. Apr-Oct, daily exc Thur and Sat. Adm charge. Tel Westerham (0959) 62206.

ROCHESTER CATHEDRAL

In centre of Rochester (Bc)

Cathedral and castle stand side by side in Rochester above the breezy waters of the River Medway, as a reminder that in the Middle Ages Church and State wielded equal power. Both buildings owe their origins to Bishop Gundulf, William the Conqueror's bishop-architect.

Gundulf began his cathedral in about 1080, and much of his sturdy round-arched Norman work survives in the crypt, in the arcading of the east end of the cathedral and in Gundulf's Tower built up against its northern side.

In later centuries the cathedral was altered and added to, the round Norman arches giving way to the pointed Gothic style in two bays. In the 13th century the monks attached to the cathedral set up a shrine to St William of Perth, a baker murdered at the start of a pilgrimage to the Holy Land, and pilgrims flocked to Rochester, bringing in money for further building. Though the west front looks medieval, its present appearance is largely due to a 19th-century restoration.

Gundulf was also responsible for the outer walls of Rochester Castle, but the mighty turreted keep was built in the 1120s by William de Corbeuil, Archbishop of Canterbury. Much of the magnificent internal Norman arcading still survives, and from the battlements there are wide views over the city and the Medway.

Cathedral: All year, daily. Free entry. Refreshments. Shop. Toilets. Tel Medway (0634) 43366. Castle: EH. All year, daily exc Sun am Oct-Mar. Adm charge. Shop. Toilets. Tel (0634) 402276.

ROMAN PAINTED HOUSE

New Street, Dover (Eb)

Redevelopment in Dover's New Street in the 1970s uncovered the remains of a remarkable Roman building. Known as the Painted House – after the frescoes that covered its walls – it stood just outside the main gate of the headquarters of the Roman fleet (the Classis Britannica), and was probably built for a high-ranking officer or as luxury accommodation for important travellers. The floors and walls of the main rooms are today displayed in a modern building, with fallen plaster fragments which have been painstakingly fitted together.

Dover Museum, in nearby Ladywell, gives a good picture of the town's history through a collection of objects ranging from bone carvings of ships made by French prisoners of war, to policemen's truncheons and boneshaker bicycles.

Painted House: Apr-Oct, daily exc Mon. Adm charge. Shop. P *(limited). Toilets. Tel Dover (0304) 203279. Dover Museum: All year, daily exc Sun and Wed. Free entry. Shop.* ♿ *Tel (0304) 201066.*

ROMNEY, HYTHE AND DYMCHURCH RAILWAY

Off A259 (Db-Da)

Far better than any road, the Romney, Hythe and Dymchurch Railway gives a complete picture of the 'lost world' of Romney Marsh, from the outskirts of Hythe to the windswept shingle and looming nuclear power station of Dungeness. It runs for 13 miles, through the meadows of the Marsh, past the back gardens of Dymchurch, St Mary's Bay and New Romney, to the foot of the twin lighthouses of Dungeness.

The railway began operations in 1927. Built to one-third scale, with a gauge of 15in, its locomotives are magnificent examples of small-scale engineering. During the Second World War the railway was taken over by the army, and in 1944 it carried material for PLUTO – the Pipeline Under the Ocean which ran from Littlestone-on-Sea to France and supplied Allied forces with fuel after D-Day. At New Romney there are displays about the railway.

Apr-Sept, daily; Mar and Oct, weekends. Fare. Refreshments and shop at Hythe and New Romney. P *Toilets. Tel New Romney (0679) 62353.*

SCOTNEY CASTLE GARDENS

Off A21, 9 miles south-east of Royal Tunbridge Wells (Ba)

Trees, grass, water and a 14th-century stone tower combine at Scotney to form what is still, despite severe damage in the storm of October 1987, one of the country's most romantic gardens. The old Tudor manor house – protected by a moat and the old castle tower – was abandoned in the 1830s when Edward Hussey built a large stone mansion up the hill from the castle. Hussey landscaped the ruins, planting masses of rhododendrons which bloom in early summer, and burying the ancient castle in roses.

NT. Apr-mid Nov, Wed-Fri; Sat, Sun and Bank Hol Mon pm. (Old Castle open May-Aug.) Adm charge. Shop. P *Toilets. Tel Lamberhurst (0892) 890651.*

SISSINGHURST CASTLE GARDEN

Off A262, 2 miles north-east of Cranbrook (Cb)

The soaring Tudor gate-tower of Sissinghurst Castle, flanked by octagonal turrets, looks as though it should lead to some vast country mansion. In fact, it forms the entrance to one of the finest gardens in Britain, the great house to which it once belonged having been demolished as long ago as 1800. The garden was created by the diplomat Harold Nicolson and his wife the novelist and poet Vita Sackville-West. They bought Sissinghurst in 1930, when the tower and garden were derelict, and over the next decade they restored the buildings and turned the garden into a series of outdoor 'rooms', all entirely different in layout and colour. The White Garden is planted entirely with white or grey plants, including white roses, artemisias, and a pear with silvery leaves.

NT. Apr-mid Oct, Tues-Fri pm; also Sat, Sun and Good Fri. Adm charge. Refreshments. Shop. P *Toilets. Tel Cranbrook (0580) 712850.*

SMALLHYTHE PLACE

On B2082, 2½ miles south of Tenterden (Cb)

Long and low, with close-set wall timbers and undulating floors, this Kentish yeoman's house was built in the early 16th century, not for a farmer but for a harbourmaster. In the Middle Ages, before the Rother Levels silted up, Smallhythe was Tenterden's port, and there was a shipyard in front of Smallhythe Place. In 1899 the actress Ellen Terry bought the house and lived there until her death in 1928. It is now a museum devoted to her memory.

NT. Apr-Oct, Sat-Wed pm. Adm charge. P *(limited). Tel Tenterden (058 06) 2334.*

TROSLEY COUNTRY PARK

Off A227, 8 miles north-west of Maidstone (Bc)

Spreading across 160 acres of the North Downs escarpment, this fine country park combines woodlands and open chalk downland, and is an ideal place for walking or picnicking. Stone Age Man travelled this way, as did later pilgrims making for Canterbury. The visitor centre has details of three circular waymarked paths, one of which leads to the Coldrum Stones, marking the burial mound of a Neolithic prince.

All year, daily. Visitor centre: Sat, Sun, Bank Hol; Aug, daily. Free entry. Shop. P *(fee). Toilets.* ♿ *Tel Fairseat (0732) 823570.*

TYRWHITT-DRAKE MUSEUM

Mill Street, Maidstone (Bc)

Across the road from the medieval palace of the Archbishops of Canterbury, a long stone barn-like building, equally ancient, was once the archbishop's stables. It now houses a unique collection of more than 50 horse-drawn vehicles in their original state. The exhibits include George III's travelling chariot, Queen Victoria's state landau, and a 19th-century state carriage.

All year, Mon-Sat; also Sun pm Apr-Sept. Adm charge. Tel Maidstone (0622) 54497.

WALMER CASTLE

On A258, 2 miles south of Deal (Eb)

Like Deal Castle just up the coast, Walmer was built by Henry VIII at a time of threatened invasion, but unlike Deal it has been domesticated, and is now the official residence of the Lord Warden of the Cinque Ports. When it was built in the 1530s it stood right beside the sea, but the shingle built up and it is now set well back. In the early 18th century it was pierced with windows and lined with elegant panelling to make it a comfortable Georgian House.

There are portraits and mementos of the Duke of Wellington, Lord Warden at the time of his death in the castle in 1852.

EH. All year, Tues-Sat and Bank Hol; also Sun pm. (Closed when Lord Warden in residence.) Adm charge. P *Toilets. Tel Deal (0304) 364288.*

WHITBREAD HOP FARM

Off B2015, 7 miles south-west of Maidstone (Bb)

Conical-roofed oast-houses, topped by white-painted cowls and set among acres of hopfields, are the most typically Kentish of all the county's sights. Nowhere are they seen to better advantage than at Beltring (near Paddock Wood), where the Whitbread Hop Farm's oasts with their 25 cowls provide the main feature of the landscape. No longer used for drying hops, these 19th-century oasts have been turned into a museum devoted to hop-growing, general agriculture and associated crafts such as coopering. A woodland pond has been set aside for fishing, and there is a craft centre and a nature trail to the Medway. Visitors can also see Whitbread's giant Shire horses.

Easter-late Oct, Tues-Sun and Bank Hol. Adm charge. Refreshments. Shop. P *Toilets. Tel Maidstone (0622) 872068 or 872408.*

COUNTY CALENDAR

February (mid-month). Gillingham: International Show Jumping Festival.

March-April (Easter Monday). Biddenden: Dole (distribution of biscuits).

May (end of month). Rochester: Dickens Festival.

June (mid-month). Allington Castle: Medieval Market. Leeds Castle: International Balloon Festival. Folkestone: International Folklore Festival. Maidstone: Summer Festival.

June (3rd week). Broadstairs: Dickens Festival.

July (mid-month). Maidstone: County Show.

July (last Sun). Whitstable: Blessing of the Waters.

July (late, to Aug). Canterbury: Chaucer Festival.

August (1st two weeks). Deal: Music Festival.

August (2nd week). Broadstairs: Folk Week.

September (1st Saturday). Canterbury: Hop Hoodening (end of hop-picking season).

September (2nd Sunday). Dunton Green: Heavy Horse Show.

September (late). Canterbury: Festival of Arts and Music.

Tourist information: Broadstairs (0843) 68399; Canterbury (0227) 766567; Deal (0304) 361161; Dover (0304) 205108; Maidstone (0622) 673581/602169; Rochester (0634) 43666; Royal Tunbridge Wells (0892) 26121.

CASTLE IN A GARDEN *A 14th-century tower is the only castle-like feature in Scotney Castle Gardens. It was built to fortify the manor house against raids by the French. The house was rebuilt in Tudor times.*

LANCASHIRE

HISTORIC HALLS AND COTTON MILLS WEST OF THE PENNINES

The Lancashire Plain spreads westwards from the Forest of Bowland, a desolate and rugged fringe of the Pennines where there are magnificent views across the plain from Beacon Fell Park. Some of Britain's finest stately homes dot the attractive countryside – some, like Astley Hall, built of local stone and others, such as the lovely Rufford Old Hall, superb examples of 'black-and-white' timber-framed building.

Lancashire has a great industrial tradition which first grew on cotton, a tradition kept alive by the Helmshore Textile Museum, the Lewis Museum of Textile Machinery and the preserved mill district called Weavers' Triangle. But industry has not totally consumed Lancashire. There are still large areas of unspoilt countryside ranging from the marshland nature reserves at Leighton Moss and Martin Mere to the country parks at Wycoller, Witton and Jumbles, and the parklands and gardens of Lever Park.

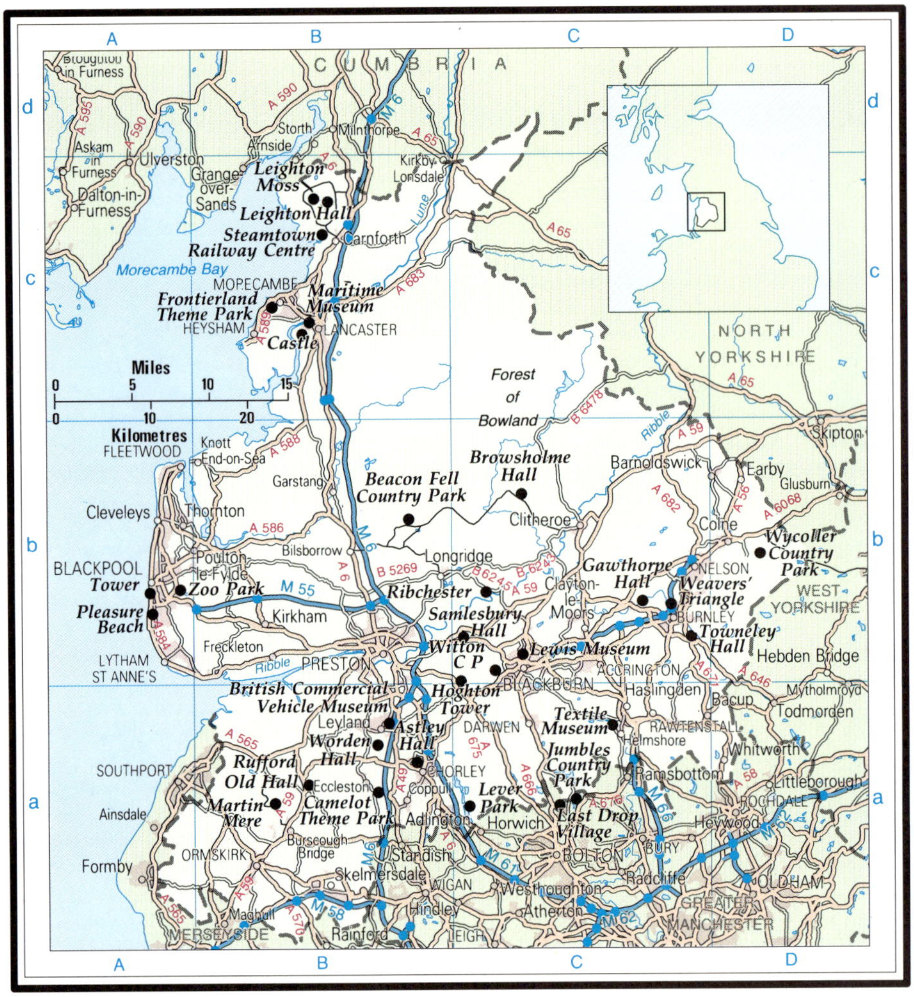

ASTLEY HALL

Just north-west of Chorley Town centre (Ba)

Like all good stately homes, Astley Hall has its ghosts: beside the lake in which she is said to have drowned appears a little girl in Elizabethan clothes, while indoors the historical figure of John Charnock, executed in 1584, is said to walk the corridors of the house in which he spent his childhood.

Ghostly visitants apart, the hall is very real, a beautiful 17th-century building which, though now run as a museum, is carefully maintained to look like a family home of 300 years ago. In the kitchen the utensils – including a massive butter churn – stand ready to prepare food for a large household. In the Great Hall stands the 'Sirloin' chair from nearby Hoghton Tower, where it is said to have been used by James I when he 'knighted' a loin of beef.

A major feature of the house is its Long Gallery. Elizabethans were fond of their walks, and when the weather was inclement they took their exercise by striding up and down the indoor gallery. Part of the furniture of the gallery is an immense shovel-board table 21ft long. The game was played like a large-scale version of shove-ha'penny – and one of the ghosts of Astley is supposed to enjoy playing it at dead of night to win a lady's hand in marriage.

A nature trail starts by the main entrance and meanders through woodlands, crossing and re-crossing the tiny River Chor. The park is noted for its variety of trees, introduced over the centuries. There are the remains of an ice-house in which ice was kept until well into the summer.

All year, daily. Adm charge. Refreshments. Shop. P *Toilets. Tel Chorley (025 72) 62166.*

BEACON FELL COUNTRY PARK

Off A6, 8 miles north of Preston (Bb)

On a clear day, views from the top of Beacon Fell take in the mountains of Wales, the Lakeland Hills – and Blackpool Tower. Its commanding position once made the site an important link in the chain of beacons giving 'early warning' of such dangers as the Spanish Armada. Even so, the fell itself is only 873ft high and easy to climb, and around it spreads a 271 acre country park consisting mainly of coniferous forest and moorland. Bird life abounds. Tawny owls live in the forest, and there are skylarks and meadow pipits on the moors. There is an information centre and nature trails, and a scenic drive goes right round the park.

All year, daily.

BLACKPOOL PLEASURE BEACH

South Promenade, Blackpool (Ab)

This vast complex of ferris wheels, helter-skelters, water chutes and 'white knuckle' rides attracts some 6½ million visitors a year. They come to enjoy the thrills of a family-run business which began in 1896 with a handful of roundabouts, a switchback steam railway, a few travelling entertainers and a gypsy band. Today, the park has millions of pounds worth of sophisticated equipment looked after by a full-time army of 175 engineers and mechanics.

Among the top attractions are the Black Hole, a high-speed ride in darkness lit only by ultraviolet strobe lights; the Steeplechase, in which the riders on mechanical horses leap fences at speeds of up to 28mph; and for children, a ride through Lewis Carroll's *Alice in Wonderland.* There is also a fleet of wooden roller-coasters, which fans claim give a more authentic and 'individual' ride than their metal successors.

In case of rain there are more than 30 covered rides and attractions – and next door to the park is the Sandcastle, an indoor entertainment centre in which it never rains and is never cold. The Sandcastle is, in effect, an enormous covered swimming pool, decorated in blue and white, with a restaurant and nightclub and a maze of shops, kiosks and bars. It holds up to 6000 people and a single ticket allows the visitor to spend the day there, moving from one attraction to the next.

Pleasure Beach: Late Apr-Oct, daily; also weekends in late Mar and early Apr and daily in Easter week. Free entry (rides charged for). Refreshments. Shop. P *Toilets.* ♿ *Tel Blackpool (0253) 41033. Sandcastle: Easter-Nov, daily; Sat-Sun in winter. Adm charge. Refreshments. Shops.* P *Toilets.* ♿ *Tel (0253) 404013.*

BLACKPOOL TOWER

Promenade, Blackpool (Ab)

For almost a century, Blackpool's world-famous tower – a glittering spire amid the autumn illuminations – has dominated the city's skyline. It was modelled on the Eiffel Tower in Paris, though about half its height, by a city that wanted a pleasure palace that would make it the envy of Europe.

At its base, between its four massive legs, the Tower Circus, decked out in crimson and gold, and the gilded Tower Ballroom were built and decorated in the ornate style of the Paris Opera. The enduring circus has thrilled audiences for decades with its high-wire artistes, stilt walkers, jugglers and acrobats. Dancing is still a daily feature in the ballroom, which retains its enormous Wurlitzer organ. A plaque commemorates its most famous organist, Reginald Dixon, 'Mr Blackpool'. At the Good Time Emporium, children have their own theatre with cartoon films and music. For the 'up to fives' there is the Tiny Tots Softplay area, where the youngsters can bounce around in perfect safety. And for the 6-12 year olds, there is Jungle Jim's Adventure Playplace – a 'forest of fun'.

An aquarium existed in Blackpool even before the tower was built. Now called Undersea World, its giant turtles and sinister piranha fish are among the principal attractions. Close by, an exhibition called 'Out of this World' features a series of startling visual effects ranging from Victorian moving pictures to modern lasers and holograms. A variety of restaurants, games rooms and play areas on four floors lead finally to the Tower lift and a dizzy 518ft ascent to the top of the Tower and its magnificent views over the city and out to sea.

Tower: Spring Bank Hol-Oct, daily; Nov-May, weekends. Adm charge. Refreshments. Shop. Toilet. ♿ *Tel Blackpool (0253) 22242. Circus: June-Oct. Tel (0253) 27776.*

BLACKPOOL ZOO PARK

Off M55, 2 miles east of Blackpool seafront (Ab)

Creatures of 114 different species, including several rarities, can be seen in superb surroundings at Blackpool Zoo Park – a zoo far removed in its safe modern design from that fictional Blackpool zoo where, in the Stanley Holloway monologue, young Albert Ramsbottom was caten by a lion. The zoo is set in 32 acres of landscaped gardens, but its compact layout makes it easy to walk round. Sea lions and penguins provide spectacular displays at feeding times, and the zoo is particularly proud of its collection of kangaroos and other pouched mammals.

Within the park is a school zoo which offers parties of children special opportunities to study animals. Apart from the zoo inmates, the park's attractions include a miniature railway and a kitchen where the animals' food is prepared.

In Stanley Park, just opposite the zoo, is Blackpool Model Village, where a small child can feel like a giant. Hundreds of craftsman-built models provide a Lilliputian version of everyday life. This is a lively village, with cricket and football matches going on and a blacksmith's shop in action; there are even firemen trying to control a blaze in one of the tiny houses. The village is set in a delightful landscape which contains waterfalls and streams. No fewer than 1500 varieties of shrubs and plants beautify the scene.

Zoo Park: All year, daily. Adm charge. Refreshments. Shop. P *Toilets.* ♿ *Tel Blackpool (0253) 65027. Model Village: Easter-Oct, daily. Adm charge. Refreshments. Shop.* P *Toilets.* ♿ *Tel (0253) 63827.*

BRITISH COMMERCIAL VEHICLE MUSEUM

King Street, Leyland (Ba)

Unlikely companions in Europe's largest museum of commercial vehicles are a splendid fire engine of the 1920s, resplendent in bright red paint and gleaming brass, and the Popemobile used by Pope John Paul II on his visit to Britain in 1982. Exhibits ranging from vehicles of the horse-drawn era to the oldest surviving steam van of 1896 are displayed in authentic period settings. Among the 40-odd vehicles on display are some still used on the roads today, for the museum realises that today's commonplace artefact is tomorrow's treasured relic.

During the summer season, steam engines are put through their paces and children have the chance of riding on carefully restored historic vehicles that are a well-remembered part of their parents' childhood.

Apr-Sept, daily exc Mon; Oct-Nov, weekends; Bank Hol Mon. Adm charge. Refreshments. Shop. P *Toilets.* ♿ *Tel Leyland (0772) 451011.*

NORTHERN LIGHTS *Etched against the night sky, Blackpool Tower presides over the seafront Golden Mile. In autumn the promenade is transformed into a glittering display of coloured lights and tableaux.*

BROWSHOLME HALL

Off B6243, 5 miles north-west of Clitheroe (Cb)

Chosen as the most appropriate location in Britain for a television series called 'History around you – a country house', Browsholme Hall is no museum, but a living home whose long history enfolds the visitor. Most of the entrance hall, for instance, dates back to the original house built about 1507; but it also contains items from almost every period onwards, from suits of armour to 19th-century stained glass. In the Velvet Room is a photograph of the estate carpenter, Richard Alston, standing beside the ornate overmantel which he himself carved in about 1900.

The descendants of the family who built Browsholme still live in it. The rooms, therefore, contain not only treasures collected over the centuries, but the domestic possessions of the present-day inhabitants which show that the house continues to be a home.

Easter, Spring and Aug Bank Hol, and Sat June-Aug. Adm charge. Shop. P *Toilets.* ♿ *Tel Stoneyhurst (025 486) 330.*

CAMELOT THEME PARK

Off M6 and A49, 4 miles south-west of Chorley (Ba)

Heralds in medieval costume welcome visitors to the legendary palace of King Arthur and his Knights of the Round Table, and the sounds of medieval jousting mingle with the splashing of a fountain near the Camelot Courtyard. Puff the Magic Dragon presides in his magical tower and the helter-skelter Derwent Water Slide deposits suitably attired visitors in a large pool. Dragons appear again in the form of two carriages of an overhead railway which weaves its way high above a large area of the park.

The Camelot theme predominates in this lively amusement park with knights on horseback, flying dragons and rides to the Kingdom in the Clouds. There is also a rope tunnel 100ft long and crossing a stream; and a Mad Monastery Dark Ride. Tearooms, inns, a children's garden, a

CATERPILLAR CAPERS *Fairy-tale castles form a medieval background for a thoroughly modern roller-coaster ride at Camelot Theme Park.*

night club and even a nappy-changing room make this very much a place for the family. A single entrance fee provides access without further payment to most of the 63 attractions.

Late May-Oct, daily; mid Apr-mid May, weekends. Adm charge. Refreshments. Shop. P *Toilets.* ♿ *Tel Eccleston (0257) 452090.*

FRONTIERLAND THEME PARK

Off A589, at southern end of Morecambe (Bc)

'Step into the world of the wild, wild west' is the slogan adopted by a theme park which re-creates the American Wild West in a colourful variety of forms. The visitor is likely to find himself in the middle of a staged 'shoot-out' between sheriff and outlaws or swept along in a crowd of whooping, rope-spinning cowboys. Funfair amusements maintain the Wild West theme, with a log flume – 'the wildest, wettest water ride ever' – a 'Wild Mouse Whirl' and a Stampede rollercoaster which belongs strictly to the 'white-knuckle' class of entertainment. A Fun House provides under-cover entertainment for children, and for adults there are the colourful Crazy Horse saloon and Ranch House Bar.

Late May-late Sept, daily; also Easter, and weekends in May and Oct. Free entry. Refreshments. Shop. P *Toilets.* ♿ *Tel Morecambe (0524) 410024.*

GAWTHORPE HALL

Off A671, 2½ miles north-west of Burnley (Cb)

This elegant 17th-century manor house has been built around the remains of the southernmost peel tower, one of the many defensive towers built for protection against marauding Scots during the 1300s. Inside the Palladian house, the drawing room with its magnificent plaster ceiling, panelling and fireplace is in its original condition; so, too, is the long gallery on the top floor. The remainder of the house, however, was substantially remodelled by Sir Charles Barry, architect of the Houses of Parliament, in the 1850s. On the ground floor is an outstanding collection of embroidery, lace and costume.

The beautiful gardens, together with the Great Barn and Estate Block, have been restored to their original appearance.

NT. Hall: Apr-Oct, pm daily exc Mon and Fri. Garden: All year, daily. Adm charge. Refreshments. Shop. P *Toilets.* ♿ *Tel Padiham (0282) 78511.*

HELMSHORE TEXTILE MUSEUM

On B6235, 1 mile south of Haslingden (Ca)

The newcomer may be surprised that a large industrial complex should have been situated in a tiny country village. Helmshore is, however, a typical product of the Industrial Revolution, when factories and mills were built where there was a suitable supply of running water. The two mills at Helmshore are both now museums. The three-storey, stone mill, built early in the last century, was originally powered by steam, but the steam engine was removed about 50 years ago. The mill was in use as a cotton condenser plant as late as 1978 and the machinery still stands in its original position, making it possible to follow the complex operation from the arrival of cotton waste to the production of finished yarn.

The neighbouring Higher Mill Museum is a fulling mill which still has its great water wheel, installed in the middle of the last century. This was working until 1954, and occasional demonstrations still take place. Water power drives the great hammers which pound the soaked woollen fibres into felt.

Apr-Oct, daily exc Sat; Mar, Mon-Fri pm; also Bank Hol weekends, and Sat pm in July and Aug. Adm charge. Refreshments. Shop. P *Toilets.* ♿ *Tel Rossendale (0706) 226459.*

HAMMER POWER *Massive wooden hammers called fulling stocks still stand in Higher Mill Museum, in Helmshore. They were used to pound the woollen cloth to remove its natural grease and mat the fibres.*

HOGHTON TOWER

Off A675, 5 miles west of Blackburn (Cb)

The approach to this stately home is as dramatic as one could wish. From every direction the house appears as a castellated crest to a steep, wooded hill, up which an impressively straight drive rises steeply for at least half a mile. It is said that when James I visited the house on a summer's day in 1617, this great drive was carpeted along its length with red velvet from the Low Countries specially woven for the occasion.

Hoghton Tower is entered through a solid, square gatehouse and divided into two main sections, each grouped around its own courtyard. Beside the inner courtyard stands the magnificent Banqueting Hall; it was in this hall that a loin of beef so delighted James I that he bestowed upon it the title 'Sirloin'. The immense table on which the sirloin rested still stands in the hall, and the menu for the meal the company ate that day is still preserved in the house.

A less happy memory of the past is to be found in the basement which held the dungeons where such malefactors as witches were incarcerated. The Tudor well-house is still preserved, together with its horse-drawn pump and oaken windlass, and outside are lovely walled gardens with wonderful views of the sea. There is also a permanent exhibition of dolls' houses and dolls.

Easter-Oct, Sun and Bank Hol pm; also Sat in July and Aug. Adm charge. Shop. P *Toilets. Tel Hoghton (025 485) 2986.*

JUMBLES COUNTRY PARK

On A676, 4 miles north of Bolton (Ca)

Although Jumbles is not very large, it offers a variety of country attractions. At its centre is a large reservoir which provides club sailing and public fishing. The reservoir lies more than 400ft above sea level and the deep water is often very cold, with strong undercurrents, so caution is necessary. Ringing the reservoir is a 1½ mile nature trail where the visitor can see waterside birds, flowers and insects. A mill once stood in the valley bottom, and although this is now covered by the reservoir, traces of its outworks

are to be found all along the trail. About half a mile away from Jumbles is Turton Tower, a fortified tower dating from 1400 which is now a museum of local history.
Park: All year, daily. Tower: All year, Sat-Wed. Adm charge.

LANCASTER CASTLE

Near centre of Lancaster (Bc)

The immense iron door swings soundlessly on its great hinges and closes with a clang. Inside, the ancient cell is totally dark, and an age seems to pass before the guide reopens the door and lets visitors to Lancaster Castle back into the world. Though the ancient cells are no longer used, much of the massive building is still a prison so only part of it is open to the public.

Begun in the 11th century, Lancaster Castle bears the additions and adaptations of 700 years of use. The tour begins in the Shire Hall, a beautiful semicircular courtroom built in the early 19th century and still doing duty as the county court. It contains one of the finest displays of heraldry in Britain, with more than 600 shields on show. The tour leads through Hadrian's Tower, a massive 11th-century structure containing instruments of punishment, including a cat o'nine tails last used in 1915. Next the visitor passes the dungeons which were rediscovered only in 1931: George Fox, founder of the Quakers, was one of many prisoners incarcerated in them. The Crown Court building, like the Shire Hall, dates from the late 18th or early 19th century, and has handsome wooden panelling. Still in place is the clamp used for restraining a felon's hand while it was branded with a hot iron. Prisoners for execution were brought to the so-called 'Drop Room'; used today as the jury room, it contains models of the gallows used at Lancaster in times gone by.

Set on the top of a steep hill, Lancaster Castle dominates the delightful little city at its feet. Immediately below it, green meadows sweep down to the River Lune, and in these meadows are part of the Roman fort which occupied the hill a thousand years before the Norman castle was built.

An extensive collection of Roman material found in and around Lancaster can be seen in the City Museum, housed in a handsome Georgian structure that was once the Town Hall. There are reminders of Lancaster's maritime past, and models of the town at various stages in its history. The building also houses the Museum of the King's Own Royal Regiment (Lancaster), whose treasures include the VCs awarded to two Lancastrians during the Abyssinian campaign of 1867-8.
Castle: Good Fri-late Sept, daily. Adm charge. Shop. Toilets. ♿ *Tel Lancaster (0524) 64998. Museum: All year, daily exc Sun. Free entry.* 🅿 *Tel (0524) 64637.*

LANCASTER MARITIME MUSEUM

St George's Quay, Lancaster (Bc)

The stylish, 18th-century stone building beside the River Lune once functioned as Lancaster's Custom House. Built between 1762 and 1764 when Lancaster was a flourishing port, the building contains the internal features which characterised custom houses throughout the country: a central Long Room where merchants and ships' owners arranged the shipping and distribution of cargoes, a Collector's Office where dues were paid, and smaller offices housing customs staff. The building has been restored to its 18th-century appearance, and today is appropriately used as a maritime museum.

LOCAL CRAFT *The Lancaster Maritime Museum includes a display on fishing around Morecambe Bay. At its centre is this locally built whammel boat, used for salmon fishing on the River Lune.*

The Collector's Office looks as though the Collector has just risen from his chair, and his flowered waistcoat still hangs on the back of it. An upper room displays the history of the port, and downstairs is an exhibition devoted to Morecambe Bay's shrimping, cockling, mussel and wet fish industries. Part of this display consists of a fisherman's cottage of the 1920s. A tape-recording recounts a local man's life as a fisherman at that time.

A riverside walk from the Maritime Museum leads to an outstanding example of 18th-century industrial architecture. This is the great aqueduct which carries the Lancaster canal high over the Lune. From beneath it resembles an immense railway arch, but from above can be seen the remarkable spectacle of water crossing water. A towpath along the canal leads back into the heart of the town.
All year, daily (Nov-Mar, pm only). Adm charge. Refreshments. Shop. 🅿 *Toilets.* ♿ *Tel Lancaster (0524) 64637.*

LAST DROP VILLAGE

Off A666, 4 miles north of Bolton (Ca)

Farm buildings dating from the 17th century have been converted to create an attractive 'village' with craft shops, a pub and a luxurious hotel whose 'Penny Farthing' conference suite was originally a tithe barn. Craftworkers share the traffic-free High Street and Market Place with a restorer of antique clocks, the ivy-clad Drop Inn and an oak-panelled tea shop where, on occasions, copper pans reflect the dancing flames of an open fire. Prints and original paintings are exhibited in the Last Drop Gallery, which is also the studio of a wildlife sculptor.

Orrell Fold Farm was derelict when Carton Walker, a Bolton businessman, bought the property in the 1960s. The village's name was suggested by a friend when he and Mr Walker were deciding who should have the 'last drop' from a bottle of wine during a meal.
All year, daily. Refreshments. Shop. 🅿 *Toilets. Tel Bolton (0204) 591131.*

LEIGHTON HALL

Off A6, 3 miles north of Carnforth (Bc)

An eagle may swoop low over the heads of visitors to Leighton Hall. The initial feeling of alarm gives way to admiration at the sight of the majestic creature banking and gliding on the air currents of the valley in which the hall is set. It is one of a number of birds introduced to Leighton Hall by the property's Falconer.

The handsome, 18th-century building is very much a family home, the ancestors of the present owners having lived there for more than 400 years. All the rooms to which the public are admitted are in everyday use, and show the little domestic touches which make the building much more than a museum. The original bell pulls used to summon the servants are still dotted around the house, and records of domestic life at Leighton show how the servants lived.

Extensive grounds include a long, narrow lawn originally laid out for archery, and the shrubbery walk that was an inseparable part of all early 19th-century gardens. In the rose garden is a sundial dated 1647, the only feature of the house that survives from before its rebuilding in 1763.
May-Sept, daily pm exc Sat and Mon. Adm charge. Refreshments. Shop. 🅿 *Toilets.* ♿ *(ground floor and gardens). Tel Lancaster (0524) 734474.*

LEIGHTON MOSS

Off A6, 3 miles north-west of Carnforth (Bc)

A freshwater marsh surrounded by low, wooded hills forms a bird reserve that is home to a wide variety of birds, mammals, insects and plants. The reserve is one of the few breeding sites in Britain of the bittern, a bird of the heron family that became almost extinct in Britain in the latter part of the 19th century but now breeds here regularly. Its presence is recognised by its deep, resonant 'boom' which can be heard as far as a mile away.

RSPB. All year, daily exc Tues. Adm charge. Shop. P *Toilets. Tel Silverdale (0524) 701601.*

LEVER PARK

Off A673, 7 miles north-west of Bolton (Ca)

Lever Park is a park built on soap. In 1884 William Lever launched his famous Sunlight Soap, which made him a fortune and earned him a peerage as Lord Leverhulme. Part of his wealth he devoted to making a dream come true, by turning 2100 acres of barren hillside into a magnificent public park and gardens. Lord Leverhulme personally designed much of the park, where long avenues and grassy footpaths lead down to a beautiful tree-fringed reservoir. One driveway leads to the eye-catching ruins of Liverpool Castle – built by Lord Leverhulme in the 1920s as a replica of the medieval castle that once stood in Liverpool.

Overlooking Lever Park are terraced gardens, which once provided the setting for Lord Leverhulme's mansion. This had to be demolished in 1947, but the gardens have been carefully restored and consist of some 45 acres of mixed woodland containing terraced walks, garden shelters, ornamental pools and even miniature waterfalls. It takes about two hours to walk around the Gardens Trail; visitors should exercise care, as many of the paths, steps and terraces become slippery in wet weather.

Towering above the gardens is the 1200ft summit of Rivington Pike, topped by its square 18th-century tower.

All year, daily.

LEWIS MUSEUM OF TEXTILE MACHINERY

Museum Street, Blackburn (Cb)

The first room that the visitor enters in this small but comprehensive museum is furnished as a cottage of the mid-18th century. This was before the great inventions of the textile industry, and pride of place is therefore given to the humble spinning wheel. Thereafter, words and phrases from the history books come to life as the visitor passes through a century and a half of the textile history. Hargreaves' 'Spinning Jenny' (named after his wife), Crompton's 'Spinning Mule' (so called because it was a cross between two earlier forms of machine) and Kay's 'Flying Shuttle' are among the many exhibits which demonstrate the production of cloth from that first simple spinning wheel to the elaborate machinery of the Industrial Revolution.

All year, Tues-Sat. Free entry. Shop. P ♿ *Tel Blackburn (0254) 667130.*

MARTIN MERE

Off B5246, 3 miles north of Ormskirk (Ba)

The visitor to Martin Mere is welcomed into a complex of buildings made from Scandinavian pine with gently sloping turf roofs, based on the traditional log houses of Norway and blending easily with the landscape. The main concourse has an immense picture window giving views of the birds on Swan Lake, and of other birds winging across to the Mere. Next door, an exhibition hall illustrates the natural history of the Mere and the work of the Wildfowl Trust which administers it.

At one time Martin Mere was the largest lake in Lancashire, but it was later drained; 20 years ago part of it was used as a rubbish dump for Liverpool. Sir Peter Scott, the naturalist, seized the opportunity to develop this rough pasture into a marvellous sanctuary for wildlife, and the Martin Mere Wildfowl Trust was established in 1975. At least 650 wild swans, of three different species, can be seen in winter, as well as flocks of up to 15,000 pink-footed geese.

All year, daily. Adm charge. Refreshments. Shop. P *Toilets.* ♿ *Tel Burscough (0704) 895181.*

RIBCHESTER

Off B6245, 10 miles north-east of Preston (Cb)

The Romans built a fort at Ribchester to guard five vital roadways through a gap in the Pennines. Excavations have revealed much of the ground plan of the fort, and some of the remains have been left exposed; for instance, the porch of the White Bull Inn in the village of Ribchester is supported by four massive pillars which probably came from the Roman bathhouse. Most of the items found at Ribchester are displayed in a museum on the site. The most famous find – a superb parade ground helmet discovered on the river bank in 1796, is in the British Museum in London, but there is an excellent replica in the Ribchester Museum.

While parents explore the Roman site, younger visitors may well linger in Ribchester's Museum of Childhood, a private collection of toys, models, dolls and dolls' houses. A working model of a fairground has 20 separate items including swings, roundabouts and steam yachts.

Roman site: Mar-Oct, daily; Nov-Feb, Sun pm. Adm charge. Shop. ♿ *Tel Ribchester (025 484) 261. Museum: All year, daily exc Mon. Adm charge. Shop.* P *Toilets. Tel (025 484) 520.*

RUFFORD OLD HALL

Off A59, 5½ miles north-east of Ormskirk (Ba)

Spectacular black-and-white timbering makes Rufford Old Hall the finest timber-framed house in Lancashire. It was built in the 15th century and is still largely unchanged. Inside, the hall has two unusual features – an immense pair of wooden sphere posts and a movable screen. The spheres were made out of enormous oak trees of slightly differing girths, and are richly carved.

An elegant brick wing, built in 1661, houses a collection of 16th-century arms and armour, as well as a folk museum. The gardens cover 14 acres.

NT. Apr-Oct, daily exc Fri. Adm charge. Refreshments. Shop. P *Toilets.* ♿ *(garden and entrance hall). Tel Rufford (0704) 821254.*

SAMLESBURY HALL

On A677, 4 miles east of Preston (Cb)

A visit to Samlesbury Hall offers three quite different attractions: the opportunity to explore an ancient building, parts of which go back to the 14th century; an opportunity to watch craftsmen at work; and an opportunity to buy or sell antiques. The original hall was built in 1325 to replace a building burnt down by Robert Bruce and his invading Scots. Its appearance today, however, is mostly that of a timbered building of the mid-16th century. The moat that once surrounded it has long since dried up, but inside there are clear traces of the hall's 600-year-old history.

All year, daily exc Mon. Adm charge. Refreshments. P *Toilets.* ♿ *(ground floor). Tel Mellor (025 481) 2229.*

BLACK BEAUTY *A superbly carved 15th-century screen adorns the Great Hall of Rufford Old Hall. Its pinnacles point upwards to a hammerbeam roof decorated with quatrefoil motifs.*

STEAMTOWN RAILWAY CENTRE

Off A6, at Carnforth (Bc)

All over the country railway enthusiasts have brought the old steam locomotives back to life, and Steamtown has about 30 preserved locomotives. Ever since 1972, when British Rail relaxed its ban on the working of steam locomotives, Steamtown locomotives have hauled special trains on British Rail lines as far afield as Chester and York.

Apart from the 30 great locomotives, on display is a Midland Railway signal box, a turntable and working cooling plant. A 15in gauge railway wanders amongst the trees for almost a mile, linking picnic areas with the main shed, while a standard-gauge line, also a mile long, connects Steamtown Halt at the north end with Crag Bank Halt.

All year, daily. Adm charge. Refreshments. Shop. 🅿 *Toilets. Tel Carnforth (0524) 732100.*

TOWNELEY HALL

On A671, 1½ miles south-east of Burnley (Cb)

Although Towneley Hall today houses an art gallery and museum, its owners, Burnley Corporation, have taken care to retain the period flavour and domestic features of a house dating mainly from the 16th and 17th centuries. The kitchen, for instance, shows how methods of cooking changed over three centuries: dominating the room is an immense medieval fireplace – but inserted into it is an early 19th-century cooking range. The servants' hall is laid out as it was when it served as the dining room for the staff of a large household. Curiously, the family dining room differs little in its furnishings, though its decoration is more opulent.

In the grounds of the hall a stone-built Brew House is now a Museum of Local Arts and Crafts. The surrounding park covers nearly 300 acres.

All year, daily exc Sat. Free entry. Refreshments. Shop. 🅿 *Toilets.* ♿ *Tel Burnley (0282) 24213.*

WEAVERS' TRIANGLE

In centre of Burnley (Cb)

The Weavers' Triangle lies along a section of the Leeds and Liverpool Canal, built between 1770 and 1816 to transport raw cotton and finished cloth. The textile mills and factories that still line the canal present a complete picture of this vitally important Lancashire industry at its peak.

This journey into the past begins at the Toll House on one bank and, after passing 31 different features, ends on the opposite bank at Nelson House, one of Burnley's few remaining Regency houses. Burnley Wharf, on which the Toll House stands, has other canal-side buildings, including the Wharf-master's House. On the wharf itself can still be seen reminders of its former use, such as rope marks on the stonework, a rope wheel and a restored 19th-century crane. A ginnel, or narrow alleyway, under the Wharf-master's House leads to brick stables which once accommodated the barge horses.

Apr-Sept, Sun, Tues, Wed pm; also most Bank Hol. Free entry. Shop. Tel Burnley (0282) 23019.

KING COTTON'S KINGDOM *Dark and brooding, but no longer Satanically belching smoke, the cotton mills lining the Leeds and Liverpool Canal form part of the preserved Victorian area called Weavers' Triangle.*

NOSTALGIA TRIP *A saddle-tank loco, built in 1942, is one of several locomotives that give free train rides at the Steamtown Railway Centre. It was once in regular use at ironstone mines in Northamptonshire.*

WITTON COUNTRY PARK

On A674, 1 mile west of Blackburn (Cb)

Witton has an interesting trail, called a 'Wayfaring Course'. Wayfaring is a woodland walk with a difference, instead of following a waymarked route or guide book, the visiting 'wayfarer' uses a map provided by the park to navigate around it by way of a series of control points. Each point is identified by a number and letter code, the letters making up a word which proves that each control has been visited. Wayfarers can proceed at their own pace, and even picnic on the way.

All year, daily.

WORDEN HALL

Just south of Leyland town centre (Ba)

This charming old country house, set in 175 acres of beautiful grounds, is appropriately enough the home of the Lancashire branch of the Council for the Protection of Rural England. What the visitor sees today is an elegant mid-18th-century building, the so-called Derby Wing which was the only part of the original house to survive a fire in 1941. Largely derelict when restoration began in the 1970s, Worden Hall now houses a visitor centre which quickly dispels any false impression that Lancashire is a predominantly industrial county.

Apr-Oct, Tues-Sun pm; Nov-Mar, Thur-Sun pm; also Bank Hol Mon. Free entry. Refreshments. Shop. 🅿 *Tel Leyland (0772) 456181.*

WYCOLLER COUNTRY PARK

Off A6068, 2½ miles east of Colne (Db)

Tucked away in a steep-sided little valley in the depths of an ancient hunting forest, Wycoller is a time capsule. Crossing the little stream called the Wycoller Beck is a single slab or 'clam' bridge dating back to the Iron Age more than 2000 years ago. Nearby are the ruins of Wycoller Hall, the original of Charlotte Brontë's Ferndean Manor in *Jane Eyre*. The little hamlet of Wycoller is a perfectly preserved 19th-century industrial village, from which cars are firmly excluded. Three trails explore the area's history, literary associations and wildlife.

All year, daily.

COUNTY CALENDAR

Good Fri Rivington Pike: Fair.

Easter Sat Bacup: Nutters' Dance (morris-style).

Easter Mon Preston: Avenham Park Egg Rolling.

May (Spring Bank Hol). Ribble River: Raft Race.

May (early). Morecambe: Music Festival.

May (late). Blackpool: Dance Festival.

July (2nd weekend). Rossendale: Country Fair.

July (late). Astley Park, Chorley: Royal Lancashire Show.

August (late, to late Oct). Blackpool: Illuminations.

August (late). Blackpool: Lions Gala.

August (late). Morecambe: Folklore Fiesta.

September (early). Morecambe: Bowling Festival.

September (1st Sun). Rawtenstall: Round the Hills Walk.

Tourist information: Blackburn (0254) 53277; Blackpool (0253) 21891; Burnley (0282) 30055; Lancaster (0524) 32878; Preston (0772) 53731.

LEICESTERSHIRE

TWO COUNTIES IN ONE, WITH CASTLES AND A MAN-MADE LAKE

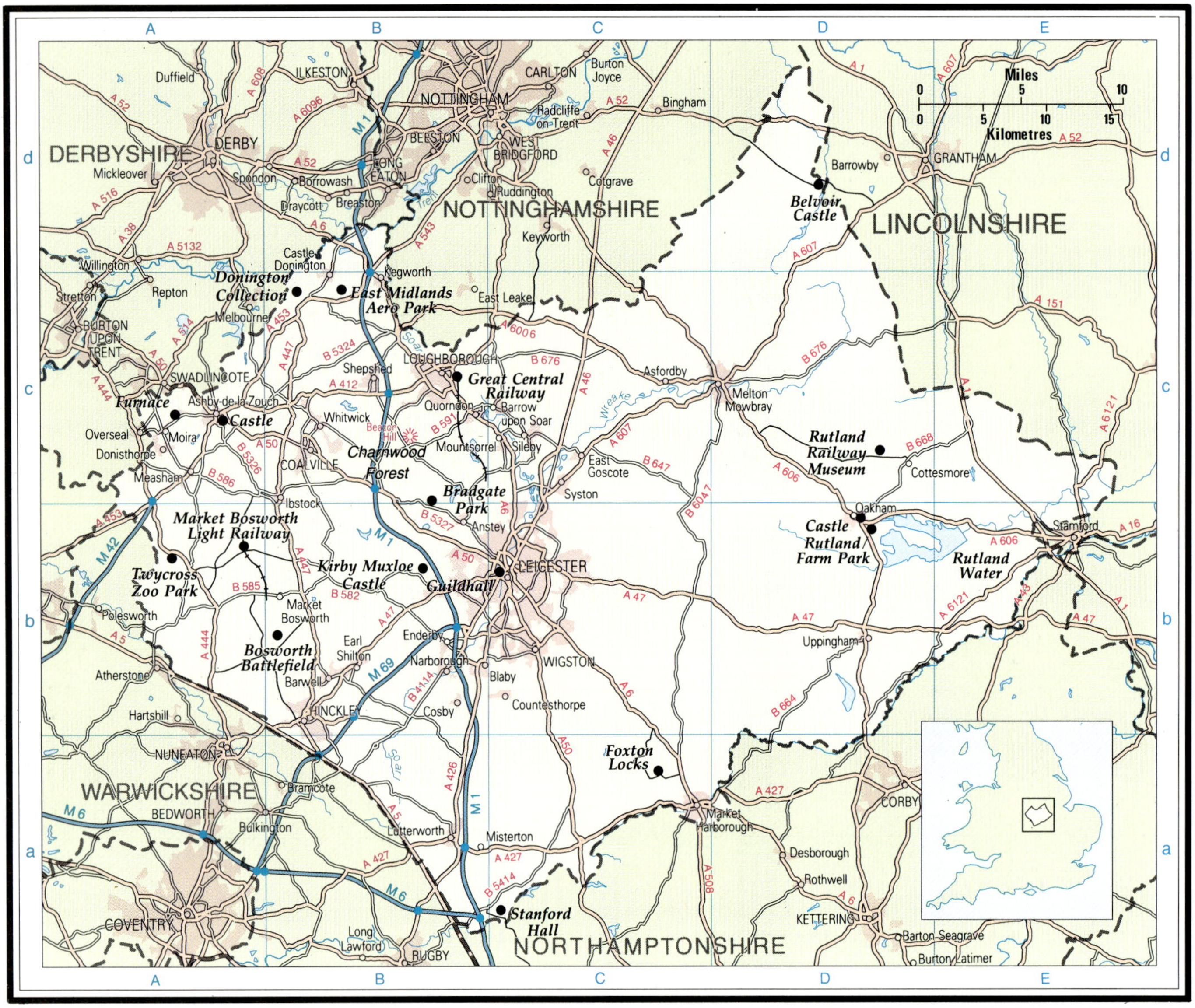

![T]his is the heart of England, a county of broad, rich, rolling landscapes. It is a small county, but packed with a surprising and varied number of attractions including four castles, three railway museums, a zoo and a famous battlefield. It includes the former county of Rutland, which doggedly refuses entirely to lose its identity and still gives its name to such attractions as the Rutland Railway Museum, Rutland Farm Park and Rutland Water. Leicester is the county town, and an industrial city, but its ancient roots can still be seen in the 14th-century Guildhall and at the Jewry Wall, built when Leicester was the Roman city of Ratae Coritanorum. In contrast Oakham, the former county town of Rutland, is a quiet little market town with a noble 12th-century hall.

ASHBY-DE-LA-ZOUCH CASTLE

In centre of Ashby-de-la-Zouch (Ac)

Sir Walter Scott set the tournament scene in his novel *Ivanhoe* in Ashby, and immediately turned public attention to the town's ancient castle ruins. The earliest parts of the castle date from the 12th century, but its most impressive feature is the tower built by the 1st Lord Hastings in the 15th century; the walls are 8ft 7in thick.

The 12th-century hall is the oldest part of the castle still standing. The solar nearby contained the private apartments of the lord and his family; it has a fine chimneypiece with moulded jambs and an elaborately carved lintel. The chapel was built by Lord Hastings between 1464 and 1483. *EH. All year, daily exc Thur and alternate Fri Oct-Apr. Adm charge.* P ♿ *(grounds only). Tel Ashby-de-la-Zouch (0530) 413343.*

BELVOIR CASTLE

Off A607, 10 miles north-east of Melton Mowbray (Dd)

This castle is not a place for faint hearts. The entrance hall is lined with ancient arms for 120 men, and near the entrance door are two star-like arrangements of cavalry sabres whose points meet in a central boss cast in the image of the Duke of Wellington. On the Grand Staircase visitors will pass a cannon captured during the First Sikh War, and a showcase in the ballroom displays the knife used to amputate the leg of Captain Lord Robert Manners, who died from wounds received in Admiral Lord Rodney's victory over the French fleet in 1782.

The dining room has two full-length portraits by Sir Joshua Reynolds, a magnificent silver punch bowl and a marble side table carved in

such a way that it appears to be covered by a white cloth. The Picture Gallery has the famous portrait of Henry VIII by Hans Holbein, and paintings by Poussin and Gainsborough.
Easter-Sept, daily exc Mon and Fri; also Bank Hol Mon. Adm charge. Refreshments. Shop. P *Toilets.* ♿ *Tel Grantham (0476) 870262.*

BOSWORTH BATTLEFIELD

Off B585, 2 miles south of Market Bosworth (Bb)

The flags of the opposing army commanders still fly over Bosworth Field where, on August 22, 1485, the last Plantagenet king, Richard III, fell defending his throne against Henry Tudor. His defeat marked the end of the Middle Ages and established Henry VII as the first Tudor monarch.

The drama and spectacle of that far-off day is recaptured today in the Battlefield Visitor Centre where replica shields, armour, flags, models and films of the battle can be seen. Visitors can follow paths and battle trails in the surrounding country park, taking in the spring where Richard drank before the battle and the spot where he was finally cut down, the positions of the opposing armies, and the path Henry Tudor took to meet the forces of his stepfather Lord Stanley who deserted Richard.
Visitor Centre: Easter-Oct, daily. Adm charge. Refreshments. Shop. P *Toilets.* ♿ *Tel Market Bosworth (0455) 290429. Country Park: All year, daily.*

BRADGATE PARK

Off B5327, 6 miles north-west of Leicester (Bc)

Visitors can walk, ride, scramble on the rocks, or simply picnic and watch the deer and other wildlife in this 1250 acre country park within Charnwood Forest. Bradgate Park comprises wonderfully varied types of countryside – bracken, woodland, parkland, grass, rocky hills and river. In the middle of it are the ruins of Bradgate House, the birthplace and home of Lady Jane Grey, great-niece of Henry VIII and Queen of England for nine days in 1553.

The surrounding Charnwood Forest is now a forest in name only, but still a fascinating place to visit. Its 30 square miles once contained Roman and Saxon settlements, and later several medieval abbeys were built there because the forest offered complete seclusion. For centuries the forest was an important source of wood for the charcoal industry, and gradually the trees disappeared. Today it consists of open heath, rocky outcrops and broken ridges, with just the occasional clump of oak trees to recall its former glory. The best viewpoints are Bardon Hill and Beacon Hill.
All year, daily.

DONINGTON COLLECTION

On A453, 7 miles north-west of Loughborough (Bc)

One man's lifelong enthusiasm for motor racing was the foundation for the collection of racing cars at Donington Park motor-racing circuit. Tom Wheatcroft fell in love with the sport when he first came to Donington Park, then in its heyday, in 1935. Now the track is his, together with almost 100 racing cars. These include many famous cars which were victorious in the Donington Grand Prix and have now been restored to the scene of their triumphs.
All year, daily. Adm charge. Refreshments. Shop. P *Toilets.* ♿ *Tel Derby (0332) 810048.*

A PHOENIX RISEN FROM THE ASHES *Beautiful Belvoir Castle stands on the site of a fortress built by Robert de Todeni, Standard Bearer to William the Conqueror. A fire in 1816 destroyed much of the castle, after which the present massive structure was built, inspired by Elizabeth, 5th Duchess of Rutland. The magnificent Elizabeth Saloon, decorated in Louis XIV style, has a ceiling painted by Thomas Wyatt using themes from Greek mythology. Its circular compartment over the great window bay (left) shows Juno in her chariot, attended by two peacocks.*

EAST MIDLANDS AERO PARK

On A453, 6 miles north-west of Loughborough (Bc)

There are few places in the country where visitors can get so close to big aircraft taking off and landing as at this aero park. A raised spectator mound stands only 60yds from the main runway and 20yds from the taxiway. All kinds of aeroplanes land at East Midlands Airport – commuter aircraft, large airliners and cargo planes – so there is always plenty to see.

In the visitor centre exhibits include a historic Whittle W2 jet engine made in 1943, while an adjoining aircraft museum includes an Avro Vulcan 'V' bomber.
All year, daily. Adm charge. Refreshments. Shop. P *Toilets.* ♿ *Tel Derby (0332) 810621.*

FOXTON LOCKS

Off A6, 4 miles north-west of Market Harborough (Ca)

An attractively landscaped picnic site is the starting point of a woodland path leading to one of the wonders of the Canal Age. In 1814, when canal builders seeking to link Leicester with London reached Foxton, they faced a problem

TIGHT SQUEEZE *A narrowboat negotiates the 7ft wide Foxton Locks, with little room to spare. The ten locks are continuous, forming a staircase, the top gate of one lock being the bottom gate of the next.*

– a 75ft rise in the space of 300yds to a summit 425ft above sea level. Their solution was the famous Foxton Staircase – ten locks arranged in two groups of five with a passing pond for barges between them.

The Staircase worked, but the locks were large enough only for one narrowboat. The problem of how to provide passage for wider boats was solved in 1900 by an even more extraordinary feat of canal engineering – the Foxton Barge Lift. Much of it was sold for scrap in 1928, but enthusiasts are now restoring it.

All year, daily. Free entry. Refreshments. Shop. P *Toilets.* ♿ *Tel Kibworth (053 753) 2285.*

GREAT CENTRAL RAILWAY

Loughborough town centre (Bc)

The starting point for steam trains of the Great Central Railway is the meticulously restored Loughborough Central Station, a wondrous scene of varnished wooden panelling and period lamps. Today's passenger can step back in time and be hauled by one of 18 steam locomotives, including the one and only No 71000 *Duke of Gloucester* – the pinnacle of express steam locomotive design in Britain.

Stations, signal boxes, bridges and viaducts along the line are all genuine Great Central structures, and the railway also boasts the only example of an original Great Central passenger steam locomotive – No 506 *Butler-Henderson*, which is part of the National Collection.

All year at weekends; also Wed in summer and Bank Hol. Adm charge. Refreshments. Shop. P *Toilets.* ♿ *Tel Loughborough (0509) 230726.*

KIRBY MUXLOE CASTLE

Off B5380, 4 miles west of Leicester (Bb)

Although it is called a castle, Kirby Muxloe is really a fortified house, complete with gunports for cannon which are among the earliest in England. It was built in the 15th century in the newly fashionable material of brick, by the 1st Lord Hastings, who had already built the castle at Ashby-de-la-Zouch. Unfortunately Hastings failed to find favour with the new king, Richard III, and was beheaded before his new castle could be completed.

The west tower is the only part of Kirby Muxloe to be completely finished. A circular stair connects the first and second floors, each of which consists of a large room, with an adjoining small room and a garderobe or latrine. The ground-floor room has six gunports, which are circular with a narrow slit above for sighting. More gunports are to be found in the gatehouse, on the right turret of which is the maunch or sleeve which formed the arms of Hastings, and above it a ship.

EH. All year, daily exc Wed and Thur Oct-Mar. Adm charge. P ♿ *Tel Leicester (0533) 386886.*

LEICESTER GUILDHALL

In centre of Leicester (Cb)

In wintertime, a bright fire of local coal burns cheerfully in the great fireplace of Leicester's ancient Guildhall. It is an endearingly domestic touch in a building which was Leicester's Town Hall until 1876 and still today plays a real part in the city's social life. The modest entrance to the building, next door to the cathedral, leads into a delightful little courtyard. On one side are cells built in the early 19th century and now a museum: peepholes in the doors give a view of the cells as they once appeared – complete with dummy prisoners. Upstairs in the Guildhall there is a small but cosy bedroom, still fitted out as it was when used by the visiting Recorder or Judge. This room leads off a library, with the books arranged on the shelves exactly as they were when first placed there about 1632. Downstairs, the Mayor's Parlour, snugly panelled in wood, has a superb Jacobean overmantel.

A reminder of an even earlier period in Leicester's history stands in the heart of the bustling modern city, where one of the largest Roman remains in Britain – the Jewry Wall – towers 30ft into the air. The origin of its name is unknown, but it probably formed the outer wall of the Roman baths, entered through the two great archways that still survive. The foundations of the various buildings are outlined in a grass lawn, and the nearby walkway gives a bird's eye view of the site. A museum displays objects found on the site, including a large section of mosaic pavement, and tableaux show 'Leicester folk' over 3000 years.

Guildhall, Jewry Wall Museum: All year, Mon-Thur and Sat; also Sun pm. Free entry. Tel Leicester (0533) 554100.

MARKET BOSWORTH LIGHT RAILWAY

Off B585, 4 miles north of Market Bosworth (Ab)

A steam-train journey through quiet countryside starts from Shackerstone Station. Completely derelict when it was bought by the Shackerstone Railway Society in 1970, the station now houses one of the finest collections of railway relics in the Midlands. Visitors can see seven steam locomotives and five diesel engines restored by the society. Most of them worked at collieries, power stations and iron works in the area. The coaches come from farther afield, such as the Corridor First, built in Swindon in 1954, and mainly used on services between Newcastle and King's Cross until it was brought to Shackerstone. The society also has several steam cranes, which are still used in laying sidings and making track alterations.

Easter Mon-Sept, Sun and Bank Hol; station also open Sat. Adm charge. Refreshments. Shop. P *Toilets.* ♿ *Tel Tamworth (0827) 880754.*

MOIRA FURNACE

Off B5003, 3 miles west of Ashby-de-la-Zouch (Ac)

In the 19th century Moira Furnace was the heart of a thriving mining village, the scene of noise, heat and activity. Now the curiously shaped building with its arched openings stands quietly in a rural setting, and it is left to the visitor's imagination to re-create the tumult of the past.

The furnace was the first of a new generation of blast furnaces built at the beginning of the 19th century, but it remained in operation for less than two years and proved an economic failure. The buildings were saved from dereliction by generations of mining families who made their homes there – in some cases up to the 1970s. The furnace remains intact, together with limekilns and the foundations of the engine house and casting shed. Displays inside the buildings explain how they worked, and a 2¼ mile industrial trail starts from the furnace.

Site: All year, daily. Buildings: Easter-Oct, weekends and Bank Hol pm. Free entry. Refreshments. Shop. P Toilets. ♿ (parts). Tel Burton upon Trent (0283) 215614.

OAKHAM CASTLE

In centre of Oakham (Db)

The Great Hall is all that survives today of this medieval fortified manor house, but it is one of the finest examples of Norman domestic architecture in England. It was built as a residence, the Great Hall being the centre of social and manorial activity. The approach to it is through a stone gateway which, although 13th century in form, was rebuilt by George Villiers, Duke of Buckingham, who bought the manor in 1621.

Inside, the hall is hung with more than 200 horseshoes, bearing the names and dates of peers and royalty who have paid the unique toll levied by the lord of the manor of Oakham on those passing through the town. The castle was also the administrative centre of Oakham and the emerging county of Rutland. Today it continues to fulfil its role as a courtroom.

All year, daily exc Mon. Free entry. Shop. ♿ Tel Oakham (0572) 3654.

CENTURIES OF DEBATE *For almost 400 years the mayor and corporation of Leicester met beneath the ancient timbers of the Guildhall. The hall was built in the late 14th century for the Corpus Christi Guild, and was bought by the town in 1563.*

RUTLAND FARM PARK

At Catmose Farm, on A6003, ½ mile south of Oakham (Db)

Parkland which previously formed part of a country estate is the setting for a varied collection of rare domestic animals, including many breeds once common on English farms but which have now almost disappeared.

Some breeds have surprisingly long histories. For example, White Park cattle probably came to Britain with the Romans. The Longhorn was developed from the medieval ox. The Soay sheep is even more ancient: bones found in New Stone Age sites are very similar to those of the present-day animal.

The park also has a collection of early tractors, horse-drawn vehicles and tools, and visitors can see the ridges and furrows which are the remains of the medieval system of cultivation; when the furrows became waterlogged, the ridges remained dry for cultivation.

Apr-Sept, daily exc Mon. Adm charge. Refreshments. Shop. P Toilets. ♿ Tel Oakham (0572) 56789.

RUTLAND RAILWAY MUSEUM

Off B668, 4 miles north of Oakham (Dc)

Any visitor who has read the Reverend W. Awdry's *Thomas the Tank Engine* will find hours of delight in this museum. It is devoted to the work of the humble tank engine and its diesel counterpart in industry generally and in ironstone quarrying in particular. The collection includes 20 steam and diesel locomotives and more than 60 wagons, vans and coaches. The museum has re-created a typical industrial yard and railway siding on which restored locomotives and stock are run. There are free train rides for visitors. There is also a lineside walk and picnic areas.

All year, daily (check for steam days). Adm charge. Refreshments (steam days only). Shop. P Toilets. ♿ Tel Stamford (0780) 62384.

RUTLAND WATER

Off A606, 3 miles east of Oakham (Db)

Wildlife and water sports abound at this man-made lake with the largest surface area in Europe: 3100 acres. Sailing and windsurfing are among the main attractions, and novice windsurfers can train on dry land on a sailboard simulator. The lake is also well known for fishing, and rainbow trout up to 10lb have been caught. A nature reserve extends around 7 miles of the shoreline. Three hides give the occasional glimpse of ospreys and terns. A visitor centre at Lyndon gives access to the 1 mile Gibbett Gorse nature trail.

An unusual feature of Rutland Water is the Water Museum, housed in a semi-submerged church. When the reservoir was created, seven farmhouses and 16 cottages were submerged, but the church was saved and its floor level raised. It now stands almost 100yds out from the shore, and is reached by a causeway. The museum is divided into two parts. One shows the history of the church and the Normanton manor estate to which it belonged. The other charts the history of the water supply, rivers and sewage disposal, and concentrates on traditional methods and equipment used before the development of new technology.

All year, daily. Recreational facilities Apr-Sept, daily. Free entry. Refreshments. Shop. P Toilets. ♿ Tel Empingham (078 086) 321.

STANFORD HALL

Off B5414, 3½ miles south-east of Lutterworth (Ca)

Visitors to this handsome William and Mary mansion will see a portrait of Sir Ambrose Cave, ancestor of the present owner, Lady Braye, with what looks like a bandage on his arm. It is, in fact, a garter belonging to Elizabeth I, which slipped from her leg one night when she was dancing. Sir Ambrose picked it up and offered it to the queen, who told him he could keep it. The good knight immediately tied it to his left arm, saying he would wear it as long as he lived.

The Cave family have lived at Stanford since 1430, and the mansion contains a collection of costumes worn by members of the family from the days of Queen Elizabeth to Queen Victoria. Among many fine paintings is a portrait of Charles II by Sir Peter Lely.

In the stable block is the Pilcher Aviation Museum. Percy Pilcher was killed at Stanford in 1899 in his flying machine *The Hawk*. In the museum there is a replica of the flying machine, looking curiously like a modern hang-glider. There is also a motorcycle museum.

Apr-Sept, Thur, Sat, Sun, Bank Hol Mon and Tues pm. Adm charge. Refreshments. Shop. Toilets. Tel Rugby (0788) 860250.

TWYCROSS ZOO PARK

On A444, 9 miles north-east of Hinckley (Ab)

Only 900 of the world's 15 million camels now live wild . . . The abbreviation 'zoo' for zoological garden was first used in a Victorian music-hall song . . . Chimpanzees enjoy colour television. Facts like these are the kind that visitors to Twycross absorb. Set in 50 acres of parkland, it has one of the largest collections of gibbons and other small apes in captivity. Visitors will learn that while all gorillas beat their chests, only males hoot, and that a lion's roar can be heard more than 2 miles away.

All year, daily. Adm charge. Refreshments. Shop. P Toilets. ♿ Tel Tamworth (0827) 880250.

COUNTY CALENDAR

Easter Mon Hallaton: Bottle-kicking and Hare-pie Scramble (traditional rugby-style game).

April (early). Loughborough: National Folk Music Festival.

May Day Hol Leicester: County Show.

May (Spring Bank Hol). Oakham: Rutland Show.

June (mid-month). Market Harborough: Carnival.

August (Sun before Bank Hol). Leicester Airport: Air Display.

August Bank Hol Leicester: Show. Belvoir Castle: Medieval Jousting Tournament.

November (early). Loughborough: Fair.

Tourist information: Leicester (0533) 556699; Loughborough (0509) 230131; Market Harborough (0858) 62649; Melton Mowbray (0664) 69946.

LINCOLNSHIRE

LANDMARKS OF BRICK AND STONE ABOVE THE FENS AND WOLDS

On the flat Lincolnshire Fens, man-made features take on a special significance. Every church spire is a landmark, windmills stretch their arms on far-off horizons and the red-brick tower of Tattershall Castle is visible for miles. Below the ever-changing skies the landscape wears a coat of many colours – the shimmering gold of cornfields, the rich green of vegetable crops, the vivid yellow of oilseed rape and, in spring, the many-hued patchwork of the tulip fields.

Lincolnshire is not all fenland, however. In the west runs the limestone ridge of Lincoln Edge, and above a gap pierced by the River Witham stands Lincoln – a queen of cities with a cathedral as its golden crown. To the east are the peaceful hills of the Wolds, beloved by Lord Tennyson whose model for his poem *Maud* lived at Harrington Hall. The Wolds descend to marshland and a breezy coastline, with wildlife havens at the Gibraltar Point and Saltfleetby-Theddlethorpe Nature Reserves, and the historic seaport of Boston whose famous 'Stump' has guided fenland travellers, sailors, and the airmen of the Second World War.

ALFORD MANOR HOUSE

West Street, Alford (Cc)

The Manor House, now a folk museum, is really a house within a house, for the original timbered building of about 1540 was encased in local red brick in the early 18th century. A model of the house in the entrance hall shows its construction.

Most of the museum's exhibits recall the Victorian age. There is a boot and shoemaker's shop of the 1860s, when a pair of boots could be made to measure for 16 shillings. Books containing recipes for well-tried pills, potions and purges are on display in the chemist's shop, and there is a schoolroom, complete with a backboard once strapped to scholars to cure round shoulders.

A peaceful waterside walk leads through the Manor House grounds, and a 'Heritage Trail' around the old town starts from the house. It passes the five-sailed mill in East Street, built in 1813 and the last of four mills in Alford. Its six-storey tower stands 95ft high. The mill is in full working order.

Manor House: Early May-late Sept, Mon-Fri. Adm charge. Shop. Tel Alford (052 12) 2484. Mill: Second Sat each month. Adm charge. Shop. P *(limited). Tel Lincoln (0522) 552222 ext 2805.*

ALVINGHAM WATER MILL

Off A16 in Alvingham, 3 miles north-east of Louth (Cc)

As many as 13 mills once worked on the little River Lud, but this one – the farthest downstream – is the only one to survive. The village has had a mill for more than 900 years, and the present building was erected in the late 17th century. Its machinery, including the great breast wheel, was probably installed in 1782, when the mill was enlarged. It prospered until about 1900, and is now restored as a working museum.

July-Aug, Mon, Thur, 2nd and 4th Sun pm; also Bank Hol Sun and Mon in summer. Adm charge. P *Tel South Cockerington (050 782) 544.*

ANIMAL GARDENS

North End, Mablethorpe (Cc)

Conservation is the main aim at Mablethorpe's Animal Gardens, and species that figure in the highly successful breeding programme include caracals (desert lynx) from Africa and India, Soay sheep from the Hebrides, sun conures and Amazon parrots from South America, and wildcats from highland Britain. The rescue and care of injured and sick animals, in conjunction with the RSPCA, is also important.

More than 70 species are represented among the 200 or so inhabitants, whose enclosures lie among colourful gardens. Monkeys include capuchins from the New World and vervet monkeys from the Old. There are birds of prey, peafowl, llamas and seals. Unusual species include giant 5ft tall sarus cranes from India and weaver birds, named for their intricately built nests.

Easter-Oct, daily. Adm charge. Refreshments. Shop. P *Toilets. Tel Mablethorpe (0521) 73346.*

AYSCOUGHFEE HALL AND GARDENS

On A1073, in Spalding town centre (Ca)

The flamboyant Gothic façade of this house, with ornate windows and doorways, pierced parapets and coat of arms, dates only from the 1840s. It hides a superb 15th-century merchant's house, complete with great hall and vaulted cellar. The house contains local history collections, and stands in lovely walled gardens where Dutch yew walks planted in the 17th century survive.

All year, daily. Free entry. Refreshments. Shop. P *Toilets.* ♿ *Tel Spalding (0775) 5468.*

BATTLE OF BRITAIN MEMORIAL FLIGHT

On A153, 15 miles north-east of Sleaford (Bb)

RAF Coningsby, an F2 Tornado base, is also the home of the Battle of Britain Memorial Flight. The Flight, whose aircraft fly regularly at displays throughout the year, is a living memorial to 'The Few' – those airmen who, when Britain stood alone after the fall of France, thwarted Hitler's invasion plans. It comprises three Spitfire Mark XIXs, a Spitfire Mark V, a Spitfire Mark II, which is believed to be the only flying survivor of the Battle of Britain, two Hurricanes, and the world's only airworthy Lancaster bomber. The aircraft are serviced by specialist groundcrew and flown by pilots, all based at RAF Coningsby.

Early Jan-mid December, Mon-Fri. Adm charge. Refreshments. Shop. P *Toilets.* ♿ *Tel Coningsby (0526) 44041.*

BELTON HOUSE

On A607, 3 miles north-east of Grantham (Ab)

A supreme example of Restoration country house architecture, Belton House remains virtually as it was built in 1688, its stonework a soft honey colour. The building is based on a simple H-plan, with long windows and a hipped roof topped by tall chimneys and graceful cupolas. In about 1830 Lady Brownlow, a descendant of the John Brownlow who built Belton, described it as 'a handsome, gentlemanlike house'.

The richly furnished interior has exquisite plaster ceilings by Edward Goudge, the 17th-century plasterer, and woodcarvings by Grinling Gibbons. There are fine paintings and silverware collected by Sir John Cust, the owner of Belton who was Speaker of the House of Commons from 1761 to 1770, and mementos of Edward VIII, to whom the 6th Lord Brownlow was lord-in-waiting and who visited Belton frequently.

The house, and formal gardens and orangery designed by Jeffry Wyatville in the 19th century, lie in a magnificently landscaped park. There is an adventure playground, and boat and miniature train rides for children in summer.

NT. Apr-Oct, Wed-Sun and Bank Hol pm, but closed Good Fri; Grounds from 11am. Adm charge. Refreshments. Shop. P *Toilets. Tel Grantham (0476) 66116.*

BURGH LE MARSH WINDMILL

On A158, 5 miles west of Skegness (Cc)

This mill is unique among Lincolnshire's surviving windmills in being 'left handed' – that is, its sails rotate clockwise to turn the millstones anti-clockwise. The five-sailed tower mill, five storeys high, was built in about 1813, although its onion-shaped cap – a style peculiar to Lincolnshire – dates only from 1947. An engine drove the stones on windless days from the late 19th century until 1960, and it is planned to install a diesel engine to drive the present four pairs of stones and other equipment.

All year, daily; working (wind permitting) 2nd and last Sun of month, and Bank Hol weekends. Adm charge. Shop. P *(limited). Tel Boston (0205) 870641.*

FLYING SALUTE *A Spitfire, Lancaster and Hurricane of the Battle of Britain Memorial Flight regularly take to the air as a continuing tribute to the airmen who fought and died during the Second World War.*

BUTTERFLY PARK

Off A17, 7 miles east of Holbeach (Ca)

The heady mixture of temperate, Mediterranean and tropical trees, shrubs and flowers, interspersed with ponds and streams and set in a vast glasshouse, is home to a wide variety of exotic butterflies. Native butterflies, moths and bees live in the outdoor British Garden, and a wildflower meadow attracts native wildlife. There is a children's adventure playground.

Apr-Oct, daily. Adm charge. Refreshments. Shop. P *Toilets.* ♿ *Tel Holbeach (0406) 363833.*

CHURCH FARM MUSEUM

Off A52, in Church Road, Skegness (Db)

The recollections of local people, who remember its days as a working farm, have enabled Church Farm to be restored to its appearance in 1900-10, and its rooms have a truly 'lived in' appearance. Most of the house dates from about 1760, but the porch, scullery, pantry and wash-house were Victorian additions. The wash-house has a hand-powered washing machine of the early 1900s. Outside are beehives, an orchard, farm implements and machinery and a traditional brick and pantile barn, whose granary is used as an exhibition gallery.

Even earlier days are recorded in the nearby Withern Cottage, a typical thatched, timber-framed Lincolnshire cottage, furnished as it would have been in 1800. The stables contain craft workshops, where there are demonstrations on most summer Sunday afternoons.

Apr-Oct, daily. Adm charge. Refreshments. P *Toilets. Tel Skegness (0754) 66658 (Apr-Oct); Lincoln (0522) 28448 (Nov-Mar).*

CROYLAND ABBEY

Off A1073, 11 miles south of Spalding (Ca)

In AD 699 a hermit, St Guthlac, set up his cell on an islet in the Fens. Many sought his counsel, including Ethelbald, a Mercian prince whose cousin had usurped his throne. Ethelbald vowed to build an abbey in memory of the saint on the site of his cell if he gained his birthright without bloodshed. This came about, and King Ethelbald founded the Benedictine abbey in 716. It soon grew, and with it the town of Crowland.

Much of the great abbey was destroyed after the Dissolution, and by Cromwell's men in 1643. However, the 15th-century north aisle survives as the parish church, with the tower and its bells – the oldest 'ring' in the country, one bell dating from the 15th century. There is also a fine Norman arch and part of the magnificently sculptured 13th-century west front.

The curious Trinity Bridge in the town centre dates from the 14th century. Its three arches, each with steps, rise up to a central point. The bridge was used by pedestrians and packhorses, but is now high and dry – the streams which it spanned were diverted long ago.

All year, daily. Free entry. Shop. P ♿ *Tel Peterborough (0733) 210499.*

DODDINGTON HALL

On B1190, 5 miles west of Lincoln (Ac)

This elegant house of brick and stone must have been something of a novelty when it was built in 1600. It does not cluster round a courtyard in the manner of earlier Elizabethan houses but looks outward through huge windows, a testimony to the security and confidence of the age, and a

ROSY VIEW *Broad windows in the west front of Doddington Hall look out on the walled West Garden, with its box-edged beds. The old-fashioned roses are at their best in late June and early July.*

hallmark of its architect Robert Smithson. Three graceful cupolas were Smithson's only decoration. His employer, Thomas Tailor, was Registrar to the Bishop of Lincoln, and though rich and successful, lived in the spartan style of the age; in 1606 there were only 83 items of furniture in the hall's 40 rooms.

The house has never been sold, but has passed by inheritance or marriage through several families, including the Delavals of Seaton. Surprisingly the exterior remains as it was in 1600, but in 1760 Sir John Delaval employed the Lumby brothers of Lincoln to redecorate the inside, and their elegant plasterwork still enhances the light, airy interior. Some rooms had double glazing – the first known use of this device in England.

Successive owners filled the hall with fine furniture, porcelain, tapestries and paintings, including two portrait groups by Reynolds. The grounds include walled formal gardens, a herb garden, 4 acres of wild gardens noted for their rhododendrons, a turf maze and a nature trail.
May-Sept, Wed, Sun and Bank Hol pm. Adm charge. Refreshments. Shop. P *Toilets. Tel Lincoln (0522) 694308.*

GAINSBOROUGH OLD HALL

Off A159, in Gainsborough town centre (Ac)

A host of eminent visitors came to this magnificent timber-framed manor house, rebuilt in 1470-80. They included Richard III, now the subject of a permanent exhibition there. Adherents of the Separatist Church, some of whom were to sail to America in the *Mayflower*, met in the house in the early 17th century. The great hall, more than 45ft long, is at the centre of the mansion, next to the enormous kitchen with its huge open fireplaces.
All year, weekdays; also Sun pm, Easter-Oct. Adm charge. Refreshments. Shop. Toilets. Tel Gainsborough (0427) 2669.

GIBRALTAR POINT NATIONAL NATURE RESERVE

Off Gibraltar Road, 3½ miles south of Skegness (Db)

Land, sea and sky merge in the infinite vistas of this carefully preserved area. It is a precarious, everchanging world. Wind-blown sand on the shore is 'fixed' by the roots of plants such as sea rocket, prickly saltwort and marram grass. The resultant dunes then provide shelter behind which deposition of finer material gradually builds mud flats into salt marshes.

Bird song pervades the air. The older West Dunes are the home of redpolls, whitethroats and willow warblers, and autumn visitors include fieldfares and redwings from Scandinavia, and thousands of waders. Plants include rare pyramidal orchids, and in summer a host of butterflies such as uncommon green hairstreaks and migrant painted ladies may be seen. Kestrels and short-eared owls hunt the short-tailed field voles that live on the salt marshes, which also attract redshanks, meadow pipits, skylarks and reed buntings. On a freshwater marsh, a public hide overlooks a man-made mere where ducks and waders breed.

The visitor centre makes a useful introduction to the 1000 acre reserve, and guided walks start from the centre on most summer days.
Visitor centre: May-Oct, daily; winter weekends. Free entry (charge for car park, May-Oct). Shop. P *(limited). Toilets.* ♿ *Tel Skegness (0754) 2677.*

GRANTHAM MUSEUM

Off A1, in Grantham town centre (Ab)

Grantham's two most famous personalities are celebrated in this museum: the physicist and mathematician Isaac Newton, who was born at nearby Woolsthorpe Manor in 1642 and attended Grantham Grammar School, and Margaret Thatcher, Britain's first woman prime minister, who was born in the town in 1925. Other displays tell the story of the town from its foundation in Saxon times, including the great days of the coaching era and the growth of its agricultural engineering industry in the 19th century. One exhibit consists of the re-creation of a room in the original museum of 1890.
Apr-Sept, daily exc Sun am; Oct-Mar, Tues-Sat. Adm charge. Shop. ♿ *Tel Grantham (0476) 66444.*

GRIMSTHORPE CASTLE

On A151, 3½ miles north-west of Bourne (Ba)

The promise of a visit from his brother-in-law Henry VIII inspired the Duke of Suffolk in 1540 to transform his medieval castle into a Tudor house of stone ranged around an open courtyard and quadrangle. In the 18th century, Sir John Vanbrugh turned the north front and courtyard into a miniature version of Blenheim Palace, his own finest creation. A little later Capability Brown landscaped the park for a fee of £105.

The west front was rebuilt in the 1840s, and extensive restoration work has been carried out this century. The castle contains fine furniture and paintings, including superb portraits.
Late July-early Sept, pm daily. Adm charge. Refreshments. P *Toilets. Tel Edenham (077 832) 205.*

HARRINGTON HALL

On A158, 7 miles east of Horncastle (Cc)

It was the terrace here which was the 'High Hall Garden' of Tennyson's poem *Maud* – in real life Rosa Baring who lived in the hall with her guardian. The 17th-century Caroline mansion of mellow red brick stands on a medieval stone base and retains its Elizabethan porch tower. Inside are panelled rooms with fine 17th and 18th-century furniture, china and paintings. There are 5 acres of gardens, noted especially for their fragrant roses, and a garden centre.

The hall lies on the edge of the Wolds, in the heart of 'Tennyson country'. The poet was born in 1809 at Somersby, 3 miles to the west, while his father was rector there. Inside the 15th-century Church of St Margaret there are mementos and a portrait bust of the poet. 'The Brook' of Tennyson's poem still flows through the village.
Hall: Easter-Sept, Thur and some Sun pm. Gardens and garden centre: Apr-Oct, Wed, Thur and some Sun and Bank Hol pm. Adm charge. P *Tel Spilsby (0790) 52281.*

HARTSHOLME COUNTRY PARK

Off B1190, 4 miles south-west of Lincoln centre (Bc)

The man-made lake in this green oasis formerly supplied water to the city of Lincoln. Hartsholme Hall, a Victorian Gothic-style mansion built in 1862 to overlook the lake, was pulled down in 1951; its 100 acre estate now forms the country park. There are several walks through grassland and woods, including a tranquil lakeside path, and a nature trail from which kingfishers may be seen.
All year, daily. Information centre: Apr-Oct, Fri-Tues. Free entry. Refreshments. P *Toilets.* ♿ *Tel Lincoln (0522) 686264.*

HECKINGTON WINDMILL

On B1394, 5 miles east of Sleaford (Bb)

This is Britain's only eight-sailed windmill to survive intact. It was built with five sails in 1830, but was repaired and given additional sails after storm damage in 1890. The mill is 100ft tall, and ground corn commercially until 1946. It is now working again.

The nearby Pearoom was built in 1890 as a pea-sorting warehouse and functioned until 1962. It is restored, and now houses workshops for crafts such as spinning and weaving, leatherwork and jewellery making.
Mill: Apr-Sept, Sat, Sun and Bank Hol pm. Adm charge. Pearoom: All year, Tues-Sat; also Sun pm. Free entry. Refreshments (weekends). Shop. P *Toilets.* ♿ *Tel (Mill and Pearoom): Sleaford (0529) 60765.*

BYGONES AND BICYCLES IN LINCOLN

There are several Lincolns, built for different times and purposes, but long meshed into a splendid whole. The Celtic fort on the hilltop became a Roman garrison town: the Newport Arch is the only Roman gateway in Britain that is still used by traffic. An Anglian town, a Danish borough, then a Norman stronghold followed. In the Middle Ages Lincoln was famed for its cloth, immortalised by the Lincoln green said to have been worn by Robin Hood; wool merchants' houses still line the streets leading down from the cathedral whose three great towers bestow a calm blessing on the city below.

Cathedral: All year, daily. Free entry. Tel Lincoln (0522) 44544. Castle: All year, daily exc Sun Nov-Mar. Adm charge. Shop. Toilets. Tel (0522) 511068. Cycle Museum, Brayford Wharf North: All year, daily. Adm charge. Shop. P Toilets. ♿ Tel (0522) 45091. Museum of Lincolnshire Life, Burton Road: All year, daily. Adm charge. Shop. P Toilets. ♿ Tel (0522) 28448.

PAVILIONED IN SPLENDOUR *From its magnificent west portals to the exquisite eight-light window at the east end (above), Lincoln Cathedral has an ethereal, dream-like quality, enhanced by its pale gold stonework, pointed Gothic arches and the delicate tracery of its tall, slender windows. It dates mostly from the 12th and 13th centuries. An earthquake destroyed much of the original Norman church, but its west front, with three elaborate Norman portals surmounted by a magnificent sculptured frieze, survived.*

RIDING HIGH *This advanced version of a 'penny farthing' bicycle, with a chain-driven gear, dates from 1884. It is one of the many exhibits in the National Cycle Museum which depicts the history of the bicycle, from a hobby horse of 1818 and springless boneshakers with solid tyres to racing cycles of the present day. There is also a collection of posters and badges.*

POINT OF VIEW *The Observatory Tower on Lincoln Castle (above) dates from the 14th century, but the upper turret was restored in 1825 as an observatory for the governor of the prison built within the castle, who was a keen astronomer. Today the tower affords fine views over Lincoln and the Trent valley.*

LIFELINES *Bygones as sharply contrasted as a 1909 steam shovel (far left) and a village post office, complete with postmistress's bicycle (left), are near neighbours in the Museum of Lincolnshire Life. A series of imaginative exhibitions shows aspects of life in the 19th and early 20th centuries.*

LOUTH MUSEUM
Off A16, in Louth (Cc)

The Louth Naturalists', Antiquarian and Literary Society had its beginnings in 1884, when four gentlemen of the town met to form a Naturalists' Club. The club and its collections grew from strength to strength, and its new museum opened in 1910. Fine collections of butterflies, moths and fossils from the area are on display. Bygones include carpets locally made in the 19th century, tapestries, dresses and gloves. Old newspapers, books and photographs relate local history, and there is a scrapbook about the poet Lord Tennyson, who with his brothers attended Louth Grammar School.

All year, Sat, Sun and Wed pm; also Mon, Tues and Thur pm, June-Aug. Adm charge. Tel Louth (0507) 603026.

MUSEUM OF BRITISH MILITARY UNIFORMS
On B1177, 8 miles south-east of Sleaford (Ba)

The feats of heroism which earned many VCs are recorded in this museum housed in an old Wesleyan chapel. There are uniforms ranging in date from the Napoleonic Wars to the present day, many of them displayed on life-size models. Mess dress, battledress, uniforms of specialist corps such as the Royal Marines and Royal Engineers, and a section devoted to the women's services are also included. The scarlet tunics of Victorian infantry and the kilts and trews of Scottish regiments give splashes of bright colour, and there is appropriately a special display on the Royal Lincolnshire Regiment.

Apr-late Sept, Thur-Sat; Oct-late Nov, Sat and Sun. Adm charge. Shop. P *Toilets.* ♿ *Tel Culverthorpe (052 95) 544.*

RUTLAND COTTAGE MUSIC MUSEUM
On B1165, 5 miles south-east of Spalding (Ca)

Time stopped in the 1950s in this museum, where all manner of mechanical musical instruments may be seen and heard, including some of the earliest Edison phonographs. There is a library of more than 10,000 records dating back to 1900, and visitors can ask to hear any of them.

The museum is the headquarters of the Fairground Society and includes fairground organs, 'rides' – the beautifully carved horses and other animals on which the public sat – and a collection of rare photographs of the fairground world.

Easter-Sept, Sat, Sun and Bank Hol. Adm charge. Refreshments. Shop. P *Toilets. Tel Holbeach St Johns (040 634) 379.*

ST BOTOLPH'S CHURCH
In centre of Boston (Cb)

During the Second World War, when bomber airfields dotted the Lincolnshire countryside, the slim, 272ft tall lantern tower of St Botolph's Church, generally called 'Boston Stump', was held in special affection by the aircrews; as they returned in the first light of morning, it pointed the way home.

St Botolph founded a monastery here in AD 654; the name of the town is simply a shortened version of Botolph's Town. Though of cathedral size, St Botolph's has never been anything other than a parish church. It stands between the River Witham and the Market Place, both of which contributed considerably to its building. In the Middle Ages, Boston was one of the principal seaports in the country, and its merchants grew rich from wine, wool and cloth.

TRAVELLERS' GUIDE *For centuries fenland travellers and sailors took their bearings from the 'Boston Stump', so called because of the stubby appearance of St Botolph's Church tower from afar. Seen at close hand, however, it is a slender creation of tall windows and graceful buttresses.*

Within, the beauty of the church owes much to its noble proportions. Its total length is just 10ft longer than the height of the tower and it has a nave that soars throughout its length. Of particular interest are the 13th-century sanctuary knocker on the tower door and the serene-faced effigy of Dame Margaret Tilney 'who layid the first stone of the goodly steple of the Paroche Church of Boston in 1309'. There are some delightful 14th-century carvings in the choir stalls, including one of a schoolmaster belabouring a boy with a birch.

The pulpit dates from 1612, the year in which the Reverend John Cotton was appointed Vicar of Boston. In 1633 he and a number of his congregation set sail for Massachusetts, where they founded a town named after the one they had left behind. Five English Bostonians later became Governors of Massachusetts and are commemorated in the church, as is John Cotton in the chapel named after him.

Another building that American visitors flock to see, because of its connection with the Pilgrim Fathers, is St Mary's Guildhall in South Street, which was built in about 1450. The guild was disbanded at the Reformation, since when the Guildhall has been courthouse and jail, Town Hall, and, latterly, a charming local museum.

The old Courtroom still has its massive dock of 1545, complete with shackles, and a circular staircase leading to the cells below. The cells are still there too, surprisingly comfortable for the period, with a plaque above them recording that William Bradford, William Brewster and others were imprisoned there in 1607 for attempting to emigrate to Holland and religious freedom. They were treated courteously, apparently, but jailed for about a month. The spot where they were arrested is marked by a monument on the river bank, some 4 miles east of Boston. In 1608 they sailed to Holland, where they stayed for 12 years before returning to England, and eventually sailed from Plymouth in the *Mayflower*.

Church: All year, daily. Tel Boston (0205) 62864. Guildhall: All year, daily exc Sun. Adm charge. Tel (0205) 65954.

SALTFLEETBY-THEDDLETHORPE NATIONAL NATURE RESERVE
Off A1301, 10 miles north-east of Louth (Cc)

Lincolnshire's only colony of natterjack toads is to be found in the freshwater marsh within the dunes of this 4½ mile long coastal reserve. These rare toads, distinguished from common toads by a yellow line down the middle of the back, are inactive by day, but emerge to feed in the evenings. In spring and early summer they move to the shallow pools to mate and spawn, and their curious churring call is heard on warm evenings.

The dunes are also noted for their sea buckthorn – a mass of bright orange berries in autumn – pyramidal and marsh orchids, badgers, nesting skylarks, warblers and linnets, and many colourful butterflies.

Grey seals produce their pups on the sandbars nearby, and these and common seals haul out to bask and rest. Part of the reserve is used sometimes by the Ministry of Defence, and visitors should observe the safety regulations displayed.
All year, daily.

SIBSEY TRADER MILL

Off A16, 5 miles north of Boston (Cb)

This stately brick-built tower mill on the edge of the Fens is one of the few surviving six-sailed windmills in England. It was one of the last mills to be built in Lincolnshire, erected only in 1877, but stands on the site of a much earlier post mill. The original machinery at Sibsey was still working in 1953, and the mill has since been restored. It contains a display about Lincolnshire mills.
EH. Apr-Sept, Mon, Thur, Fri, Sat; also Wed am and Sun pm. Adm charge. P *(limited). Toilets. Tel Boston (0205) 750036 or Cambridge (0223) 358911.*

SKEGNESS NATURELAND MARINE ZOO

North Parade, Skegness (Db)

Baby seals cast ashore from the nearby Wash are reared at this marine zoo, and most are later returned to the wild in good health. Penguins and sea lions live nearby, while the Tropical House is the home of scorpions, spiders, crocodiles, snakes, iguanas and tree frogs. Tropical butterflies, flamingos, parrots and Chinese painted quails are among the inmates of the Floral Palace, a riot of colourful tropical plants. The aquarium includes a 5000 gallon tank for rainbow trout, and striped Korean squirrels live outdoors on an island set in a pool which is home to British freshwater fish and giant Japanese carp (Koi).

At the Lifeboat Station near the Clock Tower on South Parade, visitors may look over the boat, while Skegness Model Village, in a garden nearby, has 40 buildings and 400 human figures, all one-sixteenth life size.
Zoo: All year, daily. Adm charge. Refreshments. Shop. Toilets. Tel Skegness (0754) 4345. Lifeboat station: May-Oct, daily. Free entry. Shop. Tel (0754) 3011 (am only). Model village: Easter, Spring Bank Hol-Sept, daily. Adm charge. ♿ *Tel (0754) 67805.*

SPRINGFIELDS GARDENS

On A151, 1 mile east of Spalding (Ca)

The season here opens with a colourful riot of tulips, narcissi, daffodils, hyacinths and pansies, and ends with the first hint of glorious autumn tints. More than 150,000 bedding plants, together with dahlias and roses, are the attractions from July to September. There are woodlands, 4 miles of paved walks, a lake, and glasshouses filled with tulips, geraniums and begonias. The Spalding Flower Parade visits Springfields during the parade weekend in May.
Apr-Sept, daily. Adm charge. Refreshments. Shop. P *Toilets.* ♿ *Tel Spalding (0775) 4843.*

STAMFORD MUSEUM

In Stamford town centre (Ba)

David Lambert, who topped the scales at 52st 11lb and had a girth of 9ft 4in, was Britain's heaviest man when he died in Stamford in 1809, aged 39. A life-size model of Lambert, wearing the only one of his suits to survive, stands in the museum. His grave is in St Martin's churchyard, on the other side of the River Welland.

The museum is a visitor centre for the historic market town, with displays on its archaeology and history from Roman times. Stamford was a prosperous Danish walled town by about AD 900, and there is fine Stamford ware – glazed pottery made between AD 850 and 1250.

A former brewery in All Saints Street now houses the Stamford Brewery Museum, which takes visitors back to the working world of 1900. On working days, coopers, wheelwrights and saddlers can be seen plying their trades, and a Shire horse from Samuel Smith's Tadcaster brewery can be seen. Beers from the wood can be sampled in the museum's refreshment room.
Apr-Sept, daily exc Sun am; Oct-Mar, Tues-Sat. Adm charge. Shop. Tel Stamford (0780) 55611. Brewery Museum: Apr-Sept, Wed-Sun and Bank Hol. Adm charge. Refreshments. Shop. Toilets. Tel (0780) 52186.

TALLINGTON LAKES LEISURE PARK

On A16, 4 miles east of Stamford (Ba)

This theme park is for 'water babies' of all ages. Its eight lakes set in fine parkland provide 200 acres for water sports of all kinds, from fishing and canoeing to dinghy sailing. Tuition for water-skiers and windsurfers is available. There is also a dry ski slope, a model boat harbour, and the children's adventure playground includes a beach and lagoon.
Easter-Dec, daily; also winter weekends. Adm charge. Refreshments. P *Toilets. Tel Market Deeping (0778) 347000.*

TATTERSHALL CASTLE

On A153, 3½ miles south-east of Woodhall Spa (Bb)

This lonely, moated castle keep has an exotic continental air. It was built in about 1440 for Ralph, Lord Cromwell, who as a young man had served with the English army at Agincourt in 1415. When he inherited this estate in 1419 he set about rebuilding an earlier castle on the site in the French style.

The brick tower of Tattershall now rises dramatically to 110ft above the flat countryside and commands stupendous views – on clear days as far as 'Boston Stump' and Lincoln Cathedral. The tower has four storeys above the basement, each containing one vast room with a massive, carved fireplace.

The castle became derelict about 1700, and the living quarters and curtain wall were destroyed in the 19th century. Lord Curzon, Viceroy of India, bought and restored the property, and in 1925 gave it to the National Trust.

Castle Leisure Park adjoins the castle grounds. Its 365 acres of parkland, lakes and woods provide water sports of all kinds, fishing, horse riding, pony trekking, nature walks, an adventure playground, golfing, squash and racket ball, and an indoor games room.
Castle: NT. All year, daily exc Sun am. Adm charge. Shop. P *Toilets.* ♿ *(part). Tel Coningsby (0526) 42543. Park: All year, daily. Adm charge. Refreshments. Shop.* P *Toilets.* ♿ *Tel (0526) 43193.*

WOOLSTHORPE MANOR

Off B6403, 7 miles south of Grantham (Aa)

Sir Isaac Newton, the physicist who discovered the Law of Gravity, was born in this modest farm house in 1642. His genius was recognised by his uncle, the Reverend William Ayscough, and in 1662 Newton went to Cambridge University. Though he returned to Woolsthorpe rarely, it was during a visit in 1665, made to escape the plague, that he discovered the principle of differential calculus. Newton said later: 'In those days I was in the prime of my age for invention.'

The house is much as it was in Newton's day. Graffiti on the wall of the old kitchen were reputedly drawn by Newton himself.
NT. Apr-Oct, Wed-Sun and Bank Hol pm. Adm charge. P *(limited). Toilets. Tel Grantham (0476) 860338.*

COUNTY CALENDAR

March (mid-month). Lincoln: Lincolnshire Horse Trials.

March (late). Belton House: Belton Park Horse Trials.

April/May Lincoln: Arts Festival.

May (1st or 2nd Sat). Spalding: Flower Parade.

June Lincoln: Lincolnshire Show.

July (early) Lincoln Castle: Medieval Joust and Fayre.

August Skendleby: Lincolnshire Sheepdog Trials.

Tourist information: Grantham (0476) 66444; Heckington (0529) 60765; Lincoln (0522) 29828; Spalding (0775) 5468; Spilsby (0790) 52301; Stamford (0780) 55611, Skegness (0754) 4821.

HIGH LIVING *Restoration of the moat, largely filled in during the 19th century, has restored islanded splendour to Tattershall Castle's magnificent brick keep, the main surviving part of Lord Cromwell's 15th-century home.*

MERSEYSIDE

A CITY WITH TWO NEW CATHEDRALS ABOVE A HISTORIC WATERFRONT

The heart of Merseyside is Liverpool, the small fishing village that grew to become one of the world's largest ports. Today much of the bustle of shipping which used to animate 7 miles of waterfront is stilled – but Liverpool's dockland has been reborn, with a superb maritime museum and a wide range of other exhibition centres forming a living village around the Albert Dock complex. If the maritime theme predominates, modern art and the culture of the Beatles also have honoured places.

But there is more to Merseyside than Liverpool alone. The surrounding countryside offers a choice of open-air attractions, including the beautiful Wirral Country Park, with its teeming native wildlife, and Knowsley Safari Park, where more exotic species roam. On the banks of the Mersey stands Port Sunlight Village, built by the soap tycoon Lord Leverhulme to provide ideal homes for his staff, while for those seeking out-of-the-ordinary attractions there are museums of glass-making and clock-making, and an expressively titled Large Objects Collection.

AINSDALE SAND DUNES

Off A565, 1 mile north of Formby (Bc)

A wide variety of animals and plants thrive among the Ainsdale dunes; among them are two specially protected creatures, the natterjack toad and the sand lizard. The dunes started developing in the 16th century, and by the late 19th century they formed a belt about a mile wide between Southport and Formby. Public access is restricted to protect animal and plant life, but 6 miles of pathways marked with white-topped posts enable visitors to look out over the reserve. *NCC. All year, daily (footpaths only).*

ALBERT DOCK

On dockside, Liverpool (Bb)

Nowhere else in Britain can you get a better idea of what the early Victorians were like when they began to flex their commercial muscles. The Albert Dock, opened in 1846, expresses Liverpool's total optimism in itself as a seaport; the architect, Jesse Hartley, designed buildings not merely to last, but for eternity. The basins, the walls, the gatekeepers' lodges are of granite, as are the cobbles of the quaysides. The warehouses, supported on mighty columns, are of stone and brick, cemented by iron-hard lime.

Only one thing was forgotten – the steamship, that got bigger and bigger, and required ever-deeper docks, deeper than the Albert could offer. From playing host to ocean-going square riggers, the dock declined to servicing coastal traffic and closed altogether in 1972.

But being immortal, Albert Dock and the surrounding dockland have gained a new lease of life. Granada TV News has its headquarters in the Dock Traffic Office; the Pump House has been converted into a most original pub; and the warehouse pillars now shield arcades of delightful shops selling ceramics, antiques, flowers and nursery interiors. Picturesquely piled demerara rum barrels and old, ponderous lifting gear remain as hints of older times.

Boat hire, boat trips and watersports are offered, and a Riverside Walk leads to a huge sandstone warehouse, home of the newly opened branch of London's Tate Gallery. The emphasis is on modern art; artists represented include Dali, Miró and Rothko. From the Walk there are views of ships and ferries ploughing the dark waters of the Mersey, and beyond them the cranes, docks and shipyards of Birkenhead.

The Albert Warehouse contains the Merseyside Maritime Museum, which is still very much in the making. From a historian's point of view, the nucleus is the Maritime Records Centre which has the archives of Liverpool's docks – including the original plans – and those of its shipping and dock trades. The exhibits include ship models, maritime paintings and marine engines – and there are several full-size vessels in the museum's Maritime Park – which is open from May to October. The most popular attraction is the evocative Emigrants to a New World exhibition which is dedicated to the 9 million emigrants from all parts of Europe who passed through Liverpool between 1830 and 1930 on their way to new lives in Canada, Australia and the USA. Dioramas tell of their reasons for emigrating, show the Liverpool boarding houses they stayed in, and recall the 'Street Pirate' confidence tricksters who preyed upon

them. There are also pathetic relics recovered from emigrant ships that foundered in the Irish Sea.
All year, daily. Adm charge. Refreshments. Shops. 🅿 *Toilets.* ♿ *Tel Liverpool (051) 709 1551.*

BEATLE CITY
Albert Dock, Liverpool (Bb)

A little more than a quarter of a century ago, no one outside Liverpool had ever heard of Penny Lane or Strawberry Fields. Now the world knows of them and can also appreciate the Liverpool voice and wit. It is all owed to that phenomenon of the 1960s, the Beatles, and very properly Liverpool has erected a shrine commemorating their times and talents.

Beatle City is in the new Albert Dock complex within sight of the Liver Birds, and in the liveliest manner conducts visitors through memorabilia of the childhood of John, Paul, George and Ringo, and shows how they first united in a group called The Quarrymen, being paid £3-£5 per session. There followed the Beetles (as they then spelt their name), Hamburg, the Cavern Club and manager Brian Epstein, the first great hits, world fame and Beatlemania. All these phases are recalled in reconstructions of the Cavern Club, audiovisual dioramas of Liverpool in the 1960s, reconstructions of film and recording studios, and in the endless playing of the Mersey minstrels' tapes. Lots of personal belongings – suits, guitars, Ringo Starr's Mini-Cooper, letters, accompanied by Beatle toys, posters, comics, jigsaw puzzles and the graffiti-covered front door of the Apple Corporation from London.

After all this effervescence, it's saddening to be reminded by old headlines of the Beatles' break-up, of Brian Epstein's suicide, and of the murder of John Lennon, who is represented by a bronze bust. But in Liverpool, the Beatles live on, not only in this museum, but in the driving spirit of the young groups still evolving in this musicians' breeding ground.
All year, daily. Adm charge. Refreshments. Shop. 🅿 *Toilets.* ♿ *Tel Liverpool (051) 709 0117.*

CROXTETH HALL AND COUNTRY PARK
Off A580, 5 miles north-east of Liverpool (Bb)

The atmosphere of more leisurely Victorian and Edwardian days is well preserved at Croxteth, former home of the Earls of Sefton; but there are plenty of up-to-date attractions too. This was once a vast country estate covering thousands of acres. Now fewer than 600 acres remain, but within this space there are plenty of reminders of bygone country-house life. Furnished rooms and costume groups maintain the 'Croxteth 1905' theme, and an exhibition tells the estate's story.

In the walled garden, laid out in the first half of the 19th century, are old fruit trees trained in strange shapes, figs and peaches grown under glass, and a mushroom house. Croxteth's home farm is packed with livestock and has a centre for rare breeds. Around it all, 530 acres of parkland invite walking, picnics and nature study.
Hall: Good Fri-Sept, daily. Park: All year, daily. Adm charge. Refreshments. Shop. 🅿 *Toilets.* ♿ *Tel Liverpool (051) 228 5311.*

DOCKLAND HOME *The Edwardian parlour of the lovingly restored Piermaster's House is among the highlights of the Merseyside Maritime Museum complex at Liverpool's revitalised Albert Dock.*

KNOWSLEY SAFARI PARK
Off A58 at Prescot, 10 miles east of Liverpool (Cb)

Animals from five continents contribute to the excitement and spectacle of Knowsley. Here, within sight of mighty African elephants, children can watch baby rabbits at play. Such a contrast conveys the spirit of this superb combination of zoo and park; the idea is that the animals, whilst a delight to onlookers, should live as naturally as possible.

The park had its beginnings as long ago as the early 19th century, when the 13th Earl of Derby, a noted zoologist, set up a menagerie which became one of the finest private collections in the world. The variety of animals to be seen is wide. There are lions and tigers and towering elephants; herds of African buffalo and eland; big white rhinos, gnus and zebras from Africa; wallabies from Australia; camels originating from Central Asia; and North American bison.
Mar-Oct, daily. Adm charge. Refreshments. Shop. 🅿 *Toilets.* ♿ *Tel Liverpool (051) 430 9009.*

LARGE OBJECTS COLLECTION
Princes Dock, Liverpool (Bb)

This unique museum is likely to have the strongest appeal to people who think big. All the items on show are in the heavyweight class, ranging from a Blue Streak rocket satellite launcher to the Lord Mayor of Liverpool's State Coach. The ground between is covered by such substantial objects as a 2 ton telescope, a Mersey Tunnel cleaning machine, a variety of steam-driven vehicles, and a printing press. A children's technology section explains the workings and purpose of the exhibits to youngsters.
Apr-early Sept, daily. Free entry. Refreshments. Shop. 🅿 *Toilets.* ♿ *Tel Liverpool (051) 236 0642.*

WORDS OF WISDOM *Posters and pamphlets displayed at the Merseyside Maritime Museum were designed to help the millions who sailed from Liverpool between 1830 and 1930 to seek their fortunes abroad.*

LIVERPOOL CATHEDRALS
Near city centre (Bb)

They stand at either end of the largely Georgian Hope Street, dominating – maybe overwhelming – the Liverpool skyline, and because of their size they look a lot closer to the waterfront than they really are.

They are very different. Work was begun on the Anglican Cathedral in 1904 and doggedly continued through two World Wars to the triumphant royal dedication in 1978. The already imposing size of the red-sandstone building is made all the more impressive by its siting on the edge of a rocky, wooded canyon containing the long-disused Cemetery of St James.

The cathedral is largely the work of Sir Giles Gilbert Scott, and medieval in style, though on a scale that few builders of the Middle Ages would have attempted. Within, it is grand and uncluttered, perhaps like some of the much older cathedrals before they were overwhelmed by monuments. The walls of the building are reddish-brown, the floors of black and white marble, and from the towering windows, panels of red, blue and gold glow out of the dimness.

To go directly from the Gothic of the Anglican Cathedral to the ultramodern Roman Catholic Cathedral of Christ the King takes a little adjustment. Irreverently nicknamed the Mersey funnel, with its circular nave leading up to the gigantic lantern, it does indeed somewhat resemble an upside-down funnel with flying buttresses. Before the main entrance is a 90ft separate stone wedge which is the bell tower.

As with the Anglican Cathedral, there were delays in the building. Sir Edwin Lutyens made a start with the enormous crypt – twice the size of the present church – in 1933, but by 1940 it was realised there was no chance of completing so vast a project. Work on the present, smaller building, designed by Sir Frederick Gibberd, did not begin until 1960, but five years later it was completed. It stands on the earlier crypt, half of whose roof serves as a piazza.

The interior is breathtaking – a 193ft diameter circle from which lead 13 chapels, the entrance hall and two side porches. The seating, too, is circular, centring upon the High Altar, a block of pure white marble on which stands a tall, simple bronze crucifix by Elizabeth Frink. The lighting comes from slender glass panels of red, blue and green reaching up to the 2000 ton lantern whose huge drum is filled with glass presenting all the colours of the spectrum.

Anglican Cathedral: All year, daily. Free entry. P *Tel Liverpool (051) 709 6271. Roman Catholic Cathedral: All year, daily. Free entry. Refreshments. Shop.* P ♿ *Tel Liverpool (051) 709 9222.*

LIVERPOOL MUSEUM

William Brown Street, in Liverpool city centre (Bb)

The exhibits in this fine museum range from Egyptian mummies to space exploration; from Benin bronzes to the unique Anglo-Saxon Kingston Brooch; from fish to desert animals. There are classical sculptures, plants and geological specimens from all over the world. There is also a planetarium and an aquarium.

All year, daily. Free entry. Refreshments. Shop. Toilets. ♿ *Tel Liverpool (051) 207 0001.*

MEOLS HALL

Off A5267, 1 mile north-east of Southport (Bd)

The manor of North Meols existed before the Norman Conquest, and its name was probably derived from the 'mels' or sandhills of the Lancashire coast. A house has stood on the site certainly since the reign of King John, and it has descended through 24 generations to the present occupant, Colonel Roger Fleetwood Hesketh. The Hesketh family remained Roman Catholics throughout the 17th and 18th centuries, and were periodically fined as recusants, or non-worshippers, in the established church. The house has a fine collection of pictures by artists such as Jan Bruegel, Lawrence, Romney, and Wright of Derby – as well as china, glass, silver and period furniture.

Also in Churchtown, an old part of Southport whose houses date back more than 300 years, is the Botanic Gardens Museum. A fernery and an aviary are a feature of the gardens, and the museum is a storehouse of local history.

Meols Hall: Apr-Sept, Thur and Bank Hol Mon pm. Adm charge. P *Toilets.* ♿ *Tel Southport (0704) 28171. Museum: All year, daily exc Mon, and Bank Hol Mon. Free entry. Refreshments. Shop.* P *Toilets.* ♿ *Tel (0704) 27547.*

MUSEUM OF LABOUR HISTORY

Sessions House, Islington, Liverpool city centre (Bb)

The living and working conditions of ordinary people down the ages are a subject of continued fascination. This museum attempts to show the history of the people of Merseyside, particularly in the 19th and 20th centuries – the time during which the trade union movement developed. One gallery features scenes from life in the 1840s,

FAITH IN STONE *The wedge-shaped belfry and spiky lantern tower of Liverpool's Roman Catholic Cathedral look centuries apart from the Gothic Lady Chapel in the Anglican Cathedral: yet both buildings have been completed since the Second World War.*

the 1940s and the 1980s. Another illustrates different types of work, from cargo handling in the docks to mining in St Helens.
All year, daily. Free entry. Shop. Toilets. ♿ Tel Liverpool (051) 207 0001 (weekdays); 207 1805 (weekends).

PILKINGTON GLASS MUSEUM
Prescot Road, St Helens (Cb)

The basic blend of sand, soda and limestone has been used to produce glass for 5000 years, and 90 per cent of glass made today comes from the same materials. The Pilkington Glass Museum shows the advances in glassmaking from ancient Egyptian times to the age of the laser beam. Exhibits include an Egyptian glass vessel of 1430-1340 BC, with coloured threads; a late 18th-century ceremonial goblet in opaque white glass, bearing enamel portraits; and a lighthouse optic made by a Birmingham specialist firm (now part of Pilkington) which shone for more than 50 years off Ireland's west coast.
All year, daily. Free entry. Refreshments. Shop. P *Toilets.* ♿ *Tel St Helens (0744) 692014*

PORT SUNLIGHT VILLAGE
On A41, 2½ miles south of Birkenhead (Bb)

The vision of a Victorian soap-maker has endowed Merseyside with an enduring delight. Port Sunlight Village is today a monument to the enlightened William Hesketh Lever – later the 1st Viscount Leverhulme – and has to a remarkable extent retained its original layout and character. The best starting point for any visitor is the Heritage Centre, opened in 1984.

When Lever founded his Port Sunlight factory in 1888 he had the idea of creating a community nearby. Within a year of this ideal being expressed, the first homes were built.

Most houses in the 130 acre village are fronted by unfenced garden plots. There are attractive features such as the Dell where a curved valley, once the course of a stream, now displays trees and flowerbeds and is spanned by a stone saddle-back bridge. One of the village's larger houses, Bridge Cottage, was once the home of the 1st Lord Leverhulme.

The Lady Lever Art Gallery, created by the 1st Lord Leverhulme as a memorial to his wife, who died in 1913, contains outstanding English 18th-century paintings and furniture. The Classical Renaissance building in which the gallery is housed forms an impressive centrepiece to the village. Though the village is still administered by Unilever, it is now no longer necessary to be a worker or pensioner of the company to qualify for residence.
Centre: All year, Mon-Fri; also Sat and Sun pm Easter-Oct. Adm charge. Refreshments. Shop. P *Toilets.* ♿ *Tel Liverpool (051) 644 6466. Gallery: All year, daily. Free entry. Refreshments. Shop.* P *Toilets* ♿ *Tel (051) 645 3623.*

PRESCOT MUSEUM OF CLOCK AND WATCH MAKING
In Prescot, 10 miles east of Liverpool city centre (Cb)

A great deal of time has ticked away since Prescot was the centre of an internationally famous watch and clock trade. But this museum in an attractive 18th-century house lovingly recalls the time, in the 18th and 19th centuries, when the products of South Lancashire watchmakers were highly prized. In the earliest days, the many intricate parts for watches and clocks were made in different craftsmen's workshops. Large-scale production in the area ended in 1910, but the trade continued in a small way until the 1960s. Museum displays illustrate the history of timekeeping and show something of the Lancashire clock workers' lives.
All year, daily exc Mon; also Bank Hol Mon. Free entry. Shop. P *Tel Liverpool (051) 430 7787.*

SOUTHPORT ZOO
Princes Park, Southport (Bd)

More than 800 creatures of 173 species live in pleasant surroundings at this zoo. But in the midst of this lively community the grim dodo symbol can be seen on some enclosures – a reminder that a species is threatened with extinction. The Petrie family, who run the zoo, are deeply concerned about conservation and have organised successful breeding programmes for various mammals and birds including the chimpanzee, lar gibbon, mandrill, serval, leopard cat and Humboldt's penguin.

Nearby on Southport's Promenade is Merrivale Model Village – a complete village built to the scale of 1in to 1ft, with more than 250 models and hundreds of human and animal figures. Model trains wind their way through the village.
Zoo: All year, daily. Adm charge. Refreshments. Shop. P *Toilets.* ♿ *Tel Southport (0704) 38102. Model Village: Easter-Oct, daily. Adm charge. Refreshments. Shop. Tel (0704) 42133.*

SPEKE HALL
Off A562, 7 miles south-east of Liverpool (Cb)

The beauty of a great black-and-white Tudor building can hardly be seen to better advantage than at Speke Hall, one of the best preserved half-timbered houses in Britain. It was built between 1490 and 1612 under the direction of successive generations of the Norris family. A late Elizabethan stone bridge leads the visitor to the house and its cobbled courtyard where the atmosphere of the past is enhanced by two yew trees more than 400 years old, named Adam and Eve. Inside, the great parlour has a magnificent stucco ceiling.
NT. Apr-Oct, Tues-Sun and Bank Hol Mon pm; Nov-mid Dec, Sat and Sun pm. Adm charge. Refreshments. Shop. P *Toilets.* ♿ *(ground floor). Tel Liverpool (051) 427 7231.*

WALKER ART GALLERY
William Brown Street, in Liverpool city centre (Bb)

The imposing exterior of this art gallery is matched inside by the largest collection of paintings in Britain outside London. It includes such treasures as the 14th-century painting by Simone Martini, *Christ Discovered in the Temple*, a Rembrandt self-portrait, and works by Cranach, Van Ruysdael, Degas, Poussin and Rubens. The collection is particularly strong in English painting, from Stubbs, Hogarth and Gainsborough to the Pre-Raphaelites and Turner and, in the 20th century, David Hockney, Victor Pasmore, Paul Nash and Patrick Caulfield.
All year, daily. Free entry. Refreshments. Shop. Toilets. Tel Liverpool (051) 227 5234.

PYTHON PRIESTESS *A 19th-century marble and bronze statue of the Carthaginian priestess Salammbô dancing with a black python stands in the South Rotunda of the Lady Lever Art Gallery in Port Sunlight.*

WIRRAL COUNTRY PARK
Off A540, 3 miles south-east of West Kirby (Ad)

In this happy spot for wanderers, natural beauty in many forms blends happily with the imprint of man's history. The Wirral Way has embankments with glorious views across the River Dee to the Welsh hills. Trees arch overhead, and there are cliffs, ponds and mudflats. A railway once ran here, but in the 70 years since its abandonment, a wilderness has grown up, encouraging wild plants, foxes, badgers and wading birds.
Visitor Centre: All year, daily. Free entry. P *Toilets.* ♿ *Tel Liverpool (051) 648 4371.*

COUNTY CALENDAR

April (1st Sat). Aintree: Grand National.
May (Spring Bank Holiday week). Thurstaston. Wirral Country Park Countryside Week.
June Liverpool: River Mersey Festival.
June (early). Liverpool: City Parade.
July (late). Aintree Racecourse: Royal Lancashire Show.
August Liverpool: Mersey Beatle Convention.
September Liverpool: Merseyside Marathon.
Tourist information: Birkenhead (051) 652 6106; Huyton (051) 443 3401; Kirby (051) 443 4024; Liverpool (051) 709 3631; Southport (0704) 33133.

NORFOLK

INLAND WATERS, LONELY SHORES AND A ROYAL ESTATE

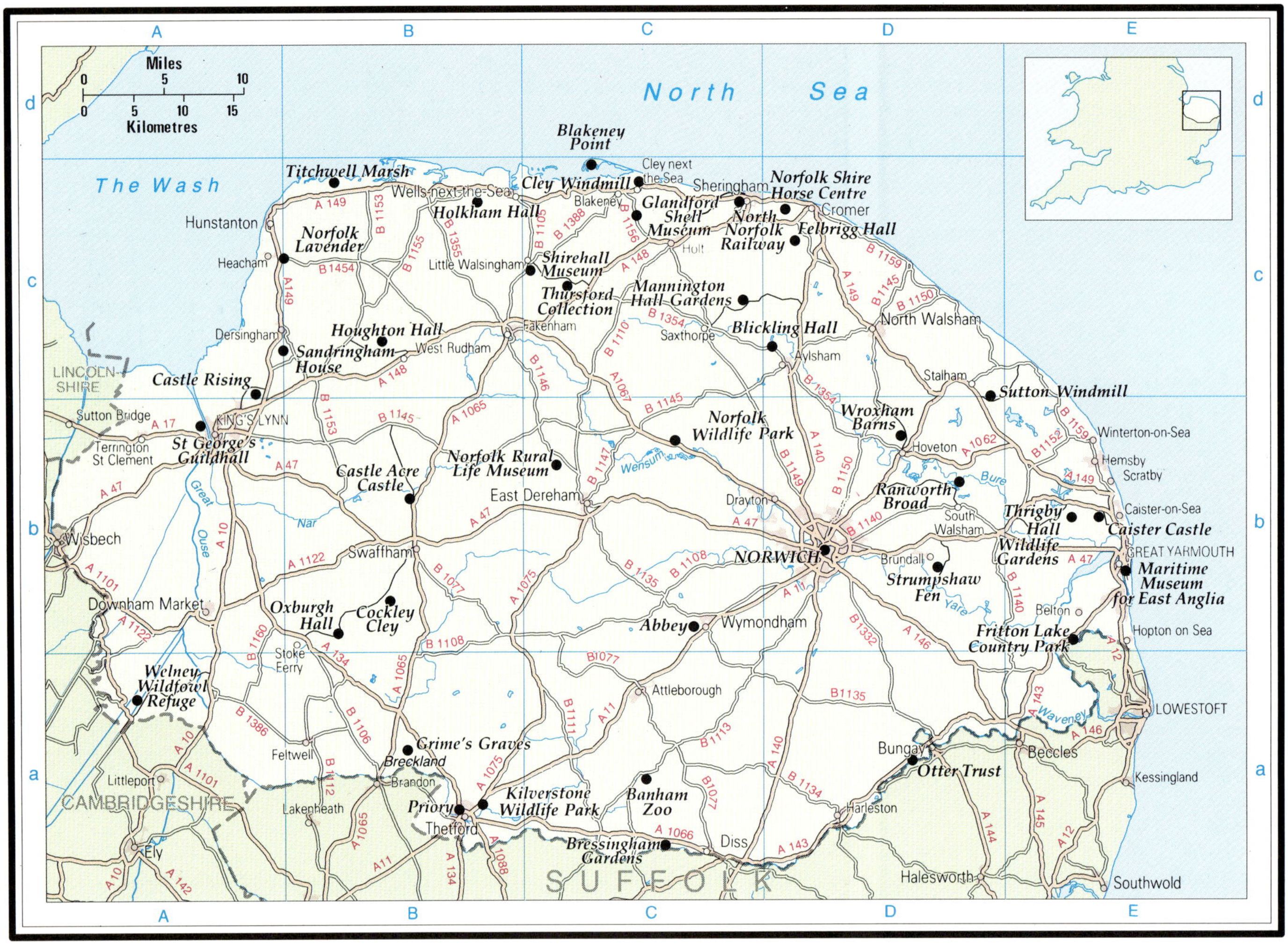

Around its central farmlands, Norfolk offers rapid changes of scenery along its hunched north-eastern shoulder, from bustling Great Yarmouth to the lonely shingle spit of Blakeney Point. Inland, the traveller comes on great country houses such as Blickling Hall and Holkham Hall; drives through the dark conifers of Thetford Forest; or skirts the reed-whispering waters of the Norfolk Broads, where sails often seem to be riding across the fields. Other sails are those of old windmills, often smartly restored.

Buildings present contrasts of colour and texture: the flint of Breckland, velvety brown carr stone around royal Sandringham, and the timber, plaster, brick and stone of King's Lynn and the cathedral city of Norwich. Echoes of history range from the flint mines of Grime's Graves to the castles of Caister, Castle Rising and Castle Acre, while museums honour the role of fishermen, lifeboatmen, weavers and merchants in Norfolk life.

BANHAM ZOO

On B1113, 9 miles north-west of Diss (Ca)

A major feature of Banham Zoo is its monkey sanctuary where rare and endangered species include the delicate white-faced saki monkey and the wistful-looking ringtail lemur. South American squirrel monkeys run free on Monkey Jungle Island. There are woodland walks, a pets corner and farmyard corner, a picnic area, a farm shop and a garden centre.

All year, daily. Adm charge. Refreshments. Shop. P *Toilets.* ♿ *Tel Quidenham (095 387) 476.*

BLAKENEY POINT

Off A149, at Cley next the Sea (Cc)

Always rustling in the wind and sometimes scoured by it, Blakeney Point is a hooked arm of shingle covering 1100 acres that provides an object lesson in the formation and shifting of sand dunes and shingle banks. Colonies of terns, oystercatchers, redshanks and ringed plovers nest on the spit of land. Summer migrants such as wheatears, chiffchaffs and sand martins add to the cheerful clamour, scurrying in and out of dune and marsh until the whole ground teems with a life of its own. There are two observation hides, and a 'discovery trail' for children. An interpretative display is mounted in Blakeney's Lifeboat House. Blakeney Point can be reached by boat from Blakeney Quay or from Morston, 1 mile west, or by a 4 mile walk along the shingle from Cley next the Sea.

NT. All year, daily. Free entry. Shop. P *Toilets.* ♿ *Tel Cley (0263) 740480.*

BLICKLING HALL

Off B1354, 1½ miles north-west of Aylsham (Dc)

The approach to Blickling from Aylsham provides a breathtaking revelation when the winding road escapes from the shadows of trees to present a vista of lawns, clipped yew hedges, and the radiant Jacobean façade of the hall, beautifully balanced by two wings of outbuildings.

The late 14th-century moated building went through many transformations at the hands of many owners, including Anne Boleyn's father and James I's Lord Chief Justice, who was largely responsible for its present appearance. In the 18th century the earls of Buckinghamshire put in hand many alterations to the grounds.

The state rooms include the Peter the Great Room, which contains a huge tapestry of the Russian ruler, presented by Catherine the Great to the 2nd earl when he was ambassador to Russia. The Long Gallery is noted for its ornate plaster ceiling, and there is a grand double staircase. In the parkland there are extensive walks, including one beside a lake populated by swans, geese and other fowl; and there is an orchard picnic site.

NT. Apr-Oct, pm daily exc Mon and Thur; also Bank Hol Mon. Adm charge. Refreshments. Shop. P *Toilets.* ♿ *Tel Aylsham (0263) 733084.*

BRESSINGHAM GARDENS

On A1066, 3 miles west of Diss (Ca)

A stranger driving beside Bressingham's extensive nursery gardens may find it incongruous to see steam and smoke rising above the trees and hear the whistle of a train. Alan Bloom, the founder of the gardens and the railway, must be unique in his dedication both to horticulture and to shovelling coal into steam engines.

The nursery fields and frames cover about 500 acres, and the meadow around the Georgian hall has been developed, with ponds, shrubs and walks under the trees, to display more than 5000 varieties of alpines, heathers, conifers and perennials. Narrow-gauge railways carry visitors round the border of the nursery, beside a lake and across the valley of the River Waveney. A magnificent collection of standard-gauge locomotives, including *Royal Scot* and *Oliver Cromwell*, are on display.

A live steam museum includes a collection of traction engines, farm machinery, and industrial engines of all kinds. In the centre of the museum area is a splendid Victorian steam roundabout, painted and maintained in full working order.

Easter, then Sun, late Apr-late Sept, Thur, early June-early Sept, Wed in Aug, and Bank Hol. Adm charge. Refreshments. Shop. P *Toilets.* ♿ *Tel Bressingham (037 988) 386.*

CAISTER CASTLE

Off A1064, 1 mile west of Caister-on-Sea (Eb)

The substantial moated remains of Caister Castle, begun by Sir John Fastolfe in 1432 and still dominated by its soaring tower, survive in a garden setting with tree walks transferred here from their original Festival of Britain site in London's Battersea Park. A museum beside the castle houses veteran and vintage cars, including an early steam car and classic models by Benz, Rolls-Royce and other great names.

Nearby is the site of a once-thriving Roman port, abandoned centuries ago as Saxon invaders swarmed in. The remains include part of the town wall, the south gateway and buildings along the main street.

EH. Castle: All year, daily. Tel Cambridge (0223) 358911. Museum: Mid May-early Oct, daily exc Sat. Adm charge. Refreshments. P *Tel Wymondham, Leics (057 284) 251.*

PROUD PULLER *Retired from years of service on the London to Glasgow line of the old LMS Railway, the 137 ton* Royal Scot *is among the gems of the steam locomotive collection at Bressingham.*

CASTLE ACRE CASTLE

Off A1065, 4 miles north of Swaffham (Bb)

The most dramatic approach to the compact hilltop settlement of Castle Acre is across the valley of the little River Nar, following a winding road which climbs steeply until it enters the village through a 13th-century stone-and-rubble bailey gate. What was once a castle bailey is now an enclosed village green called Stocks Green, and remnants of stones from old town walls and castle fortifications can be found in the walls of the trim little houses.

Although records of the castle on its huge mound begin with building work by William de Warenne, son-in-law of William the Conqueror, the earthwork itself is known to have been there long before the Normans arrived. Paths around and across the great castle mound give splendid views across the valley, and demonstrate what a fine strategic position it dominated.

Castle Acre's richness in ruins gives it not only a Norman castle but a medieval priory too. Castle Acre Priory was established by the de Warenne family, who had visited the abbey of Cluny in Burgundy and sought to establish the Cluniac order in England. Although it was intended to house only 25 monks, the buildings beside the Nar soon spread over the meadows, with a huge 13th-century church and extensive monastic quarters. The prior's lodging with its oriel windows, and a private chapel in the storey above, today houses a small museum.

But it is the priory's great west front which takes the breath away. Its 12th-century tiers of arcading must have been even more ravishing to the sight before a vast 15th-century Perpendicular window was forced into them, out of proportion to the Norman doorway below. There is further incongruity in the placing of the Tudor block alongside, covered with chequered flushwork. Yet the overall effect remains awe-inspiring, and it is possible to spend hours identifying lost walls and chambers in the stony remains preserved in well-kept lawns.

EH. Castle: All year, daily. Priory: All year, daily exc Mon and Tues mid Oct-Apr. Adm charge. P *Toilets. Tel Castle Acre (076 05) 394.*

CASTLE RISING

Off A149, 4 miles north-east of King's Lynn (Ac)

A massive Norman keep sits within equally massive earthworks which may well have been Roman in origin. The walls of the keep are

PORT WITH A PAST *The tide flows in along winding creeks to float pleasure craft at Blakeney's broad Quay, a commercial port until its estuary silted up. Opposite the Quay flat marshes stretch towards Blakeney Point.*

up to 9ft thick, and within the arched entrance a huge stone staircase leads up to a vestibule and an arch which once opened into the Great Hall, and to other rooms including a domestic chapel. Here Edward III kept his mother in reasonably comfortable imprisonment for 30 years after her part in his father's murder.

In the village nestling below the grey fortress stands the 17th-century block of Trinity Hospital almshouses, whose women pensioners still on special occasions wear bright red cloaks bearing the local Howard family arms.

Castle: EH. All year, daily exc Mon and Tues Oct-Apr. Adm charge. 🅿 *Toilets. Tel Castle Rising (055 387) 330. Hospital: All year, Tues-Thur and Sat. Free entry.*

CLEY WINDMILL

At Cley next the Sea (Cc)

Built in the early 18th century, this delightful windmill fell into disrepair in the 1920s and was later converted into a guesthouse. After the Second World War its sails were restored, and it was opened to the public in 1983. From the windmill's upper floors there are views over the coastal salt marshes, administered as a bird sanctuary by the Norfolk Naturalists Trust.

Early May-Sept, pm daily. Adm charge. 🅿 *Toilets. Tel Cley (0263) 740209.*

COCKLEY CLEY

Off A1065, 3½ miles south-west of Swaffham (Bb)

A fortified village of the Iceni tribe in Boudicca's day has been reconstructed on what is believed to have been the site of an original Iceni encampment. It is complete with timber watchtowers and drawbridge, the chief's roundhouse, chariot house, and a snake pit for malefactors. Later centuries are recalled in the remains of a Saxon church thought to date from the time of St Augustine's mission to England, and in a 15th-century cottage which houses a museum of local historical and archaeological exhibits. In a large stable block is a collection of carriages and farm equipment.

Village and Museum: Good Fri-Oct, pm daily; mid Jul-mid Sept, all day. Adm charge. Refreshments. Shop. 🅿 *Toilets. Tel Swaffham (0760) 21339.*

FELBRIGG HALL

Off A148, 2½ miles south-west of Cromer (Dc)

A great wood of oaks and other trees planted in the 17th century to act as a windbreak against North Sea gales contributes to the splendour of the huge park surrounding Felbrigg Hall. The Jacobean building was for three centuries the home of the Windham family. Furnishings and pictures from the 18th century are among its interior glories, and the windows contain insertions of medieval stained glass from St Peter Mancroft in Norwich. There is some elegant rococo plasterwork, and a Gothic library imitating one at Blickling Hall. The grounds have a walled garden, an orangery, and woodland and lakeside walks.

NT. Apr-Oct, pm daily exc Tues and Fri. Adm charge. Refreshments. Shop. 🅿 *Toilets.* ♿ *Tel West Runton (026 375) 444.*

FRITTON LAKE COUNTRY PARK

Off A143, 7 miles south-west of Great Yarmouth (Eb)

The 3 mile long lake was once a duck decoy, where wildfowl were lured by tame birds into a netted trap. In recent years a country park has been developed, with boating, windsurfing and fishing on the lake, and a spread of gardens, woodland walks and a basket-maker's workshop.

On the bank of the Waveney itself is a remnant of St Olave's Priory, with an early example of brick vaulting in its undercroft. Nearby a fragile-looking timber trestle windpump is maintained in working order.

Country Park: Apr-Oct, daily. Adm charge. Refreshments. Shop. 🅿 *Toilets.* ♿ *Tel Fritton (049 379) 208. Priory: EH. All year, daily.*

GLANDFORD SHELL MUSEUM

On B1156, 3 miles north-west of Holt (Cc)

Treasures of the seashore both local and more exotic are preserved in a Dutch-gabled building erected in 1915 to house a collection of shells made by Sir Alfred Jodrell over a period of 60 years. After his death the collection grew, with multi-hued shells coming from all over the world – as well as jewellery, stones, old pottery and a sugar bowl used by Elizabeth I. Nearby there are picnic sites on Wiveton Downs, with wide views across the surrounding countryside.

All year, daily exc Sun. Adm charge. 🅿 *Tel Cley (0263) 740081.*

GRIME'S GRAVES

Off A134, 7 miles north-west of Thetford (Ba)

Before the Breckland region was darkened with conifers to become the second largest forest in England, it was an open wasteland of sandy heath. Still longer ago, in Stone Age times, it had been densely populated by men who left behind their flint axeheads, tools and primitive ornaments. Much of that flint came from Grime's Graves, which were not graves but underground flint workings rediscovered in 1870 and explored during the 20th century.

Shafts between 13ft and 26ft deep descend sheer into the ground, dug out by those primitive inhabitants with picks made from deer antlers. On the surface a wide area is pitted with what look like bomb craters; these are shafts which were later filled in or collapsed of their own accord. There are nearly 800 of them, along with some shallower pits. From the bottom of one shaft which has been opened and made safe for visitors, galleries radiate like the spokes of a wheel, making clear the cramped conditions in which the miners had to work. In one gallery was found a small, plump figure, apparently pregnant, made out of chalk – a propitiatory offering, perhaps, to the spirit of this underworld.

EH. All year, daily. Adm charge. 🅿 *Tel Thetford (0842) 810656.*

CORN FROM CLEY *The windmill at Cley next the Sea was built around 1720 when Cley was a prosperous port, exporting wool and grain. Now the mill is a guesthouse, open to the public in summer.*

HOLKHAM HALL

On A149, 2 miles west of Wells-next-the-Sea (Bc)

On the fringe of bleak coastal salt marshes, the Palladian spread of Holkham Hall at first seems out of place. It was built in the mid-18th century by Thomas Coke on what was then little more than scrubland. The woodland, park and lake in which the hall is set are living testimony to the pioneering experiments in crop rotation and enrichment of the soil which earned their creator Thomas William Coke, great nephew of the hall's builder, the title of 'Coke of Norfolk'.

The hall itself looks classically austere from the outside; but inside it explodes into an exuberance of marble, mosaics, monuments and art treasures – including statues from Italy and paintings by Rubens, Claude, Van Dyck and Gainsborough. A collection of more than 4000 items from bygone days features fire engines, steam engines, motor cars, ploughs, tractors and tools. There is also a display of copper and pewter cooking utensils.

June-Sept, Sun, Mon and Thur; July-Aug, also Wed; Bank Hol Mon. Adm charge. Refreshments. Shop. 🅿 *Toilets.* ♿ *Tel Fakenham (0328) 710227.*

HOUGHTON HALL

Off A148, 1 mile north-west of West Rudham (Bc)

Sir Robert Walpole, England's first prime minister, who served under George I and II, commissioned this stately home built of stone shipped from Whitby. The 18th-century designer William Kent was responsible for the interior decoration, including the finely carved woodwork and marble fireplaces. The hall is set in parkland containing a herd of white fallow deer. It is the seat of the Marquis of Cholmondeley, whose collection of some 20,000 model soldiers and other militaria is on display.

Easter-end Sept, Thur, Sun and Bank Hol pm. Adm charge. Refreshments. Shop. 🅿 *Toilets.* ♿ *Tel East Rudham (048 522) 569.*

VELVET AND GOLD *Crimson velvet lines the walls of the Drawing Room at Holkham Hall. On the left hangs a portrait of Sir Edward Coke, Lord Chief Justice and founder of the Coke family's fortune.*

KILVERSTONE WILDLIFE PARK

On A11, 1½ miles north-east of Thetford (Ba)

More than 650 birds and animals from Latin America give this wildlife park its particular character. They include rare specimens of the Falabella miniature horse from Argentina. The impressive family of cats ranges from a large jaguar to the small Geoffroys cat of Argentina. An even more extensive collection of monkeys includes eight species of the acrobatic spider monkeys and 13 species of the tiny marmosets and tamarins. Bison, deer, alpacas and rheas breed regularly, and parrots squawk encouragement or abuse at passers-by. In an adventure play area there are radio-controlled vehicles and a merry-go-round, and near the lake is a miniature railway.

All year, daily. Adm charge. Refreshments. Shop. 🅿 *Toilets.* ♿ *Tel Thetford (0842) 5369.*

MANNINGTON HALL GARDENS

Off B1354, 2 miles north-east of Saxthorpe (Cc)

Set around a moated 15th-century house of battlemented flint and stone, the gardens are entered over a drawbridge. There are extensive lawns enclosed by yew hedges, with statuary busts half hidden, half watchful over visitors. One corner of the house is splashed in season with the colours of wisteria and winter jasmine, and nearby the Heritage Rose Gardens display hundreds of different roses. A lake with an attractive stone bridge borders one of the garden walks leading into the woodland, and a network of nature trails crisscrosses the estate. The house is open only by prior arrangement.

Gardens: May-Sept, Sun pm; June-Aug, Wed, Thur and Fri. Adm charge. Refreshments. Shop. 🅿 *Toilets.* ♿ *Tel Saxthorpe (026 387) 284.*

MARITIME MUSEUM FOR EAST ANGLIA

Marine Parade, Great Yarmouth (Eb)

Originally a club for seamen and a home for shipwrecked mariners, the museum has dramatic displays of seafaring life off the Norfolk coast. They include ship models, boat-building tools, fishing gear and toys and ornaments made by seamen on lightships or long voyages. On show are also some early life-saving devices. Among these are the inventions of Captain George Manby who, horrified at seeing a ship founder with all hands only 150yds offshore, devised a mortar apparatus, a breeches-buoy, and an unsinkable lifeboat.

In Tolhouse Street, 500yds west of the Maritime Museum, the Tolhouse Museum occupies a rugged, 14th-century flint building which in its time has served as a courthouse and jail: four of the original basement cells can still be seen. In the great hall or Heighning (price-raising) Chamber the corporation decreed the wholesale price of herring and took a large percentage for itself, a procedure which lasted until 1835.

Set back from South Quay is the Elizabethan House Museum, the former home of a Tudor merchant. One of its windows contains a roundel of early 17th-century Flemish glass depicting a Dutch buss, or deep-sea fishing vessel, used to catch herring. Its interior has some fine carving and, in the drawing room, an ornately moulded plaster ceiling. Displays include silver from the town regalia, old kitchen utensils, and a collection of Victorian toys.

The nearby Rows, narrow lanes running from the marketplace to the quays, suffered severely in both World Wars, but the Old Merchant's House in Row 117 and its 17th-century contemporaries in Row 111 have been preserved as characteristic town houses with fine panelling and ceilings.

Maritime Museum: June-Sept, daily exc Sat; Oct-May, Mon-Fri. Adm charge. Shop. Toilets. Tel Great Yarmouth (0493) 842267. Tolhouse Museum: June-Sept, daily exc Sat; Oct-May, Mon-Fri. Free entry. Shop. Tel (0493) 858900. Elizabethan Museum: June-Sept, daily exc Sat; Oct-May, Mon-Fri. Adm charge. Shop. Toilets. Tel (0493) 855746. Old Merchant's House (EH): Apr-Sept, Mon-Fri. Adm charge. Tel (0493) 857900.

NORFOLK LAVENDER

On A149, on edge of Heacham (Bc)

The fields around Caley Mill, the home of English Lavender, are a blaze of colour from mid-June to mid-August, when the bushes, varying in colour from white to deep purple, display their blooms. After harvesting, the lavender is distilled to produce the basis of lavender water and soap perfumes. During the flowering and harvesting season there are daily guided tours. A herb garden has all its species clearly labelled, and there is a riverside garden.

Easter-Sept, daily. Free entry. Refreshments. Shop. 🅿 *Toilets.* ♿ *Tel Heacham (0485) 70384.*

NORFOLK RURAL LIFE MUSEUM

Off B1146, 2 miles north of East Dereham (Cb)

An 18th-century red-brick workhouse contains souvenirs of farming and domestic life, with a sequence of tools and machinery displayed according to the months and seasons of the year. There are a shepherd's hut, the shop of a King's Lynn firm which supplied seeds to the region for more than 200 years, a dairy, mementos of a village school – including an infants' rocking-horse – and implements associated with carpenters, thatchers, bricklayers and other craftsmen.

Outside is Cherry Tree Cottage, a typical farm-worker's house of the early 20th century. Its brick-tile kitchen is complete with blackleaded range, a water pump, and oil lamps. Nearby is Craftsmen's Row, including a linen weaver's workshop, a smithy, a wheelwright's workshop, a saddlery, a bakery and a village store crammed with bygone goods and advertisements.

Easter-Oct, Tues-Sat; Sun pm; Bank Hol Mon. Adm charge. Shop. 🅿 *Toilets. Tel Dereham (0362) 860563.*

NORFOLK SHIRE HORSE CENTRE

Off A149, 3 miles west of Cromer (Dc)

Noble draught horses are on show here and give working demonstrations twice a day. In a barn housing a display centre there are frequent film shows and a collection of horse-drawn agricultural machinery, gypsy caravans and other rural bygones. For the energetic, a riding school offers lessons in a covered school or accompanied rides through the coastal countryside.

Easter-Sept, Sun-Fri; Bank Hol Sat. Adm charge. Refreshments. Shop. P *Toilets. Tel West Runton (026 375) 339.*

NORFOLK WILDLIFE PARK

On A1067, 10 miles north-west of Norwich (Cb)

The naturalist Philip Wayre established his wildlife park at Great Witchingham in 1961 to show animals under conditions resembling their natural environment as closely as possible. In 1978 he set up a trust to continue the work and promote the conservation of all wildlife – especially European flora and fauna. In 50 acres of parkland the spacious enclosures contain lynxes, reindeer and Barbary apes – which breed here regularly, as do otters, owls and badgers. Many such animals have later been released into their natural environment.

For children there is a pets corner, a model farm and a play area. A walk-through aviary is filled with song and chatter, and there are waterfowl lakes and picnic areas.

All year, daily. Refreshments. Shop. P *Toilets.* & *Tel Norwich (0603) 872274.*

NORTH NORFOLK RAILWAY

Sheringham Station, Sheringham (Cc)

In 1887 a railway line was opened from Holt to Cromer with a view to encouraging holiday traffic along this coast. It closed in 1964, but a section of the so-called 'Poppy Line' has been revived. Steam trains and diesel railbuses run from Sheringham along the coast to Weybourne, and then inland over Killing Heath to Holt. There is a museum of historic locomotives and rolling stock at Sheringham, complete with model railway.

Railway: Easter-Oct, trains certain days. Museum: All year, daily. Adm charge. Refreshments. Shop. P *Toilets. Tel Sheringham (0263) 822045.*

OTTER TRUST

At Earsham, on A143, 1 mile west of Bungay (Da)

Breeding pairs of British or European otters are kept in large semi-natural enclosures at Earsham, with the aim of introducing young otters into the wild wherever suitable habitat remains. The animals put on a great act for visitors, especially at feeding time, demonstrate smooth and swift swimming skills, and wander happily along the banks of their ponds and streams.

Within the extensive grounds fringing the River Waveney are three lakes with a large collection of European waterfowl, a night heronry, a nature trail and a visitor centre.

Apr-Oct, daily. Adm charge. Refreshments. Shop. P *Toilets.* & *Tel Bungay (0986) 3470.*

OXBURGH HALL

Off A134, 2½ miles north-east of Stoke Ferry (Bb)

The approach to the hall through its iron gateway and across the moat bridge is as romantic as anyone could desire. In certain lights the dusty pink brickwork of the 80ft high gatehouse sparkles with flecks of silver. The gatehouse and north front are the only surviving parts of the original exterior, most of the rest is early 19th century.

The King's Chamber above the gate – so-called because it is reputed to have been used by Henry VII – contains panels embroidered in gros point and petit point by Mary, Queen of Scots and Bess of Hardwick when the queen was in the custody of Bess's husband at Tutbury. From the roof of the tower the visitor can look down on lawns and gardens which include a formal French-style parterre.

NT. May-Sept, pm daily exc Thur and Fri; Bank Hol, Apr and Oct, weekends. Adm charge. Refreshments. Shop. P *Toilets. Tel Gooderstone (036 621) 258.*

RANWORTH BROAD

Off B1140, 1½ miles north of South Walsham (Db)

The Norfolk Broads are the flooded remains of medieval peat diggings. They have supplied long reeds for thatching and a livelihood for fowlers, as well as sustaining a variety of plants and other wildlife.

Many of these aspects of Broadland life can be studied at the Broadland Conservation Centre at Ranworth. A boardwalk nature trail, starting close to St Helen's Church in Ranworth village, leads for 400yds through dry and wet woodlands to a thatched display centre floating on pontoons, with a permanent Broadland exhibition and an upstairs gallery with binoculars. Herons, common terns and cormorants can be seen on most days.

A good overall view of the Broad can be obtained from the top of the nearby tower of St Helen's Church. Inside the church is a 15th-century painted rood screen depicting a group of saints in the company of dogs, ducks, swans and lions.

Conservation Centre: Apr-Oct, Sun-Thur; Sat pm. Adm charge. Tel South Walsham (060 549) 479. Church: All year, daily.

ST GEORGE'S GUILDHALL

King Street, King's Lynn (Ab)

The huge Guildhall of St George was used as a theatre in Elizabethan times, and it has also been a corn exchange, courthouse, powder store and wool warehouse. The brick-vaulted undercroft, now a coffee bar, was once a storage place for goods hauled straight off the quayside on the River Great Ouse. Above the undercroft is a modern theatre which still has its 15th-century roof in which beams cross diagonally like a pair of scissors, unsupported by the usual horizontal tie-beams. The whole complex, known as the Fermoy Centre after a major benefactor, has become the focal point for the annual King's Lynn Festival.

A few doors from St George's Guildhall is the Museum of Social History. In this finely proportioned Georgian town house are displays of toy soldiers, dolls, clocks, costume and glass.

Farther along King Street is the Medieval Merchant's House, a private house with a Georgian frontage; but behind that are surviving traces of earlier fabric from the 14th century onwards, including a medieval window, Tudor beams and a Tudor fireplace.

Nearby, in Saturday Market Place, is the imposing Guildhall of the Holy Trinity. Within its 15th-century flint-and-stone chequerboard walls are today the Town Hall, Tourist Information Centre and Heritage Centre. In the undercroft are the Regalia Rooms, where the town treasures are displayed. They include a sword and a silver and enamel cup associated with King John, who feasted at King's Lynn before attempting to cross The Wash and losing his baggage and treasure. The Heritage Centre, in what was once the jail, has graphic displays telling the long story of King's Lynn's love-hate relationship with the sea. Other local history exhibits are on display in the Lynn Museum, in Old Market Street.

St George's Guildhall (NT): All year, daily. Adm charge. Refreshments. Toilets. Tel King's Lynn (0553) 773578. Museum of Social History: All year, Tues-Sat. Adm charge. Tel (0553) 775001. Merchant's House: June-July, Fri and Sun; Aug, daily exc Mon, Thur and Sat; Bank Hol. Adm charge. Toilets. Tel (0553) 772454. Guildhall of the Holy Trinity: All year, Mon-Fri; end July-early Sept, Sat am. Free entry. P *Toilets. Tel (0553) 763044. Lynn Museum: All year, Mon-Sat. Adm charge. Tel (0553) 775001.*

SANDRINGHAM HOUSE

Off A149, 8 miles north-east of King's Lynn (Bc)

The 20,000 acre royal estate of heathland and forest has differing beauties to offer at every season of the year: rhododendrons in early summer, brown and golden hues in autumn, and a sense of bright remoteness on a winter's day. At its heart is Sandringham House, described by George V as 'the place I love better than anywhere else in the world'. An earlier house was converted by 1870 to its present Jacobean style. Inside there are many royal portraits, and domestic touches such as Queen Mary's tapestry work. Presents from distinguished visitors include tapestries from Alfonso XII of Spain and silver ornaments from the Russian Imperial family. The tradition of riding and shooting is illustrated in several paintings and in a collection of guns, each labelled with the name of its owner. Even the inviting views from the windows give no idea of the full extent of the gardens, with shrubberies, a heather bed, lime-tree avenue, roses, a rockery and a secluded woodland glade.

The motor museum in the grounds of Sandringham House displays vehicles used by the royal family, including a 1900 Daimler Tonneau and various Daimler shooting brakes and saloons. It also contains big game trophies, and gifts presented to the Queen during overseas tours.

In the surrounding Sandringham Country Park there are footpaths through 600 acres of

CATHEDRAL CITY BUILT ON CLOTH

Norwich Cathedral's lofty spire is one among more than 20 towers and spires that thrust above the city's rooftops. Another landmark is the tower of the 1938 City Hall, rising above the market place. The River Wensum winds round the city, enfolding narrow streets and alleys that display many an old-world shop front. Complementing the Castle Museum's art collection is the gallery of modern and ethnographic art in the Sainsbury Centre for the Visual Arts, at the University of East Anglia.

Cathedral: All year, daily. Free entry (voluntary donation). Refreshments. Shop. Toilets. ♿ Tel Norwich (0603) 626290. Strangers' Hall: All year, daily exc Sun. Adm charge. Shop. Toilets. Tel (0603) 667229. Castle Museum: All year, daily; Sun pm only. Adm charge. Refreshments. Shop. Toilets. ♿ Tel (0603) 611277.

EARLIER DAYS *The 'strangers' of Norwich's 15th-century Strangers' Hall are thought to have been immigrant Flemish weavers who worked there during the great days of the Norfolk cloth trade. Now a museum of domestic life, its rooms are furnished in the styles of different periods; they include this Victorian sitting room, a Georgian dining room and a Regency music room.*

COASTAL VIEW *John Sell Cotman's watercolour of the 74 gun warship* Mars *at anchor off Cromer is one of the works of the early 19th-century Norwich School of Painters in Norwich Castle Museum.*

HIGH LIGHTS *The tower of Norwich Cathedral – the highest Norman tower in Britain – is extended heavenward by a slender spire built in the 15th century. Inside the cathedral, the nave roof is decorated with intricately carved and brightly painted ceiling bosses (left) illustrating Biblical scenes from the Creation to the Last Judgment, which can be viewed through a mirror. Here Noah is seen planting a vine.*

REEDY MOORINGS *Pleasure craft nudge the reed-fringed banks of Ranworth Dike, a link in the chain of freshwater lakes that form the Norfolk Broads. Boats and birds share 200 miles of waterways.*

woodland, two waymarked nature trails, and a scenic drive with sheltered parking and picnic sites. Near the cafeteria is a Park Ranger's Information Centre.

From Edward VII's day until 1966 the royal family used to travel from London to Sandringham via Wolferton station, 2 miles north-west of Sandringham. The station was provided with special retiring rooms and was always kept in gleaming readiness for a royal visitor. Today the line has been taken up, but the trim little station is lovingly maintained as an independent museum.
Sandringham House, grounds, museum and Country Park: Easter-late Sept (exc when royal family in residence). Adm charge. Refreshments. Shop. P Toilets. ♿ Tel King's Lynn (0553) 772675. Station Museum: Apr-Sept, Mon-Fri; Sun pm. Adm charge. Shop. P Tel Dersingham (0485) 40674.

SHIREHALL MUSEUM

On B1105 in Little Walsingham, 6 miles north of Fakenham (Cc)

Facing Walsingham's little square, with its village pump and dignified houses,is the Shirehall, an old flint building enclosing a Georgian courtroom and lockup. In earlier times it was an almonry or pilgrim hall attached to the shrine of Our Lady of Walsingham, which from the 12th century was a centre for pilgrims from all over Europe. The Shirehall today incorporates a display illustrating the history of pilgrimages to Walsingham.

The original shrine of Walsingham was designed as a replica of the Holy House in Nazareth where the archangel Gabriel appeared to Mary. Later, more buildings sprang up as monastic orders moved into Little Walsingham. Today there remain only ruins of the medieval priory and friary, dominated by the great arch of the priory church's east window. In 1897 pilgrimages were resumed, and between 1921 and 1938 an Anglo-Catholic red-brick shrine of Our Lady of Walsingham was built in Italian style.

About a mile south of Little Walsingham, at Houghton St Giles, is a 14th-century stone Slipper Chapel where pilgrims used to leave their shoes before walking barefoot the last mile to the shrine. It was restored in the late 1890s and now has for a neighbour the modern red-brick and tile edifice of the Roman Catholic National Shrine of Our Lady and Chapel of Reconciliation.

Walsingham also plays a quite different role as the southern terminus of the Wells and Walsingham Light Railway. This 10¼in gauge line runs for 4 miles to Wells-Next-The-Sea, along part of the old Great Eastern route. The journey, through fields bright with wildflowers in summer, takes 25 minutes each way.
Shirehall: Easter-Sept, daily; Oct, Sat and Sun. Adm charge. Shop. P ♿ Tel Walsingham (032 872) 510. Abbey: Apr, Wed; May-July and Sept, Wed, Sat and Sun; Aug, daily exc Tues and Thur. Shop. Toilets. ♿ Tel (032 872) 259. Shrines: All year, daily. Tel (032 872) 255 (Anglican); 217 (Roman Catholic). Railway: Easter-mid Oct, daily. Adm charge. ♿

STRUMPSHAW FEN

Off A47, 7 miles east of Norwich (Db)

Below the gentle slope of Strumpshaw Hill, on the north bank of the River Yare, lies typical fenland country with reed and sedge beds, clumps of willow and alder, and grazing marshes and meadows where wagtails, lapwings, snipe and redshank breed. Some 5 miles of mown footpaths crisscross the reserve and pass two hides.

An information centre and hide by the entrance are reached from the level crossing near the car park, at the head of Strumpshaw Broad. Another public hide, at Buckenham Marshes, is open from October to February for viewing wigeon and one of the largest flocks of bean geese in Britain. In summer the reeds abound with warblers and buntings, and occasionally swallowtail butterflies and Chinese water deer can be seen.

Just to the south, Strumpshaw Hall Steam Museum displays a collection of steam engines which includes a showman's road engine and steam wagon, a beam engine, and a fairground organ. A small steam railway operates on Sunday afternoons during the summer season.
RSPB. All year, daily. Free entry. P Tel Norwich (0603) 715191. Steam Museum: mid May-early Oct, pm daily exc Sat. Adm charge. Refreshments. Shop. P Toilets. ♿ Tel (0603) 714535.

SUTTON WINDMILL

Off A149, 3 miles south-west of Stalham (Dc)

Britain's tallest windmill, built in 1789, is nine storeys high and offers splendid views from the top viewing gallery over a confluence of Broadland waterways. Unlike many of the abandoned tower mills in the neighbourhood, it was a corn mill and not a windpump. Its grinding machinery and sails have been rescued and restored.

The Broads Museum, next to the mill, has a collection of farm and trade tools and exhibits of hedging, thatching, woodworking and other local crafts. Among veterinary and livestock bygones are specimens of animal medicines covering the last 80 years. Nostalgia adds its appeal with collections of old cigarette packets and Second World War souvenirs.
Apr-mid May, Sun-Wed pm; mid May-Sept, daily. Adm charge. Refreshments. Shop. P Toilets. Tel Stalham (0692) 81195.

THETFORD PRIORY

Off A134 in Thetford (Ba)

The Cluniac Priory of Our Lady, founded early in the 12th century and richly endowed by the Bigod family, later became the burial place of several Dukes of Norfolk. At the Dissolution of the Monasteries, Henry VIII was petitioned to convert it into a college of secular canons; but he refused and over the centuries it fell into ruin. The most substantial remains are the 14th-century gatehouse, with its knapped flint facing, and the prior's lodging.

Thetford's black-and-white timbered Ancient House is an early Tudor building now used as a museum. Its displays cover the history and natural history of Thetford and Breckland, and the history of the local flint industry from Neolithic times onwards.
Priory (EH). All year, daily. Free entry. P Toilets. Tel Cambridge (0223) 358911. Museum: All year, Mon-Sat; end May-end Sept, Sun pm. Tel Thetford (0842) 2599.

THRIGBY HALL WILDLIFE GARDENS

Off A1064, 9 miles north-west of Great Yarmouth (Eb)

The present hall was built in 1876 upon the remains of a previous mansion, of which the red-brick cellars, garden walls and summerhouse survive. Today it is the centre of a collection of mammals, birds and reptiles – with special emphasis on Asiatic species including the Vietnamese pot-bellied pig, muntjac deer, and the alarmingly named mugger or marsh crocodile.
All year, daily. Adm charge. Refreshments. Shop. P *Toilets.* ♿ *Tel Fleggburgh (049 377) 477.*

THURSFORD COLLECTION

Off A148, 8 miles north-east of Fakenham (Cc)

Scarlet and green showman's engines, tall-funnelled traction engines, and steam engines with names such as the *Cackler*, help to make this one of the world's major collections of steam road locomotives. Barrel organs, street organs and fairground organs perform every afternoon; and a glossily preserved Wurlitzer organ, needing two rooms to accommodate its pipes and effects, is played every afternoon from July to September. The roundabout of Venetian gondolas recalls a King's Lynn inventor who patented a 'galloping horses' machine – in fact, the first roundabout. A narrow-gauge railway runs round the grounds.
Good Fri-Oct, pm daily; July-Aug, all day. Adm charge. Refreshments. Shop. P *Toilets.* ♿ *Tel Thursford (032 877) 477.*

TITCHWELL MARSH

Off A149, 8 miles east of Hunstanton (Bc)

Near an unspoilt stretch of sandy shore fringed by marshland lies a bird reserve of tidal and freshwater reedbeds, salt marsh, sand dunes and shingle. The freshwater lagoons provide a haven for passage wildfowl, and the marsh is a source of food for greenshanks, grebes, sandpipers and others. Colonies of terns and plovers breed on the shingle, and a growing colony of avocets live on the marsh. Two hides overlook this marsh and there is a third, summertime hide by the beach. There is an information centre, and a picnic area is available.
RSPB. All year, daily. Free entry. Shop. P *Toilets. Tel Brancaster (0485) 210432.*

WELNEY WILDFOWL REFUGE

Off A1101, to the east of Welney (Aa)

This 850 acre reserve at the north-east end of the Ouse Washes is a haven for nesting wildfowl. More than 60 species can be identified here, and winter counts have shown up to 30,000 wigeon, 3000 Bewick's swans, and thousands of other wildfowl. An observatory overlooking the swan lagoon, floodlit in winter, has information and identification aids. The birds are most numerous in winter flood times, but in summer wild flowers and butterflies abound. The refuge is administered by The Wildfowl Trust, founded by the naturalist Sir Peter Scott.
All year, daily. Adm charge. Refreshments. Shop. P *Toilets.* ♿ *Tel Ely (0353) 860711.*

COMFORT STATION *The station at Wolferton by which the Royal Family used to travel from London to Sandringham is now a museum. Among the curios displayed there is the toilet made for Edward VII and displaying national flags.*

WROXHAM BARNS

Off B1354, 1½ miles north of Hoveton (Db)

An attractive complex of 18th-century barns has been converted into a major centre for rural crafts in East Anglia. The barns now house studios and workshops, where the visitor can see local craftsmen and craftswomen at work, set around attractively paved courtyards.

The largest of the old barns has been transformed into a spacious gallery displaying craft products, including furniture, jewellery and knitwear, together with toys, cards and gifts. Across an arcaded piazza is a tearoom, and in the surrounding parkland are picnic areas, an adventure playground and a lake.
All year, daily. Free entry. Refreshments. Shop. P *Toilets.* ♿ *Tel Wroxham (060 53) 3762.*

WYMONDHAM ABBEY

Off A11 in Wymondham (Cb)

Two massive bell towers, one at each end, dominate the impressive remains of Wymondham Abbey, founded in the early 12th century. The beautiful octagonal tower was built by monks about 1390 to replace the original Norman tower, which was no longer safe to hold bells. Not to be outdone, the parishioners – who were restricted to the northern part of the abbey – built their own four-square tower.

The building that still stands is only about half the size of the abbey before its dissolution. Much of the interior is Norman, with sturdy columns supporting the 15th-century nave which soars up to a hammerbeam roof complete with carved angels flying out over the congregation. The ornate high altar has behind it a radiant screen surmounted by a large gold canopy shimmering with figures of Christ and the saints.

Wymondham itself is noted for its octagonal market cross raised on wooden stilts. It contains a small half-timbered room with mullioned windows, once used as a library and a market court. The town was largely rebuilt after a fire in 1615, and the Wymondham Heritage Museum tells the story of the townsfolk from medieval times to the present day.
Abbey: All year, daily. Free entry. P *(limited). Tel Wymondham (0953) 602269. Museum: Late Apr-Oct, Thur and Fri pm; Sat. Adm charge.* P *Tel Attleborough (0953) 850598.*

COUNTY CALENDAR

May Day Bank Hol. King's Lynn: May Day Celebration.

June Hunstanton: Festival of Arts.

June (late). New Costessey, nr Norwich: Royal Norfolk Show. Mannington Hall: Rose Festival.

July (last Wed). Sandringham: Flower Show.

July (and early Aug). King's Lynn: Festival.

August (1st Sun). Great Yarmouth: Raft Races.

September (early). Oulton Broad: Battle of Britain Motor Boat Championships.

November (1st two weeks). Great Yarmouth: St Andrew's Arts Festival.

Tourist information: Great Yarmouth (0493) 846345; Hunstanton (048 53) 2610; King's Lynn (0553) 763044; Norwich (0603) 666071.

NORTHAMPTONSHIRE

GREAT HOUSES IN A COUNTRYSIDE WHERE THE CANAL AGE LIVES ON

In a county still renowned both for farming and for hunting, it is not surprising to find an abundance of great houses and estates. Rockingham Castle has weathered the passage of time as royal Norman fortress, medieval castle, Tudor mansion and Victorian country house. Southwick Hall and Boughton House are also medieval survivors, while the prosperity of Elizabethan times gave rise to Althorp, Canons Ashby, Kirby Hall, Holdenby House and Sulgrave Manor.

Fine hides produced in the county made Northampton England's shoemaking centre, as the town's Museum of Leathercraft shows. The shire's rural beauty is the setting for recreational parks at Lilford and Wicksteed.

As a central English shire, Northampton had its share of ironstone to feed its once thriving steel industries, which are recalled at Hunsbury Hill Industrial Museum. It was also at the hub of England's inland waterway system, whose story is told in the Waterways Museum at Stoke Bruerne.

ACROSS THE PARK *The tall chimneys of the original Elizabethan house at Althorp were retained when Henry Holland remodelled the house in the 18th century. But he refaced the original red-brick exterior.*

ALTHORP

On A428, 5 miles north-west of Northampton (Bb)

The Spencers – the family of the Princess of Wales – came to Althorp in 1508, and their dedication has created the elegant, tasteful mansion of today. An Italian architect remodelled the original Elizabethan moated house late in the 17th century, and the inner courtyard became the lofty saloon and great staircase. The 115ft long gallery, where Elizabethans exercised on wet days, survives as the picture gallery, and it was here that a magnificent reception was given for William III during his visit there in 1695.

Soon after 1786, the architect Henry Holland altered the interior, refaced the outside with the grey-white brick of today, filled in the moat and redesigned the wooded park around the lake. Square corner towers and a grand portico were added to the elegant stable block. Restoration between 1950 and 1987 has brought the mansion's lovely Georgian rooms to life again.

Fine paintings grace the beautifully furnished house, including works by Rubens, Reynolds, Van Dyck and Lely. There is also rare porcelain from China and factories such as Sèvres and Chelsea.

All year, daily exc am Oct-June. Adm charge. Refreshments. Shop. P *Toilets. Tel Northampton (0604) 770209.*

BILLING AQUADROME

On A45, 4 miles east of Northampton (Cb)

Nine lakes beside a section of the fast-flowing River Nene are the scene of boating, fishing and windsurfing, while the surrounding 270 acres of lawns and parkland offer recreations such as picnic areas, children's rides and a miniature railway. Each of the lakes has its own characteristics, as the names imply – Willow Lake, Lily Lake, Jungle Lake and Bird Lake. The largest expanse of water is a 10 acre marina, from which boats can enter the Nene and travel to The Wash or join the Grand Union Canal system.

In one corner of the aquadrome the Billing Mill straddles the Nene, with a giant water wheel slowly turning the mill machinery.

Mar-Oct, daily. Adm charge. Refreshments. Shop. P *Toilets. Tel Northampton (0604) 408181.*

BOUGHTON HOUSE

Off A43, 3 miles north of Kettering (Cc)

The beautifully proportioned north front gives Boughton House the appearance of a French chateau. A colonnade of eight archways at the main entrance sets a classical tone; above each arch is a tall, mullioned window, with a dormer window above. This elegant façade was the work of Ralph, 1st Duke of Montagu. Nobody tried later to improve on his work, so Boughton House looks now exactly as it did in the late 17th century.

The north front does, however, mask a much older structure of enormous proportions. The house was transformed from a 15th-century monastery and stands around seven courtyards. Inside the main entrance, walls and ceilings painted by the French artist Louis Cheron surround a superb stone staircase, with a magnificent wrought-iron balustrade. Boughton is a treasure house of fine art in all its forms. There are paintings by British, Italian, Spanish and Dutch artists, French porcelain and furniture, English silverware and a collection of swords, pistols and armour.

Hall: August, daily. Grounds: May-Sept, exc Fri. Adm charge. Refreshments. Shop. P *Toilets.* ♿ *Tel Corby (0536) 515731.*

CANONS ASHBY

On B4525, 8 miles south of Daventry (Bb)

Little altered since it was built in the 16th century, this ironstone and brick manor house has fine Elizabethan wall paintings and its Jacobean plasterwork is outstanding. The ceiling in the drawing room, for example, converges on a huge, openwork pendant with four female figures like ships' figureheads. The splendour of the ceiling is almost matched, however, by the fireplace, with flanking columns and an overmantel bearing the arms of the poet Sir John Dryden, who owned the house in the 17th century. The 70 acre park can be reached through the 18th-century formal gardens.

NT. Apr-Oct, Wed-Sun. Adm charge. Refreshments. P *Toilets. Tel Blakesley (0327) 860044.*

COTON MANOR GARDENS

Off A50, 8½ miles north-west of Northampton (Bc)

In the 1960s the owners of Coton Manor added a new dimension to their already colourful gardens by introducing exotic birds, flying free, to add life and movement. Now cranes patrol the lawns, and flamingos decorate the water garden.

All this and flowers too – from rose garden, wild garden and herbaceous borders to a tropical house where palms and mimosa border a waterfall and pool.

Easter-Sept, Sun and Bank Hol Mon. Adm charge. Refreshments. Shop. P *Toilets. Tel Northampton (0604) 740219.*

DAVENTRY COUNTRY PARK

On B4036, 1 mile north of town centre (Bb)

Butterflies can be seen here in spring, for a colony of orange tips emerge as early as the beginning of May. Among the insects on the wing from early summer are lovely dragonflies and damselflies. The Daventry Reservoir lies at the heart of the park, and coarse fishing day-permits are available from the warden's office. To the south is a nature reserve where 150 species of bird have been recorded. There are hides and a nature trail on the west side of the reservoir, and the park has an interpretative centre, picnic areas and an adventure playground.

All year, daily. Free entry. P *Toilets.* ♿ *Tel Daventry (0327) 71100.*

EAST CARLTON COUNTRY PARK

Off A427, 5 miles west of Corby (Cc)

A centre dedicated to the making of steel may seem incongruous in a country park; but only a few miles away blast furnaces once produced more than a million tons of steel a year, and the bed of ironstone that provided the ore outcrops within the park. An exposure of the rock features on the park's nature trails.

The Steel Heritage Centre uses models, films and photographs to show the processes used in the making of iron and steel, and a typical steelworker's home of the 1930s is featured. In contrast with the heat and clamour of steelmaking, the 100 acre park is a peaceful place, with large areas of woodland and parkland offset by three spring-fed ponds. The centre is also home to seven craft workshops.

All year, daily. Free entry. Refreshments. Shop. P *Toilets.* ♿ *Tel Rockingham (0536) 770977.*

GUILSBOROUGH GRANGE WILDLIFE PARK

Off A50, 10 miles north of Northampton (Bc)

This park set around a Regency-style house has a friendly and informal atmosphere. A leisurely stroll round the grounds takes in some 400 animals and birds, all seen at close quarters, including lions, monkeys, seals, foxes, otters, deer and birds of prey. Garden paths lead by streams and ponds, and there are lovely views across the surrounding countryside.

All year, daily. Adm charge. Refreshments. Shop. P *Toilets.* ♿ *Tel Northampton (0604) 740278.*

HOLDENBY HOUSE GARDENS

Off A428, 6 miles north of Northampton (Bb)

Charles I walked in these gardens while a prisoner at Holdenby House, and much of what he would have seen is still there today. There are ponds, fed by a stream, Elizabethan arches and terraces and a walled border said to be the king's favourite walk. An Elizabethan garden has been replanted with plants and shrubs that would have been available when the house was built in 1580.

What the king would not have seen are the many attractions that today provide fun and interest for all the family. These include a model railway, donkey rides, rare breeds of farm animals, museum, pottery and a pets corner. Visitors can also use the croquet lawn.

Apr-Sept, Sun and Bank Hol; also Thur in July and Aug. Adm charge. Refreshments. Shop. P *Toilets.* ♿ *(part). Tel Northampton (0604) 770786.*

HUNSBURY HILL INDUSTRIAL MUSEUM

Hunsbury Hill Road, off A43 on south-west side of Northampton (Bb)

Several of Northamptonshire's former ironstone workings have been put to good use. One near Wellingborough is now Irchester Country Park, and Hunsbury Hill has been turned into a museum of our industrial past. Locomotives and wagons from workings in Northamptonshire are among the exhibits, and in summer there are rides on diesel and steam trains.

All year, Sun and Bank Hol; rides, Spring Bank Hol weekend-Sept. Adm charge. Refreshments. Shop. P *Toilets.* ♿ *Tel Northampton (0604) 499550.*

COOKING FACILITIES *The great kitchen at Canons Ashby has been restored to its appearance in Victorian times, with cast-iron range and cooking utensils at the ready to feed the busy Dryden household.*

KIRBY HALL

Off A43, 4 miles north-east of Corby (Cd)

The fascination of this Elizabethan house lies not in art treasures and finely furnished rooms, for there are none. Instead it is the richness and variety of architectural styles that hold the eye. The roofline is quite remarkable – a panorama of ornate parapets, gables, balustrades and chimneys.

The inner courtyard is entered by a seven-arched arcade, and brings into view, at the far end of the courtyard, a porch of ambitious design and proportions. Its lower arch is flanked by fluted pilasters; above them are tapered columns, and higher still is a gable of seven small columns topped by stone orbs and scallop shell motifs.

EH. All year, daily exc Mon and Tues Oct-Apr. Adm charge. P *Toilets. Tel Corby (0536) 203230.*

LAMPORT HALL

On A508, 8 miles north of Northampton (Bc)

An inscription above the frontage of Lamport Hall reads 'In things transitory resteth no glory'. There is certainly nothing transitory about this fine house, but there is much glory, beginning with the superb 17th-century façade – pleasing in its symmetry, yet breathtaking in its simplicity. By the standards of its day it is a modest building, only two storeys high, but all modesty is left behind beyond Lamport Hall's portals. Here are elegant rooms lavishly decorated and displaying fine paintings, porcelain and furniture. The grandest room of all is the High Room, with a plasterwork ceiling of flying cherubs, nymphs, mermen and swans.

The gardens and parkland are as impressive as the house, with pleasant walks and an avenue of yew trees. There is also an agricultural museum and a display of vintage tractors.

Easter-Sept, Sun and Bank Hol; also Thur in July and Aug. Adm charge. Refreshments. Shop. P *Toilets. Tel Maidwell (060 128) 272.*

UNDER THE FLAG *The Great Hall at Rockingham Castle, with its inscribed oak beams, dates from the 16th century, when a medieval fortress was converted into a comfortable Tudor home by the addition of two wings. Weapons on the walls date from the Civil War. The Flag Tower was added by Anthony Salvin in 1838.*

LILFORD PARK

On A605, 4 miles south of Oundle (Dc)

Lilford Park's 240 acres of rolling grassland and woodland, set in the lovely Nene valley, provide ample room for picnics and riverside strolls. Man-made attractions within the park include a children's farm, an adventure playground, a flamingo pool and a superb aviary containing birds from many parts of the world.

In the centre of the park stands Lilford Hall, a Jacobean gem (not open). The old stables house a craft workshop and puppet theatre.

Easter-Oct, daily. Adm charge. Refreshments. Shop. P *Toilets.* ♿ *Tel Clopton (080 15) 648.*

MUSEUM OF LEATHERCRAFT

Bridge Street, Northampton (Bb)

Statues of pupils in uniform adorn the front of this museum, for it is housed in the former Blue Coat School, built in 1812. Inside, displays tell the story of leather and its uses from ancient Egyptian times until today. Beautifully made 16th-century caskets, a coracle and a collection of leather bottles are among the exhibits, and there are displays of costumes, gloves, luggage, saddlery and harnesses.

All year, Mon-Sat. Free entry. Shop. ♿ *(ground floor). Tel Northampton (0604) 34881.*

ROCKINGHAM CASTLE

On A6003, 2 miles north of Corby (Cd)

The massive drum towers flanking the castle gateway are but a foretaste of the wonders that lie behind the mellow limestone walls of Rockingham. The castle has survived on its rocky hilltop for 900 years, and within its walls lived a self-contained community that has left marks of the styles and tastes of almost every century.

Plantagenet and Tudor kings fortified the castle, and the only time it fell to an enemy was in 1643 when Cromwell's men stormed it. More peaceful times are reflected in the Long Gallery, with its fine furniture and pictures, and in the Panel Room, its deal panelling grained to look like oak.

From the castle gardens there are views over four counties, and at the end of the Yew Walk, with a 400-year-old yew hedge clipped into elephant shapes, steps lead down to the Wild Garden, a ravine planted with more than 200 species of trees and shrubs.

Easter Sun-Sept, Sun, Thur, Bank Hol Mon; also Tues in Aug. Adm charge. Refreshments. Shop. P *Toilets. Tel Rockingham (0536) 770240.*

RUSHTON TRIANGULAR LODGE

Off A6003, 6 miles north-west of Kettering (Cc)

It has three sides, three triangular gables on each side, a three-sided chimney and triangles set in clover-leaf designs on each wall. Who was the builder, and why did he have such an obsession with triangles? The truth is that Sir Thomas Tresham's obsession was with his Roman Catholic religion, and the triangles represent the Holy Trinity. When Sir Thomas built the lodge, in 1593, his religious beliefs had already earned him many years in prison, so the building symbolises its builder's defiant faith.

No two sides of the lodge are the same, and everywhere triangles or the number 3 are incorporated. Even the Biblical quotations in Latin along the frieze each consist of 33 letters, and each side of the building is 33ft long.

In contrast the interior is plain and simple, with a large hexagonal-shaped room on each of the three storeys. Symbolic though the lodge is, it is not a folly and was used by the keeper of the rabbits on Sir Thomas's estate.

EH. Apr-Sept, daily. Adm charge. Toilets. Tel Corby (0536) 710761.

SOUTHWICK HALL

Off A427, 2 miles north of Oundle (Dd)

Three families and five centuries have moulded Southwick Hall, and though extensively altered since it was built in the 14th century, the use of the same local limestone and stone slates has resulted in a harmonious blend of styles.

To find Southwick's beginnings, stand in the courtyard and look at the circular turret with a conical roof. Its spiral staircase led to a Solar, a room where the family could enjoy privacy.

Another stair turret and a three-storey annexe were added 50 years later, and there were further additions and alterations in the 16th, 18th and 19th centuries. The later additions are best appreciated inside the house, particularly in the Hall which combines the styles of the three main building periods, in the Oak Room with its Elizabethan panelling and in the bay-windowed Parlour of the early Georgian period.
Bank Hol Sun and Mon pm; also Wed, May-Aug. Adm charge. Refreshments. P *Toilets.* ♿ *(ground floor only). Tel Oundle (0832) 74064.*

SULGRAVE MANOR

At Sulgrave, 9 miles north of Brackley (Aa)

In the top corners of the front porch are the arms of the man who built this house – two stripes and three stars. The man was Lawrence Washington, 16th-century ancestor of George Washington, first President of the USA, and his arms inspired the design of the American flag.

The house is a lovely example of a 16th-century manor, with light and airy rooms furnished in the style of the period. Though George Washington never lived there – it was his great-grandfather who emigrated to America in 1656 – the house has become a memorial to him. There are portraits of him in the Great Hall and Oak Parlour, and two small rooms contain such relics as his velvet coat and a lock of his hair.
Feb-Dec, daily exc Wed. Adm charge. Refreshments. Shop. P *Toilets. Tel Sulgrave (029 576) 205.*

WATERWAYS MUSEUM

At Stoke Bruerne, off A508, 4 miles east of Towcester (Bb)

The Grand Union Canal was once a main artery in Britain's waterways system, and colourful narrowboats plied a constant trade between London and the Midlands. The heyday of Britain's canals comes vividly to life at Stoke Bruerne, where a double-arched bridge over the canal looks down on a scene that has changed little in more than 100 years. Immediately below the bridge the massive black-and-white arms of the lock gates are still operated by muscle power, a task once performed by the bonneted and shawled boatmen's wives as their husbands navigated their craft, laden with corn or coal, through the lock. Many of those narrowboats are now pleasure craft.

Cottages and the thatched Boat Inn line the canalside. Here, in a converted corn mill, the history of the canals, the boats and the boat people is portrayed. Boat engines with gleaming brass pipework occupy much of the ground floor. There are more examples of the artefacts of everyday canal life on the upper floors: highly glazed cream and brown pottery, brightly painted buckets and cans and intricately woven ropework. On display too are the tools and equipment of the engineers who built and maintained the canals, and many photographs.

The Rural Life Collection portrays the skills and crafts used by the countrymen of south Northamptonshire in their work and home life.

There are pleasant walks beside the canal: southwards where the canal drops through seven locks into the Ouse valley, and northwards to the portal of the 3056yd long Blisworth Tunnel – England's longest canal tunnel still in use.
Canalside: all year. Waterways Museum: Easter-Oct, daily; Tues-Sun in winter. Adm charge. Refreshments. Shop. P *Toilets. Tel Northampton (0604) 862229. Rural Life Museum: Easter-mid Oct, Mon-Fri; also Sat and Sun pm. Adm charge.*

FLOATING HOME *The brightly decorated cabin of the narrowboat* Sunny Valley, *with painted roses and castles, and gleaming brass and copper, is a highlight of the Waterways Museum.*

WICKSTEED LEISURE PARK

Kettering, on A6 (Cc)

Ride the roller-coaster, roar round a racing circuit in a petrol-powered sports car, take a ride on a Western-style miniature railway or on a Mississippi steamboat, wander around Space City or use a potter's wheel – these are but a few of the attractions offered at Wicksteed. There are also quiet gardens, an arboretum, a nature trail and picnic areas, for Wicksteed Park is set in the parkland of the lovely Ise valley.
Easter-Sept, daily. Free entry. Refreshments. Shops. P *Toilets. Tel Kettering (0536) 512475.*

COUNTY CALENDAR

May (mid-month). Rothwell: Music Festival.

May (Ascension Day). Wicken: Love Feast (commemorating reconciliation of two villages).

July (mid-month). Oundle: International Organ Week.

August (3rd week). Kettering: Vintage Car Show.

September (1st week). Kettering: Horticultural Show.

October (2nd Sun). Ashton: World Conker Championships.

December (1st Sun after Dec 12). Broughton: Tin Can Band (St Andrew's Day commemoration).

Tourist information: Corby (0536) 202551; Kettering (0536) 410266; Northampton (0604) 22677; Oundle (0832) 74333.

NORTHUMBERLAND

CASTLES ON THE CLIFFS AND A WALL ACROSS A WILDERNESS

Present-day Northumbrians have created Europe's most capacious artificial lake, lying at the heart of the vast plantation of Kielder Forest; but for most of the county's history men have clung mainly to its edges, shunning the wild interior. On Holy Island, monks produced the exquisitely decorated Lindisfarne Gospels, and today, on the Farne Islands to the south, grey seals can be seen basking in the surf. But for all its rugged beauty, this 'debatable land' between English and Scots has been the most fought-over frontier in Britain. Much of Hadrian's Wall, built by Roman legionaries, lies within Northumberland. And south from Berwick's Elizabethan ramparts, the mighty stone walls of Alnwick and Bamburgh and the gaunt ruins of Dunstanburgh, Norham and Warkworth still keep watch over coast and river valleys.

ALNWICK CASTLE

Off A1068, in Alnwick (Dd)

Inside the medieval battlements of Alnwick Castle lies a world of breathtaking splendour. The talents of the finest Italian experts in architecture, design, art and sculpture were hired by the 4th Duke of Northumberland in 1854 to turn the central keep of a Norman castle into a palace in the classical style of the Renaissance. The work took 11 years to complete: some of the panels of the window shutters in the Red Drawing Room each occupied one man for a year.

A grand staircase of marble with vaulted and arched ceiling leads to the State Rooms. These are furnished with rich collections of china, furniture and pictures including works by Titian, Tintoretto, Canaletto and Van Dyck.

The castle, which dates from the 11th century, has been the home since 1309 of the Percy family, first Earls, then Dukes of Northumberland. On show is the family State Coach built for the 3rd duke, together with the principal apartments, library, armoury, guard chamber and dungeon. The weapons of the Percy Tenantry Volunteers, raised by the 2nd duke during the Napoleonic Wars and disbanded only in 1906, along with other early arms, are displayed in the entrance hall of the massive keep.

The 14th-century Abbot's Tower houses the regimental museum of the Royal Northumberland Fusiliers.

May-Sept, daily exc Sat. Adm charge. Shop. P *Toilets. Tel Alnwick (0665) 602207.*

BAMBURGH CASTLE

Off B1340, at Bamburgh (De)

Perched on a crag beside the sea, a vast curtain wall encircles the formidable keep erected in the 12th century to deter unruly barons and invading Scots. From the battlements there are superb views of the Farne Islands, Lindisfarne and the Cheviot Hills. The castle looks particularly impressive when floodlighting illuminates the weathered rocks and pink stone walls.

The outcrop on which the castle stands has been inhabited for at least 2000 years, and a well 150ft deep built in Anglo-Saxon times still survives. Finds on display in the castle museum include a gold plaque from the 7th century depicting a creature known as 'the Bamburgh Beast'.

Until Viking raiders overran the north-east, Bamburgh was one of the principal strongholds of the Anglo-Saxon kings of Northumbria. In the Middle Ages the castle survived several sieges, but in 1464, during the Wars of the Roses, it became the first English castle to fall to gunfire. After centuries of neglect, it was restored, in late Victorian days, by the 1st Lord Armstrong. Of particular note is the Great Hall, which is embellished with an elaborate hammerbeam roof carved out of solid teak.

Among the castle's treasures are exquisite Sèvres and Dresden china, Fabergé animals carved from semiprecious gemstones, and a splendid display of arms and armour.

Apr-Oct, daily. Adm charge. Refreshments. Shop. P *Toilets.* ♿ *Tel Bamburgh (066 84) 208.*

BELSAY HALL, CASTLE AND GARDENS

On A696, 12 miles south-west of Morpeth (Cc)

Few honeymoons could have been more inspirational than that of Sir Charles Monck, the 19th-century owner of Belsay. He took his bride Louise on a two-year grand tour of Europe during which their first child was born and Sir Charles conceived his plans for building Belsay Hall. The design was based largely on the classical buildings he saw, studied and sketched during a long sojourn in Greece.

The result is a honey-coloured building, standing on a slight elevation, with all the elegance and symmetry of a Greek temple. Two massive Doric columns dominate the entrance, and inside is a reconstruction of the central courtyard of a Greco-Roman house – a large open space surrounded by a pillared gallery. The theme is carried through in decorative detail on friezes and woodwork in the rooms leading off the central courtyard. The stable block was designed in similar classical style, with a central clock tower based on the Tower of the Winds in Athens. By contrast, Belsay's gardens could hardly be more English in style. They include a rose garden, a rhododendron garden, a winter garden planted with heathers, and a magnolia terrace backed by woodland of Scots pine and beech. The imaginative Sir Charles even turned the quarry from which stone was cut for the building of the hall into a wild garden.

A path winds through trees to the 14th-century Belsay Castle which once guarded the main route between Newcastle and Jedburgh from marauding Scots.

Attached to the castle is a manor house built as an extension in 1614. First the castle, then the manor house and finally the hall have been occupied since 1270 by the Middleton family – Sir Charles was born at Middleton, but took his mother's maiden name in order to inherit her family estate at Caenby in Lincolnshire.

EH. Apr-Sept, daily; Oct-Mar, Sat and Sun. Adm charge. Refreshments. Shop. P *Toilets.* ♿ *Tel Belsay (066 181) 636.*

HERALD OF PEACE *Belsay's Jacobean manor house was one of the first unfortified homes great men dared to build in strife-torn Northumberland. Out of prudence, perhaps, it was attached to the medieval castle.*

BERWICK RAMPARTS AND BARRACKS

In centre of Berwick-upon-Tweed (Cf)

From the elegant Georgian streets and squares of east Berwick, cobbled alleyways lead to a grassy common known as Magdalen Fields. From this viewpoint it is easy to understand why in 1558, with the French urging the Scots to resume their age-old war with England, Mary Tudor should order stone-faced ramparts to defend the land approaches to the town. However, the queen could not have realised that the defences would take 12 years to complete – nor that they would be the most expensive building project of the reign of her successor, Elizabeth I.

Gateways, turrets and projecting bastions add strength to the rampart walls, and from them there is a good view across the town's three bridges over the Tweed and the remains of Berwick Castle, with its stepped White Wall sloping down to the sea. Also visible from the ramparts are Ravensdowne Barracks, built during the reign of George I to house the garrison manning the ramparts. The barracks today contain an exhibition, 'By Beat of Drum', tracing the history of Britain's infantry.

Ravensdowne is also the regimental headquarters of the King's Own Scottish Borderers, and the east block contains the regiment's museum.

EH. Apr-Sept, daily. Oct-Mar, Wed and Sat. Adm charge. Refreshments. Shop. P *Toilets.* ♿ *Tel Berwick (0289) 304493. Borderers Museum: All year, Mon-Sat; also Sun pm in summer. Tel (0289) 307426.*

BRINKBURN PRIORY

Off B6344, 4½ miles south-east of Rothbury (Cc)

In a secluded spot by a bend in the River Coquet a priory was built in the 12th century as a house for Augustinian canons. The peaceful setting remains, but much of the monastery has crumbled over the centuries. The only complete surviving building is the church, built partly in late Norman and partly in Early English style, with some additions in the 14th century. Careful restoration in the 19th century included a new roof. In 1866 a bell was presented to the church, but as there was nowhere to hang it, a turret was removed and a timber bellcote built. The donor of the bell, the industrialist Sir William Armstrong, also gave the organ, which is one of the best examples of the work of the 19th-century organ builder William Hill.

EH. Apr-Sept, daily. Adm charge. Refreshments. Shop. P *Tel Longframlington (066 570) 628.*

CHESTERHOLM

Off A69, 1 mile north of Bardon Mill (Bb)

An invitation to a birthday party, a note accompanying a gift of oysters, a quartermaster's accounts, and letters to an infantry commander from his wife at home in Rome all survived about 1900 years of burial beneath the Roman fort of Vindolanda, now Chesterholm, just south of Hadrian's Wall. Though written in ink on thin wooden writing tablets, these documents were preserved by the peaty soil. A photographic exhibition of the finds, of which the originals are now in the British Museum, is a feature of the Vindolanda Museum. Boots and sandals, delicate jewellery – including a betrothal medallion engraved with a portrait of the engaged couple – and even sponges and feathers also survived in remarkably good condition, and are on display. In addition, the museum has a delightfully lifelike reconstruction of a Roman kitchen.

Outside can be seen the excavated remains of the forts erected at Chesterholm during different periods and of the civilian settlement which sprang up outside their walls, including an inn for travellers and a brewery. There is also a full-size replica of a section of Hadrian's Wall with stone and timber milecastles – and, nearby, the only Roman milestone in Britain that has survived undamaged in its original position.

All year, daily. Adm charge. Refreshments. Shop. P *Toilets.* ♿ *Tel Bardon Mill (049 84) 277.*

CHESTERS FORT AND MUSEUM

On B6318, 7 miles north of Hexham (Bb)

The Romans were a hygienic people who introduced new thoughts on bathing to the British. Just how well they provided for their troops in this respect is revealed in the remains of a building excavated from the bank of the North Tyne just outside Chesters Roman fort. It is the finest example of a Roman military bathhouse in Britain. The walls that remain, rising to 10ft in places, suggest a building that was a cross between a club and a Turkish bath. It had a large flagged entrance hall or changing room, a cold bath, two rooms for dry heat (one warm, one hot), two for moist heat and a hot bath set in a window bay. A charcoal furnace heated the water and provided hot air for the rooms.

Chesters lies close to a point where Hadrian's Wall crossed the North Tyne in one of the loveliest valleys in Northumberland. It was a garrison for a 500-strong cavalry regiment, and although much of it still awaits excavation the basic oblong shape can be seen in the visible remains of its streets and gateways. Principal buildings include the commandant's house, which had the comfort of warm-air central heating from below the floors or ducted through the walls. Relics on show in the museum on the site include the headless statue of a goddess standing on the back of a cow, a small sculpture of a reclining river god, iron tools, weapons, pottery and small items such as signet rings, beads, bone combs and a bone knife handle carved to show a greyhound chasing a hare.

EH. All year, daily. Adm charge. Refreshments. Shop. P *Toilets.* ♿ *Tel Humshaugh (043 481) 379.*

CHILLINGHAM PARK

Off B6346, 14 miles north of Alnwick (Ce)

The fierce wild cattle roaming this peaceful park are a unique herd that has lived there for 700 years or more. The cattle have thick white coats and crescent-shaped horns, and may be the direct descendants of the wild oxen that roamed the forests of Britain in prehistoric times. Since the 13th century, when a wall was built around the park to protect it from Scottish raiders, the cattle have lived in isolation. As a result, they always breed true to type and never produce coloured or even partly coloured calves.

The herd, now 50 strong, is ruled over by a king bull who reigns until defeated in combat by a younger contender. When a challenge is presented, the rival bulls stand apart from the herd, bellowing and pawing the ground. Then, after two or three rounds of butting and thrusting, the loser slinks away into temporary banishment. The cattle will not tolerate interference from human beings and, even when starving, have refused the grain and cattle cake provided.

Apr-Oct, daily exc Tues and Sun am. Adm charge. P *Toilets. Tel Chatton (066 85) 250.*

CORBRIDGE ROMAN SITE

Off B6529, ½ mile north-west of Corbridge (Cb)

The ruined walls of imposing temples, spacious granaries and a vast storehouse – the largest Roman building in Britain of which substantial traces remain – leave the visitor with no doubt about the importance of the fort of Corstopitum, which has been uncovered at modern Corbridge. Before Hadrian's Wall was built, troops were stationed here to guard a bridge over the Tyne and the junction between Watling Street, the great north-south road, and the east-west Stanegate. Later, Corstopitum was a base for the Roman invasion of Scotland.

Excavations have exposed a sunken strong-room built below the military headquarters and

SENTINEL RUINS *Stormy seas break on the shore below the gap-toothed remains of Dunstanburgh Castle: an appropriate setting for a fortress that has taken nearly seven centuries of punishment from war and weather.*

an elaborate water-supply system with a large stone tank, its sides worn down by soldiers sharpening their swords on the edges. A carved fountain head from a luxurious villa, depicting a lion savaging a deer, can be seen in the site museum. Also on display are a variety of tools, including farming and gardening implements, which indicate how little hand tools have altered since the Roman era. Other exhibits include the tombstone of a young girl tightly clutching a ball; a sculpture of a woman pounding clothes in a type of washtub still used in Northumberland; and a bronze jug which contained 160 gold coins (the coins are now in the British Museum).
EH. All year, daily. Adm charge. Shop. P *Toilets.* ♿ *Tel Corbridge (043 471) 2349.*

CRAGSIDE HOUSE AND COUNTRY PARK

Off B6341, 1 mile east of Rothbury (Cd)

A tree-lined drive opens up to reveal the dramatic features of Cragside House, a wild Victorian extravaganza perched on a wooded hillside. It began as a modest weekend retreat for the industrialist and inventor Sir William (later Lord) Armstrong. But after making a fortune in armaments Sir William turned his creative genius to developing the house and its setting. He called in the architect Norman Shaw who transformed the house, over a period of 15 years, into an elaborate mansion of mixed styles, including Gothic arches and much black-and-white 'Tudor' timbering. Armstrong also made Cragside the first house in the world to be lit by electricity derived from water power. The spit still to be seen in the kitchen was driven by hydraulics and so was the lift. Hydraulic apparatus pumped water to the house and kept pots containing fruit trees rotating in the greenhouse.

The interior of the house is as full of Victorian vigour as the exterior. It contains a lot of light oak panelling, and ranges in style from Old English to oriental. Touches of wild extravagance include a huge, two-tier Renaissance-style chimneypiece of Italian marble, weighing 10 tons, in the drawing room. Smaller rooms, in contrast, contain a clutter of charming Victoriana. The house is furnished much as it was in Sir William's time, and includes some of his paintings and his natural history specimens.

The original villa was built on a bare cliffside. Sir William surrounded it with 7 million trees and shrubs including rhododendrons and azaleas. He also created a landscape that includes several lakes, designed as much for their use in generating power as for their appearance, miles of driveway and little zigzag paths through the trees. A 6 mile scenic drive passes through the grounds.
NT. House: Apr-Sept, daily exc Mon. Adm charge. Refreshments. Shop. P *Toilets.* ♿ *Country Park: Apr-Oct, daily; Nov-Mar, Sat and Sun. Adm charge. Tel Rothbury (0669) 20333.*

DUNSTANBURGH CASTLE

Off B1339, 8 miles north-east of Alnwick (De)

Stranded on a lonely cliff-top 100ft above the sea, the ruined towers of Dunstanburgh Castle make a dramatic silhouette against the sky. When the sea is storm-driven the spray flies into the air as high as the battlements, and the rumbling of the surf echoes in a funnel-like hole near the end of the cliff.

From the fishing village of Craster, a grass track along the coast leads to the ruins. Visitors enter through an arched passage between the massive drum towers of the gatehouse keep. The original gatehouse and fortifications were built between 1313 and 1322; six decades later, the castle was further fortified by John of Gaunt and the gatehouse converted into a keep. Through his son, Henry IV, it became a Lancastrian stronghold, and was twice besieged in the Wars of the Roses and badly damaged.

Today the principal remains consist of the gatehouse-keep and three square towers, together with the ruins of the constable's house and the castle walls. Low tide reveals the foundations of the moat, hewn out of the solid rock. In a narrow inlet about a quarter of a mile to the south lies the castle harbour. Here in 1514 Henry VIII's men-of-war were discovered lying safely anchored after vanishing for three weeks during a stormy passage to the Forth.
EH/NT. All year, daily. Adm charge. Shop. P *Tel Embleton (066 576) 231.*

DUNSTAN STEADS FARM PARK

7 miles east of Embleton (De)

Harvesting, haymaking, milking, feeding the animals . . . there are a host of activities to watch at this working farm set in beautiful countryside close to the sea. In spring or early summer visitors can see new-born lambs, and watch sheep being sheared or dipped and sorted into pens. Children can feed young calves and lambs, clamber up onto the seat of a combine harvester or tractor and take home new-laid eggs still warm from the hen house.

In fine weather, visitors can take a trailer ride round the farm, follow the trails or walk to the sea. A footpath along the coast leads to Dunstanburgh Castle and the fishing village of Craster.
Apr-Sept, daily. Adm charge. Refreshments. Shop. P *Toilets.* ♿ *Tel Alnwick (0665) 76221.*

FARNE ISLANDS *The cliffs of Staple Island are white with the droppings of generations of sea birds. One fissure in its rocks is called Kittiwake Gully. On the horizon is Longstone, with its lighthouse.*

FARNE ISLANDS

1½-4 miles off coast of Northumberland (De)

These rocky outcrops have been the killers of many ships and a beloved retreat of contemplative monks. The spirit of the past broods, yet the vital force of nature is ever present. In summer, thousands of birds cluster on the cliffs, and grey seals breed on the shore. Of a total of 28 islands, about half are submerged at high tide. Only Farne Island, or Inner Farne, Staple Island and the Longstone lighthouse can be visited; these are reached in summer by boat trips from Seahouses harbour. Seen from a small boat, the 80ft cliffs are threatening, the more so in places where the sea's erosion has produced dramatic shapes.

Farne Island is forever associated with St Cuthbert, Abbot of Lindisfarne, who in AD 676 built himself a cell of stone and turf there. In 1500 Thomas Castell, Prior of Durham, erected a tower which still stands on the site of the cell, and near it is a 14th-century chapel dedicated to St Cuthbert. The tower became the islands' first lighthouse. A nature walk starting at the chapel gives a glimpse of several of the many species of birds – puffins, guillemots, cormorants, shags, eiders and terns – that have been recorded on the Farnes. From May to late July, Inner Farne and Staple Island in particular attract birdwatchers and photographers, while grey seals can be seen on the islands throughout the year; most of the young are born in November.

St Cuthbert's Chapel has a memorial to Grace Darling, daughter of the Longstone lighthouse keeper and heroine of the rescue of survivors from SS *Forfarshire* in 1838.
Islands: NT. Sailings from Seahouses to Farne Island and Staple, Apr-Sept. Refreshments. Shop. P *and toilets at Seahouses. Tel Seahouses (0665) 720424. Lighthouse: Trips from Seahouses, Easter-Sept, subject to tides. Tel (0665) 720825.*

GRACE DARLING MUSEUM

In centre of Bamburgh (De)

Even on the sunniest of days one can almost hear the storm and see the surging waves against which Grace Darling and her father, keeper of the Longstone lighthouse, battled in their epic rescue of survivors from the wrecked paddle steamer *Forfarshire* in 1838. The boat they rowed, a Northumbrian fishing coble, is preserved, together with contemporary accounts and pictures of the wrecked ship and of the rescue. Other exhibits include Grace's christening robe and cradle (she was born at Bamburgh in 1815), her personal letters and gifts sent by admirers. She died of tuberculosis at the age of 26, and is buried beneath an ornate tomb in St Aidan's churchyard.

Apr-Oct, daily. Free entry. Shop. ♿ *Tel Seahouses (0665) 720037.*

HEATHERSLAW MILL

On B6354, 10 miles south-west of Berwick-upon-Tweed (Be)

Two mills under a single roof make Heatherslaw a doubly intriguing place to visit. Left derelict for 20 years, both mills have now been restored – one as a working mill, the other as a museum of milling machinery and equipment.

Huge water wheels and gears dominate the basement in which the miller spent most of his day, manipulating sluices, set screws and turn buckles to control the functions of the mill. The milling itself takes place on the middle floor. Here visitors can watch grain being ground into flour, and see barley being hulled and polished in a special machine.

Apr-Sept, daily; Oct, Sat and Sun. Adm charge. Refreshments. Shop. 🅿 *Toilets.* ♿ *Tel Crookham (089 082) 338.*

HEXHAM ABBEY

Off A69, in Hexham (Bb)

Soaring arches, beautiful stained-glass windows and slender pinnacles, which provide a graceful contrast to the square central tower, make Hexham Abbey a masterpiece of Early English Gothic architecture. The present church was largely built between 1180 and 1250 as an Augustinian priory; however, the end of the nave was destroyed by the Scots in 1296 and only restored at the beginning of this century. Below the nave lies the crypt of an earlier church, built by St Wilfrid in AD 674, with passageways for pilgrims and an iron grille through which they could view holy relics. Other Saxon remains include St Wilfrid's Chair, beautifully carved out of a single block of stone.

In the south transept stands a memorial to a Roman standard-bearer named Flavinius: a naked Briton crouches below his rearing horse, dagger in hand, ready to dispatch the young Roman, who died in battle at the age of 25. In the same part of the church is a 'night stair' down which the monks filed from their dormitories at first light to celebrate matins.

Beyond the magnificent choir screen, near the altar, is a chapel known as Prior Leschman's Chantry which is remarkable for its delicate woodwork and rough-hewn medieval stone-carvings. These include depictions of a lady curling her hair (representing vanity), a monkey gobbling buns (gluttony) and a musician playing Northumbrian bagpipes.

Through an arch on the opposite side of Hexham's market place stands the Middle March Centre, a 14th-century jail which was used as a prison until 1824 but now houses a museum devoted to the troubled history of the Borders. It shows what life was like for people living on either side of the border as English and Scots rampaged and pillaged through one another's territory, from medieval to Tudor times.

Abbey: All year, daily. Middle March Centre: Apr-Oct, daily. Adm charge. Shop. Tel Hexham (0434) 604011.

HOLYSTONE FOREST

Off B6341, 7 miles west of Rothbury (Cd)

Cascading burns and waterfalls and a delightful variety of wild plants and birds make the wooded valley surrounding the village of Holystone an ideal place for country walks in a particularly attractive area of the Northumberland National Park. The longest waymarked walk, taking about 2½ hours, leads to Dove Crag, a large rock with a waterfall tumbling from the top.

Farm Walk, taking about an hour, passes through farmland and an oak coppice, then follows a series of small waterfalls down to the bottom of a gorge. Red squirrels hide in the tall beeches bordering the farm, curlews wheel overhead, and in winter flocks of 200 or more of them may be seen feeding in the hayfields. The half-hour Lady's Well Walk starts in an area of commercial forest, then follows part of a Roman road and crosses open farmland to an ancient well.

All year, daily. Free entry. 🅿 *Tel Rothbury (0669) 205691.*

HOUSESTEADS ROMAN FORT

Off B6318, 3 miles north-east of Bardon Mill (Bb)

Pale stone walls up to 8ft high outline the 5 acre site of Housesteads, the best preserved Roman fort in Britain. Shaped like a playing card, it stands across the top of a ridge which falls away steeply to the north. Along the crest of this ridge marches one of the most spectacular sections of Hadrian's Wall, built early in the 2nd century AD to guard Rome's northernmost frontier.

Housesteads, one of 17 forts that housed soldiers serving on the Wall, was built at a point where several Roman roads once met. It is now half a mile from the nearest road, but the steep walk is rewarded both by the insight Housesteads gives into how the guardians of the Wall lived and for the superb views across the open Northumbrian countryside.

A model of the fort, displayed in the museum on the site, shows how Housesteads might have looked in the 3rd century, with its streets, barracks, headquarters building and granaries. There is also a model of one of the massive gateways and of a typical house in the large civil settlement that spread over the slopes south of the fort. Traces remain of all four gates where troops from a 1000-strong infantry unit once stood guard. There are also remains of granaries, of the commandant's house, the headquarters building and the latrines.

On three occasions the Wall and Housesteads fort were overrun and destroyed by northern tribes. On the final occasion the end appears to have come quickly, for excavations in one of the rooms of the headquarters building revealed the remains of a smith at work making arrowheads when the building was destroyed around him.

EH/NT. All year, daily. Adm charge. Shop. Tel Bardon Mill (049 84) 363.

HOWICK GARDENS

Off B1339, 2 miles north-east of Longhoughton (Dd)

Banks of narcissi – as well as azaleas, cherries, magnolias, rhododendrons and other flowering shrubs – grow in abundance in these tree-sheltered gardens, which lie just a mile from the North Sea coast. They were created during the First World War by Lord and Lady Grey, the owners of Howick Grange, who introduced tender plants to the mansion's wooded grounds.

The gardens are seen at their best in spring and early summer, when they are a riot of colour. In autumn the trees are a mass of reds, browns and golds, and among the highlights is a group of late-flowering red-hot pokers, enclosed by a trim yew hedge. Another feature is the array of blue agapanthus along the terrace.

Apr-Sept, daily pm. Adm charge. 🅿 *Toilets. Tel Longhoughton (066 577) 285.*

HUNDAY COUNTRYSIDE MUSEUM

Off A69, 4 miles east of Corbridge (Cb)

More than 250 machines are on show at Hunday ranging from vintage tractors and early steam traction engines to a 30 ton tilling machine capable of uprooting almost anything. Some of the machines can be seen in motion, and a tractor built in 1902, one of the first powered by internal combustion, is used for ploughing demonstrations.

The entrance to the museum is through a gin gan, a wheelhouse in which horses trudged round and round to provide the power for threshing or milling. Old joiner's, blacksmith's, undertaker's and chemist's shops have been rescued and re-erected at Hunday. There is also a dairy equipped with old-fashioned churning and cheesemaking equipment; a village mill built in 1717, back in use making stone-ground flour; and, in the granary, hundreds of farming implements together with photographs showing them in use.

Hunday is also a farm, with Highland cattle, llamas, sheep and goats in the farm park. Visitors can ride on a narrow-gauge railway to a large lake with wildfowl.

Apr-Sept, daily. Adm charge. Refreshments. Shop. 🅿 *Toilets.* ♿ *Tel Stocksfield (0661) 842553.*

KIELDER CASTLE

Off B6320, 15 miles north-west of Bellingham (Ac)

In the heart of Kielder Forest, an 18th-century hunting lodge built for the Dukes of

Northumberland now houses a Forestry Commission Visitor Centre. A permanent exhibition explains the various uses of the timber grown in the commission's vast plantations, and how the trees were planted between 1926 and 1970 to form Europe's largest man-made forest.

The castle is the starting point for several waymarked walks and nature trails, and also for a 12 mile Forest Drive, for which a small toll is charged. The drive follows the course of the Kielder Burn, a tributary of the North Tyne, along which the observant eye may spot a sandpiper darting about the water's edge or a dipper perched on a midstream boulder. At Blakehope Nick the drive climbs to 1500ft, a bleak spot with views across Emblehope Moor.

The road descends for the last half of the drive, passing Witch Holes with a spectacular view down the steep bank to the burn. At the end of the drive, at Blakehopeburnhaugh, there is a waymarked walk to the Three Kings, burial stones erected 2000 years ago.

Easter-Oct, daily. Free entry. Refreshments. Shop. 🅿 *Toilets.* ♿ *Tel Bellingham (0660) 20242.*

KIELDER WATER

On B6320, 12 miles north-west of Bellingham (Ac)

The shimmering waters of one of Europe's largest man-made lakes lie in the green setting of forests climbing gentle hills. Northumbrian Water has spared no effort in landscaping the lake shore so that it blends harmoniously with the surrounding Kielder Forest, and along the southern shore are opportunities for a host of water-based recreations.

The Tower Knowe Visitor Centre, near the dam at the eastern end of the lake, provides information about all these activities, which include dinghy and board sailing, canoeing, boat hire and angling. Visitors can see an exhibition devoted to the Kielder area past and present, and a film showing how the North Tyne was dammed to create today's huge reservoir, covering 2684 acres and supplying water to a large area of north-east England.

All year, daily. Free entry. Shop. 🅿 *Toilets.* ♿ *Tel Bellingham (0660) 40396.*

MORPETH CHANTRY BAGPIPE MUSEUM

Off A1 in Morpeth (Dc)

Housed in a refurbished 13th-century chantry, the museum has one of the largest collections of bagpipes in the world. Among them are Great Highland, Border, Irish and Northumbrian small pipes, and foreign examples including Greek and Italian pipes. The chantry also contains a craft centre, local museum and a tourist information centre.

All year, Mon-Sat. Adm charge. Shop. 🅿 *(limited). Toilets. Tel Morpeth (0670) 519466.*

NORHAM CASTLE

Off B6470, 6½ miles south-west of Berwick-upon-Tweed (Bf)

The gaunt 90ft high wall of a fine Norman keep, standing high on a mound on the south bank of the swirling River Tweed, is the principal visible relic of a castle which in the 14th century was regarded as 'the most dangerous and adventurous place in Britain'. Built by a Bishop of Durham in the 12th century, the massive stone ramparts of Norham in 1318 withstood a siege by Robert Bruce lasting almost a year. The castle's west gate, now the main entrance facing the village of Norham, is known as Marmion's Gate after the English knight Sir William Marmion, hero of Sir Walter Scott's novel, who went out to prove his valour single-handed against the Scots. Considered impregnable in the 13th and 14th centuries, Norham was finally stormed by James IV in 1513.

EH. All year, daily. Adm charge. Shop. 🅿 ♿ *Tel Berwick (0289) 82329.*

OTTERBURN MILL

Off A696 at Otterburn (Bc)

The clear soft water of the streams of Redesdale has been used for centuries for washing the local Cheviot wool before making it into homespun cloth and beautiful handwoven tweeds. Otterburn Mill first appears in records for the year 1245 and has belonged to the Waddell family since 1821, when William Waddell from Jedburgh eloped with a 17-year-old schoolgirl from Edinburgh.

Today the family business includes spinning and weaving as well as fulling and dyeing. All sorts of tweed and wool garments are on sale in the showroom, including colourful rugs and handknitted sweaters, together with jewellery, ceramics and sheepskin slippers.

May-Dec, Mon-Sat; Jan-Apr, Mon-Fri. Free entry. Shop. 🅿 *Toilets. Tel Otterburn (0830) 20225.*

FRONTIER GUARDIANS *Among the many deities to whom the troops on Hadrian's Wall looked for favour was the Roman war god Mars. His statue is now in the museum at Housesteads fort, where it was unearthed. The soldiers who worshipped him patrolled ramparts (below) that still swoop impressively over the border hills at Housesteads, following the crests so that natural obstacles reinforced the man-made barrier.*

PRUDHOE CASTLE

Off A695, in Prudhoe (Cb)

Walk through the gatehouse of this medieval castle and the most imposing feature in sight is, unexpectedly, an elegant 19th-century manor house. It was built by the 2nd Duke of Northumberland whose family, the Percys, have owned the castle since 1381. Unlike the ruins around it, the building is in good condition and contains a handsome staircase and well-proportioned rooms decorated in late Georgian style. The house was built on the site of chambers occupied by former owners, and some of its interior walls are medieval. The manor's gentle features are in striking contrast to the sturdy 5ft thick walls of the 12th-century castle. Its position on a hillside above the River Tyne, commanding a major north-south route, gave the castle great strategic importance. Steep cliffs provided a natural fortification to the north, and two ditches were dug to defend it on the south side. The

HOME OF SAINTS AND SEA BIRDS

The Holy Island of Lindisfarne has attracted seekers of peace for centuries. On this windswept scrap of land, nowhere more than 1½ miles across, St Aidan, missionary Bishop of Iona, founded a priory in AD 635. A keystone of English Christianity, it was twice destroyed by Norse raiders before its final rebuilding in the 13th century. This last priory, too, is now a ruin.

Lindisfarne Castle, built in the 16th century against the Scots, never fired a shot in anger. In any case, Lindisfarne's human inhabitants have always been vastly outnumbered by the wild ducks, geese, swans and waders that teem on its shores, which are a National Nature Reserve. A causeway, under water for five hours at high tide, links the island to the mainland.

Castle: NT. Apr-Sept, daily exc Fri. Adm charge. P *Shop. Tel Berwick (0289) 89244. Priory: EH. All year, daily. Adm charge. Shop. Tel (0289) 89200. National Nature Reserve: NCC. All year, daily. Free entry.* P *Toilets.* ♿ *Tel (0289) 81305.*

FOUNT OF FAITH *A Norman priory succeeded the monastery of St Aidan and St Cuthbert.*

TRANQUIL FORTRESS *Still waters reflect Lindisfarne Castle, a ruined 16th-century fort which was converted into a private home by Sir Edwin Lutyens in 1902.*

castle was twice besieged by King William of Scotland in 1173 and 1174, but held firm on both occasions. The lower part of the gatehouse is one of the oldest parts of the castle, dating from the early 12th century. The keep, built later in the same century, still stands to symbolise the castle's strength in its heyday.

EH. Apr-Sept, daily. Oct-Mar, daily exc Wed and alternate Fri. Adm charge. Refreshments. Shop. P *Toilets. Tel Prudhoe (0661) 33459.*

ROMAN ARMY MUSEUM

Off B6318, 2 miles north-west of Haltwhistle (Ab)

Less than a spear's throw from one of the most spectacular sections of Hadrian's Wall, the museum at Carvoran re-creates the daily life of the men who guarded this lonely outpost of the Roman Empire. Some, such as Syrian archers and Spanish legionaries, came from distant countries – never to return home, since Roman soldiers had to enlist for a minimum of 20 years' service. Modern techniques have been used to bring history vividly to life. Light boxes map the Roman invasion of Britain and the building of the Wall at the touch of a button; lifelike figures display the soldiers' uniforms and weapons; and a splendid large-scale model provides a convincing reconstruction of the first Roman fort at Carvoran, built 40 years before Hadrian's Wall.

Mar-Oct, daily; Feb and Nov, weekends. Adm charge. Refreshments. Shop. P *Toilets.* ♿ *Tel Gilsland (069 72) 485.*

SEATON DELAVAL HALL

On A190, 5 miles south of Blyth (Db)

With its massive towers and porticoes, balustraded roofs and echoing arcades, the elegance and grandeur of this palatial 18th-century mansion make it instantly recognisable as the work of Sir John Vanbrugh, architect of Blenheim Palace and Castle Howard.

Although the main block has twice been gutted by fire, much of the interior has now been restored to its original splendour, including the panelling of the Mahogany Room and the magnificent sculpted chimneypiece of the Great Hall. No less impressive are the twin wings, which include a vast kitchen – with an interior window running the entire length of the east wing – and cavernous cathedral-like stables.

In the grounds is a Norman chapel, in which many of the Delaval family are buried, and in which there is a statue of Samson by the Renaissance sculptor Giambologna.

May-Sept, Wed, Sun and Bank Hol. Adm charge. Shop. P *Toilets. Tel Tyneside (091) 237 3040/1493.*

WALLINGTON HOUSE

On B6342, 16 miles west of Morpeth (Cc)

Set in a delightful park, Wallington House was built about 1688 and transformed into a more grandiose mansion during the 18th century. It contains fine Regency furniture and an outstanding collection of porcelain. The elegant plasterwork of the library, dining room and saloon, which has a magnificent rococo ceiling, dates from the 1740s. In contrast, the central hall has Pre-Raphaelite paintings and a balustrade copied from an illustration in Ruskin's *Stones of Venice*. The kitchen is pure Mrs Beeton, and in the servants' hall an outsize Victorian doll's house, with 36 rooms, electric lights and running water gives a child's-eye view of the latest developments in domestic life in the 1880s.

Allow good time to explore the outbuildings, grounds and gardens. Carriages and shooting-brakes still stand in the coach house, while the conservatory contains many exotic plants and beautiful old fuchsias – one with a stem 2ft thick. Below the house a handsome three-arch bridge, designed by James Paine, spans a river.

NT. Apr-Sept, daily exc Tues. Adm charge. Refreshments. Shop. P *Toilets.* ♿ *Tel Scots Gap (067 074) 283.*

WARKWORTH CASTLE AND HERMITAGE

On A1068, 7½ miles south-east of Alnwick (Dd)

A magnificent 15th-century keep built in the shape of a cross dominates the crumbling walls of the castle and the landscape around. It is an impressive remnant of a castle with a special place in English history. For it was here that Henry Percy, 1st Earl of Northumberland, plotted with his son Harry Hotspur to overthrow Henry IV, a plot that figures in Shakespeare's plays about that monarch. The attempted coup ended in the Battle of Shrewsbury when Hotspur was killed and Percy fled to Scotland. The angry king marched into Northumberland at the head of his army and besieged the castle, which is reputed to have surrendered after just seven shots from the royal cannon.

Plenty of stones have fallen from the walls of Warkworth since then, but the keep is remarkably well preserved and lacks only a roof and window glass. Below are the remains of graceful towers, a 12th-century great hall and the foundations of a church that was probably never completed. The Early English gatehouse, with its vaulted entry passage and guardrooms on either side, is regarded as the best piece of architecture remaining in the castle.

A half-mile walk up the River Coquet from the castle leads to a landing stage, from which a boat takes visitors to Warkworth Hermitage – a complete contrast to the castle in size, scale and setting. The hermitage dates from the 14th century. Its tiny chapel was hewn from the rocks of the river bank and has an imitation vaulted roof and an altar with a recess above, all carved from the rock. A sculpture in an arched recess represents the figure of a woman with her head supported on a square ledge and her feet against a bowl. Legend says that she represents Isabel Widdington, accidentally killed by her lover, Sir Bertram, who in expiation spent the remainder of his life as the Hermit of Warkworth.

The hermit's lodgings, built above the cliff face, offer more comfort. They include a kitchen in which can be seen the remains of an oven base, a hall with a fireplace and a large window, and an upper room with a window towards the river.

EH. Castle: All year, daily. Adm charge. Shop. P *Toilets. Tel Alnwick (0665) 711423. Hermitage: Apr-Sept, Sat and Sun. Adm charge.*

WYLAM RAILWAY MUSEUM

Off A69, in Wylam village (Cb)

In the old village schoolhouse, Wylam celebrates its most famous sons who were all pioneers of steam locomotives. George Stephenson, 'father' of the railways, was born in 1781 in a stone cottage half a mile away. The village was also the home of William Hedley, Timothy Hackworth and Nicholas Wood, whose early experiments to put Britain on the rails are recalled in models, documents and pieces of railway equipment.

The former railway bridge over the Tyne, now a footbridge, is reputed to be the first arch-rib design built to support a suspended railway track. Just across the bridge is the village railway station, one of the oldest in the world still in regular use: the Tudor-style stationmaster's house was built in 1835.

A pleasant walk beside the Tyne follows the old Wylam Wagonway, on which horse-drawn trucks trundled on wooden tracks, carrying coal from Wylam Colliery to Lemington. The Wagonway was eventually replaced by a railway, which remained in service until 1968. The footpath leads to the isolated cottage where the railway pioneer George Stephenson spent the first eight years of his life. It can hardly have been the most comfortable of childhood homes. Its floor was then bare earth, the walls were unplastered and the rafters exposed. The present staircase did not exist, and the upper floor was reached by a wooden ladder. Four families occupied the house, and with five children the Stephensons must have found it cramped.

Stephenson achieved fame as the builder of the first public steam railway, between Stockton and Darlington, and, with his son Robert, was the designer of early locomotives such as the *Rocket*. In front of his cottage ran the post road, or 'street', between Hexham and Newcastle – hence its grandiose name, 'High Street House'.

Museum: All year, Tues, Thur and Sat, pm only. Free entry. P *Toilets. Tel Wylam (066 14) 2174. Birthplace: NT. Apr-Oct, Wed, Thur, Sat and Sun, pm only. Adm charge.* P *Tel (066 14) 3457.*

COUNTY CALENDAR

April (week after Easter). Morpeth: Northumbrian Gathering.

May 1 Berwick-upon-Tweed: Riding the Bounds.

May (Spring Bank Hol). Corbridge: County Show.

June (mid-month). Morpeth: Fair. Ovingham: Goose Fair.

June (late, to early July). Alnwick: Fair.

July (3rd week). Tweedmouth: Feast, and Crowning of Salmon Queen.

August (early). Alnwick: Music Festival.

October (mid-month). Alwinton: Border Shepherds Show.

December 31 Allendale Town: Allendale Baal Fire (blazing barrels carried to light bonfire).

Tourist information: Amble (0665) 712313; Alnwick (0665) 603129; Berwick-upon-Tweed (0289) 307187; Corbridge (043 471) 2815; Hexham (0434) 605225; Morpeth (0670) 511323; Seahouses (0665) 720424.

NOTTINGHAMSHIRE

A TAPESTRY OF LEGEND AND LITERATURE, AND A LEGACY OF LACE

The romance of outlawry still clings to Castle Rock in Nottingham, among the remains of the great medieval fortress that housed the Sheriff of Nottingham and Prince John, opponents of Robin Hood. But though the city below the castle and the county around it still cherish their legends, they are built on the realities of a textile industry that dates back to the 13th century. The history of Nottingham lace, hosiery and knitwear, and of other local industries, can be traced in museums in Nottingham and at Wollaton Hall and Ruddington.

The writer D.H. Lawrence, raised in the pit village of Eastwood, reflects one aspect of the county in his novels. In contrast, Lord Byron, writing poetry and spending beyond his means amid the decaying splendours of Newstead Abbey, has become a figure of romance to rival the hero of Sherwood Forest.

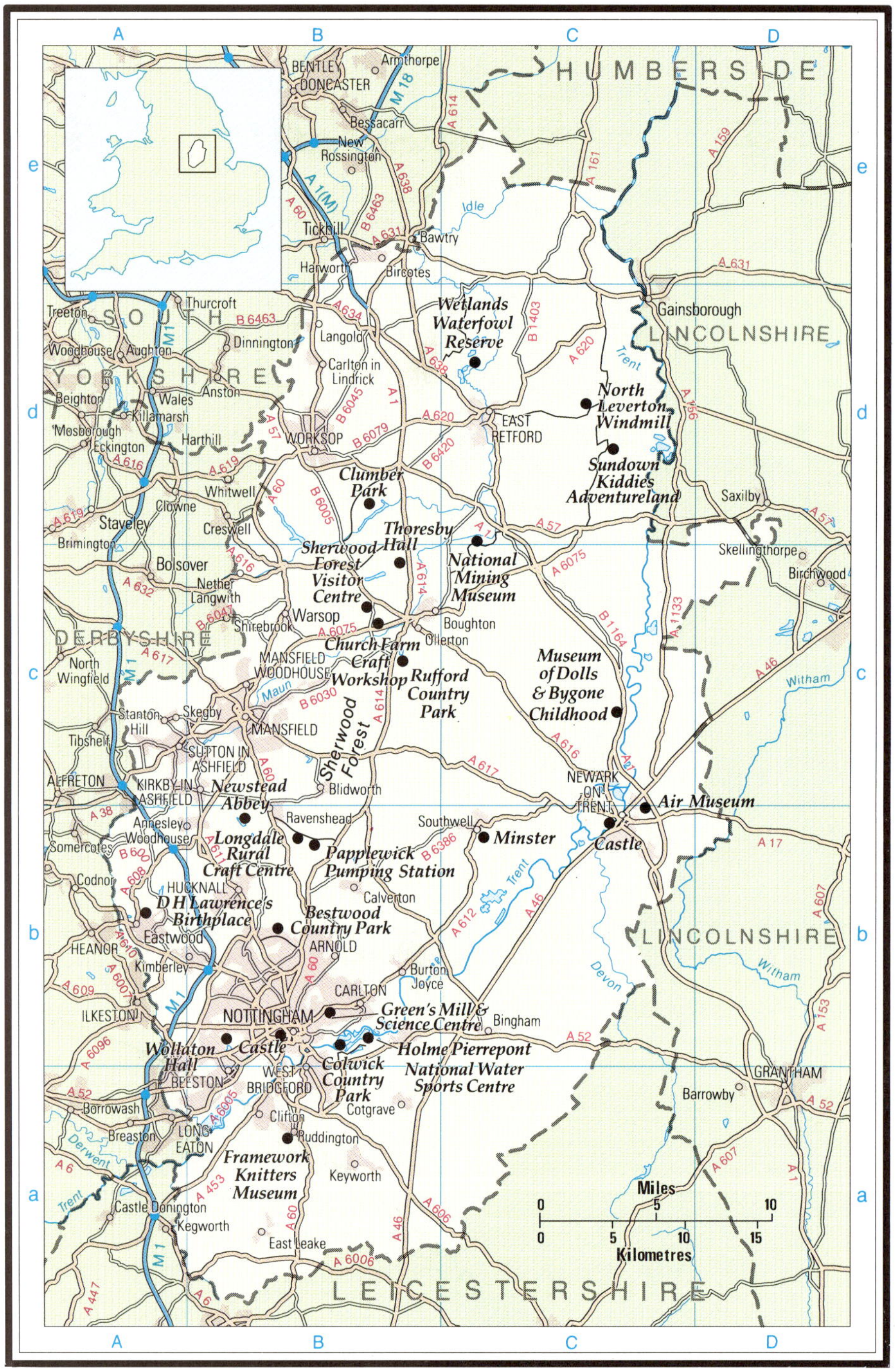

BESTWOOD COUNTRY PARK

Off A60, 4 miles north of Nottingham (Bb)

Closer to the City of Nottingham than the better known Sherwood Forest to the north, Bestwood Country Park comprises 450 acres of pleasant grassland and secluded woods. In these unspoilt surroundings, visitors can relax in shady glades or follow footpaths through the woodlands and study the birds – such as woodcocks, green woodpeckers and spotted flycatchers – and other local wildlife that abounds there. Rangers are usually on hand to explain what there is to see in various parts of the woods.

All year, daily. Free entry. P *Toilets. Tel Nottingham (0602) 273674.*

CHURCH FARM CRAFT WORKSHOPS

On A6075, 8 miles north-east of Mansfield (Bc)

The workshops, next to St Mary's Church, Edwinstowe, display a range of crafts including woodwork, model steam engines, leatherwork, brass and copperwork, lace-making, jewellery, art, flower craft, stained glass, knitwear and soft toys. Visitors can watch the craftsmen at work, and their products are on sale.

All year, Thur-Sun; some workshops daily. Free entry. Refreshments. P *Toilets.* ♿ *Tel Mansfield (0623) 824393.*

CLUMBER PARK

Off A614, 2½ miles from Worksop (Bd)

Once the country seat of the Dukes of Newcastle, the 4000 acres of Clumber Park now form a popular country park and a major haven for wildlife, the home of more than 130 different species of birds as well as many small mammals and insects. The park is big enough to satisfy the keenest walker, but bicycles can be hired from what was formerly the Duke's Garage, and there is a caravan site and a camp site. Half the park is woodland, containing a great variety of both broad-leaved and coniferous trees.

The mansion was demolished in 1938, except for the Duke's Study which now contains an exhibition about the park. There is also a spectacular range of late 19th-century glasshouses, including the Vineries, Palm House and Fig House. The 24 acres of pleasure grounds remain as they were originally designed, with grassy glades between groups of specimen trees, a 3 mile long lime avenue and a Roman temple looking across the magnificent lake to a larger Greek temple on the south side. The 2 mile long lake made by damming the River Poulton, is spanned at its narrowest point by a classical bridge, designed in the 18th century by Stephen Wright.

NT. All year, daily. Adm charge. Refreshments. Shop. P *Toilets.* ♿ *Tel Worksop (0909) 476592.*

COLWICK COUNTRY PARK
Off B686, 2 miles east of Nottingham (Bb)

In case even the wide range of recreations to be found within the park's 250 acres does not prove to be enough, it is bounded by the River Trent on one side and by Nottingham Racecourse and Greyhound Stadium on the other. The main Colwick lake in the park covers 65 acres and is stocked with trout which can be fished from boats which are available for hire. The smaller West Lake is devoted to board and dinghy sailing and coarse fishing. A third stretch of water, Colwick Hall Pool, is a quiet backwater surrounded by mature woodland which is a nature reserve. Colwick Marina adjoins the Trent. A network of footpaths, a horse trail and a 'fun and fitness course' thread through the park, which also provides ideal surroundings for a picnic.
All year, daily. Free entry.

D.H. LAWRENCE'S BIRTHPLACE
Off A608, 7 miles from Nottingham (Ab)

Admirers of the novels of D.H. Lawrence come from all over the world to visit the simple miner's cottage at 8a Victoria Street, Eastwood, where he was born in 1884. There is more to be gained from such a pilgrimage than there is from visits to the homes of many great writers, since the character of Eastwood and its surrounding countryside permeates so many of Lawrence's novels – particularly *Sons and Lovers, The Rainbow* and *Women in Love*. In later life Lawrence lived in many more exotic places – Italy, the South of France, New Mexico – but Eastwood and Nottinghamshire remained 'the country of my heart'. The house has been restored to very much its condition in Lawrence's day. Visitors can also see the nearby Breach House, at 28 Garden Road, where the Lawrence family lived from 1887 to 1891. This typical pitman's dwelling is in the area called 'The Bottoms' in *Sons and Lovers*. Also near Lawrence's birthplace is the Eastwood Craft Centre, where visitors can see a number of local craftsmen and women at work. They include potters, sculptors, stonemasons, dressmakers, photographers, french polishers, artists and designers.
Birthplace: All year, daily. Adm charge. Shop. P *Tel Langley Mill (0773) 763312. Breach House: Easter-Oct, Sun pm; other times by appointment. Free entry on Sun. Tel Ilkeston (0602) 308941. Craft Centre: All year, Mon-Fri; some at weekends. Free entry.*

GREEN'S MILL AND CENTRE
Off A612, 2 miles east of Nottingham (Bb)

One of the greatest mathematicians of the 19th century once milled flour at Green's Mill. Many years later Einstein paid tribute to the work of this great man by visiting his grave, which is near to the mill, while on a visit to Nottingham in 1933.

The mathematician George Green (1793-1841) worked in the mill as a boy and, before a brilliant career at Cambridge, took over its running from his father. Green's innovations in mathematics are now used by scientists all over the world

WRITER'S BIRTHPLACE *In 1885 David Herbert, the youngest of three sons, was born to miner Arthur Lawrence and his wife Lydia in this cottage in Eastwood. The area featured in Lawrence's novels.*

in computing, telecommunications and microelectronics. The fascinating story of his life is told in the centre attached to the mill, which also celebrates the history of windmills and offers visitors the chance to operate a number of scientific experiments for themselves, including a Van de Graaff generator, a plasma ball and experiments with light and mirrors.

A number of advanced pieces of scientific equipment are also to be seen at the centre, including weather satellite receivers. The mill itself – a five-storey, four-sailed tower mill with two pairs of millstones – is fully operational, with a resident miller. It is open to visitors, who can also buy its freshly milled flour.
All year, daily exc Mon and Tues, inc Bank Hol. Free entry. Shop. P *Toilets.* ♿ *(Centre). Tel Nottingham (0602) 503635.*

HOLME PIERREPONT NATIONAL WATER SPORTS CENTRE
Off A52, 5m east of Nottingham (Bb)

An extraordinary range of aquatic activity takes place at Holme Pierrepont. People are to be seen rowing, canoeing, windsurfing, sailing, water-skiing, power boating and angling. Others are simply watching – a pastime made all the more pleasurable by the fact that the centre is in the middle of an attractive 270 acre country park. The centre has an Olympic standard regatta course and a world-class artificial canoe slalom course. Private sailing craft, rowing boats and canoes can use the centre's facilities whenever they are not reserved for special activities, and casual anglers can buy a day ticket for coarse fishing.

Near the park is the hall built by the Pierrepont family in the early 17th century. It has a handsome facade of brick surmounted by battlements.
Water Sports Centre: All year, daily. Adm charge. Tel Nottingham (0602) 821212. Hall: June-Aug, Tues, Thur, Fri and Sun pm; Easter and Spring Bank Hol. Sun, Mon, Tues. Adm charge. Refreshments. Shop. P *Toilets.* ♿ *Tel Radcliffe on Trent (060 73) 2371.*

LONGDALE RURAL CRAFT CENTRE
Off A60, 8 miles north of Nottingham (Bb)

The chief attraction of this centre is to see artists and craftsmen practising their particular skills. Visitors can also buy the products of their labours. Among the skills on show are sculpture, painting, stained-glass window making, jewellery making, silver working, pottery, antique restoring, wood turning, bookbinding and printing. The Village Craft Museum in which all these skills are exercised is in the form of a re-created 18th-century village street. The museum also houses an extensive collection of old tools and equipment from many trades.
All year, daily. Adm charge. Refreshments. Shop. P *Toilets.* ♿ *Tel Mansfield (0623) 794858.*

MUSEUM OF DOLLS AND BYGONE CHILDHOOD
On A1, 6 miles north of Newark (Cc)

Museums like this have an irresistible appeal, since they bring back such vivid memories of long-forgotten childhood. The collection in this museum contains more than 1000 dolls, dolls' houses and other toys, together with children's clothing and baby wear, dating from the 19th century onwards. It is the private hoard of a collector, Vina Cooke, who is herself a doll-maker. It is housed in a 17th-century former rectory.
All year, daily. Adm charge. Refreshments. Shop. P *Toilets. Tel Newark (0636) 821364.*

NATIONAL MINING MUSEUM

Off A1, 5 miles south of East Retford (Cd)

When the makers of the film of D.H. Lawrence's book *Sons and Lovers* wanted to re-create the kind of pit in which the great novelist's father worked, they turned to this museum at Lound Hall. It was not only able to help, it was able to lend them the timber headstocks from the very pit in which Lawrence's father worked, and they were subsequently featured in the film.

The museum, established in 1970, is next to the National Coal Board's training centre, and the simulated underground galleries, more than 1000yds in length, which give visitors a vivid insight into conditions below ground are also used by apprentices attending the training centre. Other exhibits include an underground canal barge, locomotives, coal-cutting machines, winding equipment, pit pony harness, handtools and a range of miners' lamps including two Davy lamps made in 1825.

All year, daily exc Mon. Adm charge. Refreshments. Shop. P *Toilets.* ♿ *Tel Mansfield (0623) 860728.*

REFLECTED GLORY *Like the backdrop for a film of knightly derring-do, the solitary west wall of Newark Castle flanks the River Trent. The other walls were destroyed on Cromwell's orders after the Civil War.*

NEWARK AIR MUSEUM

Off A46, 2 miles north-east of Newark (Cc)

More than 30 aircraft are on display at the Newark Air Museum, making it one of the largest private collections in the country. It includes five Meteors, a Shackleton, a Hawker Sea Hawk, a North American Super Sabre and a Canberra B(1)8 that was used as a flying test-bed. There are also engines and other aircraft parts on view, including the remains of a V1 flying bomb.

Apr-Oct, daily; Nov-Mar, Sun only. Adm charge. Shop. P *Toilets.* ♿ *Tel Newark (0636) 707170.*

POET'S HOME *Lord Byron once declared that he would never part with Newstead Abbey, his family's home for 200 years. However, in 1817 he had to sell it for £94,000 to pay off some of his debts.*

NEWARK CASTLE

In centre of Newark (Cb)

The castle is a noble ruin, with every displaced stone speaking of its turbulent history. Only the Norman gateway – the finest surviving example in the country – and part of the west wall remain intact. But this is a place in which the imagination has space to grow. Built about 1170, it was the castle in which King John died on October 16, 1216 – probably in the bishop's room on the first floor of the gatehouse. The castle was a Royalist stronghold in the Civil War and withstood three sieges by the Parliamentarians. It was at Newark that Charles I gave himself up to the Scottish army in 1645. The castle was destroyed on Cromwell's orders, leaving it very much in the condition in which it is seen today.

In the south tower, steps lead down to a murky dungeon. Carefully preserved markings on the walls were probably made by bored guards. Carved stones now in the undercroft are the remains of an ornate archway from the Great Hall, once the scene of lavish royal banquets.

Newark's nearby Town Hall is an outstanding piece of Georgian architecture, and its ballroom is one of the finest public assembly rooms of its period in the country.

In the Millgate Folk Museum, 500yds down Castle Gate and Mill Gate from Newark Castle, social and folk-life in Newark from the mid-19th century to the Second World War is vividly re-created over three floors of a converted warehouse alongside the River Trent. The exhibits include completely furnished domestic interiors; a street of 19th-century shops, displaying the fashion and other goods of the time; and a section on the tools and implements used in local trades and businesses, including blacksmiths, brewing and farming. The craft of printing is represented by a complete 19th-century printer's workshop. The top floor of the museum contains a collection of children's books, model cars, aeroplanes, trains and other toys from the early 1900s onwards.

The Church of St Mary Magdalene, behind the Market Place in the centre of Newark, has a fascinating Treasury in a converted medieval crypt, entered through the Lady Chapel. The Treasury contains ecclesiastical silver belonging to St Mary's, amongst which pride of place goes to a set of church plate given by Lady Frances Leake in 1705; there is also a chalice of 1641.

Castle Grounds: All year, daily. Free entry. Town Hall: All year, exc Bank Hol. Free entry. Toilets. Folk Museum: Apr-Oct, daily; Nov-Mar, Mon-Fri. Free entry. Shop. P *Tel Newark (0636) 79403. Treasury: All year, Mon-Fri. Adm charge. Tel (0636) 78818.*

NEWSTEAD ABBEY

Off A60, 5 miles south of Mansfield (Bb)

Although Newstead Abbey is extremely old, having housed a community of Augustinian canons for 400 years before its dissolution under Henry VIII, it is as the home of the poet Lord Byron that it is best known. The Byron connection dates from 1540 when Sir John Byron, the poet's ancestor, bought the property and converted it into a family house.

The poet was not the first Byron to display eccentric tendencies. In the mid-18th century his great uncle, the 5th lord, known as Devil Byron, built the two mock forts by the upper lake in the splendid abbey grounds. He also kept a 20-gun warship on the water and used it to re-enact classic sea battles with his brother, a British

Navy admiral known as Foul Weather Jack.

The 19th-century entrance to Newstead leads to the 13th-century stone-vaulted crypt and late 14th-century cloister. The medieval chapter house was converted into a chapel by the Byrons, and used in the early 1800s to house part of a menagerie assembled by the poet. Byron lived in one small corner of the abbey, the rest being more or less uninhabitable by the time he inherited it. His bedroom contains some of his personal belongings, and more are to be seen down the spiral staircase in the north gallery; they included the extraordinary helmet he designed for use on his expedition to help the Greeks in 1823.

Three medieval kings, among many other famous visitors, stayed at Newstead and the Edward III room is named after one of them. It contains one of three brilliantly carved and painted 16th-century overmantels to be seen in the abbey. The bed was used by Dr Livingstone when he stayed at Newstead to write *The Zambesi and its Tributaries.*

Easter-Sept, daily. Adm charge. Refreshments. Shop. P *Toilets.* ♿ *(Parts). Tel Mansfield (0623) 793557.*

NORTH LEVERTON WINDMILL

Off A120, 4 miles east of East Retford (Cd)

Local farmers still bring their grain for milling at the last working windmill in Nottinghamshire. Most farms today use modern methods of milling, but the farmers supporting North Leverton believe the old methods still produce the best results.

Windmills are far more complicated and ingenious constructions than they might first appear, and visitors to North Leverton will be fascinated and even overawed by the complicated mechanical gadgetry that is involved in getting wind-driven sails to turn millstones. The windmill now depends for its maintenance on much voluntary help, as well as on the local farmers, many of whom are descendants of the men who founded it in 1813.

All year, daily. Adm charge. Refreshments. Shop. P *Toilets. Tel Gainsborough (0427) 880573.*

NOTTINGHAM CASTLE

In centre of Nottingham (Bb)

The first sight of Nottingham Castle may come as a shock to those steeped in the tradition of Robin Hood. Tall, elegant windows pierce the buff-coloured walls, with not a gun-port or arrow-slit to be seen, and balustrades not battlements line the rooftop. The truth is that this is not the castle of the Robin Hood legend – that disappeared after the Civil War – but a ducal palace built in 1674 by William Cavendish, 1st Duke of Newcastle.

Standing on a great rock 130ft above the city, the castle affords splendid views, with the domed and columned tower of the Council House thrusting up above the rooftops below. The castle today houses the city's museum and art gallery: ceramics, silver and glass and medieval Nottingham alabaster carvings are on show, as well as English and Continental paintings from the 14th century to the present day, including a view of Nottingham in 1830 by J.M.W. Turner.

TEMPLE TO POWER *Decorated iron columns worthy of a baroque church support the housing for the two beam engines at Papplewick Pumping Station (top). The windows of this Victorian engine house are of stained glass, and an ornate paraffin lamp hangs from the beams. The shiny brass cap of one of the engine cylinders (above), nearly 4ft across, complements the setting.*

The original castle's outer walls and gatehouse survived demolition by Parliamentarians, and the gatehouse now contains a light-hearted display depicting the exploits of Robin Hood and his Merry Men, especially as portrayed in literature and films. Nearby, the city remembers the world's most famous outlaw with a bronze statue of Robin, with longbow drawn, surrounded by bronze reliefs of scenes from his life.

Opposite the statue is a medieval building called Severns, partly devoted to Robin's chief rival for bringing world fame to Nottingham – its lace. In it the Lace Centre traces the history of lace-making and offers fine lace for sale. Round the corner in Castle Gate is the Museum of Costume and Textiles, with a series of rooms furnished in period styles as backgrounds for costumes dating from 1760 to 1960. There are also displays of lace, embroideries and tapestries.

Below the castle walls stand a group of 17th-century cottages, where aspects of daily life in Nottingham spanning 300 years are re-created in the Brewhouse Yard Museum. As well as period rooms, there is a barber's shop, surgery and chemist's shop. Also in Brewhouse Yard is the Trip to Jerusalem inn, said to date from 1189 and possibly taking its name from the Crusaders who rested there on their way to the Holy Land.

In Canal Street, a short walk away from Brewhouse Yard, a canal warehouse contains the Canal Museum, with displays based on the history of the River Trent, the Nottingham and Beeston Canal and the archaeology of the Trent Valley. The former canal basin is inside the building, and there are two narrowboats in working condition.

Castle: All year, daily. Free entry. Shop. Toilets. Tel Nottingham (0602) 411881. Lace Centre: All year, daily. Free entry. Shop. Tel (0602) 413539. Costume and Textiles Museum: All year, daily. Free entry. Tel (0602) 411881. Brewhouse Yard Museum: All year, daily. Free entry. Toilets. ♿ *(ground floor). Tel (0602) 411881. Canal Museum: Easter-Oct, Wed-Sat and Sun pm; Oct-Easter, Wed, Thur, Sat and Sun pm. Free entry. Shop.* P *Toilets.* ♿ *Tel (0602) 598835.*

PAPPLEWICK PUMPING STATION

Off A614, 7 miles north of Nottingham (Bb)

The interior of this station is like a small cathedral, complete with stained-glass windows, elaborately decorated and carved columns and hanging paraffin lamps. The Victorians treated the products of their engineering skill with reverence, and built them to last. Papplewick is one of the finest working examples of a Victorian waterworks in existence, and it houses an impressive example of Victorian engineering – a pair of massive beam pumping engines, insulated and clad with polished mahogany strip and polished brass bands, made by the famous firm of James Watt and Co in 1884. Each of these raised $1\frac{1}{2}$ million gallons of water to the surface every day, driven by six Lancashire hand-fired boilers, until electrically driven pumps were installed nearby in 1969.

Easter-Oct, Sun, and occasional open days. Adm charge. Refreshments. Shop. P *Toilets.* ♿ *Tel Nottingham (0602) 632938.*

RUDDINGTON FRAMEWORK KNITTERS' MUSEUM

Off A60, 5 miles south of Nottingham (Ba)

The invention of the handframe, a knitting machine, in 1589 by a Nottinghamshire man, William Lee, created a new industry for the region. The making of textiles and lace was to transform villages such as Ruddington from agricultural into industrial communities, and cottage craftsmen in Ruddington used Lee's machine for more than 200 years. Part of the Knitters' Museum traces the development of machine knitting from William Lee's invention to the most modern computer methods of production. A workshop full of handframes re-creates the cramped conditions in which the 19th-century knitters worked, and the noise and atmosphere as the machines were being operated. A small back-to-back cottage has been restored as a framework knitter's home of 1850.

The village museum is housed on two sites; the oldest house in Ruddington, the Hermitage, and St Peter's Rooms, part of the old village school, which contain reconstructions of a village fish and chip shop, a chemist's, a cobbler's, an ironmonger's, and a schoolroom.

Knitters' Museum: Apr-Sept, Tues and Thur. Adm charge. Shop. Toilets. Tel Nottingham (0602) 846914. Village Museum: All year, Tues am and Fri evening. Adm charge. Toilets. ♿ *Tel (0602) 211545.*

RUFFORD COUNTRY PARK

On A614, 2 miles south of Ollerton (Bc)

The ruins of a 12th-century Cistercian abbey, not open to the public, stand forlorn among the trees of this lovely park. Once a country estate, the park has woodland walks and a beautiful lake with many species of wildfowl. The abbey became derelict in the 16th century, and was replaced by a grand country house; this, too, is now a ruin, but its stable block remains and houses a craft centre. On the ground floor, visitors can browse among displays of pottery, glassware, woodwork, leatherwork, metalwork and textiles. Upstairs is a gallery where craft exhibitions are held.

Park: All year, daily. Free entry. Craft Centre: Mar-Dec, daily: Jan-Feb, Sat and Sun. Refreshments. Shop. P *Toilets.* ♿ *Tel Mansfield (0623) 822944.*

SHERWOOD FOREST VISITOR CENTRE

Off A616, 8 miles north-east of Mansfield (Bc)

Some 450 acres of the oak woodlands of Robin Hood's time survive, making Sherwood the largest area of ancient oak forest in western Europe. Waymarked paths entice the walker into its leafy glades. One marked trail starting from the visitor centre leads to the Major Oak, 30ft in circumference and safely preserved behind a wooden fence. In the hollow trunk of this oak Robin Hood's outlaws are reputed to have hidden – though as the tree is apparently no more than 500 years old it would not have been able to furnish such shelter in Robin Hood's day, 800 years ago.

The legend which has made Sherwood Forest's fame is brought to life in a display at the visitor centre called 'The Legend of Robyn Hode and Mery Scherewode', and based on the stories told in the medieval ballad *The Geste of Robyn Hode*. The first written poem mentioning Robin Hood dates from 1377, and several ballads recounting his adventures had become popular in all levels of society by the 15th century. There are

CATHEDRAL CONTRASTS *The twin-towered west front of Southwell Minster is in boldly simple Norman style. In striking contrast are the complex stone carvings inside the Minster, mainly dating from the 13th and 14th centuries. They include (right) a relief of* The Flight into Egypt.

PICTURE OF PROSPERITY *The arches of a stone gazebo frame the magnificence of Thoresby Hall – a house designed in Elizabethan style but incorporating all the comforts that its Victorian builders could provide.*

many versions of the Robin Hood legend, all with different accounts of his exploits and different claims as to his real identity, but the most popular is that he was of noble birth, that he fought against the wicked Sheriff of Nottingham, robbed the rich to give to the poor and was finally pardoned by Richard I. Today, presumably, he would be called a terrorist, but as long as stories in which Good triumphs over Evil are told, then the ballads of Robin of Sherwood will be among them.

On the northern edge of Sherwood Forest are the limestone caves of Creswell Crags, inhabited in prehistoric times and reached from a visitor centre off the B6024 in neighbouring Derbyshire.
Park and Visitor Centre: All year, daily. Free entry. Refreshments. Shop. P *Toilets.* ♿ *Tel Mansfield (0623) 823202.*

SOUTHWELL MINSTER

On A612, 12 miles north-east of Nottingham (Cb)

The cream-coloured stone and slender towers and spires of Southwell Minster have moved many people to regard it as the most beautiful church in Britain. James I, on his way south to be crowned, compared it to York and Durham. The church dates from 1108, and Norman work is much in evidence, especially in the nave with its double arches. The view from the west door is exquisite, a soaring arch framing the delicately carved screen and imposing organ case.

The minster is renowned for its Chapter House, built in 1290 and containing some of the finest examples of stone carving in England. This features different types of foliage such as maple, oak, hawthorn and vine. The identity of the medieval sculptor who created the famous 'leaves of Southwell' is unknown, though there is a stone head of a master mason that may be a self-portrait.
All year, daily. Free entry. P *Shop.* ♿ *Tel Southwell (0636) 812649.*

SUNDOWN KIDDIES ADVENTURELAND

Off A57, 6 miles east of East Retford (Cd)

Don't get lost in the secret passages leading through the Tudor Village, or waylaid by pirates in the Smugglers' Cove as you make your way to the Fantasy Castle. After all this adventure, why not relax with the donkeys, goats, pigs and sheep on the miniature farm?

Indoors on this 20 acre children's playground is a series of easy-to-operate animated tableaux illustrating scenes from children's stories and nursery rhymes. If they have any energy left, children can retire to the Noah's Ark play area.
All year, daily. Adm charge. Refreshments. Shop. P *Toilets.* ♿ *Tel Rampton (077 784) 274.*

THORESBY HALL

Off A614, 9 miles north-east of Mansfield (Bc)

This splendid Victorian re-creation of an Elizabethan mansion is the third house to be built at Thoresby, the seat of the Pierrepoint family for many generations. It was built at the peak of Victorian prosperity and reflects all the confidence and opulence of its time. Surrounding the house are 50 acres of parkland, with a river, a lake and a herd of fallow deer. Ownership of Thoresby Hall is changing, and public access and opening times are therefore also liable to change.
Tel Mansfield (0623) 822301.

WETLANDS WATERFOWL RESERVE

Off A638, 3 miles north of East Retford (Cd)

There are 40 different species of duck at Wetlands – enough to test the powers of identification of the keenest duck fancier. Given the run of 32 acres, including two lakes and some marshland, it is hardly surprising that ducks from all over the world have settled down quite happily, the Cuban tree duck living side by side with the Argentinian red shoveler, the Philippine and Patagonian ducks, the gadwall, the garganey and many more. In addition there are five different species of swan and 18 species of goose, a parrot collection, owls and flamingos.
All year, daily. Adm charge. Refreshments. Shop. P *Toilets.* ♿ *Tel Retford (0777) 818099.*

WOLLATON HALL

Off A609, 3 miles west of Nottingham (Bb)

The extravagant architecture of Wollaton Hall, with its cupolas, pinnacles, balustrades and false Dutch gables, is more like that of a Victorian mansion than the Elizabethan house it is. Its main feature is the 50ft high great hall, with a hammerbeam roof carved and coloured to look like stone and decorated with coats of arms. Two levels of rooms around the hall house Nottingham's Natural History Museum. Exhibits include mounted mammals, birds and fishes in natural settings; live insects; rocks, fossils and minerals.

The house is approached along an avenue of lime trees, with parkland on either side where red and fallow deer roam. In the formal gardens on the house's south terrace is the unusual Camellia House, built entirely of cast iron in 1823 and now fully restored.

The 18th-century stable block contains Nottingham's Industrial Museum, with fascinating exhibits that record the city's long history of industry, from lace-making to pharmaceuticals and tobacco, and some of its lesser known industries such as coachbuilding. Two 17th-century carriages on display are the oldest known English made carriages in Britain.
Natural History Museum: All year, daily. Free entry, exc Sun and Bank Hol. Shop. P *Toilets.* ♿ *Tel Nottingham (0602) 281333. Industrial Museum: Apr-Sept, daily; Oct-Mar, Thur, Sat, Sun. Free entry, exc Sun and Bank Hol. Shop.* P *Toilets.* ♿ *Tel (0602) 284602.*

COUNTY CALENDAR

April (Easter Mon). Wollaton Park: Egg Rolling.

May (1st weekend). Newark: Newark and Nottinghamshire Show.

May (Spring Bank Hol). Clumber Park: Horse Trials.

May (late, to early June). Nottingham: Arts Festival.

June (late, to early July). Worksop: Bassetlaw Festival.

July (mid-month). Holme Pierrepont: National Rowing Championships.

August (late). Tollerton Airport: Nottingham Air Show.

September (early). Wollaton Park: Nottingham City Show.

September (mid-month). Holme Pierrepont: Powerboat Grand Prix.

October (from 1st Thur). Nottingham: Goose Fair.

November (late). Laxton: Jury Day and Court Leet (traditional strip-farming ceremony).

Tourist information: Newark (0636) 78962; Nottingham (0602) 470661; Ollerton (0623) 824545; Sherwood Forest (0623) 823202; Worksop (0909) 475531.

OXFORDSHIRE

COLLEGES, PARKS AND A PALACE AMID FARMLANDS BY THE THAMES

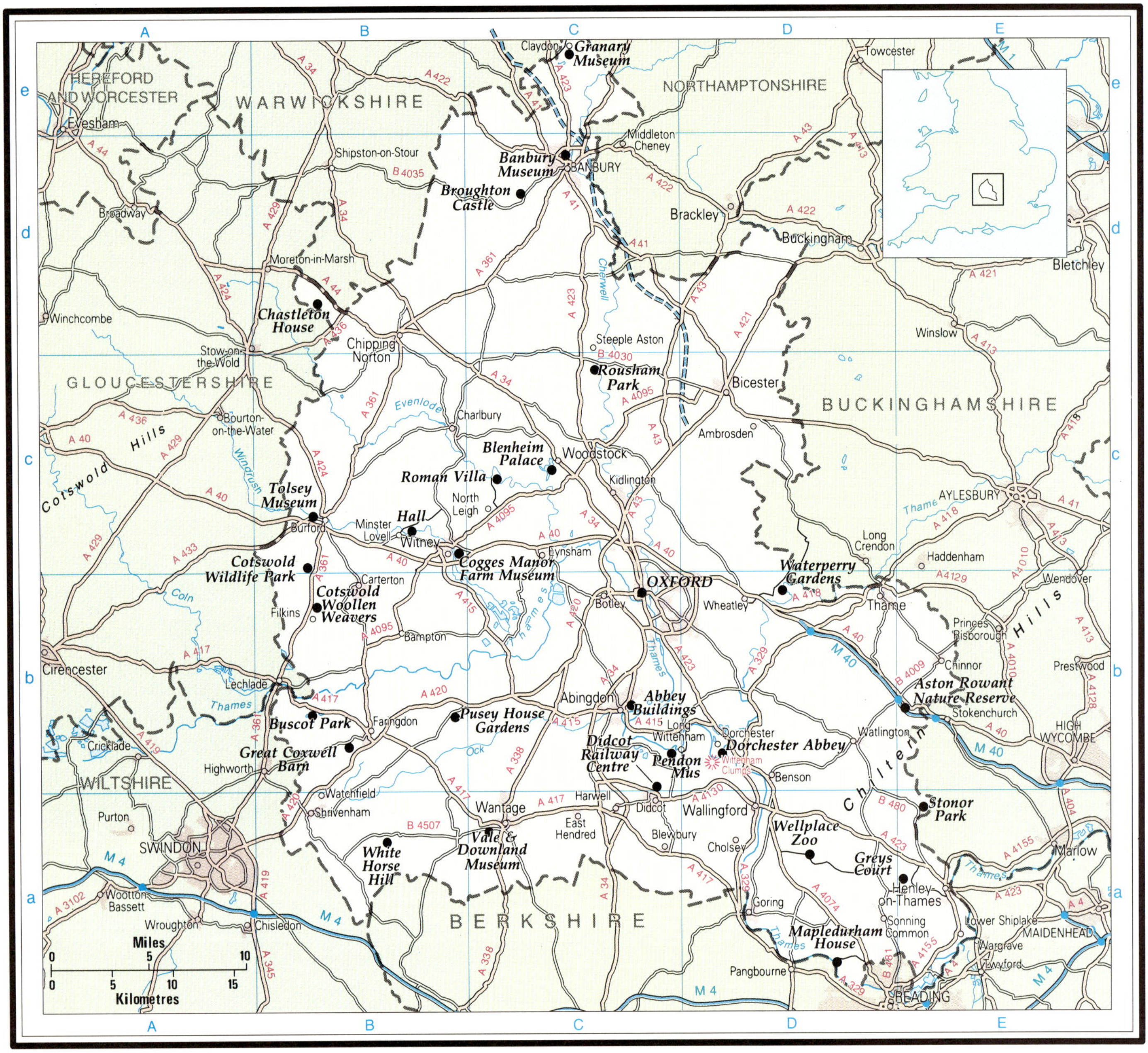

The colleges, gardens, libraries and museums of Britain's oldest university encompass a wealth of attractions in themselves. Yet beyond its walls there is much more to enjoy. Only a few miles from the city is Blenheim Palace, one of Britain's most grandiose mansions, while Broughton Castle, Buscot Park, Greys Court, ruined Minster Lovell and Rousham Park contribute further to the county's air of cultured nobility.

Oxfordshire is a primarily agricultural county. It lies in the basin of the upper Thames which, as well as serving university oarsmen, also turns the water wheel at Mapledurham's fine old mill. Cogges Manor Farm Museum recalls the bygone ways of the working countryside, whilst Banbury and Abingdon retain their integrity as market towns. Much of the traditional countryside is flat or quietly rolling, with willow-fringed meadows and hedgerows pungent with elderflower in June. Westward, though, the county creeps into the Cotswolds, where the ancient traditions of wool-weaving are kept alive at the Cotswold Woollen Weavers' mill. In 1974, Oxfordshire gained a large expanse of downland from Berkshire, including the chalk-cut White Horse of Uffington.

ABINGDON ABBEY BUILDINGS

Thames Street, Abingdon (Cb)

A small group of lay buildings, once part of the complex of Abingdon Abbey, escaped the Tudor demolition crews when Henry VIII dissolved the monasteries and stand as a reminder of that turbulent time. The entrance to the buildings is by the abbey's former bakehouse and granary; separated from them by a covered passageway is the Checker Hall, with a tall 13th-century chimney. The hall's interior has a fine timbered roof and the building serves in the summer as a theatre with an Elizabethan-style stage. From the hall an old staircase leads into the upper part of the Checker or Counting House, with a timbered long gallery.

The 15th-century abbey gatehouse also survives, with a little church on one side and a former hospital, now a guildhall, on the other. Abingdon also has a grand Market House or County Hall, which today houses Abingdon Museum. The building stands on stone arches and was built in 1678 by Christopher Kempster, one of Sir Christopher Wren's masons at St Paul's Cathedral. The museum on the first floor has displays on the town's history and some Saxon relics.

Abbey buildings: Apr-Sept, pm daily; Oct-Mar, pm daily exc Mon. Adm charge. Toilets. Tel Abingdon (0235) 25339. Museum: EH. All year, pm daily exc Bank Hol. Adm charge. Shop. Tel (0235) 23703.

ASTON ROWANT NATURE RESERVE

Off A40, 9 miles north-west of High Wycombe (Eb)

At one point between London and Oxford the M40 plunges through a deep chalk cutting, from the Chilterns' ridge down to the Thames Valley below. Here the Aston Rowant National Nature Reserve protects some 300 acres of grass downland and beechwoods, with tracts of scrub tufted with hawthorn, bramble, ash and juniper. Kestrels haunt the open skies, while the woodlands shelter badgers and fallow deer.

The 800ft Beacon Hill is a superb viewpoint which looks westward as far as the Cotswolds. At the summit is the site of the old beacon where, from ancient times, people lit warning fires in time of emergency. The reserve's centre on Beacon Hill has displays on the wildlife and vegetation of the area. Visitors should keep to the waymarked nature trail, which passes through examples of all types of countryside on the reserve.

NCC. All year, daily. Free entry. P

BANBURY MUSEUM

Horsefair, Banbury (Cd)

Housed in a turn-of-the-century building overlooking the legendary Banbury Cross, Banbury Museum has permanent displays on the town and on 'Banburyshire', the area around it. The exhibits include signboards and ovens from the original cake shop where Banbury cakes (of flaky pastry filled with dried spiced fruit) were made from the 16th century onwards. There is also a reconstructed photographer's shop of 1910.

Outside, the tall, tapered Banbury Cross is Victorian, replacing an earlier cross destroyed by the Puritans in 1602. The familiar nursery rhyme about the cross, with its 'fine lady upon a white horse', probably refers to a local girl who rode in a May Day procession.

Apr-Sept, Mon-Sat; Oct-Mar, Tues-Sat. Free entry. Refreshments. Shop. Toilets. ♿ *Tel Banbury (0295) 59855.*

BLENHEIM PALACE

In Woodstock (Cc)

Enter by the Triumphal Gate and Blenheim's great vista of lake, bridge and distant palace bursts upon the eye. The very horizon seems suddenly to widen, rolled back by the heroic perspectives of the 2200 acre park. Vast lawns swoop from a background of hanging beechwoods to the shimmering water of the lake and a poplar-plumed island which echoes to waterbirds' calls. Then, as the drive curves round towards the palace, the visitor becomes aware of the 134ft high Column of Victory, topped by its statue of the Duke of Marlborough, away to the right. Ahead are the towers of the house itself, with gilded orbs glinting above a Baroque roofscape of carved statues, urns and trophies.

PALACE BIRTHPLACE *The towers of Blenheim Palace, the great lake and Vanbrugh's Great Bridge combine in a view described as 'the finest in England' by Lord Randolph Churchill. His son, Winston Churchill, was born in the modest room (right) once occupied by the Duke of Marlborough's domestic chaplain.*

The palace was built on Queen Anne's instruction for John Churchill, 1st Duke of Marlborough, as a reward for his victory over the French at the Battle of Blenheim in 1704. It was designed by the architect Sir John Vanbrugh, and made of a warm orange-yellow stone. Vanbrugh built a grand bridge to cross the then trifling marshy stream of the River Glyme, but it was Capability Brown who, in 1764, made sense of its proportions by flooding the valley to create the superb lake there today.

The house is entered by a great hall, and visitors pass on through a suite of state rooms sumptuously ornamented with portraits, marble busts, china and fine furniture. Marlborough's military triumphs are depicted in a series of splendid tapestries, and the richness of exhibits and detailing can be overwhelming. Cooler in tone is the beautiful library, 180ft long, with stucco decoration and salmon-pink walls, with the silver pipework of an organ at the end.

Winston Churchill, a descendant of the 1st Duke, was born in a modest room of the palace and one relic here is a luxuriant lock of auburn hair clipped from his five-year-old head. Other Churchill memorabilia are displayed in adjoining rooms, while tapes play extracts from his wartime speeches. The ornate chapel leads out to the Italianate water terraces laid out by the 9th Duke in the present century. With patterning of hedge, fountains and statues they provide a formal setting from which to admire the naturalistic sweeps of woodland and water. Visitors can voyage on the lake in a motor launch, or enjoy the narrow-gauge railway, butterfly house or adventure playground.

Near the gates of Blenheim, in Park Street, Woodstock, stands Fletcher's House, a fine 16th-century building with a pleasant garden. Today it houses The Oxfordshire County Museum, which tells the story of Oxfordshire throughout the ages. The exhibits include archaeological, industrial, domestic and craft items.

Blenheim: Mid Mar-Oct, daily. Adm charge. Refreshments. Shop. P *Toilets.* ♿ *Tel Woodstock (0993) 811325. County Museum: May-Sept, daily; Oct-Apr, daily exc Mon. Free entry. Refreshments. Shop.* P *Toilets. Tel (0993) 811456.*

THE LONG SLEEP *Maidens sleep beneath an enveloping briar rose in the Garden Court, in this painting by Sir Edward Burne-Jones at Buscot Park. It is one of a series illustrating the story of Sleeping Beauty.*

BROUGHTON CASTLE

Off B4035, 2½ miles south-west of Banbury (Cd)

The homely chimneys and gables belie the term 'castle', and though crenellations are everywhere they are mainly decorative. Broughton was not built as a serious-minded military fortification. Nevertheless, with a broad encircling moat and a history of Civil War siege behind it, it has ample historic pedigree.

The original manor dates from 1300 and was built by Sir John de Broughton. He sold it in 1370 to William of Wykeham, whose great-niece married Lord Saye and Sele in 1450. The building was much enlarged in Tudor times when splendid plaster ceilings, oak panelling and fireplaces were introduced. William Fiennes, the lord at the time of the Civil War, was a Parliamentarian who held secret anti-Royalist meetings in a chamber at the top of the west stairs. After the nearby Battle of Edgehill in 1642, the castle was captured and occupied by the Royalists.

Cannonballs have been recovered from the moat but the building was not badly damaged, and the neglect of a spendthrift 19th-century heir ironically saved Broughton from too much Victorian 'improvement'. The result is a pleasing air of wholeness. The hall has arms and armour from the Civil War, and among the other rooms Queen Anne's chamber, where the wife of James I slept in 1604, is memorable for its grandiose Tudor fireplace and the 'squint' in one corner looking through to a private chapel.

Outside is a walled knot garden. The nearby parish church of St Mary dates almost entirely from the 14th century and has the painted tomb of Sir John de Broughton.

Mid May-mid Sept, Wed and Sun pm; July-Aug, Wed, Thur and Sun pm; Bank Hol. Adm charge. Refreshments. Shop. P *Toilets. Tel Banbury (0295) 62624.*

BUSCOT PARK

Off A417, 3 miles west of Faringdon (Bb)

An 18th-century house of Cotswold stone commands the high ground of a landscaped park, which includes a 22 acre lake and a chain of Italianate water gardens laid out in 1905. The house itself was carefully restored in the 1930s. With tree-lined vistas and sweeps of greensward there is much outdoors to enjoy, while indoors the supreme attraction is the art collection assembled by the industrialist Alexander Henderson, the 1st Lord Faringdon, who bought the estate in 1889.

The paintings hung throughout the house include works by Murillo, Reynolds and Gainsborough. If a single canvas holds pride of place it is certainly Rembrandt's *Portrait of a Man*, probably depicting Clement de Jongh, an early collector of Rembrandt's drawings (three examples of which can also be seen at Buscot). Lord Faringdon also collected works by English artists of his own day, and in the saloon there hangs a triumph of the Pre-Raphaelite school in *The Legend of the Briar Rose*, a celebrated series of canvasses by Sir Edward Burne-Jones portraying the story of Sleeping Beauty. The rooms are also rich in Regency and Empire furniture, Chinese porcelains and Renaissance ivories.

NT. Apr-Sept, Wed, Thur and Fri; also Good Fri, Easter Sat and Sun, and every 2nd and 4th weekend. Adm charge. Refreshments. P *Toilets. Tel Faringdon (0367) 20786.*

CHASTLETON HOUSE

Off A44, 5 miles west of Chipping Norton (Bd)

The tall Jacobean house overlooks a village of thatched cottages and forms an imposing silhouette against the sky. It was built in 1603 for a wealthy wool merchant who bought the land from Robert Catesby, one of the Gunpowder Plot conspirators. Little has changed since the 17th century: much original furniture survives, with oak-boarded floors and Jacobean plasterwork. Behind the wallpaper in one bedroom is the secret room where a Royalist, Arthur Jones, escaped detection from pursuing Roundheads. The gardens contain box bushes clipped to the shapes of birds, animals and other devices.

Good Fri-end Sept, Fri, Sat, Sun and Bank Hol pm. Adm charge. P *(limited). Tel Barton-on-the-Heath (060 874) 355.*

COGGES MANOR FARM MUSEUM

Off B4022, ¼ mile east of Witney (Bc)

The stone-built farm buildings and manor farmhouse of Cogges are an apt setting for a fascinating museum of farming and the countryside. It lies in the ancient and tiny village of Cogges, where the Cotswolds slope down to a calm valley and the willow-lined River Windrush glides gently by.

The museum tells the story of Cogges over the last 1000 years, and the farm is furnished much as it was around the turn of the century. Visitors can see the stone-flagged kitchen with its fine old range; the panelled dining room; and many interesting nooks such as the paydesk, a tiny windowed room scarcely bigger than a cupboard where on Friday afternoons the farm labourers would file past to receive their wages from the farmer. Outside is an orchard and a walled garden maintained in Edwardian style with espaliered apple trees, vegetable plots and beds edged with lavender, pinks and sweet william.

Mid Apr-early Nov, daily exc Mon. Adm charge. Refreshments. Shop. P *Toilets.* ♿ *Tel Witney (0993) 72602.*

COTSWOLD WILDLIFE PARK

Off A361, 2 miles south of Burford (Bc)

Aged yews, oaks and redwoods screen this attractive 120 acre park from the road. Behind the trees, in a green and breezy setting, is a large and varied collection of animals from all over the

TIPTOE TRIO *Small-clawed otters from Asia are among the species from warmer climates that thrive in the Walled Garden at Cotswold Wildlife Park. Near neighbours include toucans and penguins.*

world. Ostriches, zebras and rhinos roam in large, moated paddocks, while leopards and tigers prowl in grassy enclosures.

An old walled garden shelters penguins, pink flamingos, monkeys, otters and meerkats – little carnivores of South Africa's grassland whose expressive features and upright stance give them an alert and intelligent appearance. In the tropical house, visitors walk among alligator pools overhung with hibiscus and bird of paradise flowers.

In the middle of the park is a grand Cotswold manor house, built in early 19th-century Gothic style, with pinnacles and battlements. It is open to visitors. An adventure playground is sited among the trees nearby, and the outbuildings include a large butterfly house, reptile house and aquarium. A model railway provides rides.

All year, daily. Adm charge. Refreshments. Shop. P *Toilets.* ♿ *Tel Burford (099 382) 3006.*

COTSWOLD WOOLLEN WEAVERS

Off A361, 5 miles south of Burford (Bb)

Some 500 years ago, flocks of sheep covered the Cotswolds and on the wealth of their fleeces merchants built the fine wool towns and churches for which the region is noted today. Cotswold Woollen Weavers keeps the old traditions alive with a working weaving mill in a restored 18th-century barn. Visitors can tour the mill and watch its clattering looms at work, while an exhibition gallery tells the story of wool in the Cotswolds. The adjoining Cross Tree Gallery displays works by local artists and craftsmen.

All year, daily. Free entry. Refreshments. Shop. P *Toilets. Tel Filkins (036 786) 491.*

DIDCOT RAILWAY CENTRE

Off A4130, beside Didcot Station (Cb)

A typical small country halt platform is an endearing feature of this centre which looks back with affection on the golden age of steam railways. The centre was founded in 1961 by a group of local schoolboys, who set out to preserve some of the glories of the Great Western Railway, with its Brunswick-green locomotives and chocolate-and-cream carriages. The collection started in a single old engine shed, but today the centre covers 16 acres. There is a large locomotive repair shop, a coaling stage and engine turntable, and a replica of a section of the 7ft $\frac{1}{4}$in gauge trackwork – the so-called 'broad gauge' – laid down by the Great Western's engineering genius, Isambard Kingdom Brunel, in the 19th century. There is also a museum of small exhibits, ranging from nameplates to restaurant-car silverware of the 1930s.

The 20 or so locomotives on display include steam veterans such as the *Cookham Manor*, the *Dryslwyn Castle* and the *Hinderton Hall*, as well as several diesel engines. There are more than 40 coaches dating from the 1880s to the 1950s, and on certain days visitors can dine in 1930s style in the luxury saloon carriages *Princess Elizabeth* and *Queen Mary*, built originally to take boat-train passengers to Southampton en route to America.

Apr-Dec, Sat, Sun and Bank Hol, exc Christmas; Easter-Oct, Mon-Fri also. Adm charge. Refreshments. Shop. P *Toilets.* ♿ *Tel Didcot (0235) 817200.*

DORCHESTER ABBEY

Off A423, 6 miles south-east of Abingdon (Db)

Reached by a Victorian lich gate, Dorchester's abbey church of St Peter and St Paul is a 200ft long building, founded in about 1140, with fine arcades, stone tracery and stained glass. It is crammed with fascinating detail, ranging from a rare Norman lead font to an unusual 14th-century carving showing sleeping monks being woken by a devil blowing a horn. Below the altar steps is a superb tomb effigy of a 13th-century Crusader knight, Sir John Holcombe, who although recumbent reaches expressively for his sword. The abbey is noted for its 14th-century Jesse window, which depicts Christ's descent from Jesse, father of King David.

The tranquil cloister gardens have views of the oldest part of the abbey: the north wall of the nave, which is probably Saxon in its lower courses. The gardens lie on the site of the original monastery, but all that survives of the monastic buildings is the old Guest House, an amalgam of stone, brick and timber which is now the Abbey Museum. This shows patterns of settlement at Dorchester from prehistoric times, displaying Roman, Saxon and medieval finds.

Abbey: All year, daily. Free entry. Refreshments. Shop. P *(limited). Toilets.* ♿ *Tel Oxford (0865) 340007. Museum: Good Fri-Sept, pm daily. Free entry. Refreshments. Shop. Tel (0865) 340056.*

GRANARY MUSEUM

Off A423, at Claydon (Cc)

Country life in bygone days is re-created in a long, low barn crowded with agricultural implements and country craftsmen's tools, gathered together from Oxfordshire farms over the years by an enthusiastic collector. A steam roller built in 1912 is occasionally in steam. The magpie hoard of bygones spills over into a loft room beside the entrance gate. Here are the more domestic memorabilia of a lifetime's interest in other people's unconsidered trifles: old children's games and gramophones, early typewriters and wartime stirrup pumps and gasmasks.

All year, daily. Free entry. Refreshments. Shop. P *Toilets.* ♿ *(parts). Tel Banbury (0295) 89258.*

GREAT COXWELL BARN

Off B4019, $1\frac{1}{2}$ miles south-west of Faringdon (Bb)

The finest surviving medieval barn in England was described by the artist and designer William Morris as being 'as noble as a cathedral'. Dating back to the 13th century, the 152ft long structure was built of honey-coloured Cotswold stone by the Cistercian monks of Beaulieu Abbey in Hampshire. It is laid out in cruciform shape – like a church – and its oak pillars support a timber and stone-tiled roof soaring to 48ft, braced with struts and crossbeams.

NT. All year, daily. Free entry. P *Tel High Wycombe (0494) 28051.*

NIGHTS OF STEAM *A restored signal box was brought from Radstock in Somerset to re-create Didcot Halt, a typical platform halt on the old Great Western Railway. Night openings (right) at Didcot Railway Centre give enthusiasts an unusual glimpse inside the locomotive shed.*

OXFORD'S TIMELESS CHARM

Pinnacled towers and cloistered college lawns, bicycles propped against honeystone walls and the punts on the willow-fringed River Cherwell are all symbols of this venerable city whose heart still beats to its own timeless rhythms. Saxon ox drovers were the first to settle here, around a ford of the Thames, or Isis, that flows south of the city. The university itself dates from the 13th century when the first colleges were founded – University College, Merton and Balliol. Today there are 35 colleges, each with its own character and traditions. The city also has several fine museums, including the Ashmolean, Britain's oldest public museum, the Oxford University Museum and the Museum of the History of Science. Oxford's newest venture is the Oxford Story, where visitors can journey through the university's history in 'time cars'.

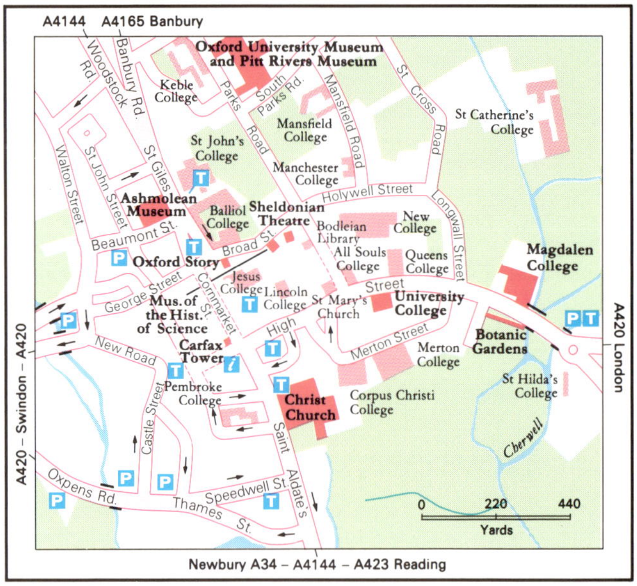

Christ Church *All year, daily. Adm charge. Shop. Toilets. ♿ Tel Oxford (0865) 276154.*

Colleges *Most open daily pm. Adm charge in some colleges. Tel (0865) 270009.*

Museum of the History of Science *All year, Mon-Fri. Free entry. Shop. Tel (0865) 277280.*

Botanic Gardens *All year, daily. Free entry. ♿ Tel (0865) 242737.*

Ashmolean Museum *All year, Tues-Sat, Sun pm. Free entry. Shop. Toilets. ♿ Tel (0865) 278000.*

Carfax Tower *Mar-Nov, daily (Sun pm). Adm charge. Tel (0865) 249811.*

Oxford Story *All year, daily. Adm charge. ♿*

University Museum *All year, Mon-Sat pm. Free entry. Shop. Toilets. Tel (0865) 272950.*

Sheldonian Theatre *All year, Mon-Sat. Adm charge. Tel (0865) 277299.*

CHRIST CHURCH

Tom Quad, the main quadrangle of Christ Church, with its bronze statue of Mercury, is the largest college quadrangle in Oxford. Its buildings date mostly from the 16th century, when the college was founded by Cardinal Wolsey, then re-founded by Henry VIII. Part of the cathedral to which the college is attached dates from the 8th century; its spire was the first to be built in England. Tom Quad takes its name from Tom Tower, the gateway to Christ Church.

MAGDALEN COLLEGE

Punts are time-honoured craft on the River Cherwell, and are especially popular with undergraduates of Magdalen College, whose greystone walls have stood by the river since the 15th century. The college was founded by William of Wayneflete, Bishop of Winchester, in 1458. Riverside walks include one named Addison's Walk, after Joseph Addison, the essayist and founder of the *Spectator,* who was a Fellow of Magdalen.

UNIVERSITY COLLEGE

The poet Percy Bysshe Shelley was a student at University College, and is commemorated there by a memorial sculpted in 1894 by Onslow Ford and showing the poet after his death by drowning in Italy in 1822. Shelley was not the college's favourite son during his lifetime – he was expelled in 1811 for publishing a pamphlet, 'The Necessity of Atheism', and in 1813 his poem *Queen Nab* attacked the monarchy, the Church and other institutions. Shelley's unpopular views forced him into exile in 1818. University College was founded in 1249 by William of Durham – though tradition says Alfred the Great founded a community there some 400 years earlier.

ASHMOLEAN MUSEUM

Richly clad hunters and their hounds disappear, through converging lines of perspective, into the bleak silence of a forest, in Paolo Ucello's haunting *The Hunt in the Forest*, one of the many masterpieces on display at the Ashmolean Museum. Named after the antiquary Elias Ashmole, the museum was opened in 1683 and is today housed in a handsome classical building of the 1840s. Its antiquities include a golden jewel said to have been commissioned by Alfred the Great.

BOTANIC GARDENS

The 17th-century Danby Gateway makes an imposing entrance to the Oxford Botanic Gardens, founded by Henry Danvers, Earl of Danby, in 1621. It is Britain's oldest botanic garden, and includes pools, alpine rockeries and greenhouses for exotic plants.

CARFAX TOWER

The quarterboys on Carfax Tower, which strike the chimes every quarter of an hour, are replicas of the 17th-century originals, now in the Museum of Oxford in St Aldates. The square tower is all that remains of a 14th-century church; there are fine views from the top.

THE OXFORD STORY

A lifelike Edmond Halley, the astronomer, is one of the many Oxford men of the past seen in the Oxford Story exhibition. Seated in 'time cars' shaped like medieval students' desks, visitors spiral upwards through a kaleidoscope of tableaux and sound effects.

OXFORD UNIVERSITY MUSEUM

The rare remains of a Dodo, the flightless bird of Mauritius that became extinct in the late 17th century (below left), and a fine collection of tropical beetles (below right) are among the exhibits in a museum dedicated mainly to zoology, entomology and geology. The museum is housed in an extraordinary Victorian Gothic building of ironwork arches under a glass roof. The design was the result of a competition held in 1854 and won by a Dublin firm; much of its design was inspired by John Ruskin, the writer and art historian. An annexe contains the Pitt Rivers Museum, which houses more than 14,000 ethnological items.

MUSEUM OF SCIENCE

A 9th-century Islamic astrolabe, used for astronomical calculations, is among the early instruments on show in a fine 17th-century building, the first home of the Ashmolean collection.

SHELDONIAN THEATRE

University ceremonies and concerts are held in the Sheldonian Theatre, the first full-scale building designed by Sir Christopher Wren, who based it on the Theatre of Marcellus in Rome. There are superb views of the city from the rooftop cupola.

GREYS COURT

Off A423, 3 miles north-west of Henley-on-Thames (Ea)

Standing among the ruined 14th-century fortifications of a 13th-century house, this gabled manor house dates mainly from the 16th century; but in the kitchen the great beams and stout posts survive from medieval times, and there is a narrow Gothic door and an old brick fireplace.

In the summer, when the grass becomes parched, the foundations of two gatehouses can be seen facing the court. The larger of them was built by Sir Francis Knollys as a suitable entrance for Elizabeth I when she visited his home. Among the outbuildings is a Tudor wheelhouse with a large donkey-wheel used for drawing water from a well 200ft deep. The gardens contain a wisteria walk and a rose garden.

NT. Apr-Sept. House: Mon, Wed and Fri pm. Garden: Mon-Sat pm; closed Good Fri. Adm charge. Refreshments. Shop. P *Toilets.* ♿ *Tel Rotherfield Greys (049 17) 529.*

MAPLEDURHAM HOUSE

Off A4074, 4 miles north-west of Reading (Da)

Inside this red-brick Elizabethan mansion the dominant feature is a magnificent oak staircase, built around a square well, with decorative pillars. The entrance hall has some unusual carved wooden heads dating from the 17th and 18th centuries. The poet Alexander Pope often visited Mapledurham in the early 18th century and dedicated some of his work to two of the ladies of the house: the beautiful sisters Martha and Teresa Blount. Among the portraits on show are those of the sisters and of Pope himself.

In 1797, the Blounts, a Catholic family, built a family chapel which survives today as a neat example of the quaint, pseudo-Gothic style then in vogue. From the grounds, visitors can see a little window gable, high up at the back of the house, which is studded with oyster shells – once a sign of safe refuge for Catholics.

A red-roofed water mill stands in the adjacent Riverside Picnic Park. Its millstones grind out wholemeal flour, which can be bought.

House, water mill and park: Easter Sun-late Sept, Sat, Sun and Bank Hol pm; also water mill winter, Sun pm. Adm charge. Refreshments. Shop. P *Toilets. Tel Reading (0734) 723350.*

MINSTER LOVELL HALL

Off B4047, 2 miles north-west of Witney (Bc)

Streaming down from the Cotswolds, the River Windrush threads its way through the lovely village of Minster Lovell, where the great ruin of Minster Lovell Hall stands secluded among the willows overlooking its banks. This 15th-century manor house, built around three sides of a quadrangle, was for generations the home of the Lovell family until Francis, Lord Lovell, a friend of Richard III, backed the losing side in the Wars of the Roses and fled abroad.

Lord Lovell returned two years later to aid the pretender Lambert Simnel, and was reportedly killed at the Battle of Stoke. However, legend has it that he survived and went into hiding at Minster Lovell, locked away in a secret vault known to only one servant; the servant died and Lord Lovell starved to death. It is recorded that during renovations in 1708, the skeleton of a man seated at a table was discovered in a cellar, 'all much mouldred and decayed'.

The manor's own decay dates to the 1740s. Nonetheless the gaunt remnant of the great hall with its kitchens, solar and south-west tower testify to former glories.

EH. All year, daily. Adm charge. P *Toilets.* ♿ *Tel Witney (0993) 75315.*

HAUNTED RUIN *Even in daylight a ghostly air hangs about the ruins of Minster Lovell, beside the quiet River Windrush. The 15th-century manor house has its legends of inhabitants trapped in secret rooms and locked chests.*

NORTH LEIGH ROMAN VILLA

Off A4095, 5 miles north-east of Witney (Cc)

Akeman Street was a major artery of Roman Britain, connecting St Albans with Cirencester, and the site of North Leigh Roman Villa lies close to the route. Excavations have revealed the remains of a 4th-century building complex with some 60 rooms grouped around a courtyard. The inhabitants lived by farming the land, and finds show that they enjoyed hot and cold baths, mosaic tiling and underfloor heating.

EH. Apr-Sept, daily exc Thur and alternate Fri. Adm charge. Tel Witney (0993) 881830.

PENDON MUSEUM

Off A415, in Long Wittenham (Cb)

The railways and rural landscapes of Britain in the 1930s form the theme of a museum which uses models of villages and stations, miniature engines and rolling stock, to re-create an almost vanished world. One scene depicts the cottages and broad farmlands of the Vale of White Horse, threaded by the Great Western Railway. A collection of transport relics includes old railway tickets, timetables and luggage labels.

All year, Sat and Sun pm and Bank Hol exc Christmas. Adm charge. Refreshments. Shop. P *(limited). Toilets. Tel Clifton Hampden (086 730) 7365.*

PUSEY HOUSE GARDENS

Off B4508, 5 miles east of Faringdon (Bb)

Reached by a drive through wooded Oxfordshire parkland, these beautiful gardens guard their secret from the road. Though extending from a noble 18th-century house, their 16 acres were created chiefly in the present century. A magnificent herbaceous border massed with delphiniums, phloxes, roses and lupins is one of the attractions, while the lawns below descend to a winding lake with a Chinese bridge, wooded banks and water garden.

Easter Sat-Oct, daily exc Mon and Fri. Adm charge. Refreshments. P *Toilets.* ♿ *Tel Buckland (036 787) 222.*

ROUSHAM PARK

Off B4030, 11 miles south of Banbury (Cc)

The entrance hall at Rousham has a mighty oak door with three shot holes in it from the Civil War; through them, the Royalist owner Sir Robert Dormer trained muskets on advancing Roundhead troops. It was Sir Robert who built the house in 1635, and the staircases and some original panelling are among the other 17th-century features which survive inside.

Rousham, though, is known especially for its later improvements by the architect and designer William Kent (1685-1748). He added pavilions to either side and gave the grey stone house its battlemented parapet and central cupola. Kent also made decorative alterations inside. One particularly fine room is his Painted Parlour on the ground floor, where grand effects are achieved in miniature through false doorways with moulded surrounds, marble fireplace, carved brackets and a ceiling painting.

Rousham's 25 acre grounds remain almost as Kent left them, with cascades, classical temples and statuary – even a sham ruin – all laid out in a naturalistic setting of woodland glades and pools which extend to the River Cherwell.

Gardens: All year, daily. House: Apr-Sept, Wed, Sun and Bank Hol. Adm charge. P *Toilets. Tel Steeple Aston (0869) 47110.*

STONOR PARK

Off B480, ½ mile north of Stonor (Ea)

Concealed by a wooded, enfolding slope of the Chilterns, this great house has been the home of the staunchly Roman Catholic Stonor family for at least 800 years. The house was a centre for Roman Catholic thought during the years of persecution; in a secret room in the roof, the 16th-century Jesuit martyr Edmund Campion printed his book *Decem Rationes* (Ten Reasons), which led to his trial, torture and execution.

The nucleus of the present house is a group of medieval buildings dating back to the late 12th century, but new parts were added over the following centuries. What visitors see today is an extraordinary jumble of rooms organised on an E-shaped Tudor plan behind a brickwork façade inset with Georgian sash windows.

During the 18th century, many parts of the interior were done up in mock Gothic style, with pointed arches and heraldic devices. The dining-room wallpaper shows panoramic views of the buildings of Paris: but perhaps the most memorable effects are found in the bedroom of the flamboyant Francis Stonor, which contains a luxurious shell-shaped bed and chairs shaped like open scallops.

Stonor has fine tapestries, pictures and Renaissance bronzes. The terrace garden, with pool and urns, looks out onto a park which has been grazed by fallow deer since the Middle Ages.

Apr, Sun pm and Easter Mon; May-Sept, Wed, Thur and Sun pm and Bank Hol Mon; also Sat pm in Aug. Adm charge. Refreshments. Shop. P *Toilets. Tel Henley-on-Thames (0491) 601587.*

TOLSEY MUSEUM

High Street, Burford (Bc)

The gabled 16th-century Tolsey, mounted on stone pillars, today houses a museum of Burford's past. Like other great Cotswold centres, the town grew on the wealth of the medieval wool trade – and the Tolsey is sited at the corner of the fittingly named Sheep Street. But Burford was a hub of more general commerce too, being especially noted for its tanning and leather trades. The Tolsey was the tollhouse where burgesses met and market rents were collected. The space between its ground-floor pillars was once walled and contained the town fire engine.

Relics on display include Burford's 13th-century seal, royal charters and silver maces.

Museum: Apr-Oct, daily. Adm charge. Refreshments. Shop. P *(limited). Tel Clanfield (036 781) 294.*

VALE AND DOWNLAND MUSEUM

Church Street, Wantage (Ca)

Housed in a converted 17th-century cloth-merchant's house, the museum tells the story of Wantage and the Vale of White Horse. Displays range from geology to rural industries such as milling, malting, wool and smithing. The Vale's dairy trade is recalled in a reconstructed farm-house kitchen and dairy, and a barn contains a collection of agricultural equipment.

All year, daily exc Mon. Free entry. Refreshments. Shop. P *Toilets.* ♿ *Tel Wantage (023 57) 66838.*

WATERPERRY GARDENS

Off A40, 2 miles north-east of Wheatley (Db)

With lawns and flowerbeds running down to the River Thame, Waterperry abounds in shrubs and climbers, conifers, roses, herbs, fruit and vegetables. Many of the products are sold in the garden shop near the estate's centrepiece – an 18th-century manor house standing among some magnificent trees. Ablaze with colour, the ornamental gardens also contain heather borders and trained fruit trees.

All year, daily. Adm charge. Refreshments. Shop. P *Toilets.* ♿ *Tel Ickford (084 47) 226.*

WELLPLACE ZOO

Off A4074, 1 mile south-east of Ipsden (Da)

Lying in the Thames valley under the Chilterns' wooded slope, this small zoo has more than 100 different varieties of bird including owls, flamingos, penguins, pelicans and rheas – flightless South American birds resembling ostriches. Other attractions range from monkeys to raccoons. The play area for children has swings, slide and sandpit, and there are donkey rides at weekends.

Easter-Sept, daily. Adm charges. Refreshments. Shop. P *Toilets. Tel Checkendon (0491) 680473.*

WHITE HORSE HILL

Off B4507, 6 miles west of Wantage (Ba)

Among the many chalk-cut horses which emblazon England's downlands only one has a truly ancient pedigree. The figure on White Horse Hill at Uffington is mentioned in a manuscript dating back to the 12th century – and a haunting, barbaric image it is with its beaky face and long, lithe body suggesting the equine spirit itself rather than the likeness of any flesh-and-blood steed.

HORSE ON THE HILL *Only from the air can the White Horse at Uffington be seen to its full advantage – making the motive and methods of its early artists a mystery. Bold chalk strokes set the creature in vigorous motion.*

Tradition holds that the figure was cut by Saxons in AD 871 to celebrate King Alfred's victory over the Danes at the Battle of Ashdown. But in reality it probably dates back much further, perhaps as long as 2000 years ago. The hill is crowned by an 8½ acre Iron Age hill-fort called Uffington Castle, and it may be that the white horse was the emblem of the inhabitants.

Uffington Castle and its slopes command sweeping vistas across the Vale of White Horse to the tree-stacked rises of Badbury Hill and Faringdon's Folly Hill. In the foreground the escarpment plunges into a beautiful downland hollow nicknamed the Horse's Manger, flanked by a flat-topped knoll called Dragon Hill. On this green platform, legend asserts, St George slew the dragon; there are patches of bare chalk where the grass never grows, and these are said to mark the places where the monster's blood spilled.

Uffington Castle lies on the prehistoric Ridgeway, and a 1½ mile walk along the hawthorn-lined track leads to Wayland's Smithy, a burial chamber of the New Stone Age, built around 2800 BC.

EH. All year, daily.

COUNTY CALENDAR

February (late). Oxford: Torpids (College rowing races).

May 1 Oxford: Dawn Choir at Magdalen College.

May (late). Eights Week (College rowing races).

May (Spring Bank Holiday). Bampton: Morris dancing.

June (Sat nearest 20th). Abingdon: Electing the Mayor of Ock Street (Morris dancing and procession).

July (1st week). Henley: Royal Regatta.

August (late). Oxford: Regatta.

September (early). Oxford: St Giles Fair.

December 24 Bampton: Mummers.

Tourist information: Abingdon (0235) 22711; Banbury (0295) 59855; Henley-on-Thames (0491) 578034; Oxford (0865) 726871; Witney (0993) 4379.

SHROPSHIRE

CASTLES, ABBEYS AND MANORS FLANKED BY BORDERLAND HILLS

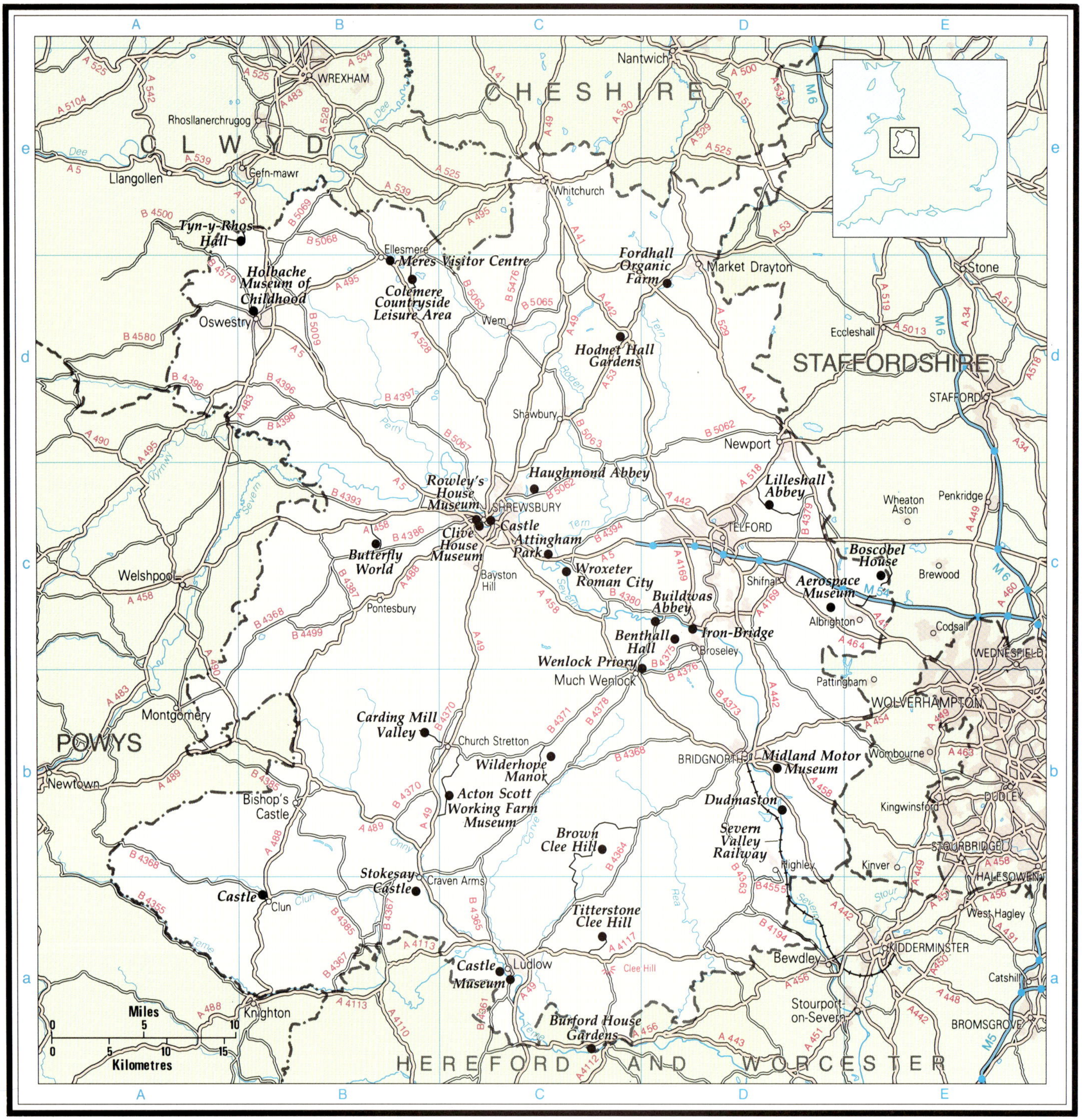

On a sunny day the peace of Shropshire's rolling hills is beguiling, but they conceal a wild history. Castles such as Clun, Shrewsbury and Ludlow had to guard the borderlands against attacks by the Welsh. Many abbeys and monasteries such as Buildwas and Wenlock suffered grievously at the hands of Henry VIII, though the ruins still evoke something of the grandeur they must once have possessed. Country houses such as Boscobel and Benthall had to survive battle and siege as the Civil War ebbed and flowed around them.

Evidence of more peaceful times can be seen in the exquisite Georgian streets of Ludlow, or houses such as Wilderhope or Attingham Park. Tranquil landscaped parks and gardens abound, as at Hodnet, Burford and Dudmaston.

When upheaval came again it was of a different kind: the Severn Gorge, with its coal and iron, was the birthplace of the Industrial Revolution, and today commemorates its past in a huge complex of museums and reconstructions centred on Iron-Bridge.

ACTON SCOTT WORKING FARM MUSEUM

Off A49, 3 miles south of Church Stretton (Cb)

Horsepower reigns supreme on this farm, which is a time capsule of the late 19th century. The working horses are heavy Shires, in daily use here until 1952 and now again to be seen drawing a plough, seed drill, reaper or Shropshire wagon. An extensive collection of 19th-century farm machinery includes a self-binding reaper developed in the 1870s to cut 10 acres of corn a day – ten times the amount a human reaper with a scythe could cut.

This is a mixed farm, producing crops and rearing livestock. Red-haired Tamworth pigs can be seen in the sties or wandering the paddocks, and Light Sussex and Dorking hens, Brecon Buff geese, Aylesbury ducks and Norfolk Black turkeys roam the farmyard. Sturdy Shropshire sheep and hardy Longhorn and Shorthorn dairy cows complete the muster. Visitors can watch the making of butter, and at certain times blacksmiths, saddlers, wheelwrights and other experts demonstrate their traditional crafts.

Apr-Oct, daily. Adm charge. Refreshments. Shop. P *Toilets.* ♿ *Tel Marshbrook (069 46) 306/307.*

AEROSPACE MUSEUM

Off A41, 8 miles south-east of Telford (Dc)

Landmarks in the story of military and civil aviation are preserved in this museum at RAF Cosford, which has more than 60 aircraft, most of them displayed under cover. The Dakota used by Field Marshal Montgomery as his personal aircraft in the Second World War takes pride of place in the military transport group, along with Hastings and York aircraft which took part in the Berlin airlift of 1948. The research and development collection includes the Hunter prototype and the Fairey Delta FD2, both of which broke world speed records.

An Azani Radial engine of the type that powered the fragile monoplane in which, in 1909, Louis Blériot made the first flight across the English Channel, is one of some 24 aero-engines on view. Items from the Second World War include a German 'doodle bug' (V1) and V2 rockets, and a Japanese Ohka suicide bomb, which used a human pilot as its control system. There is also a French Exocet air-to-surface missile of the type used by the Argentinian Air Force in the Falklands campaign of 1982. Large-scale models tell the story of pre-1939 commercial flight. They include an Argosy used in the 1920s on Imperial Airways' London-Paris 'Silver Wings' lunchtime service. An exhibition hall is devoted to the history of British Airways.

All year, daily exc Christmas-New Year period and weekends Nov-Feb. Adm charge. Refreshments. Shop. P *Toilets.* ♿ *Tel Albrighton (090 722) 4872/4112.*

ATTINGHAM PARK

On A5, 3 miles south-east of Shrewsbury (Cc)

To disguise his brick-built Queen Anne house standing in a broad curve of the River Tern, the 1st Baron Berwick in the 1780s commissioned George Steuart to create a shell for it. The result

DECORATIVE TOUCH *The top of a newly shaped block of butter is decorated by using the edge of a wooden pat in the dairy at Acton Scott Working Farm Museum.*

was this grandiose Palladian-style mansion, which is 400ft long, with a central portico upheld by four columns nearly 40ft tall. The interior is equally magnificent, with a wealth of delicate plasterwork, fine furniture, Regency silver and paintings. John Nash created the dramatic picture gallery and the circular staircase, for which he used cast iron from Coalbrookdale. The splendid park remains much as Humphry Repton landscaped it in the late 1790s.

NT. Apr-Sept, Sat-Wed pm; Oct, weekends. Adm charge. Refreshments. Shop. P *Toilets.* ♿ *Tel Upton Magna (074 377) 203.*

BENTHALL HALL

Off B4375, 4 miles north-east of Much Wenlock (Dc)

This late Elizabethan house stands less than a mile from the Severn Gorge, yet remains as serenely aloof from the valley's present-day activities as it did in the days of the Industrial Revolution. The Benthalls were Roman Catholics in the 16th century and the hall was built with a priest's hiding hole. The family was staunchly Royalist in the Civil War, and Lawrence Benthall defended his home for two years until July 1645, when Parliamentarians took it.

The stone house has mullioned and bay windows, and tall brick chimneys. Inside there is an intricately carved oak staircase, oak panelling and fine 17th-century plaster ceilings. The tranquil small garden contains crocuses from many parts of the world collected by George Maw, a 19th-century tenant.

NT. Apr-Sept, Tues, Wed, Sun and Bank Hol pm. Adm charge. P *Toilets. Tel Telford (0952) 882159.*

BOSCOBEL HOUSE

Off A41, 10 miles east of Telford (Ec)

When John Gifford converted a timber-framed farmhouse on his estate into a hunting lodge in the early 17th century he named it Boscobel, from the Italian *bosco bello*, meaning 'beautiful wood'. His family were Roman Catholics, and he incorporated in the house secret hiding places for priests. Boscobel also became a refuge for Royalists in the Civil War and in 1651, after his final defeat at Worcester, Charles II spent a day hiding from Parliamentarian pursuers in an oak tree on the estate, before escaping to France. A descendant of the oak tree survives, but the house has been much altered.

There is a collection of historical farm machinery in the farmyard.

EH. All year, daily exc Sun am. Adm charge. P *Toilets. Tel Brewood (0902) 850244.*

BROWN CLEE HILL

Off B4364, 9 miles north-east of Ludlow (Cb)

The two smooth humps of Brown Clee Hill dominate Ludlow's eastern skyline. The bracken-covered uplands rise from a busy patchwork of fields, laced with hedges and woods on rich red earth. Brown Clee is the highest point in Shropshire. Its Abdon Burf summit rises to 1772ft and is crowned by a hill-fort. The hill was a much used refuge in the Iron Age and there are two more hill-forts – one on Clee Burf summit, the other on Nordybank, the western flank of the hill. The views from the summits reach eastwards beyond Dudley and its tower blocks to the Clent Hills and Birmingham, and northwards to The Wrekin.

The Brown Clee Forest Trail – a 1½ mile circular route – starts beside a picnic area on a minor road about a mile west of Cleobury North village. It climbs a grassy slope up into conifer plantations and woods on the eastern side of the

REGENCY SPLENDOUR *A rich panel of wallpaper with an Oriental theme adorns an anteroom at Attingham Park. The rooms are furnished in the height of Regency fashion, and contain fine paintings.*

hill, which is the haunt of foxes, badgers, grey squirrels, hares, pheasants, woodpeckers, buzzards, kestrels, sparrowhawks and firecrests.
All year, daily.

BUILDWAS ABBEY

On B4378, 2 miles west of Iron-Bridge (Dc)

The ruins of the Cistercian abbey, which Roger de Clinton, Bishop of Coventry and Lichfield, founded in 1135, stand beside the quiet Severn. The abbey lies in eastern Shropshire, but was still near enough to attract the Welsh. In 1350, marauders from Powys abducted the abbot, and 56 years later followers of the Welsh prince Owain Glyndwr ravaged the abbey lands. The last abbot surrendered to Henry VIII's men in 1536.

Buildwas was a relatively small abbey, but a splendid place nevertheless. The 164ft long church is now roofless, but nearly complete. There are tall, slender windows at its eastern end and over its 14 sturdy Norman arches.
EH. All year, daily exc Sun am. Adm charge. ♿ *Tel Iron-Bridge (095 245) 3274.*

BURFORD HOUSE GARDENS

Off A456, 5 miles south-east of Ludlow (Bc)

Prettily set by the River Teme, the 4 acre gardens surround a red-brick Georgian house with a pool and summerhouse. There are many interesting trees, shrubs and aquatic plants. Clematis, though, is the speciality of the garden: more than 150 species and varieties can be seen, and the old stable block houses an exhibition devoted to the history of gardening from the 16th century to the present day.
End Mar-late Oct, daily exc Sun am. Adm charge. Refreshments. Shop. P *Toilets. Tel Tenbury Wells (0584) 810777.*

BUTTERFLY WORLD

Off B4386, 4 miles west of Shrewsbury (Bc)

In a large indoor tropical garden, colourful butterflies from all parts of the world live and breed among exotic plants. An outside garden attracts British species in season, and visitors may also see an audiovisual show about butterflies.

A display of invertebrates, including tarantulas and scorpions, is safely housed behind glass. There is also an adventure playground, a children's farm corner, a streamside area with a nature trail, and a ride around the arable farm with commentary on the crops and wildlife of the area.
Mid Apr-Oct, daily. Adm charge. Refreshments. Shop. P *Toilets.* ♿ *Tel Yockleton (074 384) 217.*

CARDING MILL VALLEY

Off A49, 1 mile west of Church Stretton (Bb)

Cataclysmic events contorted the Precambrian shales whose layers now stand on end to form the Long Mynd or 'Long Mountain'. They are about 700 million years old and are some of Britain's oldest rocks. But all is tranquil now on the Mynd's plateau top and gentle sides, which were smoothed during the last Ice Age.

The Carding Mill Valley is one of several 'secret' valleys which cut deeply into the flanks of the Mynd, and its grassy and bracken-covered sides are the haunt of many birds, including grey wagtails. The valley takes its name from the water mill built about 1812, and now converted into flats. The National Trust owns 5500 acres of the Mynd, and its Chalet Pavilion in the valley houses a café, information centre and shop. Leaflets give details of walks from the pavilion, and one of them branches up Lightspout Hollow, a side valley with the Light Spout cascade, a miniature Niagara, at its head. Another goes to Rectory Wood on the south side of the valley where there is a nature trail.

The lonely moors on top of the Mynd, where gorse, heather, sundew and bilberries grow, are the home of ravens, buzzards, white-rumped wheatears and red grouse, and provide common grazing for sheep and ponies. Prehistoric peoples used the hill as a refuge – more than 40 Bronze Age burial mounds have been found, and the ramparts of Bodbury Ring, a 2 acre hill-fort, can still be seen on the north side of the valley.
Chalet Pavilion NT: Apr-Sept, Mon-Sat pm; Bank Hol Sun and Mon; Oct, weekends; closed Fri, Apr-June and Sept. Free entry. Refreshments. Shop. P *Toilets. Tel Church Stretton (0694) 722631.*

CLIVE HOUSE MUSEUM

College Hill, Shrewsbury (Cc)

In the heart of the Georgian area of Shrewsbury, a little cobbled cul-de-sac leads to the fine 18th-century brick house occupied by Clive of India while he was Mayor of Shrewsbury in 1762. Inside is an outstanding collection of Shropshire pottery and porcelain, displayed not in glass cabinets but in authentic period settings. Outside, visitors can wander in the attractive garden.

Clive, who was also MP for Shrewsbury from 1761 until his death in 1774, is remembered too by a tall statue in The Square, in front of the Market Hall of 1596. Across the High Street from Clive's statue lies the older heart of the town, a network of tiny alleyways with names like Grope Lane, Fish Street, and Butchers' Row, lined by Elizabethan black-and-white half-timbered houses whose upper storeys almost meet overhead.
All year, daily exc Sun and Mon am. Adm charge. Shop. Tel Shrewsbury (0743) 54811.

CLUN CASTLE

Off A488, 9 miles west of Craven Arms (Ba)

The dramatic ruins of this Welsh Marchland castle stand above the little River Clun, on the motte of the earlier Saxon castle. The Norman castle built by Robert de Sav rose again after the onslaughts of the Lord Rhys (1195), Llywelyn the Great (1214) and Owain Glyndwr (1400), and parts of the Norman keep survive.

The small town originated long before the castle, in the Bronze Age. The museum housed in the town hall – built with stones from the original courthouse of the castle in 1780 – has a fine collection of even earlier flint tools from the locality, and maps of its earthworks. There are also bygones of later times.
Castle: All year, daily. Museum: Easter-Nov, Tues and Sat pm; also Sat, Mon and Tues of Bank Hol weekends. Free entry. Toilets. Tel Clun (058 84) 247.

COLEMERE COUNTRYSIDE LEISURE AREA

Off A528, 2 miles south-east of Ellesmere (Bd)

Flocks of gulls and waterfowl invade the quiet waters of the peaceful mere in winter, and migrating terns and waders arrive in season. Woodland borders two sides of Colemere, with a tangled mass of rhododendrons on the north side. There one can walk above the mere, beside the Shropshire Union Canal. There are spotted orchids, hemlock, water-dropwort and water forget-me-nots in the meadows at either end of the mere. The leisure area covers 68 acres, and is circled by miles of waymarked walks.
All year, daily.

DUDMASTON

On A442, 4 miles south-east of Bridgnorth (Db)

This estate changed hands only by inheritance from the 12th century until 1978, when it was given to the National Trust. The present William and Mary house, which was built around 1700 for Sir Thomas Wolryche, incorporates parts of a Tudor mansion, and remains an intimate family home. It contains an excellent art collection including superb 17th-century Dutch oil paintings of flowers, family portraits, botanical watercolours, and works by 20th-century artists such as Ben Nicholson, Modigliani, Augustus John, Barbara Hepworth and Henry Moore.

A shrub garden and lawns sweep gently down to the 'Big Pool' on the west side of the house, which has broad views to the Clee Hills. The Dingle, the valley of a stream which feeds the pool, is a rare survival of late 18th-century landscaping with a unique blend of tumbling waterfalls and cascades, winding paths, rustic bridges and stone niches for quiet seats.
NT. Apr-Sept, Wed and Sun pm. Adm charge. Refreshments. Shop. P *Toilets.* ♿ *Tel Quatt (0746) 780866.*

FORDHALL ORGANIC FARM

On A53, 2 miles south-west of Market Drayton (Dd)

Saxon farmers made a home on Castle Hill and drained the meadows in the lovely Tern valley below. Later generations moved westwards to a new site beside a spring which still supplies the farmhouse. The present house began as a modest cottage in the 15th century.

A nature trail follows 3 miles of the winding Tern, home to ducks, snipe, swans, kingfishers, moorhens and herons. Pastures and water meadows abound in wild flowers and herbs, and there are banks of primroses and violets in spring. Visitors can also watch the seasonal activities of the farm, which uses no artificial chemicals, or laze in one of the picnic areas in pleasant settings along the trail
All year, daily. Adm charge. Refreshments. P *Toilets.* ♿ *Tel Tern Hill (063 083) 255.*

HAUGHMOND ABBEY

On B5062, 3 miles north-east of Shrewsbury (Cc)

Like many an abbey, this one did have a life after the Dissolution. Henry VIII's representatives pulled down the abbey church in 1539, but the

14th-century abbot's house, with its great hall and kitchens, was sold and converted into a private mansion, of which there are extensive remains. In the 17th century, a fine garden gate was added, and it is through this gate that the abbey is entered today.

The Augustinian abbey was founded about 1135, on a lovely spot on the flanks of Haughmond Hill overlooking the Severn Valley. Its mid-12th-century church was built on three levels because of the sloping hillside, and it is clear from the ruins that the whole complex of buildings must have presented a magnificent spectacle. Three finely carved Norman arches at the entrance to the chapter house survive, and the splendid doorway into the former church is flanked by 14th-century statues of saints.

EH. Apr-Sept, daily exc Sun am; Oct-Mar, daily exc Sun am, Tues and alternate Wed. Adm charge. 🅿 ♿ *Tel Upton Magna (074 377) 661.*

HODNET HALL GARDENS

At junction of A53 and A442, 5½ miles south-west of Market Drayton (Cd)

A series of landscaped gardens covering more than 60 acres lie in what was once a boggy valley choked with masses of tangled growth. Natural springs were dammed to create the line of tranquil lakes which form the heart of the gardens. Lawns, ablaze with daffodils in spring, sweep down to the lakes, and stately old trees provide shade in the woodland gardens above.

FOR ALL SEASONS *Hydrangeas and lavender are planted with roses at Hodnet Hall to give a long show of colour. The whole garden, begun in 1922, has been planned to ensure fresh attractions each season.*

Colours change with the seasons. Lilacs, laburnums, azaleas, magnolias and rhododendrons follow the blossoms of early spring. Then the roses, peonies and primulas come into their own, followed by the massed borders and hydrangeas of high summer. Japonicas and clematis are among the blooms of early autumn, and presage the russet tints and bright berries of late autumn.

Special features include a water garden below a flight of waterfalls, a camellia garden, a magnolia walk, a beech avenue and kitchen gardens. A broad walk runs along the south side of Hodnet Hall – an Elizabethan-style mansion built around 1870 (not open), and from it there are magnificent views over the lakes, gardens and fields to a 17th-century dovecote.

Apr-Sept, daily pm. Adm charge. Refreshments. Shop. 🅿 *Toilets.* ♿ *Tel Hodnet (063 084) 202.*

HOLBACHE MUSEUM OF CHILDHOOD

Upper Brook Street, Oswestry (Bd)

In 1606 a certain D. Owen carved his name on an oak beam in the grammar school founded by David Holbache beside Oswestry's lovely parish church in 1407. A succession of schoolboy carvers followed Owen until 1776, when the school closed. The carefully restored building opened as a Museum of Childhood in 1983.

It contains countless treasures connected with children of the past, including more than 300 dolls from all over the world, dolls' houses, toys, a large family of teddy bears, games, books, clothes and prams. Other displays chart the changing fashions in items of dress.

Just north of the town, off Oswald Road, rises the green mound of Old Oswestry Hill-fort. The site was chosen by Iron Age people as a refuge for themselves and their flocks and herds in about 250 BC. Although only 100ft high, the flat-topped hill dominates the surrounding plain, and its steep sides, with concentric ditches and ramparts up to 14ft tall, must have been a formidable defence. The fort covers 68 acres, and was probably abandoned before the Roman invasion of AD 43.

The Oswestry district is a paradise for walkers. Five waymarked circular trails start from the car park and picnic area at the Old Racecourse on B4580, 2¼ miles north-west of the town. They take in part of Offa's Dyke Path along the rampart built by the Saxon king to mark the border of his kingdom of Mercia in the 8th century. There is also a Forestry Commission trail from the car park and picnic area at Cefn Coch, on a minor road 3¾ miles north-west of Oswestry, right on the Welsh border.

Museum: All year, Tues-Sat. Adm charge. Refreshments. Shop. 🅿 *(limited). Toilets. Tel Oswestry (0691) 650178. Hill-fort (EH): All year, daily.*

LILLESHALL ABBEY

Off A518, 4 miles south of Newport (Dc)

During the Civil War this remote religious house, founded for Augustinian canons about 1148, was for several weeks the scene of a bitter siege before falling to Parliamentarian forces. Building in local red sandstone had continued well into the 14th century, and the abbey and its land had been acquired by the Cavendish family a year after its dissolution in 1538. It was later sold to the Leveson family and it was Sir Richard Leveson who turned it into a Royalist fortress in 1645. Most of the destruction occurred then, but the ruins, which include the massive west doorway

Birthplace Of The Industrial Revolution

Six main sites, spread over 6 square miles of the banks of the River Severn, form the Ironbridge Gorge Museum, an extraordinary re-creation of the past in an area which in the 18th and 19th centuries was one of the world's busiest workplaces. On Blists Hill a typical 19th-century industrial township has been re-created, with gas-lit streets, shops, factories, and a wrought-iron foundry. Old china works now form a China Museum, and nearby is the Jackfield Tile Museum.

At Coalbrookdale is the Old Furnace of Abraham Darby, who in 1709 first smelted iron ore with coke and so revolutionised the iron-making industry. Darby's original blast furnace can be seen, and a former warehouse is now a Museum of Iron. Spanning the gorge is the Iron Bridge itself – the first cast-iron bridge in the world. There is also a visitor centre.

All sites: Mar-Oct, daily (China Museum, Visitor Centre, Museum of Iron and Old Furnace, all year). Shops. P *Toilets. Tel Iron-Bridge (095 245) 3522.*

MUSEUM PIECES *A saddle-tank locomotive built at Coalbrookdale in 1864 stands in the Museum of Iron. Decorative glazed tiles by George Maw (below) can be seen in the Jackfield Tile Museum.*

WEALTH FROM THE DEPTHS *The Blists Hill mine shaft (right), sunk in the late 18th century, reached a depth of 600ft. From it, coal and iron were supplied to the local blast furnaces, and later clay for the tile works at Jackfield. The mine was abandoned in 1941, but a winding house has been reconstructed and visitors today can see the winding gear at work, driven by a steam engine that dates from about 1870.*

HOME OF FINE CHINA *The bottle-shaped kilns of the Coalport Porcelain Company were used for glazing chinaware, fired by coal brought by barge along the Coalport Canal running parallel to the river. The original 18th-century kilns and 19th-century workshops near the head of the canal now house the Coalport China Museum, whose dazzling displays include a teapot (right) decorated in traditional Coalport style.*

BEER AND BACON *In Blists Hill's re-created Victorian High Street an enamel brewery sign decorates the wall of the New Inn, which once stood in Walsall and still serves beer in its bar, tap room and smoke room. Next door, at No 13, the butcher's shop (right) is exactly as it was when it was built in Waterloo Street, Iron-Bridge, some time before 1871. The walls are decorated with locally made tiles. The shop's slaughterhouse is close by.*

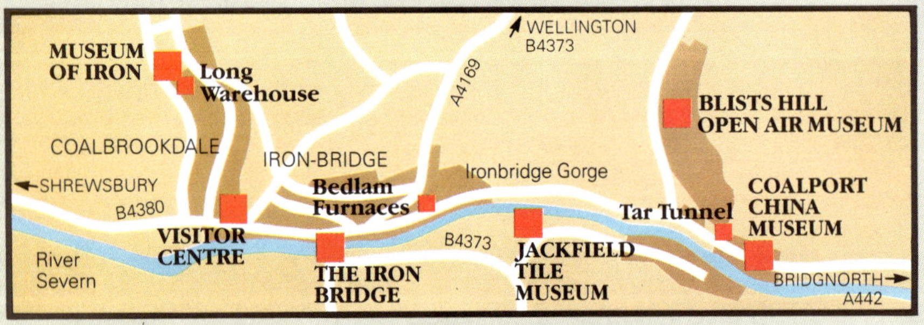

of the abbey church and the high walls of the sacristy, give a good idea of the fine, spacious building the abbey once was.

EH. Apr-Sept, daily exc Sun am. Adm charge. Tel Telford (0952) 604431.

LUDLOW CASTLE

Near centre of Ludlow (Ca)

Before entering the castle gates, spare ten minutes for a walk round the outside of the walls to get a splendid attacker's eye view of the fortress. The walk starts in the Castle Gardens – laid out, with a witty touch, with wallflowers in season. From the gardens the path dives through an arch in the castle's outer wall and past a 14th-century chapel, then drops to a leafy terrace walk circling the foot of the castle walls. Down to the left the River Teme sparkles and splashes over a weir: Ludlow means 'hill beside the loud water'. Up to the right the walls and towers of the castle rise almost sheer from the natural rock, their surface broken only by narrow windows and menacing arrow slits, a sight calculated to deter the stoutest-hearted aggressor.

After this glimpse of the castle's impregnability, inside the walls there is a corresponding sense of security. The castle was built around 1090 by a Norman knight, Roger de Lacy, to hold down the conquered Welsh. Its huge outer bailey or courtyard could have sheltered most of the townsfolk of medieval Ludlow in time of trouble; over it towers the massive keep, built up from the original gatehouse in the early 12th century. Round the inner bailey is a range of domestic buildings added in the 13th and 14th centuries by the Mortimer family, who turned the castle into a palace befitting their status; Roger Mortimer became virtual ruler of England when he helped his mistress, Queen Isabella, to murder her husband 'Edward II' and put her son on the throne as Edward III. Even in ruin the state rooms preserve their Gothic splendour, while the circular Norman chapel of St Mary Magdalene is an unusual survival from the original castle.

The oldest part of Ludlow is probably Dinham, which drops downhill from the castle towards the Teme. That it remained a coveted position until Georgian times is shown by the presence of Dinham House, built in 1716 next to the outer wall of the castle. Its inhabitants have ranged from leading Shropshire families such as the Johnes of Croft Castle to Lucien Bonaparte, younger brother of Napoleon, who was held prisoner here in 1811. The building now houses a craft centre where British crafts are on show, and craftsmen sometimes work in studios converted from the former cellars. Ludlow history is brought to life in rooms furnished as a Georgian lady's boudoir and a gentleman's study. A little lower down the hill stands the oldest remaining building in Ludlow apart from the castle. This is a tiny chapel built in 1190 and dedicated to St Thomas Becket; the plain altar stone, under a vaulted roof, can be seen through the grille at the western end.

Castle: All year exc Dec and Jan, daily. Dinham House: All year exc Jan, daily. Adm charge. Refreshments. Tel Ludlow (0584) 4240.

LUDLOW MUSEUM

In centre of Ludlow (Ca)

The 18th-century Butter Cross at the heart of Ludlow is a good place from which to start a walk around one of Britain's most attractive country towns; and the museum housed within the Butter Cross gives a useful introductory survey of the town's long history. From medieval times there is woodcarving, including the carved oak Ludlow Chest, and the official seal of the Council of the Marches of Wales, which Edward IV established at Ludlow; from Stuart times there is metalwork and pottery; and from Georgian times there are relics of the glove, ceramic and metalwork industries which sprang up to meet the demand for quality goods from Ludlow's new wealthy residents.

Radiating from the Butter Cross are streets which contain no fewer than 469 listed buildings, in an amazing prodigality of periods and styles. Towering above all is the cathedral-like Church of St Laurence, a red-sandstone giant of the 14th century whose chief glories are the misericords under the choir stalls, carved with mermaids, musicians and scenes from everyday medieval life.

The Feathers Hotel in the Bull Ring, rebuilt in 1619, is one of the finest timber-framed buildings in England. Ornamental carvings of heads, lozenges and round, Renaissance-style arches cover the three-storey façade; inside there are carved overmantels, embossed plaster ceilings and a profusion of panelling.

Broad Street, extending southwards from the Butter Cross, is Ludlow's finest thoroughfare. It has black-and-white timber-framed shops and houses of the 15th century at the narrow top end, and broadens downhill past immaculate Georgian terraces. At the southern end it squeezes through the 13th-century Broad Gate – the only one of Ludlow's seven medieval town gates to survive – before dropping to the Ludford Bridge over the River Teme.

Museum: Apr-Sept, Mon-Sat; also Sun, June-Aug. Adm charge. Shop. Tel Ludlow (0584) 3857.

MERES VISITOR CENTRE

On A495, just south-east of Ellesmere (Cd)

An interpretative centre tells the story of the north Shropshire and south Cheshire meres and mosses. These lakes and bogs occupy hollows formed when great blocks of ice melted among rock debris strewn by retreating ice sheets about 15,000 years ago. The centre has audiovisual presentations and display features, and includes a bird observatory and tourist information centre.

The building stands beside The Mere, which covers 112 acres and is Shropshire's largest. The lake's still waters surrounded by lovely parkland attract gulls, smew and goldeneye ducks in winter, terns in summer, and wigeon, great crested grebe and pochard ducks all the year. A colony of herons breed on a small island which is visible from the centre. There is a playground, and boating and fishing are available.

Easter-Oct, pm daily. Free entry. Refreshments. Shop. P Toilets. ♿ Tel Shrewsbury (0743) 252371.

MIDLAND MOTOR MUSEUM

On A458, 1½ miles east of Bridgnorth (Db)

The great days of the motor-racing circuit at Brooklands in Surrey are recalled in this museum housed in the old stable block at Stanmore Hall. On show in the museum are cars that raced at Brooklands – they include the 1925 Sunbeam Tiger 3978cc which achieved the world land-speed record of 152.33mph in 1926. There are also several cars which raced at Le Mans in the 1960s and 1970s, including Fords and Porsches.

Altogether more than 100 sports racing cars and motorcycles are on display, together with paintings, photographs and spare parts. There is a lakeside nature trail in the lovely parkland of the hall, and a terrace provides superb views over the Severn Valley to the Clee Hills.

All year, daily. Adm charge. Refreshments. Shop. P *Toilets.* ♿ *Tel Bridgnorth (0746) 761761.*

ROWLEY'S HOUSE MUSEUM

Barker Street, Shrewsbury (Cc)

The magnificent 16th-century timber-framed house jutting out defiantly between a car park and a coach park is one of the first buildings to catch the eye on a drive round Shrewsbury. Named after its builder, a Tudor merchant, it makes an appropriate starting point for a tour of the town, containing as it does a gallery devoted to the history of the town from earliest days. But the museum's main claim to fame is its collection of finds excavated from the Roman city of Viroconium at nearby Wroxeter. Items on display include a silver mirror, nearly 1ft across and probably made in an Italian workshop. The back is decorated round the edge with leaves, the fruit of the oak, apple and pine, and flowers.

Just across Hills Lane from the museum is the entrance to Shrewsbury's Victorian Arcade, a welcoming little complex of shops, all under cover, opened in 1983. Tiled passageways meet in a central courtyard with café tables under gas street lamps.

Museum: Easter-mid Sept, daily; mid Sept-Easter, Mon-Sat. Adm charge. Shop. Tel Shrewsbury (0743) 61196.

SEVERN VALLEY RAILWAY

Station, Hollybush Road, Bridgnorth (Db-Ea)

It was a telegram from the newly formed Severn Valley Railway Society that saved Bridgnorth station from destruction by a British Rail demolition gang in 1965, two years after its closure. The line from Bridgnorth to Hampton Loade along a lovely stretch of the Severn Valley reopened in 1970, and was extended in stages, reaching Kidderminster 14 years later.

Bridgnorth is the society's engineering centre, where its growing fleet of more than 40 locomotives are repaired. The loco shed bursts into activity on enthusiasts' weekends in spring and autumn when as many as ten of the magnificent locos are coaled, watered and groomed for action at the same time.

All year, most days. Trains mid May-mid Sept, daily; also Bank Hol and some winter weekends. Refreshments. Shop. P *Tel Bewdley (0299) 403816.*

SHREWSBURY CASTLE

Near centre of town (Cc)

Only a neck of land 300yds wide prevents the town of Shrewsbury from being completely islanded by the wide loop of the River Severn, and at this commanding spot stands the red-sandstone castle begun by the Normans in 1083 and rebuilt by Edward I in the 13th century. The Norman gateway still stands, and beyond it the squat, battlemented fortress presents much the same no-nonsense face to modern visitors as it must have done to rebellious Welshmen in Edward's day.

The castle last saw active service in the Civil War but today has a new type of military garrison, housing as it does the Shropshire Regimental Museum. In this collection of mementos of the three county regiments, uniforms splash the galleries with scarlet and gold, regimental colours adorn the walls, weapons glint and medals sparkle, recalling nearly 300 years of campaigns from America to Spain, India to the Sudan, Flanders to Korea.

An attractive tree-lined riverside footpath starts near the castle and follows the entire horseshoe loop of the Severn round Shrewsbury. It passes under the town's two main bridges whose names, English Bridge and Welsh Bridge, recall Shrewsbury's key position in the troubled history of the Welsh borderland. Across the river, grassy slopes rise up to Shrewsbury School.

Easter-Oct, daily; Oct-Easter, Mon-Sat. Adm charge (museum). Shop. Toilets. Tel Shrewsbury (0743) 58516.

STOKESAY CASTLE

Off A49, 8 miles north-west of Ludlow (Ba)

A timber-framed gatehouse, its plasterwork a modest ochre in shade, provides an almost cottage-like introduction to Stokesay. Through a little door the visitor emerges into a grassy courtyard, beyond which rises the contrasting stone splendour of a grand fortified manor house built around 1290 by a wealthy wool merchant, Lawrence of Ludlow. Its state of preservation after 700 years seems little short of miraculous.

The hub of social life in Lawrence's day was the Great Hall – a 52ft long chamber where the owner and his family worked, talked, played and ate. The hall still has its tall Gothic windows and soaring timbered roof, supported on its original oak crucks, each about 34ft long and marked by smoke from the central fireplace. At one end of the hall a broad wooden stairway – again the original medieval carpenter's work – leads to a bright, airy upper room at the top of the North Tower. The leaded windows are set in timber-framed recesses which project out over the stone walls of the tower on wooden brackets – a pleasantly eccentric touch by Lawrence of Ludlow which was echoed 300 years later by the Jacobean owners of Stokesay who added the timbered gatehouse.

At the other end of the hall, outside stairs rise to a solar, or withdrawing room, to which the owner and his family retired after meals. Its walls are wood-panelled, and over the fireplace is an ornate carved overmantel still showing traces of its original coloured paint. Two peepholes in wall

FORTIFIED MANOR *Much of Stokesay Castle remains just as it was first built in the 13th century, behind the timbered gatehouse added in the 1600s. Inside the castle, an upper room still has its 17th-century panelling and an ornate Flemish overmantel (right).*

niches enabled the owner to keep an eye on doings in the Great Hall below.

Even this does not exhaust Stokesay's treasures. The tall South Tower is the only really castle-like feature of the whole estate, and a staircase rising within the thickness of its walls climbs to a lookout turret 66ft high, with round chimney pots surprisingly modern in their appearance. From the top there are broad views outwards over green pastures and red ploughland, and inwards to the castle's own gatehouse, from this height diminished to the proportions of a doll's house. Just outside the dry moat surrounding the castle stands the 12th-century St John's Church, used by Stokesay's early inhabitants as their private chapel.

EH. Early Mar-Oct, daily exc Tues; Nov, weekends. Adm charge. Refreshments. Shop. **P** *Toilets. Tel Craven Arms (058 82) 2544.*

TITTERSTONE CLEE HILL

On A4117, 5½ miles east of Ludlow (Ca)

The views from the AA viewpoint on Clee Hill, just east of Cleehill village, are breathtaking. To the south-west lie the Malverns, Clows Top and Abberley Hall Tower – a needle rising between facing hills. Welsh mountains such as the Sugar Loaf near Abergavenny and the Black Mountains can be seen to the west.

At Foxwood Lodge and Bird Centre, just east of the viewpoint, more than 400 birds from all over the world are displayed in their natural settings. They include collections of parrots, birds of prey and owls. Ducks, peacocks, turkeys, pheasants and chickens wander freely in the gardens. There is a pet centre, craft shop, and a picnic area with delightful views.

Bird Centre: All year, daily. Adm charge. Refreshments. Shop. **P** *Toilets.* ♿ *Tel Ludlow (0584) 890385.*

TYN-Y-RHOS HALL

Off B4500, 4 miles north of Oswestry (Be)

A ghostly figure known as the White Lady reputedly stalks the gallery of this modest Tudor-style country seat on the Welsh border. The lady was a Miss Phillips whose family lived in the mansion from 1670 until 1922, and who in despair drowned herself in a now vanished lake on the estate when forbidden to marry the man she loved. The hall is decorated and furnished throughout in late Victorian and Edwardian styles, and has a finely carved oak staircase.

May-Sept, Sat, Sun, Wed and Thur pm. Adm charge. Refreshments. Shop. **P** *Toilets. Tel Chirk (0691) 777898.*

WENLOCK PRIORY

Off A458 at Much Wenlock (Dc)

Photographs taken a century ago were used as models for the topiary experts who restored the figures of animals and birds in clipped yew which ornament the cloister of Wenlock Priory. The attention to detail would have been appreciated by the monks who once walked here, for they belonged to the Cluniac order which set particular store on beautifying its surroundings to the glory of God.

Roger de Montgomery built the priory in the 11th century, on the site of a 7th-century abbey destroyed by the Danes, and several fine fragments of his work survived Henry VIII's depredations. The priory church was, at 350ft long, one of the longest monastic churches in England, and the end wall of its south transept still towers 70ft above the smooth lawns. A delicate pattern of interlaced arches ornaments the wall of the adjoining Chapter House. In the cloister, beside the clipped bushes, stands an elaborate lavatorium, where the monks washed before meals; carved panels depict two apostles, and Christ with St Peter.

The same mellow limestone from the hillside quarries of Wenlock Edge that was used to build Wenlock Priory went also into many of the neat little cottages in the nearby town of Much Wenlock. The town museum has displays on the history of the priory, the trades and crafts once practised in the area, and on the local wildlife and geology. There is also a section dealing with clay pipe-making, a major local industry until about 1850.

Much Wenlock's lovely half-timbered Guildhall has served the town since 1540, when a Richard Dawley was paid £13 6s 8d for 'building the Court House'. Stout oak pillars support its overhanging first floor, and inside there is fine oak panelling and furniture.

Priory EH: Apr-Sept, daily exc Sun am; Oct-Mar, daily exc Sun am, Thur and Fri. Adm charge. Shop. **P** *Tel Much Wenlock (0952) 727466. Museum: Apr-Sept, weekdays; also Sun in June-Aug. Adm charge. Shop. Toilets.* ♿ *Tel (0952) 727773.*

WILDERHOPE MANOR

Off B4371, 7 miles south-west of Much Wenlock (Cb)

This superb Elizabethan house in lovely Hopedale was built of local limestone in 1586. The valley remains quiet and secluded to this day, and the house is virtually unaltered – except for fine plasterwork ceilings, which were installed by a travelling craftsman in the 17th century. The building is unfurnished, except for a unique bow rack with room for 13 weapons over the hall fireplace, and part of it is used as a youth hostel. Several circular walks through farmland and woods start from the house, and include one along the top of Wenlock Edge just to the west.

NT. Apr-Sept, Wed and Sat pm; Oct-Mar, Sat pm. Adm charge. **P** *Toilets. Tel Longville (069 43) 363.*

WROXETER ROMAN CITY

Off A5, 5 miles south-east of Shrewsbury (Cc)

The remains of Viroconium – the fourth largest city of Roman Britain – rise from the green meadows of the Severn Valley below the whale-back hump of The Wrekin. Some idea of the size of the city is given by the fact that the entire excavated area visible today, some 100yds square, covers only the city's baths complex – the social centre of the city, where around 500 people came each day to take exercise, to relax, enjoy a good gossip, and even a meal.

The visitor passes first across the huge basilica, or exercise hall, of the baths complex, 220ft long by 65ft wide. Part of one wall of this hall, still

PRIORY PATTERNS *Tiers of overlapping arches decorate the Norman chapter house at Wenlock Priory. The monks sat on stone benches round the sides of the chapter house to discuss the daily business of the priory.*

standing 26ft high, is the most evident of Wroxeter's above-ground remains. Its massive doorway was once spanned by double doors that led to the adjoining baths themselves, to which an aqueduct brought some 2 million gallons of water each day. The foundations are visible of the elements of a sophisticated baths complex – frigidarium, or cold room; plunge baths; laconicum, or sauna; tepidarium, or wet, tepid room; caldarium, or hot wet room; and (unusual in Britain) a piscina, or open swimming pool.

Most of Viroconium was built around AD 150, on the site of a 1st-century legionary fortress whose remains have been found under those of the city. A considerable civilian community grew to serve the soldiers before the legion left in about AD 88, and it was as a tribal centre for those people that the city was founded. It prospered on trade up the Severn which brought iron and grain from the West Country and olive oil and wine from the Mediterranean area for the Romano-British city dwellers and villa owners in the surrounding countryside. The site museum displays finds from the excavations, including the honourable discharge certificate of foot soldier Mansuetus, from Trier in Germany.

EH. All year, daily exc Sun am. Adm charge. **P** *Tel Cross Houses (074 375) 330.*

COUNTY CALENDAR

May (first two weeks). Telford: Wrekin and Telford Festival.

May (mid-month). Shrewsbury: Shropshire and West Midlands Agricultural Show.

May (late). Ashton-on-Clun: Arbor Day (tree decoration).

June (late, to early July). Ludlow: Festival.

July (early). Shrewsbury: International Music Festival. Oswestry: Powis Eisteddfod.

August (early). Oswestry: Show.

September (mid-month). Shrewsbury: Poetry Festival.

Tourist information: Bridgnorth (074 62) 3358; Iron-Bridge (0952) 882753; Ludlow (0584) 3857 (summer); Oswestry (0691) 662753; Shrewsbury (0743) 50761.

SOMERSET

CAVES IN THE ROLLING HILLS THAT BORDER A MYSTIC 'ISLAND'

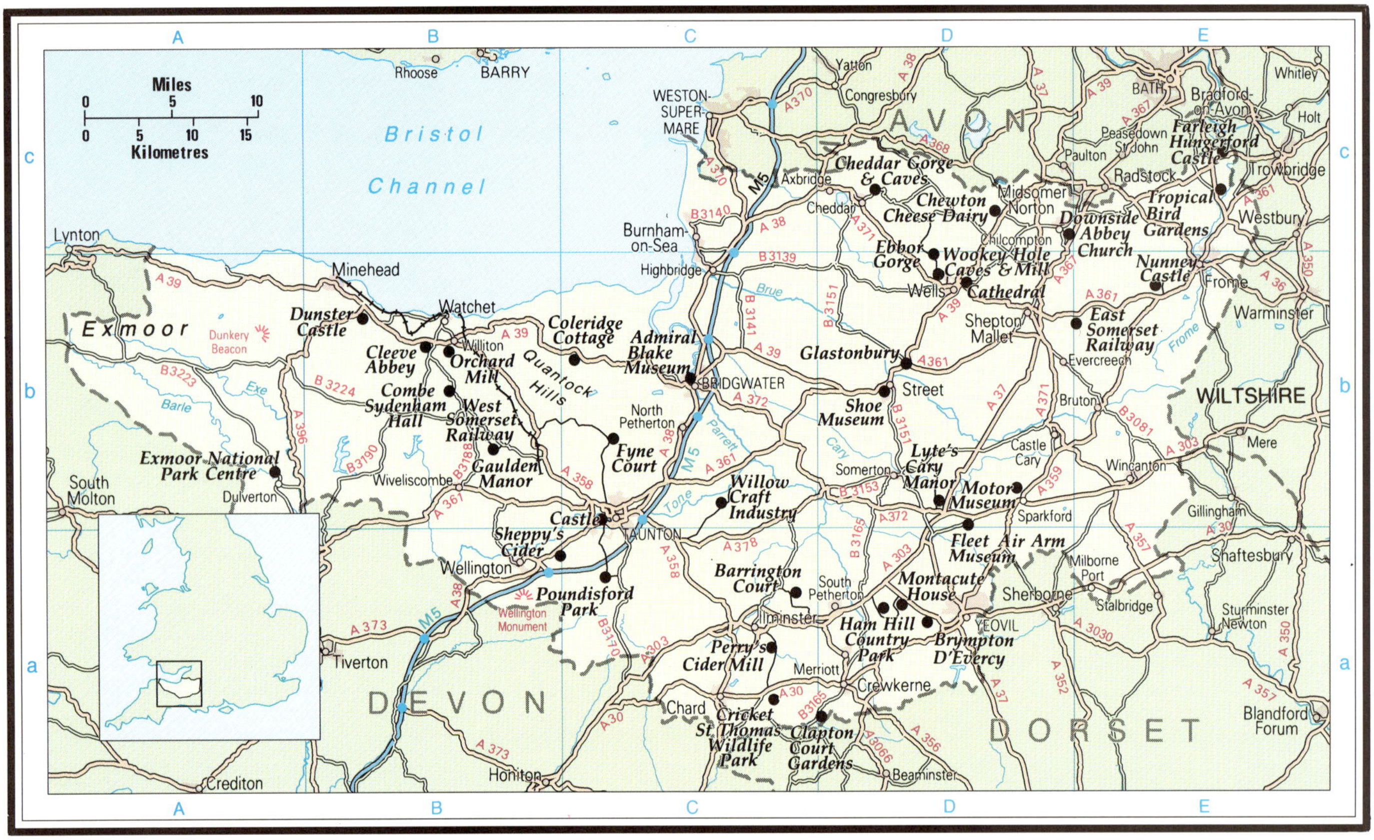

The top of Glastonbury's mysterious Tor gives a view over more than half Somerset, its level plain punctuated by landmarks such as the monumental cathedral at Wells. On the western horizon are the Quantocks, with wooded walks where Wordsworth and Coleridge dawdled; to the east are the Mendips, with great gorges at Cheddar and Ebbor and fantastic caves at Wookey Hole.

Castles abound: Dunster is a romantic restoration of a once-impregnable citadel, while Farleigh Hungerford and Nunney, ruined now, still evoke their medieval heyday. Manor houses include one of Britain's Tudor masterpieces, Montacute, and wildlife roams the historic estate at Cricket St Thomas. Two steam railways survive and traditional industries such as cider-making, cheese-making and willow crafts still flourish.

ADMIRAL BLAKE MUSEUM

Blake Street, Bridgwater (Cb)

Battlefield relics of Sedgemoor, where the Duke of Monmouth's pretensions to the throne were dashed in 1685, are among the exhibits in this museum. As well as armour and weaponry from the battle, there is a large model of the cavalry charge that routed Monmouth's rebels. The museum is housed in the birthplace of Robert Blake, the local MP who became a general in Cromwell's army in the Civil War, and subsequently a brilliant admiral. The Blake collection includes his inlaid sea chest and his compass, made in 1630. The unusual flag that flies above the museum is the Commonwealth Jack, depicting the cross of St George and the Irish standard. Flown by Blake from his masthead in the 1650s, it is 150 years older than the Union Flag.

All year, daily. Free entry. Shop. Tel Bridgwater (0278) 456127.

BARRINGTON COURT

Off B3168, 3 miles north-east of Ilminster (Ca)

The best view of this lovely Tudor mansion is from its sweeping south lawn, on the opposite side of the house from today's entrance. Built in 1514, the house is on an E-plan – unusual for such a Gothic building. The seven gable ends that form the superb façade are elaborately decorated with twisted finials and chimneys that are entirely French in style. Delightful gardens, inspired by the designer Gertrude Jekyll, include a pool of water lilies, an iris garden full of soft blues and purples in early summer, and a profusion of clematis and roses climbing over the walls of 16th and 17th-century outbuildings.

NT. Apr-Sept, Sat-Wed. Adm charge. Refreshments. Shop. 🅿 *Toilets. Adm charge. Tel South Petherton (0460) 40601.*

BRYMPTON D'EVERCY

Off A3088, 2 miles west of Yeovil (Da)

This stately mansion displays a range of architectural styles from its remarkably well preserved 14th-century Priest House – now a museum of cider-making and coopering – to the beautiful 16th-century west front. The imposing classical south front, with its asymmetric window lintels, was added in the 1670s. A superb collection of mature trees, a lake and a vineyard are features of the fine gardens, within which stands the 15th-century parish church.

May-Sept, pm daily exc Thur and Fri. Adm charge. Refreshments. Shop. 🅿 *Toilets.* ♿ *Tel Yeovil (0935) 862528.*

CHEDDAR GORGE AND CAVES

Off A371, at Cheddar (Dc)

A plunging, 2 mile cleft in the Mendip Hills presents nature at its most awesome. Soaring 400ft cliffs crowd the narrow road as if ready to slam shut in some huge seismic convulsion.

Secret streams riddle the hills, and there are more than 400 caves or holes in the area, some lit with electricity to expose their lustrous stalactites and stalagmites. Gough's Cave is the largest and most spectacular, stretching for a quarter of a mile and adorned with grandiose pillared chambers and stalagmite cascades. It was in this cave that the famous Cheddar Man – a 10,000-

CLIFFS AND CAVES *The road winding through Cheddar Gorge follows the course of the ancient river whose torrents carved the huge limestone ravine. In Cox's Cave, an illuminated forest of stalactites and stalagmites is reflected in an underground pool.*

year-old skeleton – was discovered; it is on display in the adjoining museum.

Cox's Cave is smaller but just as enticing. It displays, for example, a 'Marble Curtain' of stalactites gleaming above an underground pool. The route continues through Fantasy Grotto, man-made about 1900, with a display of animated figures. Nearby is the entrance to Jacob's Ladder, a steep flight of 322 steps up the side of the gorge.

At the head of the gorge, a leafy and peaceful contrast is provided by the Black Rock Nature Reserve. The reserve's 183 acres embrace open grassland, mature ash wood and coniferous forest. Buzzards and kestrels hunt here and the mixed terrain is home to butterflies such as the common blue and dark green fritillary.

Caves and Museum: All year, daily. Adm charge. Refreshments. Shop. 🅿 *Toilets. Tel Cheddar (0934) 742343. Nature Reserve: All year, daily.*

CHEWTON CHEESE DAIRY

On A39, 5 miles north-east of Wells (Dc)

Cheddar cheese is made by traditional methods at this dairy in the heart of the region where it was first produced in the 17th century. Visitors to the farm see all stages of the process by which a daily average of nearly 3000 gallons of milk is transformed into a ton of cheese. The store is stacked with thousands of cheeses which are kept for six to 12 months to mature.

All year, daily. Adm charge. Refreshments. Shop. 🅿 *Toilets.* ♿ *Tel Chewton Mendip (076 121) 666.*

CLAPTON COURT GARDENS

Off B3165, 3 miles south of Crewkerne (Da)

Formal and woodland gardens covering more than 10 acres include many rare and unusual trees, shrubs and plants. The season opens with a dazzling display of spring bulbs, complemented by flowering cherries and followed by rhododendrons, camellias, magnolias and azaleas. The largest ash in England, more than 200 years old and 23ft in girth, and a metasequoia, planted in 1950 and now more than 70ft tall, are two features in the woodland garden.

The formal terraces, herbaceous borders and rose garden are at their best in high summer, while streams in the wood and water garden are lined with Asiatic primulas and banks of hydrangeas. Glorious autumn colours are provided by maples and rowans. Visitors can buy rare plants, as well as several hundred varieties of pelargoniums and fuchsias.

Gardens: Feb-Nov, Mon-Fri, and Sun pm; also Easter Sat pm and Sat pm in May. Adm charge. Refreshments (Apr-Oct). 🅿 *Toilets.* ♿ *Tel Crewkerne (0460) 72200.*

CLEEVE ABBEY

Off A39, 6 miles south-east of Minehead (Bb)

The venerable buildings of a Cistercian monastery throw light on the cloistered life of its inmates 500 or more years ago. The 13th-century dormitory survives very much as it was built, even retaining traces of typical Cistercian masonry patterning and showing where the monks made their own individual alterations to the windows in their cubicles – some putting in glass, others adding shutters. The refectory range was re-modelled in the late 15th century; it has a magnificent wagon roof and, off the stairs, a parlour with wall paintings. The gatehouse also survives.

EH. All year, daily. Adm charge. Shop. 🅿 *Toilets. Tel Washford (0984) 0377.*

COLERIDGE COTTAGE

On A39, 8 miles west of Bridgwater (Cb)

Samuel Taylor Coleridge wrote his best poems, including *The Ancient Mariner*, while living here in Nether Stowey from 1797 to 1800. When writing *Kubla Khan*, his dream of Xanadu was banished by a knock on the cottage door. Wordsworth and his sister lived nearby, and the trio's moonlit rambles on the Quantock Hills which rise behind the village aroused such local suspicions that they were investigated as possible French spies, but dismissed as harmless cranks.

The cottage has been enlarged but the original parlour survives, with furniture, portraits and Coleridge documents. Castle Hill, above the village, gives views across the Bristol Channel.

To sample the 'smooth Quantocks airy ridge' that Wordsworth described, drive south-west for 2 miles along the minor road through Over Stowey to Seven Wells Bridge. This is the start of the Forestry Commission's 2½ mile waymarked Quantock Forest Trail. It leads past a picnic place at Rams Combe, through conifer plantations and across a stream by stepping-stones.

NT. Apr-Sept, Sun, Tues, Wed, Thur pm. Adm charge. Tel Nether Stowey (0278) 732662.

COMBE SYDENHAM HALL

On B3188, 3 miles south of Watchet (Bb)

The 100lb stone sphere prominently displayed in the great hall of this Elizabethan mansion is said to have won Sir Francis Drake his bride. Elizabeth, daughter of Sir George Sydenham who built the house in 1580, had promised her hand to Sir Francis, but tired of waiting for his return from sea and agreed to marry a rival suitor. At the door of the church, however, the bridal party was scattered by the descent of the great stone – in fact a meteorite. Believing the

ROCK GARDEN *Beyond this colourful corner of the rockery at Clapton Court there are further delights in the woodland, rose and water gardens. All are lovingly tended by the Loder family, who own the estate.*

missile to be a cannonball fired from Drake's distant ship, Elizabeth refused to go ahead with the ceremony. Sir Francis landed with the next tide, and married Elizabeth.

The grounds where the couple strolled are being restored to their Elizabethan glory, divided into intimate formal gardens by manicured yews. Farther afield, a series of ponds dug in Drake's time have been turned into a trout farm, and there are woodland walks through the Hall's own country park. One energetic trail rises 1000ft; the stiff climb is rewarded by breathtaking views across Exmoor and the Quantock Hills to the sea beyond.

Easter Mon-Oct, Mon-Fri. Adm charge. Refreshments. Shop. 🅿 *Toilets.* ♿ *Tel Stogumber (0984) 56284.*

CRICKET ST THOMAS WILDLIFE PARK

Off A30, 4 miles east of Chard (Ca)

The Georgian mansion is known to millions as 'Grantleigh Manor' in the TV series *To the Manor Born.* In reality it once belonged to the Hoods, a great naval family, and Lord Nelson was a frequent visitor. Peacocks which have long strutted the lawns of this historic estate have in recent times been joined by many other exotic creatures in a 1000 acre wildlife park. Other birds include storks, cranes and black swans, while there are enclosures for monkeys, raccoons and other animals. Llamas and wallabies roam free in a spacious valley.

There is a country life museum, a woodland railway, a heavy horse centre and a craft shop. A large adventure playground includes a giant fort, and there is a working dairy factory.

All year, daily. Adm charge. Refreshments. Shop. 🅿 *Toilets.* ♿ *Tel Winsham (046 030) 755.*

DOWNSIDE ABBEY CHURCH

On A367, 12 miles south-west of Bath (Dc)

Its full name is the Basilica of St Gregory the Great, and it is the church of the senior Benedictine monastery in Britain. It is also one of the largest Roman Catholic churches built in England since the Reformation. The abbey has the appearance, the character and the grandeur of a medieval foundation. In fact, the earliest part was completed in 1882 and the most recent – the nave – was designed by Sir Giles Gilbert Scott and opened in 1925. The result is a triumph of inspiration and dedication.

All year, daily. Shop. 🅿 ♿ *Tel Stratton-on-the-Fosse (0761) 232134.*

HORSE POWER *Magnificent Shire horses can be seen in harness at Cricket St Thomas Wildlife Park, which is also the home of the National Heavy Horse Centre. The horses work on the park's farmlands.*

DUNSTER CASTLE

On A39, 3 miles south-east of Minehead (Bb)

The castle rises dramatically above the pretty Exmoor village which shares its name – the perfect image of a hilltop citadel. The hill has been fortified since before the Norman Conquest, when the castle was granted to the Mohun family by King William. Dunster was sold to the Luttrells in 1376, and remained their home for 600 years. Besieged by Royalists and then by Parliamentarians, it was all but razed in the aftermath of the Civil War. A 13th-century gateway and a gatehouse of 1420 have survived, but much of the present romantic exterior is Victorian, fashioned by the architect Anthony Salvin.

Inside there are splendid furnishings from Tudor times and later; pictures include an extraordinary 16th-century portrait of Sir John Luttrell wading naked through the sea. The dining room and great staircase have ornate plasterwork ceilings of the 1680s, and the oak staircase itself is finely carved with stag-hunting scenes.

The village of Dunster, most comfortably visited out of season, has at its centre a roofed, octagonal Yarn Market, a relic of the days when Dunster was famous for its weaving.

NT. Apr-Sept, daily exc Fri and Sat; Oct, pm daily. Adm charge. Shop. 🅿 *Toilets. Tel Dunster (064 382) 1314.*

EAST SOMERSET RAILWAY

Off A361, 3 miles east of Shepton Mallet (Eb)

The restored Cranmore station is the basis for this living museum of the steam age of the railways, founded by the artist and railway enthusiast David Shepherd. Its exhibits range from the giant 140 ton steam loco *Black Prince* to the tiny 16 ton *Lord Fisher.* There are replicas of Victorian engine sheds and workshops, and on certain days visitors can ride on the reopened 2 mile line in a steam-hauled train, complete with restaurant car. The former signal box houses an art gallery, and there is a wildlife centre and children's play area.

Apr-Oct, daily; Nov-Mar, weekends. Trains Apr-Oct, Sun and Bank Hol; also Wed and Sat in July-early Sept. Adm charge. Refreshments. Shop. 🅿 *Toilets. Tel Cranmore (074 988) 417.*

EBBOR GORGE

On A371, 3 miles north-west of Wells (Db)

The caves which pit the sides of this limestone gorge in the Mendips were once the homes of Stone Age men, whose bones, tools and ornaments have been found there. Today the gorge offers attractive walks through a wilder, less-trodden ravine than the nearby Cheddar Gorge. Woodlands of ash and oak give way higher up to gleaming white limestone walls, and one track scrambles 500ft up onto the lonely Mendip plateau.

Two waymarked nature trails pass a wide variety of plants, from the mosses and ferns which thrive in the damp shade of the lower part of the gorge to salad burnet, milkwort, rock-rose, thyme and many other species higher up. The trees are the homes of grey squirrels, woodpeckers and nuthatches, and more than 30 species of butterfly have been seen in the gorge.

NT/NCC. All year, daily. 🅿

CLIMBERS' REWARD *Visitors ascending the steep wooded hill to Dunster Castle will find rare shrubs and tropical plants thriving in the mild air. The name Dunster means 'hilltop tower', and from the castle there are fine views over Exmoor and the Quantocks.*

EXMOOR NATIONAL PARK CENTRE

On B3223 at Dulverton (Ab)

Exmoor House, a Victorian workhouse, is now the headquarters and information centre for the Exmoor National Park Authority. The centre is a good starting point for walks and motoring tours into the 265 square miles of wild moors and forested hills, deep valleys and tranquil villages which fan out to the north.

One walk starting from Exmoor House leads northwards out of town past Dulverton's church and back beside the river. Waymarked walks up onto the moors include a 3 mile route to Ashway, birthplace of Sir George Williams, who founded the YMCA. A longer walk leads to the Tarr Steps, a stone crossing over the River Barle which is believed to date from prehistoric times. Suggested motoring tours starting from Dulverton include the Lorna Doone Trail, which passes through several of the places which R.D. Blackmore used as settings in his classic novel.

All year, Mon-Fri; also weekends in summer. Free entry. Shop. 🅿 *Toilets.* ♿ *Tel Lynmouth (0598) 23665.*

FARLEIGH HUNGERFORD CASTLE

On A366, 6 miles north-east of Frome (Ec)

Overlooking the wooded valley of the River Frome are the extensive ruins of a great castle built for Sir Thomas Hungerford in the 1370s. The original building had a five-storey tower at each corner, and the ruins of these still stand. The tallest is the Lady Tower, so known because one Lady Hungerford was immured in it by her husband for four years in the 1530s. The outer bailey of the castle was extended to include an existing 14th-century parish church, now the chapel. Carefully restored, this houses the tombs of Hungerfords spanning 250 years.

EH. Mar-Sept, daily; Oct-Feb, daily exc Tues. Adm charge. Shop. 🅿 *(limited). Toilets. Tel Trowbridge (022 14) 4026.*

FLEET AIR ARM MUSEUM

Off A303, 9 miles north of Yeovil (Db)

A collection of more than 50 aircraft at Yeovilton Royal Naval Air Station puts special emphasis on naval flying in both strike and rescue roles. That legendary Second World War carrier biplane the Fairey Swordfish is there; so are jets such as the Sea Vampire, and several helicopters. But the supreme attraction for many is the first British-built Concorde, 002, in its own exhibition hall. Visitors can walk through the plane, and see displays illustrating the story of supersonic flight.

All year, daily. Adm charge. Refreshments. Shop. 🅿 *Toilets.* ♿ *Tel Yeovil (0935) 840565.*

FYNE COURT

Off A38, 6 miles north of Taunton (Cb)

The Quantock countryside as it was before the changes wrought by modern farming and forestry methods is being re-created in the 26 acre grounds of what was once a grand mansion. Specimens of almost every indigenous British tree and shrub have been planted, and nature trails have been marked through the woodland.

Only a few of the old stone outbuildings and a wing remain from the original Fyne Court, which was devastated by a fire in 1898. They house the headquarters of the Somerset Trust for Nature Conservation and a visitor centre for the Quantocks.

NT. All year, daily. Free entry. Refreshments. Shop. 🅿 *Toilets.* ♿ *Tel Kingston St Mary (082 345) 587.*

GAULDEN MANOR

Off B3224, 9 miles north-west of Taunton (Ba)

John Turberville, whose noble family name Thomas Hardy used in his novel *Tess of the d'Urbervilles*, came to this tranquil retreat from London at the outbreak of the Civil War. Modest by manorial standards, the medieval house still serves the purpose for which it was built, as a working farm. The large pond in the garden was providing fish 700 years ago to the monks of Taunton Priory, proprietor of the manor from the 12th to the 16th century.

The main feature of the interior is the great hall, dominated by a spectacular Tudor plaster wall frieze which is believed to depict the life of James Turberville, Bishop of Exeter in the 16th century. Several other splendid rooms have Tudor fireplaces, some with Turberville coats of arms emblazoned above.

July-mid Sept, Sun, Wed, Thur pm; May-June, Sun and Thur pm; also Easter Sun and Mon and Bank Hol pm. Tel Lydeard St Lawrence (098 47) 213.

HAM HILL COUNTRY PARK

Off A3088, 8 miles west of Yeovil (Da)

A modest 426ft at its highest point, Ham Hill nevertheless affords panoramic views over the great chequered plain of the Somerset levels. Early settlers recognised its commanding position; the stark mounds at the crest were the ramparts of a major Iron Age fort, and even earlier there were settlements here in Stone Age and Bronze Age times.

For centuries, the golden limestone quarried at

CAMPAIGN RELIC *Argentinian aircraft captured in the Falklands campaign and displayed in the Fleet Air Arm Museum include this still-menacing two-seat Pucara ground attack aircraft.*

A SHRINE BESIDE ARTHUR'S AVALON

History and myth mingle tantalisingly in Glastonbury, a market town on the hills that rise starkly from the Somerset Levels. Joseph of Arimathea is said to have come here after the Crucifixion, to establish the first Christian church in England. A great abbey subsequently grew up, becoming among the most powerful in the land – only to meet destruction at the hands of Henry VIII at the Dissolution of the Monasteries. Under the desolate abbey ruins a mystery endures, for legend has it that King Arthur is buried there.

Glastonbury's abbots were powerful men: it was at courts held in their name in the Tribunal in High Street that itinerant judges meted out the king's justice.

Abbey: All year, daily. Adm charge. Shop. Tel Glastonbury (0458) 32267. Rural Life Museum: All year, daily. Adm charge. Refreshments. Shop. P *Toilets.* ♿ *Tel (0458) 32903. Tribunal: EH. All year, daily. Adm charge. Shop.* P *Toilets. Tel (0458) 32949.*

BARN OF MEMORIES *The magnificent abbey barn was built in the 14th century as the storehouse for the abbey's home manor. It now houses the Somerset Rural Life Museum, a collection of vintage farm wagons and machinery. The oak-timbered cruck roof is largely original, and supports 80 tons of stone tiles.*

HALLOWED ARCHES *The 13th-century walls of Glastonbury Abbey retain a sacred dignity. The abbey once held dominion over more land and lives than any other outside London. The abbey gatehouse (left) contains lovely Norman carvings from the ruins, and a section of mud plaster from the previous church on the site. There is also a model of the abbey as it might have looked just before its destruction in 1539.*

SEAT OF JUSTICE *The courtroom of Glastonbury Tribunal is on the first floor of the 15th to 16th-century building, beneath the original roof timbers. The room behind contains finds from the pre-Roman lake village discovered 1 mile to the east.*

HILLTOP CHAPEL *The ten-minute walk up to Glastonbury Tor's 525ft summit is rewarded by breathtaking views. The surrounding plain of willow-lined fields was once a great marsh, often flooded from the Bristol Channel. Glastonbury rose up from this as an island of hills, its mysticism potent enough to earn it a place in legend as the Isle of Avalon, where King Arthur came to die. The tower that caps the summit is all that remains of the 14th-century St Michael's Chapel, now empty and roofless.*

Ham Hill has been used to build beautiful homes in the area: the village and manor house of Montacute at the eastern foot of the hill are particularly fine examples. Footpaths thread their way among the old quarry workings, providing a succession of dramatic viewpoints.
All year, daily. P *Toilets. Tel Yeovil (0935) 75272.*

LYTE'S CARY MANOR

Off A372, 8 miles north of Yeovil (Db)

Set in tranquil farmland, the medieval manor house happily blends the architectural styles of six centuries. The earliest part of the house is the chapel, built in 1343. The great hall, next to it, is from a century later: open to the splendid arch-braced roof, it has a minstrels' gallery and fine plasterwork with the horses and swans that were the Lyte family's emblems. The oriel room leading off the hall, purpose-built as a dining room, is an early example of the Tudor trend away from the medieval custom of eating communally in the hall. Adjoining is the great parlour with superb 17th-century panelling and, above, the great bedroom with its original decorated plaster ceiling of 1553.
NT. Apr-Oct, Wed, Sat. P *Tel Ashcott (045 82) 23297.*

MONTACUTE HOUSE

Off A3088, 3½ miles west of Yeovil (Da)

Dramatic in its scale, Montacute is also one of the most beautiful of all mansions built in the Elizabethan period. Started in the year of the Armada, 1588, the huge H-shaped house is of local Ham Hill limestone, which gives its charmingly decorated exterior and scores of stone-mullioned windows their mellow, golden colour.

Built by Sir Edward Phelips, who became Speaker of the House of Commons, Montacute remained in his family's tenure until 1931 when it was saved from demolition by the National Trust. The many rooms which retain their original panelling and carving, plasterwork and heraldic stained glass, have been faithfully restored and contain furniture, tapestries and paintings dating back to the 15th century.

Highlights of the interior include a large plaster frieze in the Great Hall which depicts the humiliation of a village man by 'Riding the Skimmington' – a local punishment of being tied to a pole and paraded around the streets. The victim's crime: drinking on baby-sitting duty, and being caught in the act by his shrewish wife. Montacute's 172ft Long Gallery, originally an elegant venue for indoor exercise, is now home to a fine array of Tudor portraits.
NT. Apr-Oct, daily exc Tues, Good Fri. Adm charge. Refreshments. Shop. P *Toilets. Tel Yeovil (0935) 823289.*

NUNNEY CASTLE

Off A361, 4 miles south-west of Frome (Eb)

The four great towers of this ancient fortress rise more than 50ft from its deep moat, providing a fairy-tale centrepoint to a village of greystone houses. Nunney was built in the 14th century by Sir John de la Mare. During the Civil War it was a Royalist stronghold, but it eventually fell to Cromwell's cannons and was stripped of its three floors. The castle has been a ruin for 350 years, but its interior still offers interesting insights into the way its early occupants lived. Downstairs in the servants' quarters, for example, the windows are mere slits; upstairs where the owners resided, light flooded in through well-proportioned and decorative windows that look out over green and pleasant surrounding countryside.
EH. All year, daily. Free entry. P *(limited). Tel Bristol (0272) 734472.*

FRENCH FASHION *The corbels, or brackets, projecting from the towers of Nunney Castle once supported a parapet. The style is French, perhaps inspired by castles Nunney's builder had seen during military campaigns.*

ORCHARD MILL

Off A39, in Williton (Bb)

Huge wooden gears are kept turning by the great water wheel at this restored water mill in a woody dell at the foot of the Quantocks. Built in 1616, the mill is now a museum with a collection of early agricultural implements. There is also a whimsical collection of items from Victorian and Edwardian times, including examples of the earliest washing machine and vacuum cleaner.
May-Sept, daily exc Mon; Mar, Apr, Oct-Dec, daily exc Mon, Tues; also Bank Hol Mon. Adm charge. Refreshments. Shop. P *(limited). Toilets.* ♿ *Tel Williton (0984) 32133.*

PERRY'S CIDER MILLS

Off A303, 2 miles south of Ilminster (Ca)

Visitors to this cider farm in autumn can watch the age-old process of farmhouse cider being pressed from local apples in traditional style. The pressing takes place under the splendid thatch of a 400-year-old barn, set by the stream which first powered a water mill here in the 13th century. The barn also serves as a cider store and museum of rural bygones. The collection includes two venerable wooden cider presses, a dozen wagons and carts and a large number of old agricultural implements. A photographic display is devoted to village life around 1900.
All year, daily. Free entry. Shop. P *Toilets.* ♿ *Tel Ilminster (046 05) 2681.*

POUNDISFORD PARK

Off B3170, 3½ miles south of Taunton (Ca)

All the rooms on view in this entrancing Tudor house are still in regular use by the owner's family. Started in 1546 to an H-shaped floor plan, the three-storey house is, unusually, plastered externally, which sets off the golden Ham Stone mullioned windows.

Inside, the Great Hall with its remarkable Elizabethan moulded plaster ceiling is overlooked by a bay window from a gallery, where a fine collection of English and foreign porcelain is displayed. The Georgian dining room, with its ancient leaded casements, is in complete contrast to the Tudor style.
May-mid Sept, Wed, Thur, Bank Hol, also Fri in July and Aug. Adm charge. Refreshments. Shop. P *Toilets. Tel Blagdon Hill (082 342) 244.*

SHEPPY'S CIDER

On A38, 3 miles south-west of Taunton (Ba)

Kingston Black, Tremlett's Bitter and Yarlington Mill are among the picturesquely named apples harvested from 42 acres of orchards at this traditional cider farm. A small museum recalls earlier days of oak presses and stone jars, and there is a display devoted to the waning art of barrel-making, with a collection of cooper's equipment. In autumn, visitors can watch cider being made in the modern press room.
Apr-Nov, daily; Dec-Mar, daily exc Sun. Free entry. Shop. P *Toilets. Tel Bradford-on-Tone (082 346) 233.*

SHOE MUSEUM

On A39, in Street (Db)

The agonies endured by followers of fashion can well be imagined by touring this fascinating museum. In its collection of footwear from Roman times to 1970, there are winklepickers worn by fashionable young bucks around 1700, all manner of severe boots, and an extraordinary French shoe of 1895, its heel so high that the sole is almost vertical.

However, the museum, in the original C. & J. Clark factory built in the 1820s, does exhibit some more comfortable-looking alternatives: satin slippers from 1660, stylish lady's shoes from 200 years ago that could well be in fashion today – and all made long before the first machine-made footwear. One of the first such machines, patented in 1863, is also on show.
Easter Mon-Oct, daily exc Sun. Free entry. Shop. ♿ *Tel Street (0458) 43131.*

SPARKFORD MOTOR MUSEUM

On A359, ¼ mile north of Sparkford (Db)

British sports cars such as the 1937 Riley 12/4 and the 1952 Aston Martin DB2 are among the 40 glittering stars in this temple to motoring nostalgia. Vintage-car enthusiasts are treated to a 1905 Daimler limousine, complete with detachable roof, and a 1915 Model T Ford – one of 16 million produced. More recent classics include a pristine model of the 150mph E-type Jaguar, while American cars include one of the most vulgar gas-guzzlers of the 1970s, the two-ton Lincoln Continental.

All year, daily. Adm charge. Shop. P *Toilets.* ♿ *Tel North Cadbury (0963) 40804.*

TAUNTON CASTLE

Castle Bow, off North Street, Taunton (Cb)

During the Civil War a Parliamentary garrison stoutly defended this 13th-century bishop's fortress against 10,000 Royalist troops. In the process most of the town was destroyed, but the castle stood fast and some of its formidable buildings remain to this day. Entering by the walkway across the sunken garden, once a moat, visitors pass through the original gatehouse arch, altered by Bishop Thomas Langton in the 1490s and bearing his arms. Straight ahead is the Great Hall; built in 1245, this was for centuries Taunton's law court, and it was here in 1685 that some 500 men were condemned in Judge Jeffreys' 'Bloody Assize' for their part in the abortive Monmouth rebellion.

Today, the great hall has a happier function as the core of the Somerset County Museum. This houses an exhibition of Somerset arts and crafts, collections of English and Chinese pottery and, in the gallery above, geological and natural history displays. The latest addition to the museum is a military exhibition centred around the former Somerset Light Infantry. One display recalls the regiment's service at Jellalabad in Afghanistan, when half its number were killed on the way to a heroic victory. The American flag on show was captured, by the Somersets in 1813, during Britain's last war against the United States.

All year, daily exc Sun. Adm charge. Shop. P *(limited). Toilets. Tel Taunton (0823) 255504.*

TROPICAL BIRD GARDENS

Off A36 at Rode, 6 miles north of Frome (Ec)

Brilliantly coloured macaws soar high among exotic cedars and cypresses, peacocks and ornamental pheasants parade the lawns, while tall and stately cranes seem as much at home here as they would on their native African plains. The large open-air aviaries contain multicoloured cockatoos and parakeets, finches and jays. A series of lakes makes an elegant backdrop for a languid flamingo flock and an obligingly comical crowd of penguins. The gardens' remarkable collection of trees and its wide clematis collection almost rivals its birdlife for rarity and variety. A map gives a keyed and numbered guide to 150 of the finest mature trees.

All year, daily. Adm charge. Refreshments. Shop. P *Toilets.* ♿ *Tel Frome (0373) 830326.*

WELLS CATHEDRAL

In centre of Wells (Db)

The greatest gallery of medieval sculpture in Europe, a unique 600-year-old working clock and scores of delightful 12th-century carvings are among the attractions of the vast Cathedral Church of St Andrew in Wells. The famed West Front, started in 1230 – some 50 years after the main building – is honeycombed with 400 niches, most containing original medieval statues. These include larger-than-life-size figures of the 12 apostles. The only modern work here is the statue of Christ, flanked by two seraphim, in the topmost niche; it was sculpted by David Wynne, and installed in 1985.

The astronomical clock, made around 1390, is in the north transept. Its face is 6ft 4in across. The outer circle of numerals shows the hours in two sets of 12, and a gold star representing the sun acts as the 'hour hand'. A smaller star travels round the inner circle of minutes. A pointer on the central disc indicates the day of the lunar month on the innermost circle. The disc is decorated to represent the earth, and on it is a

SCISSOR SUPPORT *Beneath the central tower of Wells Cathedral, six great curves intersect in a dramatic pattern. These 'scissor arches' were added in 1338 to support the tower's weight. Above the ornate medieval clock (right), figures of four knights emerge each quarter-hour to do vigorous battle on horseback.*

medallion showing a quaint female figure representing the moon, an ingenious mechanism keeping the medallion upright as the disc turns. The exact appearance of the waxing and waning moon at any time is shown by a black and gold moon which turns in a hole in the disc opposite the medallion.

The grandeur of the cathedral's 12th-century nave is softened by the charming carvings made throughout by the original masons. These portray scenes from the life of the day, such as fruit stealers caught in the act, toothache sufferers and many beautifully depicted animals.

The newest part of the cathedral, the cloisters, completed in 1508, lead to one of the most beautiful bishops' palaces in the country. Surrounded by a wide freshwater moat – fed by the wells that give the tiny city its name – and a high castellated wall, the palace is entered through a mighty gatehouse. These formidable defences date from 1331 when Edward III stayed here and granted the bishop permission to fortify.

Within the walls, the scene is one of timeless serenity. The gabled, terracotta-coloured house built for Jocelin Trotman, first bishop of the joint see of Bath and Wells from 1219, retains its original lancet windows and, inside, the superb vaulting in its ground-floor rooms. Of the separate Great Hall, built later in the century, only the towering, crenellated walls remain, but they give a good idea of the splendour in which the medieval bishops entertained their guests.

An outstanding collection of more than 100 samplers dating back to 1740 is one of the special attractions of the Wells Museum. Here, too, are displays devoted to cave findings in the area, particularly from Wookey Hole; these include the skeleton of the so-called Witch of Wookey, a cave inhabitant of around 1000 years ago, and domestic items dating back to the Iron Age.

Cathedral: All year, daily. Refreshments. Shop. Palace: Easter-Oct, daily. Adm charge. Refreshments. Shop. Toilets. Tel Wells (0749) 78691. Museum: Apr-early Nov, daily; mid Nov-Mar, Wed, Thur, Sat and Sun. Adm charge. Shop. 🅿 *(limited). Toilets. Tel (0749) 73477.*

WEST SOMERSET RAILWAY

Minehead Station (Bb)

Nostalgic journeys by steam train are a year-round attraction on Britain's longest privately run railway. Starting at the seaside station of Minehead, the West Somerset line runs 20 miles south-east through the Quantocks to Bishops Lydeard, near Taunton.

Along the way are seven stops. First is Dunster, whose station was built for the benefit of the nobility who, at the turn of the century, flocked to play polo at the nearby castle. Next is Blue Anchor station, where the former waiting room is now a railway museum largely devoted to the heyday of the Great Western Railway. Washford station, next along the line, is home to the museum of the Somerset and Dorset Railway. After stops in the little port of Watchet and at the Doniford beach halt comes Williton, whose station of 1862 has been faithfully restored to its original style. Stogumber follows and then comes Crowcombe, a highly picturesque station in the Great Western Railway style.

Apr-Oct, daily; Nov-Mar, Sat and Sun. Adm charge. Refreshments. Shop. 🅿 *Toilets.* ♿ *Tel Minehead (0643) 4996.*

WILLOW CRAFT INDUSTRY

Off A378, 10 miles east of Taunton (Cb)

Willow beds on the Sedgemoor wetland provide the raw material for a traditional Somerset craft. A tour follows the stored, winter-harvested willows from the vast tank in which they are boiled to soften their bark and give them their mellow colour to the stripping and drying processes that produce the slim, smooth rods. In the workshop, craftsmen deftly weave willows into baskets. A visitor centre illustrates the history of the Somerset Levels – the most important wetlands to have survived in England – highlighting wildlife and the specialised industries that have grown up in the area.

All year, daily exc Sun. Adm charge. Shop. 🅿 *Toilets. Tel Taunton (0823) 490249.*

WOOKEY HOLE CAVES AND MILL

Off A371, 2 miles north of Wells (Db)

Local legend has it that two of the stalagmites among the fantastic limestone formations of these caves are the petrified remains of a witch and her dog. These fearsome denizens of the dank caverns were, according to the story, turned to stone by a monk who doused them with holy water. Moving through the caves, cut deep into the hillside by the appropriately named River Axe, it is not hard to imagine how such a myth could take hold.

DIVING AND GALLOPING

The first divers to explore Wookey Hole in 1935 used this Siebe-Gorman diving suit, displayed there today. Items from old-time funfairs on view at the caves include gaudy Victorian fairground animals, displayed on a simulated roundabout.

Visitors are guided along cave floors, tunnels and catwalks clinging to precipitous cavern walls through a series of deepening underground chambers, artfully lit to emphasise the dramatic colours of mineral seams and the bizarre convulsions of the rock. The deep pools of the silent river add to the primeval mystery of the place.

The Wookey Hole Mill manufactures handmade paper by the same methods employed here for three centuries, processing cotton by a skilled technique. In Victorian times, this was the largest paper mill of its kind in Europe, then using rags rather than new cotton.

New interests at Wookey Hole, which has been owned by Madame Tussauds since 1973, include a small waxworks exhibition devoted to the redoubtable Frenchwoman herself. There is also a collection of vintage funfair contraptions, among them an indoor replica Victorian pier with old penny amusement machines.

All year, daily. Adm charge. Refreshments. Shop. 🅿 *Toilets. Tel Wells (0749) 72243.*

COUNTY CALENDAR

January 17 Carhampton: Wassailing the Apple Tree (cider tradition).

April (1st Tues after 6th). Tatworth: Candle Auction (traditional land auction timed by burning candle).

May 1 Minehead: Hobby Horse Ceremony.

June (mid-month). South Petherton: Folk Festival. Shepton Mallet: Royal Bath and West Show.

July (starts mid-month). Minehead: Arts Festival.

August (early). RNAS Yeovilton: Air Day.

August (late). Dunster: Show.

September (mid-month). Frome: Cheese Fair.

October (last Thur). Hinton St George: Punkie Night.

November 5 Bridgwater: Bonfire Night.

Tourist information: Burnham-on-Sea (0278) 787852; Cheddar (0934) 742769; Minehead (0643) 2624; Taunton (0823) 74785; Wells (0749) 72552; Yeovil (0935) 22884.

STAFFORDSHIRE

A CHANGED FACE FOR THE POTTERIES, AND A TIMELESS CATHEDRAL

At the heart of Staffordshire is one of Britain's oldest industrial conurbations – The Potteries. Today the grimy face of the past is disappearing, as factories are transformed into living and working museums of nearly 300 years of china production. At the Gladstone Pottery Museum in Longton craftsmen display their traditional skills, while the Wedgwood Group has a gleaming modern factory set amid green fields.

Only a half-hour's drive east of Stoke-on-Trent lie the scenic wonders of the Manifold Valley, and south-east is the ancient cathedral city of Lichfield, birthplace of Samuel Johnson. Other county highlights are as diverse as Shugborough, its garden filled with monuments; Cannock Chase, one of the largest leisure areas in the Midlands; the Gothic ruin of Alton Towers, with its huge pleasure park; and the little cottage at Shallowford used by Izaak Walton, author of *The Compleat Angler*.

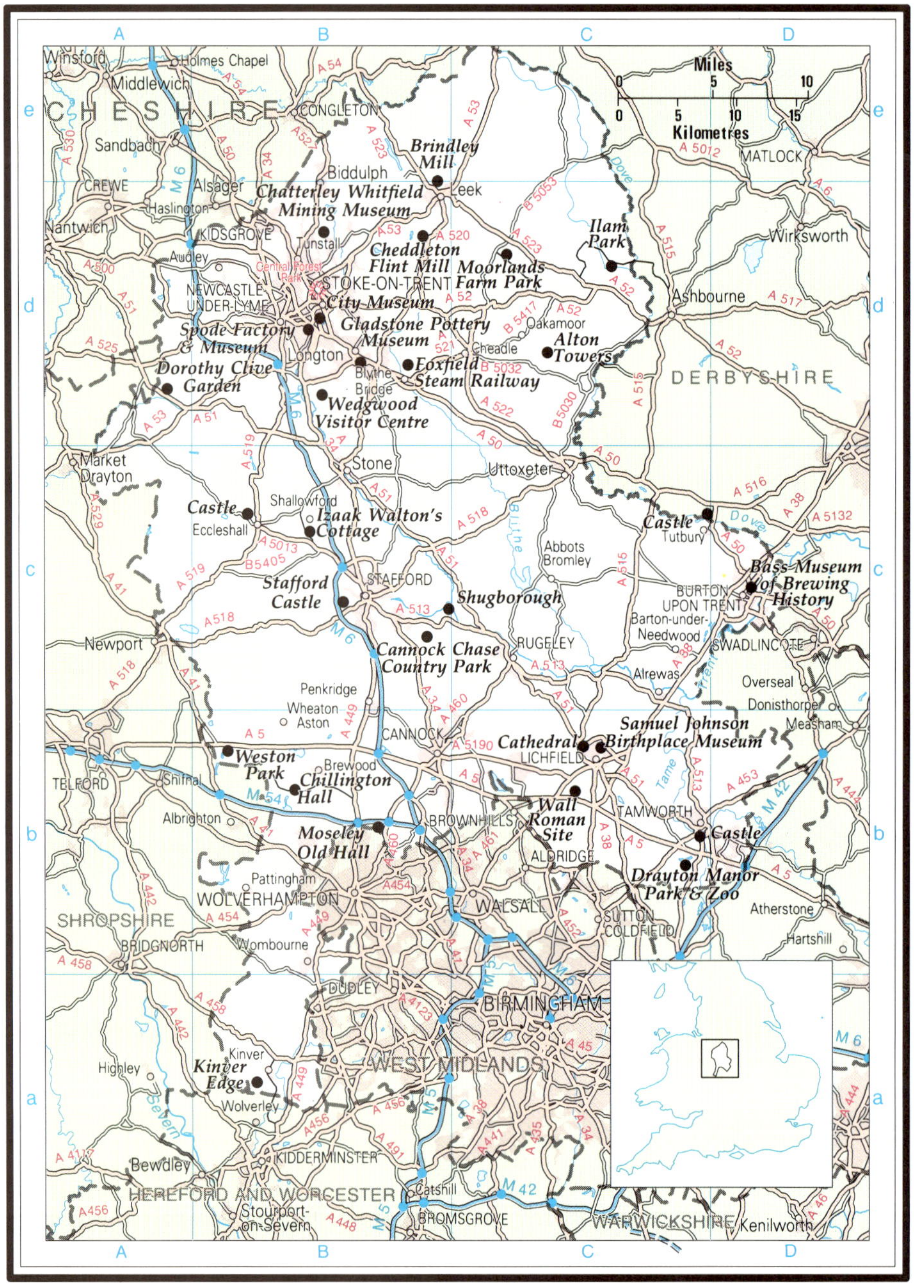

BASS MUSEUM OF BREWING HISTORY

Horninglow Street, Burton upon Trent (Dc)

When Manet painted his famous picture of the bar at the Folies Bergère in 1882 he put bottles of Bass on the counter. A century earlier Bass already enjoyed an international reputation: it was exported to Russia, where the Emperor and Empress were said to enjoy it. The museum recording the history of this well-known beer is probably the most comprehensive brewery museum in the world.

The main exhibition traces the development of brewing in Burton from the earliest times to the present day. By 1600 there were already 46 licensed victuallers in the town, each brewing his own beer; its character is said to be due to the local water, hard in quality, from its source in layers of gypsum beneath the town. The museum includes one of the largest working railway models in Europe; a reconstructed full-scale railway 'aledock', with both steam and petrol locomotives alongside it; a complete experimental brewhouse, with a magnificent Robey tandem steam compound engine of 1902, which is set in motion at weekends, and a 1916 steam Sentinel delivery dray – the oldest steam vehicle of its type still licensed and used on the roads today. It also houses the stables of the company's Shire horses.

All year, daily. Adm charge. Refreshments. Shop. P *Toilets.* ♿ *Tel Burton (0283) 45301.*

BRINDLEY MILL

Off A523, 1 mile west of Leek town centre (Bd)

James Brindley was a folk hero of the Industrial Revolution – the son of a small Staffordshire farmer who became one of Britain's greatest canal builders. Among his achievements was the Bridgewater Canal, which supplied coal to Manchester. Earlier in his career Brindley built water mills for corn, flint and textiles, each with completely different internal machinery. This corn mill, built in 1752, was Brindley's last project before he turned to the even greater problems of building waterways. It is an outstanding example of the engineering complexity already incorporated in the design of mills, from the sluice gear raising the gates to start the water wheel, to the tentering gear which adjusts the gap between the grindstones on the first floor above; the two stones, without touching, have to be close enough to grind the grain pouring from the hopper. On the second floor of the mill are displays illustrating the life and skills of James Brindley.

Easter-Oct, Sat, Sun and Bank Hol Mon; also Mon, Tues and Thur pm in July and Aug. Adm charge. Shop. P *Tel Leek (0538) 381446/384195.*

CANNOCK CHASE COUNTRY PARK

Off A513, 4 miles south-east of Stafford (Bc)

At $4\frac{1}{2}$ square miles, Cannock Chase Country Park is one of the largest in Britain, and one of the most diverse. Miles of tracks and bridlepaths wander over bracken-covered hills, through birch, oak and pine woodlands, and alongside streams such as the secluded Sherbrook Valley.

One of the major attractions of Cannock Chase is its fallow deer, which have roamed the hills for centuries. Small numbers of red deer can also be seen. There is also one plant of outstanding interest – the 'Cannock Chase berry', a rare hybrid between bilberry and cowberry which is found most commonly in this area. Other interesting plants include heath bedstraw, tormentil, bird's-foot trefoil and black medick. The Chase is home to a variety of birds, including kestrels and tawny and long-eared owls.

All year, daily. Visitor centres at Marquis Drive and Milford Common, Sat and Sun pm.

CHATTERLEY WHITFIELD MINING MUSEUM

Off A527, 1½ miles north-east of Tunstall (Bd)

Britain's first underground mining museum, Chatterley Whitfield is a real colliery where once 3000 men and boys worked. In 1936 it was the first pit in Britain to produce 1 million tons of coal. To visit the museum is to enter the coal-miner's world – both above and below ground.

The visit starts at the Lamphouse, where visitors are provided with a helmet and a lamp, and then escorted by a retired miner to the pit head; from here they descend in a cage to the shaft bottom at a speed of 10ft per second. Underground, a timbered roadway takes visitors back to the 1800s, when coal was mined by hand. Here is the Ostler's Cabin and the Stables, the home of two pit ponies now retired from active service. Passing through an airlock, visitors come forward in time to view a semi-mechanical cutter and endless haulage engine, and to take a ride on an underground locomotive.

Back on the surface, the tour passes the Robert Heath steam locomotive and the Hesketh steam winding engine, and finally there is a chance to take a miner's mug of tea in the carefully restored 1930s pit-head canteen.

All year, daily. Adm charge. Refreshments. Shop. P *Toilets. Tel Stoke-on-Trent (0782) 813337.*

PIT POWER *Brass and paint gleam on the restored steam winding engine at Chatterley Whitfield Mining Museum. It was used to raise men and coal from the pit bottom.*

CHEDDLETON FLINT MILL

Off A520, 3 miles south of Leek (Bd)

For two centuries up until 1963 the Cheddleton mill ground flint for the Staffordshire pottery industry. It is now a fascinating piece of industrial history. The flint was ground to a powder under great stones powered by water wheels, after which it was used to whiten pottery. The North Mill is preserved much as it was when it was built; the South Mill is now used for displays. Exhibits range from glaze and colour grinding pans to a 100hp drop-valve reciprocating steam engine and a narrowboat used for transporting the powdered flint to the potteries.

The North Staffordshire Railway Centre is also at Cheddleton. The centre occupies a disused station, opened in 1849 and now a museum. There is a separate locomotive museum, and short steam rides are available.

Mill: All year, Sat-Sun pm. Free entry. P *Tel Stoke-on-Trent (0782) 502907. Railway Centre: Steam days Bank Hol Sun-Mon from Easter; also Sun, June-Sept; static viewing Sun pm, Oct-Mar. Adm charge. Refreshments. Shop.* P *Toilets.* ♿ *Tel Churnetside (0538) 360522.*

CHILLINGTON HALL

Off A449, 6 miles north-west of Wolverhampton (Bb)

The present Georgian mansion is the third house the Giffard family have built on this site over the last 900 years. After arriving in England with William the Conqueror, they first built a castle, a small corner of which remains in the cellars of the present house. Elizabeth I stayed in the Tudor mansion which replaced the castle on her Royal Progress through Staffordshire. Most of the present house was designed in the 18th century, partly by Francis Smith of Warwick and partly by Sir John Soane. The best rooms are the Staircase Hall, the Morning Room with its splendid stucco ceiling, and the Saloon – Soane's best work at Chillington. The grounds are magnificent – 1100 acres of park and woodlands, landscaped by Capability Brown.

May-mid Sept, Thur; also some Sun, inc all in Aug. Adm charge. P *Toilets.* ♿ *Tel Brewood (0902) 850236.*

DOROTHY CLIVE GARDEN

On A51, 11 miles north-west of Stone (Ad)

It was in 1939 that Colonel Harry Clive began turning a disused quarry into a garden for his wife Dorothy. It lay in woodland at the top of the grounds of their house, Elds Gorse, with magnificent views into Shropshire and Cheshire.

The garden includes a quarry garden noted for rhododendrons and azaleas, an alpine garden and a water garden. Its spectacular seasonal displays include camellias in spring, shrub roses in summer and autumn-flowering bulbs.

Mar-Nov, daily. Adm charge. P *Toilets. Tel Pipe Gate (063 081) 237.*

DRAYTON MANOR PARK AND ZOO

Off A4091, 2 miles south of Tamworth (Cb)

Some 160 acres of parkland at Drayton include an extraordinary variety of entertainments and a zoo covering 15 acres. More than 30 man-made diversions range from the Looping Roller Coaster to the Pirate Ship. The zoo has an impressive collection of primates, reptiles, big cats, bears, birds and paddock animals.

Apr-Oct, daily. Adm charge. Refreshments. Shop. P *Toilets.* ♿ *Tel Tamworth (0827) 287979.*

ECCLESHALL CASTLE

Off A519, ¼ mile north of Eccleshall (Bc)

Cromwell's soldiers demolished most of Eccleshall Castle during the Civil War, but it makes a most romantic ruin. One unusual nine-sided tower survives, together with the moat walls, from the original 13th-century building in which Queen Margaret of Anjou, wife of Henry VI, took refuge after the Battle of Blore Heath in 1459. The moat was drained in the 18th century and now forms attractive formal gardens. The castle is in the grounds of a handsome William and Mary house of 1690 which contains fine porcelain, paintings and furniture.

Easter-Sept, Sun and Bank Hol Mon and Tues; also Thur, June-Sept, and Tues in Aug. Adm charge. Refreshments. Shop. P *Toilets.* ♿ *Tel Eccleshall (0785) 850250.*

FOXFIELD STEAM RAILWAY

Off A50 at Blythe Bridge, 5 miles south-east of Stoke-on-Trent (Bd)

Originally built for the transport of coal from Foxfield Colliery, this standard-gauge railway is now operated strictly for pleasure, carrying passengers up and down a series of steep gradients and sharp curves of a boldness usually found only on narrow-gauge lines. It all makes for a thrilling 4 mile ride, with the three passenger coaches drawn by any one of a number of steam locomotives. Altogether the line owns 24 locomotives and a great deal of rolling stock.

Apr-Sept, Sun and Bank Hol. Adm charge. Refreshments. Shop. P *Toilets. Tel Stoke-on-Trent (0782) 314532.*

GLADSTONE POTTERY MUSEUM

Off A50 in Longton, 3 miles south-east of Stoke-on-Trent (Bd)

Four giant bottle ovens dominate the cobbled yard of this complete Victorian 'potbank', which is now a living and working museum of British pottery. The purpose of the museum is not only to preserve the buildings and tools used by the industry in past times, but also to maintain the traditional skills. Consequently visitors can see a wide range of items being made, from huge garden pots to delicate china.

The museum also contains a series of galleries devoted to the history of the Staffordshire potteries; decorative tiles, and ceramic colour and decoration. A gallery devoted to sanitaryware includes a working replica of the first water-closet, designed by Sir John Harington for Elizabeth I.

FUN AND FANTASY AT ALTON TOWERS

Entertainment with the spice of adventure, and some of the loveliest gardens in Britain, attract more than 2 million visitors to Alton Towers Leisure Park every year. The 800 acre estate was the home of the Earls of Shrewsbury, and it was Charles Talbot, the 15th earl, who in 1814 began to landscape the grounds. Today the gondolas of a space-age Skyride, carrying visitors high above the tree-tops, give a bird's eye view of the park and more than 100 entertainments it offers. The entrance ticket pays for all attractions, so on public holidays the queues for the more popular rides and shows can be long.

Adventurous visitors head for the Corkscrew Rollercoaster, which has become the symbol of the park; its riders loop the loop twice under forces three times that of gravity. A close rival in popularity is the Log Flume, an aqueduct at tree-top level so angled that the water carries canoes along at great speed, and in places plunges them from a height. The Black Hole hurls riders at seemingly immense speed through the blackness of interstellar space, while Cine 2000 whirls its audience down the Grand Canyon or high into aerobatic manoeuvres.

There are quieter attractions too. When it was completed in the 19th century, the neo-Gothic mansion of Alton Towers was the largest private house in Europe, with a ground floor covering 6½ acres. Today it is largely a ruin, but parts of it have been restored and visitors can marvel at the spacious rooms, which include a banqueting hall with superb stained-glass windows.

The building forms the centre of the third major feature of the park – the display area. This includes the elegant Talbot Street, lined by reconstructed 19th-century houses, in one of which a water ballet is performed by fountains synchronised with lighting and music.

Items in the Dolls' Exhibition include the throne in which the present Prince of Wales sat for his investiture, Queen Victoria's mourning dress and veil, ancient Oriental puppets and mechanical tin toys from the 19th century.

Almost one-third of the attractions of Alton Towers are under cover. Outdoors there are picnic areas and three waymarked nature trails, from 1 to 3 miles long. Regular live entertainments include a daily parade.

Off M1 and M6, 12 miles east of Stoke-on-Trent (Cd). Grounds: All year, daily. Entertainments: Late Mar-Oct, daily. Adm charge. Refreshments. Shop. P *Toilets.* ♿ *Tel Oakamoor (0538) 702200.*

GARDEN FOR ALL SEASONS *The Rock Garden of Alton Towers is vibrant with colour throughout the year. Terraces, statuary, pools, fountains, colonnades and a Chinese temple all add to the glory of the gardens.*

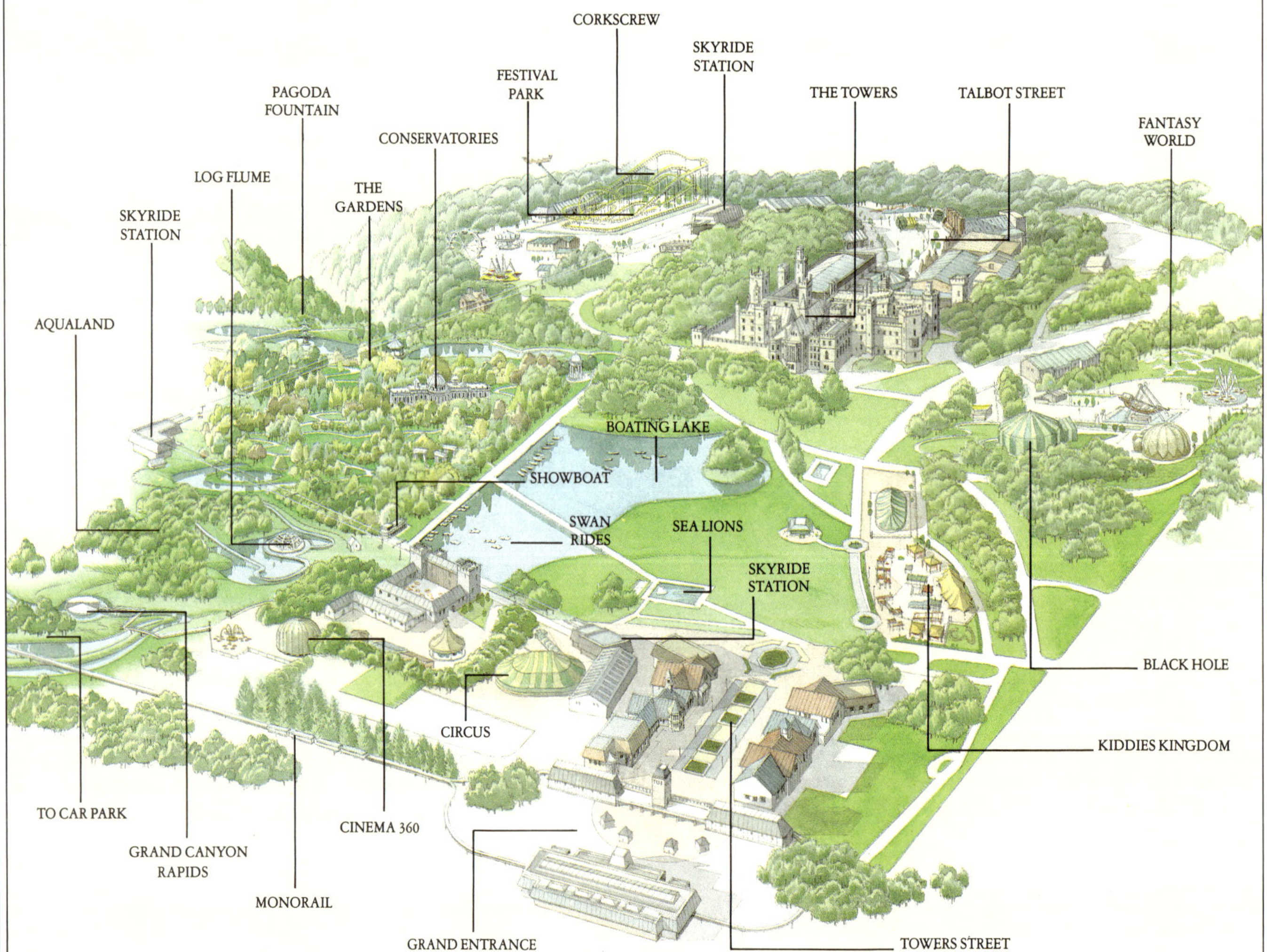

At the nearby John Beswick Studios of Royal Doulton, in Gold Street, visitors can see how the famous character and Toby jugs are designed and made, along with a range of ceramic sculptures, including the Beatrix Potter figure collection.
Gladstone Museum: All year, daily exc Mon, Nov-Feb. Adm charge. Refreshments. Shop. P *Toilets.* ♿ *Tel Stoke-on-Trent (0782) 319232. John Beswick Pottery: All year, Mon-Fri exc annual factory hol; appointments preferred. Adm charge. Shop. Toilets. Tel (0782) 313041.*

ILAM PARK

Off A523, 18 miles east of Stoke-on-Trent (Cd)

The valley of the River Manifold holds one of Britain's natural wonders: a disappearing river. From late autumn to spring the Manifold is a sparkling upland stream, rushing between high banks. But in the drier months it disappears underground for some 4 miles, emerging again at Ilam Hall. This is limestone country, and when the water table falls it takes the river underground with it.

The scenic wonders of the Manifold Valley can be enjoyed on an attractively varied walk up the valley from Ilam Hall, owned by the National Trust. The hall itself is a youth hostel, but the grounds are open to the public. Even the most energetic walker is tempted to linger here, for it is laid out like a private garden with emerald-green lawns sweeping down to the river. The so-called Paradise Walk in the park continues along the river for about 1 mile, then begins to ascend the steep moorlands, along a metalled track, to the ruins of Throwley Hall. Although there is no signpost, the footpath continues through a farmyard and brings the walker out to a stupendous view. Below, the moorland falls rapidly away down to the riverbed, while towering above is the massive limestone cliff called Beeston Tor.

From here on, the valley presents its most dramatic face as the cliffs on either side rise to form a narrow gorge. About 1 mile beyond Beeston Tor is Thor's Cave, an immense limestone cavern high above the river. Steps have been built up to it and the long climb is well worth the effort, for at the mouth of the cathedral-like cave the whole valley opens out to view. The riverside walk continues to Wetton Mill, where the river disappears in the drier months, to reappear downstream in the hall grounds. The 16th-century corn mill ceased working in 1857, but the covered mill race still runs under the farmyard. The farm belongs to the National Trust.

Wetton Mill is also the starting point of another Manifold Valley walk, which is particularly suitable for the disabled. Before the First World War an over-optimistic railway company built a narrow-gauge railway along most of the valley, with stations remarkably close together; the remains of one are still visible at Beeston Tor. It proved an economic failure, however, and was abandoned. In 1937 the county council metalled the railway track so that today it is a narrow, totally traffic-free road running for over 8 miles. This track branches off to the right at Beeston Tor to emerge at last at Waterhouses.
All year, daily.

IZAAK WALTON'S COTTAGE

Off A5013, 5 miles north-west of Stafford (Bc)

The author of *The Compleat Angler* – the most famous book on fishing ever written – lived to the age of 90, thereby becoming in himself the best of all recommendations for the sport he loved. The 17th-century cottage was part of a farm he owned at Shallowford, where he spent some of his leisure when he was not working as Steward to the Bishop of Worcester.

The cottage is no longer thatched as in Walton's time, but the interior is typical of the late 17th century when he stayed there and contains many items of interest to fishermen.
Mar-Oct, daily exc Wed and Thur; Oct-Mar, weekends only. Adm charge. Refreshments. Shop. P *Toilets.* ♿ *(garden). Tel Stafford (0785) 40204.*

KINVER EDGE

Off A449, 5 miles north of Kidderminster (Ba)

From the summit of this red-sandstone escarpment, which falls dramatically away down to the little town of Kinver, five other ranges of hills can be seen: the Clents, the Cotswolds, the Malverns, the Habberleys and the Clees. It is a perfect spot for a picnic.

People have been coming to Kinver Edge for thousands of years. Iron Age tribes occupied it 2500 years ago, and the earthworks of a hill-fort are still visible. Over the succeeding centuries, wherever the soft sandstone formed a suitable cliff, cave dwellings and rock houses were scooped out. The most spectacular of these are in Holy Austin Rock at the northern end where some dwellings, with brick fronts and tiled gables, continued to be occupied until about 1950.
NT. All year, daily.

LICHFIELD CATHEDRAL

In centre of Lichfield (Cb)

Although only a few minutes' walk from a busy shopping centre, Lichfield Cathedral seems to occupy a world of its own. The sense of isolation is partly the effect of two lakes, the Minster Pool and the Stowe Pool, which separate the cathedral from the town and form one of Lichfield's most distinctive and beautiful features. The three spires of the cathedral, towering above the houses of the close and delightfully nicknamed the 'Ladies of the Vale', survived even the cannonades of the Civil War when the cathedral was besieged first by the Parliamentarians and then by the Royalists. The cathedral dates from the 13th century, and though the interior was altered by James Wyatt in the 18th century, it retains much of its medieval grandeur because Gilbert Scott sensitively restored it in the 19th century. In the ante-room to the Chapter House are stone benches for people waiting to do business inside.

A medieval mason at work on Lichfield Cathedral is the subject of one of the tableaux in the Lichfield Heritage and Treasury Exhibition at the nearby St Mary's Centre. The centre is brilliantly converted from the Church of St Mary, made redundant as a result of the declining

ENDURING WORDS *An elaborate illumination opens the Gospel of St Matthew in an early manuscript which has been in Lichfield Cathedral for nearly 1250 years. It is on display in the Chapter House.*

population in the town centre. A series of lifelike tableaux illustrates Lichfield's history over some 2000 years. Outstanding is the collage showing an ancient ceremony, the Bower Procession. This collage is based on an 18th-century engraving but the procession, whose origins are long since forgotten, still takes place each year, on Spring Bank Holiday. The sword and mace used in it are on display in the Treasury Exhibition.
Cathedral: All year, daily. Free entry. Refreshments. Shop. Toilets. ♿ *Heritage exhibition: All year, daily. Adm charge. Refreshments. Shop.* P *Toilets.* ♿ *Tel Lichfield (0543) 256611.*

MOORLANDS FARM PARK

Off A523, 5 miles south-east of Leek (Cd)

There is nothing modern or commercial about this farm: all the breeds of animals on view are commercially extinct. They are museum pieces – historically important for their contribution to the development of modern breeds, but valuable still only as a gene bank on which livestock breeders may need to call in the future. Here are the ancient Longhorn cattle, along with the White Galloway, the Shorthorn, Dexter, Dun Galloway and Highland. There are 12 breeds of sheep, including the ancient Soay, and old-fashioned pigs like the Tamworth and Gloucester Old Spot; pygmy goats, Breckon Buff geese and Partridge Cochin poultry.
Apr-Oct, daily. Adm charge. Refreshments. Shop. P *Toilets.* ♿ *Tel Ipstones (053 871) 479.*

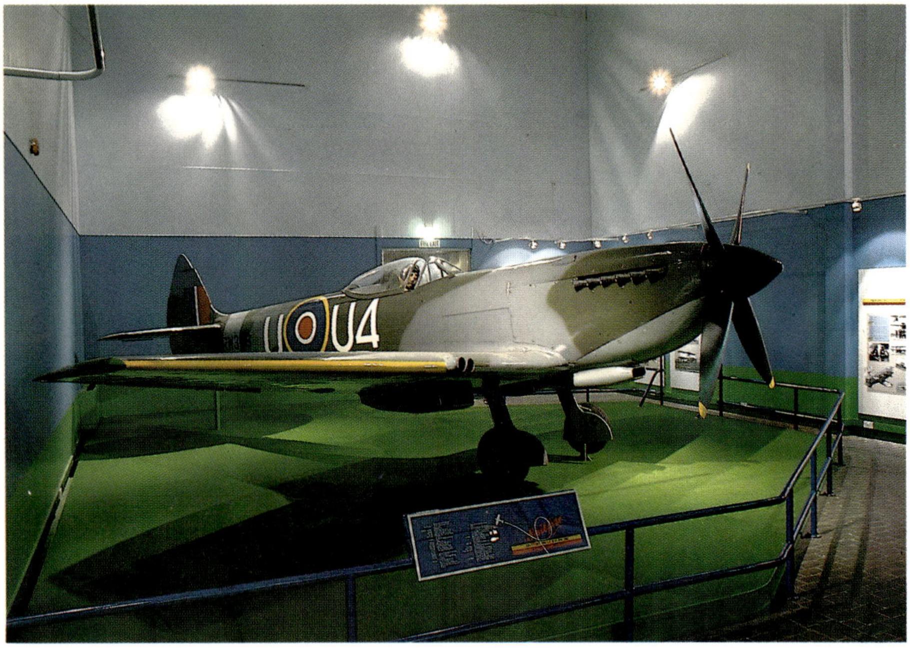

WARTIME WINNER *A Mark XVI Spitfire of the Second World War has a proud place in Stoke's City Museum. The fighter's designer, Reginald Mitchell, was born in Longton in 1895. He died in 1937, before his planes played their vital wartime role.*

MOSELEY OLD HALL

Off A460, 5 miles south-west of Cannock (Bb)

There may be finer Elizabethan houses in the country, but few have such an interesting history. Charles II arrived at the hall on the morning of September 8, 1651, dressed as a woodcutter, after leaving his army defeated at the Battle of Worcester five days earlier. In the King's Room at Moseley is the four-poster bed in which he slept, and the hiding place, concealed within a cupboard, in which he spent an uncomfortable time while Cromwell's soldiers questioned the owner of the house.

On the wall in the corridor is a document of September 10, 1651, offering a reward of £1000 for the king's capture. From the little study over the front porch Charles watched the sad remnants of his army pass on their long walk back to Scotland. A showcase in the entrance hall contains a letter written by Charles to Jane Lane, sister of a local landowner, thanking her for her assistance in helping him to escape to France. Charles reached the Continent about five weeks after his departure from Moseley.

NT. Mar-June, Sat and Sun pm; July-mid Sept, Wed-Sun; mid Sept-Oct, Sat-Sun. Adm charge. Refreshments. Shop. P *Toilets.* ♿ *Tel Wolverhampton (0902) 782808.*

SAMUEL JOHNSON BIRTHPLACE MUSEUM

Breadmarket Street, Lichfield (Cb)

'Every man has a lurking desire to appear considerable in his native place', said Dr Samuel Johnson. The great lexicographer has certainly achieved his ambition in Lichfield, where he was born in 1709. Both Johnson's statue and that of his biographer Boswell stand in the delightful little marketplace.

A stone's throw away is the house where Johnson was born, the son of a bookseller, and where he lived until he left to seek his fortune. It is now a museum, laid out as far as possible as it was when Johnson was a boy, but also containing exhibits from his later years when he was nationally famous. The tour starts in the parlour, the 'best room' of the house in Johnson's day and used only when guests were entertained; normally the family lived on the floor below. In the family bedrooms upstairs are exhibits relating to Johnson's education in Lichfield, his attempt to start a school and the early years of his marriage. The room in which Johnson was born is used today to illustrate his fame as a writer, pride of place being given to his great *Dictionary of the English Language*.

May-Sept, daily; Oct-Apr, daily exc Sun. Adm charge. Shop. Tel Lichfield (0543) 264972.

SHUGBOROUGH

Off A513, 6 miles east of Stafford (Bc)

While the house is undeniably handsome, beautifully set in 900 landscaped acres, Shugborough is even more celebrated for the monuments in its park. They were all constructed in the 18th century – at a time when rich English country gentlemen were full of enthusiasm for the 'Greek revival' trend in architecture. At Shugborough this resulted in a fine collection of monuments being built to adorn the landscape, including a grand romantic Ruin, a Doric Temple, a Chinese House, a Triumphal Arch, The Tower of the Winds (based on the design of the original building in Athens) and the Lanthorn of Demosthenes.

The Red Drawing Room, designed by Samuel Wyatt, is the finest room in the house, with outstanding plasterwork by Joseph Rose, Adam's favourite plasterer. The house, which is the home of the Earl of Lichfield, contains fine collections of 18th-century ceramics, silver, paintings and French furniture.

The old servants' quarters at Shugborough are now the home of the Staffordshire County Museum, which contains authentic reconstructions of bygone times in Staffordshire. Nostalgia is the theme also of Shugborough Park Farm, one of the most complete re-creations in England of 19th-century agricultural life. The farm buildings remain much as they were in 1805 and include a working corn mill. There is a range of livestock breeds originating in Staffordshire. They include the Tamworth pig, Longhorn cattle and the Bagot goat.

NT. Apr-Dec, daily. Adm charge. Refreshments. Shop. P *Toilets.* ♿ *Tel Little Haywood (0889) 881388.*

SPODE FACTORY AND MUSEUM

Church Street, Stoke-on-Trent (Bd)

Josiah Spode is famous for two contributions to the development of ceramics. In 1784 he perfected the process for transfer printing in blue on earthenware, which led to British decorated pottery becoming prized throughout the world. He followed this with the most important discovery in the history of English pottery – bone china. The brilliant whiteness and delicate translucency of this new material inspired new standards of artistry and craftsmanship and created a new, world-wide demand.

A tour of the Spode factory gives the visitor an opportunity to see the skills and processes involved in producing fine bone china, many of which have remained unchanged since the 18th century. The Spode Museum has an outstanding collection of rare and precious pieces from the factory's output over the past 200 years.

All year, Mon-Sat. Adm charge for tours (by appointment). Shop. P *Toilets. Tel Stoke-on-Trent (0782) 744011.*

STAFFORD CASTLE

Off A518, on western side of Stafford (Bc)

One of the earliest and largest Norman castles in Britain, Stafford Castle was originally built four years after the Norman Conquest. It was partly demolished by the Parliamentarians in the Civil War and remained a ruin until 1800, when parts were rebuilt. The earthworks are among the best preserved of their kind in Britain, and include the site of a Norman settlement. An illustrated trail leads through the castle grounds.

All year, daily. Free entry. Refreshments. Shop. P *Toilets.* ♿ *Tel Stafford (0785) 223181.*

STOKE-ON-TRENT CITY MUSEUM

Bethesda Street, Hanley, Stoke-on-Trent (Bd)

The importance of Stoke-on-Trent as the centre of English pottery making from the 17th century to the present day is appropriately the principal theme of the town's main museum. The ceramics galleries illustrate the technique of pottery making, and the history and development of Staffordshire pottery.

The museum also honours one of Staffordshire's most famous sons – Reginald Mitchell, the designer of the Spitfire. Mitchell,

who was born in Longton, became personal assistant to the managing director of the Supermarine Aviation Works in Southampton, where he rapidly progressed to become Chief Engineer. The museum's Spitfire Gallery celebrates the whole of Mitchell's brief but brilliant career.
All year, daily. Free entry. Refreshments. Shop. Toilets. ♿ *Tel Stoke-on-Trent (0782) 202173.*

TAMWORTH CASTLE

In centre of Tamworth (Cb)

This fine Norman motte-and-bailey castle, with its herringbone curtain wall, is thought to date from the 1180s. The shell-keep has a square tower set into its walls and contains Tudor and Jacobean apartments. The fine timber-framed Great Hall dates from the mid-15th century. In the Long Gallery are museum displays, including models of Tamworth's Saxon fortifications and silver pennies from the town's mint, and visitors can see an audiovisual presentation on the town and castle. Collections of period furniture can be seen in some of the rooms. Fine views may be had from the tower roof, which is open in good weather.

The 'good Lord Marmion', celebrated in Sir Walter Scott's poem, once lived at the castle. Several medieval kings visited it, and later James I stayed there three times. The keep is reputedly haunted by two female ghosts.
All year, daily exc Sun am and Fri. Adm charge. Shop. 🅿 *Toilets.* ♿ *Tel Tamworth (0827) 311222.*

TUTBURY CASTLE

On A50, 4 miles north-west of Burton upon Trent (Cc)

Mary, Queen of Scots did not like Tutbury Castle, but her views were undoubtedly coloured by the fact that she was twice imprisoned there by Elizabeth, Queen of England. Mary complained of the cold, and the lack of privacy, and the smell from the privies (one of which was under her window). But even she must have admired the view, since the castle stands on a steep, isolated rock from which vast areas of surrounding countryside can be seen. The castle was also visited several times by Mary's son James I, and by Charles I. After Charles I's departure in June 1646 the castle was besieged by Parliamentarian soldiers and largely destroyed.

The oldest parts of the castle's remains are the 12th-century chapel and 14th-century gateway. Most of the surviving parts date from the 15th century, including the South Tower, the North Tower and most of the castle wall.
Apr-Oct, daily exc Thur; Sat, pm only. Adm charge. Refreshments. Shop. 🅿 *Toilets.* ♿ *Tel Burton upon Trent (0283) 812129.*

WALL ROMAN SITE

Off A5, 2 miles south-west of Lichfield (Cb)

One of the most complete examples of a Roman town bath-house in Britain adjoins the remains of a *mansio*, or lodging house for official travellers. In Roman times Wall was the substantial settlement of Letocetum, a posting station on the main road known as Watling Street from London to Chester, where horses could be changed and accommodation found. The walls of the elaborate bath-house, which served townspeople as well as travellers, still stand to a considerable height. Many finds from excavations, including some military equipment, are in the site museum.
EH. Mar-Oct, daily; Oct-Mar, Wed-Sun. Adm charge. Shop. 🅿 *Toilets.* ♿ *(museum). Tel Shenstone (0543) 480768.*

WEDGWOOD VISITOR CENTRE

Off A34, 4 miles south of Stoke-on-Trent (Bd)

One of the fascinations of this centre is to see craftsmen at work making the Jasper ware – raised white figures on a blue background – for which Wedgwood is famous. But there is much more to see, starting with one of the six black basalt vases which Josiah Wedgwood personally made to celebrate the opening of his factory at Etruria in 1789. There is also a 'first edition' Portland Vase dated 1793.

The centre is set in 550 acres of parkland and contains a comprehensive collection of early and modern Wedgwood. A variety of skills are on display in the crafts demonstration hall, including pot-throwing, turning on the lathe, the forming and application of classical ornaments and the casting of figurines and other finely detailed ornamental pieces. There is also an art gallery.

At nearby Barlaston Hall, visitors can see many other traditional craft skills in operation in the restoration of this fine Palladian building. The 18th-century hall was built for Thomas Mills, an attorney of Leek, at the height of the rococo fashion in England and has elaborate plasterwork and decoration which is being restored to its original state.
Wedgwood Centre: All year, daily exc Sun. Adm charge. Refreshments. Shop. 🅿 *Toilets.* ♿ *Tel Stoke-on-Trent (0782) 204318. Barlaston Hall: All year, Sat and Sun. Free entry. Tel London (01) 228 3336.*

WATER AND WOODLAND *Rhododendrons dot the banks of the Temple Pool in Weston Park. The pool and nearby Temple Wood are among the beauties praised over the years by visitors – including Benjamin Disraeli.*

WESTON PARK

Off A5, 11 miles west of Cannock (Bb)

The house, built in 1671, is one of the best examples of Restoration period architecture in the country. It has been the home of the Earls of Bradford for nearly 300 years and contains Aubusson and Gobelins tapestries, and pictures by Holbein, Van Dyck, Reynolds, Stubbs and Gainsborough. The grounds combine superb landscaping by Capability Brown with a delightful variety of ornamental buildings, including a Roman Bridge and Temple of Diana designed about 1760 by James Paine. There are nature and architectural trails, and a narrow-gauge miniature railway. There is also a craft pottery, a museum of country bygones, an aquarium, a pets' corner and an adventure playground.
Apr-May, Sat, Sun and Bank Hol; June-July, daily exc Mon and Fri; July-Aug, daily; Sept, weekends only. Adm charge. Refreshments. Shop. 🅿 *Toilets.* ♿ *Tel Weston-under-Lizard (095 276) 20722.*

COUNTY CALENDAR

March (early). Lichfield: Shrovetide Fair, Pancake Race.

May (Ascension Day). Lichfield: Beating the Cathedral Bounds.

May (late). Bingley Hall, Stafford: County Show.

May (Spring Bank Hol). Lichfield: Court of Arraye and Greenhill Bower (Crowning of Bower Queen).

June (mid-month). Stoke-on-Trent: National Craft Fair.

July (early). Lichfield: Arts Festival.

September (Mon following 1st Sun after 4th Sept) Abbots Bromley: Horn Dance.

September (Sat nearest 18th). Lichfield: Dr Johnson Commemoration.

October (mid-month). Stoke-on-Trent: Beer Festival.

December 24 and 25 Uttoxeter: Mumming Play.

Tourist information: Burton upon Trent (0283) 45454; Lichfield (0543) 252109; Stafford (0785) 40204; Stoke-on-Trent (0782) 411222.

SUFFOLK

HEATHS, WOOL TOWNS AND VINEYARDS BEYOND THE STOUR

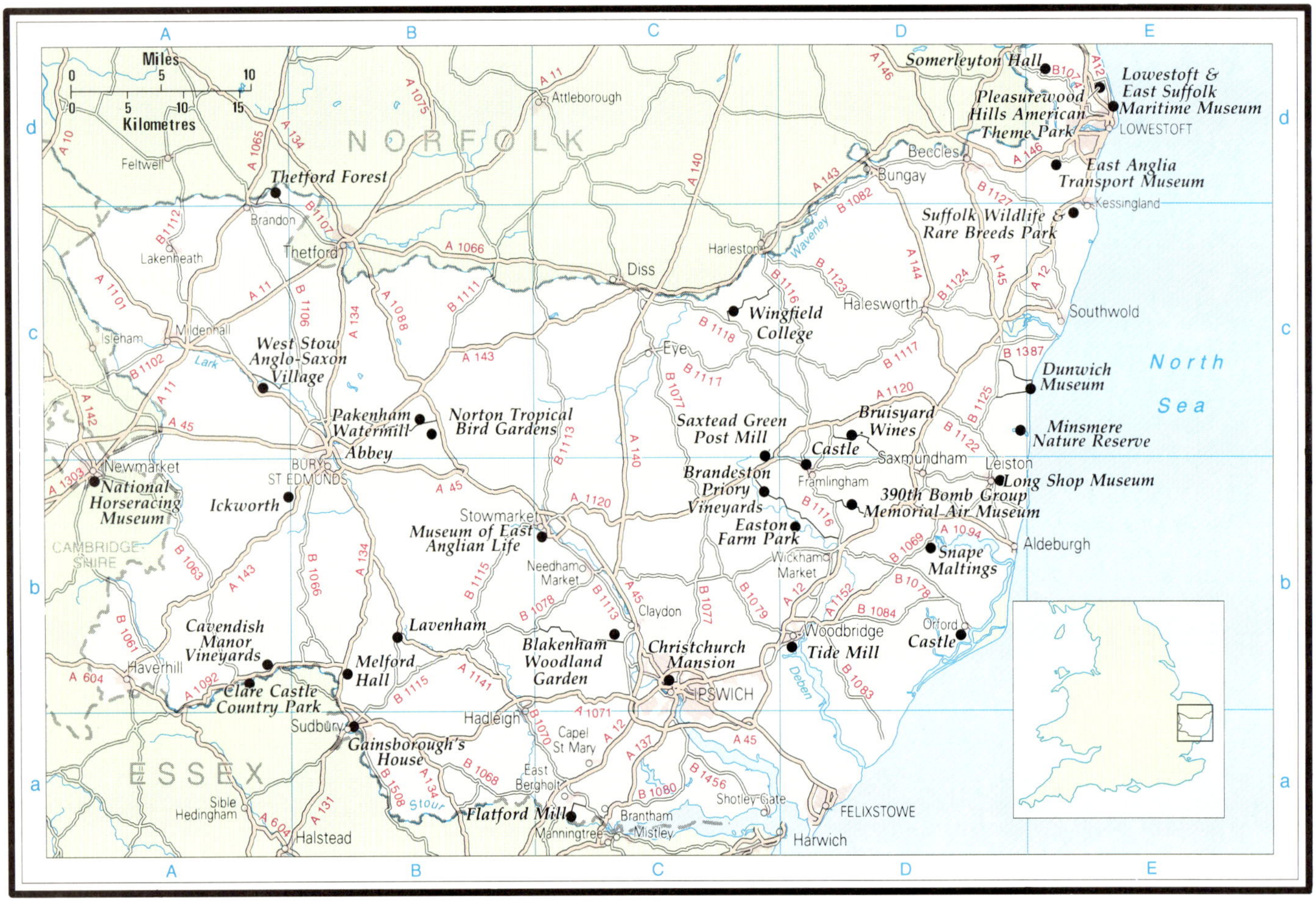

Between the River Stour in the south and the River Waveney along its northern border, Suffolk presents a patchwork of different landscapes. In the west lie sandy heathlands near the abbey town of Bury St Edmunds; and lush grasslands around Newmarket where racehorses gallop. The estuaries of the Deben and Stour cut into the county's south-east coast, and between them are the rich farmlands commemorated in the paintings of the Suffolk artists John Constable and Thomas Gainsborough. Journeys inland lead to working water mills and to busy vineyards producing light white wines. Stately buildings include Christchurch Mansion, Ickworth and Melford Hall, and there are seasoned and historic castles at Framlingham and Orford.

For birdwatchers, Minsmere Nature Reserve is a paradise, and devotees of old cars, trams and trolleybuses will make for the East Anglia Transport Museum near Lowestoft. A vivid glimpse of a more remote past is provided by the West Stow Anglo-Saxon village, built on an ancient pagan site.

BLAKENHAM WOODLAND GARDEN

Off B1113, 4 miles north-west of Ipswich (Cb)

Set at the top of a field, with grassy parking for cars, the beauties of the woodland garden are revealed the moment one steps through the gate. It was created by John Blakenham between 1950 and 1982 in the hope, according to a plaque in the rustic shelter, that visitors would derive as much pleasure from it as he had found in laying it out. It is hard to believe anyone could fail to do so.

Seen at its best in bluebell time, when the blue carpet seems in danger of swallowing up everything else, the garden has been planted with camellias, azaleas, wild roses, tulip trees and a variety of shrubs which provide a calculated contrast of colours and textures throughout the seasons yet leave an impression of charming informality.

Apr-Sept, Wed, Thur and Sun pm. Adm charge. P ♿

BRANDESTON PRIORY VINEYARDS

Off A1120, 12 miles north-east of Ipswich (Cb)

The symbol of Brandeston Priory Vineyards represents a man hanging from a gibbet, grimly commemorating the hanging in 1646 of a 90-year-old vicar of the parish by Matthew Hopkins, the Witchfinder-General who conducted a Puritan reign of terror during the Civil War. Present surroundings are less sinister. The converted 16th-century priory is surrounded by formal and informal gardens with a yew walk, scented rose garden, herbaceous borders, and the vineyards which produce a light, fruity white wine, on sale in the shop. There is a woodland walk and a wooded picnic area.

May-Oct, Mon-Fri and Bank Hol. Adm charge. Shop. P *Toilets.* ♿ *Tel Earl Soham (072 882) 462.*

BRUISYARD WINES

Off B1119, 4 miles north-west of Saxmundham (Dc)

The name of the village which is the home of Bruisyard Wines derives from a quite different fermented product: it was one of the first places in England where hops were planted for beer making, and was then known as 'Brewer's Yard'. Grapes from the 10 acre vineyard, which was planted in the mid-1970s, are processed in a winery adapted from the old milking parlour of what was once Church Farm. Wine can be tasted in the sheltered courtyard, and there is a picnic area.

Easter-Nov, daily. Adm charge. Shop. P *Toilets.* ♿ *Tel Badingham (072 875) 281.*

BURY ST EDMUNDS ABBEY

In centre of Bury St Edmunds (Bb)

The town's name and crest recall that the remains of the East Anglian King Edmund were lodged in a small monastery here after he was martyred by the Danes in AD 870. Another historic event took place on St Edmund's Day, November 20, 1214, when disaffected barons swore at the high altar of the abbey that they would force from King John a charter of rights, Magna Carta.

Today the ruins of the once vast abbey are little more than warped clumps of stone rearing up like prehistoric monsters from the abbey gardens beside the River Lark. However, two impressive entrances survive: a Norman tower complete with belfry, and the 14th-century Great Gate or Abbey Gate. The grounds encompass colourful flowerbeds, an aviary, a garden with plants chosen for their scent and a rose garden.

Beside the abbey ruins stands the new St Edmundsbury Cathedral, until 1913 the parish church of St James. A large modern extension to the cathedral was consecrated in 1970, the 1100th anniversary of St Edmund's death. Among specially designed features some of the most colourful are rows of tapestry hassocks, within whose basic design and blue background schools and local organisations from all over the county stitched individual motifs.

It was King Canute who, in penance for earlier Danish depredations, gave a charter in 1021 for the building of the original Benedictine abbey. A copy of the charter is exhibited in Moyse's Hall Museum, in Cornhill, along with other relics of the town's history. The 12th-century flint-and-rubble building on Cornhill has in its time been a synagogue, an abbey guesthouse, a tavern, wool hall, jail, police station and a Great Eastern Railway parcels office. Its collections include archaeological finds, restored barrel organs and a 'poaching corner' with some terrifying mantraps. Relics of William Corder, who murdered Maria Marten in the Red Barn at Polstead in 1827, include a book bound in his skin.

Framed on one wall is the Lord Chamberlain's licence for the first performance of *Charley's Aunt* at the Theatre Royal in Westgate Street, poorly attended on its first night but later a worldwide success. The theatre is one of the only three surviving Georgian playhouses in the country. Soon after the First World War the building was bought and used as a barrel store, but it was restored and reopened in 1965, and its graceful auditorium is usually open to visitors.

Angel Corner, on Angel Hill, is a Queen Anne house leased to the town for the display of clocks and watches bequeathed by the cellist Frederick Gershom Parkington as a memorial to his son John, killed in the Second World War. All kinds of time-keeping equipment are on show, such as table clocks, lantern clocks, longcases by Vulliamy, Tompion and others, watches and watch movements, sundials and sand glasses.

Abbey: EH. All year, daily. Free entry. Cathedral: All year, daily. Moyse's Hall; Clock Museum (NT): All year, daily exc Sun am. Free entry. Shop. P *(limited). Tel Bury St Edmunds (0284) 763233.*

CAVENDISH MANOR VINEYARDS

On A1092, 5 miles north-west of Sudbury (Ab)

Sturdily timbered Nether Hall, near Cavendish church, is one of the prosperous merchants' houses built during the 15th-century heyday of the Suffolk wool trade. The wool industry later declined, but this dignified house is now the centre of a new industry – that of wine production. Within three years of Cavendish Manor Vineyards' first planting at Nether Hall in 1972, a prizewinning white wine had been produced. Visitors can tour the house and gallery, study the production cycle in the museum, follow a vineyard trail, and taste the wines. The grounds include a collection of rural bygones and a picnic site.

Below the vineyards and the church, the road descends to a wonderful sweep of village green. The 16th-century Old Rectory, near the pond, is the home of the philanthropist Sue Ryder, and in the Sue Ryder Foundation Museum are displays showing the work done on behalf of the sick and disabled – and the work still to be done.

Vineyards: All year, daily. Adm charge. Shop. P *Toilets.* ♿ *Tel Glemsford (0787) 280221. Museum: All year, daily. Adm charge. Refreshments. Shop.* P *Toilets.* ♿ *Tel (0787) 280252.*

CHRISTCHURCH MANSION

Christchurch Park, Ipswich (Cb)

Set in extensive parkland, Christchurch Mansion was built in the 16th century and has some 40 rooms furnished in various periods, from the fine Tudor bedroom to the sumptuous 18th-century state rooms. It houses a splendid exhibition of Lowestoft china, while costumed figures lend vitality to the re-created servants' wing of the house, with its large array of cooking and domestic utensils. The Wolsey Gallery, named after the Cardinal born in the town, displays Gainsborough and Constable treasures, including the best known of Constable's studies of Willy Lott's Cottage at Flatford.

All year, daily exc Sun am. Free entry. Shop. Tel Ipswich (0473) 53246.

CLARE CASTLE COUNTRY PARK

On A1092, 7 miles north-west of Sudbury (Ab)

Outrage was expressed in 1865 when the newly arrived railway cut a gash through the old bailey of Clare Castle. Today the abandoned station platforms are themselves historic monuments, preserved so that youngsters can play trains along the springy grass surface where once the rails lay. Clare Castle Country Park has been developed around the site with picnic areas, a children's play area, and a history trail which spirals uphill to the jagged remains of the ivy-choked keep. A longer nature trail follows the bank of the River Stour, past clusters of wild flowers, wildfowl ponds and a butterfly garden.

The nearby Clare Priory dates back to the 13th century, when Augustinian friars were established here in their first English priory by Richard de Clare, one of Henry III's most powerful barons. At the Dissolution most of the buildings were converted to domestic use or served as farm outhouses. One barn became the hall of a boys' school during the 19th century, but in 1953 friars returned and began to restore the hall as a church, and salvaged much of the prior's house, cloisters and refectory ruins.

The Ancient House in Clare High Street, traditionally known as the Priest's House,

OLD AND ORNATE *The Ancient House in Clare, which stands beside the churchyard, is noted for its elaborate 17th-century pargeting, or ornamental plasterwork. The house bears the date 1473 on the west gable.*

contains a museum of local archaeological finds.
Country Park: All year, daily. Free entry. Shop. P *Toilets.* ♿ *Tel Clare (0787) 277491. Priory: All year, daily. Free entry. Shop.* P *Tel (0787) 277326. Ancient House: Easter-Sept, Wed-Sun and Bank Hol pm; also Sun am. Adm charge. Shop.* P ♿ *Tel (0787) 277865.*

DUNWICH MUSEUM

Off B1125, 5 miles south of Southwold (Ec)

Little remains of the once proud port of Dunwich, in Norman times a town of 5000 inhabitants, for its harbour, markets and churches were swallowed up by the sea many stormy centuries ago. The museum in the tiny fragment of village remaining chronicles the history of the place since Roman times, and has several other exhibits concerning local wildlife and habitats.
Mar-Oct, Sat and Sun pm; also Tues and Thur pm May-Sept and pm daily in Aug. Free entry. Shop. P *Tel Westleton (072 873) 358.*

EAST ANGLIA TRANSPORT MUSEUM

On A146, 3 miles south-west of Lowestoft (Ed)

Enthusiastic volunteers have spent some years laying out a period street scene complete with old tram-stop signs and other street furniture, to which it is hoped in due course to add authentic houses and shops from bygone days, rescued like the vehicles from many parts of the country. The visitor can see transport equipment, old cars and commercial vehicles, some of them battery-powered, as well as trams and trolleybuses.
Easter; May-Sept, Sun and Bank Hol; also Sat June-Sept and daily in Aug. Adm charge. Refreshments. Shop. P *Toilets.* ♿ *Tel Lowestoft (0502) 69399.*

EASTON FARM PARK

Off B1116, 5½ miles north of Woodbridge (Db)

Set by the quiet upper reaches of the River Deben, the buildings are those of a model farm built by the Duke of Hamilton about 1870. Although still a working farm, it has been adapted to present a picture of farming methods past and present, enabling visitors to compare modern milking methods with the earlier world of the cool, charming Victorian dairy. There are working animals, tame nanny goats and ponies, and an aviary with rare breeds of poultry, ornamental pheasants and peacocks. There is also a collection of country bygones.
Easter-Oct, daily. Adm charge. Refreshments. Shop. P *Toilets.* ♿ *Tel Wickham Market (0728) 746475.*

FLATFORD MILL

Off B1070, 12½ miles south of Ipswich (Ca)

Although Flatford Mill and Willy Lott's Cottage, so often painted by John Constable, form part of a Field Studies Centre and are not open to the public, the buildings can be clearly seen from the outside, looking their best from the towpath on the opposite bank of the River Stour. Visitors are welcome at Bridge Cottage, grandly re-thatched and housing an exhibition of 'John Constable at Flatford', and at the adjoining National Trust information office and shop; there is also a tea-room on the river bank. Boats can be hired nearby, and there are weekend river trips.

NO PLACE LIKE IT *Willy Lott's Cottage beside the River Stour at Flatford was named after a farmer who was born there and lived to the age of 88 without spending more than four days away from his home.*

Along the lane stands the Granary Museum, with a collection of farming implements from Constable's time, old cycles and photographs and a number of mezzotints of the painter's work.
Bridge Cottage: NT. Apr-Nov, Wed-Sun; June-Aug, daily. Free entry. Refreshments. Shop. P *Toilets.* ♿ *Tel Colchester (0206) 298260. Museum: Easter-Nov, daily. Adm charge. Tel (0206) 298111.*

FRAMLINGHAM CASTLE

On B1119, 7 miles west of Saxmundham (Db)

Winding roads converge on Framlingham across the undulating Suffolk farmlands; and from each of them there is a glimpse of the high walls and towers and Tudor chimneys of Framlingham Castle. At closer quarters can be seen the dry ditch and outer moat, and the complexity of the towers, 13 in all. Inside the shell of the bailey a narrow, dizzying walk high up behind the parapets gives views over the sparkling little town and meadows.

The first simple palisaded castle was built around 1100 by one of the Bigod family. During centuries of disputes between lords and kings the castle changed hands many times; its most celebrated owner was Mary Tudor, who rallied her supporters there when the threat arose of Lady Jane Grey being put on the throne of England. During Elizabeth I's reign the castle was used as a prison for dissenting priests. In the 17th century it was bequeathed to Pembroke Hall, Cambridge, who converted the hall into a poorhouse and pulled down most of the internal buildings.

The outlines of what remains today are those of an outer court or bailey, an inner court, and a lower court on the western side with a prison tower. The poorhouse on the site of Roger Bigod's great hall, used during the 19th and early 20th centuries as a county court and drill hall, is a patchwork of different architectural periods. A museum within the castle has a display of historical photographs, paintings, and other memorabilia of the everyday life in Framlingham.
Castle: EH. All year, daily. Adm charge. Shop. P *Toilets.* ♿ *Tel Framlingham (0728) 723330. Museum: Easter-Sept, daily exc Sun am and Fri. Adm charge.* P *Tel (0728) 723330.*

GAINSBOROUGH'S HOUSE

In centre of Sudbury (Ba)

The 18th-century painter Thomas Gainsborough was born in this house and lived here until he went to study in London, returning with his young wife to work for a time as a local portrait painter. The house contains more works by Gainsborough than any other gallery, along with contemporary furniture, china and personal relics. The lower bow room galleries are devoted to varying exhibitions, and modern sculpture is often displayed in the secluded garden at the back, from which one can see the characteristic weavers' windows on the upper floor. Gainsborough's cloth-merchant father used the premises as a family home and a weaving business.
All year, Tues-Sat; also Sun and Bank Hol pm. Adm charge. Shop. P *Toilets. Tel Sudbury (0787) 72958.*

ICKWORTH

Off A143, 3 miles south-east of Bury St Edmunds (Ab)

Huge as it is, the mansion is hidden by tall trees until a curve in the drive suddenly reveals the great oval rotunda and splayed wings of one of the most grandiose extravagances of late 18th-century self-indulgence. The Hervey family had by then owned the estate for some 300 years, but it was not until the arrival on the scene of Frederick Augustus, Bishop of Derry and 4th Earl of Bristol, that the rich incomes of his many estates were channelled into the creation of this combination of home and art gallery.

The 4th earl was an ardent collector, spending lavishly during tours of Europe. Seeking a worthy setting for his accumulation of art treasures, he commissioned the building of a rotunda which was to be his home, with two curving wings to hold his acquisitions. When Frederick Augustus died in 1803 the interior of the rotunda was no more than an empty shell, and most of the treasures he had planned to house in the wings had been captured in Rome during Napoleon's 1798 campaign. His son adapted the east wing as living quarters and displayed the remaining items of the collection in the rotunda. The contents today include Regency and 18th-century French porcelain, silver and paintings exhibited in sumptuous state rooms.

Inviting features of the grounds are a formal garden, walled garden, and the Albana Walk through woodlands later named after Elizabeth Albana, whom the 5th earl married in 1826.

NT. May-Sept, pm daily exc Mon and Thur; Apr and Oct, weekend and Bank Hol pm. Adm charge. Refreshments. Shop. 🅿 *Toilets.* ♿ *Tel Horringer (028 488) 270.*

LONG SHOP MUSEUM

On B1119, in Leiston (Db)

The Garrett family business in late 18th-century Leiston developed from simple beginnings in a local forge to the manufacture of ploughs, threshers and cast-iron work, and then exploited the new market for steam-powered units in factories, mills and farms. Richard Garrett III visited the United States to study mass production, and returned with the idea of building his own assembly hall. Known as the Long Shop (or locally as 'the cathedral'), this helped to expand construction of road rollers, steam tractors and steam engines. During the Second World War the firm made shell lathes, gun mountings, and sections of the Mulberry harbour, used in the Normandy landings.

The works closed in 1980 but the Long Shop has been restored as an industrial museum, its huge timber columns supporting galleries from which assemblies and machine parts were once fed onto engines moving down the centre aisles. Among historic Garrett manufactures preserved on the site are road haulage tractors and rollers, an 1846 fire engine, a trolley bus, a thresher and seed drills.

Apr-Sept, daily. Adm charge. Shop. 🅿 *Toilets.* ♿ *Tel Leiston (0728) 832189.*

IN THE ROUND *The spacious rotunda at Ickworth contains the mansion's drawing room, dining room, library and entrance hall. The decorations of the Pompeian Room (below) are based on ancient wall paintings found at the Villa Negroni in Rome.*

LOWESTOFT AND EAST SUFFOLK MARITIME MUSEUM

Sparrow's Nest Park, Lowestoft (Ed)

The long seafaring tradition of Lowestoft, perched beside the tumultuous North Sea on the easternmost tip of the British Isles, can hardly be forgotten in streets and alleys whispering or howling with the salt-tanged wind. In Sparrow's Nest Park the flinty building of the Lowestoft and East Suffolk Maritime Museum houses exhibits of different aspects and different generations of trawling, drift net fishing, lifesaving and boat-building. The large collection of ship models includes sailing drifters and a herring lugger, accompanied by historical photographs and marine paintings.

During both World Wars the park served as headquarters of the Royal Naval Patrol Service, which now has its own museum with ship models, uniforms, naval documents and photographs. In Belle Vue Park above it is the monument erected by the Imperial War Graves Commission to men of the RN Patrol Service who have 'no grave but the sea'. Lowestoft Archaeological and Local History Society's Museum includes a collection of Lowestoft china, fossils, flints, and medieval finds from local sites.

Maritime Museum: May-Sept, daily. Adm charge. Shop. 🅿 ♿ *Tel Lowestoft (0502) 61963. RN Patrol Service Museum: May-Oct, daily. Free entry. Refreshments. Shop.* 🅿 *Toilets.* ♿ *Tel (0502) 86250. Lowestoft Museum: May-Sept, daily. Adm charge. Shop. Toilets.* ♿ *Tel (0502) 511457.*

MELFORD HALL

On A134, 3 miles north of Sudbury (Bb)

Red-brick turrets rise above the high wall of Melford Hall, built in the 16th century around what had been a hunting lodge for the wealthy abbots of Bury St Edmunds. Its creator was William Cordell, a cunning lawyer who became Master of the Rolls and contrived to keep well in with Henry VIII and both his daughters. The property eventually became the home of the Parker family, three of whom distinguished themselves as admirals. Their descendants still live in the house.

Rooms of various periods include the original banqueting hall, a Regency library and a Victorian bedroom. Among the items on display are a collection of Chinese porcelain captured from a Spanish ship in 1762, period furniture, fine panelling, and family and maritime paintings. One room features paintings by Beatrix Potter, who was a cousin of the present baronet's grand-

LAVENHAM, MEDIEVAL WOOL TOWN

Timber and plaster buildings, which have been preserved since the Middle Ages, are a feature of East Anglian towns. Lavenham has perhaps the richest legacy, with more than 300 buildings listed as being of architectural and historical interest, but Kersey, Thaxted and Saffron Walden also have their gems. Wealth from the medieval woollen cloth-making industry built the splendid houses and reared the proud churches – such as the almost cathedral-size church in Lavenham whose 141ft tower dominates the town. In Henry VIII's reign, 33 separate broadcloth businesses flourished in the town, and a tax assessment of 1524 shows it to have been the 14th richest town in England.

Priory: Apr-Oct, daily; Nov, Dec, Mar, Sat-Mon. Adm charge. Refreshments. Shop. P *Toilets. Tel Lavenham (0787) 247417. Church: All year, daily. Shop.* P *Tel (0787) 247244. Guildhall: NT. Early Apr-Oct, daily. Adm charge. Refreshments. Shop. Toilets.* ♿ *Tel (0787) 247646. Little Hall: Easter Sat-mid Oct, Sat, Sun and Bank Hol Mon pm. Adm charge. Shop.* P *Tel (0787) 247179.*

THE PRIORY *This basically 13th-century house never was a priory, although Benedictine monks did live there until the Dissolution of the Monasteries by Henry VIII in 1536. Later it was occupied by a wool merchant and by rectors of Lavenham. The pargeting, or raised ornamental plasterwork, is the finest in the town.*

TOWERING TRIBUTE *The medieval Church of St Peter and St Paul was built largely out of funds provided by local clothiers. Among them was Thomas Spring, who is buried in the church and whose coat of arms appears 32 times on the tower. Inside is a rare 14th-century rood screen and some finely carved choir stalls with misericords.*

CLOTHIER'S LEGACY *Lavenham's Guildhall was built in 1529 as the meeting place of a guild of clothiers, founded to maintain the standards of the craft. When the industry was ousted by imported worsteds, the building was in turn a jail, a workhouse and almshouses. It is now a museum of crafts and local history.*

OAK IS FOREVER *Assembled by medieval craftsmen and cemented by time, Lavenham's timber-framed and plaster-walled buildings seem as permanent as the Pyramids. Show and function were balanced in their design. Fine carving adorns the door of the house in Barn Street (left), and the capitals of 10-11 Lady Street (above). The arch at the lower end of this building is actually a Tudor shopfront, whose customers would have been grateful for the shelter of the overhanging upper storey.*

A HALL RESTORED *The timber-framed home of a family of medieval clothiers and farmers, Little Hall was restored in the 1930s. It had originally a high hall, occupying the central part of the house, warmed by a central hearth, and a solar or bedroom over the parlour, or family room, now the library. An upper floor was added in the 16th century over what is now the dining room, to store cloth. In the Second World War evacuees slept there, and painted their names on the chest of drawers.*

mother and who frequently stayed at the hall.

Across the main road lies the broad slope of Long Melford's village green, culminating in the magnificent spread of Holy Trinity Church, itself awesomely long. Its dazzling exterior has some of the richest flushwork in Suffolk, a county specialising in these intricate patterns of knapped flint and freestone. Many Roman remains have been found beside Melford's main street, and it is believed that the original church was set on the site of a Roman temple; but no Roman columns could ever have been as graceful as the pillars and arches of the bright interior, flooded with light from the elegant clerestory windows.

The Clopton family were the principal founders and benefactors of the church. Beside their chapel is the Kentwell Aisle, so called after their family home, Kentwell Hall, which can be seen from the churchyard through the trees. A splendid lime avenue provides a noble approach to the moated Tudor mansion with its extensive lawns and gardens.

Melford Hall: NT. Apr-Sept, Wed, Thur, Sat, Sun and Bank Hol Mon, pm. Adm charge. P *Toilets.* ♿ *Tel Sudbury (0787) 70000. Kentwell Hall: Good Fri, then mid Apr-mid June, Thur and Sun, pm; mid July-Sept, pm daily exc Mon and Tues; Bank Hol. Refreshments. Shop.* P *Toilets.* ♿ *(parts). Tel (0787) 310207.*

MINSMERE NATURE RESERVE

Off B1125, just south-west of Dunwich (Dc)

One of Britain's major bird reserves, Minsmere has a variety of habitats – including shingle seashore, sand dunes, freshwater reedmarsh, lagoons, mixed woodland and heath. These provide nesting places for more than 100 species of birds. The breeding birds include avocets, bitterns, marsh harriers, nightjars and nightingales. Among regular visitors to Minsmere are purple herons, spoonbills, spotted redshanks and many other waders.

There are several nature trails through the reserve, as well as hides overlooking the marsh. A good parking place is at Dunwich Heath, which has a small information centre and shop.

RSPB. All year, daily exc Tues. Adm charge. Shop. P *Toilets.* ♿ *Tel (072 873) 281. Heath: All year, daily.*

MUSEUM OF EAST ANGLIAN LIFE

In centre of Stowmarket (Cb)

The 70 acre estate of Abbot's Hall between Stowmarket's modern shopping precinct and the banks of the little River Rattlesden has been developed over the years as a repository for East Anglian agricultural, industrial and domestic items which might otherwise have been lost forever. When there was a danger of Alton water mill near Ipswich being drowned under a new reservoir, it was shifted piece by piece and carefully reconstructed on this site. In 1986 a large exhibition building was fashioned from the Robert Boby engineering workshop transported from Bury St Edmunds. It now contains craft workshops demonstrating the skills of wheelwright, rake maker, basket maker, cooper, harness maker and printer, as well as a steam traction engine and models of steam engines.

There are exhibitions connected with gypsies, travelling showmen, poachers and gamekeepers, and with the domestic life of the region, including room settings of different periods. Horse-drawn rides are provided in a vehicle drawn by a Suffolk Punch, the heavy horse of the region. At least one of the five steam engines on site is in steam on the first Sunday in each month of the season.

Mar-Nov, daily. Adm charge. Refreshments. Shop. P *Toilets.* ♿ *Tel Stowmarket (0449) 612229.*

NATIONAL HORSERACING MUSEUM

In centre of Newmarket (Ab)

All roads approaching Newmarket present the hazard of strings of horses waiting to cross the road from stud or riding school to grassy gallops, and views of horses trotting or galloping across the glowing green countryside. The entire town and its surroundings are virtually dedicated to horseracing. In 1983 the Queen opened a more formal museum in an elegant Regency building in the High Street. Its collections include mementos of famous mounts, owners, jockeys and patrons, including the skeleton of the great racehorse Eclipse. There are paintings by Stubbs and Munnings, and delightful bronzes by John Skeaping.

The galleries of the museum tell the whole story of racing at Newmarket. It ranges from the days when Richard II rode on the Heath against the Earl of Arundel, through the period of James I, Charles I and Charles II, who lodged Nell Gwyn in the town and whose amorous exploits earned him the name of 'Old Rowley' after a stallion of that name; the main racecourse at Newmarket is still called The Rowley Mile. The story concludes with an account of the Jockey Club next door, and the foundation of an Equine Research Station and the National Stud. A video programme shows Shergar, Red Rum and other horses in many famous races.

Mar-Dec, daily exc Mon. Adm charge. Refreshments. Shop. P *Toilets.* ♿ *Tel Newmarket (0638) 667333.*

NORTON TROPICAL BIRD GARDENS

On A1088, 7 miles east of Bury St Edmunds (Bc)

The gardens combine an abundance of plants and trees with well-spaced aviaries and enclosures of mainly tropical birds. Peacocks strut and display; flamingos paddle delicately through their pool; there are cranes and a colourful collection of waterfowl; and as well as the squawks of parrots there are frequent comments from mocking, mimicking myna birds. Spring offers an array of flowering bulbs, and in summer the air is heavy with the scent of some 500 rose bushes.

All year, daily. Adm charge. Refreshments. Shop. P *Toilets.* ♿ *Tel Pakenham (0359) 30957.*

ORFORD CASTLE

On B1084, in Orford (Db)

The three-storeyed keep on its grassy mound is all that remains of a fortress set up by Henry II to watch over the sea approaches to the then flourishing port of Orford and also to uphold royal authority over the surrounding lands. It remained an important royal stronghold for two centuries, seized by the French after King John's death and changing hands several times during baronial upheavals.

The stone walls of the bailey disappeared long ago, but their outlines can be traced in the undulating earthworks about the keep. The tower itself is cylindrical inside but polygonal outside, with three rectangular turrets commanding every possible angle over its surroundings. Its main material is a local clayey limestone called septaria, the large blocks of which have been seriously eroded over the centuries. Caen stone was imported for the plinth and battlements. Inside there are spacious halls on two floors above the basement, and a fine spiral staircase in the southern turret.

In Front Street, the craft shop houses the Dunwich Underwater Exploration Exhibition, showing the results of recent explorations by divers of the ruins of old Dunwich on the seabed, with details of structures located and artefacts recovered from the depths.

Castle: EH. All year, daily. Adm charge. Shop. P *Tel Orford (0394) 450472. Exhibition: All year, daily. Adm charge. Refreshments. Shop.* P *Toilets. Tel (0394) 450678.*

PAKENHAM WATER MILL

Off A143, 6 miles north-east of Bury St Edmunds (Bc)

Pakenham can be proud of retaining two working mills, both grinding corn in traditional style – a lofty, finely preserved tower windmill, and a water mill restored by the Suffolk Preservation Society. The Domesday survey recorded a water mill on this site in 1086 and there seems to have been an unbroken history of milling here: excavations of the foundations in recent years exposed remnants of a Tudor mill which was replaced by the present building late in the 18th century. This worked until 1974, but was in danger of dereliction until restoration work began in 1978.

Water to turn the wheel comes from a small tributary of the Black Bourn, channelled to provide a 10ft drop. The water wheel was originally wooden, but around 1900 it was replaced by a large new iron wheel. With increasing demand for white flour, a midget roller mill was introduced, driven by an auxiliary oil engine; but current taste has reverted to stone-ground wholemeal flour, and Pakenham water mill is again working at its old product.

Easter; May-Sept, Wed, Sat, Sun and Bank Hol. Adm charge. Refreshments. Shop. P *Toilets.* ♿ *Tel Lavenham (0787) 247179.*

PLEASUREWOOD HILLS AMERICAN THEME PARK

Off A12, 2 miles north of Lowestoft (Ed)

Set in parkland within easy reach of Corton Cliffs and the sandy shore, the park offers more than 50 rides and other attractions, nearly all included in the entrance fee. There is a roller-coaster, a boating lake, crazy golf, a pirate ship and model fairground, as well as music-hall performances and sea-lion shows. Picnic sites and free use of barbecues are provided, and there are play areas

for younger children. Wide views of the whole area are offered from the miniature railway and Western-style train, and from the higher vantage point of a chairlift.
Apr, Sat, Sun, Bank Hol; May-Sept, daily. Adm charge. Refreshments. Shop. P *Toilets.* ♿ *Tel Lowestoft (0502) 513626.*

SAXTEAD GREEN POST MILL

Off A1120, 2½ miles north-west of Framlingham (Cc)

One of the finest surviving post mills in England stands on an ideally exposed site where there is known to have been a windmill as early as the late 13th century. Records show that the present mill was working in 1796, and was rebuilt in 1854. It went on producing flour until the end of its commercial life in 1947 – though after the First World War it was used mostly for grinding animal foodstuff.

The post mill is so called because the whole body or 'buck' containing the machinery and carrying the sails revolves around a central post, kept facing into the wind by fantails, or wind vanes fixed at right angles to the main sails.
EH. Apr-Sept, daily exc Sun. Adm charge. Tel Framlingham (0728) 82346.

SNAPE MALTINGS

Off B1069, 4 miles south-east of Saxmundham (Db)

The concert hall built in Garretts' old maltings beside the River Alde became in 1967 the main venue for performances in the annual Aldeburgh Festival established by the late Benjamin Britten and Peter Pears. Around it have grown up a number of workshops and galleries, including craft shops, wholefood, farm and garden shops, a piano repair shop, and tearooms. The subjects of craft courses and activity holidays include printing, painting, embroidery, quilting and wildlife studies. A walk towards Iken cliff gives the chance to see avocets and other birds.
Shops and Galleries: All year, daily. P *Tel Snape (072 888) 303.*

SOMERLEYTON HALL

Off B1074, 4 miles north-west of Lowestoft (Ed)

The original Elizabethan hall was rebuilt in the middle of the 19th century by the railway contractor Sir Morton Peto. One of the treasures of the house is a large Flemish tapestry. The range of glasshouses was designed by Sir Joseph Paxton, architect of the Crystal Palace. The clock in the tower of the stable block was originally intended for the Houses of Parliament, but it proved too elaborate and had to give way to the present world- famous clock, whereupon Morton Peto acquired it for himself.

The gardens, which cover 12 acres, are more than three centuries old and have many ancient trees. There is a maze, a garden trail, a rose walk, and a lime avenue. A miniature railway runs for a quarter of a mile through the grounds.
Hall, Gardens and Maze: Easter-late May, Thur, Sun and Bank Hol, pm only; late May-late Sept, Sun, Tues-Fri and Bank Hol, pm only. Adm charge. Refreshments. Shop. P *Toilets.* ♿ *Tel Lowestoft (0502) 730224.*

SUFFOLK WILDLIFE AND RARE BREEDS PARK

On A12, at Kessingland (Ec)

Rare and endangered species of cattle, sheep, pigs and poultry are a major concern of this animal collection – but at the same time the familiar attractions of lynx, leopard, lion, tiger and Barbary ape are not forgotten. A children's pet corner allows visitors to stroll among tame animals in natural surroundings, and touch them. A startling contrast is provided between miniature horses from Argentina and a giant Shire mare. Among other unusual animals are miniature cows less than 3ft high, and tailless Manx Rumpie chickens. A lake set in the 70 acres of parkland displays waterfowl, including varieties of swans and geese.

The Suffolk Miniature Light Railway runs for almost 1½ miles through the grounds. Its four steam engines and two diesels operate regular trips in summer.
Park: Easter-Oct, daily. Adm charge. Refreshments. Shop. P *Toilets.* ♿ *Tel Lowestoft (0502) 740291. Railway: May-Sept, daily exc Sat in May and June.*

THETFORD FOREST

Off B1107, 2 miles east of Brandon (Ad)

Although a large part of Thetford Forest lies in Norfolk, the Forestry Commission district office and information centre lies just within Suffolk, at Santon Downham. From the centre the Commission has laid out a 2 mile forest trail, with seats at intervals. The route begins in broadleaved woodland planted in 1880, then skips several decades to enter the 1969 Jubilee Plantation of Corsican pine and oak planted by schoolchildren, parish councils and members of the United States Air Force from neighbouring airfields, to commemorate the jubilee of the Forestry Commission's birth.

One of the most appealing parts of the trail is the lime avenue which accompanies the road leading out towards Thetford. The original trees were planted in 1880, but about 90 of them are felled and new trees planted every ten years to maintain the avenue in its radiant condition. There is also a 3½ mile bird trail along which woodlarks and nightingales, among other species, may be seen and heard.
FC. Centre: All year, Mon-Fri. Free entry. Shop. P *Toilets. Tel Thetford (0842) 810271. Forest trails: All year, daily.*

390TH BOMB GROUP MEMORIAL AIR MUSEUM

Off B1116, 5 miles south-east of Framlingham (Db)

In May 1981 the restored control tower of the Second World War United States Air Force airfield outside the village of Parham was dedicated as a museum 'in grateful tribute to the Allied airmen who, in valour, gave their lives to the victory that made real the challenge for world peace and unity'. The American 390th Bomb Group (Heavy) was based here from July 1943 to August 1945, during which time it flew more than 300 operations and lost 176 aircraft.

Among the exhibits on the two floors of the tower are engines and other material recovered from crashed planes such as Flying Fortresses, Liberators and fighter escorts. Some of the fragments lay buried deep underground until as late as the mid-1970s, when they were uncovered by aviation enthusiasts on organised digs.
Mar-Oct, Sun and Bank Hol pm. Free entry. Shop. P *Toilets.* ♿ *Tel Felixstowe (0394) 70203.*

WEST STOW ANGLO-SAXON VILLAGE

Off A1101, 5 miles north-west of Bury St Edmunds (Ac)

During excavations of a low hill beside the River Lark at West Stow the footings of some 80 Anglo-Saxon houses were found, together with personal and domestic items such as bone combs, bronze brooches and dress fasteners, weaving pins, pottery fragments and animal bones. From the evidence available it has been possible to

AS GOOD AS OLD *The Anglo-Saxon village of West Stow has been reconstructed from the remains of the original buildings. The houses were rebuilt using the tools and techniques available to Anglo-Saxon farmers.*

FIRST AND LAST *The late 18th-century Tide Mill at Woodbridge was the first such mill to be built in England and the last to cease turning – almost 200 years later. It was saved from rust and decay in 1968, and today is once again in good working order. Originally the mill operated for two hours on either side of low tide, so the miller found himself working irregular hours.*

reconstruct a group of thatched wooden houses and a communal hall, using only the tools and techniques which the Anglo-Saxons would have known. The village is at the centre of the 125 acre West Stow Country Park, where footpaths wind round a lake frequented by migrant birds, through woodland and over the sandy Breckland heath. A nature trail draws attention to plants, animals and birds to be seen.

Village: Apr-Oct, pm daily exc Mon; also Sun and Bank Hol am. Adm charge. Shop. P *Toilets.* ♿ *Tel Culford (028 484) 718. Park: All year, daily.*

WINGFIELD COLLEGE

Off B1118, 7 miles east of Diss (Cc)

The addition during the late 18th century of a new façade and false interior walls and ceilings disguised for many years the existence of an early 14th-century timber-framed great hall and the chambers and dormitories of the original chantry college. Rediscovery of the true nature of the building had to wait until 1971, when the present owner uncovered the basic fabric. Now the rooms provide a setting for collections of prints and textiles and for concerts and recitals. The grounds include a moat garden and a topiary garden. The collegiate church has a mounting-block before it, and inside is kept a parson's shelter used when conducting funeral services in bad weather. From the village's wide green, Wingfield Castle (not open to the public) presents a romantic sight, with its 14th-century gatehouse, turrets and stone frontage joined to a colourful Tudor wing, all reflected in the broad moat.

Easter-Sept, Sat, Sun and Bank Hol Mon pm. Adm charge. Refreshments. P *Toilets. Tel Stradbroke (037 948) 505.*

WOODBRIDGE TIDE MILL

On Deben estuary at Woodbridge (Db)

Seen from the train, from the road skirting the Deben estuary, or from the deck of a boat in the estuary itself, one of the most conspicuous landmarks is the quayside tide mill.

A mill operated not by the action of river water but by tidal power has been recorded at Woodbridge since the 12th century. The present mill was built around 1793; it operates for two hours on either side of low tide, so the miller found himself working irregular hours. The mill continued working until 1957, though latterly it was driven by a diesel engine. Neglected for years, it has now been restored and the machinery operates at certain times, driven by water from a millpond filled by the tide. Inside, drawings and photographs explain the history and processes of the mill. Windows high up command views over the River Deben, the yacht harbour which now occupies what was once the millpond, and the mysterious heathland towards Sutton Hoo.

Woodbridge Museum, on Market Hill, houses collections of local interest, including mementos of famous inhabitants such as Edward Fitzgerald, translator of the *Rubáiyát of Omar Khayyám*. One room is devoted to the story of the excavations at Sutton Hoo, with a scale model of the famous Anglo-Saxon burial ship and details of recent excavations and theories.

Buttrums Mill, standing a little way back from Burkitt Road, is a six-storey red-brick tower mill built in 1835 which worked until about 1928. Suffolk County Council has restored it with four fully shuttered sails, a fantail, and all the machinery intact. It can be visited by appointment through Ipswich council offices.

Tide Mill: July-Sept, daily; also certain other days in summer. Adm charge. Tel Woodbridge (039 43) 2548. Museum: Easter-Oct, Thur-Sat and Bank Hol; also Sun pm. Adm charge. Shop. ♿ *Tel (039 43) 3599.*

COUNTY CALENDAR

May (early). Bury St Edmunds: South Suffolk Show.

May (late). Ipswich: Suffolk Show.

June (2nd and 3rd weeks). Aldeburgh: Festival.

June (mid-month). Ipswich: East Coast Boat Show.

July (mid-month). Ipswich: Flower Show.

July (late). Beccles: Regatta.

October (1st Sun). Bury St Edmunds: Harvest Festival.

Tourist information: Aldeburgh (072 885) 3637; Bury St Edmunds (0284) 64667; Ipswich (0473) 58070; Lowestoft (0502) 65989; Sudbury (0787) 72092.

SURREY

HILLS, HEATHS AND GREAT HOUSES BEYOND LONDON'S FRINGE

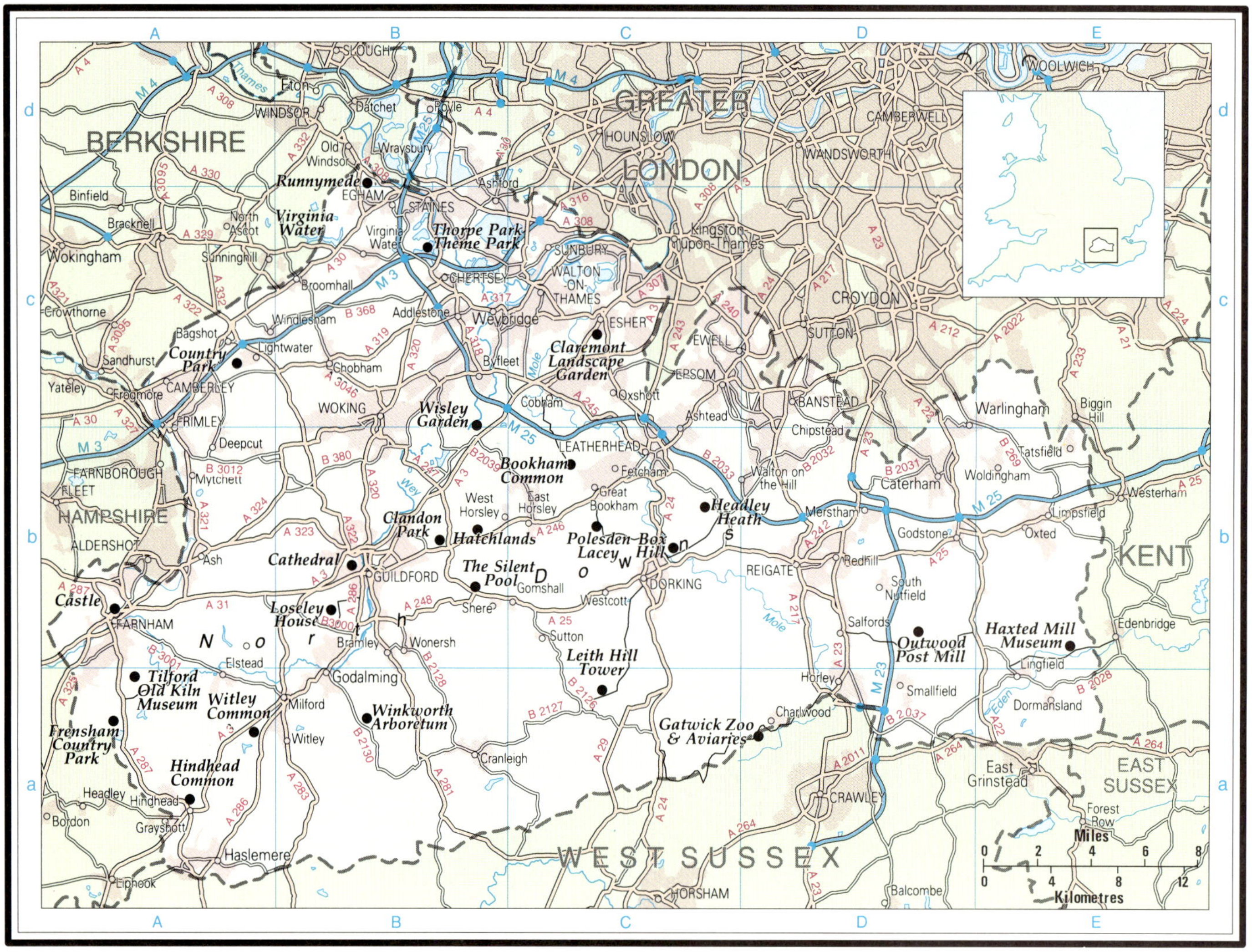

Wooded hills sweeping across north Surrey climb to spectacular viewpoints at Box Hill, a popular picnic spot for three centuries, and Leith Hill, the highest point in South-east England, with a panorama that extends from St Paul's Cathedral to the South Downs. To Surrey belongs the south bank of the River Thames around historic Runnymede, while the tributary River Wey flows gently through Guildford, a county town whose well-preserved old houses complement a fine modern cathedral.

Stately homes built by the earliest aristocratic 'commuters' in countryside so temptingly close to London include the Tudor Loseley House and the classically styled Clandon Park and Hatchlands. To traditional open-air forms of recreation by lakesides, on heaths and in famous gardens, Thorpe Park adds a whole new range of modern entertainments in a single 500 acre theme park.

BOOKHAM COMMON

Off A245, 2½ miles west of Leatherhead (Cb)

Footpaths and bridleways crisscross the common, which covers almost a square mile and is a mixture of grassland, scrub, woods, ponds and streams. Some 500 species of wild flowers have been recorded, and the woodlands teem with bird life. The ponds and streams sometimes attract kingfishers, herons and wagtails. Small mammals such as voles, mice and shrews are preyed upon by weasels and stoats.
NT. All year, daily.

BOX HILL

Off A24, 1 mile north-east of Dorking (Cb)

Above the valley cut through the North Downs by the River Mole stands Box Hill, a dramatic escarpment rising 400ft from the river. The box trees that give the hill its name have grown there for centuries, though it is the magnificent beechwoods that are the hill's crowning glory today. They climb the steep cliff, part of which is known as 'The Whites' from the patches of chalk showing through the trees, to the plateau which is cut by steep-sided valleys.

The Zig-Zag Road winds Alpine-fashion between grassy slopes to the top, views becoming more and more spectacular. The main viewpoint at the top looks down on the town of Dorking, and beyond it across the Weald to the South Downs with, on a clear day, the coronet of trees on Chanctonbury Ring. The North Downs Way long-distance path climbs to this summit viewpoint after crossing the River Mole by steppingstones. To the west there is another wide and impressive view across the Mole Valley to Ranmore Common.

But there is more to Box Hill than just the views. There are the woods, where roe deer may be seen in the evening or early morning, or a fox crossing a footpath, and among the bird life are woodpeckers, owls, jays and magpies. There are also buildings on the hill, some of them oddities and some with an interesting history, such as the Swiss Cottage where the television pioneer John

Logie Baird conducted some of his early experiments. Among the oddities is a fort, built in the 1880s as part of a defence network for London against a fear of invasion by the French; derelict for years, it is now being restored. A former tool store now houses a National Trust Information Centre.

Nearby is the gravestone of Major Peter Labellière, who died in 1880 and asked to be buried on Box Hill – upside down. He regarded the world as topsy turvy, and considered he would one day be right way up. The simple stone may not actually mark his burial spot, as it is said his body was later removed and reburied elsewhere – though which way up is not known.

Like all the best hills, Box Hill has its folly. It stands above Zig-Zag Valley: a round flint tower built in 1814 by Thomas Broadwood, a member of the piano-making family, and known as Broadwood's Folly.

NT. All year, daily. Free entry. Refreshments. Shop. P *Toilets. Tel Dorking (0306) 885502.*

CLANDON PARK

On A247, 3 miles east of Guildford (Bb)

The tall pilasters on the south front of this fine Georgian house and the Venetian windows on the ground floor are the work of Giacomo Leoni, the Venetian architect who built the house about 1733, and beyond are impressive rooms, with the magnificent Marble Hall serving as an overture. Two chimneypieces have relief tableaux in different-coloured marbles depicting sacrificial scenes, and on the ceiling the plaster figures seem to cling precariously to the ornate frieze.

Clandon Park also houses the Gubbay Collection of porcelain, furniture, jade, metalwork and textiles, left to the National Trust by Mrs David Gubbay in 1968. The collection includes Bow, Chelsea, Wedgwood and Meissen porcelain, Chinese enamelware and English and Continental furniture. The gardens contain a flint and brick grotto and – a little incongruous in this setting – a reconstructed Maori house from New Zealand.

NT. Apr-Oct, daily exc Thur and Fri. Adm charge. Refreshments. Shop. P *Toilets. Tel Guildford (0483) 222482*

CLAREMONT LANDSCAPE GARDEN

On A307, ½ mile south of Esher (Cc)

To wander through Claremont's garden, with its lake, island pavilion, grotto and amphitheatre, is to make a passage through the history of the English landscape garden. Here can be seen the work of four men whose names are synonymous with the English garden – Sir John Vanbrugh, Charles Bridgeman, William Kent and Capability Brown. Begun by Vanbrugh and Bridgeman before 1720, it was soon hailed as 'the noblest of any in Europe'; after Vanbrugh's death in 1726 the work was continued by Kent and later by Brown.

Today Claremont is the earliest surviving English landscape garden, but its survival owes much to a massive restoration operation undertaken by the National Trust between 1975 and 1980, for since the 1920s the garden had become derelict, the lake had silted up and trees and shrubs had grown rampant. The restoration revealed much of the original work – Vanbrugh's pretty Belvedere Tower, for example, standing on a knoll at the head of an avenue of trees, and Bridgeman's turf amphitheatre above the lake. The lake, now dredged and its outlines defined, was Kent's, as are the woodland groves of beech, chestnut and yew. Brown made few alterations, but he designed the nearby house for Clive of India; it was not completed until after Clive's death in 1774, and is now a private school.

Garden: NT. All year, daily. Adm charge. Refreshments. P *Toilets.* ♿ *Tel Bookham (0372) 57223. House: Feb-Nov, first full weekend, pm. Adm charge.* P *Toilets. Tel (0372) 67841.*

FARNHAM CASTLE

On A287, ½ mile north of Farnham (Ab)

Most Norman castle keeps were built on a motte, or mound, and were surrounded by an outer curtain wall. In Farnham's case the mound itself also has a wall around it, and the ground within the walls is 37ft higher than outside. Only the foundations of the square keep that stood on the mound remain, and in the centre is a deep well, now covered by a concrete slab. Steps lead down to an observation platform below the slab, where the floodlit well, some 13ft square, can be seen.

The approach to the castle is through a 17th-century gateway, and across a courtyard steps lead up to the great brick tower, built in the 15th century. Its top is decorated with one of the earliest and best examples of patterned brickwork in England. The tower was built by Bishop Wayneflete of Winchester, who lived at the castle; the castle remained the residence of the Bishops of Winchester until 1927, and of the Bishops of Guildford until 1955.

The local museum in Willmer House, a fine Georgian building, includes a display on William Cobbett, author of *Rural Rides*, who was born in Farnham in 1763.

Castle: EH. Apr-Sept, daily. Adm charge. P *Tel Farnham (0252) 713393. Museum: All year, Tues-Sat. Free entry. Shop.* ♿ *Tel (0252) 715094.*

FRENSHAM COUNTRY PARK

On A287, 4 miles south of Farnham (Aa)

The combination of two lakes with sandy beaches and the heathland of Frensham Common makes this country park a perfect 'get-away-from-it-all' haven. The park offers good walking, with a conservation trail and a nature reserve, while the less energetic can stretch out on the banks of the Great Pond, or its smaller neighbour Little Pond, and watch the swans, grebes and coots that glide and dart on the mirror-like surface.

All year, daily.

VENETIAN MEDLEY *Styles are mixed in the exterior of the square, red-brick house at Clandon Park, rebuilt in the 1730s for Thomas, 2nd Lord Onslow. Classical columns add an Italian touch to the south front.*

GATWICK ZOO AND AVIARIES

Off A217 at Charlwood, 2 miles north of Crawley (Da)

Enclosures and aviaries within 10 acres of landscaped grounds contain hundreds of animals, birds and butterflies. Some of the birds, such as macaws, are free-flying and tame. Many of the animals have been bred at the zoo, including a large group of squirrel monkeys whose island home is shared with a pair of spider monkeys. There is a butterfly garden where tropical specimens can be seen on the wing in jungle-like conditions.

Apr-Oct, daily. Adm charge. Refreshments. Shop. P *Toilets.* ♿ *Tel Crawley (0293) 862312.*

GUILDFORD CATHEDRAL

Off A31, ½ mile west of Guildford (Bb)

In the tradition of the great cathedrals of the past, Guildford Cathedral stands on a hill. Unlike the medieval cathedrals, however, the town at its feet did not grow up around it for it was already there before the cathedral was built. The lovely red-brick building in a simplified Gothic style was designed by Sir Edward Maufe and consecrated in 1961. The traditions of earlier cathedrals are echoed in the long nave with its arches of honey-coloured stone, the tall lancet windows set with stained glass, and the creamy marble floor. A brass stag set in the floor beneath the tower marks the point at the top of Stag Hill around which the building was designed. Below the cathedral spread the buildings of part of the University of Surrey.

The centre of Guildford is dominated by the ruined keep of its castle, a rare example of Norman and early Plantagenet work since it was never expanded and little modified in later periods. It stands on a mound and was built to overawe the town; how well it did so can be seen from the top of the spiral staircase in the north-west corner, which today also affords a fine view of the cathedral.

TURNING ON *A water wheel some 150 years old is still driving Haxted Mill, near Edenbridge on the Surrey-Kent border. The well-restored mill dates in part from the 16th century; there is a record of a mill on the site in the 14th century.*

ARCHES OF GLORY *Soaring arches, delicately touched by light, frame the south aisle of Guildford Cathedral. The building is a newcomer among English cathedrals, much admired for its simplified Gothic style.*

Guildford Museum, in Quarry Street, is devoted to local history and archaeology. It includes a collection of items connected with Charles Lutwidge Dodgson, better known as Lewis Carroll, the creator of *Alice in Wonderland.* He died in Guildford in 1898 and is buried in Mount Cemetery.

Cathedral: All year, daily. Free entry. Refreshments. Shop. P *Toilets.* ♿ *Tel Guildford (0483) 65287. Castle: Apr-Sept, daily. Adm charge. Shop. Tel (0483) 505050. Museum: All year, Mon-Sat. Free entry. Shop. Toilets.* ♿ *Tel (0483) 503947.*

HATCHLANDS

Off A246, 2 miles east of Guildford (Bb)

A long, sweeping drive past a lake and across parkland leads to Hatchlands, a friendly looking, welcoming house of mellow red brick. It was built in 1758 by Admiral Boscawen, probably to his own designs, and was financed out of the prize money he had gained in naval actions in the Seven Years' War against France. Certainly it has the appearance of being influenced by a man used to tidiness and uniformity, and its only concession to ornamentation is the white pilastered entrance added by a later owner.

Only the ground-floor rooms are open to the public, but in two of them, the drawing room and library, can be seen the earliest-known work by Robert Adam, the then little-known architect whose superb designs were later to appear in many great houses. In both rooms the wall panels, ceilings, fireplaces and chimneypieces are exquisite examples of Adam's enormous talent.

In contrast, the Music Room added in 1903 by Lord Rendel is very much in the Edwardian style. It contains paintings by Henry Lamb, an official war artist during the First World War.

NT. Apr-mid Oct, Wed, Thur, Sun and Bank Hol Mon. Adm charge. Refreshments. P *Tel Guildford (0483) 222787.*

HAXTED MILL MUSEUM

Off B2028, 3 miles west of Lingfield (Eb)

This painstakingly restored water mill, part 16th century and part 18th century, stands by the River Eden which, until 1945, drove the millstones that ground corn for flour and meal for animal foods. Now the wheel is turning again, and the double-fronted timber building houses a mill museum. Among the working exhibits are a Cornish tin-mine wheel and a pumping water wheel that once supplied water to a Sussex manor. There are old postcards, photos and drawings of water mills long gone and, on the three upper floors, a range of other exhibits illustrating the history and development of water power.

June-Sept, daily; Apr-May, Sat, Sun and Bank Hol. Refreshments. Shop. P *Tel Edenbridge (0732) 862914.*

HEADLEY HEATH

On B2033, 3 miles south-east of Leatherhead (Cb)

This wide expanse of heathland on the northern slope of the North Downs owes its present wooded state to the Second World War. During that time the heath was an open wilderness, once grazed by sheep, and was used as an army training ground. This so disturbed the soil that dormant birch seeds were able to germinate, and within a short time the young trees were flourishing. Oaks, beeches and rowans make up the rest of the woods, accessible by footpaths and riding tracks. The National Trust plans to re-establish the older areas of heather. There is a picnic area beside the ancient Brimmer Pond. Wildlife abounds, including great spotted, lesser spotted and green woodpeckers, and the rare chalkhill blue butterfly.

NT. All year, daily. P *Tel Bookham (0372) 53401.*

HINDHEAD COMMON

On A3, east of Hindhead (Aa)

High above the Weald are the wild heathlands, pinewoods and steep valleys that make up Hindhead Common, some 1400 acres of which are owned by the National Trust. Linked by a network of footpaths, each area offers walks in sylvan surroundings, in places with magical and sometimes puzzling names, such as Polecat Copse, Hurt Hill, Golden Valley and Stoatley Green. Supreme among them is the Devil's Punch Bowl, a vast hollow some 2 miles long and half a mile wide scooped out of the hills by streams and springs. Its steep sides plunge 350ft to a stream that flows into the River Wey. At the north-west corner of the hollow three humps, known as the Devil's Jumps, are where the Devil is said to have taken his daily exercise, by jumping from one to another.

The Portsmouth road that crosses the common was once the haunt of thieves and highwaymen, and on the 895ft summit of Gibbet Hill stands a granite cross marking the spot where the gibbet stood. Three villains who murdered a sailor on the hill ended up on the gibbet in 1787, and a stone marks the murder site. Glorious panoramas extend northwards to the dark line of the North Downs; in the opposite direction the South Downs form the misty horizon.

NT. All year, daily.

LEITH HILL TOWER

On B2126, 4½ miles south-west of Dorking (Ca)

In the 18th century there was an obsession among some landowners to raise buildings with no function other than to satisfy the whim of their creators. Leith Hill Tower is one such folly, though it was built for looking from rather than at. A road winds up wooded Leith Hill to a car park just below the crest of the hill, and from there it is a short walk to the turreted medieval-looking tower. A tablet in Latin above the door says that Richard Hull built the tower in 1766 so that he and his friends could admire the view from the top; Hull was buried beneath the tower in 1772. As Leith Hill stands 965ft high, the highest point in South-east England, Hull's 64ft tower raises the viewpoint to more than 1000ft. From here it is claimed that on a clear day 13 counties can be seen. The hill itself has paths among shady woods – severely damaged by the storm of October 1987 – and, in season, carpets of bluebells and clumps of rhododendrons.

NT. Tower: Apr-Sept, Wed, Sat, Sun and Bank Hol Mon. Adm charge.

LIGHTWATER COUNTRY PARK

Off A322, 2 miles south-east of Bagshot (Ac)

On this wild stretch of Bagshot Heath it is not difficult to believe the legend that this was once the haunt of the highwayman Dick Turpin. Gorse, heather and bogs, with groups of pine and silver birch, make up most of the heath, which rises from three lakes near the car park to High Curley Hill. There are two waymarked footpaths – one a short stroll of about 1 mile and the other a 1½ mile climb to High Curley – and a nature trail that takes in the changes in the terrain and their varied wildlife.

All year, daily.

LOSELEY HOUSE

On B3000, 2 miles south of Guildford (Bb)

This is Elizabethan building at its best – all gables, tall chimneys, stone mullioned windows and mellowed stonework. Loseley has the air of a house much favoured by majesty: Elizabeth I stayed there three times, James I was a frequent visitor and Queen Mary came to the house in 1932. The house has other royal connections too, for the panelling in the Great Hall and a marble table came from Henry VIII's Nonsuch Palace when it was demolished, and the rooms abound with royal portraits and other regal items, such as the two chairs in the drawing room with cushions believed to have been sewn by Elizabeth I.

The chairs flank a remarkable chimneypiece. Carved out of a solid block of chalk it stands the full height of the room, with fluted columns on either side of the fireplace and carved figures supporting an ornate frieze. In the centre are six delicately worked panels bearing coats of arms. Also beside the fireplace is a rare 16th-century German cabinet of pinewood inlaid with pearwood, rosewood, beech, sycamore and ash.

The bedrooms are mostly furnished with 16th or 17th-century furniture. The room used by James I has a handsome four-poster bed, 17th-century wall tapestries and a carpet with Tudor rose, crown and thistle motif laid in the king's honour.

May-Sept, Wed-Sat; also Spring and Summer Bank Hol Mon. Adm charge. Refreshments. P *Toilets.* ♿ *Tel Guildford (0483) 571881.*

TUDOR SPLENDOUR *Green-velvet lawns sweeping almost to the doorstep make a simple stage for the theatre-set splendour of Loseley House. The manor has played host to three British monarchs.*

OUTWOOD POST MILL

Off A23, 5 miles south-east of Reigate (Db)

The oldest working windmill in England, Outwood Mill was built in 1665 when Charles II was on the throne. Its huge sails were turned by the same breeze that fanned the Great Fire of London. On its hilltop site on Outwood Common the mill still grinds corn the way it did 300 years ago. Not only the sights of the miller's trade are here but the sounds as well – the sighing of the wind through the sails, the creaking of timbers and the rumble of the grindstones. In Outwood Mill the shafts, wheels and cogs of a bygone age still turn – but time has stood still. There is a small museum of farming bygones.

Easter-Oct, Sun and Bank Hol Mon pm. Adm charge. Shop. P *Tel Smallfield (034 284) 3458.*

POLESDEN LACEY

Off A246, 1½ miles south of Great Bookham (Cb)

This Regency-style house, built in 1824, has all the embellishments of its period, but behind the colonnade and roughcast, yellow-washed walls lies a very different world. Here the atmosphere is strongly Edwardian, a legacy of the world of social weekends and the country house hostess. From 1906 until the outbreak of the Second World War Polesden Lacey's hostess was The Honourable Mrs Ronald Greville, who lavishly furnished and decorated the house to impress her many friends, among whom she numbered Edward VII, George V, George VI and Queen Elizabeth who, as Duke and Duchess of York, spent their honeymoon there in 1923.

Mrs Greville was a woman of good taste, as can be seen in the dining room with its crimson silk brocades, English, French and Chinese furniture, Georgian silver and a collection of English portrait paintings. She was also an admirer of 17th-century woodcarvings, and the richly carved oak screen in the hall was originally in Sir Christopher Wren's St Matthew's Church in the

City of London. The drawing-room walls are adorned with carved and gilded panelling that may once have graced an Italian palace.

The house stands on high ground amid lawns and terraces, herbaceous borders, statues, clipped box hedges and yews. To the south lies Ranmore Common, 472 acres of woodland owned by the National Trust and accessible by footpaths from Polesden Lacey.

NT. Apr-Oct, Wed-Sun; Mar and Nov, Sat and Sun. Refreshments. Shop. P *Toilets.* ♿ *Tel Bookham (0372) 58203.*

RUNNYMEDE

On A308, 2 miles north-west of Egham (Bd)

These broad water meadows beside the Thames are famous throughout the free world as the place where King John put his seal to Magna Carta in 1215, and wrote above it, in Latin, 'Given by our hand in the meadow that is called Runnymeade'. Here the river flows at an unhurried pace between reed and willow-fringed banks, and the scene has probably changed little since the king was forced by his barons to agree to the document that guaranteed liberty for his subjects.

The precise spot where the historic meeting took place is not known, but a small classical temple near the river is a memorial to the occasion. The memorial was built in 1957 by the American Bar Association. Only six years later, America lost a fighter for freedom when President John F. Kennedy was assassinated. A memorial to him, a block of Portland Stone, stands near the Magna Carta Memorial in an acre of land given to the people of the United States by the people of Britain.

The Kennedy Memorial stands on the lower slope of Cooper's Hill, on top of which is the Air Forces Memorial, also dedicated to the defence of democracy. It commemorates the 20,456 airmen of the Allied Forces who died during the Second World War and have no known grave. Their names are recorded in the cloister that forms part of the building.

NT. All year, daily.

FIRE AND WATER *Autumn brings its special beauty to the Seven Acres Lake at Wisley Garden. The russet leaves are those of* Cotinus coggygria, *whose purple summer flowers give it the name 'smoke tree'.*

THE SILENT POOL

On A25, 1 mile west of Shere (Bb)

A path from a car park on the main road leads after 100yds to two tranquil pools; one, called the Silent Pool, is remarkable for the clarity of its water, springing from the chalk downs above. If it seems a slightly haunted spot even on the brightest day this may be an echo of the tragedy which, according to legend, occurred here in 1193. A maiden bathing naked was disturbed by Prince John (later King John). She retreated deeper and deeper into the water until she lost her footing and drowned.

West of the Silent Pool the road climbs to the lofty viewpoint of Newlands Corner, which looks down over the wooded slopes of the North Downs and across the valley of the Tilling Bourne. Islanded on its hilltop can be seen St Martha's Church, connected to Newlands Corner by a stretch of the North Downs Way.

All year, daily. P

THORPE PARK THEME PARK

On A320, 1 mile north of Chertsey (Bc)

Shoot the rapids on a river of white water, hurtle through black space on a roller coaster or take a trip among things that go bump in the night: these are some of the attractions offered at this theme park set out in 500 acres, half of which is covered by water. There are lakes large enough for windsurfing, water-skiing and waterbus trips; beside one lake there is a nature trail.

The park's centre area is occupied by a skilful blend of gardens, fountains, shops and cafés. One garden has scale models of world-famous buildings such as the Eiffel Tower, the Statue of Liberty, the Taj Mahal and the Sydney Opera House. Close by, the visitor can take a lightning trip through centuries of British architecture in a street where each house front represents a different period – Tudor, Georgian, Victorian. In fact the house fronts are merely façades behind which some of Thorpe Park's ride attractions are cunningly hidden. A Victorian doorway leads suddenly into the world of the astronaut, with a roller coaster waiting to transport the visitor to Space Station Zero; behind the timber-framed walls of the Tudor house, slow-moving cars glide through Phantom Fantasia where skeletons dance, witches cast their spells and the phantom of the opera plays on the organ. After the thrills of a ride in space or the chills of a macabre underworld, there is the relaxing contrast of a gentle cruise along a millstream meandering between grassy banks, past the slowly turning water wheel and into the fairyland of the Magic Mill.

For refreshment, European Square has restaurants and cafés in Bavarian, Italian, Dutch, French and Belgian styles, and at the lakeside there is a restaurant on a Mississippi riverboat. From one lakeside jetty, ferryboats leave at regular intervals for Thorpe Farm, where the bustle of rides and sideshows is exchanged for a scene of rural tranquillity. Grouped around a duckpond are a farmhouse, old barns and animal pens where sheep, goats, cattle, calves and pigs are to be seen. A craft centre displays such crafts as spinning, basketwork and pottery.

The return trip can be made by a 'land-train', drawn by a replica steam tractor, or again by the ferry which passes 'Our Heritage', a fascinating collection of buildings re-creating a Stone Age cave, Roman ruins, a Saxon hut, a medieval castle and, moored at the lakeside, a Roman galley.

June-mid Sept, daily; also Easter, then Sat and Sun to end May and in late Sept. Adm charge. Refreshments. Shop. P *Toilets.* ♿ *Tel Chertsey (093 28) 62633.*

TILFORD OLD KILN MUSEUM

Off A287, 4 miles south of Farnham (Aa)

A pair of splendid gates, comprising four iron wheels in wrought-iron frames, stands at the entrance to the museum, which has an impressive collection of agricultural implements, a smithy, a wheelwright's shop and a bakery. The workshops are the real thing, taken from other parts of Surrey and re-erected here, as are the fittings in the bakery, including a gas-heated stand that was used for making muffins and crumpets. Among the wagons and carts on display are a Surrey wagon, a Wiltshire wagon and a timber wagon from the Forest of Dean. An arboretum has more than 100 species of trees from all over the world.

Apr-Sept, Wed-Sun. Adm charge. Shop. P *Toilets.* ♿ *Tel Frensham (025 125) 2300.*

THEME PARK PARADE *A full-size replica of a Roman galley and a miniature Bavarian castle are among the attractions at Thorpe Park. The galley is part of the 'Our Heritage' display and can be boarded; the castle is one of many scale model buildings set among the gardens of Model World.*

VIRGINIA WATER

On A329, 4 miles west of Chertsey (Bc)

Woods of beech, sweet chestnut, oak and pine border this lovely lake, and in spring and summer azaleas and rhododendrons add their brilliant hues to the many shades of green. The lake stretches in a glistening sheen for some 2 miles, its waters speckled with wildfowl, and at the eastern end cascades over a waterfall. Seats hollowed from the trunks of chestnut trees provide a chance to sit and take in the view and breathe the sweet, pine-scented air.

For the walker, however, Virginia Water has some curiosities waiting to be discovered. Not far from the waterfall stand columns from the Roman city of Leptis Magna, in Libya, which were brought to England in 1816 and presented to the Prince Regent. They were intended for the portico of the British Museum, but instead ended up here to form a picturesque ruin that blends perfectly with its sylvan surroundings. In complete contrast is the Totem Pole, which jabs a slender finger skyward on the northern side of the lake. It is 100ft tall and its mythical Red Indian figures were carved from a 600-year-old Western red cedar. This emblem of ancient tribes, so far from home, was erected in 1958 to mark the centenary of British Columbia.

Also on the northern side are two superb gardens. The Valley Garden, bordering the lake, has some 200 species of heather, which ensures that there is a heather in flower at all times of the year. A large collection of rhododendrons and other flowering shrubs covers 50 acres and floods the landscape with colour. Massed hydrangeas add their colours in season. Farther north, in a corner of Windsor Great Park, is the Savill Garden, laid out in 1932 by Sir Eric Savill, then the park's deputy ranger. Containing two stream-fed ponds it is known especially for its rhododendrons and azaleas. Lilies and primulas rise from the damp hollows. The Alpine Meadow and Dry Garden are devoted to colourful denizens of the Mediterranean and similar climatic regions.

All year, daily. Free entry (adm charge for Savill Garden only).

WINKWORTH ARBORETUM

On B2130, 2 miles south of Godalming (Ba)

Shrubs and trees, many of them rare, cover this 97 acre corner of Surrey, much of which consists of steep hillside plunging down to a valley and two enchanting lakes. Though there are walks among glades and woods there is nothing park-like in the arboretum, and although the setting is natural each section has been carefully planned to make the most of the seasons: the reds, oranges and golds of autumn, the rich greens of summer and the awakening colours of spring, enhanced by carpets of bluebells and daffodils.

The two lakes, called Rowe's Flashe and Phillimore Lake, mirror the profusion of multi-coloured foliage and flowers on the hillside above. On Rowe's Flashe a boathouse on stilts at the water's edge stands near an old log cabin, almost smothered by a magnificent wisteria. Nearby are the Azalea Steps, with hydrangeas at the foot and azaleas of every hue flanking the 106 steps to the top of the hill.

NT. All year, daily. Adm charge. Refreshments. Shop. P *Toilets.* ♿ *Tel Hascombe (048 632) 477.*

WISLEY GARDEN

Off A3, 8 miles north-east of Guildford (Bc)

Keen gardeners with a problem, would-be gardeners needing advice or inspiration, or people who simply enjoy wandering among gardens that range from formal to informal will find satisfaction at Wisley, the garden of the Royal Horticultural Society. There are staff on hand to give expert advice on every kind of gardening problem. For the beginner there are examples of what plants grow best in particular situations, and how to provide colour in a garden all year round. Mindful of the fact that many people have only a small plot to cultivate, the society has set out small gardens showing how to make the best of limited space. One of the model gardens was designed and planted for the television series *Gardener's Calendar,* and there is also a garden showing what can be achieved by disabled or elderly people.

For the carefree wanderer Wisley offers a dazzling display that includes banks of heather, a rock garden, massed clusters of rhododendrons and azaleas, a wild garden, herbaceous borders and stately oaks and redwoods. In front of the laboratory, housed in a Tudor-style building which in fact dates only from 1915, there is a formal pool dappled with water lilies and flanked by trim, ruler-straight lawns.

RHS. All year, Mon-Sat (Sun, members only). Adm charge. Refreshments. Shop. P *Toilets.* ♿ *Tel Guildford (0483) 224234.*

WITLEY COMMON

On A286, 1¼ miles south-west of Milford (Aa)

The best way to get to know the common is to explore it by one of the three waymarked nature trails. The astonishing variety of habitats, ranging from pine and birch woodland to wet and dry heathland, and the wildlife they support is due largely to the construction of army camps here during the Second World War. The soils and other materials brought in to build the now-demolished camps enriched the ecology of the common which was once almost barren and desolate heathland.

NT. Apr-Oct, daily exc Mon and Fri. Free entry. Shop. P *Toilets.* ♿ *Tel Wormley (042 879) 3207.*

COUNTY CALENDAR

March (1st Thur). Guildford: Dicing for Maids' Money (ceremony dating from 17th-century bequest).

May (mid-month). Tilford: Bach Festival. Guildford: County Show.

June (1st Wed). Epsom Downs: Derby Day.

June (early). Dorking: Boxhill Music Festival.

June (mid-month, to early July). Polesden Lacey: Open-Air Theatre season.

July (1st half). Guildford: Festival.

July (3rd full week). River Thames, upriver from Sunbury: Swan Upping (annual marking ceremony).

July (2nd half). Haslemere: Music Festival (Dolmetsch early instruments).

August (early). Cranleigh: Home Counties and Cranleigh Show.

August Bank Hol weekend Egham: Egham and Thorpe Royal Show.

Tourist information: Farnham (048 68) 4104; Guildford (0483) 575857; Walton-on-Thames (0932) 228844.

EAST SUSSEX

DOWNLAND AND FOREST BEHIND A COASTAL PLAYGROUND

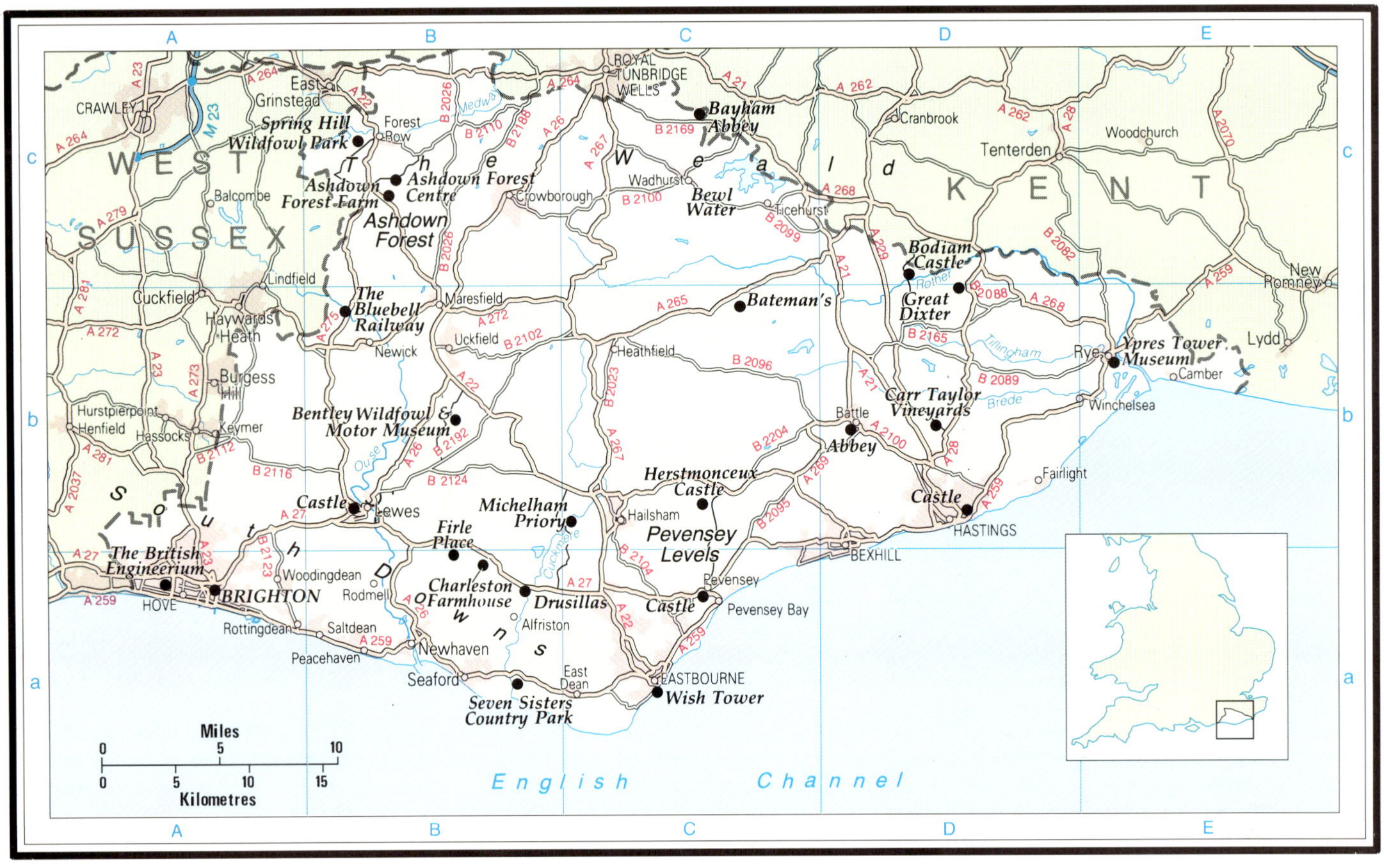

The great bare whaleback of the South Downs is England's doorstep, dropping sheer to the sea at Beachy Head and the Seven Sisters in cliffs as white as anything Dover can present. In other places the South Downs stand back, leaving room along the coast for a series of towns, each with a distinctive personality and a separate tale to tell. They include Brighton, elegant and theatrical; Eastbourne, wholesome and respectable; Hastings, one of the Cinque Ports that once guarded our shores; and Pevensey that the Romans knew and that later witnessed the arrival of William the Conqueror.

William's heel ground heavily on East Sussex. At Battle, he wrested England from Harold, and for miles about he and his followers raised their castles, at Hastings, Lewes and Pevensey, followed by a later generation of fortresses at Bodiam, Rye and Herstmonceux.

Newer attractions of East Sussex include theme parks and open-air museums – the Ashdown Forest Farm, for example, Drusillas, near Alfriston, and the famous Bluebell Railway. Few writers have expressed their love for their chosen county more clearly than Rudyard Kipling, who lived at Bateman's.

ASHDOWN FOREST CENTRE

Off A22, 3 miles south of Forest Row (Bc)

Set in the heart of the Sussex Weald, the conifer-studded heathland of Ashdown Forest forms a striking contrast to the rich farmland that surrounds it. The Ashdown Forest Centre consists of three ancient oak-framed barns, two used by the Conservators and Rangers who run the 6500 acre forest, and one housing a visitor centre.

Displays explain how in the past Ashdown Forest's trees provided charcoal to power the furnaces of the Wealden ironworks, while kings and noblemen hunted the deer. The storm of October, 1987 took a heavy toll among the remaining trees. Most of the forest is open to the public, who may glimpse fallow deer crossing the paths.

Forest: All year, daily. Visitor centre: Apr-Sept, pm daily. Oct-Mar, Sat and Sun. Free entry. Shop. P *Toilets.* ♿ *Tel Forest Row (034 282) 3583.*

ASHDOWN FOREST FARM

Off A22, 3 miles south of Forest Row (Bc)

Rare breeds of animals and poultry that have disappeared from most modern farms roam this farm in the heart of Ashdown Forest. A member of the Rare Breed Survival Trust, its rarities include the middle white pig, the Dorking hen said to have been brought to Britain by the Romans, Wensleydale sheep with their long silky ringlets, and Dexter cattle, the smallest British breed.

All year, daily. Adm charge. Refreshments. Shop. P *Toilets. Tel Nutley (082 571) 2040.*

BATEMAN'S

Off A265 at Burwash, 6 miles east of Heathfield (Cb)

Just below the picture-postcard village of Burwash on its ridge, the little River Dudwell flows through a peaceful valley. In 1634 a wealthy Sussex ironmaster built himself this dignified stone house not far from the river; it was bought in 1902 by Rudyard Kipling, who lived here until his death in 1936. At Bateman's, Kipling wrote some of his best-known books, among them *Puck of Pook's Hill*, inspired by the locality.

Bateman's is still very much as it was in Kipling's day, full of his furniture and mementos. Upstairs in his study his worktable is laid out with pen and inkwell ready for a hard day's writing. The garden was largely planned and laid out by Kipling and his wife. By the river is an 18th-century water mill, which Kipling converted to provide electricity for Bateman's. In the 1970s it was restored to its ancient role and now produces stoneground flour for sale.

NT. Apr-Oct, daily exc Thur and Fri. Adm charge. Refreshments. Shop. P *Toilets.* ♿ *Tel Burwash (0435) 882302.*

BATTLE ABBEY

In centre of Battle (Db)

Though Hastings has given its name to the best-known conflict in English history, the actual battle between William the Norman and Harold the Saxon took place some 7 miles inland, on October 14, 1066, at the spot now marked by Battle Abbey. Built about 1070 by William, the abbey extends along a low ridge – roughly where Harold drew up his troops to await the Norman onslaught. The high altar marks the spot where Harold fell.

Before exploring the remains of the abbey, it is worth making the circuit of the battlefield, which is explained by notices placed at intervals round it. For all its key role in our history, the battle was on a tiny scale by modern standards, with about 7000 Saxons fighting the same number of Normans. Though there are more trees there now than there were in 1066, it is easy to visualise the Norman cavalry battling up the slope towards the Saxon infantry, their mock retreat which lured the Saxons to chase them down the hill, and their final triumph as evening fell.

The splendid 14th-century gatehouse is the finest of the medieval remains. Little of the great church is left, apart from the foundations, but a good deal of the monks' dormitory survives, with its vaulted rooms below still intact.

Across the road from the abbey, the leisurely days of Victorian shopping are revived in Buckley's Museum of Shops. Housed in a 600-year-old building, the museum displays more than 10,000 items from every type of shop.

Abbey: EH. All year, daily. Adm charge. P *Toilets. Tel Battle (042 46) 3792. Museum: Easter-Dec, daily. Adm charge. Shop. Tel (042 46) 4269.*

AUTHOR'S DEN *The study in Rudyard Kipling's home, Bateman's, is kept much as he left it. The walls are lined with his favourite fiction, and with the reference books he combed for the backgrounds to his stories.*

BAYHAM ABBEY

Off B2169, 5 miles east of Royal Tunbridge Wells (Cc)

Standing in beautiful and remote countryside beside the slow-flowing River Teise, Bayham Abbey was built early in the 13th century and survived without incident until it was dissolved by Henry VIII. A good deal of the gatehouse survives, facing north across the river, while the remains of some of the arches and piers at the east end of the church show what a superb building it must have been at the height of its glory, despite its incorporation in 18th-century 'landscaping' by Humphry Repton.

EH. Apr-Sept, daily. Adm charge. Shop. P *Toilets.* ♿ *Tel Lamberhurst (0982) 890381.*

BENTLEY WILDFOWL AND MOTOR MUSEUM

Off B2192, 8 miles north-east of Lewes (Bb)

Some 100 species of geese, swans and ducks honk, quack and dabble in a series of artificial ponds fed from a spring. Visitors can walk freely among the birds, which include black swans, Australian shelducks and eastern greylags. Among rare wildfowl successfully bred at Bentley are ne-ne or Hawaiian geese and white-winged wood ducks from Thailand; stocks of both species have been returned to their native countries.

Other attractions include a formal garden, laid out as a series of open-air 'rooms' separated by yew hedges, and a motor museum. This is a changing assembly of veteran and vintage cars, almost all in running condition, lent by private owners.

There is also a grassy picnic spot – from which a woodland walk leads to a small plantation – and a children's play area.

Apr-Oct, daily; Oct-Dec and Feb-Mar, Sat and Sun. Adm charge. Refreshments. Shop. P *Toilets.* ♿ *Tel Halland (082 584) 573.*

MONKS' REST *Fine stone vaulting supports the ceilings of the common room, novices' room and library of Battle Abbey, where up to 70 monks studied and took their ease. They slept in the dormitory above.*

BEWL WATER

Off A21, 8 miles south-east of Royal Tunbridge Wells (Cc)

When the River Bewl, on the Kent-East Sussex border, was dammed in the 1970s to make the Bewl Bridge reservoir, three small valleys were flooded, forming a trident-shaped stretch of water. With an area of 770 acres and a shoreline of 13 miles, Bewl Water provides a variety of lakeside footpaths. An information centre explains the workings of the reservoir, where recreations include trout fishing and 45 minute cruises on the SS *Frances Mary*.

All year, daily. Adm charge. Refreshments. P *Toilets.* ♿ *Tel Lamberhurst (0982) 890661.*

THE BLUEBELL RAILWAY

On A275 at Sheffield Park Station, 9 miles north of Lewes (Bb)

Every day throughout the summer, and at weekends during the rest of the year, 5 miles of peaceful Sussex valley echo with the whistles and snorts of engines getting up steam, while the again-familiar plumes of smoke drift over the trees. The Bluebell Railway, opened in 1960, was the pioneer of steam passenger lines rescued by a band of enthusiasts from the British Rail cuts of the 1950s and 1960s. The line runs from Sheffield Park to Horsted Keynes.

Popular with the public and with makers of television films who want to recapture the

BRIGHTON, PRODUCT OF A ROYAL FANCY

Belief in the benefits of bathing in and drinking seawater had already transformed a fishing village called Brighthelmstone into a seaside resort when the Prince Regent visited the town in 1783, liked it and decided to make a home there. High fashion followed, transforming Brighton into 'London by the sea', and the town still retains a singular blend of charm and raffishness in its Regency architecture, antique shops, yacht marina, idiosyncratic museums and busy promenades.

Royal Pavilion: All year, daily. Adm charge. Refreshments. Shop. Toilets. ♿ Tel Brighton (0273) 603005. Volk's Railway: Apr-Sept, daily; some winter weekends. Adm charge. Tel (0273) 681061. Aquarium: All year, daily. Adm charge. Refreshments. Shop. Toilets. ♿ Tel (0273) 604234. Booth Museum: All year, daily exc Thur. Free entry. Shop. ♿ Tel (0273) 552586. Brighton Museum: All year, daily exc Mon. Free entry. Refreshments. Shop. Toilets. Tel (0273) 603005.

PRINCE'S PLEASURE *The onion domes of the Royal Pavilion suggested to the Regency wit Sydney Smith that the dome of St Paul's in London had come to Brighton and pupped. A simple classical villa when first built for the Prince Regent, its exterior was redesigned by John Nash in 1815-22 in the 'Indian style'. The interior, including the Banqueting Room (left), was lavishly decorated in the 'Chinese style'. Restoration work may temporarily close some rooms, and conceal parts of the exterior.*

MORE THAN A MOORING *Brighton Marina, with its chandlers' stores and moorings for 2000 boats, is undergoing a transformation. Already the largest man-made harbour in Europe, it is being supplemented by 800 houses and flats, superstore, water theme park, sports complex, a 'village square' of shops and moorings for still more boats.*

BY THE SHORE *Volk's Electric Railway, built in 1883 as Britain's first electric seafront railway, still runs between the Palace Pier and the Marina. A yellow-tailed blue damselfish (right) is among the attractions of the Aquarium and Dolphinarium, which also include alligators, performing sea lions, dolphins, and an aquatic adventure playground.*

STILLED SPLENDOUR *The glory of an Abyssinian roller's plumage lives on in the Booth Museum of Natural History in Dyke Road, founded by the sportsman Edward Booth in 1874 to house his collection. Birds of every size from golden eagles to bramblings are preserved, together with butterflies from around the world and the fossilised bones of a dinosaur, the iguanadon.*

FRIENDLY FELINE *A cheerful china cat, made in France about 1880, is among the pottery and porcelain on show in Brighton's Museum and Art Gallery in Church Street. There are displays of Art Nouveau and Art Deco furniture and decorative art, collections of paintings, drawings and musical instruments, and a Fashion Gallery that tells the history and meaning of costume down the centuries.*

flavour of the age of steam, the Bluebell Railway now has 30 historic locomotives and an extensive stock of coaches and wagons. The station at Sheffield Park has been restored in the 1880s style of the London, Brighton and South Coast Railway, while Horsted Keynes is in the 1930s style of the Southern Railway.

Half a mile north of Sheffield Park station, Sheffield Park Garden is a splendid Capability Brown landscape, laid out in the late 18th century around a T-shaped series of lakes. Ageing trees were devastated by the gales of October, 1987, but the remainder still bravely fly their autumnal colours, and the spring daffodil display is as breathtaking as always.

Railway: Spring Bank Hol-Sept, daily; May and Oct, Sat, Sun, Wed; Nov-Dec, Mar-Apr, Sat, Sun; Jan-Feb, Sun. Adm charge. Refreshments. Shop. P *Toilets.* ♿ *Tel Newick (082 572) 3777. Garden: NT. Apr-early Nov, daily exc Mon, Good Fri and Tues following Bank Hol. Adm charge. Shop.* P *Toilets.* ♿ *Tel Danehill (0825) 790655.*

BODIAM CASTLE

Off A229, 11 miles north of Hastings (Dc)

Round corner towers, battlemented walls and a gate-tower reflected in a tranquil moat, make Bodiam Castle the perfect fortress of a child's imagining. Though it seems to be in a pointless situation today, tucked away in a valley a dozen miles inland from the sea, when it was built in 1385 it was in a highly strategic position, as the Rother was navigable right up to Bodiam Bridge. However, its strength was never put to the test, as French coastal marauders did not penetrate so far upriver. Within the walls a good deal survives, or can be easily traced, including the great hall, chapel, kitchen and 'Ladies' Bower'. A model shows the castle as it was in its heyday in the 15th century.

NT. Apr-Oct, daily; Nov-Mar, daily exc Sun. Adm charge. Refreshments (Apr-Oct). Shop. P *(charge). Toilets.* ♿ *Tel Staplecross (058 083) 436.*

THE BRITISH ENGINEERIUM

Off Nevill Road, Hove (Aa)

In Victorian times the Engineerium, built well above the seafront on the lower slopes of the South Downs, was the pumping station that provided water for Brighton and Hove. With its 100ft chimney and ornamental brickwork it is an impressive building, and is even more so inside, where the massive 1876 beam engine that once pumped the water is 'in steam' on Sundays and Bank Holidays. The 2000-plus exhibits include a collection of old fire engines.

All year, daily. Adm charge. Shop. P *Toilets. Tel Brighton (0273) 559583.*

CARR TAYLOR VINEYARDS

Off A28 at Westfield, 5½ miles north of Hastings (Db)

Iron-ore shale, from which cannonballs were smelted, provides the bedrock for this 21 acre vineyard. Visitors can sample the six different still white wines produced, as well as Britain's first wine produced by the *méthode champenoise* (champagne method), a sparkling wine fermented in the bottle. There are conducted tours round the vineyard and winery.

Easter-Dec, daily. Adm charge. Shop. P *(limited). Toilets.* ♿ *Tel Hastings (0424) 752501.*

CHARLESTON FARMHOUSE

Off A27, 6 miles east of Lewes (Ba)

Tucked away below Firle Beacon on the northern fringe of the downs, this unpretentious farmhouse seems an unlikely setting for the literary and artistic achievements of the brilliant Bloomsbury Group. From 1916 until her death in 1961 Charleston was the country home of Vanessa Bell, one of the artists of the group. Sister of the novelist Virginia Woolf, she was married to the art critic Clive Bell, and their visitors down the years included T.S. Eliot, E.M. Forster and Benjamin Britten.

Together with Duncan Grant and other friends, Vanessa Bell decorated every possible surface at Charleston – fireplaces, cupboards, tables, bedheads – as well as producing book jackets and illustrations in the studio. Duncan Grant lived on at Charleston until his death, aged 93, in 1978. Charleston's beautiful flint-walled garden has been restored to its original cottage-garden style.

Nearby Berwick church is decorated with murals by Vanessa Bell, Duncan Grant and Vanessa's son, Quentin Bell. Monk's House in the beautiful little village of Rodmell, beside the Ouse south of Lewes, was the home of Virginia Woolf from 1919 until her suicide there in 1941.

Charleston: Apr-Oct, Wed, Thur, Sat, Sun, Bank Hol Mon, pm only. Adm charge. P *(limited). Toilets. Tel (Charleston only) Ripe (032 183) 265. Monk's House: NT. Apr-Oct, Wed and Sat pm. Adm charge.*

DRUSILLAS

Off A27, at Alfriston (Ba)

A cluster of cottages and converted barns just north of the Downland village of Alfriston forms one of the most varied entertainment complexes in East Sussex. Beginning life some 60 years ago as tearooms, Drusillas now has a zoo, a miniature railway, a children's adventure playground, a traditional pub, a butterfly house, and a Japanese garden. It is also the headquarters of the English Wine Centre, with its own vineyard, cellars and wine museum.

Nearby Alfriston is a gem of a Sussex village, full of timbered medieval inns and weather-boarded cottages, and crammed with antique shops. Beside the church is the half-timbered Clergy House – the first building acquired by the National Trust, who bought it in 1896 for £10. Built about 1350, it had fallen derelict and was saved by the Trust from demolition.

Drusillas: All year, daily. Adm charge. Refreshments. Shop. P *Toilets.* ♿ *Tel Alfriston (0323) 870234. Clergy House: NT. Apr-Oct, daily. Adm charge. Shop. Tel (0323) 870001.*

EASTBOURNE WISH TOWER

King Edward's Parade, Eastbourne (Ca)

Immediately above Eastbourne's shingle foreshore, two relics of the Napoleonic Wars have been turned into museums of military history. Prominent on the seafront is the so-called Wish Tower, No 73 in the chain of Martello towers built around the south coast in the early 1800s to counter Napoleon's threats of invasion. It has been fully restored, with displays showing what life was like in these squat forts when 'Boney' was expected daily. At the eastern end of the front, the more substantial Redoubt Fortress, built at much the same time, is now the home of the Sussex Combined Services Museum.

Farther along Royal Parade is Eastbourne's

ARTISTS' RETREAT *Tiles, pottery and paintings by members of the Bloomsbury Group adorn the shelves, walls and even the fireplace of Charleston Farmhouse, the country home of Clive and Vanessa Bell.*

Butterfly Centre, where visitors can walk among exotic butterflies, free-flying in a covered tropical garden.
Wish Tower: Easter-Oct, daily. Adm charge. Shop. Tel Eastbourne (0323) 33952. Fortress: Easter-Nov, daily. Adm charge. Refreshments. Shop. P (limited). Toilets. ♿ Tel (0323) 33952. Butterfly Centre: Easter-Oct, daily. Adm charge. Shop. ♿ Tel (0323) 645522.

FIRLE PLACE

Off A27, 5 miles east of Lewes (Ba)

The tree-covered escarpment of the South Downs looms above this dignified mansion, set in a spacious park. Though it looks from the outside like a large 18th-century country seat, the core of Firle is a Tudor house, built round a courtyard, with a great hall as its main room. The home of the Gage family for almost 500 years, it was built by Sir John Gage in the late 1400s. It was greatly altered and adapted to the new Georgian style in the years up to 1744, when the hammerbeam roof of the great hall was concealed by a plaster ceiling, and new rooms such as the elegant Palladian drawing room were created. There is a fine collection of Sèvres porcelain, and paintings by Van Dyck, Correggio and many other masters.
June-Sept, Wed, Thur, Sun, Bank Hol. Adm charge. Refreshments. Shop. P Toilets. Tel Glynde (079 159) 335.

GREAT DIXTER

Off A28 at Northiam, 11 miles north of Hastings (Db)

Standing above the Rother Valley at the northern end of the village of Northiam, Great Dixter is a magnificent 15th-century timber-framed manor house. It was bought in 1910 by the architectural historian Nathaniel Lloyd, who commissioned Sir Edwin Lutyens to restore it and lay out the garden. Though it looks all of a piece, it in fact consists of three separate parts: the original house, to the right of the entrance porch; the Lutyens extension, left of the porch; and a 16th-century yeoman's hall, behind the extension.
Apr-mid Oct, daily exc Mon. Adm charge. Shop. P Toilets. Tel Northiam (0797) 743160.

HASTINGS CASTLE

Near centre of Hastings (Db)

High on West Hill, above the old town and modern seaside resort, fragments of stone walls and a few arches are all that survive of William the Conqueror's great castle. William's first Hastings Castle was probably a prefabricated wooden structure set up on a motte or artificial mound in 1066; the stone castle, built a year or two later, lasted only until 1287, when colossal storms swept away most of the building.

Below the curtain wall are caves tunnelled in the sandstone, said to have been used as dungeons in the Middle Ages. A short way inland, the more extensive St Clement's Caves cover 4 acres below West Hill. Used in the 18th century for storing smugglers' contraband, they were enlarged in the 19th century, and served as air-raid shelters during the Second World War. Both the castle and the caves can be reached by road, or by the West Hill Cliff Railway. At the foot of East Hill, the Fishermen's Museum, in a converted Victorian chapel, has a Hastings fishing boat, or lugger, as its centrepiece. Nearby, the Shipwreck Heritage Centre is a reminder of the perils of this stretch of coast. Based on a group of wrecks visible on the shore at low tide, it covers 3000 years of maritime history using audiovisual presentations. Visitors can operate the centre's radar equipment to monitor shipping in the Channel.

The Old Town Hall in the High Street, built in 1823, is now a museum of local history highlighting the growth of tourism, together with famous people who lived in the Hastings area, such as John Logie Baird, the inventor of television. The present Town Hall, in Queens Road, displays the Hastings Embroidery. Made in 1966 to commemorate the 900th anniversary of the Battle of Hastings, its 27 needlework panels depict the major events of British history.

From East Hill eastwards to Fairlight stretch the 520 acres of Hastings Country Park. Deep glens gouge the sandstone hillside, covered with trees and gorse, while from the rolling grassland above the cliffs the coast of France can be seen on a clear day. Several nature trails lead over the hills. Below Fairlight church are a car park and a visitor centre.
Castle: Apr-mid Oct, daily; Oct, weekends. Shop. Tel Hastings (0424) 722022. Caves: Apr-mid Oct, daily; mid Oct-Mar, Sat, Sun. Adm charge. Shop (Apr-mid Oct). Toilets. ♿ Tel (0424) 722022. Fishermen's Museum: Spring Bank Hol-Sept, daily exc Sat. Free entry. ♿ Tel (0424) 424787. Shipwreck Centre: Easter-Oct, daily. Adm charge. Shop. ♿ Tel (0424) 437452. Old Town Hall: Easter-Sept, daily exc Sun. Adm charge. Tel (0424) 721209. Town Hall: June-Sept, daily exc Sun; Oct-May, daily exc Sat and Sun. Adm charge. Shop. Toilets. ♿ Tel (0424) 722026. Country Park: All year, daily. (Centre, Easter-Sept, weekend pm.) P Toilets. ♿ Tel (0424) 424242.

LUTYENS GARDEN *The garden of Great Dixter, laid out by the architect Sir Edwin Lutyens, restorer of the house, exhibits a rich diversity of blooms as well as more formal clipped yew hedges and topiary.*

HERSTMONCEUX CASTLE

Off A271, 5 miles east of Hailsham (Cb)

This palatial 15th-century castle, unusual in being built of brick instead of stone, has for more than 30 years been the headquarters of the Royal Greenwich Observatory, which moved to Sussex in the 1950s because of increasing atmospheric pollution in London. Though the giant 98in Isaac Newton telescope was moved to the still clearer atmosphere of the Canary Islands in 1979, Herstmonceux remained the nerve centre of British astronomy. It is planned to move the observatory to Cambridge in 1990.

Built by Sir Roger Fiennes, a veteran of Agincourt, in the 1440s, the castle's exterior is virtually unaltered. Visitors can wander round the 200 acres of parkland, and study the latest developments in astronomy at an exhibition in the green-domed buildings east of the castle.
Good Fri-Sept, daily. Adm charge. Refreshments. Shop. P Toilets. ♿ Tel Eastbourne (0323) 833171.

LEWES CASTLE

In centre of Lewes (Bb)

Lewes Castle stands commandingly at the high point of the town, giving wide-ranging views both inland and down the River Ouse towards Newhaven and the sea beyond. Built by William de Warenne soon after 1066, it is unusual among English castles in having two mottes, or artificial mounds, on which wooden and later stone keeps were constructed. The finest medieval survival is the great Barbican or outer gatehouse, added in the 14th century.

Outside the castle walls the Barbican House Museum is the headquarters of the Sussex Archaeological Society, and houses collections ranging from Saxon jewellery to ancient kitchen utensils. Nearby the Lewes Town Model and Living History Centre offers audiovisual displays of the town's history, from its beginnings as a Saxon *burh* to its heyday as a fashionable Georgian resort.

The Military Heritage Museum in West Street illustrates the history of the British Army from the 17th century to the First World War, with displays of weapons, uniforms and equipment.

In Southover, the southern part of Lewes, Anne of Cleves House is now the local history museum of the Sussex Archaeological Society. This rambling timber-framed house, built around 1500, was given to Anne of Cleves as part of her divorce settlement from Henry VIII.

Castle and Barbican House Museum: Apr-Oct, daily; Nov-Mar, daily exc Sun. Adm charge. Shop. Toilets. Tel Lewes (0273) 474379. Town Model: Mar-Oct, daily. Adm charge. Shop. ♿ Tel (0273) 474379. Military Heritage Museum: All year, daily. Adm charge. Shop. Tel (0273) 473137. Anne of Cleves House: Apr-Oct, daily; Nov and Mar, daily exc Sun. Adm charge. Shop. Toilets. Tel (0273) 474610.

MICHELHAM PRIORY

Off A22, 2 miles west of Hailsham (Cb)

The black-robed figure of an Augustinian prior seated at his desk adds a realistic medieval touch to Michelham, which stands, surrounded by a moat, in beautiful and peaceful countryside by the River Cuckmere. The priory was built by the Augustinians in 1229, and though most of it was destroyed at the Dissolution of the Monasteries in 1536, the spacious Prior's Room survives, as does the vaulted undercroft, or cellar, below it, and the tall gate-tower by the moat.

Behind the priory a 'physic garden' has been laid out, containing herbs used in the Middle Ages for cooking and medicine. Among the small plots are herbs for the eyes, ears and teeth, for depression, insomnia and nightmares, and for childbirth and children's diseases. The monks' water mill, powered by water carried by a leat, or channel, cut from the Cuckmere, has been restored and produces and sells stone-ground flour.

Late Mar-Oct, daily. Adm charge. Refreshments. Shop. P *Toilets.* ♿ *Tel Hailsham (0323) 844224.*

PEVENSEY CASTLE

Off A259, at Pevensey (Ca)

Though old Pevensey village is now a mile inland, in former centuries it stood right on the shore, strategically placed on a vulnerable stretch of coast. The village is dominated by the mighty walls of Anderida, one of the Forts of the Saxon Shore built by the Romans in about AD 300 to guard the coast against Saxon raiders from across the Channel. William the Conqueror came ashore somewhere near Pevensey in 1066, and soon after the Conquest his half-brother, Robert of Mortain, built a medieval castle inside the Roman walls. It was fortified again during the Second World War, when the medieval towers were made habitable and pillboxes were constructed on the keep.

EH. All year, daily. Adm charge. P ♿ *Tel Eastbourne (0323) 762604.*

SEVEN SISTERS COUNTRY PARK

On A259, 2 miles east of Seaford (Ba)

East of the winding Cuckmere River, the undulations of the Seven Sisters chalk cliffs form a gentle prelude to the mighty bastion of Beachy Head. Behind the cliffs, a beautiful 700 acre stretch of water meadow and downland forms the Seven Sisters Country Park. Part of the Sussex Heritage Coast, it is owned by the East Sussex County Council and one of the few lengths of unspoilt coastline in Sussex. At Exceat, beside the main road, a superb group of barns houses a permanent exhibition of live creatures.

All year, daily. (Centre: Easter-Sept, daily; Oct-Easter, Sat, Sun.) Adm charge (exhibition). Shop. P *(limited). Toilets.* ♿ *Tel Alfriston (0323) 870280.*

MONASTIC MEMORIES *Michelham Priory was among the monasteries dissolved by Henry VIII. Later, a farmer built a great barn (above) over its ruins. A surviving fragment of the original priory is the gatehouse beside the moat (left).*

SPRING HILL WILDFOWL PARK

Off A22 at Forest Row (Bc)

On the northern fringe of Ashdown Forest, not far from the Weir Wood Reservoir, the 14 acre grounds of a 15th-century house have been turned into a reserve for a large collection of exotic birds. Among them are flamingos and cranes, ostriches and Indian blue peacocks, and rare species of geese, swans and ducks.

All year, daily. Adm charge. Refreshments. Shop. P *Toilets.* ♿ *Tel Forest Row (034 282) 2783.*

YPRES TOWER MUSEUM

Gun Garden, Rye (Eb)

Set on a terrace that commands the level ground between Rye and the sea, the rugged stone walls of the Ypres Tower are a reminder of centuries of war with the French. Built as Rye's castle around 1250, it lost its importance as the Rother silted up and Rye declined as a port. Until well into the 19th century it was used as the town jail, and later as a mortuary. It was damaged in the Second World War by a German bomb, but in the 1950s it was restored and became the local museum. Among the exhibits are displays on shipping and shipbuilding, and on Rye's pottery industry, past and present.

Lamb House, in the heart of the old town, is a superb Georgian mansion facing down a cobbled street. Built in 1723 by James Lamb, a member of a leading Rye family, it was the home of the American novelist Henry James in the early years of this century. A later author who lived there was E.F. Benson, whose 'Mapp and Lucia' novels were set in and around Rye, and filmed for television there.

Museum: Easter-mid Oct, daily. Adm charge. Tel Rye (0797) 223254. Lamb House: NT. Apr-Oct, Wed, Sat, pm only. Adm charge. Tel (0797) 223763.

COUNTY CALENDAR

January (1st two weeks). Hastings: Chess Congress.

March Hastings: Musical Festival.

April (mid-month). Brighton: Southern Garden Show.

May (1st three weeks). Brighton: Arts Festival.

May (1st week). Eastbourne: Folk Festival.

May (from mid-month). Battle: Festival.

May (late, to late Aug). Glyndebourne: Festival Opera.

May (late). Hastings: Blessing the Sea.

May (Spring Bank Hol). Rye: Mayoring Day.

June (3rd week) Eastbourne: Women's International Tennis Tournament.

August (early). St Leonards: National Town Criers' Championships.

August (2nd and 3rd weeks.) Michelham Priory: Music and Arts Festival.

September (early). Alfriston: English Wine Festival.

November (1st Sun). London to Brighton RAC Veteran Car Run.

November 5 Lewes: Bonfire Celebrations.

Tourist information: Battle (042 46) 3721; Brighton (0273) 23755; Eastbourne (0323) 2747; Hastings (0424) 722022; Rye (0797) 222293.

WEST SUSSEX

A ROMAN PALACE AND GREAT GARDENS BELOW THE DOWNS

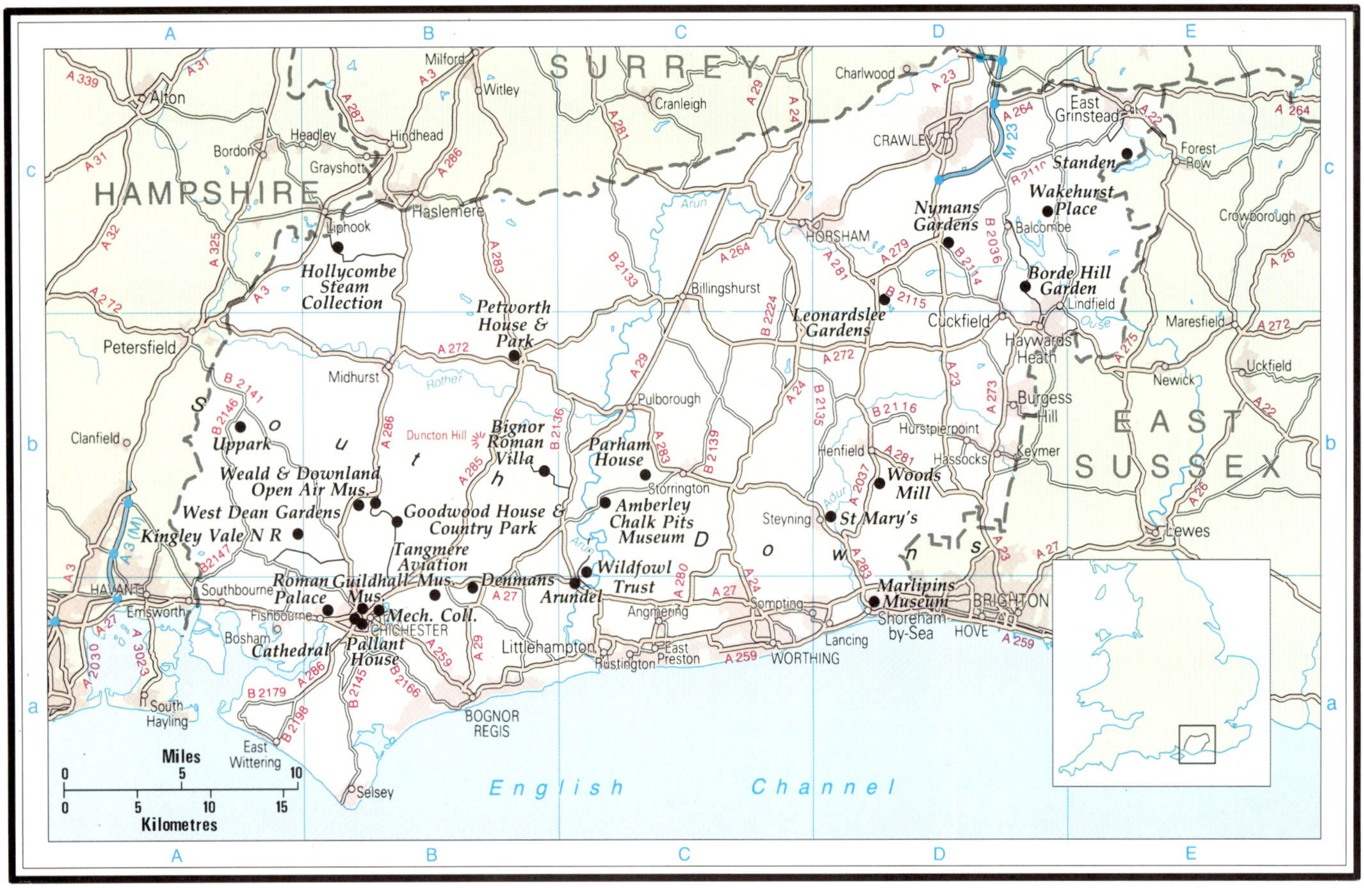

A rich plain sweeping down to the sea and divided by rivers made western Sussex a natural point of arrival for invaders. During the Roman occupation, one of the most sumptuous palaces in northern Europe was built at Fishbourne, and the land was farmed around villas such as Bignor. The Romans founded a walled city on their line of march into the interior: known today as Chichester, it is the natural county town, with a cathedral in which old and new gracefully combine, and a guildhall which was once the chancel of a priory church. Equally impressive is Arundel Castle, built by the Normans to guard the gap where the River Arun curves through the South Downs. The castle walls tower over a town of elegant Georgian and Edwardian streets.

Inland, the broad, smooth ridge of the South Downs provides excellent walks and superb views. In their shelter thrive famous gardens such as Leonardslee and Nymans, lovingly tended over the generations. Stately homes such as Goodwood and Petworth are stored with treasures, while humbler historic buildings are guaranteed survival at the Weald and Downland Open Air Museum.

AMBERLEY CHALK PITS MUSEUM

Off B2139, 5 miles north of Arundel (Cb)

Gleaming white cliffs of chalk form the background to this unusual museum, for it is set in an immense pit quarried out of the downs between the 1840s and the 1960s. The quarried chalk was burnt to produce lime, and most of the museum's buildings were erected for this purpose. Some buildings have been rescued from other places and re-erected on the site.

The theme of the museum is the industrial past of the South of England. Visitors arrive at what used to be the goods yard of Amberley station, and the path follows the former track-bed of the railway through the quarry. Horse transport played an important role in the quarry's life, and the buildings on show include a blacksmith's shop. One exhibition shows the evolution of road construction since Roman times, and there is a display of omnibuses, and a country bus garage of the 1920s. The old bagging shed now houses an exhibition showing the uses of concrete – including such oddities as a concrete bow which fires arrows, and a floating concrete canoe. The top of the quarry gives a view over the site.

Apr-Oct, Wed-Sun and Bank Hol Mon, also Mon and Tues in school summer hol. Adm charge. Refreshments. Shop. P *Toilets.* ♿ *Tel Bury (0798) 831370.*

BIGNOR ROMAN VILLA

Off A29, 5 miles south-west of Pulborough (Bb)

The mosaics are the glory of this Roman farmstead. For more than 1500 years these glowing pictures in multicoloured stones lay buried beneath the fields. Then, in 1811, a farmer's plough struck a large stone – and in moving the stone he uncovered a mosaic depicting a child being borne aloft by an eagle. The Ganymede mosaic, as it is now known, is one of the first sights to confront visitors entering the villa through what used to be the triclinium, or dining room. Nearby are the remains of an elegant hexagonal fountain surrounded by mosaics of dancing girls with flying veils.

The villa is one of the largest discovered in Britain, with traces of 65 rooms apart from outhouses for cattle. Some of these rooms have been reburied, while those with the principal mosaics have been roofed over. In the North Portico is an 82ft length of formally patterned mosaic, the longest mosaic on display in Britain, while the principal dining room holds one of the finest mosaics in Europe – a representation of Venus with, below her, a row of gladiators.

June-Sept, daily; Mar-May and Oct, Tues-Sun and Bank Hol Mon. Adm charge. Refreshments. Shop. P *Toilets.* ♿ *Tel Sutton (079 87) 259.*

PANOPLY AND PLAYTHINGS IN ARUNDEL

The road into Arundel from the south runs, straight as a die, over the fast-flowing River Arun to climb the steep hill upon which the little town is built. Crowning the hilltop are two enormous stone buildings, the castle and the cathedral. Architecturally separated by many centuries, they are nevertheless closely related through the family which built or rebuilt them: the Howard family, Dukes of Norfolk and Earls Marshal of England since the titles were conferred on Sir John Howard by Richard III in 1483.

A useful starting point for a visit to Arundel is its Museum and Heritage Centre, which has excellent topographical models and displays on the story of Arundel from the Stone Age to the present day. One gallery is entirely devoted to Arundel's history as a port, from the Norman Conquest onwards. No less interesting is the charming Toy and Military Museum, which often has displays of model soldiers.

Heritage Centre, High St: Apr-Oct, daily. Adm charge. Shop. Tel Arundel (0903) 882268. Castle: Apr-Oct, pm daily exc Sat. Adm charge. Refreshments. Shop. P Toilets. ♿ Tel (0903) 883136. Cathedral: All year, daily. Free entry. Shop. P (limited). ♿ Tel (0903) 882297. Toy Museum, High St: All year, weekends; June-Aug, school hol and Bank Hol, daily. Adm charge. Shop. Tel (0903) 883101.

VALUED VOLUMES *The library is one of the glories of Arundel Castle. Built by the 11th Duke of Norfolk in 1800, it is entirely fitted out in carved Honduras mahogany, and designed to resemble a church. Even the great stone fireplaces, made for the 15th duke in 1900, are made to look like chapels. The library contains 10,000 books mainly collected by the 9th and 11th dukes. On view in the castle are two of the most poignant relics (right) of the Fitzalan-Howard family's Roman Catholic past: the prayer book and golden rosary carried by Mary, Queen of Scots at her execution and bequeathed by her to the family.*

PICNIC PARTY *Teddy bears which have 'posed' for many a book illustrator find a home in Arundel's Toy and Military Museum. The little Georgian building – which itself looks like a giant doll's house – is crammed with a collection of treasures dating from the 19th century onwards, amassed by the owners and augmented by gifts from visitors.*

LIGHT IN THE WEST *A great rose window dominates the west front of Arundel's Roman Catholic Cathedral, which was built by the same 15th Duke of Norfolk who commissioned the re-construction of Arundel Castle. Begun in 1869, its designer was Joseph Hansom, inventor of the Hansom cab, whose use of the medieval style gave the cathedral a spacious, light interior. The principal memorial in the cathedral is the shrine to St Philip Howard, an ancestor of the Duke of Norfolk who died for his faith in 1595.*

BORDE HILL GARDEN

Off B2036, 1½ miles north of Haywards Heath (Dc)

This is a 'gardener's garden' – it was here the famous camellia called 'Donation' was raised and earned the highest awards from the Royal Horticultural Society. But Borde Hill has been so well laid out that the visitor who has only the slightest knowledge of botany can nevertheless enjoy its beauties. For nearly 90 years, successive owners have maintained and added to the collection of rare or exotic plants and trees.

A series of walks and individual gardens are arranged according to species and themes. The Azalea Ring comes to vivid life in late May; the South Lawn has plants from the mountains of Burma and North China; the Long Walk, with its hardy Chusan palm trees, leads to the Old House Garden with some unusual hybrid plants.

Late Mar-late Oct, Tues-Thur, Sat, Sun and Bank Hol. Adm charge. Refreshments. P *Toilets.* ♿ *Tel Haywards Heath (0444) 450326.*

CHICHESTER CATHEDRAL

In centre of Chichester (Ba)

Although more than 900 years old, Chichester Cathedral owes much of its present fame to a 20th-century man, Walter Hussey, who was Dean from 1955 to 1977. Dean Hussey, a connoisseur of art, believed in enrolling art in the service of the Church, and the cathedral is in consequence a treasure house of modern painting, sculpture and stained glass.

The cathedral stands at the very centre of the Roman city: recent excavations near the high altar uncovered a mosaic pavement which has been left exposed beneath a glass cover. Most of the present building was completed by the year 1123, and the cathedral contains two of the most important Norman sculptures surviving in Britain: the *Raising of Lazarus* and *Christ arriving at Bethany*, both sculpted around 1125. The interior of the great building, with its vast Romanesque columns towering up to a vaulted ceiling, has probably changed little in appearance over the intervening centuries.

Against the soft, honey-coloured stone the modern works stand out vividly. Dominating all is the tapestry by John Piper behind the High Altar, with its central splash of crimson fading off into sombre blues and browns. In the Chapel of St Mary is a startlingly modern representation by Graham Sutherland of Christ appearing to Mary Magdalen, while a window in the north aisle is by the French painter Marc Chagall. More traditional arts are represented by the 14th-century misericords – the lively carvings under the hinged seats of the choir stalls – and the 16th-century panels in the south transept showing Henry VIII and notable figures of his reign.

Outside the cathedral, the area between the cloisters and the main building, which used to be a graveyard, is now a delightful garden. Vicars' Hall, which dates from the 12th century, is now a restaurant, while between these ancient buildings and the outside world is a tangle of lanes.

All year, daily. Free entry. Refreshments. Shop. P *Toilets.* ♿ *Tel Chichester (0243) 782595.*

CHICHESTER GUILDHALL MUSEUM

Priory Park, Chichester (Ba)

Unlike most historic cities, Chichester never bothered to build its own guildhall, but made do with an existing building. This was the church of the Greyfriars' Priory, which was sold to the People of Chichester by Henry VIII when he ordered the dissolution of the priory. All the other buildings of the priory have disappeared, but the chancel of the church survives as a museum.

Entering by the west door the visitor is immediately impressed by its great height and by the five tall lancet windows at the east end. Slotted into the side walls are seats for the friars – some worn away over the centuries. The Guildhall is now a branch of Chichester District Museum (at 29 Little London).

Priory Park is tucked into a bend of the city walls, near which is all that remains of the Norman castle. It consists today simply of a green mound which, though low, allows an excellent view of the priory grounds, with the church at its centre. From here it is easy to reach the encircling city walls, from which there is an unforgettable view of the city.

June-Sept, Tues-Sat pm. Free entry. Shop. Tel Chichester (0243) 784683.

DENMANS

Off A27, 4 miles east of Chichester (Ba)

Visitors to the gardens at Denmans pass first through the estate's former Home Farm, where teas, plants, dried flowers, herbs and other country products are on sale in the old dairy and other buildings. From 1946 the 19th-century estate was transformed into a series of ornamental gardens. These include the Walled Garden, noted for massed perennials, herbs and old-fashioned roses in high summer. The Gravel Stream, planted with grasses, bamboo and shrubby willow, leads down to a water garden, and beyond is a 'wild garden'. The lawns of the tree-girt South Garden erupt with spring flowers.

Mar-Oct, Tues-Sun and Bank Hol Mon. Adm charge. Refreshments. Shop. P *(limited). Toilets. Tel Eastergate (024 368) 2808.*

SECOND SPIRE *The slender spire of Chichester Cathedral was rebuilt in 1861. Beside the cathedral stands the 15th-century bell tower. John Piper's tapestry behind the High Altar represents the Trinity.*

MYTH IN MOSAIC *A winged sea-horse forms part of the design of a mosaic floor in the North Wing of Fishbourne Roman Palace. The wing, comprising 23 rooms, was added to the palace in about AD 150.*

FISHBOURNE ROMAN PALACE

On A27, 1¼ miles west of Chichester (Ba)

Standing in what was once the garden of a Roman palace, the visitor can see two worlds separated by nearly 2000 years. On the left is a modern housing estate: it was during the ground work for a planned extension to it in 1960 that the

North Wing of the palace was discovered, when a trench cut to lay a water main uncovered Roman ruins. In front stand the covered remains of what was probably the most splendid Roman building north of the Alps.

Fishbourne was the residence of a pro-Roman local king, and its interior was accordingly sumptuous. The mosaics are world-famous for they are both extensive and sophisticated, employing advanced techniques of perspective.

Modern museum techniques have been used brilliantly at Fishbourne. In the garden, for instance, excavations have determined the position and shape of the original Roman flowerbeds, and these have been replanted with the type of plants the Romans would have grown. At the entrance to the palace, a model shows how Fishbourne would have appeared in about AD 75, when the first building phase was complete. The sea was much nearer then, and another model shows this and the routes to the palace's busy quay. Other displays show the objects which were discovered on the site, and their significance in the palace's history.

The route through the North Wing is by a series of walkways which protect the mosaics. Here and there can be seen charred material – evidence of the fire which destroyed the palace in the late 3rd century. There remain many traces of the building details, such as a hypocaust for underfloor heating and an oven.

Mar-Nov, daily; Dec-Feb, Sun. Adm charge. Refreshments. Shop. P *Toilets.* ♿ *Tel Chichester (0243) 785859.*

GOODWOOD HOUSE AND COUNTRY PARK

Off A286, 3½ miles north-east of Chichester (Bb)

'Glorious Goodwood' has entered the language as a description of an exhilarating sporting occasion. Races continue to be held at Goodwood Racecourse on its beautiful site high on the South Downs – the winning post is 700ft above sea level – as they have been for nearly 180 years. But there are far more open-air activities these days. The 60 acre country park includes a golf-course, an airfield and motor circuit.

Tsars, kings and queens made Goodwood House their home every July for the horseracing and all left a thank you in the form of jewellery or other rich presents, still to be seen in the house. Charles II was the father of the 1st Duke of Richmond, ancestor of the present owner, and the house has been 'royally' embellished over the years. The 3rd duke, for instance, was a great traveller and collector, and it was he who brought back the priceless collections of Sèvres porcelain and Gobelins tapestries. He also planned the great ballroom as a gallery in which to display to advantage the portraits of his ancestors. They are still on view, in the exact positions he sketched out for them, and form a nationally important collection of works by some of England's most famous portrait painters, among them Reynolds, Lely and Kneller.

Easter weekend; early May-early Oct, Sun and Mon pm; also Tues, Wed and Thur pm in Aug. Adm charge. Refreshments. Shop. P *Toilets.* ♿ *Tel. Chichester (0243) 774107.*

LAKESIDE SPLENDOUR *Hammer ponds dating back to 17th-century iron-smelting days are a feature of the woodland gardens at Leonardslee. The tall trees around them shelter banks of azaleas and rhododendrons.*

HOLLYCOMBE STEAM COLLECTION

Off A3, 2 miles south-east of Liphook (Bc)

At Hollycombe the visitor has the chance to relive the romantic age of steam, in a beautiful woodland setting, with walks and superb views. There are three main rides: the Quarry Railway runs for 1½ miles with views of the South Downs, the Burrell Traction Engine hauls carriages through the woods, and there is a miniature railway. Other attractions include a reconstruction of an early travelling cinema, backed up by a magnificent steam organ; the huge engine from the paddle steamer *Caledonia;* and the oldest surviving showman's engine, the Burrell 'Emperor' built in 1894. The Woodland Gardens offer a blaze of azaleas in spring and spectacular autumn colours.

Easter-mid Oct, Sun and Bank Hol pm; mid-end Aug, pm daily. Adm charge. Refreshments. Shop. P *Toilets. Tel Liphook (0428) 724900.*

KINGLEY VALE NATURE RESERVE

Off B2146, 6 miles north-east of Chichester (Ab)

This is a national nature reserve under the protection of the Nature Conservancy Council, for it is not only one of the last of Britain's yew forests but the finest in Europe. The first trees grew at least 500 years ago, and about 20 of these ancient trees still survive – giants up to 15ft across. The rest of the forest grew naturally from berries dropped by birds, and the rich soil also encouraged the growth of a large variety of other trees and shrubs. Each has its attendant bird and insect residents, so that the reserve is a fascinating 'laboratory' of wildlife.

There is a nature trail through the reserve, and in addition to natural history there are historical and archaeological sites to look out for. The oldest of all the yew trees, for example, are on the site where a battle was fought against the Vikings in AD 859. Higher up the slope are Stone Age flint mines and earthworks, while the four humps known locally as the 'Devil's Humps' are in fact Bronze Age tombs.

All year, daily. Free entry. P *(limited). Tel East Marden (024 359) 286.*

LEONARDSLEE GARDENS

Off A281, 5 miles south-west of Crawley (Dc)

In a county renowned for its beautiful gardens, Leonardslee is outstanding. The 80 acre estate, at its best in spring, lies in a valley with a chain of lakes and waterfalls. In April the collections of camellias and magnolias are in bloom. These beautiful and graceful plants have been grown at Leonardslee for 150 years, and the older specimens have reached tree-like proportions. They are followed by a blaze of rhododendrons and early azaleas: the fragrant rhododendron Loderi for which the garden is famous usually flowers during the second week of May. The Rock Garden, with its waterfall and wishing well, is also then at its best.

In late May the deciduous azaleas begin to bloom in their shades ranging from pink through yellow to deep orange, the yellow variety scenting the gardens. Then, in October, maples add to the rich tints of autumn. In this peaceful valley a herd of wallabies have thrived for 100 years; in spring and summer, females can often be seen with babies in their pouches.

Mid Apr-late June, daily; July-Sept, Sat and Sun pm; Oct, Sat and Sun. Adm charge. Refreshments. Shop. P *Toilets. Tel Lower Beeding (040 376) 212.*

MARLIPINS MUSEUM

High Street, Shoreham-by-Sea (Da)

A handsome, 12th-century building in chequerboard flint, Marlipins has been used as a Custom House, bonded warehouse and courthouse.

Today it contains a museum illustrating the history of Shoreham from the 1600s onwards. Sketches and paintings show the town as it looked in pre-Victorian days, and its growth after that time is captured in a large collection of photographs and postcards.

The displays cover road and rail transport in the district, but the emphasis is on the sea and shipping. An upstairs room is devoted to Shoreham's maritime past, complete with prints, paintings, charts, maps and models of locally built ships and those which regularly docked at the port.

May-Sept, daily exc Sun am. Free entry. Shop. Tel Shoreham-by-Sea (0273) 462994.

MECHANICAL MUSIC AND DOLL COLLECTION

Off A27, 1 mile east of Chichester (Ba)

Housed in a former Victorian church in the eastern outskirts of Chichester, this unusual museum has a comprehensive collection of mechanical musical instruments from the Victorian period. It includes mechanical pianos, fairground organs, musical boxes, horn gramophones and barrel organs, all of which are in working order and demonstrated to visitors. The doll collection ranges from china and wax Victorian dolls to dolls of the 1920s made of velvet and felt.

Easter-Sept, daily; Oct-Easter, Sat and Sun. Adm charge. Shop. P *Tel Chichester (0243) 785421.*

NYMANS GARDEN

On B2114, 4½ miles south of Crawley (Dc)

This is one of the great gardens of the Sussex Weald, though the storm of October 1987 wrought severe damage among its 30 acres of rare and beautiful trees and plants collected from all over the world. The walled garden, the sunken garden, the laurel walk, the ancient bank of bird cherries, the azaleas, rhododendrons, hydrangeas and magnolias make Nymans a delight all through the spring, summer and autumn. The picturesque ruins of the house overlook the lawns with their topiary and fine old cedars.

NT. Apr-Oct, Tues-Thur, Sat, Sun and Bank Hol Mon. Adm charge. Refreshments. Shop. P *Toilets.* ♿ *Tel Handcross (0444) 400321.*

PALLANT HOUSE

In centre of Chichester (Ba)

The Pallants are a complex of streets that form a tiny city within the city of Chichester, and their centre is a large and handsome house built in 1713, which takes its name from the area. Although today it harmonises with its surroundings, when first built it must have been conspicuous in an area then largely occupied by brewhouses, wash-houses and other industrial premises. The builder of the house was a wealthy wine-merchant, Henry Peckham, who wanted to advertise his success by erecting an opulent family home. It was turned into local government offices in 1919, but in 1979 was restored and converted into an art gallery.

The main aim of the restorers has been 'authenticity': even the paints used have been mixed according to 18th-century recipes. Henry Peckham would certainly recognise the grand entrance hall with its original panelling, its flamboyant carved oak staircase and its stone-flagged floor. On the left-hand side of the hall is a dining room which to modern eyes seems cold and austere, with its uncarpeted floor and flimsy looking chairs. The kitchen is set out as it would have been around the year 1900: there is even a patent mousetrap of the period and on the mantelpiece a glass wasp-trap which used to be baited with watered jam.

The elegant long room on the other side of the hall has been set out as a gallery housing the collection bequeathed by Walter Hussey, the Dean of Chichester who commissioned most of the modern works of art in the Cathedral. Among them is a preliminary drawing by John Piper for the great tapestry now in the cathedral. There is also a portrait of Walter Hussey by Graham Sutherland. Upstairs, the Cabinet or Tearoom has been restored as an early 19th-century art collector's room. There are wide views over the rooftops of the city to Chichester Cathedral.

All year, Tues-Sat. Adm charge. Shop. Toilets. Tel Chichester (0243) 774557.

BIRD IMPRESSIONS *The birds which flank the entrance to Pallant House are meant to be ostriches, as portrayed in the builder's family crest, but the sculptor had never seen an ostrich, and his impression earned the house the nickname of 'The Dodo House'.*

PARHAM HOUSE

On A283, 2½ miles south of Pulborough (Cb)

The approach to this gracious Elizabethan manor house is along a drive which rises gently along the back of Windmill Hill – crowned by a causewayed ramp and Bronze Age barrows – and then descends towards the house. As the drive bends round the foot of the hill so the greystone house comes into view with, as backdrop, the slopes of the South Downs about half a mile away. The deer which amble across the drive are descendants of those which were established at Parham at least as early as the 16th century.

The heart of the house is the Great Hall on the ground floor, and it was here that Elizabeth I dined in state in 1593. At the east end of the hall is the carved oak screen put in when the house was built. Above the screen are two windows belonging to the Steward's Room; these enabled him to keep in touch with activities in the Great Hall when his duties took him upstairs.

Scattered through the house are many historic paintings, the most unusual of which is that of a kangaroo by George Stubbs; painted from a skin brought back from Australia by Sir Joseph Banks, it was the first representation of a kangaroo ever seen in Europe. In the 160ft Long Gallery at the very top of the house the Elizabethans took exercise in bad weather. Its ceiling is modern, by Oliver Messel, and display cases contain mementos of the house's history. Outside are a walled garden, a herb garden, an orchard, and grounds enhanced by statues and a lake.

Easter Sun-early Oct, pm Sun, Wed, Thur and Bank Hol Mon. Adm charge. Refreshments. Shop. P *Toilets. Tel Storrington (090 66) 2021.*

PETWORTH HOUSE AND PARK

On A272, 7 miles east of Midhurst (Bb)

Although there has been a building on the site of Petworth House since the early 14th century, most of the present building was the work of the extraordinary 6th Duke of Somerset. His work includes the West Front, begun in 1688, whose magnificence reflects the character of the man who was nicknamed the Proud Duke; he expected to be served on bended knee, and even his children had to stand when speaking to him. By contrast the back of Petworth House is a hotchpotch of styles; only the chapel and the cellars survive from the original building.

The 6th duke's successors continued what he began. In the 18th century the woodcarver Grinling Gibbons was commissioned to create the Carved Room. Here are now displayed Gibbons's superb carved limewood picture frames, emphasising in particular the portraits of the Proud Duke and his wife. The frames are virtually sculptures in their own right, the distinctive flowers and fruit standing out from the background. The Turner Room is devoted entirely to the works of the painter J.M.W. Turner, who was a frequent visitor to Petworth around the 1830s.

The grounds were laid out in 1751 by Capability Brown, whose achievement was to make a man-made layout look entirely natural.

NT. House: Apr-Oct, pm Tues-Thur, Sat, Sun and Bank Hol Mon. Adm charge. Refreshments. Shop. P *Toilets.* ♿ *(ground floor). Park: All year, daily. Free entry.* P *Tel Petworth (0798) 42207.*

ST MARY'S, BRAMBER

On A283, ½ mile east of Steyning (Db)

This beautiful, half-timbered house bears evidence of seven centuries of architectural history. Underfoot lie the foundations of a 12th-

GREEN GLOBES *Old-fashioned herbaceous borders flank the paths leading to the Italian Fountain at Nymans Garden. The fountain is framed by topiary yews, finely sculpted to the shape of hollow globes.*

century building erected by the Knights Templar. The present building was erected in about 1470 as the guesthouse in which the monks of a nearby priory lived and gave shelter to travellers; what is visible today comprises the wing on the eastern side of the old courtyard. One of the original carved entrance arches is on show. On display, too, is a remarkable 'shutting window' in 12 folding sections, bound and hinged with elaborate ironwork; it is the only known example of its kind.

Throughout the house is a wealth of carving and artefacts from its long history, but even in this richly decorated house the famous Painted Room stands out. The panelling of the room is a masterpiece of trompe l'oeil work in which the unknown artist has created the impression of arches leading off into the distance. The room was decorated for the visit of Elizabeth I in 1585, and appears today exactly as it would have done four centuries ago. Outside, the lovingly restored grounds show the traditional English garden at its best, complete with amusingly executed topiary work, and a Monks' Walk once trodden by the monks who were also Wardens of the Bridge over the nearby River Adur.

By contrast, Bramber's House of Pipes is a 'smokiana' museum, whose 40,000 items tell the history of smoking in 180 countries over the past 1500 years. On entering the museum, the visitor finds himself in a replica of a 19th-century shopping arcade, in which is displayed an amazing array of pipes, holders, matches, lighters, snuff boxes, cigars, cutters, cards and coupons.

St Mary's: Early Apr-late Oct, Sun and Bank Hol Mon, and Mon and Thur pm; also early July-Aug, Tues, Wed and Fri pm. Adm charge. Refreshments. Shop. P *Toilets. Tel Steyning (0903) 816205. House of Pipes: All year, daily. Adm charge. Refreshments. Shop.* P *Tel (0903) 812122.*

STANDEN

Off B2110, 2 miles south of East Grinstead (Ec)

A wealthy Victorian gentleman's country villa, Standen is the only house designed by Philip Webb, friend and colleague of William Morris, to have survived with most of its original decoration and furniture intact. Many of the textiles and wallpapers are by William Morris, and are so vulnerable to sunlight that window blinds are in use throughout the house.

Outside, the house appears a solid four-square structure with a curious, squat tower. Webb's design was influenced by his determination to incorporate into the new house the medieval farmhouses that stood on the site. Inside, however, Standen belies the usual conception of a Victorian house, for the rooms are light and airy, and the Morris wallpapers rich and delightful. The wallpaper in the lobby, incorporating birds drawn by Webb, was the first Morris designed. Webb attended to all the details, even down to designing the electric light fittings in the drawing room. Three of the 12 bedrooms and the two dressing rooms can also be seen.

In the 1930s the garden – with its fine views over the Medway valley – became heavily overgrown; but the National Trust has restored Webb's open and restful design.

NT. Apr-Oct, Wed-Sun pm. Adm charge. Refreshments. Shop. P *Tel East Grinstead (0342) 23029.*

TANGMERE MILITARY AVIATION MUSEUM

Off A27, 3 miles east of Chichester (Ba)

A Hawker Hunter jet of 1956 guards the entrance to this former RAF fighter aerodrome, a key station during the Battle of Britain and now the home of a museum of aviation history.

The Tangmere Hall tells the story of the station through its 50-odd years of existence, and includes a display on the intrepid Lysander pilots who flew secret agents into and out of Occupied Europe. There are also later exhibits from the Falklands campaign.

The Battle of Britain Hall displays the remains of aircraft, personal effects, photographs and paintings as lasting reminders of the critical air battles of 1940. A new extension to the museum includes a reconstruction of the famous raid on the Mohne Dam by the 'Dambusters' of 617 Squadron.

Mar-Oct, daily. Adm charge. Shop. P *Toilets. Tel Chichester (0243) 775223.*

UPPARK

On B2146, 5 miles south-east of Petersfield (Ab)

The Duke of Wellington was offered this elegant 17th-century house by a grateful nation in 1816, but promptly declined it when he saw the steep road climbing to it. He calculated that if he lived at the top of such a hill he would have to buy new horses every 18 months. But the climb is well worth it for, from the crest of the hill, the view stretches beyond Chichester to the sea and the Isle of Wight 20 miles away. It was doubtless this superb situation which persuaded the 1st Earl of Tankerville to build here in 1690.

Visitors approach the house along an arcaded

HOMES FROM THE PAST ON THE DOWNS

Curving hills surround a 40 acre bowl which is the setting for a remarkable collection of domestic architecture and country workshops, trades and machinery gathered from all over south-east England. The Weald and Downland Open Air Museum is a perpetual rescue operation that seeks out native buildings of historic importance and re-erects them at Singleton.

The collection includes a reconstructed 14th-century cottage only slightly less primitive than a cave, and the 15th-century Bayleaf Farm with its original lavatory and smoky fireplace. There is also a charcoal-burner's camp complete with a thatched, wooden kiln.

Off A286, just west of Singleton (Bb). Apr-Oct, daily; Nov-Mar, Wed, Sun and Bank Hol. Adm charge. Refreshments (Apr-Oct). Shop. P *Toilets.* ♿*(part). Tel Singleton (024 363) 348.*

LESSONS OF THE PAST *Scarred bench desks, slates, inkwells and an abacus in the reconstructed village school from West Wittering arouse wonder or misty affection in visitors. Originally a cart shed, the building was converted into a schoolroom for the teaching of six poor children of the parish under a charitable trust of 1702.*

HORSE'S HOME *This type of timber-framed, weather-boarded building has been the standard Sussex stable or byre since time immemorial. This example from Watersfield now houses a glossy, mightily thewed carthorse; its winter feed waits in a haystack thatched in traditional style.*

COUNTRY LIVING *This group of buildings (top picture) from various parts of south-east England includes medieval houses, a 16th-century market hall and a 15th-century shop. The Victorian carpenter's shop (above) is complete with well-worn tools and a delicious smell of new-planed timber.*

NATURE'S POWER *The wind pump by the duck pond (right) was originally employed to drain a clay pit. Nearby is a water mill powered by a wheel turning in a mill race, and its splendidly ponderous machinery (far right) has been restored to full working order. Visitors may buy stone-ground wholemeal flour, biscuits and details of country recipes.*

corridor designed by Humphry Repton in 1811. Though the domestic rooms of the house have changed over the years, the ceremonial rooms still look very much as they would have done in the 18th century. The faded, mellow quality of the interior of the house is part of its charm. Wallpapers and curtains, some more than 200 years old and very delicate, are protected from light by drawn blinds. An excellent example of 18th-century taste is the red drawing room with its flock wallpaper, original festoon curtains and rococo furniture. Uppark has a fine collection of European paintings.

NT. Apr-Sept, Wed, Thur, Sun and Bank Hol Mon pm. Adm charge. Refreshments. Shop. P *Toilets.* ♿ *(parts). Tel Harting (073 085) 317.*

WAKEHURST PLACE

On B2028, 6 miles north of Haywards Heath (Dc)

The garden at Wakehurst Place was founded more than 80 years ago and is now at its peak. It consists, in effect, of a series of gardens each devoted to a specific theme or type of plant or tree. The Memorial Garden, dedicated to Sir Henry Price who left the estate to the nation in 1963, is laid out as an old-fashioned, walled cottage garden whose flowers are all in delicate pastel shades. The Himalayan Glade, by contrast, contains plants such as rhododendrons and mountain gentians that are usually to be found above 10,000ft in the Himalayas.

Bloomers Valley and Bethlehem Wood contain such exotic strangers as the giant Californian redwood and a monkey-puzzle tree from Chile. Many fine trees were lost during the storm of October 1987. The oldest garden is the Heath Garden, established in the 1880s and containing plants brought from Australia and South America.

Among all these handsome plants from the far corners of the world is one area devoted not simply to British plants but to native Sussex plants. They grow in a delightful little valley called The Slips, down which a stream meanders to fall at last into the Water Garden. Just beyond is one of the spectacular sites of Wakehurst. Called simply The Ravine, its steep slopes are covered with rhododendrons which in early spring become one great blaze of colour.

NT. All year, daily. Adm charge. Refreshments. Shop. P *Toilets.* ♿ *Tel Ardingly (0444) 892701.*

WEST DEAN GARDENS

On A286, 5 miles south of Midhurst (Bb)

The gardens date back at least to 1622, but around 1768 they were transformed into the landscape style fashionable at the time. Further planting was carried out in 1895, and at the turn of the century many trees were planted by visiting royalty and European aristocracy. In 1911 Harold Peto designed the colonnaded Italianate pergola some 300ft long. The pergola, its pillars draped with roses, honeysuckle and clematis, leads to a gazebo which has an extraordinary floor of knapped flints interspersed with horses' molars. Today the gardens cover some 35 acres, set in a bowl of the South Downs. Flowering trees include foxglove and tulip.

West Dean House, built in 1804 entirely of flint, is now a college of arts and crafts and not open to the public.

Apr-Sept, daily. Adm charge. Refreshments. Shop. P *Toilets.* ♿ *Tel Singleton (024 363) 301.*

WILDFOWL TRUST, ARUNDEL

Mill Road, Arundel (Cb)

Below the immense cliff crowned by Arundel Castle, a series of small lakes or meres provide natural havens for some 1200 wildfowl. A viewing gallery looks out over the central mere, Swan Lake, where diving and sea ducks abound, and hides dotted around the Wildfowl Trust's 55 acres give a close view of water rails, teals, snipes, redshanks and greenshanks. Alternatively, visitors can follow the winding gravel paths which lead from one mere to another. Most of the birds are surprisingly tame, and approach close to be fed. Only one species is entirely enclosed: this is the blue duck from New Zealand, which has its own waterfalls and rushing streams.

All year, daily. Adm charge. Refreshments. Shop. P *Toilets.* ♿ *Tel Arundel (0903) 883355.*

WOODS MILL

Off A2037, 1 mile south of Henfield (Db)

An 18th-century water mill with its turning wheel houses a wildlife and countryside exhibition, among the highlights of which is a model of an oak tree, 25ft tall, showing its life cycle and attendant bird, animal and insect life. There is also an aquarium, a vivarium for harvest mice and an observation beehive. The displays feature local geology and the history of the mill, and two audiovisual programmes illustrate the county's wildlife.

Outside, in the 15 acre nature reserve, marked trails wind through woodland, past meadow and marsh, across streams and around a lake. There are also trails laid out for youngsters, and a pond in which children may catch and identify specimens.

Good Fri-Sept, Tues, Wed, Thur and Sat pm; Sun and Bank Hol. Adm charge. Shop. P *Tel Henfield (0273) 492630.*

COUNTY CALENDAR

Good Fri Tinsley Green: Marbles Championship.

April (early). Bognor Regis: Clown Convention.

June (mid-month). Ardingly: South of England Show.

July 25 Ebernoe: Horn Fair.

July (late). Chichester: Southern Cathedrals Festival, every third year from 1989.

July (late, to early Aug). Goodwood: Race Meeting.

August (early). Littlehampton: Grand Arun Charity Bath Tub Race.

August (late). Bognor Regis: International Birdman Rally.

August (late, to early Sept). Arundel: Arts Festival.

September (late). Ardingly: Antiques Fair.

October (late). Singleton: Steam threshing and ploughing with horses.

Tourist information: Arundel (0903) 882268; Bognor Regis (0243) 823140. Chichester (0243) 775888; Worthing (0903) 210022.

TYNE AND WEAR

A SPECTACULAR COAST AND A CITY WHERE INDUSTRY FLOURISHED

Two arches catch the spirit of Tyne and Wear. The great steel arch of the Tyne Bridge, soaring over the river at Newcastle, is a symbol of the city's engineering skills, while on the coast the limestone arch of Marsden Rock is a piece of natural sculpture on the grand scale.

In Newcastle, the Museum of Science and Engineering celebrates some of the county's most inventive sons and the days when Tyneside built the liner *Mauretania* and the battleship *Nelson*. The fort of Arbeia at South Shields recalls the importance of the River Tyne in Roman times, when Hadrian's Wall started near Newcastle. In the 7th century the Venerable Bede made St Paul's Monastery at Jarrow one of the most famous centres of learning in Europe. A Jarrow writer of modern times, Catherine Cookson, has evoked Tyneside life in more than 60 best-selling novels, and her work is celebrated in the South Shields Museum.

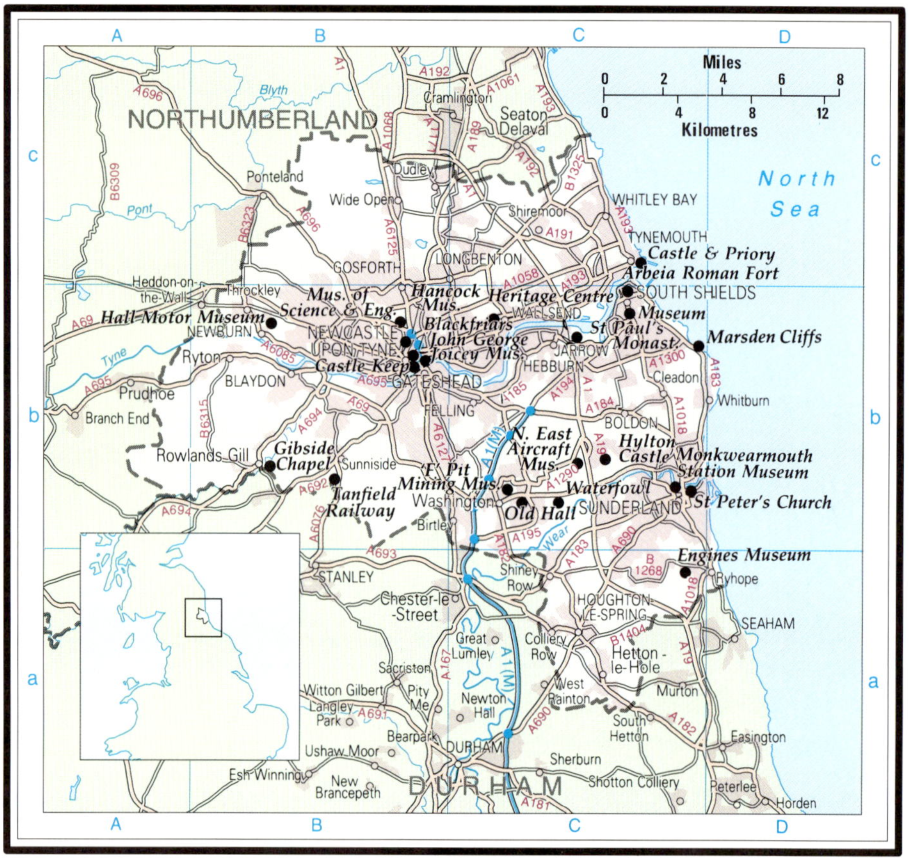

ARBEIA ROMAN FORT

Baring Street, South Shields (Cb)

A full-size reconstruction of a Roman gateway stands beside the excavated remains of a fort dating from AD 163. Every detail of the gateway, down to the hinges and locks, is based upon authentic Roman features. In Roman times the fort guarded the vulnerable eastern flank of Hadrian's Wall and protected supplies coming into the River Tyne for the garrisons along the Wall.

Visitors can see the excavated foundations of the headquarters building, granaries and barracks. A small museum contains objects found during excavations, including the tombstone of a woman called Regina, who lived at the fort with her husband, Barates, a standard bearer from Palmyra in Syria. She is shown sitting in a wicker chair with a wool basket beside her.

May-Sept, daily. Oct-Apr, daily exc Sun. Free entry. Shop. **P** *Toilets.* ♿ *Tel Tyneside (091) 456 1369.*

BLACKFRIARS

In centre of Newcastle upon Tyne (Bb)

Only a short walk from Newcastle's busy Eldon Square stands one of the city's oldest buildings. Founded in the 13th century, Blackfriars is one of the most complete Dominican friaries surviving in England. After the Dissolution of the Monasteries the building became a meeting place for craft guilds, and it is in some of their halls on the upper floor that an exhibition illustrates the development of Newcastle by models, audio-visual displays and wall panels.

The former Chapter House, on the ground floor, contains an exhibition that follows the history of Blackfriars through its three phases – as a medieval friary, its occupation by the guilds and its 20th-century restoration. In keeping with the crafts tradition, Blackfriars now houses several craft workshops, where leatherwork and engraving are carried on.

All year, daily. Free entry. Refreshments. Shop. Toilets. Tel Tyneside (091) 261 5367.

CASTLE KEEP

Quayside, Newcastle upon Tyne (Bb)

In 1080 the Normans built a 'new castle' to guard the strategic crossing of the River Tyne. Its keep still stands, a rugged, four-square tower of time-blackened stone, chequered with the pale grey of many restorations. As the Normans intended, the view from the ramparts is panoramic, especially to the south where Newcastle's six bridges span the river – each a milestone in the industrial history and growth of the prosperous city.

The High-Level Bridge was the first of Newcastle's 'modern' bridges, built in 1846-9 to carry the railway high enough above the river for the tall ships to pass beneath it. Below the railway a lower deck carries road traffic. The bridge dwarfs its close neighbour, the Swing Bridge, which squats close to the water and has a centre section that can pivot to allow ships to pass through. The Newcastle-born engineer William Armstrong built it in 1876, using hydraulics to drive the pivot mechanism.

Both these bridges, however, are dominated by the Tyne Bridge which carries the A6127 into the heart of the city. Opened in 1928, its soaring rainbow of steel has become Newcastle's most famous landmark. Farther upriver the yellow carriages of Newcastle's Metro railway trundle across a network of girders that almost obscure the King Edward VII railway bridge, opened in 1906, while in the distance traffic flies high on the slender arches of Redheugh Bridge, opened in 1983.

In Broad Chare, just off the Quayside, the Trinity Maritime Centre is a delightful little museum crammed with ship models which illustrate Newcastle's maritime heritage, both as a port and as a shipbuilding centre.

Castle Keep: All year, daily. Adm charge. Tel Tyneside (091) 232 7938. Maritime Centre: All year, Tues-Fri. Adm charge. ♿ *Tel (091) 261 4691.*

GIBSIDE CHAPEL

Off A694, 6 miles south-west of Gateshead (Bb)

Designed by the architect James Paine, the chapel looks more like an elegant Palladian villa than an 18th-century church. Its honey-coloured sandstone façade, with its Ionic columned portico, looks down an avenue of Turkey oaks to the statue of British Liberty at the top of a 140ft column. The chapel and the column are the only parts of a grand 18th-century scheme of buildings on the Gibside estate to remain intact.

A raised saucer dome, surmounting a high drum supported by four arches with Corinthian capitals, covers the central area of the chapel, which is decorated with fine plasterwork. Under the chapel is the mausoleum containing the remains of members of the Bowes family, and of the Bowes Lyon family, Earls of Strathmore.

NT. Apr-Oct, Wed, Sat, Sun and Bank Hol. Adm charge. Refreshments. Shop. P ♿ *Tel Consett (0207) 542255.*

HANCOCK MUSEUM

Claremont Road, Newcastle upon Tyne (Bb)

An elegant late Victorian building has for more than 100 years housed the museum of the Natural History Society of Northumbria. It takes its more familiar name from two brothers, John Hancock, whose collection of stuffed birds formed the nucleus of the museum, and Albany Hancock, a researcher into marine life. In the 'Magic of Birds' gallery, the stuffed exhibits are shown in lifelike pose against natural backgrounds. There are also displays showing how birds fly, how they survive and their migration patterns.

A light-hearted display aimed mainly at children is Abel's Ark. Abel Chapman, a Northumbrian naturalist, collected specimens from all over the world. His collection of animals can be seen in a side room, some crowding the decks of the ark, while others wait patiently to go on board. Abel sits by the gangplank and can be heard talking to his charges – accompanied by their growls, roars and grunts.

Across the road from the Hancock Museum is the Museum of Antiquities, where the emphasis is on the Roman altars, tombstones and artefacts from excavations on the sites of Hadrian's Wall. Almost 2000 years separate the Wall from Newcastle's Civic Centre, whose square tower topped by a copper-clad lantern rises majestically to 156ft, well above the rest of the building of Portland stone and red brick. On one wall, by the main entrance, is a 16ft high bronze sculpture of the river-god Tyne, with water pouring from his upstretched hand. The sculptor was David Wynne, whose bronze *Swans in Flight* takes to the air from a pool in the centre's quadrangle. There are conducted tours of the building, which is lavishly decorated with Italian marbles, superb tapestries and crystal chandeliers.

Hancock Museum: All year, daily. Adm charge. Shop. P *Toilets.* ♿ *Tel Tyneside (091) 232 2359. Museum of Antiquities: All year, daily exc Sun. Free entry.* ♿ *Tel (091) 232 8511.*

HYLTON CASTLE

Off A1231, 4 miles south-west of Sunderland (Cb)

A Norman castle on this site was built to defend a ford on the River Wear against the Scots. The present castle was begun in the 14th century by Sir William Hylton, and its imposing early 15th-century keep-gatehouse survives. Its special glory is the west façade, which is broken by four square turrets and topped by battlemented parapets, and has a splendid array of medieval heraldry. This includes canopied banners showing the Arms of Henry IV, and those of the Hylton family and the Percys, Dukes of Northumberland.

EH. All year, daily. Adm charge. Shop. P ♿ *(grounds). Tel Sunderland (0783) 495048.*

DOMED CHURCH *Arches with classical columns support the drum and dome of the 18th-century Gibside Chapel. It is still a consecrated building, where services are conducted by the Earl of Strathmore's chaplain.*

JOHN GEORGE JOICEY MUSEUM

City Road, Newcastle upon Tyne (Bb)

In a quiet byway below the level of bustling City Road stands a 17th-century almshouse, formerly the Holy Jesus Hospital and the only surviving Jacobean brick building in Newcastle. On the ground floor an arcade of 30 arches runs along the entire length of the building, forming a covered walkway. The building now houses a museum funded by the bequest of John George Joicey, a Gateshead coal owner, and devoted mainly to the social history of the city. It also includes an exhibition of relics of the Northumberland Hussars and the 15th/19th The King's Royal Hussars.

Displays illustrate aspects of Newcastle's history, including a sound and visual presentation of the Tyne Flood of 1771 and the Great Fire of 1854. There are also exhibits featuring 19th and 20th-century sporting guns of the north-east, and the German swordmakers who settled at Shotley Bridge.

The Laing Art Gallery, in nearby Higham Place, is a building of lavish Baroque detail and a perfect setting for the art treasures it contains. They include paintings by Reynolds, Landseer and Burne-Jones, and displays of glass, pottery and Newcastle silver.

Joicey Museum: All year, Tues-Sat. Free entry. Shop. Toilets. Tel Tyneside (091) 232 4562. Laing Art Gallery: All year, daily exc Mon. Free entry. Tel (091) 232 7734.

MARSDEN CLIFFS

Off A183, 2 miles south-east of South Shields (Cb)

High limestone cliffs surround Marsden Bay and an exhilarating path runs along their grassy tops; take care not to go too near the edge, for the rock is fragile. The cliffs are home to thousands of sea birds, including kittiwakes, fulmars, guillemots, razorbills and terns. Marsden Rock, a natural arch, is a breeding ground for cormorants.

At the foot of the cliffs is the Grotto, originally a cave gouged out by the sea and turned into a home by an 18th-century miner known as 'Jack the Blaster', while he was working at Marsden Quarry. It is said to be haunted by the ghost of John the Jibber, a local smuggler who betrayed his comrades to the excise men. In revenge they suspended him in a bucket halfway up the cliffs, and left him to starve to death.

The Grotto has been a pub since 1828. It is reached either by a lift or by nearby steps down to the beach.

NT (land). All year, daily. Free entry. Refreshments. P *Tel Tyneside (091) 455 2043 (Grotto).*

NATURAL ARCH *Framed by the wave-carved 100ft arch of Marsden Rock is a rock pillar, left when the sea washed away softer rock between the pillar and the limestone cliffs beyond. The arch itself will eventually collapse, leaving another pillar.*

MONKWEARMOUTH STATION MUSEUM
North Bridge Street, Sunderland (Cb)

The grand classical façade of Monkwearmouth's station, on the line between Newcastle and Sunderland, was built in 1848, at the height of the railway boom. Sunderland's member of parliament at the time was George Hudson, the 'Rail way King', who controlled more than 1000 miles of railway. The station makes the ideal setting for a railway museum, since it has hardly changed since it was opened. The ticket office is much as it was in 1866, and the barrows and trunks on the platform date from the steam age.

All year, daily. Free entry. Shop. P *Toilets.* ♿ *Tel Sunderland (0783) 77075.*

MUSEUM OF SCIENCE AND ENGINEERING
Blandford Square, Newcastle upon Tyne (Bb)

In a handsome Victorian Gothic building, Newcastle displays its place in Britain's industrial history and pays tribute to the local men who played an important part in it. They include Joseph Swan, pioneer of electric light; Charles Parsons, inventor of the steam turbine; the railway engineers George and Robert Stephenson and the industrialist and inventor William Armstrong.

The Motive Power gallery illustrates the development of power harnessed to ships, motor cars and aircraft. In a gallery telling the maritime history of the Tyne, pride of place goes to models more than 12ft long of the largest ships built on the Tyne: the Cunarder RMS *Mauretania*, 762ft long, and the Royal Navy's battleship HMS *Nelson*.

All year, daily exc Sun. Free entry. Tel Tyneside (091) 232 6789.

NEWBURN HALL MOTOR MUSEUM
Off A69, 2 miles west of Newcastle upon Tyne (Bb)

Apart from the large collection of veteran, vintage and post-vintage cars which this museum displays in its main exhibition hall, one of the biggest attractions is the opportunity to see restoration work in progress. Some of the cars on show have appeared in films and television series, including *Chariots of Fire* and *Brideshead Revisited*.

All year, daily exc Mon. Adm charge. Refreshments. Shop. P *Toilets.* ♿ *Tel Tyneside (091) 264 2977.*

NORTH EAST AIRCRAFT MUSEUM
Off A1290, 3 miles west of Sunderland (Cb)

The museum has a collection of some 25 aircraft, including an Avro Vulcan bomber of the type used in the Falklands Campaign, as well as a range of aero engines covering almost the full span of aviation history. It also displays relics of both British and German aircraft of the Second World War that crashed in the north-east. There is also an interesting range of military vehicles, including fire engines.

May-Oct, daily; Oct-May, Sun and Bank Hol. Adm charge. Refreshments. Shop. P *Toilets.* ♿ *Tel Seaham (091) 581 3602.*

RYHOPE ENGINES MUSEUM
Off A1018, 3 miles south of Sunderland (Ca)

The two 100hp beam engines at Ryhope Pumping Station were built and installed in 1869 at a cost of £9000 and ran for the next 100 years, delivering 3 million gallons of water per day from deep wells at Ryhope. The engines and their boilers are still housed in the pumping station, which has now been converted into a museum. This also contains a light-hearted but fascinating display of sanitary fixtures and fittings called 'Clean and Decent'.

Easter-Dec, Sat and Sun pm. Adm charge. Shop. P *Toilets. Tel Sunderland (091) 521 0235.*

ST PAUL'S MONASTERY
Church Bank, Jarrow (Cb)

The chancel of the present parish church of St Paul was part of the very monastery church in which the Venerable Bede, 'Father of English History' and one of the greatest scholars of the Christian world, first prayed when he came to Jarrow as a boy of 12 more than 1300 years ago. Bede wrote his *Ecclesiastical History of the English People* only a few years after the monastery was dedicated in AD 685.

The church has the oldest stained glass in Europe, contained in a window unaltered since AD 681 and made up of glass from the monastery workshop. The monastery was destroyed by Vikings in AD 794, but remains of the cloisters survive.

The Bede Monastery Museum in nearby Jarrow Hall, an 18th-century house, has finds from the monastery excavations, and displays and an audiovisual presentation about the great religious house and the life of its monks.

Monastery: EH. All year, daily. Church: All year, daily. Free entry. Refreshments. Shop. P ♿ *Tel Tyneside (091) 489 7402. Museum: All year, daily exc Mon. Adm charge. Refreshments. Shop.* P *Toilets.* ♿ *Tel (091) 489 2106.*

MONK'S CHURCH *Some 1300 years ago, monks took stone from abandoned Roman buildings to create St Paul's Church at Jarrow. A modern statue of their most famous brother, the scholar Bede, gazes on their work.*

ST PETER'S CHURCH
St Peter's Way, Sunderland (Cb)

This beautiful church was part of a monastery which was once one of the world's greatest centres of Christian learning, and the site remains one of the most important in the early Christian history of Britain. The monastery was built in AD 674 by St Benedict Biscop, a Northumbrian nobleman who later founded St Paul's at Jarrow. The Venerable Bede was born in Wearmouth (now part of Sunderland) and entered the joint community in 681.

The main Saxon parts of the church still surviving are the tower, with its carved stone porch, and the west wall. Showcases contain a fine selection of carved stonework, and there is an audiovisual display on the 1300 year history of the church.

Apr-Oct, Mon-Sat. Free entry. Shop. P *Toilets. Tel Wearside (091) 567 3726.*

SOUTH SHIELDS MUSEUM
Ocean Road, South Shields (Cb)

This museum has re-created the frontage of part of William Black Street, East Jarrow, lovingly described by the best-selling novelist Catherine Cookson in her book about her mother, *Our Kate*. Thousands of visitors every year now make a literary pilgrimage to the museum's Catherine Cookson Gallery to wander down the 'street'. There is a reconstruction of the kitchen in which the authoress spent many of her childhood hours. A popular additional attraction for children is Affleck's old-fashioned sweet shop.

The museum also has a maritime section, whose displays on local shipbuilding include a model of the first purpose-built lifeboat. William Wouldhave designed the boat, which was built in Newcastle in 1789.

All year, daily exc Mon. Free entry. Shop. P *Toilets.* ♿ *Tel Tyneside (091) 456 8740.*

TANFIELD RAILWAY
Off A6076, 1 mile south of Sunniside (Bb)

A passenger service was introduced here as early as 1842, but the lifeblood of Tanfield was its haulage work for the local collieries, and their closure from 1945 onwards led to the gradual decline of the line; the last working section closed in 1981. By then enthusiastic amateurs had already begun their bid to preserve the line. Carriages have been specially built to ferry

HOLY FORTRESS *The formidable ruins of Tynemouth Priory tower over the Tyne estuary. The commanding position of the original Norman church led to its conversion into one of England's biggest castles.*

passengers between Sunniside and Marley Hill, and the entire line to East Tanfield is scheduled for completion by 1990.

All year, daily; steam trains Sun, June-Aug, and Bank Hol, Easter-Aug. Fares. Refreshments. Shop. P *Toilets.* ♿ *Tel Tyneside (091) 274 2002 (evgs).*

TYNEMOUTH CASTLE AND PRIORY

In Tynemouth, near North Pier (Cc)

The headland that forms the north side of the mouth of the Tyne, with steep cliffs and the sea on three sides, was a site of great importance both as a religious centre and as a coast and border castle from the 7th century onwards. It was regularly attacked and plundered by the Danes between AD 800 and 1000.

Near the castle and priory, at Spanish Battery, is the Watch House of the Tynemouth Volunteer Life Brigade. Founded in 1864, the brigade was Britain's first Life Brigade, and the model on which HM Auxiliary Coastguard Service was based.

Castle and Priory: EH. All year, daily. Adm charge. Shop. Toilets. ♿ *(Castle only). Tel Tyneside (091) 257 1090. Watch House: All year, daily exc Mon. Free entry.* P *Toilets. Tel (091) 257 2059.*

WALLSEND HERITAGE CENTRE

Buddle Street, Wallsend (Cb)

For years Wallsend was famous for building big ships, including what was once the biggest ship in the world – RMS *Mauretania*, which for 23 years held the Blue Riband for the fastest Atlantic crossing. The 31,938 ton liner had a service speed of 31mph. But the town's claim to fame goes much farther back than the launching of the *Mauretania* in 1906. Its name literally means 'the end of the wall' – Hadrian's Wall – and the Heritage Centre celebrates Wallsend's Roman past with a display of finds from the Roman fort of Segedunum. A separate gallery is devoted to the history of coal-mining in the district.

All year, daily. Free entry. Shop. P *Toilets.* ♿ *Tel Tyneside (091) 262 0012.*

WASHINGTON OLD HALL

Off A1231, in Washington (Cb)

American presidents have visited Washington Old Hall, the home of George Washington's direct ancestors for five generations and of the Washingtons and their descendants for 430 years. The Hall is a typical example of a small English manor house of the early 17th century.

The stone sundial on the terrace is the gift of a former American Ambassador in London, Mr Walter Annenberg, while the Jacobean woodwork in the Panelled Room, from the Old Manor House, Abbots Langley, was the gift of Miss Mabel Choate, in memory of her father who was once American Ambassador to Britain.

NT. Apr-Sept, daily exc Fri; Oct, Wed, Sat and Sun. Adm charge. Shop. P *Toilets. Tel Tyneside (091) 416 6879.*

WASHINGTON 'F' PIT MINING MUSEUM

Off A182, Albany Way, Washington (Cb)

The first shaft was sunk at this pit in 1777 and the last coal drawn from it in 1968 – by an 1888 horizontal steam winding engine, the last one in the Durham and Northumberland coalfield. This outstanding example of 19th-century engineering, built by the Grange Iron Company of Durham, can be seen at the museum, operated for demonstration by an electric motor.

Apr-Oct, daily exc Mon. Adm charge. P *Toilets. Tel Tyneside (091) 232 6789.*

WASHINGTON WATERFOWL PARK

Off A1231, 1 mile east of Washington (Cb)

More than 100 different types of wildfowl – ducks, geese and swans – from every continent of the world can be seen at the Wildfowl Trust's reserve at Washington. One of the biggest attractions is a flock of elegant Chilean flamingos. The reserve is made up of 100 acres of ponds, lakes and woodland. Paths lead visitors to hides overlooking bird-feeding stations.

All year, daily. Adm charge. Refreshments. Shop. P *Toilets.* ♿ *Tel Tyneside (091) 416 5454.*

COUNTY CALENDAR

June (mid-month). Newcastle upon Tyne – South Shields: Great North Run (charity marathon).

June (late, to Aug). South Shields: South Tyneside Cookson Country Mardi Gras.

June (last week). Newcastle upon Tyne: Newcastle Hoppings (annual fair).

July (late, to early Aug). Newcastle upon Tyne: Tyneside Summer Exhibition.

August (mid-month). South Shields: South Tyneside Festival and Flower Show.

November (early). Newcastle upon Tyne: Festival.

Tourist information: Gateshead (091) 477 3478; Newcastle upon Tyne (091) 261 0691; South Shields (091) 454 6612; Sunderland (091) 565 0960.

WARWICKSHIRE

PROUD CASTLES AND STATELY HOMES AT ENGLAND'S HEART

A county at the heart of England whose attractions span the centuries, Warwickshire has appropriately at its own heart a county town with one of England's greatest medieval castles, some fine timber-framed buildings and a wealth of handsome Georgian houses. Only a few miles to the north of Warwick stands Kenilworth Castle, its crumbling sandstone walls still beautiful on its grassy knoll. Kenilworth suffered during the Civil War, whose opening Battle of Edgehill is commemorated at Farnborough Hall.

Throughout the county there are great houses, ranging from the Elizabethan elegance of Charlecote Park and Arbury Hall to the Georgian grandeur of Farnborough Hall and Stoneleigh Abbey. But Warwickshire's most famous building is a humble dwelling in Stratford-upon-Avon where, in 1564, William Shakespeare was born.

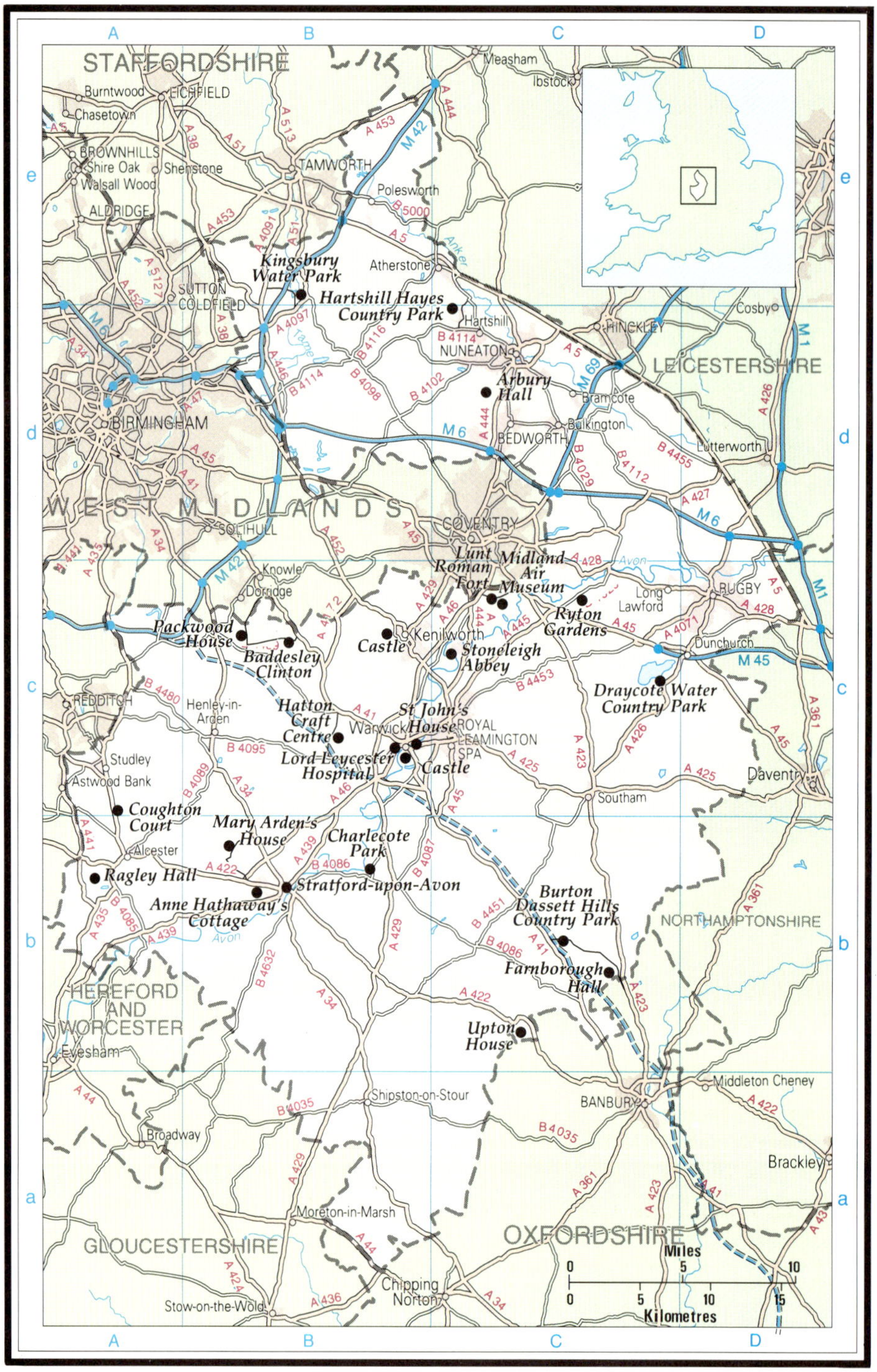

ANNE HATHAWAY'S COTTAGE

Off A439, 1 mile west of Stratford-upon-Avon (Bb)

Even if this were not the birthplace of William Shakespeare's wife, the cottage would still hold its own as an architectural gem, with irregular timber-framed walls and tiny latticed windows beneath a trim, thatched roof. Little has changed since Shakespeare strolled through the herb-scented garden to woo the woman he was to marry in 1582. Inside he would have seen rooms furnished much as they are today, with the wooden settle in the living room where, it is said, William and Anne sat when courting.

All year, daily. Adm charge. Shop. P *Toilets. Tel Stratford-upon-Avon (0789) 204016.*

ARBURY HALL

Off B4102, 2 miles south-west of Nuneaton (Cd)

Behind Arbury Hall's lovely Elizabethan façade is a remarkable interior in which the hall's 18th-century owner, Sir Roger Newdigate, indulged his enthusiasm for the Gothic Revival style. The soaring fan-vaulted ceilings, plunging pendants and filigree tracery were described by the writer George Eliot, who was born on the estate, in her book *Mr Gilfil's Love Story*. Substituting 'Cheverel Manor' for Arbury she wrote of 'architectural beauty, like a cathedral' in the dining room, and described the saloon as 'elaborate in its tracery, which was like petrified lacework'.

Easter-Sept, Sun and Bank Hol Mon pm; also Tues and Wed pm, July-Aug. Adm charge. Refreshments. Shop. P *Toilets.* ♿ *Tel Nuneaton (0203) 382804.*

BADDESLEY CLINTON

Off A41, 7½ miles north of Warwick (Bc)

One of the finest medieval moated houses in England, Baddesley Clinton has changed little since 1634, and its stone walls rise sheer from the broad moat that completely surrounds it. There is only one way into the house – across the brick-built bridge and through the handsome gatehouse that rises to rooftop height. Beyond lies a courtyard laid out with yews and a lawn set with flowers in the form of the arms of the Ferrers, owners of Baddesley Clinton until 1939.

An unusual feature of the house is the 'priest-hole' built into a drain in the kitchen, which can be seen through a glass panel in the floor. Other rooms contain fine fireplaces, especially in the Great Hall where the massive carved stone chimneypiece bears a coat of arms made up of four branches of the Ferrers family. Shields in the stained-glass windows record family marriages.

NT. Late Mar-Oct, Wed-Sun pm. Adm charge. Refreshments. Shop. P *Toilets.* ♿ *(ground floor). Tel Lapworth (056 43) 3294.*

BURTON DASSETT HILLS COUNTRY PARK

Off A41, 10 miles south-east of Warwick (Cb)

Approached from any direction, the hills are dramatic, thrusting up from the flat surrounding countryside in rugged grassy humps. They evoke an irresistible urge to explore the old iron-ore quarries on their sides, to inspect the quaint little beacon tower perched on Windmill Hill and to savour the views from Magpie Hill.

The quarries date from the 19th century and now, grass-grown and weathered, offer adventure for children and shelter for picnickers. Above them, footpaths lead to the beacon tower, possibly used in 1642 to signal the start of the first Civil War battle at nearby Edge Hill. Magpie Hill, 630ft up, has a view indicator which identifies the landmarks visible on a clear day – including Warwick Castle, the city of Coventry and the Malvern Hills.

At the southern end of the 100 acre park is Burton Dassett's Church of All Saints, built on a hillside. It dates from the 12th century, and its builders coped with the terrain simply by giving the building a slope of 15ft from end to end. Inside, wide steps lead up to the altar, flooded with light from tall, clear glass windows.

All year, daily. Free entry. Refreshments. P *Toilets. Tel Warwick (0926) 493431.*

CHARLECOTE PARK

Off B4086, 5 miles east of Stratford-upon-Avon (Bb)

Charlecote's gatehouse sets the scene for the lovely house beyond. Built of brick which four centuries have mellowed to a rosy pink, it is pure Elizabethan both in style and origin. The gatehouse was the one part of Charlecote that escaped the attentions of its 19th-century owner George Lucy who, despairing of the many alterations that had taken place over the centuries, restored the interior of the house in the 'Elizabethan Revival' style.

Nevertheless, the exterior of Charlecote Park still has that magical atmosphere that the Elizabethans were able to create with red brick and grey stone, its tall bay windows, corner towers, gabled roof and elegant porch all blending into a harmonious whole. The house is further ennobled by its gardens, the winding River Avon below and a deer park landscaped by Capability Brown. Herds of red and fallow deer roam the park, as they have done since the young William Shakespeare, it is said, suffered the wrath of Sir Thomas Lucy, Charlecote's builder, by poaching his deer. All seems to have been forgiven, however, and one garden contains flowers mentioned in his plays.

Inside the house the rooms contain fine paintings, sculptures and furniture acquired by George Lucy during his time at Charlecote and arranged as they were 150 years ago. The outbuildings include a brew house with its original brewing equipment, and a coach house where carriages used by the Lucys are on display.

NT. Apr-Oct, daily except Mon and Thur. Adm charge. Refreshments. Shop. P *Toilets.* ♿ *Tel Stratford-upon-Avon (0789) 840277.*

HATHAWAY HOME *This lovely timber-framed cottage, with its brick chimneys and old-fashioned English garden, was the birthplace of Anne Hathaway, who in 1582 married the 18-year-old William Shakespeare.*

COUGHTON COURT

Off A435, 2 miles north of Alcester (Ac)

The most imposing feature of Coughton Court is its gatehouse, beautifully proportioned with tall bay windows set between slender octagonal towers. It was built early in the 16th century and through its archway horses and wagons once passed. In the 18th century, however, this archway was transformed into the front hall. It has a fan-vaulted ceiling, and the walls are hung with 17th-century Flemish tapestries.

The rooms above the front hall include the Tower Room in the north-east turret, which had two secret compartments beneath its floor for hiding priests in times of trouble. The Throckmorton family, who have lived here for five centuries, have always been Roman Catholics, and it was in the drawing room of Coughton Court that the wives of the Gunpowder Plotters are said to have heard of the plot's failure.

NT. May-Sept, pm daily exc Mon and Fri; Apr and Oct, Sat and Sun pm. Adm charge. Refreshments. Shop. P *Toilets.* ♿ *(parts). Tel Alcester (0789) 762435.*

READING ROOM *Charlecote Park's library contains books collected by Sir Thomas Lucy in the early 17th century. In front of the bookcases two high-backed ivory-inlaid chairs are illuminated by a shaft of sunlight.*

DRAYCOTE WATER COUNTRY PARK

On A426, 2 miles south-west of Dunchurch (Cc)

A country park of some 21 acres lies on the south side of Draycote Water, and includes Hensborough Hill which makes a good vantage point for watching the sailing races on the reservoir below. There is a car park at the top of the hill, which also has a picnic area. There is an adventure playground near the park entrance.

All year, daily. Free entry. P *Toilets. Tel Warwick (0926) 493431.*

FARNBOROUGH HALL

Off A423, 6 miles north of Banbury (Cb)

In the 18th century the Grand Tour of Europe was popular among young men of means, and many came back to England impressed with the architecture they had seen, particularly in Italy, and with their baggage crammed with fine paintings and sculptures. One such young man was William Holbech, owner of Farnborough Hall from 1717 until 1771. On his return he set about remodelling the hall on the lines of a Palladian villa, and filled it with classical sculptures and paintings by Canaletto and Panini. To set off these treasures he employed a Yorkshireman, William Perrit, to provide rococo plasterwork that ranks among the finest in Britain.

The house's showpiece is undoubtedly the Dining Room, where Perrit's work adorns picture frames and mirrors, the white marble fireplace, the door surrounds and ceiling. Plasterwork panels illustrate Holbech's interest in hunting and music.

Holbech also laid out a Terrace Walk three-quarters of a mile long south-east of the house, and flanked it with an Ionic Temple and an Oval Pavilion. The walk leads to a tall, slender obelisk, whose base is carved with the initials of Italian prisoners of war, who were at Farnborough when it was a military hospital during the Second World War. From the obelisk there is a panoramic view across the Warwickshire Plain towards Edge Hill.

A barn in the grounds of Farnborough Hall houses the Edgehill Battle Museum, devoted to the events of October 23, 1642, when, 3 miles to the west, Englishmen fought Englishmen in an inconclusive engagement, in which both sides suffered heavy casualties. Arms, armour and costumes of both armies are displayed – the weapons and finery of King Charles's Cavaliers contrasting vividly with the Parliamentarians' poor equipment. Maps and dioramas show the battle lines and how the battle progressed.

For a view of the actual battlefield, drive west along a minor road to Edge Hill itself, the sandstone ridge where Charles I raised his standard before the battle. A century later an octagonal tower was built on the spot by Sanderson Miller, a local architect and landowner. Today it is part of the Castle Inn, from which paths descend through beechwoods to the village of Radway.

House and Grounds: NT. Apr-Sept, Wed and Sat pm; grounds only, Thur, Fri and Sun pm. Adm charge. P (limited). Toilets. Museum: Apr-Oct, Wed, Sat, and Spring Bank Hol pm. Free entry. Refreshments. Shop. P Toilets. ♿ Tel Banbury (0295) 89202.

HARTSHILL HAYES COUNTRY PARK

Off B4114, 4 miles north-west of Nuneaton (Cd)

On a ridge overlooking the Anker Valley, this park encompasses 136 acres of open hilltop and woodland. There are panoramic views across four counties – a patchwork of fields and hedgerows, farms and villages, with the Derbyshire Peak and Charnwood Forest visible on a clear day. The many trails include two waymarked woodland walks, each taking about one hour.

All year, daily. Free entry. P Toilets. Tel Nuneaton (0203) 395141.

HATTON CRAFT CENTRE

On A41, 3 miles north-west of Warwick (Bc)

This award-winning craft centre occupies 19th-century farm buildings where an extensive range of work is displayed. There are some 30 workshops, about 20 of which have items for sale, including corn dollies, silk flowers, needlecraft, country clothes, candles, pottery and model locomotives. Nearby is a pick-your-own fruit farm.

A short walk from the craft centre leads to Hatton Locks, on the Grand Union Canal. There are 21 locks, the longest flight in Britain, 17 to the east of the bridge crossing the canal and four to the west.

All year, daily. Free entry. Refreshments. Shop. P Toilets. ♿ Tel Claverdon (092 684) 2436.

KENILWORTH CASTLE

On B4103, in Kenilworth (Bc)

The red-sandstone castle keep stands foursquare on a grassy slope, aloof from the bustling market town below, serene in its own world. Though its towers are crumbling and its windows as blank as sightless eyes, it still retains the imposing strength and grandeur that made it one of England's chief strongholds in Norman times.

The best approach to the castle on foot is across the causeway that leads from the car park on the south side. Here much of the castle's outer wall still stands; beyond it the Norman keep stands alone, separated by the ravages of war, time and weather from the buildings added to it in later centuries. Only the walls remain of the great banqueting hall built by John of Gaunt in the 14th century, and little more of the buildings added by Robert Dudley, Earl of Leicester, in the 16th century.

The best preserved parts of Kenilworth are Dudley's gatehouse, which was designed to impress distinguished visitors and still impresses with its tall corner towers and battlemented parapets, and the stables, which are built of dressed stone with a timbered upper storey. Dudley's castle certainly impressed Elizabeth I, who was a frequent visitor to Kenilworth. During the Civil War the castle was held by the Roundheads, who destroyed the keep's north wall after the war. The castle has not been lived in since the Restoration.

EH. All year, daily. Adm charge. P Toilets. Tel Warwick (0926) 52078.

PAST GLORIES *Tall windows rise beside a massive fireplace in the 14th-century Great Hall of Kenilworth Castle. The hall was once the scene of lavish banquets, with Elizabeth I as guest of honour.*

KINGSBURY WATER PARK

On A4097, 6 miles south of Tamworth (Be)

There is water galore in Warwickshire's 'little lake district', comprising 20 lakes – former gravel pits – in 600 landscaped acres alongside the River Tame. The lakes are linked by winding footpaths that lead through woodlands and along the water's edge. Visitors can take their own canoes or inflatable boats onto the water, or just watch the sailing, hydroplaning or windsurfing. Nature trails lead to quieter areas of woodland, and there is a nature reserve with hides. There is ample space for picnicking, and there is also a children's adventure playground.

All year, daily. Adm charge. Shop. P Toilets. ♿ Tel Tamworth (0827) 872660.

LORD LEYCESTER HOSPITAL

High Street, Warwick (Bc)

Standing shoulder to shoulder against Warwick's medieval West Gate, the Lord Leycester Hospital consists of a group of timber-framed buildings of 1383, their dark brown timbers and weathered stonework supporting gabled upper storeys that lean alarmingly over the cobbled pavement. The 'hospital' was founded as a charitable institution in 1571 by Robert Dudley, Earl of Leicester, as a retirement home for his aged retainers and their wives. The buildings still serve as almshouses, and their occupants today, the 'Brethren', are eight ex-servicemen and their wives.

Next door is the Chapel of St James, founded in 1383 and still lit by candles in candelabras. In 1450 Richard Neville, Earl of Warwick, built the adjoining Guildhall, a superbly timbered room which has a collection of swords brought back by previous Brethren from their foreign campaigns. The hospital's Great Hall is also notable for its magnificent oak roof. The buildings cluster around a tiny courtyard where brightly painted coats of arms decorate an overhanging gallery.

All year, daily exc Sun. Adm charge. Refreshments (summer). Shop. Toilets. ♿ (ground floor). Tel Warwick (0926) 492797.

LUNT ROMAN FORT

Off A423, 2 miles south-east of Coventry (Cc)

An impressive reconstruction stands on the site of the original Roman fort built after the rebellion of the Iceni tribe under Queen Boudicca in about AD 60. The site is on high ground overlooking the River Sowe. The gateway is based on that carved on Trajan's column in Rome, and erected in the fort's original post-holes. Another reconstructed building is the granary, where all finds from the site are displayed. But the most impressive feature of the fort is the Gyrus, a great fenced ring in which the Romans trained their horses for battle.

June-Sept, daily exc Mon and Thur. Adm charge. Shop. P Toilets. ♿ Tel Coventry (0203) 25555, ext 241.

MARY ARDEN'S HOUSE

Off A34, 3 miles north-west of Stratford-upon-Avon (Bb)

Of the two women who figured largest in William Shakespeare's life, his mother, Mary Arden, is the less well-known, and her home at Wilmcote the least familiar of the houses associated with him. Yet it is perhaps the most fascinating, for it was continuously occupied until 1930 and is preserved in almost its original condition.

The Ardens were farmers, and the house is a typical Tudor farmstead with a dairy, dovecote and outbuildings. These now contain the Farming Museum, which has a vast collection of farming tools, machinery and domestic articles, some dating from Shakespeare's time. In the rickyard there are farm wagons, a horse-drawn fire engine and two gipsy caravans.

Apr-Oct, daily; Nov-Mar, Mon-Sat. Adm charge. Shop. P Toilets. ♿ Tel Stratford-upon-Avon (0789) 204016.

MIDLAND AIR MUSEUM

Off A423, 2½ miles south-east of Coventry (Cc)

In terms of size, the biggest attraction of this museum is the mighty Vulcan bomber purchased after its retirement from the RAF. Visitors can climb up into the crew area of this famous plane, which once carried Britain's H-bombs. There are more than a score of aircraft on display at this open-air museum, including five built nearby at the Armstrong Whitworth factory – the Sea Hawk, Meteor, Argosy, Javelin and Hunter. The museum also has the only Lockheed Starfighter on display in this country. Sir Frank Whittle, pioneer of the jet engine, was born in Coventry, and there is a centre devoted to his work.

Easter-Nov, Sun, Thur and Fri. Adm charge. Shop. P Toilets. ♿ Tel Coventry (0203) 301033.

PACKWOOD HOUSE

On B4439, 9 miles north-west of Warwick (Bc)

The most distinctive features of Packwood House are its tall, steep-sided gables, massive chimneystacks and stone mullioned windows. Such features are common in 16th-century timber-framed houses, but at Packwood the timbers lie buried behind a brick and rendered façade added some time around 1800. Inside the house there are additions and alterations of even later dates, such as the superb oak floor in the Hall, laid in 1931, the oak floored and panelled Long Gallery, added in the same year, and the magnificent timber-roofed Great Hall, fashioned from a barn and added to the house in 1925.

Packwood has had its share of famous visitors – though the much-travelled Elizabeth I seems to have passed it by – and the rooms where they slept are named after them. Henry Ireton, the Parliamentarian general, slept there before the Battle of Edgehill in 1642, and Queen Mary, wife of George V, was there in 1927.

Packwood is justly famous for its garden, and especially the Yew Garden where clipped yew trees are said to represent the Sermon on the Mount. One large tree is called 'The Master', and on each side are the Evangelists and Apostles. Smaller trees represent the listening Multitude.

NT. Apr-Oct, Wed-Sun and Bank Hol Mon pm. Adm charge. Shop. P Toilets. ♿ (parts). Tel Lapworth (056 43) 2024.

GRAND DESIGN *The magnificent mural on the South Staircase at Ragley Hall – thought to be the world's largest 20th-century mural – shows Lord and Lady Hertford and their family looking down into the hall from the top landing.*

RAGLEY HALL

On A435, 2 miles south of Alcester (Ab)

Few great houses can boast such elegance and grandeur as this house designed by Robert Hooke, in the Palladian style, in 1680. Seventy years later it was further embellished by the dazzling plasterwork of James Gibbs, and in 1780

James Wyatt added the magnificent portico and was responsible for the decoration of some of the rooms.

Though the work of Gibbs can be seen in almost every room, he excelled himself in the Great Hall, where slender pilasters climb to a richly carved frieze and delicate, two-dimensional carvings adorn the pale pink walls. In the centre of the 40ft high ceiling, Britannia rides in a chariot drawn by winged lions.

In 1969, the artist Graham Rust began painting his mural *The Temptation* on the walls and ceiling of the South Staircase. It took him 14 years to complete.

The mural begins on the ground floor and culminates in an open-topped dome painted on the flat ceiling, through which is seen the Mount of Temptation with the Devil offering Christ the world's riches.

Ragley Hall's gardens and park, landscaped by Capability Brown, contain a children's adventure wood, amusements, a nature trail and lake.

Apr-Oct, pm daily exc Mon and Fri. Adm charge. Refreshments. Shop. P *Toilets.* ♿ *Tel Alcester (0789) 762090.*

RYTON GARDENS

On B4029, 5 miles south-east of Coventry (Cc)

In a world where gardeners make free use of chemical fertilisers and pesticides, Ryton is unusual in avoiding their use altogether. Since 1986 Ryton has been the National Centre of Organic Gardening, and every plant is grown according to organic principles, using manures and composts. On view are extensive vegetable gardens, a rose garden, a herb garden, a shrub walk and fruit trees. There are demonstrations of composting and natural pest control methods, of how to kill weeds without using weedkillers and of how to grow vegetables without digging.

All year, daily. Adm charge. Refreshments. Shop. P *Toilets.* ♿ *Tel Coventry (0203) 303517.*

ST JOHN'S HOUSE

Coten End, Warwick (Bc)

This 17th-century mansion houses a branch of the Warwickshire County Museum. On the ground floor are displays of domestic life in room settings, as well as costume and crafts; one room is a replica of a Victorian schoolroom.

The upper floor of the building is devoted to the museum of the Royal Warwickshire Regiment, with an impressive display of uniforms, badges, medals, trophies and regalia. One room contains weaponry of two World Wars. There are also mementos and relics of Field-Marshal the Viscount Montgomery, the regiment's colonel from 1947 until 1963; they include one of his uniforms and his famous black, two-badge beret.

All year, Tues-Sat and Bank Hol Mon; also Sun pm, May-Sept. Free entry. Shop. P *Tel Warwick (0926) 410410.*

STONELEIGH ABBEY

On A444, 5 miles south of Coventry (Cc)

Though parts of Stoneleigh Abbey date from the 16th century, it is the 18th-century West Wing that catches the eye, with its handsome porch, tall windows and fluted pilasters climbing three storeys high to the balustraded roof. Inside the house the rooms contain much of its original furniture, complemented by superb oak panelling, plasterwork and marble fireplaces and columns.

The gardens, landscaped by Humphry Repton, now include a nature trail, an adventure playground and a miniature railway that runs at weekends. There are pleasant walks through woodlands and gardens by the River Avon. Beyond the grounds 600 acres of land are leased to the Royal Agricultural Centre, the scene of research into farming techniques, and the venue for the Royal Show every July.

May-Aug, daily exc Tues and Sat. Adm charge. Refreshments. Shop. P *Toilets.* ♿ *Tel Kenilworth (0926) 52116.*

UPTON HOUSE

On A422, 10 miles south-east of Stratford-upon-Avon (Cb)

Though extensively remodelled in 1927-9, this late 17th-century house retains its classical elegance and provides a perfect setting for its contents. The house is virtually an art gallery, and it was to house the vast collection of the 2nd Lord Bearsted that Upton House was remodelled. The superb collection includes paintings by Canaletto, El Greco, Reynolds and Stubbs, Brussels tapestries, Chelsea and Sèvres porcelain and 18th-century furniture.

The steeply terraced garden is colourful with herbaceous plants, and descends to pools and a bog garden in the valley below.

NT. Apr-Sept, Mon-Thur pm; also some weekends pm in May, July, Aug. Adm charge. P *Toilets.* ♿ *Tel Edge Hill (029 587) 266.*

UPTON TREASURE *The painting* Christ taken in Captivity *by El Greco which hangs in Upton House is thought to have been a model for the Spanish artist's altarpiece in Toledo Cathedral, painted in 1577-9.*

WARWICK CASTLE

On A41, in Warwick (Bc)

The view of Warwick Castle across the willow-fringed River Avon was thought by Sir Walter Scott to be unsurpassed in England. Looking at that view today it is easy to sympathise with the romantic novelist, for there are few castles more romantic than Warwick, and no river more English than the sweet Avon that flows softly beneath its walls. Here is no ancient monument of crumbling walls and towers, haunted only by ravens; Warwick Castle is as alive and vibrant now as at any time during its 600 year history, and part of that history is vividly portrayed in a series of waxwork tableaux set out in the rooms. Other exhibits include a helmet worn by Oliver Cromwell and an elaborately wrought executioner's axe.

Called 'A Royal Weekend Party, 1898', the display depicts a visit by the Prince of Wales and other distinguished guests during the summer of 1898, when the Earl and Countess of Warwick were hosts at many such parties. Guests who stayed at the castle in earlier times and less happy circumstances are recalled in the castle dungeon, with its grisly display of instruments of torture. In the magnificently appointed State Rooms are the castle's art treasures, furniture collection and displays of arms and armour.

Close to Warwick Castle, in Castle Street, are models of a different kind. The Doll Museum has a fascinating collection of antique dolls, dolls' houses, prams, toys and puzzles contained in a superb black-and-white house of 1550 which was the home of Thomas Oken, a benefactor of the town.

Castle: All year, daily. Adm charge. Refreshments. Shop. P *Toilets.* ♿ *Tel Warwick (0926) 495421. Doll Museum: Mar-Nov, daily; Dec-Feb, weekends. Adm charge. Tel (0926) 495546.*

COUNTY CALENDAR

March (Shrove Tues). Atherstone: Shrovetide Football (village custom).

April (Sat nearest 23rd). Stratford-upon-Avon: Shakespeare's Birthday procession.

May Day Bank Hol. Kenilworth Castle: Carnival and Country Craft Fair.

June (mid-month). Kenilworth Lions Show (carnival).

July (1st week). Stoneleigh: Royal International Agricultural Show.

July (2nd week). Royal Leamington Spa: Carnival.

July (last two weeks). Stratford-upon-Avon: Town Festival.

August Bank Hol. Stoneleigh: Town and Country Show.

October (12th, or Mon following). Stratford-upon-Avon: Mop Fair.

October (mid-month). Warwick: Mop Fair and Ox Roast.

December (Sat before 25th). Kenilworth Castle: Open-air Carol Concert. Warwick Castle: Candlelit Carol Concert.

Tourist information: Kenilworth (0926) 52595; Leamington Spa (0926) 311470; Stratford-upon-Avon (0789) 293127; Warwick (0926) 492212.

THE BIRTHPLACE OF THE BARD

There are few places more English than Stratford-upon-Avon, the charming market town where William Shakespeare was born. Something of the character of Shakespeare's time still clings to the lovely timbered houses and old-world gardens he knew, infuses the air along the willowed banks of the river he loved, and lingers in the foundations of New Place, his last home.

Modern technology plays its role in re-creating Elizabethan times in audiovisual displays of the World of Shakespeare. Vintage motor cars and butterflies also give the Bard some competition for visitors' attention.

Shakespeare's Birthplace: All year, daily. Adm charge. Tel Stratford-upon-Avon (0789) 204016. Hall's Croft: All year, daily exc Sun Nov-Mar. Adm charge. Tel (0789) 204016. New Place: All year, daily, exc Sun Nov-Mar. Adm charge. Tel (0789) 204016. World of Shakespeare: All year, daily. Adm charge. Shop. Toilets. ♿ Tel (0789) 69190. Holy Trinity Church: All year, daily. Adm charge for Shakespeare's grave. Shop. ♿ Tel (0789) 66316. Motor Museum: All year, daily. Adm charge. Shop. Toilets. ♿ Tel (0789) 69413. Butterfly Farm: All year, daily. Adm charge. Shop. ♿ Tel (0789) 299288.

BLESSED PLOT *Beside the Avon rises the tall spire of Holy Trinity Church. Here William Shakespeare was baptised in 1564, and buried in 1616. Beside him lie his wife, Anne, and his eldest daughter, Susanna.*

BID TIME RETURN *Figures from different levels of Elizabethan society, from courtier to vagabond, form the first of 25 life-size tableaux in the World of Shakespeare. Shakespeare's home town is seen bustling with activity as the queen visits nearby Kenilworth.*

SWEET THUNDER *Some of the great cars of the 1920s and 1930s, such as this 1934 Rolls-Royce Phantom II (left), recall the golden age of motoring in Stratford's Motor Museum.*

WHERE THE BEE SUCKS *Borders of old English flowers and the lovely half-timbered Hall's Croft combine to create the atmosphere of a typical Elizabethan house and garden. Here lived Dr John Hall, the husband of Shakespeare's eldest daughter, Susanna. In the house is the doctor's dispensary, complete with apothecary's jars, pestles and mortars.*

TIMELESS MEMORIALS *The half-timbered house where Shakespeare was born looks today much as it did in his time. It is simply furnished in Elizabethan style; simplest of all is the birthroom, with its oak bedstead and wooden cradle. Some 300 years after Shakespeare's death the Royal Shakespeare Theatre was opened and regular productions of his plays blaze brightly from its boards.*

BUTTERFLY SAFARI *An Atlas moth from west Java is among hundreds of moths and butterflies that fly free among exotic plants, trees and flowers at the Stratford Butterfly Farm. Visitors can walk around the hothouse, following paths beside pools and waterfalls, and visit the insect house, whose residents eye them from behind glass.*

WEST MIDLANDS

MUSEUMS OF INDUSTRY AROUND THREE CATHEDRALS

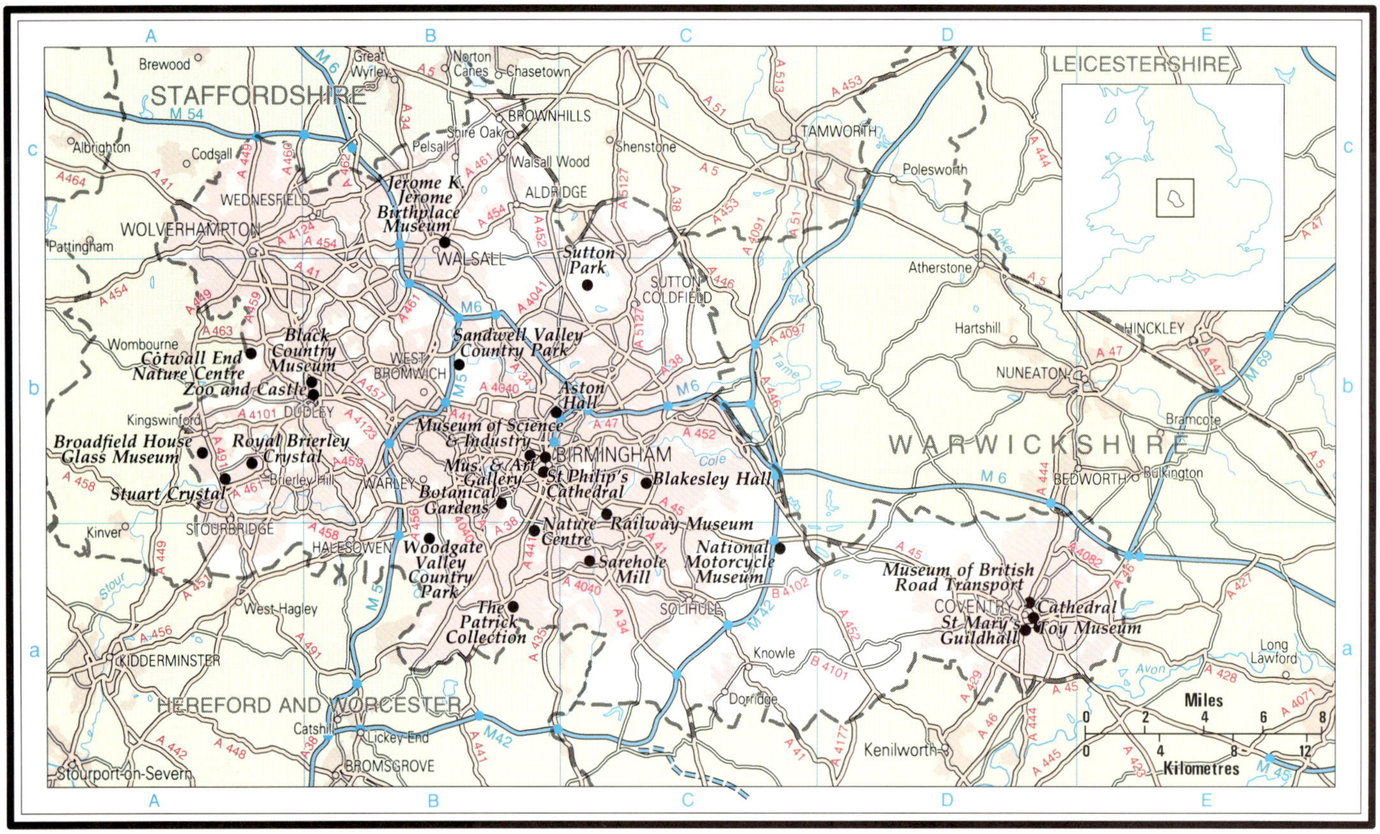

Birmingham, Britain's second biggest city, dominates the West Midlands. The area is traditionally associated with the bustling energy of the Industrial Revolution, and museums today commemorate its 19th-century role as one of the great workshops of the world. Most of the scars of industry have now healed, enabling today's visitors to appreciate Birmingham's many noble buildings and beautiful parks. Coventry grew again after its fierce blitzing in the Second World War; the ruins of its old cathedral stand beside Sir Basil Spence's impressive new building.

Much of the West Midlands was once covered by the Forest of Arden, where Shakespeare set *As You Like It*. Patches of attractive country survive, providing homes for wildlife not far from the city streets, and Sutton Park houses a museum of the English countryside.

ASTON HALL

Off A4040, 2 miles north of Birmingham (Bb)

This is among the last of the great Jacobean houses to be built in England. It was much admired by Horace Walpole who copied details from it for his house at Strawberry Hill, Twickenham. The Great Stairs, Long Gallery, and Great Dining Room frieze are major examples of early 17th-century decoration. The cantilevered oak staircase has an intricately carved balustrade, while the 135ft Long Gallery has a fine strapwork ceiling and arcaded oak panelling. The exterior is equally ornate, with a host of turrets, gables and octagonal chimneys.

Mar-Oct, pm daily. Free entry. Shop. P *Toilets. Tel Birmingham (021) 327 0062.*

BIRMINGHAM BOTANICAL GARDENS

Off A456, 2 miles south of Birmingham (Bb)

This delightful oasis seems a world away from the busy centre of Birmingham. The Tropical House has a 24ft wide lily pool and its lush vegetation includes banana, cacao and other economically important trees. Palms, tree ferns, orchids and insectivorous plants are displayed in the Palm House. There is a wide variety of citrus trees in the Orangery, and the Cactus House shows a desert scene with giant agaves and opuntias. Outside are colourful terrace beds and rhododendron and azalea borders, a rose garden, rock garden and more than 400 trees.

All year, daily. Adm charge. Refreshments. Shop. P *Toilets.* ♿ *Tel Birmingham (021) 454 1860.*

BIRMINGHAM MUSEUM AND ART GALLERY

Chamberlain Square, in city centre (Bb)

The most famous picture in the art gallery is probably the Pre-Raphaelite painting by Ford Madox Brown *The Last of England*, depicting a couple departing for Australia. As well as its world-famous Pre-Raphaelite paintings, the gallery has Turners and Constables. The prize work in the European section is Bellini's magnificent *Madonna and Child* altarpiece, while the museum also contains a major collection of coins and medals. Other treasures include glass and ceramics.

All year, daily exc Sun am. Free entry. Refreshments. Shop. P *Toilets.* ♿ *Tel Birmingham (021) 235 2834.*

BIRMINGHAM MUSEUM OF SCIENCE AND INDUSTRY

Newhall Street, in city centre (Bb)

Fascinating machines on display in this museum range from one of the world's oldest working steam engines – the Smethwick Engine of 1779 built by Boulton and Watt – to John Cobb's World Land Speed Record Car. The museum pioneered the running of steam engines, and the prize exhibit in the Locomotive Hall is the 1257 ton Coronation Class Stanier Pacific locomotive *City of Birmingham*, which is moved along its track by an hydraulic system once every hour. Some of the engines in the Engineering Hall are run every day, and many of the automatic manufacturing machines on display can be operated by push-button.

All year, daily exc Sun am. Free entry. Refreshments. Shop. Toilets. ♿ *Tel Birmingham (021) 236 1022.*

BIRMINGHAM NATURE CENTRE

Off A441, 3½ miles south of Birmingham (Ba)

The aim of the centre is to enable young city-dwelling visitors to observe a variety of British and European wildlife in a natural setting. Species to be seen range from badgers, foxes and tawny owls to reptiles, fish and insects. There is a fish pond with underwater viewing windows, and an observation beehive. The butterfly house is filled with British and European butterflies and moths and their caterpillars. There are mammal and reptile houses, aviaries and paddocks, and one area which has deliberately been left wild.

Mar-Oct, daily. Free entry. Refreshments. Shop. P *Toilets.* ♿ *Tel Birmingham (021) 472 7775.*

BIRMINGHAM RAILWAY MUSEUM

Off A41, 3 miles south-east of Birmingham (Cb)

Alongside the impressive collection of working steam locomotives great and small are several items of great interest even to visitors who are not steam enthusiasts. There is a saloon carriage from the royal train, built in 1940 and used as a mobile office for Sir Winston Churchill and General Eisenhower during the Second World War. Another saloon carriage was part of the royal train built for Edward VII and Queen Alexandra. The travelling post office ambushed by the Great Train Robbers can also be seen, while two of the museum's great locomotives, *Clun Castle* and *Kolhapur*, run on special excursions on British Rail main lines.

All year, daily. (Steam days, Easter-early Oct, Sun and Bank Hol Mon.) Adm charge. Refreshments. Shop. P *Toilets. Tel Birmingham (021) 707 4696.*

BLACK COUNTRY MUSEUM

On A4037, 1 mile north of Dudley (Bb)

On 26 acres of what was once derelict land the life and work of the heart of industrial Britain are being re-created. Visitors can ride an electric tram, past a replica of the world's first steam engine and a small colliery, to reach a village where craftsmen can be seen at work in buildings brought from all over the Black Country. Here are shops, homes, a bakery and a pub – all looking as they did in the 1880s.

Across the cast-iron bridge of 1879 spanning the canal can be found Gregory's Store – a 19th-century shop selling items ranging from butter to paraffin and drapery – a chainmaker's house, a glasscutter's workshop and a fully equipped chemist's shop. Electric narrowboats run trips through Dudley Tunnel.

All year, daily. Adm charge. Refreshments. Shop. P *Toilets.* ♿ *Tel Birmingham (021) 557 9643.*

BLAKESLEY HALL

Off A4040, 4 miles east of Birmingham (Cb)

The life of 17th-century country gentry has been reconstructed in the rooms of Blakesley Hall, following an inventory of the house made in 1684. The substantial timber-framed house, built a century earlier, was a family home for more than 350 years. The large hall has its original long table where the family dined before relaxing in the great parlour beside it. Upstairs is the Painted Chamber, decorated with 16th-century wall paintings rediscovered in the 1950s.

Apr-Oct, pm daily. Free entry. Shop. P *Toilets. Tel Birmingham (021) 235 2834.*

BROADFIELD HOUSE GLASS MUSEUM

Off A491, 2½ miles north of Stourbridge (Ab)

The brilliance and ingenuity of its glassmakers made Stourbridge famous throughout the world in the 19th century. This museum in an elegant Georgian mansion records the development of the glassmaker's art from Roman times to the present day, and the leading part Stourbridge firms have played in it over the last 400 years. Some of these firms are still household names – Royal Brierley, Stuart Crystal, Thomas Webb. The museum contains many paintings, prints, photographs and pieces of traditional equipment which explain some of the intricate manufacturing and decorating processes.

All year, Tues-Sun and Bank Hol pm; Sat am. Free entry. Shop. P *Toilets. Tel Kingswinford (0384) 273011.*

COTWALL END NATURE CENTRE

Off A459, 4 miles south of Wolverhampton (Ab)

Although it is less than 15 minutes' drive from Dudley and Wolverhampton the centre is truly rural in atmosphere, comprising 15 acres of grass and woodland with views down the Cotwall End Valley to the Malvern Hills. More than 80 species of wild birds visit the valley and, in a good year, more than 20 species of butterfly. In the paddocks a variety of domestic animals, including many ancient breeds, are kept.

All year, daily. Free entry. Refreshments. Shop. P *Toilets.* ♿ *Tel Sedgley (090 73) 74668.*

COVENTRY CATHEDRAL

Off Broadgate, in city centre (Da)

The great charred cross which stands on the altar in the ruins of the old cathedral – destroyed by fire bombs during the longest single air raid suffered by any British city during the Second World War – has long been world famous. It

CHRIST IN GLORY *The mighty tapestry behind the high altar of Coventry Cathedral was designed by Graham Sutherland. Between the feet of Christ is man, and four symbolic creatures give worship. The ruins of Coventry's medieval cathedral (below) have been preserved as a reminder of its destruction by German bombs on the night of November 14, 1940.*

VINTAGE SUPERBIKE *Looking rather like a drawing-room sofa on wheels, this splendid 880cc Wilkinson model of 1912 is one of some 800 machines on display at the National Motorcycle Museum.*

was made from two beams from the roof, and with the Cross of Nails is recognised as a symbol of reconciliation and renewal. Since its consecration in 1962 the new cathedral, linked to the old by a canopy, has become a place of pilgrimage. Although no longer new as modern architecture goes, Coventry Cathedral is still capable of astonishing visitors by the simplicity, boldness and coherence of vision of the architect, Sir Basil Spence, and by the brilliant effects achieved by some of the artists employed. Of these the most spectacular are the enormous tapestry – the largest in the world – by Graham Sutherland, and the blaze of colour of the baptistry window designed by John Piper, the largest piece of stained glass made this century. Another is the great wall of glass engraved with religious figures by John Hutton, while outside, on the south wall, is the bronze sculpture of St Michael and the Devil by Jacob Epstein.
All year, daily. Free entry. Refreshments. Shop. Toilets. ♿ Tel Coventry (0203) 27597. Visitor Centre: All year, daily. Adm charge. Tel (0203) 24323.

COVENTRY TOY MUSEUM
Much Park Street, in city centre (Da)

The ancient face of Coventry, much damaged by the savage bombing of the Second World War, still survives in buildings like the Toy Museum, which is housed in Whitefriars Gate, the 14th-century entrance to what was once a great Carmelite Friary. The museum contains some 4000 toys of every description, ranging from a 1690s' wooden doll to models and games from the 1950s.

The Herbert Art Gallery and Museum, in nearby Jordan Well, contains sketches by Graham Sutherland for the great tapestry in Coventry Cathedral. There are also displays on the history of the city through the ages, on its crafts and industries, and on two famous local ladies – Lady Godiva and Mary Ann Evans, who is better known as the novelist George Eliot.
Toy Museum: All year, daily exc am Oct-Mar. Adm charge. Refreshments. Shop. P Tel Coventry (0203) 27560. Art Gallery and Museum: All year, daily. Free entry. Shop. P Toilets. ♿ Tel (0203) 833333.

DUDLEY ZOO AND CASTLE
On A459 in town centre (Bb)

Set in 40 acres of attractively wooded grounds, the zoo contains a comprehensive collection of wildlife from all over the world. There is a children's corner, and other attractions with a special appeal to the young, including a farmyard housing rare breeds of sheep, pigs, goats and poultry. A miniature railway gives rides, and a chairlift takes visitors up to Dudley Castle. Only the stone keep, gatehouse and parts of the curtain wall remain of the 13th-century castle, but there is also an impressive range of Tudor buildings, including the Great Hall, living quarters, kitchens, pantry and buttery, which are now being restored.
All year, daily. Adm charge. Refreshments. Shop. P Toilets. Tel Dudley (0384) 52401.

JEROME K. JEROME BIRTHPLACE MUSEUM
On A4148 in Walsall (Bc)

Since it was first published in 1889, people all over the world have enjoyed *Three Men in a Boat*, Jerome K. Jerome's deceptively simple story of three friends on a rowing holiday – not forgetting the dog, Montmorency. Jerome was born in 1859 in this spacious town house, now a museum dedicated to his life and to his sense of the ridiculous. One room has been decorated and furnished as a parlour of the period. There is also a collection of inscribed first editions and personal items, and a craft gallery.
All year, Tues-Sat. Free entry. Shop. P (limited). Tel Walsall (0922) 21244.

MUSEUM OF BRITISH ROAD TRANSPORT
Off Hales Street, Coventry (Da)

As might be expected from a museum created in the heartland of the British car industry, there are many famous and some unique models to be seen here, covering the development of the motor car from its earliest days to the present. Cars from the formative years of motoring are set in period street scenes, and the Royalty on the Road exhibition features cars once owned by Queen Mary and George VI. Also on view is Thrust 2, which broke the world land speed record in 1983 with a speed of 633.468 mph.
Easter-Sept, daily; Oct-Easter, Fri, Sat and Sun. Adm charge. Refreshments. Shop. P Toilets. ♿ Tel Coventry (0203) 832425.

NATIONAL MOTORCYCLE MUSEUM
On A45, 8½ miles south-east of Birmingham (Ca)

The gleaming ranks of powerful machines with names like Norton, Matchless and Triumph make this museum a magnet for motorcycle enthusiasts. Arrayed in chrome and nickel splendour, models from 1902-1961 trace 'Sixty Glorious Years' of mechanical development – the theme for Hall One of the museum. In another hall are assembled competition models, trials machines, scramblers, sprinters, road racers and record breakers. There are six more halls and some 800 machines are on display.
All year, daily. Adm charge. Refreshments. Shop. P Toilets. ♿ Tel Hampton-in-Arden (067 55) 3311.

THE PATRICK COLLECTION
Lifford Lane, off A441, King's Norton, Birmingham (Ba)

Motor cars from most periods of their development are on show in two large halls. Exhibits include the original Singer Le Mans of 1934 and the car which inspired many James Bond-type dreams, the Aston Martin Zagato. The early days of motoring are depicted in a 1920s street scene, which includes cars of the period and a genuine barrel organ. By contrast, racing cars of the 1980s are on show in the museum's Mansell Hall.
Apr-Nov, daily exc Tues. Adm charge. Refreshments. Shop. P Toilets. ♿ Tel Birmingham (021) 459 9111.

ROYAL BRIERLEY CRYSTAL
Off A461 at Brierley Hill (Ab)

Scottish silica sand, Australian red lead oxide, potassium carbonate and nitrate from France make up 99 per cent of the formula for the Royal Brierley Crystal made exclusively here. The remaining 1 per cent of the ingredients, and the element which gives the glass its unique clarity and lustre, remains a secret known only to a handful of Brierley craftsmen. The men who blow, cut, polish and fashion the glass can be seen at work, in teams called 'chairs'.
Shop: All year, daily. Factory: All year, Mon-Fri (exc last week July, first week Aug, last week Sept). Free entry. Refreshments. Shop. P Toilets. ♿ Tel Brierley Hill (0384) 70161.

ST MARY'S GUILDHALL
Coventry city centre (Da)

Coventry's 14th-century Guildhall of St Mary is one of the finest in the country. Although its timber roof was destroyed by enemy bombs in the Second World War, the carved figures and

CRYSTAL CLEAR *A craftsman puts the foot on a vase at the Royal Brierley Crystal factory, noted for the exceptional clarity of its glass. Glassmaking came to the West Midlands with Huguenot refugees around 1700.*

bosses on the oak ceiling in the Great Hall are all original, dating from the reign of Richard III. One of the guildhall's finest features is the Great North Window, which was installed together with the Arras Tapestry for the visit in 1500 of Henry VII. The tapestry shows the king and his queen, Elizabeth, accompanied by their lords and ladies. The Minstrels' Gallery contains a collection of medieval armour, while the Old Council Chamber has a Guild Chair of about 1450.
Easter-Oct, daily. Free entry. Shop. Toilets. Tel Coventry (0203) 833333.

ST PHILIP'S CATHEDRAL

Colmore Row, in centre of Birmingham (Bb)

The Pre-Raphaelite painter Edward Burne-Jones was baptised in what is now Birmingham's Cathedral of St Philip, which contains four great stained-glass windows designed by him and made in the workshops of William Morris. The cathedral was built in the 18th century in the English Baroque style, to which were added a number of humorous and grotesque features. Looming from the carved foliage surrounding the windows above the west doors, for example, is a series of terrifying faces.

St Chad's Cathedral, in Queensway, was the first Roman Catholic cathedral to be built in England after the Reformation. It is the work of the pioneer of the Victorian-Gothic revivalist style, Augustus Pugin, and was completed in 1841.
Both cathedrals: All year, daily. Free entry.

SANDWELL VALLEY COUNTRY PARK

Off A41 at West Bromwich (Bb)

An oasis of farmland and woods has at its heart the excavated remains of a 12th-century Benedictine Priory. The priory was demolished at the Dissolution and on its site was built Sandwell Hall, home of the Earls of Dartmouth until 1853. This was demolished in 1927, but the home farm of the estate is today being restored as a smallholding typical of the early 1900s, with Longhorn cattle, black pigs and other old breeds. The nearby woods, lakes, ponds and streams abound with birds, plants and wildlife, and there are waymarked nature trails.
All year, daily. Free entry. Refreshments. Shop. P *Toilets.* ♿ *Tel Birmingham (021) 553 0220.*

SAREHOLE MILL

Off A34, 3½ miles south-east of Birmingham (Ca)

It is difficult to think of Birmingham now in terms of corn mills and ducks paddling peacefully on millponds, but Sarehole Mill is a historic reminder of the city's rural past. It is the last working water corn mill surviving within the city boundaries. Sarehole Mill produced corn commercially from the 1760s until 1919, then fell into disrepair until its restoration in the 1960s. The process of corn grinding can be followed on all three floors of the mill, while one of its two water wheels is usually in operation. The bakehouse across the yard still has its large bread oven, and the granary displays cover local agriculture and rural life.
Mar-Nov, daily. Free entry. Shop. P *Tel Birmingham (021) 777 6612.*

MILL SURVIVOR *The mellow brick Georgian buildings of Sarehole Mill add their colour to the banks of the River Cole. The chimney belongs to an engine house added in the 1850s to supplement water power from the river.*

STUART CRYSTAL

On A491 1 mile north of Stourbridge (Ab)

The Redhouse Cone is a famous local landmark – the only traditional glass furnace in the Stourbridge area, which for centuries has been the centre of English crystal glass production. Now a museum, it features regular displays of glass-making and engraving, together with fine examples of Victorian and Edwardian decorative glassware. Tours of the modern factory enable visitors to observe all the processes involved in glass-making.
All year, daily; factory tours Mon-Fri. Free entry. Refreshments. Shop. P *Toilets.* ♿ *Tel Brierley Hill (0384) 71161.*

SUTTON PARK

Off A5127 at Sutton Coldfield (Ab)

At the time of the Domesday Book, Sutton Park was a Royal Hunting Ground; now it is a 3 square mile museum of the English countryside, just a short journey from industrial Birmingham. John Vesey, 16th-century Bishop of Exeter, who lived nearby at Sutton Coldfield, persuaded Henry VIII to grant the park to the local people and set up a trust to protect the land.

In the east is an encampment of the ancient Britons; in the west lies a well-preserved 1½ mile stretch of the Roman Ryknild Street. Sutton Park is also a naturalist's delight, with two nature trails offering a sight of rare plants such as pink flowering bog bean and great spearwort.
All year, daily. (Visitor Centre: Tues, Wed, Thur and Sun; Sat pm). Free entry. Refreshments. Shop. P *Toilets.* ♿ *Tel Birmingham (021) 355 6370.*

WOODGATE VALLEY COUNTRY PARK

Off A456, 5½ miles south-west of Birmingham (Ba)

There are more than 450 acres of natural countryside here, and miles of waymarked footpaths to suit all tastes and capabilities. Guided tours at weekends start from the visitor centre, and pony trekking, riding for the disabled and free donkey trap rides for the elderly are available at Hole Farm.
All year, daily. Free entry. Refreshments. P *Toilets.* ♿ *Tel Birmingham (021) 421 7575.*

COUNTY CALENDAR

March (mid-month). Birmingham: Steam Weekend.

April (early). National Exhibition Centre: International Antiques Fair.

May (early). National Exhibition Centre: National Classic Motor Show.

May (mid-month). Birmingham: Canal Festival.

June (mid-month). National Exhibition Centre: Royal International Horse Show.

July (1st weekend). Handsworth: Caribbean Festival.

August Bank Hol. Birmingham: Superprix Motor Race.

October (mid-month). National Exhibition Centre: International Motor Show.

Tourist information: Birmingham (021) 643 2514; Coventry (0203) 20084; Dudley (0384) 50333; Wolverhampton (0902) 312051.

WILTSHIRE

STONES OF MYSTERY ON A PLAIN RINGED BY GREAT HOUSES

The bare expanses of Salisbury Plain and the Wiltshire downs form the hub of southern England's chalk uplands. Here stand the awesome stone circles of Stonehenge and Avebury, the ancient man-made mound of Silbury Hill and the numerous barrow tombs of long-dead chieftains. Equally alluring, in their livelier way, are two great Wiltshire houses: Longleat, famed for its lions, and Littlecote, where jousting contests are among the present-day attractions. Stourhead and Bowood House are known for their superb landscape gardens, whilst Lacock offers an abbey house and its village almost untouched by the 20th century.

But not all of Wiltshire was bypassed by the machine age. The Great Western Railway turned Swindon into a clamorous railway centre, and museums there recall the locomotive boom years. Earlier, the Kennet and Avon Canal was cut through the county; it is now being restored for leisure purposes, with a display centre at Devizes.

Nevertheless, Wiltshire remains an essentially rural county, its unspoilt character caught in the city of Salisbury. Many English cathedrals have found themselves islanded by busy roads and 20th-century buildings, but Salisbury's great church rises from spacious, baize-green lawns surrounded by some of England's most beautiful town houses.

AVEBURY

On A4361, 6 miles west of Marlborough (Cd)

From the leafy approaches hummocky green embankments suddenly startle the eye, and ancient grey slabs loom up singly or in groups like ghostly sentinels.

Avebury, a very English village of thatch and brick, is necklaced with the largest prehistoric stone circle in the world. The earthwork rampart surrounding it encloses an area of more than 28 acres, which is divided into four parts by roads entering the village. The embankment rises to 18ft, swooping into an 11ft ditch, and a walk around the rim leads for almost a mile. The site speaks of a colossal deployment of labour among the prehistoric farmers on Wiltshire's upland.

The stones themselves are sarsens – hard sandstone blocks from the nearby Marlborough Downs, of which the largest weighs nearly 60 tons. They were raised in about 2400 BC and there were originally 180 of them, arranged in a big circle enclosing two smaller circles, one of which contained a yet smaller ring. Of the total, only 49 stones survive above ground today, for many were buried or broken up by medieval villagers who disliked their brooding pagan presence. None of the stones has been shaped by man, but the monument-builders favoured two basic types: thin and straight-sided or flat diamond-shape.

The Avebury area is strewn with important prehistoric sites, and two avenues marked by a double row of megaliths once led off from the great circle. The so called Beckhampton Avenue has now vanished, but the West Kennet Avenue has been partially restored and can be seen heading south from the village to Overton Hill, site of the concentric stone and timber circles known as The Sanctuary.

Finds from the Avebury area can be seen in the Alexander Keiller Museum, just outside the earthwork rampart. The collection owes its name to Alexander Keiller who excavated half of the big stone circle in the 1930s. A model shows how the great blocks were erected, and besides Stone Age hammerheads, antler picks and bag-shaped pottery there is a macabre exhibit: displayed in a glass-paned recess in the floor is the skeleton of a young child, found at the Windmill Hill site, 1½ miles to the north-west.

The 17th-century thatched Great Barn nearby houses the Museum of Wiltshire Folk Life – with displays on traditional crafts such as coopering, shepherding and thatching – and a tourist information centre.

Stone Circle: EH/NT. All year, daily. Museum: EH. All year, daily. Adm charge. Shop. 🅿 *Tel Avebury (067 23) 250. Great Barn: Late Mar-Oct, daily; Nov-late Mar, Sat pm, Sun. Refreshments. Shop.* 🅿 *Toilets. Tel (067 23) 555.*

BARTON FARM COUNTRY PARK

On western edge of Bradford-on-Avon (Bc)

The country park covers 36 acres of meadowland set in the wooded valley of the River Avon and centring on the complex of Barton farmhouse with its medieval outbuildings and packbridge.

STONE SYMBOLS *The prehistoric stones at Avebury – straight-sided or diamond-shaped – may have been chosen as male and female symbols. It is possible that the circle was once the scene of fertility rites.*

The stone-built tithe barn is among the finest in England, having a stone tiled roof supported by splendid timber joists, and huge doors of feathered oak planks hung on the original iron hinges. Cruciform ventilations in the walls contribute to its church-like appearance. It contains a collection of farm implements from the 18th and 19th centuries.

Tithes and farm materials arrived by the old packbridge, which is today the starting point of a pleasant 1½ mile walk to Avoncliff. The country park lies on the edge of Bradford-on-Avon, where beautiful buildings of Bath stone scramble down a slope to the river. The Saxon Church of St Lawrence survives from a monastery founded in the 7th century; two sculptured angels fly above its tall, thin chancel arch.

Park: All year, daily. Tithe Barn: EH. Apr-Oct, daily. Adm charge.

BOWOOD HOUSE AND GARDENS

Off A4, 2½ miles west of Calne (Cd)

Home of the Shelburne family for more than 230 years, Bowood was once effectively two houses. The 'Big House' of 1755 proved too expensive to run after the Second World War and was demolished in 1955. What visitors see today is only the 'Little House' which once adjoined it. But the golden stone building is neatly proportioned and, having a palatial Robert Adam wing and standing in superb landscaped grounds, survives in its own right as one of Wiltshire's noblest houses.

Bowood's library houses 5000 volumes and in a small room known as the laboratory, Dr Joseph Priestley, librarian and tutor to the first marquis's sons, discovered oxygen gas in 1774. The family chapel was designed in 1821 by C.R. Cockerell. Adam's Orangery of 1769 now houses a picture collection. Elsewhere in the house, visitors can see collections of sculpture, jewellery, Indian artefacts and Victoriana. Costumes are displayed too, the prize exhibit being the Albanian dress in which Lord Byron posed in a painting of 1814 by Thomas Philips.

In the 1760s Capability Brown dammed two streams to create the lovely serpentine lake seen today. Additions include a rock-ledged cascade and a 'hermit's cave' insinuated into the setting by the amateur landscapist Charles Hamilton in 1785. The grounds also include a lakeside temple and an austere Adam mausoleum. There is a children's adventure playground, and in the rhododendron season a separate woodland garden is open to the public.

Apr-mid Oct, daily. Adm charge. Refreshments. Shop. 🅿 *Toilets.* ♿ *Tel Calne (0249) 812102.*

BRATTON CAMP

Off B3098, 2 miles east of Westbury (Bc)

It was to the downland refuge of this Iron Age hill-fort that the Danes fled in disorder after their defeat by Alfred the Great in the Battle of Ethandun in AD 878. Surrounded here, on the western edge of Salisbury Plain, the Danes were forced to surrender, and to leave Wessex for good. The hill rises to 755ft and commands superb views over the Bristol Avon valley. Cut into the chalk just below the ramparts is the Westbury White Horse. Tradition holds that it was branded into the hillside to commemorate Alfred's victory; however, the present figure is known to have been carved in the 18th century, and there is no firm evidence that an earlier figure ever existed.

EH. All year, daily.

COATE WATER COUNTRY PARK
Off A4259, on south-east edge of Swindon (Dd)

The heart of the park is a Y-shaped lake which has been used for recreation and regattas since Victorian times. At one end is a 20 acre wetland nature reserve where kingfishers and sandpipers are seen, and the nightingale is a summer visitor. Elsewhere are facilities for angling, boating and golf, and a play area for children. A model railway runs nearby, and there are two museums close to the park. The Richard Jefferies Museum commemorates the naturalist and author who featured Coate Water in his novel *Bevis*, among other writings. The Agricultural Museum displays old farm wagons and machinery.
Park: All year, daily. Jefferies Museum: All year, Wed, Sat and Sun pm. Free entry. Shop. Tel Swindon (0793) 26161. Agricultural Museum: Easter-Oct, Sun pm. Free entry. Refreshments. Shop. P Toilets. Tel (0793) 22837.

CORSHAM COURT
In centre of Corsham (Bd)

An Elizabethan manor dating from 1582, Corsham was substantially altered in the 18th and 19th centuries and rises today in a fine array of gables and pinnacles from spacious gardens laid out by Capability Brown. The supreme attractions, though, are the contents which include furniture, china and, above all, an exceptional collection of old master paintings in the Georgian state rooms. The collection was begun by Sir Paul Methuen (1672-1757) and left to a cousin who acquired Corsham specifically to house it. Pride of place, perhaps, is occupied by a celebrated *Annunciation* (1463) by Fra Filippo Lippi.
All year, pm daily exc Mon and Fri; also Bank Hol pm. Adm charge. P Toilets. ♿ Tel Corsham (0249) 712214.

CROFTON BEAM ENGINES
Off A338, 6 miles south-east of Marlborough (Dc)

The two oldest working beam engines in the world still to be seen in steam are housed at the Crofton pumping station on the Kennet and Avon Canal. They are a Boulton and Watt of 1812 and a Harveys of Hale of 1845, which were installed to pump water to the upper level of the canal. Trips on the narrowboat *Jubilee* are available during steam weekends. At the hamlet of Wilton nearby, visitors can see Wiltshire's only working windmill, rising from a 550ft high chalk ridge. A five-storey brick tower mill, the Wilton Windmill was built in 1821 and operated until 1911; it has now been fully restored.
Beam Engines: Apr-Oct, Sun; 'in steam' certain weekends. Adm charge. Refreshments. Shop. P Toilets. Tel Marlborough (0672) 870683. Windmill: Easter-Sept, Sun and Bank Hol Mon pm. Adm charge. Shop. P Tel (0672) 870268.

GREAT CHALFIELD MANOR
Off B3107, 3 miles south-west of Melksham (Bc)

A pleasing assemblage of mellow stone buildings, with house, outbuildings and parish church all encircled by a moat, Great Chalfield lies in quiet country near the River Avon. The present manor was built in about 1480 for Thomas Tropnell, a Wiltshire businessman. The approach is by the north front, with its pretty symmetry of gables and oriel windows, and inside is a two-storey great hall with staircases to the north bedroom and solar. Squints or spy windows, hidden behind stone masks, overlook the hall and another unusual feature is the very early screened-off dining room; in the 15th century meals were usually eaten in the main hall.
NT. Early Apr-late Oct, Tues-Thur pm. Adm charge. P Tel Melksham (0225) 782239.

GREAT WESTERN RAILWAY MUSEUM
Faringdon Road, Swindon (Dd)

Before the coming of the Great Western Railway in 1841, Swindon was a sleepy little market town. Then as the site of the GWR's main engineering works, it became a railway boom town whose population increased more than twentyfold by the end of the century. The Great Western Railway Museum is housed in a twin-towered Victorian Gothic building constructed as a lodging house for unmarried railway workers. It once served as a Wesleyan chapel and has a fittingly ecclesiastical appearance for a shrine to the GWR – 'God's Wonderful Railway' as it is known to enthusiasts.

Isambard Kingdom Brunel started to build the railway in 1835, creating for it his unique 7ft $0\frac{1}{4}$in gauge track. A room in the museum is devoted to the great engineer, and there is a full-size replica of the famous *North Star*, the first locomotive to run successfully on the railway. There is also a 1934 diesel railcar in the GWR's distinctive chocolate-and-cream livery, with a buffet.

Next door, 34 Faringdon Road survives from Swindon's planned Victorian railway village and has been refurbished inside and out as it would have been around 1900. Lit only by gas and oil lamps, Swindon Railway Village Museum, as the house is called, is a perfect period piece in every detail, from the iron bedsteads upstairs to the outside WC.
Both museums: All year, daily. Adm charge. Shop. Toilets. Tel Swindon (0793) 26161.

KENNET AND AVON CANAL EXHIBITION
The Wharf, Devizes (Cc)

The 87 mile long Kennet and Avon Canal passes through 104 locks to connect the River Kennet at Reading with the Avon at Bath. Extended by the Thames and Avon, it also links London with Bristol. It was opened in 1810, but after only 40 years its traffic had moved to the faster and more flexible railways, and the canal fell into disuse.

The Kennet and Avon Canal Trust was founded in 1962 with the aim of achieving the complete restoration of this historic waterway by 1990. It has its office in a restored wharf building in Devizes, where an exhibition illustrates every aspect of the canal's story. It lays special emphasis on the characters involved: the navvies and engineers who built the canal, the boatmen and lock-keepers who operated it. There is a public right of way along the whole length of the canal towpath in Wiltshire; some of the prettiest stretches lie east of Devizes, where the waterway meanders through the Vale of Pewsey.
Easter-Oct, daily. Adm charge. Refreshments. Shop. P Toilets. ♿ Tel Devizes (0380) 71279.

BACK TO WORK *Built in 1812, this Boulton and Watt engine at Crofton pumping station is one of the world's oldest working beam engines in steam. It pumped water to the upper level of the Kennet and Avon Canal.*

LACOCK ABBEY
Off A350, 3 miles south of Chippenham (Bd)

The village of Lacock is among the most photogenic in England – and there is an appropriateness in that. For it was at Lacock that

SNAPSHOT *In 1835 this oriel window at Lacock Abbey became the subject of the world's first known negative. It was made by the pioneer of photography, William Fox Talbot, one of whose early cameras, (right) can be seen at the Fox Talbot Museum in Lacock.*

William Henry Fox Talbot, owner of the fine old abbey, made his pioneering photographic experiments in the 1830s. His negative of an oriel window there is the oldest in existence, and many other early photographic studies of his home can be seen in a museum at the abbey gates.

The house is reached through an airy Gothic-style arch of 1775, and the main hall is framed in the same style. Both were designed by the architect Sanderson Miller and are among the earliest examples of the Gothic revival in Britain. The hall ceiling is emblazoned with heraldic devices, and in the pinnacled wall niches are some curious 18th-century terracotta figures, among them an angel, a skeleton and a horned bull.

Several authentic medieval rooms still exist, however. There is a fine cloister court where, in one corner staircase, timeworn steps lead up to a squint, or spyhole, from which the abbess could watch her nuns in the cloisters below. The abbey's octagonal tower was built in the 16th century by William Sharington, who also built the striking brewery where visitors can see the huge mash tun, cooling trough and fermentation vat. William Fox Talbot (1800-77) gave the abbey the three oriel windows on the south front, and the central one is shown on his famous negative. He was also an eminent botanist, and the grounds contain several of his plantings including tulip trees, swamp cypress and plane trees. The Fox Talbot Museum, in a 16th-century barn, has displays which tell the pioneer photographer's story, with an audiovisual presentation and much vintage photographic equipment. An old-fashioned *camera obscura* projects the image of the trees outside onto a glass screen. Talbot's contemporaries traced such an image with pencil; the inventor instead coated paper with light-sensitive silver nitrate and fixed the image with a solution of salts.

Lacock village, like the abbey, is owned by the National Trust. It grew at the gates of the 13th-century religious house and prospered through the wool trade. Its buildings date almost entirely from the 13th to the 18th century.

Abbey: NT. Apr-Oct, pm daily exc Tues. Adm charge. Shop. P *Toilets. Tel Lacock (024 973) 227. Fox Talbot Museum: NT. Mar-Oct, daily exc Good Fri. Adm charge. Shop.* P ♿ *(ground floor). Tel (024 973) 459.*

LITTLECOTE PARK

Off B4192, 2½ miles north-west of Hungerford (Ed)

Sweeping in from the gate, visitors to Littlecote see first the gaudy pennants of the hilltop tournament field; then a fine gabled Tudor house of brick and flint which lies long and low in its landscape. Henry VIII courted Jane Seymour here; at Littlecote, too, William of Orange rested during his advance on London in 1688. This is a truly historic home and yet, with mock jousting and a miniature steam railway among its attractions, it is also a modern leisure park.

From 1415 Littlecote was the home of the Darrell family, but after 'Wild' William Darrell – a man of notorious reputation – was killed in a hunting accident it passed to Sir John Popham in 1580. A celebrated judge, Popham was the Lord Chief Justice who presided at the trials both of Sir Walter Raleigh and Guy Fawkes. It was he who built Littlecote's handsome south entrance front. Relics in the house include his finger stock – a restraining device which he took with him when travelling on assizes, by which prisoners awaiting trial were locked in place by a single finger.

Popham's descendants were Puritans who supported Cromwell in the Civil War, and the house today re-creates its appearance in July 1642, when Colonel Alexander Popham returned to his home with some 60 armed cavalry troopers to escort his wife Katherine to a place of safety. Visitors pass through a series of oak-panelled ground-floor rooms in which life-size wax effigies have been set: here troopers clean their pistols; there stands a bearer of dispatches. Among the rooms is the only surviving example of a Cromwellian chapel – a plain, balconied chamber lacking both altar and wall decoration. The walls, ceiling and door of the Dutch parlour are covered with vibrant 18th-century paintings which include scenes from the story of Don Quixote, while the Great Hall contains Britain's only original Civil War armoury.

Throughout Littlecote, staff go dressed in period costume (which may be hired by visitors too). Displays of falconry are given, and jousting entertainment is mounted daily in summer on the tournament field. Additional attractions include horse-drawn wagon rides, an adventure playground, a pets' corner and a working farm.

Apr-Oct, daily. Adm charge. Refreshments. Shop. P *Toilets.* ♿ *(parts). Tel Hungerford (0488) 84000.*

LONGLEAT HOUSE AND SAFARI PARK

Off A362, 4½ miles south-east of Frome (Bb)

In 1949 Lord Bath became the first peer of the realm to open his country home to the public on a commercial basis. Longleat House is a superb

STARS IN STRIPES *Zebras are among the animals that bring the sights of the African plain to England at Longleat Safari Park. Motorists can drive through 600 acres of wooded game reserves.*

Elizabethan building of mellow Bath stone which stands in parkland landscaped by Capability Brown. It was soon attracting thousands of visitors every year, but the costs of upkeep remained daunting. So in 1966 the marquis opened a new attraction: a drive-through reserve where 50 lions were allowed to roam free. The scheme caused a furore, for nothing comparable had been attempted in Britain before. But it endured – and today the 'Lions of Longleat' remain one of the grandstand attractions of Britain's leisure industry.

The safari park now also includes drive-through reserves of giraffes, elephants, rhinoceroses, monkeys, tigers and wolves. All are set in the deep peace of the Wiltshire countryside, amid rolling hills wooded with oak, beech and chestnut.

The house itself retains great dignity, set in Brown's beautiful landscape of suave green slopes, water and woodland. The building was constructed by Sir John Thynne, ancestor of the marquis, and is sumptuously decorated inside in Italian Renaissance style. The walls are hung with Thynne family portraits, there is much good furniture and the ceilings are almost overwhelming in their gilded and ornamented grandeur. Highlights of a tour include the stone-flagged Great Hall with its antler-bedecked panelling, and the Red Library containing 6000 volumes. Three dining rooms can also be seen, their tables laid for breakfast, luncheon and dinner.

Formal gardens with an orangery and neatly disciplined hedging can be seen outside the house, while tucked discreetly to the rear are a wealth of further attractions among the outbuildings. The kitchens, for example, have been restored to their Victorian condition, with figures in period costume. Visitors can admire collections of dolls' houses, bygones and vintage vehicles. There is a maze and a butterfly garden and – perhaps the most unusual offering – a permanent exhibition devoted to the BBC television series *Doctor Who* with push-button exhibits which include a full-size Dalek.

A miniature railway takes visitors alongside the lake, where safari boats cruise. Seals and hippos swim free alongside the craft, whilst an island on the lake has a colony of gorillas.

House: All year, daily. Park: Mid Mar-Oct, daily. Refreshments. Shop. P *Toilets.* ♿ *Tel Maiden Bradley (098 53) 551 (house); 328 (park).*

LYDIARD COUNTRY PARK

Off A3102, 3 miles west of Swindon (Cd)

Lydiard Mansion was the country home of the St John family for more than 500 years before being bought by the former Corporation of Swindon in 1943. It has since been much renovated. The classical design results from extensive remodelling in the 1740s, and the main rooms include a handsome hall, library, drawing room and state bedchamber. The house and 13th-century Church of St Mary are set in a 260 acre country park, with woods, farmland, lakes and children's play area.

All year, daily. Free entry. Refreshments. Shop. P *Toilets.* ♿ *Tel Swindon (0793) 771419.*

WHITE GIANTS *A covering of snow adds to Stonehenge's air of awesome mystery. It was perhaps built as a place of sun worship – the Heel Stone in the foreground stands on the axis of sunrise at the summer solstice.*

MONKTON FARLEIGH MINE

Off A363, 4 miles east of Bath (Bc)

At a depth of 100ft below the surface of a Wiltshire hillside lie the remains of Europe's biggest Second World War underground ammunition depot. Monkton Farleigh was created out of an abandoned stone mine and once held over 12 million tons of ammunition. The bomb-proof labyrinth of tunnels and chambers covered 80 acres and was served by an arterial system of conveyors and narrow-gauge track, connected by a mile-long tunnel to the main railway. Air-conditioned and electrically lit by giant whirring dynamos, the mine amounted to a subterranean metropolis. Displays are mounted in the reception building, and hour-long guided tours conduct visitors through the eerie underworld.

Good Fri-Oct, daily; Nov-Good Fri, Sat and Sun. Adm charge. Refreshments. Shop. P *Toilets. Tel Bath (0225) 852400.*

OLD SARUM

Off A345, 2 miles north of Salisbury (Db)

The ruins of Old Sarum – a 56 acre site containing the foundations of a Norman castle, cathedral and bishop's palace – stand on a breezy hilltop. The buildings were the work of Bishop Osmund, who in 1078 chose a hill-fort site which had been known to Iron Age tribes and the Romans. In the 13th century, due to water shortages and quarrels between clergy and soldiers, it was decided to move the bishop's see down to the valley where a new cathedral was built – and the city known as New Sarum, or Salisbury, came into being. Meanwhile, Old Sarum languished and fell derelict. Today the castle's inner bailey can be reached by a wooden footbridge over a deep moat. There are sweeping views over to Salisbury and its cathedral.

All year, daily. Adm charge. Shop. P *Toilets. Tel Salisbury (0722) 335398.*

SAVERNAKE FOREST

On A346, 3 miles south-east of Marlborough (Dc)

Covering 200 leafy Wiltshire acres, Savernake was a hunting ground of the Norman kings and today it is the only English forest still in private hands; even the roads running through it are closed once a year to preserve their private status.

The forest had fallen into such bramble-strewn decay by the late 17th century that a navy surveyor found only three or four trees fit for use as timber; a rare survivor among the truly ancient trees is the 'big-bellied oak' on the Andover road. The older trees seen today date back mostly to the 18th century, when the forest was refurbished by Capability Brown. It was Brown who designed the 4 mile Grand Avenue, a beech-lined drive which cuts a ruler-straight diagonal through the forest, evoking the columned grandeur of a cathedral aisle. Other avenues include the curving 2 mile walk known as Long Harry.

Scattered among the deep woods are green glades and open scrubland, and the forest has a flourishing wildlife. Primrose, anemone and wood sorrel colour the woodland in spring, to be followed in summer by wood sage, archangel and rosebay willowherb. Fallow, roe and muntjac deer frequent the forest's quiet places, lying up by day in oak thickets and coming out to feed at dusk.

FC. All year, daily.

SHELDON MANOR

Off A420, 2 miles west of Chippenham (Bd)

A delightful stone manor house, Sheldon is all that remains of an abandoned medieval village and has served for seven centuries as a family home. Much of the gabled building dates from 1659, but the house also possesses a large and remarkable two-storey porch surviving from the 13th century. Inside are collections of local Nailsea glass, porcelain, Persian saddle bags and much good oak furniture. Outside are terraced gardens, ancient yew trees and a water garden.

Mar-Oct, Sun, Thur and Bank Hol pm. Adm charge. Refreshments. Shop. P *Toilets.* ♿ *(ground floor). Tel Chippenham (0249) 653120.*

SILBURY HILL

On A4, 1 mile South of Avebury (Cd)

Hard by the main road looms the flat-topped green cone of Silbury Hill, a baffling landmark which is the largest artificial mound raised in prehistory to be found anywhere in Europe. The grass-grown monument rises to 130ft and covers 5½ acres at its base; it has been calculated that 8¾ million cubic feet of chalk rubble, clay and other material must have been moved to make it. The mound was set up in about 2500 BC and required the labour of at least 700 men, working over a period of ten years.

What was it for? One theory suggests it was a burial mound – yet the central area has now been fully explored without finding any evidence of burial. The prehistoric engineers, moreover, seem to have been obsessed with the stability of their structure. Silbury was built as a stepped cone, with successive drum-shaped layers of chalk walling having concentric and radial walls, infilled with raked and compacted chalk rubble. So solid is the result that almost nothing has been lost by erosion in 4500 years.

Much more is understood about the nearby West Kennet Long Barrow, a gigantic chambered tomb 350ft long. This was a collective place of burial, the largest of its kind in England or Wales, which was built in about 3250 BC and in use for over 1000 years. The remains of 46 skeletons, including a dozen children, have been recovered from part of the long barrow.

EH. *All year, daily.*

STONEHENGE

Off A303, 2 miles west of Amesbury (Cb)

As the main road from Amesbury sweeps over one of Salisbury Plain's gently curving ridges the mysterious stone circle looms in clear view ahead. The plain's wide, prairie-like horizon diminishes the scale of the structure, and only when the eye catches human figures among the stones do the massive proportions become apparent. Stonehenge then seems the work of giants; and one can almost believe the assertion by the 12th-century historian Geoffrey of Monmouth that the wizard Merlin was involved in its creation.

From a car park visitors pass through a tunnel to reach the monument. A rope barrier protects the stones, but the visitor is close enough to them to experience their magic. Some blocks have been squared off with extraordinary precision; others are more weatherbeaten and haggard. Starlings and jackdaws flutter under the gigantic lintels and the whole monument is lichen-spattered with the result that many fallen stones, embedded in the ground, seem almost to grow from the landscape.

No comparable prehistoric monument exists elsewhere in Europe. Stonehenge is incredibly ancient, it was begun in about 3100 BC – before Egypt's pyramids were built. Like a medieval cathedral, it was much remodelled after its foundation. The monument grew in three main phases over about 1300 years, beginning as a ditch-and-bank circle. In phase two a double circle of bluestones was added; there are 80 of these, each weighing about 2 tons, and they were brought 200 miles from the Preseli Hills of south-west Wales, probably by raft across the Bristol Channel and on by river.

In the third phase the bluestones were displaced and the colossal sarsen stones were added, sandstone boulders each weighing more than 50 tons which were hauled from the Marlborough Downs 20 miles away. The sarsens were set up in an outer ring and inner horseshoe topped with lintels, and remarkable skill was employed in cutting the horizontal blocks so that they were curved to fit the circle and jointed with mortise holes to fit tenons, or protruding knobs, on the uprights. The highest upright is 21ft and its tenon is clearly seen in silhouette against the sky.

In its final form, Stonehenge included a re-arrangement of the bluestones. The completion date was about 1550 BC, so there can be no question of the monument being 'built by Druids', for the Druids were priests of Celtic peoples who reached Britain only in about the 3rd century BC.

Why was Stonehenge built? From the beginning the main axis of the monument was aligned with the midsummer sunrise, and it is possible that many other orientations were keyed to the position of the sun on the horizon at different times of the year. Stonehenge, then, was possibly a holy ceremonial centre celebrating the sun and marking the calendar of the seasons. It lies in an area rich in prehistoric burial mounds, many of them the graves of wealthy Bronze Age chieftains, and Woodhenge is also nearby.

A leaflet available at the car park bookshop suggests walks over National Trust land to various barrow sites, as well as to the enigmatic sweep of ground known as The Cursus which may have been a processional way – or even a ceremonial racecourse. Stonehenge itself teems with visitors throughout the summer, but these walks are much less frequented. Skylarks trill high above the chalk downland, and looking back at the crowds at the foot of the monument it is possible to imagine how Stonehenge may have looked when other, ancient, peoples congregated there.

EH. *All year, daily. Adm charge. Refreshments. Shop.* P *Toilets.* ♿ *Tel Bristol (0272) 734472.*

PLEASURE GARDENS *The London banker Henry Hoare, known as 'Henry the Magnificent', created the lake and bridge at Stourhead in 1741. A grass-covered walk crosses the Turf Bridge.*

STOURHEAD

Off B3092, 3 miles north-west of Mere (Bb)

It is often supposed that Capability Brown in the 1750s somehow 'invented' the English landscape garden with its informal vistas of lawns, woodland and water. But the master had precursors, notably in Henry Hoare (1705-85). A member of a London banking family, he created at his Wiltshire home of Stourhead one of the finest landscape gardens to be seen anywhere in the world – and he began work in the 1740s, a decade before the illustrious Brown.

West of his house, Hoare dammed springs of the River Stour to create a sweeping lake with

AROUND SALISBURY CATHEDRAL

Salisbury grew up around its graceful cathedral, which rises from the sward of a spacious and secluded close. Begun by Bishop Herbert Poore in 1220, the cathedral was completed 38 years later and is noted for its Early English pointed arches and tall windows. The cathedral's crowning glory, its tower and slender spire, soars 404ft into the sky, the tallest spire in England.

The Close is entered through medieval gateways and contains some fine ecclesiastical and private residences. To the north, by Choristers Green, is Mompesson House, a dignified, stone-faced building with half a dozen rooms furnished in 18th-century style. Nearby, streets of gabled inns, bow-windowed shops and half-timbered houses are laid out on a grid pattern.

Cathedral and Chapter House: All year, daily. Adm charge. Refreshments. Shop. Toilets. ♿ Mompesson House: Apr-Nov, daily exc Thur and Fri. Adm charge. Tel Salisbury (0722) 335659. Salisbury and South Wilts Museum: All year, Mon-Sat; July-Aug, Sun pm. Adm charge. Refreshments. Shop. Toilets. ♿ Tel (0722) 332151. Regimental Museum: Apr-Oct, Sun-Fri; Feb, Mar, Nov, Mon-Fri. Adm charge. Shop. Toilets. Tel (0722) 336222.

SACRED STONES *The graceful central column of the Chapter House (top) of Salisbury Cathedral was renewed in 1856 when the octagonal building was restored to its original 13th-century splendour, complete with fan-vaulted roof. The building is now an exhibition area. The cathedral's west front (left) was the last part of the building to be completed in 1258. Its rows of niches contain statues of saints, which are Victorian replacements of the originals. Among the many fine monuments in the high-vaulted nave is the tomb (above) of William Longespée, 3rd Earl of Salisbury, who laid one of the foundation stones in 1220. Six years later he became the first person to be buried in the cathedral.*

ANCIENT BONES *The skeleton of one of the so-called Beaker Folk, who inhabited Britain in the Bronze Age, is among the exhibits of early man in the Salisbury and South Wiltshire Museum. The Beaker Folk were often interred along with their tools and domestic utensils – especially their bell-shaped pottery beakers, from which they get their name – in round burial barrows. There is also a Stonehenge Gallery, containing finds from the site and describing how and when the standing stones were raised. The museum is in Salisbury Cathedral Close at The King's House, named after James I who was a visitor there in 1610 and 1613.*

COLOUR PARADE *The ceremonial colours of the Duke of Edinburgh's Royal Regiment – the county regiment of Wiltshire and Berkshire – are laid up in Salisbury Cathedral. The Regimental Museum in Cathedral Close tells the story of 250 years of military history in displays of silver, medals and uniforms.*

wooded islands; around the sheet of water he disposed classical temples and bridges in an attempt to re-create the dreamy, idealised landscapes seen in the paintings of Claude Lorrain and Gaspar Poussin. A stone bridge was added to set off the romantic sweep of water.

Hoare's garden survives in layout much as he planned it, but the plantings today include many varieties of trees and shrubs unknown in his day. Exotic masses of azalea and rhododendron provide gaudy displays on the lawn south of the house in May and June. Elsewhere, paths wander from one delightful spot to another: from the shaded grotto with its statues of Nymph and River God to high vantage points such as The Shades and the Temple of Apollo which command dramatic views from above. The house itself, built in plain 18th-century Palladian style, contains a picture gallery, a collection of family portraits and Chippendale furniture.

NT. Garden: All year, daily. House: May-Sept, pm daily exc Fri; Apr and Oct, pm daily exc Thur and Fri. Refreshments. Shop. P *Toilets.* ♿ *Tel Bourton (0747) 840348.*

STOURTON HOUSE GARDEN

Off B3092, 3 miles north-west of Mere (Bb)

Tucked away near the car park of its celebrated neighbour Stourhead, Stourton House Garden is a privately owned and pleasantly informal 4 acre spread for plant lovers, with grass paths leading among shrubs and trees. Attractions include a herbaceous garden and a small woodland garden. Hydrangeas are a speciality, and special days are designated for viewing daffodils, azaleas and delphiniums in season. Stourton House is known, too, for its bouquets of dried garden flowers. More than 20 varieties of hydrangeas are on sale, as well as a selection of rare plants.

Apr-Nov, Wed, Thur, Sun and Bank Hol Mon. Adm charge. P *Toilets. Tel Bourton (0747) 840417.*

SWINDON AND CRICKLADE RAILWAY

Off A419, 4 miles north-west of Swindon (Ce)

Gleaming steam and diesel locomotives – and lovingly preserved rolling stock – are running again along part of the former Midland and South Western Junction Railway. Since 1979 members of the voluntary Swindon and Cricklade Railway Society have been laying new track for the trains. So far about three-quarters of a mile of line is in use, with Blunsdon station serving as the first stage in the reconstruction of the railway between Moredon (a suburb of Swindon) and Cricklade – an eventual run of about 4½ miles.

There are passenger rides over part of the relaid track on the second Sunday of certain months and on Bank Holidays. The museum at Blunsdon station has an evocative collection of guards' lamps, station clocks, pressure gauges, and plates and silverware from Pullman restaurant cars. The station is open every weekend for visitors to watch the restoration work in progress.

Trains and museum: Apr-Oct, second Sun and Bank Hol. Adm charge. Refreshments. Shop. P *Tel Swindon (0793) 771615.*

WESSEX SHIRE PARK

Off B3089, 7 miles west of Wilton (Ca)

The park covers 130 acres of countryside near the thatched village of Teffont Magna, and incorporates the site of Wick Ball Camp, a 3000-year-old Celtic site. The park's theme is farming through the ages: carts and wagons of bygone times are displayed, and there is a farming area where visitors can see Shire horses and even try their hand at driving a horse in harness. Cart and tractor rides offer further attractions, and a play area has been laid out for children. The park also includes a rhododendron walk and wildlife trail, while the summit of Spyglass Hill has panoramic views which sweep from the spire of Salisbury Cathedral to the Regimental Badges cut into the chalk downs near Fovant.

Easter-Oct, daily. Adm charge. Refreshments. Shop. P *Toilets.* ♿ *Tel Salisbury (0722) 76393.*

WILTON HOUSE

Off A30, at Wilton (Ca)

Huge, stately cedars rise from the lawns of Wilton House, home for 400 years of the Earls of Pembroke. It is a place rich in historic associations. Shakespeare is said to have given the first performance of *Twelfth Night* at the house; Charles I is said to have 'loved Wilton above all places'; and much later, during the Second World War, Wilton was HQ of Southern Command, scene of the planning of the D-Day invasion.

The present building dates from the time of William Herbert, 1st Earl of Pembroke, in the 1540s. But the fine south front was created in the 17th century with advice from Inigo Jones, who also contributed to the design of the eight splendid state rooms which are on view. For palatial grandeur none surpasses the 60ft long Double Cube Room (so-called because it is twice the size of the adjoining cube-shaped room).

The house contains various old master paintings, including works by Rubens, Rembrandt, Reynolds and Bruegel. Chippendale furniture and classical sculptures lend further distinction. The river Nadder flows through the grounds and is spanned by a Palladian bridge of 1737.

Easter-mid Oct, daily exc Mon; Bank Hol Mon. Adm charge. Refreshments. Shop. P *Toilets.* ♿ *Tel Salisbury (0722) 743115.*

WILTON ROYAL CARPET FACTORY

Off A36, at Wilton (Ca)

Wilton carpet is known for its velvety surface texture, and Wilton Royal, established on its present site since 1655, is probably the oldest carpet factory in the world.

The factory is set around its 17th-century courtyard. One of the original weaving sheds, creeper-clad today, houses a working exhibition showing some of the carpets which have flourished over more than 300 years of manufacture on the site. Display cases contain some of the finest handmade items, and there is a collection of looms and ancillary machinery such as tuft-cutters and bobbin winders, most of which are in working order and demonstrated by staff. A visit also includes a tour of the modern factory, showing processes from the dyeing of yarn to the final inspection in the finishing department.

All year, Mon-Sat exc Bank Hol. Adm charge. Refreshments. Shop. P *Toilets.* ♿ *Tel Salisbury (0722) 742441.*

WINDMILL HILL

Off A4361, 1½ miles north-west of Avebury (Cd)

The hill rises gently to some 640ft above sea level and is crowned by a 21 acre enclosure with three concentric rings of banks and ditches. It is known as a 'causewayed enclosure' because the ramparts are interrupted for access, and is famed both for its exceptional size and as the first of its type to be investigated. Excavated in 1925-29, Windmill Hill has given its name to a certain type of Stone Age pottery and provided some of the first true insights into Stone Age life. It was found, for example, that the ditches had been dug out with antler picks; that crops grown were a primitive form of wheat with some barley and flax; that dogs were kept and cattle were raised in numbers. Begun in about 3250 BC, the enclosure probably served as a communal gathering place and pen for cattle barter.

EH. All year, daily.

WOODLAND PARK AND HERITAGE MUSEUM

Off A3098 at Brokerswood, 1 mile west of Westbury (Bc)

Part of the ancient forest of Selwood, the park covers 80 acres of natural broadleaved woodland and has a lake with wildfowl. Roe and muntjac deer haunt the quieter glades; bluebells and the early purple orchid are among the flowers which brighten the forest floor. This too is a working woodland, where hazels are coppiced, according to a seven-year cycle, yielding pea and bean sticks as a crop.

The Woodland Heritage Museum contains displays of forestry, conservation and wildlife.

All year, daily. Adm charge. Refreshments. Shop. P *Toilets.* ♿ *Tel Westbury (0373) 822238.*

COUNTY CALENDAR

Good Fri. Devizes to Westminster International Canoe Race.

May 29. Great Wishford: Grovely Forest Rights (procession and decoration of houses).

May Day Bank Hol. Downton: Cuckoo Fair (Maypole dancing).

June (early). Swindon: Thamesdown Games.

June 21. Stonehenge: Druids' Dawn Ceremony.

July (late). Salisbury: Southern Cathedrals Festival (every three years, from 1988).

August (mid-month). Wilton: Sheep Fair.

August Bank Hol. Lacock: Village Fair.

September (early). Salisbury: Arts Festival.

October (mid-month). Marlborough: Mop Fair. Salisbury: Charter Fair.

Tourist information: Bradford-on-Avon (022 16) 2495; Chippenham (0249) 657733; Salisbury (0722) 334956; Swindon (0793) 30328.

NORTH YORKSHIRE

LONELY ABBEYS AND SCENIC WONDERS OF MOORS AND DALES

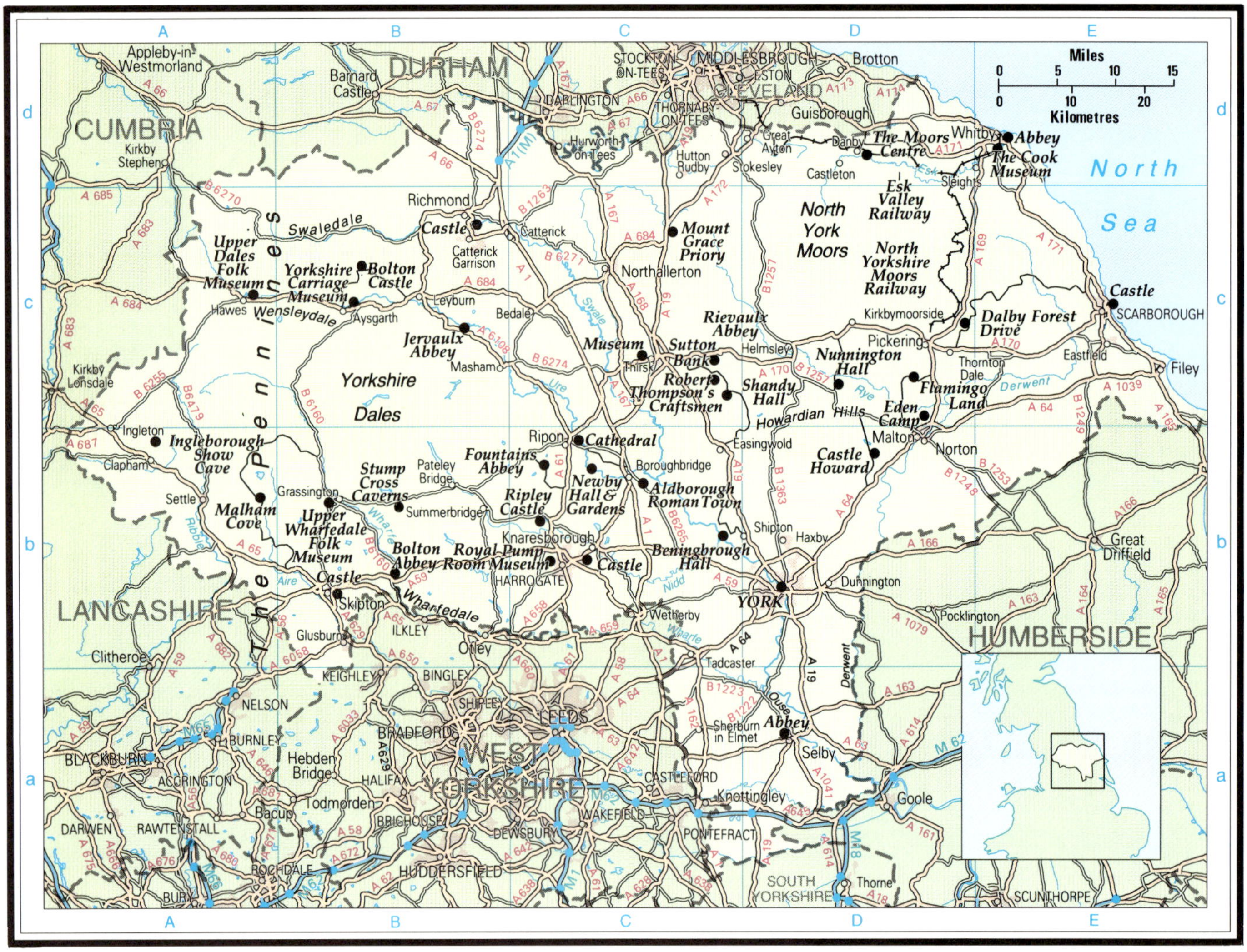

The moors and dales that make up most of North Yorkshire spread from the Pennines to the sea – a landscape as varied as anywhere in England, and dotted with some of the country's loveliest and most historic towns and cities. Medieval monks built their abbeys – Bolton, Fountains, Jervaulx and Rievaulx – in the broad dales and the Vale of York, watered by crystal-clear rivers spilling down from the Pennines. Though ruined now, the abbeys are still lovely sights, standing in their peaceful settings below hills where sheep graze amid an embroidery of dry-stone walls.

North of the historic city of York lie the Howardian Hills, setting for the lordly Castle Howard. Beyond, the land rises to a heather-clad plateau and the dramatic escarpment of Sutton Bank. Eastwards moorland extends to the coast, where a fringe of high cliffs is broken by towns as contrasted as Whitby and Scarborough.

ALDBOROUGH ROMAN TOWN

Off B6265, 1 mile south-east of Boroughbridge (Cb)

The small village of Aldborough lies within the area of what was once Isurium Brigantum, capital of the Brigantes, the largest tribe in Roman Britain. Isurium followed the usual pattern of a Roman town, having a regular grid of streets with the forum near its centre. Remains include parts of the town wall and two mosaic pavements which formed part of a large town house.

Aldborough's museum houses relics from Isurium, and also a replica of a lamp in the form of a sleeping boy, the original of which is in the British Museum.

EH. Apr-Sept, daily exc Sun am. Adm charge. Shop. P *Toilets. Tel Boroughbridge (090 12) 2768.*

BENINGBROUGH HALL

Off A19, 2½ miles west of Shipton (Cb)

Lifestyles in an English country house – from the splendour of an 18th-century state bedroom to the starkness of a Victorian laundry – are shown in this beautifully restored early Georgian house. The main fronts are aglow with warm red brick, punctuated by door and window frames of mellow stone. Inside, the highlights are a vast two-storey hall and a cantilevered oak staircase leading to a magnificent saloon adorned with gilded Corinthian pilasters. Outside, the working life of the laundry and stable block is described in portraits and audiovisual displays. Around the house are gardens and wooded parkland.

NT. Easter week pm, and Sat and Sun pm in Apr; May-Oct, pm daily exc Mon and Fri; Bank Hol Mon pm; Nov, Sat and Sun pm. Adm charge. Refreshments. Shop. P *Toilets.* ♿ *Tel York (0904) 470666.*

BOLTON ABBEY

On B6160, 4 miles east of Skipton (Bb)

A gateway in the wall that runs beside the road at Bolton Abbey leads into a vanished past. The River Wharfe meanders between sheep-grazed meadows, and softly contoured fells climb gently beneath a wide sky. Half hidden by trees are the gaping arches and windows of a ruined priory church built by Augustinian canons more than 800 years ago. Follow the path down to the riverside and the priory comes into full view, when it can be seen that not all the building is a ruin. This was due to the foresight of Prior Richard Moone who, at the time of the Dissolution of the Monasteries, built a wall between the choir and the nave. This barrier saved the nave, which became, and still is, the parish church.

The west tower, begun in 1520, was not completed and stood derelict for 450 years. But in 1984 it was restored and its warm, honey-coloured stone makes a splendid entrance to the church. A pointed Gothic arch leads to the nave, tastefully restored in the late 19th century. The south windows were designed by Augustus Pugin, the 19th-century architect, and contain 36 stained-glass panels. A series of 11 paintings on the east wall above the altar are floral designs symbolising events in the life of Christ: barley, olive, vine, passion flower, wild rose and palm tree. The panels are interspersed with the madonna lily, symbol of St Mary to whom the church is dedicated.

Upper Wharfedale begins at Bolton Abbey, and waymarked nature trails starting near the abbey run along the river and through Strid Wood to the narrow gorge of The Strid.

All year, daily. Free entry. P ♿ *Tel Bolton Abbey (075 671) 238.*

BOLTON CASTLE

Off A684, 4 miles west of Leyburn (Bc)

Bolton Castle stands on the northern slopes of Wensleydale, and seen from the valley below looks almost intact. Its massive square towers, though crumbling at their tops, stand 100ft high. Many of the castle's rooms are roofed, and leaded-glass windows glint from its buff-coloured walls. It was built in the late 14th century as the fortress home of Richard le Scrope, Chancellor of England during the reign of Richard II.

Bolton Castle was the prison for six months of Mary, Queen of Scots after her defeat at Langside in May 1568. One of the rooms in the south-west tower is called Mary's Room, though it is doubtful whether this was the actual room she occupied. More likely she would have had a state chamber in the north-west tower, its five storeys now floorless and roofless. Though virtually a prisoner, the queen would certainly have enjoyed greater comfort than inmates of the dungeon in the basement of the north turret – a grim chamber with only one entry – a square trap through which the victims were dropped.

Mar-Oct, daily. Adm charge. Refreshments. Shop. P *Toilets. Tel Wensleydale (0969) 23674.*

THE COOK MUSEUM

In Grape Lane, Whitby (Ed)

It was to this house that the navigator James Cook came in 1746 at the age of 18 as an apprentice to its owner John Walker. Cook learnt his seamanship on Walker's North Sea and Baltic colliers over the next three years, and lived in the house while ashore. It is now restored as a museum, with two ground-floor rooms meticulously re-created in their 18th-century style. The first floor is devoted to Cook and his Pacific voyages, and displays include letters, documents and ship models.

May-Oct, daily exc Wed am and Tues. Adm charge. Shop. Tel Whitby (0947) 601900.

DALBY FOREST DRIVE

Off A170, 3 miles north of Thornton Dale (Dc)

Miles of fine walking await the nature lover in the Dalby Forest area. The key to exploration is the information centre at Low Dalby, near the start of the Dalby Forest Drive, a 9 mile scenic link between Thornton Dale and Hackness. Along the drive are several parking areas from which waymarked walks radiate.

The walks provide an insight into the operation of a working forest and an introduction to its varied wildlife. A favourite walk is the Snever Dale Forest Walk, which starts just north of Low Dalby and is about 3 miles long, though a short cut can reduce it to 1 mile.

FC. Drive: All year, daily. Information centre: Apr-Sept, daily. Drive toll. Shop. P *Toilets.* ♿ *Tel Pickering (0751) 72771.*

EDEN CAMP

Off A64, 2 miles north-east of Malton (Dc)

Visitors to this former prisoner-of-war camp experience the sights, sounds and smells of Britain during the Second World War. There are moments of dread and horror. In one display, a family with their cat are gathered round their radio to hear the declaration of war on that first Sunday morning of September 1939. In another 'frozen moment', the wheel of a smashed bicycle still turns in the blitzed street where a bomb has just fallen. The acrid smell of burning and the noise of explosions and wailing sirens fill the air.

There are lighter moments too. In the puppet theatre wartime stars give variety shows, and fashions of the 1940s are also on parade. Other aspects of life on the 'Home Front' include evacuation, rationing, the black market, propaganda, the black-out, the Home Guard and the life of women on farms and in factories.

Mid Feb-Christmas, daily. Adm charge. Refreshments. Shop. P *Toilets.* ♿ *Tel Malton (0653) 697777.*

ESK VALLEY RAILWAY

From Middlesbrough Station to Whitby Station (Dd)

Scenically, this 35 mile route is one of the loveliest train journeys in Britain. Historically, it is linked with the country's very first railway; it was the extension of the Stockton-Darlington railway in 1830 that turned the village of Middlesbrough into a thriving industrial town. The journey between Middlesbrough and Whitby takes in 15 country stations, all offering temptations to the traveller to linger. They include Marton, birthplace of Captain Cook.

Trains all year, daily exc Sun Oct-Easter. Tel Middlesbrough (0642) 225535.

FLAMINGO LAND

Off A169, 5 miles north of Malton (Dc)

The zoo here has a fascinating range of inmates, and many of them, including flamingos, capuchin monkeys and dama-wallabies, result from a highly successful scientific breeding programme. There are dolphins, sea lions and parrots, circus shows, and more than 50 rides and slides, including a looping roller coaster.

Mid Apr-Sept, daily. Adm charge. Refreshments. Shop. P *Toilets.* ♿ *Tel Kirby Misperton (065 386) 287.*

FOUNTAINS ABBEY

Off B6265, 1½ miles west of Ripon (Cb)

Visitors approaching the ruined 12th-century Cistercian abbey past the Elizabethan-style Fountains Hall enjoy a staggering view of the

ABBEY BUILT ON WOOL *Sunset pierces the delicate lancet windows of the great church at Fountains Abbey. Cistercian monks prospered through the wool trade and built one of the finest abbeys in England.*

abbey's west face, with the jagged silhouettes of guesthouses in the foreground and a lofty, crenellated tower thrusting above a background of trees Inside, a long, narrow nave with gloriously arched aisles leads to the roofless Chapel of the Nine Altars, which has slender pillars and graceful arches. Ranged against the west wall of the nave is the longest line of cloisters in existence, extending for 312ft and magnificently vaulted in 22 double bays. Most of the abbey stands on the north bank of the River Skell, but the lay brothers' refectory stretches across the water to the south bank like a small bridge.

Studley Royal is the abbey's landscape garden, which was laid out in the 18th century and is a riot of follies, ornamental temples, water gardens, waterfalls and statues. It is bounded on its northern edge by a lake and by 400 acres of parkland where deer roam. The rise and fall of the abbey is the theme of an exhibition and video film in Fountains Hall.

NT. Abbey and Gardens: All year, daily. Adm charge. Refreshments. Shop. P *Toilets. Tel Sawley (076 586) 333. Fountains Hall exhibition: All year, daily. Tel (076 586) 333.*

INGLEBOROUGH SHOW CAVE

Off A65, 1¾ miles north of Clapham (Ab)

The Yorkshire Dales are riddled with caves and underground passages, and three spectacular cave systems lie within a few miles of each other. The Ingleborough Show Cave offers a journey through a wonderland of stalactites and stalagmites, with picturesque and descriptive names such as The Beehive, Sword of Damocles, The Skittles and the Mushroom Bed. To the north of the cave is Gaping Gill, a cavern where the Fell Beck tumbles 340ft into a chamber 100ft wide and 110ft high. It can be entered only by descending in a bosun's chair and winch, operated at Spring and Summer Bank Holidays.

Mid Feb-mid Jan, daily. Adm charge. P *Tel Clapham (046 85) 242.*

JERVAULX ABBEY

Off A6108, 4 miles north-east of Masham (Be)

This abbey stands in beautiful parkland and is especially attractive in late spring, when aubrieta splashes the grey walls with purple. There is still much to remind the visitor of the Cistercian monks who built and occupied it – humble men always seeking a simpler way of life. The heart of the abbey was the church, which can be entered through the south-west door, a fine piece of 12th-century architecture. Among other parts to be seen are the cloister, the abbot's lodging, the dining hall and two infirmaries.

All year, daily. Adm charge. Refreshments. Shop. P *Toilets. Tel Bedale (0677) 60226.*

KNARESBOROUGH CASTLE

In centre of Knaresborough (Cb)

The vast cliff-top castle of Knaresborough – in its medieval heyday the fort and playground of kings – fell victim to Cromwell's forces in 1648. Only a petition from local townspeople won remission for the keep, which was maintained as a prison for many years. Its formidable walls, 15ft thick, enclose a dimly lit dungeon which was probably built as a safe storage area for food and water supplies in times of siege.

On the keep's first floor is the King's Chamber, where Richard II is believed to have been held before he was taken to Pontefract Castle and murdered. The carved stone handrails on the spiral stairway from below and the outer stairway are unusual features specially designed by the master mason when the castle was built. Near the keep is the 14th-century courthouse. Its upper storey, added before 1600, now houses the Courthouse Museum which contains furniture from the original Tudor Court. There are two tunnels for secret entry and exit.

Castle: Easter, then May Day Bank Hol, and Spring Bank Hol-Sept, daily. Museum: Apr-Sept, daily; Oct-Mar, Sun pm. Adm charge. P *(limited). Toilets. Tel Harrogate (0423) 503340.*

MALHAM COVE

Off A65, 7 miles east of Settle (Ab)

The road through Malhamdale twists and turns through a landscape of wild fells above fields embroidered with grey-white ribbons of dry-stone walls – a typical landscape of the Yorkshire Dales National Park. On a slight rise the grey cottages of Malham village come into view, and beyond is the white cliff of Malham Cove, a vast semicircular wall of craggy limestone, carved out of the green hills.

PAVED BY TIME *Thousands of years of weathering of cracks and fissures in the rock have created the gigantic blocks that make up the spectacular limestone plateau, or 'pavement', above Malham Cove.*

There is a car park in the village, beside the National Park Information Centre which gives details of walks and drives in the park. From the information centre it is a 1 mile walk to Malham Cove, first along the road and then along a footpath that leads to the cliff. The approach gives the opportunity to study the dramatic scale of this phenomenon – a towering wall 300ft high and some 900ft across. Once a stream flowed over the cliff, but now it flows underground and emerges from the base, a crystal clear watercourse that eddies around a rocky pool before making its chattering, pebble-strewn way across the fields, through the village and on to join the River Aire.

A steep path and steps curve up the western flank of the cove. At the top of the cove is an expanse of gigantic limestone blocks between which grow plants such as hart's-tongue fern, herb-robert, enchanter's nightshade and wood-sorrel. The view down Malhamdale is wonderful, a vista of rumpled fields dotted with lonely farmsteads.

Just over 1 mile to the north of the cove is Malham Tarn, a 150 acre lake formed by melting glaciers during the Ice Age. Its peat-bordered waters are a haven for wildlife, and nearby is the Malham Tarn Field Centre where natural history is researched and taught. To the east of Malham village a path runs for 1½ miles to another scenic wonder – Gordale Scar, where water cascades through a narrow ravine.

All year, daily. Free entry.

THE MOORS CENTRE, DANBY

Off A171, 2 miles east of Castleton (Dd)

The North York Moors National Park covers 553 square miles of beautiful countryside, and the Moors Centre at Danby is an excellent starting point for exploring this wild and unspoilt landscape of moors, forest, rivers and lakes.

Danby Lodge is a former shooting lodge built in the 17th century, and stands on the banks of the River Esk in 13 acres of parkland. There are nature trails through woods and by the river, and the lodge is also the starting point for waymarked walks onto the moors.

Easter-Oct, daily; winter, Sun pm. Free entry. Refreshments. Shop. P *Toilets.* ♿ *Tel Castleton (0287) 60654.*

MOUNT GRACE PRIORY

Off A19, 7 miles north-east of Northallerton (Cc)

Below the tall, battlemented tower of its monastic church, a fascinating picture of the austere, solitary lives of Carthusian monks can be built up at Mount Grace. Founded in 1398, it is the best preserved of all the Carthusian monasteries, or Charterhouses, of the order in England. Unlike other Western orders, the Carthusians rejected the fully communal religious life in favour of a hermit-like existence. At Mount Grace visitors can see what remains of individual cells where the monks spent most of their time. These cells and their gardens made the cloister of a Charterhouse much larger than that of any other sort of monastery – in the case of Mount Grace, more than 200ft from side to side.

EH. All year, daily exc Sun am. Adm charge. Shop. P *Toilets. Tel Osmotherley (060 983) 249.*

NEWBY HALL AND GARDENS

Off B6265, 3 miles south-east of Ripon (Cb)

Newby Hall's gardens are planned to delight throughout the seasons. In early summer laburnums splash the scene with gold, and a

NOBLE PALACE IN A GREEN FRAME

The approach to Castle Howard is by ruler-straight, tree-lined avenues, and where they meet stands a 100ft high obelisk. This bears a lengthy inscription commemorating Charles, 3rd Earl of Carlisle, who was responsible for the great house and its parklands. Set amid trim lawns where peacocks strut, surrounded by parkland whose boundaries are the distant horizons, Castle Howard has all the majesty and nobility of a palace, which is exactly what the 3rd earl and his architect Sir John Vanbrugh had in mind in 1699. On its hilltop site the house dominates the landscape, a piece of classical architecture on the grand scale with pilastered façades, tall arched windows, a balustraded parapet and, crowning the central block, a 70ft high dome topped with an octagonal lantern. The dome was the first in England to be built on a private house, and it is no coincidence that it resembles the dome on St Paul's Cathedral, for Vanbrugh's assistant at Castle Howard was Nicholas Hawksmoor, a student of Sir Christopher Wren.

LADY'S CHAMBER *The bedroom of Lady Georgiana, wife of the 6th Earl of Carlisle, remains as she left it when she died in 1858. The bed dates from 1770; pictures of relatives line the walls.*

This house – familiar to television viewers as the setting for many scenes in *Brideshead Revisited* – was the first building which Vanbrugh designed. He did so with little regard to convention and much attention to opulence and splendour – nowhere more so than in the Hall. Cathedral-like in its loftiness and awesome in its proportions, it has a dome supported on tall arches with carved and fluted pillars. On the dome's ceiling the horses of the Sun frisk and gallop among billowing clouds, and in the four corners between the arches are mythological subjects. On one side of the Hall a great chimneypiece dwarfs a cast-iron fireplace that could never have been large enough to heat such a vast space. The chimneypiece, the work of Italian stuccoists, is a riot of carvings in scagliola, a mixture of plaster and marble chips.

Though the Hall is Vanbrugh's masterpiece, there is much to see and admire in the other rooms. In one bedroom stands a four-poster bed, with hangings of painted Chinese silk, that Queen Victoria slept in, and in the Long Gallery and Tapestry Room there are paintings by Van Dyck, Holbein, Gainsborough, Romney and Reynolds. The Music Room has a Broadwood piano dating from 1796, and this room is also remarkable for its carved pinewood cornice, frieze and door surrounds.

WATERY WORLD *The fountain by John Thomas in Castle Howard's formal gardens shows Atlas bearing the globe. The trumpet-blowing figures were shown at the Great Exhibition of 1851 in London.*

In the grounds are lawns, trim hedges, lakes, a walled garden and a magnificent fountain. In the park beyond South Lake stand the domed Temple of the Four Winds, designed by Vanbrugh, and Hawksmoor's Mausoleum, a circular building with a tall colonnade which many claim to be his finest work. The Great Lake covers 70 acres, and bathing and fishing are allowed. The stable block houses a display of costumes from the 17th century to modern times in period settings.

Off A64, 15 miles north-east of York (Db). Mar-Oct, daily. Adm charge. Shop. Refreshments. Toilets. P ♿ *Tel Coneysthorpe (065 384) 333.*

variety of old-fashioned roses bloom in June. Later the herbaceous borders present the display for which Newby Hall is famous, and in autumn a host of end-of-season plants appears.

The house was built mainly in the late 17th century and enlarged in the 18th century, with Robert Adam as one of the architects. Its treasures include Gobelins tapestries, classical statues and Chippendale furniture. There is a miniature railway.

Apr-Oct, Tues-Sun and Bank Hol Mon. Adm charge. Refreshments. Shop. 🅿 *Toilets. Tel Boroughbridge (090 12) 2583.*

NORTH YORKSHIRE MOORS RAILWAY

Pickering Station (Dc)

Nostalgia and nature combine to give a special character to a journey on the North Yorkshire Moors Railway. As well as the never-failing attraction of steam travel on a line built in the 1830s, passengers on the 18 mile trip between Pickering and Grosmont can alight at stations on the way for a walk through moorland countryside which beautifully reflects the changing seasons.

Deer may be seen as the train passes through Blansby Park, the medieval deer park of Pickering Castle. Skelton Tower, looming over the line, looks like part of a ruined castle, but in fact it was erected by a Victorian clergyman who used it for seclusion. Passengers can also see the famous Fylingdales 'golf balls' – domes protecting the radar scanners of the Ballistic Missile Early Warning System.

Some 200yds from the station in Pickering, a handsome Regency residence houses the Beck Isle Museum of Rural Life. The printer's shop has a large press which was built in 1854 and is still in working order, and there are also a barber's, an outfitter's and a cobbler's.

Railway: Apr-Oct, most days; Christmas specials. Fares. Refreshments. Shops. 🅿 *Toilets.* ♿ *Tel Pickering (0751) 72508. Beck Isle Museum: Apr-Oct, daily. Adm charge. Shop.* 🅿 *Tel (0751) 73653. Castle: EH. Adm charge. Shop.* 🅿 ♿ *Tel (0751) 749899.*

NUNNINGTON HALL

Off B1257, 4½ miles south-east of Helmsley (Dc)

A classical doorway and carved stone window surrounds give a stately air to the south front of this manor house on the bank of the River Rye. The building dates partly from the 16th century, but is largely the creation of Lord Preston, an ardent supporter of the Stuart cause who tried to bring back James II after he had fled the country in 1688. In his retirement at Nunnington, Preston remodelled the south side of the house and laid out the formal walled garden.

A number of rooms are decorated in typical late 17th-century style, with moulded panelling and doorcases. An unusual attraction at Nunnington is the Carlisle Collection of 22 miniature rooms, one-eighth normal size and furnished and decorated in different period styles.

NT. Apr and Nov, Sat and Sun pm; May-Oct, Tues-Thur, Sat, Sun and Bank Hol Mon pm. Adm charge. Refreshments. Shop. 🅿 *Toilets.* ♿ *Tel Nunnington (043 95) 283.*

UNCHALLENGED DEFENDER *Norman lords built Richmond Castle as a defence against enemies who never came. Even the Wars of the Roses and the Civil War passed it by, and time has been its main assailant.*

RICHMOND CASTLE

In Richmond town centre (Bc)

Set magnificently on a crag high above the River Swale, the Norman castle towers dramatically over Richmond's cobbled marketplace. Its rectangular keep, built in the 12th century, is 100ft high and one of the finest in England, and there are walls dating from the 11th century. Alan the Red, a Breton follower of William the Conqueror, built the castle on land given to him by the king. For some time the castle and estate retained links with the dukedom of Brittany, but they eventually passed to the Crown.

Richmond also has the most authentic public 18th-century Georgian theatre to be seen today. It was built as the Theatre Royal in 1788 by the actor-manager Samuel Butler, and many great 19th-century actors, including Edmund Kean and William Macready, trod its boards. The theatre closed in the 1840s and the building was used as a corn chandler's, a furniture store and an auction room before a group of enthusiasts took it over in the 1930s and restored it. Attached to the theatre is a museum with displays of playbills and photos.

Much military history in these parts concerns the Green Howards, whose regimental museum is housed in part of an old church in Richmond's market square. The Green Howards were formed in 1688 to fight for William of Orange against James II, and some of the arms and equipment of that time can be seen.

Around Richmond lies the beautiful area known as Richmondshire. This has its own museum in the town, with displays showing the development of the region since the 11th century. James Herriot enthusiasts can see the set of the vet's surgery built for the television series *All Creatures Great and Small.*

Castle: EH. All year, daily exc Sun am Oct-Mar. Adm charge. Shop. Toilets. Tel Richmond (0748) 2493. Theatre: May-Sept, pm daily; also Sat and Bank Hol Mon am. Adm charge. Shop. Tel (0748) 3021. Green Howards Museum: Apr-Oct, daily; Feb-Mar, Nov, Mon-Sat exc Sat in Feb, some weekends. Adm charge. Shop. Tel (0748) 2133. Richmondshire Museum: Easter-Nov, pm daily. Adm charge. Shop. Tel (0748) 5611.

RIEVAULX ABBEY

Off B1257, 2¼ miles west of Helmsley (Dc)

The majestic, hauntingly beautiful ruins of this great Cistercian abbey stand beside the River Rye, below wooded hills. The abbey's earliest buildings had all the austerity for which the Cistercians were famous, and this is especially noticeable in the 12th-century nave and transepts of the abbey church. The extensive remains still convey something of the days when the abbey was prosperous and influential.

Rievaulx was founded in 1132, and its first monks were from the abbey of Clairvaux in France. The community grew until in the latter part of the 12th century it contained 140 monks and more than 500 lay brothers. Later, the community dwindled, and by the time the monasteries were dissolved Rievaulx had only 22 monks and probably no lay brothers. A small museum tells the abbey's history.

Rievaulx Terrace, which overlooks the abbey, offers a contrasting enchantment. The half-mile grassy strip was laid out in the 18th century and is bounded at each end by a classical temple. The whole scene was the creation of Thomas Duncombe in the late 1750s, and it may have been his intention to link it with a similar combination of terraces and temples already gracing his home at Duncombe Park, about a mile down the River Rye. The link-up never took place, but the Rievaulx Terrace is a delight in its own right. One of the buildings is known as the Doric or Tuscan rotunda and the other as the Ionic Temple. The latter is elaborately furnished and contains an exhibition of landscape designs and pictures.

Ryedale Folk Museum, in Hutton-le-Hole, has a fine range of exhibits covering the area's history from prehistoric times. In the museum's extensive grounds is a reconstruction of an Elizabethan glassmaker's furnace.

Abbey: EH. All year, daily exc Sun am Oct-Mar. Adm charge. Shop. P Toilets. ♿ Tel Helmsley (043 96) 228. Terrace and Temples: NT. Apr-Oct, daily. Adm charge. Shop. P Toilets. ♿ Tel (043 96) 340. Folk Museum: Mar-Oct, daily. Adm charge. Shop. P Toilets. ♿ Tel Lastingham (075 15) 367.

RIPLEY CASTLE

On A61, 3½ miles north of Harrogate (Cb)

The lives of the Ingilby family, owners of Ripley Castle for more than six centuries, are closely woven into the fabric of their lovely home. Portraits of beloved ancestral dogs flank the entrance hall, while the painting on oak panelling of Edward III, with a boar's head above it, recalls the proud moment when Thomas Ingilby won his knighthood by saving the king's life during a hunting party.

Only the arched 15th-century gatehouse and the 16th-century tower, which contains the fine Knight's Chamber and authentic 'priest's hole', now remain from earlier days. The 'new' building, with gardens designed by Capability Brown sloping down to a lake and deer park, and the model village of Ripley beside it, date from the 18th century and are in perfect keeping. The castle's splendid rooms contain Chippendale and Hepplewhite chairs, Lalique glass, maiolica, tapestries and fine paintings.

June-Oct, daily exc Mon; Apr and May, Sat, Sun and Mon. Adm charge. Refreshments. Shop. P Toilets. Tel Harrogate (0423) 770152.

RIPON CATHEDRAL

In centre of Ripon (Cb)

Parts of Ripon Cathedral prove it to be one of Britain's oldest Christian buildings. According to the Venerable Bede, a small mission was built in the village of Rhypum around AD 655, and later in the same century this was enlarged by Bishop Wilfrid of York into a monastery and church dedicated to St Peter. The church was wrecked and the monastery vanished during the 9th century; but the crypt of the old church survives as one of the few Saxon structures left in England. The present building was begun towards the end of the 12th century, and over the years much has been changed and added.

Near the cathedral, in St Marygate, the Prison and Police Museum occupies a 17th-century building designed to bring 'rogues, vagabonds and sturdy beggars to work and correction'. In the 19th century it was enlarged to take other prisoners, but in 1877 it became a police station. Now it contains mementos, and equipment used by parish constables and policemen from the 17th century onwards.

Cathedral: All year, daily. Free entry. Shop. Tel Ripon (0765) 2072. Museum: May-Sept, Tues-Sun and Bank Hol pm. Adm charge. Shop. P Tel (0765) 3706.

ROBERT THOMPSON'S CRAFTSMEN

Off A170, 8 miles east of Thirsk (Cc)

The master woodcarver called the Mouseman of Kilburn has enriched many buildings in Britain and abroad. Robert Thompson's trademark, or signature carving, was a mouse – carved on a sudden impulse, he said, when a colleague talked of being poor as a church mouse. The son of a carpenter, Thompson was born in 1876 at Kilburn. Inspired by medieval craftsmanship, he resolved to produce furniture of the same fine quality. Among the buildings graced by his skills are Westminster Abbey and York Minster. Thompson died in 1955, but his family and other craftsmen continue his work.

All year, daily exc Sat pm, Sun and Bank Hol. Free entry. Shop. P Toilets. ♿ Tel Coxwold (034 76) 218.

ROYAL PUMP ROOM MUSEUM

Royal Parade, Harrogate (Cb)

Sulphur wells which lie in the basement of the Royal Pump Room Museum are the reason for Harrogate's existence. The water was believed to cure a wide variety of skin diseases, digestive disorders and rheumatic complaints, and the Royal Pump Room was built in 1842 and extended in 1913 to accommodate a growing number of visitors. It has recently undergone major restoration, during which the distinctive copper roof dome has been replaced.

It is still possible to taste the waters in the museum, which celebrates the many aspects of Harrogate's history as a spa. Regular patronage by royalty made Harrogate fashionable. In 1911 three queens were resident in Harrogate – Queen Alexandra, her sister the Empress of Russia, and Queen Amelie of Portugal.

All year, daily exc Sun am. Adm charge. Shop. P Tel Harrogate (0423) 503340.

MIGHTY MOUSE *Craftsmen in the Robert Thompson workshop still carve the founder's trademark of a mouse on their work, proudly carrying on the tradition of fine quality woodcarving that he set.*

MUSEUMS BESIDE A MINSTER

A 13th-century city wall 3 miles long still guards the medieval heart of York, gathered around its magnificent Minster – one of Europe's greatest cathedrals. 'The history of York is the history of England', said George VI of a city on which Romans, Saxons, Vikings and Normans have left their mark. Modern York owes much to the city's leading role in the 19th-century railway boom, celebrated in one of the finest of its many museums.

York Minster *All year, daily. Free entry. Shop. Toilets. ♿ Tel York (0904) 624426.*

Treasurer's House *NT. Apr-Oct, daily. Adm charge. Refreshments. Shop. Toilets. Tel (0904) 624247.*

York City Art Gallery *All year, daily exc Sun am. Free entry. Shop. Toilets. ♿ Tel (0904) 623839.*

Merchant Adventurers' Hall *All year, daily, exc Sun in winter. Adm charge. Toilets. ♿ Tel (0904) 654818.*

York Castle Museum *All year, daily. Adm charge. Refreshments. Shop. Toilets. ♿ (part). Tel (0904) 653611.*

Jorvik Viking Centre *All year daily. Adm charge. Shop. Toilets. ♿ Tel (0904) 643211.*

Guildhall *All year, Mon-Sat. Free entry. Toilets. ♿ Tel (0904) 613161.*

Yorkshire Museum and Multangular Tower *All year, daily exc Sun am. Adm charge. Shop. Toilets. ♿ Tel (0904) 629745/6.*

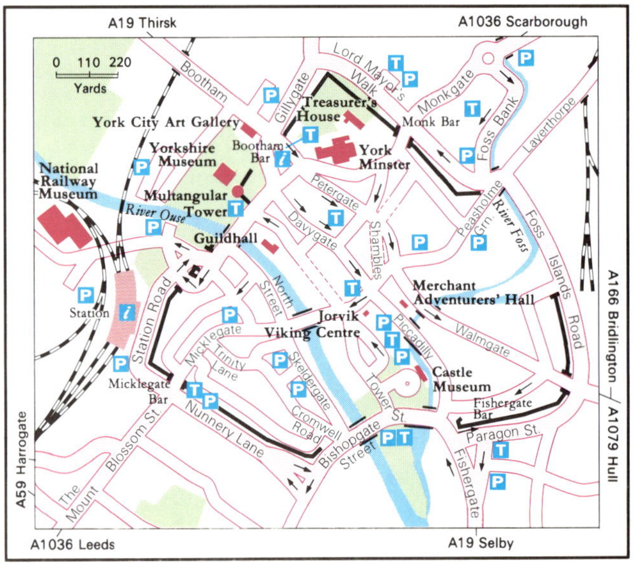

National Railway Museum *All year, daily. Adm charge. Refreshments. Shop. P Toilets. ♿ Tel (0904) 621261.*

YORK MINSTER

The word 'minster' is Anglo-Saxon for 'a large central church' – in York's case, a modest definition of the largest Gothic church in Northern Europe. The fourth cathedral to stand on the site, it was begun in 1220 and took more than 250 years to build.

PINNACLES OF PERFECTION One of the soaring twin towers of the west front and the immense, delicately carved window that divides them illustrate the peaks of perfection achieved in building York Minster. They were completed in 1472, just before the final masterpiece – the 197ft lantern tower. The Minster is 519ft long and 249ft across the transepts. Its treasures include more than 100 stained-glass windows, some of them 800 years old.

THE ARCHBISHOPS The effigy of Tobias Matthews (1606-28) is among many of past Archbishops of York; Walter de Grey, who began the Minster, is carved in Purbeck marble.

HIGH POINT No central pillar supports the high, vaulted ceiling of the octagonal Chapter House, built in wood in the late 13th century. The building measures 66½ft from floor to ceiling.

CLOCK MEMORIAL The astronomical clock in the north transept is a memorial to 18,000 airmen of the RAF, stationed in the north-east, who were killed during the Second World War.

TREASURER'S HOUSE

A view from the Chapter House of York Minster reveals the glory of the Treasurer's House behind its high wall. This was the cathedral treasurer's home until that office was abolished in 1547 (to be revived in the 19th century). It passed into private hands and was altered to its present form in the 17th and 18th centuries. The last owner gave it to the National Trust in 1930, with a collection of fine period furniture.

YORK CITY ART GALLERY

A collection of works by the York-born artist William Etty (1787-1849) is a feature of the gallery. Etty was famed for his nudes, as mythological characters on huge canvases. His portraits include (right) *Mlle Rachel,* a French tragic actress of the 19th century.

YORKSHIRE MUSEUM

A fine collection of local pottery in the Yorkshire Museum includes this delightful Castleford teapot. There are also finds from Roman, Saxon and Viking York; one unusual exhibit is the auburn hair of a girl who lived in Roman Britain.

MULTANGULAR TOWER

The massive Roman Tower off Museum Street formed one corner of the wall surrounding the fortress-city of Eboracum, established by the Romans in the 1st century AD. Later the tower became part of the medieval city wall. The chisel marks made by the Roman masons can still be distinguished.

NATIONAL RAILWAY MUSEUM

A local draper, George Hudson, rode to riches on the 19th-century railway boom, and made York an important railway centre. So the city is an appropriate location for a museum telling the story of the railways in Britain. The gleaming *Gladstone* of 1882 is one of a vast collection of locomotives, from *Agenoria* of 1824 to the 126mph steam-speed record holder *Mallard* of the 1930s. Rolling stock includes Queen Victoria's carriage and a Travelling Post Office.

JORVIK VIKING CENTRE

Viking invaders settled in York, or 'Jorvik', in AD 867, and their life is re-created today in a display on the site of their original settlement. 'Time cars' carry visitors past tableaux – complete with sounds and smells – of market, houses and wharf.

GUILDHALL

York's great stone Guildhall, a meeting place built in 1448 by the city and the Guild of St Christopher and St George, was burnt out in an air raid in 1942. In 1960 it was carefully restored to the original design, even to the colourful, sometimes bizarre carvings (right) on the beautifully carved timber roof. Supporting columns are fashioned from solid oak tree trunks. Some genuine 15th-century craftsmanship in the inner council chamber escaped the flames. There are two secret doors in the panelled walls, and the ceiling carvings include grotesque figures.

MERCHANT ADVENTURERS' HALL

The Merchant Adventurers emerged as the most powerful of the many medieval guilds controlling commerce in York. 'God grant us rewarding ventures', says the motto on their coat of arms displayed over the entrance to their hall in Fossgate. The chair (below) was made by an apprentice around 1620.

YORK CASTLE MUSEUM

Three cobbled streets lined with shops and buildings of the gaslight and horse-drawn carriage era are re-created in a museum occupying two 18th-century jails. The shops are stocked with goods of the period. Visitors can also see the condemned cell where Dick Turpin spent his last night.

SCARBOROUGH CASTLE

On Marine Drive, in Scarborough (Ec)

The first fortress at Scarborough was built by the Normans in 1158, and its massive square keep, barbican and curtain wall still stand. Kings held court at Scarborough Castle, and in 1312 it became the refuge of Piers Gaveston, Earl of Cornwall and favourite of Edward II. In 1557, during the reign of Mary, the castle was seized by Sir Thomas Stafford, who proclaimed himself Protector of the nation; but it was retaken and Stafford was executed.

Wood End Museum, in The Crescent, is on the site of a house once occupied by a famous literary family – the Sitwells. They lived there for 60 years from 1870, and the west wing has been restored as nearly as possible to its original state. It contains an almost complete collection of the published works of Dame Edith, Sir Osbert, Sir Sacheverell and their father, Sir George.

Castle: EH. All year, daily exc Sun am Oct-Mar. Adm charge. Shop. Toilets. ♿ Tel Scarborough (0723) 372451. Wood End Museum: All year, Tues-Sat; also Sun pm Spring Bank Hol-Sept. Free entry. Shop. Tel (0723) 367326.

SELBY ABBEY

In centre of Selby (Da)

The ambitions of a fortune-seeking French monk gave the north of England one of its finest churches. Selby Abbey dates back to Norman times when the monk Benedict absconded from Auxerre in France, bearing the dried finger of St Germain. His sacred relic so impressed Hugh, Sheriff of Yorkshire, that in 1069 he persuaded the king to grant Benedict a royal charter to build a monastery and abbey church.

Selby owes its cross shape to its second abbot, Hugh, under whose auspices the greatest phase of building began around 1100. The majestic nave and Hugh's Pillar on its south side are of this period. During a later phase of fine Gothic building the Norman choir was removed and a lofty and graceful choir was added.

All year, daily. Shop. Tel Selby (0757) 703125.

SHANDY HALL

Off A170, 11 miles east of Thirsk (Cc)

The mellow-bricked building in Coxwold, at the foot of the Hambleton Hills, was the home, in the 18th century, of the village parson Laurence Sterne, who here wrote much of his experimental novel, *The Life and Opinions of Tristram Shandy, Gentleman.* The runaway success of his book – which is peppered with one-sentence chapters, blank pages and other typographical eccentricities – prompted him to call the house Shandy Hall; and while living there he produced *A Sentimental Journey*, a humorous account of a tour through France and Italy, published in 1768.

Sterne's book-lined study has been lovingly preserved, and the hall is filled with books, pictures and memorabilia that tell the story of the Irish-born author and his work.

Coxwold has a second building of note in Newburgh Priory, half a mile to the south, built by Augustinian monks in the 12th century. It contains the tomb of Oliver Cromwell, and in the grounds are a beautiful water garden and rock and alpine plants.

Hall: June-Sept, Wed and Sun pm. Adm charge. Shop. 🅿 (limited). Toilets. Tel Coxwold (034 76) 465. Priory: Mid May-late Aug, Wed and Sun pm. Adm charge. Refreshments. 🅿 Toilets. Tel (03476) 435.

SKIPTON CASTLE

In centre of Skipton (Bb)

Happily surviving Cromwellian destruction and escaping Victorian restoration, Skipton Castle is one of the best preserved medieval fortresses in England. Dating from the late 11th century but largely rebuilt in the 14th, it was the home of the powerful Clifford family.

The castle's conduit court, from which water was supplied, is a place of great beauty, exemplifying the early Tudor architectural style. Here stands a yew tree planted by Lady Anne Clifford in the mid-17th century. Lady Anne's restoration of the castle, after it had been besieged and occupied by Parliamentarian forces in the Civil War, contributed substantially to its survival.

All year, daily exc Sun am. Adm charge. Shop. Toilets. Tel Skipton (0756) 2442.

STUMP CROSS CAVERNS

Off B6265, 6 miles west of Pateley Bridge (Bc)

This underground wonderland of stalactites and stalagmites which probably began forming some 500,000 years ago was not discovered until the mid-19th century, by miners prospecting for lead. Today some 400yds of paths, artfully floodlit, wind past rocks named after their shapes.

Easter-Oct, daily; Nov and Dec, Sun. Adm charge. Refreshments. Shop. 🅿 Toilets. Tel Grassington (0756) 752780.

UP HILL, DOWN DALE *At Sutton Bank the wild, heather-clad scenery of the North York moors changes dramatically, with limestone cliffs plunging 700ft to the pastoral counterpane of the Vale of York.*

SUTTON BANK

On A170, 5½ miles west of Helmsley (Cc)

Set in a commanding position above the Vale of York, Sutton Bank offers breathtaking views extending to Swaledale, Wensleydale and the Pennines. Gliders soar aloft on the air currents forced up by the escarpment. A walk leads to the White Horse of Kilburn. This gigantic figure, 314ft long and 228ft high, appeared on the limestone face of the Hambleton Hills in 1857. It was carved by a local schoolmaster, John Hodgson, with the help of pupils and 30 village men.

Information centre: Apr-Oct, daily; some Sun out of season. Free entry. Refreshments. Shop. 🅿 Toilets. ♿ Tel Thirsk (0845) 597426 (summer); Helmsley (0439) 70657 (winter).

THIRSK MUSEUM

16 Kirkgate, Thirsk (Cc)

Thomas Lord, the founder of Lord's Cricket Ground, was born in 1755 in this oak-beamed cottage off Thirsk's market square. Cricketing memorabilia are among the exhibits in the restored building, which also records the town's history, industry and local life.

A Victorian kitchen is evocatively reconstructed, complete with period equipment, including a hand-operated washing machine invented by a Thirsk man. Appropriately in the town in which the writer James Herriot had his veterinary practice, there is a display of veterinary equipment.

Easter, then May-Sept daily exc Sun am; Oct, Sun pm, Sat and Mon. Adm charge. Shop. 🅿 Tel Thirsk (0845) 22755.

UPPER DALES FOLK MUSEUM

On A684, in Hawes (Ac)

The hand-powered wheel once used to twist the fibres at the nearby Hawes ropeworks is one of the exhibits in a museum illustrating the old ways of life in the Upper Dales. There are farm tools and equipment used for peat digging, cheese and

butter making, sheepshearing and lead-mining. There is a section on local crafts, with the tools of a cabinet-maker, shoemaker, clogger, blacksmith and wheelwright. At the factory of W.R. Outhwaite, visitors can see rope being made by traditional methods.
Museum: Easter-Sept, daily exc Sun am. Adm charge. Shop. P *Toilets. Tel Hawes (096 97) 494. Ropeworks: All year, Mon-Fri. Free entry. Tel (096 97) 487.*

UPPER WHARFEDALE FOLK MUSEUM

The Square, Grassington (Bb)

Two cottages built for lead miners in the early 18th century in Grassington's leafy, cobbled square have been joined to form a museum which tells the domestic and working history of Wharfedale through the centuries. Exhibits include a mangle of 1885, a cobbler's bench, tools and materials, farming tools, geological specimens including Grassington minerals such as galena (an ore of lead), and a medieval whetstone. There are also prehistoric stone arrowheads and bones from the Ice Age.

Near the museum is an information centre for the Yorkshire Dales National Park. Grassington is a good starting point for exploring Wharfedale, a countryside of stone villages and fertile valleys crisscrossed with dry-stone walls.
Museum: Apr-Oct, pm daily; Nov-Mar, Sat and Sun pm. Adm charge. Refreshments. P *(limited). Tel Grassington (0756) 752800. Centre: Easter-Oct, daily. Free entry. Shop.* P *Toilets.* ♿ *Tel (0756) 752748.*

WHITBY ABBEY

East Cliff, Whitby (Ed)

The jagged sandstone ruins of Whitby Abbey loom dramatically on a cliff top above this old fishing port. Standing on the site of an abbey founded by St Hilda in AD 657, the church was built after the Norman invasion by Benedictines, and was abandoned in 1539 when Henry VIII dissolved the monasteries. It fell into decay and in 1830 the central tower collapsed, leaving the abbey much as it is today.

At night, the skeleton of the abbey can take on a sinister aspect, and it was one of the settings for Bram Stoker's vampire novel *Dracula*, published in 1897. The most photographed aspect of the abbey is its lofty east front, with three rows of narrow, pointed windows behind which lie the nave, rebuilt in the 13th century, and the tall north transept.

On the other side of the River Esk is Whitby Museum, set among the gardens of Pannett Park. A display devoted to the Yorkshire-born navigator Captain James Cook tells of his training in seamanship in the town and displays models of the Whitby-built ships – *Endeavour*, *Discovery* and *Resolution* – which took him on his voyages of discovery in the Pacific. There are also displays of intricately carved jewellery made from jet – a dense, black form of coal – gathered on the nearby shore.
Abbey: EH. All year, daily exc Sun am Oct-Mar. Adm charge. Shop. P *Toilets.* ♿ *Tel Whitby (0947) 603568. Museum: All year, daily exc Mon and Tues am Oct-Mar, and Sun am. Adm charge. Shop.* P *Toilets. Tel (0947) 602908.*

SHELL-SHOCKED SHELL *Henry VIII was not the only despoiler to contribute to the ruinous state of Whitby Abbey. Its walls were hit by shells from German warships during the First World War.*

YORKSHIRE CARRIAGE MUSEUM

On A684 at Aysgarth (Bc)

Horse-drawn carriages and a haunted cab are among the exhibits in a former cotton mill. Coaches, bread vans and milk floats are also on view. Many of the exhibits have been featured in films and television productions such as *Far From the Madding Crowd* and *All Creatures Great and Small.*

Near the mill is the Yorkshire Dales National Park Centre. Its displays illustrate the remarkable rock formations which created the Aysgarth Falls, less than a mile away, where the River Ure pours over three huge limestone steps. The upper falls are best seen from the 16th-century bridge spanning the river, the two lower falls are reached by a footpath on the north bank.
Museum: Good Fri-Oct, daily. Adm charge. Shop. Tel Richmond (0748) 3275. Centre: Easter-Oct, daily. Free entry. Shop. P *Toilets.* ♿ *Tel Aysgarth (096 93) 424.*

COUNTY CALENDAR

January (Sat following 1st Mon after 6th Jan). Goathland: Plough Stots Dance (sword dance and blessing of plough).

February (Shrove Tues). Scarborough: Pancake Bell and Shrovetide Skipping Festival.

April (late). Harrogate: Spring Flower Show.

May (Ascension Eve). Whitby: Planting the Penny Hedge (traditional penance to a murdered monk).

May (mid-month, to early June). Swaledale: Festival.

June (end of month). Northallerton: North Yorkshire Agricultural Show.

July (early). York: Early Music Festival.

July (mid-month). Harrogate: Great Yorkshire Show.

August (1st two weeks). Harrogate: International Festival.

September (early). Richmond: First Fruits of Harvest.

December (Boxing Day). Ripon: Sword Dance Play.

Tourist information: Harrogate (0423) 525666; Richmond (0748) 3525 (summer); Ripon (0765) 4625 (summer); Scarborough (0723) 373333; Selby (0757) 703263; Skipton (0756) 2809; Whitby (0947) 602674; York (0904) 21756.

SOUTH YORKSHIRE

LIVING MUSEUMS AROUND A CITY WHERE STEEL IS KING

Sheffield's busy modern heart still finds time and space to recall the history of the steel-making which earned the city a worldwide reputation, and to display with pride some of the finest wares produced in its factories over the years. Outside the city, too, monuments of the Industrial Revolution are painstakingly restored for the enjoyment of today's visitors. Industrial prosperity gave the area several dignified Georgian buildings; a Norman castle still overlooks the Don; and wildlife in plenty can be seen in walks through Howell Wood or by the shores of Worsbrough Canal Reservoir.

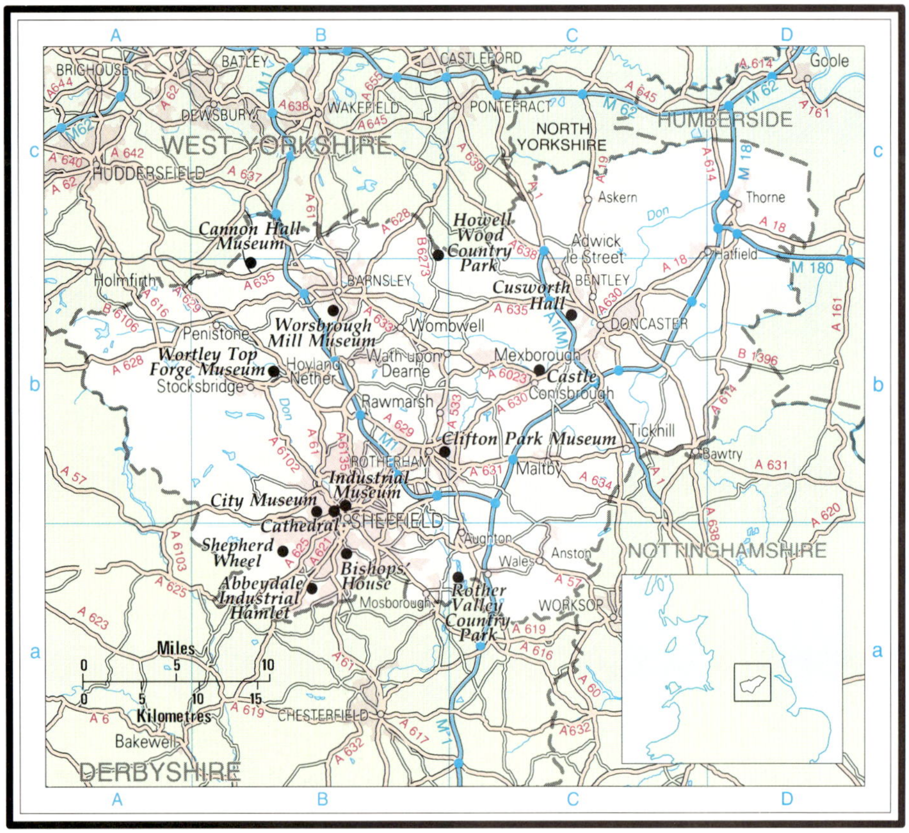

ABBEYDALE INDUSTRIAL HAMLET

On A621, 3½ miles south-west of Sheffield (Ba)

Once one of the largest water-powered industrial sites on the River Sheaf, Abbeydale is today one of the country's best-preserved monuments of the Industrial Revolution. Abbeydale's main products were scythes and other agricultural tools such as grass hooks and hay knives. The works closed in 1933, but today the workshops have been reconstructed to present a complete picture of foundry work in the 19th century.

Fast-flowing water and abundant iron ore and coal ensured Sheffield's early prominence as a steel-making centre. Abbeydale became a self-contained community whose craftsmen lived alongside their workshops in terraced cottages and made as many as seven dozen scythe blades a day. Today's visitor can see regular demonstrations of the process.

All year, daily. Adm charge. Refreshments. Shop. P *Toilets.* ♿ *(parts). Tel Sheffield (0742) 367731.*

BISHOPS' HOUSE

Meersbrook Park, Sheffield (Ba)

Tradition says that two brothers, John Blythe, Bishop of Salisbury, and Geoffrey Blythe, Bishop of Lichfield and Coventry, lived here at the turn of the 15th and 16th centuries. Standing at the highest point of Meersbrook public park's grounds, in the leafy shade of a grove of trees, the simple L-shaped house is the most complete example of a black-and-white timber-framed house surviving in Sheffield.

UNDER THE HAMMER *The finest Abbeydale scythes were made by welding a piece of steel between two pieces of wrought iron under the hammers of this tilt forge. The hammers struck more than 120 blows a minute.*

In the west wing were the family's private apartments, chief of which was the Great Parlour which is still furnished as it was in Tudor and Stuart times. In the east wing is the hall, once the centre of household life and open to the roof, but now an exhibition area.

All year, Wed-Sun. Adm charge. Shop. Toilets. Tel Sheffield (0742) 557701.

CANNON HALL MUSEUM

Off A635, 5 miles west of Barnsley (Bb)

Once nicknamed Roast Beef Hall because of the generous hospitality of its 19th-century owner Sir Walter Spencer Stanhope, Cannon Hall is a typical Georgian country house: solid, dignified and above all comfortable, and set in serene parkland. Now a museum, the hall's rooms are furnished in a variety of styles from Jacobean to Victorian. Their sumptuous elegance reaches its peak in the spacious, Jacobean-style ballroom with its fine oak-panelled walls, minstrels' gallery and elaborate fireplace. A glassware collection includes such 19th-century oddities as glass rolling pins and walking sticks.

Cannon Hall also houses the regimental museum of the 13th and 18th Royal Hussars, whose part in the Charge of the Light Brigade in 1854 is recalled in a series of displays.

All year, daily. Free entry. P *Toilets.* ♿ *(ground floor). Tel Barnsley (0226) 790270.*

CLIFTON PARK MUSEUM

Clifton Lane, Rotherham (Bb)

In the elegant drawing room of this former town house, with its polished floor, tasteful furniture and upright piano, the Victorian ironmaster Joshua Walker would have relaxed in front of a roaring fire after a hearty meal. The kitchen, crammed with crockery, pots and pans, still has the air of its 19th-century hustle and bustle, and on the first floor is a reconstructed Victorian child's bedroom.

A short walk away, in Drummond Street, the York and Lancaster Regimental Museum tells the history of the regiment from 1758 to its disbandment in 1968. Exhibits include a collection of almost 1000 medals.

All year, daily exc Fri. Free entry. Shop. Toilets. ♿ *(ground floor). Tel Rotherham (0709) 382121.*

CONISBROUGH CASTLE

Off A630, in Conisbrough (Cb)

Overlooking the River Don, the mighty stone keep of Conisbrough Castle towers over an impressive medieval English fortress. Originally

100ft high, it is one of the finest existing examples of late Norman defensive architecture. Although much of the circular keep is now in ruins, there is still evidence of several rooms, including the first-floor chamber with its open fireplace.
EH. All year, daily. Adm charge. Shop. 🅿 ♿ *(parts). Tel Rotherham (0709) 863329.*

CUSWORTH HALL MUSEUM

Off A638, 3 miles north of Doncaster (Cb)

Cedars, strawberry trees, larches, cypress, fig, yew and bamboo still grow in the Pleasure Grounds of this imposing mansion. With its fine ornamental doors and windows and Palladian pavilions, Cusworth is an excellent example of early Georgian architecture. Inside, the rooms are decorated with elaborate plasterwork, panelling and carved marble chimneypieces. The hall is now a museum of local life. Items as diverse as children's dolls, a whalebone corset and decorated chamber pots illustrate life in South Yorkshire over the past 200 years.
All year, daily exc Fri (grounds daily). Free entry. Shop. 🅿 *Toilets.* ♿ *(grounds). Tel Doncaster (0302) 782342.*

HOWELL WOOD COUNTRY PARK

Off B6273, 8 miles east of Barnsley (Bc)

Jays, woodcocks, stoats, weasels, brown hares, foxes and grey squirrels are among the inhabitants of Howell Wood. An unusual feature of the wood is an ice house used by the 19th-century residents of nearby Burntwood Hall to preserve their food. A cylindrical well 18ft deep was packed with ice from the adjoining lake in winter; double brick walls and the shade of overhanging oaks and yews kept the ice frozen for up to three years.
All year, daily.

ROTHER VALLEY COUNTRY PARK

Off A618, 12 miles east of Sheffield (Ca)

Opencast coal mines have been flooded to create a world of wildlife in the valley of the River Rother. The park is a birdwatcher's delight: visitors include tufted ducks and grey herons, while birds of prey to be seen include the occasional osprey. The restored Bedgreave Mills illustrate the development of mill working, from water to steam power.
All year, daily. Free entry. Refreshments. Shop. 🅿 *Toilets.* ♿ *Tel Sheffield (0742) 471452.*

SHEFFIELD CATHEDRAL

In centre of Sheffield (Bb)

Sheffield Cathedral is seen at its best on a fine summer's day, when sunlight streams through its magnificent stained-glass windows. One of the finest is the Te Deum window, by Christopher Webb, which portrays Christ flanked by the prophets and apostles, saints and martyrs down the ages. Six windows in the Chapter House tell the history of Sheffield and its 15th-century church over the centuries. It became a cathedral in 1914. John Wesley, the founder of Methodism, is depicted on one of these windows, and his preaching desk is in the sacristy.
All year, daily.

ON THE REBOUND *The six wedge-shaped buttresses of Conisbrough Castle's keep allowed missiles dropped by defenders to ricochet off onto any attackers who had penetrated the battlemented outer curtain wall.*

SHEFFIELD CITY MUSEUM

Weston Park, Sheffield (Bb)

A dagger which shoots bullets and a knife 4ft long are two of the unusual items in the large collection of Sheffield cutlery on display behind the City Museum's handsome neoclassical façade. There is also a collection of Old Sheffield Plate and ceramics. A Wildlife Gallery has displays on urban wildlife and exotic species, and includes aquaria and an ant house. An Anglo-Saxon warrior's helmet is also on display.
All year, daily. Free entry. Shop. Toilets. ♿ *Tel Sheffield (0742) 768588.*

SHEFFIELD INDUSTRIAL MUSEUM

Kelham Island, Sheffield (Bb)

A former 19th-century generating station is the setting for a museum which tells the story of Sheffield's industrial development through the centuries. It stands on an island created in the 12th century by the channelling of water from the River Don to drive a corn mill. The museum illustrates the diversity of the city's products: from penny-farthing bicycles to steam engines, from engineer's tools to pocket watches, from silver-plated candelabra to lawn mowers.
All year, Wed-Sun; also Bank Hol. Adm charge. Refreshments. Shop. 🅿 *(limited). Toilets.* ♿ *Tel Sheffield (0742) 722106.*

SHEPHERD WHEEL

Off A625, 2½ miles south-west of Sheffield (Ba)

In tiny rural workshops such as Shepherd Wheel, skilled craftsmen forged, ground and hafted the steel which earned Sheffield a worldwide reputation. Set on the River Porter, the Wheel and its outbuildings are a good example of the functional, straightforward industrial architecture of the 18th century. Shepherd Wheel was probably used for the grinding of domestic knives and pocket knives. Its two workshops were powered by a single water wheel which operated ten grindstones made of local sandstone.
All year, Wed-Sun. Free entry. ♿ *Tel Sheffield (0742) 367731.*

WORSBROUGH MILL MUSEUM

On A61, 2½ miles south of Barnsley (Bb)

The mill's cast-iron water wheel of 1864 still uses water from the River Dove to turn the millstones which grind corn from neighbouring farms into flour. The clatter of cartwheels and the sound of horses' hooves as they deliver sacks of flour and grain recall a simpler, more peaceful age. The area of the Dove Valley in which the mill stands is now a country park, while the Worsbrough Canal Reservoir is the home of a variety of birds.
All year, Wed-Sun; also Bank Hol. Adm charge. Shop. 🅿 *Toilets.* ♿ *Tel Barnsley (0226) 203961.*

WORTLEY TOP FORGE MUSEUM

Off A629, 10 miles north of Sheffield (Bb)

A cluster of simple terraced buildings in the Upper Don Valley embraces a foundry, a blacksmith's and a joiner's shop, a furnace site and three water wheels. Together they form an open-air museum telling the story of iron-making in the area. A re-created 19th-century workshop recalls the early days of the Industrial Revolution, when the railway axle replaced the cannonball as the forge's main product. The forge has its original water-powered hammers and cranes.
All year, Sun. Adm charge. Shop. 🅿 *Toilets.* ♿ *Tel Sheffield (0742) 847201.*

COUNTY CALENDAR

June (early). Sheffield. Lord Mayor's Parade.

July (mid-month). Barnsley: Vintage Vehicle Rally.

September (early). Nr Doncaster, RAF Finningley Air Display.

September (1st full week). Doncaster: St Leger Festival.

December 26 Grenoside and Handsworth: Longsword Dancing.

Tourist information: Doncaster (0302) 734309; Rotherham (0709) 382121; Sheffield (0742) 734671.

WEST YORKSHIRE

MILL MUSEUMS AND MANSIONS AMONG THE PENNINE MOORS

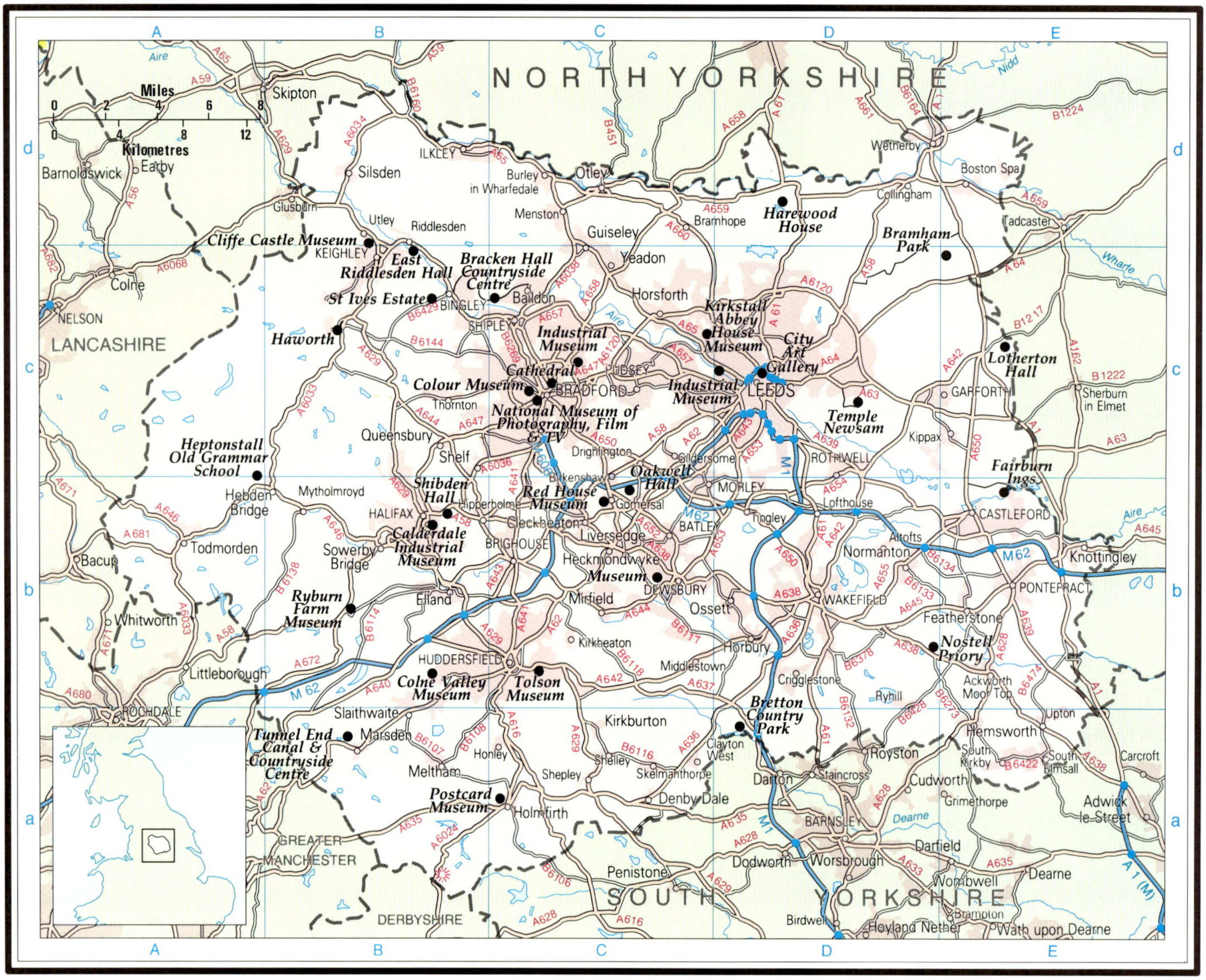

The West Yorkshire area has been associated with wool since medieval times, and the developing techniques of its industry are graphically re-created in 'living museums' at Bradford, Calderdale and Leeds. The little worsted town of Haworth has another claim to fame as the home of the Brontë family of authors. Wealthy textile moguls built Cliffe Castle and Red House, and the life of their workers is re-created at Kirkstall Abbey. Harewood House is a monument to another source of wealth: the sugar trade.

The same dynamic spirit that built up the textile industry inspired the establishment in Bradford of the National Museum of Photography, Film and Television. By contrast, the scenery and wildlife of the countryside are protected at Fairburn Ings, Bracken Hall and Oakwell Hall.

BRACKEN HALL COUNTRYSIDE CENTRE

Off A6038, 4 miles north of Bradford (Cc)

In the lovely, leafy Shipley Glen it is hard to realise that Bradford's busy centre is less than 5 miles away. The Bracken Hall Countryside Centre stands at the top of the glen, below Baildon Moor, and has displays about the scenery, history and wildlife of the area. There are guided nature walks, and paths lead to the wide, airy moors.

A 15 minute walk leads down to Roberts Park beside the River Aire. Alternatively, visitors can take the Shipley Glen Tramway, an unusual 386yd cable tramway which opened in 1895 over the steepest part of the route: the fare was then 'a penny up and a halfpenny down'.

On the opposite bank of the Aire stands the small town of Saltaire, a monument to the Victorian era. It was the creation of one man, Sir Titus Salt, who made a fortune from a loom that could make cloth out of long-fibred alpaca wool. In 1853 Salt opened a six-storey, 545ft long mill whose top floor, running the full length of the building, is still one of the largest rooms in the world. At full pressure, Saltaire Mill produced 30,000yds of cloth a day and employed 3000 people, whom Sir Titus housed in the town he built around it. It has 22 streets, named after members of his large family and composed of handsome little stone houses. Salt also provided almshouses, an Institute – which now contains a library and a fine organ museum – a school and a church.

Countryside Centre: Apr-Oct, Wed-Sun and Bank Hol; winter, weekends. Free entry. Shop. P *Toilets. Tel Bradford (0274) 584140. Tramway: All year, Sat pm, Sun and Bank Hol; also Wed in June and July. Fare. Tel (0274) 685532.*

BRADFORD CATHEDRAL
In centre of Bradford (Cc)

The interior is small as cathedrals go, with an intimacy and an air of informal friendliness very much in keeping with the spirit of the city. The parish church of St Peter was raised to cathedral status in 1919. Modern additions are highly successful: see especially the simple chapels of St Aidan and the Holy Spirit, with their beautifully embroidered altar frontals. The story of the city is told in the carvings and monuments of its cathedral. The provost's stall is surmounted by a carving of St Blaize, patron saint of woolcombers, and a plaque nearby shows how the tower was hung with woolpacks to protect it from Royalist cannon during Civil War sieges.

The rigours of the 20th century included, for Bradford, the slow death of the textile industry. The city's resilience is nowhere better expressed than in Little Germany, behind the bank on which the cathedral stands. The name of this mid-city gathering of majestic Victorian architecture is derived from the German cloth merchants who set up businesses there about a century ago. A hundred years' grime has been removed to reveal the buildings' ornate features, and they are being put to new uses as flats and offices.
All year, Mon-Sat, and Sun pm.

BRADFORD INDUSTRIAL MUSEUM
Off A658, north-east of centre of Bradford (Cc)

An imposing gateway set in high walls leads to the vast four-storey Moorside mills, which today house an exciting museum devoted to Bradford's industrial heritage. The city was the 'worsted capital' of the world in the 19th century, and the remarkable machines which turned raw wool into cloth may be seen in the museum – and even heard and felt when they pound into action on 'steam' days. Bradford-made railway equipment, cars, trams and motorcycles are on show in the transport gallery, and the mill manager's house is furnished as a prosperous middle-class home.

The collections of the West Yorkshire Transport Museum in Mill Lane, south of the city centre, include a wide variety of trams, trolley buses, motorbuses, commercial vehicles, railway locomotives and rolling stock. Other vehicles include a rare Barford Perkins road roller of 1911 which runs on petrol or paraffin.
Industrial Museum: All year, Tues-Sat and Bank Hol Sun and Mon; steam days, Wed and 1st Sat in month. Free entry. Refreshments. Shop. P *Toilets.* ♿ *Tel Bradford (0274) 631756. Transport Museum: All year, 1st Sun pm in month. Free entry. Refreshments. Shop.* P *Toilets. Tel (0274) 736006.*

BRAMHAM PARK
Off A1, 5 miles south of Wetherby (Ec)

This superb Queen Anne mansion stands in formal gardens – with avenues, broad walks, vistas, ponds and cascades – and across the park lie wooded 'pleasure grounds'. The estate was conceived as a whole by Robert Benson at the beginning of the 18th century, and has been lovingly preserved by nine generations of his family.

A fire destroyed much in 1828, but, although rebuilding had to wait for 78 years, Benson's elegant masterpiece with two wings linked to the main block by tall colonnades was finally recreated. The house contains fine furniture, porcelain, silver and paintings, and the old kitchen is now a museum and photograph gallery.
Mid June-Aug, Sun, Tues, Wed, Thur and Bank Hol, pm. Garden: Also Easter and Spring Bank Hol weekends, pm. Adm charge. P *Toilets. Tel Boston Spa (0937) 844265.*

BRETTON COUNTRY PARK
On A637, 5 miles south-west of Wakefield (Da)

It was in the 18th century that the passion for creating classical landscapes grew among the owners of Europe's country estates. Sir Thomas Blackett of Bretton Hall was no exception, and by 1810 his lovely deer park, with picturesque cascades and lakes, was well established. Some 96 acres of it now form a country park. Three waymarked trails take visitors across a nature reserve between the lakes, where more than 150 Canada geese live, along with coots, great crested grebes, mallards and tufted ducks.

The nearby Yorkshire Sculpture Park is an unusual outdoor art collection whose exhibits, including part of Barbara Hepworth's 'Family of Man' series and Elizabeth Frink's powerful *Atlas*, stand dramatically amid the parkland and formal gardens. There is a trail for the disabled.
Country Park: All year, daily. Free entry. Refreshments. P *(limited). Toilets.* ♿ *Tel Bretton (092 485) 550. Sculpture Park: All year, daily. Free entry. Refreshments. Shop.* P *Toilets.* ♿ *Tel (092 485) 302.*

CALDERDALE INDUSTRIAL MUSEUM
Square Road, Halifax (Bb)

The sights, sounds and smells of life in Halifax after the coming of the Industrial Revolution in about 1760 are re-created in a 19th-century mill. The streets of the town in the 1840s are vividly portrayed, and there are working machines of all kinds, including a spinning jenny, a flying shuttle loom, knitting machines and early washing machines. Visitors may 'clock in' at a mill entrance, and experience the harsh working conditions in a reconstructed coal mine.

Adjoining the museum is the magnificent Piece Hall, where three storeys of colonnaded and galleried rooms surround a vast Italian-style piazza. It was to Piece Hall, erected in 1779, that the cottage weavers of the surrounding district brought their lengths, or 'pieces', of cloth to be sold, either in the 315 merchants' rooms or in the central court. The hall now houses the Pre-Industrial Museum and Art Gallery. This tells the story of cloth production before 1760, from wool fleece to finished piece, and exhibits include a spinner's cottage, a weaver's loom chamber and a refurbished room where a prosperous merchant may be seen selling his cloth.

The National Museum of the Working Horse is not far away in Dobbin's Yard, off South

HARMONY IN STONE *The nave and tower of Bradford Cathedral date from the mid-15th century. Additions 400 years later matched the original, as the builders all used the same pale local stone.*

TOFFEE DE LUXE *This window in Calderdale Industrial Museum came from Mackintosh's factory in Halifax. The display shows stages in the production of toffee, made in the town since the 18th century.*

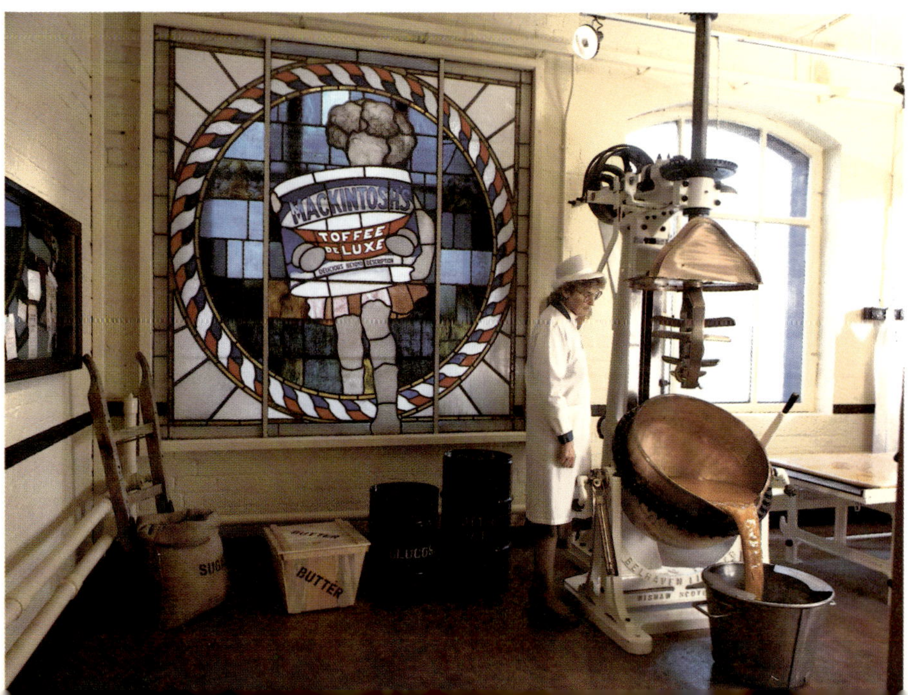

Parade. The yard and its stables are authentically restored, and the horses, both heavyweight Shires and lighter cobs, may be seen during grooming and harnessing, and at work pulling vehicles. Period photos help recall the days when the horse was vital to the urban community. There are horse-drawn rides.
Industrial Museum: All year, Tues-Sat; also Sun pm and Bank Hol. Adm charge. Shop. Toilets. ♿ Tel Halifax (0422) 59031. Piece Hall: All year, daily. Free entry. Refreshments. Shops. Toilets. Tel (0422) 59031. Horse Museum: Mar-Sept, daily; Oct-1st week Jan, pm daily. Adm charge. Refreshments. Shop. P Toilets. ♿ Tel (0422) 46835.

CLIFFE CASTLE MUSEUM

Off A629, ½ mile north-west of Keighley (Bd)

Having rebuilt and glorified his family home after a gas explosion in 1874, the wealthy worsted manufacturer Henry Butterfield changed its name from Cliffe Hall to Cliffe Castle to suit its new grandeur. The magnificent Victorian mansion has now been converted into a museum, which includes a suite of finely decorated reception rooms furnished with French furniture.

The museum's displays tell the geological story and history of Airedale, and include the reconstructed workshops of a hand-loom weaver, oat-bread maker and clog maker. There are also natural history exhibits.
All year, Tues-Sun and Bank Hol Mon. Free entry. Refreshments. Shop. P (limited). Toilets. ♿ Tel Keighley (0535) 664184.

COLNE VALLEY MUSEUM

Off A62, 2½ miles west of Huddersfield (Bb)

The life and working world of local people in the last century are vividly brought to life in this museum, which is housed in three 19th-century weavers' cottages. There is a weaver's living room of 1850, complete with hefty utensils of cast iron and earthenware, and a loom chamber with working hand looms incorporating the flying shuttle mechanism and a spinning jenny. A clogger's shop of 1910 sells locally made clogs, and staff demonstrate different crafts, including spinning, weaving, clogging and lace-making.
All year, Sat, Sun and Bank Hol, pm. Adm charge. Refreshments. Shop. Toilets. Tel Huddersfield (0484) 659762.

COLOUR MUSEUM

Grattan Road, Bradford (Cc)

The intention of this museum is to make people think about colour. How important is it? What function does it play? Numerous interactive exhibits allow visitors to investigate colour vision and blindness, the effect of mixing colour, and how colours are deliberately chosen by artists, designers and ourselves to warn, excite or calm the onlooker. Another part of the museum looks at colour and textiles, past and present. Displays chart the history of dyes and dyeing from ancient Egypt to the present day, the development of textile printing from its Chinese origins, and the importance of colour for today's fashions.
All year, Tues-Sat. Free entry. P Shop. Toilets. ♿ Tel Bradford (0272) 725138.

VENETIAN AIR *The paintings in this Italianate Drawing Room at Harewood House include works by Venetian artists such as Titian, Tintoretto and Veronese. The ceiling design is Robert Adam's.*

DEWSBURY MUSEUM

Heckmondwike Road, 1 mile south-west of town centre (Cb)

Childhood is the theme of this museum housed in Crows Nest mansion – an 18th to 19th-century house amid an attractive park. The desperate plight of children in textile mills and coal mines in the 18th and 19th centuries is portrayed in the gallery devoted to 'Children at Work'. On a happier note, games, toys and dolls fill the 'Children at Play' gallery and there is also a reconstructed 1940s classroom.
All year, daily exc Sun am. Free entry. Refreshments. Shop. P Toilets. Tel Dewsbury (0924) 468171.

EAST RIDDLESDEN HALL

On A650, 1 mile north-east of Keighley (Bc)

James Murgatroyd, a rich clothier from Halifax, gave his ornate Jacobean manor house in the Aire valley an unusual main entrance in the form of a two-storey porch with a round window on the upper floor. The fish pond, which once provided food for the monks of Bolton Abbey, survives beside the house. Inside, superb 17th-century oak panelling and plasterwork grace the rooms, which contain fine pewter and traditional Yorkshire oak furniture. There is a magnificent 120ft long medieval tithe barn.
NT. Apr and Nov, weekend pm. May-Oct, Wed-Sun and Bank Hol, pm. Adm charge. Refreshments. Shop. P Toilets. Tel Keighley (0535) 607075.

FAIRBURN INGS

Off A656, 3 miles north-east of Castleford (Eb)

The name of this bird reserve harks back to the days when the Vikings ruled northern England, for 'ing' comes from an Old Norse word for a meadow. Today, meadows survive in the west of the reserve. Elsewhere there are shallow ponds, open stretches of deeper water, and mounds of coal-mining waste covered by dense masses of hawthorn, birch and wild flowers.

The reserve is a haven for wildfowl and waders migrating across the Pennines. Some 170 to 180 species of birds are seen every year, and about 70 have been known to breed, including mallard, teal, shovelers, gadwalls, tufted duck and pochard. Mute swans and Canada geese visit in summer, and whooper swans, wigeon, goldeneyes, goosanders and great flocks of gulls are seen in winter. A viewing hide near the information centre gives fine views over the reserve, and three more hides are reached by the footpath from Fairburn village (off A1, just east of the reserve). Visitors must keep to the footpaths. There is a long boardwalk designed for disabled visitors.
RSPB. All year, daily. Information Centre, weekends. Free entry. Shop. P (limited). Toilets. ♿

HAREWOOD HOUSE

On A61, 7 miles north of Leeds (Dd)

A palace rather than a house, Harewood offers much more than the regal splendour of its rich fabric and contents. To reach the house the visitor has to run the gauntlet of a host of competing attractions. There is an Adventure Playground of massive, many-levelled complexity, including a slide shaped like a gigantic serpent, while close by a Woodland Garden glows imperial purple and scarlet at rhododendron time.

A Bird Garden is arranged beside the lake in a stepped series of large aviaries encompassing medium-sized trees and other plants; and the Penguin Pond has a glass wall, through which visitors can see the birds swimming underwater. Other favourites are the great Indian toucans with massive heads like large bunches of bananas, Cereopsis geese from Australia that chat with the visitors in tones exactly like those of pigs, and the snowy owl, whose expression changes from the haughty to the outraged in an instant. In the Paradise Garden, small tropical animals, birds and reptiles live in close approximations of their natural habitats.

On the terrace of Harewood, a 9ft bronze statue of Orpheus looks out over the lake and park, one of Capability Brown's less-restrained creations, while the backdrop is the lovely southern front of the house itself. Most of Harewood dates from the early 1770s, when building began at the order of Edwin Lascelles, 1st Lord Harewood, who made a fortune in the West Indies. He spent it wisely, commissioning Robert Adam to design the interiors and Thomas Chippendale to make the furniture; most of their work still remains. Major additions were made in the 1850s by the 3rd Earl of Harewood, and between the two World Wars by the 6th earl, who married the daughter of King George V.

Visitors move at their own speed through the house, and there is plenty to linger over among the luscious interiors, the paintings and the porcelain. Highlights include the Spanish Library, its walls covered with 17th-century Spanish leather, the library with its ornate Adam ceiling and Yorkshire landscapes by Turner, and the Rose Drawing Room, where the star and circle pattern of the carpet is echoed by the ceiling. The Gallery is the house's greatest triumph, with a 76ft long Adam ceiling, moulded and patterned and incorporating 16 paintings of gods and goddesses. The magnificent window frames were carved by Chippendale, and the richly draped taffeta pelmets are in fact made of wood, and were carved in his workshop. Chinese porcelain is on show in the gallery, and the walls are lined with family portraits. Among them the Reynolds portraits of the 1st Lord Harewood's stepdaughters who, even after 200 years of changing fashions in beauty, are still lovely enough to turn heads.

Apr-Oct, daily; Feb, Mar and Nov, Sun only. Adm charge. P *Refreshments. Shops. Toilets.* ♿ *Tel Leeds (0532) 886225.*

HEPTONSTALL OLD GRAMMAR SCHOOL

Off A646, 1 mile north-west of Hebden Bridge (Ac)

The early 17th-century school building in Heptonstall is today a museum telling the story of one of Yorkshire's loveliest villages. Its sturdy stone houses cling to a steep hillside below Pennine moors, and overlook Hebden Bridge and the Rochdale Canal in the Calder valley below. Displays explain Heptonstall's farming and crafts, and especially its days as a major hand-loom weaving centre before the Industrial Revolution. Early school furniture survives, much marked with carved initials and names.

Visitors can watch craftsmen making clogs by traditional methods in a 19th-century mill beside the Calder about a mile south-east of Hebden Bridge. F Walkley (Clogs) Ltd is Britain's only surviving clog mill.

The Keighley road north from the town centre leads to Old Town. There in Billy Lane is Automobilia, a vintage car museum, where early Austin and Morris cars and old bicycles are displayed on a hillside with lovely views.

Old Grammar School: May-Aug, Mon, Wed, Thur, Fri; also Sat and Sun, pm; Sept-Apr, Sat and Sun, pm. Adm charge. Shop. P *Toilets. Tel: Halifax (0422) 843738. Clog Mill: All year, daily. Free entry. Refreshments. Shop.* P *Toilets.* ♿ *Tel (0422) 842061. Automobilia: Apr-Sept, pm exc Mon; Oct-Mar, Sat and Sun, pm. Adm charge. Refreshments. Shop.* P *Toilets. Tel (0422) 844775.*

HOLMFIRTH POSTCARD MUSEUM

Off A635, in town centre (Ca)

Terraces of neat houses line the steep, cobbled alleys and streets of Holmfirth, a small, bustling town in the heart of the lovely Pennine moors which provided the setting for the BBC television series *Last of the Summer Wine*. The house of Nora Batty can be seen in Scarfold, and nearby is the café meeting place of that redoubtable trio of senior citizens – Compo, Clegg and Foggy (later replaced by Seymour).

AS SEEN ON TV *The Holmfirth house of Nora Batty (alias Kathy Staff), the indefatigable lady of the concertina stockings, is recognisable by enthusiasts of the television series* Last of the Summer Wine.

Curiously, this town 80 miles from the sea is also the setting of a museum devoted to the saucy postcard associated with seaside holidays. The family firm of Bamforth was founded in the town to produce lantern slides in 1870, and in 1902 began making postcards with pictures printed from their slides. Artist-drawn cards became fashionable after the First World War, and soon thousands of the cheeky variety were on sale.

Postcards became popular collectors' items after the Second World War, and Major Scherer, a retired officer of the US Air Force, amassed one of the world's finest collections of Bamforth cards. This is now on show in Holmfirth Library, and forms the core of the Postcard Museum.

All year, daily exc Sun am. Free entry. Shop. P *(limited). Toilets.* ♿ *Tel Huddersfield (0484) 682231.*

KIRKSTALL ABBEY HOUSE MUSEUM

On A65, 3 miles west of Leeds (Cc)

The Great Gatehouse of Kirkstall Abbey, a Cistercian house built between 1152 and 1182, was later converted into a fine dwelling known as Abbey House. It now houses a museum which takes visitors back into another age, containing as it does streets of 18th and 19th-century cottages, workshops and shops. Most of them are from the Leeds area, and furnished as they would have been a century or more ago.

There is an inn, with its cluttered Victorian parlour upstairs, and a chemist's, whose window displays four large containers of green, yellow, red and blue liquid to represent the elements – Earth, Air, Fire and Water – on which medicine was once based.

BLUSHING BRIDE *An early Victorian wax doll dressed as a bride is part of the large collection of bygones at Kirkstall Abbey House Museum. Dolls on show range in age from the 17th century to modern times.*

The museum also has items from the abbey excavations, a large collection of costumes and accessories dating from 1760 to the present, and a vast collection of toys. The Folk Galleries illustrate the life of ordinary local people over the last century, with the everyday items they used for cooking, laundering, lighting and heating.

The abbey church, with a finely carved west doorway, was completed in the 1160s and survives almost intact. The remainder of the buildings, however, fell into disrepair after the Dissolution. In the 18th and 19th centuries, the romantic ruins, then overgrown with trees and ivy, appealed to a host of painters and poets, among them J.M.W. Turner, John Cotman, Thomas Gray and Robert Southey.

All year, daily exc Sun am. Adm charge for museum. Refreshments. Shop. P *Toilets.* ♿ *Tel Leeds (0532) 755821.*

VILLAGE OF THE BRONTËS

There are two Haworths: the old village with the church and parsonage on the hilltop, and the mill town on the Keighley and Worth Valley Railway in the valley below. The two are linked by Main Street, steeply cobbled and flanked by shops, many of them named after the famous literary Brontës of Haworth Parsonage, itself now a museum. Nearby is the Haworth Museum of Childhood. *Railway: All year, Sat and Sun; July-Aug and Bank Hols, daily. Adm charge (Oxenhope Museum and Haworth Workshop). Refreshments. Shops.* 🅿 *Toilets. Tel Haworth (0535) 43629. Parsonage: All year, daily exc Feb. Adm charge. Shop.* 🅿 *Tel (0535) 42323. Country Park: All year, daily. Museum of Childhood: Easter-Dec, daily; Jan-Easter, Sat and Sun. Adm charge. Shop.* 🅿 ♿ *Tel (0535) 43825.*

STEAM VETERAN *A Keighley and Worth Valley grand old lady of steam plies the 5 mile line to Oxenhope. The railway closed in 1961, but reopened in the hands of a preservation society seven years later. Its headquarters are at Haworth, which has a pretty little station and the line's workshop. Splendid veteran steam locomotives include* Bellerophon *of 1874, and* City of Wells, *which once hauled the Golden Arrow. Oakworth station, now restored to Edwardian perfection, starred on television and in the film* The Railway Children.

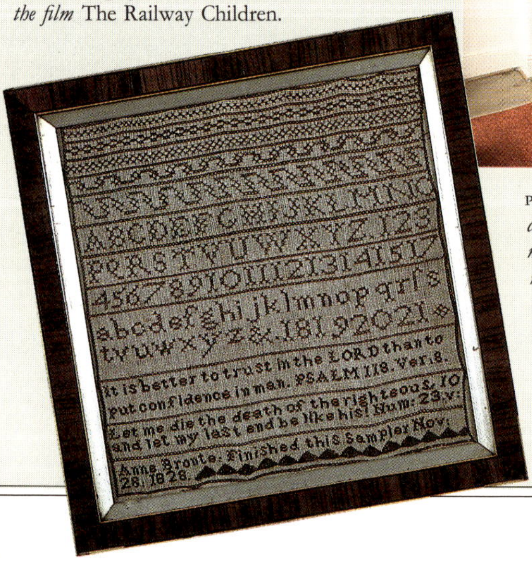

POWERHOUSE OF GENIUS *Anne Brontë's writing desk lies on the dining-room table at the Brontë Parsonage (above) where the family did most of their writing. A pastel portrait of Charlotte hangs over the mantelpiece. Anne finished the sampler (left) in 1828, when she was only eight. Bleak, beautiful Haworth Moor nearby inspired the Brontës, and the view from Penistone Hill Country Park (top picture) shows the village of Stanbury beyond the morning mist. A 1½ mile heritage trail around the park starts at Moorside car park. Victorian and Edwardian dolls and an endearing array of teddy bears (right) are among the inhabitants of the Haworth Museum of Childhood, along with working models of toy trains.*

LEEDS CITY ART GALLERY

The Headrow, Leeds (Dc)

With its mighty columns, pillared dome, allegorical figures and gilded ceilings, Leeds Town Hall celebrates the soaring northern prosperity and pride of achievement of the mid-19th century. Its dignity is not at all diminished by the chess players who today set up their games – played with knee-high chessmen – in its shadow. Next door is another token of civic pride, the Art Gallery, which is of national, and even world-wide, significance. Most famous are its modern collections – paintings by Francis Bacon, Warhol, Ben Nicholson, Lowry, Augustus John, Wyndham Lewis, Sutherland and Piper, and sculpture by Moore, Epstein and Barbara Hepworth. But best-loved, perhaps, are the Victorian narrative paintings that launched the gallery: Frank Holl's *The Village Funeral*, Holman Hunt's *Shadow of Death*, Waterhouse's *Lady of Shalott*, and Lady Butler's *Scotland for Ever!*, depicting the charge of the Royal Scots Greys at Waterloo.

In the adjoining City Museum visitors are greeted by a large tiger of ferocious aspect that figured in the Great Exhibition of 1851 in Hyde Park, London, and before that as a sporting trophy of a Captain Reid of the Ghurkas. This introduces a large collection of stuffed animals mounted against realistic backgrounds, a theme that is continued with life-sized models of peoples around the world – Afghans, Japanese, Zulus, Red Indians, Eskimos – in appropriate costumes.

Art Gallery: All year, daily. Free entry. Shop. Toilets. ♿ Tel Leeds (0532) 462495. Museum: All year, Tues-Sat. Free entry. Shop. Tel (0532) 462633.

LEEDS INDUSTRIAL MUSEUM

Armley Mills, Canal Road, Leeds (Dc)

Many of the most important industries of the Leeds district are represented at Armley Mills. The most spectacular survival of local industry is the building itself. The splendid Georgian stone-built fulling mill, which dates from 1806, towers over a mill pond and watercourses which provide power for the mill water wheels. Although the mill was initially waterpowered, steam engines were later added to increase the power, and a working example can be seen in its purpose-built engine house.

Inside the mill, visitors walk through stone-floored rooms lined with iron columns and see large carding engines and spinning mules on which yarn is spun at daily demonstrations. All around are photographs of the workers who once spent long hours in Yorkshire mills. Other galleries take visitors through a labyrinth of streets re-creating that part of Leeds where Irish and Jewish immigrants worked alongside local people in the 'sweat-shops' and early tailoring factories. Visitors can follow the development of ideas, skills and machines which led to the large multiple tailoring factories of Hepworth, Montague Burton and many others whose shops became well known in high streets all over the country.

The optical and cinematograph industries also flourished in Leeds in the early 20th century, and there are displays about these too. Visitors can enjoy early films in a reconstructed 1920s cinema, complete with gas lighting, purpose-built projection box and cinema piano.

The city was also a world-renowned producer of locomotives, and Leeds-built engines from many parts of the world have been collected at Armley Mills. They include locomotives built to work underground in coal mines or in the sugar plantations of India. Some of the engines operate on a small demonstration track on special days.

The only trans-Pennine canal in the country, the Leeds and Liverpool, passes alongside the mill. The canal and waterways displays illustrate the life and work of the people who lived and worked on the canal barges and occupied the canal-side cottages and workshops.

Many products of Leeds engineering, transport and other trades can be seen. There are several picnic sites around the site, and visitors can also enjoy the wildlife which now inhabits the mill pond and races.

All year, Tues-Sat and Bank Hol; also Sun pm. Adm charge. P *Shop. Toilets. ♿ Tel Leeds (0532) 637861.*

LOTHERTON HALL

On B1217, 9 miles east of Leeds (Ec)

An amazing array of some 200 species of birds from all over the world live in the bird garden here at Lotherton Hall. Many of them are rare or endangered, and Lotherton has a full conservation and breeding programme designed to re-introduce birds into the wild. Some birds are in large, landscaped aviaries, while others roam freely. The variety is enormous. The parrots alone range from 4ft long hyacinthine macaws to pygmy parrots only 4in long, and there are African glossy starlings and Himalayan monals with iridescent plumage. Birds of prey include giant Andean condors – the largest of all flying birds, with a wingspan of nearly 10ft. Bizarre-beaked toucans and crowned cranes from Africa cut a dash, and large flightless birds such as rheas and emus stalk their pens.

The rambling Edwardian mansion is a treasure house of paintings, silver, Chinese ceramics, porcelain, modern ceramics and furniture, including a magnificent bedroom suite made of papier-mâché in 1851. Attractive gardens laid out during the Edwardian years include a formal walled garden, rose garden and Japanese garden, all graced by fine statuary.

Bird Garden: May-Oct, Tues-Sun and Bank Hol. Park: All year, daily. House: All year, Tues-Sun and Bank Hol. Adm charge for house. Refreshments. Shop. P *Toilets. ♿ Tel Leeds (0532) 813068.*

NATIONAL MUSEUM OF PHOTOGRAPHY, FILM AND TELEVISION

In centre of Bradford (Cc)

The exterior, though modern, bears a more than passing resemblance to a cinema of the Golden Era, and a lively statue of J.B. Priestley, entertainer, broadcaster and Bradford's favourite son, stands smack outside the front door. Within, an extraordinarily realistic model of Lord Lichfield

HERE IS THE NEWS! *The director and his assistants assemble a television news broadcast from the multitude of pictures from many sources displayed on monitor screens, in the mock-up of a control room in the National Museum of Photography, Film and Television in Bradford. In earlier days news photographers had to jostle for pictures while holding bulky cameras like the Auto Graflex plate reflex camera of 1908 (right).*

making a pleasant speech of welcome makes the visitor aware that he is entering not so much a museum as a brand new branch of showbiz.

From the foyer, the visitor walks through a gigantic model of a Victorian camera to a gallery that illustrates the principles of photography and film processing by means of all kinds of devices including a working, 6ft high camera. There follows a display of 'Beyond Photography' – of fibre optics that can peer inside engines and the human body, and of cameras that photograph models of bridges and viaducts to estimate stresses on the real structures. The wonders of satellite weather forecasting are illustrated by a receiver on the roof which picks up signals from a satellite 20,000 miles out in space and transmits them as pictures to a screen in the gallery.

A mock-up of a newspaper's picture desk opens a discussion on news photography. The visitor sees stills and newsreels of events such as the killing of Lee Harvey Oswald or the SAS attack on the Iranian Embassy, and is asked to judge which medium he finds more effective. He is shown, too, how cunning cropping and depth of print can entirely alter the emphasis of a news picture.

The television section begins with a re-creation of a television news room on the lead-up to the *Nine o'Clock News*. Real recent news items flicker on the monitor screens, and the recorded voices of the studio crew add urgency and realism. Nearby, TV drama is illustrated in a similar way by a set of *Beauty and the Beast*, in which the voices of director and cameraman accompany changing lighting effects and camera angles to show how the maximum movement may be got out of a small stage.

Children can make a telerecording of themselves reading real news items, or sit on a Magic Carpet, watch a TV screen and see themselves riding the carpet through mountains, over a safari through the African bush, among Eastern minarets or around the towers of an English stately home. There is a history of British television from 1936 onwards, and a nostalgic stroll through ancient TV sets showing programmes appropriate to their years of construction – *Wakey-Wakey!, Six-Five Special, That Was The Week That Was, Dr Finlay's Casebook*, and other trips down memory lane.

The climax of the whole show is the IMAX cinema, with its five-storey wrap-around screen and six sound channels. The 40 minute films shown are mostly about aviation, since that shows off the tricks of IMAX best. From the moment the curtains part, the spectator is realistically within the film, the sound seeming to come from inside one's head as one overshoots the deck of an aircraft carrier, skims along a river – and, with clammy-palmed vertigo, falls out of a biplane into and down The Grand Canyon.

All year, Tues-Sun; also Bank Hol Mon and evening cinema performances. Adm charge for cinema. 🅿 *Refreshments. Shops. Toilets.* ♿ *Tel Bradford (0274) 727488.*

NOSTELL PRIORY

On A638, 6 miles south-east of Wakefield (Db)

More than 100 pieces of work by Thomas Chippendale at Nostell Priory form England's finest collection of the great cabinet-maker's work. Chippendale, a former apprentice on the Nostell estate, was commissioned in 1766 to furnish the house of Sir Rowland Winn, which had been built near the site of the medieval priory. Robert Adam was commissioned to add the east wing and decorate the interior, and the combination of his design, Chippendale's furniture and wall paintings by the Venetian artist Zucchi made each state room a masterpiece. The house also contains fine paintings, silver and porcelain, a set of exquisite Brussels tapestries, and an 18th-century doll's house.

In the grounds are the 16th-century Wragby church, rose gardens, a lakeside walk and an adventure playground.

NT. Easter-Oct, Sat pm, Sun and Bank Hol; also Mon-Thur in July and Aug. Adm charge. Refreshments. Shop. 🅿 *Toilets.* ♿ *Tel Wakefield (0924) 863892.*

OAKWELL HALL AND COUNTRY PARK

Off A652, 5 miles south-east of Bradford (Cb)

Charlotte Brontë described this Elizabethan moated manor house as 'Fieldhead', the home of Shirley Keeldar in *Shirley*. The novelist knew Oakwell in the 1840s, when friends of hers ran it as a boarding school, and little has changed since then. The 15th-century, timber-framed house on the site was encased in stone in 1583, and retains its fine great hall with a magnificently carved screen. The manor is now restored and furnished in the style of the 17th and 18th centuries.

Formal gardens surround the house, and beyond lies an 87 acre country park, which includes an arboretum and wildlife garden. There are several nature trails and woodland walks, and the old farm buildings house a visitor centre, with craft workshops.

The Bagshaw Museum, in nearby Wilton Park, is housed in an imposing Victorian Gothic mansion built in 1875 by a local woollen cloth maker. One room is decorated in Egyptian style, with stencilled shutters and finely painted ceiling. Another has a spectacular frieze painted in medieval fashion with hunting and harvesting themes. The museum displays local history, natural history, Egyptology, ethnography and fine Oriental works of art.

Hall: All year, daily exc Sun am. Free entry. Refreshments. 🅿 *Toilets.* ♿ *Tel Batley (0924) 474926.*
Museum: All year, daily exc Sun am. Free entry. Shop. 🅿 *Toilets. Tel (0924) 472514.*

RED HOUSE MUSEUM

Oxford Road, Gomersal (Cb)

When William Taylor, a prosperous cloth merchant, built this red-brick house in 1660 it must have been an extraordinary innovation in an area where buildings were traditionally made of the plentiful local stone. Alterations produced the Regency country residence where Charlotte Brontë often stayed with her friend Mary Taylor and which appears as 'Briarmains' in her novel *Shirley*.

Red House is now fitted out as it would have been in the 1820s, complete with a cheerful parlour. There are displays relating to the Luddite riots which swept the West Riding in 1812 and on which *Shirley* is based.

All year, daily exc Sun am. Free entry. Refreshments. Shop. P *Toilets. Tel Cleckheaton (0274) 872165.*

RYBURN FARM MUSEUM

On B6113, 5 miles south-west of Halifax (Bb)

The early days of the Industrial Revolution, when sheep farming and the production of woollen cloth went hand-in-hand, are re-created here. The farm lies high on the Pennine moors in the centre of Ripponden, and is equipped as it would have been in the 19th century. There are typical tools and equipment in the dairy and barn adjoining the house, and upstairs is the loom chamber for the weaver.

Mar-Oct, Sat, Sun and Bank Hol, pm. Adm charge. P *Tel Halifax (0422) 54823.*

ST IVES ESTATE

On B6429, ½ mile south-west of Bingley (Bc)

There are magnificent views across the Vale of Harden from this lovely country park on the edge of the Pennine moors. A nature trail takes in parkland, farmland, woods, moorland and watersides. Coppice Pond is home to black-headed gulls, mallards, pochards, tufted ducks and teal in winter. In summer, dabchicks, coots and moorhens nest among the bankside plants and banks of rhododendrons erupt around the ponds and woods.

All year, daily.

SHIBDEN HALL

On A58, 1½ miles east of Halifax (Bb)

This house owes its appearance largely to one remarkable woman – Anne Lister, who inherited the property in 1826. The modest half-timbered 15th-century gentleman's home had been in her family since the 16th century, but Anne wanted something much grander. She altered the interior and put in a new staircase, added the 'Norman' tower and 'Gothic' servants' wing, changed the windows, terraced the gardens and created a lake. These projects were funded by Anne Lister's business enterprises in local minerals and an hotel and casino.

Now the Folk Museum of West Yorkshire, the main rooms are furnished and equipped as they would have been in the 17th or 18th centuries, and give the impression that the occupants have only just left. For instance, a meal typical of about 1700 is set out in the dining room: it comprises snails, salmon, chicken, pie and cold meat, and syllabub, all accompanied by wine.

The vast 17th-century Pennine barn houses old farm tools and a fine array of horse-drawn vehicles, including a brightly painted gypsy caravan of about 1880. Other buildings around the cobbled courtyard re-create a 19th-century village centre, with estate worker's cottage, bar, apothecary's shop, brewhouse, pot shop and pottery dealer's cottage. There are the workshops of a clogger, saddler, blacksmith, wheelwright and basket maker, where occasional demonstrations are given.

Feb, Sun pm; Mar-Nov, daily exc Sun am. Adm charge. Refreshments. Shop. P *Toilets. Tel Halifax (0422) 52246.*

TEMPLE NEWSAM

Off A63, 5 miles east of Leeds (Dc)

The Knights Templar owned this estate from the 12th to early 14th centuries and gave it the first part of its name. The Newsam derives from the Domesday survey of 1086, where buildings were recorded at *Neuhusu* – 'at the new houses'.

The present house, begun around 1500, is an elegant Tudor and Jacobean mansion of red brick, with tall windows and parapet of white stone. It is beautifully decorated inside, and has a splendid suite of Georgian rooms, and impressive collections of furniture, silver, porcelain and paintings. Capability Brown landscaped the 1000 acre park in the 1760s. It now includes woodland and avenues, seven spectacular gardens and a Home Farm with rare breeds of livestock.

ORIENTAL SPLENDOUR *The Chinese Drawing Room at Temple Newsam has been restored to its appearance when redecorated in the 1820s. The Chinese wallpaper was a gift from the Prince Regent.*

All year, Tues-Sun and Bank Hol Mon. Adm charge. Refreshments. Shop. P *Toilets. Tel Leeds (0532) 647321 or 641358.*

TOLSON MUSEUM

On A642, 1½ miles east of Huddersfield (Cb)

Ravensknowle Hall – a mansion built around 1860 as a more modest version of Osborne House, Queen Victoria's Italianate home on the Isle of Wight – stands in lovely parkland. It was briefly the home of Legh Tolson, a local textile-maker, who in 1919 gave it to the people of Huddersfield as a museum to commemorate his two nephews killed in the First World War. It includes natural history and geology collections, displays on local history and folk life, textiles, toys and horse-drawn and vintage vehicles.

All year, daily exc Sun am. Free entry. Shop. P *(limited). Toilets.* ♿ *Tel Huddersfield (0484) 530591.*

TUNNEL END CANAL AND COUNTRYSIDE CENTRE

Off A62, in Waters Road, Marsden (Ba)

Standedge Tunnel cuts through more than 3 miles of hard Pennine rock and carries the Huddersfield Narrow Canal, which linked the city with Manchester. It is the longest canal tunnel and the highest section of canal in the country. There is no towpath through the tunnel, so laden boats were 'legged' by two bargemen lying on their backs and 'walking' along the roof.

The Countryside Centre housed in the former tunnel-keeper's cottage has mementos from the great days of the canal, and interpretive displays about the lovely Pennine countryside.

The Marsden to Slaithwaite section of canal is being restored, and its towpath is an idyllic spot for walkers in the beautiful Colne valley. There are boards giving information about the canal's wildlife, which includes dippers, kingfishers, trout and marsh marigolds.

All year, Wed-Sun; also Tues pm and Bank Hol. Shop. P *(limited). Toilets. Tel Huddersfield (0484) 846062.*

COUNTY CALENDAR

Good Fri Upper Calder Valley: Pace Egg Play (children's street theatre).

May (1st Sat). Gawthorpe: Feast (May Day procession).

May (mid-month). Leeds: Tetley Brass Band Championships.

June (mid-month). Harewood House: Northern Horse Show and Country Fair.

June (last Sat). Leeds: Lord Mayor's Parade.

July (1st Sun). Oxenhope: Straw Race.

August (Bank Hol weekend). Bramham Park: Leeds and District Traction Engine Rally.

August (early). Leeds: Show.

August (1st weekend). Wakefield: Show.

September (early). Keighley: Show. Sowerby Bridge: Rushbearing Festival.

September (2nd half). Leeds: International Piano Competition (every 3 years, 1990).

Tourist information: Bradford (0274) 753678; Halifax (0422) 68725; Haworth (0535) 42329; Holmfirth (0484) 684992; Ilkley (0943) 602319; Leeds (0532) 462454; Wakefield (0924) 370211; Wetherby (0937) 62706.

WALES

A make-believe Mediterranean fishing village . . . a steam train crawling beetle-like up the shoulder of Britain's second-highest mountain . . . a military museum in an underground wartime bomb store: Wales is a land where man-made surprises abound, amid the scenic wonders of great national parks. Wales is famed for its castles – Harlech, Caernarfon, Conwy – built by Edward I to overawe the Welsh. Other stories of the past reside in the Roman remains at Caerleon, abbeys at Tintern and Valle Crucis, and country houses such as Plas Newydd and Bodrhyddan Hall. Visitors descend into pits where miners once toiled for slate, lead, copper, coal and gold; they watch electricity being generated from rushing waters; and they become 'Seawatch' coastguards monitoring the radio messages of ships in the busy Bristol Channel.

Portmeirion, Gwynedd

CLWYD

TWO VALES WITH CASTLES, ABBEYS AND A TOUCH OF OLD IRON

A sandy coast dotted with holiday resorts borders a county whose inland hills, valleys and forests provide some of the wildest – and finest – scenery in Britain. All around, too, are reminders of the region's past links with industry. At Bersham, for instance, John Wilkinson made cannons for 18th-century wars, and at Chwarel Wynne slate was once quarried in extensive caverns which can be toured by today's museum visitors.

Castles at Chirk, Ewloe, Denbigh and Rhuddlan are reminders of the turbulent Middle Ages, while among many country houses in Clwyd one of the finest is the black-and-white timbered mansion of Plas Newydd. It stands near Llangollen, a town in the lovely Dee Valley. The town is an ideal centre for delightful journeys by canal boat, steam train or on foot, and every July it hosts its renowned International Eisteddfod.

BERSHAM INDUSTRIAL HERITAGE CENTRE

Off B5098, 2½ miles west of Wrexham (Cb)

One permanent exhibition at this centre is devoted to John 'Iron-Mad' Wilkinson (1728-1808), who brought international fame to the Bersham ironworks. His cannons were used in the American War of Independence and his cylinders helped to develop James Watt's steam engine for industrial use. Another display records the achievements of the Davies brothers, gatesmiths of nearby Croesfoel, who in 1721 made the wrought-iron gates for Chirk Castle.

The centre is on the Bersham and Clywedog Industrial Trail – an 8 mile open-air museum charting industrial life in the area from Roman times. On summer Saturdays guided tours can be arranged.

Easter-Oct, Tues-Sat and Bank Hol; also Sun pm; Nov-Easter, Tues-Sat. Free entry. Shop. P *Toilets.* ♿ *Tel Wrexham (0978) 261529.*

BOD PETRUEL VISITOR CENTRE

Off B5105, 9 miles south-west of Ruthin (Bb)

Few places insulate the visitor more effectively from the pressures of urban civilisation than a 15,000 acre forest. The Clocaenog Forest lies across gently undulating high moorland west of the Vale of Clwyd. Apart from being amply provided with trees of all kinds, from larch, spruce and pine to beech, oak and ash, it also encloses two huge man-made lakes – the Alwen and Llyn Brenig reservoirs.

From the visitor centre there are a number of clearly marked forest walks, ranging from a half-mile riverside stroll to the secluded valley of the upper River Clwyd, to much longer walks taking the visitor out of the forest and up onto unplanted moorland. Many colourful damselflies and butterflies, including orange tips, small heaths and small tortoiseshells, can be seen by the lake at the visitor centre.

FC. Apr-Sept, daily. Free entry. P *Toilets. Tel Clawdd-newydd (082 45) 208.*

BODRHYDDAN HALL

Off A5151, 4 miles south-east of Rhyl (Bc)

A 3000-year-old Egyptian mummy is the unlikely occupant of a small room in this handsome, mainly 17th-century house. Brought from Egypt in 1836 by the present owner's great grandmother as a honeymoon memento, it was later identified as a junior priest in the Temple of the God Amun at Thebes.

Much of the armour in the front hall of Bodrhyddan came from Rhuddlan Castle after it was dismantled by Parliamentarian forces in the Civil War. A glass-topped table contains the Charter of Rhuddlan, granted by Edward I in 1284. In the pretty White Drawing Room the panels surrounding the two fireplaces are from the chapel of one of the ships of the Spanish Armada wrecked off the coast of Anglesey.

June-Sept, Tues and Thur, pm. Adm charge. Refreshments. Shop. P *Toilets.* ♿ *Tel Rhuddlan (0745) 590414.*

CHIRK CASTLE

Off B4500, ½ mile west of Chirk (Ca)

The outside of this border castle – ranged around a central courtyard – has changed little since it was built by Edward I in 1310. It was once the home of Sir Thomas Seymour, who married Henry VIII's widow, Catherine Parr, and of Robert Dudley, Elizabeth I's favourite, and it has been lived in continuously for almost 670 years. Set in spacious formal gardens with clipped yews and a variety of flowering shrubs, the castle is a treasure house of portraits, tapestries, elaborate plasterwork and superb Adam-style furniture.

NT. Apr-Sept, pm daily exc Mon and Sat; Oct, Sat and Sun, pm. Adm charge. Refreshments. Shop. P *Toilets. Tel Chirk (0691) 777701.*

CHWAREL WYNNE MINE MUSEUM

On B4500, 6 miles west of Chirk (Ca)

There are 2½ miles of underground caverns at Chwarel Wynne, some of them vast – over 60ft high – and all of them created almost entirely by hand by miners quarrying for slate. The mine was continuously worked from 1750 to 1928, producing more than 2000 tons of roofing slates a year.

OUTDOOR GIRLS *Haymakers in Victorian dress help to re-create the period atmosphere during a farming demonstration at Erddig Country Park Visitor Centre.*

Visitors are given a guided 30 minute tour of the underground workings, during which methods of mining and processing the slate are explained.

In the museum itself a film tells the history of the slate industry in North Wales. Tools, photographs and documents relating to the mine are displayed, together with objects relating to the life and times of a slate-quarrying village at the turn of the century.

Apr-Oct, daily. Adm charge. Refreshments. Shop. 🅿 *Toilets.* ♿ *(museum only). Tel Glyn Ceiriog (069 172) 343.*

DENBIGH CASTLE

Near centre of Denbigh (Bb)

The castle, built on the orders of Edward I in 1282, stands at the top of a rocky hill dominating the ancient market town of Denbigh and the Vale of Clwyd. Eight of its great towers remain, together with its impressive Great Gatehouse. The Great Kitchen Tower has two fireplaces, each 16ft wide, on the ground floor. Among the famous residents was Henry Percy – the 'Hotspur' of Shakespeare's *Henry IV* plays – who in 1402 occupied the castle in support of Owain Glyndwr against the claims of Henry IV.

The town walls of Denbigh were built at the same time as the castle and are still for the most part intact. They include three impressive towers.

Cadw. All year, daily exc Sun am mid Oct-mid Mar. Adm charge. Shop. 🅿 *Toilets. Tel Denbigh (074 571) 3979.*

ERDDIG

Off A534, 2 miles south of Wrexham (Cb)

For anyone seeking a complete picture of the 'upstairs-downstairs' life of the traditional country house, a visit to Erddig could hardly be bettered. Downstairs, the original laundry still has its box mangle – a huge box of stones moved over wooden rollers. In the stable yard are the household's various carriages – a governess or tub cart, a gig and two phaetons. Later means of transport are represented by a 1907 Rover and a 19th-century bicycle. All these were owned by members of the Yorke family, who lived at Erddig for more than 200 years, until 1973. The Servants' Hall is decorated with portraits of Erddig staff from the 18th and 19th centuries.

The 'upstairs' part of Erddig has outstanding furniture, including sets of silver, walnut chairs and pier glasses, and a magnificent state bed. The house and gardens are surrounded by a country park of almost 2000 acres in which there is a waterfall known as the Cup and Saucer, built in 1774. A visitor centre, open at weekends, explains the workings of the estate.

NT. Apr-Oct, pm daily exc Fri. Adm charge. Refreshments. Shop. 🅿 *Toilets. Tel Wrexham (0978) 355314.*

EWLOE CASTLE

Off B5125, 3½ miles north of Buckley (Cb)

The great interest of this early 13th-century castle is that it is entirely Welsh, built by the Welsh princes before Edward I conquered North Wales in the second half of that century. Hidden in a wooded hollow, it is identified by its characteristically Welsh D-shaped tower. The tower is well preserved, although the walls of the castle are in ruins. Begun by Llywelyn the Great about 1210, it was finished by Llywelyn the Last about 1257.

Cadw. All year, daily. Free entry. Tel Cardiff (0222) 465511.

RELIC OF WAR *A German Pak 40 antitank gun of the Second World War has its last resting place in a former British bomb store in the underground galleries of the Grange Cavern Military Museum.*

GEOLOGICAL MUSEUM OF NORTH WALES

Off A525, 5 miles north-west of Wrexham (Cb)

The rocks of North Wales are some of the oldest in Britain, and the museum tells, briefly but graphically, their story over the last 600 million years. Visitors will learn the difference between such curiously named rocks as horneblende gabbro and mica schist. There is a section on industrial relics, ranging from winding wheels to blast furnaces, and one on fossils, featuring that formidable early carnivore, the dinosaur *Tyrannosaurus rex*.

Outside the museum, the Bwlchgwyn Geological Trail leads through a large disused silica (quartz) quarry.

All year, Mon-Fri; also Sun, June-Aug. Adm charge. Refreshments. Shop. 🅿 *Toilets. Tel Wrexham (0978) 757573.*

GRANGE CAVERN MILITARY MUSEUM

Off A5026, ½ mile north-west of Holywell (Bc)

During the Second World War this cavern was used as a store for more than 11000 tons of bombs, including the famous 'Bouncing Bombs' used by the 'Dambusters' in their raid on the Ruhr valley. Appropriately the cavern now houses one of the largest collections of historic military equipment in Britain, in 2½ acres of disused limestone workings 100ft below ground.

The collection includes more than 70 military vehicles, including a Long Range Desert Group Chevrolet truck believed to be the only known survivor of its type from the Second World War. Displays range from a First World War trench to a section on the Falklands campaign.

Apr-Oct, daily; Feb-Mar, weekends only. Adm charge. Refreshments. Shop. 🅿 *Toilets.* ♿ *Tel Holywell (0352) 713455.*

GREENFIELD VALLEY HERITAGE PARK

Off B5121 at Holywell (Cc)

There are 1½ miles of lakeside and wooded walks in this park, which stretches from the market town of Holywell down to the ruins of historic Basingwerk Abbey by the River Dee. There are five reservoirs, an adventure play park, guided walks and nature trails. A large collection of old farm tools and machinery is displayed in the Abbey Farm Agricultural Museum, which also has a collection of animals.

The park also includes seven scheduled national monuments, including St Winefride's Holy Well – where, according to legend, the severed head of St Winefride fell in the 7th century – and the buildings which form the remains of the valley's once thriving copper industry. Basingwerk Abbey, at the north-east corner of the park, was founded around 1132 and was the home and workplace of Cistercian monks for 400 years until the Dissolution of the Monasteries.

Park: Apr-Oct, daily. Adm charge. Refreshments. Shop. P *Toilets. Abbey: All year, daily. Free entry. Tel Holywell (0352) 714172.*

LLANGOLLEN STEAM RAILWAY

The station, Llangollen (Ca)

A return journey on this little standard-gauge line takes about 40 minutes, passing through some of the loveliest parts of the Dee Valley. Passenger trains run from Llangollen station to Berwyn, 2 miles to the west, steaming across the River Dee bridge, where trees lean lazily over the track.

The line was originally part of the old Great Western Railway route between Barmouth and Ruabon, which operated from 1865 to 1968. The track and fittings were then removed for scrap, and the station buildings fell into disrepair. In the late 1970s a local preservation society took over the line and raised the money – partly by collecting and selling waste paper – to transform it into the delight it is today. As well as steam engines, diesels are also in service – and more will be needed when the line is eventually extended to Corwen, 10 miles from Llangollen.

Dominating the skyline above Llangollen are the ruins of an old Welsh fortress, Castell Dinas Bran. A stronghold has stood on top of the castle's 1000ft high limestone hill since the days of the ancient Britons, and the present stone building dates from the 12th century.

A mile east of Llangollen, reached by a towpath along the River Dee, are the Horseshoe Falls, a man-made weir on the Dee built by the engineer Thomas Telford in 1830 to provide water for the Shropshire Union Canal.

In Llangollen's Canal Museum, the visitor walks through a reproduction of a 19th-century coal mine before seeing how coal and other cargoes used to be transported around the country.

Railway: Displays, all year, daily. Trains, late May-late Sept, daily; also weekends and Bank Hol, Easter to mid-May and Oct. Fares vary. P *(limited). Toilets. Tel Llangollen (0978) 860951. Castle: All year, daily. Free entry. Tel (0978) 860828. Canal Museum: Late Apr-Sept, daily. Adm charge. Shop.* P *(limited). Tel (0978) 860702.*

CANAL STYLE *The interior of an old narrowboat, reproduced at Llangollen's Canal Museum, shows the artistic touch cultivated on the waterways. Below is a boatman's model of a narrowboat.*

LLYN BRENIG

Off B450, 4 miles north of Cerrigydrudion (Bb)

The 919 acres of water called Llyn Brenig which occupy two valleys high on Mynydd Hiraethog are primarily a reservoir, but they also provide facilities for fishing, sailing, canoeing and windsurfing. Visitors can follow two nature and two archaeological trails; guides are available from a visitor centre. The short nature trail covers about 1½ miles and the long trail about 3½ miles, each providing ample opportunity to observe the range of wetland, moor and forest wildlife in the Brenig Valley. The archaeological trails pass a Stone Age camp, a Bronze Age burial mound and ring cairn, and a 16th-century hut settlement.

All year, daily. Free entry. Refreshments. Shop. P *Toilets.* ♿ *Tel Corwen (049 082) 463.*

LOGGERHEADS COUNTRY PARK

Off A494, 3 miles south-west of Mold (Cb)

Contrary to its name, Loggerheads is one of the most peaceful spots imaginable, with the lovely River Alyn running through its 72 acres, set on the eastern edge of the Clwydian Range. The composer Felix Mendelssohn was inspired to write his 'Rivulet' music after musing over the river at the Leete – a man-made waterway which once operated waterwheels at mines in the valley.

On the other side of the river, near the car park, is Pentre Water Mill, a 19th-century working corn mill. A nature trail leads along the river and through woodland.

High above the park to the west is Moel Famau, one of the finest viewpoints in Wales. From the car park at its foot – on an unclassified road off the A494 – two footpaths lead to the summit, more than 1800ft high.

Country Park: All year, daily. Free entry. Mill: Apr-Sept, Sat and Sun. Adm charge. Refreshments. Shop. P *Toilets.* ♿ *Tel Llanferres (035 285) 586.*

LADIES' LEGACY *Carved panelling flanks the handsome staircase at Plas Newydd, where the two eccentric 'Ladies of Llangollen' entertained celebrities of their day. Gifts from guests helped to furnish the house.*

PISTYLL RHAEADR

On minor road, 3½ miles north-west of Llanrhaeadr-ym-Mochnant (Ba)

One of the traditional Seven Wonders of Wales, this spectacular waterfall drops 240ft, making it the highest waterfall in Britain south of the Highlands. After a near-vertical drop of 120ft the water surges through a natural arch in the rock to complete the remaining half of its journey. Its Welsh name means 'spout waterfall'.

Apr-Oct, daily; Nov-Mar, Sat and Sun. Refreshments. P *Toilets.* ♿ *Tel Llanrhaeadr (069 189) 392.*

PLAS NEWYDD

Off Butler Hill, ¼ mile south-west of Llangollen (Ca)

From 1780 to 1829 this elegant, black-and-white timbered mansion, set in its own grounds, was the home of Lady Eleanor Butler and Miss Sarah Ponsonby. Generally known as the 'Ladies of Llangollen', the two inseparable companions dressed in dark riding habits and starched neckcloths and soon established themselves as a pair of eccentrics. They corresponded with some of the leading thinkers, and celebrities of the time – the poets Robert Southey and William Wordsworth, the novelist Sir Walter Scott, the playwright Richard Brinsley Sheridan and the Duke of Wellington – all visited them.

When the two ladies first moved in, Plas Newydd was little more than a glorified cottage. But they soon transformed it into an elaborate residence complete with projecting oriel windows with stained glass and rooms filled with dark, fancifully carved oak furniture and panelling. Afterwards more rooms, including a kitchen and brewhouse, were added, and visitors can see

all these – as well as the Gothic library and the bedroom and dressing room. The Elizabethan-style timbering which gives the house its dramatic black-and-white façade was added by a later owner, General John Yorke.
May-Sept, daily. Adm charge. 🅿 *(limited). Toilets. Tel Ruthin (082 42) 2201.*

RHUDDLAN CASTLE

Off A547 at Rhuddlan, 3 miles south of Rhyl (Bc)

Towering majestically over the River Clwyd, this late 13th-century castle has concentric curtain walls and massive twin gatehouses enclosing a square. Rhuddlan was the second major fortress built by Edward I in his efforts to subjugate North Wales, and is now the home of an exhibition on the 15 Welsh castles erected or strengthened during his reign. Rhuddlan Castle was partly destroyed during the Civil War.
Cadw. All year, daily exc Sun am mid Oct-mid Mar. Adm charge. Shop. 🅿 *Toilets.* ♿ *Tel Rhuddlan (0745) 590777.*

RUTHIN CRAFT CENTRE

Off Park Road, in Ruthin (Bb)

A purpose-built craft centre in the heart of the Vale of Clwyd houses 13 craftsmen working in their own studios around a landscaped courtyard. Galleries have changing exhibitions, and products for sale include work in glass, leather, wood, ceramics, jewellery and textiles.

The old market town of Ruthin is set in a ring of wooded hills, some more than 1000ft high, in the lovely Vale of Clwyd. In the marketplace is the Maen Huail, the stone on which, according to legend, King Arthur had Huail, brother of Gildas the historian, beheaded as a rival in love.
All year, daily. Free entry. Refreshments. Shop. 🅿 *Toilets.* ♿ *Tel Ruthin (082 42) 4774.*

ST ASAPH CATHEDRAL

In centre of St Asaph (Bc)

Standing stoutly on a hill overlooking meadows beside the River Elwy is Britain's smallest medieval cathedral. Its peaceful setting belies its long and turbulent history. The first cathedral on the site was built in 560, ruined by Henry III's troops in 1245 and again destroyed by Edward I in 1282. In 1402 it was burnt down during a rebellion against the English, and it was restored in 1482.

Among its many treasures are the clerestory windows dating from 1403, a first edition of the William Morgan Bible in Welsh of 1588, which was used at the Investiture of the Prince of Wales in 1969; the William Salisbury New Testament of 1567; and a 1549 prayer book that belonged to Roger Ascham, Elizabeth I's tutor, which has notes in his handwriting.
All year, daily. Free entry. 🅿 *Toilets.* ♿ *Tel St Asaph (0745) 583429.*

VALLE CRUCIS ABBEY

On A542, 1½ miles north-west of Llangollen (Cb)

Set in a narrow valley by the Eglwyseg River, and surrounded by rolling, wooded hills, this Cistercian abbey was founded in 1201 by Madoc, Prince of Powys. Much of the abbey remains, including its strikingly original east end with its five lancet windows. The façade at the west end, with its three Early English windows and later rose window above, also survives largely intact, as does the richly carved west door.

The east range of the cloister was rebuilt in the 14th century, and the fine chapter house remains. There are sculptured memorial slabs.
Cadw. All year, daily exc Sun am mid Oct-mid Mar. Shop. 🅿 ♿ *Tel Llangollen (0978) 860326.*

WELSH MOUNTAIN ZOO

Off A547, 1½ miles south of Colwyn Bay (Ac)

From its vantage point 500ft above sea level, the zoo is a magnificent setting for animals and plants from all over the world, with fine views over mountains and the sea.

The biggest attractions for visitors are the feeding of the sea lions and the regular free-flying displays of the zoo's collection of eagles – even more impressive when seen in a natural mountain setting. The zoo's breeding programme involves endangered species such as the American bald eagle, the European otter, the Persian leopard and the Mongolian wild horse.
All year, daily. Adm charge. Refreshments. Shop. 🅿 *Toilets.* ♿ *Tel Colwyn Bay (0492) 532938.*

COUNTY CALENDAR

January (mid-month). Llangollen: Dee River Race.

April (mid-month). Llangollen: Craft Fair.

May (last week). Rhyl: Community Festival.

June (mid-month). Delyn: Festival of Arts and Culture.

July (early). Llangollen: International Musical Eisteddfod. Wrexham: Show.

August (mid-month). Rhyl: Denbighshire and Flintshire Show.

September (mid-month). St Asaph: North Wales Music Festival.

Tourist information: Colwyn Bay (0492) 530478; Llangollen (0978) 860828 (summer only); Rhyl (0745) 55068; Ruthin (082 42) 3992.

PICTURE OF PEACE *The roofless ruins of Valle Crucis, 'Valley of the Cross', Abbey stand on a wooded slope leading down to the Eglwyseg River. In the 13th century the abbey suffered a disastrous fire.*

DYFED

SHRINES, CASTLES AND A STEAM RAILWAY IN ST DAVID'S LAND

After the departure of the Romans, who mined gold at Dolaucothi, Dyfed became a haven of saints, and their hermit sites at Caldey and St David's eventually held great religious houses. The Normans left a ring of castles, and from fortresses such as Pembroke and Haverfordwest they made westernmost Dyfed the 'Little England Beyond Wales'.

The region's great beauty inspired a poet, Dylan Thomas, and an artist, Graham Sutherland. It is seen to perfection from the Vale of Rheidol Railway, at Llyn Brianne, and in the Cardigan and Pembrey parks. Traditional industries are recalled at Llywernog and in the Museum of the Welsh Woollen Industry.

ABERYSTWYTH CASTLE

Off New Promenade, Aberystwyth (Cc)

The dignified ruins of Aberystwyth's 13th-century coastal castle include the twin-towered Great Gatehouse and several towers. Built on a promontory beside the Rheidol estuary, it was the first castle erected in Wales by Edward I. Aberystwyth grew up around it, and the resort is today the home of a college of the University of Wales, whose older buildings dominate the seafront.

The main college – a bright, multi-levelled building at Penglais, in the north-east outskirts of the town – houses the Aberystwyth Arts Centre. This contains galleries with changing exhibitions of painting, photography, prints and sculpture. There is a permanent exhibition of ceramics, and another charting the evolution of graphic art from the 15th century to today.

Castle: All year, daily. Arts Centre: All year, Mon-Sat. Free entry. Refreshments. Shop. P *Toilets. Tel Aberystwyth (0970) 4277.*

CALDEY ISLAND

Off coast, 3 miles south of Tenby (Ba)

Caldey is a small island with a long religious history. Its abbey is the successor to religious settlements stretching back 1500 years to the earliest Celtic saints. The old priory and St Illtud's Church stand on the site of a 6th-century hermits' chapel; the church contains the ancient Caldey Stone, with inscriptions in Latin and Ogham.

The monastery, a red-roofed Italianate building, was built between 1910 and 1912. Inhabited by Cistercian monks, it is furnished with simplicity and austerity. There are guided tours of the monastery, for men only, but the perfumery, where the monks manufacture perfume from the local gorse and lavender, is not open. There is a small museum.

Boats from Tenby, mid May-late Sept, Mon-Sat. Free entry. Refreshments. Shop. Toilets. Tel Tenby (0834) 2632.

CARDIGAN WILDLIFE PARK

Off A478, 2 miles south-east of Cardigan (Bb)

This 50 acre stretch of wood and grassland combines a natural park with a wildlife sanctuary. There are the remains of 19th-century slate quarries beside the river, and restored quarrymen's cottages house a visitor centre. Enclosures contain bison, wild boars and other rare breeds.

All year, daily. Adm charge. Refreshments. Shop. P *Toilets.* ♿ *Tel Cardigan (0239) 614449.*

CAREW CASTLE

On A4075, 4 miles east of Pembroke (Ba)

Gerald de Windsor, Henry I's Constable of Pembroke, founded this castle beside the Carew River around 1100, and his descendants have owned it ever since. A tower built around 1200 is the oldest part of the present castle; subsequent extensions transformed it into a medieval fortress and then into an Elizabethan mansion, with handsome windows. The castle was abandoned around 1690, but is now being restored.

Carew Tidal Mill dates from the 19th century and is the only Welsh mill of its kind still intact.

Easter-Oct, daily. Adm charge. Shop. P *(mill only). Tel Carew (064 67) 782 (castle); 657 (mill).*

CARREG CENNEN CASTLE

Off A483, 3 miles south-east of Llandeilo (Ca)

Ruined but still impressive, Carreg Cennen stands on a high, windy crag above the River Cennen, its south-facing ramparts perched on the edge of a vertical 330ft limestone cliff. An English stronghold from 1277, Carreg Cennen was briefly occupied by the Welsh leader Owain Glyndwr during the early 15th century. Later it played a part in the Wars of the Roses, and Yorkists ordered its destruction after taking it in 1462. The demolishers must have been half-hearted in their work, for Carreg Cennen's walls still command wonderful views south-east across the Black Mountain. A passage beneath the foundations leads to a cavern in which have been found the skeletons of prehistoric people.

Cadw. All year, daily. Adm charge. Shop. P *Tel Cardiff (0222) 465511.*

DOLAUCOTHI GOLD MINES

On A482, 7 miles south-east of Lampeter (Cb)

Deep in the hills of south-west Wales is the only site in Britain where it is known for certain that the Romans mined for gold. In a wooded hillside jagged bands of rock, hewn by Roman slaves, lie hidden among the foliage, with remnants of an elaborate aqueduct system.

Authentic 1930s mining equipment, workshops and trams in full working order show how the mines operated up until the Second World War. Visitors should start at the exhibition centre, then follow the 'Miners' Way'. Guided tours include some of the underground workings.

NT. Apr-Sept, daily. Adm charge. Shop. P *Toilets.* ♿ *(part). Tel Pumsaint (055 85) 359.*

JOUSTING GROUND *The stately ruins of Carew Castle overlook the Carew River. In 1507, the fortress and nearby meadows were the scene of the last great medieval tournament held in Wales. Beyond is a tidal mill.*

DYLAN THOMAS'S BOATHOUSE
Off A4066, at Laugharne (Ca)

This house on stilts overlooking the Taf estuary was the home of Dylan Thomas and his wife Caitlin from 1949 until his death on November 9, 1953, aged 39. It is now a museum dedicated to his life and work. From the windows, visitors can gaze across the waters and the 'heron-priested shore' that inspired some of Thomas's best-known works. His tempestuous progress from young Bohemian to poet of international stature is recalled with manuscripts, family photographs and an audiovisual programme.

Thomas locked himself away to write in a shed – known as 'The Shack' – along the path to the boathouse. Here he wrote 'Under Milk Wood'. Visitors can peer into the sparsely furnished 'study', with Thomas's papers strewn about. The poet's grave in the churchyard of St Martin's Church is marked by a simple white cross.

In Duncan Street, in the centre of Laugharne, is Little Treasures, a doll museum in a converted 18th-century barn.

Boathouse: Easter-early Nov, daily. Adm charge. Refreshments. Shop. Toilets. Tel Laugharne (099 421) 420. Little Treasures: Easter-Oct, daily. Adm charge. Shop. P *(limited).* ♿ *Tel (099 421) 554.*

FELIN GERI
On B4333, 1 mile north-west of Newcastle Emlyn (Cb)

This 16th-century water-powered flour mill, long derelict, has been restored to working order and today produces stone-ground flour by traditional means. It lies in a tranquil valley beside the Ceri, a tributary of the River Teifi. In the surrounding meadows farm animals are on view, and there is a craft workshop, a museum of rural life, trout pools, picnic sites and walks.

Easter-Oct, daily. Adm charge. Refreshments. Shop. P *Toilets.* ♿ *Tel Newcastle Emlyn (0239) 710810.*

GRAHAM SUTHERLAND GALLERY
Off A40, 6 miles east of Haverfordwest (Ba)

The gallery housed within the courtyard of Picton Castle contains a superb collection of works by the artist Graham Sutherland, including large works painted specially for the gallery. Much of Sutherland's work was inspired by the natural beauty of Pembrokeshire. He first worked there in 1934, and throughout his life returned 'to benefit from the clear and transparent light'.

Apr-Sept, Tues-Sun, Bank Hol. Adm charge. Refreshments. Shop. P *Toilets.* ♿ *Tel Rhos (043 786) 296.*

GWILI STEAM RAILWAY
Off A484, 2 ½ miles north of Carmarthen (Ca)

The first standard-gauge preserved railway to operate in Wales, the Gwili Railway is a living reminder of a Great Western Railway branch line which retains its rural character. Steam trains haul holiday passengers for just over $1\frac{1}{2}$ miles by the Gwili river from Bronwydd Arms to a riverside station at Llwyfan Cerrig, where there is a picnic area, a children's activity centre and a nature trail. The railway is run entirely by volunteers.

Trains: Bank Hol; June, Sun; July, Wed, Sat and Sun; late July-late Aug, daily exc Fri. Refreshments. Shop. Toilets. Tel Maesteg (0656) 732176.

HAVERFORDWEST CASTLE MUSEUM
Off A40, in centre of Haverfordwest (Ba)

The shell of a 12th-century Norman castle built to guard the ford over the Western Cleddau river crowns a steep 80ft hill overlooking the ancient town's streets. It was slighted in the Civil War, later becoming the county jail. In 1820 a new jail was built in the Outer Ward; this now houses the Castle Museum, which covers Haverfordwest's great days as a thriving seaport and former county town of Pembrokeshire.

All year, Tues-Sat; also Mon in summer. Adm charge. Shop. P *Toilets. Tel Haverfordwest (0437) 3708.*

KIDWELLY CASTLE
Off A484, in town centre (Ca)

The towering three-storey gatehouse and massive round towers and curtain walls of Kidwelly Castle stand tall and almost complete. The castle was built in the early 12th century on a rocky ridge above the Gwendraeth Fach river, and guarded a ford on the main road westwards. The earliest part of the present fortress – the inner quadrangle – was erected in the 1270s, and a chapel was built out over the river bank in 1300. The outer walls were added soon after to make a concentric 'walls-within-walls' defence.

In the 18th century Kidwelly became an industrial centre noted for its tinplate works. A 164ft chimney marks the remnants of the old works complex just north-east of the town, where tinplate was made by hand. Here today, in the Kidwelly Industrial Museum, much of the machinery can still be seen.

Castle: Cadw. All year, daily. Adm charge. Shop. P *(limited). Toilets.* ♿ *Tel Kidwelly (0554) 890104. Museum: Easter-Sept, daily, exc Sat and Sun am. Adm charge. Refreshments. Shop.* P *(limited). Toilets.* ♿ *(part). Tel (0554) 891078.*

LLANGLOFFAN FARMHOUSE CHEESE CENTRE
Off A487, 5 miles south-west of Fishguard (Bb)

Milk from Jersey cows is turned into farmhouse cheese by traditional methods in this carefully restored dairy, where the original cheese presses, wooden moulds and curd knives are still in use. Visitors can watch the entire process, which takes a morning to complete; they can also stroll among the farm's cows, chickens and pigs. The cheese can be tasted, and is on sale.

May-Sept, daily exc Sun, and some other days. Adm charge. Refreshments. Shop. P *Toilets.* ♿ *Tel St Nicholas (034 85) 241.*

LLYN BRIANNE
Off A40, 10 miles north of Llandovery (Db)

Water thunders down the 1312ft spillway of the Llyn Brianne reservoir at up to 60 mph, entering the River Tywi in a cloud of spray. Llyn Brianne stretches back 4 miles behind the dam, and a scenic road runs along its eastern side, through the conifer plantations of the Tywi Forest and northwards to the spectacular Abergwesyn to Tregaron mountain road.

About a mile below the dam, on the minor road from Llandovery, is the information centre for the Dinas Reserve. A boardwalk takes visitors over marshy land to the reserve itself – a conical hill where the Tywi cascades through a splendid gorge.

Reservoir: All year, daily. P *Toilets (summer).* ♿ *Tel Llandovery (0550) 20693. Reserve: RSPB. All year, daily. Information Centre: Easter-Aug, daily.* P *Tel Rhandirmwyn (05506) 276.*

LLYWERNOG SILVER-LEAD MINE
On A44, 10½ miles east of Aberystwyth (Dc)

It is hard to realise that the lovely country on the flanks of the mighty Plynlimon, with wild, lonely slopes and isolated sheep farms, was once a flourishing mining area. The first prospectors arrived at Llywernog in the 1740s, and production at the water-powered mine did not end until the 1880s. The mine stood derelict until it was restored in the early 1970s as an open-air museum.

Old buildings have been re-erected, and machinery and water wheels re-created. A Miners' Trail around the 7 acre site includes a short underground section through a prospecting tunnel. There is an audiovisual show, and a 'California of Wales' exhibition.
Easter-Sept, daily; Oct, some days. Adm charge. Refreshments. Shop. P *Toilets. Tel Ponterwyd (097 085) 620.*

MAESLLYN WOOLLEN MILL MUSEUM
Off A486, 11½ miles east of Cardigan (Cb)

A mill built in 1881 and providing flannel until after the First World War has been revived as a museum of the Welsh weaving industry. The renovated machinery now produces flannel again, and also tweed. Next to the 19th-century machines are earlier hand-operated looms, and audiovisual displays explain the production process. The mill sells woollen clothes and rugs, and a nature trail winds its way through woods.
Easter-Oct, daily exc Sun am; winter, Mon-Fri. Adm charge. Refreshments. Shop. P *Toilets.* ♿ *Tel Rhydlewis (023 975) 251.*

MANORBIER CASTLE
On B4585, 5 miles south-west of Tenby (Ba)

'In all the broad lands of Wales, Manorbier is the most pleasant place by far.' So said the medieval writer Giraldus Cambrensis (Gerald of Wales) who was born there in 1146. The castle's mellow limestone ruins crown a steep sandstone spur in a green valley running down to the sea. To Old Tower and hall were later added a vast gatehouse, two towers, the curtain walls and the chapel, which retains some of its painted plaster.
Easter-Sept, daily. Adm charge. Shop. P *Toilets.* ♿ *(gardens). Tel Manorbier (083 482) 394.*

MANOR HOUSE WILDLIFE PARK
On B4318, 3 miles north-west of Tenby (Ba)

Enclosures in the park surrounding an 18th-century manor house contain sika deer, wallabies, chimpanzees, emus and llamas, while pens in the walled gardens shelter monkeys, marmosets, penguins, macaws, parrots and flamingos. Birds fly free among exotic plants in the tropical house, and there is a snake house and aquarium. Manor House has a fine collection of birds of prey, and falconry displays are given most afternoons. There is also a model railway.
Easter-Sept, daily. Adm charge. Refreshments. Shop. P *Toilets.* ♿ *Tel Carew (064 67) 201.*

MARINE LIFE CENTRE
On A487, just south-east of St David's (Aa)

A fascinating journey through the underwater world of the St David's Peninsula may be made here in a simulated cave system, complete with a shipwreck. More than 60 species of sea creature may be seen. Ship models, finds from local wrecks, items from the oil and gas industry and diving and rescue equipment are also on view.
Mar-Oct, daily. Adm charge. Refreshments. Shop. P *Toilets.* ♿ *Tel St David's (0437) 721665.*

PILGRIMAGE AND GRACE *Pilgrims have visited St David's for a thousand years. The gracefully vaulted ceiling (left) is in the tower of St David's Cathedral (below), where the tombs of the famous include that of Edmund Tudor, father of Henry VII.*

MUSEUM OF THE WELSH WOOLLEN INDUSTRY
Off A484, 4½ miles east of Newcastle Emlyn (Cb)

At the turn of the century, the Teifi Valley was Wales's chief textile-producing area. This museum is housed in the old water-powered and later gas engine-driven Cambrian Mills, established around 1900 in Drefach Felindre.

The growth of the Welsh woollen industry from the Middle Ages is recalled through old machinery and handtools, photographs and documents. Demonstrations are given of hand-carding and spinning, and hand and power-loom weaving. Visitors can see present-day production methods at Melin Teifi, the working mill incorporated in the museum, and a factory trail guides visitors around the sites.
Apr-Sept, Mon-Sat; winter, Mon-Fri. Free entry. Refreshments. Shop. P *(limited). Toilets.* ♿ *Tel Felindre (0559) 370929.*

NANT EOS
On A4120, 3 miles south-east of Aberystwyth (Cc)

This Georgian mansion completed in 1739 stands in spacious grounds, surrounded by green pastures and low hills. After long neglect, Nant Eos is being restored; it is noted for its magnificent music room, with an Italian marble fireplace and a lovely rococo plaster ceiling.
All year, daily. Adm charge. Refreshments. Shop. P *Toilets.* ♿ *(part). Tel Aberystwyth (0970) 617756.*

NATIONAL MUSEUM OF GYPSY CARAVANS, ROMANY CRAFTS AND LORE
Commons Road, Pembroke (Ba)

This enchanting collection of gypsy memorabilia ranges from cooking utensils to the colourfully decorated horse-drawn caravans in which gypsies lived and travelled. The museum also covers the history of gypsies and the Romany lifestyle.
Easter-Sept, Sun-Fri. Adm charge. Shop. P ♿ *Tel Pembroke (0646) 681308.*

PEMBREY COUNTRY PARK
Off A484, 6 miles west of Llanelli (Ca)

Pine forests and grassland lead down to dunes and sands beside Carmarthen Bay. The beach has good fishing and swimming and magnificent views to the Gower. There are bridleways, nature trails, picnic and barbecue areas, a dry ski slope, a bird hide, and a narrow-gauge railway.
All year, daily.

PEMBROKE CASTLE
Off B4320, just west of the town (Ba)

Once past the Great Gatehouse of Pembroke Castle, visitors face a large expanse of grass dominated by a massive round tower. This Great Keep, 100ft high, and Norman Hall stand within the inner ward, a defended area at the tip of a promontory jutting into the Pembroke River. The entire castle is contained by well-preserved walls defended by stout towers. There are more fortifications outside, for the town walls were a 13th-century extension of the castle defences.

The present castle dates mainly from the late

12th and 13th centuries. In 1457 Henry Tudor, who defeated Richard III to become Henry VII, was born in the tower named after him.
All year, daily. Adm charge. Shop. Toilets. ♿ Tel Pembroke (0646) 681510.

ST DAVID'S CATHEDRAL

On A487, in city centre (Aa)

The cathedral lies in a grassy hollow, its square tower below the roof level of nearby cottages, but is suddenly revealed in all its glory as visitors pass through the ancient gatehouse. St David's stands on the site of a small monastic community founded in the mid-6th century by Dewi Sant, St David, the missionary-monk who became Wales's patron saint. His base became an influential religious house and shrine, two pilgrimages to St David's equalling one to Rome.

The present building was begun soon after 1178. Restoration and improvements, especially in the 13th century, produced a magnificent building, predominantly Decorated Gothic in style. Behind the mellow, purple-hued stone exterior are many glories, including an ornately carved 16th-century oak ceiling of supreme craftsmanship in the original Norman nave.

The cathedral's neighbour in the walled close is the Bishop's Palace. This is now a shell-like ruin, but in the early 16th century it was a grand and desirable residence. Fine rows of arcaded parapets run along the main wings, and there is much decorative stonework.
Cathedral: All year, daily. Free entry. Shop. P Toilets. ♿ Tel St David's (0437) 720456. Palace: Cadw. All year, daily. Adm charge. Shop. Toilets ♿ (part). Tel (0437) 720517.

SCOLTON MANOR MUSEUM

On B4329, 5½ miles north-east of Haverfordwest (Ba)

A well-proportioned late Georgian mansion looks out across an attractive country park. Rooms decorated and furnished in mid-19th century style contain displays relating to costume, photography and medicine and to the house and its owners. In the former stables, the skills of the smith, wheelwright and cobbler are recalled by collections of tools and equipment. In the walled garden an imaginary Pembrokeshire village from bygone times is being created.

Displays in the Countryside Centre, which adjoins the manor, provide an introduction to the surrounding country park.
Museum: May-Sept, Tues-Sun. Park: All year, Tues-Sun. Adm charge. Refreshments. Shops. P Toilets. ♿ Tel Clarbeston (043 782) 328 (museum); 457 (park).

SOLVA NECTARIUM

On A487, 2½ miles east of St David's (Aa)

The owners of this butterfly farm coined their own word for it: 'nectarium' appeared in no dictionary before this establishment opened in the 1980s. A hot, humid 'tropical forest' environment contains butterflies from many parts of the world, including the rain forests of India, Malaysia and the Amazon.
Easter-Sept, daily. Adm charge. Refreshments. Shop. P (limited). Toilets. Tel St David's (0437) 721323.

PLEASURE HAVEN *The remains of Tenby Castle crown the site of a Welsh predecessor, whose name meant 'Little Fort of the Fish'. Both guarded the harbour below – now used mainly by pleasure craft.*

STRATA FLORIDA ABBEY

Off B4343, 14½ miles south-east of Aberystwyth (Db)

A boldly decorated Norman archway frames a tranquil scene at this grey ruin, tucked away in the foothills of the Cambrian Mountains. The remains are sufficient to evoke images of the abbey in its medieval heyday, when it was the 'Westminster Abbey of Wales'; several members of Welsh royal houses are buried there,

The abbey of Strata Florida – or Ystrad-fflur, 'Plain of Flowers' – was founded for Cistercians in 1164. Despite its remoteness, it suffered in the Welsh wars of the Middle Ages, but its wealth kept it going until the Dissolution.
Cadw. Mid Mar-mid Oct, daily. Adm charge. P Tel Cardiff (0222) 465511.

TENBY CASTLE

Off A478, just south of harbour (Ba)

The remains of Tenby Castle, begun in the 12th century, stand on a headland jutting into Carmarthen Bay. Below, rows of fine Georgian and Regency buildings overlook the harbour. The town walls are the most complete in South Wales, with one gate and six towers surviving.

The town's medieval and seafaring past both feature in Tenby Museum on Castle Hill, and seafaring days are also recalled in the Tudor Merchant's House in Quay Hill.
Castle: All year, daily. Free entry. Museum: Apr-Oct, daily; Nov-Mar, Mon-Sat pm. Adm charge. Shop. Toilets. Tel Tenby (0834) 2809. Merchant's House: NT. Easter-Sept, Mon-Fri, Sun pm. Adm charge. Tel (0834) 2279.

VALE OF RHEIDOL RAILWAY

From Aberystwyth station (Cc)

One of the 'Great Little Trains of Wales', the steam-powered Vale of Rheidol Railway runs from Aberystwyth to Devil's Bridge, 12 miles and 1 hour away, where the River Mynach plunges 300ft to join the Rheidol below. The line's three sturdy locomotives were built around 1921 and are more than 8ft wide – yet they work a narrow-gauge track with rails only 1ft 11½in apart, hauling carriages up steep inclines cut into the valley's southern hillside.

At Capel Bangor a minor road forks off the A44 to pass the Cwm Rheidol Reservoir, part of the vast Rheidol hydro-electric scheme. Just above the 700ft long Cwm Rheidol Dam, a reception centre marks the start of the Cwm Rheidol Nature Trail, a 2½ mile walk circling the reservoir. The trail also passes the power station, which has an information centre; guided tours are available.
Railway: Mid Apr-Oct, daily. Refreshments. Shop. P Toilets. Tel Aberystwyth (0970) 612378. Mynach Falls and Nature Trail: All year, daily. Adm charge. Refreshments. Shop. P Toilets. Tel Ponterwyd (097 085) 233. Power Station: Easter-Sept, daily; Oct pm daily. Adm charge. Refreshments. Shop. P Toilets. ♿ Tel Capel Bangor (097 084) 667.

COUNTY CALENDAR

June (mid-month). Saundersfoot: Edwardian Week.

July (late). Fishguard: Music Festival. Aberystwyth: Summer Music Festival.

August (mid-month). Carmarthen: United Counties Show. Haverfordwest: Pembrokeshire Show.

August (late). Cilgerran: Coracle Races.

Tourist information: Aberystwyth (0970) 612125; Cardigan (0239) 613230 (summer). Tenby (0834) 2402.

THE GLAMORGANS

FAIRY-TALE CASTLES AND INDUSTRIAL RELICS AMONG THE VALLEYS

High peaks, forests, lakes, plunging waterfalls and lovely valleys are among the natural attractions of South Wales which can be viewed with little effort from the trains of the Brecon Mountain Railway or from easy walks in the Afan Argoed Country Park and at Aberdulais Falls. Man-made wonders include ancient castles such as Caerphilly and Oystermouth and latter-day imitators such as Castell Coch and Cardiff Castle.

South Wales rural life is the theme of the Gower Farm Museum, on the Gower peninsula, renowned for its spectacular coastal scenery, while the mining and heavy industry for which Glamorgan has always been noted are explained at Afan Argoed and at Cyfarthfa Castle. Most aspects of South Wales life are covered in the national capital, Cardiff, with an Industrial and Maritime Museum in the old docklands and a celebrated Folk Museum at St Fagans.

ABERDULAIS FALLS

On A465, 3 miles north-east of Neath (Cb)

The force of the falls on the River Dulais as they thunder through a shady, boulder-strewn ravine makes an impressive spectacle. As early as 1584 the power of the falls was harnessed by water wheel to drive the bellows of a copper smelting works, the start of more than 300 years' industrial use of the site.

Although only a stone's throw away from a busy main road the site is secluded and peaceful. The old buildings are being restored and footpaths laid, and a visitor centre tells the story of the area's industrial past. Just across the road is the Aberdulais Basin, the meeting point of two canals which once carried coal and iron. The disused basin, now landscaped, is a pleasant place for a picnic or a towpath walk.

NT. All year, daily. Adm charge. Shop. ♿ *Tel Neath (0639) 56674.*

AFAN ARGOED COUNTRY PARK

On A4107, 6 miles north-east of Port Talbot (Cb)

This is a country park with a view, for it straddles the narrow, wooded Cwm Afan, a valley known locally as 'Little Switzerland'. This scenic vale was the site of industrial exploitation from the 17th century, though today the mine tips are grassed over and the mines and metal works themselves have all but disappeared.

Much of the park is on Forestry Commission land, where the trees are mainly conifers. But there are woods of oak and birch, open moorlands and streams which tumble down stony valleys. Iron Age hill-forts and settlements can be seen among the hill farms of the park and its surrounds, where sheep have been raised for more than 2000 years.

The richest wildlife occurs in the oakwoods of the Cwm yr Argoed, though foxes, herons and badgers may be seen throughout the park. Water and woodland birds abound, and fallow deer may be glimpsed as they feed in the early morning and evening. Five short, circular forest walks over relatively easy slopes start from the Countryside Centre.

The centre shares its building with the Welsh Miners' Museum. It is well placed, for there were more than 25 collieries in the Cwm Afan in 1912. The last, at Glyncorrwg, closed in 1970. The museum's exhibits forcefully communicate the harsh realities of 'coal getting' in South Wales. There is a simulated coalface, and a section devoted to child mineworkers. There are also records of mining disasters, including Britain's worst, when 439 men died at Senghenydd, in Taff Vale, in 1913. Domestic and social life in the pit communities is also featured in displays which include a re-creation of a miner's cottage interior.

Park: All year, daily. Countryside Centre and Museum: Apr-Oct, daily; Nov-Mar, Sat and Sun. Adm charge (museum). Refreshments. Shop. P *Toilets.* ♿ *Tel Cymer (0639) 850564.*

BRECON MOUNTAIN RAILWAY

Pant Station, Merthyr Tydfil (Dc)

A 2 mile narrow-gauge railway running from Pant to Pontsticill station, in the foothills of the Brecon Beacons National Park, follows the route of the old Newport and Brecon railway closed in 1964. Brecon Mountain's engines, resplendent in their polished maroon liveries, chuff northwards out of the Pant terminus. Soon, the track rounds a sharp hillside curve to reveal a magnificent panorama. On a clear day, the razor-sharp profile of Pen y Fan – at 2906ft the highest peak in South Wales – dominates the horizon. Below are open hillsides, coniferous forest and Pontsticill Reservoir.

The narrow-gauge locomotives have been brought from many parts of the world – East and West Germany, Spain, South Africa – and were all built between 1894 and 1936. The carriages have been constructed from the frames of wagons last used by the South African Railways. The line at present ends at the halt beside the Pontsticill Reservoir which is a good base from which to explore the southern slopes of the national park. A 5 mile footpath encircles the water.

Summer, daily. Fares. Refreshments. Shop. P Toilets. ♿ Tel Merthyr Tydfil (0685) 4854.

CAERPHILLY CASTLE

Off A469, in town centre (Db)

Right at the centre of an unassuming, unpretentious town stands one of the Western world's great castles. After restoration, its massive grey-green walls and towers stand to their full height, its water defences are filled, and it looks as formidable as it did 700 years ago.

The castle was largely the work of Gilbert de Clare, a Norman lord under threat from the Welsh prince Llywelyn ap Gruffudd. Llywelyn destroyed Clare's first castle, begun in 1268, but after more strife, Clare managed to complete another fortress by 1283. His castle occupies a 30 acre site, and in area it is the second largest British castle after Dover.

Caerphilly's concentric inner and outer walls surround a central strongpoint. All is ringed by a sophisticated system of water defences – a series of lakes. Within the well-protected inner ward, the most striking feature is the Great Hall. Also conspicuous is one ruined tower which manages to remain upright while out-leaning the famous Tower of Pisa; it has been leaning since Cromwell's troops tried to blow it up with gunpowder during the Civil War (1642-8).

Cadw. All year, daily, exc Sun am mid Oct-mid Mar. Adm charge. Toilets. ♿ Tel Caerphilly (0222) 883143.

CARDIFF CASTLE

On A4161 in city centre (Ea)

The decorative embellishments and ornate clock tower of Cardiff Castle are obviously of Victorian origin. But the castle is in fact a three-in-one historic site, part Roman fort, part medieval stronghold, part 19th-century mansion.

Sections of Roman wall can still be seen in the outer wall, and are part of the third Roman fort on the site which was built around AD 250 and covered 8 acres. Beyond the gatehouse, the castle grounds are watched over by the sturdy shell of a mid-12th-century keep on its steep mound. A new castle was begun in the following century, when the Black Tower was built. Additions and restorations were made until, by the mid-19th century, the building was more mansion than castle.

In the 1860s came a glorious transformation, wrought by the eccentric genius of architect William Burges and the wealth of the 3rd Marquess of Bute. The marquess, owner of Cardiff's booming docklands and reputedly the richest man in the world, poured some of his fortune into turning the castle into a romantic re-creation of the Middle Ages. Its lavish wealth of detail and flamboyant decor are regarded as stunning by some, excessive by others. The Arab Room, a mock Moorish extravaganza, has a gilded ceiling, cedarwood cupboards and a chimneypiece of white alabaster inset with lapis lazuli. The lofty Banqueting Hall has a gold-embellished timber-vaulted ceiling and fine murals. 'Medieval' banquets are held in the castle, which also houses the Welch Regiment Museum and The Queen's Dragoon Guards Regimental Museum.

The National Museum of Wales, near the castle, contains exhibits on a wide range of themes including geology, archaeology and natural history, and a splendid art collection. There is also an industrial section. The Welsh Industrial and Maritime Museum in Bute Street displays huge steam engines which powered the coal mines, iron and steel works and tinplate mills, all restored to working order.

Castle: All year, daily (Guards Museum, Mar-Oct). Adm charge. Refreshments. Shop. Toilets. Tel Cardiff (0222) 822083. National Museum: All year, Tues-Sat; Sun pm. Free entry. Refreshments. Shop. P Toilets. ♿ Tel (0222) 397951. Industrial and Maritime Museum: All year, Tues-Sat; Sun pm. Free entry. Refreshments. Shop. P Toilets. ♿ Tel (0222) 481919.

LASTING IMPRESSION *Renoir's* A Parisian Girl *(right) is among the French Impressionist paintings in the National Museum of Wales in Cardiff. A more crowded background was favoured by William Burges in his Summer Smoking Room in Cardiff Castle (below), which has a silver, copper and brass Earth inlaid in its floor and a chandelier representing the Sun.*

THE LONG VIEW *The water lily canal leads the eye across the gracious lawns of Dyffryn Gardens to the mansion at their heart. The fountain in the centre of the canal is an oriental bronze, the Dragon Bowl.*

CASTELL COCH

Off A470, 5 miles north-west of Cardiff (Db)

A trio of towers peeping out above the trees in a steep-sided wooded gorge is the first view of this fairy-tale castle. The towers are circular, with conical roofs, and built in the rosy stone which gives the castle its name, meaning 'Red Castle'.

There is more fairy tale inside, beyond the drawbridge. The rooms surrounding the small courtyard are elaborately decorated. The walls and ceiling of the drawing room, for example, are covered with fantastic murals depicting, among other themes, Aesop's Fables; it is possible to pick out a frog holding a bottle of medicine for the 'frog' in his throat.

THREE FATES *Carved figures of the goddesses believed by the Greeks to control man's destiny adorn the overmantel of Castell Coch's drawing room. The heads below them represent the Three Ages of Man.*

Though it stands on a rocky ledge once occupied by a genuine medieval stronghold, Castell Coch is a Victorian whimsy, the work of the eccentric genius William Burges, who designed it for his wealthy, landowning client, the Marquess of Bute. Begun in 1875, Castell Coch is a companion piece to the even more outrageously decorative Cardiff Castle. Burges's fertile imagination even provided a mock dungeon, which featured in BBC TV's production of *The Prisoner of Zenda* in 1984.

Cadw. All year, daily, exc Sun am Oct-Mar. Adm charge. P *Toilets. Tel Cardiff (0222) 810101.*

CEFN COED COLLIERY MUSEUM

On A4109, 5 miles north of Neath (Cb)

The next best thing to an authentic underground tour of a mine is on offer here, for the museum – next to Blaenant Colliery, a working mine – has a realistic underground mining gallery through which visitors can walk. The rest of the museum occupies the surface buildings of the Cefn Coed pit, which closed in 1968. Once the deepest anthracite mine in the world, it reached a depth of 2262ft. Among the pit machinery preserved is a massive winding engine.

Apr-Oct, daily. Adm charge. Shop. P *Toilets.* ♿ *Tel Crynant (0639) 750556.*

CYFARTHFA CASTLE MUSEUM

Off A470, 1 mile north of Merthyr Tydfil (Dc)

Grand, baronial Cyfarthfa Castle is a monument to the wealth of 19th-century industrial South Wales. It stands in its own park above a vanished kingdom – the Cyfarthfa Iron Works, once ruled by the ironmaster William Crawshay. The castellated, greystone mansion in mock-medieval style which Crawshay built in the 1820s is today partially open as a museum and art gallery.

Paintings on show include an arresting canvas that depicts the Merthyr of old, its night sky aglow with the white heat of its iron foundries. Fine collections of furniture, including Welsh country furniture, porcelain, silver and glass are also displayed. One section traces Merthyr's role as the iron and steel 'capital of the world' in the early 19th century, when it was the largest town in Wales. There are also models of Richard Trevithick's steam locomotive, which ran along the Taff valley from Abercynon to Pen-y-Darren just north of Merthyr in 1804 – a full 20 years before Stephenson's famous *Rocket*.

For a glimpse of the other face of the Industrial Revolution, compare the grandeur of Cyfarthfa Castle with the insanitary terrace of workers' cottages built by Crawshay around the same time at nearby Chapel Row beside the Glamorganshire Canal. One has been turned into a museum commemorating the prolific Welsh composer Dr Joseph Parry, who was born there in 1841. Many of his 400 or so hymn tunes and his splendid Te Deum are still used today.

Castle: All year, Mon-Sat; also Sun pm. Adm charge. Shop. P *Toilets (in park).* ♿ *Tel Merthyr Tydfil (0685) 3112. Museum: All year, Mon-Fri am. Free entry.* P *(limited). Tel (0685) 73117.*

DYFFRYN GARDENS

Off A48, 6 miles south-west of Cardiff (Da)

These landscaped gardens, a mixture of the formal and informal, bring a blaze of colour to the green pastures of the Vale of Glamorgan. Within Dyffryn's 50 acres there are rare plants, exotics from the Orient, an arboretum, beautiful walks and picnic sites. The seasonal bedding displays, rose garden, herbaceous borders, ponds and individually designed smaller gardens, such as the Roman garden, are among the highlights. Dyffryn is also famous for its statuary, and hot houses filled with tropical and subtropical species such as orchids, palms and cacti. Dyffryn House, a grand late 19th-century mansion is now a conference centre.

Late Mar-late May, pm daily; end May-end Aug, daily; end Aug-late Sept, pm daily; Oct, Sat and Sun pm. Free entry in winter. Refreshments. Shop. P *Toilets.* ♿ *Tel Cardiff (0222) 593328.*

GLAMORGAN NATURE CENTRE

Off B4281, 3 miles north-west of Bridgend (Cb)

Moorhens breed around Park Pond, the tranquil, willow-fringed pool beside the centre. The willows are home to tits and finches, and visiting snipe are often seen in the surrounding marsh and meadow. The pond lies in the Glamorgan Wildlife Trust's Cwm Risca Reserve – an area of mainly oak woodland. The centre is the trust's headquarters, and its displays cover not only the reserve, but the wildlife of the three Glamorgans.

All year, Mon-Fri am. Free entry. Shop. P *Toilets.* ♿ *Tel Bridgend (0656) 724100.*

GOWER FARM MUSEUM

Off A4118, 12 miles west of Swansea (Ab)

Old agricultural tools, and – more fascinating still – personal details of a long-established farming family, paint an informative picture of life on

WELSH FOLK LIFE AT ST FAGANS

The stars of the unusual Welsh Folk Museum are its open-air exhibits – 30 rural buildings of bygone days brought from all over Wales and meticulously re-erected in the 100 acre park of St Fagans Castle, near Cardiff. A complex of modern museum galleries completes the scene.

Kennixton farm from the Gower catches the eye with vibrant pillar-box red walls beneath its thatch. It dates from about 1630 and contains furniture of the period. The back kitchen is complete with butter churn and butter-working table. Capel Pen-rhiw, a small, severely functional chapel building from west Wales, dates from about 1770, during the early days of Welsh Nonconformism: the preacher must have had a tight squeeze to fit into its tiny pulpit. Maestir School served a village near Lampeter from 1880 to 1916. Youngsters of five to 14 years were taught in its single classroom, where the master's desk looms above those of his pupils.

St Fagans Castle is an elegant mansion built around 1580 to the typical Elizabethan E-plan. Oak panelling and tapestries are the main decorative features inside, and each room is a reminder of the comfortable, privileged way of life. The Great Chamber was the main reception room, and its 17th-century furniture includes a fine gilt cabinet. The kitchen has two large fireplaces, one with a dog-driven spit. The fishponds in the grounds are once more stocked with carp, bream and tench, as in the 17th century. Ancient metal-wheeled tractors, now restored, stand next to old threshing and haymaking machines in the Agricultural Gallery. In the Costume Gallery, tableaux of the effervescent 1920s and of sober Victorian society make a striking contrast. The Gallery of Material Culture covers domestic, social and cultural life in rural Wales, with collections ranging from love spoons and harps to swords and Welsh dressers.

Off A48, 4 miles west of Cardiff city centre (Da). Apr-Oct, daily; Nov-Mar, daily exc Sun. Adm charge. Refreshments. Shop. P *Toilets.* ♿ *Tel Cardiff (0222) 569441.*

BARREL CRAFT *A cooper can be watched at his work in the coach house at St Fagans, together with a woodturner. Other craftsmen show their skills in the corn mill, the smithy, the saddler's shop, the bakehouse and the woollen mill, and many of the goods they make are on sale.*

DUAL PURPOSE *The farmer and his family used this kitchen and a living room and two bedrooms at one end of the Cilewent long house; their cattle occupied the other end. The building once stood on the Powys moors.*

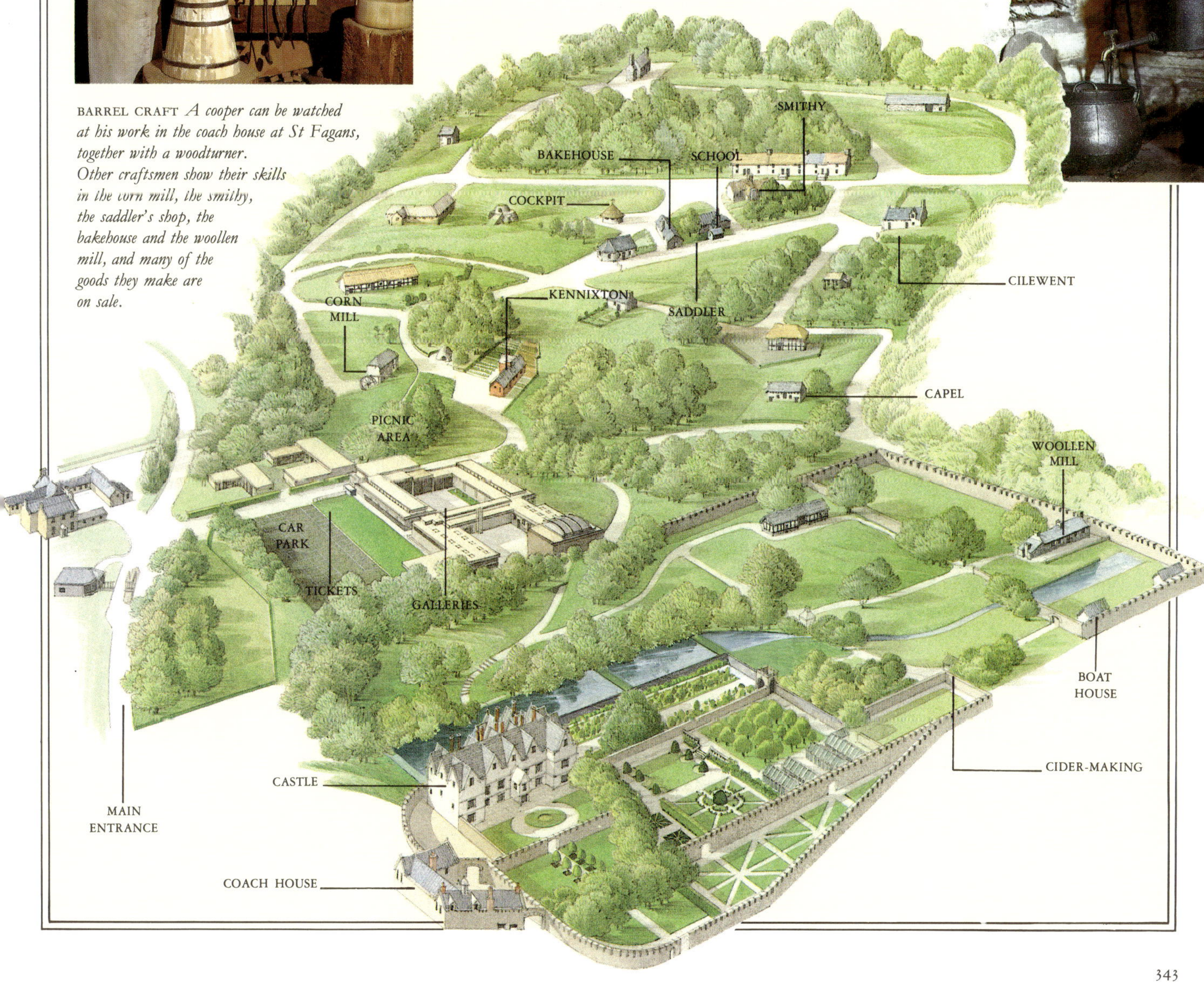

the Gower peninsula before the arrival of mechanisation and tourism. The museum at Lake Farm near Llanddewi centres around the Watter family, whose documents, photographs, household goods and farming implements cover a 100 year span.

It is also possible to compare today with yesterday, for the museum is the starting point of a farm trail which introduces visitors to today's farming methods. Young visitors may handle some of the farm animals.

All year, daily. Adm charge. Refreshments. Shop. 🅿 *Toilets.* ♿ *Tel Gower (0792) 391195.*

KENFIG POOL AND DUNES

Off B4283, 2½ miles north of Porthcawl (Ca)

This wilderness beside Swansea Bay, comprising some 1000 acres of dunes and a 70 acre freshwater lake fed by underwater springs, has an exceptional range of flowering plants – more than 550 species have been recorded.

Sedge, reed and willow warblers breed around the pool, where mute swans, great crested grebes, coots, tufted ducks and mallards live. Winter brings pochards, teal and Bewick's and whooper swans, which can be seen from a hide on the south shore. Foxes, hares, harvest mice and water shrews may be seen. The reserve centre has permanent displays about Kenfig wildlife.

Part NCC. All year, daily. Free entry. Shop (weekends). 🅿 *Toilets.* ♿ *Tel Porthcawl (0656) 743386.*

TUFTED DIVER *The tufted duck, named after its purplish head feathers, thrives on Kenfig Pool. Its ducklings swim within hours of hatching.*

LLANDAFF CATHEDRAL

Off A4119, 2 miles north-west of Cardiff (Da)

Unlike most cathedrals, this lofty building does not tower above the rooftops but hides in a deep, shady hollow, its tall spire and solid tower rising barely higher than road level. Externally, it has the pure lines of a traditional place of worship. Within, it contains a modernistic statue of Christ in Majesty by the sculptor Sir Jacob Epstein. Llandaff also boasts ancient features, expressing practically every style of medieval ecclesiastical architecture. The west front of 1220 – excluding the tower and spire – is one of the finest pieces of medieval stonework in Wales.

Llandaff was originally a religious settlement founded by the 6th-century monastic leader St Teilo. The present building was started in Norman times and was complete by 1500. Later Llandaff suffered neglect, even serving as an ale house for Parliamentarian troops in the Civil War, a cattle pen and a post office. Rebuilding in classical style commenced in the 18th century, but 100 years later, work to restore the cathedral's medieval splendour began.

In 1941 the cathedral was severely damaged by a German landmine. Once again, major rebuilding took place. By 1958, Llandaff was restored to its former glory – with two striking additions: the Welch Regiment Chapel and, dominating the cathedral's interior, Epstein's statue. This severe sculpture in unpolished aluminium graces the side of the organ case, which stands on a massive parabolic arch of reinforced concrete across the nave.

All year, daily.

PASSION KILLER *Grotesque medieval gargoyles adorn the outside of Llandaff Cathedral. The hideous beasts were intended to remind those entering God's house that they must renounce all evil passions and vices.*

MARGAM COUNTRY PARK

On A48, 4 miles south-east of Port Talbot (Cb)

Only a stone's throw from the busy M4, this tranquil 850 acre park contains a remarkable combination of man-made and natural treasures. Below the Iron Age hill-fort of Mynyddy Castell are the remains of a Cistercian monastery founded in the 12th century. The abbey church was restored in the 19th century, and has superb stained glass, including windows by William Morris. Across the churchyard, the Margam Stones Museum contains locally found inscribed stones and Christian crosses dating from the 5th to 11th centuries.

After the dissolution of the abbey in 1536, Sir Rice Mansel, a local landowner, turned the remainder of the abbey into a fine country house. In 1786 Thomas Mansel Talbot began the glory of Margam – the magnificent 327ft long Orangery, part of which now houses exhibitions. His son built the castellated Gothic mansion known as 'The Castle' around 1835. This too is now ruined but buildings around its courtyard contain a visitor centre and the Coach House Theatre which shows films about the estate and its wildlife.

The bracken-covered and wooded Craig y Lodge and Ton Mawr uplands in the north of the park, with waymarked trails and walks, overlook the landscaped parkland and gardens of the south. More than 40 sculptures adorn the park, and the maze beside the kitchen gardens covers an acre; its 3250 conifers were planted in 1982.

Park: All year, daily exc Mon and Tues Oct-Mar. Adm charge. Refreshments. Shop. 🅿 *Toilets.* ♿ *Tel Port Talbot (0639) 881635. Abbey: All year, daily. Free entry. Tel (0639) 891067. Museum: Cadw. Easter-Sept, daily. Adm charge.* 🅿 ♿ *Tel Kenfig Hill (0656) 742678.*

OXWICH NATIONAL NATURE RESERVE

Off A4118, 11 miles south-west of Swansea (Ab)

The reserve beside one of Gower's many pretty crescent-shaped sandy bays includes not only shoreline but also dunes, salt and freshwater marsh and woodlands. It is well served by footpaths, boardwalks and viewing hides. More than 600 species of flowering plant, 160 bird species and 34 butterfly species have been recorded there. The reserve centre offers advice, leaflets and maps, and sometimes displays, but visitors should ring first to check its opening times. There are regular guided walks in summer.

NCC. All year, daily. Free entry. 🅿 *Toilets.* ♿ *(centre only). Tel Gower (0792) 390320.*

OYSTERMOUTH CASTLE

On A4067, 4½ miles south-west of Swansea (Bb)

Even the secluded Gower did not escape the medieval wars between the Welsh and English. This castle – the stronghold of the Braose family, Norman Lords of Gower – must have been a tempting prize to the Welsh. They burnt the original wooden castle in the 1180s, and sacked its stone replacement a century later. Even so, its sturdy walls of local pale grey limestone still stand to their original height. The ruined gatehouse, chapel and great hall top a grassy mound above the pretty sailing centre of The Mumbles. They command wide views over Swansea Bay and Mumbles Head.

Apr-Sept, daily. Adm charge. 🅿 *Tel Swansea (0792) 50821, ext 2815.*

PENSCYNOR WILDLIFE PARK

Off A4230, 3 miles north of Neath (Cb)

Hundred of birds and animals brought from all over the world live in a park occupying 16 acres of a wooded hillside. The chimpanzees perform for the public, the penguins are friendly and the deer will eat from visitors' hands. Tropical birds feed in the warmth of their own house, and South American monkeys have their own woodland quarters. There is an aquarium, and trout ponds. A chairlift takes visitors to the top of an Alpine bobsleigh ride, which swoops down the hillside.

All year, daily. Adm charge. Refreshments. Shop. 🅿 *Toilets.* ♿ *Tel Neath (0639) 2189.*

PONTYPRIDD HISTORICAL AND CULTURAL CENTRE

Bridge Street, off A470 in town centre (Db)

Many old chapels in the South Wales valleys now present a neglected face. Not so the Tabernacl in Pontypridd, for this fine Welsh Baptist chapel, built in 1861 and closed as a place of worship some 120 years later, has been given a new lease of life as a custodian of the past. The interior has been converted into display and gallery areas, and archive material on the Glamorganshire Canal and misty photographs of old Pontypridd paint a picture of the place as it was in the 18th and 19th centuries, when coal was king.

All year, Tues-Sat and Bank Hol. Adm charge. Refreshments (summer). Shop. Toilets. ♿ *Tel Pontypridd (0443) 402077.*

SEAWATCH CENTRE

Off B4265, 2¼ miles south-east of Llantwit Major (Da)

This is a marvellous place from which to observe the ships that pass along the busy Bristol Channel. The tidal range reaches 45ft – the second largest in the world, after the Bay of Fundy in Canada. The centre is housed in a converted coastguard station. From a 'ship's bridge' visitors can listen to ships' radio messages and plot their courses on Admiralty charts, using radar. They can also use the centre's meteorological instruments to forecast the weather or state of the sea. There is a 'Rescue at Sea' display, and the centre is an ideal spot for birdwatching.

All year, daily. Free entry. 🅿 *Toilets. Tel Southerndown (0656) 880157.*

SWANSEA MARITIME MUSEUM

Off Victoria Road, in city centre (Bb)

The renovation of Swansea's South Dock, which ceased industrial operation in the 1920s, renews Swansea's links with the sea. Its centrepiece is a 600 berth marina. One of the original wharf buildings has been converted into a Maritime and Industrial Museum with exhibits recalling the city's great seafaring days. A collection of veteran vehicles and locomotives includes a cab of a train of the Mumbles Railway, which ran along the seafront from 1804 to 1960.

Other sections of the museum relate to manufacturing and agriculture. The most unusual exhibit is a complete set of weaving machinery, rescued from a local mill which was closing and now in use again producing high-quality wool, blankets and rugs.

The Swansea Museum, in Victoria Road, was built in the late 1830s in heroic neoclassical style. Of special interest among the diverse exhibits are fine collections of Swansea porcelain and of Nantgarw pottery. Another section recalls the sad fate of Petty Officer Edgar Evans (from nearby Gower) who perished on Scott's ill-fated South Polar expedition in 1912.

The stumpy remains of Swansea's Old Castle date from the 13th century. The ruined New Castle, built in the following century, towers above the Strand – as it once dominated both

BRAVE LITTLE SHIPS *The lightship* Canning *and the former Mumbles lifeboat* William Gaunt *are among the outdoor exhibits at Swansea Maritime Museum which visitors may board in summer. The ewer and plate in Swansea Museum were made in the 1850s at Landore, now a north-eastern suburb of the city.*

town and harbour. Cromwell's troops destroyed most of the castle in 1647, during the Civil War. In its time, it served several purposes, including Norman mint, medieval bishop's palace and Victorian debtors' prison.

Maritime and Industrial Museum: All year, daily. Free entry. Shop. Toilets. ♿ *Tel Swansea (0792) 50351. Swansea Museum: All year, Tues-Sat. Adm charge. Shop.* 🅿 *(limited). Toilets. Tel (0792) 53763. Castle: Cadw. All year, daily. Tel (0792) 468321.*

WALES AIRCRAFT MUSEUM

Off A4226, 9½ miles south-west of Cardiff (Da)

Some of the aircraft parked beside Cardiff (Wales) Airport's terminal building are not about to fly anywhere – they are exhibits of the Wales Aircraft Museum. More than 30 propeller and jet aircraft and helicopters are on display including naval planes, Vulcan and Canberra bombers, a Hawker Hunter fighter and US Airforce jets. Visitors can sit in the cockpit of a Seahawk jet, or take refreshments inside an old Viscount airliner.

June-Aug, daily; Sept-May, Sat and Sun pm. Adm charge. Refreshments. Shop. 🅿 *(at airport). Tel Cardiff (0222) 757767.*

WELSH HAWKING CENTRE AND WILDLIFE PARK

On A4226, 8 miles south-west of Cardiff (Da)

Flying demonstrations by birds of prey are a major attraction here. They take place every afternoon weather permitting and merlins, buzzards, kestrels, owls and eagles are all flown free. More than 200 birds of prey are kept, some in breeding aviaries, others in covered areas or in the open. Breeding is an important part of the work, and the centre also cares for injured birds. There is a conservation area, explored by a waymarked nature trail.

All year, daily. Adm charge. Refreshments. Shop. 🅿 *Toilets.* ♿ *Tel Barry (0446) 734687.*

COUNTY CALENDAR

May (1st week). St Fagans: Old May Day Fair.

June (mid-month). Cardiff: Gwyl Ifan (Welsh folk dance festival). Port Talbot and Swansea: Margam Festival.

June (late). Pontypridd: Flower and Music Festival.

July (mid-month). Penarth: Jazz Festival. Cardiff: Welsh Proms.

August (late). Pontardawe: International Music Festival. The Mumbles: Swansea Bay Week.

September (mid-month-October). Swansea: Festival of Music and The Arts.

Tourist information: Cardiff (0222) 27281; Swansea (0792) 468321; Barry (0446) 747171 (summer); Caerphilly (0222) 851378 (summer).

GWENT

CASTLES, MONASTERIES AND ROMAN REMAINS BY THE WYE

The green, wooded valley of the Wye is one of the glories of Gwent, while the river itself forms a quiet-flowing frontier with England. Today's peaceful countryside is dotted with castles such as Abergavenny, Chepstow, Grosmont and Penhow which are monuments to years of strife between the Welsh and their Norman conqueror-barons. At Caerleon are the ruins of a Roman amphitheatre, where gladiators fought sword to sword and criminals were matched against savage beasts.

Not all of Gwent's ancient buildings were built for military purposes. Augustinian monks created Llanthony Priory, and Cistercian monks erected Tintern Abbey – both of which, though ruined, retain their beauty and grace. Other aspects of Gwent's history are commemorated in the Gwent Rural Life Museum at Usk, in the Model Farm Museum near Chepstow, and in The Valley Inheritance at Pontypool, where tourists can now explore an underground world once seen only by coal miners.

ABERGAVENNY CASTLE

Castle Street, Abergavenny (Bc)

One of William the Conqueror's barons pressed the local people into building the first motte-and-bailey castle in Abergavenny in 1090. On Christmas Day 1177 the castle was the scene of a terrible act of vengeance. The Norman lord of the castle, William de Braose, invited the Welsh Chieftain Sitsyllt – who had killed De Braose's uncle – and his followers to a banquet to mark a truce between them. After plying their unarmed guests with food and drink, the Normans massacred them as they sat at table.

Although the castle is now in ruins, an early 19th-century hunting lodge built within its walls is the unusual setting of Abergavenny Museum. The museum traces the history of the town from its origins as a Roman fort to the present day through lively displays of crafts, costume, industry and archaeology. Highlights include a complete saddler's shop and traditional Welsh kitchen, tools used in the industries of the area over the ages and examples of the products manufactured around Abergavenny.

All year, daily exc Sun, Nov-Feb. Adm charge. Shop. P *Tel Abergavenny (0873) 4282.*

BEAUFORT BIRD GARDENS

Off B4293, 5 miles north-west of Chepstow (Cb)

Beautifully situated at Devauden Green, on the edge of the Wye Valley, the gardens contain more than 300 birds in custom-built aviaries. The collection centres around some rare ornamental pheasants, including golden, silver and Lady Amherst's. Many of the 30 species of birds on show – such as the Himalayan monal – are listed as endangered species in their native lands; and among the more secure species are the Indian blue peafowl and the black-shouldered and all-white peafowls.

Children will be fascinated by the peacocks, parakeets, lovebirds, finches, budgerigars and varieties of doves, and by the large enclosure of rabbits and guinea pigs.

All year, daily. Adm charge. Refreshments. Shop. P *Toilets. Tel Wolvesnewton (029 15) 346.*

BIG PIT MINING MUSEUM

Off B4248, ½ mile west of Blaenavon (Bc)

Visitors to this 'living museum' are kitted out like working miners with safety helmets and lamps, and descend 300ft in a pit cage for a guided tour that gives a vivid impression of mining life. The Big Pit – so called because of the width of the shaft – opened in 1880, incorporating galleries already 70 years old, and closed only in 1980. Many of today's guides once worked in the colliery as miners, and so have a lively repertoire of first-hand memories. Warm clothing and sturdy shoes are recommended for the hour-long tours, which take visitors through narrow tunnels to the galleries where miners hacked out coal. Cut into the walls of the main tunnels at intervals are niches in which miners took shelter as lines of wagons filled with coal trundled past on tramlines to the pit shaft.

At the time the colliery closed nearly 80 pit ponies were still in service, and the tour includes a visit to the underground stables, where names such as Prince and Tiger can still be seen on the stalls.

Above ground there is plenty to see, too, including the pit baths, sawmill and forge, as well as the colliery workshops and the winding gear that lowers and raises the cage. The pithead railway, with its steam and diesel locomotives, is still in occasional use, and in the former baths complex there is an exhibition about the pit's history that includes a lifelike reconstruction of a miner's living room and backyard.

Only a few minutes from the Big Pit is Blaenavon Ironworks, opened in 1798 and remarkably well preserved. It was near here that Sidney Thomas, the works chemist, and his

cousin Percy Gilchrist perfected the method for removing phosphorus from iron ore that led to the wider use of the Bessemer process for making steel. The whole site can be seen from a viewing area, and there are guided tours of the blast furnaces, casting-houses and ironworkers' cottages.
Big Pit: Mar-Dec, daily. Adm charge. Refreshments. Shop. P *Toilets. Tel Blaenavon (0495) 790311. Ironworks: Apr-Sept, daily. Free entry (charge for tours).* P *Tel Pontypool (049 55) 52036.*

CAERLEON ROMAN FORTRESS

On B4236, in Caerleon (Cb)

The impressive remains of the amphitheatre, baths and barracks of the 1900-year-old fortress of Isca make Caerleon one of the most important Roman military sites in Europe. Established in AD 75, Isca was the headquarters of the 2nd Augustan Legion, one of the three regiments of front-line troops permanently stationed in Britain, the others being based at Chester and York.

Only discovered in 1964 and excavated during the past decade, the fortress's baths and exercise hall formed a leisure complex the size of a cathedral. Richly decorated with wall paintings, carvings and mosaics, they acted as the social centre of the fort, a place where soldiers could spend their off-duty hours playing board games.

The baths were also used by the women and children of the camp. Hair pins, jewellery, milk teeth and a richly inlaid copper strigil, or body scraper used for scraping off massage and bath oil, have been recovered from the drains. These and other finds are displayed at the spacious Legionary Museum in the High Street of Caerleon. At the site itself an exhibition using artists' reconstructions, recorded commentaries and computer graphics gives a lively impression of the baths in Roman times.

The most spectacular of the remains at Caerleon are those of the amphitheatre, similar in construction to a modern sports stadium and large enough to seat a large proportion of the garrison of 6000.

A Town Trail round Caerleon also takes in the Mynde, or mound, where according to legend King Arthur built a huge tower so that Queen Guinevere could see the hills of Somerset.

At Caerwent, 11 miles away, are the remains of Venta Silurum, the capital and main market town of Roman South Wales. Houses, shops and a temple, all laid out in traditional Roman grid pattern, have been excavated here, as well as a long section of the massive town walls.
Cadw. All year, daily. Adm charge. Shop. P ♿ *Tel Caerleon (0633) 422518 (fortress); 423134 (museum).*

CALDICOT CASTLE

Off A4245, 5 miles south-west of Chepstow (Cb)

This carefully restored medieval castle, surrounded by acres of attractive parkland, dates back to the 11th century, when it was built by the Normans to guard the road from Chepstow into South Wales. The keep was erected by Humphrey de Bohun, Earl of Hereford, in the 12th century, and soon afterwards he added the unusual De Bohun Gateway, based on a design

INTO THE ARENA *As many as 5000 spectators once crowded into the Roman amphitheatre at Caerleon to watch gladiatorial combat and animal baiting. The arena was also used as a parade ground for drill. The ivory mask (right), found at Caerleon, dates from the 2nd or 3rd century.*

brought back from the Holy Land by Crusaders.

The imposing gatehouse through which visitors enter was built by the youngest son of Edward III, Thomas Woodstock, who, after marrying ten-year-old Alianore de Bohun, transformed Caldicot into a luxurious royal residence. In 1397, jealous of Woodstock's power, his nephew Richard II arranged for his murder.

The castle now houses a museum which includes furniture, costumes, and items from one of Nelson's flagships, the *Foudroyant*.
Mar-Oct, daily. Adm charge. P *Toilets.* ♿ *(gardens). Tel Caldicot (0291) 420241.*

CHEPSTOW CASTLE

In centre of Chepstow (Db)

The long grey walls of this formidable fortress rise dramatically from the steep cliffs flanking the River Wye; on the opposite side, the castle is protected by a deep ravine. Chepstow was built by William FitzOsbern, a childhood friend of William the Conqueror who gave him the Earldom of Hereford – together with the task of pushing the Norman conquest into Wales. A later owner, Roger Bigod, one of Edward I's most powerful barons, built two Great Halls – one for his own household, the other for important visitors.

After the Civil War – during which it was twice besieged and captured – the castle was used as a prison, its longest-serving inmate being Henry Marten, who had been rash enough to sign Charles I's death warrant. Condemned for treason, he spent 12 years in the tower named after him.

Near the castle are the town's local history museum – whose displays include a fine collection of artists' views of the Wye Valley spanning 200 years – and the glass studio of Stuart Crystal where visitors can watch craftsmen gilding and engraving handmade crystal.

An enjoyable way of seeing some of the magnificent scenery of the Wye Valley is to follow part of the Lower Wye Valley Walk, which starts from the Chepstow Leisure Centre and runs for 54 miles up the river to Hereford.
Castle: Cadw. All year, daily. Adm charge. Shop. P *Toilets. Tel Chepstow (029 12) 4065. Museum: Mar-Oct, daily. Adm charge. Shop.* P *Toilets.* ♿ *Tel (029 12) 5981. Stuart Crystal: All year, daily. Free entry. Shop.* P *Toilets.* ♿ *Tel (029 12) 70135.*

STANDING FIRM *Some 600 years of military architecture are represented in Chepstow Castle, built by the Normans shortly after the Battle of Hastings. It is thought to be Britain's first stone castle, and was extended and added to up to the mid-17th century.*

CWMCARN FOREST DRIVE

On B4591, 8 miles north of Newport (Bb)

A 7 mile drive winding through dense woodland and over tree-clad mountainsides gives motorists the chance to enjoy the beauty of the Ebbw Forest from the comfort of their cars. However, it is worth leaving the car at one of the seven car parks to follow waymarked footpaths into the forest and climb to the Iron Age hill-fort at the top of Twmbarlwm, from which there are spectacular views of the Brecon Beacons and across the Bristol Channel to the Mendips.

The forest is home to dozens of species of woodland birds, and sometimes buzzards and kestrels can be seen soaring overhead. A visitor centre at the entrance to the drive has an exhibition about the forest, and nearby is the start of a nature trail that follows the course of a gently flowing stream.

Within easy reach of Cwmcarn are two ancient churches. St Tudor's, dating back to the 14th century but extensively restored in the 1820s, stands on the western slope of Mynyddislwyn, overlooking the Sirhowy Valley. In the churchyard is the so-called 'Drinkers and Gamblers' tombstone, decorated with what look like beer glasses and dominoes. The glasses are in fact chalices and the domino marks were left after the removal of a brass plate.

The 13th-century Church of St Sannan's in the tiny hamlet of Bedwellty also has an interesting churchyard, with an iron tombstone and the grave of an American slave who found her way to Bedwellty, where she died in 1875. The church is unusual in having two parallel naves separated by a remarkable arcade of five pointed arches supported by sturdy stump-like pillars.

Easter-Sept, daily. Adm charge. Refreshments. P *Toilets.* ♿ *Tel Newport (0633) 400205.*

FOURTEEN LOCKS CANAL CENTRE

Off B4591, 1 mile west of Newport (Bb)

With its 72 locks and an intricate network of channels, sluices, ponds and weirs, the Monmouthshire and Brecon Canal is an impressive example of the engineering skills of the Industrial Revolution. Dug in the 1790s by navvies using picks and shovels, the twin branches of the canal, each 11 miles long, transported coal, iron and other products to Newport for export or shipment to other parts of Britain.

The Canal Centre stands beside the top pond of the western arm of the canal, which joined Newport to Crumlin, at the start of a staircase of 14 locks. Nearby is the junction with the eastern arm of the canal, which runs to Pontnewynydd, near Pontypool. An exhibition traces the history of the canal and provides some fascinating facts and figures about the locks and water storage system. From the picnic area beside the Canal Centre there are two waymarked canalside walks, about 2 miles and 3 miles in length, and a half-mile trail around part of the 14-lock section.

Apr-Sept, daily exc Tues and Wed. Free entry. Shop. P *Toilets.* ♿ *Tel Newport (0633) 894802.*

GROSMONT CASTLE

Off B4347, 15 miles north-east of Abergavenny (Cd)

The tree-shadowed ruins of this robust castle stand – as its Norman name suggests – on a large hill overlooking the small village of Grosmont. One of the 'Three Castles of Gwent', with Skenfrith and White Castle, Grosmont was completely rebuilt in the 13th century by Hubert de Burgh, King John's all-powerful 'Justiciar' or chief officer of state. In the wars between the Welsh chieftain Owain Glyndwr and the young Prince Hal, later Henry V, the castle and neighbourhood were the scene of much fighting.

The impressive remains include substantial parts of the Great Hall and imposing south-west tower. An ornamented chimney rising from the block of princely apartments built by the Earls of Lancaster in the 14th century gives an idea of the castle's former decorative splendour.

Below the castle stands the village church, its large size recalling a time 500 years ago when Grosmont was the third largest town in Monmouthshire. Beneath the church wall lies the grave of Jack O'Kent, a wizard who figures prominently in local folktales. According to legend, the Devil swore that he would carry off the wizard's soul no matter whether he was buried inside or outside the church. To cheat the Devil, Jack was buried neither in nor out.

Cadw. All year, daily. Free entry. ♿

GWENT RURAL LIFE MUSEUM

On A472, at Usk (Cb)

Near the river in the small market town of Usk stands an ancient malt barn with a Victorian cottage built onto the back. Together the two buildings house a fascinating country life museum.

Inside the barn the visitor's eye is drawn to two brightly painted wagons and to the walls, on which are illustrated the four seasons of the countryman's year. Visitors can step inside a country kitchen, an old-fashioned laundry and a dairy with a variety of butter and cheese-making equipment. Inside the museum are all manner of intriguing utensils and paraphernalia – ranging from blacksmith's tools to horse ploughs, while outside in the yard is a splendid assortment of larger farm machines, such as vintage tractors and binders.

Usk lies astride the waymarked Usk Valley Walk, which offers magnificent views of the Brecon Beacons. The 25 mile walk starts at the Ship Inn in Caerleon and ends at Usk Bridge in Abergavenny. Walkers pausing to rest their feet at the pumping station near Great Estavarney farm are standing on the oldest rocks in Gwent, estimated to be 430 million years old.

Apr-Sept, daily exc Sat and Sun am; Mar and Oct, daily exc Sat; Nov-Feb, Mon-Fri. Adm charge. Shop. P *Toilets.* ♿ *Tel Usk (029 13) 3777.*

LLANTHONY PRIORY

Off A465, 13 miles north of Abergavenny (Bd)

The substantial remains of this monastic settlement are dominated by the square central tower of its church. The Augustinian monks who founded the building were driven out at the Dissolution of the Monasteries in 1538, and it had a succession of owners until 1807, when it came into the hands of the poet Walter Savage Landor. By then, one of its towers had been turned into a shooting box, in which Landor lived for a time. But his grandiose plans for the estate – including planting 10,000 cedars of Lebanon and importing merino sheep from Spain – made him bankrupt, and the building was neglected until the 1950s.

A team of masons worked for several years to conserve the remains, which include the north and south transepts, the presbytery and the nave. The ruins extend under the nearby Abbey Hotel, where there is a cellar bar in part of the original buildings – and outside, across a field to the west of the church, is the old priory gatehouse.

All year, daily. Free entry. Refreshments. P *Toilets.* ♿ *Tel Crucorney (0873) 890487.*

MODEL FARM FOLK MUSEUM

Off B4235 at Wolvesnewton, 8 miles north-west of Chepstow (Cb)

Horse-drawn wagons and a Victorian cottage bedroom complete in every detail can be seen in this delightful folk museum set in rolling countryside between the Usk and Wye valleys.

Housed in an unusual cross-shaped barn and other buildings belonging to a model farm created by the Duke of Beaufort in the 18th century, the museum has a wide collection of antique toys and early medical instruments. There are also domestic and agricultural utensils, equipment and bric-a-brac spanning a hundred years of social history from Queen Victoria to Queen Elizabeth II.

Art exhibitions are held in a gallery in the old mill, and visitors can watch craftsmen at work around the mill courtyard. Outdoors there are pure-bred waterfowl and poultry, and a picnic area with magnificent views of the Black Mountains and Wolvesnewton Valley; indoors an audiovisual show gives an entertaining picture of Victorian life.

Apr-Sept, daily; Oct-Nov, Sat and Sun. Adm charge. Refreshments. Shop. P *Toilets.* ♿ *Tel Wolvesnewton (029 15) 231.*

MONMOUTH MUSEUM

Priory Street, Monmouth (Dc)

Nelson's fighting sword and a detailed model of his flagship at Trafalgar, HMS *Victory*, are among Monmouth Museum's most treasured possessions. The Nelson Collection was started by Lady Llangattock, the mother of Charles Rolls, the co-founder of Rolls-Royce, who grew up near the town. It includes many relics of Nelson, including gifts and letters exchanged with his mistress, Lady Hamilton. The museum also has a local history section, part of it devoted to Charles Rolls's exploits in early motor cars, aeroplanes and balloons.

Just outside Monmouth, the summit of a steep wooded hill known as the Kymin provides fine views over the Wye Valley. The small battlemented Round House on the hill was built in 1793 as a banqueting place for a dining club formed by the 'first gentlemen' of the town. In 1800 a Naval Temple was erected nearby, crowned by a statue of Britannia and adorned with red and blue medallions commemorating the victories of great British admirals. When Nelson accepted an invitation to breakfast there during a surprise visit to Monmouth, he was greeted with a salute from the four naval cannons that now stand outside the Round House.

Museum: All year, daily. Adm charge. Shop. P *Tel Monmouth (0600) 3519. Kymin: NT. All year, daily.*

NEWPORT MUSEUM AND ART GALLERY

John Frost Square, Newport (Bb)

Roman ornaments, mosaics and other finds unearthed at Caerwent, formerly Venta Silurum, the Roman capital of South Wales, are on show in Newport Museum, in a square named after John Frost, the Chartist leader and former mayor of the town. In 1839, a band of 5000 armed men led by Frost marched into Newport demanding a People's Charter, including fair elections and universal male suffrage. Ten of them were shot dead by soldiers and the three leaders, including Frost, were sentenced to be hanged, although their sentences were eventually commuted to transportation. The museum has an exhibition about the Chartists and the Newport Riots. In the same building is an art gallery with an attractive collection of English and Welsh watercolours of the 18th and 19th centuries – as well as some Staffordshire pottery figures.

Near the museum is Newport's famous transporter bridge across the River Usk, built in 1906. There is only one other bridge of this kind in Britain, in Middlesbrough, and only two others in Europe.

All year, daily exc Sun and Bank Hol. Free entry. Shop. P ♿ *Tel Newport (0633) 840064.*

PENHOW CASTLE

On A48, 5 miles east of Newport (Cb)

Believed to be the oldest inhabited castle in Wales, Penhow was built as one of a ring of fortresses erected to protect the Welsh Marches, or border country, and is the only one that has survived intact. Its attractive buildings, grouped round a stone-flagged courtyard, span more than 800 years – ranging from the 12th-century keep to a Restoration wing with a fine canopied doorway and a kitchen filled with Victorian cooking equipment.

RURAL RELICS *An earthenware water purifier dominates Victorian relics at Gwent Rural Life Museum. Other items include red-painted bars from a draught-horse's collar and some corn dollies.*

WARM WELCOME *Visitors to the Keep Room in Penhow Castle can warm themselves by an open fire and admire the gleaming oak table. The room has been restored to its appearance in the early Middle Ages.*

In medieval times Penhow was owned by the St Maur family, from the village of the same name in the Loire Valley, who came over from France with William the Conqueror. Their name quickly became corrupted to Seymour and it is from one of the early owners of Penhow, Sir Roger de St Maur, that Jane Seymour, the wife of Henry VIII, and the Dukes of Somerset are descended.

The castle has undergone a remarkable programme of reconstruction, after more than 250 years of dereliction during which the Tudor wing was used as a farmhouse and several of the buildings as barns or stables. Today all the rooms have been restored and refurnished – including the 15th-century Great Hall and the Seymours' chamber on the second floor of the keep, which has a shutter designed to protect the window from missiles hurled by attackers bold enough to scale the ramparts. From the battlements, which can be reached by a stairway built within the walls of the keep, there are splendid views over the marshland of the Severn Estuary.

Easter-Sept, daily exc Mon and Tues, and Bank Hol; Oct-Easter, Wed. Adm charge. Refreshments. Shop. P *Toilets. Tel Newport (0633) 400800.*

ROYALIST FORT *The sturdy six-sided Great Tower of Raglan Castle was the target of daily bombardment by the cannonballs of Parliamentarian forces during the Civil War. It fell after a ten-week siege.*

RAGLAN CASTLE

On A40, 7½ miles south-west of Monmouth (Cc)

Boldly silhouetted against the sky, the ruins of this handsome moated castle are visible from several miles away. Stately living apartments grouped around two courtyards, shapely towers and a double-fronted gatehouse all contribute to an effect of harmonious beauty.

The present castle was begun by Sir William Thomas, the local lord of the manor, who was knighted for his service in the Hundred Years' War by Henry VI. Fearing that his retainers were not to be trusted, he built a self-contained tower for his family, isolated from the rest of the castle by the moat. Security was not the only consideration. Sir William also set out to create an impressive residence in keeping with his enhanced status – an ambition completed by his son, William Herbert, Earl of Pembroke.

During the Civil War Henry Somerset, Marquis of Worcester, whose family had acquired the castle by marriage, held Raglan for the Royalist cause. In the summer of 1645 Charles I played bowls on the bowling green, which is still in good condition; less than a year later, after a ten-week siege, Somerset surrendered when Sir Thomas Fairfax surrounded the castle with 3500 men.

In the 19th century another member of the Somerset family and owner of the castle, Lord Raglan, achieved military fame of a different kind. As Commander-in-Chief of the British Army during the Crimean War, he gave the ambiguous order, misunderstood by his subordinates, that led to the ill-fated Charge of the Light Brigade.

Cadw. All year, daily. Adm charge. Shop. P Toilets. ♿ Tel Raglan (0291) 690228.

SIRHOWY VALLEY COUNTRY PARK

Off A4048, 6 miles north-west of Newport (Bb)

Motorists can drive to the park through lush green countryside, leave their cars at the Full Moon Visitor Centre and from there explore almost 1000 acres of parkland stretching along 4 miles of the lower Sirhowy Valley. A network of waymarked paths leads through extensive conifer plantations broken up by ancient oak and beech woods, and passes the haunts of buzzards, rabbits, squirrels and the occasional fox. Land-Rover safaris occasionally explore much of the terrain, and for the more energetic there is a wayfaring course and a fitness circuit. There are picnic sites and walks along the banks of the River Sirhowy.

All year, daily. Free entry. P Tel Ynysddu (0495) 270991.

SKENFRITH CASTLE

On B4521, 10 miles north-west of Monmouth (Cd)

The stately ruins of this once-powerful castle stand in a beautiful riverside setting at the heart of the tranquil village of Skenfrith. Together with Grosmont and White Castle, Skenfrith was one of the 'Three Castles of Gwent' – a triangle of fortresses erected to command the open border country between the Wye Valley and the hills of Wales.

Originally the castle was mainly of timber construction, but early in the 13th century the chief

TRANQUIL TINTERN *The calm and seclusion which led Cistercian monks to build Tintern Abbey on a remote site by the River Wye still invest the tall ruins.*

officer of state, Hubert de Burgh, Earl of Kent, who had been given the three castles by King John, rebuilt Skenfrith completely in stone. The well-preserved keep is guarded by a curtain wall with projecting towers and was once surrounded by a wide moat, now grassed over to form the village green.

Nearby stands the sturdy square-towered village church, which dates from the same period and is built from the same warm-hued local sandstone.

Cadw. All year, daily. Free entry. ♿ Tel Cardiff (0222) 465511.

TINTERN ABBEY

On A466, 5 miles north of Chepstow (Db)

Whether seen against a cloudless summer sky or the red and gold tints of autumn, the soaring arches and delicate tracery of the empty windows make Tintern one of the most beautiful of ruined abbeys. With its backdrop of steep woods and lofty cliffs sloping down to the River Wye, the 'wild secluded scene' inspired a famous poem by Wordsworth and some of Turner's most evocative paintings.

Although now roofless, the great abbey church – built by white-robed Cistercian monks around the start of the 14th century – has survived remarkably intact. The layout of the abbey is plainly visible as the visitor wanders among the labyrinthine ruins of the monastic buildings and abbot's quarters.

Not far from the ruins is the Anchor Inn – once the abbey's watergate, with a slipway down to the river – and an old railway station that is now a picnic site and a countryside information centre, with an exhibition of pre-1918 photographs tracing the early history of the Wye Valley Line, which closed in 1964. The Wye Valley is an Area of Outstanding Natural Beauty, and there is some delightful walking country around Tintern. A variety of short circular walks start and end at the railway station, and the 54 mile Lower Wye Valley Walk passes the abbey.

Cadw. All year, daily. Adm charge. Shop. P Toilets. ♿ Tel Tintern (029 18) 251.

TREDEGAR HOUSE

Off A48, 2 miles south-west of Newport (Bb)

Surrounded by a beautiful park with magnificent wrought-iron gates and a large lake, Tredegar was the country home of the Morgan family for more than 500 years. The house was almost completely rebuilt around 1670, and today has been carefully restored and refurnished in period styles ranging from the 17th to the 20th centuries.

Among the numerous family portraits is a painting of Godfrey, 1st Viscount Tredegar, who, with his horse, survived the Charge of the Light Brigade (his horse lies buried in the grounds). Another portrait is of Evan, the colourful 2nd Viscount, who was the last Morgan to live at Tredegar. During the 1930s, celebrities ranging from the writer H.G. Wells to the Satanist Aleister Crowley were regular guests at the viscount's lively weekend parties.

The most spectacular of the house's 40 rooms is the Gilt Room, with its painted stucco ceiling and ornate gilt chimneypiece flanked by twisted black pillars. The most intimate is the charming Cedar Closet, which has a sundial painted on one of the windowpanes and cupboards for valuables concealed in the panelling.

The servants' quarters and outbuildings, including the orangery and stables, contain colourful records of life at Tredegar.

Besides delightful walled gardens and woodland walks, there are carriage rides, fishing and boating on the lake, an orienteering course, an adventure playground and workshops where visitors can watch craft demonstrations.

Easter-Sept, daily exc Mon and Tues. Adm charge. Refreshments. Shop. P Toilets. ♿ Tel Newport (0633) 62275.

THE VALLEY INHERITANCE

Park Buildings, Pontypool (Bb)

An elegant Georgian building which was formerly the stable block of Pontypool Park House is now a lively modern exhibition centre devoted to the industrial heritage of the South Wales valleys. Old photographs, films, audiovisual shows and displays of industrial relics bring to life the story of the valleys – including the iron and coal industries over the years.

The exhibition centre is run by a conservation trust which has rescued several important buildings and sites in the Torfaen Valley, on the edge of the beautiful Brecon Beacons National Park. The trust's Torfaen Trail of History includes two major attractions: the Big Pit – where visitors are taken on an underground tour of a coal mine – and an 18th-century ironworks, both at Blaenavon.

Also part of the Trail of History are the early 19th-century ironworkers' cottages of Forge Row in Cwmavon; Llanyrafon Farm, where the trust maintains a 16th-century water mill and a 17th-century manor house; and Junction Cottage, a tollkeeper's lodge at the Pontymoel canal basin, which houses an exhibition about the waterways system of South Wales.

All year, daily. Adm charge. Shop. P Toilets. ♿ Tel Pontypool (049 55) 52036.

WHITE CASTLE

Off B4521, 7 miles north-east of Abergavenny (Cc)

The towers and curtain walls of this sturdy ruined castle on a windswept hilltop rise dramatically from a deep water-filled moat. Once the walls were covered with shimmering white plaster, and here and there traces of the plaster coating can still be seen.

Together with Grosmont and Skenfrith, White Castle was one of the 'Three Castles of Gwent' – a triangle of fortresses within 5 miles of one another that protected the border against the Welsh. Although earthworks and foundations from earlier castles on the same site are still visible, the magnificent towers were added late in the 13th century.

The castle consists of two circular wards built in a figure-of-eight pattern, and to reach the inner ward visitors cross a wooden bridge high above the moat.

White Castle played a curious role in 20th-century history. During the Second World War, Hitler's deputy, Rudolf Hess, was confined in a nearby mental hospital and from time to time was brought to the castle to feed the swans that glide majestically round the moat.

Cadw. All year, daily. Adm charge. P (limited). ♿ (part).

GILDED FRAME *The Gilt Room at Tredegar House presents a glittering spectacle. Above the ornate chimneypiece is a portrait painted in 1650 of Sir William Morgan, whose grandson rebuilt the house.*

COUNTY CALENDAR

March (late). Newport: Drama Festival.

April (late). Abergavenny: Llantilio Crossenny Festival of Music and Drama.

May Day Hol Caldicot Castle: May Day Spectacular.

May (late). Abergavenny: Steam Rally. Crosskeys: Islwyn Folk Festival.

May (early, to late July). Abergavenny: Midsummer Welcome (carnival, fête, music, drama and medieval market).

July (mid-month). Usk: Festival. Abergavenny: Agricultural Show.

August (early). Chepstow: Agricultural Show.

August (mid-month). Abergavenny: Llanthony Valley Show.

August (late). Monmouth: County Show.

September (mid-month). Usk: Show.

Tourist information: Abergavenny (0873) 3254 (summer); Blaenavon (0495) 790122; Chepstow (029 12) 3772 (summer); Monmouth (0600) 3899; Newport (0633) 842962.

GWYNEDD

HIGH PEAKS AND MIGHTY CASTLES IN WILD SNOWDONIA

In this dramatic corner of Wales, the jagged crests of Snowdonia cluster around their mother peak like silent sentinels. Many are more than 3000ft high, with the majestic Snowdon rising 3560ft to its rocky summit. In these wild mountains there are precipitous cliffs, plunging to deep valleys that sparkle with crystal lakes and foaming waterfalls. In the passes stand castles such as Dolwyddelan, built by the Welsh in defiance of the invading English. When defiance turned to defeat in the 13th century, Edward I built his own chain of castles to subdue the fiery Welsh; these still stand, with Beaumaris, Caernarfon, Conwy and Harlech as noble and awesome today as when they were built.

Six centuries later the mountains were exploited for slate for the building industry. Quarries such as Gloddfa Ganol and Llechwedd now offer a fascinating journey into the working life of the men who tunnelled deep into the mountains in Victorian days. The slate industry also gave birth to quaint little narrow-gauge railways, such as the Ffestiniog Railway, which now carry visitors through spectacular scenery.

BALA LAKE RAILWAY

On B4403, 7 miles south-west of Bala (Db-Dc)

It is possible to row the 4 mile length of Bala Lake, but for visitors short of time or energy a trip on the railway running alongside the largest natural lake in Wales is a relaxing alternative. The return trip takes an hour, in a train hauled by one of three 'Alice' class steam locomotives – one of which, *Holy War*, was the last working slate quarry locomotive. The journey can be broken in Bala, or at other stations, for picnics, swimming or fishing. The main station is at Llanuwchllyn, at the western end of the lake, where a display of historic industrial locomotives and wagons can be seen.

Easter-Oct, daily. Refreshments. Shop. P *Toilets.* ♿ *Tel Llanuwchllyn (067 84) 666.*

BANGOR CATHEDRAL

In centre of Bangor (Cd)

The cathedral occupies one of the most ancient ecclesiastical sites in Great Britain. A church has stood there since AD 525 – 70 years before Canterbury Cathedral was founded. The present cathedral is mainly 13th century, much restored by Sir Gilbert Scott and his son Oldrid in the 19th century. Among the cathedral's treasures are a 15th-century font, the carved oak figure of 1518 known as the Mostyn Christ, and some medieval tiles. The cathedral library has an outstanding treasure: the Bangor Pontifical – a book containing those services that only a bishop can perform – compiled by Bishop Anian II around 1310. The Bible Garden, beside the cathedral, contains many plants mentioned in the Bible that have been able to withstand the Welsh climate; they include the fig and the Judas tree.

Opposite the cathedral stands the Museum of Welsh Antiquities, which covers the development of North Wales from prehistoric times to the present. It has a collection of furniture and porcelain from the 17th to 19th centuries, some of which is seen in period settings, including a farmhouse kitchen and a country house.

Cathedral: All year, daily. Free entry. P ♿ *Tel Bangor (0248) 370693. Garden: All year, daily. Free entry. Museum: All year, Tues-Sat pm. Free entry.* P ♿ *Tel (0248) 353368.*

BEAUMARIS CASTLE

Castle Street, Beaumaris (Cd)

The last of eight great castles built by Edward I in North Wales to contain the rebellious Welsh, Beaumaris represents the pinnacle of medieval military architecture in Britain. It is based on a concentric pattern of defences, instead of the traditional Norman keep and bailey. In building it the architect, Master James of St George, was helped by the chosen site, consisting of flat marshland facing the sea.

Surrounding the castle was an 18ft wide moat, most of which still remains, with a tidal dock for shipping connected by a channel to the sea. An iron ring where vessels of up to 40 tons used to tie up can still be seen in the castle wall. The low outer curtain wall, with 16 towers, provided the next line of defence. The inner walls are 43ft high and nearly 16ft thick, with three great towers on the east and west sides and gateways to the north and south. To reach the inner ward attackers had to overcome 14 separate and formidable obstacles. The best views can be obtained from the northern gatehouse. The elegant chapel on the first floor of the Chapel Tower has a fine vaulted Gothic ceiling.

Cadw. All year, daily exc Sun am. Adm charge. P *Toilets.* ♿ *Tel Beaumaris (0248) 810361.*

CHILDISH THINGS *Ornaments and dolls in the Beaumaris Museum of Childhood include favourites such as Mickey Mouse. Among the pottery figures is one of James Watt experimenting with a kettle.*

BEAUMARIS COURTHOUSE AND GAOL

In centre of Beaumaris (Cd)

It is easy for the visitor to this well-preserved courthouse to put himself into the position of a prisoner in the dock in the 17th century. The building dates from 1614 and much of the original structure remains. It was in this courtroom that in 1773 Mary, wife of Richard Hughes, was sentenced to be transported for seven years for stealing a bed-gown valued at sixpence. From the dock she would have been taken to the nearby Beaumaris Gaol where, in the 18th century, men, women and children were herded together in the same room to sleep on filthy straw and eat whatever they could afford to buy. Prisoners sentenced to hard labour spent their days breaking stones, or working on the treadmill which pumped water to rooftop tanks for the gaol's water supply. The treadmill is the only one in Britain still in its original position. The present gaol, however, is the result of the Gaol Act of 1823 which sought to improve prison conditions. Visitors can see the laundry room, the drunks' cell, the workroom, the kitchen, the punishment room (sound-proofed and pitch dark) and the condemned cell. A wooden ramp led to a platform above the street where the gibbet was placed in view of the crowds.

By contrast, a glimpse of the gentler side of Victorian life is provided by the charming Museum of Childhood in Castle Street. A glass sweet jar containing seaside rock made in Morecambe in 1880 is typical of the museum's ability to conjure up images of childhoods long since gone. The museum has one of the largest collections of money boxes and mechanical iron banks in Britain, including many ingenious Victorian devices to instill the saving habit in children, such as the William Tell Bank in which the child's coin shoots the apple off the head of a little cast-iron boy. The museum has more than 300 model trains and cars, a large collection of music boxes and magic lanterns, as well as dolls, games, samplers and needlework pictures.

Courthouse and Gaol: June-Sept, daily. Adm charge. Shop P *Tel Beaumaris (0248) 810367 (courthouse); 810921 (gaol). Museum of Childhood: Mar-Jan, daily exc Sun am. Adm charge. Shop.* P *Tel (0248) 810448.*

BODNANT GARDEN

On A470, 8 miles south of Llandudno (Dd)

A great garden is more than a collection of plants: it is like a stage set, which needs to be carefully designed if the characters which inhabit it are to be seen at their best. At Bodnant the design of the set has been a constant preoccupation of the Aberconway family since 1875. They started with the great natural advantage of a situation above the Conwy Valley with distant views of Snowdonia, and built a series of terraces stepped into the hillside and leading down from the west front of the house to the Hiraethlyn, a tributary of the Conwy. At the entrance to the gardens is the astonishing Laburnum Arch, overhung by shimmering cascades of yellow. The curved walk beneath is 180ft long, between trees twined over an arched framework.

The first terrace has a great lawn flanked by cedars with a pool filled with water lilies. The next contains a paved rose walk, and below that there is a splendid 18th-century garden house called Pin Mill. The terraces are connected by

MOUNTAIN GREENERY *Water lilies dapple a pool set in velvet lawns on the great terrace at Bodnant. Beyond a greenwood fringe lies the Conwy Valley and the cloud-capped peaks of Snowdonia.*

pergolas and flights of steps with balustrades, wall fountains and ornaments. Below is one of Bodnant's chief glories – a collection of camellias, rhododendrons, azaleas and magnolias.

NT. Mar-Oct, daily. Adm charge. Refreshments. P *Toilets.* ♿ *Tel Ty'n-y-groes (049 267) 460.*

BRYNKIR WOOLLEN MILL

Off A487, 3½ miles north-west of Porthmadog (Bc)

The whole process of producing traditional Welsh woollen cloth, from teasing the newly shorn wool from local sheep to the final weaving of the cloth, can be seen at this mill, which has been in continuous production for 150 years. The water wheel still turns, though it now provides electric power for the mill rather than directly driving its machinery. Among the processes to be seen are carding, spinning, doubling and hanking, warping, winding and weaving. In the shop a whole range of woollens can be purchased, from socks to tapestry bedspreads.

All year, daily exc Sat and Sun. Free entry. Shop. P *Toilets.* ♿ *(part). Tel Garndolbenmaen (076 675) 236.*

CAERNARFON CASTLE

In centre of Caernarfon (Bd)

The soaring walls, fortified gatehouses and lofty towers of this massive and well-preserved castle have dominated Caernarfon since the late 13th century, when it was founded by Edward I. He built it as both fortress and royal palace, and there in 1301 installed his son as the first Prince of Wales. The first royal investiture was held in the castle in 1911, when the future Edward VIII became the new prince; and in 1969 it saw the investiture of the present Prince of Wales.

Edward meant Caernarfon to be the mightiest of his Welsh castles, and to ensure this he modelled the greystone walls on those of Constantinople, the modern Istanbul. On nights when they are floodlit, with the castle ramparts reflected in the calm purple waters of the River Seiont, they take on a romantic, fairy-tale aspect. The castle's ground plan is roughly in the shape of an hour-glass and is divided into a Lower Ward and Upper Ward. At either end the town walls extend into those of the fortress, and the seven main towers have views over the Menai Strait and Anglesey; and from the top of Queen's Tower (named after Edward's wife, Eleanor) the vista stretches to the rugged peaks of Snowdonia.

Queen's Tower is the home of the Royal Welch Fusiliers Regimental Museum, whose exhibits include relics of the Napoleonic Wars, Crimean War, Indian Mutiny and the two World Wars – as well as eight of the 14 Victoria Crosses won by members of the regiment. The Chamberlain Tower has an exhibition of 'The Castles of Edward I'; the North-East Tower houses the 'Prince of Wales Exhibition', including his Robing Room; and in the Eagle Tower there is an audiovisual programme on the history of Caernarfon.

Outside the castle, a short walk along the promenade leads to the whitewashed Maritime Museum. The museum's centrepiece is the 1807 ton steam dredger SS *Seiont II*, built in 1937 for Caernarfon Harbour Trust and a rare working survivor of the days of coal-fired steamships.

On the south-eastern edge of Caernarfon, on the A4085, are the remains of the Roman fort of Segontium, built around AD 78 as part of a chain by which the Romans hoped to contain the Welsh tribes led by Caractacus. There were four gates to the rectangular fort, which housed an auxiliary cohort of 1000 men and was surrounded by a civilian settlement. Next to the north-west entrance is the workshop and commandant's house. In the centre of the fort is the *principia*, or headquarters building. Channels for the underfloor heating system are still visible. The site museum contains finds from the excavations, including an altar to Minerva.

Castle and Regimental Museum: Cadw. All year, daily exc Sun am. Adm charge (joint). Shops. Toilets. Tel Caernarfon (0286) 77617 (castle); 3362 (museum). Maritime Museum: Easter weekend; May-Sept, pm daily. Free entry (adm charge to board ships). Shop. P *Tel (0286) 830932. Segontium: Cadw. All year, daily exc Sun am. Free entry. Shop. Toilets.* ♿ *Tel (0286) 5625.*

COED-Y-BRENIN FOREST

On A470, 8 miles north of Dolgellau (Cb)

Miles of forest cover the riverside and slopes and stretch up towards craggy peaks. Coed-y-Brenin was planted by the Forestry Commission in 1922, and is one of the oldest and largest forests in North Wales, full of subtle contrasts and spectacular views. Six parking areas are the starting points of 50 miles of waymarked paths and tracks. At the visitor centre north of Ganllwyd, displays and audiovisual programmes describe the wildlife of the area and the Forestry Commission's work there. Fallow deer run in parts of the high woodland, and there are badgers, foxes, squirrels and rabbits.

Close by, the Eden Valley trail starts from a picnic spot in a wooded glade and leads along a river bank to a tumbling tributary. Another walk climbs through the wood to a viewpoint and then on to the Rhaeadr Mawddach and Pistyll Cain waterfalls.

FC. All year, daily; Visitor Centre, Easter-Sept. Free entry. Refreshments. Shop. P *Toilets.* ♿ *Tel Dolgellau (0341) 40666.*

CONWY CASTLE

Near centre of Conwy (Dd)

Seen from across the river, with the foothills of Snowdonia providing a magnificent backdrop, Conwy Castle is a thrilling sight. Built by Edward I in five years from 1282, it has eight massive round towers, and barbicans at either end. Two of its most interesting features are the 125ft long Great Hall, the scene of great banquets when the king was in residence, and the royal apartments. Both these are now roofless and bare-walled, but there is a beautiful little chapel with some of its fine decoration still preserved.

Medieval Conwy was a garrison town. The walls which protected it are still intact and are among the finest of their kind in Europe – nearly 1 mile in extent, with 22 towers and three original gateways. The history of Conwy is the subject of an exhibition in the 14th-century timber-and-plaster Aberconwy House in Castle Street, one of the oldest houses in Wales.

Castle: Cadw. All year, daily exc Sun am. Adm charge. P *(limited).* ♿ *Tel Aberconwy (0492) 592358. Aberconwy House: NT. Apr-Sept, daily exc Tues. Adm charge. Shop. Tel (0492) 592246.*

CORRIS CRAFT CENTRE

Off A487, 7 miles south of Dolgellau (Ca)

How to design and make a jigsaw puzzle, fire a handmade pot and mould a candle are just a few of the mysteries revealed to visitors by craftsmen at this centre set in magnificent countryside. Among other crafts practised are jewellery making and pyrography – decorating wood with artistic scorch marks.

All year, daily. Free entry. Refreshments. Shop. P *Toilets.* ♿ *Tel Corris (065 473) 343.*

CRICCIETH CASTLE

Off A497, at Criccieth (Bc)

The 13th-century castle is worth visiting for the view alone. It stands on a hill overlooking the little seaside town and provides magnificent views of Cardigan Bay, the Lleyn Peninsula and Snowdonia.

The original castle, including the imposing twin-towered gatehouse, with towers pierced by arrow-slits, was built by the Welsh prince Llywelyn the Great about 1220, and added to by his grandson Prince Llywelyn the Last. In 1283 Edward I added an Engine Tower – now in ruins – to the north end of the castle. The castle was sacked and burnt by Owain Glyndwr in 1404 in the last Welsh uprising against the English crown. It now houses an exhibition on the castles of the Welsh princes.

Cadw. All year, daily exc Sun am. Adm charge. P *Toilets. Tel Criccieth (076 671) 2227.*

ARTISTRY IN STONE *Caernarfon Castle's turreted Eagle Tower, on the left, and the smaller Queen's Tower are reflected in the waters of the River Seiont. The castle walls, decorated with bands of red sandstone, were inspired by the 5th-century walls of Constantinople.*

CWM IDWAL NATURE TRAIL

Off A5, 7 miles south-east of Bangor (Cd)

This nature trail makes a 2 mile circuit of Llyn Idwal, taking in a rich variety of plants and scenery carved by glaciers. The most spectacular formation is the great rock cleft known as the 'Devil's Kitchen'. Stumps of trees preserved in peat are evidence that woodland probably reached as high as 2000ft in Snowdonia a few thousand years ago. The lake is visited by herons, cormorants and whooper swans, and the Idwal Slabs, huge steep slabs of rock, attract rock climbers.

NCC. All year, daily.

DOLBADARN CASTLE

On A4086, 7½ miles south-east of Caernarfon (Cd)

The castle still dominates the mountain pass of Llanberis which, in medieval times, was the main route from Caernarfon to the upper Conwy Valley. All the determination of the Welsh to defy the English invader is embodied in this castle, even to the adoption of the English round keep, which proved so effective against medieval weaponry. Built by the great Welsh prince Llywelyn the Great about 1200, ironically only this most English-looking structure remains; the remainder is in ruins. The castle has a romantic setting, overlooking the waters of Llyn Peris.

Cadw. All year, daily exc Sun am. Adm charge. P *Tel Caernarfon (0286) 76475.*

DOLWYDDELAN CASTLE

On A470, 6 miles south-west of Betws-y-Coed (Cc)

Rising dramatically from a rocky hill in the shadow of Moel Siabod mountain, the castle once played a key part in the defence of North Wales against the invading English. It was built by the Welsh prince Llywelyn the Great around 1200 to guard the mountain pass from Meirionnydd to the Vale of Conwy. In 1283 it fell to Edward I, who reinforced its defences by building a second tower; this is now in ruins, but the original square keep of Llywelyn still stands, its crenellated battlements restored in the 19th century. From them there are marvellous views, while an exhibition inside the keep tells the story of Dolwyddelan.

Cadw. All year, daily exc Sun am. Adm charge. P

FAIRBOURNE RAILWAY

On A493, 10 miles north of Tywyn (Cb)

Some splendid coastal and mountain scenery can be enjoyed from this narrow-gauge railway, which also presents an unusual challenge. Ask to be dropped off at Gorsafawddacha'idraigodanheddogleddollônpenrhynareurdraethceredigion. It may require a little practice to get the pronunciation right – it boasts the longest place-name in the world – but in return the visitor gets the longest railway ticket ever issued. The name means in English: 'Station by the Mawddach alongside the dragon's teeth on Penrhyn drive north by the golden sands of Cardigan Bay'.

The route follows the coast to Porth Penrhyn on the Mawddach Estuary, with the pretty town of Barmouth on the northern bank reached by ferry. The terminus at Gorsaf Newydd also houses the Fairbourne Butterfly Safari, containing exotic live butterflies.

Apr-Nov, daily. Fares. Refreshments. Shop. P *Toilets.* ♿ *Tel Dolgellau (0341) 250362.*

FFESTINIOG POWER STATION

Off A496, 1 mile west of Blaenau Ffestiniog (Cc)

A spectacular Alpine-style drive leads 1000ft up the mountainside to the Stwlan Dam above the power station, offering superb views over Snowdonia as well as an exhibition, a cinema, a shop, a café, a picnic site and a variety of walks. There are also guided tours round the power station itself, bookable at the station's information centre at Tanygrisiau.

Ffestiniog was the first pumped storage scheme in the country, and is capable of supplying 360,000 kilowatts of electricity to the national grid in just under a minute. The water used in the generating process is pumped back up the mountain at off-peak times for re-use.

Easter-Oct, daily. Adm charge. Refreshments. Shop. P *Toilets.* ♿ *Tel Blaenau Ffestiniog (0766) 830310.*

FFESTINIOG RAILWAY

From Porthmadog station (Cc)

The little trains of the Ffestiniog Railway run from Porthmadog, on the Glaslyn estuary, through the lovely Vale of Ffestiniog, into the mountains and on to Blaenau Ffestiniog. It is a meandering, happy-go-lucky journey of some 14 miles.

The narrow-gauge track at first carried horse-drawn wagons from the slate mines to Porthmadog's harbour. Steam came to the line in the 1860s, and some of the locomotives built at that time are still in service. The *Prince* is one, a pretty saddle-tank engine. Some of the passenger coaches are just as old, and include buffet and observation cars.

The line starts on Porthmadog's harbourside, where a museum houses some of the railway's retired engines, including *Prince's* sister, *Princess*. The single track first crosses the Cob, a causeway built across the Glaslyn estuary in 1811, with marvellous views of the Snowdon range. It passes the Boston Lodge works where many of the locomotives were built, then starts its long climb in great looping curves around Llyn Mair.

Clinging precariously to the mountainside the trains run through a 60yd tunnel and then climb to Campbell's Platform, where wild goats roam the hills, and on to Dduallt. Here the track spirals upwards to gain height to run above the Tanygrisiau reservoir, then it makes another stiff climb to Blaenau Ffestiniog, 710ft above sea level. Passengers can alight at stations along the route, to admire the view down the Vale of Ffestiniog, or to follow the nature trail at Tan-y-Bwlch.

Another narrow-gauge railway, the Welsh Highland Railway, runs from Porthmadog to Pen y Mount, a short trip of just under a mile. Before the line closed in 1937 it ran some 22 miles to Dinas, its route taking in some of the most spectacular scenery in Wales. The re-opened line is being restored, and it is hoped that eventually it will once again run its original distance.

SOUND AND FURY *Rushing down through Gwydyr Forest from the mountains of Snowdonia, the River Llugwy becomes a torrent of white water as it thunders over the boulder-strewn Swallow Falls.*

Ffestiniog Railway: Mar-Nov, daily. Museum: Mar-Nov, daily. Free entry. Refreshments. Shop. P *Toilets.* ♿ *Tel Porthmadog (0766) 512340. Welsh Highland Railway: July and Aug, daily; Apr-June and Sept-Oct, Sat and Sun. Refreshments. Shop.* P *Toilets.* ♿ *Tel (0766) 513402.*

GREAT ORME COUNTRY PARK

Off A546, 1 mile west of Llandudno (De)

A limestone headland rising 679ft from the sea at the western end of Llandudno, the Great Orme is noted for the curly horned wild goats that scramble around its rocks and grassland; they are descendants of a pair from the Windsor royal herd released on the Orme around 1900. The Orme also attracts many smaller forms of wildlife which can be spotted along a 3½ mile nature trail which passes through heathland, over rocky sections, and through grassland where rockrose, wild thyme and quaking grass can be seen. The wild flowers attract butterflies, and the cliff ledges are the nesting places of guillemots, razorbills and kittiwakes. Migratory birds such as wheatears, golden plovers and wood warblers stop at the Orme to take advantage of its well-stocked larder of insects. A church has stood on the Orme since the 6th century when Tudno, a Welsh missionary, built the first chapel. The present 12th-century church was restored in 1855.

The top of the Orme can be reached on foot, by car, by Victorian tramway or by cable car. The less energetic can enjoy the Happy Valley, a grassy slope with terraced gardens and an open-air theatre.

The Doll Museum in Masonic Street has more than 1500 dolls dating from the 16th century onwards and collected from many countries. One room houses a working scale model railway in a landscaped setting.

Park: All year, daily. Visitor Centre: Apr-Oct. Free entry. Refreshments. Shop. P *Toilets.* ♿ *Happy Valley: All year, daily. Free entry. Refreshments. Shop.* P *(limited). Toilets.* ♿ *Museum: Good Fri-Sept, daily exc Sun am. Adm charge. Shop.*

GWYDIR CASTLE

Off B5106, ½ mile south of Llanrwst (Dd)

Peacocks on the lawns, doves fluttering among the trees and flower-filled gardens greet visitors to this creeper-clad castle. It is more a much-loved home than a castle, although there has been a fortification on the site since AD 600. Even the trees are ancient – a magnificent cedar was planted in 1627 to commemorate the wedding of Charles I.

The castle contains a secret room, once hidden by a sliding wooden panel, a manorial court with cold, dank dungeons below it, a long gallery containing fine hammerbeams, ancient stone carvings – and the ghost of a monk said to have been trapped in a tunnel leading from the secret room.

Easter-Oct, daily. Adm charge. Refreshments. Shop. P *Toilets. Tel Llanrwst (0492) 640261.*

GWYDYR FOREST

Off A5, at Betws-y-Coed (Dd)

Visitors calling at the Snowdonia National Park Visitor Centre in Betws-y-Coed before a walk in Gwydyr Forest have been known to spend the whole day enjoying its various attractions. These range from a local waterlife exhibition, with aquaria containing fresh and seawater fish, to a wildlife tunnel down which children can crawl to inspect the homes of moles, badgers, foxes and mice. There are exhibitions on a year in the life of Gwydyr Forest, on local farming, including a talk from a robot farmer, craft demonstrations and a Royal Society for the Protection of Birds exhibition on Wild Snowdonia.

The centre is the natural starting point for a dozen waymarked walks through the 20,000 acre forest, where wildlife flourishes amid spectacular scenery. Among the outstanding sights of the area are Swallow Falls, where the River Llugwy cascades through a wooded ravine; the Giant's Head precipice; Summerhouse Crag, with its marvellous views across the forest; and High Parc, with panoramic views of Snowdonia.

Easter-Oct, daily. Free entry.

HARLECH CASTLE

Near centre of Harlech (Cb)

Of all the castles built by Edward I to contain the rebellious Welsh, Harlech is perhaps the most impressive, designed to withstand any assault weapon which the ingenuity of medieval man could devise. Rising 200ft on a rocky promontory once skirted by a tidal creek, it remains largely intact, its stone towers still capable of overawing visitors by their enormous bulk and strength.

The chief threat of attack was from the eastern, landward side. This was protected first by a great ditch, then by a curtain wall and finally by a four-towered massive gatehouse, which housed the main private accommodation. Harlech was designed to be victualled from the sea; a gated and heavily fortified stairway was built for this purpose, and visitors can still use it to enter the castle.

Cadw. All year, daily exc Sun am. Adm charge. P *Toilets. Tel Harlech (0766) 780552.*

LLANFAIR QUARRY SLATE CAVERNS

Off A496, 1 mile south of Harlech (Cb)

A Welsh Lady can easily be held in the hand. It has precise dimensions – 16in by 8in – and is invariably made of slate. Roofing slates ranged in size from Ladies to Princesses measuring 24in by 14in. Llanfair quarry has provided millions of roof slates, not only for the rapidly expanding towns in Britain in Victorian times, but also for other parts of Europe. The quarry has nine caverns, all of which can be visited, and a stairway of broad stone steps known as Jacob's Ladder emerges to a splendid view of the Cambrian coast.

Apr-Oct, daily. Adm charge. Refreshments. Shop. P *Toilets. Tel Harlech (0766) 780247.*

LLOYD GEORGE MUSEUM

On A497, 2 miles west of Criccieth (Bc)

The lion-maned 'Welsh wizard' remained deeply attached to the village of his boyhood. David Lloyd George was born in Manchester in 1863, but after his father died he lived with his mother

INTO A MOUNTAIN OF SLATE

Slate makes its presence felt as soon as the road into Blaenau Ffestiniog begins to descend between the high mountains that ring the town. It is everywhere, rising in jagged tiers from the roadside and cladding the hills with a grey armour. This is the waste slate of 100 years of slate-mining, in Blaenau Ffestiniog's two great mines of Llechwedd and Gloddfa Ganol. Both invite visitors to take a journey into the past, to see how the miners of 100 years ago blasted and hewed the slate from the rockfaces, working by candlelight in vast caverns deep inside the mountains.

At Llechwedd Slate Caverns a cable railway descends hundreds of feet into Deep Mine which has an underground lake.

At Gloddfa Ganol Slate Mine visitors can take a Land-Rover trip to a tunnel cut high in the mountainside. They can watch, too, the slatesplitters at work, deftly cleaving the slabs into wafer-thin slices, and visit the cottages where the miners once lived.

On A470, at Blaenau Ffestiniog (Cc). Llechwedd Slate Caverns: Apr-Oct, daily. Free entry (charge for tours). Refreshments. Shop. P Toilets. Tel Blaenau Ffestiniog (0766) 830306. Gloddfa Ganol Slate Mine: Easter-Sept, Mon-Fri; also Sun mid July-Aug. Adm charge. Refreshments. Shop. P Toilets. Tel (0766) 830664.

HOME AND WORKPLACE *Perched high on a mountainside (top right) are the buildings of the Gloddfa Ganol Slate Mine, including cottages whose rooms (top left) show the sparse but snug living conditions of the miners. The mineshafts were tunnelled into the mountainside, and a half-mile walk into one of them leads to the caverns where the slate was worked. A converted miners' train (left) takes visitors to the mineshaft entrance, passing on the way one of the mine's early steam locomotives (above).*

TREASURE FROM THE DEPTHS *At Llechwedd a slatesplitter (above) demonstrates his craft, using methods employed for more than 100 years. Several hundred feet underground are the awesome chambers hewn out by miners in Victorian times. In Deep Mine, reached by a steep tramway, the conditions in which the miners worked are evoked by sound and lighting effects, and by lifelike figures of miners working on rockfaces high above the chamber floor. Some galleries extend to join up with another chamber below, giving a rockface of 200ft or more. Most spectacular of all is the underground lake (right), its glass-smooth surface mirroring the rugged walls and towering roof of a gigantic cavern.*

and his uncle, a shoemaker, in a cottage in Llanystumdwy which is now a museum. Displays tell the story of his progress, to the office of Prime Minister – with victory in the First World War as the crowning triumph. There are reminders, too, of the great Liberal's later years in the political wilderness.

In 1944 Lloyd George returned to live in the village. The next year, soon after accepting an earldom, he died. He is buried on the banks of the River Dwyfor, not far from the museum.

July-Sept, daily. Adm charge. Shop. P *Toilets.* ♿ *Tel Criccieth (076 671) 2071.*

LLYN PADARN COUNTRY PARK

Off A4086, at Llanberis (Cd)

In addition to its superb natural setting, this country park offers a scenic lakeside railway and a museum devoted to slate-mining. The Llanberis Lake Railway runs for 2 miles along the shore of Llyn Padarn, through some of the finest lake and mountain scenery in Wales.

The Welsh Slate Museum is established in the former workshops of the Dinorwig slate quarry which, until its closure in 1969, was one of the biggest slate quarries in Wales. The museum preserves the workshops, machinery and plant as it was when in use, including the machinery for sawing, splitting and trimming slate; the foundry; the smithy with its four hearths, where a blacksmith can usually be seen at work; and the water wheel, the biggest in Wales, which once drove the workshop machinery. The Vivian Trail takes visitors round the old quarry workings and the 50ft deep quarry pool.

Park: All year, daily. Free entry. Refreshments. Shop. P *Toilets.* ♿ *Tel Llanberis (0286) 870892. Railway: Apr-Sept, daily. Fares. Refreshments. Shop.* P *Toilets. Tel (0286) 870549. Museum: Easter-Sept, daily. Adm charge. Shop.* P *Toilets.* ♿ *Tel (0286) 870630.*

MAES ARTRO TOURIST VILLAGE

On A496, at Llanbedr, 3 miles south of Harlech (Cb)

This is a novel adaptation of a wartime RAF camp, set in 10 acres of fields and woodland close to the beautiful Cambrian coast. Attractions include a large marine aquarium, a model village, a re-created 19th-century Welsh village street and a variety of craft shops selling handmade goods. Additional attractions for children include an adventure playground, and a Wild West fort.

Apr-Oct, daily. Adm charge. Refreshments. Shop. P *Toilets.* ♿ *Tel Llanbedr (034 123) 467.*

MEIRION MILL

Off A470, 10 miles south-east of Dolgellau (Db)

In a delightful setting beside the River Dovey, looms clank in a weaving shed converted from part of a railway station that closed in 1951. The mill produces traditional wool tweeds and tapestry, and its shop sells bedcovers, knitwear, knitting wool and gifts. Visitors can see the looms on which the cloth is made. The station house has been converted into a coffee shop, and there is a walk along the old railway track.

Apr-Oct, daily. Free entry. Refreshments. Shop. P *Toilets.* ♿ *Tel Machynlleth (065 04) 311.*

CASTLE COMFORT *Elaborate carving and plaster decoration cover the walls and ceiling of Penrhyn Castle's sumptuous library. The castle and its rooms were designed by the architect Thomas Hopper.*

ORIEL ERYRI

Off A4086, 7 miles south-east of Caernarfon (Cd)

One of the biggest permanent attractions at this museum, which is part of the National Museum of Wales, is the pictures taken live and direct from the Meteosat weather space satellite and displayed on television screens. A short film about Meteosat and its launching, prepared for the European Space Agency, can also be seen. The museum has exhibitions on the natural life and environment of Wales, and an audiovisual theatre showing how the scenery of Snowdonia was formed over more than 400 million years.

May-Sept, daily exc Sun am. Free entry. Shop. P *Toilets.* ♿ *Tel Llanberis (0286) 870636.*

PENRHYN CASTLE

On A5122, 1 mile east of Bangor (Cd)

The wealth derived from sugar plantations in Jamaica and invested in the Penrhyn slate quarries enabled G.H. Dawkins Pennant in 1820 to build himself a Norman castle on a scale which befitted his affluence. The exterior boasts the crenellated walls and towers of a real medieval fortress, while the interior is designed on a scale and lavishness that is almost Byzantine; the Great Hall, with its polished sandstone floor, was modelled on Durham Cathedral. The house contains fine paintings, some 800 dolls and, in the stables, industrial locomotives.

NT. Apr-Oct, pm daily exc Tues. Adm charge. Refreshments. Shop. P *Toilets.* ♿ *Tel Bangor (0248) 353084.*

PLAS NEWYDD

On A4080, 3 miles south-west of Menai Bridge (Bd)

There is a cavalry museum at Plas Newydd, most appropriate in a house which has a statue of Field-Marshal the Marquis of Anglesey in the grounds, gazing across the Menai Strait to Snowdonia. In the museum are a boot and mutilated trousers worn by the 1st marquis at the Battle of Waterloo, when he was involved in that famous desultory exchange with the Duke of Wellington: 'By God, Sir, I've lost my leg' – 'By God, so you have.'

The architect of the 18th-century house was James Wyatt. It is an imaginative and highly decorative building in the Gothic style. The artist Rex Whistler was a frequent visitor and painted an outstanding *trompe l'oeil* decoration in the dining room.

NT. Apr-Sept, pm daily exc Sat. Adm charge. Refreshments. Shop. P *Toilets.* ♿ *Tel Llanfairpwll (0248) 714795.*

PLAS-YN-RHIW

Off B4413, 4 miles east of Aberdaron (Ab)

From the verandah of this late Tudor house the visitor can look across the vast expanse of Cardigan Bay, past the wild cliffs of Hell's Mouth to Cardigan. The family which built the house were descendants of the 9th-century Welsh King Ferfyn Frych. Some of the walls are more than 6ft thick, and beside a big open fireplace is a large cavity in the wall with a stone spiral stairway above it. The house has been carefully restored to preserve a bygone way of life in the Welsh countryside. A cobbled yard, with a waterfall, leads to a group of buildings which once comprised the dairy, saddle room and stable. The garden is surrounded by some 325 acres of farmland and woodland.

NT. Apr-Sept, pm daily exc Sat. Adm charge. P *Toilets.* ♿ *Tel Rhiw (075 888) 219.*

PORTMEIRION

Off A487, 1 mile south-east of Porthmadog (Cc)

Its architecture is startling yet sublime, its atmosphere cosmopolitan yet urbane – Portmeirion is a village that takes the imagination by the scruff of the neck. From its Italianate gatehouse to the truly English hotel down by the seashore, this joyful jumble of colour-washed houses and cottages, pavilions and towers, statues and columns, fountains and pools, arches and arcades stemmed from the dream of the architect Clough Williams-Ellis, who saw no reason why the architecture of many lands should not stand side by side on the beautiful wooded peninsula he chose for its site.

Williams-Ellis began to realise his dream in 1926. Several of the buildings were rescued from demolition in other places: the Colonnade overlooking the piazza, for instance, dates from 1760 and once graced a house in Bristol. The domed Pantheon that dominates the village was Williams-Ellis's design – but its façade was the upper half of the fireplace of a Cheshire mansion built in 1883. The 14th-century Town Hall has a barrel-vaulted plasterwork ceiling depicting the life and labours of Hercules.

Many film-makers have been attracted to Portmeirion, but the village is no filmset; its buildings are real and many of the lovely cottages are used for hotel or self-catering accommodation. Those who stay there see Portmeirion at its best, when the daytime visitors have gone.

Apr-Oct, daily. Adm charge. Refreshments. Shops. P *Toilets.* ♿ *Tel Penrhyndeudraeth (0766) 770228.*

SNOWDON MOUNTAIN RAILWAY

Llanberis station (Cd)

The little steam trains puffing up Snowdon are now accepted as part of the scenery, like friendly insects on the face of the highest mountain in Wales and England. The extraordinary railway, built between 1894 and 1896, presented a mighty challenge to Victorian engineering skills. A track of 4⅝ miles had to be built over an ascent of 3140ft, finishing only 67ft below the 3560ft summit. It is the only public railway in Britain operating on the rack-and-pinion system familiar in the Alps. Its toothed central racks are gripped by cogged wheels, or pinions, and the train is pushed upwards tooth by tooth.

The trip up the mountain, starting from Llanberis, is an exhilarating experience. From the summit, on a clear day, it may be possible to see into England, Scotland and Ireland.

Mar-Oct, weekdays and most weekends. Fares. Refreshments. Shop. P *Toilets.* ♿ *Tel Llanberis (0286) 870223.*

SYGUN COPPER MINE

Off A498, just east of Beddgelert (Cc)

An old water wheel on the River Glaslyn just outside Beddgelert is a relic of a 19th-century copper mine where men once worked ten hours a day, six days a week, digging into the hillside in search of the elusive ore. The mine was abandoned in 1903 but has recently been opened up and restored. Visitors can step into the tunnel driven into the hill and discover an amazing world of caverns festooned with stalagmites and stalactites. They emerge on a hill with glorious views of the Gwynant Valley and Snowdonia. Artefacts, models and photographs and an audio-visual presentation can be seen at the visitor centre.

Apr-Oct, daily; Nov-Mar, Sat, Sun. Adm charge. Refreshments. Shop. P *Toilets. Tel Beddgelert (076 686) 595.*

TALYLLYN RAILWAY

Wharf station, Neptune Road, Tywyn (Ca)

Half-size steam engines pull old-style carriages along a single narrow-gauge track through some of the wildest scenery in Wales. The trains climb from the coast through mountain foothills with a distant view of Cadair Idris, over a deep gorge and along mountain ledges. The return trip of 14 miles to Nant Gwernol takes about two hours, with a short halt; but passengers can break their journey at Dolgoch Falls or Abergynolwyn.

At Dolgoch, a deep wooded gorge contains three waterfalls, paths and an old slate mine. At Abergynolwyn there is a quarry museum, and at Nant Gwernol there are forest paths, picnic sites and a path to the abandoned slate quarry.

The railway runs on a track built in 1865 to carry slate from the quarries to the coast; the carriages are a mixture of historic relics and modern versions built in the old style. A museum at Tywyn Wharf station contains gleaming narrow-gauge locomotives, wagons and signalling equipment, and visitors can operate the controls of the Victorian steam locomotive *Jubilee 1897*.

Railway: Easter-Sept, daily; Oct, daily exc Fri. Fares. Refreshments. Shop. P *Toilets.* ♿ *Tel Tywyn (0654) 710472. Museum: Apr-Oct, daily. Adm charge. Refreshments. Shop.* P *Toilets. Tel (0654) 710472.*

TREFRIW WOOLLEN MILL

On B5106, 1 mile north of Llanrwst (Dd)

The old Victorian mill used the waters of the River Crafnant both to drive two water wheels which powered the machinery, and also to wash the wool. The wheels have long since gone, but the traditional manufacturing process of turning raw wool into tapestries and tweed continues. Visitors can watch the carding, spinning, dyeing, warping and weaving, and see how the cloth is tailored into garments. Wool products are sold in the shop, where a film explains the manufacturing process.

All year, Mon-Fri, exc Bank Hol and two weeks at Christmas. Free entry. Refreshments. Shop. P *Tel Llanrwst (0492) 640462.*

WYLFA POWER STATION

Off A5025, 1½ miles north-west of Cemaes (Bc)

Perched on the rugged north-west coast of Anglesey, and clad in tinted brown and green metal sheeting to help it merge with the landscape, is a nuclear power station. Tours are arranged through the information centre on the site. The station may also be observed from a nearby headland, where an observation tower contains an exhibition on nuclear power; there is also a picnic site and a nature trail.

All year, Mon-Fri. Free entry. Shop. P *Toilets. Tel Cemaes Bay (0407) 710471.*

COUNTY CALENDAR

May Day Hol weekend. Llandudno: Victorian Festival.

May (mid-month). Llangefni: Eisteddfod Mon. Llanedwin: Anglesey Steam Rally.

May (late). Beaumaris: Arts Festival.

June (mid-month). Holyhead: Leisure Island Festival.

July (mid-month). Snowdon: International Race to Summit. Blaenau Ffestiniog: Festival of Transport and Energy.

July (late). Beaumaris Castle: Medieval Fayre. Menai Strait: Regattas. Bala: Carnival.

August (early). Caernarfon: North Wales Show.

August (mid-month). Holyhead: RAF Valley Open Day. Mona: Anglesey County Show.

August (late). Dolgellau: Merioneth County Show.

September (early). Bala: Watersports Festival.

October (early). Caernarfon: Folk Dance Festival.

Tourist information: Bangor (0248) 352786 (summer); Betwys-y-Coed (069 02) 426 (summer); Blaenau Ffestiniog (0766) 830360 (summer); Caernarfon (0286) 2232 (summer); Holyhead (0407) 2622 (summer); Llandudno (0492) 76413; Llangefni (0248) 724666.

PEAK PERFORMANCE *Dusted by feathery clouds, Snowdon (centre) and her sister peaks rise in grey grandeur beyond the placid, green-fringed waters of Llynnau Mymbyr.*

POWYS

MOUNTAINS, LAKES AND CAVES IN THE HEART OF WALES

Magnificent vistas of mountains and moorlands that give Powys its air of wild romanticism give way in places to softer, rolling farmlands and gentle river valleys. The two tallest mountains in South Wales – Pen y Fan and Corn Du – can be seen from the Brecon Beacons Mountain Centre, while thrusting deep into a hillside to the north of Abercraf are the spectacular Dan-yr-Ogof Caves. To the natural landscape, man has added the mighty earthwork of Offa's Dyke – the first man-made frontier between Wales and England, and the subject of a special heritage centre in Knighton.

The industrial face of South Wales – past, present and future – is represented by the Bryn Tail Lead Mine, the Cambrian Factory where wool is spun and woven, and the futuristic Centre for Alternative Technology. Museums commemorate the area's two most famous sons: the social reformer Robert Owen and the Welsh freedom fighter Owain Glyndwr, who in the early 15th century made Machynlleth his capital.

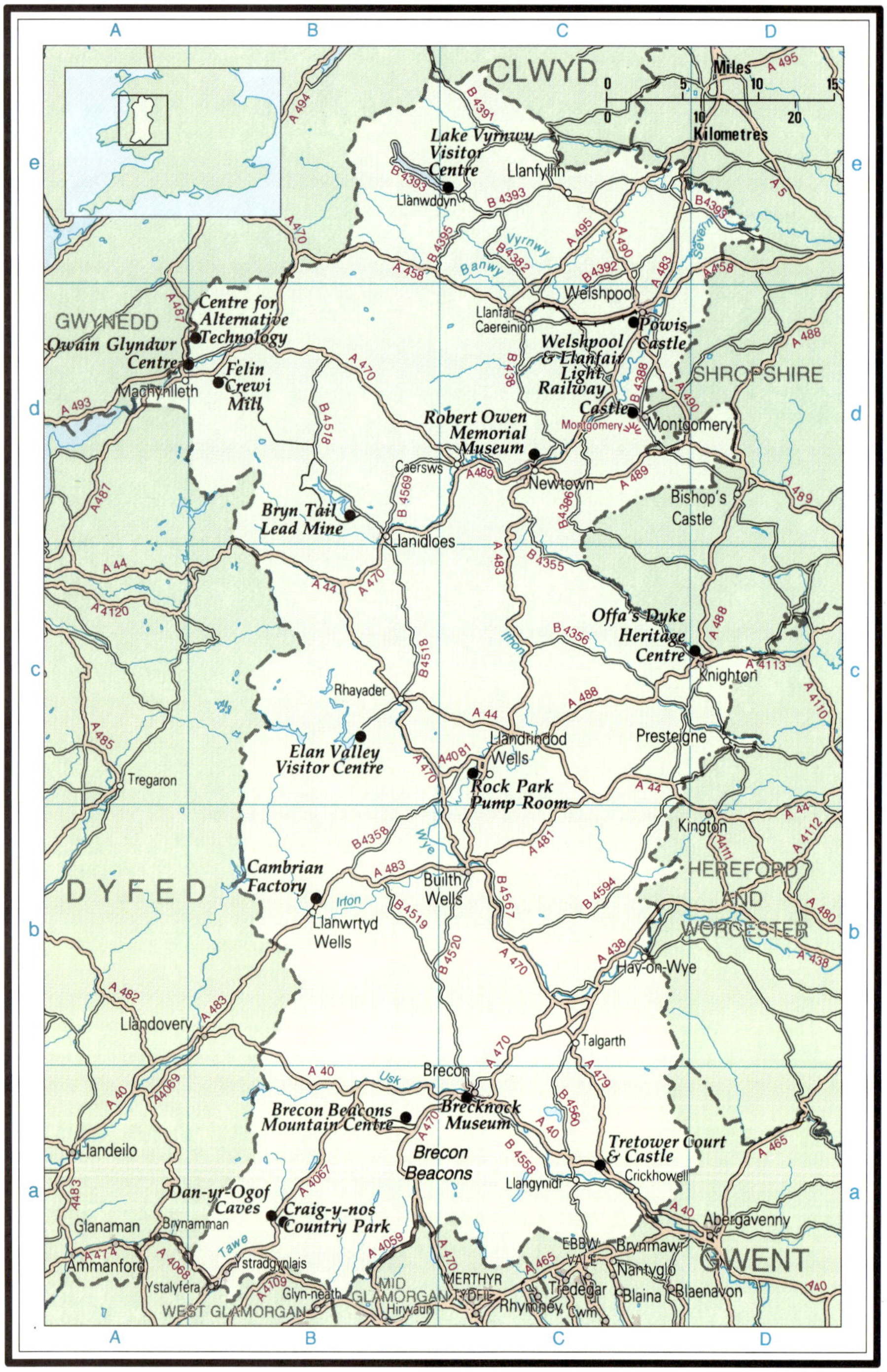

BRECKNOCK MUSEUM

Captain's Walk, Brecon (Ca)

The splendid classical façade of Brecknock Museum is a fitting showcase for the treasures within. The white stone building, with its grand portico, once served as the Shire Hall; inside, the old Victorian assize court is preserved intact. An archaeology gallery displays early Christian inscribed stones, monuments from Roman times and an ancient dug-out canoe found in nearby Llangorse Lake. A traditional Welsh kitchen has been re-created, and includes a collection of intricately carved lovespoons, symbols of betrothal in the rural Wales of old.

Another museum in Brecon, beside the Barracks, is devoted to the South Wales Borderers. Military relics span the regiment's 280 year history, the Zulu War Room recalling its heroic defence of Rorke's Drift in 1879, when 141 Borderers held off 4000 Zulu warriors.

On the hill above Brecon stands its cathedral, dating largely from the 14th century. Its interior is notable for its fine Early English chancel arch and impressive vaulting. The former priory church was elevated to cathedral status in 1923.

Brecknock Museum: All year, daily exc Sun. Free entry. Shop. P *(limited). Toilets.* ♿ *Tel Brecon (0874) 4121. Borderers Museum: Apr-Sept, daily; Oct-Mar, Mon-Fri. Adm charge. Shop.* P *(limited). Toilets.* ♿ *Tel (0874) 3111 ext. 310. Cathedral: All year, daily.*

BRECON BEACONS MOUNTAIN CENTRE

Off A470, 5½ miles south-west of Brecon (Ba)

The view from the balcony of the Mountain Centre is one of the finest in the Brecon Beacons National Park. The centre stands on a grassy shoulder of land right in the middle of the park more than 1000ft up on Mynydd Illtud, a stretch of open moorland which commands panoramic views of the park's four mountain ranges. To the south-east the horizon is dominated by the distinctive twin peaks of Pen y Fan (2970ft) and Corn Du (2863ft), whose triangular summits are the highest in South Wales.

The centre's displays, exhibition panels and guide books are an excellent source of information on the entire 519 square mile park, and a good introduction for anyone wishing to explore its various upland ranges. The Mountain Centre is the starting point of a number of easy walks across Mynydd Illtud – a gently undulating common where hardy mountain ponies graze – and has details of the routes.

All year, daily. Free entry. Refreshments. P *(Fee). Toilets.* ♿ *Tel Brecon (0874) 3366.*

SONGBIRD'S RETREAT *Ringed by wooded hills and fields, Craig-y-nos Castle was the country retreat in the late 19th century of the 'Queen of Song' – opera singer Adelina Patti, who gave private performances there.*

BRYN TAIL LEAD MINE

Off B4518, 3 miles north of Llanidloes (Bd)

It is hard to imagine a time when the silent, green hills of Mid Wales were busy with industry. Bryn Tail, on the hillside above the shores of Llyn Clywedog, is one of the few 19th-century lead-mining sites that have been preserved; it is now an open-air museum whose relics and displays re-create its vanished past. A number of different processes are covered, from the extraction of the lead ore from the rocks to its crushing to extract the valuable mineral. Bryn Tail's peak year was in 1851, when nearly 400 tons of ore were mined; it closed in 1884.

Cadw. All year, daily. Free entry. P *Tel Cardiff (0222) 465511.*

CAMBRIAN FACTORY

On A483, ½ mile east of Llanwrtyd Wells (Bb)

Sorting, dyeing, carding, spinning, warping, winding and weaving are among the processes in wool manufacturing that can be viewed at this roadside mill deep in the Welsh hills. The factory, a sizable one considering its remote location, manufactures tweeds traditionally spun and woven from pure new Welsh wool. All the workshops are open to visitors, who can buy the fabrics made in them.

All year, Mon-Fri. Free entry. Refreshments. Shop. P *Toilets.* ♿ *Tel Llanwrtyd (059 13) 211.*

CENTRE FOR ALTERNATIVE TECHNOLOGY

On A487, 3 miles north of Machynlleth (Bd)

In an abandoned slate quarry deep in the Welsh hills, this so-called 'Village of the Future' puts into practice a host of theories on energy conservation and self-sufficiency. The centre's location among thickly forested slopes can be identified by the tall, windmill-like structure standing out above the trees. This is an aerogenerator, a machine for generating electricity from wind power to supply the centre. It is typical of the many ingenious devices employed at the centre to harness natural resources in a non-polluting way. Some of the devices are of Heath Robinson-like complexity while others are disarmingly simple; all are designed to exploit alternative, and renewable, sources of heat, light and power.

Water turbines and a water wheel make the most of Mid-Wales's high rainfall. When the sun does shine, solar panels are ready to trap the sun's energy to heat water, to power a steam engine and to provide more electricity. At a heavily insulated energy-saving house, visitors can pick up tips for reducing their own heating bills, while organic methods of growing vegetables can be seen in the centre's garden.

All year, daily. Adm charge. Refreshments. Shop. P *Toilets.* ♿ *Tel Machynlleth (0654) 2400.*

CRAIG-Y-NOS COUNTRY PARK

Off A4067, 5 miles north of Ystradgynlais (Ba)

The large Gothic mansion of Craig-y-nos Castle looks down onto the ornamental grounds and open meadowlands of this lovely country park. The castle (not open to the public) and park were the 19th-century country home of the internationally acclaimed soprano Adelina Patti, who died in 1919.

Madame Patti's 40 acre 'Pleasure Grounds' are laid out in a sheltered valley below the rambling old mansion. The great attractions of Craig-y-nos ('Rock of the night') lie in the variety of habitats within its relatively limited space and the contrast this formal, man-made park presents with the rugged hills on its doorstep.

An arboretum of specimen trees selected for their colour, fragrance or fruit merges into thick beechwoods leading down to the River Tawe, and a tributary, the Llynfell. Visitors can stroll by an ornamental pond, venture along riverbank and woodland footpaths, with peaceful picnic sites, or step back into the heyday of the estate in the 1890s through the display in a restored pavilion.

All year, daily. Free entry. P *(Fee). Toilets.* ♿ *Tel Abercraf (0639) 730395.*

CATHEDRAL CAVE *Soaring upwards for 70ft, and extending for 160ft, Cathedral Cave at Dan-yr-Ogof is the largest single chamber in any British show cave. Exploration of the cave complex began in 1912.*

DAN-YR-OGOF CAVES

Off A4067, 7 miles north of Ystradgynlais (Ba)

Weird and wonderful cave formations, stalactites and stalagmites can be seen on a guided tour within the steep boulder-strewn hillside at Dan-yr-Ogof in the Upper Tawe valley. The caves' evocative names describe the spectacle – 'Frozen Waterfall', 'Alabaster Pillar', 'Dagger Chamber' and 'Cauldron Chamber'. There is even a 'Flitch of Bacon', a translucent curtain formation that resembles a streaky rasher. The labyrinth of underground features was created over 'millions' of years by streams and percolating water in the limestone rock. Visitors enter Dan-yr-Ogof's main show cave, the longest in Britain, near a point where the River Llynfell returns to the surface after an underground journey of some 14 miles.

In the thickly wooded gorge above lies the entrance to Ogof-yr-Esgyrn, the Bone Cave. Imaginative displays – of animals, for example,

and of a prehistoric family – and an audiovisual sequence tell the story of man the early cave dweller. Dan-yr-Ogof's many attractions are not all below ground. The extensive site also contains a Dinosaur Park populated by life-size models of these prehistoric beasts, a museum and a 350ft dry ski slope with ski tow.
Caves: Easter-Oct, daily. Adm charge. Refreshments. Shop. P *Toilets. Ski Centre: Nov-Mar. Adm charge. Refreshments. Shop.* P *Toilets. Tel Abercraf (0639) 730284.*

ELAN VALLEY VISITOR CENTRE

Off B4518, 6 miles south-west of Rhayader (Bc)

In the folds of the starkly beautiful Cambrian Mountains lies a 9 mile long chain of delightful man-made lakes, created earlier this century when the valleys were flooded to create four huge reservoirs to provide water for Birmingham. The Elan Valley Visitor Centre, run by Welsh Water, tells the story of the remote and rugged valley from earliest times to the present.

Vast, empty stretches of moor and mountainside today rise from the lakes. But the area was not always so sparsely populated. As exhibitions and an audiovisual show explain, the valley has been inhabited since Bronze Age times, and in the Middle Ages Cistercian monks established a Monks' Road across the wilderness. A wide range of animals and birds find a haven there; in particular it is the home of the rare red kite.

Welsh Water, the authority which runs the centre, provides a graphic description of the building of the reservoirs, the first of which were completed in 1904, and their vital role today. The centre also has an attractive picnic area.
Easter-Oct, daily. Free entry. Refreshments. Shop. P *Toilets.* ♿ *Tel Llandrindod Wells (0597) 810880.*

FELIN CREWI MILL

Off A489, 2 miles east of Machynlleth (Bd)

The cast-iron water wheel is turning again and the mill stones are grinding at this old, beautifully restored mill. Felin Crewi is a solid, slate-roofed group of 18th-century buildings, finished in attractive rough-hewn local stone that dazzles with whitewash. It dates from the 18th century and is now one of the few working corn mills in Wales. The mill produces 12 grades of flour, the products of which can be sampled in its café.
Apr-Sept, daily; Oct-Mar, Mon-Fri. Adm charge. Refreshments. Shop. P *Toilets.* ♿ *Tel Machynlleth (0654) 3113.*

LAKE VYRNWY VISITOR CENTRE

On B4393, 8 miles east of Llanfyllin (Cc)

The original village of Llanwddyn was flooded in the late 19th century to create the dramatically beautiful Lake Vyrnwy – a reservoir almost 5 miles long and up to half a mile wide. A new settlement was built at the foot of the dam, together with a chapel – Capel Bethel – which now houses a visitor centre. This tells the story of the lake's creation, and describes the bird and animal life to be found on its forested shores.
Easter-Spring Bank Hol, weekends; Spring Bank Hol-Sept, daily. Free entry. P *Toilets.* ♿ *Tel Llanwddyn (069 173) 688.*

RUSTIC REVELS *Festive shepherds and shepherdesses pipe and dance on the balustrade of a terrace above the orangery at Powis Castle. The statues are made of lead and painted white to resemble marble.*

MONTGOMERY CASTLE

In centre of Montgomery (Cd)

The ruined fortress stands in a lofty, strategic spot on an outcrop above the Severn valley, its stumpy stonework and fractured walls looming over the handsome little town round its base. Montgomery Castle was built by Henry III in the early 13th century and last saw active service in the Civil War, after which it was dismantled. Some evidence of its original strength still remains in its large, twin-towered gatehouse and the formidable rock-cut ditch. Finds from excavations at the castle are on show in the museum in the town.
Cadw. All year, daily. Free entry. P *Tel Cardiff (0222) 465511.*

OFFA'S DYKE HERITAGE CENTRE

West Street, Knighton (Dc)

Created by King Offa of Mercia in the 8th century, Offa's Dyke formed the first official border between the Welsh and the English, and the huge earthwork snakes from Prestatyn in North Wales to Chepstow in the south. A 168 mile long-distance footpath now follows the line of the dyke, keeping close to it wherever possible.

Some idea of the monumental construction effort involved in building the dyke, and details of its history, can be obtained in the Offa's Dyke Heritage Centre. Those who want to see the real thing do not have to travel far, for well-preserved sections of the earthwork survive in a long, unbroken stretch in the hills just to the north-west.
June-Sept, Mon-Sat; Apr, May and Oct, Tues-Sat. Free entry. Toilets. Tel Knighton (0547) 528753.

OWAIN GLYNDWR CENTRE

In centre of Machynlleth (Ad)

In this stone and half-timbered building along Machynlleth's main street the last great Welsh rebel, Owain Glyndwr, is said to have presided in 1404 at the first – and only – Welsh parliament. Today the building houses an exhibition devoted to the life of this enigmatic folk leader, the mercurial 'great magician, damned Glendower' of Shakespeare's *Henry IV* who led a Welsh uprising in the early 15th century. Next door, an information centre tells the history of the region and the story of Welsh slate.
Easter-Sept, Mon-Sat. Free entry. Shop. ♿ *Tel Machynlleth (0654) 2401.*

POWIS CASTLE

On A483, 1 mile south of Welshpool (Cd)

Perched on a steep ridge above the balustraded terraces of its Italianate gardens, Powis might be taken for a papal villa, rather than a medieval Welsh border castle. Although it began life, in 1200, as a simple stone fortress, it evolved in opulence over the centuries to become the mansion of deep red stone, mock-military turrets, towers and battlements which visitors see today.

The transformation was largely wrought in the late 17th century by the 3rd Baron Powis, who also created the formal gardens. In 1784, Lord Clive – son of Clive of India – married into the family, bringing the Clives' vast wealth to Powis. The Clives enriched the castle's store of treasures with fine paintings, furniture and memorabilia from their years in India; these are on show in the Clive of India Museum. Other treasures include a 16th-century table from Florence, inlaid with marble and semiprecious stones, and a canopied four-poster bed fit for a king. Outside, clipped yews overhang the terraced gardens, which have steps, statues and pavilions, and colourful plants at every level. Below the bottom terrace a grassy bank descends to a great lawn.

In nearby Welshpool, the Powysland Museum explores the history of this part of the borderlands. Kitchen and dairy implements give an insight into bygone domestic life, and there are displays of textiles and country crafts.

Powis Castle and Garden: NT. July-Aug, daily exc Mon; mid Apr-June, Sept and Oct, daily exc Mon and Tues; also Bank Hol. Adm charge. Refreshments. Shop. 🅿 *Toilets. Tel Welshpool (0938) 4336. Museum: All year, daily exc Sat am, Sun and Bank Hol. Free entry. Shop. Tel (0938) 4759.*

ROBERT OWEN MEMORIAL MUSEUM

Broad Street, Newtown (Cd)

The remarkable story of Robert Owen, who was born in Newtown in 1771, is told through displays of his works and possessions. He began as a shop boy and became manager of the great cotton mills at New Lanark in Scotland, where he built world-famous schools, and fought for Poor Law reform and for restriction of child labour. His writings on social reform through universal education and community living brought him many followers, and inspired the modern Co-operative Movement.

By the 19th century his home town had become known as 'the Leeds of Wales' on the strength of its thriving woollen industry. Old hand looms, machinery and items of social history from the heyday of flannel production are on display at the nearby Textile Museum, which is housed in an old weaving shop.

Robert Owen Museum: All year, Mon-Sat exc Sat pm and Bank Hol. Free entry. Shop. Tel Newtown (0686) 26345. Textile Museum: All year, Tues-Sat. Free entry.

ROCK PARK PUMP ROOM

In centre of Llandrindod Wells (Cc)

Gout, rheumatism, anaemia and dyspepsia are among the numerous complaints that the healing waters of Llandrindod Wells are said to treat. The tranquil little town, 700ft above sea level, is a perfectly preserved Victorian spa. Today's visitors can sample three types of spa water in Edwardian style, at the Rock Park Pump Room, which stands in 18 acres of wooded parkland. The Victorian and Edwardian heyday of this and other Welsh spas is recaptured in a pictorial history displayed at the Bath House next door.

The Town Hall Gardens are the setting for the Llandrindod Wells Museum. Amongst the museum's exhibits are items excavated from the Roman camp at nearby Castell Collen, and a charming doll collection.

Another side of Victorian life is explored at the Automobile Palace, in the town centre. Penny-farthings, solid-tyred 'boneshakers', motorised bicycles and an early tandem tricycle are on display next to brand-new cars.

Pump Room: Mar-Oct, daily. Free entry. Refreshments. 🅿 *Toilets.* ♿ *Tel Llandrindod Wells (0597) 4307. Museum: All year, Mon-Sat exc Bank Hol and Sat pm Oct-Mar. Free entry. Shop.* 🅿 *Tel (0597) 4513. Automobile Palace: All year, Mon-Sat exc Bank Hol. Free entry.* 🅿 *Toilets.* ♿ *Tel (0597) 2079.*

TRETOWER COURT AND CASTLE

Off A479, 3 miles north-west of Crickhowell (Ca)

Tretower takes its visitors back into two different periods of history. The Court is a substantial medieval manor house, commodious and comfortable by the standards of its period. Across the green meadows stands another, older Tretower, a greystoned tall round tower which is the shell of an early military stronghold.

Tretower's fascination lies in the contrast, expressed in stone and timber, between the bellicose early medieval period in Wales and the more settled late 14th and 15th centuries. The former era finds expression in the stark round tower and fragments of fortified wall, both of which are Norman. The Court, ranged around a grassy courtyard, was clearly designed for purposes other than war. Its spacious rooms and stout oak timbers convey the flavour of gracious living. The gallery's sliding wooden shutters, the gallery itself and the panelled timber partition in the hall are notable examples of woodwork.

Tretower was the home of the Vaughan family whose best known member was the 17th-century metaphysical poet, Henry Vaughan.

Cadw. All year, daily exc Sun am. Adm charge. Toilets. ♿ *Tel Brecon (0874) 730279.*

WELSHPOOL AND LLANFAIR LIGHT RAILWAY

Off A458, 9 miles west of Welshpool (Cd)

This charming narrow-gauge steam-powered line runs through rich, rolling border country between the market town of Welshpool and the village of Llanfair Caereinion. The 8 mile line links the wide Severn valley to the narrower Banwy valley and the start of the Welsh hills proper, climbing to 603ft on the way.

Each of Wales's 'Great Little Railways' has its own distinctive personality. The character of the Welshpool and Llanfair comes from its idyllic route and its cosmopolitan collection of rolling stock. The railway boasts an international line-up of steam engines from places as far apart as Austria, Africa and the West Indies. Pride of place, though, goes to *The Earl* and *The Countess*, two of the locomotives built for the opening of the line in 1903. Passengers ride on vintage coaches from Austria or modern examples from Africa.

The Llanfair Line was built early this century to carry country people and their produce to market. It died with the advent of buses and lorries, the last passenger train running in 1931 and the final goods train in 1956. By the early 1960s trains were once again back on the tracks, thanks to the efforts of volunteer enthusiasts.

Mid July-mid Sept, daily; mid June-mid July, daily exc Mon and Fri; also Spring Bank Hol Week, and Sat and Sun from Easter to Oct. Adm charge. Shop. 🅿 *Toilets (Llanfair).* ♿ *Tel Llanfair Caereinion (0938) 810441.*

COUNTY CALENDAR

May (late). Welshpool: Agricultural Show.

June (mid-month). Llanwrytd Wells: Drovers' Walk.

July (mid-month). Welshpool: Festival of Transport. Builth Wells: Royal Welsh Show.

August (1st Sat). Brecon: County Show.

August (1st week). Llanwrtyd: Festival.

August (late). Llanwrtyd Wells: District Show

August (Bank Hol Mon). Llanwrtyd Wells: World Bog Snorkelling Championships.

September (early). Sennybridge: Agricultural Show.

September (1st two weeks). Llandrindod Wells: Victorian Festival.

Tourist information: Knighton (0547) 528753; Llandrindod Wells (0597) 2600; Llanwrtyd Wells (0591) 3391; Machynlleth (0654) 2401; Welshpool (0938) 2043.

STILL WATERS *Man added to the scenic beauty of the Welsh hills in the 1880s by creating Lake Vyrnwy as a source of water for Liverpool. The Gothic tower is the start of a 68 mile pipeline.*

SCOTLAND

Centuries of history abide in the mighty castles of Edinburgh, Stirling and Glamis; in glorious abbeys at Melrose, Kelso and Jedburgh; and in grim Border strongholds such as Smailholm. Legends cling to Loch Ness and Dunvegan Castle, while ghosts of the real past still haunt Bannockburn, Culloden and brooding Glencoe. Scotland's climate has produced spectacular gardens at Inverewe, Logan and Pitmedden. Ospreys nest at Loch Garten, and lions and tigers roar at Blair Drummond. Indoors there are museums of clan history, Highland life, fisheries and whisky, and Glasgow's Burrell Collection is one of the grandest treasure houses of art in Britain. Visitors intent on scenic wonders will head for the great nature reserves of the north – craggy Beinn Eighe, and the ancient worn landscapes of Torridon and Inverpolly.

Edinburgh Castle: the Military Tattoo

BORDERS

CASTLES AMONG THE HILLS THAT INSPIRED TWO WRITERS

Hermitage Castle and Smailholm Tower evoke the warring centuries on the Scottish Border before 1700, and museums in Jedburgh and Selkirk tell the stormy history of two Border towns. The medieval Traquair House is believed to be Scotland's oldest inhabited home, while at Jedburgh and Melrose impressive remains of great abbeys have survived the ravages of the centuries. Later peaceful times saw Floors, Thirlestane and Neidpath castles transformed into gracious mansions. The Border hills inspired Sir Walter Scott, whose home was at Abbotsford, while another writer who loved Tweeddale is recalled in the John Buchan Centre.

ABBEY ST BATHANS

Off B6355, 10 miles north of Duns (Cc)

Bronze Age people, Picts, Celts and early Christians have all been settlers in this beautiful and secluded valley between the Lammermuir Hills and the sea. Today the traces of hill-forts, hut settlements and a Pictish broch survive in an undisturbed woodland setting. The abbey itself, close to Whiteadder Water, was destroyed by Henry VIII's forces, but its church survives. A craft centre and gallery displays work by Scottish craftsmen and artists. Salmon fishing, a trout farm and the sight of deer are among the other attractions of Abbey St Bathans today.

Visitor Centre: Easter-Sept, daily. Free entry. Refreshments. Shop. P *Toilets. Tel Abbey St Bathans (036 14) 242. Trout farm: All year, daily.*

ABBOTSFORD

Off A7, 2 miles east of Galashiels (Bc)

The passion for Scotland's history which found expression in Sir Walter Scott's novels and poems is reflected also in the historical mementos that still adorn the house in which he spent the last years of his life. Among them are Rob Roy's broadsword and dagger, Robert Burns's tumbler with some of his verses scratched on it, and Bonnie Prince Charlie's drinking cup.

When the Scott family first moved to Abbotsford, they lived in a farmhouse named Cartley Hall. In 1822 Sir Walter pulled this down and built an imposing mansion with turrets, battlements, and a gateway fit for a castle. In the entrance hall and armoury is a fine collection of arms and armour, including a sword with a calendar of saints' days engraved on the blade.

Among the paintings in the drawing room are Raeburn's portrait of Sir Walter (another version is at Bowhill) and a delightful study of his dog, Ginger, by Landseer. In the south courtyard stands a sculpture of his deerhound, Maida, which served as a mounting block. Maida died in 1824 and lies buried beneath the effigy.

Mar-Oct, daily. Adm charge. Refreshments. Shop. P *Toilets.* ♿ *Tel Galashiels (0896) 2043.*

BOWHILL

Off A708, 3 miles west of Selkirk (Bb)

Set in beautiful woodland against a backdrop of heather-clad hills, this rambling Georgian mansion, Border home of the Dukes of Buccleuch, is a treasure house of rich furnishings and superb paintings, including works by Canaletto, Gainsborough and Reynolds. By contrast, the macabre relic of the shirt in which the Duke of Monmouth was executed after his ill-fated uprising against James II recalls Monmouth's links with the family as husband of Anne, heiress to the Scotts of Buccleuch.

The 4th Duke of Buccleuch's friendship with Sir Walter Scott is commemorated by Raeburn's famous portrait of the poet, the 5th duke's 65 years at Bowhill are recalled by gifts and letters from Queen Victoria and an album of Victorian valentines. There are two woodland nature trails – one skirting two small lochs and another leading down to Yarrow Water.

House and Grounds: July-mid Aug, pm daily. Grounds: May-mid July, pm daily exc Fri. Adm charge. Refreshments. Shop. P *Toilets.* ♿ *Tel Selkirk (0750) 20732.*

COLDSTREAM MUSEUM

Market Square, Coldstream (Cc)

Wrought-iron gates fashioned by a local blacksmith provide an impressive entrance to this small museum honouring the feats of the Coldstream Guards. During the harsh winter of 1659 General Monck, Commander of the Army in Scotland, set up his headquarters in the Guards House at Coldstream – now the museum. His troops braved the cold with such a cheerful spirit that they became known as 'the Coldstreamers'. After Cromwell's death Monck marched his hardy band south, restoring order and paving the way for the restoration of Charles II.

The cap badges of many Scottish regiments are on display, and the ground floor of the museum is devoted to local history. There are relics from a flour mill, a Victorian country kitchen and a collection of old agricultural machinery.

At the western end of Coldstream, a lakeside farmstead houses the Hirsel Homestead Museum and Craft Centre. On display are the implements of blacksmiths, fishermen, farmworkers and laundrymaids in bygone days. The museum also traces the history of the Home family, the Hirsel's

owners since 1611; one notable descendant, Sir Alec Douglas-Home, later Lord Home, was Prime Minister in 1963-4. In summer, resident craftsmen weave, turn wood and set gems.
Coldstream Museum: Easter, July-Oct, pm daily; mid May-June, pm daily exc Mon. Adm charge. P *Tel Coldstream (0890) 2630. The Hirsel: All year, daily. Entry by donation. Refreshments (Sun and Bank Hol). Shop.* P *Toilets.* ♿ *Tel (0890) 2834.*

DAWYCK BOTANIC GARDEN

On B712, 6 miles south-west of Peebles (Ac)

Thousands of daffodils line the drive of Dawyck House in spring, and from April to June many varieties of rhododendron flower along the Rhododendron Walk. Administered by the Royal Botanic Garden, Edinburgh, the arboretum has trees from every part of the world, including a noted collection of Chinese conifers.

Near the house stands an unusual beech with upright branches like a poplar, discovered growing on the estate in the 1830s and christened the Dawyck Beech. In autumn the beeches and maples provide a spectacular blaze of colour.
Apr-Sept, daily. Adm charge. P *Toilets.* ♿ *Tel Peebles (0721) 6254.*

DRYBURGH ABBEY

On B6356, 1 mile north of St Boswells (Cc)

Two famous Scotsmen lie buried among the majestic ruins of Dryburgh Abbey: the writer Sir Walter Scott and Field-Marshal Earl Haig, commander of the British Army in France during the First World War. Built around 1150 by the White Canons, the abbey has lain in ruins since the 16th century, when it was burnt down and the town of Dryburgh destroyed by a 700-strong raiding party from across the Border. Arches and doorways are still visible in the ruins of the abbey church, and the west wall of the refectory still has the framework of a rose window.
HBM. All year, daily exc Sun am. Adm charge. Shop. P *(limited). Toilets. Tel Edinburgh (031) 244 3101.*

POET'S CORNER *A statue of Sir Walter Scott and some of his belongings lie on his study desk at Abbotsford. In 1935, two secret drawers in the desk yielded dozens of letters which the writer and his wife exchanged before and after their marriage.*

EYEMOUTH MUSEUM

Market Place, Eyemouth (Dc)

On Eyemouth's 'Black Friday', October 14, 1881, a freak storm caught the town's fishing fleet at sea and 189 fishermen were drowned – nearly half the adult male population of Eyemouth. The victims are commemorated in this museum by a tapestry showing scenes of the shipwrecks and the names of the lost sailors. A re-creation of a 19th-century fisherman's cottage shows the lifestyle of those who made their living by the sea, and a modern fishing boat gives evidence of Eyemouth's continuing existence as a port.
Easter-Oct, daily exc Sun am. Adm charge. Shop. P *(limited).* ♿ *(part). Tel Eyemouth (0890) 50678.*

FLOORS CASTLE

Off A6089, 1 mile north of Kelso (Cc)

The dramatic roofscape of turrets, domes and clustered chimneys makes Floors look more like a chateau on the Loire than a castle on the Tweed. Originally it was a plain Georgian country house built for the 1st Duke of Roxburghe in the 1720s by William Adam. In the 1840s the 6th Duke commissioned William Playfair to turn Floors into the castle of his dreams. The result was the palatial residence which today's filmgoers may recognise as the ancestral home of the Earl of Greystoke – better known as Tarzan.

The ballroom and dining room contain exquisite porcelain and French furniture, mainly collected by May, the American wife of the 8th Duke. It was May, too, who remodelled the drawing room to accommodate a magnificent set of Brussels tapestries brought from her family's Long Island mansion. More unexpected are the splendid collections of stuffed birds and of parasols, and a model of the castle made from icing sugar and matchsticks by the chef in 1851.

The walled garden has beautiful herbaceous borders and rosebeds. Several varieties of carnation, including the 'Duchess of Roxburghe', have been created at Floors and many of the plants grown there are on sale at the garden centre.
Easter, May-July, Sept, daily exc Fri and Sat; July-Aug, daily exc Sat. Adm charge. Refreshments. Shop. P *Toilets.* ♿ *Tel Kelso (0573) 23333.*

HALLIWELL'S HOUSE MUSEUM

Halliwell's Close, Market Place, Selkirk (Bb)

Mousetraps, fishing tackle, chamberpots and coffin handles jostle for space on the shelves of a reconstructed ironmonger's shop stocking every tool or gadget a housewife, handyman or country gentleman of Edwardian times could have needed. Ironmongers lived and sold their wares in Halliwell's Close – named after a wigmaker who owned the buildings in the 18th century – for more than 150 years. The museum also has displays on the turbulent history of the ancient Royal Burgh of Selkirk.

BLACK FRIDAY *Fishermen battle the great storm of 1881, on the Eyemouth Tapestry in the town's museum, opened in 1981. Local people took more than two years to cover the 15ft canvas with nearly a million stitches.*

Selkirk's association with the novelist Sir Walter Scott is recalled in Sir Walter Scott's Courtroom in the old town hall. From 1799 until his death in 1832 Scott served as Sheriff, or judge, of Selkirk, hearing cases ranging from disputes over wagers to salmon-poaching and sheep-stealing. Visitors can see his Bench and chair.
Museum: Apr-Oct, daily exc Sun am; Nov and Dec, pm Sun-Fri and Sat am. Adm charge. Shop. P *Toilets. Tel Selkirk (0750) 20096. Courtroom: July-Aug, pm Mon-Fri. Free entry.* P *Toilets. Tel (0750) 20096.*

HERMITAGE CASTLE

Off B6399, 15 miles south of Hawick (Bb)

Standing stark and four-square on a grassy platform, Hermitage Castle has kept watch over miles of surrounding moorland for five centuries. Its lonely setting, and a violent history which includes murders by starvation, drowning and boiling alive, give the towering pile an eerie atmosphere even on the brightest day.

A 14th-century tower built by the Douglases still survives, but round it have been added over the centuries four massive towers with connecting walls, looking outwardly almost intact to this day. It was to Hermitage that Mary, Queen of Scots, in 1566, rode 25 miles from Jedburgh to see the wounded Bothwell, her lover and later her third husband, and returned to Jedburgh in a high fever that nearly killed her.
HBM. All year, daily exc Sun am. Adm charge. P *Tel Edinburgh (031) 244 3101.*

JEDBURGH ABBEY

In centre of Jedburgh (Cb)

This abbey of rich red sandstone has survived a turbulent history to maintain its place as one of Scotland's most beautiful buildings. Its 84ft tower rises above a nave which at first sight looks almost intact but is in fact roofless and windowless. Founded by King David I in 1138, the abbey was a retreat of Augustinian monks. Being so close to the English border, it was the target of much sacking and pillaging over the years. Even so, parts of it were still being used for public worship in Victorian times. When a new church was founded in 1875 the remains of the abbey, with a magnificent west door, were restored.

High above the town of Jedburgh where a castle once stood, the former castle jail is now a museum of Victorian prison life, with a section devoted to the social history of the town. The separate, heated cells, open exercise yard and prison kitchen – little changed since the 1820s – show what conditions were like after the prison reforms introduced by John Howard in 1774. In nearby Queen Street, a 16th-century house where Mary, Queen of Scots is said to have stayed in 1566 is now a visitor centre giving an interpretation of her life through the work of local craftsmen and relics of the tragic queen.

Abbey: HBM. Apr-Sept, daily exc Sun am; Oct-Mar, Mon-Wed, Thur am, Sun pm. Adm charge. Shop. P *Toilets. Tel Edinburgh (031) 244 3101. Jail: Easter-Sept, daily exc Sun am. Adm charge.* P *(limited). Toilets. Tel Jedburgh (0835) 63254. Mary, Queen of Scots' House: Easter-Oct, daily. Adm charge.* P *Tel (0835) 63301.*

JIM CLARK MEMORIAL ROOM

Newtown Street, Duns (Cc)

A Japanese samurai helmet and a large cowbell with an embroidered leather halter are two of the more unusual trophies assembled in the memorial room dedicated to the Scottish racing driver Jim Clark, who died in an accident in 1978. More than 120 trophies presented to Clark are on display.

Clark lived in Chirnside, about 6 miles from Duns, and is buried in the churchyard there. In 1963, at the age of 27, he became the youngest driver ever to win the World Championship. His record total of 25 Grand Prix successes was broken in 1973 by his close friend Jackie Stewart, but his record of seven wins in one season still remains unbeaten.

Apr-Oct, daily. Adm charge. P *Toilets.* ♿ *Tel Duns (0361) 82600.*

JOHN BUCHAN CENTRE

Off A701, at Broughton (Ac)

The little church in Upper Tweeddale where the writer John Buchan often worshipped is now a museum devoted to his life and achievements. Although he was born in Perth and grew up in Fife and Glasgow, Buchan frequently spent his summer holidays in Broughton, where his grandfather farmed. A keen fisherman and hill-walker, Buchan loved Tweeddale and chose the title Lord Tweedsmuir when he became a peer. On display in the museum are photographs and personal possessions, copies of Buchan's books and mementos from his career, which included the post of Governor-General of Canada.

Easter-mid Oct, pm daily. Adm charge. P *(limited). Toilets.* ♿ *Tel Biggar (0899) 21050.*

BORDER LOOKOUT *The dramatic ruin of Smailholm Tower overlooks a small loch and the fertile Tweed plain. Sir Walter Scott described it as 'that mountain'd tower, Which charm'd my fancy's wakening hour' in* Marmion.

JOHN WOOD COLLECTION

Fishers Brae, Coldingham (Dd)

A garage in the seaside village of Coldingham is the unlikely setting for a remarkable collection of Victorian and Edwardian photographs. In 1983, in a shed belonging to a retired market gardener, a garage owner named Robert Thomson stumbled upon two boxes of glass plate negatives coated with grime. After painstakingly cleaning them he was able to make pin-sharp prints of ploughmen, soldiers, stonemasons, sheep-shearers, blacksmiths, and early motor vehicles.

The pictures were taken by a local photographer named John Wood. After Wood died in 1914, a village handyman carted away from his studio two truck-loads of plates to use for glazing greenhouses. Thousands of Wood's photographs were lost, but the 600 that have survived provide a marvellous record of rural life in the late 19th and early 20th centuries.

Apr-Oct, daily exc Sun. Free entry. Shop. P *Toilets. Tel Coldingham (089 07) 71259.*

KAILZIE GARDENS

On B7062, 2½ miles south-east of Peebles (Bc)

The gardens provide a splendid contrast between the cultivated and the wild, since they are set within 15 acres of woodland, burnside and laburnum walks. A walled garden has a collection of old-fashioned shrub roses. There is also a waterfowl pond and an art gallery. The estate lies beside the River Tweed, with hills all around.

Apr-Oct, daily. Adm charge. Refreshments. P *Toilets.* ♿ *Tel Peebles (0721) 20007.*

KELSO ABBEY

Bridge Street, Kelso (Cc)

A porch towering so high that it dwarfs the surrounding trees bears silent witness to the former splendour of this spectacular ruined abbey. Founded in 1128 for monks from Chartres, the abbey was built in the unusual form of a double cross surmounted by twin towers. Inside it had 12 altars and was divided by a transverse wall to create an area at the back reserved exclusively for chanting monks. The abbey was largely destroyed in the 16th century, but sizable sections of the porch, west tower and transepts have survived, with the outer parlour and part of a handsome Romanesque nave arcade.

HBM. All year, daily. Free entry. Tel Edinburgh (031) 244 3101.

MANDERSTON

Off A6105, 2 miles east of Duns (Cc)

Edwardian extravagance, craftsmanship and fine materials went into the rebuilding in 1901 of this 18th-century country house. The ballroom, hung with embossed velvet and curtains embroidered in gold and silver, contains Louis XVI-style furniture upholstered in primrose and white – the racing colours of Sir James Miller, the house's owner. Miller's equine interests are further reflected in the stables, with their arched roof and stalls made of teak, brass halter rings and marble floor. Nor were the cows neglected: the dairy has a fountain designed by Italian and French craftsmen to resemble a Roman cloister.

Rare species of rhododendrons and azaleas grow in the 56 acre garden. The formal garden is entered through a gateway that Sir James gilded so that it would blaze in the setting sun.

Mid May-Sept, Thur and Sun pm; Spring Bank Hol and Aug Bank Hol, pm. Adm charge. Refreshments. Shop. P *Toilets. Tel Duns (0361) 83450.*

MELLERSTAIN HOUSE

Off A6089, 7 miles north-west of Kelso (Cc)

Exquisite Adam ceilings coloured in delicate pastels and iced with decorative white stucco are

an outstanding feature of this graceful Georgian mansion built in 1770 by Robert Adam for the Baillie family. Busts of Lady Grisell Baillie and her daughter Lady Murray complement the fine Adam ceiling and fireplace and classical friezework of the library, Mellerstain's finest room. The decor throughout the house is set off by elegant 18th-century furniture and paintings by artists such as Gainsborough and Allan Ramsay. The view over the Italianate terraced gardens extends over rosebeds and broad lawns to a lake and the Cheviot Hills beyond.
May-Sept, pm daily exc Sat. Adm charge. Refreshments. Shop. P *Toilets.* ♿ *(ground floor only). Tel Gordon (057 381) 225.*

MELROSE ABBEY

Main Square, Melrose (Cc)

An ornate church encircled by the tombs of former monks, Melrose Abbey was rebuilt in the late 14th century upon the ruins of a 12th-century structure. The ornamented wall arcades of the cloister are richly carved with berries, flowers and the clam-shell emblem of St James. A niche in the westernmost buttress contains a fine medieval sculpture of the Virgin and Child; this was mutilated by iconoclasts in 1649, but according to legend, the head of Christ fell on the arm of the man who struck it off, paralysing the arm for life. Carvings round the doorway include a kneeling figure with clasped hands, curly-haired angels playing musical instruments and a cook holding a ladle. A visitor centre has displays on the abbey's history.

Near the abbey is Priorwood Garden, where the monks grew fruit. There are old damson and cherry trees, pears and gages, and an 'apple walk' traces the history of apple-growing in Britain.

Melrose Motor Museum displays a splendid variety of vintage cars, motorcycles, signposts and motoring accessories. Most of the vehicles have been restored to working order, and many of them have featured in cinema and television films, including *Dr Finlay's Casebook*.
Abbey: HBM. All year, daily exc Sun am. Adm charge. Shop. P *(limited). Toilets.* ♿ *(part). Tel Edinburgh (031) 244 3101. Garden: NTS. Apr-Dec, daily. Free entry. Shop.* P *Tel Melrose (089 682) 2965. Motor Museum: mid May-mid Oct, daily. Adm charge. Shop.* P *Toilets.* ♿ *Tel (089 682) 2624.*

NEIDPATH CASTLE

On A72, 1 mile west of Peebles (Bc)

The massive tower and turrets of Neidpath Castle rise dramatically from a rock high above the Tweed valley. Built as a laird's stronghold in the 14th century, the castle was converted into a more comfortable home in the 17th century. Nevertheless, it still has much of its medieval character, retaining its rock-hewn well, massive walls, and a pit prison which was used as late as the 16th century by the Lords of Hay of Yester, hereditary Sheriffs of Tweeddale.

Footpaths extend each side of the river in both directions, and roe deer and other animals are often seen.
Easter weekend, May-mid Oct, daily exc Sun am. Adm charge. P *Toilets. Tel Aberlady (087 57) 201.*

SMAILHOLM TOWER

Off B6404, 7 miles west of Kelso (Cc)

Perched on a windswept crag with a precipitous drop on three sides, this bleak and lonely tower was built in the 15th century as a fortified farmhouse which also served as a watchtower. The top storey has a wall-walk with a seat for the watchman and a recess for his lantern. The tower stands five storeys high, with walls 7ft thick, but even so, the lands it protected were frequently ravaged by English raiders.

In 1635 Smailholm was sold to Sir William Scott of Harden – a direct ancestor of Sir Walter Scott – and it was to Sandyknowe, the nearby farmhouse, that Walter was sent as a 'wee, sick laddie' in need of country air. At Sandyknowe, Walter's grandmother and Aunt Janet amused him with songs and tales which, together with the grim, romantic tower, inspired him with ideas for his Border *Ballads*. Today the tower houses an exhibition of tableaux from the ballads.
HBM. Apr-Sept, daily exc Sun am. Adm charge. P *Tel Edinburgh (031) 244 3101.*

THIRLESTANE CASTLE

Off A68 at Lauder (Bc)

The crescendo of shapely roofs and pointed turrets gives Thirlestane Castle an aura of power and grandeur. Built on the foundations of a medieval fortress, the castle was remodelled in the 17th century by Sir William Bruce, and its extravagant appearance was further augmented in Victorian times. The interior is equally unrestrained. Garlands of leaves, flowers, fruit and even musical instruments cascade from the plasterwork ceilings of the two drawing rooms, and the dining-room ceiling is patterned in white and gold.

The man who commissioned the refurbishment was John Maitland, Duke of Lauderdale, who was created Secretary of State for Scotland by Charles II and ruled the country as uncrowned king for 20 years. The castle has remained the home of the Maitlands, and a vast collection of family portraits includes paintings by Gainsborough and Romney.

In the south wing, the Border Country Life Exhibition includes sections on monastic life, veterinary work and the wildlife of the Tweed valley, and re-creations of a gamekeeper's hut and a country tailor's shop. A fine collection of toys is displayed in the old nurseries. The castle has attractive formal gardens, and woodland and riverside walks in the grounds.
July-Aug, pm daily exc Sat; May, June and Sept, Wed, Thur, Sun, Bank Hol Sun and Mon, pm. Adm charge. Refreshments. Shop. P *Toilets. Tel Lauder (057 82) 430.*

TRAQUAIR HOUSE

Off B709, 1 mile south of Innerleithen (Bc)

At the end of the tree-lined approach to Traquair House stands a pair of wrought-iron gates flanked by gateposts crowned with snarling heraldic bears. The gates have not been opened since 1745, when Bonnie Prince Charlie passed through them, never to return, and the Earl of Traquair swore they would remain closed until the Stuarts regained the throne of England. Believed to be the oldest inhabited house in Scotland, Traquair has been the Stuart family home since the 15th century. The rooms are filled with paintings, embroideries and other historic treasures of the Royal House of Scotland – among them a rosary and crucifix which belonged to Mary, Queen of Scots.

In the grounds are riverside and woodland walks and a maze. Stables have been converted into workshops where pottery, silk-screen printing and wood-turning are practised. In the 18th-century brewhouse, Traquair Ale is made.
Apr-mid Oct, pm daily; also am July-mid Sept. Adm charge. Refreshments. Shop. P *Toilets.* ♿ *Tel Innerleithen (0896) 830323.*

HIGH NOTE *The harpsichord in the High Drawing Room at Traquair House was made in Antwerp in 1651 by Andreas Ruckers, and retains its original decoration. The room has fine 17th-century painted beams.*

REGIONAL CALENDAR

February 2 Jedburgh: Jethart Ba' (street handball).

May (Sun before Bank Holiday). Kelso: Great Tweed Raft Race.

June (early). Coldstream: Borders Country Fair. West Linton: Whipman Play (Common Riding and sports).

June (mid-month). Peebles: Beltane Festival (week of celebrations including Riding the Marches).

June (late). Jedburgh: Callants Festival. Galashiels: Braw Lads Gathering.

July (early). Duns: Reivers Week (Common Riding).

July (3rd week). Innerleithen: St Ronans Games and Cleikum Ceremony (procession).

July (late). Lauder: Common Riding. Kelso: Civic Week.

August (early). Coldstream: Civic Week.

Tourist information: Coldstream (0890) 2607; Eyemouth (089 07) 50678; Hawick (0450) 72547; Peebles (0721) 20138; Selkirk (0750) 20054.

CENTRAL

STRONGHOLDS OF KINGS AND PATRIOTS IN SCOTLAND'S HEARTLAND

Much of Scotland's history can be traced where the Lowlands end and the Highlands begin, with a battle relived at Bannockburn's heritage centre and audiovisual displays at Stirling Castle and the Wallace Monument. Castles loom over the once troubled countryside, now rich in parks set in woodlands and beside shimmering lochs. There is a hint of the great mountains to the north in the lovely Trossachs, with steamer trips on Loch Katrine and walks in the woodlands that inspired Sir Walter Scott and sheltered the outlaw Rob Roy MacGregor.

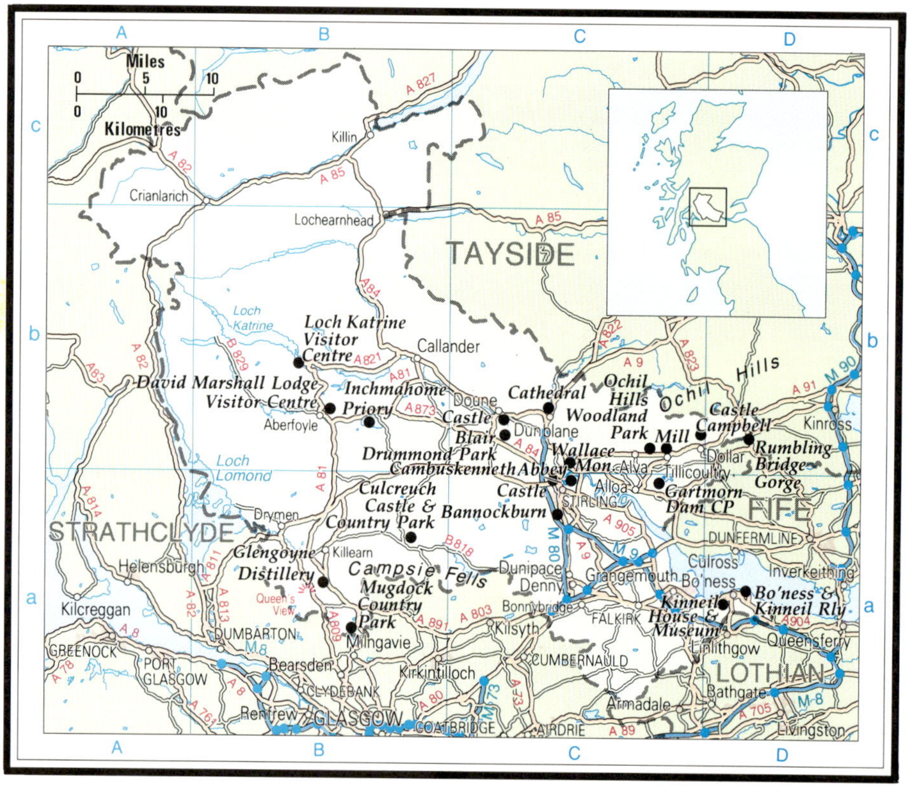

BANNOCKBURN

Off A872, 2 miles south-east of Stirling (Ca)

The scene of an old battle can stir the imagination powerfully. Centuries after the conflict, the warlike sights and sounds can be conjured up at the Bannockburn battle site on the edge of the little town. Here, on June 24, 1314, Scotland won its most glorious victory: King Robert Bruce and his men routed English troops, commanded personally by Edward II, who were vastly superior in numbers and equipment.

Scots have lovingly preserved part of this battlefield where their nation established its independence. At Borestone Brae, where Bruce had his headquarters, is a heritage centre where the whole story is dramatically told. A giant mural of the battle rivets attention, and there is a theatre where a sight-and-sound presentation recreates the action. Here, too, are many exhibits of historical interest. The area has been landscaped and drained; it is no longer the boggy terrain where the English floundered. And a great bronze equestrian statue of Bruce was unveiled by the Queen on the battle's 650th anniversary in 1964.

Bannockburn was Scotland's revenge for England's long domination. The great patriot William Wallace had been defeated by Edward I's army at Falkirk in 1298 and hanged seven years later. At this point the Scots seemed on the brink of surrender. But the crowning of Robert Bruce at Scone in 1306 – the year before Edward II succeeded his father in England – was a signal for Scotland to fight back. Towns and fortresses occupied by the English were taken. By the spring of 1314 few castles remained in English hands, the most important of these being Stirling Castle.

King Robert's brother, Sir Edward Bruce, laid siege to Stirling. Under the laws of chivalry he made an agreement with the castle's governor that it would be surrendered if not relieved by June 24, Midsummer Day. Edward II decided it must be relieved on time. However, with about 5500 trained men to face an English army of some 20,000, Bruce prepared a strong defensive position astride the Falkirk-Stirling road, with the line of the Bannockburn stream as the main obstacle to the enemy.

On June 23, the English 'great van' of cavalry, foot soldiers and archers advanced, only to be thrown back in disorder across the burn. On the next day the English, forced to fight on a narrow front, were pushed farther back, and King Edward sought refuge in Stirling Castle. When the Royal Standard was seen leaving the field the army was plunged into confusion. Finally the castle was surrendered and Edward, with an escort of nobles, escaped to Dunbar and then to Berwick.

NTS. Site: All year, daily. Centre: Apr-Oct, daily. Adm charge. Refreshments. Shop. P *Toilets.* ♿ *Tel Stirling (0786) 812664.*

ON THE ALERT *A group of South American llamas, incongruous against the Scottish baronial architecture, peer inquisitively at visitors driving through Blair Drummond Safari and Leisure Park.*

BLAIR DRUMMOND SAFARI AND LEISURE PARK

Off A84, 2 miles south-east of Doune (Cb)

Set amid superb scenery, this park covers 120 acres and has 3 miles of road running through it, enabling animals to be seen in safety at close quarters. There are unusual sights, such as shaggy animals called yakmacs, which are a cross between a yak and a Highland cow. The monkey jungle is fascinating, and there is a boat safari to Chimp Island. Sea lions show off their grace, speed and skills, and the penguin pool and waterfall make a delightful attraction. A safari bus is available for visitors without suitable transport.

The park has many other attractions. These include an adventure playground and Cinema 180, where three-dimensional films provide heart-in-the-mouth sensations. A cable trip across the lake is another exciting experience.

Apr-Sept, daily. Adm charge. Refreshments. Shop. P *Toilets.* ♿ *Tel Stirling (0786) 841456.*

BO'NESS AND KINNEIL RAILWAY

Off Union Street, Bo'ness (Da)

The magic of steam is back in Bo'ness, thanks to the Scottish Railway Preservation Society. On a site to which British Rail steam locomotives were 'retired' in the 1960s, the society has set up a railway centre and station where veteran stock is on show – and still in service. Among the attractions are a vintage Swedish train, hauled by the largest engine to be seen in Scotland, and the society's mascot locomotive, CR No 419, which dates from 1908 and served with the Caledonian Railway.

Rolling stock from all Scotland's original railway companies is here, too. Trips by steam train, starting at the new station, run for 2 miles, providing fine views across the Firth of Forth and the old town of Bo'ness.

Centre: All year, daily. Trains: Easter-Sept, Sat and Sun; also some weekdays July and Aug. Free entry (fares for trips). Refreshments. Shop. P *Toilets.* ♿ *Tel Bo'ness (0506) 822298.*

CAMBUSKENNETH ABBEY

Off A907, 1 mile east of Stirling (Ca)

Standing in a position which commands breathtaking views over the Forth valley, Cambuskenneth Abbey was founded in 1147, probably by David I of Scotland. It was colonised by Augustinian monks and became one of the richest abbeys in Scotland, thanks to gifts of money, goods and livestock. The proximity of Stirling Castle, where the king lived, added to its prestige. Later, during the wars with England in the reign of David II, the abbey was often pillaged. Little now remains of the buildings except their foundations, the western doorway and the unusual free-standing belfry in the style of an Italian *campanile*; the date of the belfry is uncertain, but a document of 1361 records it being struck by lightning.

HBM. Apr-Sept, daily exc Sun am. Adm charge. Tel Edinburgh (031) 244 3101.

CASTLE CAMPBELL

Off A91, 1 mile north of Dollar (Cb)

The ruins of a castle where powerful chieftains once ruled loom romantically above some of Scotland's finest countryside. What can be seen of it today comprises buildings of the 15th, 16th and 17th centuries, but there may have been a timber castle on the site in the 11th or 12th century. The 15th-century tower is structurally the most complete of the remaining buildings. Long known as Castle Gloom, this was the lowland headquarters of successive Earls of Argyll. During Charles I's reign it was a stronghold of the Covenanters – Protestants opposed to the king's religious policies. The 8th Earl and 1st Marquis of Argyll, one of the leading Covenanters, was executed as a traitor after the Restoration. Wooded Dollar Glen offers a fine scenic walk to Castle Campbell, but rain can make the path dangerous.

HBM. All year, daily exc Sun am; also closed Thur pm and Fri Oct-Mar. Adm charge. Refreshments. P *Toilets. Tel Dollar (025 94) 2408.*

CULCREUCH CASTLE AND COUNTRY PARK

On B818 at Fintry, 6 miles east of Killearn (Ba)

Culcreuch has been likened to Brigadoon, the Scottish ghost village in the musical show, because the less attractive features of this century seem to have passed it by. The castle, set among hills, moorland, woods and water, is one of the oldest still inhabited in Scotland, and was for more than 300 years a seat of the Galbraith clan.

Within the castle walls, splendid carved furniture can be seen in the Carved Hall – part of an extension built in 1721. Here, too, are old swords and a variety of items collected from overseas. The Picture Drawing Room has, as well as its pictures and mirrors, a fine collection of china. The strangest room of all is the Chinese Bird Room, its walls decorated with Chinese wallpaper bearing hand-painted designs of colourful birds and exotic palms. The furniture here is mostly French, and there is a well-documented ghost – said to be good-humoured.

The surrounding 2000 acres of parkland, woods and fells provide a choice of beautiful walks. The walled castle garden and a pine plantation can be visited. A tradition of banquets at Culcreuch which dates back to the 13th century is kept alive by special 'Taste of Scotland' feasts.

All year, daily. Free entry. Refreshments. P *Toilets.* ♿ *Tel Fintry (036 086) 228.*

DAVID MARSHALL LODGE VISITOR CENTRE

Off A821, 1 mile north of Aberfoyle (Bb)

The rolling scenery of The Trossachs has inspired many writers – notably Sir Walter Scott and Dorothy Wordsworth. It has also been a setting for the activities of colourful characters in Scottish history such as the clan chief and outlaw Rob Roy MacGregor. The David Marshall Lodge is an ideal point at which to start taking in the landscape and the folklore. It is a centre where visitors can get information, see an exhibition – and eat. Outside stretches the green vastness of the Queen Elizabeth Forest Park, with a wealth of splendid forest walks and trails and facilities for pony trekking, fishing and boating.

Near the lodge is the entrance to the Achray Forest Drive, a 7 mile route through fine scenery, with opportunities for observing wildlife. This is a working forest which produces timber. The trees are mostly coniferous, but in autumn others – notably birch – provide a spectacle of breathtaking colour. There are parking places, picnic sites and waymarked walks.

Lodge and Forest Drive: Easter-Sept, daily. Park: All year, daily. Free entry (charge for drive). Refreshments. Shop. P *Toilets.* ♿

UNHAPPY VALLEY *The ruin of Castle Campbell stands between two ravines, in which flow the Burn of Care and the Burn of Sorrow – the reason, perhaps, why the fortress was once called Castle Gloom.*

DOUNE CASTLE

On A820, 9 miles north-west of Stirling (Cb)

One of Scotland's best preserved 14th-century castles, Doune remains substantially what it was when it was built by Robert Stewart, Duke of Albany. It has stayed with his descendants, the Earls of Moray, and was extensively restored in the 1880s by the 14th earl. Its huge keep-gatehouse rises to 95ft and the main block contains four full storeys and a garret. A walk along the castle walls affords magnificent views.

The castle is of great importance historically; it was an ideal base for controlling the route to the Highlands. Stuart kings and queens, including Mary, Queen of Scots, dined and slept here; Bonnie Prince Charlie kept prisoners here after the Battle of Falkirk in 1745.

Nostalgia for the more recent past can be indulged at the neighbouring Doune Motor Museum, with its array of vintage cars belonging to the Earl of Moray. Apart from such favourites as Rolls-Royce, Frazer Nash and Morgan models, there are fascinating rarities. These

FRENCH CONNECTION *This 1923 Citröen 5CV in the Doune Motor Museum was one of the many French cars sold in Britain during the 1920s. More than 40 cars, built between 1905 and 1968, make up the collection.*

include the Hispano-Suiza Ballot, a 1934 hybrid, and the JP Special 500cc of 1950 – Scotland's only volume-production racing car.

Castle: HBM. All year, daily exc Sun am; also closed Fri and alternate Sat Oct-Mar. Adm charge. P *Tel Edinburgh (031) 244 3101. Motor Museum: Apr-Oct, daily. Adm charge. Refreshments. Shop.* P *Toilets.* ♿ *Tel Doune (0786) 841203.*

DUNBLANE CATHEDRAL

In centre of Dunblane (Cb)

The art historian John Ruskin said of Dunblane Cathedral: 'I know not anything so perfect in its simplicity and so beautiful, as far as it reaches, in all the Gothic with which I am acquainted.' He was particularly impressed by a small oval window at the top of the west gable – now called the Ruskin Window. The lower storeys of the tower are all that is left of the Norman cathedral; the present one dates mainly from the 13th to 15th centuries. Late in the 16th century the roof of the nave fell in, and it was not replaced until a general restoration began in 1889. In the cathedral precincts is the Dean's House, dating from 1624, which is now a museum of local history.

Cathedral: HBM. All year, daily. Free entry. P *Tel Dunblane (0786) 825388. Museum: June-Sept. Mon-Sat; also some Sun pm. Free entry. Refreshments. Shop.* P *Toilets. Tel (0786) 822217.*

GARTMORN DAM COUNTRY PARK

Off A908, 2 miles north-east of Alloa (Ca)

This 215 acre stretch of countryside is centred on Scotland's oldest man-made reservoir still in public use; it was built in 1713 to provide water power for Alloa's industries. Bird life is abundant. Among the residents are mallards, oystercatchers, jays, goldfinches, pochards and great crested grebes. Summer visitors include swallows, wheatears, green sandpipers, redshanks and willow warblers. An information centre is housed in an old pumphouse.

Park: All year, daily. Centre: Apr-Sept, Mon-Wed; also Sat and Sun pm. Free entry. Shop. P *Toilets.* ♿ *Tel Alloa (0259) 214319.*

GLENGOYNE DISTILLERY

On A81, 3 miles south of Killearn (Ba)

Lying beneath the Campsie Hills, this small distillery has a view northwards to Ben Lomond and Loch Lomond. Early in the 19th century it was recorded as Burnfoot of Glenguin, and a local historian wrote excitedly of the smoke rising from its stills in the early morning. Its whisky, though highly prized, was then illicit and girls smuggled it into Glasgow in containers strapped under their skirts. Today Lang Brothers produce a choice malt whisky to which the old skills are applied. Visitors can tour the distillery and taste its product.

Apr-Oct, Mon-Fri. Free entry. Shop. P *Toilets. Tel Glasgow (041) 332 6361.*

INCHMAHOME PRIORY

Off B8034, 4 miles east of Aberfoyle (Bb)

In its tranquil island setting, this Augustinian priory is one of the best relics of medieval monastic life left in Scotland. It stands on Inchmahome, one of three islands in Lake of Menteith – not called a loch, it is said, because of a map-maker's mistake. Built in the 13th century, the priory gave shelter to the famous during its 400 years of religious activity. Robert Bruce is said to have visited it before his victory over the English at Bannockburn in 1314. Mary, Queen of Scots, as a child, was taken there for her safety in 1543; there is a belief that a group of box trees, called Queen Mary's Bower, was planted by her. A ferry to the island runs from a pier near The Lake Hotel at the north-east corner of the lake.

HBM. Apr-Sept, daily exc Sun am. Ferry charge. Shop. P *Toilets. Tel Stirling (0786) 50000.*

HEAVENLY LIGHT *The glow of the setting sun bathes Dunblane Cathedral in a golden flood, highlighting the Gothic glory of the west front with its tall lancet windows. Inside, the cathedral is notable for its magnificent woodcarvings, especially on the choir stalls (right), which are among the finest examples of medieval craftsmanship in the country.*

KINNEIL HOUSE AND MUSEUM

Off A904, 1 mile west of Bo'ness (Da)

The 16th-century house was on the point of being demolished in 1936 – until wall paintings of the 16th and 17th centuries were found in two of its rooms. The earliest of these date from the mid-16th century and can be seen in the Parable Room. They illustrate the parable of the Good Samaritan and other Biblical subjects.

Kinneil Museum, housed in the renovated

stable block of the estate, has displays illustrating the history of Bo'ness, a contraction of Borrowstounness; local pottery is prominent. Also in the museum are exhibits telling the story of the Kinneil estate since Roman times. Kinneil House stands on the line of the Antonine Wall, once the north-west frontier of the Roman Empire, and a nearby Roman fortlet has been excavated and partly rebuilt.

Kinneil House: HBM. Daily, exc Sun am; also closed Tues pm and Fri Oct-Mar. Adm charge. P *Tel Edinburgh (031) 244 3101. Museum: May-Oct, daily exc Sun; Nov-Apr, Sat. Free entry. Shop.* P *Tel Bo'ness (0506) 824318.*

LOCH KATRINE VISITOR CENTRE

Off A821, 10 miles west of Callander (Bb)

Loch Katrine has retained its romantic beauty despite its use as a reservoir supplying Glasgow. It lies amid superb Trossachs scenery rich in oak and birch woodlands – country where the outlaw Rob Roy MacGregor evaded his enemies. Sir Walter Scott drew inspiration from this area for his novel *Rob Roy* and his long poem *The Lady of the Lake*. The visitor centre at The Trossachs pier is a good starting point for a walk through the woods, while the steamer *Sir Walter Scott* takes visitors on a delightful voyage over the 9 mile length of the loch.

May-Sept, daily. Free entry. Refreshments. Shop. P *Toilets.* ♿ *Tel Trossachs (087 76) 275; (steamer) Glasgow (041) 336 5333.*

MUGDOCK COUNTRY PARK

Off A81, 9 miles south of Killearn (Ba)

The 500 acres of this park offer a wide variety of scenery and wildlife. In addition to the parkland of the old Craigend and Mugdock estates there are walks through undisturbed ancient woodland and around Mugdock Loch and its surrounding marshes. The park contains the remains of the 14th-century Mugdock Castle, once the seat of the Grahams of Montrose. A Countryside Ranger Service operates in the park, and rangers can arrange walks and talks for groups.

All year, daily. Free entry. P *Toilets.* ♿ *Tel Glasgow (041) 956 6100.*

OCHIL HILLS WOODLAND PARK

Off A91, ½ mile east of Alva (Cb)

These 50 acres of mixed woodland were originally an informal garden around Alva House. This was the seat of Sir John Erskine, who made a fortune in silver-mining in nearby Silver Glen in the early 18th century, and later of the Johnstone family, great benefactors of the district. A careful planting programme introduced a variety of trees, including ash, oak, birch, sycamore, sweet chestnut, larch, pine and yew. The driveway leading into the park has a fine array of shrubs. Alva House itself has long since vanished, but the stable block, designed by the Adam brothers, survives as a listed building. From the wooded park there are wide views, and bird life within the park is abundant, the green woodpecker being one of the star inhabitants.

All year, daily. Free entry. P *Tel Tillicoultry (0259) 52176.*

TUNES OF GLORY *The great drum towers of Stirling Castle, headquarters of the Argyll and Sutherland Highlanders, make an evocative setting for a parade by a Scottish pipe band.*

RUMBLING BRIDGE GORGE

Off A823, 7½ miles east of Dollar (Db)

A double bridge crosses the River Devon as it flows through a narrow chasm. Here the river, dashing over precipices and bounding from rock to rock, produces a hollow, rumbling sound which gives the gorge its name. Within the moist, shady gorge liverwort, mosses and ferns thrive; paths lead to good viewpoints.

All year, daily. Free entry. P

STIRLING CASTLE

Near centre of town (Ca)

Formidable on a 250ft high rock, Stirling Castle has played a major role in Scotland's history. The castle changed hands repeatedly in the wars between the Scots and English in the 12th and 13th centuries. From the late 14th to 16th centuries it was a residence of the Stuart kings, and most of today's main buildings date from that time. James V was responsible for the royal palace, with its ornate stonework largely cut by French masons. It ceased to be a royal residence in 1603, when James VI left to become James I of England as well.

The visitor centre gives a clear picture of the castle's long history, by means of a multi-screen theatre and an exhibition. The castle also contains the museum of the Argyll and Sutherland Highlanders regiment, with fine displays of regimental silver, uniforms and medals.

Castle: HBM. All year, daily exc Sun am. Adm charge. Refreshments. Shop. P *Toilets. Tel Stirling (0786) 62517. Museum: Apr-Oct, most days. Covered by castle adm charge.* P *Tel (0786) 75165.*

TILLICOULTRY MILL

Off A91, 3 miles south-west of Dollar (Cb)

Scotland's tweed, tartans and knitwear are as famous as its whisky. One area noted for its traditional woollen industry lies among the beautiful Ochil Hills, with Tillicoultry as its centre. The Clock Mill in Tillicoultry, built in 1824, now houses a tourist information centre and a display of looms and other equipment; in its craft workshops traditional skills – including kilt-making – can be watched. Also in Tillicoultry are Paton's Mill, once reckoned to be the largest in Scotland, and Sterling Mill, now a furniture warehouse. A Mill Heritage Trail for motorists, centred on the Clock Mill, takes in other mills at Alva, Dollar and Lochleven.

Clock Mill Centre: Apr-Sept, daily. Free entry. Shop. P *Toilets.* ♿ *Tel Tillicoultry (0259) 52176.*

WALLACE MONUMENT

Off A907, 2 miles north of Stirling (Cb)

Scots admit that it took a long time to raise an impressive monument to their hero of independence, Sir William Wallace – hanged and quartered by the English in 1305. But when this great landmark was built in the 1860s its grandeur more than compensated for the delay. Standing 600ft up the Abbey Craig above Stirling, the tower – itself 220ft high – appears to have grown out of the rock. The monument commands views of seven battlefields – among them Stirling Bridge where Wallace's forces beat the English in 1297, and Bannockburn, scene of Robert Bruce's victory in 1314. In the Sword Room is his giant two-handed sword.

Feb-Oct, daily. Adm charge. Refreshments. Shop. P *Toilets. Tel Stirling (0786) 72140.*

REGIONAL CALENDAR

May (late). Drymen: Agricultural Show.

June (early). Kinlochard and Tyndrum: Sheepdog Trials.

July (early). Alva: Highland Games.

July (mid-month). Stirling: Tartan Week. Killin: Pipe Band Display. The Trossachs: Highland Festival.

July (late). Lochearnhead: Balquhidder and Strathyre Highland Games. Airth: Highland Games.

July (late, to early Aug). Stirling: District Festival.

August (early). Bridge of Allan: Highland Games. Stirling Castle: Beating of Retreat.

Tourist information: Aberfoyle (087 72) 352 (summer); Callander (0877) 30342 (summer); Killin (056 72) 254; Stirling (0786) 750194; Tyndrum (083 84) 246 (summer).

DUMFRIES AND GALLOWAY

GREEN HILLS AND RUINED CASTLES IN THE GENTLE LOWLANDS

Some of Scotland's gentlest and most beautiful scenery lies in this sprawling Lowlands region. The forests of Galloway and Glen Trool clothe the hillsides with a rich green mantle, and there are pockets of colour in fine gardens such as Ardwell, Galloway House and Threave. The region is studded with castles and grand houses such as Caerlaverock Castle, Drumlanrig Castle, and Maxwelton House, the home of Annie Laurie, and it has two ruined but imposing abbeys in Glenluce and the romantically named Sweetheart Abbey.

The region's history is reflected in several unusual museums, including the Museum of Scottish Lead Mining at Wanlockhead and the Duncan Savings Bank Museum near Annan. There is also a Robert Burns Centre in Dumfries, and the birthplace of the writer Thomas Carlyle is preserved at Ecclefechan. But the best known of the region's buildings remains the Old Blacksmith's Shop at Gretna Green – the scene in the past of many an 'anvil marriage', and still a place where newly married couples delight to be photographed.

ARBIGLAND

Off A710, 12 miles south of Dumfries (Db)

In an area of Galloway where the climate is very much like that of Torquay, 400 miles farther south, the 1400 acres of Arbigland estate include formal gardens with roses, banks of rhododendrons, azaleas and camellias – and a water garden called Japan. Arbigland's 'top 100 plants' are labelled and located on a map of the gardens.

The nearby Paul Jones' Cottage was the birthplace in 1747 of the first commander of the United States Navy. His father was head gardener when Arbigland was laid out.

May-Sept, Tues, Thur, Sun pm. Adm charge. Refreshments. Shop. P *Toilets.* ♿ *Tel Kirkbean (038 788) 283.*

ARDWELL GARDENS

Off A716, 11 miles south-east of Stranraer (Ab)

Informal gardens surrounding an 18th-century mansion merge into woodland on an estate set back from Luce Bay. Ardwell has a walled garden and greenhouses, and a path around a large pond has views over the bay to the Galloway hills. Rock plants are a speciality.

Mar-Oct, daily. Adm charge. P *Toilets.*

BLOWPLAIN OPEN FARM

Off A712, 2 miles east of New Galloway (Cc)

Near the head of Loch Ken is a high-level farming district of humpbacked fields – known locally as 'drums' – whose dry-stone walls lead the eye towards the skyline hills of the Galloway Forest Park. In the heart of this rolling countryside, Blowplain offers guided tours which show the workings of a stock-rearing farm.

Easter-Oct, daily exc Tues and Sat. Adm charge. P *Toilets.* ♿ *Tel New Galloway (064 42) 206.*

BROUGHTON HOUSE

High Street, Kirkcudbright (Cb)

This elegant Georgian mansion with sheltered gardens reaching down to the River Dee was originally the town house of the Murrays of Broughton and then, much later, the home of Edward Hornel, leader of the local artists' colony. It is now a museum and art gallery, with a fine collection of paintings and a library of 15,000 books and manuscripts.

The district around Kirkcudbright is known as the Stewartry, and the Stewartry Museum in a Scottish Baronial building of 1891 in St Mary Street illustrates its long history.

Broughton House: Mid Mar-mid Oct, daily exc Tues. Adm charge. Shop. Toilets. Tel Kirkcudbright (0557) 30437. Museum: All year, daily exc Sun. Adm charge. Toilets. Tel (0557) 30797.

CAERLAVEROCK CASTLE

Off B725, 9 miles south of Dumfries (Dc)

One of the great strongholds within easy reach of the border between Scotland and England, this castle was started some time before 1300. It is triangular in plan, with single round towers at two corners and a massive twin-towered gatehouse at the third. Huge red-sandstone curtain walls rise from a still water-filled moat. Caerlaverock was built for the Maxwells, who owned it until the Civil War. After Robert Maxwell was created Earl of Nithsdale in 1612, the Nithsdale apartments were built in the heart of the castle; their fine Renaissance walls and carved stone panels remain features of the ruined fortress.

Near the castle, 6 miles of Solway salt marshes are protected as a national nature reserve. Behind it, The Wildfowl Trust's 1400 acre Eastpark Farm has three observation towers and 20 hides, approached by sunken pathways.

Castle: HBM. All year, daily. Adm charge. P (limited). Toilets. Tel Edinburgh (031) 244 3101. Nature Reserve: NCC. All year, daily. Free entry. Tel Alexandria (0389) 58511. Wildfowl Trust: Mid Sept-Apr, daily. Adm charge. P Toilets. Tel Glencaple (038 777) 200.

BORDER STRONGHOLD *Despite its stout walls and wide moat, Caerlaverock Castle changed hands many times during border clashes between the Scots and English, and was once almost demolished.*

CARLYLE'S BIRTHPLACE

Off A74, at Ecclefechan (Ec)

A journey to Diogenes Teufelsdröckh's home in Entepfuhl is not as non-Scottish as it sounds. These were names invented by the 19th-century philosopher and historian Thomas Carlyle, in his early satirical book *Sartor Resartus*, to disguise both himself and the village of Ecclefechan. A museum devoted to Carlyle occupies the house, built by his stonemason father, where he was born in 1795. In later life Carlyle lived in Chelsea, but when he died in 1881 his wishes were respected, and he was brought home to be laid to rest in the parish churchyard at Ecclefechan.

NTS. Easter-Oct, pm daily. Adm charge. P (limited). Tel Ecclefechan (057 63) 666.

CASTLE KENNEDY GARDENS

Off A75, 3 miles east of Stranraer (Ab)

The finest privately owned gardens in Galloway were laid out in the 18th century by soldiers from the Royal Scots Greys and the Inniskilling Fusiliers, diverted from military duties by their commander, the 2nd Earl of Stair. Having also been ambassador to France, he wished to create a garden based on the one at Versailles. He picked a splendid site: the isthmus between the freshwater White Loch and Black Loch, where there are now almost a mile of woodlands, viewpoints, formal beds, avenues and footpaths.

Castle Kennedy itself, a 15th-century ruin, stands at one end. At the other is Victorian Lochinch Castle, home of the present earl and Countess of Stair.

Apr-Sept, daily. Adm charge. Refreshments. Shop. P Toilets. ♿ Tel Stranraer (0776) 2024.

CRAIGCLEUCH COLLECTION

On B709, 2 miles north-west of Langholm (Ec)

From the outside, Craigcleuch looks characteristically Scottish: a baronial mansion in wooded grounds in the heart of beautiful Eskdale. Woodland walks head down to the winding riverside and give a fine view towards the gap in the hills known for generations as 'the Gates of Eden'.

Inside, the atmosphere changes completely. There are magnificent displays of jade and ivory, sculptures and wooden figurines, masks, fabric paintings and wall-hangings brought back by explorers from North-west Canada, Africa and the Far East. Ornate American Indian peace pipes form a striking exhibit.

Easter, then May-Sept, Mon-Sat. Adm charge. Shop. P Toilets. ♿ Tel Langholm (0541) 80137.

CREETOWN GEM ROCK MUSEUM

Off A75, at Creetown (Bb)

Apparently dull-coloured rocks which under ultraviolet light suddenly come alive in a blaze of reds and greens are a main feature of this remarkable collection housed in the old Creetown school. Jades, agates, rose quartz, rock crystals and fine examples of lapidary work stand beside samples of local rocks and minerals. Curiosities include an agate inside which a 200 million year-old drop of water can be seen.

Goldsmiths and silversmiths work elsewhere in the village, and the Craft Centre in the square produces gemstones and jewellery.

Museum: Easter-Dec, daily. Adm charge. Refreshments. Shop. P Toilets. ♿ Tel Creetown (067 182) 357. Craft Centre: Mar-Dec, daily. Free entry. Shop. P ♿ Tel (067 182) 373.

DRUMLANRIG CASTLE

Off A76, 3 miles north of Thornhill (Dc)

Set in wooded parkland, this splendid stately home looks out over the most beautiful part of upper Nithsdale. It is the Dumfriesshire home of the Duke of Buccleuch and Queensberry, built for one of his Douglas ancestors during the 17th

ROYAL RELICS *Personal possessions of Bonnie Prince Charlie – including his money box, camp kettle and a swatch of Flora MacDonald's tartan – are displayed in the bedroom he once used in Drumlanrig Castle.*

century. Its pink sandstone was quarried nearby and at the main entrance a horseshoe staircase rises from arched colonnades. The main part of the castle is quite severely proportioned, but at roof level it blossoms out with balustrades, gargoyles, stone carvings and cupolas.

Drumlanrig's public rooms are richly furnished. One of the finest private art collections in Britain includes works by Rembrandt and Leonardo and the castle's silver is rare and valuable. The bedroom in which Bonnie Prince Charlie slept during the Jacobite campaign of 1745 retains its Brussels tapestry wall-coverings.

Outside, peacocks tread imperiously across the gardens. There are woodland walks and nature trails. A former stables block has been converted into a visitor centre for video shows and displays, and a craft centre, where artists produce woodwork, knitwear, leather goods, puppets and porcelain jewellery.

May-late Aug, daily exc Fri. Adm charge. Refreshments. Shop. P *Toilets.* ♿ *Tel Thornhill (0848) 30248.*

DUMFRIES MUSEUM

The Observatory, Dumfries (Dc)

The museum stands on a hilltop in western Dumfries and is housed in a splendid 18th-century windmill later converted into an observatory, with a camera obscura in the tower. Originally meant for observing sunspots, the camera obscura is now used simply for admiring the countryside all around – in clear conditions, as far south as the Old Man of Coniston in the Lake District.

The burgh is more than 800 years old, and the museum has displays on its shoe and clog-making, fine silverware, watch and clock-making; on old-style farming life; on its one-time status as a port trading with the American colonies; and on its prisons, from which comes the death mask of Robert Smith, hanged here in 1868 at the last-ever public execution in Scotland.

A short walk downhill, the Old Bridge House Museum is in a building of 1660 at the west end of the much older and very attractive red-sandstone bridge over the Nith. While its exhibits are generally more domestic – toys, dolls and household furnishings – it also has a re-created dentist's surgery from around 1900.

Dumfries Museum: Apr-Sept, daily; Oct-Mar, daily exc Sun and Mon. Shop. Toilets. ♿ *Tel Dumfries (0387) 53374. Old Bridge House Museum: Apr-Sept, daily. Free entry. Shop. Tel (0387) 56904.*

DUNCAN SAVINGS BANK MUSEUM

Off B724, 6 miles west of Annan (Dc)

A single-street village among the Solway farmlands, Ruthwell hardly looks like a financial centre to rival the City of London. But it was here in 1810 that the Reverend Henry Duncan founded the Ruthwell Savings Bank which brought investment possibilities, for the first time, within the orbit of people whose savings were too small to be accepted by the existing banks of the day. The original whitewashed cottage is now a museum of the trustee savings bank movement.

All year, daily. Free entry. Shop. P *Toilet.* ♿ *Tel Dumfries (0387) 87640.*

DUNDRENNAN ABBEY

On A711, 6 miles south-east of Kirkcudbright (Cb)

Cistercian monks began building Dundrennan in 1142. While not neglecting their religious duties, they established a flourishing export trade in wool, with their own ships sailing from their own Solway harbour. Dundrennan is a handsome and substantial ruin, with many fine memorials. In 1568 Mary, Queen of Scots spent her last night on Scottish soil here.

HBM. All year, daily. Adm charge. Tel Edinburgh (031) 226 2570.

BRUCE STONE *A granite memorial overlooking Loch Trool marks the site where Robert Bruce's forces ambushed the English, at the start of his campaign for Scottish independence.*

ELLISLAND FARM

Off A76, 6½ miles north-west of Dumfries (Dc)

Robert Burns rented this peaceful Nithsdale farm from 1788 until 1791; but, although he introduced up-to-date farming methods, Ellisland never made money, even after he turned to dairying so that his wife could look after the cattle while he worked as an excise officer. Relics of their years here are still on display, as well as exhibits on 18th-century farming.

All year, daily. Free entry. P *(limited). Toilets. Tel Dumfries (0387) 74426.*

FLEET FOREST TRAILS

Off B727, at Gatehouse of Fleet (Cb)

On the outskirts of Gatehouse of Fleet, a Forestry Commission nursery grows millions of spruce, pine and larch seedlings for the vast hill plantations of Galloway. Around it, older broadleaved woodlands are still carefully maintained. Footpaths and waymarked trails pass through lovely oak, ash, beech and sycamore woods.

A landmark to the south-west is the four-storey ruin of Cardoness Castle, reached by the B727. The 15th-century hilltop tower, the stronghold of the McCulloch family, has fine stonework.

Forest: FC. All year, daily. Free entry. P ♿ *Tel Gatehouse (055 74) 280. Castle: HBM. All year, daily. Adm charge. Tel Edinburgh (031) 244 3101.*

GALLOWAY HOUSE GARDENS

Off B7004, at Garlieston (Bb)

Ideal for a walk on a windy day, these sheltered and informal gardens in coastal woodlands near the harbour village of Garlieston were originally laid out in the 1740s as the pleasure grounds of Galloway House, not open to visitors. Grassy paths wander past banks of rhododendrons and azaleas, the walled garden features a camellia house, and botanical rarities include a handkerchief tree. There is an old-established heronry in the grounds.

All year, daily. Adm charge. P *Toilets.* ♿ *Tel Garlieston (098 86) 225.*

GLENLUCE ABBEY

Off A75, 2 miles north of Glenluce (Bb)

Late in the 12th century, Cistercian monks chose a quiet and pleasant location for this abbey founded by brethren from Dundrennan. The best-preserved feature of the abbey ruins is the chapter house, with its fine vaulted ceiling and Gothic windows. Many kings and queens of Scotland visited Glenluce, sometimes with other motives than pilgrimages in mind. James IV played bowls with the abbot, suggested a modest wager on the result – and lost.

HBM. All year, daily. Adm charge. P *Toilets.* ♿ *Tel Edinburgh (031) 244 3101.*

GLEN TROOL

Off A714, at Bargrennan (Bc)

The entrance to this long glen is at Stroan Bridge, over the Water of Minnoch. Foaming, peat-tinted water dashes down a granite ravine where pathways lead onto exposed rocks beside waterfalls. From the bridge, four waymarked forest walks wander through plantations of spruce and larch. Halfway up the glen, the Forestry Commission's Caldons campsite is an access point for more walks. Scotland's longest long-distance footpath, the Southern Uplands Way, passes through on its 212 mile route from sea to sea.

The public road ends beside a hilltop viewpoint at the Bruce Stone, the traditional site of Robert Bruce's command post at the Steps of Trool. In this engagement in 1307, his men ambushed a party of 2000 English troops by hurling boulders down on them.
All year, daily.

HODDOM ESTATE

Off B725, 2 miles west of Ecclefechan (Dc)

The visitors' lodge beside Hoddom Bridge on the River Annan explains the running of a 10,000 acre farming and forestry estate, and notes the animals, birds and wildflowers to be seen on it. Waymarked walks of quite different kinds spread out from the lodge. To the east, forest trails circle the hill called Woodcock Air, once a hunting ground of Scottish and English kings. On its far side, wind-felled trees lie among the plantations of oak and beech, spruce, larch and pine. Lower down, there is a view across the Annan to the site of the 6th-century church established by St Kentigern.
All year, daily. P *Toilets. Tel Ecclefechan (057 63) 244.*

LOGAN BOTANIC GARDEN

Off B7065, 14 miles south of Stranraer (Ab)

So close to the Irish Sea, across which the prevailing south-westerly winds sweep with often considerable force, Logan seems an unlikely location for any botanic garden, let alone one which specialises in trees, plants and flowering shrubs from the warm temperate regions of the world. But Logan has a micro-climate of its own. Temperatures are moderated because of its peninsular situation, with the sea less than 2 miles away both west and east. Those south-westerly winds come over an ocean warmed by the North Atlantic Drift. Shelter belts of woodland and high interior walls mean that the heart of the extensive garden is as protected as it possibly can be without being roofed over. So species from South Africa, California, Australasia and the Pacific islands, the Canaries and South America flourish out of doors.

There is an avenue of Chusan palms near the entrance to Logan. Within the walls there are water and tree-fern gardens, and a fine display of the New Zealand cabbage palms, which are not related to either palms or cabbages. In the woodland there is a gunnera bog where these huge Brazilian plants spread their 6ft leaves.
Apr-Sept, daily. Adm charge. Refreshments. P *Toilets.* ♿ *Tel Ardwell (077 686) 231.*

MABIE FOREST

Off A710, 3 miles south of Dumfries (Dc)

Some of the finest views of Nithsdale and the Solway Firth are from the waymarked trails in

SUMMER GLORY *Exotic shrubs bloom beneath tropical palms in Logan Botanic Garden. The garden was created in the late 19th century in the grounds of a ruined medieval castle.*

the hillside forest based on the old amenity woodlands of Mabie House. They start from a picnic place beside an arboretum, then spread upwards through beech and oakwoods, alder, elm, wild cherry and ash into plantations of spruce and larch, Western hemlock and the aromatic grand fir, crossing tumbling burns.
All year, daily.

MAXWELTON HOUSE

Off B729, 2 miles east of Moniaive (Cc)

Scots all over the world sing the ballad of *Annie Laurie* probably not knowing that it was published as a fund-raiser for widows and orphans of the Crimean War. Anna Laurie of Maxwelton was courted in the early years of the 18th century by a neighbour, William Douglas. But as he was a Jacobite, Anna's Hanoverian father forbade any marriage, and the young couple parted. Douglas wrote the first version of the song, much later amended into its present form.

Maxwelton is a handsome 14th to 15th-century house, completely restored in the 1960s. One of the rooms is the boudoir traditionally given Annie Laurie's name. In the courtyard is a small museum of kitchen, dairy, farm and garden implements.
House and Museum: July-Aug, Mon-Thur pm. Adm charge. P *Toilets. Tel Moniaive (084 82) 385. Garden: Apr-Sept, Mon-Thur pm. Adm charge.*

MOTE OF MARK

Off A710, 5 miles south of Dalbeattie (Cb)

The hilltop Mote of Mark is one of the most important archaeological sites on the Solway coast. Overlooking the tidal inlet of Rough Firth, it was once a Celtic fortress. Although the excavations have been covered over, the grassy summit remains a splendid viewpoint. Meandering footpaths surround the Mote and follow the shore. Higher up, the wider Jubilee Path links the

ANNIE'S ROOM *Warmth and comfort are the keynotes of Annie Laurie's boudoir in her Maxwelton House home. The lofty ceiling is vaulted and the parquet floor was made from the wood of a yew tree in the garden.*

villages of Rockcliffe and Kippford. Close at hand, Rough Island is linked to the mainland by a shingle bank called the Rack. This is uncovered at low tide; after taking advice about when it is safe to make the crossing, a walk to the island allows visitors to explore a bird sanctuary.

NTS. All year, daily. Free entry. Tel Castle Douglas (0556) 2575.

MULL OF GALLOWAY

Off A716, 20 miles south of Stranraer (Bb)

Scotland's south-western tip is this dramatic peninsula where a lighthouse crowns a grassy headland flanked by 250ft cliffs. In clear weather, it offers a spectacular view to the mountains of the Lake District, the Isle of Man and the Antrim hills of Northern Ireland.

The Mull of Galloway is a nature reserve where guillemots, kittiwakes, razorbills, shags and fulmars can be seen nesting at different levels on the colourful sandstone cliffs. More majestic than these local birds, gannets cruise by on fishing expeditions from their own remoter breeding colony on the isolated rock stacks called the Scares.

RSPB. All year, daily. Free entry. Lighthouse at discretion of keeper. Tel Stranraer (0776) 84211.

MUSEUM OF SCOTTISH LEAD MINING

Off B797, at Wanlockhead (Dd)

Crouched in a windy hollow of the Lowther Hills, Wanlockhead is the highest village in Scotland, almost 1500ft above sea level, and the open-air museum is devoted to the industry which has brought men to the Lowthers since Roman times.

The museum occupies a series of sites in the valley of the Wanlock Water, which flows alongside Goldscaur Row between steeply rising grass and heather grouse moors. Its visitor centre, in a restored blacksmith's forge of 1764, uses maps, models, photographs and life-size tableaux to explain the theory and practice of lead-mining.

There are many tools of the miner's trade, which survived here until 1959. And railway enthusiasts appreciate the display on the Elvanfoot to Wanlockhead Light Railway which operated from 1902 until 1938. At 1498ft above sea level, in the cutting above Wanlockhead, it crossed the highest summit of any standard-gauge railway in Britain. Part of it is relaid as a narrow-gauge line for diesel trains.

From the visitor centre, an outdoor trail wanders along the valley of the Wanlock Water. There are stops at the sites of individual mines and a smelt mill, and at the Wanlockhead Beam Engine of the Straitsteps Mine. This is a rare survivor of an ingenious water pump which predated the steam engines used for keeping the mine galleries free of flooding. Pride of place on the trail, however, goes to the walk-in Lochnell Mine. Guided tours take visitors along the 18th-century passage called Williamson's Drift, about 7ft high and 4ft wide. The vein of lead can still be seen, and, at the far end, a tableau shows 18th-century miners drilling a hole for a gunpowder charge.

Museum: Good Fri-Sept, daily. Adm charge. Shop. P *Toilets.* ♿ *Tel Leadhills (065 94) 387.*

SILVER STREAK *Grey Mare's Tail Burn plunges 200ft down through a steep glen from Loch Skeen to join Moffat Water. The fall, one of Scotland's highest, is on the A708, 10 miles north-east of Moffat.*

OLD BLACKSMITH'S SHOP

At Gretna Green (Ec)

Generations of runaway young couples were married at the Old Blacksmith's Shop – the first house over the border and one with a special 'marriage room'. In the past Scotland's lax marriage laws allowed youngsters over the age of 16 to be married without parental consent simply by declaring their intentions before an official – such as a blacksmith – and two witnesses. Elsewhere, the age of consent was 21. Weddings performed over the anvil by 'blacksmith priests' became increasingly popular; but in 1940 an Act of Parliament stopped the 'anvil marriages'.

Today the shop's visitor centre has a fine exhibition of horse-drawn carriages, including the state landau of William IV.

All year, daily. Adm charge. Refreshments. Shop. P *Toilets.* ♿ *Tel Gretna (0461) 38224.*

PALGOWAN OPEN FARM

Off A714, 11 miles north of Newton Stewart (Bc)

North of Glentrool Village, the 7000 acres of Palgowan widen out to climb the green and rounded but wild-looking hills, and its grazing land extends all the way to the summit of the Merrick, at 2765ft the highest point in Galloway. Palgowan is the biggest hill farm in south-west Scotland. It raises Black and Belted Galloway, Luing and Highland cattle, and thousands of Blackface sheep. Guided tours explain the working of the farm, the story of the 24 miles of dry-stone walls – first built in 1710 – which divide the grazing areas, and the making of ram's-horn walking sticks.

Easter week, then mid June, Sept and Oct, Tues, Wed and Thur; July-Aug, Mon-Fri. Adm charge. Refreshments. Shop. P *Toilets.* ♿ *Tel Bargrennan (067 184) 227.*

QUEEN'S WAY

A712, New Galloway to Newton Stewart (Cc-Bb)

Named at the time of the Queen's Silver Jubilee in 1977, this stretch of the A712 links several Forestry Commission visitor attractions in the 240 square mile Galloway Forest Park. Sheltered by a stand of pines and other trees from the winds which whisk across the reservoir of Clatteringshaws Loch, the Galloway Deer Museum has displays on the red and roe deer of the forests, the otters, wild goats and varied birdlife. The workings of the Galloway Hydro Electric Scheme – of which Clatteringshaws is a part – are explained, along with the process by which the forest timber is planted, harvested and used.

South of the museum, the Queen's Way winds down through a cutting to a bridge over the rock pools of the Dee. Along the left bank of the river the 10 mile Raiders Road forest drive recalls the 18th-century hill-country cattle thieves who used this route to hurry home cattle rustled from lowland Galloway farms. Beyond the start of the Raiders Road, a Red Deer Range occupies a wide stretch of rumpled and rocky hillside. Here, too, is a Wild Goat Park, with its adjoining car park, and beyond it, in a secluded glen, a pretty waterfall.

Opposite nearby Craigdews Hill a low-level footpath runs along the rowan-marked bank of the Palnure Burn, then curls through the forest to a clearing beside the lonely cottage of Dunkitterick. This ruined house has been partly rebuilt as a memorial to Alexander Murray, a shepherd's son born here in 1775. Too short-sighted to work on the hill, he began to teach himself languages and eventually became Professor of Oriental Languages at Edinburgh University.

Forest Park: All year, daily. Free entry. Refreshments. Shop. 🅿 *Toilets.* ♿ *Tel Newton Stewart (0671) 2420. Deer Museum: Apr-mid Oct, daily. Free entry.* 🅿 *Toilets.* ♿ *Tel New Galloway (064 42) 285.*

ROBERT BURNS CENTRE
Mill Road, Dumfries (Dc)

Although he was born and brought up in Ayrshire, Robert Burns spent his latter years as an excise officer in Dumfries, and his statue stands outside Greyfriars Church. The Robert Burns Centre is housed in the mellow red-sandstone Old Town Mill built in 1781 and in operation during his lifetime. Displays recall Burns's years in Dumfries, not just as a government official and productive poet and songwriter, but also as somebody involved in the affairs of the town: for instance, his signature is shown on a petition supporting a local schoolmaster.

Of Burns's two homes in Dumfries, the second and larger one is Burns House, a two-storey building in the street now named after him. One small room was the study in which, often after a hard day's work as a horse officer in the excise service, he continued with his writing. Burns died in this house in July 1796, and was buried in the nearby St Michael's churchyard, with full military honours. A more cheerful memorial to Burns's time in Dumfries is the Globe Inn, in an alleyway off the High Street. Much of the low-ceilinged interior remains as he knew it.

Burns Centre: Apr-Sept, daily; Oct-Mar, daily exc Sun and Mon. Free entry. Refreshments. Shop. 🅿 *(limited). Toilets.* ♿ *Tel Dumfries (0387) 64808. Burns House: Apr-Sept, daily; Oct-Mar, daily exc Sun and Mon. Adm charge.* 🅿 *Tel (0387) 55297.*

SWEETHEART ABBEY
On A710, at New Abbey (Dc)

This 13th-century red-sandstone abbey gave its name to the familiar term of endearment. Its founder, the widowed Devorgilla, carried with her till her death a silver and ivory casket containing the embalmed heart of her husband, the vastly wealthy landowner John Baliol, founder of Balliol College at Oxford. When she died in 1290, the casket was buried beside her, and that 'sweet heart' became the abbey's name.

Towards the end of the 18th century the abbey ruins were bought by two local speculators to be used as a quarry for housebuilding in the village of New Abbey which had grown up nearby. But the walls of the Abbey Kirk survive to a substantial height, still showing their pointed-arch Gothic window design. The present New Abbey corn mill, built in the closing years of the 18th century, has been restored and is open to visitors.

New Abbey's third main attraction, in a mid-Victorian Scottish Baronial mansion, is Shambellie House Museum of Costume. It displays items from its 2000 piece collection, mostly of British and continental women's fashions from the late 18th century to Edwardian times.

Abbey and Mill: HBM. All year, daily. Adm charge. 🅿 *(limited). Toilets. Tel Edinburgh (031) 244 3101. Costume Museum: Mid May-mid Sept, daily exc Tues and Wed. Free entry.* 🅿 *Tel (031) 225 7534.*

THREAVE GARDEN
Off A75, 1 mile west of Castle Douglas (Cb)

The National Trust for Scotland created this 60 acre garden virtually from scratch after being given Threave's 1500 acre estate. A tour starting at the visitor centre takes in a rose garden, walled and woodland gardens, a nursery, peat and heather gardens, an arboretum, an orchard and a garden approached through a laburnum arch.

Another part of the estate is given over to the Trust's Threave Wildfowl Refuge, along the banks of the River Dee. Four main observation points have been provided, overlooking favourite wintering areas for wild geese and ducks. Hundreds of mallards and teal, goosanders and goldeneyes, and thousands of wigeon and greylag geese winter in the district.

From a car park on the edge of the reserve a half-mile footpath leads to a ferry which takes visitors to the handsome ruin of Threave Castle, a 14th-century stronghold of the Douglases.

Garden: NTS. All year, daily. Adm charge. Refreshments. Shop. 🅿 *Toilets.* ♿ *Tel Castle Douglas (0556) 2575. Wildfowl Refuge: Nov-Mar, daily. Free entry.* 🅿 *Tel (0556) 68242. Castle: HBM. All year, daily. Adm charge. Tel Edinburgh (031) 556 8400.*

WHITHORN PRIORY AND MUSEUM
Off A746, at Whithorn (Bb)

One of the most intriguing archaeological digs in Scotland, and the only one regularly open to visitors, was started in 1986 on the oldest Christian site in Scotland. St Ninian built a church at Whithorn some time around the end of the 5th century. It was a place of pilgrimage for over 1000 years, and the barrel-vaulted crypts where relics of the saint were kept are still complete. The roofless nave of a medieval cathedral survives alongside the modern parish church. Lower

COLOUR SCHEME *Despite the sometimes harsh climate and heavy soil, the rock garden at Threave (above) is designed to be in colour most of the year. Chestnut-headed teal (right), Britain's smallest duck, winter at Threave Wildfowl Refuge nearby.*

down, excavations have uncovered foundations of a Viking trading settlement and coins and gaming pieces from still earlier Anglo-Saxon times. There are guided tours of the site and a viewing platform.

HBM. Apr-Sept, daily; Oct-Mar, Sat and Sun. Adm charge. 🅿 *(limited). Toilets* ♿ *Tel Edinburgh (031) 244 3101.*

REGIONAL CALENDAR

June (mid-month). Lockerbie: Gala and Riding of the Marches. Dumfries: Guid Nychburris (Good Neighbours' Week).

July (early). Annan: Common Riding. New Galloway: Gala Week.

July (mid-month). Moffat: Gala Week. Kirkcudbright: Summer Festivities.

July (late). Gatehouse of Fleet and Newton Stewart: Gala Week. Palnackie: World Flounder Tramping Championships.

July (last Fri). Langholm: Common Riding.

August (early). Parton: Scottish Alternative Games (unusual contests). Dumfries: Show. Wigtown: Agricultural Show. Stranraer: Galloway Highland Games. Castle Douglas: Stewartry Agricultural Show.

Tourist information: Castle Douglas (0556) 2611; Dumfries (0387) 53862; Kircudbright (0557) 3094; Moffat (0683) 20620; Newton Stewart (0671) 2431.

FIFE

ROYAL PALACES, ABBEYS AND TOWNS OF AN ANCIENT KINGDOM

B y 1600 the ancient Kingdom of Fife, home of Scottish kings for more than five centuries, contained no fewer than 14 of the 66 Scottish Royal Burghs. Their proud legacy can be seen today in St Andrews, and in Dunfermline and Falkland, both of which had royal palaces. Culross preserves the palace-like home of a descendant of Robert Bruce. Castles include Earlshall and Kellie, both restored by the Scottish architect Robert Lorimer who also rebuilt the mansion at Hill of Tarvit.

Fife's indented coastline provides fine scenery, seen at its best in sites such as Cambo Country Park. Fishing harbours include Anstruther, the home of the Scottish Fisheries Museum. Among Fife's famous sons are Adam Smith the economist, who is featured at Kirkcaldy Museum, and the explorer McDouall Stuart, whose birthplace is preserved at Dysart.

ABERDOUR CASTLE

Off A921, 7 miles east of Dunfermline (Ba)

The glory of this castle overlooking Aberdour harbour is its gardens, which were among the earliest castle gardens in Scotland. Terraces, now restored, were laid out in the 16th century, and a fine beehive-shaped dovecote with room for some 600 birds was built below. The walled garden dates from the following century.

The powerful Douglases owned this castle from 1342. It began as a tower house in the 13th or 14th century, and additions were subsequently made. By 1700 it was ruinous and the Douglases abandoned it in 1725. However, it continued in use; the east wing is now the home of the custodian. Nearby stands the little Church of St Fillan. It is a gem of Norman and 16th-century architecture, with fine stained glass.

HBM. All year, daily exc Thur pm and Fri, Oct-Mar. Adm charge. P *(limited). Tel Edinburgh (031) 244 3101.*

CAMBO COUNTRY PARK

On A917, 7 miles south-east of St Andrews (Ec)

The clear Cambo Burn makes its way to the sea by pools and waterfalls in a glen filled with trees and flowering shrubs and offering lovely woodland walks and an adventure play area. The beach – safe and sandy – is a wildlife haven, with rock pools and sea birds, including herons and gannets. Near the glen, at Cuddle Corner, children may get to know tame farm animals, and there is a nature trail around the park.

May-Sept, daily; Mar-Apr, Sat and Sun. Adm charge. Refreshments. Shop. P *Toilets.* ♿ *Tel Crail (0333) 50810.*

CULROSS

Off B9037, 9 miles west of Dunfermline (Aa)

Small red-tiled houses line the cobbled streets of Culross, the most complete surviving example of a Scottish burgh of the 18th and 19th centuries. It owes its present appearance to continuing restoration by the National Trust for Scotland, which has a visitor centre in the 17th-century Town House.

In the 6th century Culross was an important religious centre, and it is honoured as the birthplace of St Mungo, patron saint of Glasgow. The ruins of a chapel dedicated to St Mungo can still be seen.

The later prosperity of Culross was based on coal and salt, and the peak of its prosperity was reached in the days of George Bruce, a descendant of Robert Bruce's family. A brilliant mining innovator, Bruce took over Culross colliery in 1575 and made it possible for men to work 240ft under the sea. A great storm destroyed the under-sea workings in 1625. But the decline of the town's prosperity came later. Quarrying, linen weaving and shoemaking could not take the place of mining and salt panning; Culross seemed stranded in time.

In 1932 the National Trust for Scotland bought Culross Palace, a house built by Bruce between 1597 and 1611, which has stood virtually unaltered since its completion – an outstanding example of a rich merchant's home of the period. Now the trust owns more than 20 properties in Culross, which can be seen on a tour trail beginning at the car park at the east end of the town.

Culross Abbey was founded for the Cistercians by Malcolm, Earl of Fife, in the 13th century; there was some new building in the 16th century. After the Reformation the choir of the abbey church remained in use as a place of worship for local people, and it formally became the parish church in 1633. It was restored in 1823 and 1905. *Visitor Centre: NTS. Easter-Sept, daily. Adm charge.* P *Toilets. Tel Newmills (0383) 880359. Culross Palace: HBM. All year, daily. Adm charge.* P *Tel Edinburgh (031) 244 3101. Culross Abbey: HBM. All year, daily. Adm charge. Tel (031) 244 3101.*

DUNFERMLINE ABBEY

In centre of Dunfermline (Ba)

The Norman nave of Dunfermline Abbey, with its heavily incised columns, is one of the great architectural treasures of Scotland. The abbey was founded by David I in the 12th century as a Benedictine monastery and became one of the most magnificent establishments in Scotland, finally replacing Iona as the royal burial place.

The nave remained in use throughout the centuries as a parish church. The rest of the abbey fell into decay and much of it is now occupied by the new parish church built in the 1820s. The guest-house of the abbey became one of the favourite royal palaces of the Scottish kings, and Charles I was born here in 1600. Only a wall, tower and archway remain.

Next to the palace is Pittencrieff Park, one of the finest parks in Scotland, covering 76 acres. The 17th-century Pittencrieff House has an exhibition of local history on the first floor and a Costume Gallery above it. House and park were bought for Dunfermline by the town's most famous son, Andrew Carnegie. The son of a local hand-loom weaver, Carnegie emigrated to

ROYAL RESTING PLACE *Six kings are buried in Dunfermline Abbey. They include Robert Bruce, Scotland's hero who reigned from 1306 to 1329 and defeated the English at Bannockburn in 1314.*

America in 1848 at the age of 12 to become 'King Steel' and the richest man in the world. During his lifetime he gave away over $350 million, including many benefactions to his home town. These included the Pittencrieff estate and the Carnegie Library, the first of nearly 3000 libraries he gave to communities world wide.

The weaver's cottage where Carnegie was born is now a museum, furnished as it would have been when he was a boy. A display tells the story of his life, with mementos and pictures. *Abbey and Palace: HBM. All year, daily. Free entry.* P *Tel Edinburgh (031) 244 3101. Pittencrieff House and Park: May-Sept, daily exc Tues. Free entry. Shop.* P *Toilets.* ♿ *Tel Dunfermline (0383) 721814. Carnegie Museum: All year, daily. Shop.* P *Toilets.* ♿ *Tel (0383) 724302.*

EARLSHALL CASTLE

Off A919, 6 miles north-west of St Andrews (Dc)

This sturdy Lowland castle survives very much as it was when Sir William Bruce built it in 1546 and entertained Mary, Queen of Scots. Few changes were made and in 1891 the owner employed the young Scottish architect Robert Lorimer to carry out a sympathetic restoration.

The castle remains what it has always been – a family home. Its glory is the Long Gallery, more than 50ft in length, with a ceiling intricately painted with the Seven Virtues and other themes. The panelled rooms contain fine furniture and porcelain, and one of the world's largest collections of Scottish armour. *Easter Sat, Sun and Mon, pm; Apr-late Sept, Thur-Sun pm. Adm charge. Refreshments. Shop.* P *Toilets. Tel Leuchars (033 483) 205.*

FALKLAND PALACE

Off A912, in High Street (Cc)

In a lovely setting below the Lomond Hills, this royal domain was a favourite residence of Mary, Queen of Scots, who spent much of her time in the years from 1561 to 1565 there, and like her predecessors enjoyed hunting and hawking in the hills.

There was a castle or 'Great Tower' on the site long before the palace, and the murder there of

YEW ALLEY *The walled gardens at Earlshall Castle contain this fine example of topiary work. They were planned in 16th-century style by Robert Lorimer, the architect who restored the castle for Robert Mackenzie in the 1890s.*

FAITH AND GOLF AT ST ANDREWS

Almost 1000 years of proud Scottish history have made St Andrews a hallowed place of religious belief and of academic learning – and a sportsman's paradise. It has the oldest university in Scotland, the dramatic ruins of a 12th-century cathedral and of a 13th-century castle, and the world's oldest and most famous golf course, the Old Course.

The town's blend of medieval, Victorian and Edwardian streets is dotted in term-time with the rich, red robes of St Andrews University undergraduates. On the northern side, miles of sandy beaches face the open sea. Although golf is the town's best-known recreation, a wealth of other diversions range from sailing and fishing to strolling through parks and gardens and viewing historic landmarks such as the ancient West Port, the gateway to the old city. The Botanic Garden off The Canongate has rock and peat gardens beside a stream and ornamental lake.

University: July-Aug, daily guided tours. Adm charge. Tel St Andrews (0334) 76161. Royal and Ancient Courses: Apr-Oct, daily exc Sat, by advance booking. P *Tel (0334) 75757. Castle: HBM. All year, daily. Adm charge.* P *(limited). Tel Edinburgh (031) 244 3101. Botanic Garden: Apr-Oct, daily; Nov-Mar, Mon-Fri. Adm charge.* P *Tel (0334) 72361.*

GOD'S HOUSES *The 108ft high, flat-topped tower of St Regulus (left) is all that is left of a 12th-century church dedicated to the Greek monk who, in the 4th century, founded the first Christian settlement at St Andrews. Nearby are the substantial ruins of the 12th-century St Andrews Cathedral (above), around which the town grew. Visitors can wander through the nave, sanctuary, transepts, chapter house, cloister and monastic buildings.*

ACADEMIC OASIS *The spacious quadrangle of St Salvator's College – which with nearby St Mary's College make up St Andrews University – lies off North Street. Removed from the bustle of the town's traffic, the quadrangle is an oasis of academic calm. The rambling, ivy-clad building was built in 1450 by Bishop Kennedy, one of the young James III's regents. In the chapel is a pulpit from which John Knox preached.*

RULING HOUSE *As large and dignified as a palace, the clubhouse of the Royal and Ancient Golf Club at St Andrews (left), built in 1854, is the headquarters of world golf. The club was founded in 1754, and the rules of the modern game were first drawn up there. Many of the game's finest players have competed on the 15th-century Old Course. The public are not admitted to the clubhouse, but can play on the Old Course and three other courses.*

LETHAL WARNING *The jagged ruins of St Andrews Castle cling to a low, grassy cliff on the coast. The castle was founded about 1200 as a bishop's fortified palace, and much of it was dismantled in the 16th century to provide stones to repair the town harbour. In 1546 Reformists entered the castle and hung the murdered body of Cardinal Beaton from a window of the Fore Tower, overlooking the beach, as a warning against the 'sins' of Catholicism.*

the young Duke of Rothesay in 1402 is described by Sir Walter Scott in *The Fair Maid of Perth*. The castle passed to James II in 1437, and it was he who began the palace and made Falkland a royal burgh. His great-grandson James V used French and Scottish craftsmen to embellish the building in superb Scottish Gothic style, adding the magnificent twin-towered gatehouse. It was for James V that the real tennis court was built in 1539. It is Britain's oldest, and is still used. The palace, built around three sides of a courtyard, has been restored by successive keepers and by the National Trust for Scotland. The Chapel Royal has a superbly painted wooden ceiling, and the royal arms of Scotland of James V's day are painted large over the fireplace of the sumptuous King's Bed Chamber.

Lawns give a clever illusion of long vistas in the walled garden, which was laid out in 1945 to a Stuart plan.

NTS. Apr-Sept, daily; Oct, Sat and Sun. Adm charge. Shop. Toilets. Tel Falkland (0337) 57397.

HILL OF TARVIT

On A916, 2 miles south of Cupar (Cc)

Frederick Sharp, a wealthy jute manufacturer of Dundee, bought the mansion house at Hill of Tarvit in 1904 to house his art collections. The building had been begun in 1696, and Sharp commissioned the architect Sir Robert Lorimer to remodel and enlarge it. The result is an elegant mansion of mellow, cream-coloured stone set among hillside gardens harmoniously planned by Lorimer. The drawing room, with plaster and woodwork in 18th-century French style, contains French furniture, and two of the treasures among the Dutch masters in the house: winter landscapes by Bruegel and Adriaen Van der Velde.

A 15 minute walk leads from the gardens to the summit of Tarvit Hill, where a monument commemorates Queen Victoria's Diamond Jubilee in 1897. There is also a viewpoint indicator to the breathtaking panoramas all around. To the south stand the cylindrical Hill of Tarvit dovecote, built in the 17th and 18th centuries, and Scotstarvit Tower, a striking 16th-century tower house.

NTS. House: May-Sept, pm daily; Easter weekend, pm; Apr and Oct, Sat and Sun, pm. Garden: All year, daily. Adm charge. Refreshments. P *Toilets. Tel Cupar (0334) 53127.*

KELLIE CASTLE

Off B9171, 3 miles north-west of Pittenweem (Dc)

The Lorimers first came to Kellie as summer visitors in 1878, and the family bought the castle only in 1948, yet it is this artistic family which made it what it is today – a magnificently restored example of 14th to 17th-century Scottish Lowland architecture. By 1878, the massive, square, turreted building was a shambles of neglect, and restoration work began at once, aided early this century by the architect Robert Lorimer. The austere façade belies the light and airy interior. There is superb plasterwork in most rooms, and the Withdrawing Room has 64 wall panels painted with romantic scenes of the reign of Charles II. The kitchen is equipped as it was in the early 1930s, the last great age of country house entertaining.

NTS. Castle: May-Sept, pm daily; Easter weekend, pm; Apr and Oct, Sat and Sun, pm. Garden: All year, daily. Adm charge. Refreshments. Shop. P *Toilets.* ♿ *Tel Arncroach (033 38) 271.*

KIRKCALDY MUSEUM AND ART GALLERY

By railway station in town centre (Cb)

In 1847 Michael Nairn began his floor-covering factory in Kirkcaldy, and the burgh soon became the 'linoleum centre of the world'. Today the industry produces mostly vinyl flooring.

This is just one of the themes of this museum's section on local industries. The museum also covers the geology, natural history, prehistory and history of Kirkcaldy district. There is a display devoted to Adam Smith, the political economist, who was born in Kirkcaldy in 1723, and the art gallery has a fine collection of Scottish and English 18th and 19th-century paintings.

All year, Mon-Sat, exc Bank Hol; Sun pm. Free entry. Shop. P *Toilets. Tel Kirkcaldy (0592) 260732.*

MCDOUALL STUART MUSEUM

Off A955, 2½ miles north of Kirkcaldy (Cb)

The birthplace in Dysart in 1815 of the explorer John McDouall Stuart now contains a museum devoted to him. After qualifying as a civil engineer, Stuart set out for Australia at the age of 23. He spent some years as a surveyor with Captain Sturt, the famous explorer, and between 1858 and 1862 led six expeditions of his own. His greatest achievement came in 1862, when he became the first man to cross Australia from the south coast to the north.

June-Aug, pm daily. Free entry. Shop. P *Tel Kirkcaldy (0592) 260732.*

WRITER RECALLED *A two-volume first edition of Adam Smith's 1776 treatise* The Wealth of Nations *is among the relics of the economist in Kirkcaldy Museum. The profile medallion is a rare portrait made in Smith's lifetime.*

VETERANS OF THE SEA *Old boats and fishing gear lie in the courtyard of the Scottish Fisheries Museum, Anstruther. It stands on the site once occupied by the 15th-century Chapel of St Ayles.*

SCOTTISH FISHERIES MUSEUM

Off A917, at Anstruther (Db)

The museum is housed in old buildings overlooking a harbour used for fishing since the early 14th century, and its displays cover the whole history of Scottish fisheries and the communities following the fortunes of the sea. The museum is, among other things, a tribute to their skill and courage, and one room is kept as a memorial to those lost at sea.

Among the exhibits are reconstructions of a fisherman's house around the turn of the century and of a fishing boat's wheelhouse. There is a fine array of model boats, and actual vessels can be seen in the courtyard and in the nearby harbour. There is also a well-stocked aquarium.

All year, daily. Adm charge. Refreshments. Shop. P *Toilets. Tel Anstruther (0333) 310628.*

REGIONAL CALENDAR

March (late). St Andrews: Festival of Food and Wine.

May (late). Balcormo Mains: Fife Agricultural Show.

June (early). Strathmiglo: Highland Games.

June (late). Falkland: Festival. Dunfermline: Civic Week.

July (early). Cupar: Highland Games.

July (late). Auchtermuchty. Folk Festival. St Andrews. Highland Games.

August (1st Thur). Inverkeithing: Lammas Fair.

August (mid-month). Newburgh: Festival. St Andrews: International Golf. Aberdour Castle: Drama Festival.

September (mid-month). Leuchars: Air Display.

Tourist information: Anstruther (0333) 310628 (summer); Cupar (0334) 55555 (summer); St Andrews (0334) 72021.

GRAMPIAN

CASTLES AMONG THE HILLS AND A GRANITE CITY BY THE SEA

A region of green plains between dark, dramatic mountains, Grampian is also the home of a series of spectacular castles, some of them – such as Balmoral, the Queen's Highland home, Braemar and Dunnottar – resounding with historical associations. Grand country houses include Fasque, beloved by the Prime Minister William Gladstone, and Leith Hall, with one of the region's loveliest gardens. Spiritual foundations that welcome the visitor range from the restored 13th-century Pluscarden Abbey to the Findhorn community, very much of the 20th century with its organic garden and cultural centre.

Winding routes following river valleys such as those of the Dee and the Don lead also to distilleries where age-old processes can be watched; to folk museums where the past is brought vividly to life; to country parks set amidst magnificent Highland scenery; and to nature reserves that give sanctuary to a host of birds.

ADEN COUNTRY PARK

Off A950, 10 miles west of Peterhead (Ed)

The parkland and woods of the former private Aden estate now form a 230 acre country park, through which the South Ugie Water winds sedately between overhanging trees. There are secluded picnic spots, children's play areas and craft centres where country craftsmen can be seen at work. A heritage centre portrays everyday life on the estate in the 1920s, and its displays include a panorama of farming techniques from the ox

MAJESTIC HOME *The Royal Standard fluttering over Balmoral Castle shows that the Queen is in residence at her Deeside home. The light grey granite, quarried on the estate, gleams in the summer sun.*

teams of the past to the four-wheel-drive tractors of today.

Park: All year, daily. Free entry. Refreshments. Shop. P *Toilets.* ♿ *Heritage Centre: May-Sept, daily; Apr and Oct, Sat-Sun. Tel Mintlaw (0771) 22857.*

ARBUTHNOT MUSEUM

In centre of Peterhead (Ed)

Polar bears and seals bring a tang of the sea to this largely maritime museum, which is housed in Peterhead's public library. Founded in the 1890s, it was based on the wildlife collections of Adam Arbuthnot, a local trader. As well as Arctic animals, its displays tell of the town's days as an important centre of the whaling and seal fishing industries.

All year, Mon-Sat. Free entry. Shop. P *Tel Peterhead (0779) 77778.*

BALMORAL CASTLE

Off A93, 8 miles east of Braemar (Bb)

The Queen's holiday home is Scottish baronial at its romantic best, a castle set amid wooded hills on a curve of the salmon-silver Dee. A 15th-century castle, called *Bouchmorale* – Gaelic for 'majestic dwelling' – stood here when Queen Victoria first paid a visit in 1848. She instantly fell in love with a place where, she said, 'all seemed to breathe freedom and peace'.

Prince Albert bought the castle for £31,000 in 1852, and spent three years rebuilding it. The massive tower, with pepper-pot turrets at each corner, is 100ft high; more pepper pots peep above the main roofline, and large mullioned windows flood the interior with light. The dining room, library and billiards room are on the ground floor; so is the ballroom, nearly 70ft long and 25ft wide, which houses a changing exhibition of pictures and other items from the Queen's private collection.

Outside, in the formal gardens, wide herbaceous borders lead the eye onto wild moorland scenery beyond. Crathie Church, where the royal family worship, is opposite the bridge leading to the castle's main gate. Queen Victoria laid the foundation stone of the church in 1893.

May-July, Mon-Sat. Adm charge. Refreshments. P *Toilets.* ♿ *Tel Crathie (033 84) 334.*

BALVENIE CASTLE

Off A941, 1 mile north of Dufftown (Bd)

The impressive ruins of Balvenie Castle, set on a grassy mound above the River Fiddich and protected by a dry moat, are the remains of a 13th-century fortress from which the Comyns guarded strategic mountain passes. Its imposing curtain wall, 25ft high and 7ft thick, still surrounds the large courtyard. Later owners, the Stewart Earls of Atholl, in the 16th century added a stately three-storeyed mansion with a grand tower, and this tower still stands.

HBM. Apr-Sept, daily exc Sun am. Adm charge. P *Tel Edinburgh (031) 244 3101.*

BENNACHIE FOREST RESERVE

Off B993, 7 miles west of Inverurie (Cc)

From the 1698ft summit of Mither Tap the panoramic views are breathtaking – for those who have any breath left after the steep walk up. Walks leading to it range from 3 miles to 6¼ miles, and start from the four car parks. At the summit, an indicator identifies sights of interest, including the Caithness hills more than 80 miles north-west. Other splendid colour-coded walks starting from the car parks include one of only half a mile. The Donview Visitor Centre in the south provides information on walks, forestry and wildlife.

FC. Donview Visitor Centre: Easter-Oct, daily. Free entry. Tel Aberdeen (0224) 632727.

BRAEMAR CASTLE

On A93, ½ mile north-east of Braemar (Ab)

Viewed from the main road – with its rugged walls, dominating round tower, gun-slits and barred windows – Braemar Castle looks every inch a fortress. To the west, however, the walls are pierced by spacious windows, and the building presents itself as a private home – that of the Farquharsons of Invercauld – complete with memorabilia collected during their 200 years of occupation.

The L-plan castle was originally built in 1628 by the Earl of Mar and was attacked and burnt in 1698 by the so-called 'Black Colonel', John Farquharson of Inverey. Farquharson of Invercauld bought it as a ruin in 1732 and turned it into a charming private residence. Today the tower is one of the highlights of the castle. Other notable features are the barrel-vaulted ceilings, massive iron yett, or gate, underground prison, and the star-shaped defensive curtain wall.

The living quarters contain a varied collection of furniture, and historic relics include a piece of plaid said to have been worn by Bonnie Prince Charlie, and what is probably the world's largest cairngorm – a semiprecious stone found in the Cairngorm Mountains and weighing 52lb.

May-early Oct, daily exc Fri. Adm charge. Shop. P *Toilets. Tel Braemar (033 83) 219.*

BRODIE CASTLE

Off A96, 4½ miles west of Forres (Ad)

Outside, all is battlemented towers with gun loops and arrow-slit windows, a legacy of the 1560s when Scottish lairds built with security in mind. Inside, a bowl of flowers set tastefully at the end of a low, vaulted entrance hall sets the domestic tone of a building which is still the family home of the Brodies.

The ground-floor library contains the family archives which crowd every shelf. The more formal rooms are on the first floor. They comprise a light, airy drawing room; a red drawing room hung with Dutch 17th-century paintings; and a dining room whose ceiling is one of the castle's glories – a riot of ornamental plasterwork depicting flowers, fruits and mythical creatures.

NTS. Easter; May-Sept, daily exc Sun am. Adm charge. Refreshments. P *Toilets.* ♿ *Tel Brodie (030 94) 371.*

Silvery Gems Of Aberdeen

Proudly known as the 'Granite City', Aberdeen gets its nickname from its handsome grey-granite buildings – many of them speckled with mica – which shine like silver in the sunlight. Here the old and the new live comfortably together, with some streets and houses dating from the 16th century – and still more from the 19th century, when fishing was the city's principal industry. The North Sea oil boom of the 1970s and early 1980s created the city's new prosperity.

The most attractive sights in Aberdeen, however, are the unchanging ones. They include ancient dwelling places such as Provost Skene's House, the two imposing cathedrals of St Andrew and St Machar, and a hallowed university with its colourful botanic garden.

Botanic Garden: All year, Mon-Fri; also Sat and Sun, pm May-Sept. Free entry. P *Tel Aberdeen (0224) 272000. Provost Skene's House: All year, Mon-Sat. Free entry. Refreshments. Shop.* P *Toilets. Tel (0224) 641086. St Andrew's Cathedral: June-Sept, Mon-Fri and service times. Free entry. Shop.* P *Tel (0224) 640290. St Machar's Cathedral: All year, daily. Free entry. Shop.* P *(limited). Toilets. Tel (0224) 485988.*

HARBOUR LIFE *Sturdy local fishing boats rub shoulders in Aberdeen's bustling harbour with foreign cargo vessels and supply ships for the North Sea oil rigs. The port has flourished since the end of the 13th century, when it sent fish, timber, hides and wood to England and Europe.*

FULL FLOWER *The wooded green slopes and trim lawns of Cruickshank Botanic Garden (left) include flowerbeds, flowering shrubs, aquatic and marsh plants, a rock garden and a long herbaceous border. The garden, founded in 1898 and expanded from the 1960s onwards, covers 11 acres of ground in Old Aberdeen.*

CHAPEL ROYAL *The crown tower of King's College Chapel was erected in honour of James IV of Scotland, the co-founder and first patron of the college, which is now part of Aberdeen University. The chapel, completed in 1505, forms one side of a grassy quadrangle and looks down on the memorial of Bishop Elphinstone, the college's other founder.*

PROVOST'S HOUSE *The 17th-century Restoration Room in Provost Skene's House is overlooked by an oval painting above the fireplace called simply* The Scottish Lady. *The building – named after Sir George Skene, a late 17th-century Provost, or Chief Magistrate, of the city – dates from 1545.*

TRANSATLANTIC LINK *The east window of St Andrew's Cathedral, with its central figure of Christ, was completed in 1945. One shield bears the city's coat of arms, and the other the United States flag; the first American bishop was consecrated here in 1784.*

TOWERING ADDITION *The twin towers of St Machar's Cathedral (right) jab the sky above the old quarter of the city. The cathedral dates from the 14th and 15th centuries, but the tower's spires – each of them surmounted by a cross – were added by Bishop Dunbar between 1518 and 1532.*

BUCKIE MARITIME MUSEUM
In centre of Buckie (Be)

Buckie's long association with the sea is reflected in a wide range of maritime themes: fishing methods, lifesaving, navigation, coopering, and the work of people in related industries – including women engaged in the gutting and packing of fish. The museum also has 800 paintings by the 20th-century artist Peter Anson, whose canvases provide a lively picture of the fishing industry.
All year, Mon-Sat. Free entry. Shop. P *(limited). Tel Forres (0309) 73701.*

BULLERS OF BUCHAN
On A975, 5½ miles south of Peterhead (Ec)

Above a high-cliffed bay, a razor-edged path leads along a dizzy route about 200ft above a boiling cauldron of water. The word 'bullers' comes from the old Scottish word for 'boilers', and at one point the surging sea has carved a cave in the inlet. The path is no place for children or those with no head for heights.
All year, daily.

CASTLE FRASER
Off B993, 3 miles south of Kemnay (Db)

Turrets, crow-stepped gables and coats of arms set high on the walls give Castle Fraser something of the appearance of a French chateau. It is in fact a typical baronial tower house of the 16th century, and was mainly the work of the 6th laird, Michael Fraser, in the 1570s. His son Andrew in 1633 became the 1st Lord Fraser and embellished the castle as an expression of his status.

Inside the castle, a winding staircase leads up to a bright, white-walled Great Hall which is sometimes the setting for concerts of 18th and early 19th-century music, the scores for which were found in the castle library. A cosy smoking room is lined with peacock-patterned 19th-century wallpaper, and from it a wooden covered stairway leads to the Green Room, home of the obligatory family ghost – that of a princess allegedly murdered in the room. From the round tower there is a fine view over the castle's 26 acres of wooded parkland, which includes a walled formal garden.
NTS. Grounds: All year, daily. Castle: May-Sept, pm daily. Adm charge. Refreshments. P *Toilets. Tel Sauchen (033 03) 463.*

CORGARFF CASTLE
Off A939, 12 miles south of Tomintoul (Bb)

Built in the mid-16th century as a small tower house, Corgarff Castle was turned into a military barracks after the defeat of Bonnie Prince Charlie at Culloden. It became one of the strongholds on the new military road from Blairgowrie to Fort George on the Moray Firth. The tower was gutted and rebuilt with an officer's room and kitchen on the ground floor, and cramped barrack rooms – with eight double beds to each room – on the two upper floors. The cobbled courtyard was enclosed by a star-shaped wall with loopholes, so that the little barracks could hold out against musketry attack, but not artillery. Today the stronghold looks much as it did more than 200 years ago, with recesses for muskets, enormous stone fireplaces and replica cot beds in the barrack rooms.
HBM. Apr-Sept, daily; Oct-Mar, see keykeeper. Adm charge. P *Tel Edinburgh (031) 244 3101.*

HAPPY HOUSE *Winter gives a dramatic frame to Brodie Castle. It was built in 1567 by Alexander, the 12th Brodie of Brodie, and its present owner – the 25th laird – calls it a 'happy house', without a family ghost.*

CRAIGIEVAR CASTLE
On A980, 4 miles south of Alford (Cb)

At first sight, the pink, roughcast walls of this handsome castle seem to have grown out of the green hillside on which it stands. It was built in the early 17th century in Scottish baronial style for the Forbes family, and today it is as proud and imposing as ever, with its sturdy central tower and overhanging turrets built to give flanking fire along the walls.

The castle's only entrance is through one guarded doorway in the tower. This leads to a paved vestibule, off which is a barrel-vaulted chamber once used as a dungeon. On the first floor is the musicians' gallery, with a door bearing the arms and initials of Master William Forbes, first owner of the castle, his wife Margaret Woodward, and, nearby, the date 1612.
NTS. May-Sept, daily. Adm charge. P *Tel Lumphanan (033 983) 635.*

CRATHES CASTLE
Off A93, 3 miles east of Banchory (Db)

Majestic woodlands typical of Royal Deeside line the approach to Crathes Castle. The square turrets and conical pepper-pot towers of the 16th-century tower house peep out above lime trees that are comparative newcomers, being only 200 years old. Stories and legends cling to a castle that was lived in by a single family, the Burnetts, for more than 350 years.

The ghost of Crathes, said to have been sighted even in the sceptical 1980s, is that of the Green Lady who carries in her arms a baby girl supposed to have met her death in the castle. The Room of the Nine Nobles is named after ceiling decorations which are a feature of the castle, showing great heroes of the past such as Julius Caesar, Alexander the Great and King Arthur.

Eight small individual gardens are contained within the walled garden at Crathes, and provide a succession of dazzling colours from spring to autumn. The surrounding estate has five wood-

HIGH ART *Grotesque faces, weird designs, coats of arms and moral exhortations are among the well-preserved 16th-century ceiling decorations in the Green Lady's Room in Crathes Castle.*

land walks ranging from 1½ miles to 6 miles, including one trail suitable for disabled visitors which leads to a viewpoint overlooking the Dee.
NTS. Gardens: all year, daily. Castle: mid Apr-Sept, daily; Oct, weekends. Adm charge. Refreshments. Shop. P *Toilets.* ♿ *(gardens only). Tel Crathes (033 044) 525.*

DARNAWAY FARM VISITOR CENTRE

Off A96, 3 miles west of Forres (Ad)

The development of a Victorian farmsteading into a modern dairy farm can be seen by visitors to Darnaway. From an elevated walkway, visitors can see how the present-day herd of dairy cows is kept – and watch them being milked every afternoon. To portray the past there is a collection of bygone farm implements and a graphic exhibition of the history of Darnaway, with its castle and forest.

On Wednesday and Sunday afternoons in summer a minibus runs from the centre to the castle, where one of the highlights of the conducted tour is the magnificent medieval hammer-beam roof in the hall. There are also conducted tours of the surrounding countryside, including the broadleaved and coniferous forest.
June-late Sept, daily. Adm charge. Refreshments. P *Toilets.* ♿ *Tel Forres (030 94) 469.*

DRUM CASTLE

Off A93, 4 miles west of Peterculter (Db)

A splendid tree-lined avenue leads uphill to a ridge from which Drum Castle overlooks its parkland. For more than 650 years Drum Castle was the home of the Irvine family, and their flag – white, with three sprigs of holly – still flutters over the battlements of the medieval keep. The castle consists of a Jacobean mansion house with a Victorian extension. The mansion house was built by Alexander Irvine and his wife, Marion Douglas, and the date is inscribed on one of the stones of its dormer windows – however, as the masons could not read or write, they carved the date '6191' instead of '1619'. Inside, the rooms are magnificently furnished in a variety of styles.
NTS. May-Sept, daily. Adm charge. Refreshments. P *Toilets. Tel Drumoak (033 08) 204.*

ARTIST AS ANGEL *A large picture of the Archangel Gabriel dominates the library at Drum Castle. The model for the painting was the artist himself – Hugh Irvine, the brother of the 18th Laird of Drum.*

DUFF HOUSE

Off A98, ½ mile south of Banff (Dd)

Standing uninhabited and unfurnished amidst a sweep of ornamental parkland, Duff House seems haunted by the ghosts of its glorious past, when grand social gatherings mustered in surroundings of lordly splendour. Its spacious, high-ceilinged rooms have been carefully restored; and moving through them it is possible, with a little imagination, to picture how Highland noblemen and their families of the 18th and 19th centuries lived and entertained in style.

The house was designed by William Adam for the socially ambitious William Duff (later 1st Earl of Fife), and building work began in 1735. But it was not until 1870 that the second classical wing was added – and after that the house drifted into decay and disrepair. The pictures, books and ornate furniture were removed and, after renovation, the house served as a hotel and later a sanatorium. In the Second World War it housed captured German merchant navy officers.
HBM. Apr-Sept, daily; Oct-Mar, see keykeeper. Adm charge. Shop. P *Tel Edinburgh (031) 244 3101.*

DUFFUS CASTLE

Off B9012, 6 miles north-west of Elgin (Be)

When built in about 1150, Duffus was one of Scotland's main defensive strongholds, and for more than 500 years it served as a fortress-residence. But by the time it was abandoned in 1705 it had become little more than a ruin. Originally built of timber on a hillock, the castle was rebuilt in stone in the 14th century. Still standing are a gateway, the curtain wall, part of the tower, the ground floor of the keep, and parts of a kitchen and great chamber.
HBM. All year, daily. Free entry. P *(limited). Tel Ardersier (0667) 62777.*

DUNNOTTAR CASTLE

On A92, 2 miles south of Stonehaven (Da)

The castle ruins squat pugnaciously on a vast, flat-topped, isolated rock that rises 160ft sheer above the sea. There has been a fortress here since the 9th century, much altered and added to over the centuries. Visitors enter the castle by a steep path from the beach. The two most substantial remains are the keep and gatehouse. The chapel retains part of its 13th-century pointed windows, and with the quadrangle, churchyard, bowling green, store and stables shows that Dunnottar once accommodated a sizable, self-contained community. A gloomy underground vault is little changed since 1685, when 167 Covenanters were imprisoned there because of their Presbyterian beliefs.
Apr-Oct, daily; Nov-Mar, daily exc Sat. Adm charge. Shop. P *Toilets. Tel Stonehaven (0569) 62173.*

ELGIN CATHEDRAL

Cooper Park, Elgin (Bd)

Once known as the Lantern of the North, the 13th-century cathedral is Elgin's most revered monument, standing in parkland in the east of the town. The twin towers of the cathedral's west front present an elegant face to the world, although the interior walls bear the marks of a fire in 1390 which gutted the building. Despite major repairs, the cathedral fell into decay and in 1711 the central tower collapsed, leaving the shell much as it is today. However, much of the original interior work remains, including the transept and choir. At the west end of the choir is a 9th-century Celtic cross-slab carved with a lively hunting scene and Pictish symbols. The octagonal chapter house stands intact to the east.
HBM. All year, daily. Adm charge. Shop. P *(limited). Tel Edinburgh (031) 244 3101.*

FALCONER MUSEUM

In centre of Forres (Ad)

Although the Falconer Museum is Italianate in design, its lines are now very much a part of the Forres townscape. It was built between 1868 and 1871 and was the inspiration of two local brothers, Alexander and Hugh Falconer, who wanted to establish a museum for 'objects of art and science'. Hugh Falconer was one of the leading botanists and geologists of his day, and the exhibits include fossils from many parts of the world, minerals and stuffed birds. There are also collections of local household items and antiquities.
July-Aug, daily; mid May-June, Sept, Mon-Sat; Oct-mid May, Mon-Fri. Free entry. Shop. P *Tel Forres (0309) 73701.*

FASQUE

On B974, 7 miles north-west of Laurencekirk (Ca)

The British prime minister W E Gladstone made Fasque his country home from 1830 to 1851, and many of his diary entries tell how fond he was of it. He loved long hill walks around the estate, and enjoyed the shooting.

Today, the palatial house looks much as it did in Gladstone's time, and is still lived in by his descendants. It was built in 1809, although the façade of the central tower and the top storey of the servants' east wing were added later. Among the relics of Gladstone is a selection of the hundreds of illuminated addresses presented to him during his career – including some from women who supported his unsuccessful efforts to give them the vote.

May-Sept, daily exc Fri. Adm charge. Shop. P *Toilets.* ♿ *Tel Fettercairn (056 14) 201.*

FINDHORN FOUNDATION

Findhorn Bay Caravan Park, Findhorn (Ad)

Organically grown vegetables, flowers and wholefood products are grown at this international spiritual community. Since its birth in 1962, the garden at Findhorn has flourished. Despite poor soil and frequently fierce weather the Foundation claims this as 'impressive evidence of the power of working in harmony and cooperation with the nature realms'. Today the community is some 200 strong. Half-day tours include a visit to the strikingly modern Universal Hall Centre for Arts and Culture and to Findhorn's food and craft shop.

June-Sept, pm daily; Oct-May, Mon, Thur and Sat, pm. Free entry. Refreshments. Shop. P *Toilets.* ♿ *Tel Findhorn (0309) 30311.*

FOCHABERS FOLK MUSEUM

High Street, Fochabers (Bd)

A former church is the setting of this unusual museum. Upstairs, the church has been converted to hold one of the largest collections of horse-drawn vehicles in Scotland. Downstairs there is an Aladdin's Cave of articles connected with the village and the surrounding countryside, including clocks, wedding dresses, model engines, and pictures and representations of bygone personalities, events and settings – including a replica of an early village shop.

All year, daily. Adm charge. Shop. P *Tel Fochabers (0343) 820362.*

FORVIE NATURE RESERVE

Off A975, 12 miles north of Aberdeen (Ec)

Motorists can see eider ducks in the summer and flocks of geese in the winter as they pass this sand-and-moorland coastal reserve. Covering some 2550 acres, Forvie is a regular breeding ground for more than 40 species of birds including sandwich terns, shelducks, kittiwakes and fulmars. Despite the cold winds that often whip in off the North Sea there is a colourful butterfly and moth population, and migrant species such as the painted lady have been recorded.

The Forvie Centre is at Collieston, at the northern end of the reserve, and here visitors can obtain information about the area through audiovisual presentations, various displays and a scale model.

All year, daily. Free entry. P *Toilets.* ♿ *Tel Collieston (035 877) 330.*

FYVIE CASTLE

Off A947, 8 miles south-east of Turriff (Dd)

The castle's five great towers which dominate the surrounding countryside are monuments to the five families who have owned Fyvie over the last 500 years. Each tower is named after one of the families: the Prestons, the Meldrums, the Setons, the Gordons and the Leiths. The oldest part of the castle dates from the 13th century, and behind its stout walls is a labyrinth of rooms and passages rich in Edwardian furnishings and 16th-century tapestries.

The great wheel-stair, perhaps the finest in Scotland, rises dramatically on 10ft wide steps through five floors to the drawing room in the lofty Gordon Tower. According to legend, the Gordons once rode their horses all the way up the stairs for a wager. Nearby is the music room in which King Alfonso of Spain and his bride Queen Victoria Eugenie danced a night away on their honeymoon in the castle in 1906.

About a mile south of the castle, off B9005, is the early 19th-century Fyvie parish church. It is dominated by its beautiful east window, created at the beginning of this century by Louis Tiffany, the American artist who specialised in decorative glass work. It depicts a life-size St Michael poised on a wheel, wearing armour, and holding in his right hand a flaming sword and in his left the banner of the Cross. It commemorates Percy Forbes-Leith, who died at the age of 18 during the Anglo-Boer War. There is also a smaller Tiffany window in the laird's pew. The unusual oak pulpit is carved in the shape of a huge wineglass.

Castle: NTS. May-Sept, daily. Adm charge. Refreshments. P *Toilets.* ♿ *Church: May-Sept, Sat and Sun, pm.* P *Tel Fyvie (065 16) 266.*

BABE IN ARMS *A detailed reconstruction of a Victorian living room – complete with aspidistra and a model of a mother nursing her baby – is among the domestic exhibits at the Fochabers Folk Museum.*

GLENBUCHAT CASTLE

On A97, 2½ miles west of Glenkindie (Bc)

A stone inscription above the entrance to this stronghold states that it was built in 1590 to mark the marriage of John Gordon of Cairnburrow to Helen Carnegie. The castle is Z-shaped, with

PIPE MUSIC *A large, self-playing pipe organ is set below the ceiling in The Gallery, or Music Room, at Fyvie Castle. The gallery was built in the Leith Tower in 1900, and its walls were hung with Brussels tapestries.*

round and square turrets, projecting stair towers, steep gables and tall chimney stacks. A gun-slit in the turret by the entrance rakes downwards to defend the only door. Inside, a circular stone staircase leads up to the laird's apartment on the first floor – complete with hall, retiring room, bedchamber and sizable fireplace. The last laird quit the castle in the 1730s.

HBM. All year, daily. Free entry. P *(limited). Tel Ardersier (0667) 6277.*

GLENFIDDICH DISTILLERY

On A941, ¼ mile north of Dufftown (Bd)

Glenfiddich is the only distillery in the Highlands where malt whisky is bottled on the premises, and visitors can watch the entire process.

The distillery was founded in 1886 by William Grant, a former cattle-herder and shoemaker, and he and his seven sons built it stone by stone with their own hands. On Christmas Day 1887 Grant watched the first whisky run from the stills, and Glenfiddich has been owned by the Grant family ever since. Today the distillery complex covers 60 acres, and its warehouses can hold up to 18½ million gallons of Scotch. In the theatre the story of the whisky's growth is told.

Glenfiddich is one of seven distilleries which are joined by a signposted road tour, the Malt Whisky Trail, through 70 miles of magnificent Grampian scenery. At each of them visitors can watch the distilling process and buy the product. Other distilleries on the trail include The Glenlivet, Glen Grant, Glenfarclas, Strathisla, Tamdhu and Tamnavulin.

Glenfiddich: All year, Mon-Fri; also Sat and Sun June-Sept. Free entry. Shop. P *Toilets.* ♿ *Tel Dufftown (0340) 20373. Glenfarclas: All year, Mon-Fri; also Sat July-Aug. Other distilleries: Easter-Sept, Mon-Fri, some Sat.*

BETTER BY DESIGN *Over the centuries the lairds of Leith Hall have embellished the house – a drum tower here, a pavilion there, a rash of chimneys in the 19th century giving it a jaunty appearance.*

GRAMPIAN TRANSPORT MUSEUM

In centre of Alford (Cc)

About 100 vehicles of all kinds – cycles, motorcycles, steam engines, fire engines, lorries, sledges, horse-drawn carriages, and veteran, vintage and classic cars – are on proud display here. They include several late 19th-century 'horseless carriages' – among the first to be seen in Scotland – and an 1896 horse tram, used in Aberdeen. But the museum's most cherished exhibit is the Craigievar Express – a cross between a steam engine and a three-wheeled cart – built in 1895 by a local postman.

From the village station the brightly painted green-and-red engines and coaches of the Alford Valley Railway take passengers through lush forest where the trees almost meet overhead and tall grass threatens to grow over the tracks. This 2ft narrow-gauge railway makes half-hour long trips to Haughton Country Park and on to Murray Park. The station has been rebuilt to look as it did in the 19th century.

Transport Museum: Apr-Sept, daily. Adm charge. Refreshments. Shop. P *Toilets.* ♿ *Tel Alford (0336) 2292. Railway: June-Aug, daily; Apr, May and Sept, Sat and Sun. Adm charge. Shop.* P *Railway Museum: Apr-Sept, daily. Adm charge. Tel (0336) 2052.*

HADDO HOUSE

Off B9005, 10 miles north-west of Ellon (Dc)

A magnificent stone staircase, supported by pillars, sweeps across the front of this handsome house, rising to the first floor and passing over the broad front door. Designed by William Adam, and owned by the Gordon family for more than 250 years, the house is an impressive mixture of architecture and design from the 18th to the 20th centuries – with works of art, books, ceramics and furnishings dating from the 1600s. Attached to the north wing is a late 19th-century chapel with a fine stained-glass window by Sir Edward Burne-Jones.

The outlying country park has a tree trail from which roe deer can often be seen grazing in woodland clearings.

NTS. House: Easter, Apr weekends, pm; May-Sept, pm daily. Adm charge. Refreshments. Shop. P *Toilets.* ♿ *Tel Tarves (069 15) 440. Park: All year, daily. Free entry.* P *Toilets.* ♿ *Tel (065 15) 489.*

HUNTLY CASTLE

In northern outskirts of Huntly (Cd)

The crowning glory of the castle is the tall 'frontispiece' carved over the main door in the tower. It stretches upwards, starting with the arms of the 6th Earl of Huntly (created 1st Marquis of Huntly in 1597) and his lady, Henrietta Stewart. Above this are the royal arms of Scotland and those of James VI's queen, Anne of Denmark. Above this again is a panel showing the Five Wounds of Christ and two supporting figures, probably St Mary and St John. Over this is a circular panel depicting the Risen Christ in His Glory, haloed by clouds. At the summit is the figure of St Michael, the warrior archangel, triumphing over Satan on the day of Last Judgment. The elaborate piece of masonry was commissioned by the 1st marquis soon after 1600.

Set in 8 acres of wooded parkland, the now ruined castle is approached by a fine avenue. Inside the main door, stairs plunge down to a graffiti-lined corridor leading to a prison – the graffiti include drawings of men and women in 16th-century garb.

HBM. All year, daily. Adm charge. P *(limited). Tel Edinburgh (031) 244 3101.*

LEITH HALL

On B9002, 5 miles north-east of Rhynie (Cc)

The first view of Leith Hall from the long, tree-lined drive is of the white-faced west wing, added in the late 19th century. The home of the Leith family from 1650 to 1945, the four-storeyed hall is a treasure trove of relics, tracing the Leiths' long and turbulent history.

The handsome, oak-ceiling entrance hall was built at the beginning of this century by Charles Leith-Hay, whose portrait dominates the space. The inner hall is a 1756 addition and contains some late 18th-century elm chairs. Upstairs on the south landing is an early 18th-century long-case clock which runs for a year – and, by family tradition, is rewound on August 12. The Leith bedroom, in the oldest part of the house, has furniture dating from George III's reign.

Despite all these indoor treasures, the hall's chief beauty is perhaps its series of gardens, each sheltered by a hedge or wall and each having its own individual character. A carpet of blue catmint fills an entire border, and there are colourful rose beds and herbaceous borders.

NTS. May-Sept, pm daily. Adm charge. P *Toilets.* ♿ *Tel Kennethmont (046 43) 216.*

PITMEDDEN GARDEN

On A920, 6 miles west of Elton (Dc)

The doorway leading into the Great Garden of Pitmedden bears the date of its foundation – May 2, 1675 – and just above it on the lintel are the initials of its founders, SAS and DML: Sir Alexander Seton and Dame Margaret

REWARDING WORK *Box hedges are a feature of Pitmedden Garden, with Latin mottoes along the borders. These include the legend* Merces Haec Certa Laborum – *'This Sure Reward of Our Labours'.*

Lauder, his wife. The dignified formal garden, inspired by one created near Paris for Louis XIV, fell into neglect after the house was badly damaged by fire in 1818. The present building was erected in 1860 and Sir Alexander's great garden was re-created between 1955 and 1974.

A fountain forms the focal point for the garden. Around it is an attractive split pebble pavement, beyond which the garden stretches out in four great rectangles, outlined by box hedges and divided by turf paths.

By Pitmedden House is an outdoor Museum of Farming Life consisting of a furnished farmhouse, a bothy or workmen's hut, a stable with hayloft, a byre and a turnip shed.

NTS. Garden: All year, daily. Adm charge. Refreshments. 🅿 *Toilets.* ♿ *Tel Udny (065 13) 2352. Museum: May-Sept, daily. Free entry.*

PLUSCARDEN ABBEY

Off B9010, 5½ miles south-west of Elgin (Ad)

Sheltering at the foot of a steep and thickly wooded hill, this remote, 13th-century abbey retains its atmosphere of quiet and godly reflection. The old Pilgrim Road to Pluscarden swept round to the imposing North Gate of the abbey – one of only 16 monasteries of Benedictine monks in Britain. Today, the abbey complex is dominated by the massive block of the central tower. The buildings fell into ruins after the suppression of the Scottish monasteries in 1560, and religious life did not recommence until 1948, when the white-robed monks again took up residence. In 1955 the tower was re-roofed and the bells of Pluscarden once more rang out.

All year, daily. Free entry. 🅿 *Toilets. Tel Dallas (034 389) 257.*

STORYBOOK GLEN

Off B9077, 5 miles west of Aberdeen (Db)

The old woman who lived in a shoe . . . Old Macdonald who had a farm . . . Humpty Dumpty . . . Jack and Jill . . . Goldilocks and the Three Bears . . . these are some of the favourite fairy-tale and nursery-rhyme characters waiting to meet visitors to this world of make-believe set in the heart of Royal Deeside, and adults can relax among acres of plants.

All year, daily. Adm charge. Refreshments. Shop. 🅿 *Toilets.* ♿ *Tel Aberdeen (0224) 732941.*

TOLBOOTH MUSEUM

North Pier, Stonehaven (Da)

Prisoners about to be hanged for stealing a few bags of meal were kept in the tolbooth in the 17th and 18th centuries. Others found guilty of theft, and dealt with less severely, were scourged through the town, branded on the shoulder or bored through the ears with a red-hot awl. To perform these duties Stonehaven employed an 'executioner, hangman and scourger', who worked from the tolbooth, now the town's oldest building. It was built in the late 16th century as a storehouse for cargoes on their way to nearby Dunnottar Castle, and in 1600 it became the town's courthouse and prison. Carefully restored, its exhibits include the town's unusual stocks – with seven holes!

June-Sept, daily exc Tue. Free entry. Shop. Tel Peterhead (0779) 77778.

REGIONAL CALENDAR

January 11 Burghead: Burning the Clavie (Old New Year's Day custom).

April (mid-month). Aberdeen: Indoor Highland Games.

June (mid-month). Aberdeen: Highland Games.

June (late). Burghead: Highland Games and Pipe Band Championships. Drumtochty: Highland Games.

July (early). Forres, Elgin: Highland Games.

July (mid-month). Stonehaven: Highland Games.

July (late). Dufftown: Highland Games. Peterhead: Scottish Week.

August (early). Aboyne: Highland Games.

August (late). Ballater, Lonach: Highland Games.

September (1st Sat). Braemar: Royal Highland Gathering.

October (early). Dufftown: Highland Dancing Festival.

Tourist information: Aberdeen (0224) 632727; Ballater (0338) 55306 (summer); Braemar (033 83) 600 (summer); Peterhead (0779) 71904 (summer); Stonehaven (0569) 62806 (summer).

HIGHLAND

CASTLES AND BATTLEGROUNDS AMONG THE RUGGED HEIGHTS

Majestic mountains, bewitching lochs and noble castles combine to make the Scottish Highlands a region of dramatic spectacle, which has often been the backcloth to bloody clan feuds and fierce battles. Culloden provides a lasting memorial of Bonnie Prince Charlie's final defeat by George II's troops in 1746, while Fort George still stands as the legacy of Hanoverian fears of further campaigns for the Stuart cause. Meanwhile the haunted mountain pass of Glencoe evokes memories of the horrifying massacre of the Macdonalds in 1692.

But the Highland Region does not live on the past alone. A modern phenomenon has been the development of Aviemore as a leisure resort, while other attractions include Britain's only herd of reindeer roaming free in Glenmore Forest; a craft community village on Cape Wrath; a Spey Valley Whisky Centre near Aviemore; and an exhibition at Loch Ness in honour of the most famous monster of them all.

ARDTORNISH

Off A884, 2½ miles north of Lochaline (Ba)

A 28 acre woodland garden of conifers, azaleas and rhododendrons has been sculpted out of a rocky hillside above Loch Aline. It forms part of the Ardtornish estate, whose 60 square miles also include Kinlochaline Castle, a 14th-century tower house much restored in 1890; a small fireplace on the roof is said to have been used for heating oil or water to pour down onto attackers.

Apr-Oct, daily. Adm charge. P *Toilets. Tel Morvern (096 784) 288.*

AVIEMORE CENTRE

Off A9, 12 miles north of Kingussie (Dc)

Before 1960 Aviemore was just a quiet village. Then, in the Cairngorm snows, Scottish skiing began to develop and later, as well as being packed with skiers in winter, Aviemore became a bustling resort for sports, including golf, squash, riding, curling and water sports on two lochs. For informal recreation, there are walks in the splendour of the Spey Valley.

The Spey Valley is also noted for its whisky production, the subject of the Whisky Centre and Museum at Inverdruie, just south of Aviemore. On display are hundreds of brands of whisky, along with the equipment used in distilling, past and present. Visitors can taste samples of whisky, and a map shows distilleries open to the public.

Aviemore Centre: All year, daily. Free entry. Refreshments. Shop. P *Toilets.* ♿ *Tel Aviemore (0479) 810624. Whisky Centre: All year, daily. Adm charge. Shop.* P *Toilets. Tel (0479) 810574.*

BALNAKEIL CRAFT VILLAGE

Off A838, 1 mile north-west of Durness (Cf)

Amid the wild beauty of Cape Wrath, craftsmen and craftswomen form the north-westernmost community of mainland Britain, the first village of its kind to be established in the country, and the only one owned by its residents. The site was originally a Ministry of Defence 'early warning' station. But in 1964, when the station buildings were derelict, Sutherland county council invited people with skills to move in. Among the activities at Balnakeil today are pottery, weaving, jewelcraft, woodwork and marquetry.

Apr-Sept, daily. Free entry. Refreshments. Shop. P *Tel Durness (097 181) 346.*

BEINN EIGHE NATIONAL NATURE RESERVE

Off A832, 2 miles north-west of Kinlochewe (Bd)

On the southern shore of Loch Maree stands a remnant of the old Caledonian forest, Coille na Glas Leitire, 'the wood on the grey slope'. The slope rises to the craggy, 3000ft peaks of Meall a'Ghiubhais, and farther south are the peaks of the Beinn Eighe range. Some 10,000 acres of mountain, moorland and forest between Loch Maree and Beinn Eighe form a National Nature Reserve, the first in Britain when it was established in 1951.

The main access to the reserve is from the road that runs alongside the loch, about 2 miles from Kinlochewe and the Aultroy Visitor Centre. The centre, housed in a converted 19th-century cottage, has an exhibition about the reserve, and the 1 mile Glas Leitire Nature Trail, which starts from the centre, provides an introduction to its scenic splendours. Beside the start of the trail the Allt na Airidhe burn flows into Loch Maree. The trail then climbs between pines and birches, and at about 300ft there are views across the 12 mile vista of Loch Maree to the mountains to the north, dominated by the 3215ft peak of Slioch.

Beinn Eighe has been designated by UNESCO as a Biosphere Reserve, thereby making it one of the premier nature reserves in the world. A European Diploma awarded by the Council of Europe has linked it with other protected areas of European interest.

NCC. May-Sept, daily exc Sun. Free entry. P *Tel Kinlochewe (044 584) 258.*

CAWDOR CASTLE

On B9090, 5½ miles south-west of Nairn (Dc)

This majestic fortress, rising out of the Nairn valley woods, has a colourful history which William Shakespeare – aided by myth – has coloured even more. In *Macbeth* it is the scene of King Duncan's murder, but in the 11th century, when Macbeth and Duncan lived, the castle had not been built; in any case, Duncan was killed in combat.

The castle has a turreted 14th-century tower, flanked on one side by a gully and on the other by a dry moat. Since the 17th century it has been developed as a spacious family mansion, and it remains the home of Cawdor earls – members of the Campbell clan. The gracious drawing room has an attractive 17th-century fireplace carved with the family buckle and hart's head. Among the portraits is one of Nelson's mistress, Emma Hamilton. The Tapestry Bedroom has a Venetian bed, with velvet hangings, and 17th-century tapestries of Biblical and pastoral scenes. Outside the castle are three gardens, each with a distinc-

PIPE POWER *Colourful dress and the skirl of bagpipes provide a stirring pageant at Aviemore's International Highland Games. In the quieter surroundings of nearby Glenmore Forest Park (below), Britain's only herd of reindeer, bred from Swedish stock, feed in the snow.*

CAWDOR KITCHEN *Lamplight gleams on the burnished copper utensils in a kitchen at Cawdor Castle. The kitchen was first used around 1640, though parts of the castle are 300 years older.*

tive character and providing a wealth of colours and scents. There are four nature trails.
May-Oct, daily. Adm charge. Refreshments. Shop. P *Toilets.* ♿ *Tel Cawdor (066 77) 615.*

CLAN DONALD CENTRE, SKYE

Off A851, 1½ miles north-east of Ardvasar (Bb)

Scenic beauty and a wealth of history centred on the Macdonalds reward a visit to this part of the Isle of Skye. Here, on the beautiful Sleat peninsula, more than 40 acres of the Macdonald estate can be explored by woodland walks and nature trails. A variety of trees, shrubs and flowers grow on an estate where the hand of man has assisted nature. Dr Samuel Johnson, on his visit in 1773, remarked on the tall ash trees – appreciated all the more because, he noted, 'a tree in Scotland is as rare as a horse in Venice'.

On the estate are the ruins of Armadale Castle, a comparatively modern structure in which the Macdonald family lived until 1925. It was bought, along with woods and farmland, by the Clan Donald Lands Trust in 1972. The oldest remaining part of the castle was built in 1795; this now contains a museum, telling the story of Clan Donald's part in Scotland's history. The stables have been turned into a visitor centre.
Apr-Oct, daily. Adm charge. Refreshments. Shop. P *Toilets.* ♿ *Tel Ardvasar (047 14) 227 or 305.*

CLAN MACPHERSON MUSEUM

On A86, at Newtonmore (Db)

One of Scotland's most colourful families is the subject of this fascinating collection. Highland battle mementos include the Black Chanter (the melodic pipe which plays the bagpipes), said to have fallen from heaven at the Battle of North Inch of Perth in 1396, and the Green Banner which brought the clan their victories. Also on display is the fiddle on which James Macpherson played before he was unjustly hanged at Banff, and the silver epergne which commemorates one of the Macpherson chief's escapes after Culloden.
May-Sept, daily. Free entry. Shop. P *(limited). Toilets.* ♿ *Tel Newtonmore (054 03) 332.*

CORRIESHALLOCH GORGE

On A835, 12 miles south-east of Ullapool (Cd)

The waters of the Falls of Measach plunge 150ft in this spectacular mile-long gorge, whose sheer rock walls are linked by a suspension bridge built by John Fowler, one of the designers of the Forth Bridge. Farther downstream a viewing platform provides an excellent view of the falls.
NTS. All year, daily. Free entry. P *Tel Inverness (0463) 232034).*

CULLODEN BATTLEFIELD

On B9006, 3 miles east of Inverness (Dc)

In the last battle to be fought on British soil, the armies of Prince Charles Edward Stuart and the forces led by the Duke of Cumberland faced each other across Culloden Muir on April 16, 1746. Within an hour, the Prince's force of 5000 Highlanders was routed by the 9000 Government troops, and the Stuart dynasty had lost its last chance of regaining the British throne.

In recent years trees on the battlefield site have been felled and a road has been re-routed, restoring the landscape to something like its appearance in 1746. At the visitor centre, an audiovisual display vividly brings to life the battle in which more than 1000 men died. A memorial cairn, 20ft high, commemorates 'The gallant Highlanders who fought for Scotland', while an English stone bears the inscription 'The

FRENCH TOUCH *Towering above sloping gardens, Dunrobin Castle has the appearance of a French chateau. The regalia of the Sutherland family is set out in the Billiards Room (above); on the wall behind is the banner of Edward VII when Prince of Wales.*

English were buried here' – although no grave site has ever been recorded.
NTS. Visitor Centre: Apr-Oct, daily. Adm charge. Refreshments. Shop. 🅿 *Toilets.* ♿ *Tel Inverness (0463) 790607.*

DORNOCH CRAFT CENTRE

On A949, in centre of Dornoch (Dd)

The seaside resort of Dornoch is a place where, unusually, visitors are encouraged to go to jail. For a craft centre is housed in the old town prison; it specialises in tartans, which visitors can see being woven. An exhibition on the premises is a reminder of the building's original purpose, showing as it does the harshness of prison life in Victorian times.

Dornoch Cathedral, founded in 1224, was partly rebuilt in the 17th century, restored in the 1830s and completed in 1924 to mark the 700th anniversary of its foundation. The building contains some fine workmanship, notably in its memorial windows.
Craft Centre: Easter-June, daily exc Sun; July-Sept, daily; Oct-Easter, Mon-Fri. Free entry. Refreshments. Shop. 🅿 *Toilets.* ♿ *Tel Dornoch (0862) 810555. Cathedral: All year, daily.*

DOUNREAY EXHIBITION

Off A836, 10 miles west of Thurso (Df)

The 'golfball' nuclear reactor at Dounreay is a familiar landmark on the flat Caithness coast, its sphere having a diameter of 135ft – more than 20ft larger than the dome of St Paul's Cathedral. In 1962 this became the first fast reactor in the world to produce electricity for public use; but it closed down in 1977 and is dwarfed by the massive square block of the new Prototype Fast Reactor (PFR).

Dounreay's chief function is to develop the technology of fast reactors, which can produce energy from uranium 50 times more efficiently than a conventional nuclear power station. The Dounreay Exhibition tells the story of nuclear power, and there are guided tours.
Easter-Sept, daily. Free entry. Refreshments. Shop. 🅿 *Toilets. Tel Thurso (0847) 62121.*

DUNROBIN CASTLE

On A9, ½ mile north of Golspie (Dd)

Occupied since the 14th century, the ancestral home of the Earls and Dukes of Sutherland is one of Britain's oldest continuously inhabited houses. But the white stone building surrounding the castle's heart owes its existence to the 2nd Duke of Sutherland, who had lived in France as a boy and loved French architecture. In 1840 he commissioned Sir Charles Barry, chief architect of the Houses of Parliament, to transform Dunrobin following French patterns; and among the changes was the setting out of gardens in the formal style of Versailles.

The high-ceilinged rooms of the castle, leading directly into each other, contain many fine paintings and examples of exquisite craftsmanship. In the main entrance hall is a bronze statue of the 3rd duke as a boy; he appears, too, with his sister in a portrait by Sir Edwin Landseer. The dining room was re-designed, along with other rooms, by the Scottish architect Sir Robert Lorimer after a fire in 1915; the ceiling is a fine example of Lorimer's work. The room contains several portraits, some by George Romney.

The drawing room has a ceiling designed by Lorimer, paintings of Venetian scenes by Canaletto, portraits by Sir Joshua Reynolds and Sir Thomas Lawrence, and some fine Louis XV furniture.
June-Sept, daily. Adm charge. Refreshments. Shop. 🅿 *Toilets. Tel Golspie (040 83) 3177.*

POWER HOUSE *Eilean Donan Castle was built in the 13th century in a strategic position to keep out the Danes. The reconstruction of the castle in 1932 faithfully followed the original pattern.*

DUNVEGAN CASTLE, SKYE

On A850, 1 mile north of Dunvegan (Ae)

This noble square-towered castle has remained in the hands of one family, the MacLeods, for its entire history of more than 750 years. The MacLeods are descended from Leod, one of the last Norse kings of Man and the North Isles. Leod built his fort at Dunvegan in the 13th century, and sections of it remain. The keep dates from the mid-14th century. At the end of the 18th century the 23rd chief, Norman, set about making the house more comfortable, but the outside is largely the result of a Victorian restoration carried out between 1840 and 1850.

The castle contains many portraits, books and MacLeod family treasures. These include a drinking horn holding the equivalent of two bottles of wine, which a 12th-century chief is said to have drained at a draught. Dunvegan also has its Fairy Flag, said to have the power of serving the clan if waved at moments of great danger.
Castle: Apr-Oct, daily exc Sun; times vary. Adm charge. Refreshments. Shop. 🅿 *Toilets.* ♿ *Tel Dunvegan (047 022) 206.*

EILEAN DONAN CASTLE

Off A87, 11 miles east of Kyle of Lochalsh (Bc)

A lone sentinel among tree-clad hills, the formidable Eilean Donan Castle stands guard on a promontory where three lochs meet. Visitors pass over a stone arched causeway to the forecourt, through the main doorway under the portcullis and into the courtyard. Within are two magnificent chambers faithfully restored to their former splendour by MacRae descendants of the castle's original 16th-century constables.

Walls 14ft thick enclose the Billeting Room, furnished with a fine Chippendale gaming table, a Sheraton writing bureau and paintings of the warring Highlanders. The Banqueting Hall is decked out with trophies and souvenirs, including drinking cups made of cannonballs.

Good Fri-Sept, daily. Adm charge. Shop. 🅿 *Toilets. Tel Dornie (059 985) 202.*

FORT GEORGE

Off B9006, 11 miles north-east of Inverness (Dd)

One of the finest artillery fortifications in Europe, Fort George is an awesome reminder of how seriously the government of George II took the Jacobite threat in Scotland. After Bonnie Prince Charlie's campaign ended with his defeat at Culloden in 1746, it was decided that any new attempts to overthrow Hanoverian rule should be doomed from the start. In the latter stages of the Jacobite Rising, General George Wade's small Highland forts had shown their weakness. There were humiliating surrenders by the garrisons of the first Fort George at Inverness Castle and Fort Augustus; in both cases the defences were blown up and the buildings burnt.

So in 1747 a great new coastal fort was planned as an impregnable base for the army. Its buildings were designed to accommodate the governor and other officers, an artillery detachment and some 1600 infantry. The fort also had a magazine, a bakehouse, a brewery and a chapel. Work on the fort was not completed until 1769. By then the Highlanders were peaceful and local people regarded the new fort as a costly mistake, but after Prince Charles's campaign it could not have been forseen that the threat of war would vanish so soon. The fort has remained in military use ever since.

The great distinction of Fort George today is the amount of it that survives intact – not only the bastioned defences with their outworks, but also the interior buildings, which are fine examples of military architecture. From 1881 to 1961 the fort was the depot of the Seaforth Highlanders, now amalgamated with the Camerons to form the Queen's Own Highlanders whose regimental museum is housed in the former home of the fort's governor. It includes uniforms, medals, colours, pipe banners, paintings, documents and photographs covering the period from 1778 to the present day.

Fort George: HBM. All year, daily. Adm charge. Shop. 🅿 *Toilets.* ♿ *(part). Tel Edinburgh (031) 244 3101. Regimental Museum: Apr-Sept, daily; Oct-Mar, Mon-Fri. Shop.* 🅿 *Toilets. Tel Inverness (0463) 224380.*

GLENCOE VISITOR CENTRE

On A82, 1¾ miles east of Ballachulish (Cb)

A visitor centre set amid the wild, dramatic beauty of Glencoe explains the background to the notorious massacre of February 1692, which resulted from bitter feuds between Highland clans and the English government's difficulty in keeping them under control. The Macdonalds of Glencoe failed to swear allegiance to William III within a set time, so troops were sent to the glen with orders to root out the clansmen and take no prisoners. In command was Captain Robert Campbell, whose clan bore a fierce grudge against the Macdonalds; about a dozen men of his force were also Campbells. Some 38 people were slaughtered.

The area is rich in stories of giants, monsters and witches – and for those undisturbed by such tales it offers some of the finest walking and climbing country in the Highlands. There is an abundance of wildlife including red deer, wildcats and golden eagles. The visitor centre provides information on walks, and presents an audiovisual programme.

In Glencoe village a thatched building houses the Glencoe and North Lorn Folk Museum. This has a collection of costumes, weapons and relics of the Jacobite Rising and clan wars. Local crafts and industries also figure in the displays.

Visitor Centre: NTS. Apr-Oct, daily. Adm charge. Refreshments. Shop. 🅿 *Toilets.* ♿ *Tel Ballachulish (085 52) 307. Folk Museum: mid May-Sept, daily exc Sun. Adm charge. Shop.* ♿

GLEN OF HISTORY *Dark peaks called The Three Sisters of Glencoe look down on the scene of the infamous 17th-century massacre of Macdonald clansfolk. Burns cut silver threads down the mountain slopes.*

GLENFINNAN MONUMENT

On A830, 18 miles west of Fort William (Bb)

Against a glorious background of mountains and loch on the famous Road to the Isles, the statue of a Highlander looks out from the top of a 65ft pillar. The monument commemorates the day – August 19, 1745 – when Prince Charles Edward Stuart launched the campaign which, though it ended in failure, occupies a special place in Scottish history. At Glenfinnan the handsome young man, surrounded by his army of fearsome-looking Highlanders, raised his standard in hope of regaining the throne of Britain for the Stuarts. Eight months later, defeated by the Duke of Cumberland's forces, he became a fugitive.

The monument was built in 1815 by Alexander Macdonald of Glenaladale as a tribute to the 'generous zeal, the undaunted bravery and the inviolable fidelity' of those who fought for the prince's cause. The figure of the Highlander, sculpted by John Greenshields, was added in 1834. A visitor centre has displays and commentaries on the prince's campaign from Glenfinnan to Derby and back to his final defeat at Culloden.

NTS. Apr-Oct, daily. Adm charge. Refreshments. Shop. 🅿 *Toilets.* ♿ *(centre only). Tel Kinlocheil (039 783) 250.*

GLENMORE FOREST PARK

Off B970, 5 miles east of Aviemore (Dc)

Spread around three sides of Loch Morlich, this magnificent forest park sweeps gradually up from its shores to the 4000ft summits of the Cairngorms. It covers much of the land that was once the domain of the mighty Gordons, but today the fiercest creature the visitor is likely to encounter is a roe deer, red squirrel, fox or possibly a badger. Diving ducks live on the loch, whooper swans come from Iceland in the winter, and there may be a glimpse of a golden eagle.

Eight marked walks – ranging from 2 miles to 10 miles – start from the car park at the north-east corner of the lake. The nearby information centre has displays on the Caledonian pine forests and the local plant and animal life. Because of its altitude, about half of the park is treeless; but the other half is rich in alder, Douglas fir, larch, Scots pine and Sitka spruce.

Beyond the car park the road climbs through the forest and into the Cairngorm foothills. From here chairlifts rise in two stages to near the 4084ft summit of Cairngorm.

The wildlife of the Glenmore Forest Park includes Britain's only herd of reindeer, descendants of a small herd brought from Sweden in 1952. This was a reintroduction to Scotland, for there is a record of reindeer being hunted in Caithness 800 years ago. Each morning visitors leave Reindeer House, above the Glenmore camp site, to accompany the keeper on his daily check of the animals. People can mingle freely with the tame herd.

Park: FC. All year, daily. Free entry. Refreshments. Shop. P *Toilets.* ♿ *Tel Cairngorm (047 986) 271. Reindeer: All year, daily. Adm charge.* P *Toilets. Tel (047 986) 228.*

HIGHLAND FOLK MUSEUM, KINGUSSIE

Off A9, 12 miles south-west of Aviemore (Db)

Scottish Highland and island relics in this museum give a fascinating picture of how the region's people lived and worked in the past. The reception building is an 18th-century shooting lodge. In the grounds are an Isle of Lewis black house – designed for people and animals – and water mill. The lighter side of Highland life is recalled in a collection of musical instruments played at ceilidhs.

A mile south of Kingussie, on the B970, stand the ruins of Ruthven Barracks. The Government barracks were captured by Bonnie Prince Charlie's Highlanders in the Jacobite Rising, and after the prince's defeat at Culloden in April 1746 it was hoped he would raise his standard again at Ruthven. Instead he sent a farewell message to his supporters.

Folk Museum: Apr-Oct, daily. Adm charge. Shop. P *Toilets.* ♿ *Tel Kingussie (054 02) 307. Ruthven Barracks: HBM. All year, daily. Adm charge. Tel Edinburgh (031) 244 3101.*

HIGHLAND WILDLIFE PARK

On A9, at Kingussie (Db)

Wild boars, wolves and great brown bears have returned to an area of the Scottish Highlands that was their natural habitat centuries ago. Visitors driving through more than 200 acres of parkland will also spot red deer, European bison and mouflon and Soay sheep. Reindeer, arctic foxes, lynx and polecats, together with eagles, owls and buzzards, can be seen in the park's walk-through area.

Some 12,000 years ago, ancestors of today's wolves roamed in packs as their prey, the reindeer, oxen, antelopes and wild horses, grazed on the first lichens and mosses after the Ice Age. As the climate warmed, a forest of pine, birch and aspen covered the lower hills, gradually giving way to oak, ash and lime with a rich underlayer of hazel, hawthorn, holly and wild raspberries.

Wild cattle, bison, red and roe deer were abundant in this luxurious forest – until man arrived on the scene, felling trees and burning the undergrowth to plant fields of wheat and barley and raise domesticated cattle, sheep and pigs. By the 18th century, the forest, its animals and plants had almost disappeared. Hundreds of thousands of sheep destroyed any remaining young trees, and the wooded slopes became pastures of grass and heather. In the 19th century, hunters killed off the little wildlife that remained.

Today, the Royal Zoological Society of

COSY PARLOUR *The parlour of stonemason Hugh Miller's Cottage in Cromarty is furnished in the style of the early 19th century. The kettles and utensils in the fireplace are similar to those in daily use then.*

Scotland, as keeper of the park, is breeding and planting in a bid to recapture something of the area's past and to protect it for the future.

Apr-Oct, daily. Adm charge. Refreshments. Shop. P *Toilets.* ♿ *Tel Kincraig (054 04) 270.*

HUGH MILLER'S COTTAGE

Church Street, Cromarty (Dd)

The long, low, thatched cottage in which Hugh Miller was born in 1802 recalls a bygone age of Cromarty. Miller was a local stonemason who became a renowned geologist, writer and churchman. His birthplace, built in 1711 by his great-grandparents, is the last fishertown cottage of its era and has been furnished in early 19th-century style as a memorial to Miller's varied achievements. Visitors can browse through Miller's letters and the evangelical newspaper which he edited, and examine a selection of the fossils unearthed, including the *Pterichthys milleri*, a fossil fish named after him.

NTS. June-Sept, daily; Easter-June, daily exc Sun. Adm charge. P *(limited). Tel Cromarty (038 17) 245.*

INVEREWE GARDENS

On A832 at Poolewe (Bd)

One man's vision and a natural phenomenon have transformed this northern headland from heathery hags, peat bogs and strewn rocks into a varied and luxuriant wooded garden. Entering it today, along a path framed with foliage and flowers, it is hard to envisage the barren ground which faced its creator, Osgood Mackenzie, in 1862 when he began a task that would absorb him for 60 years.

Mackenzie recognised that despite the shallow soil and vicious south-westerly gales, the influence of the warm North Atlantic Drift in this northerly spot provided a frost-free environment suitable for growing an abundance of exotic plants and trees. The scarlet flowers of the Chilean lantern tree that blaze today on the walls of the gate lodge and the splendid Tasmanian eucalyptus by the house illustrate the accuracy of his vision.

Thanks to the sheltering windbreak of Corsican and Scots pine planted by Mackenzie, the borders are a mass of colour for most of the year. Paths meander through the trees around a small pond and peat banks enclosing a lime-free bed where a deep pink Madeiran orchid and delicate rare plants from Tibet, Italy and China bloom in summer.

An enclosed area to the north-east is dubbed Bambooselem because of its shelter of bamboos. Beyond the towering eucalyptus and larch, the Japanese umbrella tree unfurls its strap-shaped leaves, but the centrepiece is a splendid 50ft magnolia tree which blossoms in spring with deep pink flowers.

NTS. All year, daily. Adm charge. Refreshments. Shop. P *Toilets.* ♿ *Tel Poolewe (044 586) 229.*

COTTAGE INDUSTRY *An 18th-century weaving loom from South Uist forms part of an exhibition of cloth-making at the Highland Folk Museum, Kingussie. A model sits at the spinning wheel.*

KNOCKAN VISITOR CENTRE
Off A835, 12 miles north-east of Ullapool (Cc)

The visitor centre is a welcoming introduction to the huge Inverpolly National Nature Reserve, covering almost 27,000 acres and the second largest reserve in Britain after the Cairngorms. Two well-marked trails start near the car park, and there are pointers explaining how the great forest which once covered the area gradually gave way to moss, heather and peat. The nature trail leads some 1500ft up to the crest of Knockan Cliff, which looks out over starkly dramatic rocks, bogs and moorland – and onto the sandstone peaks of Stac Pollaidh, Cul Beag and Cul Mor.

Golden eagles and red deer can sometimes be seen and there are regular sightings of golden plovers, greenshanks and curlews. The reserve abounds in foxglove, bell heather, cross-leaved heath and yellow mountain saxifrage.

May-Sept, Mon-Fri. Free entry. P *Toilets. Tel Strathkanaird (085 486) 254.*

LAIDHAY CROFT MUSEUM, DUNBEATH
On A9, 21 miles south-west of Wick (Ee)

The croft occupies a special place in the Scottish folk memory, and well-preserved examples are always an attraction. This long-house type of crofter's dwelling is furnished and equipped as it would have been in the early years of this century – with byre, kitchen, living room and box beds. A cruck barn at the rear of the house contains early farm machinery.

Easter-Sept, daily. Adm charge. P *Toilets.* ♿ *Tel Dunbeath (059 33) 244.*

LANDMARK VISITOR CENTRE
On B9133, ¼ mile south of Carrbridge (Dc)

In an uncompromisingly modern building, the Landmark Visitor Centre brings alive the history and natural history of the local countryside. In a circular auditorium a three-screen display tells the story of man and the Highlands, and a sound and light display interprets the history of Strathspey. Outside the centre are a tree-top trail along a catwalk 20ft above ground, a nature trail, an adventure playground and a pine forest nature centre. The Scottish Forestry Heritage Park tells the story of the industry in Scotland, and includes a steam-powered sawmill, 60ft viewing tower and five exhibition halls.

All year, daily. Adm charge. Refreshments. Shop. P *Toilets.* ♿ *Tel Carr Bridge (047 984) 613.*

LOCHALSH WOODLAND GARDEN
Off A87, 3 miles east of Kyle of Lochalsh (Bc)

This garden has grown in beauty and variety over the years. Lochalsh House (not open) was built in 1887, and the first trees were planted about that time. Now there is a tree canopy of immense variety within the garden's 6½ acres. The garden being developed under the canopy has a number of interesting exotic plants. The Coach House exhibition serves as a focal point for walks.

NTS. All year, daily. Exhibition: Apr-Oct, daily. Adm charge. P *Tel Balmacara (059 986) 207.*

LOCH GARTEN
Off B970, 12 miles north-east of Aviemore (Dc)

The nature reserve here is renowned for its regular nesting pair of ospreys, which can be observed from a hide overlooking the pine-tree eyrie. Provided the birds are in residence, the hide is open from mid-April to August, and powerful binoculars and telescopes allow close views of the ospreys. In a breeding season only one family is reared – probably consisting of two or three young. Watchers particularly enjoy seeing the parent birds bringing home fish for the family.

The reserve, covering 2949 acres, is rich in other wildlife. Regular breeding birds include the crested tit, Scottish crossbill, capercaillie, black grouse, redstart, siskin and several birds of prey; sometimes golden eagles are seen around the osprey site. Teal, wigeon and little grebes frequent the Garten and Mallachie lochs. Resident mammals include red squirrel, pine marten, wildcat, otter and red and roe deer.

RSPB. Osprey observation, mid Apr-Aug, daily. Free entry. Shop. P ♿ *Tel Boat of Garten (047 983) 694.*

LOCH NESS MONSTER EXHIBITION
On A82, at Drumnadrochit (Cc)

Scotland's favourite legend has drawn thousands of curious visitors to Loch Ness for centuries. Sightings of the famous monster said to lurk in its peat-darkened depths have been recorded on many occasions since St Columba rebuked the beast for terrorising a monk in the 6th century.

Drumnadrochit now has an exhibition centre illustrating old and new searches for Nessie in pictures, audiovisuals, film and other exhibits. It also describes the natural history of the massive loch, which covers some 13,900 acres and has been estimated to drop to 754ft at its deepest point.

All year, daily. Adm charge. Refreshments. Shop. P *Toilets.* ♿ *Tel Drumnadrochit (045 62) 573.*

ROTHIEMURCHUS ESTATE
On B970, 1½ miles south-east of Aviemore (Dc)

A visitor centre near the entrance to the Rothiemurchus estate is the introduction to a gloriously varied stretch of countryside between the River Spey at Aviemore and the summits of the Cairngorms. Within its boundaries lie farmlands and woods, forestry plantations, lochs and heath-clad hills. Rangers are available with advice on exploring the countryside, which is criss-crossed by miles of waymarked footpaths. A recommended family jaunt is the two-hour estate tour by tractor and trailer, with red deer, Highland cattle and other animals to be seen. There are ranger-guided walks and birdwatching with an ornithologist.

In the heart of Rothiemurchus lies beautiful Loch an Eilein, which has its own information centre. The loch has an island with a ruined castle and is surrounded by native pinewoods. The area teems with wildlife, and early morning visitors may see roe deer, foxes and pine martens. In the loch is an abundance of brown trout, pike and eels, and herons may be seen darting on their prey. A trail round the loch runs through Scots pine woodland, comprising part of the ancient Caledonian Forest. Crested tits and crossbills can be seen.

All year, daily. Free entry. Shop. P *Toilets.* ♿ *Tel Aviemore (0479) 810858.*

MONSTER MYSTERY *A rainbow strikes into Loch Ness beyond Urquhart Castle, the scene of many claimed sightings of the loch's 'hidden treasure', the fabulous monster. One such sighting (inset) was photographed in 1934 by a London surgeon, Mr R. Wilson.*

SKYE MUSEUM

On A855, 7 miles north of Uig (Ad)

The hard, self-reliant life of island crofters around a century ago is mirrored in this cluster of thatched croft cottages, including a weaver's house and a smithy. The people who lived in houses like these spent most of their time outdoors and did not hanker after home luxuries. James Boswell, visiting Skye with Dr Johnson in 1773, noted: 'We had no rooms that we could command, for the good people here had no notion that a man could have any occasion but for a mere sleeping-place.' But there was singing and storytelling beside the peat fire at night. All these buildings, including a weaver's house and a smithy, present a fascinating picture of old times.

Nearby, under an impressive Celtic cross, is the grave of the Highland heroine Flora MacDonald. In June 1746, when she was 24, this Skye girl risked her life to help the defeated Bonnie Prince Charlie elude the army of George II. She married another MacDonald in 1750 and they went to live in America. But they spent their last years in Skye, where Flora died in 1790.

Museum: Apr-Oct, daily exc Sun. Adm charge. Shop. P *Toilets.* ♿ *Tel Duntulm (047 052) 279.*

STRATHPEFFER DOLL MUSEUM

Off A834, 4 miles west of Dingwall (Cd)

The village of Strathpeffer, developed in the 19th century as a spa, now has a doll museum in what remains of the baths complex. Here are dolls, teddy bears, toys and games spanning some 150 years. Other features of the Victorian nursery, such as baby clothes, lace and cradles, are included in the collection built up by the museum's owner, Mrs Angela Kellie.

Strathpeffer owes its development largely to Dr Thomas Morrison who found the local springs beneficial. As a health resort it enjoyed a boom after a railway station was opened in 1862, and some impressive buildings remain as a reminder of the spa's heyday. A visitor centre in a restored Victorian railway station has an audiovisual show on the wildlife of the northern Highlands.

Doll Museum: Easter-Oct, Mon-Fri; June-Aug, some weekends. Shop. P ♿ *Tel Strathpeffer (0997) 21549. Visitor centre: Easter-Oct, Mon-Sat. Shop.* P *Toilets.* ♿ *Tel Kessock (046 373) 505.*

STRATHSPEY RAILWAY

Off B9152 at Aviemore or Boat of Garten (Dc)

After visiting Strathspey in 1860, Queen Victoria wrote: 'It was very beautiful – fine wooded hills – the high Cairngorm range . . . and the broad Spey flowing in the valley, with cultivated fields and fine trees below.' Passengers aboard the restored Strathspey Railway enjoy much the same views today as they travel 800ft above sea level through exquisite Highland countryside for 5 miles between Aviemore and Boat of Garten.

The enthusiasts of the Strathspey Railway Association, who have operated the line since its 1978 reopening, have effectively re-created the era of steam at its most picturesque. The rebuilt terminus at Aviemore is largely an authentic Scottish country station moved from Dalnaspidal, 25 miles south. Locomotives and rolling stock in their original Strathspey colours of green engines and purple and white carriages date back to Victorian and Edwardian times.

July-Aug, daily exc Fri; May, June, Sept, early Oct, Sat and Sun; most Bank Hol. Fares. Refreshments. Shop. P *Toilets.* ♿ *Tel Boat of Garten (047 983) 692.*

TORRIDON MOUNTAINS CENTRE AND DEER MUSEUM

On A896, 8 miles east of Shieldaig (Bc)

Red deer and the occasional roe deer can be seen roaming the red-brown sandstone mountain slopes of Torridon. Appropriately Torridon also has a museum devoted to deer, with exhibits ranging from magnificent antlers to the cruel snares set by poachers. Displays explain the life cycle of the deer in the Highlands, and the need for careful management to prevent overpopulation and the consequent destruction of the local habitat.

A countryside centre has an audiovisual presentation on Torridon wildlife. From the centre visitors can take a variety of scenic routes to discover a wealth of animal and plant life, including spectacular alpine rock gardens.

NTS. Museum and Centre: June-Sept, daily. Adm charge. P *Toilets (nearby).* ♿ *Tel Torridon (044 587) 221.*

URQUHART CASTLE

On A82, 1½ miles south of Drumnadrochit (Cc)

Since the Iron Age, strongholds have been built on a strategic point jutting out into Loch Ness. Parts of the present Urquhart Castle ruins date back to Norman times, but it has often been pulled down and rebuilt.

The 16th-century residential tower at the northern end of the promontory is the only part of the ruins in which distinctive architectural detail is preserved.

HBM. All year, daily. Adm charge. P *Toilets. Tel Drumnadrochit (045 62) 551.*

WEST HIGHLAND MUSEUM

Cameron Square, Fort William (Cb)

This museum spans the history of the region from the Stone Age to modern times, but is especially noted for its relics of the Jacobite campaigns. It has a remarkable treasure in an unusual portrait of Prince Charles Edward Stuart. This trick picture, by an unknown 18th-century artist, at first appears to be a meaningless blur of paint. But the blur, when reflected in a polished cylinder, reveals an excellent likeness of the prince.

There are bagpipes recovered from the field of Culloden, and visitors are reminded how young Flora MacDonald helped the prince to escape to Skye by disguising him as her maid; a picture shows him in this role. Clan feuds, for so long a feature of Highland life, are recalled in a formidable array of weapons, including broadswords, dirks and pistols.

Fort William is overlooked by Ben Nevis, at 4406ft Britain's highest mountain. In the town, the Scottish Crafts and Ben Nevis Exhibition serves as a kind of shrine to the mighty peak; even its telephone number is significant. The exhibition is dominated by a large relief model of the mountain, and a video show takes viewers up the tourist path.

HIDDEN PRINCE *This 'secret portrait' of Bonnie Prince Charlie in the West Highland Museum reveals its subject only when reflected in a polished cylinder. It was made for Jacobites at a time when possessing a picture of the prince was dangerous.*

West Highland Museum: All year, Mon-Sat, times vary. Adm charge. Shop. Toilets. Tel Fort William (0397) 2169. Scottish Crafts and Ben Nevis: Apr-Oct, Mon-Sat; June-Aug, Sun. Adm charge. Shop. ♿ *Tel (0397) 4406.*

WICK HERITAGE CENTRE

On A9, at Wick (Ee)

Wick has been a fishing port for centuries, and a herring fleet of more than 1000 vessels once operated from its harbour. The heritage centre near the harbour preserves the town's history and heritage. Photographs record 115 years of the port's history, and there is a cooper's workshop, a working fish kiln, a complete blacksmith's shop and foundry, and a restored fisherman's cottage. There is also a collection of toys and 19th-century costumes. The centre's terraced gardens give panoramic views across the town.

Hand-blown glass of modern design produced at Caithness Glass, on the south side of Wick, has achieved an international reputation. Visitors may watch the fascinating process of glass-blowing, and buy the finished products from the well stocked factory shop.

Heritage Centre: June-Sept, Mon-Sat. Adm charge. P *Toilets. Tel Wick (0955) 3268. Caithness Glass: All year, Mon-Fri (shop also Sat). Free entry. Refreshments.* P *Toilets.* ♿ *Tel (0955) 2286.*

REGIONAL CALENDAR

March (1st week). Aviemore: International Curling.

April 18. Culloden Muir: Commemorative Service.

May (late). Kingussie: Badenoch Folk Festival.

June (late). Grantown-on-Spey: Highland Games.

July (mid-month). Inverness: Highland Games.

July (late) Durness: Highland Games. Beauly: Gala Week. Aviemore: International Highland Games.

July (last Sat). Fort William: Lochaber Highland Games.

August (1st Mon). Mallaig: Highland Games.

August (early). Abernethy, Dornoch and Newtonmore: Highland Games.

August (late). Drumnadrochit: Glenurquhart Highland Games. Inverness: Piping Championships.

Tourist information: Aviemore (0479) 810363; Dornoch (0862) 810400; Fort William (0397) 3781; Grantown-on-Spey (0479) 2779; Inverness (0463) 234353; Portree, Skye (0478) 2137; Wick (0955) 2596.

ISLANDS AREAS

ROCKY OUTPOSTS WHERE VIKINGS LEFT THEIR MARK

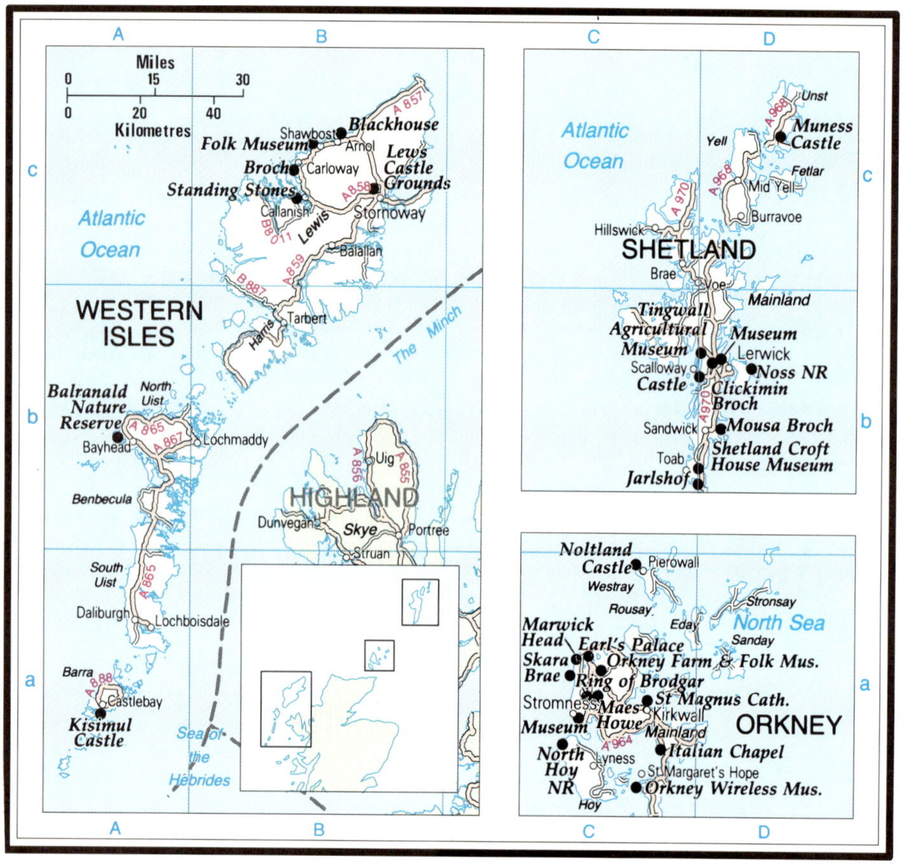

The islands off Scotland's northern coast – Orkney, Shetland and the Western Isles – are among the most remote and romantic parts of Britain. They were also among the oldest to be settled by man; several eerily atmospheric ancient sites include Maes Howe and Skara Brae on Orkney, Jarlshof on Shetland, and Callanish on the Western Isles, with its famous Standing Stones.

Centuries of invasions and raids have left a rich legacy of castles. Some are ruined, such as Muness and Scalloway on Shetland and Noltland on Orkney, while Kisimul in the Western Isles has been painstakingly restored. Religious buildings include the mighty cathedral of St Magnus at Kirkwall, Orkney, and the ornate Italian Chapel, a few miles to the south-east.

ORKNEY

EARL'S PALACE

Off A966, 20 miles north-west of Kirkwall (Ca)

The gaunt ruins of this once grand palace dominate the village of Birsay and its bay. It was built around a courtyard for a 16th-century Earl of Orkney, on a tiny island linked to the shore by a causeway. There are also traces of 7th and 8th-century Pictish dwellings and more substantial relics of a 12th-century Norse settlement, including the ruins of a church. A small museum contains artefacts found on the site.

HBM. All year, daily. Adm charge. P *(limited). Tel Edinburgh (031) 244 3101.*

ITALIAN CHAPEL

Off A961, 7 miles south-east of Kirkwall (Ca)

On the bleak campsite that was their island home during the Second World War, Italian prisoners of war created this gem of a chapel from two Nissen huts, driftwood, scrap and concrete. To hide the bare outline of the huts, the gifted artists built a façade that could belong to any Italian village church, with an arch supported by columns, a belfry and decorative Gothic pinnacles. Windows of decorated glass and, above the entrance, a thorn-crowned head of Christ moulded in red clay complete the picture. The mood continues inside with a magnificent wrought-iron sanctuary screen, an altarpiece of the Madonna and Child surrounded by cherubs, painted windows showing St Francis and St Catherine and medieval-style wall paintings. An imitation vaulted ceiling hides the hut roofs.

The little masterpiece – together with a statue of St George made from barbed wire and concrete which stands nearby – is all that is left now of Camp 60 where 550 prisoners were housed during the latter years of the war while they built the causeways, known as the Churchill Barriers, that now link Mainland with several smaller islands.

All year, daily. Free entry. P ♿

MAES HOWE

On A965, 5 miles north-east of Stromness (Ca)

Beneath the great green cone-shaped mound of Maes Howe is a 3000-year-old chambered tomb generally regarded as the finest example of prehistoric architecture in Britain. An entrance on the south-west side of the 24ft high mound opens into a stone-lined passageway leading to a 14ft square burial chamber shaped like a beehive. It is formed of huge stone slabs weighing up to 30 tons, each carefully levelled and plumbed; the roof of the chamber is given extra support by projecting piers in the four corners. Burial cells are let into three of the walls. The stone blocks that once fitted closely over their entrance now rest on the floor below them.

The tomb was built for an important chief and was periodically raided by the Vikings, who scratched graffiti on its stones. Some inscribed their names, others left messages: one of these blames Crusaders for carrying off the tomb's treasure.

HBM. All year, daily. Adm charge. P *(limited). Tel Edinburgh (031) 244 3101.*

MARWICK HEAD

Off B9056, 10 miles north of Stromness (Ca)

Seabirds galore breed on the rugged cliffs of Marwick Head. One census counted over 35,000 guillemots and almost 10,000 pairs of kittiwakes crowded into less than a mile of seashore. A footpath along the cliff provides excellent viewing of this bird haven, which is also home for fulmars, razorbills and lesser numbers of ravens, rock doves and twites. Sea campion, thrift and spring squill grow among the rocks, and otters have been spotted at the southern end of the head. A monument at the top is dedicated to Lord Kitchener, who was drowned nearby when HMS *Hampshire* was sunk by a German mine in 1916.

RSPB Reserve: All year, daily. Free entry. P *(limited). Tel Kirkwall (0856) 850175.*

NOLTLAND CASTLE

Off B9066, ½ mile west of Pierowall (Ca)

Overlooking the harbour at Pierowall are the gaunt walls of what was once one of the most heavily fortified castles in Scotland. It was built in the 16th century as a bolt hole for Gilbert Balfour, Master of the Household to Mary, Queen of Scots, and constant plotter on her behalf. There are 71 gunloops ranged in tiers in the walls – far more than in any other Scottish castle. The castle's Z-shaped design gives all-round protection against attack. The main staircase is one of the finest in Scotland.

HBM. All year, daily. Free entry. Tel Ardersier (0667) 62777.

MIRACLE WORKERS *The concrete altar and wrought-iron sanctuary screen are among the marvels of the Italian Chapel. It was built by Italian prisoners of war out of two Nissen huts and pieces of scrap material.*

NORTH HOY NATURE RESERVE

Off B9047, 14 miles north-west of Lyness (Ca)

Some of the highest sea cliffs in the British Isles provide spectacular nesting sites for fulmars, guillemots and kittiwakes and smaller numbers of razorbills, puffins, shags and herring gulls. Great skuas are common, while Arctic skuas nest in the two main valleys. The area's most famous landmark is the 450ft sandstone stack, the Old Man of Hoy. This once formed part of a rock arch carved out by the sea; its top disappeared in the early 19th century.

RSPB. All year, daily. Free entry. P *Tel Hoy (085 679) 298.*

ORKNEY FARM AND FOLK MUSEUM

Off A986, 10 miles north-east of Stromness (Ca)

A glimpse of Orkney's ancient farming traditions is provided by a museum housed in two restored farmsteads, 5 miles apart.

Kirbuster in Birsay is the last surviving Orkney farmhouse with its hearth built in the middle of the floor, the smoke escaping through a hole in the roof. A stone bed is built into the wall. The 19th-century house at Corrigall has a gable fireplace and wooden box beds.

The farm buildings have been restored with roofs made of local flagstones insulated with turf and heather ropes. Floors and shelves are of stone, as are the stalls for cattle. A hand-weaving loom and a grain-drying kiln are also on show.

Between Kirbuster and Corrigall, off the B9057 2 miles north-east of Dounby, stands Orkney's last remaining horizontal corn mill. A small, stone and turf-roofed building, this so-called 'click-mill' gets its name from the sound made as a wooden tongue attached to the grain tray strikes a stone projection to keep the grain moving along the tray.

Museum: Apr-Sept, daily. Adm charge. Shop. P *Toilets.* ♿ *(part). Tel Kirkwall (0856) 3191. Mill: HBM. All year, daily. Free entry. Tel Edinburgh (031) 244 3101.*

ORKNEY WIRELESS MUSEUM

Church Road, St Margaret's Hope (Ca)

Nostalgia rules for wireless buffs in this cottage museum, with exhibits ranging from an early crystal set to a modern transistor. There are handsome wireless sets from the 1930s, horn loudspeakers, toy tin gramophones from the 1920s and old records. Many exhibits show how wireless was used to defend the area during the last war, and there is a NAAFI issue wireless set.

Apr-Sept, daily. Adm charge. P ♿ *Tel St Margaret's Hope (085 683) 462.*

RING OF BRODGAR

Off B9055, 5 miles north-east of Stromness (Ca)

Overlooking the southern end of Loch of Harray is a circle of tall, upright stones, precisely spaced, erected by prehistoric man around 2000 BC. Of the original 60 stones, 27 remain upright, like sentinels keeping a timeless watch over the moor and the water. They average about 7ft high, and two have inscriptions.

Close by are the Standing Stones of Stenness, which may have formed a similar, but smaller, circle. Only four of the original 12 stones remain, the tallest being 18ft high. Little is known of the circles' origins, but one theory is that they may have been used for astronomical observations.

HBM. All year, daily.

ST MAGNUS CATHEDRAL

Broad Street, Kirkwall (Ca)

The red-sandstone cathedral of St Magnus has dominated the bustling town and harbour of Kirkwall for 850 years. Although weathered, it is one of the best-preserved medieval cathedrals in Scotland, its unusual colour giving a warm glow to the magnificent nave with its massive stone columns and wealth of round, Norman arches.

Magnus was a Norse martyr who died trying to bring peace to the islands. He was declared a saint in 1135, and work on the cathedral started two years later. During renovation work in 1919 the skeleton of Magnus was discovered in a casket hidden in the south arcade of the choir. An axe cut in the skull accords with the story of his death as told in the old sagas.

Near the cathedral stand the ruins of two palaces. The Bishop's Palace, dating from the 12th century, has had pieces added to it over the years, including the impressive Bishop Reid's round tower of the 1540s. The final reconstruction merged it with the new palace built by the tyrannical Earl Patrick Stewart in the early 17th century. The Earl's Palace has massive turrets and a great hall regarded as one of the noblest state rooms in any private castle in Scotland.

The elegant Tankerness House, also in Broad Street, is now a museum surveying Orkney's rich archaeological and social history. The house dates from the 16th century, but its contents go back more than 5000 years.

Cathedral: All year, Mon-Sat; Sun, services only. Free entry. Palaces: HBM. Apr-Sept, daily. Adm charge. P *Tel Edinburgh (031) 244 3101. Tankerness House: All year, daily exc Sun. Adm charge. Shop.* P *Toilets.* ♿ *(part). Tel Kirkwall (0856) 3191.*

SKARA BRAE

Off B9056, 7 miles north of Stromness (Ca)

On the wild shores of the Bay of Skaill lies a snug little village carved by Stone Age man 4500 years ago out of a huge rubbish tip and remains of earlier houses. From the top of the tip, now covered in grass, today's visitors can peer into the roofless homes. Some of the walls are 8ft high, and all six excavated houses are linked by a covered passageway.

The village was built from local flagstones. Each of the one-roomed homes has a central hearth framed by four kerb stones, stone beds with recesses above for personal effects, and a stone dresser. The entrances are about 4ft high, and probably had doors, and each house has a small cell let into the thick walls where residents kept treasures such as carved implements.

Skara Brae is believed to have been abandoned after a freak storm covered it in sand around 2500 BC. The village owes its remarkable state of preservation to the sand, and the weather-proofing mound of peat-ash, shells, animal bones and other rubbish that covered the houses up to their rooftops. It was another freak storm, in 1850, that ripped off the top grass to reveal the buildings.

HBM. All year, daily. Adm charge. Shop. P *(limited). Tel Edinburgh (031) 244 3101.*

TALL MAN *The rose-pink rock stack called the Old Man of Hoy, rising to 450ft on the north-west coast of Hoy, was first climbed in 1966. The pillar helps to explain the island's name, which is Norse for 'high island'.*

STROMNESS MUSEUM
Alfred Street, Stromness (Ca)

Orkney's rich maritime history is re-created in the museum in this picturesque old town with its twisting paved streets, gabled stone houses and private jetties. There are displays on fishing and boat-building – once thriving industries in the town. Also recalled are the salvaging of the German fleet which was scuttled in Scapa Flow in 1919, and local links with the Hudson's Bay Company.

The Pier Arts Centre, in a building in Victoria Street which was once the main recruiting centre for the Hudson's Bay Company, houses a fine collection of 20th-century British art, including works by Ben Nicholson and Barbara Hepworth. *Museum: All year, Mon-Sat. Adm charge. Shop.* P *Tel Stromness (0856) 850025. Arts Centre: All year, Tues-Sat; also Sun June-Aug. Free entry.* P *(limited). Toilets.* ♿ *(part). Tel (0856) 850209.*

SHETLAND

CLICKIMIN BROCH
In Loch of Clickimin, 1 mile south of Lerwick (Db)

At the end of a causeway reaching into the Loch of Clickimin are the circular remains of one of the best preserved and excavated brochs in Scotland. The round tower was built in Bronze Age times to defend the small community of 40 to 80 people who lived in half-timbered houses within its walls. The 4th-century BC broch builders carried stones from the beach to build the tower, which once stood 40 to 50ft high. Like similar brochs on the islands, it was partially demolished in the 2nd century AD by later settlers who used its stones for 'wheelhouse' homes like those at Jarlshof. *HBM. All year, daily. Free entry. Tel Edinburgh (031) 244 3101.*

IN THE ROUND *The prehistoric 'wheelhouse' homes at Jarlshof are the most intact in Britain. Widespread in north-west Scotland, they were probably lived in until the Vikings arrived in the 9th century AD.*

JARLSHOF
Off A970, 1 mile south of Toab (Cb)

Among grassy hillocks close to the airport at Sumburgh are the remains of stone buildings that were the homes of the earliest settlers in Shetland. The seashore site was occupied continuously for nearly 3000 years, from the Stone Age through the Bronze and Iron Ages and then by Vikings and medieval farmers and landowners. The earliest preserved ruins are of Bronze Age houses, in which thick buttresses create cells round an open space. In one is a smithy in which mould fragments were found for casting axeheads, swords and ornaments.

Iron Age immigrants from the Continent later took over the site and built a broch, or massive stone defence tower. This was taken apart a century later by the so-called 'wheelhouse builders'. They used the stones from the tower to build circular houses divided by partition walls – like thick spokes – which converge onto a central hearth space. The stone slab roofs at Jarlshof are intact, making these the best preserved 'wheelhouses' in Britain.

On the crest of the mound is a 17th-century hall built by Earl Patrick Stewart in the late 16th century. A laird's house was later added, and this is now the best preserved building on the site. Two centuries later, Sir Walter Scott was so impressed by the house that he named it Jarlshof and used the setting in his novel *The Pirate*. What neither he nor anyone else then knew was that the ruin hid a great secret. This was revealed in 1905 when a violent storm ripped the surface off the south face of the mound, showing the walls of the ancient houses below.
HBM. All year, daily. Adm charge. P *(limited). Tel Edinburgh (031) 244 3101.*

MOUSA BROCH
By boat from Sandwick (Db)

The uninhabited island of Mousa is the site of the most complete Iron Age broch in existence. The circular tower, built for defence, rises 60ft above the grass-covered remains of the outer ramparts. Built of local stone by the Picts, it has two circular walls, one inside the other, and a stone staircase between the walls leads to the parapet. From the top, where Pictish guards once patrolled, there are magnificent views over the island and across the sea to Mainland.
HBM. All year, daily. Free entry. P *(limited). Tel Ardersier (0667) 62777.*

MUNESS CASTLE, UNST
Off A968, 6 miles east of Belmont (Dc)

The bleak ruins of Britain's northernmost castle dominate the lonely reaches of the south-east tip of Unst. When it was built in 1598, the castle was three storeys high and surrounded by outbuildings around a courtyard. Now only the main rectangular building stands, without most of its top storey. The castle was built on the Z plan, with two projecting circular towers at diagonally opposite corners. This enabled defenders to cover two sides of the building without exposing themselves to the fire of attackers. The castle fell into disuse within a century of its completion and was burnt by privateers or a vengeful neighbour.
HBM. All year, daily. Free entry. Tel Ardersier (0667) 62777.

NOSS NATURE RESERVE
By ferry from Bressay (Db)

More than 100,000 breeding seabirds nest on the wedge-shaped Isle of Noss, which has spectacular sandstone cliffs, caves and stacks. The residents of Noss include large colonies of great skuas, kittiwakes and guillemots, and smaller numbers of Arctic skuas, razorbills and puffins. Gannets nest on the horizontal ledges around The Noup where cliffs rise 600ft from the sea.
NCC. Mid May-Aug, daily exc Mon and Thur. Adm charge. P *Toilets. Tel Lerwick (0595) 3434.*

SCALLOWAY CASTLE
In centre of Scalloway (Db)

The gaunt ruins of the castle, which dominate the town of Scalloway and its harbour, are a grim reminder of the darkest days of Shetland's history. The castle was built in 1600 by the oppressive Earl Patrick Stewart, whose notoriety spread when he set about replacing Viking law with a feudal system of rule by the Scottish mainland. Both the earl and his son Robert were eventually executed at Edinburgh. The key to the castle can be obtained from the cottage opposite the entrance.
HBM. All year, daily. Free entry. Tel Ardersier (0667) 62777.

SHETLAND CROFT HOUSE MUSEUM
Off A970, 4 miles north of Toab (Db)

The self-reliant Shetlanders had life well organised inside this snug, low stone-and-thatch croft perched amid grassland overlooking the sea. The croft has been restored to show how a typical family and their livestock would have lived in the mid-19th century. Authentic furnishings of the period include box beds, butter churns, chests, a spinning wheel, lamps and furniture made from driftwood.
May-Sept, Tues-Sun. Adm charge. P *(limited). Toilets. Tel Lerwick (0595) 5057.*

SHETLAND MUSEUM
In centre of Lerwick (Db)

The building is modern but the exhibits inside create a fascinating picture of Shetland life dating back to Stone Age times. The main displays cover archaeology, folk life, maritime history and Shetland textiles. There are also replicas of Celtic church treasures found on St Ninian's Isle, off Mainland. Maritime exhibits include ships' figureheads, models of ships, and shipwreck relics recovered from the seabed.

Nearby, the high walls and gun ports of Fort Charlotte look out to sea. Built in the late 17th century to protect the Bressay Sound, it was burnt in 1673 by the Dutch – who also set fire to the town – and was rebuilt in the early 1780s.
Museum: All year, Mon-Sat. Free entry. Tel Lerwick (0595) 5057. Fort: HBM. All year, Mon-Sat. Free entry. Tel Edinburgh (031) 244 3101.

TINGWALL AGRICULTURAL MUSEUM

Off A971, 5 miles west of Lerwick (Db)

In the granary, cottage and stables of a modern working croft is a fascinating collection of household, agricultural and fishing equipment commonly in use on Shetland during the last century. They include tushkars and flaachter-spades which were used for cutting peat, heavy horse-drawn implements, tools – and the means for baking the daily bread.
May-Sept, daily exc Mon and Fri. Adm charge. Shop. P Toilets. Tel Gott (059 584) 344.

WESTERN ISLES

BALRANALD NATURE RESERVE

Off A865, 3 miles north-west of Bayhead (Ab)

Long white sandy beaches, lonely marshes and rich inland meadows attract rare birds to this reserve. It is one of the last strongholds of the corncrake, and is occasionally visited by red-necked phalaropes. Lapwing, snipe, oyster-catchers, ringed plover and dunlin nest in large numbers on the sandy beaches while teal, shoveler, gadwall, wigeon and mute swans nest in the marshes. There are waymarked paths.
RSPB. Apr-Aug, daily. Free entry. Tel Lochmaddy (087 63) 321.

BLACKHOUSE

Off A858, at Arnol (Bc)

With double stone walls 6ft thick and a low, thatched roof tied with ropes weighed down by stones, the Tigh Duth, or 'black house', was a snug refuge for families living on the windswept shores of the Outer Hebrides. One of these traditional crofts has been preserved as a museum.

The long, low humped building provided a home for three generations of a family and their farm animals. Family life centred on the kitchen, where a peat fire burned in the centre – with no chimney to allow the smoke to escape. The furnishings are strictly functional: a dresser, a long wooden settle and stools. In the sleeping room are three straw-filled box beds. Utensils used until 40 years ago are also displayed.
HBM. All year, Mon-Sat. Adm charge. P (limited). Tel Edinburgh (031) 244 3101.

CALLANISH STANDING STONES

Off A858, at Callanish (Bc)

On bleak moorland at the southern end of the township of Callanish stands one of the great wonders of the British Isles. The upright stone slabs, which are up to 12ft high, rival those of Stonehenge in stature – and in mystery. They are placed roughly in the shape of a Celtic cross, with 19 stones arranged as an avenue 270ft long leading to a circle of 13 monoliths. The tallest stone of all stands at the centre of the circle, overlooking a chambered cairn which was once a burial chamber.

CIRCLE OF MYSTERY *The Callanish Standing Stones were probably built for astronomical purposes – but they almost certainly served also as a centre for religious rites and as a meeting place for prehistoric people.*

The Standing Stones were quarried locally and raised to their present positions around 4000 years ago. Nobody knows the meaning of the formation, although it appears to be aligned with other smaller groups of standing stones in the area. The most favoured theory is that they served as an astronomical observatory.
HBM. All year, daily. Free entry. Refreshments. P (limited). Tel Edinburgh (031) 244 3101.

CARLOWAY BROCH

Off A858, at Carloway (Bc)

On a crag overlooking the township of Carloway are the massive remains of an Iron Age broch, or defensive tower, built between 100 BC and AD 300. It is the best preserved in the Western Isles, with double walls, 10ft to 12ft thick, rising on one side to a height of 30ft. Several chambers at the base can be entered from a central courtyard. Narrow stone steps twist and climb up the interior to galleries at three levels, ending suddenly where the walls have fallen away.
All year, daily. Free entry. Tel Stirling (0786) 62421.

KISIMUL CASTLE

Off A888, in Castle Bay (Aa)

Although its walls rising out of the sea in Barra's Castle Bay present a sombre spectacle, the story of Kisimul Castle's restoration is as romantic as any in Scottish folklore. Robert Lister Macneil, 45th Chief of the Clan Macneil, dreamed of restoring the castle, but he had to wait nearly 30 years – until 1937 – before he could start. The war years interrupted the work, but by the early 1960s the dream was a reality.

Centuries ago the Macneils were pirates wreaking terror through the Western seas, and the docking place of their great war galleon can still be seen. The castle dates from the early 11th century and is now a pleasing blend of the old and the new. Inside the curtain wall are the watchtower, the great hall which now has beams that were once railway sleepers – the chapel, the great tower and the kitchen house.
Boats from Castlebay, Apr-Sept, Wed and Sat pm. Adm charge.

LEWS CASTLE GROUNDS

Near harbour, Stornoway (Bc)

Two nature trails starting from the porter's lodge of Lews Castle lead through lush woodland, over moors and along shrub-hung riverbanks. The grounds were laid out just over a century ago by a merchant, Sir James Sutherland Matheson, who bought the then treeless island in 1844.

Many of the trees and shrubs were transported from the Far East and from Canada. Some of these specimens survive, including a rare sarawa cypress, an ash-leaved maple or box elder, and Western Himalayan fir and spruce.
All year, daily. Free entry. P (limited). ♿ Tel Stornoway (0851) 2002.

REGIONAL CALENDAR

January 1 Kirkwall: New Year's Day Ba' Game (traditional street contest, Uppies v Downies).

January (late). Lerwick: Up-Helly-Aa (Viking Festival).

April (late, to May). Shetland Folk Festival.

May (late). Stromness: Orkney Folk Festival.

June (mid-month). Kirkwall: St Magnus Festival.

July (late). Lewis: Highland Games.

August (early). Kirkwall: Orkney County Show.

August (mid-month). Kirkwall: St Magnus Fair. St Margaret's Hope, S Ronaldsay: Festival of the Horse, and Boys' Ploughing Match (beach custom).

Tourist information: Barra (087 14) 336; Lewis (0851) 3088; North Uist (087 63) 321; Orkney (0856) 2856; Shetland (0595) 3434.

LOTHIAN

MANSIONS AND CASTLES AROUND SCOTLAND'S HISTORIC HEART

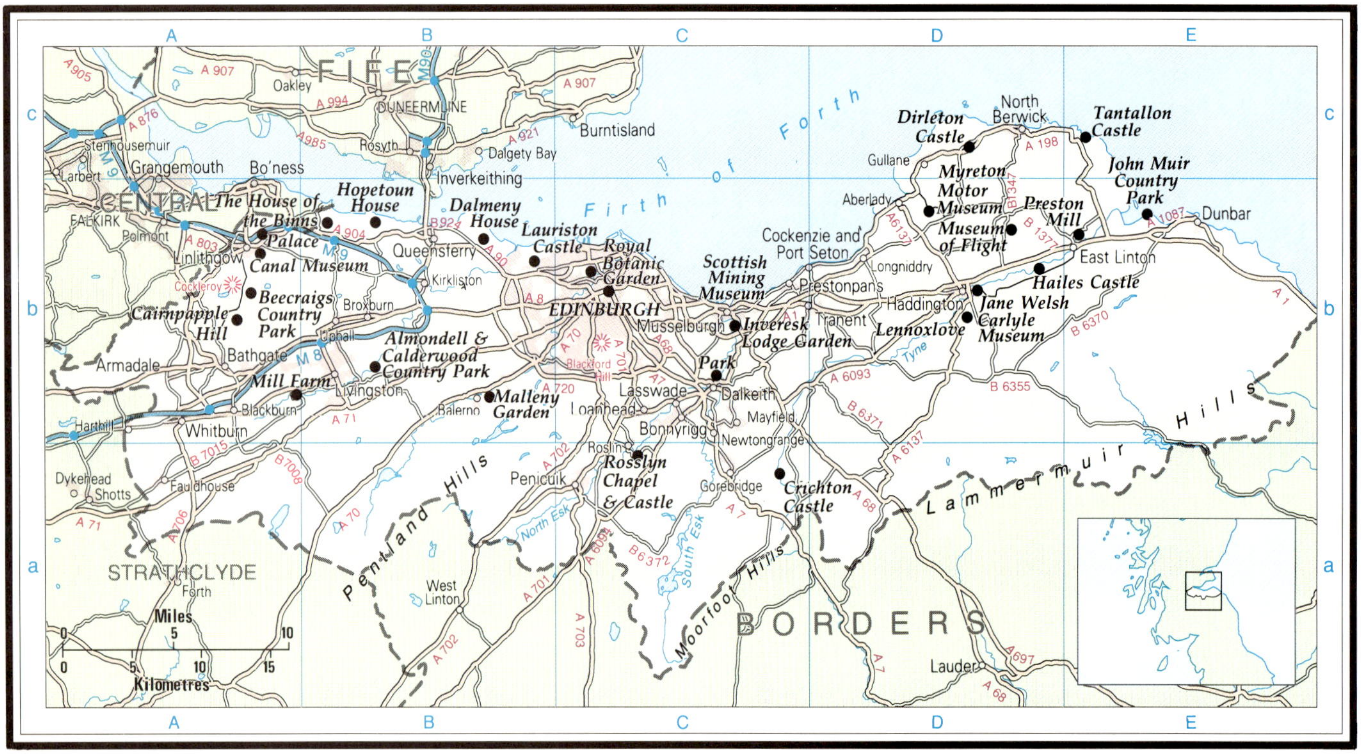

A host of medieval fortresses lie within easy reach of Edinburgh, Scotland's historic capital, which has its own spectacular castle and palace. They include Crichton, Dirleton and Tantallon, and the mighty Stuart palace at Linlithgow. Later, more settled times led to the building of great houses such as Dalmeny, Hopetoun and Lennoxlove.

This Scottish heartland on the Firth of Forth has great natural beauty, which is tended and embellished in the Beecraigs, Dalkeith and John Muir parks, and in the Inveresk Lodge Garden and the Royal Botanic Garden. Lothian also has a varied industrial heritage, recalled in the Linlithgow Canal Museum, Livingston Mill Farm and the Scottish Mining Museum.

ALMONDELL AND CALDERWOOD COUNTRY PARK

Off B7015, 2 miles south of Broxburn (Bb)

Beside the River Almond, and the Murieston and Linhouse Waters which flow into it, lies an area of great natural beauty. The park is formed from two adjoining estates. Calderwood, to the west, is a mixture of woodland and open spaces criss-crossed by tracks. Almondell, though largely wooded, is planted with colourful daffodils, rhododendrons and azaleas.

Almondell and Calderwood Country Park contains a number of picnic areas, a barbecue site and miles of quieter woodland and riverside paths. The visitor centre contains aquaria with native waterlife, and also displays covering the history and wildlife of the park. Free ranger-guided walks start from the centre in summer.

Park: All year, daily. Free entry. P *(limited). Toilets.* ♿ *Tel Mid Calder (0506) 882254. Centre: All year, daily exc Fri and Sat. Free entry.*

BEECRAIGS COUNTRY PARK

Off A803, 2 miles south of Linlithgow (Ab)

Set amid the delightful uplands of the Bathgate Hills, Beecraigs Loch and the surrounding forest offer a choice of activities. The park's 500 acres of woodland are crisscrossed by waymarked paths and nature trails.

The Park Centre near the loch has a small exhibition area, and demonstrations of crafts, such as pottery, woodcarving and spinning, are held there on Sundays in summer. Nearby are trout and deer farms, where visitors can see the fish at the various stages of their life cycle and watch red deer in their natural environment from a special walkway and viewing platforms.

A gentle climb from the west car park leads to the 912ft summit of Cockleroy, from which there are 360 degree panoramic views across the breadth of Scotland.

All year, daily. Free entry. Shop. P *Toilets. Tel Linlithgow (0506) 844516.*

CAIRNPAPPLE HILL

Off B792, 3 miles north of Bathgate (Ab)

On the summit of this bleak, windswept hill, Stone Age man erected an oval ring of upright stones. Later, during the Bronze and Iron Ages, when Cairnpapple Hill became a burial ground, the standing stones were uprooted and used for building tombs. Nevertheless, the holes dug for them more than 4000 years ago are still visible; some of the packing blocks used to keep the stones upright are still in place; and one of the cairns, or mounds, has been restored so that visitors can enter the burial chambers.

Excavations at the site have yielded many finds; these include a food vessel and a funeral urn discovered virtually intact, and fragments of polished stone axes made as far away as the Lake District and North Wales. Although it is a short, easy climb to the top, the view from the summit extends across the entire breadth of this part of Scotland, from the mountains of Arran in the west to Bass Rock in the east.

HBM. Apr-Sept, daily exc Sun am. Adm charge. Shop. P *(limited). Tel Edinburgh (031) 244 3101.*

CRICHTON CASTLE

Off B6367, 5 miles south-east of Dalkeith (Ca)

The imposing ruins of this medieval castle, built around a rectangular tower house, stand on a prominent plateau overlooking Tyne Water near Crichton village. In the 15th century it was the home of the Lord Chancellor of Scotland, Sir William Crichton, a bitter enemy of the local Douglas family. In 1440 Crichton lured the young Earl of Douglas and his brother to a feast in Edinburgh Castle where they were brutally murdered. In revenge, their kinsmen kept Sir William under siege in Edinburgh, while their followers stormed Crichton Castle. Shortly afterwards, the chancellor remodelled and enlarged it, to make it less vulnerable to attack.

In the 16th century the castle was owned by the 4th Earl of Bothwell, third husband of Mary, Queen of Scots. Later that century, his wild and much-travelled kinsman, Francis Stuart, Earl of Bothwell, brought from the Continent an Italian architect who created the unusual inner courtyard which, with its shady arcades and diamond-patterned walls, resembles an Italian piazza.

The castle has four kitchens; below one of them, in the 14th-century tower, is a dismal prison pit barely 7ft square. Standing apart from the keep are the massively buttressed stables.
HBM. Apr-Oct, daily exc Sun am. Winter, Sat, Sun pm. Adm charge. Tel Edinburgh (031) 244 3101.

DALKEITH PARK

Off High Street, Dalkeith (Cb)

In the grounds of historic Dalkeith Palace, owned by the Duke of Buccleuch, are 5 miles of nature trails and a woodland adventure playground for children. The nature trails follow the courses of two rivers – the North Esk and the South Esk – for part of the way, cross a bridge designed by Robert Adam in 1792 and pass the former orangery.
Apr-Oct, daily. Adm charge. Refreshments. Shop. P *Toilets. Tel Edinburgh (031) 663 5684.*

DALMENY HOUSE

Off B924, 7 miles west of Edinburgh (Bb)

Napoleon's ornate shaving stand and the cushion placed beneath his head when he lay in state are among the Napoleonic mementos collected by the 5th Earl of Rosebery which are on display at Dalmeny. Although the estate has belonged to the Earls of Rosebery since the 17th century, the present mansion designed by William Wilkins dates from 1817 when the family moved from Barnbougle Castle, half a mile to the west.

The house has a flamboyant Gothic façade – but the interior is even more impressive. The entrance hall has a set of tapestries designed by Goya for the royal palaces of Spain, and the large Savonnerie carpet in the drawing room was ordered by Louis XIV for the Louvre.

The 5th Earl, who succeeded Gladstone as prime minister, married Hannah Rothschild, daughter of Baron Meyer de Rothschild. The Baron collected art treasures on a grand scale, and before the contents of Mentmore, his palatial mansion in Buckinghamshire, were auctioned in 1977, some of the finest French furniture was moved to Dalmeny, together with a collection of porcelain. Madame de Pompadour once filled a whole room with perfumed porcelain flowers as a present for Louis XV: two vases of these flowers and a Sèvres porcelain portrait of Marie Antoinette playing with her children are among the pieces on show at Dalmeny.

The house has a splendid collection of paintings, including works by Rembrandt, Gainsborough and Reynolds.

In the village of Dalmeny, 1½ miles to the west, stands the Romanesque parish church of St Cuthbert. Built in the middle of the 12th century, it has outwardly changed little since then – although the stout, square western tower was rebuilt in 1816. At the same time the interior was refurbished, new seats and galleries being fitted; it was generally restored in 1926.
House: May-Sept, Sun-Thur, pm. Adm charge. Refreshments. P *Toilets.* ♿ *Tel Edinburgh (031) 331 1888. Church: All year, daily.* P ♿ *Tel (031) 331 1869.*

BROODING RUIN *The striking appearance of Crichton Castle, described in Scott's* Marmion, *is largely due to Francis Stuart, Earl of Bothwell, who rebuilt it around 1585, and entertained James VI there.*

DIRLETON CASTLE

In Dirleton, 2 miles west of North Berwick (Dc)

Visitors naturally expect a castle such as this, massively built in the 13th century on an outcrop of solid rock, to have a colourful history. Dirleton does not disappoint. Now a romantic ruin, it was first battered by the great stone catapults of England's Edward I, then recaptured for Scotland by Robert Bruce and, much later, wrecked by Cromwell when it was held in the Royalist cause. In 1649 a group of men and women accused of witchcraft were imprisoned in the castle, then strangled and burnt at the stake there. The terrible prison pit in which the victims were kept can still be seen.

The main features of the castle are three 13th-century drum towers, the chapel, the kitchen and the ruins of the great hall. The attractive gardens contain a 17th-century bowling green. The nearby waymarked Yellowcraig Nature Trail covers a square mile of woodland, dunes and seashore between Dirleton and the sea.
Castle: HBM. All year, daily exc Sun am. Adm charge. P *(limited).* ♿ *Tel Edinburgh (031) 556 8400. Nature Trail: All year, daily.* P *Toilets. Tel North Berwick (0620) 21970.*

HAILES CASTLE

Off A1, 2 miles south-west of East Linton (Db)

A 16th-century master of Hailes Castle was James, 4th Earl of Bothwell, who married Mary, Queen of Scots after plotting the murder of her second husband Lord Darnley. Two hundred years earlier, his ancestors had enlarged a castle which was built in the 13th century: surviving parts of the original building are the base of the tower – which contains a vaulted prison pit – the lower parts of the curtain wall and a vaulted stairway to a well. A pit prison can also be found in the 14th-century western tower, which has a vaulted basement with living rooms above. Between the towers is a basement bakehouse. In the chapel over it, the remains of a large tracery window can be seen.
HBM. Apr-Sept, daily exc Sun am; Oct-Mar, daily exc Sun am, Wed pm and Thur. Adm charge. Tel Edinburgh (031) 244 3101.

ARCH ENEMIES *A bust of Napoleon as King of Italy stands in Dalmeny House. The red campaign chair nearby belonged to the Duke of Wellington, and from it he planned Napoleon's final defeat at Waterloo.*

ROYAL MILE AND NEW TOWN

As early as the 5th century AD, Din Eidyn, 'Eidyn's fort', stood on Castle Hill, and it was around this that Edinburgh grew, to become Scotland's capital in 1124 by decree of David I. The backbone of Edinburgh's Old Town is the Royal Mile, a series of narrow streets running eastwards from the castle to the Palace of Holyroodhouse. The palace was begun around 1500 by James IV, the monarch who made the city famous throughout Europe as a place of learning. Notable buildings along the Royal Mile include St Giles' Cathedral, a mainly 15th-century kirk on a 9th-century church site. To the north, beyond Princes Street, lies the 18th-century New Town.

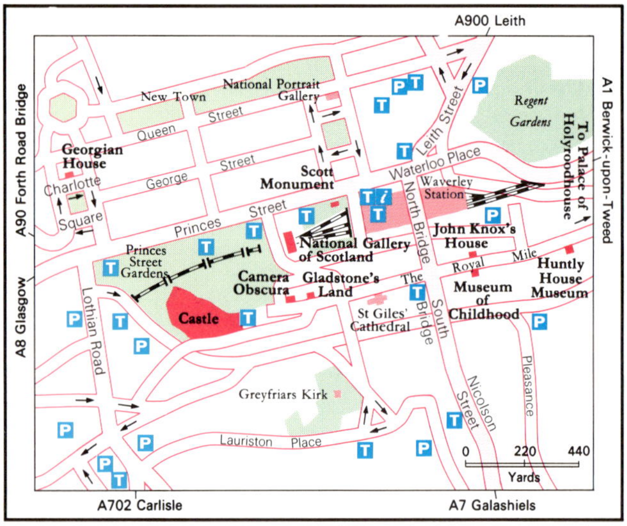

Camera Obscura *All year, daily. Adm charge. Shop. Tel Edinburgh (031) 226 3709.*

Huntly House Museum *All year, Mon-Sat and Bank Hol. Free entry. Shop. Toilets. Tel (031) 225 2424 ext 6689.*

Scott Monument *All year, Mon-Sat. Adm charge. Tel (031) 225 2424 ext 6596.*

John Knox's House *All year, Mon-Sat. Adm charge. Refreshments. Shop. Tel (031) 556 6961.*

National Gallery of Scotland *All year, daily exc Sun am. Free entry. Shop. Toilets. ♿ Tel (031) 556 8921.*

Palace of Holyroodhouse. *All year, daily exc 2 weeks in late May, 3 weeks late June-July, and Sun in winter. Adm charge. Refreshments. Shop. P (limited). Toilets. ♿ (part). Tel (031) 556 7371.*

Gladstone's Land *NTS. Apr-Oct, daily exc Sun am; Nov, Sat, and Sun pm. Adm charge. Shop. ♿ (ground floor). Tel (031) 226 5856.*

The Georgian House, *7 Charlotte Square, NTS. Apr-Oct, daily exc Sun am: Nov, Sat and Sun pm. Adm charge. Shop. Tel (031) 225 2160.*

Edinburgh Castle *HBM. All year, daily. Adm charge. Shop. P (limited). Toilets. ♿ (part). Tel (031) 225 9846.*

Museum of Childhood *All year, Mon-Sat. Free entry. Shop. Toilets. ♿ Tel (031) 225 2424.*

St Giles' Cathedral *All year, daily. Free entry. Refreshments. Shop. P (limited). Toilets. Tel (031) 225 4363.*

CAMERA OBSCURA

A fascinating all-round view of Edinburgh (left), received through a revolving mirror, is focused onto a white concave surface in the Outlook Tower. There are also displays of holograms, and the rooftop gives panoramic views over the city and beyond.

HUNTLY HOUSE MUSEUM

Edinburgh glass on display in Huntly House includes a superb cut-glass epergne, or table centre (right), made at the Holyrood Glass Works to commemorate Queen Victoria's accession in 1837. The restored 16th-century mansion has displays on local history and relics of Field-Marshal Earl Haig, who was born in Edinburgh in 1861 and commanded British forces in the First World War. Edinburgh silver, Scottish pottery, long-case clocks and quaint old shop signs are also on view.

SCOTT MONUMENT

A marble figure of the Scottish writer Sir Walter Scott (1771-1832) sits under a graceful Gothic spire more than 200ft tall. A competition for the best design for a monument was won by George Meikle Kemp; it was finished in 1844.

JOHN KNOX'S HOUSE

Two sundials, topped by a figure of Moses pointing to the Sun's golden disc, grace this finely restored 15th-century house. Whether John Knox (1505-72) lived there is doubtful, but he certainly lived nearby. The spire of St Giles' Cathedral, where he preached, can be seen from the study window, and relics of Knox are on view in the house.

MUSEUM OF CHILDHOOD

A clockwork chauffeur-driven saloon made in Germany in about 1930, and a British board game of some 20 years earlier, are among the museum's treasures. The collection includes toys, games, dolls and teddy bears, and displays on children's clothes, food and health.

GLADSTONE'S LAND

A 17th-century cloth-merchant's booth (right) has been reconstructed on the ground floor of the 16th to 17th-century house, originally the home of an Edinburgh burgess, Thomas Gledstanes. The house, has been restored and refurnished in period style; the Painted Chamber has an exquisitely decorated ceiling.

THE GEORGIAN HOUSE

Edinburgh's elegant 'New Town' grew up when citizens no longer needed to huddle near the castle for protection. Robert Adam designed Charlotte Square, built between 1793 and 1805. The lower rooms of No 7, including the dining room (above), are furnished as they might have been then. An audiovisual show tells the story of the New Town.

EDINBURGH FESTIVAL

A cavalcade of bands, decorated floats, dancers, jugglers and many more (below) marks the opening of the Edinburgh Festival in August. During the next three weeks, music, drama, dance and exhibitions are provided, both by festival artistes and by the increasingly popular 'Fringe' performers. Film and jazz festivals also flourish, and the Castle Esplanade is the scene of a Military Tattoo with a display by massed pipe bands (far right).

NATIONAL GALLERY OF SCOTLAND

An off-duty cleric, Robert Walker, skated into immortality as the subject of this striking portrait by Sir Henry Raeburn (1756-1823), which is among the gallery's unrivalled group of works by Scottish artists. The neoclassical building houses a fine collection of European paintings dating from the 14th century.

PALACE OF HOLYROODHOUSE

The Queen's official residence in Scotland was begun in 1498 by James IV, and rebuilt by order of Charles II. Mary, Queen of Scots spent six years of her reign there, and in the palace in 1566 her Italian secretary David Rizzio was murdered. The picture gallery contains portraits depicting 89 Scottish kings of history and legend, and fine tapestries and 18th-century furniture grace the state apartments.

HOPE AND GLORY *This magnificent Baroque painting was discovered in the cupola of Hopetoun House only in 1984. Its cherubs and angels support the crest and coat of arms of the owners, the Hope family.*

HOPETOUN HOUSE

Off A904, 2½ miles west of Queensferry (Bb)

The symmetrical elegance of this palatial classical mansion can best be appreciated from the avenue leading to the house. Built by the Scottish architect Sir William Bruce for the 1st Earl of Hopetoun in 1699, the house was enlarged by William Adam, who added the front façade, and twin wings linked to the main block by curving colonnades in the 18th century.

After William Adam's death in 1748, the interior was decorated by his two sons, Robert and John. Several of the rooms have rich, silk wall-coverings, magnificent ceilings and paintings by masters such as Canaletto and Gainsborough. The Wainscot Room and Great Ballroom are hung with fine French and Belgian tapestries, and set into the panelling beside the carved pine staircase are murals painted by the Scottish artist William McLaren in 1970.

Two unusual features of the house are the 18th-century strongroom with heavy iron doors and shutters, where visitors can inspect estate books and deed boxes dating from that period, and the serving room, where food was warmed after travelling to the State Dining Room from the huge kitchen by way of a steam-heated railway and a lift.

At the top of the house there is an observatory with splendid views over the Firth of Forth and a museum devoted to the history of the Hope family – which includes the Earls of Hopetoun and the Marquesses of Linlithgow. The large park has attractive walled gardens, a nature trail, deer and four-horned St Kilda sheep.

Easter; May-mid Sept, daily. Adm charge. Refreshments. Shop. P *Toilets.* ♿ *Tel Edinburgh (031) 331 2451.*

THE HOUSE OF THE BINNS

Off A904, 4 miles west of Queensferry (Bb)

A delightful country mansion ornamented with turrets and elegant dormer windows, the House of the Binns owes its name to the twin hills, or 'binns' in Old Scots, on which it stands. It was built between 1612 and 1630 by Thomas Dalyell (pronounced 'Dyell'), who made his fortune in London at the court of James I. Over the next 200 years the house was enlarged, and in 1826 Sir James Dalyell erected the tower on the hill behind it.

The house is dominated by the colourful personality of General Tam Dalyell. When Charles I was beheaded, the general swore that he would never cut his hair or shave until the monarchy was restored. Known as 'Bluidy Tam', he became Commander-in-Chief under Charles II.

Displayed in the dining room is the sword given to the general by the Tsar during a period of service in Russia, his Bible (a rarity because of a misprint in the Book of Ruth where God is referred to as 'She'), and the huge comb with which he kept his uncut hair and beard tidy.

The elaborate ceilings in the High Hall and King's Room date from 1630 when the Dalyells lavished money on the house, hoping that Charles I would stay with them during a royal progress through Scotland. Many of the rooms contain handsome Scottish furniture and fine Chinese and European porcelain.

NTS. Easter; May-Sept, pm daily exc Fri. Adm charge. P *Toilets. Tel Philipstoun (050 683) 4255.*

INVERESK LODGE GARDEN

On A6124, 6 miles east of Edinburgh (Cb)

Through a wrought-iron gate beside the 17th-century Inveresk Lodge lies a charming garden which looks over Doocot Park and beyond it towards Arthur's Seat. No one knows who laid out the original beds, but plans of 1851 showing the garden's semi-formal structure came to light when it was being replanted in the early 1960s.

A conservatory protects glasshouse plants in winter and contains a small collection of exotic birds. Beside it a border flowers throughout the year, and shrub and species roses bloom nearby. A pure white flowering cherry and a bushy crab apple are among the trees and shrubs in the half-moon beds. Distinctive trees in the lawn include a Himalayan birch with white bark, and a Japanese rowan, brilliant scarlet in autumn.

NTS. All year, daily exc Sun am and Sat. Adm charge. P *(limited). Tel Edinburgh (031) 336 2157.*

JANE WELSH CARLYLE MUSEUM

Lodge Street, Haddington (Db)

It was in this house where she was born that the 19th-century historian Thomas Carlyle first met Jane Welsh and immediately fell in love with her. It led to a five-year courtship and an exchange of letters which is one of the treasures of English literature. As well as being instantly taken by the 19-year-old Jane, Thomas was very impressed with the house, his only reservation being that it might contain 'a superfluity of elegant whim-whams'. Jane, too, fell in love and devoted the rest of her life to her husband and his work. Their home in Chelsea became the centre of a brilliant literary circle which included Tennyson, Thackeray, Dickens, Leigh Hunt and Ruskin. While Carlyle wrote his histories, Jane wrote her letters. They met in the evening when she was 'the rainbow of his dripping day'. When she died, after 40 years of marriage, Carlyle said the light of his life had gone out. The museum records all the phases of Jane's childhood and her life with Carlyle in an extensive display of paintings and engravings of scenes and people from the Carlyle circle, as well as furniture of the period.

Jane's tomb is in St Mary's Collegiate Church, the squat 500-year-old tower of which is known as the 'Lamp of Lothian'. It is one of the largest Scottish churches built in the late 14th and 15th centuries, with an elaborately carved exterior.

Museum: Apr-Sept, Wed-Sat pm. Adm charge. P *(limited). Toilets. Tel Haddington (062 082) 3738. Church: Easter; Apr-Sept, daily exc Sun am. Free entry. Refreshments. Shop.* P *Toilets.* ♿ *Tel (062 082) 5111.*

JOHN MUIR COUNTRY PARK

Off A1087, just north-west of Dunbar (Eb)

A glorious expanse of wild countryside extending for 8 miles along the coast west of Dunbar, including the estuary of the River Tyne, is named after the pioneer conservationist John Muir, who was born in Dunbar in 1838.

The woodland and coastal area are full of interest for naturalists and birdwatchers. Eider ducks and shelducks nest on the dunes. In autumn, after the last flowers have faded, the estuary springs to life as an important staging post for migrating birds. It also provides a haven for sea birds and waders that fly south to winter in Britain. Both children and adults can enjoy following the cliff-top nature trail or searching the rockpools along the shore for scarlet sea anemones, crabs and starfish. In summer, the Ranger Service organises guided walks.

After emigrating from Dunbar to the USA with his parents at the age of 11, John Muir spent much of his life campaigning to preserve the wild places of America. A number of them now bear his name, including Lake Muir in California and Muir Glacier in Alaska.

The three-storeyed house in which Muir was born – John Muir House, in Dunbar's High Street – is now a shrine to his memory. It is furnished much as it was in his early childhood, with a tin bath in the kitchen for family use on Friday nights, and an iron range on which the bath water was boiled. Upstairs, the best bedroom contains the family Bible and a washstand with tortoiseshell toilet set. A special exhibition room, complete with audiovisual display, tells the story of Muir's life and achievements.

Country Park: All year, daily. Adm charge. P *Toilets.* ♿ *Tel East Linton (0620) 860556. John Muir House: June-Sept, daily exc Wed and Sun. Free entry. Tel Dunbar (0368) 63353.*

LAURISTON CASTLE

Cramond Road South, on north-west edge of Edinburgh (Bb)

To set foot in Lauriston Castle is to step back to the days of Edwardian house parties and croquet on the lawn. For when the last private owners, William Reid and his wife, died more than 60 years ago, they left their home to the nation on condition that it should be preserved unchanged.

William Reid was the proprietor of an Edinburgh cabinet-making firm, and a tireless collector. All the rooms are filled with furniture and objets d'art collected by him – including nearly a hundred Blue John ornaments made from the translucent mineral found in Derbyshire.

Lauriston consists of a 16th-century castle incorporated into a roomier neo-Jacobean mansion built in 1827. From the Oak Room, once the principal apartment of the castle, a narrow staircase hidden within the wall leads to a secret chamber with a listening hole for eavesdropping and a peephole for spying on the room below.

Apr-Oct, daily exc Fri; Nov-Mar, Sat and Sun pm. Adm charge. Shop. P *(limited). Toilets. Tel Edinburgh (031) 336 2060.*

LENNOXLOVE

Off B6369, 1 mile south of Haddington (Db)

Set among thick woodland, and looking out towards the Lammermuir Hills, this ruggedly handsome house was named after Frances Stewart, Duchess of Lennox, who in the 17th century was the model for the figure of Britannia used on Britain's coinage. She was known as 'La Belle Stewart', and there is a full-length portrait of her in the Yellow Room; while the Petit Point Room, lined with 17th-century damask, contains a mother-of-pearl inlaid workbox, a gift from her ardent but unsuccessful suitor, Charles II.

Since 1946 the house has belonged to the Dukes of Hamilton, and is rich in treasures and historical relics brought from Hamilton Palace. The Ante Room is devoted to Mary, Queen of Scots, and contains her death mask and a French silver casket given to her by her first husband, Francis II of France, and said to have once contained documents incriminating her in the murder of her second husband, Lord Darnley. The 20th Century Room downstairs contains the map and compass carried by Rudolf Hess, Hitler's deputy, who flew solo to Lanarkshire in 1941, apparently in an attempt to involve the Duke of Hamilton in negotiating a peace between Britain and Germany.

Easter; May-Sept, Wed, Sat and Sun pm. Adm charge. P *Toilets. Tel Haddington (062 082) 3720.*

LINLITHGOW CANAL MUSEUM

Manse Road Basin, Linlithgow (Ab)

A stable which once sheltered canal horses now houses a museum devoted to the development of the Union Canal which runs for 31 miles between Edinburgh and Falkirk. Original documents, photographs and artefacts record the construction of the canal, which involved building three aqueducts, digging out a 696yd tunnel and 11 locks. A table lists notable events in the canal's history, and an aquarium and audiovisual programme illustrate the wildlife in and around the canal. On summer weekends, boat trips down the canal from the basin can be taken aboard *Victoria*, a diesel-powered replica of a Victorian steam packet boat.

Easter-Sept, Sat and Sun pm. Free entry (boat fare). Shop. P ♿ *(museum). Tel Linlithgow (0506) 843621.*

LINLITHGOW PALACE

Off High Street, in Linlithgow (Ab)

One of Scotland's four royal palaces, Linlithgow was built in the 15th century for James I of Scotland. The building was gutted by fire when it was occupied by soldiers of the Duke of Cumberland in 1746. While the fire and subsequent neglect destroyed the roof and interiors, the shell of the building remains largely intact, surrounding a

ROYAL ENDING *The death mask of Mary, Queen of Scots is displayed in the Ante Room of Lennoxlove. Mary was executed for treason in England in 1587 and her death mask was brought home to Scotland.*

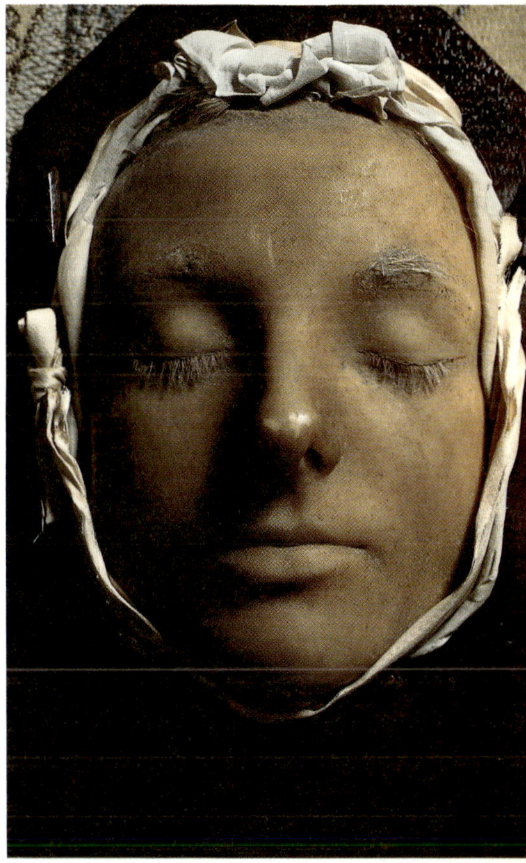

ROYAL BEGINNING *The romantic ruin of Linlithgow Palace stands beside Linlithgow Loch. James V was born in the palace in 1512, and 30 years later it was the birthplace of his daughter Mary, Queen of Scots.*

large inner courtyard in which there is an elaborate stone fountain. The Great Hall, the Chapel and the Presence Chamber can still be seen, and a climb up the 140 steps of the Queen's turnpike tower leads to Queen Margaret's Bower, a small vaulted apartment from which the Grampians can be seen on a fine day.
HBM. All year, daily. Adm charge. Shop. 🅿 *Toilets.* ♿ *(part). Tel Edinburgh (031) 244 3101.*

LIVINGSTON MILL FARM
Off B7015, 1½ miles south of Livingston (Ab)

This countryside museum preserves the local way of life down on the farm 100 years ago. It comprises a restored 18th-century water mill and 6 acres of farmland along the River Almond, complete with horses, cows, sheep, goats and other traditional farm animals, and collections of traditional farm equipment.
Easter-Sept, daily. Adm charge. Refreshments. 🅿 *Toilets.* ♿ *Tel Livingston (0506) 414957.*

MALLENY GARDEN
Off A70, 3 miles south-west of Edinburgh (Bb)

The fragrant scent of shrub roses makes the garden of Malleny House a delightful place to visit in midsummer – though earlier callers will enjoy a spectacular blaze of colour from the massed rhododendrons. Although the house itself is not open to the public, its round stone tower and elegant Georgian wing provide a pleasing focal point for the garden; so does the rustic dovecote, which is unusual in having the nesting holes on the north side, instead of the south. The earliest recorded owners of Malleny were the Knychtsoune family. In 1603 they planted 12 yew trees, of which four trimly clipped specimens survive.
NTS. All year, daily. Adm charge. 🅿 ♿ *Tel Edinburgh (031) 336 2157.*

MUSEUM OF FLIGHT
Off B1347, 4 miles south of North Berwick (Db)

The most famous aircraft associated with East Fortune Airfield, the home of this museum, can be seen only in photographs. This is the airship R34, which made the first non-stop double crossing of the Atlantic from East Fortune in July

RALLY VETERAN *This grand old 1902 5hp Wolseley in the Myreton Motor Museum has taken part in the RAC London to Brighton Rally several times. It cost £225 when delivered to its first owner.*

MIRRORED MILL *Preston Mill, with its beautiful riverside setting, conical-roofed kiln and mellow pantiled roof, has attracted generations of artists. Its great iron water wheel is 13ft across.*

1919. But the museum has many other famous models which can be seen, from Percy Pilcher's Hawk glider of 1896 to a giant Vulcan delta-wing heavy bomber, one of two used in the attack on Port Stanley during the Falklands campaign.

The oldest aircraft in the collection is a 1930 De Havilland Puss Moth, the first of its type to fly to Australia. It also possesses the only surviving example of the first British all-metal light aircraft – the General Aircraft Cygnet – and Sheila Scott's Piper Comanche 'Myth Too' in which she set 94 world records in the early 1970s.
June-Aug, daily. Free entry. Refreshments. Shop. 🅿 *Toilets.* ♿ *Tel North Berwick (0620) 88308.*

MYRETON MOTOR MUSEUM
Off A198, 1½ miles west of Aberlady (Db)

The vehicles on show in the Myreton Museum are not rare or exotic specimens in showroom condition, but cars and trucks that were once produced in large numbers and were in regular use on the roads. The earliest exhibit is an 1896 French Leon Bolle model, once owned by C.S. Rolls, the co-founder of Rolls-Royce Ltd in 1904. All the vehicles are in working condition and some are driven in rallies and film-making. Historic road signs, motoring accessories, motorcycles and bicycles, and Second World War military vehicles are also displayed.
All year, daily. Adm charge. 🅿 *Toilets.* ♿ *Tel Aberlady (087 57) 288.*

PRESTON MILL
On B1407, in East Linton village (Eb)

The water-driven grain mill was grinding corn until 1957, and has now been restored to working order. It dates from the 17th century, but its circular kiln is 200 years older. Nearby is the 16th-century Phantassie Doocot, or dovecote. Doocots were once common in Scotland, providing a supply of pigeons for the pot in winter when fresh meat was scarce. The massive circular walls are cut off at the top to create a sloping, sheltered horseshoe-shaped roof for the pigeons to land and perch on.
NTS. Apr-Nov, daily exc Sun am. Adm charge. 🅿 *Tel East Linton (0620) 860426.*

ROSSLYN CHAPEL AND CASTLE
Off B7003, 1½ miles south of Loanhead (Ca)

Dramatically situated between a rocky headland and the rushing waters of the North Esk, the ornately carved and pinnacled Rosslyn Chapel was originally intended as part of a vast cruciform church. Built in the 15th century, it is notable for its lofty chancel, dignified south aisle, and charming lady chapel. The exquisitely wrought Apprentice Pillar is said to be the work of the apprentice of a master mason who was abroad at the time. On his return, the mason was so jealous of the apprentice's work that he struck him dead with his mallet.

High up in the woods above the chapel can be seen the ruins of Rosslyn Castle, a medieval stronghold reached by a narrow bridge. This was the home of the builder of the chapel, William Sinclair, 3rd Earl of Orkney.
Chapel: Apr-Oct, daily exc Sun am. Adm charge. Refreshments. Shop. 🅿 *Toilets.* ♿ *Tel Edinburgh (031) 440 2159. Castle: Apr-Oct, Sat am. Free entry.* 🅿 *(limited). Tel (031) 440 2159.*

ROYAL BOTANIC GARDEN
Inverleith Row, just north of centre of Edinburgh (Cb)

This is the second oldest botanic garden in Britain, having been founded in 1670, 49 years after the one at Oxford. It contains a superb rock garden, with plants from a variety of climates, from high mountains and Arctic permafrost to the Mediterranean; a Rhododendron Walk which also provides shelter for many smaller plants, especially peonies; an arboretum; and a series of exhibition plant houses and palm houses.

The Tropical Aquatic House contains a viewing chamber, which enables visitors to view the pool and its plants and fish from below. The outstanding summer attraction in the pool is the huge flowers and disc-shaped leaves of the Victoria water lilies from South America. The Exhibition Hall presents displays on the plant kingdom. There is also a visitor centre with changing exhibitions in Inverleith House, a 17th-century mansion in the centre of the garden.

All year, daily. Free entry. Refreshments. Shop. 🅿 *Toilets.* ♿ *Tel Edinburgh (031) 552 7171.*

SCOTTISH MINING MUSEUM

Off B1344, 5 miles east of Edinburgh (Cb)

The museum is spread over two former collieries, one of which is the birthplace of Scottish coal mining. A charter was granted to work coal at Prestongrange 800 years ago. Today it is linked to Lady Victoria Colliery – the other half of the museum – by a Coal Heritage Trail through the heart of the former Lothian coalfield.

Prestongrange tells the story of Scottish mining from the earliest times to 1800. It features a historic collection of mining equipment and material, including the Giant Beam Engine, dominating the site, which was installed at Prestongrange in 1874.

The Lady Victoria Colliery carries the story of mining to the early days of the 20th century. Talking tableaux in the visitor centre introduce the personalities of the pit, and the working and living conditions of the miners and their families in the 1890s. Visitors can also see the giant winding gear in operation, and tour the pithead.

All year, Tues-Fri; Sat and Sun pm. Adm charge. Refreshments. Shop. 🅿 *Toilets.* ♿ *Tel Edinburgh (031) 663 7519.*

TANTALLON CASTLE

Off A198, 3 miles east of North Berwick (Ec)

'Broad, massive, high and stretching far' was how Sir Walter Scott, in his poem *Marmion*, described the ruins of Tantallon, with its towering red-sandstone walls, poised on the edge of rugged cliffs, still as spectacular today.

Built in the 14th century, the castle provided the 'Red' Douglases with a strong base from which they pursued bitter feuds against the rival 'Black' Douglases, and sometimes against the Crown. Nevertheless, James V managed to storm Tantallon in 1528 after a three-week siege. In 1651 General Monck, Cromwell's commander in Scotland, captured it with the help of six battering rams after 12 days' gruelling artillery bombardment. Surprisingly, substantial parts of the towers and hall block are still standing. Visitors can climb up to the battlements, from which there are fine views, by way of a remarkable arched stairway built inside the curtain wall.

HBM. Apr-Sept, daily exc Sun am; Oct-Mar, daily exc Sun, Wed and Thur am. Adm charge. 🅿 *(limited). Tel Edinburgh (031) 244 3101.*

REGIONAL CALENDAR

March (late). Edinburgh: Folk Festival.

April (late). Edinburgh: Antiques Fair.

May (end of month). Musselburgh Links: Shooting for The Silver Arrow (Archers Competition dating from 17th century).

June (mid-month). Ingliston: Royal Highland Show. Linlithgow: Riding of The Marches. Livingston: Gala Day.

August (Friday before 2nd Sat). Queensferry: The Burry Man & Ferry Fair (man dressed in burrs parades around the town on eve of fair).

August (last 3 weeks). Edinburgh: Arts & Fringe Festival; Military Tattoo; Film Festival; Jazz Festival.

November (late). Edinburgh: International Curling Competition.

December (early). Ingliston: Scottish Agricultural Winter Fair.

Tourist information: Dunbar (0368) 63353; Edinburgh (031) 577 2727; Linlithgow (0506) 844600; North Berwick (0620) 2197.

CLIFFTOP FORTRESS *The ruins of Tantallon Castle, sandstone stronghold of the Douglas family in the 14th and 15th centuries, straddle a windswept promontory surrounded on three sides by the sea.*

STRATHCLYDE

LAND OF LOCHS AND LAIRDS BEYOND A POET'S BIRTHPLACE

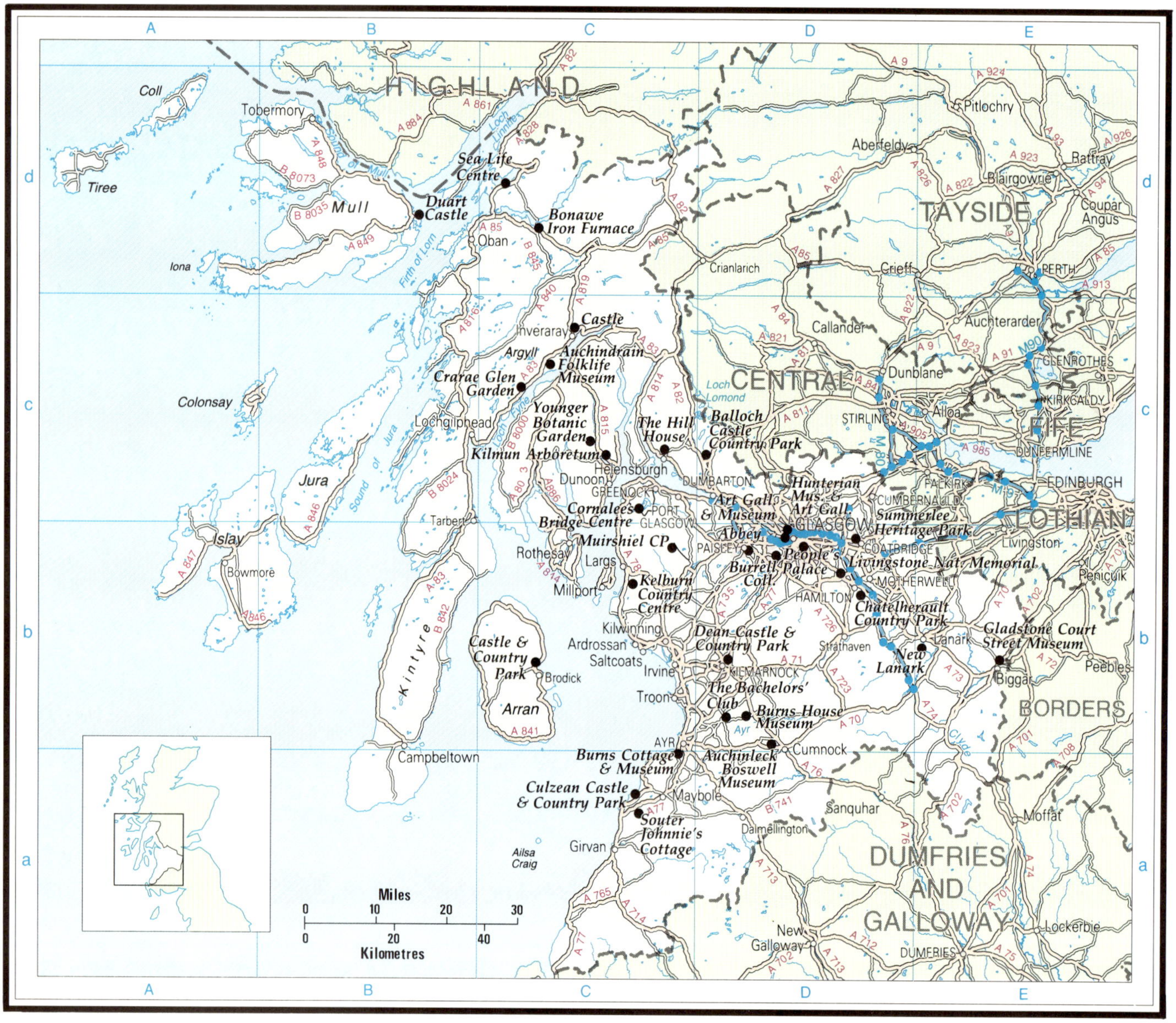

Glasgow is at the heart of Strathclyde, and the bustle of city life can quickly be left behind for the delights of an inspiring and romantic countryside. It certainly inspired Robert Burns, whose birthplace at Alloway is now a museum, as are The Bachelors' Club he attended in Tarbolton, his wife's house at Mauchline and the cottage near Maybole of Souter Johnnie, immortalised in Burns's ballad *Tam o' Shanter*. Few could fail to be inspired by the serene beauty of Loch Lomond or the rugged charm of castles such as Culzean, Duart and Inveraray. Glasgow itself has much to offer, with its museums and art galleries, and at nearby New Lanark are the restored buildings of an 18th-century cotton-mill village.

AUCHINDRAIN FOLKLIFE MUSEUM

On A83, 5½ miles south-west of Inveraray (Cc)

Clusters of cottages and barns in acres of rough grazing land survive at Auchindrain, the last farm in Scotland to have been worked on the once-widespread communal tenancy system, in which several families, instead of one, shared the rent and the labour. Auchindrain was still being farmed in this way as late as 1935.

The MacCallums, Campbells, MacCoshams, Munros and others who worked the land over the centuries had 4000 acres of hill grazing. Most of that has today disappeared under conifer plantations. The cottages and barns are furnished and equipped as in past centuries, and a visitor centre illustrates the hard work and simple recreations of the farming families mentioned in estate records as long as 500 years ago.

June-Aug, daily; Apr, May and Sept, daily exc Sat. Adm charge. Refreshments. Shop. **P** *Toilets. Tel Furnace (049 95) 235.*

AUCHINLECK BOSWELL MUSEUM

On A76, 1½ miles north-east of Cumnock (Db)

It was from James Boswell's family home, Auchinleck House, that he and Dr Johnson set off in 1773 on their tour of the Hebrides. The old parish church is now a Boswell museum, with portraits and mementos. James himself lies buried in the family mausoleum alongside. The museum also commemorates another son of Auchinleck: William Murdoch, the 18th-century pioneer of gas lighting.

Apr-Sept, Mon-Fri. Free entry. **P** *Tel Cumnock (0290) 21185.*

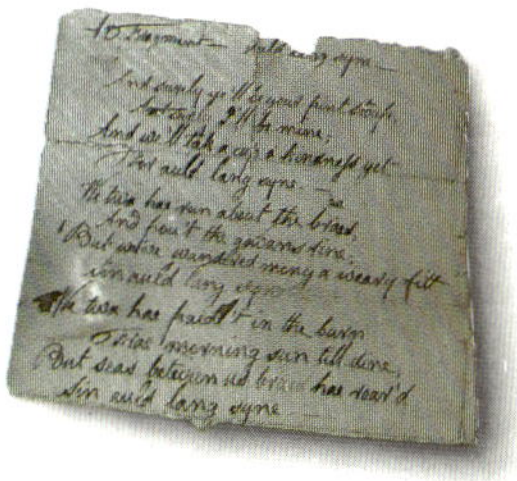

AULD LANG SYNE *The song sung the world over on New Year's Eve was written by Robert Burns, and a fragment of his original manuscript is on display in the Burns Cottage Museum.*

THE BACHELORS' CLUB

On B730 at Tarbolton, 9 miles east of Ayr (Db)

During his twenties Robert Burns, the poet and local farmer's son, spent much of his leisure time in Tarbolton. In an upstairs room in a building close to the village inn, he attended a dancing class and founded a weekly debating society called The Bachelors' Club. The thatched and whitewashed building is now a Burns museum. There are relics of the company-loving poet here, and a reminder that his first satire, *Death and Dr Hornbrook*, was about the Tarbolton schoolmaster's optimistic belief in his own skills as an apothecary.

NTS. Apr-Oct, pm daily. Adm charge. Toilets. Tel Tarbolton (0292) 541940.

BALLOCH CASTLE COUNTRY PARK

Off A811, 4 miles north of Dumbarton (Dc)

There was a confident air about the city fathers of Glasgow during the First World War; in the middle of hostilities they bought the Loch Lomondside estate around Balloch Castle, and it has remained a public park ever since. The present castle, built in 1808, serves as a visitor centre.

A colourful walled garden is half-hidden in the grounds, unusual specimen trees flourish in the ornamental woodlands, and sweeping picnic lawns offer beautiful views of Loch Lomond and its surrounding mountains.

All year, daily (Visitor Centre, Easter-Sept). Free entry. Refreshments. P *Toilets.* ♿ *Tel Alexandria (0389) 58216.*

BONAWE IRON FURNACE

Off B845, 12 miles east of Oban (Cd)

In an unexpected setting beside a sea loch in the mountains, Bonawe was the most successful of the Highland charcoal ironworks. It was founded in 1753 by a company from Furness in Lancashire, which shipped in the ore from Ulverston; the furnace was heated by charcoal made in the local oak and birchwoods.

Most of the buildings on the hillside site have been carefully restored. An exhibition describes charcoal-fired iron smelting, as well as life at Bonawe and how the woodlands of nearby Glen Nant were harvested to provide the charcoal.

HBM. Apr-Sept, daily. Adm charge. P *(limited). Tel Edinburgh (031) 244 3101.*

BRODICK CASTLE AND COUNTRY PARK

On A841, 1½ miles north of Brodick, Isle of Arran (Cb)

For generations Brodick Castle was the heart of the Isle of Arran estate of the wealthy Dukes of Hamilton. The striking red-sandstone building is noted for fine plasterwork ceilings, furniture, porcelain, portraits and silver.

Brodick's 60 acre gardens include one of the finest rhododendron collections in Europe. Footpaths wander past a Victorian rose garden, through woodlands where red squirrels live safely in territory not yet invaded by the grey. A more strenuous footpath climbs over open ground to the 2866ft summit of Goatfell.

Near the castle entrance, the Isle of Arran Heritage Museum's buildings include a blacksmith's shop, stables and a harness room, a milk house and a turn-of-the-century cottage.

Castle: NTS. Mid Apr-Sept, daily; early Oct, Mon, Wed and Sat, pm. Adm charge. Refreshments. Shop. P *Toilets.* ♿ *Country Park: NTS. All year, daily. Adm charge. Refreshments. Shop.* P *Toilets.* ♿ *Tel Brodick (0770) 2202. Museum: May-Sept, Mon-Fri. Adm charge. Refreshments.* P *Toilets.* ♿ *Tel (0770) 2636.*

BURNS COTTAGE AND MUSEUM

On B7024 at Alloway, 3 miles south of Ayr (Cb)

Few literary figures are so inextricably connected with a single place, in both life and work, as Robert Burns is with Alloway. Scotland's national poet was born on January 25, 1759, in the cottage his nurseryman father had built. Thatched and whitewashed, the cottage still has some of the family's original furniture, while the adjoining museum houses many of Burns's manuscripts, letters and books.

The nearby Land o'Burns Centre explains the way of life of the Ayrshire farming community in which Burns grew up.

Cottage, Museum: All year, daily exc Sun Nov-Mar. Adm charge. Refreshments. Shop. P *Toilets.* ♿ *Tel Alloway (0292) 41215. Land o'Burns Centre: All year, daily. Free entry. Refreshments. Shop.* P *Toilets.* ♿ *Tel (0292) 43700.*

BONNIE BANKS *From Conic Hill, north-east of Balloch Castle, there is a magnificent view of snow-capped mountains crenellating the skyline on the western banks of Loch Lomond, Britain's largest lake.*

HOOFS TO THE PLOUGH *Traditional methods are still used to till the land around Auchindrain Folklife Museum. Fields now being reclaimed used to be shared by several families working in partnership.*

BURNS HOUSE MUSEUM

On A76 at Mauchline, 7 miles north-east of Cumnock (Db)

Robert Burns farmed for a time at Mauchline, and wrote some of his best-remembered verses there. He rented part of a stone-built house in the village for his wife Jean Armour, and the building is now the Burns House Museum. Jean's upstairs room has been kept intact and furnished in the style of the period, and there is a large collection of Burnsiana and folk objects.

Easter-Oct, daily. Adm charge. Refreshments. Shop. P *Toilets. Tel Mauchline (0290) 50045.*

BURRELL COLLECTION

Pollok Country Park, Glasgow (Db)

Glasgow was amazingly fortunate in the benefactions which grouped the 8000-piece Burrell Collection in the same 361 acre parkland as Pollok House. Sir William Burrell's art collection – of ceramics, bronzes, Oriental jade, tapestries, silver and glassware, furniture, needlework, prints and paintings – is the most valuable ever handed over freely into the public domain.

Sir William's original gift was in 1944, but it

DANCING FEET *The painting* The Rehearsal *by the French artist Edgar Degas is one of the treasures of the Burrell Collection. Degas found in the world of ballet the subjects for many of his finest paintings.*

was only in 1983 that a purpose-built gallery was completed to house it. And the gallery itself is a work of art. Ornamental doorways and arches from the collection fulfil their original functions in its inner and outer walls, and many pieces from the extensive stained-glass collection are mounted against south-facing windows.

Round three sides of a courtyard, the main rooms of Sir William's home at Hutton Castle have been re-created. The courtyard centres on the Warwick Vase, reconstructed from fragments of a massive garden ornament which used to stand in the grounds of Emperor Hadrian's villa at Tivoli near Rome.

The problem of finding a site for a Burrell gallery was solved in 1966 when the Maxwell Macdonald family made a gift of the fine Georgian mansion of Pollok House and the woods and parkland around it. The house itself is now a museum with one of the most important collections of Spanish paintings in Britain.

The remainder of the estate forms Pollok Country Park, centred on the Old Stables Courtyard beside a weir on the White Cart Water. An interpretation centre explains and illustrates Pollok's history and wildlife, and its natural-history trails.

Burrell Collection: All year, daily exc Sun am. Free entry. Refreshments. Shop. P *Toilets.* ♿ *Tel Glasgow (041) 649 7151. Pollok House: All year, daily. Free entry. Refreshments. Shop.* P *Toilets.* ♿ *Tel (041) 632 0274.*

CLIFFTOP CASTLE *Towers, turrets and battlements give an air of fairy-tale splendour to Culzean Castle. Within the romantic shell is a sumptuous Georgian mansion built by Robert Adam for the 10th Earl of Cassillis.*

CHATELHERAULT COUNTRY PARK

Off A72, 1½ miles south-east of Hamilton (Db)

The Dukes of Hamilton are also Dukes of Chatelherault in France, so it was not eccentric for the 5th Duke to give a French name to the highly ornate shooting lodge William Adam designed for him in 1732. It still stands in Hamilton High Parks, all ornamental archways and roof decorations, the centrepiece of one of Scotland's newest country parks. A visitor centre has been built in the old dog kennels. Open hillside slopes gently up to the lodge, while behind it the winding 2 mile gorge of the Avon Water, wooded to the skyline and with 10 miles of footpaths, makes it hard to believe that Scotland's industrial heartland is only a few minutes' drive away.

All year, daily.

CORNALEES BRIDGE CENTRE

Off A78, 8 miles south of Greenock (Cc)

A brilliantly engineered water scheme opened in 1827 to supply Greenock's textile mills and other industries. Its reservoirs, sluices and 'cuts' or narrow water channels were designed by Robert Thom. The original outflow was through a series of sluices at Cornalees Bridge. The story of the whole imaginative scheme is explained and illustrated in the visitor centre here – one of several in the 30,000 acre Clyde Muirshiel Regional Park – and there are also displays on the local wildlife.

All year, daily.

CRARAE GLEN GARDEN

On A83, 10 miles south-west of Inveraray (Cc)

Three generations of 20th-century Campbell lairds created one of Scotland's finest woodland gardens in a glen down which a West Highland burn tumbles to Loch Fyne. Rhododendrons abound and the taller sheltering trees have been thinned to open up the garden floor. Footbridges link up networks of pathways on both sides of the glen.

All year, daily. Adm charge. P *Toilets.* ♿ *Tel Minard (0546) 86633.*

CULZEAN CASTLE AND COUNTRY PARK

Off A719, 12 miles south-west of Ayr (Ca)

On a clifftop site 150ft above the sea and backed by more than 500 acres of gardens, fields and woodlands, Culzean is one of the finest Scottish properties open to the public. The castle, once the home of the Kennedy Marquises of Ailsa, contains some of Robert Adam's most splendid work, including the supremely elegant oval staircase he created in what was originally a gloomy and sunless courtyard between two buildings.

BLACK SHEEP *Relics in Duart Castle tell the story of James Maclean, who turned to highway robbery in the 18th century and became known as 'The Gentleman Highwayman'. He was hanged at Tyburn in 1750.*

Among the lavishly furnished public rooms, probably the star attraction is the circular first-floor Saloon, with windows looking out over the Firth of Clyde to the granite stack of Ailsa Craig, from which the Kennedys took their title.

Adam also designed the attractive Home Farm complex round four sides of a courtyard, which has been renovated as the visitor centre for Culzean Country Park. The ground floor of one building, originally a cart house, includes a model of the estate. In the upper rooms – once a tractorman's house and a hayloft – presentations trace the history of the Kennedy family and the creation of the present-day estate.

Culzean's extensive grounds include walled and terraced gardens, and ornamental estate buildings such as the Victorian acetylene Gas House. Its woodlands are crisscrossed by 17 miles of footpaths. Jays, warblers, woodcock and woodpeckers are all established here, and the Swan Lake also has nesting colonies of moorhen, mallard, coot and grebe.

NTS. Apr-Oct, daily. Adm charge. Refreshments. Shop. P *Toilets.* ♿ *Tel Kirkoswald (065 56) 274.*

DEAN CASTLE AND COUNTRY PARK

Dean Road, Kilmarnock (Db)

The Lords of Kilmarnock held sway over their estates from this 14th-century stronghold on the outskirts of the town. The castle was burned out in 1735, remained in ruins until Edwardian times and then was meticulously restored. Although a modern copy of a 16th-century gatehouse was added for effect, the restoration respected the integrity of the original castle, built around a courtyard of which the stone keep of 1350 forms one side. The first floor, for instance, retains not only the Great Hall with its minstrels' gallery but also the entrance to a fearsome dungeon. In the castle are valuable collections of Brussels tapestries, of arms and armour, and of fine early musical instruments.

The restored Dower House contains the visitor centre for a 200 acre country park, with waymarked nature trails, a walled garden and a pinetum.

All year, daily. Adm charge. Refreshments. Shop. P *Toilets.* ♿ *(parts). Tel Kilmarnock (0563) 26401 or 34580. Park: Free entry. Tel (0563) 22702.*

DUART CASTLE

Off A849, at Duart Point, Island of Mull (Bd)

The Clan Maclean chiefs' stronghold was built on a low clifftop where Loch Linnhe, the Firth of Lorn and the Sound of Mull form an impressive and significant junction of seaways. Duart is visited by Macleans from all over the world, and its Scout Exhibition recalls that the present Lord Maclean was Chief Scout of the Commonwealth.

Earlier this century, when Duart Castle was rebuilt from a tumbledown ruin, the Victorian Duart House across the bay was renamed Torosay Castle. It has pleasant walled and terraced gardens with fine seaward views. Also on Mull, 20 miles north of Duart, is the Old Byre Heritage Centre, with displays of crofting and farming life before and after the Highland Clearances.

BOXES, BOTTLES AND BINS *A reconstructed grocer's shop from the late 19th century in Gladstone Court Street Museum recalls the days when household goods were measured out on brass scales.*

Duart Castle: May-Sept, daily. Adm charge. Refreshments. P *Toilets.* ♿ *(parts). Tel Craignure (068 02) 309. Torosay Castle: Apr-Sept, daily (garden all year, daily). Adm charge. Refreshments. Shop.* P *Toilets.* ♿ *(part). Tel (068 02) 421. Old Byre: Easter-mid Oct, daily. Adm charge. Refreshments. Shop.* P *Toilets. Tel Dervaig (068 84) 229.*

GLADSTONE COURT STREET MUSEUM

Off High Street, Biggar (Eb)

This museum includes many old-style shopfronts from the town. The reduced-size shops behind are furnished as they were when used by the local grocer, printer, druggist, watchmaker, ironmonger, dressmaker, joiner and photographer.

Moat Park Heritage Centre recalls the history of the surrounding district in books, documents and illustrations, and the story of the dangerous times when Church and State came into violent conflict in 17th-century Scotland is told in the Greenhill Covenanter's House. Biggar's original coal-burning gasworks, built in 1839, is also preserved as a museum.

Museum: Apr-Oct, daily. Adm charge. Shop. P *Toilets.* ♿ *Tel Biggar (0899) 21050. Centre: All year, daily. Adm charge. Shop.* P *Toilets.* ♿ *Tel (0899) 21050. House: Apr-Oct, daily. Adm charge. Shop.* P ♿ *(parts). Tel (0899) 21050. Gasworks Museum: July-Sept, daily. Free entry. Shop.* P ♿ *Tel Edinburgh (031) 225 7534.*

GLASGOW ART GALLERY AND MUSEUM

Kelvingrove Park, Glasgow (Db)

Canvases by Rembrandt and Giorgione are among hundreds of paintings from major British and European schools housed in this red-sandstone building in Kelvingrove Park. The gallery also contains the Art Nouveau furniture designs of Charles Rennie Mackintosh and displays of glass, porcelain, pottery and silver. The exhibits in the museum include fossils of dinosaurs and other creatures.

All year, daily. Free entry. Refreshments. Shop. P *Toilets.* ♿ *Tel Glasgow (041) 357 3929.*

THE HILL HOUSE

Upper Colquhoun Street, Helensburgh (Cc)

Standing high above the Firth of Clyde, this is – inside and out – one of the finest house designs by the architect Charles Rennie Mackintosh. It was completed in 1904 for the publisher Walter Blackie, and includes neat little details such as an alcove where the children of the house could dress up and put on plays.

NTS. All year, pm daily. Adm charge. P *Tel Helensburgh (0436) 3900.*

HUNTERIAN MUSEUM AND ART GALLERY

University Avenue, Glasgow (Db)

Opened in 1807, the Hunterian in Glasgow University houses one of the world's finest collections of coins and medals, going back more than 2000 years. The museum's other main displays include archaeological and geological finds. The Hunterian Art Gallery, in a separate building opposite the university, has paintings by Chardin, Rembrandt, Reynolds, Pissarro, Sisley and Stubbs.

Museum: All year, Mon-Fri; also Sat am. Free entry. Refreshments. Shop. P *(limited). Toilets. Tel Glasgow (041) 330 4221. Art Gallery: All year, Mon-Fri; also Sat am. Free entry. Shop.* P *(limited). Toilets.* ♿ *Tel (041) 330 5431.*

INVERARAY CASTLE

Off A819, at Inveraray (Cc)

In the 18th century, the Dukes of Argyll commissioned a new castle at Inveraray and replaced the

MODEL VILLAGE ON THE CLYDE

Emptied of cars and people, the view of New Lanark today could easily be an early 19th-century artist's picture. The cluster of 18th-century buildings in the steeply wooded valley below the Falls of Clyde is being preserved as a living memorial to what was once the largest cotton-spinning complex in Britain, and a place of pioneering social experiment.

The idea of harnessing the Falls of Clyde to power a mill was the inspiration of David Dale and Richard Arkwright, inventor of the spinning frame. But New Lanark is better known as the place where Dale's son-in-law Robert Owen, who became manager in 1800, developed his revolutionary social theories. Owen's workers, though strictly disciplined, were provided with good housing and dormitory accommodation for the apprentices, a cooperative store, an excellent school, and an adult education and social centre with the resounding name of 'New Institution for the Formation of Character'. In the context of its time, this was enlightened capitalism indeed.

The mills closed in 1968, but nearly all the major buildings – in elegant Georgian style – survive. Up to 2500 people lived in the village and there is still a resident population – so this is no seasonal museum piece. The Institution and Mill Number 3 have been converted into a visitor centre, with displays on the cotton industry and the social history of New Lanark. Owen's school, in which children from one to ten were taught with kindness and without punishments, can still be seen; so can the Mill Lade, a 300yd tunnel which brought water from the Clyde to power New Lanark's mill wheels.

The village dyeworks now forms a visitor centre of another kind, illustrating the natural history of the Falls of Clyde Nature Reserve, which includes both banks of the wooded gorge through which the Clyde reaches New Lanark. The centre is just downstream from the lowest fall, Dundaff Linn. Binoculars are provided, and visitors may see dippers bobbing up and down on the flat rocks immediately outside or splashing down for food in the river. Woodland walks follow both banks of the gorge, which is spanned by a bridge above Corra Linn and Bonnington Linn, out of sight of the village. Some paths skirt the water's edge, and others follow the rim of the gorge.

In normal conditions, Bonnington and Corra Linns are bypassed as part of a hydro-electric scheme, and only a trickle of water passes through the upper gorge. However, on four advertised days every year – usually in April, June, August and September – the tunnels are closed and suddenly the majestic gorge is filled with spray and crashing water.

Off A73, 1/2 mile south of Lanark (Eb). Village Centre: HBM. All year, daily. Free entry. Refreshments. Shop. P *Toilets. Tel Lanark (0555) 61345. Reserve Centre: Easter-Oct, daily; Oct-Easter, Sat and Sun. Adm charge. Shop.* P *Toilets.* ♿ *Tel (0555) 65262.*

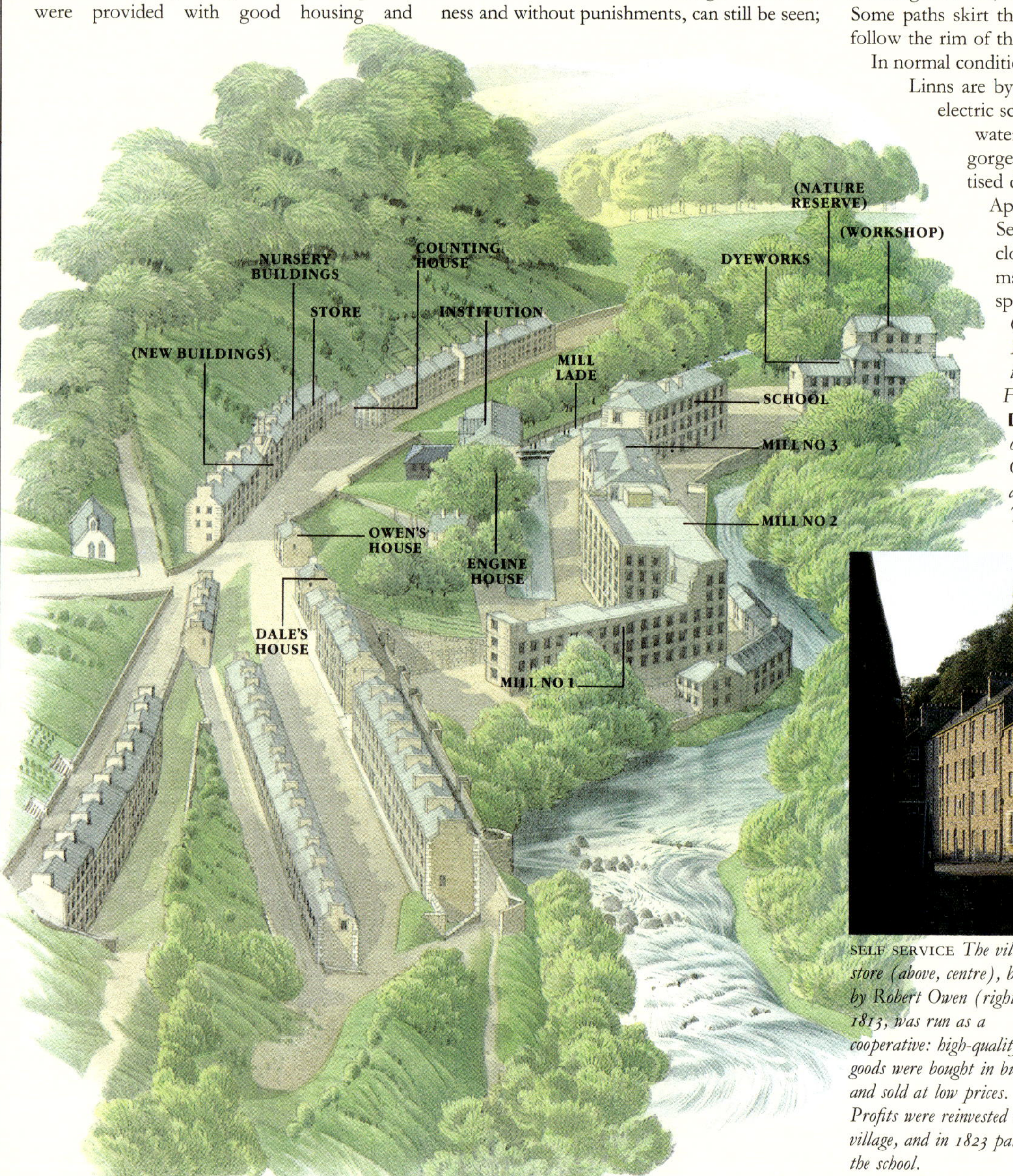

SELF SERVICE *The village store (above, centre), built by Robert Owen (right) in 1813, was run as a cooperative: high-quality goods were bought in bulk and sold at low prices. Profits were reinvested in the village, and in 1823 paid for the school.*

ramshackle settlement which had cluttered the site with a planned town on the shore of Loch Fyne. The castle's State Dining Room and Drawing Room have beautiful ceiling decorations, tapestries and wall panellings in a style fashionable in pre-Revolutionary Paris. Circular turret rooms include one with a fine display of Derby, Meissen and Oriental porcelain. The airy, light-painted Armoury Hall displays more than 1300 pole-arms, muskets, dirks and fearsome Lochaber axes, and its high ceiling is painted with Campbell armorial shields.

At Cherry Park, close to the castle, is a Combined Operations Museum. With photographs, models, guarded contemporary newspaper reports and later reminiscences, this tells the remarkable story of Inveraray's Second World War role as HMS *Quebec*, where a quarter of a million soldiers, sailors, airmen and marines were trained in coastal assault techniques.

Castle: July-Aug, daily; May-June and Sept-mid Oct, daily exc Fri. Adm charge. Refreshments. Shop. P *Toilets.* ♿ *Tel Inveraray (0499) 2203. Museum: July-Aug, daily; May-June, Aug-Sept, daily exc Fri. Adm charge. Shop.* P *(limited). Toilets.* ♿ *Tel (0499) 2203.*

KELBURN COUNTRY CENTRE

Off A78, 1 mile south of Largs (Cb)

This historic estate of the Earls of Glasgow lies in a steep and wooded glen down which the Kel Burn cascades from moorland 1000ft above. There are beautiful winding walks and spectacular views over the Firth of Clyde. There is a walled garden known as The Plaisance and a formal Children's Garden. Kelburn Castle, the focal point of the estate, has been the home of the Boyle family – since 1703 the Earls of Glasgow – for more than 800 years.

Easter-Sept, daily; Oct-Easter, Sat and Sun. Castle: late Apr-late May only, daily guided tours. Adm charge. Refreshments. Shop. P *Toilets. Tel Fairlie (047 556) 685.*

KILMUN ARBORETUM

On A880, 5 miles north of Dunoon (Cc)

Plots first planted in 1930 sweep up sharply from the Holy Loch. Pathways climb through plantations of larch, spruce, hemlock, cypress, cedar and pine, to glorious viewpoints. There is a fine collection of dawn redwoods – trees which were known only from fossil remains until living specimens were discovered in 1945 in China.

FC. All year, daily. Free entry.

LIVINGSTONE NATIONAL MEMORIAL

Off A724 at Blantyre, 4½ miles north of Hamilton (Db)

The Victorian missionary-explorer David Livingstone was born and bred in Shuttle Row, an 18th-century block of mill tenements, which has been lovingly restored among lawns and parkland by the River Clyde. He lived there as a schoolboy and while studying to be a doctor. The building now contains maps, models, murals, tableaux and audiovisual displays of his journeys from Scotland to the heart of Africa.

All year, daily. Adm charge. Refreshments (Easter-Oct). Shop. P *Toilets.* ♿ *Tel Blantyre (0698) 823140.*

MUIRSHIEL COUNTRY PARK

Off B786, 9 miles south of Port Glasgow (Cb)

Set in a high valley above moorland, the park consists of conifer and deciduous woods mixed with rhododendron thickets. One waymarked trail from the visitor centre explores woodlands in which roe deer can be seen; another takes in Muirshiel's varied habitats, ranging from pond and woods to rocky riverside.

All year, daily. Free entry.

PAISLEY ABBEY

High Street, Paisley (Db)

This abbey, founded in 1163, has been carefully restored in the present century, with soaring nave and choir, fine stone carvings and woodcarvings, beautiful modern stained-glass windows and one of the finest church organs in Europe.

Paisley Museum houses a display of more than 800 Paisley-pattern shawls, based on designs which can be traced back more than 2000 years. The Sma' Shot Cottages have been restored as a typical Victorian artisan's house. The 'small shot' was a hidden linking thread in the cloth.

Abbey: All year, daily. Free entry. Shop. Toilets. ♿ *Tel Glasgow (041) 889 7654. Museum: All year, daily exc Sun. Free entry. Shop. Tel (041) 889 3151.*

PEOPLE'S PALACE

Glasgow Green, Glasgow (Db)

Opened in 1898 as a cultural centre for Glasgow's East Enders, this handsome red-sandstone museum recalls the city's many industries, from the 18th-century tobacco and textile trade with the American colonies, through pottery and printing to stained glass, ornamental ironwork and heavy engineering. But the main theme of the displays is political. Broadsheets, posters, documents, flags and banners recall the days when the city was heavily involved in the fight for trades unions, the extension of the franchise and the cause of the suffragettes.

All year, daily. Free entry. Refreshments. Shop. P *Toilets. Tel Glasgow (041) 554 0223.*

SEA LIFE CENTRE

On A828, 10 miles north of Oban (Cd)

Visitors to this imaginatively laid-out aquarium may come to feel that their function is to keep the 2000 or so inmates interested, and not the other way round, for eye-to-eye contact with fiercer specimens like the razor-toothed conger eel can be chilling. The centre is built on several levels, and one stairway leads down to the transparent side of the seal tank. Another area explains the increasingly successful West Highland industry of fish-farming.

Apr-Oct, daily. Adm charge. Refreshments. Shop. P *Toilets.* ♿ *Tel Ledaig (063 172) 386.*

SOUTER JOHNNIE'S COTTAGE

On A77, 4 miles south-west of Maybole (Ca)

In the summer of 1775 young Robert Burns caroused in Kirkoswald's inn with a lively crew, which included the farmer, maltster and smuggler Douglas Graham, of Shanter Farm, and the local souter, or shoemaker, John Davidson. Many years later, Burns put them both into his popular ballad *Tam o'Shanter*. Davidson's thatched cottage is now a Burns museum, with relics of his time and lifelike figures of Souter Johnnie, Tam, the innkeeper and his wife.

NTS. Apr-Oct, pm daily. Adm charge. Toilets. Tel Kirkoswald (065 56) 603.

SUMMERLEE HERITAGE PARK

West Canal Street, Coatbridge (Db)

From the mid-18th century onwards, Coatbridge developed into virtually the iron and steel capital of Scotland. The furnaces are long since cold, but the old Summerlee Ironworks has today been transformed into an industrial heritage park. A huge new exhibition hall houses restored machinery from furnaces, foundries and coal mines, working tinsmith's and brassfounder's shops, and reconstructed Victorian houses. Outside, a tramway runs round the 25 acre site, and a branch of James Watt's 18th-century Monklands Canal has been reopened.

All year, daily. Adm charge. Refreshments. Shop. P *Toilets.* ♿ *Tel Coatbridge (0236) 31261.*

YOUNGER BOTANIC GARDEN

Off A815, 7 miles north-west of Dunoon (Cc)

Overlooked by the mountains beside Loch Eck, this beautiful, 120 acre garden, an out-station of the Royal Botanic Garden, Edinburgh, has more than 250 species of rhododendron, and the stately soft-barked giants of its Wellingtonia avenue soar to an impressive 150ft. Trees such as Scots pine, spruce and larch have been planted here since 1820, and by 1883 the slopes of the surrounding valley were clothed with almost 6½ million trees. Waymarked walks lead round the garden, past a pond where golden orfe dart and up to a lofty viewpoint over Holy Loch.

Apr-Oct, daily. Adm charge. Refreshments. P *Toilets.* ♿ *Tel Dunoon (0369) 6261.*

REGIONAL CALENDAR

May (early). Oban: Music and Dance Festival.

May (late). Cardross: Dumbarton County Show.

June (early). Ayrshire: Burns Arts Festival.

June (mid-month). Glasgow: Horse Show and County Fair. Lesmahagow: Highland Games.

June (2nd week). Lanark: Lanimer Day (horse racing, Highland Games).

July (mid-month). Balloch and Inveraray: Highland Games.

July (late). Luss, Tobermory and Taynuilt: Highland Games. Culzean Castle: Country Fair.

August (mid-month). Bute: Highland Festival. Culzean Castle: Festival of Flowers and Music.

August (late). Irvine: Marymas Festival. Dunoon: Cowal Highland Gathering.

September (mid-month). Ayr: Gold Cup race. Glasgow: Marathon.

December 31 Biggar: Ne'erday Bonfire.

Tourist information: Ayr (0292) 248196; Glasgow (041) 227 4880; Girvan (0465) 4950; Kilmarnock (0563) 39090; Largs (0475) 673765; Oban (0631) 63122.

TAYSIDE

CRADLE OF SCOTTISH NATIONHOOD AMID A CIRCLET OF CASTLES

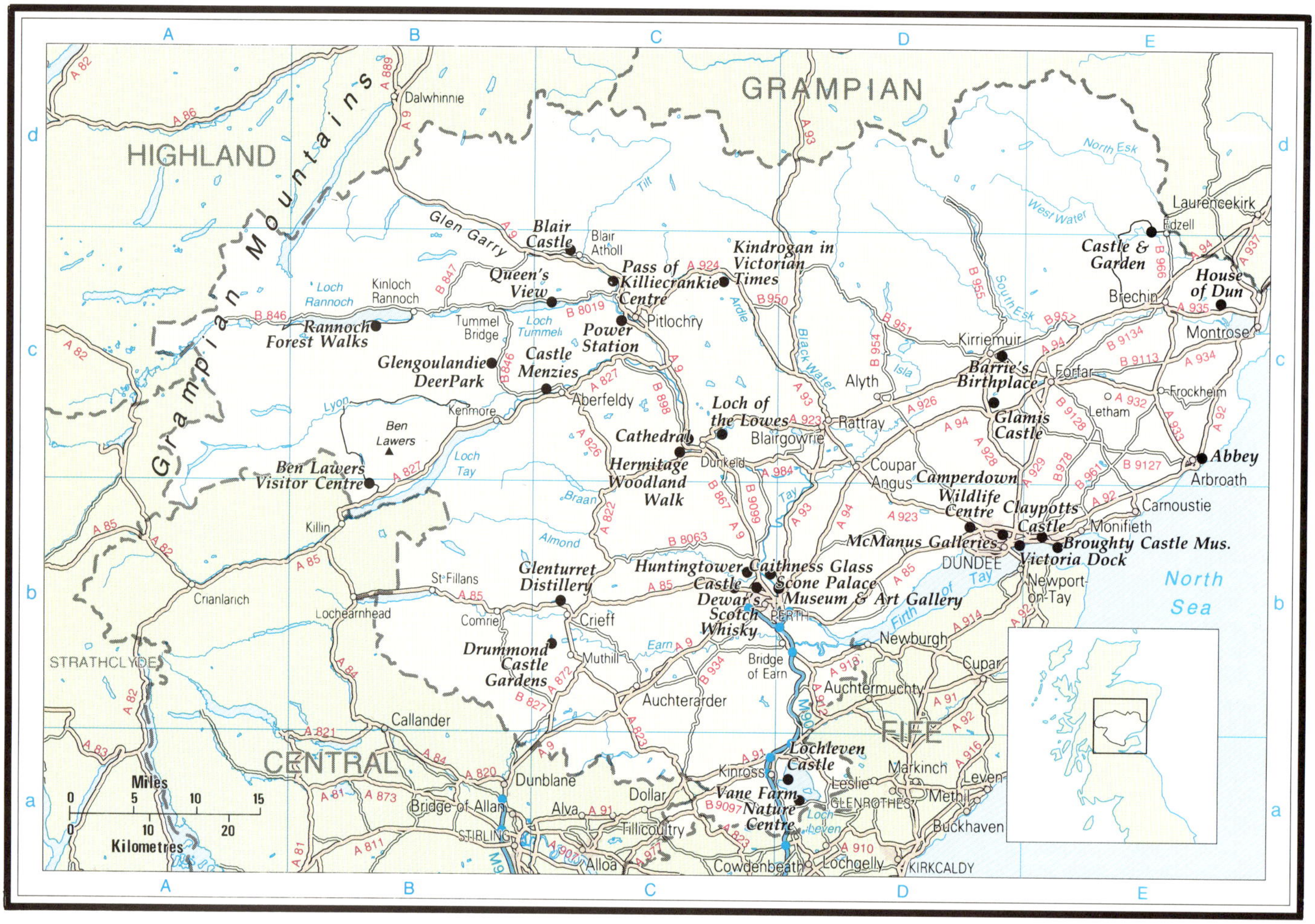

No region has closer associations with the history of Scotland as an independent nation than Tayside. At Arbroath Abbey, Robert Bruce signed Scotland's Declaration of Independence; at Scone the new nation's monarchs were crowned; at Lochleven Castle, Mary, Queen of Scots was imprisoned. In later years the Jacobites won a famous victory at the Pass of Killiecrankie, only to be repelled at Dunkeld.

But Tayside has a gentler face too. Wooded hills, where deer roam, slope up from Loch Tummel and Loch Rannoch. Set in commanding positions are a series of great houses with lovely parks and gardens – among them Blair Castle, home of Britain's only private army, and Glamis Castle, childhood home of the Queen Mother.

At the coast there are reminders of whalers and of warships in the golden age of sail, and the little town of Kirriemuir preserves a permanent memorial to J.M. Barrie, the writer best known as the creator of the immortal Peter Pan.

ARBROATH ABBEY

In centre of Arbroath (Ec)

Although the 12th-century Arbroath Abbey fell victim to neglect and plundering in the 17th century, enough of it remains to testify to its former grandeur. The towering gable of the south transept with its high circular window – the 'O of Arbroath', once lit as a mariners' beacon – is richly ornamental with three tiers of wall arcading. Its one surviving great gateway was designed both as a stout defence and an indication of the magnificence that lay inside. Parts of the nave and presbytery have survived, as well as much of the sacristy, off which can be found the so-called Jenny Batter's Hole – a chamber where lunatics were locked away in the 18th century.

The abbey was founded in 1178 by King William the Lion, who lies buried in front of the high altar. In 1320, Robert Bruce signed Scotland's Declaration of Independence in the abbey.

Beside Arbroath's harbour, a museum in the former signal tower to The Bellrock Lighthouse traces the history of the town. It covers the building of the lighthouse and local industries such as fishing, linen-weaving, shoemaking and engineering.

Abbey: HBM. All year, daily. Adm charge. P *(limited). Tel Edinburgh (031) 244 3101. Museum: July-Aug, daily; Jan-June, Sept-Dec, daily exc Sun. Free entry. Shop.* P *Toilets. Tel Arbroath (0241) 75598.*

BARRIE'S BIRTHPLACE

9 Brechin Road, Kirriemuir (Dc)

On May 9, 1860, James Matthew Barrie – Scotland's greatest playwright and the creator of Peter Pan – was born in this four-roomed cottage in a modest corner of the town known as the Tenements. The youngest son of a hand-loom weaver, he spent the first eight years of his life in the house – which had an upstairs kitchen next to his parents' bedroom, and his father's linen-making workshop on the ground floor. Barrie died in 1937 and was buried in the hill cemetery at Kirriemuir, a short walk from his birthplace. Today his old home has been lovingly preserved as a museum; its original cottage atmosphere has been retained and the outside wash-house, with its original wash boiler and wooden stool, still stands.

NTS. Easter weekend, then May-Sept, daily. Adm charge. Refreshments. Tel Kirriemuir (0575) 72646.

BEN LAWERS VISITOR CENTRE

Off A827, 16 miles south-west of Kenmore (Bb)

The national nature reserve lies on the southern flanks of the Lawers range, which rises to 3984ft above sea level. It is noted for its rich variety of alpine plants and wide selection of mammals and birds. The visitor centre, beneath the looming mass of Beinn Ghlas, has an audiovisual programme and displays on the geology and flora of the area. A nature trail starts at the centre.
NTS NCC. Apr-Sept, daily. Adm charge. P *Toilets. Tel Killin (056 72) 397.*

BLAIR CASTLE

Off B847, 1 mile north of Blair Atholl (Cc)

A great avenue of lime trees leads from the main road to the white, roughcast façade of a storybook castle set beneath forest-clad mountains above the River Garry. Over the past 700 years, Blair has changed its architectural appearance several times, reflecting the tastes of different generations and making good the damage done by various attackers. Standing unchanged is the main tower, named Cumming's Tower after John Cumming of Badenoch, who began building the castle in 1269. Today, Blair's 32 rooms are packed with fine furniture, paintings, arms and costumes which present a stirring picture of Highland life from the 1500s to the present day. The castle is the home of the 10th Duke of Atholl, the commander-in-chief of Britain's only private army, the Atholl Highlanders.

In the lofty entrance hall is a large collection of rifles, swords, crossbows and powder horns; and on a table by the door is a framed section of the flooring from the top of Cumming's Tower bearing the marks of the red-hot shot fired at the roof during a siege by the Jacobites in 1746. It was the last castle in Britain to be besieged.

Blair Castle Craft Centre, by the entrance to the castle grounds, sells locally made jewellery, horn spoons and cutlery, shepherds' crooks and horn-handled walking sticks, and knitwear in Arran and Icelandic wools. Next door is the Atholl Country Collection, recalling the daily life of villagers in Glen Garry in bygone times. Exhibits include a blacksmith's 'smiddy', a crofter's stable and byre, and his living room with its box bed.

A short distance away, down by the River Garry, is Blair Atholl Mill, a working water mill dating from 1613. Visitors can see the milling room, where oatmeal and wholemeal are milled in the traditional way, and freshly baked bread and scones can be bought.
Castle: Easter week; mid Apr, Sun and Mon; end Apr-mid Oct, daily. Adm charge. Refreshments. Shop. P *Toilets.* ♿ *Tel Blair Atholl (079 681) 207. Craft Centre: June-Oct, daily. Free entry. Shop.* P *Tel (079 681) 409. Country Collection: Late May-mid Oct, pm daily; also am July and Aug. Adm charge. Shop.* P *Toilets.* ♿ *Tel (079 681) 232. Mill: Apr-Oct, daily exc Sun am. Adm charge. Refreshments. Shop. Toilets. Tel (079 681) 321.*

BROUGHTY CASTLE MUSEUM

At Broughty Ferry, 5 miles east of Dundee (Eb)

Standing on a rocky spur overlooking the River Tay, Broughty Castle was a military strongpoint from 1547 to 1945. Its occupants once levied tolls from ships entering the Tay and controlled the lucrative ferry linking it with Fife. The story of Broughty Ferry, and of Dundee's former whaling industry, is told in the castle's museum, which also has exhibits of seashore wildlife and the natural history of the Tay.
HBM. All year, Mon-Thur and Sat; also Sun, July-Sept. Free entry. P *Tel Dundee (0382) 23141.*

CAITHNESS GLASS

At Inveralmond, just north of Perth (Cb)

The intricate art of glass paperweight-making can be watched in this factory. On weekdays visitors can watch craftsmen shaping molten glass into the delicately patterned paperweights. There is a collectors' gallery, and a factory shop selling glassware and other local craft products.
Visitor Centre: All year, daily. Free entry. Refreshments. Shop. P *Toilets.* ♿ *Tel Perth (0738) 37373.*

CAMPERDOWN WILDLIFE CENTRE

Off A923, 3 miles north-west of Dundee (Db)

The rare European brown bear, usually found only in remote mountain regions, is one of the main attractions of a wildlife centre covering some 400 acres of wooded parkland. There are roe deer, weasels, stoats, squirrels, owls, kestrels and woodpeckers, and examples of other now extinct British species, ranging from reindeer to northern lynx. The North American raccoon scoops fish from shallow water with its paws.
All year, daily. Adm charge. Refreshments. Shop. P *Toilets. Tel Dundee (0382) 623555.*

CASTLE MENZIES

On B846, 1 mile west of Aberfeldy (Cc)

The tall, 16th-century castle commanding the road to Loch Rannoch and Loch Tay is the seat of the Chiefs of Clan Menzies. With two towers, a central block and four storeys, the fortress was spacious. The vaulted chambers of the ground floor contained the kitchen and guard rooms; the large hall on the first floor was the castle's social centre, while the private apartments and guest chambers above include the room in which Bonnie Prince Charlie slept on his way to

PICTURES AND MUSIC *Quadrilles dedicated to the Duchess of Atholl lie open in the drawing room of Blair Castle. Above is a portrait of the 4th duke.*

STORYTELLER *J.M. Barrie's photograph, books, spectacles, pipe, tobacco pouch and tobacco jar are among the mementos of the writer on view at his birthplace in Kirriemuir.*

Culloden in 1746. A copper cast of his death mask is on display.

The castle was built in 1488, and added to over the next 400 years – and its 18th-century entrance has a Victorian porch. To the right of it is the much smaller original entrance, with a 16th-century marriage shield above it. Inside, the large main rooms have been restored and, with their decorated plaster ceilings, look much as they did in the early 17th century.

Apr-Sept, daily. Adm charge. Shop. P *Toilets. Tel Aberfeldy (0887) 20982.*

CLAYPOTTS CASTLE

Off A92, 1 mile north-west of Broughty Ferry (Eb)

Tall, round towers capped by square garrets give this small and well-preserved fortress its distinctive appearance. It was built in the late 16th century as a family home by John Strachan, and to ensure its safety he had holes strategically placed in the walls so that missiles could be fired from them across the face of the building. Built with domestic comfort in mind, the castle's ground floor is dominated by the kitchen, with its vast arched fireplace. The main living quarters fill most of the first floor. The castle's sole entrance is a small doorway on the west front.

HBM. Apr-Sept, daily. Adm charge. Shop. Tel Edinburgh (031) 244 3101.

DEWAR'S SCOTCH WHISKY

Off A9, on north-west edge of Perth (Cb)

A blending and bottling plant now capable of filling up to 350,000 bottles of whisky a day grew from modest headquarters set up in Perth's High Street in 1846 by the company's founder, John Dewar, a former carpenter. Today the company's master blender decides, by the simple act of 'nosing', or sniffing, how up to 40 different malt whiskies are to be blended to give the flavour to Dewar's Scotch. The complete whisky-making process is shown to visitors during twice-daily tours of the plant.

All year, daily exc Bank Hol and first fortnight in July. Free entry. Shop. P *Toilets.* ♿ *Tel Perth (0738) 21231.*

DRUMMOND CASTLE GARDENS

Off A822, 2½ miles south of Crieff (Cb)

An exotic obelisk sundial with 50 different faces, designed to tell the time in most European capitals, rises up from the centre of Drummond's bushes and blooms. The instrument was built by Charles I's master mason for the Earl of Perth in the 17th century. It stands on a circular plot of black-and-white pebbles and from it bold lines of parallel and diagonal paths trace an appropriate St Andrew's Cross.

The 13 acre garden, created in the 17th century and decorated with Italian figures and statues around 1830, drops away steeply from Drummond Castle's stark medieval keep. Viewed from the highest terrace, the gardens' etched beds and lawns, circular hedges and sculpted shrubs form an elaborate geometrical pattern, stretching towards the woodlands beyond.

May-Aug, daily. Adm charge. P *Toilets. Tel Muthill (076 481) 257.*

BOWES-LYON LION *A great stone beast that echoes the Queen Mother's family name guards Glamis Castle. The first 'Lyon' of Glamis was Sir John, who was given the estate by Robert II in 1372. His castle was rebuilt in the 17th century in the style later called Scottish Baronial. The Queen Mother's sitting room (right) contains fine tapestries and Chinese and Dutch porcelain.*

DUNKELD CATHEDRAL

Cathedral Street, Dunkeld (Cc)

Below the wooded slopes of the Perthshire hills, the cathedral of Dunkeld stands in quiet dignity on the banks of the River Tay. Half of the cathedral, which is dedicated to St Columba, is still in use as a church; the other half is a ruin which is being restored.

The choir, completed in 1350, is the oldest part of the original church. The early Norman style gave way to Gothic as the nave, south porch, Chapter House and Tower were built a century later. The cathedral was plundered in 1560 during the Reformation, and was further damaged by fire in 1689, during the Battle of Dunkeld, when the Cameronians held the town against Highland supporters of James II. Look out for the pre-12th-century Ionic cross and Pictish Apostles' Stone behind the carved oak screen, and the Leper's Squint by the pulpit.

In Cathedral Street and High Street are 20 restored 17th-century artisans' houses, owned by the National Trust for Scotland which has a shop in Ell House, a former weaver's cottage.

HBM. All year, daily. Free entry. P *(limited). Tel Edinburgh (031) 244 3101.*

EDZELL CASTLE AND GARDEN

Off B966, 6 miles north of Brechin (Ec)

The red-stone ruins of this largely 16th-century castle are dominated by a square tower house and the walls of the spacious great hall, built over a kitchen with a massive arched fireplace, cellars and a vast oven. Edzell was built for the Lindsay family, who lived in it until the end of the 17th century, after which it fell into disrepair.

The castle's crowning glory is its formal walled garden. A jaunty stone summerhouse at one corner was used as a retreat from the main building and has its own small banqueting room, in which sweetmeats were served after a feast.

HBM. All year, daily exc Sun am. Adm charge. Shop. P *(limited). Toilets. Tel Edinburgh (031) 244 3101.*

GLAMIS CASTLE

Off A928, 5 miles south of Kirriemuir (Dc)

Approaching along a tree-lined avenue, visitors are confronted by a breathtaking vista of spires, turrets and towers as Glamis Castle rises majestically into view. The avenue passes between statues of James VI and his son Charles I and past two small forts, all that is left of the outer defences. Set in immaculate grounds, and framed by the imposing Grampian Mountains, the castle is the family home of the Earls of Strathmore and Kinghorne, and has been visited and lived in by royalty since the 14th century. The Queen

Mother spent much of her childhood at Glamis, and Princess Margaret was born there.

Visitors enter the castle by a north door, and a broad stone staircase leads to the dining room with an elaborate fireplace and huge oak armorial overmantel. The crypt has a medieval air with armour, axes, swords and pistols – and a bricked-in secret chamber. The most magnificent room is the 60ft drawing room, which has a splendid arched ceiling of early 17th-century plasterwork. Duncan's Hall is traditionally the scene of King Duncan's murder in Shakespeare's *Macbeth*.

The Royal Apartments are a suite set aside for the Queen Mother in 1923 when, as Lady Elizabeth Bowes-Lyon, she married the future George VI. The Queen Mother's bedroom has an elegant four-poster bed with fluted columns capped by gilt fretwork.

Outside is an Italian Garden which the Queen Mother's parents created at the beginning of the century. Its 2 acres are enclosed by high yew hedges, and there are two stone gazebos in 17th-century style and a fountain.

In the village of Glamis, the Angus Folk Museum is a row of 17th-century cottages housing a collection of early furnishings, clothing, domestic utensils and agricultural tools.

Castle: May-Sept, pm daily exc Sat. Adm charge. Refreshments. Shop. P *Toilets.* ♿ *Tel Glamis (030 784) 242. Museum: NTS. May-Sept, pm daily. Free entry. Shop.* P *(limited). Toilets. Tel Montrose (0674) 73232.*

GLENGOULANDIE DEER PARK

Off B846, 5½ miles north-east of Aberfeldy (Bc)

Spread out below Schiehallion peak, the park is crossed by a scenic road along which visitors can stop at will to admire the magnificent herd of red deer. The park is also the home of Highland cattle, and rare breeds of sheep such as the prehistoric Soay and the ancient four-horned Jacob. Elsewhere in the park peacocks strut and display their thousand-eyed tails.

May-Sept, daily. Adm charge. Shop. P *Toilets. Tel Kenmore (088 73) 509.*

GLENTURRET DISTILLERY

Off A85, 1 mile north of Crieff (Cb)

Glenturret was established in 1775 on the site of five illicit stills, and draws its water from the River Turret which curves through the glen. Visitors can watch the whisky-making process stage by stage, and sample whiskies up to 21 years old. An old warehouse has been converted into an audiovisual theatre, and the Smugglers' Restaurant recalls the 'rogue' distillers who kept a lookout for the authorities from two high hills on either side of the river.

Mar-Dec, Mon-Fri; also Sat Apr-Oct. Adm charge. Refreshments. Shop. P *Toilets.* ♿ *Tel Crieff (0764) 2424.*

HERMITAGE WOODLAND WALK

Off A9, 2 miles west of Dunkeld (Cc)

This beautiful wooded area contains numerous exotic trees, such as Chile pine, as well as Norway spruce, Scots pine and Douglas firs. The walk starting from the car park passes beneath a 19th-century railway bridge and along the banks of the twisting River Braan, beneath the shade of old yews, oaks and alders. Farther on, a charming 18th-century bridge spans a narrow gorge below the Black Linn fall. Just beyond the bridge is The Hermitage, a folly built in 1758 by the future 3rd Duke of Atholl. It is open to the public on most days in summer.

NTS. All year, daily. Free entry. P *(charge). Tel Pitlochry (0796) 3233.*

HOUSE OF DUN

On A935, 3 miles west of Montrose (Ec)

The outstanding feature of this handsome house designed by William Adam in the early 18th century is the exuberant plasterwork in the saloon, which occupies the central three bays of the south front. The work consists of the armorial bearings of Lord Dun, a series of mythological scenes, and an array of naval and military trophies.

Outside, a potting shed contains a selection of early 20th-century tools and a life-size figure of a gardener at work. In a gamekeeper's hut a gamekeeper can be seen checking his traps. There are wooded walks in the surrounding parkland.

NTS. Grounds and Courtyard Buildings: May-Sept, pm daily. House: July-Sept, pm daily. Adm charge. Refreshments. P *Tel Bridge of Dun (067 481) 264.*

FORMAL GARDEN *Edzell Castle still has its 17th-century enclosed garden, or pleasance, divided into geometrically laid out beds and surrounded by walls with recesses for flower boxes and nesting birds. Trimmed boxwood hedges spell out the Lindsay family motto:* Dum Spiro Spero *(While I Breathe I Hope).*

HUNTINGTOWER CASTLE

Off A85, 3 miles north-west of Perth (Cb)

Two medieval tower houses joined by some late 17th-century stonework form the substantial remains of this fortified family house. The eastern tower is the older of the two and has one of the finest and oldest painted ceilings in Scotland, dating from the early 1500s. The ceiling timbers and supporting beams are also highly decorative, bearing scrolls, fruit and the faces of dragons and other weird animals. The plastered walls show fragments of colourful paintings, including a lion and a hare.

Before the towers were joined, the space between them was known as The Maiden's Leap from a daring jump made by a daughter of the 1st Earl of Gowrie in the 15th century. About to be discovered in the chamber of the man she planned to marry, she ran to the roof and leaped 9½ft from one tower to the other, heedless of the 60ft drop, to reach her own bedroom.

HBM. All year, daily. Adm charge. P *(limited). Tel Edinburgh (031) 244 3101.*

KINDROGAN IN VICTORIAN TIMES

Off A924, 3 miles north of Kirkmichael (Cc)

A plaque by the banks of the River Ardle marks the spot where Queen Victoria stopped to have tea on her way from Balmoral to Dunkeld in October 1866. The woods and the three-storeyed

ROYAL PRISON *Islanded in its loch, Lochleven Castle was a strategic fortress and a state prison from the 14th century. Mary, Queen of Scots was held prisoner in the castle for nearly a year in 1567-8.*

manor house of Kindrogan itself have been kept looking much as they did in Victoria's time. Many of the plants in the garden were introduced from abroad in the late 19th century.

A riverside and woodland walk passes places admired by Queen Victoria, including the bridge over Donald McCoull's Burn, named after an early 19th-century local sheep stealer.

All year, daily. Free entry. P *Toilets. Tel Blairgowrie (0250) 81286.*

LOCH OF THE LOWES

Off A923, 2 miles north-east of Dunkeld (Cc)

Each April ospreys return here after wintering in Africa, and some 30,000 people a year come to see the sharp-taloned predators, which feed on the loch's trout and pike. A visitor centre is set on the western shore. Among the other birds that breed here are great crested grebes, tufted ducks and goosanders. The woodland skirting the centre is a good place for spotting roe and fallow deer. There is an observation hide by the water, and the centre has a wildlife exhibition and several small aquaria.

Apr-Sept, daily. Free entry. Shop. P *Toilets. Tel Dunkeld (035 02) 337.*

LOCHLEVEN CASTLE

Castle Island, Loch Leven (Da)

The romantic ruins of Lochleven Castle rise jaggedly from the waters of Loch Leven, across which boats ferry summer visitors out to the island from the jetty in Kinross. The castle owes its place in history to Mary, Queen of Scots who was imprisoned there in June 1567, after her defeat at the Battle of Carberry. Together with a doctor, cook and two ladies-in-waiting, she remained in the castle until her escape in May 1568 with the aid of Willy Douglas, the keeper of the castle's boats.

The nucleus of the castle is the 14th-century tower house, which although roofless is one of the best preserved buildings of its type in Scotland. In the courtyard are the scanty remains of the 16th-century great hall and kitchen.

HBM. Apr-Sept, daily. Adm charge (including ferry). P *(limited). Tel Edinburgh (031) 244 3101.*

MCMANUS GALLERIES

Albert Square, Dundee (Db)

Jute, jam and journalism – the industries which created Dundee's wealth – have appropriate coverage in the city's McManus Galleries. The galleries' celebration of the city's vibrant life includes reconstructions of an old bar and shop, and souvenirs of local 'worthies' such as the noted poet of bad verse, William McGonagall. Exhibits trace the Dundonians back to their Stone Age ancestors, while in the galleries and beneath the vaulted roof of the grand Albert Hall a wealth of porcelain, clocks, musical instruments and paintings are on display.

The nearby Barrack Street Museum is largely devoted to Scottish wildlife, from the Highlands to the sea. The skeleton of the Great Tay Whale is on display, as well as stuffed specimens of more exotic species including the lion, crocodile and duck-billed platypus.

In Balgay Park, on the north-western edge of Dundee, stands the Mills Observatory, an imposing sandstone building with a papier-mâché dome which opens up to reveal the night sky. On clear winter evenings, visitors can use the fine 10in Cooke refracting telescope to observe the moon, planets and distant galaxies.

McManus Galleries: All year, daily exc Sun. Free entry. Shop. Toilets. ♿ *Tel Dundee (0382) 23141. Barrack Street Museum: All year, daily exc Sun. Free entry. Shop. Toilets. Tel (0382) 23141. Observatory: All year, daily exc Sun. Free entry. Shop.* P *(limited). Toilets. Tel (0382) 67138.*

PASS OF KILLIECRANKIE VISITOR CENTRE

Off A9, 3 miles north of Pitlochry (Cc)

Weather-beaten rowans and birches and moist, fern-clad crevices are found in this rugged gorge. The pass was the scene of the Battle of Killiecrankie in 1689, when Highland soldiers led by 'Bonnie Dundee' routed government troops under General Hugh Mackay. The visitor centre includes a display about the battle, and from it a path leads to the site of the fighting. Nearby is the Soldier's Leap, named after a government soldier who was trapped there by Highlanders and escaped by jumping across a deep gully.

NTS. Apr-mid Oct, daily. Adm charge. Refreshments. Shop. P *Toilets. Tel Pitlochry (0796) 3233.*

PERTH MUSEUM AND ART GALLERY

George Street, Perth (Cb)

Beneath the dome of the Marshall Monument – the Victorian heart of Perth's city museum – is a fine collection of 19th and 20th-century Scottish paintings, many of which also provide a record of Perthshire from 1820 to the present day. Perth art glass, known as Monart and Vasart, features in the glass collections, and there is a fine Perth silver collection.

Close to the museum, in Curfew Row, is the house which Sir Walter Scott chose as the home of Catherine Glover, the romantic heroine of his historical novel set in the 14th century, *The Fair Maid of Perth.* Today's Fair Maid's House dates back to the 1600s when the glovers of Perth used it as their hall; their motto 'Grace and Peace' appears above the door.

Scott's 'Fair Maid' was instrumental in saving the great St John's Kirk, in the heart of the city. For it was the novel's publication in 1828 that reawakened interest in the Middle Ages and prompted Perth to improve the dilapidated 15th-century church. Outside, St John's today looks much as it did in medieval times, its central tower a landmark for miles around. Inside, its spacious dignity is enhanced by the positioning of the choir on a higher level than the nave. The organ, bell tower, War Memorial Shrine and vividly translucent stained-glass windows are 19th and 20th-century additions.

Just south of the kirk, in Marshall Place, is the Round House, a Victorian rotunda which once

RIDING HIGH *Striped great crested grebe chicks ride on the back of their parent on Loch of the Lowes. The crest is raised by both sexes at the height of the courting display. The birds nest on a platform of weeds in shallow water near the loch side.*

housed the city's waterworks. Built in classical style, the waterworks functioned for 133 years before falling into disrepair. Following restoration, visitors can now enter it to watch a slide show of Perth projected onto its walls.
Museum and Art Gallery: All year, daily exc Sun. Free entry. Shop. P Toilets. ♿ Tel Perth (0738) 32488. Fair Maid's House: All year, daily exc Sun. Free entry. Shop. Tel (0738) 25976. Church: Mar-Dec, daily; Jan-Feb, Sun services only. Free entry. P ♿ Tel (0738) 26159. Round House: June-Sept, daily; Apr-May, daily exc Sun; Oct-Mar, Mon-Fri. Free entry. Shop. ♿ Tel (0738) 38353.

PITLOCHRY POWER STATION

Off A9, at Pitlochry (Cc)

When Pitlochry Power Station was built in the late 1940s it created the beautiful Loch Faskally by damming the salmon-swarming River Tummel. The dam itself is some 85ft high and 1673ft long, and a fish ladder beside it lets the salmon battle their way upstream to spawn.

From an observation room in the adjacent visitor centre it is sometimes possible to see the fish swimming by – usually in the spring and early summer, but occasionally as late as September. There is also a display devoted to the salmon, which describes the life cycle of the fish and the efforts to protect them.
Visitor Centre: Late Mar-late Oct, daily. Shop. P Tel Pitlochry (0796) 3152.

QUEEN'S VIEW, LOCH TUMMEL

On B8019, 6 miles north-west of Pitlochry (Cc)

High above the wooded Tummel Valley as it unfolds westwards towards the 3547ft high Schiehallion peak is a viewpoint christened Queen's View after a visit by Queen Victoria in 1866. Here the Forestry Commission has built a visitor centre which presents an exhibition of forestry throughout the ages. Three waymarked trails begin at the Allean car park, to the west. A picnic spot overlooks Loch Tummel, and a short but steep circular waymarked trail leads down through woods and along the lochside.
Visitor Centre: FC. Apr-Oct, daily. Free entry. Refreshments. Shop. P Toilets. ♿ Tel Pitlochry (0796) 3123.

RANNOCH FOREST WALKS

On Lochside Road, 4 miles west of Kinloch Rannoch (Bc)

Lying to the south of Loch Rannoch, the forest consists mainly of Scots pines and Douglas firs with pockets of birch and oak. Three walks begin from the Carie car park on the west side of Carie Burn, sharing a single uphill path until they reach an old stone wall. The Carie walk proceeds for three-quarters of a mile downhill to Carie Burn; the Kilvrecht walk extends for 2 miles along the banks of the Carie and Bogair Burns; and the Allt-na-Bogair walk is a 5 mile hike high into the hills above the loch where red deer may be seen.
All year, daily.

SCONE PALACE

Off A93, 2 miles north-east of Perth (Cb)

Peacocks strut on the lawns facing this stalwart, pink-stone palace, which for some 500 years was the crowning place of the Kings of Scotland. It is renowned for its superb collections of French furniture, china, ivories and clocks. The drawing room has a writing table made for Marie Antoinette and stamped with the French queen's personal cipher. The library displays a priceless collection of 18th and 19th-century porcelain, while the Long Gallery has a highly polished oak floor on which, in 1842, Queen Victoria and Prince Albert practised the sport of curling.

The palace was once the home of the Stone of Scone, on which Scottish monarchs were crowned, but in 1296 Edward I of England carried the Stone to its present resting-place in Westminster Abbey. The palace is surrounded by extensive grounds which include a woodland garden, a magnificent pinetum with giant sequoias, and a lime avenue. Modern additions include a children's playground and a picnic place. On Moot Hill, at the front of the palace, there is an elaborately decorated chapel, and down by Catmoor Burn is a friars' den, where monks once relaxed and fished. The grounds are also noted for their Highland cattle and a collection of veteran agricultural machinery.
Easter-mid Oct, daily. Adm charge. Refreshments. Shop. P Toilets. ♿ Tel Perth (0738) 52300.

PERTH CRAFTS *Silver snuffboxes are among the Perth-made objects that are the treasures of the Perth Museum. The Perth glass on display includes an inkwell (left). There are also archaeological finds, costumes, maps and photographs illustrating the city's past.*

VANE FARM NATURE CENTRE

Off B9097, 3 miles south-east of Kinross (Da)

Overlooking the southern shores of Loch Leven, the nature centre is a perfect place from which to observe a wide range of birds, including great crested grebes, herons, mallards, greylag geese, pink-footed geese, swans, oystercatchers, redshanks and black-headed gulls. The converted farm building has an observation room equipped with telescopes that between them sweep the waters of the loch. There is a public hide on the shore, a taped commentary on seasonal bird news, and a nature trail.
RSPB. All year, daily. Adm charge. Shop. P Toilets. Tel Kinross (0577) 62355.

VICTORIA DOCK, DUNDEE

Just east of Tay Road Bridge, Dundee (Db)

The figurehead of a wooden unicorn leaps out from the prow of the frigate *Unicorn*, the oldest British-built warship afloat. The *Unicorn* belongs to the golden age of sail and occupies a historic place between the traditionally built HMS *Victory* and Brunel's first iron ship, SS *Great Britain*.

Built in 1824, after the Napoleonic Wars, the 46-gun frigate never saw action, and she was laid up in reserve at Chatham. By 1857 sailing warships were outclassed by steam power, and *Unicorn* became successively a gunpowder storage hulk and a drill ship, arriving in Dundee in 1873. Dismayed by the Ministry of Defence's decision to scrap the frigate in 1968, local people formed a preservation society and began the long task of restoration. When it is complete, the 150ft long vessel will be fully rigged.

Exploring the decks and exhibition area, visitors gain a vivid impression of 19th-century sea life when daily rations were maggot-ridden and sailors slept in 18in of hammock space, and risked a flogging for substandard work. The captain, by contrast, had his own plumbed-in shower and an elegant, spacious cabin – shared with four 18-pounder guns.
Apr-mid Oct, daily. Adm charge. Shop. P Toilets. Tel Dundee (0382) 21558.

REGIONAL CALENDAR

March (mid-month). Perth: Indoor Highland Games.

April (late). Blairgowrie: Folk Festival.

May (mid-month, to Oct). Pitlochry: Festival Theatre.

May (late). Perth: Festival of the Arts. Blair Castle: Atholl Gathering.

June (early). Blair Castle: Atholl Highlanders Parade.

July (early). Dundee: Highland Games.

August (early). Perth: Highland Games.

August (mid-month). Crieff: Highland Gathering.

August (late). Blairgowrie: Highland Gathering.

September (mid-month). Pitlochry: Highland Games.

October (late). Blair Castle: Piping Championships.

December 31 Comrie: Flambeaux Procession.

Tourist information: Arbroath (0241) 72609; Blairgowrie (0250) 2960; Dundee (0382) 27723; Perth (0738) 22900; Pitlochry (0796) 2215.

INDEX

Page numbers in **bold** type indicate a main entry, often accompanied by an illustration on the same page. Page numbers in *italics* indicate other illustrations. Page numbers in light roman type denote shorter text references.

— A —

— B —

— C —

— D —

— E —

— F —

— G —

— H —

— I —

— J —

— K —

— L —

— M —

— N —

— T —

— U —

— V —

— W —

— Y —

— Z —

ACKNOWLEDGMENTS

The photographs in this book came from the sources listed below. Those commissioned by Reader's Digest appear in *italics*.

The position of illustrations on each page is indicated by the letters after the page number:

T = top; B = bottom; L = left; C = centre; R = right

Front dust jacket and cover *Richard Surman.* Back dust jacket: TL Noel Habgood/Derek Widdicombe; TC The Charleston Trust; TR Wales Tourist Board; CR *Neil Holmes;* BR *Barry Hitchcox.* **6-7** *Skyscan.* **8-9** Angelo Hornak. **11** T Visionbank Library Ltd & England Scene; B The National Maritime Museum. **12** TL, BL & BR *Neil Holmes;* TR Bath Assembly Rooms; C The Holburne Museum, Bath. **13** *Neil Holmes,* except for BL, postcard of Victorian song sheet reproduced by permission of Frank Staff; BR Post Office Rifles Association. **14** Exploratory Hands-on-Science Centre, Bristol. **15** Robert Harding Picture Library. **17** T Bedfordshire County Council; C Woodmansterne Ltd; B Richard Jemmett. **18** Patrick Thurston. **19** Richard Jemmett. **21** T Robert Harding Picture Library; C *Peter Keen;* B Institute of Agricultural History and Museum of English Rural Life. **22** TL Adam Woolfitt/Susan Griggs Agency; TR Woodmansterne Ltd; BL, BR The Royal Collection. **23** T Mark Fiennes/The Household Cavalry Museum, Windsor; CL, CR The Royal Collection; B Andy Williams. **24** *Neil Holmes.* **25** T By permission of the Trustees of the Stanley Spencer Gallery; B Keystone/Photo Source. **27** *Patrick Thurston.* **29** T Adam Woolfitt/Susan Griggs Agency; B The National Trust/Woodmansterne Ltd. **30** Woodmansterne Ltd. **31** T *Keith Morris;* B The National Trust/Woodmansterne Ltd. **33** L Trevor Wood/The Image Bank; R Cromwell Museum, Huntingdon. **34** All, except for R, reproduced courtesy of the Syndics, Fitzwilliam Museum, Cambridge/Woodmansterne Ltd; R Cambridge and County Folk Museum. **35** TL, TR, CL, CR Patrick Thurston; CT, cb Woodmansterne Ltd; BR John Bethell; B Richard Jemmett. **36** Tim Woodcock. **37** *Neil Holmes.* **38** Robert Estall. **39** Tim Woodcock. **41** Visionbank Library Ltd & England Scene. **42** T Visionbank Library Ltd & England Scene; B David Reed/Impact Photos. **43** T Robert Harding Picture Library; B Spectrum Colour Library. **45** Sefton Photo Library. **46** L Michael Freeman/Bruce Coleman Ltd; TR Woodmansterne Ltd; BR Matchbox International Collectors' Association. **47** Grosvenor Museum, Chester, except for TC, BL *Jon Wyand;* CR Robert Estall/Malcolm Aird. **48** Aspect Picture Library. **49** TL Woodmansterne Ltd; TR Sefton Photo Library. **50** L Macclesfield Sunday School Heritage Centre; R Richard Surman. **51** The National Trust/Woodmansterne Ltd. **53** The National Trust. **55** Robert Harding Picture Library. **56** Biofotos. **57** *Jon Wyand.* **58** Biofotos. **60** Visionbank Ltd & England Scene. **61** *Jon Wyand.* **62** *Jon Wyand.* **63** Biofotos. **64** T Andy Williams; B Pamla Toler/Impact Photos. **65** T *Jon Wyand;* B Britain on View. **67** Richard Surman. **68** T, C The Wordsworth Trust, Dove Cottage; lc, lb Cressida Pemberton-Pigott; BR Brian Shuel; CT *Neil Holmes;* BC *Cressida Pemberton-Pigott.* **69** Richard Jemmett. **70** T The National Trust/Woodmansterne Ltd; B R.W. Hourd and Son Ltd. **71** Robert Harding Picture Library. **72** T Neil Chase; B Graham Edwards/Museum of Lakeland Life and Industry. **73** Visionbank Library Ltd & England Scene. **75** *John Vigurs.* **76** L, R *Richard Surman;* C By permission of the Trustees of the Chatsworth Settlement. **77** Jason Smalley. **78** T Tim Woodcock; B The National Trust. **79** Biofotos. **80** T Robert Estall; B The J. Allan Cash Photo Library. **83** Andy Williams. **84** Jeremy Marks/Woodmansterne Ltd. **85** Michael Holford. **86** Derek Widdicombe. **87** *Nigel Cassidy.* **88** *Nigel Cassidy.* **89** T Andrew Lawson; B Eric Crichton/Bruce Coleman Ltd. **90-91** *Jon Wyand.* **92** Earl of Devon/Woodmansterne Ltd. **94** Michael Holford. **95** T *Nigel Cassidy;* L Colin Molyneux; C Adrian Davies/Bruce Coleman Ltd; BR *Neil Holmes;* BL *Patrick Thurston.* **96** T Geoff Dore/Bruce Coleman Ltd; B The National Trust/Woodmansterne Ltd. **97** The National Trust. **99** John Heseltine/Susan Griggs Agency. **100** Clive Friend/Woodmansterne Ltd. **101** T Woodmansterne Ltd; B Andy Williams. **103** Beamish North of England Open Air Museum. **104** Tim Woodcock. **105** Derek Widdicombe. **107** T Michael Holford; B English Heritage. **109, 111** *Barry Hitchcox.* **113** Woodmansterne Ltd. **114** *Neil Holmes.* **115** T Michael Holford; B Michael Freeman/Bruce Coleman Ltd. **116** Patrick Thurston. **117** T Robert Opie Collection; B John Bethell. **118** Andrew Lawson. **119** The National Trust/Woodmansterne Ltd. **121** T Richard Bryant/Arcaid, rest Michael Holford. **122** Imperial War Museum. **123** Department of the Environment. **124** T British Museum (Natural History); CL Reproduced by permission of the Trustees of the Science Museum; CR By courtesy of the Trustees of the Victoria and Albert Museum; B The Natural History Museum. **125** Department of the Environment. **126** National Maritime Museum. **127** T Spectrum; BL English Heritage; BC By permission of the Director of the Greenwich Hospital/Woodmansterne Ltd; BR Robert Harding Picture Library. **128** London Transport Museum. **129** T Museum of London; BL, BR Madame Tussaud's Ltd. **130** L Department of the Environment; C, R Crown Copyright, by permission of the Controller of Her Majesty's Stationery Office. **131** The National Gallery. **132** Tim Woodcock. **133** TR Arcaid; CR Kew Bridge Steam Museum; CL The National Trust; C Department of the Environment; CR English Life Publications Ltd; BL Marble Hill, Twickenham (English Heritage); BC M. Gilroy/Aquila; BR British Motor Industry Heritage Trust. **134** Theatre Museum/By courtesy of the Trustees of the Victoria and Albert Museum. **135** Jarrold and Sons Ltd. **137** The National Trust/Woodmansterne Ltd. **138** Patrick Thurston. **139** *Jon Wyand.* **141** The National Motor Museum, Beaulieu. **142** © Broadlands (Romsey) Ltd. **143** Trevor Wood/The Image Bank. **144** T M.P.L. Fogden/Bruce Coleman Ltd; B Jeremy Marks/Woodmansterne Ltd. **145** T Patrick Thurston; B Jeremy Marks/Woodmansterne Ltd. **146-7** *Neil Holmes,* except for D-Day Tapestry, D-Day Museum, Portsmouth. **148** Lucinda Lambton/Arcaid. **149** Pitkin Pictorials. **151** T Malcolm Osman/Woodmansterne Ltd; B © Skyscan. **152** *John Sims.* **153** Clive Friend/Woodmansterne Ltd. **154** Jennifer Fry/Bruce Coleman Ltd. **156** L © Worcester Museum and Art Gallery; C Nicholas Servian/Woodmansterne Ltd; R Heart of England Tourist Board. **158** Tania Midgley. **159** Aspect Picture Library. **160** T Andy Williams; B Visionbank Library Ltd & England Scene. **161** *Neil Holmes.* **162** TL, TR *Neil Holmes;* BL, BR The National Trust. **163** *Neil Holmes.* **164** Visionbank Library Ltd & England Scene. **165-7** *Jon Wyand.* **168** Howard C. Moore/Woodmansterne Ltd. **169** Patrick Thurston. **170** Woodmansterne Ltd. **171** Godshill Model Village. **173** TL, B English Heritage; TR John Bethell. **175** The National Trust. **176** L Woodmansterne Ltd; C Angelo Hornak; R *Philip Llewellin.* **177** TL Heritage Projects (Canterbury Ltd); TC, BL John Bethell; TR, BR, CR The Royal Museum and Art Gallery, Canterbury; CL *Philip Llewellin;* CR Buffs Museum, Canterbury. **179** T Jeremy Marks/Woodmansterne Ltd; B Hever Castle. **180** The National Trust. **181** Jeremy Marks/Woodmansterne Ltd. **182** T *Skyscan;* B Port Lymne Zoo Park. **183** The National Trust. **185** T John Vigurs; B Visionbank Library Ltd & England Scene. **186** Derek Widdicombe. **187** *John Vigurs.* **188** Jeremy Marks/Woodmansterne Ltd. **189** *John Vigurs.* **191** Belvoir Castle. **192** Michael E. Ware. **193** *Mike St Maur Sheil.* **195** Richard Winslade. **196** *Jon Wyand.* **197** T Neville Fox-Davies; TL, BL, C *Neil Holmes;* R *Martyn Chillmaid.* **198** Woodmansterne Ltd. **199** Michael Holford. **201-3** *Jon Wyand.* **205** T Bressingham Steam Museum; B Neville Fox-Davies. **207** Jarrold and Sons Ltd. **209** TL Patrick Thurston; TR Neville Fox-Davies; BL Jeremy Marks/Woodmansterne Ltd; BR Clive Friend/Woodmansterne Ltd. **210** Neville Fox-Davies. **211** Tim Woodcock. **212** By permission of the Earl Spencer, Althorp. **213** The National Trust. **214** T Rockingham Castle; B Visionbank Library Ltd & England Scene. **215** Waterways Museum. **217** *Neil Holmes.* **218** Visionbank Library Ltd & England Scene. **219** Clive Friend/Woodmansterne Ltd. **221** T Patrick Thurston; B Andrew Lawson. **222** T *Andrew Lawson;* B Ian Howes. **225** Visionbank Library Ltd & England Scene. **226** T Robert Harding Picture Library; B Eric Crichton/Bruce Coleman Ltd. **227** Clive Coote. **228** Jeremy Marks/Woodmansterne Ltd. **229** Visionbank Library Ltd & England Scene. **231** Jeremy Whitaker. **232** The National Trust. **233** L Patrick Thurston; R Great Western Society. **234** L Rod Williams/Bruce Coleman Ltd; C John Bulwer/Susan Griggs Agency; R Angelo Hornak. **235** T Ashmolean Museum, Oxford; CL John Bethell; C *Tony Evans;* CR Heritage Projects; BL, BC Oxford University Museum; bcr Museum of the History of Science, Oxford University; BR Eric Crichton/Bruce Coleman Ltd. **236** Visionbank Library Ltd & England Scene. **237** Dr Georg Gerster/John Hillelson. **239** T Visionbank Library Ltd & England Scene; B The National Trust. **241** Andy Williams. **242** Ironbridge Gorge Museum, except for L Skyscan. **242-3, 243** Ironbridge Gorge Museum. **244** Patrick Thurston. **245** Aspect Picture Library. **247** T David Reed/Impact Photos; B Tania Midgley. **248** BL Cricket St Thomas. **248-9** The National Trust. **249** BR Fleet Air Arm Museum. **250** TR *Malcolm Aird;* TL, CR, BL Tim Woodcock; BR The National Trust. **251** Robert Harding Picture Library. **252** T Woodmansterne Ltd; B Jeremy Marks/Woodmansterne Ltd. **253** T Wookey Hole Caves Ltd; B Unichrome (Bath) Ltd. **255** Derek Widdicombe. **256** Andy Williams. **257** Jeremy Marks/Woodmansterne Ltd. **258** City Museum and Art Gallery, Stoke-on-Trent. **261** Aspect Picture Library. **262** Eric Crichton/Bruce Coleman Ltd. **263** Jeremy Marks/Woodmansterne Ltd. **264** TL, TR, CL *Anthony Lambert;* C, CR Neville Fox-Davies. **266** *Nigel Cassidy.* **267** John Topham Picture Library. **270** T Woodmansterne Ltd; B Nicholas Servian/Woodmansterne Ltd. **272** Tania Midgley. **273** *Neil Holmes.* **275** TL, CR, BL The Royal Pavilion, Art Gallery and Museums; TR Michael Holford; CL Robert Harding Picture Library; C *Philip Dowell;* BR Jarrold and Sons Ltd. **276** T Visionbank Library Ltd & England Scene; B The National Trust. **277** The Charleston Trust. **278** Roger Scruton/Impact Photos. **279** Judges Postcards Ltd, Hastings. **281** T Clive Friend/Woodmansterne Ltd; BL Patrick Thurston; CR *Anthony Howarth;* B Arundel Toy Museum. **282** T Michael Holford; B Pitkin Pictorials. **283, 284, 285** Sheila & Oliver Mathews. **286, 287** *Eric Meacher.* **289** T The National Trust; B Patrick Thurston. **290** Derek Widdicombe. **291** Colin Molyneux/Bruce Coleman Ltd. **293** Lucinda Lambton/Arcaid. **294** Patrick Thurston. **295** Jeremy Whitaker. **296** The National Trust. **297** TL, CR Andrew Lawson; TR John Wright; CL Stratford Motor Museum; BL Robert Harding Picture Library; BC Andy Williams; BR Alain Compost/Bruce Coleman Ltd. **299** T Pitkin Pictorials; B Patrick Thurston. **300** T National Motorcycle Museum; B John Melville/Heart of England Tourist Board. **303** Robert Estall. **304** Clive Coote. **305** T Eric Crichton/Bruce Coleman Ltd; C The National Trust; B Jarrold and Sons Ltd. **306** Geoff Dore/Bruce Coleman Ltd **307** The Northern Picture Library. **308** T Angelo Hornak; CL Salisbury & S Wilts Museum; C Norman Tomalin/Bruce Coleman Ltd; CR Robert Harding Picture Library; B The Duke of Edinburgh's Royal Regiment. **311** T Photo Library International; B Sheila & Oliver Mathews. **312** Derek Widdicombe. **313** L Castle Howard; R *Trevor Wood.* **314-15** *Jon Wyand.* **315** Roger Scruton/Impact Photos. **316** TL Richard Jemmett; TC *Philip Llewellin;* TR Clive Friend/Woodmansterne; BL Britain on View; BR Sefton Photo Library. **317** TR *Mike Freeman;* Jorvik, York Archaeological Trust; rest *Trevor Wood* and *Philip Llewellin.* **318** Colin Molyneux. **319** Images Colour Library Ltd. **320** Patrick Thurston. **321** *Penny Tweedie.* **322** T Neil Holmes; B Bankfield Museum. **324** Harewood House. **325** Derek Widdicombe. **326** TL Simon Warner; BL Brian Seed/John Hillelson Agency; C © The Brontë Society. **326-7** both Simon Warner. **328** Neil Holmes. **329** Leeds City Art Galleries. **330-1** *Colin Molyneux.* **333** T Wales Tourist Board; B David Tease. **334** T Tim Woodcock; B Wales Tourist Board. **335** Robert Harding Picture Library. **338** *Colin Molyneux.* **339** Colin Molyneux/The Image Bank. **341** T National Museum of Wales, Cardiff/Bridgeman Art Library; B Lucinda Lambton/Arcaid. **342** Wales Tourist Board. **343** *Philip Evans.* **344** Robert Harding Picture Library. **345** *Neil Holmes.* **347** T Celtic Picture Library; B Robert Estall. **348** Andy Williams. **349** T Penhow Castle; B Wales Tourist Board. **350** T Tim Woodcock; B Andy Williams. **351** Newport Leisure Services. **353** Lucinda Lambton/Arcaid. **354** Andy Williams. **356** *Adam Woolfitt.* **357** *Neil Holmes.* **356** T The National Trust; B Robert Harding Picture Library. **359** John Cleare/Mountain Camera. **361** Wales Tourist Board. **362** Tim Woodcock. **363** Andy Williams. **364-5** Adam Woolfitt/Susan Griggs Agency. **367** Scottish Tourist Board. **368** Sheila and Oliver Mathews. **369** Jeremy Marks/Woodmansterne Ltd. **370** Jarrold and Sons Ltd. **372** TL Henderson Graphics; TR, B Friends of Dunblane Cathedral. **373** Scottish Tourist Board. **375** By permission of the Duke of Buccleuch. **376** Scottish Tourist Board. **377** T Royal Botanic Garden, Edinburgh; B Maxwelton House. **378** Britain on View. **379** National Trust for Scotland. **381** T Britain on View; B Scottish Tourist Board. **382** TR, CR *Neil Holmes;* CR, BL *Colin Molyneux;* TR *Philip Llewellin.* **383** T Scottish Fisheries Museum; B Scottish Tourist Board. **385** Andy Williams. **386** T, CR, BR *Philip Llewellin,* rest Aberdeen Tourist Board. **387** T The National Trust for Scotland; B Robert Harding Picture Library. **388** National Trust for Scotland. **389** T Fochabers Folk Museum; B National Trust for Scotland. **390** Scottish Tourist Board. **391** Britain on View. **393** T George Young; B Malcolm Aird/Robert Estall. **394** Britain on View. **395** T Andy Williams; B Britain on View. **396** Noel Habgood/Derek Widdicombe. **397** T Britain on View; B Scottish Tourist Board. **398** Scottish Tourist Board. **399** T R. Matassa, Fort William; B Colin Molyneux/The Image Bank. **401** T Robert Harding Picture Library; B Chris Bonington/Bruce Coleman Ltd. **402** Scottish Tourist Board. **403** Sheila Thomlinson. **405** T Britain on View; B Scottish Tourist Board. **406** L Outlook Tower and Camera Obscura; C, R *Philip Llewellin.* **407** TL John Kegan/Susan Griggs Agency; CR, CR Adam Woolfitt/Susan Griggs Agency; TR Museum of Childhood, Edinburgh; BR *Philip Llewellin;* CR, National Trust for Scotland; BL National Gallery of Scotland. **408** Jeremy Marks/Woodmansterne Ltd. **409** T Duke of Hamilton; B Britain on View. **410** Scottish Tourist Board. **411** Britain on View. **413** TL Britain on View; TR Scottish Tourist Board; B Loch Lomond, Stirling and Trossachs Tourist Board. **414** T The Burrell Collection, Glasgow Museums and Art Galleries; BL National Trust for Scotland; BR Jarrold and Sons Ltd. **415** Britain on View. **416** © New Lanark. **417** Royal Botanic Garden, Edinburgh. **419** Scottish Tourist Board. **420** T Adam Woolfitt/Susan Griggs Agency; B Britain on View. **421** *Ian Howes.* **422** Scottish Tourist Board. **423** Perth Museum.

Typesetting: Vantage Photosetting Co Ltd, London
Separations: Colourscan Co Pte Ltd, Singapore
Paper: Townsend Hook Ltd, Snodland
Printing: Jarrold Printing Ltd, Norwich
Binding: Hazell, Watson & Viney Ltd, Aylesbury

NORTHERN BRITAIN

The 54 counties of England and Wales and the 12 regions and islands areas of Scotland into which this book is divided, together with the Isle of Man and the Channel Islands, are shown on the two endpaper maps. A detailed map of each section appears on the page indicated. The endpaper maps also mark places that are the subjects of special features, many of which have their own maps.

- County/Region Boundary
- Special feature with town centre plan
- Other special feature
- Other city or town
- Urban area
- Motorway
- Major road
- Car ferry

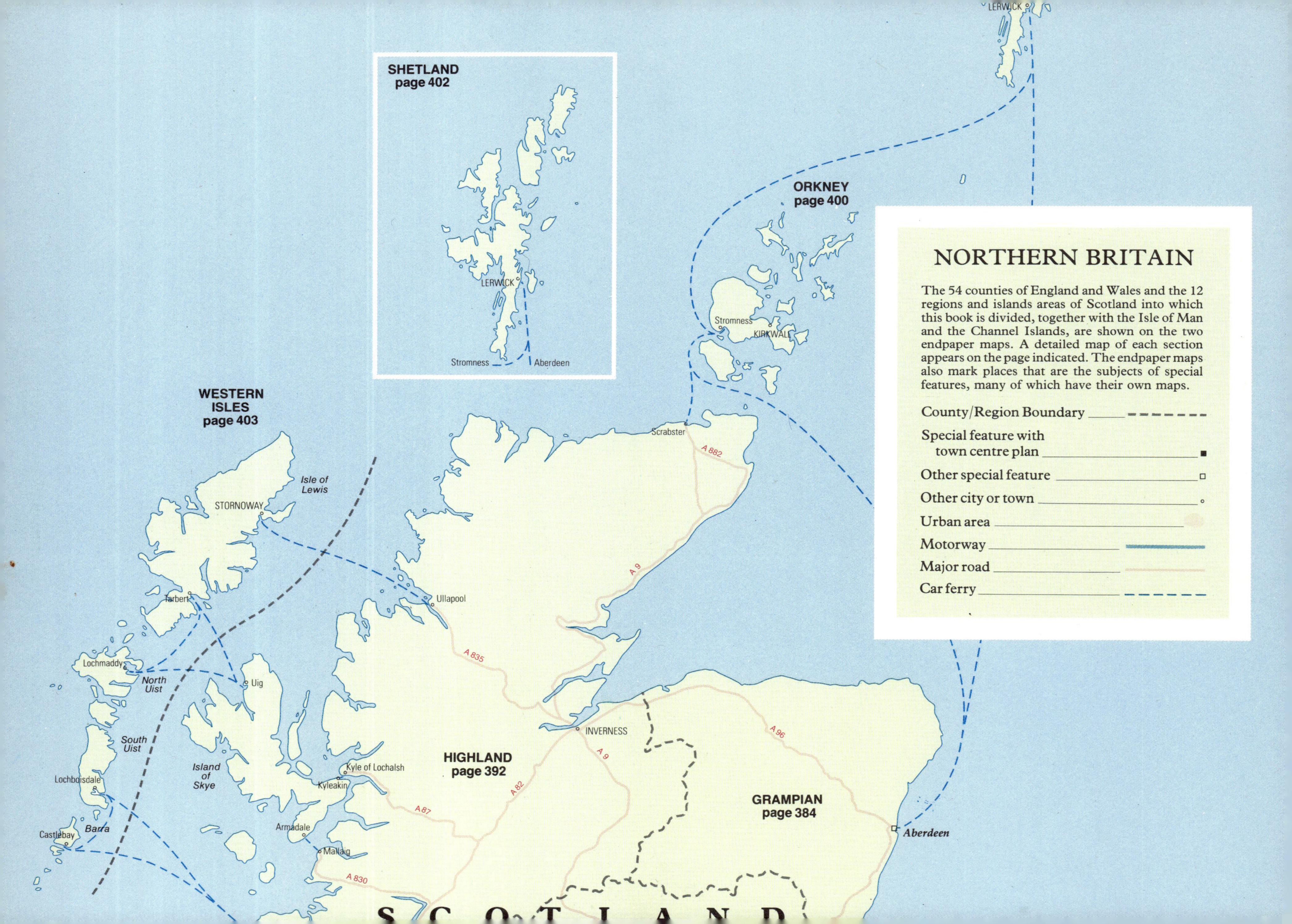